Surrender to the King of Babylon

ÖSTERREICHISCHE BIBLISCHE STUDIEN

Herausgegeben von Georg Braulik

BAND 56

Berlin - Lausanne - Bruxelles - Chennai - New York - Oxford

Salvatore Maurizio Sessa

Surrender to the King of Babylon

Jeremiah's "Prophetic Choice" in the Face of Jerusalem's End (Jer 21:1-10; 27–28; 38:14-28a)

Translated by Denver Michelle Beattie

Berlin - Lausanne - Bruxelles - Chennai - New York - Oxford

Library of Congress Cataloging-in-Publication Data
A CIP catalog record for this book has been applied for at the Library of Congress.

Bibliographic information published by the Deutsche Nationalbibliothek.
The German National Library lists this publication in the German National Bibliography; detailed bibliographic data is available on the Internet at http://dnb.d-nb.de.

Vidimus et approbamus ad normam Statutorum
Pontificii Instituti Biblici de Urbe.
Romae, die 16 mensis novembris 2022.
Prof. BOVATI Pietro
Prof. ABREGO DE LACY José María

ISSN 0948-1664
ISBN 978-3-631-88976-3 (Print)
E-ISBN 978-3-631-89790-4 (E-PDF)
E-ISBN 978-3-631-89791-1 (EPUB)
DOI 10.3726/b20601

© 2024 Peter Lang Group AG, Lausanne
Published by Peter Lang GmbH, Berlin, Germany

info@peterlang.com - www.peterlang.com

All rights reserved.
All parts of this publication are protected by copyright.
Any utilization outside the strict limits of the copyright law, without the permission of the publisher, is forbidden and liable to prosecution.
This applies in particular to reproductions, translations, microfilming, and storage and processing in electronic retrieval systems.

To my father and my mother,
to my brother Sergio and sister Laura,
to all my friends
who have accompanied me
on this long and fascinating journey.
To all the prophets
who have taught me to discern
the time for battle,
the time for hiding,
the time for resistance,
and the time for surrender.

Contents

Acknowledgements 23

General Introduction 25

1. Searching for Meaning. Starting from the rubble 25
   - 1.1. The enigma of the end and the rereading of history 25
   - 1.2. After the end: The efficacy and crisis of an interpretive model 26
   - 1.3. Before the end: Jeremiah and the call for "consignation to the king of Babylon" 29
   - 1.4. The submission-surrender to Babylon and its interpretations. *Status quaestionis* 30
     - 1.4.1. The political perspective 31
     - 1.4.2. The political-redactional perspective 35
     - 1.4.3. The ethical perspective 38
     - 1.4.4. The theo-political perspective 40
2. The principal guidelines of my working hypothesis 41
   - 2.1. Beyond and within the contradictions: Revelation and the prophetic assumption of the Meaning 41
   - 2.2. The meaning of history: What YHWH reveals, how to respond to YHWH 43
   - 2.3. The surrender as a "prophetic choice" 44
3. On meaning and its complexity: Definition of the object of study and the principal methodologies of inquiry 45
   - 3.1. Faced with the text 45
   - 3.2. A first definition of the theme: Structuring elements and significant relationships 46
   - 3.3. Implications: Research paths and general notes on method 50
     - 3.3.1. Text, history, and the world of the text 50
     - 3.3.2. Communicative phenomenon and communication theory ... 53
     - 3.3.3. The world of the text as a world of signs (and symbols) 55
     - 3.3.4. A passageway beyond semantics: The pragmatic dimension of language as interaction between words and the world 56

Contents

3.3.5. A pragmatic revisitation of the notion of "context" 60

3.3.6. Exegesis, interpretive cooperation, and language sciences 64

4. Genesis, development, and articulation of the research: The stages of a (dual) path 67

4.1. Ordo inventionis: A path of discovery 67

4.2. Ordo expositionis: A path of (re-)reading 68

PART I
"Up leaps the lion from his thicket"
Emergenc(i)es.
Literary emergences – Historical emergencies 73

CHAPTER I The thematic emergence of the surrender to the king of Babylon. Orientative literary-hermeneutical coordinates 75

1. Introduction 75

2. Overall literary organisation of the book of Jeremiah and hermeneutical notes 76

2.1. The three major sections of the book (between "poetry", "prose", and some communicative peculiarities) 76

2.2. Fundamental hermeneutical coordinates 81

2.2.1. My approach to the book of Jeremiah: A starting point 81

2.2.2. The unity of the book: An underlying problem 82

2.2.3. Some literary-critical theories: A metacritical note on epistemological foundations 84

2.2.4. Aporias and alternative paths of research 90

2.3. The "symbolic" approach of Louis Stulman: Towards a new perspective for inquiry 92

2.4. Semiotic *arcatas* and the architecture of meaning 94

2.4.1. Historical-critical exegesis and (Semitic) rhetorical analysis ... 94

2.4.2. A transemiotic notion with heuristic significance 101

2.4.3. Semiotic *arcatas* and narrative analysis 108

3. The texts relevant to the theme of the surrender to the king of Babylon 111

3.1. Criteria for the textual "decoupage" 111

3.2. Selected texts 112

Contents

4. The framing of the texts within the literary organisation and thematic interweaving of the book of Jeremiah 114

   4.1. The textual portions 6:1–8, 22–30; 21:1–10, and 25 within the first part (1–25) 114

      4.1.1. Overview 114

      4.1.2. Articulation of the structuring elements 115

   4.2. The textual portions 27–28; 29; 38; 42–43:7 within the second part (26–45) 119

      4.2.1. Overview 119

      4.2.2. Articulation of the structuring elements 123

5. General composition and thematic insertion: First hermeneutical observations 125

   5.1. The necessity of surrender to Babylon: A far from marginal theme 125

   5.2. A scribal explication of the prophetic preaching 126

CHAPTER II Facing the might of the Babylonian empire. Historical international emergencies as the pragmatic context of the call to surrender 129

1. The historical-literary context as the pragmatic-cognitive context of the surrender 129

   1.1. Preliminary notes on the epistemology of history 129

   1.2. Towards a focalisation of the pragmatic context underlying the Jeremianic message 132

2. Babylon is victorious (605 B.C.) and becomes the new global threat. A general historical contextualisation 135

   2.1. How a geopolitical scenario changes 135

      2.1.1. Prophecy and history in the shadow of the great empires ... 135

      2.1.2. Babylon *resurgens*, the disappearance of the Neo-Assyrian empire, and the Egyptian manoeuvres 138

      2.1.3. Nebuchadnezzar and the collapse of the Egyptian hegemony over Palestine 141

   2.2. Winds of rebellion 147

      2.2.1. The capitulation and trauma of 597: On the brink of the abyss 147

      2.2.2. Political instability and international plots in Jerusalem (594) 149

10 Contents

2.3. The fall of Jerusalem and disappearance of the kingdom of Judah 156

2.3.1. The situation precipitates: It is the end 156

2.3.2. Amidst the rubble of the Davidic kingdom: New disobedience of the prophetic word, flight to Egypt, a new germ of hope 159

3. The City and its destiny, between resistance and surrender. A particular historical-theological contextualisation 161

3.1. History, narration, and theology 161

3.2. Surrender or resist? People and opposing politico-theological orientations in the turmoil of history 163

3.2.1. Jeremiah and the option to *surrender*: Supporters and motivations 165

3.2.1.1. Supporters 165

3.2.1.2. Motivations 179

3.2.2. The *resistance* option and its "prophets": Motivations and supporters 179

3.2.2.1. Motivations 179

3.2.2.2. The supporters 192

3.2.3. For a synthetic assessment 195

3.3. Surrender: The solution of a "realist"? 197

3.3.1. Isaiah and Jeremiah, between utopia and realism. The emblematic interpretation of F.J. Gonçalves 197

3.3.2. Some critical notes: Redefining the category of "realism" in light of the historic context 199

3.3.2.1. Then, now 199

3.3.2.2. Submission 199

3.3.2.3. Surrender 200

3.3.2.4. Escalation 201

3.3.2.5. Emblematic examples 209

3.3.2.6. Scorched earth 218

3.3.2.7. Reasons 220

3.3.3. Towards an alternative solution: Surrender as a "prophetic act" 220

Contents 11

PART II
"Bow your necks beneath the yoke of the king of Babylon!"

Texts
Words – Actions – Significations 223

CHAPTER III Jer 21:1–10. The surrender as acceptance of
the end: A symbolic-narrative prolepsis
and hermeneutical key to an entire history ... 225

1. Introduction: Orientative coordinates 225

    1.1. Literary context and intertextual references as devices for
    meaning 225

    1.2. Specific objectives and articulation of the study of Jer 21:1–10 226

2. A first approach to the textual data 227

    2.1. Hebrew text, translation, and philological-exegetical notes on
    Jer 21:1–10 227

    2.2. Contextual insertion and demarcation of the communicative
    unit 229

    2.3. Composition 230

3. The broad context: The necessity of surrender as the "first" word of
    Jeremiah 233

    3.1. The problem of the literary context: An altogether unusual
    positioning 233

        3.1.1. Disorientations 233

        3.1.2. Proposals for a solution 236

        3.1.3. New indications of meaning 238

    3.2. Introductive and proleptic function of Jer 21:1–10 239

        3.2.1. Entering into a story. The figure of the king (מֶלֶךְ) and
        destiny of the nation 239

        3.2.2. Saying it both before and after: Semiotic *arcatas*
        (starting from Jer 23:1–8) 241

        3.2.3. The intermediary semiotic *arcata* of Jer 21:1–10 and Jer
        23:9–40: The opposition between true and false prophecy ... 244

        3.2.4. The most extreme semiotic *arcata* of Jer 21:1–10 and Jer
        24: New elements and other connections 246

12 Contents

3.2.5. The negation of *suspense*. In search of the meaning and strength of the pragmatic context of an already familiar story 248

3.3. A hermeneutical key for entering into the logic of God's judgement 250

3.4. A content-related synthesis and focalisation of thematic saliencies 251

4. Study of the fundamental themes: Surrender, the inevitable end, and possible life 252

4.1. The announcement of the end through reuse of the symbolic coordinates of the origins 252

4.1.1. The communicative and political-religious context of the pericope 252

4.1.2. The wonders of the Exodus 255

4.1.2.1. Now is not the time. An invitation to "surrender" for Baruch as well 255

4.1.2.2. With outstretched hand and mighty arm, but against Jerusalem! 262

4.1.2.3. The scourge of the plague (דֶּבֶר) is no longer for Egypt 267

4.1.3. The (inverted) symbolic coordinates of the "holy war" and the *herem* 269

4.1.4. The curses of the Covenant 279

4.2. Anti-Exodus, new Exodus, and new Covenant. A new prospect for salvation 282

4.2.1. The two paths: The ethical option (Deut) and the "prophetic choice" 282

4.2.2. The gesture of surrender as "life as war booty" 290

5. Conclusions: Surrender as a "prophetic choice" on the basis of semiotic-literary coordinates 295

5.1. Accepting the end of one (hi)story so there can still be any (hi)story. Principal acquisitions 295

5.2. Holy wars and side effects. Some secondary conclusions 296

Contents 13

Chapter IV Jer 27–28. The world beneath the yoke of the king of Babylon: The multi-levelled *ante factum* of the prophetic call to surrender 299

1. Introduction 299

2. Jer 27–28: A first approach to the textual data 302

   2.1. Jer 27: Hebrew text, translation, and philological-exegetical notes 302

   2.2. Jer 28: Hebrew text, translation, and philological-exegetical notes 308

   2.3. Contextual insertion and delimitation of the communicative unit ... 312

   2.4. Compositional arrangement 314

      2.4.1. Rhetorical analysis of Jer 27. Universal perspective and particular focalisation 315

      2.4.2. Rhetorical analysis of Jer 28. Resumption of the particular perspective and return to the universal dimension 319

      2.4.3. Elements of unity and overall structure of chs. 27 and 28. Jerusalem and the nations, true and false prophecy 322

   2.5. Content-related synthesis and focalisation of thematic saliencies 324

3. "Make yourself straps and yoke crossbars and put them on your neck" (27:2). The general communicative importance of an emblematic symbolic gesture in the book of Jeremiah 326

   3.1. Preliminary considerations: Verbal communication and non-verbal communication in studies on biblical prophetism 326

   3.2. For an interdisciplinary revaluation of the synergetic unity between gesture and word 331

   3.3. From the sign of the yoke to the (symbolic) act of surrender to Babylon 333

   3.4. From semantics to pragmatics. Beyond the information, the relation. To surrender "prophetically" 338

   3.5. When words are no longer enough. The time of crisis and urgency of its language 342

4. "Bend your neck beneath the yoke of the king of Babylon!" (27:12). Between wisdom and prophecy: Surrender as a universal theology of history 347

   4.1. The response to the design of God anticipated and requested by means of the gesture of the yoke. Semantic-pragmatic analysis 347

4.1.1. The gesture of the yoke and its literary structure 347

4.1.2. The gesture of the yoke and its historical context 347

4.1.3. Two literary resonances: The relationship with 1 Sam 11:7 and 1 Kgs 22:11 348

4.1.4. The lexicon and tool of the yoke in Jer 27–28 in the light of the cultural context of the ancient Near East: Between agricultural *frame* and military *frame* 350

4.1.5. The figurative use of the yoke and its various *frames* of reference in the context of the ancient Near East 358

4.1.6. The image of the yoke in the HB and in the book of Jeremiah. Paths of meaning between slavery, liberation, transgression, and new promises 362

4.1.7. The "iron yoke" and the curse of Deut 28:47–48. Levels of meaning and possible paths of salvation 369

4.2. The universal dominion of YHWH, the world subjected to the yoke of the king of Babylon: Sapiential dimension and prophetic dimension 371

4.2.1. The *ante factum* of Jer 21:1–10. A historical-theological flashback essential for the foundation and comprehension of the theme of surrender to the king of Babylon 371

4.2.2. The theme of creation in the HB and the book of Jeremiah. The *status quaestionis* 372

4.2.3. A notion having foundative value in the book of Jeremiah. The *status creationis* 375

4.2.4. A creation that is complete and thus continually underway, in a fragile equilibrium. *Creatio continua* and the risk of de-creation 376

4.2.5. "I made the earth, the human beings, and the animals [...]" (27:5a). YHWH: The only God creator of the universe (sapiential dimension) 377

4.2.6. "And I give it to whomever seems right in my eyes" (27:5b). YHWH, creator and Lord of history (sapiential dimension and prophetic aperture) 383

4.2.7. "And *now* I have delivered all these lands into the hand of Nebuchadnezzar, my servant" (27:6a). YHWH: The Lord of *this* history (prophetic dimension) 391

4.3. Jer 27–28: To submit without any motivation? A pragmatic-intertextual solution perspective 405

4.3.1. The terms of the problem 405

4.3.2. Still on the decisive importance of the communicative context for a correct exegesis: Dramatisation, pragmatics, intertexuality. And a pertinent example 406

4.3.3. "Drink!" (שְׁתוּ) [...] "You shall surely drink!" (שָׁתוֹ תִשְׁתוּ). The nations faced with the (motivated) imperative of surrender to Babylon 409

4.3.4. A look at the oracles on the nations 414

4.3.5. YHWH in Jer 27–28: A cosmic God or an ethical God? The prophetic synthesis of the Jeremianic message 421

5. "They prophesy lies to you, do not listen to them!" (27:16–17). True and false prophecy in the face of crisis and threat of the end 424

5.1. True and false prophecy in the book of Jeremiah: A fallacious distinction or fallacious negationist argumentation? 424

5.1.1. The problematic position of M.J. de Jong 424

5.1.2. Some critical notes 428

5.2. "Do not listen to your prophets..." (27:9): The Jeremianic prophetic message and its implications 434

5.2.1. To obey (the Word) means to dis-obey (other words) 434

5.2.2. The truth of the prophetic mission as an authentic relation to the Origin 436

5.3. "And the prophet Jeremiah went on his way" (28:11). Jeremiah's "surrender" before Hananiah: A "symbolic gesture" even more eloquent than that of the yoke 440

5.3.1. The preparation of the scene. MT and LXX: Two different paths of meaning towards the same mystery of the "surrender"? 440

5.3.2. The public dispute with Hananiah 447

5.3.3. The "surrender" of Jeremiah: The mystery of God's silence and the submission to the enemy 450

5.3.4. "Whoever consigns themself [...] will live!" (21:9). Yet another (different) paradigmatic anticipation of a possible path of salvation within the horizon of the end of Jerusalem 457

6. Conclusions: Jer 27–28 as an analepsis and multileveled paradigm with respect to the injunction of the surrender in Jer 21:1–10 and 38:14–28a 460

6.1. Jeremiah beneath the yoke: A symbolic paradigmatic gesture to signify and physically take on the meaning of history in obedience to YHWH 462

16 Contents

6.2. YHWH as creator and Lord: Origin and foundation of a universal theology of history and paradoxical salvation, between a sapiential horizon and a prophetic focalisation 463

6.3. Between Word and anti-Word: Criteria for discernment of the meaning of history, before it is (once again) too late 465

CHAPTER V Jer 38:14–28a. Jeremiah and Zedekiah: The final colloquy. A paradigmatic dramatisation of human-divine communication 471

1. Introduction 471

2. A first approach to the textual data 472

2.1. Hebrew text, translation, and philological-exegetical notes 473

2.2. Immediate contextual placement (Jer 38) and unity of the composition being studied 476

2.3. Internal articulation of Jer 38:14–28a (rhetorical analysis) 479

2.4. Semiotics of the literary architecture (I): The long-distance relationship between Jer 26–27(-29) and the diptych of Jer 38 (v. 1–13 and 14–28a) 481

2.5. Semiotics of the literary architecture (II): A new overview of section chs. 26–45 483

2.6. Content-related synthesis and focalisation of the thematic salencies 488

3. Exegetic focalisations 489

3.1. First part (vv. 14b-18): The need to surrender to the king of Babylon 489

3.1.1. The king (מֶלֶךְ) and the prophet (נָבִיא): The final and decisive secret consultation 489

3.1.2. The "surrendered" and taken (√לקח) prophet and the semiotics of space 498

3.1.3. The request of the king (√שאל) and relation between the urgency of salvation and need for truth 503

3.1.4. A space for the Word 505

3.1.5. The secret oath (√שבע). An underlying ambiguity 509

3.1.6. The radicality of choice: More on the way of life and the way of death 511

Contents

3.1.7. Going out (√יצא) towards the leaders of Babylon. Exodus, anti-Exodus, and new Exodus 513

3.1.8. The end is here, or not. An extreme possibility of salvation for the City as well? 520

3.2. Second part (vv. 19–23): Objection and response 524

3.2.1. Fear (√ראה): The reaction of one, sign of objection of all 524

3.2.2. Humiliation (√עלל): A king's greatest fear 526

3.2.3. Nuances: To listen/to recognise (√שמע) the voice of God in the human word? 530

3.2.4. Analogies (1:4–19 and 38:14–28a): A new "prophetic vocation"? 533

3.2.5. Considerations: In view of further investigations 540

3.2.6. Vision (√ראה): A communicative event in real time? 541

3.2.7. Pre-vision (I): Weakness and truth 546

3.2.8. Pre-vision (II): Fire and responsibility 549

3.3. Third part (vv. 24–27): From the Word to words, towards the silence of the end 552

3.3.1. First impression: Vain wisdom and a futile interrogation ... 552

3.3.2. Jeremiah and the silencing of the prophecy: Picking back up and developing a problematic theme 554

3.3.3. Epilogue: The City falls, the Word is fulfilled, the end sets the Meaning free 557

4. Conclusions: The king and the prophet, a paradigmatic dramatisation of human-divine communication 558

4.1. One in front of the other. Literary context and semiotic polarisations 559

4.2. One against the other, one for the other. Thematic-actantial polarisations, analogical relationships, and communicative dynamics 560

PART III
Whoever surrenders [...] shall live!

Hermeneutics
Handing oneself over to the king of Babylon: phenomenology and interpretation 563

Contents

CHAPTER VI The gesture of the surrender: Phenomenology and symbolic apertures 565

1. Phenomenology and symbolism. Starting from the linguistic and extralinguistic context 565

2. Preliminary considerations: The surrender and its *frame* of reference in a pragmatic and symbolic perspective 565

3. The (sub-)frame of the surrender in the context of the HB and the ancient Near East 567

    3.1. The frame of war in the ancient Near East: Ideology and war typology 568

    3.2. The prodromes of a surrender: An enemy, a war, and a siege. Lexical traces of the biblical context 573

    3.3. Imbalance of forces, negotiations, and admission of inferiority. The objective fact 578

    3.4. Mortal danger, fear, and desire for salvation. The subjective fact 583

    3.5. The act of surrender 587

    3.6. Overview 594

4. Structure of the symbol and polysemic apertures of meaning. Surrender as a "symbolic gesture" 594

    4.1. Introductory hermeneutical notes: Literal meaning does not exist 594

    4.2. The symbol is within the body of the "letter", not outside of it 598

    4.3. Fundamental symbolic irradiations implicated by the act of surrender 601

        4.3.1. The symbol of the yoke and the yoke of the symbol 601

        4.3.2. The gate and walls of the City. To go out and (to let) enter ... 602

        4.3.3. The goods, the land, the temple, and the loss of possession ... 605

        4.3.4. The stranger, his order, and his gods 609

    4.4. Overview 610

CHAPTER VII The surrender to the king of Babylon as a "symbolic-prophetic choice" 611

1. The surrender to the king of Babylon as a "symbolic-prophetic choice" (and not only) 611

    1.1. From the symbol to the (prophetic) sign. From the proposal to the (prophetic) response 611

Contents

1.2. The symbolic-prophetic sign and its context in the light of the inferential model of communication 613

2. Incipit. Jer 1 as a "cognitive map" for access to the Jeremianic semiosphere 617

2.1. Point of departure 617

2.2. The form of the text and originary semiotic paradigms 620

3. In the semiosphere: First guidelines for mapping the symbolic levels of the book of Jeremiah. Towards the identification of a new hermeneutical category 622

3.1. Level of microstructural signification. The prophetic language and the signs of the overflowing of meaning 623

3.2. Level of macrostructural signification. The general architecture of the book and its semiotic *arcatas* 626

3.3. Level of signification of the prophetic ministry. The figure of Jeremiah and his interlocutors 626

3.3.1. Symbolic-prophetic oracles 626

3.3.2. Symbolic-prophetic visions 627

3.3.3. Symbolic-prophetic gestures (rhetoric-didactic and biographical) 628

3.3.4. The celibacy of Jeremiah as an extreme symbolic-prophetic gesture 629

3.3.5. A symbolic-prophetic life (vocation and "passion" of Jeremiah) 631

3.3.6. Symbolic-prophetic choices/acts of obedience requested of Jeremiah 632

3.3.7. Symbolic-prophetic choices/acts of obedience requested of the people 634

4. The surrender as Prophetic-Obediential ConSign*A(c)tion* (*POC*) 636

4.1. A synthetic definition 636

4.2. A category to be understood in a prototypical sense 638

4.3. Some possible examples of reference (in view of further research) 640

CHAPTER VIII The surrender to the king of Babylon as "Prophetic-Obediential ConSign*A(c)tion*" (POC) 641

1. A hermeneutical synthesis as a new working hypothesis 641

2. A choice. A free choice carried out in a story of revelation 643

3. Signified by an action with profound anthropological implications 647
   3.1. Historical-temporal implications. The duration or
        irreversibility of the choice presented 648
   3.2. Socio-affective implications. The intensity of the relational
        repercussions 650
   3.3. Dramatic implications. The entity of the mortal risk 654
4. Commanded by God to the prophet or the people at a precise point
   in time 658
   4.1. Beyond the strategic-political dimension 658
   4.2. Beyond the ethical-moral dimension 663
   4.3. Beyond the religious dimension of the cult 666
   4.4. Beyond the rhetorical-didactic dimension 668
5. Expression of a significative and prophetic option (regarding the
   Covenant and the meaning of history) 670
   5.1. It is an obedience of faith (within a history of covenant) 670
   5.2. It is the emergence of the unsaid (the foreigner who saves) 673
   5.3. It is the acceptance and concrete manifestation of the
        meaning of history (revealed by God here and now) 677

General conclusions (and apertures) "But what will you do when the end comes?" (Jer 5:31) 679

1. The whole meaning (of history) in a (symbolic-prophetic) gesture 679
   1.1. Final synthesis: The gesture of surrender and its
        communicative context 679
   1.2. The configuration of the background context: Facing the
        failure of the Covenant and imminence of the end 680
   1.3. The pragmatic orientation of the gesture: The surrender as
        signification and assumption of the meaning of history 681
2. "What do you see, Jeremiah?" Contextual pertinence and
   interpretive cooperation 683
   2.1. The surrender and the literary context (between synchrony
        and diachrony) 684
        2.1.1. Synchronic level 684
        2.1.2. Diachronic level 686
   2.2. The surrender and the pragmatic-cognitive context of the
        communication 690
        2.2.1. The historical-literary context 691

Contents

2.2.2. The surrender and its phenomenology, between language and encyclopaedic experience 694

2.3. The surrender in the context of the symbolic-pragmatic communication 695

2.3.1. Symbolic gestures and digital communication 695

2.3.2. Symbolic irradiations of the literality 695

3. The surrender in the context of the Jeremianic semiosphere. A new interpretive proposal 696

3.1. The surrender as a "symbolic-prophetic gesture" of response 696

3.2. The surrender as "Prophetic-Obediential ConSignA(c)tion" (POC) 697

3.3. The surrender and its isomorphic manifestations (Jer 29; 42–43:7) 698

3.3.1. Eradication: Accepting the end of a history to inhabit a new relationship with God 698

3.3.2. Radication: Accepting to let oneself be planted anew in the land of the Covenant 699

4. Theological horizons on the threshold of the end 700

4.1. The urgency of the discernment, between true and false prophecy 700

4.2. For a theology of the history, between wisdom and prophesy 701

4.3. The risks of a "theology of surrender" (without the option of "resistance") 704

4.4. Two paradigms of free will in the face of the end (human will and divine will) 706

4.5. "To hand oneself over to the king Babylon": The horizon of the end and its overcoming 709

4.5.1. The end of politics 710

4.5.2. The end of religion 711

4.5.3. The end of ethics 712

4.5.4. The end of rhetoric 714

5. The last king of Israel and the fulfilment of the kingship (in the act of surrender) 715

Abbreviations and sigla 719

Bibliography ... 739

1. Hebrew text and ancient versions ... 739
   1.1. Hebrew text ... 739
   1.2. Ancient versions ... 739

2. Other sources ... 740
   2.1. Texts from the ancient Near East ... 740
   2.2. Classical historiography ... 741
   2.3. Other classics ... 742
   2.4. Dead Sea texts ... 743
   2.5. Rabbinical and Jewish texts ... 743

3. Photographic Repertories ... 744

4. Instruments ... 744
   4.1. Grammar and syntax books ... 744
   4.2. Dictionaries, encyclopedias, concordances, and other instruments ... 744
   4.3. Online/information technology resources ... 746

5. Commentaries and other studies ... 746

Acknowledgements

While containing a few later updates, the present study makes available to a wider audience the original dissertation submitted in Italian to obtain the doctorate in Biblical Studies at the Pontifical Biblical Institute in Rome and defended on 21 June 2017. This paragraph, on the other hand, is dedicated to giving thanks. Despite its brevity and later writing, it is, in a sense, of the greatest importance since it allows me to express, at least in a symbolic form, the purpose itself of every human journey according to biblical revelation, that is, praise, gratitude, the Magnificat (cf. Luke 1:46–55; 24:52–53).

In this movement of turning back to retrace the steps taken (cf. 2 Kgs 5:15; Isa 38:19; Luke 17:15) through the countless stages the work has undergone, I can recollect faces, encounters, and precious friendships. These are meaningful moments and individuals whose contributions have made this long academic endeavour a fascinating and fruitful existential adventure. They are like the sacred places of the Patriarchs where altars or other memorials are erected to honour the Lord of Life (cf. Gen 8:18; 12:7–8; 13:18; 28:18; 31:45; 33:20; Josh 4:20; etc.).

My first thanks can go to none other than my thesis supervisor, the man who has been my paternal guide within the fascinating world of biblical prophecy and the Jeremianic microcosm in particular, namely Prof. Fr Pietro Bovati SJ. From the very first steps I took at the Pontifical Biblical Institute, he has been for me a constant source of intellectual and spiritual stimuli, inspiration, and encouragement to fearlessly assume responsibility for talents received. For him, I hold immense gratitude. I also thank the second speaker, Prof. P. José María Abrego de Lacy SJ, and other members of the commission, Profs. Fr Michael Francis Kolarčík SJ, Fr Peter Dubovský SJ, and in particular, the late Prof. P. Stephen Pisano SJ for his interest and appreciation of my contribution. I would also like to thank all the personnel of the Pontifical Biblical Institute and notably, the Secretary General Carlo Valentino, a precious point of reference for his readiness and care of every student.

All research paths are indebted to the countless travel companions who often times one can confront only amongst the stacks of the library, consulting their works. But here, I express my gratitude to all those whom I have been able to meet in person and who have contributed in different ways to this work, often on the basis of sincere friendship. A special thanks thus goes to Prof. Paolo Merlo for reviewing the historical part and for his advice on the sources of the Ancient Near East, Prof. Robyn Anne Carston, professor of Linguistics at University College London, for our exchange and her encouragement in the study of Pragmatics and Relevance Theory, Prof. Mark Avila for his lively lessons in Akkadian and cordial friendship, Prof. Georg Fischer, a great expert on Jeremiah, Prof. Jean Louis Ska, Prof. Federico Giuntoli, Prof. Maura Sala, and prof. Gwen Griffith-Dickson. The advice I received from each of them was quite valuable. I cannot fail to mention my dear companions in study and life Claudio Arletti, Lorenzo Gasparro, Maurizio Volante, Emanuele Meconcelli, and Diego Zanda, whose fraternal friendship has always been a precious gift over these years.

Special recognition is due to the late Card. Achille Silvestrini for having wanted me as his special secretary and spiritual assistant at the Domenico Tardini College of Excellence Community (Villa Nazareth). May the Lord reward him for his great heart. I cherish fond memories of those years and all the people I met, both students and members of the Villa Nazareth Association, and special thanks in this regard also goes to H.E. Msgr. Claudio Celli.

Going back even further, I feel great filial gratitude towards Fr Valfredo M. Zamperini, founder of the Missionaries of Mary, who desired this path of formation for me, the specific direction of which was also encouraged by the prophetic word of the late Msgr. Mansueto Bianchi. His passionate and exciting lessons on the prophets and the Johannine Writings are always alive in my memory. A sincere thanks also to Sr Donatella Camarlinghi for her support.

I give infinite thanks to my parents, my brother Sergio, and my sister Laura – gifts that are wellsprings of still more gifts. For you, blessings from Heaven without end. Finally, a word about the present translation: a monumental undertaking that would have been impossible without the dedication, professionalism, and theological-literary sensitivity of Denver Michelle Beattie. To her, all my gratitude. A heartfelt thanks also to all those who made it possible for this work to see the light, in particular to the Tonani family, Belinda Theis, Kemalova-Pollo Poesio family.

There are so many more names still to be mentioned, but those who have lent even a small contribution towards this achievement know that my thanks go out to them as well. This work is yours, too. Even the obstacles, of all kinds, have contributed to this result. For all things, praise to the Lord, for all has been, is, and will be grace. And this grace is to be shared in the communion of the Spirit.

General Introduction
"Where are your own prophets who prophesied to you saying: 'The king of Babylon will not attack you or this land'?" (Jer 37:19)

Ainsi l'échec et l'espoir ne sont-ils pax deux moments espacés de l'œuvre divine; il sont inhérents l'un à l'autre, comme deux pôles opposés, et un seul et même terme exprime leur simultanéité, de telle sorte que, dans le texte biblique, l'échec et l'espérance se lisent dans le même mot, se captent dans la même charnière de l'aventure biblique.[1]

1. Searching for Meaning. Starting from the rubble

1.1. The enigma of the end and the rereading of history

"In the tenth month of the ninth year of Zedekiah, king of Judah, Nebuchadnezzar, king of Babylon, and all his army marched against Jerusalem and placed it under siege. In the fourth month of the eleventh year of Zedekiah, the ninth of the month, the city wall was breached [...]" (Jer 39:2; cf. 52:6–7; 2 Kgs 25:1–4). It is the beginning of the end. Jerusalem is destroyed, the temple of YHWH burned down, and the Davidic reign of Judah erased from history. The survivors are deported to Babylon (cf. 39:9; 52:15), the certainties they once had like sand and rubble in their hands. All is lost. All appears to be lost. In the end, the catastrophe – threatened by some prophets, negated by others, and exorcised in vain by rituals, theological conventions, and political choices – really did come. Death entered through the windows, it penetrated the palaces, it wreaked havoc on the promises of youth (cf. 9:20) and the time when Israel followed YHWH through the desert, its firstfruits tended with burning jealousy (cf. 2:2–3). And today, as then, the underling question remains the same: *Why* did it happen? "Why has the Lord pronounced all this great disaster against us?" (16:10). Indeed, it is these queries in the context of the trauma of the exile[2] that gave life to that intertwining of voices, provocations, and questions and answers that makes up the book of Jeremiah.[3]

As far as modern historiography is concerned, the facts referred to in the testimony of biblical narrative need be considered within the framework of the ancient Near East's geopolitical dynamics. Therewithin, the collapse of modest state entities is a

---

1 A. Neher, *L'exil de la parole. Du silence biblique au silence d'Auschwitz*, Paris 1970, 255.
2 On this theme, I refer to D.L. Smith-Christopher, *A Biblical Theology of Exile*, Minneapolis 2002.
3 "To read the book of Jeremiah is to enter a colloquy of voices. These voices contend with one another to give meaning to a national tragedy so devastating that it defies simple explanation and rational analysis" (K.M. O'Connor, «Jeremiah», in: *The Oxford Bible Commentary*, eds. J. Barton – J. Muddiman, Oxford 2001, 487–528; here, p. 487). The nature of and "contention" between these voices is an argument that is still up for discussion, and through the study of my topic, I will engage in precisely this.

26 General Introduction

predictable outcome of the power struggles that existed between the great, dominant political entities of the time, or could constitute an inevitable systemic collapse,[4] a consequence typical of other transitional processes as well. Indeed, historical science is wont to programmatically dismiss the dimension of transcendence as impertinent, by virtue of its methodological presuppositions concerning the reconstruction of past events and of the Jewish religion itself.[5] But the entire biblical text and its world vision is permeated by the correlation between the human horizon and the divine one. The question of *historical truth* is thus attributed to being a *theological truth*. And it is therefore no coincidence that for countless generations, at the annual Jewish memorial for the catastrophe celebrated on the ninth day of the month of Ab, not annalistic chronicles but rather the Lamentations are recited.[6] Rereading the past in this (intercultural) perspective[7] has a much higher pretence than does that of conducting an assessment of crude facts. In Israel, the destiny of this modest capital of this even more modest remote kingdom is considered a *parabolic event* of universal value.[8] In it, the balance of creation is put back into play (cf. 4:23–25) and the very Meaning of history as it regards all nations is revealed (cf. 18:1–15; 25; 46–51).

1.2. After the end: The efficacy and crisis of an interpretive model

The general interpretative schema of biblical historiography can be attributed in particular to influences of the so-called Deuteronomistic tendency,[9] which strives

---

4   This is the perspective adopted e.g. by L. TATUM, «Jerusalem in Conflict: The Evidence for the Seventh-Century B.C.E. Religious Struggle over Jerusalem», in: *Jerusalem in Bible and Archaeology.* The First Temple Period, *eds.*, A.G. VAUGHN – A.E. KILLEBREW, SBLSymS 18, Atlanta 2003, 291–306, which suggests interpreting the decline and end of the reign of Judah not as the simple monocausal result of contingent invasions by hostile empires, but rather starting from the "secondary state collapse" model (pp. 291–294), utilised in the anthropological field with other denominations to describe determinate processes of socio-political change (headed towards structural collapse) common to the history of a series of ancient states and/or cultures. I will defer some brief critical notes on this interpretation to ch. II, n. 24 of my dissertation.
5   Cf. e.g. F.M. CROSS, «Introduction to the Study of the History of the Religion of Israel», in: *Inspired Speech.* Prophecy in the Ancient Near East. Essays in Honor of Herbert B. Huffmon, *eds.* J. KALTNER – L. STULMAN, JSOT.S 378, London – New York 2004, 8–11.
6   Cf. Y. GITAY, «The Poetics of Exile and Suffering: Memory and Perceptions. A Cognitive-Linguistics Study of Lamentations», in: *Exile and Suffering.* A Selection of Papers Read at the 50th Anniversary Meeting of the Old Testament Society of South Africa OTWSA/OTSSA, Pretoria August 2007, *eds.* B. BECKING – D. HUMAN, OTS 50, Leiden – Boston 2009, 203–212.
7   On this subject, see the contributions compiled in N.C. LEE – C. MANDOLFO, *eds.*, *Lamentations in Ancient and Contemporary Cultural Contexts,* SBLSymS 43, Atlanta 2008.
8   "[...] an analysis of the design of the poetry of Lamentations, its use of language and its metaphoric depiction sheds light on its quality and ability to perpetuate the trauma of the people not as a single event but as a universal phenomenon which is presented in a moving, shocking manner" (Y. GITAY, «The Poetics of Exile», 212).
9   Beginning with M. NOTH, *Überlieferungsgeschichtliche Studien.* Die sammelnden und bearbeitenden Geschichtswerke im Alten Testament, Tübingen 1942, ²1957 (from which the definition of "deuteronomistisches Geschichtswerk" derives); cf. J. VAN SETERS, *In Search of History.* Historiography in the Ancient World and the Origins

to reinterpret the entire history of Israel, from after Moses bids farewell (in Deut) and Israel is established in the land of Canaan (with Josh), through to its tragic end (2 Kgs 25).[10] It does this on the basis of some fundamental theological coordinates: the notion of "election" placed within the framework of the reciprocity of the Covenant and, above all, the relation between *sin* and *punishment*. This causal relation is a hermeneutic that is simple, effective, and also rather persuasive, probably due to its being part of an original anthropological experience tied to the processes of evolutionary adaptation (with their reflection in educational practices; cf. e.g. Prov 13:24; 19:18; 22:15; etc.; Eph 6:4; Heb 12:6–7; etc.). These processes forgive no errors and "sanction" every deviation from the physio-biological laws, by which life is possible only under certain conditions. The model is a ubiquitous one, especially in the ancient Near East, even if in Israel the context it falls into is a peculiar one, where faith in YHWH, the only and righteous Lord of history, does not consider the real possibility of evil being attributable to other rival forces, whether these be other gods (conceived regardless as inferior, if not actually non-existent) or a blind Fate superior to any human-divine intentionality.

Despite there being several obscure knots that prove hard to untangle within this hermeneutical context, not the least of which would be pious Josiah's embarrassing exit from the scene, the retributive model and attempt to justify YHWH's actions seem to pervade prophetic literature in its entirety. This is true to such an extent that this literature has been defined as an impressive proposal of *theodicy*,[11] in which history

---

of Biblical Historiography, New Haven 1983, Winona Lake [2]1997; R. ALBERTZ, *Die Exilszeit. 6. Jahrhundert v. Chr.*, BE 7, Stuttgart 2001, 210–260; R.F. PERSON, Jr., *The Deuteronomic School. History, Social Setting, and Literature*, SBL.SBL 2, Atlanta 2002; T. RÖMER, *The So-Called Deuteronomistic History. A Sociological, Historical and Literary Introduction*, London – New York 2007.

10 As a result of this pervasiveness, many have discussed "pandeuteronomism". In this regard, see the contributions collected in L.S. SCHEARING – S.L. McKENZIE, eds., *Those Elusive Deuteronomists. The Phenomenon of Pan-Deuteronomism*, JSOT.S 268, Sheffield 1999.

11 'Within the biblical canon the Former Prophets constitute a monumental theodicy, an almost heroic attempt to exonerate the deity for permitting the defeat of Jerusalem and the exportation of a large number of Judeans to Babylonia" (J.L. CRENSHAW, «Theodicy and Prophetic Literature», in: *Theodicy in the World of the Bible, eds. A. LAATO* – J.C. DE MOOR, Leiden – Boston 2003, 236–255). On the topic of theodicy, see also J.L. CRENSHAW, «Introduction: The Shift from Theodicy to Anthropodicy», in: *Theodicy in the Old Testament, ed.* J.L. CRENSHAW, IRT 4, Philadelphia 1983, 1–16; R.P. CARROLL, «Theodicy and the Community: The Subtext of Jeremiah v 1–6», in: *Prophets, Worship, and Theodicy. Studies in Prophetism, Biblical Theology, and Structural and Rhetorical Analysis, and on the Place of Music in Worship. Papers Read at the Joint British-Dutch Old Testament Conference Held at Woudschoten, 1982*, OTS 23, Leiden 1984, 19–38; J.L. CRENSHAW, *Defending God. Biblical Responses to the Problem of Evil*, Oxford 2005; J. BARTON, «Historiography and Theodicy in the Old Testament», in: *Reflection and Refraction. Studies in Biblical Historiography in Honour of A. Graeme Auld, eds.* R. REZETKO – T.H. LIM – W.B. AUCKER, VT.S 113, Leiden – Boston 2007, 27–33; D. ROM-SHILONI, «Theodical Discourse: Theodicy and Protest in Sixth Century BCE Hebrew Bible Theology», in: *Theodicy and Protest: Jewish and Christian Perspectives, eds.* B. EGO et al., SKI.NF 13, Leipzig 2018, 55–74.

28 General Introduction

gets reread as an attempt to ultimately achieve a plausibility of meaning following the experience of meaninglessness inherent in every disaster.[12] With the destruction of Jerusalem, however, one finds oneself before a *cognitive dissonance*[13] of apparently unmanageable consequences: an entire religious vision of the world seems to have shattered. For this reason, the traditional hermeneutical schema is called into question in a way that is so radical that the test of its interpretive strength could either definitively legitimise its validity or, instead, affirm its structural insufficiency in elucidating history as an organic process. We are well aware that in the wisdom tradition, what seriously jeopardises this schema is the question of the righteous sufferer (with the case of Job, above all). But already placed within the pages of a great prophetic book like Isaiah are the stages of a mysterious path of humiliation in which the sore lot of

---

12 With regard to the book of Jeremiah, see: Cf. K.M. O'CONNOR, «Surviving Disaster in the Book of Jeremiah», *WW* 22 (2002) 369–377; ID., «The Book of Jeremiah: Reconstructing Community after Disaster», in: *Character Ethics and the Old Testament. Moral Dimensions of Scripture*, *eds.* M.D. CARROLL R. – J.E. LAPSLEY, Louisville 2007, 81–92; D. ROM-SHILONI, «Facing Destruction and Exile: Inner-Biblical Exegesis in Jeremiah and Ezekiel», *ZAW* 117 (2005) 189–205; D.J. REIMER, «Redeeming Politics in Jeremiah», in: *Prophecy in the Book of Jeremiah*, *eds.* H.M. BARSTAD – R.G. KRATZ, BZAW 388, Berlin 2009, 121–136; K.M. O'CONNOR, *Jeremiah*. Pain and Promise, Minneapolis 2011, 29–34; L. STULMAN, «Reflections on the Prose Sermons in the Book of Jeremiah: Duhm's and Mowinckel's Contributions to Contemporary Trauma Readings», in: *Bible through the Lens of Trauma*, *eds.* E. BOASE – C.G. FRECHETTE, SemeiaSt 86, Atlanta 2016, 125–139. Cf. also K. BERGE, «Is There Hope in the Deuteronomistic History?», in: *New Perspectives on Old Testament Prophecy and History*. Essays in Honour of Hans M. Barstad, *eds.* R.I. THELLE – T. STORDALEN – M.E.J. RICHARDSON, VT.S 168, Leiden 2015, 264–277; L.J. CLAASSENSIN, «Jeremiah. The Traumatized Prophet», in: *The Oxford Handbook of Jeremiah*, *eds.* L. STULMAN – E. SILVER, Oxford 2021, 358–373.

13 The theory of "cognitive dissonance" (of a socio-psychological matrix) was proposed by L. FESTINGER, *A Theory of Cognitive Dissonance*, Stanford 1957 (cf. also L. FESTINGER – H.W. RIECKEN – S. SCHACHTER, *When Prophecy Fails*. A Social and Psychological Study of a Modern Group that Predicted the Destruction of the World, Minneapolis 1956, ²2008; L. FESTINGER, *Conflict, Decision, and Dissonance*, Stanford 1964). It was applied in the biblical field to the theme of the so-called "failed prophecies" (in a way that was problematic, in my opinion) in two interesting contributions by R.P. Carroll (ID., *When Prophecy Failed*. Reactions and Responses to Failure in the Old Testament Prophetic Traditions, London 1979; ID., «Prophecy and Dissonance: A Theoretical Approach to the Prophetic Tradition», *ZAW* 92 [1980] 108–119). The underlying idea is that when an irreconcilable contradiction between two cognitions occurs in a subject, the subject itself is automatically induced to search for a resolution of the discomfort either by intervening in reality, by modifying its behaviour, or by altering its own cognitive schema of approach to the experience. For a more recent example of its use (in the realm of the apocalyptic), see e.g. A.C. MERRILL WILLIS, *Dissonance and the Drama of Divine Sovereignty in the Book of Daniel*, LHBOTS 520, London – New York 2010. For a critical note, cf. S.D. O'LEARY, «When Prophecy Fails and when It Succeeds. Apocalyptic Prediction and the Re-Entry into Ordinary Time», in: *Apocalyptic Time*, *ed.* A. BAUMGARTEN, SHR 86, Boston 2000, 341–362, who rightly emphasises the limiting way in which the concept of "failure of a prophesy" has been considered.

Searching for Meaning. Starting from the rubble

a Righteous One (the servant of YHWH) opens up altogether unprecedented perspectives. The fact is that if single individuals can also be representative of a collective destiny (cf. also the figure of the "son of man" [v. 13: בַּר אֱנָשׁ] in Dan 7), then it is difficult to see, in the history of a people in alliance with YHWH, a path entirely free of fault or infidelity capable of making the retributive schema obsolete. The question thus remains an open one, and the book of Jeremiah confronts it in a way all its own.

1.3. Before the end: Jeremiah and the call for "consignation to the king of Babylon"

The prophets had announced peace (שָׁלוֹם), but peace did not come (cf. 4:10; 6:14; 8:11; 14:13; 23:17; etc.). They had given assurance that the king of Babylon would not be a threat and that the Lord would break his yoke, ripping it from the neck of all the nations. Instead, his armies devastated and annihilated the kingdom of Judah (cf. 27:9; 28:1–4.11; 29:9; 37:19; Ezek 22:28; Lam 2:14; etc.). The eternal covenant between YHWH and his people appears to have been terminated, and with it, the promises of the permanency of the Davidic throne, possession of the land given to the Fathers, and the very dogma of election made visible by the earthly dwelling place of God amidst his people (cf. Isa 40:27; 49:14; Jer 33:24; Ezek 33:10; 37:11; Ps 44:14; 89:39–40; Lam 3:54; etc.).

The *failure*[14] of Israel's history seems radical and incomprehensible, above all bearing in mind the contradiction between the theme of its *election* and that of its *punishment*. This punishment has been made manifest in a tragedy, a castigation so harsh that it could be read as the negation of the election itself. And yet, during the exile and post-exile, it is the search for meaning in the face of the enigma of the end that identifies, in the figure of Jeremiah, an emblematic anchoring. However one might consider him today (as a historical character, literary project, or fictional figure), a word of truth is regained in him that sets him apart from all the other pre-catastrophe voices. And it sets him apart from the other prophetic figures and traditions (in particular, those of Isaiah and Ezekiel) as well. Whilst a fruitful intertextual dialogue with the most important biblical traditions is evident throughout the Jeremianic corpus,[15] it is to Jeremiah alone that a *precise* indication of meaning by which the catastrophe might have been avoided through the actualisation of a concrete political option, however unprecedented, can be attributed. The prophet had not only foretold the arrival of the enemy from the North and then demonstrated the historical concretisation of this in the Babylonian invasion, but in the name of YHWH, he had also presented an inexorable alternative: to either continue to *resist* the king of Babylon by opposing him to the bitter end, or to *surrender* to this foreign power and remain alive. The scope of my research is to try my hand at addressing the hermeneutical challenge posed by the subversive potential of this prophetic gamble on a political and theological level.

Moreover, the theme of "consignation to the king of Babylon" is by no means a marginal aspect of the theological-literary complexity of the book of Jeremiah. On

---

14 On the relevance of this category, see J.A. LOADER, «Understanding of Failure and Failure of Understanding: Aspects of Failure in the Old Testament», *HvTSt* 70 (2014) 1–11 [DOI: 10.4102/hts.v70i1.2657].

15 In this regard, see the observations by G. FISCHER, «Il libro di Geremia, specchio della cultura scritta e letta in Israele», *RivBib* 56 (2008) 393–417.

30 General Introduction

the contrary, it is a recurring motif that is presented in various circumstances and to various recipients. These are so diverse and representative of the totality of Israel that I am drawn to consider that this message, delivered in a specific theological-political context, is destined to assume a "universal" value. Universal value implies universal responsibility. And in fact, Jeremiah addresses the nations (27:2–11), the king Zedekiah (27:12–13), the priests and all the people (27:16–17), the exiles of the first deportation (29:4–7), the people once again (38:2–3), Zedekiah once more (38:17–23), and finally, even the remaining population left behind in the country after the fall of Jerusalem (42:10–18). Certainly, the main culprit for the tragedy will be the monarchy, but it will most definitely not be alone. Indeed, this option for survival and salvation is addressed to all.

It is thus not by chance that the experience of the exile leads to a retrospective consideration of this prophetic word and its implications. Once again in the Jeremianic corpus, the sin of the people and its governors is called into question. But this is not merely a repeating or re-elaborating of the bare bones of doctrinal content. It wants, first of all, to present and listen once more, as I have said, to a *parable of life* that runs through the end and beyond. In this "parable", the prophetic oracles on the one hand, and the history of a (no less prophetic; cf. 1:5) "body" on the other, move together synergistically upon the stage of the text and of history. A doctrine is listened to, a drama lived, or re-lived. For this reason, from the very beginning of Jeremiah and throughout its disorienting literary organisation, the book engages its listeners/readers in the same descending parabola that its protagonists experience. And the outcome of this is well known. What is now most interesting to learn is not only *why*, but even more so *how* they got to that point. And what is most pressing to know is if, from this failure, or even from *within this failure*, a germ of new *hope* can come forth.

"Where are your own prophets [...]?" (37:19) Jeremiah asks his interlocutors, rendering the falsity of their words manifest. The entire book is fruit of a *retrospective gaze* that originates from the revelatory nature of the impact with reality, which it attests within its own literary perimeter. So the prophet's invitation to stop along the paths of men to scrutinise the wisdom derived from past experiences (cf. 6:16) does not regard the people of his time alone. Faced with the enigma of the end, one looks back because before that end, the most grave disobedience was not only that of refusing to walk the way of *moral good* (דֶּרֶךְ הַטּוֹב) but also that of not wanting to recognise a (human-divine) communicative event taking place and read its *grammar of significa-tion* (cf. 6:17: "I raised up watchmen for them: 'Pay attention [√קשׁב hi.] to the sound of the trumpet! [לְקוֹל שׁוֹפָר]'. But they said, 'We will not pay attention! [√קשׁב hi.]' "). An exploration of the Meaning therefore demands the dedication of renewed attention to the dimension of signs and symbols, to all those faint traces or clear communicative provocations that require a hermeneutical act. And it requires, still further, *obedience*. Here as well, what is asked of the prophet from the outset (cf. 1:11, 13: "what do you see, Jeremiah?") is asked of each and every reader of the book of Jeremiah. And before us, numerous others have grappled with this fascinating and challenging undertaking.

1.4. The submission-surrender to Babylon and its interpretations. Status quaestionis

Everyone and no one. An initial response, with regard to the focalisation of the *status quaestionis* of my topic, could be reduced to this succinct expression. In fact, every

Searching for Meaning. Starting from the rubble

commentator of the Jeremianic text discusses the question and confronts it in one way or another since over the course of the book of Jeremiah the prophetic injunction explicitly calling for submission-surrender[16] to Babylon is inevitably encountered several times. It is however surprising that no one thus far, to my knowledge, has dedicated a monographic study to it. At most, the theme can be found in a few articles, treated according to various perspectives.

My dissertation intends foremost to bridge this hermeneutical gap, attempting to conduct a study that combines exegetical inquiries of an analytic sort on the relevant texts with a synthetic global vision and a personal interpretive proposal. As a point of departure, a clear focalisation of the most prevalent and significantly beaten tracks to date will be useful, since my work will present itself as a critical dialogue with respect to them, albeit using different modalities, given the heterogeneity of these contributions. Indeed, given their variegated and fragmentary nature, it seems opportune that I group these various proposals together according to the distinct hermeneutical perspectives shared by their most representative authors, at least in terms of their background horizons.

1.4.1. The political perspective

The elements of a political nature contained in the book of Jeremiah have long been identified.[17] The choice to submit or surrender to a foreign power is clearly an act that concerns the government of a state entity[18] performed by its supreme leaders and those who can influence the decision-making power. In the kingdom of Judah at the time of Jeremiah and in the contemporary context of the ancient Near East, the governance of public life was the prerogative of the figure of the sovereign, who availed himself of ministers and other professional figures.

Generals, advisors, scribes, priests, prophets, haruspices, astrologers, and other power agents make up, in one way or another and in different measure, the administrative workings of the court in the majority of state aggregations (above all, in those that are most complex and structured, such as the Neo-Assyrian empire and, following, the Neo-Babylonian one). For these entities, information that is human and information deriving from the divine sphere constituted the basis for every decision-making process, whether for the individual or the highest state positions. In this respect, speaking of "politics" as an art of governance by an urban collective runs the risk of

---

16 Even though in reference to the Jeremianic preaching the concepts of "submission" and "surrender" are not always immediately superimposable, throughout the course of the present dissertation, to simplify the terminology, I will mostly use the term "surrender", to be understood in a broad sense. I refer further specification in this regard to ch. II, § 3.2 (and respective note 123).

17 Cf. e.g. A.C. WELCH, Jeremiah. His Time and His Work, London 1928, Oxford ²1951, even if he then attributes Jeremiah's positions to entirely religious motivations.

18 If the term "politics" as used today refers principally to the experience of the Greek polis, "It is undeniable that the range of phenomena which allowed the development of complex societies (the origin of the state, the city, writing, and so on) first appeared in the Near East, and that the reconstruction of the history of their transmission to our time is complex, yet possible" (M. LIVERANI, The Ancient Near East. History, Society and Economy, London – New York 2014, 4).

being anachronistic if one does not carefully contextualise this field of action within the relevant socio-cultural horizon in which myths, religious beliefs, and governance practices are imbricated dimensions.[19] Even with this caution, it is nevertheless possible to identify a decisional space in which *pragmatic* grounds, inspired by what we can call balanced "realism", could have prevailed.[20] Indeed, a certain strand of interpretation of the Jeremianic option seems to be marked by precisely this category, even if the terms in which it does so are, in my opinion, reductionistic.

According to Francolino José Gonçalves, for example,[21] the injunction to accept the yoke of Babylon (cf. 27–28) would not have been attributable by Jeremiah to any specific theological motivation other than that of it being the impenetrable design of YHWH on history. The necessity to submit to the imperial hegemony of the moment would thus have nothing to do at all with either the relational dynamic of the Covenant in general or with the sin-punishment nexus in particular (thematised especially by the Deuteronomistic tradition). Jeremiah would have therefore spoken and acted as a member of the pro-Babylonian party, manifesting, albeit in the name of YHWH, merely a "réalisme politique", to be counterposed with the "irréalisme absolu" of Isaiah who on the contrary, faced with the Assyrian threat, asked to confide in the help of YHWH.[22]

Burke O. Long, in a study on the social roots of the prophetic conflict with regard to the stance to be taken towards Babylon,[23] had already complained about the excessive significance assigned by commentators to the theological dimension of the question. In his opinion, the issue would be entirely political, and not theological at all. He sustained this based solely on the fact that both representatives of the contending groups, the pro-Egyptian and pro-Babylonian, would have been invoking YHWH as an instrumentality.[24] This frankly simplistic position, in my view, results in an erroneous

---

19 Cf. M. HUTTER, «Politik. III. Politik und Religion. 1. *Religionswissenschaftlich*», *RGG⁴* VI, 1453–1454.

20 With regard to ancient Israel, both on the inextricable relationship between religion, morale, law, and politics, and at the same time on the possibility of identifying more specific areas of competency, see e.g. Z.W. FALK, «Religion and State in Ancient Israel», in: *Politics and Theopolitics in the Bible and Postbiblical Literature, eds.* H.G. REVENTLOW – Y. HOFFMAN – B. UFFENHEIMER, JSOT.S 171, Sheffield 1994, 49–54 (esp. p. 50). The political elements involved in biblical prophecy are not, in any case, easily identifiable (as noted e.g. R.P. CARROLL, «Prophecy and Society», in: *The World of Ancient Israel.* Sociological, Anthropological and Political Perspectives. Essays by Members of the Society for Old Testament Study, *ed.* R.E. CLEMENTS, Cambridge 1989, 203–225 [here p. 214]), given the complex relationship on the textual level between historical data and the communicative intentions involved in any literary production.

21 See F.J. GONÇALVES, «Isaïe, Jérémie et la politique internationale de Juda», *Bib.* 76 (1995) 282–298.

22 *Ibid.*, 297.

23 B.O. LONG, «Social Dimensions of Prophetic Conflict», in: *Anthropological Perspectives on Old Testament Prophecy, eds.* R.C. CULLEY – T.W. OVERHOLT, Semeia 21, Chico 1982, 31–53.

24 Along the same lines, particularly with regard to the Isaianic oracles concerning Assyria, see J. HØGENHAVEN, «Prophecy and Propaganda. Aspects of Political and Religious Reasoning in Israel and the Ancient Near East», *SJOT* 1 (1989) 125–141, which speaks about prophetic activity in general (historically speaking) in terms of "political propaganda" (p. 130).

overturning of cause and effect. In the book of Jeremiah, it is not the differing political positions (the motivations of which, by admission of the author himself, would remain obscure)[25] that call upon different prophetic words for support. It is prevalently, instead, the diverse perceptions of the *theological* meaning of the history taking place, that is, the different interpretations of YHWH's actions and revelation of himself within the frame of the Covenant, that determine the counterposed political options. My underlying thesis is this. I hasten to note that on the basis of these perspectives of political reductionism represented by B.O. Long and F.J. Gonçalves, the prophetic message attested in the Jeremianic work would be reduced, problematically, to an anecdotal fact and completely arbitrary position that would have revealed itself to be that most forward-looking for the well-being of the state only.

Nevertheless, and without even presenting in-depth argumentation, other authors express themselves along these same lines. Amongst these is William L. Holladay. In his monumental commentary on the book of Jeremiah, while justly underscoring that the survival of the people in 21:8–10 is a fact detached from any ethical imperative, he refers to the Jeremianic perspective as "simple prudence".[26] The prophet is thus counted, even if extemporaneously, as one of the numerous technical advisors to the king, as if he were the director of a subordinate sector capable of identifying the most opportune strategic choices.

Specific attention should be given to Hedwige Rouillard-Bonraisin who, albeit while expressing positions that are actually quite similar, dedicates a specific article expressing nuances of her own on the regal politics of the kingdom of Judah in relation to the positions taken by Isaiah and Jeremiah.[27] In her opinion, the prophet from Anathoth, while remaining convinced of the power of YHWH, would have comprehended the uselessness of military resistance to the Babylonian empire to the bitter end (conceived as a mere substitute for the Assyrian threat) with his *political acumen*.[28] In other words, she still presents the question as one of realism and prudence,[29] even if cloaked in a theological-prophetical structure. This time, however, Jeremiah would find himself in line with the likewise realist Isaiah, gifted instead with "acuité politique exceptionelle"[30] because believed capable of correctly evaluating the situation of the

---

25 B.O. LONG, «Social Dimensions», 49–50.

26 W.L. HOLLADAY, *Jeremiah 1.* A Commentary on the Book of the Prophet Jeremiah. Chapters 1–25, Hermeneia, Philadelphia 1986, 574.

27 Cf. H. ROUILLARD-BONRAISIN, «Ésaïe, Jérémie et la politique des rois de Juda», in: *Prophètes et rois.* Bible et Proche-Orient, ed. A. LEMAIRE, LeDiv.HS, Paris 2001, 177–224.

28 *Ibid.*, 221–222. Jeremiah would simply be acting as a political advisor (at least in 38:15, 17–18) also according to N. KILPP, *Niederreißen und aufbauen.* Das Verhältnis von Heilsverheißung und Unheilsverkündigung bei Jeremia und im Jeremiabuch, BThSt 13, Neukirchen-Vluyn 1990, 92.

29 Always as regards the defence of the national identity guaranteed by the Davidic monarchy, even if subservient to a foreign power. According to D.S. VANDERHOOFT, *The Neo-Babylonian Empire and Babylon in the Latter Prophets,* HSM 59, Atlanta 1999, 135, as well, the finality for which Jeremiah pushed for capitulation before the Babylonian power was preservation of the nation's religious and cultural autonomy.

30 H. ROUILLARD-BONRAISIN, «Ésaïe, Jérémie», 198.

balance of power in play on the geopolitical scene. The Jeremianic position would, however, go further. Not only would he have wisely (and not so much "prophetically") foreseen the ineluctability of the end of Jerusalem in case of resistance, but he would have also consequently put forth an invitation to enter into a collective collaboration with Babylon. And he would have done this thanks to a "réflexion politique clairvoyante" that was combined with faith in YHWH, in-depth study of the situation, and an accurate understanding of the Babylonian inclination towards defeated populations. Upon removal of the theological-prophetic paludament,[31] Jeremiah (as well as Isaiah) would reveal himself to be basically a polished analyst of international relations.[32] To me, this perspective seems inappropriate and far from the communicative intentionality of the prophetic tradition. As already observed, this tradition cannot content itself with reporting horizontal readings of the course of history in terms of chronicle. It wants rather to address the question of YHWH's self-revelation in the interweaving of human events and under the pretence that this can be comprehended only within the covenant relationship in which Israel is protagonist.

The socio-political approach proposed by Edward Silver is also, in my view, a problematic one. In a contribution dedicated to the image of the yoke in the context of political communication in the ancient Near East and its symbolic function in the request of submission to Babylon in chs. 27–29,[33] he rightly maintains that the symbolic gesture of Jeremiah cannot be seen as merely a rhetorical device nor be interpreted simply as a generic reference to a necessary acceptance of the Babylonian power.

His search for a more adequate interpretation, however, leads him to believe that the question has to do with the intentional and "liberating" recovery of a system of socio-economic values, evoked specifically by the rural work instrument of the "yoke" and rooted in the context of decentralised social organisation, the only dimension that would have been capable of surviving beyond the disintegration of the political institutions and the geographical dispersion of the people.[34] His reading certainly has the merit of advocating the need for a study that takes into consideration

---

31   *Ibid.*, 222–224.

32   See, in this regard, what David J. Reimer emblematically states. Having downgraded the claim of the prophets to be spokespersons of the divine as a pre-critical and "irrational approach" (even if he then denies that the prophets can be understood as "advisors on domestic or foreign affairs"), he presents the possible hermeneutical alternative by which "prophets' politics were shaped not so much by the divine will as by the depth of insight of the prophet into the workings of the world based on their observations of it. Some prophets lived intimately within the power structures of the day, and served the interests of the regime; others were isolated from these structures and acted as political critics. Perhaps the contrasting tasks of the politician's Press Secretary and the freelance journalist provide a reasonable analogy to these two prophetic roles. In either case, the decisive factor in this account is native wit, not divine revelation" (D.J. REIMER, «Political Prophets? Political Exegesis and Prophetic Theology», in: *Intertextuality in Ugarit & Israel*. Papers Read at the Tenth Joint Meeting of The Society for Old Testament Study and Het Oudtestamentisch Werkgezelschap in Nederland en België, held at Oxford, 1997, *ed.* J.C. DE MOOR, OTS 40, Leiden 1998, 126–142, here, p. 127).

33   Cf. E. SILVER, «Performing Domination/Theorizing Power: Israelite Prophecy as a Political Discourse beyond the Conflict Model», *JANER* 14 (2014) 186–216.

34   *Ibid.*, 202.

the communicative complexity and grammar of the world of signs and symbols. Nevertheless, according to this Jeremianic theory of power, the prophet would still be a "subaltern political actor" set on subverting the logic of the imperial power through the valorisation of individual freedom.[35]

In E. Silver's view, the empire (here, the reference is to Assyrian attestations and not Babylonian ones), wanting to control the body of its subjects, makes propagandistic, self-celebratory use of the metaphor of subjugation under the yoke. Assuming a position against the empire, Jeremiah would invite Israel to take action valorising its ability to manage its own physical dimension. By evoking another microcosm of values instead, while expressing external obedience, they would actually be subtracting themselves from the meaning that the empire wants to impress upon it. The problem is that it truly seems hardly relevant to consider a resignification that is readable solely in a socio-economic key. I therefore believe that a rereading of the symbolic gesture of the yoke would be best founded on a more accurate contextualisation of the "sign vectors" and symbolic vectors evoked by it, keeping in mind that their reorientation comes about within the world of signification instituted by the *entirety* of the Jeremianic corpus and not just by one of its many aspects.

1.4.2. The political-redactional perspective

In the wake of the approach just highlighted, a series of scholars pick up on the focalisation of the Jeremianic message in a political key, but take their start from the classical historical-literary methodology that seeks to reconstruct the history of the composition of the text using a diachronic approach. Indisputably, contributing towards this development configures a type of research that is particularly pertinent in the case of the book of Jeremiah, given the factual evidence of its dual textual form (MT and LXX).

With regard to my topic, we can speak of a political-"redactional" perspective (with all the reservations or generalisations that such a reference to the work of one or more "redactors" or actual "authors" may bring with it)[36] that hypothesises and believes to have found textual traces of the existence of opposed redactional circles. Each of these circles would be ascribable to the distinct communities that arose from the Babylonian deportations, each with its own political agenda: the Palestinian one, that exiled in Babylon, and that taking refuge in Egypt.[37] Then, however, *two conflicting groups* would fundamentally be identified,[38] corresponding to two mutually antagonist

---

35 "In Jeremiah's hands, the yoke represents not subjugation to foreign exploiters but a return to basic forms of social organization and ordered, self-sufficient agrarian labor. [...] With this performance, Jeremiah accomplishes a remarkable bifurcation of the self. Externally, he engages in normative, submissive behaviors. Internally, however, these actions are motivated by concerns that were orthogonal to those of the dominant elite" (*Ibid.*, 216).

36 See what has been observed on this subject in ch. I, § 4.2.1, n. 124.

37 E W. NICHOLSON, *Preaching to the Exiles*. A Study of the Prose Tradition in the Book of Jeremiah, Oxford 1970, particularly underscores the Deuteronomistic provenance of the Babylonian redaction.

38 And this can already be seen in the now classic work by K.-F. POHLMANN, *Studien zum Jeremiabuch. Ein Beitrag zur Frage nach der Entstehung des Jeremiabuches*,

36 General Introduction

redactions: the Jewish one and the pro-*gôlâ* one (cf. e.g. 24:5–7 with 42:10–12). The book of Jeremiah would thus attest, as Robert P. Carroll asserts,[39] not so much to a firm political stance of the historical prophet, but rather to the post-exilic interests and attempts at self-legitimisation of different editorial communities. In this sense, historical research should regard only the ideology or theology (for him, synonymous) of the producers of "Jeremiah", and his figure be understood as merely a literary construct.

As far as my specific theme is concerned, exegetes like Christopher R. Seitz[40] and William McKane[41] (in addition to R.P. Carroll himself[42]) hold the view that within the textual material relating to the epoch of King Zedekiah, a still more ancient literary layer exists (denominated by C.R. Seitz as the "Scribal Chronicle"), in which the prophet would envision the possibility of salvation for the kingdom of Judah, and for Jerusalem in particular, binding it, in fact, to submission to the king of Babylon. This positive openness would then be subject to a radical revisitation, evident in a successive redactional intervention (the "Exilic Redaction") in which Jeremiah becomes the improbable proclaimer of an ineluctable end.

That this is, from a historical point of view, an unreliable (or *ex eventu*) version of the prophetic phenomenon would be made evident, according to Matthijs J. de Jong,[43] by studying the divinatory phenomenon typical of the ancient Near East, of which biblical and extrabiblical prophetism would be only some of the many and diversified expressions. In this context, the specialistic function of the prophetic oracles would make no sense unless conceived within a fundamental, positive intentionality towards the state and national society, of which the prophets themselves were an integral part.[44]

FRLANT 118, Göttingen 1978; cf. one of the more recent works on the subject: D. Rom-Shiloni, «Group Identities in Jeremiah: Is It the Persian Period Conflict?», in: *A Palimpsest: Rhetoric, Ideology, Stylistics, and Language Relating to Persian Israel*, eds. E. Ben Zvi – D. Edelman – F. Polak, PHSC 5, Piscataway 2009, 11–46.

39   Cf. R.P. Carroll, *Jeremiah*. A Commentary, OTL, London 1986, 102, 104. For the author, the historical Jeremiah simply disappears "behind the activities of redactional circles and levels of traditions which have created the words and story of Jeremiah ben Hilkiah of Anathoth" (p. 48).

40   Cf. C.R. Seitz, *Theology in Conflict*. Reactions to Exile in the Book of Jeremiah, BZAW 176, Berlin 1989, 203–291. Also worthy of mention is the reworking of these theories by C.J. Sharp, *Prophecy and Ideology in Jeremiah*. Struggles for Authority in the Deutero-Jeremianic Prose, London – New York 2003.

41   Cf. W. McKane, *Jeremiah*. Vol. II: Commentary on Jeremiah XXVI–LII, ICC, Edinburgh 1996, 875–877, 965–966, 971.

42   Cf. R.P. Carroll, *Jeremiah*, 641–643.

43   Amongst the various contributions in which the author confronts the thematic, one can see, in particular, M.J. de Jong, «Why Jeremiah is Not Among the Prophets: An Analysis of the Terms נביא and נביאים in the Book of Jeremiah», *JSOT* 35 (2011) 483–510 (esp. pp. 504–508); Id., «Rewriting the Past in Light of the Present: The Stories of the Prophet Jeremiah», in: *Prophecy and Prophets in Stories*. Papers Read at the Fifth Meeting of the Edinburgh Prophecy Network, Utrecht, October 2013, eds. B. Becking – H.M. Barstad, OTS 65, Leiden – Boston 2015, 64–75.

44   One of the conclusions reached by the study of M.J. de Jong, *Isaiah among the Ancient Near Eastern Prophets*. A Comparative Study of the Earliest Stages of the Isaiah Tradition and the Neo-Assyrian Prophecies, VT.S 117, Leiden – Boston 2007, is summarised as follows: "Both the Assyrian prophets and Isaiah functioned as *guardians of the state* and fiercely turned against those perceived as enemies of the state"

Thus, the historical Jeremiah would have been concerned exclusively with saving the kingdom of Judah. He would have advised acceptance of the Babylonian hegemony both for pragmatic reasons and in the name of YHWH. Thus, he would have never either foretold or desired the end of his country, as would have been expected of any officer of divination in the (direct or indirect) service of the royal power and national interests.[45] Only after the catastrophe, ascertaining the rationality of the Jeremianic option, would his words and figure have been re-evaluated, and he have been redressed in the clothes of a prophet, enemy of the (corrupt) state and proclaimer of its end caused by the sins of the people and their rulers. And thus, in order to survive in a certain geopolitical situation, the successive re-elaboration would have then linked a specific interpretation of the fall of Jerusalem to the original, simple Jeremianic message regarding the need to submit to Babylon. By this, the fall would have been caused by disobedience towards the prophet himself and divine wrath for the sins of the people, a universally diffused motif in the context of the ancient Near East.[46]

The aspect of this reconstruction that is in my opinion problematic concerns, in the first place, the intrinsic fragility of the basic methodological principles upon which literary criticism in general is founded, in relation to the scarcity of documentational evidence. On the one hand, wanting at all costs to reconnect textual contradictions or narrative tensions to a coherent overall logic may, at times, reveal itself to be inaccurate. On the other, however, it can be simplistic to prescind from the question of whether the contradictions and tensions present could actually be *just that* (and not only for the modern reader) and if they might be "resolved" (supposing that the producer[s] of the text did not intend to create an *ad hoc* effect) by turning to different sources and other ideologically oriented redactional layers. One needs to keep well in mind that a text without "tensions" would be the very negation of both narrativity and poetry.[47]

(p. 456, my italics). The ideological support ensured the royal dynasty, as the same author had already noted in the wake of the studies done by A. MALAMAT, «A Mari Prophecy and Nathan's Dynastic Oracle», in: *Prophecy. Essays Presented to Georg Fohrer on his Sixty-Fifth Birthday, 6 September 1980, ed.* J.A. EMERTON, BZAW 150, Berlin 1980, 68–82 (here, pp. 79–82), and T. ISHIDA, *The Royal Dynasties in Ancient Israel.* A Study on the Formation and Development of Royal-Dynastic Ideology, BZAW 142, Berlin 1977, 90–92, is characteristic of the *historical prophets* (to be distinguished from the figures of "classical prophets", seen as tardive literary profiles) both in Israel (cf. 2 Sam 7:5–17) and in Mari and Assyria (cf. p. 33).

45   "He neither foretold nor intended the destruction of his country. Instead, he acted as was expected of a diviner: he revealed the divine will with regard to a matter of major importance in order to provide the information necessary for the political decision-makers to act wisely to secure the common welfare" (M.J. DE JONG, «Rewriting the Past», 134).

46   Cf. *Ibid.*, 138–139.

47   See e.g. the contribution of J. DUBBINK, «Jeremiah: Hero of Faith or Defeatist? Concerning the Place and Function of Jeremiah 20.14–18», *JSOT* 86 (1999) 67–84, who argues in favour of the traceability of a theological compositive logic regarding the relationship between the curses pronounced by Jeremiah in 20:14–18 (often considered by the exegetes to be a distinct textual unit) and their immediate context (the famous passage of the Confessions of 20:7–13). In conclusion, the author notes: "Thus it appears that the depth of the book of Jeremiah is often underestimated. The book

38 General Introduction

In this particular case, in fact, aside from possible critiques[48] of the "standard" thesis of K.-F. Pohlmann that there be two counterposed redactions, the underlying assumption of M.J. de Jong would need to be verified from the exegetic point of view in order to establish if, and to what measure, one can actually speak in the book of Jeremiah of a condemnation without appeal ("irrevocable punishment") of Jerusalem and all the people, and if the figure of Jeremiah (whether literary or not) be truly (solely) that of the proclaimer of an inevitable, complete end. Could his threat not have simply been finalised just for the "well-being of the state", and thus be a special communicative form, however extreme? As the case of 26:18–19 suggests, it would seem more than legitimate to presume so.

It is not clear why, moreover, if the relationship between (human) crime and (divine) punishment were a ubiquitous hermeneutical schema of antiquity, as M.J. de Jong himself asserts, this could not itself already be innervated in the prophetic preaching of the "historic Jeremiah" regarding the necessity (in this case, also implicitly motivated) of "consignation to the king of Babylon", rather than only be a successive scribal expansion. Is it then realistic to believe that amongst all the "specialists in divination" of the time, to use the author's words once again, only for a sole figure like that of Jeremiah must the salvation of the state have needed to pragmatically pass through surrender? Without then considering that this option might already have at its origin some sort of meaning within the relational logic of the Covenant? Was it indeed really only about the fact that abandonment of the Holy City could only take place if allowed and commanded by YHWH? In short, even this interpretation of the Jeremianic message does not seem resolutive. And the *minimalist semantic* of the prophetic call to surrender that it proposes (even if it were no more than a mere successive re-elaboration) does not seem to account for the complexity and wealth of meaning of the Jeremianic tradition.

1.4.3. The ethical perspective

Setting aside questions of textual composition, another study perspective begins by taking on the book of Jeremiah in its actual form (MT) and reflecting on its prophetic message according to ethical categories. Let us consider, for example, the emblematic position taken and articulated by Daniel L. Smith,[49] who focuses on the "letter to the exiles" included in ch. 29. The text in question is a literary perimeter within which, as we will later see,[50] the Jeremianic message of surrender that was previously addressed

---

expects much from its readers and does not make it easy for them. It presupposes readers who are prepared to look beyond a one-dimension theology of a God who saves out of every need, and even beyond the image of the suffering righteous one who is given as an example for the reader. The theology of the book of Jeremiah is full of contrasts in which praise and curse keep standing beside each other, critically explain each other, but do not neutralise each other in advance" (pp. 81–82).

48 See e.g. those put forth by C. LEVIN, *Die Verheißung des neuen Bundes.* In ihrem theologiegeschichtlichen Zusammenhang ausgelegt, FRLANT 137, Göttingen 1985, 66 and R. ALBERTZ, *Israel in Exile.* The History and Literature of the Sixth Century B.C.E., SBL.SBL 3, Atlanta 2003, 308.

49 D.L. SMITH, «Jeremiah as Prophet of Nonviolent Resistance», *JSOT* 43 (1989) 95–107.

50 In ch. II, § 3.2 of the present dissertation, at least in a way that is introductory.

to the inhabitants and ruling class of Jerusalem as well as to the kingdom of Judah in general is merely adapted for other recipients and for another situation. In fact, following the exile of 597, Jeremiah calls out to the deported. He tells them to not give way to facile hopes of a rapid return home, but to accept their present situation instead: the need is "to seek" (√שׁדר) "the peace" (שָׁלוֹם: i.e. "the well-being") of Babylon and "to pray" (√פלל hitp.) for it (cf. 29:4–7).

D.L. Smith denominates this existential statute "nonviolent social resistance".[51] He emphasises that this option is all but simplistic. According to him, these indications should be reread in the light of the military context and war exemptions provided for in Deut 20 (and to also be linked with Deut 28 and Isa 65). In this sense, reusing the Deuteronomistic vocabulary, Jeremiah would be declaring a sort of "armistice" on the community of the exiled.[52] The question is thus brought back to what stance to adopt before the Babylonian power. Indeed, this is the issue at hand during the clash between Jeremiah and Hananiah in ch. 28, which I will be addressing in detail. This polemic would reflect the psychological tension and ideological clash that exists within every community reduced to the condition of being a minority subject to external power. The conflict is between those who would opt for a form of collaboration and social resistance, and those set on an explicit, violent rebellion. In the frame of this paradigmatic social context, Jeremiah would propose something quite different from pacifism (and/or cowardly behaviour) which, for example, R.P. Carroll[53] and John Bright[54] (justly) consider to be an inadmissible interpretation. The question would instead be that of the first emergence of a *non-violent* Jewish ethic, one cautious and attentive to the more appropriate strategic options with regard to socio-religious survival within a system in which they are the minority. This would be evident in the book of Daniel, in the ancient practice of the Pharisees, and in primitive Christianity.[55]

Other commentators assume this underlying ethical perspective while diversifying tonality, focuses, and hermeneutical implications. Amongst these, I will make particular note of Oliver O'Donovan, if for none other than his (not inappropriate) focus on the theme of historical events as a manifestation of the "judgment of YHWH" (and in particular, on the Davidic monarchical institution).[56] Also to be mentioned are Terence E. Fretheim who, in his monographic contribution on Jeremiah, instead raises once again the value-ethical dichotomy between violence and non-violence,[57] and the reflections of Joseph Jensen, conducted within the framework of research that focuses specifically on the ethical dimensions contained in the prophetic tradition and their impact on the formation of the conscience of Israel.[58]

---

51 D.L. Smith, «Jeremiah», 95.
52 'Jeremiah is not simply advising a settled existence, but using the Deuteronomic exemptions from warfare to declare an «armistice» on the exilic community" (D.L. Smith, «Jeremiah», 102).
53 Cf. R.P. Carroll, *From Chaos to Covenant*. Prophecy in the Book of Jeremiah, New York 1981, 275–276.
54 Cf. J. Bright, *Jeremiah*, AncB 21, Garden City 1965, cviii–cix.
55 D.L. Smith, «Jeremiah», 104.
56 Cf. O. O'Donovan, *The Desire of the Nations*. Rediscovering the Roots of Political Theology, Cambridge 1996.
57 T.E. Fretheim, *Jeremiah*, S&HBC, Macon 2002, 386–387.
58 J. Jensen, *Ethical Dimensions of the Prophets*, Collegeville 2006, 141–142.

40 General Introduction

Without entering, at least for now, the various arguments in detail, I will simply anticipate here that according to my line of interpretation, it seems inappropriate to reduce the complexity of the Jeremianic message to a merely ethical level, as if it were almost just a generic necessity of "penitence". On the other hand it is true that one is often accustomed to seeing precisely in the synthetic category of "repentance", that is, in "moral conversion", the lowest undifferentiated common denominator of almost all prophetic literature. In the book of Jeremiah in particular, this has been done significantly, for example, by John H. Walton, in a schematic synthesis about the oracular signs provided in the various prophetic books of the OT.[59] But it is precisely the specificity of the Jeremianic call to surrender to Babylon that invites going beyond this general interpretive framework of a moral nature, and in particular, that which reads into his prophetic call the promotion of an ethic of non-violence.

1.4.4. The theo-political perspective

To isolate and define another hermeneutical perspective as theo-political could seem, at a first glance, redundant or even superfluous. Indeed, no commentator sticking to the text would negate that the message of Jeremiah regards both of these dimensions simultaneously. And yet, as I have briefly mentioned, beyond making this reference to the sphere of transcendence that I could call "conventional", some interpretations truly seem to reduce the theological value of his message (even if only that of a supposed "historical Jeremiah") to a mere political-pragmatic level on which opposing party politics (whether pro-Babylonian versus pro-Egyptian, or exiled versus non-exiled) call each other into question. And these politics would be the fundamental hermeneutical key for understanding the presumed rival theological perspectives believed to be retraceable in the book of Jeremiah.[60] I am convinced, and I am not the only one, that this interpretive choice is a reductionism that does not favour an adequate interpretation of the complexity of the Jeremianic message.[61] Many other scholars, in fact, call attention to the peculiar, decisive religious dimension of the context within which the communicative event being studied is structured. And I believe that this is the right direction to take. That is, that it is right to *not* isolate the two dimensions, the political one and the theological one,[62] setting them in opposition, but rather to begin from an assumption of their mutual, indivisible relationship within the prophetic tradition.

---

59 Cf. J.H. Walton, *Ancient Near Eastern Thought and the Old Testament*. Introducing the Conceptual World of the Hebrew Bible, Grand Rapids 2006, 245–247.

60 According to the basic belief expressed by R.P. Carroll, *Jeremiah*, 104, for which "Party politics is the key to understanding these features of the book of Jeremiah".

61 Such as, e.g. J.R. Lundbom, *Jeremiah Closer Up*. The Prophet and the Book, HBM 31, Sheffield 2010, 105: "Jeremiah's theology cannot be reduce to a political viewpoint, i.e., which would be that because Jeremiah preaches subservience to Nebuchadnezzar he is 'pro-Babylonian'". And the same D.J. Reimer, referring to his previous (and already cited) contribution («Political Prophets?») recalls having claimed that "the 'political' and 'theological' are indissolubly connected in the Jeremiah tradition" (Id., «Redeeming Politics», 121).

62 Positions similar to those expressed, e.g. by A.C. Welch, *Jeremiah*, all centred on the theological dimension, do not take into due consideration the contingent aspects in which the protagonists of the Jeremianic text find themselves living and deciding.

As is programmatically expressed from the incipit of the book (cf. 1:4–19), Jeremiah unifies his ministry, and thus also his call for submission to the Babylonian power, with the prophetic authority he has received from YHWH. Hence, "consignation to the king of Babylon" and generally speaking the question of how to relate to adverse, foreign power within the context of faith in YHWH who is the Lord of history is without doubt a theo-political fact, as Walter Brueggemann efficaciously underscored.[63] Situated along the axis that ideally unites the two conceptual polarities, at differing distances and with precise, distinct accents, are the various authors who either allude to the religious and prophetic nature of the Jeremianic message in a generic sense or intend to valorise it through specific focal points. In his contribution on the topic, W. Brueggemann, for example, takes on the category of "mercy" as a core one, on the basis of a targeted selection of texts. But beyond his proposal, which draws attention to a specific theme, the questio in my view is that of understanding *in what relationship* these two dimensions, the political one and the theological one, find themselves.[64] And the issue is then to address *what modality* is most appropriate for their articulation in a study that unites a (founding) moment of an analytic-exegetic type with a (consequent) one of a synthetic theological nature. The intent of my path of inquiry fits precisely in this perspective, and I will seek to propose both an approach and a hermeneutical key attentive to multiple dimensions of meaning.

2. The principal guidelines of my working hypothesis

2.1. Beyond and within the contradictions: Revelation and the prophetic assumption of the Meaning

Focalisation of the *status quaestionis* regarding the interpretation of the Jeremianic message has clarified the diversified positions of modern commentators, some of which are in complete opposition. In a certain sense, these can simply be considered the expansion and projection along the axis of time of a hermeneutical question that is already entirely contained within the book of Jeremiah itself. Indeed, I am convinced that one of the aims of the Jeremianic work is precisely that of explicitly putting forth the question itself of the discernment of the true prophetic word. And I believe that it does so by having the reader/listener actively participate in the hermeneutical

---

63 He rightly notes that "Israel's rhetoric at the interface of God and empire is a concrete attempt to hold together the inscrutable reality of God (which is at the center of its rethought world) and the raw power of the empire (which is a daily reality of its life). Israel's self-identity, presence in the world, and chance for free action depend upon how these two are held together" (W. Brueggemann, «At the Mercy of Babylon: A Subversive Rereading of the Empire», *JBL* 110 [1991] 3–22, here, p. 4).

64 For a reflection on the dialectical essence of the concept of "theo-politics", see Y. Hoffman, «Reflections on the Relationship between Theopolitics, Prophecy and Historiography», in: *Politics and Theopolitics*, 85–99 (pp. 93–98 deal particularly with Jeremiah, expressing the belief that the genuinely and formally theo-political elements contained in the book be ascribed only to those parts in prose, and that these be likely attributable to later authors who would have, in any case, retrospectively made explicit Jeremianic ideas and positions, especially those expressed in the oracles against the nations).

42 General Introduction

dynamic through the juxtaposition of seemingly contradictory themes, narrative dramatisation, and the overall architecture of the Jeremianic work. Its twofold general arrangement (according to the MT and LXX) already makes the action of different symbolic-compositional *intentionalities* apparent.

What figure are we then to see in Jeremiah? A true prophet or a false one? A nationalist concerned with the welfare of the kingdom of Judah, or a fifth columnist being paid off for the interests of a foreign power? An astute court counsellor, or a cynical defeatist who is a danger to the morale of the soldiers sacrificing their lives to defend the City? An authoritative re-reader of the prophetic tradition and defender of divine rights within the framework of the Sinaitic Covenant, or a blasphemous destroyer of the holiest dogmas of Yahwism?

On the ("literal") semantic level, the message of Jeremiah is clear and simple: submission and/or surrender to the king of Babylon is a necessity. And yet, at the same time ("the fourth year of the reign of Jehoiakim [יְהוֹיָקִים][65]"), when the irruption of his overwhelming power is proclaimed (cf. 25:1; 36:1; 45:1; 46:2), Jeremiah announces the end of Babylon (cf. 51:59–64), which in the final oracles of the book is severely condemned (cf. 50–51:1–58). The same could be said about other important prophetic expressions that concern the kingdom of Judah and the other nations in general: there is a word of destruction and a word of reconstruction (cf. 1:10). YHWH hurts, YHWH heals (cf. 30:12–14 with 30:15–17). A promise of life and well-being (שָׁלוֹם) is addressed to every human being, but then appears to be contradicted by experiences of suffering and death (cf. 1:5 with 20:7–18; and also 4:10; 6:14; 14:19; etc.). The need to "hand oneself over to Babylon"[66] and the horizon of the end (both threatened and realised) seem to negate not only the fundamental theological category of the election of Zion and the Davidic dynasty, but also the founding event of Israel's freedom, the Exodus.

My underlying thesis is that it be possible to reconcile these formally contradictory expressions in a coherent hermeneutical framework, the structuring principle of which can be identified precisely via a more adequate rereading of the theme of the surrender to Babylon. Entering along that interpretative route that takes on the dialectic and interweaving of the political and theological dimensions as ineluctable, I believe that the Jeremianic message should be reunderstood according to its explicit *"prophetic" dimension*. It should be comprehended, in other words, according to the "claimed" *revelative valence of the Meaning of the history* of Israel and of all nations. Whilst not configured as research to be inserted primarily along the channels of those studies that have been done on the history of the text's composition, those contributions will still be borne in mind and, if necessary, discussed. My study intends therefore to question the particular *communicative nature* of the book of Jeremiah as a whole: a work in which both historical vestiges and semiotic-literary intentionality, while not being easily distinguishable from each other,[67] do coexist. And it is these aspects

---

65 For the transcription of proper names, I will abide by this rule: upon first mention, I will also present the original Hebrew, but the English will conform to the choices made in the most widespread translations.

66 From this point on, I will use this expression interchangeably with "to consign oneself". Though the latter is slightly more awkward in English, its specific meaning will reveal itself to be significant in ch. VIII.

67 Along the wavelength of a general paradigm shift that occurred in studies of biblical prophetism, namely in a "Prozess 'vom Prophetenwort zum Prophetenbuch'" (E.

The principal guidelines of my working hypothesis   43

themselves that testify to the possibility of diversified manifestations of the spirit of prophecy: that of unrepeatable, originary personal experiences, that of the disciples, that of the scribes and all the listeners who then transmit that same prophetic word. This process then engages today's reader, who is called on to participate, with their own hermeneutical act, in the same dynamism of *revelation* and prophetic *assumption* of the Meaning.

2.2. The meaning of history: What YHWH reveals, how to respond to YHWH

From what has been said thus far, the appeal of a thorough study on the theme of "consignation to the king of Babylon" seems evident to me. In addition to its recursion in the Jeremianic work and displacement in strategic points (as we shall see), it is precisely the theme's *uniqueness* within the panorama of prophetic literature that ought to attract a greater measure of attention and demand a rigorous, multidisciplinary study.

As D.J. Reimer[68] has pointed out, unlike other likewise Jeremianic themes that can be found in other books and from which the "author" of Jeremiah seems to draw, however ingeniously and creatively[69] (consider, e.g. of the attention devoted to Egypt), the theme of the surrender to Babylon has no direct terms of comparison. To explain its nature and origin, we cannot resort to other prophetic traditions, whether the minor ones or the great books of Isaiah or Ezekiel.[70] There is an entirely Jeremianic specificity that depends on the *uniqueness of the historical conjuncture*[71] (which, despite or precisely thanks to its uniqueness, will assume a paradigmatic value in several respects). This peculiarity is, in my opinion, an invitation to take the *revelatory value* of the prophetic word seriously. History is not seen as merely an anonymous, undifferentiated flow of worthless, jumbled acts and human intentionality dominated by chance. History is rather the place visited by the divine word that not only calls things into existence, but

---

ZENGER *et al.*, *Einleitung in das Alte Testament*, KStTh 1.1, Stuttgart 1995, [6]2006, 513), by which interest passed from that in (certain, presumed, or probable) historical prophets and from an attempt to identify their *ipsissima verba*, to the study of their respective "books" as literary works, at this point, studies on Jeremiah have also renounced a historicising pretence (on this topic, see the observations and bibliographic indications of L. STULMAN, *Order amid Chaos*. Jeremiah as Symbolic Tapestry, BiSe 57, Sheffield 1998, 13–19 and M. NOBILE, «Il profetismo biblico. Il dibattito su un tema ancora discusso», in: *"Ricercare la sapienza di tutti gli antichi" [Sir 39,1]*. Miscellanea in onore di Gian Luigi Prato, *eds.*, M. MILANI – M. ZAPPELLA, SRivBib 5[6], Bologna 2013, 271–283).

68   "[..] we could not explain the choices evidenced in Jeremiah by appeal to the Isaiah or Ezekiel traditions. Although the rejection of Egypt, for instance, is part of a wider political/theological movement in the Hebrew Bible and makes a contribution to an evaluation of Jeremiah, it is not sufficient to explain the precise shape of politics in Jeremiah" (D.J. REIMER, «Political Prophets?», 141).

69   Cf. G. FISCHER, «Il libro di Geremia».

70   Although, as I will point out, a certain reference for comparison can be made with the siege of Jerusalem and the discourses of the Assyrian commander (Rabshakeh) in 2 Kgs 18:13–37–19:1–37; //Isa 36–37.

71   Cf. B.O. LONG, «Social Dimensions», 45.

44 General Introduction

also establishes a relationship with a subject who is elevated to responsible partner (i.e. one capable of responding). For this reason, cosmic events, geopolitical dynamics, the vicissitudes of peoples, and the human adventures of individuals become, in the book of Jeremiah, scenarios in which the Meaning can reveal itself and solicit a response.

The gesture of surrender is to be explored as the emergence of a complex dynamic of manifestation and assumption of this meaning of history revealed by YHWH in a way that is precise, *here* and *now*. We must therefore ask ourselves anew, and on a level that is deeper still, about both the specific *content* of prophetic signification that Jeremiah (as a literary architecture and as an intradiegetic prophet) intends to impress upon the choice that all are called to make (surrender), as well as what *modalities* and *relational dynamics* are called into question through this gesture. Because in my view, the book of Jeremiah intends to configure a *relational paradigm* that tells the reader, retrospectively, not only *what* and *how* YHWH speaks within history, but also *how to respond* to YHWH and *what* needs to be signified with the concreteness of one's body in that specific temporal horizon.

2.3. The surrender as a "prophetic choice"

From the first chapter of the book, Jeremiah is presented as the paradigmatic figure of the one called to prophecy. Fundamentally, this means nothing other than that he is the figure of the human being, of every person in Israel, called to listen to and obediently receive the divine word. For this reason, what happens to him becomes meaningful for others, for his interlocutors, for all of Jerusalem. For this reason, his vocation coincides with the invitation, which gets reflected upon the reader/listener themself, to receive the discipline of prophetic discipleship. "What do you see, Jeremiah?" (cf. 1:11, 13). It is clear that this apprenticeship has, as its fundamental object, that of learning to see history and reality according to the perspective of YHWH.

The history of Israel (and, in this case, of the kingdom of Judah) is a small matter inserted in the history of the nations and the great history of the empires of that time. And yet, it is referred to in the biblical text as a story that purports to house the Lord himself of *every story*. And yet, paradoxically, the parable that we witness plummets dramatically to its conclusion. To its failure. It overflows with infidelity, falsehood, and an abuse of power. The gravity of the situation is "revealed" precisely by the fact that the injustice is hidden, lurking and breeding in the shadows of the sacred space of the Covenant rendered visible by worship at the temple, under the gaze of the Davidic dynasty, and within the reassuring nest of the theology of election and impregnability of Zion. At a certain point, prophetic threats no longer seem to suffice. And it is here that, according to my working hypothesis, right in the option of surrender to Babylon in which the threat of the end materialises, the book of Jeremiah ultimately formulates what I can for the moment call a "*prophetic choice*". Using the same grammar of the call to prophecy, this means that it signifies the *meaning of the history* taking place: the acceptance of the righteous punishment of YHWH, the recognition of one's failure, and new and unconditional faith in the Lord of history. Everything is condensed in this choice. And this choice, I believe, is proposed as an *extreme path of salvation* that exceeds both the political and sapiential dimensions. It even exceeds the *ethical imperative* so dear to the Deuteronomistic tradition.

To discern, and then choose. To accept, and decide. In other words, it is necessary to grasp and accept the meaning of history as it occurs in order to respond to YHWH, and thus choose the path of life instead of that of death. My working hypothesis is that the call to surrender to Babylon need be understood within these general hermeneutical coordinates.

3. On meaning and its complexity: Definition of the object of study and the principal methodologies of inquiry

3.1. Faced with the text

Communicating means entering into the world of meaning and its complexity. This is always irreducible, since, based on the polysemy of natural language, it is never entirely formalisable.[72] On the other hand, as was observed at the beginning of the nineteenth century by the great linguist Karl Wilhelm von Humbolt, language provides us with finite methods for infinite uses. And this renders the structural limit of the human condition itself astonishing. One discovers that the human being is equipped with a striking ability to produce and comprehend the universe of signification, in which textuality and interpretation are generated ceaselessly.

Practicing ἐξήγησις means meeting a critical need regarding texts and their meaning. Conducting biblical exegesis means attempting to give an explanation, in a methodologically coherent manner, of a meaning inscribed within a given sign system, a human product (also or above all) inserted within a specific historical-literary context. The complexity is ineludible: one can concentrate on one aspect more than another, but that dimension that always remains incumbent on the hermeneutical act cannot be dismissed. At least, this cannot be done without consequences.

Multiple elements are in reciprocal relationships: questions about origin, about the "how", the "why", the "from whom", and the "when". There are questions about the circumstances of the production and re-elaboration of the texts and their meaning (diachrony). And together, these elements address the decipherment of the linguistic code, the study of the morphology, syntax and semantic, rhetorical strategies, and countless other aspects that are inherent to the "world of the text" (synchrony).[73] This

---

72   The renowned Polish logician Alfred Tarski asserted the impossibility of elaborating a coherent semantic for the natural languages due precisely to their extreme complexity (cf. ID., *Logic, Semantics, Metamathematics*. Papers from 1923 to 1938, New York 1956, Indianapolis [2]1983, 403: "[...] it is only the semantics of formalised languages which can be constructed by exact methods"). Towards the end of the Sixties, on the other hand, with Donald Davidson and Richard Merett Montague, the possibility of arriving at a rigorous semantic theory of the natural languages is acknowledged (the so-called formal or modelistic semantic). A counterposition to this orientation was taken by the philosophers of ordinary language (latter Wittgenstein, Friedrich Waismann, John Austin, Herbert Paul Grice, Peter Strawson), giving birth to contemporary pragmatics (cf. C. BIANCHI, *Pragmatica del linguaggio*, Bari 2003, [8]2010, 12–13). Fluctuation in vocabulary and the contemporary presence of different meanings are, after all, characteristics of versatility that are essential for the development of knowledge and human interactions (cf. T. DE MAURO, *Minisemantica dei linguaggi non verbali e delle lingue*, STLa 87, Bari 1982, [10]2011, 105–106, 118–119, 133–141).

73   On the hermeneutical need for dialogue between diachronic and synchronic approaches, see e.g. H. UTZSCHNEIDER – S.A. NITSCHE, *Arbeitsbuch literaturwissenschaftliche*

46 General Introduction

complexity calls for contributions from multiple disciplines, which each have different assumptions and precomprehensions. And all these factors actually, inevitably, channel together.

This premise is necessary for a path of research that promises to be as fascinating, for the meaning that it lets us glimpse, as it is challenging, for the multiplicity of exegetic instruments and interdisciplinary insights required case-by-case, depending on the object under scrutiny. To best illustrate this, I will begin with some elementary considerations that can serve as guidelines for the necessary methodological assumptions.

3.2. A first definition of the theme: Structuring elements and significant relationships

The delineation of a theme and circumscription of autonomous, well-defined textual units within a broader communicative process is one of the responsibilities entrusted to the reader. The exegete, then, has the ulterior task of justifying these (or modifying their boundaries) with adequate methodological instruments as an obligatory path for comprehending the text's meaning.

At this stage, however, it is more opportune to simply "simulate" the *experience* of a *first reading* of the book of Jeremiah in its entirety, thus limiting ourselves to a precursory reconnaissance of the Jeremianic theme of "consignment to the king of Babylon". In doing so, I will draw forth some general indications of method. I therefore renounce providing a rigorous definition of the topic at this point, as this could not but be the result of my entire path of inquiry. I will simply attempt to give a few descriptions of it from the outside having an operative valence. For the same reason, I will postpone the use of a more technical vocabulary until a point further on, when the analytical instruments implemented will have been made explicit.

At this point, we will therefore remain at a level of empirical observation, focusing on the book segments where our theme emerges in its *most evident* form. I can thus easily isolate the following texts for now: 21:1–10; 27–28; 38:14–28a. In addition to our precomprehensions (which make any investigation of reality possible), in the act of reading, several categorical fields that contribute to the theme's denotation and connotation can be intuitively recognised (and channelled towards a unity of meaning, at least as a first interpretive hypothesis). I can make these explicit, keeping in mind that the theme of the surrender to Babylon can be traced back to some identifying aspects of both a formal type (characteristic vocabulary and phraseology) and a contenutistic type (i.e. within the narrative structure), and be studied on the basis of some fundamental relationships that are traceable according to different levels of contextual pertinence (intra- and extratextual).

I will now briefly present one (cf. Figs. 1 and 2) of the many different schematic summaries possible so that it can become clear which methodological approaches I believe to be most adequate (cf. Fig. 3) for a working hypothesis for the search for meaning untainted by a preconditioned or excessive separation of disciplinary fields.[74]

Bibelauslegung. Eine Methodenlehre zur Exegese des Alten Testaments, Gütersloh 2001, 21.

74 While an elevated degree of specialisation is indispensable for a serious scientific approach (in my case, exegetical), the risk of conducting inquiries in a way that is

On a first exploration, the theme presents itself as:

A. A phenomenon of (prophetic) *communication*. This is its fundamental dimension.[75]
B. A communication with a content (the message of surrender) that:
   a) *expresses a significance* that *reads the meaning* of history, beginning with the overall interpretive context of the book of Jeremiah: YHWH strikes his people through Nebuchadnezzar because of their infidelity
   b) *imposes a decision* (to accept this reading of history) that is to be expressed in a precise *behaviour*: to surrender (pragmatic level)

   This requested behaviour (submit-surrender) has, in turn:
   a) a meaning, both "literal" and "symbolic-prophetic" (semantic level)
   b) a salvific effect, on both the human level as well as that of the relationship with YHWH (pragmatic level)
C. A communication given within a *context*, through a *sender* (Jeremiah), for specific *recipients* in *two interrelated forms*[76]:
   a) Through the *non-verbal* channel (the *sign* of the yoke in Jer 27–28)
   b) Through the *verbal* channel (the oracular content of the Jeremianic message)
D. This is a communication that assumes a *narrative form (story)*
E. This is a narrative communication in the form of *written text*

---

excessively autonomous is not infrequent. The risk is that a scarce interest in the results obtained in disciplines that work making use of other methods and a different technical vocabulary ends up depriving that same research of important heuristic instruments.

75 The fundamental aspect that I want to highlight with this schematisation is the *communicative dimension*. Its importance is not in order to give greater or lesser relevance with respect to the other elements, but rather in the fact that it substantiates all of them according to their lowest common denominator. Text, narration, words and gestures, message, semantic level, and pragmatic effects are, after all, merely particular manifestations, in reciprocal relation, of a complex process of interaction that involves multiple elements. In the present diagram, I cite only those most immediately relevant to the identification of the methodologies I adopt for the present research.

76 I emphasise the dual modality of communication (also in the diagram following), not because the concepts of issuer, context, and recipient are less important. On the contrary, they are all essential dimensions of the communicative event. But it is the dual channel of communication that is particularly emphasised by a central text like Jer 27–28, and this suggests the need for a specific, in-depth study.

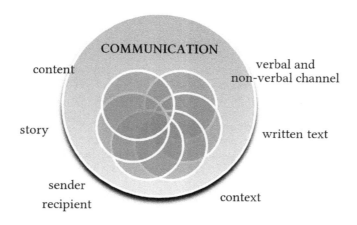

Fig. 1: The theme and its structural elements

The theme, considered as a communicative phenomenon, is part of (or insertable within) broader communicative phenomena (cf. Fig. 2) that can likewise be considered *contextual levels* of reference for different paths of interpretation:

a) The materiality of the *book* (or *books)*[77] *of Jeremiah* (MT/LXX)
b) The literary unity that the book forms can be considered, in turn, as part of the broader HB and/or OT "sign system"
c) This textual area is, in turn, inserted or insertable (from the point of view of a figural type of biblical theology),[78] within the broader *Bible/Holy Scriptures* "system",

---

77 Cf. K. SCHMID, «Schrift und Schriftmetaphorik in der Prophetie des Jeremiabuches», in: *Metatexte. Erzählungen von schrifttragenden Artefakten in der alttestamentlichen und mittelalterlichen Literatur*, eds. F.-E. FOCKEN – M.R. OTT, MTK 15, Berlin – Boston 2016, 123–144.

78 I am referring to the teleological (or typological) model of figural (or structural) exegetics elaborated by Paul Beauchamp, in which the instance of the "fulfilment" of the Scriptures (elicited from within itself), together with the idea of "totality" and "rereading/recapitulation" ("deuterosis"), substantiates the interpretive act, which is thus placed in continuity with the spirit of patristic (and medieval) exegetics. See P. BEAUCHAMP, *L'un et l'autre Testament. Essai de lecture*, Paris 1976; ID., *Le récit, la lettre et le corps. Essais bibliques*, CFi 114, Paris 1982, ²1992; ID., *L'un et l'autre Testament. 2. Accomplir les Écritures*, Paris 1990. For a summary of his proposal of biblical theology: ID., «Théologie biblique», in: *Initiation à la pratique de la théologie*. I: Introduction, eds. B. LAURET – F. REFOULÉ, Paris 1982, 189–237; ID., «Accomplir les Écritures. Un chemin de théologie biblique», *RB* 99 (1992) 132–162; ID., «Lecture christique de l'Ancien Testament», *Bib.* 81 (2000) 105–115. Here in particular, I refer to the concept of "récit totale" (cf. *L'un et l'autre Testament. 2*, 225) by which, in a theologically oriented comprehension of Scripture, as it is accepted and believed in the ecclesial setting, from Genesis to Revelation a single great narrative is unravelled as it strives towards its Christological fulfilment.

hermeneutically understood as a "récit totale", including the NT "system" and having the "Christ event" as its culmination and decisive key to interpretation
d) The entirety (or the single parts) is insertable within a context that is even more general (even if of a different nature), that is, the historical horizon, reconstructible starting from the totality of extrabiblical documentation

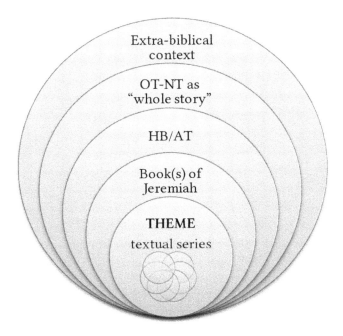

Fig. 2: The theme and the different contextual areas

The entirety of that which we can already define as a *system of signic relationships* (the theme in its structuring elements, which are in a reciprocal relationship) can be placed in relation with other "signic systems" (some of which have just been introduced), according to other fundamental guidelines (cf. Fig. 3). I can thus highlight:

A. The text's relationship with the *historical dimension*, which can be broken down into:
   a) The history of the composition of the text (diachronic approach)
   b) The question of the historicity of the information provided by the text (both in reference to extrabiblical data, for its verification, and in order to attempt to reconstruct a plausible historical context)
B. The relationship, of an *exclusively literary nature*, of the fragment with the entirety seen as an organically given whole (synchronic approach). That is, the relationship between the text (understood as a textual series containing the theme) and the text of the book of Jeremiah, which can, in turn, be considered in relationship to:
   a) the HB/OT (and potentially, intertestamental literature)
   b) the totality of the Bible/Sacred Scriptures understood as a "récit totale"

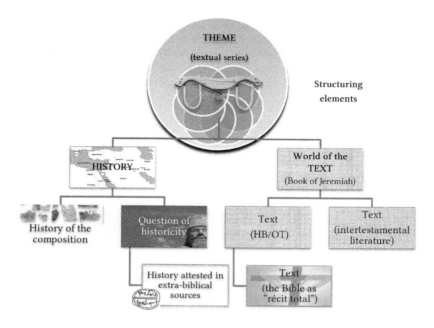

Fig. 3: The theme in relation to some fundamental hermeneutical dimensions

3.3. Implications: Research paths and general notes on method

On the basis of the structuring elements that emerge from the literary presentation of the theme and in reference to the textual or extratextual dimensions with which I believe a fruitful hermeneutical relationship can be established, I will now briefly present the paths of research and methodological approaches that I intend to follow. My challenge lies in developing an *ad hoc* methodological system that can enable the various disciplines to which I will refer to establish a fruitful dialogue between them in order to gain a better comprehension of the meaning.

3.3.1. Text, history, and the world of the text

The theme of the surrender to Babylon traced in the textual series indicated can be studied according to *two fundamental directives* (cf. Fig. 3). While from a methodological point of view these may be distinct, I believe that they can be articulated in a way that will prove fruitful for my research.

1) One way of reading the text, which then coincides with the very birth of exegetics itself as a scientific discipline, consists in drawing an interrogative relationship with the *historical dimension*. This can be done on at least two principal levels. The first, classical level regards, above all, the question of the history of the text's composition.[79]

---

79 This concerns, more precisely, the *pre*history and the literary genesis of the biblical texts (at least the major part of which), conceived as the outcome of numerous

On meaning and its complexity 51

The second, instead, presents the problem of the relationship between the historical facts contained within the text and the succession of events contemporary to it that can be traced following the methodologies of the historical-archaeological sciences. I hasten to state that the objective of my research is not that of providing and testing a new hypothesis of *Redaktionskritik* (and/or of *Redaktionsgeschichte*). I will certainly take into account, when necessary, the contributions and propositions of scholars in this field. But I will engage with this methodological perspective chiefly on the level of its epistemological foundations (above all, in relation to the overall compositional dynamic of the book of Jeremiah; cf. ch. II, § 1.2) and will only indirectly – almost as a consequence of the exegetical analysis – address some specific problematics and specific textual areas.

The theme of the surrender to Babylon assumes eminently political implications and is located in a context of international conflicts, to which the book of Jeremiah provides an interesting set of coordinates. For precisely this reason, I must dedicate a congruous space to the question of the relationship between the text and the historical references. The issues of whether the option of "surrender" was or was not practicable and advantageous within the geopolitical framework of the Babylonian hegemonic ambitions, by whom and why it was sustained or opposed within the establishment of the kingdom of Judah, and whether or not it made political sense, need to be addressed. In my opinion, all of these questions are by no means trivial for comprehension of the text/theme.

It will be necessary to consult extrabiblical sources from the ancient Near East and specialised studies about these, to form conjectures about dates and wartime scenarios, to attempt to intuit political and military strategies, and to formulate hypotheses on the meaning of the events and decisions of the people at the time. As we will see, the current *trend* of Jeremianic studies seems to judge such an approach, which was until recently preponderant, as being on the par with a somewhat *vintage* catwalk. Georg Fischer, for example, considers it to be undermined by its intrinsic impossibility of attaining certain results. And whilst considering the question of historicity entirely legitimate, he excludes it from his commentary.[80]

Aware of the limits of this approach (which I will, in any case, frame in a coherent interpretive proposition of my own), I remain, however, convinced that an attempt to provide a plausible reconstruction of the historical (socio-politico-religious) context, by having the facts offered by the book of Jeremiah interact with the document-based acquisitions available and the relative interpretive hypotheses, is important for an adequate understanding of my object of inquiry. I will seek to specify the meaning,

---

redactions, rereadings, and subsequent reworkings (cf. C. NIHAN, «L'analyse rédactionnelle», *Manuel d'exégèse de l'Ancien Testament*, ed. M. BAUKS – C. NIHAN, MoBi 61, Genève 2008, 137–189, here 137–138).

80 Cf. G. FISCHER, *Jeremia 1–25*, HThKAT, Freiburg im Breisgau 2005, 39; ID., *Jeremia. Der Stand der theologischen Diskussion*, Darmstadt 2007, 113–130 (esp. p. 117: "Unabhängig davon [the reference is to the author's own perplexity regarding this approach], und das sei eigens betont, bleibt die Frage der Historizität offen"). For the same reason, his comment remains coherently on the level of literary analysis and does not have the traditional, classic historicistic configuration typical of the German mould, often marked, if not exclusively, with the exception of some recent shifts, by an interest in matters of *Redaktionsgeschichte*.

52 General Introduction

modalities, and results of this path in the chapter where I specifically deal with the question, which will be, in any case, propaedeutic to my interpretive proposition, articulated to the historical dimension but situated prevalently on a literary and linguistic level.

2) Another legitimate hermeneutical option, upon which the central part of my dissertation is founded, consists in privileging a literary dimension of the *synchronic* sort.[81] This involves studying the theme in relation to the entire book of Jeremiah assumed as a narrative context (or scenario)[82] of a symbolical-theological type constructed *a posteriori* by its (author or) authors. In this case, I will speak of the "*world of the text*", to wit, of a coherent hermeneutical horizon resulting from a unity of meaning that can be analysed remaining on the level of its internal structural relationships, also in relation to the broader context of Old-Testamentary literature[83] (and/or inter-testamentary, and/or the entire corpus of biblical writings).

The world of the text is thus definable, in more precise terms, as a "possible world".[84] It is a universe whose laws, logical structures, and internal organisation can certainly coincide with our concept of reality or with historical-archaeological reconstructions of a given time (such as that acting as a background to the Jeremianic message). But they can also differ from this, both in part or completely, without losing coherency of meaning, for this reason.[85] It is precisely this coherence, postulated by the material

---

81 This affirmation serves more than anything else to distinguish the two approaches conceptually, since it is in fact impossible to derogate entirely from the historical dimension, even if wanting to remain on a purely linguistical-literary level. This is so if for no other reason than the fact that the code that transmits the meaning to be interpreted is that of a language from the past, whose semantics need to be attained through a technical-hermeneutical proficiency related to its world, a cultural universe whose distance from our own is determined also, or above all, by the temporal factor.

82 This involves hermeneutical categories that are acquired during studies of narrative analysis, such as: contract of reading, narrator, author (Model and empirical), reader (Model and empirical), fabula, plot, dialogues, narrative mode (telling), scenic mode (showing), and many others that I will define only when necessary. One can already observe, however, that the individual texts or individual pericopes in which the theme can be discerned certainly have a temporal coherence, but this local linearity is often times contradicted by abrupt and apparently unmotivated transitions. The entire book of Jeremiah then, while containing vast sections in prose and individual stories, hosts other portions ascribable in a certain sense to the "poetic" genre, and does not seem to present itself, in its complexity, as (only) a coherent narrative.

83 This is e.g. the methodological approach behind the great commentary by G. Fischer (cf. ID., *Jeremia 1–25*; ID., *Jeremia 26–52*, HThKAT, Freiburg im Breisgau 2005).

84 On this concept applied to the creative force of literary texts, see J. LYONS, *Semantics*, Cambridge 1977, 161–167; U. ECO, *Lector in Fabula. La cooperazione interpretativa nei testi narrativi*, TasB 27, Milano 1979, [10]2006; 122–173; T. ALBALADEJO, *Teoría de los mundos posibles y macroestructura narrativa. Análisis de las novelas cortas de Clarín*, Alicante 1986 (considerations examined in further depth in: ID., *Semántica de la narración. La ficción realista*, Madrid 1992); L. DOLEŽEL, *Heterocosmica. Fiction and Possible Worlds*, Baltimore – London 1998; L. VITACOLONNA, *Per un paradigma semiotico del testo*, Chieti 1989, 17–47; ID., «Los textos literarios como mundos posibles», *CEsL* 16 (1991) 189–212.

85 Cf. J. LYONS, *Semantics*, 167: "Statements or propositions, which might be held to be contradictory, or absurd, in a more or less scientific discussion of the physical world

On meaning and its complexity 53

unity of the book itself, that provides the manoeuvring space for this sort of exegetic analysis. Despite the polysemic nature of the literary texts (not to be confused with the concept of ambiguity) and contrary to the deconstructionist theories that dissolve the *intentio operis* within the infinite range of possible interpretations on the part of the single readers,[86] I believe, along with Umberto Eco, that a proposition of meaning[87] can be put forth and subjected to verification beginning right from a study of the text's own internal articulations.

In this case as well, the necessary elaborations and reference to the most significant contributions will be presented in the part of the dissertation where I will make use of the pertinent conceptual instrumentations. Here, it suffices to state that the hermeneutical approaches I will apply to the literary dimension (and proceed to explicate in the paragraphs following) are those that substantiate the epistemological skeleton of the entire work. This methodological sort of foundation is opportune not only because the historical reconstruction will be followed by the central part of the study, which is dedicated to a series of precise textual analyses, but also because that very same focalisation of the extratextual context, obtained from the confrontation and interweaving of the extrabiblical facts with those derived from the book of Jeremiah, will then be taken on as a particular (or possible) con-textual extension of reference (a sort of pragmatic context or "widened text of reference"), endowed with its own interpretative autonomy. And in the light of this, I will then be able to re-comprehend the theme of the surrender to Babylon. What will be important is to maintain as clear and distinct the various levels of reference to the different textual units (theme-text of the book of Jeremiah/other texts; theme-historical reconstruction/broader context), so as to be able to correctly identify the specific relevance of every consideration in merit.

3.3.2. *Communicative phenomenon and communication theory*

On the basis of the foregoing considerations, and thus placing us distinctly within the realm of the literary approach, I will now return to the first reconnaissance of the

---

      may be regarded as perfectly acceptable in a mythological or religious context, in poetry, in the narration of a dream, or in science fiction."

86   Consider the extreme positions taken by Jacques Derrida (and by the Yale Critics) and the absolute "empire" of the reader postulated by the approach of Reader-response criticism (cf. M. FERRARIS, *La svolta testuale*. Il decostruzionismo in Derrida, Lyotard e gli "Yale Critics", Milano 1986).

87   "The reader's initiative consists in making a conjecture about the *intentio operis*. This conjecture must be approved by the entirety of the text as wholly organic. This does not mean that one and only one conjecture can be made on a text. In principle, an endless number can be made. But in the end, the conjectures will be tested by the text's coherence, and the textual coherence cannot but disapprove of certain rash conjectures" (translated from U. Eco, *I limiti dell'interpretazione*, Milano 1990, 34. As in this case, where an official translation has not been available, I have provided a translation myself). Obviously, as U. Eco himself highlights, defending this principle of interpretability ("interpretanza") presupposes a close connection (i.e. a fruitful hermeneutical circle) between the *intentio operis* and the *intentiones lectoris* (cf. *Ibid.*, 38).

54 General Introduction

theme, which now proves to be situated clearly within precisely that interpretative track, distinct, but not alternative, and indeed, articulable to that of a historical kind.

The nature of the structuring elements identified and, in particular, the fact of having highlighted the (prophetic) *communicative dimension* in reference to my theme (cf. Fig. 1), already implies being positioned within the literary work and accepting its rules. Indeed, what we are dealing with is, first and foremost, a text. We do not have an observable communicative event before us, but rather a literary representation in which a *man* communicates a *message* to some *recipients*. It hardly matters, though, that this man is defined as a *prophet* (Jeremiah) who purports to speak in the name of a *deity* (YHWH) who asks for *obedience*. At least from a methodological point of view. At least at first instance.

An all-encompassing anthropological phenomenon of the human being is, in fact, in play: that of *communication*. This is a dimension that has in turn its own rules and dynamisms, in which the particulars of the written text are clearly included. This evidence is often overlooked as being so obvious that it risks, in exegetic use, being treated or implicated in a way that is almost *naïf*, without the interdisciplinary contribution that sector studies can provide in support of the specific and traditional (or not) exegetical methodologies. It therefore seems appropriate to read the theme in relation to the science called *communication theory*. In this way, the customary exegetical instruments can better grasp the theme's semantic (and pragmatic) density.

If the first inquiries into communicative phenomenon date back to ancient Greece (with Plato's Cratylus and Aristotle's *Perí hermeneías*), it is only from the second half of the twentieth century that this interest has gradually assumed a scientific status. It is a very broad field of study, afferent to different disciplines,[88] each of which has elaborated its own paradigms and different definitions of the concept of "communication". For this reason, it is actually preferable to speak in the plural of "communication theories"[89] that are concerned with what appears like a variegated mosaic.[90]

---

88   Albeit at times in a rather eclectic way, this can involve philosophy, sociology, pedagogy, mathematics, engineering, economics, politics, statistics, aesthetics, ethics, law, etc. (cf. D. GRONOWSKI, *Introduzione alla teoria della comunicazione,* Roma 2010, 7).

89   Given the vast amount of literature on the subject, I point out only some contributions of reference important for the present work, according to different perspectives of inquiry, such as the series of articles contained in B. DERVIN *et al.,* eds., *Rethinking Communication.* Volume 1: Paradigm Issues, Thousand Oaks 1989; P. COBLEY, *ed., The Communication Theory Reader,* New York 1996; S. GENSINI – F. CIMATTI, *eds., Manuale della comunicazione.* Modelli semiotici, linguaggi, pratiche testuali, Roma 1999; L. ANOLLI, *ed., Psicologia della comunicazione,* Strumenti, Bologna 2000; P. COBLEY *et al., Communication Theories,* London 2006; the entries (those relevant to our topic, given the ample interdisciplinary array of the collections) by W. DONSBACH, *ed., International Encyclopedia of Communication,* Oxford 2008; S.W. LITTLEJOHN – K.A. FOSS, *Encyclopedia of Communication Theory,* Thousand Oaks 2009. For an initial orientation, see E. GRIFFIN, *A First Look at Communication Theory,* New York 1991, [8]2012; for an excellent introduction to the specificity of the discipline, with a detailed overview of its multiple theoretical variations (from the most classic to the most recent) and of their reciprocal interconnections, see S.W. LITTLEJOHN – K.A. FOSS, *Theories of Human Communication,* Belmont 1981, [10]2011 (with an impressive updated bibliography). A useful reference is also R. WEST – L.H. TURNER, *Introducing Communication Theory.* Analysis and Application, New York 2000, [4]2010.

90   Cf. J.T. WOOD, *Communication Mosaics.* An Introduction to the Field of Communication, Boston 2006, [6]2011, 5: "Communication is an intricate mosaic composed of basic

3.3.3. The world of the text as a world of signs (and symbols)

According to the metamodel elaborated by Robert T. Craig,[91] seven principal theoretical traditions can be identified in the vast field of communication studies, whose reciprocal relation is both of complementarity and of dialectical tension: the rhetorical, semiotic, phenomenological, cybernetic, socio-psychological, socio-cultural, and critical traditions.

Having highlighted in my theme, amongst other things, the interpenetration between the narrative dimension and a dynamism of interaction founded upon the exchange of signs (typical of both verbal and non-verbal language), I will direct our attention initially, though not exclusively, to the *semiotic tradition*. My interest is not so much in its "generative" or "structural" development,[92] however (if not for some occasional foray), but rather in its "interpretive" development, aimed at the texts' comprehension.[93] My choice is more operational than theoretical, aware that, even within this address, diversified and not homogeneous schools and tendencies have developed. In other words, I basically share the methodology adopted by the semiotician Ugo Volli in his presentation of a series of conceptual instruments useful for textual analysis:

> The non-trivial challenge underlying this choice is that these different concepts not be related to the conceptual *systems* of their authors, but that their analytical validity hold, even in the absence of the large theoretical assumptions that have influenced their formation, because from our point of view they are effective models for finding and describing *different levels of articulation actually present in the texts*.[94]

> processes and skills that are relevant to the range of situations in which we interact. In any particular context, some aspects of communication stand out, and others are subdued [...] as a mosaic made up of different tiles whose appearance varies by context."

91 Cf. R.T. CRAIG, «Communication Theory as a Field», *ComT* 9 (1999) 119–161; R.T. CRAIG – H.L. MULLER, *Theorizing Communication*. Readings Across Traditions, London 2007. See also J.A. ANDERSON, *Communication Theory*. Epistemological Foundations, New York 1996. For a general overview of their definitions of communication, the inherent problems they propose to address, and their metavocabulary, see also S.W. LITTLEJOHN – K. A. FOSS, *Theories*, 33–62.

92 This trend is marked by the founding contribution of the Swiss linguist Ferdinand de Saussure, and the further contributions of Louis Hjelmslev, the anthropologist Claude Lévi-Strauss, and the semiologist Algirdas J. Greimas.

93 Developed beginning with works by Charles Sanders Peirce and Umberto Eco. For a brief overview of the relationship between semiotics and biblical studies, see L. PANIER, «Semiotica e studi biblici. Evoluzioni metodologiche e prospettive epistemologiche», in: *Destini del sacro. Discorso religioso e semiotica della cultura*, eds. N. DUSI – A. MARRONE, Meltemi.Edu 115, Roma 2008, 11–25.

94 Translated from U. VOLLI, *Manuale di semiotica*, MBa 13, Bari 2000, ⁶2007, x: "La scommessa non banale sottostante a questa scelta è che questi diversi concetti non siano legati ai *sistemi* concettuali dei loro autori, ma che la loro validità analitica regga anche in assenza delle grandi assunzioni teoriche che ne hanno condizionato la formazione, perché dal nostro punto di vista essi sono modelli efficaci per reperire e descrivere *diversi livelli di articolazione effettivamente presenti nei testi*."

In accordance with this hermeneutical perspective, I will resume from an awareness of what every text *is*: interweaving, *textum* (from the Latin *texere* "intertwine"), that is "that which communicates something with a system of signs" and which, through juxtaposition or coordination between several units, determines complex intertextual webs.[95] I will not, however, stop at only "the totality of the linguistic characters organised within the writing".[96] I instead aim for the world of complex signic and symbolic references that, beginning with this system, move forward composing and structuring bit by bit before the reader's eyes. These references engage and provoke an intelligent reading, to wit, one that can read *intus*, within, as well as *beyond* the mere literality of the text. A text assumed as a symbolic fact is perceived as being inhabited by an analogical tension that pushes, thanks to the letter (and within the letter), beyond itself towards an extralinguistic dimension that arises at the boundary "between language and life".[97]

The world of signs and symbols has had and continues to have its explorers, its already charted courses, and ever-operative construction sites. A confrontation with these coordinates, and integration of some of their hermeneutical models will inspire my exegetic analysis in various ways. My aim will be to highlight some of the most important semiotic-symbolic interactions contained in the book of Jeremiah, which I adopt as *a single* world structured and inhabited by a complex set of signs or symbolic systems that relate to one another on multiple levels. In other words, I consider it to be a literary work that is the fruit of an extraordinary creative capacity. In this respect, the fact that the theme of the submission to Babylon is plastically announced with a provocative "symbolic gesture" in Jer 27–28 assumes, from my point of view, a very important relevance, which will open the way for my research towards a focalisation of a complex dynamism of signic references within which my theme will acquire a distinctive valence of meaning.

3.3.4. *A passageway beyond semantics: The pragmatic dimension of language as interaction between words and the world*

What has just been asserted about the excess of symbolic dynamism with respect to the mere textual fact, which orients the fulfilment of the interpretive act *beyond the "letter"*, is actually valid in a certain sense even before and in a way that is more radical for the linguistic tool itself and for the way in which, communicating, we produce and comprehend meanings. Indeed, there are cases in which it is clear that mere knowledge of a language's semantic conventions is not sufficient for correctly understanding the meaning of a sentence. It is necessary, in other words, to pass beyond the traditional semantic paradigm, which identifies the meaning with the truth-conditions of the sentence in question. I will clarify the meaning of this affirmation by introducing another

---

95   Cf. G. AICHELE, *Sign, Text, Scripture*. Semiotics and the Bible, Sheffield 1997, 99–105.

96   G. FERRONI, *Profilo storico della letteratura italiana,* vol. I, Milano 1992, xiv.

97   Obviously, the delicate question of the definition and distinction between the concepts of sign, analogy, symbol, and metaphor remains to be addressed. In this regard, I will interact with the most recent developments and with the reflections of philosophical hermeneutics elaborated by Paul Ricœur in relation to the symbolic phenomenon. The reference here is to P. RICŒUR, «Parole et symbole», *RevSR* 49 (1975) 142–161 (p. 153).

On meaning and its complexity 57

important branch of studies of human communication that can be either situated within or straddle across the socio-cultural tradition (ethnomethodology)[98]: *cognitive pragmatics,* and, in particular, the *Relevance Theory.*[99]

My brief analysis of the structuring elements of the theme of the surrender to Babylon (cf. Fig. 1) presented the general dimension of "communication" as their basic common foundation. It was then necessary to anticipate certain categorical differentiations, such as that between the *semantic* level and the *pragmatic* one. It is now opportune to succinctly clarify the epistemological foundations of these. I will interpret them in the light of the aforementioned contemporary perspective of the philosophy of language.

According to the classic model that has been handed down to us from Aristotle, to communicate means to be able to encode and decode messages. The assumption is that there be a correspondence between mental representations (concepts, thoughts, etc.) and linguistic signs (words, utterances, etc.). This *code* model has been passed down through the centuries substantially unchanged. In recent times, thanks to the contributions of the British philosopher and linguist Herbert Paul Grice,[100] the so-called *inferential model* has been counterposed (or, for the new and the post-Gricean, associated) to it. According to this perspective, the act of communicating and comprehending is not reducible to a system of codification or decodification of data, but rather always implies a process of manifestation, attribution, and recognition of *intentions,* starting from a series of clues, of both a linguistic and *extralinguistic* nature, provided by either the speaker or the context of reference. Human communication, therefore, always entails an inferential process (of an abductive sort),[101] with relative evaluation, confirmation, or falsification of interpretive hypotheses. In other words, for the hermeneutical act, it is necessary to attribute a decisive importance to the *pragmatic* dimension based on the language's *context of use,* opening a passageway that goes beyond the traditional semantic paradigm, by which what is instead fundamental is the conventional meaning of a linguistic nature (with only a limited pragmatic share being derived from deictic elements that generate a semantic underdetermination),[102]

---

98 Cf. S.W. LITTLEJOHN – K.A. FOSS, *Theories,* 164–169.

99 I orient myself in this field mainly thanks to the studies by D. SPERBER – D. WILSON, *Relevance.* Communication and Cognition, Oxford 1986, [2]1995; C. BIANCHI, *Pragmatica del linguaggio;* ID., *Pragmatica cognitiva. I meccanismi della comunicazione,* ML 273, Bari 2009; S.C. LEVINSON, *Presumptive Meanings.* The Theory of Generalized Conversational Implicature, Cambridge 2000; R. CARSTON, *Thoughts and Utterances. The Pragmatics of Explicit Communication,* Oxford 2002.

100 The most important contributions were assembled in H.P. GRICE, *Studies in the Way of Words,* Cambridge 1989; ID., *The Conception of Value,* Oxford 1991; ID., *Aspects of Reason,* eds. B. HALE – C. WRIGHT, Oxford 2001.

101 While *deductive reasoning* draws a sure conclusion from a rule that is likewise certain (but this, in and of itself, does not advance knowledge, since the result is already implicit in the premises) and *inductive logic* attempts to trace back to a (unknown) general rule starting from an isolated (known) phenomenon (case), with *abduction* (according to C.S. Peirce), the present case is connected by a hypothetical route to a rule and result that are well known and certain. Wherever a true interpretive act is in process, there is abduction, that is, a "gamble" that requires field testing. Often however, due to objective limitations, we must settle for a greater or lesser degree of plausibility (cf. U. VOLLI, *Semiotica,* 138–141).

102 For a summary of the components of this traditional paradigm, see C. BIANCHI, *La dipendenza contestuale.* Per una teoria pragmatica del significato, Napoli 2001, 71.

58   General Introduction

Syntax, semantics, and pragmatics are the three great classical disciplinary subdivisions of interest to linguistics[103] (apart from phonology, morphology, and lexicology). Syntax regards the study of the correct modalities through which linguistic expressions can interface amongst themselves, according to a purely grammatical perspective independent from the significance. Semantics, instead, regards the significance of words or phrases in relation to objects in the world. Pragmatics has long been defined negatively as the receptacle of every sort of linguistic anomaly that is unresolvable from a syntactic or semantic point of view,[104] or is identified with the phenomena of *deixis* or *indexicality*. But seen in a more positive light, pragmatics can be defined as

> the study of the relations between signs and speakers, between linguistic expressions and those who make use of them to communicate thoughts, [...] the study of the ways in which it is possible to use sentences in concrete situations. In other words, while syntax studies the combinatorial apparatus of the expressions of a language, and semantic the interpretive apparatus, pragmatics deals with how a speaker makes use of the combinatorial and interpretive apparatuses within a specific communicative situation.[105]

When, for example, Jeremiah asks besieged Jerusalem, in the person of the king Zedekiah, to surrender to the generals of the Babylonian sovereign as the only guarantee of survival (cf. 38:14–28a), it is only by way of the focalisation of the "context/occasion of use",[106] and therefore through the ascertainment of the relevant clues strategically disseminated in significant points of the book, that we can infer a correct interpretation of the prophetic word with the most adequate degree of approximation (given, in any case, the temporal distance and specificity of a written communication). In this way, as we shall see, it will be possible to avoid confining the Jeremianic message within a solely political plan and to not reduce it to a stance that is ultimately utterly arbitrary or anecdotal.

Therefore, in order to understand what that request in that specific context was meant to signify, it is necessary, in my opinion, for us to not limit ourselves to an analysis of a semantic sort, but rather implement one that is also pragmatic. This because, as can be observed, the literary form in which the theme of the surrender to Babylon is developed in the book of Jeremiah is that of the narrative register, and this

---

103   Cf. C. BIANCHI, *Pragmatica del linguaggio*, 4–7.
104   Such as deixis, irony, metaphor, et cetera.
105   Translated from C. BIANCHI, *Pragmatica del linguaggio*, 6–7: "[...] lo studio delle relazioni fra segni e parlanti, fra espressioni linguistiche e coloro che se ne servono per comunicare pensieri, [...] lo studio dei modi in cui è possibile usare le frasi in situazioni concrete. In altri termini, mentre la sintassi studia l'apparato combinatorio delle espressioni di un lingua, e la semantica l'apparato interpretativo, la pragmatica si occupa di come un parlante si serva degli apparati combinatorio e interpretativo in una particolare situazione comunicativa."
106   Cf. *Ibid.*, 19–20: "The conventional meaning of an utterance, in absence of the particular occasion of its use, determines, in a way that is incomplete, the conditions of truth of that utterance: the meaning of a linguistic expression depends on the *use* made of the expression – it depends on what one wants to do with that expression. This is the *pragmatic dimension* of language."

On meaning and its complexity 59

is always articulated – and significatively so – as a *conversational context.*[107] By this, it is apparent, in my opinion, that this is one of the clearer cases in which, to gain the ultimate truth of the meaning, syntax and semantics are insufficient. In other words, it will be necessary to take other knowledge into account. And this knowledge, perhaps implicit, regards the "world" and not only language. For "world", or extralinguistic context, it is necessary to understand (and articulate) both its historical representation or reconstruction, and that which is defined on a literary level by the creative force of the author(s) of the book of Jeremiah. In this sense, we need to consider, as a virtually pragmatic and in a broader sense extratextual space, all the data and thematic references (useful for defining a pertinent interpretive context) that are situated beyond the limits of the single pericopes explicitly circumscribing the Jeremianic injunction to "surrender to the king of Babylon".

Thus far, I have nevertheless introduced only one of the paths of research of meaning involved in the pragmatic dimension of language: the *influence of the context* (or world) *on the word.* No less important and, on the contrary, in many ways decisive for the comprehension of my topic, is a second essential aspect: the *influence of the word on the context,* or, put another way, the force that the communication has on the re-creation of reality.[108] Indeed, it will not suffice to ask ourselves what the act requested by Jeremiah consists in or signifies per se. We must likewise ask, from the point of view of exegetic analysis, what impact that same request had (or had wanted to have)[109] on his listeners, and what consequences (salvific in the fullest sense) had been guaranteed for those who decided to freely obey his word by going out and handing themselves over to the generals of the king of Babylon.[110]

The methodological perspective to be implemented will, in this case, be that which regards the performative dimension of language, studied by John Austin in particular, and revised by John Searle. Language is not, in fact, only an instrument for communicating something about reality; it also has an impact *on that reality* itself. Initially, J. Austin's theory of linguistic acts distinguished between statements having descriptive importance and those having a performative force, for which the truth/falsehood

---

107 I emphasise this point because when it is time (in regard to the study of 38:14–28a in ch. V), I will also need to introduce the category of "conversational implicatures", which contribute to clarify the pragmatic framework within which the request for surrender is placed in the book of Jeremiah.

108 C. Bianchi summarises the two complementary dimensions of the pragmatic theory thus: "1) on the one hand, it deals with the influence the context has on the word: the interpretation of language must take into account information about the situation of the discourse, and therefore, the world; 2) on the other hand, it studies the influence the word has on the context; speakers make use of language to modify the situation of the discourse, particularly to influence the beliefs and actions of their interlocutors". ID., *Pragmatica del linguaggio,* 11.

109 The question is, yet again, one that is both historic as well as merely literary (i.e. verifiable according to the clues offered by the book of Jeremiah itself).

110 These salvific effects, as we will see, are anticipated in a paradigmatic way in the events concerning the prophetic body and in the figures of Baruch and Ebed-melech. Cf. E. CHAUTY, *Qui aura sa vie comme butin?* Échos narratifs et révélation dans la lecture des oracles personnels de Jérémie, BZAW 519, Berlin 2020, 205–206, 225–226.

criterion has no relevance. In his latter university lectures,[111] however, the American philosopher then recognises an illocutionary force in every sort of utterance, which can be explicit or implicit. By integrating the perspective of analytical philosophy in this way, the attention on language shifts from its descriptive function to its performative efficacy.

This methodological direction, however, in my view, ought not to be limited to verbal language. It should *be extended to the communicative microcosm of non-verbal language*, a dimension that is central to my topic, albeit necessarily taken up in its narrative form. With the prophetic call to surrender, in fact, in addition to the propositional level of communicative exchanges (and to the expressive one), another fundamental function of human communication is called into question: the *relational function*. In other words, it must be borne in mind that the act of communicating involves a number of diverse relational modalities of the participants in the communicative event. And in this "total communication", along with the verbal dimension, the bodies themselves of the communicator (the prophet) and the recipients (the actants) are elevated to become interactive corporeal enunciations. Indeed, it is within this horizon that the drama of the Covenant and the destiny of Jerusalem in the face of the historical emergency brought on by the Babylonian hegemony and military offensive play out.

3.3.5. *A pragmatic revisitation of the notion of "context"*

It should be self-evident that a rigorous study of biblical texts must be founded and measured against a contextualisation of the linguistic data and extralinguistic references contained within these. But this is not always the case. Often, in fact, the extensional (or denotive) determination of the term "context" to which different scholars refer is not clear in the least, given that prior in-depth reflection is rarely dedicated to it. The risk is that the notion of "context" underlying exegetic analyses be conceived in a way that is static, or worse yet, in reference to a horizon of meaning that has been arbitrarily predetermined by the interpreter but not made explicit to the reader. And yet, invariably, it will be precisely the contextual background and not only the method employed that will determine the results of the interpretive act.

Well known in this regard, and ever relevant, are the severe criticisms directed by James Barr at the methodological assumptions upon which many modern philological and lexicographical research projects in the biblical field are founded.[112] The way in which these, for example, resort to etymologies and comparative linguistics can often risk being misleading for correct comprehension of the lexemes.

In counterposition to the traditional truth-conditional paradigm (the so-called "code model"), contextualistic contributions of a pragmatic-cognitive matrix instead emphasise that the semantic is dependent, in a binding sense, upon the real contexts of use of the speakers (or writers). It is worth emphasising, along with Luigi Anolli, that there is in other terms no embedded linguistic meaning in words that would be

---

111 Collected in J.O. URMSON – M. SBISÀ, *eds., How To Do Things With Words*. The William James Lectures delivered at Harvard University in 1955, Cambridge 1962, ²1975.
112 See chiefly J. BARR, *The Semantics of Biblical Language*, London 1961.

immutably preserved by the etymology or by roots interconnected by a more or less common evolutive history.

> The context is to be understood as the totality of the biological, spatio-temporal, relational, institutional, and cultural restrictions and opportunities of the *hic et nunc* that, together with a given text, generate a certain message endowed with meaning. An indefinite number of available contexts thus exist in reference to precisely the same text, and vice versa. They are "incapsulated" one within the other, hierarchically. Like in a matryoshka. This inclusion of the contexts radically changes the meaning of the message, on the level of the event itself.[113]

As I have emphasised, the determination of the meaning of an expression or, even more so, of a broader communicative (textual) unit, is always a *process of inference* of an abductive sort, in which the effect of its semantic potential on its real context of use need be assessed. Indeed, speaking of "semantic potential" means becoming aware that the communicative act is founded first and foremost upon the existence of a common cognitive platform rather than on predetermined meanings and conventions in an abstract sense (i.e. of a "dictionarial" sort). This platform is composed of specific rational dynamics of *pertinentisation* and the ability to make conceptual cuts within the experiential flux (which will together form the personal "encyclopaedia"[114] of a subject). This is what, in turn, determines the fact that the dynamic of human communication, while still requiring a linguistic code (even non-verbal), is not reducible to a linear phenomenon of emission, reception, and "translation" of a message, but is instead an act of expression and inference that has, as its object, the manifestation and recognition of its own *intentions* or those of others.

According to the so-called (and by now classic) model developed by Claude E. Shannon and Warren Weaver (originally elaborated by C.E. Shannon[115] alone for communicative devices, but then also applied on a large scale to the field of theories

---

113   Translated from L. ANOLLI, *Fondamenti di psicologia della comunicazione*, Manuali, Bologna 2006, ²2012, 116: "Il contesto va inteso come l'insieme delle restrizioni e delle opportunità biologiche, spaziotemporali, relazionali, istituzionali e culturali dell'*hic et nunc* che assieme a un dato testo genera un certo messaggio dotato di senso. Esiste, quindi, un numero indefinito di contesti a disposizione in riferimento al medesimo testo e viceversa. Essi sono 'incapsulati' uno dentro l'altro in modo gerarchico. Come in una matrioska. Questa inclusione dei contesti cambia radicalmente il significato del messaggio, a parità dell'evento."

114   In semiotics, the term "encyclopaedia" (from which comes the notion of "encyclopaedic competence") assumes a technical sense. It corresponds to the "background of meaning for every communicative event" (cf. U. VOLLI, *Semiotica*, 67: "sfondo di senso per ogni evento comunicativo") that is comprised of the knowledge and beliefs relating to the world that are shared within a certain society at a certain time. To what measure this deposit of knowledge adheres to reality or not is not as relevant as is the fact that this sharing of context be the key to the success of a communicative event. Only by the measure in which we become competent regarding the encyclopaedia of Dante (and the society in which he lived) can we hope to comprehend the Divine Comedy.

115   C.E. SHANNON, «A Mathematical Theory of Communication», *BSTJ* 27 (1948) 379–423, 623–656.

62 General Introduction

of human communication of the linguistic type[116]), the communicative process develops on a linear scale through stages. These stages are: 1) stimulus; 2) message; 3) coding; 4) transmission (through a *channel* subjected to *"noise"* conditioning); 5) reception; 6) decodification; 7) recomposition of the original message; 8) and finally, in the linguistic field, conceptualisation. In an attempt to better adapt it to the phenomenon of human communication, the linguist Roman Jakobson has subjected this scheme to a more accurate re-elaboration.[117] The six elements mentioned instead by Jakobson can be applied (and, in this case, are actually applied first) to the written text of the book of Jeremiah as literary communication. Thus: the *code* is the Hebrew language and the language conventions used ("poetry", "prose", literary genre); the *message* is made up of all the elements confined to the perimeter of the text (characters, actions, themes, etc.); the *contact* is the very materiality of the physical support that has transmitted the text; the *context* will regard the history of the composition of the written work in relation with spatial-temporal, social, etc. coordinates; the *recipient* is the reader/listener (that implied in the text, either implicit, real, collective, individual, etc.); the *sender* is the author (or authors). R. Jakobson identifies each factor as the focal point of just as many respective relationships, or functions, which become established between the factor itself and the message: 1. referential function (the information transmitted by the message); 2. emotional (expresses the experience of the issuer); 3. conative (aims to act upon the recipient); 4. phatic (controls the functioning of the communicative channel); 5. metalinguistic (thematises the code itself); 6. poetic (concentrates the attention on the message itself). I will not delve into this question further since it will not strictly concern my own analysis, but I will note that real messages usually cause more functions to interact amongst each other simultaneously. In the case of Jer 27–28, for example, the referential, conative, and metalinguistic dimensions prevail (since affirmations are made on the authority-veracity of the prophetic message itself).

The application of these notions to biblical text requires further clarification, however, precisely because it is a literary text and not a conversational dynamic of an oral type taking place. It is not, to use U. Eco's words, the determination of the *intentio auctoris* that is in question. This remains fundamentally undeducible (due also to the not uneasy application of this category to the complexity of the biblical text). While the objective of countless exegetic efforts may be precisely this, and despite the fact that some hypotheses of intentionality concerning entire books or single insertions limited to single verses can correspond to reality, one must acknowledge that these are almost always mere conjectures that are, more often than not, indemonstrable, since they are based on facts that are too uncertain. Attention should thus be moved instead to *intentio operis*,[118] that is, to the communicative unit at hand, which is of a written kind. This presumes, however, that the interest in its diachronic evolution (reconstructible only with large margins of hypotheticality)[119] is to be conjoined and

---

116 The divulgated version was presented in C.E. Shannon – W. Weaver, *The Mathematical Theory of Communication*, Urbana 1963.
117 See R. Jakobson, «Linguistics and Poetics», in: *Selected Writings III. Poetry of Grammar and Grammar of Poetry*, The Hague – Paris – New York 1981, 18–51.
118 In this regard, see U. Eco, *I limiti dell'interpretazione*, 22–25, 110–125.
119 It is sufficient to look at the history of studies on the formation of the Pentateuch to realise this, unless one still wants to present as a normal dynamism of the scientific method the systemic collapse of old and new hypotheses, often replaced only by

On meaning and its complexity

even subordinated to its current synchronic state. The text, intended as an identifiable signic perimeter, if not subjected uncritically to the *intentio lectoris*, reveals the elements that determine its meaning itself, independent of its author's intent.

In the linguistic field, the contextualist approach has by now generated reconsideration of the determinative function of the context, so this can no longer be considered as merely a *facilitator* of the comprehension of the meaning, but must rather be considered its own virtual *source*.[120] The problem is that in the field of biblical studies, as Gene L. Green[121] observes, the paradigm shift is late in being noticed. On-going attempts are, nonetheless, in my opinion, promising,[122] and they encourage the opening of new paths of research in a number of directions. My study of the Jeremianic call to surrender to Babylon fits, therefore, within this perspective, wanting to thematise the specific cognitive valence of the pragmatic context of reference, at least as an underlying methodological attention. I am aware of the difficulty presented by the multifactorial distance that separates us, as secondary readers, from the biblical text. But I regardless consider it possible, and in fact appropriate, to take on the challenge of a confrontation with the question of the correct pertinentisation of the prophetic message of Jeremiah.

---

new theories endowed more than anything else by momentary convergences of "authoritative" consensus. It would obviously be ungenerous to negate that, as in this case, the history of criticism had not indeed contributed to a more adequate understanding of the evolution of the biblical text (as has occurred for other ancient texts, and one thinks e.g. of the renowned case of the diachronic reconstruction of the Epic of Gilgamesh). The problem is that a solid epistemology for this kind of study is lacking, given the scarcity of information available, and thus incontrovertible results are rarely guaranteed.

120 As does M. Silva, *Biblical Words and Their Meaning*. An Introduction to Lexical Semantics, Grand Rapids 1994, 139.

121 See G.L. Green, «Lexical Pragmatics and the Lexicon», *BBR* 22 (2012) 315–333, which, in its opening, notes how "recent research in the field of lexical pragmatics, currently discussed among those working on Relevance Theory (RT) and other cognitive approaches to linguistics, gives important new guidance to orient our use of the lexicon and offers valuable insights that can help shape their future design. Lexical pragmatics points to a new, more context-oriented and dynamic approach to understanding the relationship between lexemes and concepts, and the nature of concepts as ad hoc constructions, in the communication of meaning" (p. 315). For the specific relationship with biblical exegesis, see also his previous contribution: G.L. Green, «Lexical Pragmatics and Biblical Interpretation», *JETS* 50 (2007) 799–812.

122 On Jeremiah, I think e.g. of the (very technical) contribution by E.R. Hayes, *The Pragmatics of Perception and Cognition in MT Jeremiah 1:1–6:30*. A Cognitive Linguistics Approach, BZAW 380, Berlin – New York 2008, or more generally, to the work by V.H. Matthews, *More than Meets the Ear*. Discovering the Hidden Contexts of Old Testament Conversations, Grand Rapids 2008 (see esp. pp. 151–162, the presentation of the "social space theory" in reference to the course undergone by the Jeremianic scroll), and to the monograph by M. Guidi, *"Così avvenne la generazione di Gesù Messia"*. Paradigma comunicativo e questione contestuale nella lettura pragmatica di Mt 1,18–25, AnBib 195, Roma 2012 (with a large introductive treatise of a methodological nature on pp. 39–136). In this regard, see also M. Grilli, «Parola di Dio e linguaggio umano. Verso una pragmatica della comunicazione nei testi biblici», *Gr.* 94 (2013) 525–547.

64 General Introduction

That which is relevant is information that produces cognitive effects by strengthening, modifying, or contradicting existing assumptions. As secondary readers of the biblical text, we ask questions regarding which assumptions both the author and readers could have supplied.[123]

The context of reference should therefore be reconsidered to be a cognitive horizon or backdrop organised in *frames* or "scripts" of experience that each subject can immediately draw upon as a personal "encyclopaedia" (to use the words of U. Eco) by which to interpret the world. Underlying this are the regularity with which certain "type" situations repeat themselves and the human capacity to carry out abstractions or interconnections.[124] Hence, the semantic that derives from it is *encyclopaedic* and not "dictionarial". In other words, it is tied to narrative representations of the world and not to crystallised meanings in an univocal staticity. Over the course of my inquiry, the attention I give to the processes of communication and the implications that have arisen from recent research done on ordinary language mentioned briefly in these methodological notes will be translated into the utilisation of theoretical methods that I judge as having the most effective heuristic value and to which I will refer, specifying them, as necessary.

3.3.6. *Exegesis, interpretive cooperation, and language sciences*

The methodological guidelines highlighted thus far should be conceived within the perspective of that fundamental "principle of cooperation", already formulated by H.P. Grice and re-elaborated by U. Eco,[125] upon which the communicative intent of human relations bases itself.

For U. Eco, the literary text "postulates the cooperation of the reader as its condition of actualisation" and thus requires the help of the interpreter in order to generate meaning. We are dealing with "a product whose interpretive fate must be a part of its generative mechanism".[126] According to this perspective, it does not suffice to limit one's attention to what is explicitly said and lexicalised, but is rather necessary to also consider the *unsaid*, the silences, the spaces intentionally left blank by the protagonists of the communication.[127]

---

123 G.L. Green, «Lexical Pragmatics», 807.
124 Cf. P. Violi, *Significato ed esperienza*, Milano 1997, 281–282.
125 In the sociolinguistic field, according to the founding contribution of H.P. Grice, «Logic and Conversation», in: *Syntax and Semantics*, vol. III: *Speech Acts*, eds. P. Cole – J. Morgan, New York 1975, 41–58 (= in: H.P. Grice, *Studies in the Way of Words*, Cambridge 1989, 22–40; these are the *William James Lectures* held at Harvard in 1967), the interaction between people mediated, in particular, by an interview (but also by any voluntary sort of cooperation in general, even literary) falls under this implicit prescript: "Make your conversational contribution such as it is required, at the stage at which it occurs, by the accepted purpose or direction of the talk exchange in which you are engaged" (p. 45). An important re-elaboration in the semiotic-textual field is instead thanks to the aforementioned U. Eco, *Lector in fabula*, which deals with the reflection on "interpretive cooperation in narrative texts" (above all, in ch. III).
126 Translated from U. Eco, *Lector in fabula*, 54.
127 Cf. what I highlight, esp. in ch. IV, § 5.3.3.

On meaning and its complexity 65

The text is thus interwoven with blank spaces, gaps to be filled, and the one who put it out there foresaw that these would be filled, and left them blank for two reasons. First of all, because a text is a lazy (or economic) mechanism that lives on the added value of meaning that gets introduced by the recipient. Only in cases of extreme fussiness, extreme didascalic concern, or extreme repressivity does the text complicate itself with redundancies and ulterior specifications – to the extent that the normal rules of conversation be violated.[128] And secondly because, as it passes gradually from the didactic function to the aesthetic one, a text wants to leave the interpretative initiative to the reader, even if it usually wants to be interpreted with a sufficient margin of uniqueness. A text wants someone to help it function.[129]

While I disagree with the reductive interpretation that U. Eco gives the phenomenon of "redundancy", which is, amongst other things, an aspect of particular hermeneutical importance in the book of Jeremiah, based on his considerations, I do however take the constitutively *provocative* disposition of the text as a given (whilst finding his definition of it as "a lazy machine" or "economical", however, most unfortunate). The question is that of seeing *what* actually wants to be provoked, regardless.

For these reasons, an exegesis that programmatically aims to reduce the search for meaning (intended as conceptualisation) to a truistic analytical computation of lexical elements considered in a more or less isolated way (the single lexemes or the syntagms considered the most significant), risks precluding itself of the text's comprehension. This risk is valid above all for biblical text, which is constructed entirely of processes of metaphorisation, the art of allusion, and multiple symbolical relationships, with ample

---

128 The reference is to the *conversational maxims* of H.P. GRICE, «Logic and Conversation», 41–58. It should be noted that, as with the "principle of cooperation", the formulation of these "maxims" is subject to cultural conditioning and cannot have an absolute value. They are, in any case, valid for establishing the (variably modulated) cooperative necessity as the essential foundation of human interactions. For this very reason, the very violation of such implicit norms can be used in an intentional way, either for fraudulent purposes or for conveying particular meanings (beyond the mere letter of the text, and thus according to a pragmatic dimension) that are intelligible by way of inference (H.P. Grice calls them *implicatures*). I will discuss this more in-depth in the ch. dedicated to the exegesis of 38:14–28a. For an interesting collection of studies on the subject, see e.g. E. ROLF, *ed.*, *Pragmatik*. Implikaturen und Sprechakte, LBSo 8, Wiesbaden 1997. On the Gricean maxims as expressed by H.J. HERINGER, «Gricesche Maximen und interkulturelle Kommunikation», *Sprache und Literatur* 74 (1994) 40–49 (quoted more extensively in the introduction to the same collective work, on p. 7): "Eine der größten linguistischen Entdeckungen dieses Jahrhunderts sind nach meiner Meinung die Griceschen Maximen" (here p. 40).

129 Translated from U. ECO, *Lector in fabula*, 52: "Il testo è dunque intessuto di spazi bianchi, interstizi da riempire, e chi lo ha emesso prevedeva che essi fossero riempiti e li ha lasciati bianchi per due ragioni. Anzitutto perché un testo è un meccanismo pigro (o economico) che vive sul plusvalore di senso introdottovi dal destinatario, e solo in casi di estrema pignoleria, estrema preoccupazione didascalica o estrema repressività il testo si complica di ridondanze e specificazioni ulteriori – sino al limite in cui si violano le normali regole di conversazione. E in secondo luogo perché, via via che passa dalla funzione didascalica a quella estetica, un testo vuole lasciare al lettore l'iniziativa interpretativa, anche se di solito desidera essere interpretato con un margine sufficiente di univocità. Un testo vuole che qualcuno lo aiuti a funzionare."

recourse to that which is unsaid (ellipses and enthymemes), rhetorical structures that open on to meaning by way of the form, and paradigmatic figures offered as heuristic instruments for penetrating the textual surface.

It is worth noting, furthermore, that if one wanted to study, for example, the theme of "sin" with exegetic operations based on such reductionistic linguistic presuppositions, then logic would dictate the exclusion of Gen 3 (the renowned story of "original sin") from the treatise simply because the term חַטָּאת cannot be found therein. Or, one would need to say that the "new heart" in Ezek 11:19; 18:31 and 36:26 has nothing to do with the motif of the Covenant since the term בְּרִית does not appear. In this same vein, which tends to undervalue the distinction between conceptual segmentation of phenomena and their linguistic expression, Elijah, one of the greatest prophets remembered by the tradition of Israel, is seen by some scholars as being, more than anything, a sort of "shaman", since there is not any sort of technical prophetic title indicated when his figure is presented in 1 Kgs 17:1.

Analogously, if the theme of the surrender to Babylon is studied by isolating the texts that are immediately pertinent from the network of signic relations in which they are included, then one would need to agree with those who exclude every link to the themes of the Covenant or YHWH's punitive measures, which are instead typical of that relational dynamism and are specifically attested in the book of Jeremiah. But as we shall see, there is no sense in doing this. These methodological prejudices, which at times have radical outcomes and other times take more mild positions, are unfortunately also found in authoritative publications in the exegetic field. In that sense, biblical studies are still conditioned by them.[130] Ultimately, it seems exceedingly

---

130 The same applies for the inopportune and misleading methodological distinction between the "profane" use and "sacred" use of Hebrew vocabulary upon which all lexicographic research of authoritative collective works is based, such as *ThWAT, THAT, HALAT*, which have marked and continue to mark exegetic research with their merits and defects (in this sense not negligible). And this is not a little bit surprising, as pointed out by P. BOVATI, *Geremia 1–6*. Dispense ad uso degli studenti. Pontificio Istituto Biblico, Roma 2005–2006, 89, because even E. Jenni, in the introduction to *THAT* (p. XIX) asserts: "Eine strenge Abgrenzung zwischen "profan" und "theologisch" ist hinsichtlich der Wortbedeutung *in den wenigsten Fällen möglich* [...]" (my italics). For this reason, P. Bovati also remarks, "in addition to being an objectively inaccurate treatment, the consequence becomes that of detaching the theological meaning from its anthropological context, and of losing sight of the fact that the whole religious discourse is metaphorical, that is, dependent upon the comprehension of the profane meaning" (*ibid.*; my translation). In my opinion moreover, behind this artificial separation of fields is the failure to assume the metaphorical value not only of religious language (which can be easily proven), but of language itself, on its every level as a communicative instrument that cannot do without, in a constitutive way, the process of metaphoricalisation. Scholars of cognitive linguistics have long highlighted not only the pervasiveness of this process in our natural and everyday language (cf. G. LAKOFF – M. JOHNSON, *Metaphors We Live By*, Chicago 1980), but also that our conceptual system itself, the foundations of our thinking and speaking, are of an essentially metaphoric nature (cf. ID, *Philosophy in the Flesh*. The Embodied Mind and Its Challenge to Western Thought, New York 1999). For this purpose, these scholars introduce the notion of "conceptual metaphor", and for an exemplificative idea of this, it is sufficient to think of how, in many cultures, the idea of time is in fact expressed *metaphorically* in spatial terms, or how metaphors linked to the

opportune to me, above all for my research, to implement an approach to the texts that instead gives serious consideration to the most evolved hermeneutical acquisitions and perspectives that have arisen from recent theories of communication in general, and from the science of language in particular.

4. Genesis, development, and articulation of the research: The stages of a (dual) path

4.1. Ordo inventionis: A path of discovery

From the perspective of the path of inquiry (*ordo inventionis*), my research was initially stimulated, other than by a general interest in the theological richness of the book of Jeremiah, by the original and likewise paradoxical form the Jeremianic message takes with regard to what attitude to adopt towards the Babylonian threat. Within the horizon of the end of Jerusalem, a moment as dramatic as it was enigmatic for the history of Israel and the development of biblical revelation, the so-called "symbolic gestures" of the prophets likewise drew my attention. These effective non-verbal communication devices come into play to function together with the oral message in a way that is far from auxiliary in the revelation of the meaning of the present moment, and to indicate the most appropriate ways to respond to the God of the Covenant. This is particularly true in Jeremiah and Ezekiel, excellent witnesses of both the lordship of YHWH in history and the end of Jerusalem.

A specific working hypothesis thus took form: that from precisely the convergence of these two different dimensions, namely, the historical-political one and the theological-communicative one mediated by non-verbal communication, a new, fruitful path of inquiry could open up. And I believe that this path could serve to better understand the Jeremianic injunction, since the most common interpretations seem unsatisfactory to me. Their different hermeneutical perspectives aside, their most conspicuous limit seems to be due precisely to a methodological reductionism that is, in fact, inadequate before a theme that is too complex to not invoke a multi-, inter-, and even transdisciplinary study.[131]

For this reason, and in accordance with the particular nature of the object of study, I have conducted in-depth study and research aimed at several directives. My starting point has always been that of precise textual units, *in primis* Jer 21:1–10. Here, the

---

semantic field of wartime conflict have become widely used in every communicative field, albeit unconsciously (cf. G.J. STEEN, *Finding Metaphor in Grammar and Usage. A Methodological Analysis of Theory and Research*, Amsterdam – Philadelphia 2007, 8–10).

131 On the reciprocal relationships amongst these approaches, see F. BRAND – F. SCHALLER – H. VÖLKER, *eds.*, *Transdisziplinarität. Bestandsaufnahme und Perspektiven*. Beiträge zur THESIS-Arbeitstagung im Oktober 2003 in Göttingen, Göttingen 2004 (in particular, the contribution of H. VÖLKER, «Von der Interdisziplinarität zur Transdisziplinarität?», 9–28); B. NICOLESCU, «Transdisciplinarity – Past, Present and Future», in: *Moving Worldviews – Reshaping Sciences, Policies and Practices for Endogenous Sustainable Development, eds.* B. HAVERKORT – C. REIJINTES, Leusden 2006, 142–166; and R. FRODEMAN, *Sustainable Knowledge. A Theory of Interdisciplinarity*, New York 2014.

theme of the surrender to Babylon appears on the scene of the text explicitly for the first time, and it seemed evident to me immediately that, for its particular configuration, it would require multi-perspectival treatment capable of making sense of textual, contextual, linguistic, historical, communicative, and symbolical aspects. It was therefore necessary, beginning with this *case study*, to test my working hypothesis by studying the question of "symbolic gestures" in-depth and simultaneously verifying the historical-theological plausibility of the call to surrender as a possible option in the geopolitical context evoked by the historical-literary dramatisation reconstructed in the book of Jeremiah.

From the clues and evidence that progressively emerged, I saw the hypothesis becoming better defined and reinforced: The act of the surrender to the king of Babylon that Jeremiah requests is not to be understood as an arbitrary political option, but rather needs to be read as a call to pose a "prophetic choice", that is, an act capable of symbolically interpreting (and expressing) the significance of a precise historical moment. At the same time, this act needs to realise a concrete (and paradoxical) path of obedience to YHWH, whose nature cannot be abruptly reduced to either the ethical or sapiential sphere. Speaking of "prophetic choice" means introducing a (new) specific category as a key to interpretation, one that has been unconsidered by scholars until now. The justification of its plausibility and adequate illustration of its pertinence and heuristic value for the comprehension of other parts of the book of Jeremiah as well (and of the phenomenon of biblical prophetism itself) has constituted the challenge, and even prior, the discovery, of the present path of study.

4.2. Ordo expositionis: A path of (re-)reading

The present dissertation consists of eight chapters, in which the different phases of study and extensive data and elements of meaning that emerged from the research on my topic (conducted on diversified fronts) are reorganised for presentation according to a logical sequential relationship that takes the shape of a unified path of reasoning. While this proposal of (re-)reading progresses as a continuum, it seemed however appropriate to distinguish *three parts* characterised by distinct, albeit intrinsically consequential, perspectives.

The FIRST PART, denominated EMERGENC(I)ES, thematises, by way of a single synonymic categorisation (that of "emergency/emergence", in fact), two different contextual focalisations of the prophetic Jeremianic message regarding the surrender to Babylon. The first reconnaissance, the subject of ch. I, concerns the literary emergence of the theme. Namely, it concerns the question of the theme's "emersion" upon the textual surface in relation to the global context of the book of Jeremiah. The second perspective is, instead, of a historical-literary type. This focuses on the geopolitical context that serves as a background and, in fact, deeply informs the meaning of the prophetic request. This international scenario is dominated by a *general state of emergency,* as it sees the sudden irruption of the new Babylonian imperial power on the Syro-Palestianan political theatre. This power will overturn the balances that were, until that moment, consolidated, and will impose controversial and not easy political choices on the modest kingdom of Judah.

Chapter I. The thematic emergence of the surrender to the king of Babylon. Orientative hermeneutical-literary coordinates. Having emphasised, beginning with the present General Introduction, the fundamental importance of the contextual anchoring of every communicative act, I could not but dedicate the beginning of my research to the study and focalisation of the principle hermeneutical and literary coordinates within which my interpretive proposal is situated. It has thus been necessary to propose a first *general mapping* of the book of Jeremiah, the unity and compositive structure of which commentators have highly discordant positions. The question of its literary organisation is, after all, one of the most problematic of the entire HB, and this indirectly calls into question the different *hermeneutical presuppositions* of scholars, who seldom pause to explicate them and discuss the plausibility of their respective epistemological foundations. On the basis of this panoramic view, accompanied by some hermeneutical notes and a presentation of our own precomprehensions, it will be possible to comment on the meaning of the strategic positioning of the texts in which the theme of "consignment to the king of Babylon" emerges.

Chapter II. Facing the Babylonian Empire. Historic international emergencies as a pragmatic context of the Jeremianic text. In this second chapter, the contextual question regards the historical and historical-literary level of the book of Jeremiah, which is taken on according to a specifically *pragmatic* valence. The influence of the world on the text, as an essential background for the comprehension of every communicative act, renders it opportune as an appropriate first step to attempt an *historical reconstruction* of the last phases of the kingdom of Judah. These phases will be considered within the broader framework of the political upheavals that affected all of the ancient Near East around the sixth century. It is precisely within this scenario that Jeremiah's prophetic request assumes its full meaning. And it is on the basis of deeper knowledge of military strategy in that period that the option of submission-surrender, as it was explicitly put forth at the time of Zedekiah and the second Babylonian invasion that will lead to the destruction of Jerusalem in 587, can also be evaluated as having been a realistic proposition or not. In the stage of in-depth analysis that then follows, I will concentrate on the historical-literary dimension of the Jeremianic request. This request will be considered in the light of the *decisional labour of a theological-political nature* that must have anguished the people and authorities of Jerusalem being faced with the emergency of Babylon's excessive power. Here, references to the historical context will be more stringently interfaced with the literary data offered by the Jeremianic text in order to study the opposing relationship between the option to surrender and that of resistance and rebellion. One immediately senses that both options had to have had supporters and detractors, but only an accurate analysis of the elements available will enable me to better clarify the historical situation and the contextual configuration of it elaborated in the book of Jeremiah, where the surrender to Babylon assumes a significance that is quite specific.

The SECOND PART of the dissertation, denominated TEXTS, is devoted to analytical study of the textual units that I consider most pertinent and aims to achieve a more adequate understanding of the prophetic request. From the *emergenc(i)es of historical contingencies*, one then passes to the *emergency of the choice to make and signify*. The central assumption, which will be subject to demonstration throughout the various phases of our study, is that the surrender be proposed (by Jeremiah) and, at the same time, requested (of the people of the king and all of Jerusalem) basically as *an act of non-verbal signification* finalised to express, in a "prophetic" manner, the meaning of the history taking place. On the scene that is patched together by the Jeremianic texts, words resonate and gestures, symbolic acts, and significa(c)tions are sketched out. In particular, the passages studied present three different *significant actions*. First of

70 General Introduction

all, at least in the logical-chronological sense, (1) that of the prophet himself, who in 27:1–3 receives the command from YHWH to build a "yoke" for himself and to send several more as well to the ambassadors of the nations close to the kingdom of Judah who have gathered together in Jerusalem before Zedekiah. The revelation of the divine lordship over history is thus translated into a symbolic gesture that demands, in turn, (2) the symbolic-political and above all "prophetical" act of universal *submission* to the yoke of the king of Babylon. The Jeremianic request is eventually (3) expressed in the indication of the gesture of *surrender*. This, too, is an act of signification that is to be placed on the same semiotic level, but with specific expressive-pragmatics of its own.

Chapter III. Jer 21:1–10. The surrender as acceptance of the end: symbolic-narrative prolepsis and hermeneutical key to an entire story. Following the communicative flow established by the current structure of the MT, I will immediately take on the call to surrender presented in what is clearly the most dramatic phase of the kingdom of Judah. The king of Babylon is waging war against Jerusalem, and the king Zedekiah sends some of his dignitaries to consult Jeremiah, or better still, to solicit his intercession so that YHWH will renew his salvific wonders towards his people. This is the first time that the theme emerges explicitly in the book of Jeremiah. And I am persuaded that it is not by chance that this be presented at the beginning of a new section (given in chs. 21–24), where the narrative sequentiality is subjected to disorienting dischronies: first, with the last king of Judah, the prospect of the end, and then, in chronological order, reference to a series of previous kings. It is precisely this surprising textual placement of the passage in question that will provide me with a way to interrogate the sort of signification that the book of Jeremiah seems to want to establish, even on the level of its structural organisation, from its broader sections to its more minor ones (given, in this case, in chs. 21–24). The first phase of the research will therefore be dedicated to the *semiotic of the textual insertion* of the theme of surrender in relation to the textual units that follow. The second phase will then seek to account for the wealth of *thematic-symbolic references* that inform the prophetic message. This is another peculiarity specific to this passage which, by limiting historical-narrative references to a minimum, expresses, even on this different level, an intention of signification that goes beyond the simple textual surface and, by inverting them, evokes the thematic motifs of biblical traditions with foundational significance. The call to surrender is thus configured as a symbolic-prophetic act designated to express and accept the (failed) meaning of an entire history of alliance. So that a new hope may be given, purely as a gift, by YHWH.

Chapter IV. Jer 27–28. The world under the yoke of the king of Babylon: the multi-level ante factum of the prophetic call to surrender. If in Jer 21:1–10 mention to historical anchoring is barely given, in chs. 27–28 the reader finds themself instead in the historical-narrative frame that precedes the temporal (and theological) context assumed by 21:1–10, as well as that reprised in 38:14–28a. The Jeremianic message is brought into focus here in its first logical-chronological expression by way of the *symbolic gesture* of the yoke. The category of *anteriority* thus assumes a central function, but on *different levels of meaning,* which I propose to study. In the first instance, I will deal with the peculiar non-verbal communication device used by the prophet in coordination with the locutionary act. Conceptual aspects and relational dimensions are interwoven to impress upon the Jeremianic request a valence that goes beyond the pure rhetorical function to which commentators usually reduce the gesture's meaning. The second level will instead examine the prophetic message in relation to its

Genesis, development, and articulation of the research

recipients and to a reading of the history underway: the lordship of YHWH over his creation and over human events challenges not only the *specific destiny* of the kingdom of Judah, but also the *universal* destiny of the nations. It will thus be necessary to verify whether this reference allows for a reading of the call to submission to the king of Babylon in which it holds a meaning that goes beyond a pure manifestation of divine arbitrariness in historical upheavals. A last, but no less relevant, question will be that of the *relationship between true and false prophecy*. On this level as well, Jer 27-28 is configured therefore as the paradigmatic-hermeneutical *ante factum* of the Jeremianic communication. The reader is, in fact, faced with the question of discernment, a problem that is inherent to every purported prophetic locution, but all the more urgent and dramatic as it relates to the horizon of the end and the destiny of an entire people.

Chapter V. Jer 38:14–28a. Jeremiah and Zedekiah: the final colloquy. A paradigmatic dramatisation of human-divine communication. The theme of recognition of the true prophetic word capable of leading to life and saving from death according to the promises of the Covenant assumes a dimension in this text that is entirely intimate and personal. Here, in fact, with the fall of Jerusalem imminent, we find placed the theme of the *secret meeting* between Jeremiah, imprisoned for his preaching, and Zedekiah, who has the prophet called for a final and decisive consultation. The dramatisation staged by the story then intentionally places the *king* and the *prophet* face to face in the solitude of their respective symbolic-narrative roles. The man who presents himself before the king is in turn being presented to the reader in a way that is *paradigmatic*. He is himself the very message that he has been called to deliver, rendered visible before the definitive point of no return. And in turn, the king who is, and not by chance, the lone recipient of the prophetic word at this juncture, becomes in a certain sense an icon of human liberty and the humankind's travail before the call and the mystery of God who reveals himself in history.

In the THIRD PART of the dissertation, denominated HERMENEUTICS, I will return to the complexity of the facts highlighted by the exegetical analysis to attempt an overall summary of a more reflective nature, thus achieving the most complete configuration of my interpretive proposal of the Jeremianic prophetic message. The gesture of surrender will, in fact, be analysed first of all on a sematic-pragmatic level according to a *phenomenological dimension* based on the biblical testimonies and the most relevant extrabiblical documentation. After that, I will delimit the *symbolic dimension* evoked by the factuality of the act that is requested and be able to highlight how the Jeremianic injunction of surrender to Babylon can amount to a *"symbolic-prophetic choice"* This general categorisation, presented in relation to a first mapping and articulation of the complex devices of signification structuring the book of Jeremiah, will consent me to establish the possibility of a further and even *more specific categorical definition*. This interpretive outcome will be the point of arrival for my research. And at the same time, it will take the shape of a *new working hypothesis* whose heuristic value, overflowing the literary confines of the book of Jeremiah to become of interest to the phenomenon of biblical prophetism on the whole, will require further elaboration.

Chapter VI. The gesture of the surrender: phenomenology and symbolic openings. After having studied the Jeremianic message of surrender established by its first occurrence (21:1–10) in its problematic contextual insertion, and having focalised the source point of the programmatic gesture of the yoke (chs. 27–28), now the final demonstration of this series of references (38:14–28a) will lend itself to a study that highlights two interrelated aspects of the gesture of surrender: the *phenomenological* aspect and the *symbolic* aspect. In this phase, I will therefore concern myself first with studying, by means of *semantic-pragmatic analysis*, which dimensions of meaning evoke on a "literal"-factual level the Jeremianic injunction to "surrender to the king of Babylon", that is, what shape the act of the surrender takes in general, beginning from the relevant contexts available. Then, on this basis, I will be able to focalise the fundamental *symbolic vectors* activated by the prophetic message, going beyond the standard distinction between literal meaning and figurative meaning. The symbolic dimension is, in fact, already innervated within the letter of the gesture, and is inconceivable as only a secondary meaning.

Chapter VII. The surrender to Babylon as a "symbolic-prophetic choice". After the previous preparatory phase, in this chapter and that following, I will enter into a more specifically hermeneutical phase. This phase will present an overall interpretation of the option of surrender considered according to its own "prophetic" dimension. Achieving a correct representation of the act of surrender by interfacing the relevant context of the ancient Near East, that of the HB, and the attestations of the book of Jeremiah, still does not account for the peculiar features of the prophetic message. This message utilises the evocative force of the symbol to configure a complex synthetic communication in which verbal and non-verbal aspects are coordinated. In my opinion, this communicative horizon must be placed in relation to that of the so-called "symbolic gestures" of the prophets (already introduced in ch. IV of my dissertation, in § 3), but earlier still, with the Jeremianic semiosphere, of which Jer 1 constitutes the hermeneutical gateway. Proceeding by identifying and differentiating between the various semiotic-symbolic levels of the book of Jeremiah, I will come to define the gesture of surrender as a "symbolic-prophetic choice", and then, in a more technical sense, will assign it a new and promising interpretive category: that of the "Prophetic-Obedential ConSignA(c)tion"

Chapter VIII. Surrender as "Prophetic-Obedential ConSignA(c)tion". In this last phase of my research, I will seek to present a conclusive hermeneutic of the option of the surrender to Babylon, starting precisely from the foundation of the potential heuristic of the category introduced in the preceding chapter. Having offered a specific and concise definition, its constituent traits will be analysed in-depth, looking beyond the book of Jeremiah as well. On the one hand, a *new working hypothesis* will be shaped, given that for a fully satisfactory justification, a mapping of the semiosphere I have sketched needs to be further elaborated and verification done in other biblical contexts as well; on the other, I can bring the path of research carried out thus far to a close, enucleating the most relevant elements of meaning that I believe make sense of the most accurate signification of the Jeremianic message.

With the General conclusions (and openings), I will complete this long itinerary of exegetic rereading. I will be able to take up the most relevant elements that have emerged from the research while avoiding, however, limiting myself to a *tout-court* repetition of what the reader will find in greater detail within the conclusions of the various chapters. While in several respects, the meaning of the act of surrender can be clarified, it will be likewise possible to indicate further, feasible paths of inquiry in a number of directions. It is of no surprise that what the "Jeremiah-*prophet*" promises to those who listen in the moment when everything seems to collapse, comes about also for those who let themselves be led by the "Jeremiah-*prophetic book*" to scrutinise the drama of the end: unexpectedly, new horizons of meaning unfold.

PART I

"UP LEAPS THE LION FROM HIS THICKET"

EMERGENC(I)ES
LITERARY EMERGENCES – HISTORICAL EMERGENCIES

> *Up leaps the lion from his thicket,*
> *the destroyer of nations has set out,*
> *he has gone out from his place,*
> *to turn your land into desolation:*
> *your cities will be destroyed,*
> *they will be left with no inhabitants (Jer 4:7).*

Chapter I
The thematic emergence of the surrender to the king of Babylon. Orientative literary-hermeneutical coordinates

L'énergie nait de l'image, mais doit en sortir. C'est sans doute pourquoi les textes bibliques donnent tant à penser à l'esprit le plus exigeant, sans jamais penser à sa place. Ils propulsent leur lecteur vers le moment redoutable où il devra interpréter à son propre compte.[1]

1. Introduction

Study on a topic as complex as the message of Jeremiah regarding the need to surrender to the king of Babylon, attested in a vast array of texts and diverse historical-literary contexts, cannot do without a preliminary orientative hermeneutical assessment, which can be gained from careful consideration of the specific textual positioning of the pertinent pericopes. While it is true that the principal textual blocks emerge fairly clearly, a *general mapping* of the book that would consent an accurate overall vision and thus help us to grasp the meaning of the minor textual units as well is not, however, a prerequisite to which one can refer as a given, for the question of the literary organisation of the Jeremianic material, scholars unanimously concur, is one of the most intricate and controversial of the HB.

Closely linked to this problem, which obviously does not regard only approaches of a synchronic sort (nor can it be resolved exclusively from this perspective), is also, I believe, the question of the *hermeneutical presuppositions* upon which no small number of literary-critical studies base themselves in their attempt to respond to the question of the book's unity according to customary diachronic modalities. These hypotheses that have been formulated about the history of the composition intersect, in a certain sense, with my own topic, albeit from a different angle. Amongst the attempts to make sense of the peculiar Jeremianic message is, in fact, the suggestion (or conviction) that it can be explained (in its various components) by interpreting the textual data as the tendentious expression of self-interested politico-religious factions fighting amongst themselves, each attempting to legitimise their own authority.

For these reasons, before developing the various stages of my study, which will be characterised by distinct and interrelated methodological approaches targeting the texts that relate to the theme of surrender, it seems opportune that I first clarify the *general literary coordinates* of the book of Jeremiah upon which my own study is based and explicate the *hermeneutical precomprehension* that will guide my path of inquiry.

From this initial analysis concerning the question of the inclusion of the texts under scrutiny within their broader literary context, it will become clear how the theme of

---

1 P. BEAUCHAMP, «Préface», in: *L'analyse rhétorique*. Une nouvelle méthode pour comprendre la Bible, *ed.* R. MEYNET, Paris 1989, 12.

76 Orientative literary-hermeneutical coordinates

the surrender, in its various articulations, emerges as being far from marginal in the redactional economy of the book. Indeed, we will see how its sapient *positioning* in certain strategic points signals its relevance and suggests interesting paths of interpretation that call for careful exegetical study in order to gain a more comprehensive understanding of the entirety of the prophetic message of Jeremiah.

2. Overall literary organisation of the book of Jeremiah and hermeneutical notes

2.1. The three major sections of the book (between "poetry", "prose", and some communicative peculiarities)

Based on formal and content-related criteria, literary-critical studies, and a confrontation with the text of the LXX, *three major sections* in the book of Jeremiah (MT) can be identified. These sections are recognised and considered distinct for their substantial literary homogeneity by the vast majority of exegetes.[2]

---

2 Some of the more important authors who support this subdivision are: W. RUDOLPH, *Jeremia*, HAT 12, Tübingen 1947, [3]1968, xix-xxii; A. WEISER, *Das Buch Jeremia*. I: Kapitel 1-25,14, ATD 20, Göttingen 1952, [7]1976, xxxviii-xliii; W. THIEL, *Die deuteronomistische Redaktion von Jeremia 1-25*, WMANT 41, Neukirchen-Vluyn 1973, 289: distinguishes between 1-25 (*Worte*) and 26-45 (*Berichte*); ID., *Die deuteronomistische Redaktion von Jeremia 26-45*, WMANT 42, Neukirchen-Vluyn 1981; W.L. HOLLADAY, *Jeremiah 1*; ID., *Jeremiah 2. A Commentary on the Book of the Prophet Jeremiah*. Chapters 26-45, Hermeneia, Philadelphia 1989; W. McKANE, *Jeremiah*. Volume I: Introduction and Commentary on Jeremiah I-XXV, ICC, Edinburgh 1986; ID., *Jeremiah*. Volume II; W. BRUEGGEMANN, *To Pluck Up, To Tear Down. A Commentary on the Book of Jeremiah 1-25*, ITC, Grand Rapids – Edinburgh 1988; ID., *To Build, To Plant. A Commentary on the Book of Jeremiah 26-52*, *ibid.* 1991; P.C. CRAIGIE – P.G. KELLEY – J.F. DRINKARD, Jeremiah 1-25, WBC 26, Dallas 1991; G.L. KEOWN – P.J. SCALISE – T.G. SMOTHERS, *Jeremiah 26-52*, WBC 27, Dallas 1995; G. WANKE, *Jeremia*. Teilband 1: Jeremia 1,1–25,14, ZBK.AT 20.1, Zürich 1995; G. FISCHER, *Jeremia 1-25*, 84-87. As is always the case with questions of this sort, not all scholars concur in recognising this general structure. In particular, I note the following divergent positions: R.P. CARROLL, *Jeremiah*, 38, who identifies 4 parts: I) 2-25; II) 25:15-38 and 46-51; III) 26-36, with a subdivision in 27-29 and 30-31 (plus 32-33 as appendices) and the narratives of 26; 34; 35; 36; IV) 37-45; C.R. Seitz, «The Prophet Moses and the Canonical Shape of Jeremiah», ZAW 101 (1989) 3-27, for reasons of content, proposes marking out the sections as 1-20; 21-36; 37-45; 46-52; this organisation is essentially also found in the commentary by J.R. LUNDBOM, *Jeremiah 1-20. A New Translation with Introduction and Commentary*, AncB 21A, New York 1999; ID., *Jeremiah 21-36*, *ibid.* 2004; ID., *Jeremiah 37-52*, *ibid.* 2004. For his part, A. ROFÉ, «The Arrangement of the Book of Jeremiah», ZAW 101 (1989) 390-398, identifies 6 distinct units: I) 1-24; II) 25-36, which, in turn, includes: III) 30-33; IV) 37-45; V) 46-51; VI) 52. Amongst those who do not recognise there being a caesura after ch. 25, I will point out A.J.O. VAN DER WAL, «Toward a Synchronic Analysis of the Masoretic Text of the Book of Jeremiah», in: *Reading the Book of Jeremiah. A Search for Coherence*, *ed.* M. KESSLER, Winona Lake 2004, 13-23 (who provides an overview of several proposals for the structuring), and more recently, R.D. WEIS, «The Structure of MT Jeremiah, with Special Attention to Chapters 21-45», in: *Partners with God. Theological and Critical Readings of the Bible in Honor of Marvin A. Sweeney*, *eds.* S.L.

First section: Jer 1–25. These are prevalently oracles (traditionally ascribed to the literary genre of "poetry") against Israel, Judah, and Jerusalem. The narrative parts (in "prose") are sporadic and complementary to the prophetic word. I will note straight off that these parts also recount some *gestures and narratives of a symbolic nature* (the one about the linen loincloth in 13:1–11; celibacy and other abstentions of a socio-religious nature in 16:1–9; the "acted-out parable" of the potter in 18:1–12; and the broken flask in ch. 19). This section also contains the renowned "confessions" of Jeremiah. According to classic studies in literary criticism[3] still cited today in the introductions of the most prestigious commentaries, this textual block would contain the authentic oracles of the prophet himself.

Second section: Jer 26–45. This contains the narration (once again, in "prose") of the final days of Jerusalem and the "passion of Jeremiah". Of note is the unique case of chs. 30–31, an assemblage of oracles (in "poetry") of consolation and hope, whose central positioning is problematic in terms of both form and content, given their heterogeneous character with respect to the immediate context.[4] Within this same textual perimeter, it is also interesting to note the relationship between the two different communicative styles, which also convey two apparently opposed and discontinuous themes. The theme of the *end*, within which the surrender motif is placed, and the theme of the *new beginning* beyond the *end*, are placed in a relationship that will require in-depth examination.

Third section: Jer 46–51 (52). This consists of a cohesive block containing the oracles (in "poetry") against the nations.[5] This major part of the book of Jeremiah also regards,

---

BIRDSONG – S. FROLOV, CSHBS 2, Claremont 2017, 201–224 (who, for formal motives, in my opinion unconvincing, opts for this tripartition: 1–20:18; 21:1–45:5; 46–51:64a).

3   I refer, of course, to the well-known commentary by B. DUHM, *Das Buch Jeremia*, KHC 11, Tübingen – Leipzig 1901, and to his theories on the composition of the book of Jeremiah, refined by S. MOWINCKEL, *Zur Komposition des Buches Jeremia*, Kristiania 1914. This autho takes inspiration, to a certain extent, from Julius Wellhausen's theory of the Pentateuch "sources", identifying a source A: the original oracles of the prophet, in poetry; a source B: "biographical" accounts about the prophet in third person; a source C: prose discourses in a style that closely recalls the Deuteronomist (homiletic/paraenetic) style; and a source D: chs. 30–31. In a subsequent study (ID., *Prophecy and Tradition.* The Prophetic Books in the Light of the Study of the Growth and History of the Tradition, ANVAO.HF 3, Oslo 1946, 62, 105, n. 61), the same author no longer speaks of ' sources" but rather of "cycles of traditions", thus reassessing the oral tradition. S. Mowinckel's theories were later organically re-presented (and further elaborated) by W. RUDOLPH, *Jeremia,* and by J.P. HYATT, «Jeremiah and Deuteronomy», *JNES* 1 (1942) 156–173 (= in: *A Prophet to the Nations.* Essays in Jeremiah Studies, eds. L.G. PERDUE – B.W. KOVACS, Winona Lake 1984, 113–127), who was the first to advance the theory of a Deuteronomistic redaction of Jeremiah, in ID., «The Deuteronomic Edition of Jeremiah», *VStH* 1 (1951) 71–95 (= in: *A Prophet to the Nations.* Essays in Jeremiah Studies, eds. L.G. PERDUE – B.W. KOVACS, Winona Lake 1984, 247–267). In this regard, I also recall the position of W. MCKANE, *Jeremiah,* I, l-lxxxiii, who considers chs. 1–25 to be the development of a small collection of Jeremianic oracles produced by many authors and produced over a long period of time (in his words, the theory of the "rolling-corpus").

4   As is well emphasised, e.g. in A. ROFÉ, «The Arrangement», 395.

5   Differently from the MT, the LXX places this section after 25:1–13 (which announces the judgement against the nations). According to various authors, this would have been

78 Orientative literary-hermeneutical coordinates

in a certain sense, the prophetic injunction of surrender to Babylon, given that in 27–28, this is presented as a "universal" necessity. It is followed by ch. 52,[6] a narrative account (in "prose") of the end of Jerusalem and the fate of the king Jehoiachin (יְהוֹיָכִין).

By presenting very summarily the overall organisation and content of the book of Jeremiah, I have wanted to highlight how the two forms of expression in which this prophetic writing has been handed down to us, that is, in "poetry" and "prose",[7] together contribute to form *a single literary corpus* that is recognised and accepted in the Canon by the Tradition. On the one hand, it is not difficult to highlight the distinct prevalence of prophetic oracles in "poetry" with respect to parts in proper narrative "prose" (and vice versa) and to trace these back through the respective macro-sections of the book. But one need note that it is not, on the other hand, equally simple to reach ulterior delimitations in detail, given that the distinction between the two literary genres (poetry and prose) is not so obvious. It is not, generally speaking, in modern literature, as Northrop Frye[8] has pointed out, nor is it in the HB. And it

---

its original placement; cf. e.g. A. WEISER, *Das Buch Jeremia*. II: Kapitel 25,15–52,34, ATD 21, Göttingen 1954, ⁴1966, 222–223; B. GOSSE, «La place primitive du recueil d'Oracles contre les Nations dans le livre de Jérémie», *BN* 74 (1994) 28–30. This part of the book of Jeremiah is considered "secondary" by the majority of authors (starting from S. Mowinckel, who excludes it from his analysis). For a comparison between the structuring of the book of Jeremiah identifiable in the LXX and in the MT, see the proposition of R.D. WEIS, «An Analysis of the Structure of LXX of Jeremiah with a Comparison to that of MT of Jeremiah», in: *A Necessary Task*. Essays on Textual Criticism of the Old Testament in Memory of Stephen Pisano, eds. D. CANDIDO – L.P.S. DA PINTO, AnBib.St 14, Roma 2020, 245–267.

6 This is commonly held to be a late addition. There are three main reasons for this: 1) ch. 51 ends at v. 64 with the colophon: עַד־הֵנָּה דִּבְרֵי יִרְמְיָהוּ ("Thus far the words of Jeremiah"); 2) it is absent from the LXX; 3) we find it, practically identical, in 2Re 24:18–25, 30, that is, in what was indubitably its original position. In particular, for a discussion on ch. 52 MT as a secondary insertion drawn from the Second Book of Kings, cf. S. DELAMARTER, «Thus Far the Words of Jeremiah: But Who Gets the Last Word?», *BiRe* 15 (1999) 34–45, 54–55. For the characteristics that make it regardless a text firmly anchored in the logic of the book of Jeremiah, see G. FISCHER, «Il libro di Geremia», 394–396. See also H. DE WAARD, *Jeremiah 52 in the Context of the Book of Jeremiah*, VT.S 183, Leiden 2020, and H. DE WAARD, *Jeremiah 52 in the Context of the Book of Jeremiah*, VT.S 183, Leiden 2020.

7 The possibility that the two genres might be readily distinguishable in the book of Jeremiah was already maintained by R. LOWTH, *De sacra poesi Hebraeorum praelectiones academicae Oxonii habitae*, Oxford 1753, but a first systematic distinction is due to B. BLAYNEY, *Jeremiah and Lamentations*. A New Translation with Notes Critical, Philological, and Explanatory, Oxford 1784, London ³1836. For a recent reprise of this criterion of delimitation, cf. J.R. LUNDBOM, «Delimitations of Units in the Book of Jeremiah», in: *The Impact of Unit Delimitation on Exegesis*, eds., R. DE HOOP – M.C.A. KORPEL – S.E. PORTER, Pericope 7, Leiden – Boston 2009, 146–174.

8 See, in this regard, his renowned entry *Verse and Prose* written for *Princeton Encyclopedia of Poetry and Poetics* (ed. A. PREMINGER, Princeton 1965, ²1974, 885–890; in the fourth and most recent edition of 2012 [eds. R. GREEN *et al.*] the same entry, on pp. 1507–1512, is instead by T. Steele), still considered to be "una pietra miliare nella teoria dei generi letterari" ["a milestone in the theory of literary genres"], recently retranslated into Italian and annotated (her quote) by Sara Sullam (N. FRYE, «Verso e Prosa», *Entymema* 5 [2011] 17–30). According to the author, the only essential difference between poetry and prose would be their difference in rhythm.

Overall literary organisation of the book of Jeremiah and hermeneutical notes   79

most certainly is not so in Jeremiah, where the distinction remains quite fragile or, at least, object of debate.

Generally speaking, biblical poetry is identified primarily by its use of parallelism, a recognisable rhythm, and a refined, elliptical style that deliberately omits articles, relative pronouns, and accusative indicators.[9] But a close look reveals that actually, on more than a few occasions, the boundary does not appear to be so clear. One need question if we are not imposing irrelevant literary conventions on Hebrew text. Recent scholarly contributions, for example, have extended our definition of what is considered "poetic" in Scripture, precisely with respect to biblical narrations.[10] As far as the book of Jeremiah is concerned, it was Helga Weippert[11] who drew attention to the literary particularities of its prose (which she defines as "Kunstprosa"), the characteristics of which blur the boundary between the two genres to the extent that it is, at times, entirely unrecognisable. The typographical presentation of the Jeremianic text (whether in Hebrew or in translation) in the contributions of scholars reflects their respective diverse approaches. For example, both the critical publication on Jeremiah by Rudolf Kittel (in the BHK[1]–[2] [1906, 1913] and in BHK[3] [1929–1937]), and that done by Wilhelm Rudolph (in the BHS [1970]) categorically distinguish those parts considered prose from those considered poetry by way of a distinctive typographic layout of the Hebrew text. Thus doing, they propose a rhythmic reading and a division of verses. G. Fischer, on the other hand, in his commentary, renounces making any distinction whatsoever.[12]

For my part, I believe that despite the above-mentioned observations and with all due caution, a certain distinction between the two genres cannot be abolished entirely. A poetic register does exist in the HB, regardless, and its peculiarities (both stylistic[13] and theological[14]) can be studied. It is, however, certainly true that sensing this difference is far simpler than is theorising about it in full. In fact, by and large, one can say that the distinction between Hebrew poetry and prose is more an issue of quantity than of quality,[15] since poetic elements can be detected in the prose and vice versa.

---

9   Cf. G. FISCHER, *Jeremia 1–25*, 57.

10   See, e.g. J.L. KUGEL, *The Idea of Biblical Poetry,* New Haven 1981 (on the "poetry" of some psalms that take the form of "prose"); M. STERNBERG, *The Poetics of Biblical Narrative*. Ideological Literature and the Drama of Reading, Bloomington 1985 and D.M. GUNN – D. FEWELL, *Narrative in the Hebrew Bible,* Oxford 1993, 147–148, 190, where it is noted that while in the composition of a text in modern prose, we seek in every way to avoid the phenomenon of repetition (which, by our standards is more suitable for the poetic genre), in Hebrew prose, on the other hand, it is considered an appropriate and effective literary device.

11   In H. WEIPPERT, *Die Prosareden des Jeremiabuches*, BZAW 132, Berlin 1973.

12   Cf. G. FISCHER, *Jeremia 1–25*, 56–57. For further examples of different arrangements of the text, cf. S.E. GILLINGHAM, *The Poems*, 19–21.

13   Cf. L. ALONSO SCHÖKEL, *Manual de poética hebrea*, Madrid 1987; J.P. FOKKELMAN, *Reading Biblical Poetry*. An Introductory Guide, Louisville 2001.

14   Cf. P.D. MILLER, «The Theological Significance of Poetry», in: *Language, Theology, and the Bible*. Essays in Honour of James Barr, *ed.* S.E. BALENTINE – J. BARTON, Oxford 1994, 213–230; S.E. BALENTINE, «The Prose and Poetry of Exile», in: *Interpreting Exile*. Displacement and Deportation in Biblical and Modern Contexts, *eds.* B.E. KELLE – F.R. AMES – J.L. WRIGHT, SBL.AIL 10, Atlanta 2011, 345–363.

15   Thus e.g. S.E. GILLINGHAM, *The Poems and Psalms of the Hebrew Bible*, Oxford 1994, 42–43: "It would appear that the over-categorising of Hebrew poetry and prose is a

In the book of Jeremiah, for example, it is unthinkable that a text like the initial *rîb* against the beloved City in 2:1–19 and the account of the sufferings undergone by the prophet in 38:1–13 (and his subsequent final argument with Zedekiah on the topic of surrender) could be placed on the same level. So one can say that there are different ways of reaching the reader, and that through these, the reader, in turn, feels differently engaged, though they may not immediately know the reason (modelled by an exhaustive theory) for this. We head into poetic territory when the textuality favours a regular, characteristic metre and rhythm, causing us to distance ourselves simultaneously from both the intriguing nature of the narrative and its chronological order. It is in this way that the poetic-prophetic oracle calls upon us directly, making us leap over great temporal and spatial (and, obviously, cultural) distances.[16] The narrative text, on the other hand, renders the reader participant in the facts narrated through suspense, curiosity, and surprise,[17] while still maintaining a certain *distance*, deliberately. In this way, particularly in the book of Jeremiah, attention is drawn to the interplay of alternations and reciprocal relationships between the two stylistic modalities. This interplay probably exposes an *intentional* compositional and/or communicative process in which the reader is on the one hand being kept at a distance, precisely to favour their freedom and discernment of the situation at hand. Meanwhile, on the other, they are being called directly into account by a word that intends to engage them and impel them to take a stance.

Lingering further on the question of poetry-prose also reveals some additional impacts that this has on my topic of study in relation to its literary context. One can observe, in fact, that a good number of commentaries, above all the "classic" ones, beginning with Bernhard Duhm's contribution, establish a privileged relationship between the literary genre of the prophetic oracle and the poetic form, which is generally considered more *authentic* (i.e. and erroneously so, more noble or "significant" from the viewpoint of biblical revelation). In the case of Jeremiah, these commentaries show an elective attention towards the first part of the book (1–25). Thus, the story of the prophet and the events involving him (in section 26–45), including the question of the surrender to Babylon, is frequently attributed instead as being the (secondary,

---

> result of our modern assumptions about poetry in general. If we examine the material as much as is possible from the Semitic context itself, we are left with more questions than answers concerning whether there are distinctive forms of prose and poetry in the biblical literature. What we have overall are 'poetic components' within the prose accounts, and 'prose-like tendencies' within the poetry. The distinction is more quantitative than qualitative, more of degree than of kind."

16   Cf. J.P. FOKKELMAN, *Reading Biblical Narrative.* An Introductory Guide, Louisville 1999, 171–187.

17   These are the essential elements that define narrativity, according to M. STERNBERG, «Telling in Time (II): Chronology, Teleology, Narrativity», *Poetics Today* 13 (1992) 463–541: "I define narrativity as the play of suspense/curiosity/surprise between represented and communicative time (in whatever combination, whatever medium, whatever manifest or latent form). Along the same functional lines, I define narrative as a discourse where such play dominates: narrativity then ascends from a possibly marginal or secondary role (e.g. as a temporal force governed by the space-making, descriptive function that always coexists with it [...] to the status of regulating principle, first amongst the priorities of telling/reading" (p. 529).

Deuteronomistic) work of some devoted scribe[18] to whom the form of the story is due. And in fact, these often do not receive the same exegetical appreciation and interest.

On the basis of what I have observed about the opportunity to maintain a fairly fluid relationship between poetry and prose, however, this perspective proves problematic. The prevalence of one genre or another can certainly be observed in the major sections of the book, but detailed examination will require a case-by-case assessment. Thus, ultimately, to the measure in which the differences between the two genres fade and their tight interdependence can be detected, so also does the theme of the surrender to Babylon cease to be an isolated or "secondary" *motif* (without going a step further to say that from a "historical" perspective, this relationship could actually be inverted entirely[19]). On the other hand, to the measure in which the difference in communicative effects between narrativity and non-narrativity becomes evident, one can focalise the unique, complementary significance of the provocation directed at the reader to discern and make a choice.

2.2. Fundamental hermeneutical coordinates

2.2.1. *My approach to the book of Jeremiah: A starting point*

Beginning from the just highlighted ascertainment of the stylistic interweaving that makes up the fabric of this single book, I will now touch upon the fundamental *hermeneutical presupposition* that will guide us down our path of research. My intent is not that of performing an *archaeology* of the text(s), in search of those words that would form Jeremiah's (original) announcement regarding a precise political option (surrender). Nor is it to isolate hypothetical redactional layers in order to elaborate a model that would give an account of the history of the book's composition. My intent is rather to delve into the *revelatory* (theological) nature of the written text at hand (MT), as it can be read in its *present final form*, while still bearing in mind the knowledge acquired and hypotheses derived from literary-critical studies.

We shall see, in fact, how in the pericopes of interest to us (though, naturally, not in these exclusively), the "oracle" element is presented prevalently within the narrative mode of expression. This element is often associated elsewhere with the (more "authentic") poetic form, and the narrative mode commonly judged to be "secondary". But within this narrative, people and events are brought into the scene of the text within the framework of the articulation of a "story". And this story does not

---

18 It has actually even been thought that he be Baruch himself; cf. J.P. HYATT, «Jeremiah and Deuteronomy», 156–173; J. MUILENBURG, «Baruch the Scribe», in: *Proclamation and Presence. Old Testament Essays in Honour of Gwynne Henton Davies, eds.* J.I. DURHAM – J.R. PORTER, Richmond 1970, 215–238 (= in: *A Prophet to the Nations. Essays in Jeremiah Studies, eds.* L.G. PERDUE – B.W. KOVACS, Winona Lake 1984, 229–245). The section to which I am referring (26–29; 34–45), e.g. is entitled "Die Bericht Baruks" by C. WESTERMANN, *Jeremia*, Stuttgart 1967, 17. Others prefer to think of some other scribe. For details on this and other hypotheses, cf. W.L. HOLLADAY, *Jeremiah 2*, 286.

19 Cf. the points noted in the General Introduction (§ 1.4.2) with regard to the position of M.J. de Jong, who attributes ("normalising it") the Jeremianic injunction of surrender to the perspective of the divination professionals typical of the ancient Near East concerned about the well-being of the state.

82 Orientative literary-hermeneutical coordinates

contradict the oracular-poetic message but rather presumes it and expresses the same fundamental concepts that it does, only in a different way. In other words, we could say that the message and the story of the messenger (or "prophetic body") shed light upon each other reciprocally, and in the present form of the book of Jeremiah, these both strive together inextricably to proclaim a singular Word.[20]

2.2.2. *The unity of the book: An underlying problem*

While identification of the principal textual blocks of Jeremiah may not be a particularly arduous task for scholars, it need be acknowledged that it is not only the less expert readers who are left fairly disconcerted after an initial, in-depth "reconnaissance" of the book. Even the exegetes themselves are taken aback by its lack of clear literary coherence, apparently illogical running-around of passages, and sections in poetry and prose, oracles, and stories or speeches, all with an absence of narrative development built along any linear temporal axis.

The more recent studies of Jeremiah[21] seek to recompose the dialectic between this perception of chaos and some organising principles.[22] But the fact is that in their commentaries, a number of specialists first confirm this perception arising from an initial impact with the text, and then found judgements upon it that seem to leave no space for differing interpretations.[23] So we are dealing primarily with reconstructions of the

---

20 I therefore believe it inappropriate to wish to attribute greater importance to one expressive form or the other, such as, e.g. dedicating privileged consideration to the poetic-oracular genre because it is considered more archaic and thereby more "authentic".

21 See, in this regard, the critical review by C.E. CARROLL, «Another Dodecade», 162–182, which takes up and updates that of R.P. CARROLL, «Surplus Meaning and the Conflict of Interpretations: A Dodecade of Jeremiah Studies (1984–95)», *CR.BS* 4 (1996) 115–160 (cf. also ID., «Century's End: Jeremiah Studies at the Beginning of the Third Millennium», *CR.BS* 8 [2000] 18–58).

22 For some examples, one can look at the collection of studies contained in M. KESSLER, ed., *Reading the Book of Jeremiah*. A Search for Coherence, Winona Lake 2004.

23 See, e.g. J. BRIGHT, «The Date of the Prose Sermons of Jeremiah», *JBL* 70 (1951) 21, and his assessment of the book of Jeremiah (in ID., *Jeremiah*, lvi–lxiii), considering it "a hopeless hodgepodge thrown together without any discernible principle of arrangement at all"; and, in particular, the claim by R.P. CARROLL, «Halfway through a Dark Wood: Reflections on Jeremiah 25», in: *Troubling Jeremiah, eds.* A.R.P. DIAMOND – K.M. O'CONNOR – L. STULMAN, JSOT.S 260, Sheffield 1999, 75: "I am still of the opinion that the book of Jeremiah is a very difficult, confused and confusing text" (already of the same opinion was McKANE, *Jeremiah*, I, xlix–l and, more recently, S.A. MEIER, *Speaking of Speaking*. Making Direct Discourse in the Hebrew Bible, VT.S 46, Leiden 1992, 258, 272; S. GESUNDHEIT, «The Question of LXX Jeremiah as a Tool for Literary-Critical Analysis», *VT* 62 [2012] 29–57 (for this author, it is precisely the incoherencies of the MT compared with the LXX that would allow for study of the text's development). This perception is also reflected in the difficulties that other authors have in grasping the "unitary" face of God about which the book of Jeremiah speaks (one thinks, e.g. of W. BRUEGGEMANN, *Jeremiah*, 270, 283, according to whom it would be impossible to reconcile the "God who judges" with the "faithful God", or of L. STULMAN, *Order amid Chaos*, 186, for whom "the jumbled character of God pulsates with tensions and contradictions"). That the problem exists is, regardless, evident

Overall literary organisation of the book of Jeremiah and hermeneutical notes   83

"original text" that are as laboured as they are hypothetical, consequent attempts at recomposition,[24] research done on the text's various editorial stratum, and mere juxtapositions of passages or single verses considered to be in contradiction. Generally, these portions of text are identified (on the basis, largely speaking, of fairly disputable criteria) as the *tendentious "ideological" expressions of distinct communities* (ordinarily, the post-597 exilic community and the Palestinian community) with different visions of history and counterposed theological-political aims. Both, however, are characterised as being animated by a one and the same desire to self-legitimise their own authority at the expense of the adversarial group.[25]

This last perspective in particular definitely warrants a critical note, seeing as it inspires contributions that also concern, in a certain sense, my own thematic area of study and the question of the book's present arrangement. This type of interpretation, however, is based on (implicit) criteria for the reading of texts that differ profoundly from my own corresponding basic hermeneutical precomprehension.[26] Within the realm of paths of literary-critical inquiry dedicated to the book of Jeremiah, in fact,

---

(already S. Mowinckel in *Zur Komposition*, 5, spoke of «auffälliger Planlosigkeit») as reiterated by L.G. PERDUE, «Jeremiah in Modern Research: Approaches and Issues», in: *A Prophet to the Nations. Essays in Jeremiah Studies, eds.* L.G. PERDUE – B.W. KOVACS, Winona Lake 1984, 12: «By far the most complicated and controversial issue in Jeremiah studies involves the analysis of the literary composition and development of the book». There are also those who, in my opinion, attempt in a rather forced way to interpret the impression of disorder imparted by the book of Jeremiah as a *desired* effect, that "fait ressentir au lecteur, de manière assez concrète, le chaos qui règne dans la population et dans les esprits à Jérusalem" (I am referring here to E. DI PEDE, *Au-de là du refus: l'espoir*. Recherches sur la cohérence narrative de Jr 32–45 [TM], BZAW 357, Berlin 2005, vi, 121, 163–164, 325 [I quote from here], etc., who takes up a suggestive observation of A. NEHER, *Jérémie*, Paris 1960, vi). That the arrangement could somehow reflect a labour of composition dependent, in its turn, on historical contingency is in my opinion plausible (along these lines, cf. also K.M. O'CONNOR, «The Book of Jeremiah», 89); that it be a predetermined effect, however, seems less plausible. It is more probable, instead, as I shall seek to demonstrate, that faced with the composite material, there has been an attempt to organise it in its entirety according to some ordering principles, working chiefly from the basis of the more significant textual blocks.

24   See Di PEDE, E., *Au-de là du refus*, 139–152, for an annotated synopsis of the textual rearrangements on a chronological basis made by three classic commentators on section 32–45 (C.H. CORNILL, *The Book of the Prophet Jeremiah*. Critical Edition of the Hebrew Text Arranged in Chronological Order with Notes, SBOT 11, Leipzig 1895; ID., *Das Buch Jeremia*, Leipzig 1905; J. STEINMANN, *Le prophète Jérémie*. Sa vie, son œuvre et son temps, LeDiv 9, Paris 1952; J. BRIGHT, *Jeremiah*).

25   For an updated general overview of the studies of a critical-redactional matrix on the book of Jeremiah, see M.A. SWEENEY, «The Prophets and the Prophetic Books, Prophetic Circles and Traditions – New Trends, Including Religio-psychological Aspects», *HBOT* III/2, 500–530 (pp. 519–523; with bibliography).

26   By the term "precomprehension", I herein intend the conceptual world consciously thematised by the interpreter themself, the summation of the problems and solutions they already establish before each interpretation, as a basis for further questioning, research, and understanding. Cf. C. BADOCCO, «Precomprensione», *EF* IX, Milano 2006, 8896–8897.

84 Orientative literary-hermeneutical coordinates

there are a whole series of studies[27] that propose interpretive solutions that seem to me to be based on premises taken for certain far too hastily. Indeed, despite their development of extremely complex analyses and argumentation, (one need acknowledge) that often, they do not place their premises under any preliminary scrutiny whatsoever.[28]

2.2.3. Some literary-critical theories: A metacritical note on epistemological foundations

For every discipline that wants to call itself scientific and every afferent research sector, the problem arises of the epistemological statute of the type of "knowledge" it intends to establish. The question is a crucial one, for a theoretical foundation concerns not only the elaboration of the methodological criteria of the research itself but also, and even beforehand, the *conditions of validity* of its presuppositions. These ought to be object of prior discussion and not negligently taken for granted.[29] To ascertain that apt foundations be present and be capable of sustaining the demonstrative structure and fruitfulness of the research to be done is no small matter. This is especially true if one intends to build an impressive theoretical edifice or wants, as in the case of a

---

27 Along the line inaugurated for the book of Jeremiah by K.-F. POHLMANN, *Studien*, see, e.g.: C.R. SEITZ, «The Crisis of Interpretation over the Meaning and Purpose of the Exile. A Redactional Study of Jeremiah xxi-xliii», *VT* 35 (1985) 78–97; ID., *Theology in Conflict*; C. HARDMEIER, *Prophetie im Streit vor dem Untergang Judas*. Erzählkommunikative Studien zur Entstehungssituation der Jesaja- und Jeremiaerzählungen in II Reg 18–20 und Jer 37–40, BZAW 187, Berlin 1990; H.-J. STIPP, *Jeremia im Parteienstreit*. Studien zur Textentwicklung von Jer 26,36–43 und 45 als Beitrag zur Geschichte Jeremias, seines Buches und judäischer Parteien im 6. Jahrhundert, BBB 82, Frankfurt am Main 1992; R.P. CARROLL, «Synchronic Deconstructions of Jeremiah: Diachrony to the Rescue», in: *Synchronic or Diachronic? A Debate on Method in Old Testament Exegesis, ed.* J.C. DE MOOR, Leiden 1995, 39–51; J. APPLEGATE, «The Fate of Zedekiah: Redactional Debate in the Book of Jeremiah», *VT* 48 (1998) 137–160, 301–308; C.J. SHARP, *Prophecy*; M. LEUCHTER, *The Polemics of Exile in Jeremiah 26–45*, Cambridge 2008 (for the latter, the communities in conflict would be made up of the different groups of exiles: that of 597 in opposition with that formed subsequently with the deportations of 587 and 582); D. ROM-SHILONI, *Exclusive Inclusivity*. Identity Conflicts between the Exiles and the People Who Remained (6th-5th Centuries BCE), LHBOTS 543, London – New York 2013.

28 I share, in this sense, the critical standpoint of D. ROM-SHILONI, «From Prophetic Words to Prophetic Literature: Challenging Paradigms That Control Our Academic Thought on Jeremiah and Ezekiel», *JBL* 138 (2019) 565–586, who openly recognises "the importance of exposing background arguments and overall preconceptions that drive our scholarly thoughts and work" (p. 583) as part of her research journey.

29 According to the definition of G. Basti, Filosofia della Natura e della Scienza. 1: I Fondamenti, Roma 2002, 233, "By epistemology we mean that logical and philosophical subject area that studies the methods of 'scientific knowledge' (from the Greek ἐπιστήμη) and in particular the basis of its being *scientific* and *certain*. Epistemology is not the same as *gnoseology*, or 'philosophy of knowledge', which, instead, studies knowledge *in general terms*, in its variations and in its psychological bases within the human mind. It is also different from *meta-logics* and *meta-mathematics* that study the foundations of logic and mathematics, i.e., of such semantic notions as the *consistency* or *truth* of formal languages" (translation by Philip Larrey).

Overall literary organisation of the book of Jeremiah and hermeneutical notes   85

method wishing to call itself historical or critical, to designate its single perspective of inquiry as having absolute priority over others. As Paul Ricœur duly noted, no "innocent"[30] method free of precomprehensions and presuppositions truly exists. But recognition of these precomprehensions and presuppositions helps one to not fall into ideological postures. Let me specify that I certainly do not intend to confront herein the issue of the criteria of scientificity of literary criticism *tout-court*, but I do, however, wish to pose the problem of the application of this method to the book of Jeremiah, with particular reference to the principal paths attempted to date.

In this particular case, the operative dispositions derived from its set of axioms are well known. Through this line of research, real or presumed conceptual discord, thematic and literary tensions, and more or less evident traces of a history of the text's composition get explained as being evident signs or *proof*. And it is held that this proof would indubitably reveal the misleading and manipulative (redactional or pseudepigraphical) editorial activity of *conflicting power groups* fighting each other for the *legitimation of their own politico-religious authority* at the expense of the opposing community. As a rule, these two groups would be the exiles in Babylon after the first deportation of 597 and the community that remained in Jerusalem or elsewhere in the territory of Judah before and after the second deportation of 587.

I will put forth some critical observations in this regard. That behind the biblical texts there (also) be the whole vortex of passions, limits, and contingent human intentions goes without saying, and it would be naive to deny or even belittle the consequences of these on a hermeneutical level. That it be possible, in particular with regard to my theme, to reconstruct the scenarios of some of the conflictual post-exilic situations that took place (or even pre-exilic situations between different politico-religious groups) based on some biblical texts seems evident or at least plausible (one thinks, e.g. of the scenario derived from the books of Ezra and Nehemiah, or even earlier, of texts like Jer 24 or the insertion of vv. 16–20 in ch. 29, which are absent from the LXX; or even Ezek 11:15–17). But that it actually be possible to identify *with certainty* within the book of Jeremiah which textual elements are in radical, reciprocal conflict for thematic reasons, and to systematically see within these (presumed) tensions the reflection of precise political contrapositions that existed between the specific power groups, of whom an accurate social, ideological profile could also be sketched, as far as I am concerned, remains *still entirely to be proven*. And yet, notwithstanding the absence of any real empirical basis for these models, the confidence held in them is remarkable, even when the very disparity of opinions on the subject, despite their being founded on the same basic premises, ought to itself suggest a more cautious approach.[31]

---

30   Every method, in fact, presupposes a theory of meaning that has not yet been fully acquired, which is in itself problematic. In this regard, see P. Ricœur «Esquisse de conclusion», in: *Exégèse et Herméneutique, eds.* R. Barthes *et al.*, Paris 1971, 286–287.

31   If it is true that all research must necessarily begin from some presuppositions, then it should rest equally true that these then be accepted as *working hypotheses* to be therein verified (or proven wrong), and not as pre-constituted certainties. Otherwise all the research, while it may even achieve the elaboration of a system that could be coherent, would do so with wholly uncertain guarantees of veracity (i.e. in correlation to reality).

86 Orientative literary-hermeneutical coordinates

Let me elaborate further. The assumption that underlies these studies is – as I have said – that two different and opposed power groups (of a politico-religious nature) within the people of Israel had waged a battle for the legitimation their own authority. This battle was to have taken place by means of redactional interventions on the "Jeremianic tradition"[32] or by dint of *ex-nihilo* creations of more or less extensive portions of text of a propagandistic nature. One needs question however if this *a priori* assumption regarding the book of Jeremiah really has sufficient elements of verisimilitude. In my opinion, the answer is negative. It is true that the reorienting of authoritative ancient texts handed down through the tradition on the basis of present necessities (above all, exilic or post-exilic) is indeed a practice that can be traced through the MT.[33] But in this specific case, it is not clear who would have really had the need to legitimise themself (and before what audience) as the authentic heir of the Jeremianic tradition during the brief time span between the first deportation and the decades that follow the second. At this time, the tradition *in fieri* was anything but normative for the faith of Israel. In what way and to what extent would the "antagonist" group have presented a threat? Would the traumatic nature of these events and subsequent existential precariousness that they inflicted really have left time and energy for the *immediate* rise of these concerns and for a literary undertaking of this sort[34]?

---

32 Not only on the texts in prose, but ultimately aimed at the predominantly poetic section as well. See e.g. the work of C.J. SHARP, *Prophecy.*

33 See, e.g. the doctoral dissertation by F. GIUNTOLI, *L'officina della tradizione.* Studio di alcuni interventi redazionali post-sacerdotali e del loro contesto nel ciclo di Giacobbe (Gen 25:19–50; 26), AnBib 154, Roma 2003.

34 As indicated by W.M. SCHNIEDEWIND, *How the Bible Became a Book.* The Textualization of Ancient Israel, Cambridge 2004, 91–117; 139–164, the clues that can be obtained from archaeological investigations demonstrate that only favourable socio-economic conditions and an elevated degree of urbanisation could guarantee significant processes of "textualisation". This is what happens in Jerusalem during the last stage of the Davidic monarchy (this is, moreover, a correlation diffused amongst many cultures, as has been observed by one of the most renowned contemporary anthropologists; cf. J. GOODY, *The Logic of Writing and the Organization of Society,* Cambridge 1986). From this point of view, however, the Exilic and post-Exilic periods can certainly not be considered the most favourable historical periods. Along the same lines, B.T. ARNOLD, «What has Nabuchadnezzar to do with David? On the Neo-Babylonian Period and Early Israel», in: *Mesopotamia and the Bible.* Comparative Explorations, *eds.* M.W. CHAVALAS – K.L YOUNGER, Jr., JSOT.S 341, London 2002, 330–355. After having pointed to how, amongst the ancient Semitic cultures, precisely those that were able to establish stable national power would subsequently also experience a significant flowering of literary production, he observes: "Curiously, among Old Testament scholars such a possibility has been denied for ancient Israel. Some scholars deny Israel ever had dominant and successful monarchs like David and Solomon [Garbini]. For those scholars who still admit the existence of David and Solomon, the age of literary greatness is nonetheless assumed to be the exile, though this would be an unparalleled situation among ancient Semitic peoples. A close and unbiased comparison of these ancient Semitic cultures – Israel and Neo-Babylonia – suggests that the literary traditions of Israel preserved in the Old Testament genuinely reflect the architectural and literary activities of Israel's United Monarchy" (p. 343). The theses of W.M. Schniedewind are obviously widely debated. As I have shown in the General Introduction to my work with regard to the genesis of the book of Jeremiah,

Overall literary organisation of the book of Jeremiah and hermeneutical notes   87

And then, above all, to conceive the composition of the book of Jeremiah as a "redactional debate"[35] – one that would have even taken place while the "historical Jeremiah" himself was still alive! – between two groups divided by a distance of thousands of kilometres, both grasping with the grave contingent problems of sheer survival, seems highly improbable. It is hardly plausible to even think that a "debate" would have been carried out, moreover, in the shape of a common literary support (or in an oral tradition) used as a base upon which and through which to counterattack, or as a starting point from which to insert their own responses and accusations against their adversaries.[36] And this would then still not explain who would have tied all these disparate and counterposed positions back together to form the "unstable" unity of a single book like that of Jeremiah (and for what motive). It is as if there were a single, chimerical, basic textual Jeremianic *corpus* (or lumping together of tradition) to which each group could have added their own texts and perspectives, in turn and at pleasure, in response to those of their adversaries. They would have tampered indiscriminately, as it suited them, moreover, with redactional interventions (of which the "ideology", persuasive power, and self-legitimisation seem at times to truly be anything but evident, even on the basis of the very basic criteria that the various scholars themselves present).[37]

Not to mention that if these groups, or the so-called "winning group" (i.e. the exiles in Babylon under the auspices of the royal family of Jehoiachin), were to have had such open access to the Jeremianic tradition, in both a creative and redactional function, then it isn't clear why they would have engaged in tacking clumsy interpolations onto the page in response to criticism from the opposing party. Why they

---

it can be precisely the most critical conditions that catalyse a great hermeneutical-literary effort to safeguard the meaning of events from the flood of chaos that every tragedy bears within itself. This does not, however, implicate a literary creation *ex novo* or the invention of stories, facts, and characters that are entirely fictitious.

35 A problematic expression that acts as Leitmotiv in the article by J. APPLEGATE, «The Fate of Zedekiah». But one could cite other similar expressions in other studies.

36 Redactional interventions of this kind would be conceivable in a history of the composition that is drawn out over a prolonged period of time, with a text received already substantially established and canonised, to which literary material can only be added and not removed (except to a limited extent).

37 Various voices and protagonists in dialectical tension, an enormous distance between them but a single communicative basis upon which to freely intervene with close conversational exchanges, and all in a very short span of time: this is a hermeneutical model that is (too) much like the modern *forums* on the *web*. In these, once a *thread* (i.e. a topic of discussion that generates a sequence of contributions on the theme in question) has been created by a site moderator, every user can have his say by adding a *post* in support of his ideas and/or in opposition to one or the other *posts* of another user, thus building up the body of the thread itself until the discussion is closed. This model of communication and comparison is certainly interesting (typical e.g. of social networks), but is one that, to me, seems to have truly very little to do with the temporal frame, complexity, and dramatic nature of the historical context in which the events and themes of the book of Jeremiah are involved. According to this model, the (supposed) intervention into the Jeremianic text would actually have had to be made on a single manuscript (and the others?), without explaining how a "correction" or comment would have been laid down.

88   Orientative literary-hermeneutical coordinates

did not simply expunge and purge whole textual portions or individual verses that were problematic or perceived to be detrimental to their own desire for authority[38]? Furthermore, with the rapid end of the Babylonian Empire at the hand of the Persians, and once the decree of Cyrus was issued, it is not clear then on what grounds and for what purpose it would have been opportune to put the theme of the surrender to Babylon in the mouth of Jeremiah with such emphasis.

Sincerely, the whole thing seems quite unrealistic. And yet, even more daring and creative theories exist, such as that of C. Hardmeier[39] (validated and re-elaborated by R. Albertz[40] and J.-H. Stipp[41]), who goes so far as to propose as a plausible hypothesis the notion that not only in the already relatively brief time span between 597 and 587[42] but even specifically during the *very brief* suspension of the siege (to be placed in the summer of 588), the "national-religious party" would had wanted and been able to compose, for ideological purposes, what would subsequently become the "account of Hezekiah". C. Hardmeier believes to have found this story within the literary perimeter of 2 Kgs 18:9–19:37. Denying any direct historical reference to Hezekiah or to the prophet Isaiah, he maintains that this text would actually be a propagandist one intended to demolish Jeremiah's (and Ezekiel's!) position, and that in fact, a situation entirely (?) similar to that in Jeremiah be described in this story, that is, the Assyrian siege of 701, later miraculously lifted.[43] According to C. Hardmeier, the narration put

---

38   In order to remove a textual tension between two elements in conflict, simply eliminate one. If someone had the authority to amend or reshape the Jeremianic tradition at will, why was this not done? These questions remain substantially unanswered. The tendency to conserve pre-existing text is a well-known fact, but it is valid with respect to *ancient* traditions. In the case of Jeremiah, however, it would have been a question of operations carried out on a newly created text and within a tradition that had a history behind it that was too brief or almost non-existent to have the power to impose itself regardless. On the other hand, considering the preservative power of memory regarding facts that in this particular case were fairly recent and well known, it seems implausible that scribal interventions would have easily introduced truly significant modifications to that attested by the incipient tradition regarding the prophet Jeremiah and his historical context. In other words, the book of Jeremiah cannot be conceived as a sort of *blockchain*, that is, as a log of data in blocks, concatenated according to a chronological order that progressively increases due to a multiplicity of subjects, creating a structure that is, at the same time, both shared and immutable.

39   Cf. C. HARDMEIER, *Prophetie*, 287–408.

40   Cf. R. ALBERTZ, *Religionsgeschichte Israels in alttestamentlicher Zeit*. Teil 1: Von den Anfängen bis zum Ende der Königszeit, ATD 8/1, Göttingen 1992, 370–372. More recently, it has been revived by A. BARUCHI-UNNA, «The Story of Hezekiah's Prayer (2 Kings 19) and Jeremiah's Polemic concerning the Inviolability of Jerusalem», *JSOT* 39 (2015) 281–297.

41   Cf. H.-J. STIPP, «Zedekiah in the Book of Jeremiah: On the Formation of a Biblical Character», *CBQ* 58 (1996) 627–648 (see esp. pp. 632, 645–646).

42   Just as does e.g. clearly C.J. SHARP, *Prophecy*, 12, n. 31.

43   C. Hardmeier ought to at least express a doubt however, on specifically the very grounds of his own methodology, about whether the suspension itself of the siege described in the book of Jeremiah be an actual historical fact (as he implicitly suggests) or merely another tendentious text invented by some group to meet its own political ends instead.

Overall literary organisation of the book of Jeremiah and hermeneutical notes   89

the principal themes of the Jeremianic preaching regarding the surrender on the lips of the enemy general, thus stigmatising them as underhanded and perverse anti-nationalist propaganda.

Several questions immediately arise, however: Who would those in power have needed to manipulate? The people? But how many of these people actually knew how to read, even considering the evolution of literacy that characterises the last stage of the reign of Judah[44]? Was there really time available to write it, elaborate it, and render the operation politically effective? How would this text have been physically distributed amongst the people? And last but not least: if the "account of Hezekiah" really were a phoney document with a polemic, anti-Jeremianic function, how then would one explain its permanence after the facts of 587 had already proven Jeremiah right (and he had been recognised, at least in hindsight, as having been a true prophet)?[45] One could go on, but I believe that what has been highlighted thus far is beyond sufficient to express my personal assessment of the insufficient level of anchoring in truth of similar literary-critical theories. While certainly clever and perhaps fascinating to consider, they seem to push well beyond the limit of plausibility suggested by the documented data available to us.

In short, I by no means negate the evident traces of a history of the text's composition (which, however, appears to have come about over a long span of time and not during the immediate and overwhelming succession of events relating to the last phase of the kingdom of Judah, nor in the first decades following the end of Jerusalem). But it seems problematic to me, to say the least, that interpretive models having such a low level of historical plausibility[46] be indubitably presumed. It is clear that the critical

---

44 This process of "textualisation" is highlighted by W.M. SCHNIEDEWIND, *How the Bible*, 91–117.

45 To justify its survival in the biblical text and thus bring the circle to a close, C. Hardmeier believes that this propagandistic document was later and erroneously reinterpreted as being historical. Due to precisely his own presupposition that its origin be so late, this hypothesis seems quite improbable. On this question, see also the critical observations of C.R. Seitz by C. HARDMEIER, *Prophetie*, in *JBL* 110 (1991) 511–513, and P.S. EVANS, *The Invasion of Sennacherib in the Book of Kings*. A Source-Critical and Rhetorical Study of 2 Kings 18–19, VT.S 125, Leiden – Boston 2009, 9–10.

46 I place myself in the wake of the same doubts expressed by G. Fischer in this regard. Amongst his various critical findings, in which he highlights how several questions remain unresolved and how much these literary-critical hypotheses lack solid foundations, given that they are absolutely unable to convincingly explain the present textual configuration, he states (in reference to the work of H.-J. Stipp, but clearly, not only): "Fraglich ist jedoch, ob dafür mehrere Gruppen bzw. Autoren anzunehmen sind, und wer auf welche Weise die kontrastierenden Standpunkte dann dennoch in *einem* Buch zusammengeführt hat" (see G. FISCHER, *Jeremia*, 107). And after having reviewed the various contributions on the subject, whilst admitting different perspectives within the book of Jeremiah, ones similar however to the musical grammar of a score (pp. 103–104) that literally evolves in "Synthensen" and "Mosaiken" (p. 113), he thus concludes lapidarily but incisively: "Die Argumentation mit Schichten oder Redaktionen für die Entstehung von Jer führt nicht weit und vermag den vorliegenden Textbefund nicht zu erklären" (p. 110). The concept of the "mosaic" was already used by B. DUHM, *Jeremia*, 10, but in a negative sense (cf. also K. SEYBOLD, *Der Prophet Jeremia*. Leben und Werk, CTB 416, Stuttgart – Berlin – Köln 1993, 40). Instead, in a positive sense, in J. KRISPENZ, «Die Einsetzung des Jeremia. Ambivalenz als

assessment I have presented of the epistemological bases underlying the studies cited is merely a sketch, and that more adequate development would be required. But it is likewise evident that the scholars who have undertaken this sort of research have adequately motivated neither their presuppositions nor the conclusions of their theories. Therefore, I believe that it has sufficed to put the problem forth, at least for this initial phase of my dissertation.

2.2.4. Aporias and alternative paths of research

The interpretative lines that I have mentioned can perhaps be attributed to a certain absolutisation of some procedures that characterise the historical-critical method. Until not long ago, these procedures or methodologies seemed, in their attempt to provide a diachronic reconstruction of the text, to be those most appropriate (if not the only ones) for exegetical science.[47] These studies certainly retain the merit of having drawn attention to the undeniable impact of history on the literary corpus. But I believe I can say that today, they seem increasingly fragile, at least in the biblical field.[48] This results from their having to rely on knowledge that is almost always partial

---

Mittel der Sinnkonstitution», in: *Schriftprophetie*. Festschrift für Jörg Jeremias zum 65. Geburtstag, *eds.* F. HARTENSTEIN – J. KRISPENZ – A. SCHART, Neukirchen-Vluyn 2004, 203–219 (here, pp. 214, 219). As regards reliability of the traditional redaction-critical research in Old Testament studies and its claim to be able to clearly identify previous layers in the final texts, see the severe criticism from B. ZIEMER, *Kritik des Wachstumsmodells*. Die Grenzen alttestamentlicher Redaktionsgeschichte im Lichte empirischer Evidenz, VT.S 182, Leiden 2020. Regarding his own redactional-critical hypothesis on the formation of the book of Jeremiah (and the fundamental assumption of his whole work), see the subsequent observations by H. -J. STIPP, «Überlegungen zu ausgewählten Aspekten der Behandlung des Jeremiabuchs in der Monographie von Benjamin Ziemer "Kritik des Wachstumsmodells" (2020)», *BZ* 65 (2021) 191–215.

47 It is no accident that I speak of "some procedures that characterise the historical-critical method" rather than of the historical-critical method *tout-court*. Indeed, it is my impression that too often this complex discipline (essential for the study of ancient documents) has actually been identified with diachronic reconstruction of the history of the text and the effort to approach the chimera of the "original/authentic text" (or the no less elusive "intentio auctoris") as much as possible. Instead, the historical-critical method, however, involves a whole series of procedures. And it is up to the exegete, on the basis of the text and the questions posed in its regard, to identify the most appropriate methodological procedure(s). Cf., e.g. H. SIMIAN-YOFRE, *ed.*, *Metodologia dell'Antico Testamento*, StBi(Bo) 25, 1994 Bologna, esp. pp. 79–119, where the author prefers to speak, significantly, not of a "method" but of "historical-critical methods".

48 See, in this regard, the collection of studies J. TIGAY, *ed.*, *Empirical Models for Biblical Criticism*, Philadelphia 1985, where the majority of the contributions, aside from the exception noted by E. Tov (pp. 97–130), show an inability to found literary-critical theories on any empirical evidence. This is not the case in the compilation of some extrabiblical texts from the ancient Near East (cf. esp. J. TIGAY, *The Evolution of the Gilgamesh Epic*, Philadelphia 1982). See also, on the difference between historicism and pseudo-historicism, B.D. SOMMER, «Dating Pentateuchal Texts and the Perils of Pseudo-Historicism", in: *The Pentateuch*. International Perspectives on Current Research, *eds.* T.B. DOZEMAN – K. SCHMID – B.J. SCHWARTZ, FAT 78, Tübingen 2011,

Overall literary organisation of the book of Jeremiah and hermeneutical notes 91

and disputable in anything involving strata, sources, traditions, dating, author, redactor, attribution of a distinctive lexicon, and every other historical question concerning the book's formation and the facts presented by it or that can be correlated to it.

Maintaining steadfast the need for proper rigour in every inquiry aspiring to be considered "scientific", other methodological perspectives ultimately seem to offer points of view and alternative or complementary solutions that open new, interesting horizons. Of principal interest to me is the plausibility of a *non-random arrangement* (redactional or not) of the texts physically belonging to a single book.[49] An arrangement of this sort would seem to obey more the demands of a profound theological understanding of the prophetic phenomenon or a prophetic reading of history in general (even if only scribal) than it would aspirations of socio-politico accreditation.

In other words, without wanting to disregard the contributions of literary-critical studies and their respective theories on the composition's history, my own exegetic work will seek to take elements of a symbolic and semiotic nature into consideration. This set of communicative elements is always involved and brought into play when conceptual content passes from the oral level to the written form.[50] Thus all the more reason why, I believe, these should be examined here in the specific case of the book of Jeremiah, which was clearly subject to multiple readjustments and sagacious rereadings successively, over a long period of time.

According to this perspective, and contrary above all to the authors who judge the process that led to the present Hebrew form of the book of Jeremiah as having been substantially random in nature, I hold the belief that its literary organisation be a significant vehicle of meaning irreducible to that of the result of unlikely and incidental "intratextual" or "redactional" debates between rival political factions moved

---

85–108. He rightly points out two main fallacies that pervade many biblical studies: 1) "the assumption that if an idea or text is especially relevant to a particular historical period, then the idea or text must have originated in that period", and that 2) "when scholars claim that a text is obviously appropriate for a particular moment in history, they are often correct, but they fail to acknowledge that the idea or text is equally appropriate for some other moment as well" (p. 94).

49 Other studies done along these lines inc. e.g. J.M. ABREGO, *Jeremías y el final del reino*. Lectura sincrónica de Jer 36–45, Institución San Jerónimo, EstAT 3, Valencia 1983; ID., «El texto hebreo estructurado de Jeremías 36–45», *CuaBi* 8 (1983) 1–49; A.R. DIAMOND, *The Confession of Jeremiah in Context*. Scenes of Prophetic Drama, JSOT.S 45, Sheffield 1987; C.R. SEITZ, «The Prophet Moses», 3–27; M.S. SMITH, *The Laments of Jeremiah and their Contexts*. A Literary and Redactional Study of Jeremiah 11–20, SBLMS 42, Atlanta 1990; R.E. CLEMENTS, «Jeremiah 1–25 and the Deuteronomistic History», in: *Understanding Poets and Prophets*. Essays in Honor of G.W. Anderson, ed. A.G. AULD, JSOT.S 152, Sheffield 1993, 93–113; W. BRUEGGEMANN, «The "Baruch Connection": Reflections on Jer. 43: 1–7», *JBL* 113 (1994) 405–420; M.E. BIDDLE, *Polyphony and Symphony in Prophetic Literature*. Rereading Jeremiah 7–20, SOTI 2, Macon 1996; L. STULMAN, *Order amid Chaos*; R.R. WILSON, «Poetry and Prose in the Book of Jeremiah», in: *Ki Baruch Hu*. Ancient Near Eastern-Biblical and Judaic Studies in Honor of Baruch A. Levine, *eds*. R. CHAZAN *et al.*, Winona Lake 1999.

50 Cf. G. BAUMANN, *The Written Word*. Literacy in Transition, Oxford 1986. With regard to the complexity of the communicative process underlying the prophetic phenomenon, cf. esp. M. NISSINEN, «Spoken, Quoted, and Invented: Orality and Writtenness in Ancient Near Eastern, SBLSymS 10, Atlanta 2000, 235–271.

by the desire to accredit themselves before a phantom, socio-religious audience (to be manipulated at will). In my opinion, the present arrangement of the MT instead attests a very particular semiotic-redactional intentionality. This must have left a significant imprint on the literary organisation of the text as a whole after 561 (in fact, the rehabilitation of Jehoiachin narrated in ch. 52 dates back to this year, a text which is also implicitly referred to in 1:3) and must have assumed a form that was more or less definitive, or at any rate fairly stabilised, probably not before the fourth century.[51]

In fact, I believe that it is possible to demonstrate, even solely on the basis of the specific theme that is the object of my study, how the current arrangement of the book of Jeremiah according to the MT suggests an intentional unitary theological design. I believe this to be the fruit of an elevated mastery and faculty of re-elaboration and "discussion" of more ancient texts and of the entire Jeremianic tradition.[52] The corpus that we have before us today appears to be a sophisticated scribal interweaving of varied available textual materials that, while still conveying different tones, voices, and accents, wittingly intend to reflect and illuminate the meaningful intricacy of a story handed down through time. In it, the human and the divine intertwine and become indistinguishable, delivering the reader a *surplus* of theological meaning that is imprinted upon the final work. This arrangement discreetly offers a hermeneutical key able to introduce a coherent comprehension of both the figure of the prophet Jeremiah and his message. My study of the theme of the surrender to Babylon and its profound implications, in relation to the other fundamental themes of the book of Jeremiah and to the unitary theological meaning of the Jeremianic corpus, lies precisely in this (alternative) direction.

2.3. The "symbolic" approach of Louis Stulman: Towards a new perspective for inquiry

At least in some respects, my perspective shares the approach to the issue of the book's structure developed by Louis Stulman, in particular.[53] In reference to the book

---

51 This starting point, which I share, was pointed out by G. FISCHER, *Jeremia*, 111; ID., «Il libro di Geremia», 395; 413, n. 71.

52 As was very clearly shown by G. FISCHER, «Il libro di Geremia», 393–417 and, previously, also by K. VAN DER TOORN, *Scribal Culture and the Making of the Hebrew Bible*, Cambridge (MA) 2007, 173–204, who in the seventh chapter programmatically defines the book of Jeremiah as a "Scribal Artifact".

53 See L. STULMAN, *Order amid Chaos* (as well as ID., «The Prose Sermons as Hermeneutical Guide to Jeremiah 1–25: The Deconstruction of Judah's Symbolic World», in: *Troubling Jeremiah, eds.* A.R.P. DIAMOND – K. O'CONNOR – L. STULMAN, JSOT.S 260, Sheffield 1999, 34–63), which, in turn, is based on the insights of R.E. CLEMENTS, «Jeremiah 1–25», 94–108, according to whom the macrostructures of Jer 1–25 would closely follow the essential points of the Deuteronomistic reflection on the fall of the kingdom of the North found in 2 Kings 17:7–23. Nevertheless, the work of L. Stulman represents a strand of research that believes it be possible to retrace a particular theological meaning in the diversity of the various textual elements (which, for the devotees of literary criticism, would refer instead only to their "sources" and to different and opposing ideologies). More recently, W. BRUEGGEMANN, *The Theology of the Book of Jeremiah*, New York 2007, in introducing the complexity of the book of Jeremiah, identifies three principal hypotheses of solutions, represented respectively by 1) the conservative position of W.L. Holladay, who claims that most of the material

Overall literary organisation of the book of Jeremiah and hermeneutical notes　93

of Jeremiah, he speaks of a "symbolic tapestry" that is not so much an "unreadable" textual bundle, fruit of a random assemblage or incongruent development, but rather the literary reflection of mindful redactional strategies, of a complex hermeneutical process of reinterpretation and adaption carried out in the spirit of *substantial fidelity* to the Jeremianic preaching.[54]

According to his thesis, precisely the insertion of the texts belonging to the C "source" (the so-called prose discourses)[55] would carry the significant structural force to provide the necessary coordinates to give adequate intelligence to the entirety (namely, the remaining A and B "sources", which identify, respectively, the passages in poetry and autobiographical prose).[56] More specifically, these passages would function a bit like midrash, introducing (or recalling), clarifying, and "codifying" the themes expressed in the immediate context. This context is characterised above all in 1–25, by the typical (often disorienting) freedom of its "poetic" style.[57] The complex and "wild" symbolic system evoked by the poetry and crystallised in literary material arranged apparently without a precise logic, would therefore be re-expressed, linked back, and placed in harmonious relation within the whole corpus (*Sitz im Buch*) through these "symbolic connections" in prose informed by a specific theological meaning.[58]

---

be "genuine" and thus the parts in poetry and prose intimately interconnected; 2) the diametrically opposite position maintained by R.P. Carroll, for whom direct access to the historical figure of the prophet is impossible, given the predominant ideological intervention of a Deuteronomistic hand in the prose that obscures the more original material contained in the poetry; 3) the author I cited, L. Stulman, for whom, on the contrary, it is precisely some of the prose texts that serve as guide to the reading of the book as an organic whole.

54　"Contrary to the dominant voice in biblical scholarship which understands Jeremiah as a random collection of prophetic materials with a disjointed character, the book, it seems to me, is a rather carefully constructed composition with a purposeful theological design. To put it more modestly, in spite of the book's untidiness this literature is readable, not primarily by standards of linear logic and coherence, but as a symbolic tapestry of meanings with narrative seams" (L. STULMAN, *Order amid Chaos*, 17).

55　I refer to this subdivision, assuming only its conventional value, given that more recent studies in literary criticism strongly dispute the possibility of there being a clear distinction between the literary material once attributed to "source" B and that attributed to "source" C.

56　This statement (cf. L. STULMAN, *Order amid Chaos*, 18) could actually be entirely valid only with regard to chs. 1–25, given that amongst the texts in prose in which the author recognises a particular structuring intensity (chs. 26; 45; 52; cf. *ibid.*, 63), only ch. 45 is attributed by S. MOWINCKEL, *Zur Komposition*, 40 to "source" C. In fact, ch. 26 would be part of "source" B (cf. *ibid.*, 24), while ch. 52 is a late addition (cf. *ibid.*, 16).

57　Cf. L. STULMAN, *Order amid Chaos*, 52–55.

58　It seems evident that the attempt to understand the book of Jeremiah as a totality that is "redactionally" (and theologically) structured follows along the lines of the so-called synchronic approaches. However, this certainly does not mean reading the text according to the intents that R.P. Carroll somewhat arbitrarily seems to attribute to this perspective, which – as he sees it – would merely claim to consider the book "as a *narrative representation* of the closing decades of the Judean state, with lengthy poetic discourses, in terms of the behaviour and utterances of the prophet Jeremiah" (cf. ID., «Synchronic Deconstructions», 49). My perspective also deviates from the hermeneutics of a devotee of *Rhetorical Criticism,* as is J.R. Lundbom. I am persuaded,

94   Orientative literary-hermeneutical coordinates

The book of Jeremiah would essentially take the shape of a two-part drama, corresponding to the first two major literary blocks that compose it. The first would thematise the dismantling of the symbolic-sacral microcosm of the religion of Judah (1–25). In the second, signs of a new beginning would appear, seeds germinating from amidst the ruins of a politico-religious system marked by the end (26–45).[59]

My reference to L. Stulman's contribution, more than be a sharing of method (in fact, in § 4.1.2, I will mention the problematic aspects of this), represents a concrete exemplification of how the problems posed by the composition of the book of Jeremiah can be approached through an alternative perspective, one far more sensitive to that extra *quid* of a theological nature that got imprinted through the redactional workings of dislocating the various textual clusters to then create new links between them. Ultimately, the question is that of making explicit a postulation that I believe ought to be borne in mind (and which I will seek to substantiate), above all during the stage in which the texts most relevant to the present dissertation are being presented in relation to their (significative) placement within the literary perimeter of the Jeremianic corpus.

2.4. Semiotic *arcatas* and the architecture of meaning

In the hermeneutical perspective that I am illustrating, it is not only the *history of the composition* of the text that interrogates the reader's intelligence, but also (and above all) the *compositional form* given by the *present* arrangement of its parts. This is most significantly true on the level of the textual blocks that are much larger than a single verse or pericope.

2.4.1. Historical-critical exegesis and (Semitic) rhetorical analysis

With its classical diachronic methodologies,[60] historical-critical exegesis has helped to draw attention to small textual units, highlighting (or believing to highlight and account for) significant tensions and fractures present within the various books of the Bible. Today, after two centuries of genetic sorts of inquiries, a study of biblical texts

---

that the determination of the final form of the text, in the case of the structure of the book of Jeremiah, be not *only* a question of mnemonic demands, or of a stylistic balancing of the textual units or rhetorical devices that belong to the *ars retorica* typical of oral preaching (cf. ID. *Jeremiah: A Study in Ancient Hebrew Rhetoric*, SBLDS 18, Missoula 1975, Winona Lake ²1997, 147–149, 152–154), but rather – primarily – of the intent to shape the final structure with a theological meaning deduced from the various materials used for its arrangement (and even pushed "beyond"). This could be demonstrated by highlighting "semiotic *arcatas*" (which I will discuss in the following paragraph), that is, relevant and convincing thematic-lexical connections. This operation, given the aim of my work, will particularly regard the case of 21:1–10, a text that I will also study in the light of its relation to its proximal literary context.

59   Cf. L. STULMAN, *Order amid Chaos*, 18, 56–57.

60   In this regard, see W. STENGER, *Biblische Methodenlehre*, LeTh 18, Düsseldorf 1987, 65–85; H. SIMIAN-YOFRE, *ed.*, *Metodologia*, 79–137 and J.-N. ALETTI – M. GILBERT – J.-L. SKA – S. DE VULPILLIÈRES, *Vocabulaire raisonné de l'exégèse biblique. Les mots, les approches, les auteurs*, Paris 2005, 39–69; M. BAUKS – C. NIHAN, *eds.*, *Manuel d'exégèse de l'Ancien Testament*, MoBi 61, Genève 2008, 95–190.

Overall literary organisation of the book of Jeremiah and hermeneutical notes   95

that prescinds from a critical assumption of their historical character and defends their compositional unity in a way that is ingenuous or pre-scientific can be deemed unthinkable.

At the same time, however, the "traditional" application of these kinds of methodologies without the contribution of an accurate reflection on their very epistemological foundation has often resulted in a number of reconstructions being marked by a highly elevated degree of speculativeness. This is hardly compatible with the claims of "objectivity" that have accompanied the efforts of many scholars. This fact cannot be minimised. Let me clarify. It is obvious that the dialectic between working hypotheses and demonstrative argumentations, with their relative confirmations, denials, and adjustments, be the unique characteristic of every rigorous (and in this sense "scientific") research that is done.[61] But it is equally indubitable that aside from a relative consensus on the more macroscopic questions, this field of study is generally distinguished by a striking and permanent divergence of opinions. The suspicion is that many conclusions may be mostly just (respectable) *conjectures* and not the direct and cogent results of a reliable methodology. Due to its own intrinsic epistemological limits, this methodology would regardless be incapable of exhausting, on its own, the wealth of meaning found on the biblical page.

In response to a type of research in which the dimension of fragmentariness is simultaneously both a stimulus and a limit of the research itself, I believe that it is necessary to reintroduce the question of its meaning as a "totality". This allows us to recuperate an ability to grasp in synchronic perspective, that is, in the semiotic unity derived from the single biblical books, the long-distance *relationships* between micro and macro thematic-lexical elements. The issue is that of seeing if the redactional/authorial (or simply scribal) intentionality that has presided over the actual shaping of the biblical books might in fact be something radically more complex than what was traditionally conceived when referring to the notion of "stitching" together redactional insertions and their relative theological reorientations.

At the local level, it is clearly apparent that the concatenation of the textual discourse makes wide use of *grammatical parallelism* ("parallelismus membrorum")[62] and of *parataxis*.[63] This is typical of biblical literature in general and, above all, that of the "poetic" sort. The Semitic thought that shapes the Scripture prefers *juxtaposition* between elements that are different and/or similar, and leaves the burden of a multiperspectival interpretive synthesis to the reader. It appears, in other words, to proceed and express itself in a manner that is different from that of a Greek matrix, which is founded instead on deductive logic and hypotactic phraseology. This phenomenon has deep cognitive anthropological roots that are by no means reducible to

---

61 It is obvious that the description "scientific", which can be attributed to historical research or to the human sciences in general, is of an entirely different nature than that, paradigmatic, of the so-called "exact sciences", where the principle of Popperian falsifiability and empirical-experimental verification reigns.

62 In this regard, see e.g. R. ALTER, *The Art of Biblical Poetry*, New York 1985, 3–26; L. ALONSO SCHÖKEL, *Manual de poética hebrea*, 69–85; M.P. O'CONNOR, *Hebrew Verse Structure*, Winona Lake 1980, ²1997, 88–96.

63 "Ce mot barbare signifie simplement que les choses sont posées l'une à côté de l'autre, sans que leur rapport soit explicité" (R. MEYNET, *Lire la Bible*, Paris 1996, ²2003, 94).

the field of poetic expression,[64] so it is not surprising that its binary nature (reinterpreted by P. Beauchamp as "deuterosis")[65] is encountered on more levels than solely that of the word or the discourse. It exercises a force of structural organisation that can be traced through the entire body of the individual biblical books to the level of the Scripture as a whole, both that which is only Jewish and that which is Christian, given the structural relationship between the Old and New Testament, where the first Genesitic creation finds its recapitulative fulfilment in the new creation announced in the book of Revelation.[66]

The study of Semitic rhetoric conducted by (biblical) "rhetorical analysis"[67] has made a particular contribution to the formalisation of a series of criteria or rules able

---

64 As shown, e.g. in A. WAGNER, «Der Parallelismus membrorum zwischen poetischer Form und Denkfigur», in: *Parallelismus membrorum, ed.* A. WAGNER, OBO 224, Göttingen 2007, 1–26. Already, G. von Rad, had spoken of "Stereometrie", while more recently, it has been specified as a question of a general attitude of Hebrew thought (cf. in this regard, above all H.W. WOLFF, *Anthropologie des Alten Testaments,* München 1973, 22 e B. JANOWSKI, *Konfliktgespräche mit Gott.* Eine Anthropologie der Psalmen, Neukirchen-Vluyn 2003, ²2006, 13–21). In particular, the adjective "stereometric" refers analogically, aside from to the fundamental anthropological polarities, to the binocular vision of three-dimensional objects. In this sense, it is a question of having an ability to grasp and explain the truth of things in a pluridimensional way, starting with their reciprocal relationship (and then unified by a cognitive synthesis).

65 It was P. Beauchamp (in *L'un et l'autre Testament,* 150–163) who coined this neologism to refer to the phenomenon not so much of "repetition", understood in the literal sense, but rather as "recapitulation", that is, of the "pliure du discours sur lui-même" (p. 162): "La deutérose se présente dans la loi comme un impératif dont le contenu est replié sur lui-même puisqu'il enjoint d'observer la loi, dans les prophètes comme une parole de Dieu dont le contenu est que Dieu parle et qu'il est Dieu, dans les sages comme une invitation qui a pour centre ces mots: 'Commencement de la Sagesse: acquiers la Sagesse'" (p. 150). It is, indeed, "an unusual term in the exegetic field, precisely because no one had highlighted the phenomenon of rewriting, of resuming, of repetition as the principle of intelligence of the structure of the Old Testament and as pivotal in the relationship between the one and the other Testament" (P. BOVATI, «Deuterosi e compimento», *Teol[M]* 27 [2002] 20–34, here, translated from p. 20). Nonetheless, it should be stressed with P. BOITANI, *Prima lezione sulla letteratura,* Roma – Bari 2007, XII, that the phenomenon of "rewriting" is the principle that governs the growth of that gigantic tree that is literature itself.

66 "Rather than be a final moment, a recapitulation is a moment in its own right, when the perspectival point from which, in view of the future of the text, everything that has previously occured is read. In other words: on the one hand, a recapitulation brings everything that has already been produced up to that point to a closure; on the other, it opens up a new understanding that arises from the new 'centre of gravity' that it itself offers for future reflections" (G. BORGONOVO, «Primo Testamento», in: *AsSaggi biblici.* Introduzione alla Bibbia anima della teologia, *ed.* F. MANZI, Milano 2006, 51–138 (here, translated from p. 110).

67 I refer in particular to the studies and methodology systematically elaborated by Roland Meynet (see, esp.: ID., *L'analyse rhétorique.* Une nouvelle méthode pour comprendre la Bible, Paris 1989; *Traité de rhétorique biblique,* RhSem 4, Paris 2007, ²2013) starting from a line of research that already has its own history (from the middle of the eighteenth century, with *De sacra poesi hebraeorum praelectiones academicae Oxonii habitae* by Robert Lowth), but a limited number textual investigations. I shall

Overall literary organisation of the book of Jeremiah and hermeneutical notes   97

to identify important *clues to the text's composition*, be it on the level of the single clause or in broader sections of text, up to the entire book. This methodology, which has its roots in the linguistics matrix, is still in a phase of development and calibration[68] and is not to be adopted in a conclusive manner. It ought rather be taken as *one* of the multiple procedures of the exegetic method. Specifically, it is the procedure that approaches the general question of the text's meaning by focalising attention on its organisation (or "shape") and by raising the question of the potential meanings this may have.[69]

On the general level, relationships of sameness or opposition between different linguistic elements set at variable distances are categorised by R. Meynet using the basic notion of "symmetry". To use his terminology, this "symmetry" can be of the "total", "partial", or "concentric"[70] sort. This concept does have considerable hermeneutical implications, since it can refer not only to the conformation of living organisms defined by biology, but also to the profound structure of reality as described by modern physics.[71] In my opinion, however, its adoption in this field of study is not

---

make use of the basic applications of this methodology in presenting the compositional organisation of the texts I am studying. If, on the one hand, in the devotees of this methodology at times a certain tendency to push the method to extremes can be observed, it is, in my opinion, right to accept the invitation to take the peculiarities of the compositional processes typical of the Semitic culture (different from those of Graeco-Latin rhetoric) into due consideration, as well as the need to be equipped with a rigorous research methodology (with truly verifiable formal and content criteria), the lack of which often renders more than a few suggestions for the textual organisation approximate.

68   In this regard, see the critical insights and reflective proposals of P. BOVATI, «Il centro assente. Riflessioni ermeneutiche sul metodo dell'analisi retorica, in riferimento specifico alle strutture prive di centro», in: *Retorica biblica e semitica 1*. Atti del primo convegno RBS, *eds.* R. MEYNET – J. ONISZCZUK, RBSem 1, Bologna 2009, 107–121. In particular, P. Bovati rightly observes how rhetorical analysis should be considered only *one* of the possible tools of the exegetical method, and, therefore calls to "reassess its claim of being the methodologically rigorous explicitation of the only manner of structuring biblical texts", by entering into dialogue with other methodologies of textual analysis (translated from pp. 112–113). On the other hand, if the form mediates the meaning, rhetorical analysis can be configured as only a passage (a "way", to wit, a method) that must carry one beyond the letter without remaining prisoner of meticulous analyses that are an end in themselves or of undue "predilection for concentric structuring" (translated from p. 118).

69   This axiom of P. Beauchamp whereby "la forme est la porte du sens" (ID., «Préface», 8) is by now renowned. This postulate obviously does not only concern the structural configuration of the text that the rhetorical analysis sets its sights on studying, but is valid at any communicative level (cf. *ibid.*, 7) and, according to various perspectives, for any exegetic process (from the study of "morphology" to *Formgeschichte*, up to analysis of the most complex modulations and expressions of signification). In this regard, see the observations of P. BOVATI, «Il centro assente», 107–121 (esp. pp. 107–108).

70   For the technical vocabulary adopted by rhetorical analysis, see esp. the methodology proposed by R. MEYNET, *Traité de rhétorique biblique*.

71   But in truth, both on a biological and physical level, it is precisely the breaking of a symmetry that generates the multiplicity and dynamic complexity of reality. Take,

entirely satisfactory on the heuristic level, on the one hand for reasons of referential semantic pertinence, while on the other, for precisely the type of phenomenon that I intend to bring to the foreground over the course of my study.

In fact, the concept of symmetry rigorously regards the mutual specular correspondence between *identical elements*. This is, however, exactly the contrary of what is expressed by the "basic" device of *parallelismus membrorum*. This device is, a close look reveals – aside from its syntactic construction – by nature, *asymmetrical*, since it bases its communicative strength on the *synonymic* (or *antonymic*) representation of *formally distinct*[72] lexical elements. For example, if whoever speaks in the Scripture repeats what they have said a second time but in a way that differs (or is even opposite), it is logical that they do not want to uselessly reduplicate the same concept. They intend, rather, to convey a more complex idea, one that only the totality of a semantic plexus can offer. On the other hand, one need simply look at the examples adopted by R. Meynet to realise that by the notion of "symmetry", he is actually referring to formal literal and fundamentally *asymmetrical* cross-references, even when so-called "complete symmetries"[73] are in question. Ultimately, it could not be otherwise, given that the event of communication (be it poetic or narrative) is not associable to the static nature of a perfect figure, but rather a dynamic phenomenon generated quite specifically by the breaking of an initial or ideal symmetry (and thus, from a stasis).

In other words, while there is no lack of expressions or terms repeated to the letter in the figures that emerge from the biblical page (which can most certainly be important clues of rhetorical composition), the question is more that of textual organisations having an evident level of *proportionality* that comes from the "balanced tension" established amongst their components. For this reason, in my view, it would be more appropriate to speak of phenomena of *regularity* expressed in correspondence to *analogous semantic relationships* (for the synonymous references) or in *semantic oppositions* (for the antithetical relationships).

Referring, above all, to levels and textual units that are higher than single phrases, we can say that if the repetition does not normally occur in the sign of the identical but rather in the analogous, then we are in the presence of a series of back and forth references of a *symbolic* nature. These references are suggested and proposed to the

---

for example, the functional asymmetry of the two cerebral hemispheres and the cosmological theory of the beginning of the universe as the breaking of a symmetry that was originally perfect. In the linguistic field as well, recently, with the theory of "Dynamic Antisymmetry", the hypothesis has been posed that syntactic movement has the function of "breaking the symmetry" of syntactic structures to allow the linearisation of the linguistic signal. In this regard, see A. Moro, *Dynamic Antisymmetry*, LIM 38, Cambridge (MA) 2000; Id., *The Boundaries of Babel. The Brain and the Enigma of Impossible Languages*, CSL, Cambridge (MA) 2008, 203–227.

72   This is very clear when beyond the form (of the lexemes) there is an emphasis on their quantitative-numerical referentiality, subject to a law of "intensification" when two contiguous phrases are set in parallel (cf. e.g. Deut 32:30 and 1 Sam 18:7).

73   See e.g. the phrases of Song 4:6: "(a) Léve-toi (b) *Aquilon* / (a') accours (b') *Autan*", that of Luke 19:38: "(a) Dans le ciel (b) *paix* / (b') et *gloire* (a') dans les hauteurs", and of Ps 59:2: "(a) *Délivre-moi* (b) de-mes-ennemis (x) MON-DIEU, (b') de-mes-agresseurs (a') *protège-moi*", given as demonstrative examples, respectively, of "total symmetry", "mirror symmetry", and "concentric composition", in R. Meynet, *Traité*, 218–219.

reader's intelligence so that they may be the one who says the "unsaid" in the text (i.e. what the text does not explicitly say, but rather implies). It is to be the reader who extracts the meaning from the relationships suggested between the various elements and within the most relevant context for their correct interpretation. The question, as can be seen, is one of *cognitive pragmatics*: in virtue of the principle of interpretive cooperation,[74] the circumstanced semantic analysis of the single lexemes and single pericopes is not sufficient for comprehending the surplus of meaning that arises from their reciprocal relationship in a given context. This occurs precisely because that meaning comes about (or in other words, is adequately understood) only outside of the literalness of the text itself. In other words, it is within the act of the interpreter who is conscious of the contextual amplitude of an *intra-* as well as *extratextual* nature that the text itself desires to be interpreted.

Fig. 4. Two physical (and pragmatic) constitutive dimensions of the biblical text of the OT: the unrolling and rolling along a continuous vertical axis; the succession of elements or vertical geometrical spaces placed in parallel ("columns"). Here, an illustrative example: the thirteenth century Biella Torah, one of the oldest and complete Pentateuchal scrolls still suitable (kosher) for public reading by a Jewish community (Biella Synagogue, Italy).

It need be emphasised, in any case, that a "symbol" is not something "symbolic" in an erroneous sense of the "immaterial" (or even purely "conventional")[75] to which

---

74   I refer here to what U. Eco (in the third chapter of his *Lector in fabula*) re-develops on the level of textual semiotics starting from the sociolinguistic contribution by H.P. Grice. According to the Ecoian perspective, the text should be understood as an economic, incomplete mechanism that requires its own Ideal Reader, establishing blank spaces within itself that a correct interpretation on the part of the reader will later need to fill in. Only by means of this work of textual cooperation between the author and the reader does the text fully assume its own meaning.

75   I am referring, therefore, to a concept of "symbol" diametrically opposed to that employed by C.S. Peirce, for whom the dimension of the symbolic has no objective

this concept is often reduced. Far from it. The symbol, in and of itself inexhaustible and irreducible to definitive conceptualisations, refers to a "beyond", to an "other than itself" (the reality being signified), but in the concreteness of a "body/object" (signifier) that *already* renders it in some way present and accessible in its own physicality.[76] To say (something) twice in a way that is slightly varied or analogous, or in inverse order; to rewrite, recapitulate, and repeat differently: all this, mediated by the concept of "deuterosis", far from evanesces into abstraction. Indeed, the fundamental reference here is to the *physicality* of the support structure used by the books of the Hebrew Bible (cf. Fig. 4), namely, the very scroll itself, which basically obliges its reader to grow accustomed to the movement of a text unrolling and then folding back up on itself. Wrapping itself around its *umbilicus*, that is, the pivot (or pivots) around which the parchment or papyrus is rolled, it returns to the *caput* in a way that is new.[77] To unroll the scroll is to write it or read it, while to wind it back up means preparing oneself to read it again or rewrite it. To re-understand the beginning, starting from the end. An unrolled scroll traces a horizontal axis. And actually, at the same time, it also lays out a succession of vertical geometric elements in a way that is *parallel*, lining them up one beside the next. These are the *columns* of text of which the scroll is composed (cf. Fig. 5).[78] Through the horizontal unrolling of the scroll, which mirrors the "linearisation" of the linguistic sign[79] and the consequent diachronic linearity of the act of its reading, another principle of access to its meaning is in fact introduced. This principle derives instead from the synchronic consonance of distant (similar or deliberately antithetical) elements. Through this, a fruitful hermeneutical relationship is established (or better, suggested), one based on specific formal and substantive

---

relationship with the referent but rather involves an arbitrary and conventional signification.

76   I shall take up this theme in ch. V, § 4.3 of my dissertation.

77   Cf. G. Borgonovo, «Primo Testamento», 110–114.

78   The scribal practice of organising literary texts to form a geometrical arrangement in "columns" to be repeated in an equal or variable degree is attested as far back as the clay tablets with cuneiform writing and in the ancient Egyptian scrolls, and is a common characteristic of all the biblical and extrabiblical texts from Qumran. The technical term of the Lachish Ostraka is דלת (Ost. 4:3–4) and in the HB, it is attested, in this sense, precisely in the book of Jeremiah, in the plural, in the emblematic episode concerning writing, destruction, and rewriting of the prophetic scroll (cf. Jer 36:23). The root meaning of the term is "door" or "door leaf". The original reference in the literary field, even taking into consideration the translation of the LXX (which has the term σελίς), should be to the wooden tablet support. For further information on this subject, see E. Tov, *Scribal Practices and Approaches Reflected in the Texts Found in the Judean Desert*, StTDJ 54, Leiden 2004, 82–99.

79   In linguistic circles, "linearisation" in the technical sense is used to indicate the linear structure of the code of verbal expression, subject to the monodimensionality of time. To speak, in fact, means to emit sounds in temporal succession (and to write means to represent the chain of the acoustic signifier with a spatial line of graphic signs). As expressed by the renowned linguist Ferdinand de Saussure: "Le signifiant, étant de nature auditive, se déroule dans le temps seul et a les caractères qu'il emprunte au temps: a) *il représente une étendue,* et b) *celle étendue est mesurable dans une seule dimension*: c'est une ligne" (Id., *Cours de linguistique générale*, eds. C. Bailly – A. Séchehaye, Paris 1916, 103).

elements. This phenomenon, in turn, echoes yet another that is, in a certain sense, much more profound: codified, in the linearity of the linguistic signs, is a non-linear structure, that of the syntactical relationships.

Fig. 5. The "columns" of the text are arranged in succession along the horizontal axis, traced by the unrolling of the scroll, sign of the reader-oriented diachrony typical of the act of reading. Between these significant textual portions, rhetorical clues that suggest a synchronic reading able to identify "semiotic arches" – that is, distant relationships that convey a more elaborate architecture of meaning – are discernible. Here, a scroll mislabelled by an archivist in 1889 as dating from the seventeenth century, but rediscovered in 2013 at the University Library of Bologna and identified by Italian professor Mauro Perani as the oldest complete scroll of the Tôrâ in the world. The text may have been written more than 850 years ago (photo from M. PERANI, ed., The Ancient Sefer Torah of Bologna. Features and History, SJHC 59, Leiden – Boston 2019, 55, Fig. 3.1). https://www.herald.co.zw/worlds-oldest-torah-scroll-found-in-italian-archive/

2.4.2. A transemiotic notion with heuristic significance

From this perspective, which delineates a genuine *architecture of meaning,* this too having its foundation in the physicality of the text that assumes the form of the scroll, I thus introduce the conceptual category of the "semiotic *arcata*". By this notion, I intend to refer to a series of discernable connections made between textual units placed at short, medium, and even long distances that invite the re-reader to an interpretive act capable of explaining the elements of meaning generated by these relationships.

In Italian, the lexeme "arcata" refers, in the proper or figurative sense, both to the typical architectonic curvilinear, load-bearing element whose extremes rest on door jambs or columns (i.e. in English, the "arch"), as well to the more complex structure formed by a series of several arches in succession (i.e. the "arcade"). The implications of the semiotic *arcata* are to be understood in this twofold sense of the word. The use of a metaphorical sort of reference to the world of architecture to try to describe compositional phenomena typical of literature is nothing new. And the inverse is true as well.

Between the two semiotic systems, in and of themselves heterogeneous, there are reciprocal relationships and possible correlations that are often underestimated.[80] I believe that it is worth noting that Ulrich Berges and Jacques Vermeylen referred to the book of Isaiah as a "literarische Kathedrale" or "literary cathedral",[81] thereby assuming architectural realisations that are apparently extraneous to the biblical or Semitic world in general as a heuristic model.[82] The structural complexity of the book of Jeremiah in which the theme of the surrender to Babylon is situated is no less impressive, with its broad tripartition containing, in turn, further minor subdivisions on several levels. And this, in fact, finds an unexpected analogical correspondence on the level of interpretative modelling, as I will repeatedly attempt to suggest throughout my study, precisely through an abundant utilisation of elements of bridging and covering in arches or vaults in use in both the facades and internal structuring of cathedrals and medieval duomos (cf. Fig. 6).

Fig. 6. The facade of the cathedral of Saint George the martyr in Ferrara (Italy). Its typical arched structure and other connecting elements, one atop the other, recalls the tripartitian of the book of Jeremiah and its complex subdivisions. (photo licensed under the Creative Commons CC0 1.0 Universal Public Domain Dedication).

For most exegetes, considerations of this sort are usually cause for alarm. Everything that does not find immediate and evident textual evidence seems to not be relevant for

---

80 See, in this regard (albeit in a modern interpretation, since the methodology of comparison between different semiotic systems that are artistic in nature is still at an early stage): R. CASARI et al., eds., *Testo letterario e immaginario architettonico*, Milano 1996 and D. SPURR, *Architecture and Modern Literature*, Ann Arbor 2012.
81 See U. BERGES, «Das Jesajabuch als literarische Kathedrale. Ein Rundgang durch die Jahrhunderte», *BiKi* 61 (2006) 190–197 and J. VERMEYLEN, *Le livre d'Isaïe. Une cathédrale littéraire*, LeDiv, Paris 2014 (esp. pp. 11–58).
82 On the relationships between textuality and art (with reference to the use of images that have come from the ancient Near East), cf. also J.M. LEMON, «Iconographic Approaches: The Iconic Structure of Psalm 17», in: *Method Matters. Essays on the Interpretation of the Hebrew Bible in Honor of David L. Petersen*, eds. J.M. LEMON – K.H. RICH, SBLRBS 56, Atlanta 2009, 143–168.

the correct interpretation of the text itself. And yet, as the most recent linguistic interpretations in cognitive pragmatics demonstrate, it is precisely that which is by nature extratextual (encyclopaedic knowledge) that makes the most satisfactory comprehension of a communicative exchange possible, whether this be verbal or crystallised in a written form.[83] The actual arcade (or arch), as an element of comparison between the two semiotic systems, is absent from the text, and some would be surprised to hear it being referred to in the field of ancient Near East architecture since it is generally associated with Roman engineering. The Romans – as is well known – made intense, admirable use of it in numerous types of architecture. It is true that the most ancient system of construction, which is also the basis of the classic architectonic orders, is the trilithic one (two vertical elements and one horizontal element). And yet, the arch has been utilised since the third millennium B.C. It was employed both in Egypt (especially for tombs and vaults) and in Mesopotamia[84] (and one thinks of what an incredible sight it must have been, even for the exiles of the kingdom of Judah, to see the famous royal Ishtar Gate, the principal access to the city of Babylon built by Nebuchadnezzar). The arch is understandably fairly rare in the realm of ancient Near Eastern monumental architecture, since it is a structure usually built using clay bricks and hence, in and of itself, in any case more vulnerable than other structures to the passage of the centuries. Yet there is no lack of significant attestations of its presence in the Syro-Palestinian area as well. The most ancient ones (even in an absolute sense) are definitely the three-arched city gate of Tel Dan (cf. Fig. 7)[85] and the gate of Tell Mumbaqat,[86] both dating back to the Middle Bronze Age (1900–1500 B.C.). Also worth noting is Building I of Tell Jemmeh (cf. Fig. 8), an Assyrian palace from the Late Iron Age II (IIB and IIC, ca. 923–550 B.C., probably dating back to the beginning of the seventh century) with its triple-arched vault.[87]

---

83 "In advanced societies, external symbolic storage entails highly complex storage media that require extensive training of the young. Such training can actually change the operational architecture of cognition in the individual by influencing the developing brain. The continuing interplay between material culture and cognition creates new cognitive opportunities, changing how members of a society represent reality, both individually and collectively" (M. Donald, «Material Culture and Cognition: Concluding Thoughts», in: *Cognition and Material Culture. The Archaeology of Symbolic Storage*, eds. C. Renfrew – C. Scarre, Cambridge 1998, 181–187 [here, p. 181]).

84 See G. Leick, *Dictionary of Ancient Near Eastern Architecture*, London 1988, 16–17; A.L. Palmer, *Historical Dictionary of Architecture*, HDLA 29, Lanham 2008, 27–30.

85 See A. Biran, «The Triple-Arched Gate of Laish at Tel Dan», *IEJ* 34 (1984) 1–19; A.A. Burke, *Walled Up to Heaven. The Evolution of Middle Bronze Age Fortification Strategies in the Levant*, SAHL 4, Winona Lake 2008, 250–254 (and esp. pp. 252–253).

86 Cf H. Kühne – H. Steuerwald, «Das Nordost-Tor von Tell Mumbaqat», in: *Le Moyen Euphrate: Zone de contacts et d'échanges*. Actes du Colloque de Strasbourg 10–12 mars 1977, ed. J.C. Margueron, Leiden 1980, 203–215.

87 See, in this regard, the study by D. Ben-Shlomo, «Results from Field IV: The Iron II and Later Periods», in: *The Smithsonian Institution Excavation at Tell Jemmeh, Israel, 1970–1990*, eds. D. Ben-Shlomo – G.W. Van Beek, Washington 2014, SCAn 50, 403–641 (esp. pp. 519–523); and also Id., «Tell Jemmeh, Philistia and the Neo-Assyrian Empire during the Late Iron Age», *Levant* 46 (2014) 58–88 (esp. Fig. 16, p. 73). Amongst

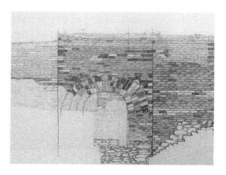

Fig. 7. Sketch of the front arch of the great city gate of Tel Dan (from A. BIRAN, «The Triple-Arched Gate», 5).

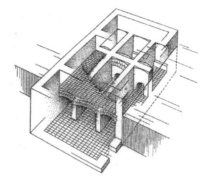

Fig. 8. Reconstruction and sectioning of building I at Tel Jemmeh (from D. BEN-SHLOMO, «Tell Jemmeh», 517).

As mentioned above, there is obviously no actual arch (or other element used to connect distances) present in the (Jeremianic) text. But this cannot dismiss the fact that structures using arches were clearly present in the cognitive frame of the authors/redactors of the biblical texts and of the populations of the land of Canaan in general, certainly from the Middle Bronze Age onward. On the other hand, with the exception of a few limited examples, most all architectonic roofing elements, whether these be beams, vaulted ceilings, or arches, have not remained standing even on archaeological sites. Archaeologists, starting with the foundations of the vertical vestiges of the buildings, discern their presence, at times finding evident traces of them, and attempt their reconstruction. They propose graphic re-elaborations that

---

the various examples that could be cited from outside the Syro-Palestinian area, cf. the arched structures discovered at the Nush-i Jan site in Iran, documented in D. STRONACH – M. ROAF, *Nush-i Jan I. The Major Buildings of the Median Settlement*, Leuven 2007, 184–185, 190–191, pl. 43a-b.

prolong the remaining elements, first in the mind and then on paper or in 3D virtual archaeology reconstructions.[88]

Research progresses by trying to fill out, with its interpretive act, that which today is missing on a material level. It reconstructs those architectural links that the ancient people had put into place and with which they were quite familiar. The semiotic environment of the written text, with its horizontal arrangement made up of a succession of columns, differs from that in architecture for the fact that structurally, there were not any actual physical connections between distances, if not those written as reciprocal references in given textual "columns". The references and relationships had to have been clear to whoever compiled and organised the texts, and the "*arcatas*" that joined together certain supporting structures were hermeneutical acts put into writing and signified within the text itself. This is why the challenge placed before readers today becomes that of learning to *read* this particular grammar of signification.

Fig. 9. The renowned Hebrew mᵉnôrâ *with seven arms, carried in triumph by the Romans as spoils of the war of* A.D. *70, in a detail of the relief designs of the Arch of Titus (photo, here cropped, by Gunnar Bach Pedersen, available under the Creative Commons CC0 1.0 Universal Public Domain Dedication).*

I will therefore assume, as a working hypothesis, that something similar occurs for biblical literature, albeit in inverse terms with respect to that asserted by Walter Benjamin for architecture in general when he stated that it reflected the latent mythological universe of its artificers ("Architektur als wichtigstes Zeugnis der latenten 'Mythologie'").[89] That is, the Semitic way of thinking and composing, characterised by a dynamic that proceeds by making juxtapositions and remote connections, seems to reflect or be reflected in the architectural and/or artistic imagery of the *arcata* and/or, looking closely, even in the particular structure of the overturned concentric arches that typify the renowned candlestick (the *mᵉnôrâ*; cf. Fig. 9) used in temple worship. It is interesting to note, moreover, that the translation of the architectural arch and

---

88 See, e.g. B.L. MOLYNEAUX, *ed.*, The Cultural Life of Image. *Visual Representation in Archaeology*, London – New York 1997 (esp. S. JAMES, «Drawing Inferences: Visual Reconstructions in Theory and Practice», 22–48); R.M. VAN DYKE, «Seeing the Past: Visual Media in Archaeology», *AmA* 108 (2006) 370–375.

89 W. BENJAMIN, *Gesammelte Schriften*. Band 5: Das Passagen-Werk. 2 Teilbände, Frankfurt am Main 1991, 1020.

column elements makes an explicit appearance in some modern Hebrew manuscripts, albeit with an ornamental scope. One example of this is the copy of the scroll of Esther made in Venice in 1564 by Stellina. Here the columns of text are flanked by caryatids and are placed under decorated arcades (cf. Fig. 10).

Fig. 10. Detail of the fully decorated Esther scroll made by Stellina (Venice, 1564), the only early modern megillah *that we know to have been created by a woman (Zürich, Braginsky Collection, S102).*

Given this hermeneutical framework, I believe that the notion of the "semiotic *arcata*" has particular heuristic value for study of the book of Jeremiah, even if I can propose only a few examples of it herein (cf. in particular chs. III and V of the present dissertation). As I have observed, the notion is a metaphorical one, at least insofar as it refers to a specific element that makes a physical connection,[90] the *arch* or the *arcade*. However, since what is called into question here is *semiosis*, that is, the process of signification, I will rely on a pragmatic consideration of the context, one of an extratextual nature.[91]

Just as a musical score does not coincide with the act of the musical reading during an execution, which is always an *interpretation*, likewise, a text gives indications, provides clues to its structuring, and builds its main pylons and minor columns. These devices are not to be banally reduced to that of phenomenon of inclusion or concentric organisation that would mark some textual areas as being *more significant*, to the detriment of others. The question is rather that of a process of *pertinentisation* able to grasp the meaning of the thematic and formal relationships that serve, above all, to create a dialogue between texts that are either placed a distance away, or significantly delimited within a space that allows for the emergence of a specific signification, broader in nature or on a level superior to the local one (that of single phrases or minor units).

---

90 Obviously, metaphorical meaning must be supported by some fact of objective knowledge, otherwise transference from one semantic domain to another is not even conceivable.

91 The consequences on the hermeneutical level will be explicated according to a different perspective in the next chapter, dedicated to the historic contextualisation of the Jeremianic message of submission-surrender to Babylon.

Paradoxically, the final purpose of a frame, thus understood, is not so much an operation of closure as it is a function of dialogue and interchange between the work and the surrounding world, favouring the entrance of the audience into the world of the art and the comprehension of its meaning.[92]

In other words, the semiotic *arcata* coincides with a hermeneutical act on the part of the reader and for this reason, it can only be *suggested*. Hence, in the case in point, the linear disposition of the Jeremianic scroll displays, not only virtually but also physically, a vertical succession of "columns" (lit. "door" or "door leaf": דְּלָתוֹת) of text (cf. 36:23). Between these columns, the reader themself, rather than proceed in the disrespectful and irreverent manner of the king Jehoiakim, brandishing a penknife to cut and section the scroll,[93] is called upon to build a bridge or *arcata* (or at times, simply a beam) instead. That is, the reader is to build an interpretive arch between structural elements that may even be distant. And by doing so, they gain access to an underlying theological meaning that is neither appreciable nor easily perceivable via other analytical or philological methodological instruments.

By way of a more macroscopic example, that is, one that concerns the overall structuring of the book of Jeremiah, the subdivisions that I have already proposed as semiotic *arcatas* can be envisaged (and illustrated).[94]

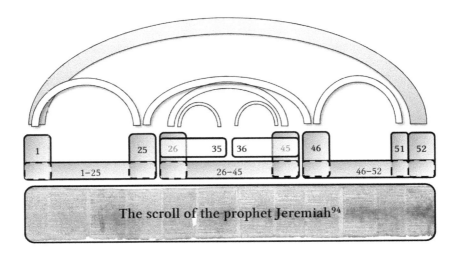

---

92 Translated from C. GOTTARDI, «La porta, il ponte, l'architrave. L'idea di cornice nel sistema performativo», *Venezia Arti* 27/24 (2014) 58–64, here p. 58: "Paradossalmente, la funzione ultima di una cornice così intesa non è tanto una operazione di chiusura quanto una funzione di dialogo e interscambio tra l'opera e il mondo circostante, favorendo l'ingresso dello spettatore all'interno del mondo dell'arte e la comprensione del suo significato."
93 Emblem of an act of reading that destroys the scroll itself because there is no intention of obeying it.
94 Having not attained an intact scroll of the book of Jeremiah from the Qumram texts, as an example-suggestion I will insert, as the background, part of the image of the Great Isaiah Scroll (1QIsaᵃ). Photo by The Israel Museum (public domain).

As we can see, they are precisely this: proper semiotic *arcatas*. More than be (or even before being) textual segmentations, they serve as connections endowed with a particular value according to the productivity of meaning that can be recognised on a level higher than that of their local signification. While I am unable to develop an adequate demonstrative system of an analytical nature herein, I will limit myself to the proposition and utilisation of this noetic instrument of heuristic value whenever necessary. It will suffice to emphasise that recognising a "semiotic *arcata*" means building a bridge on distinct columns (or portions of text) through inference. Doing so ignites a spark of interpretation between the two polarities that the text itself creates and proposes, triggering the hermeneutical act. While by nature, these may be "virtual" relationships, since left to the acumen (but not the imagination) of the reader, the challenge will be to demonstrate, insofar as is possible, that the question is by no means that of unduly placed arbitrary interpretive schemas within the text. These are rather relationships that better explain the particular phenomenon of significations connected with the peculiar (or problematic) structuring of the book of Jeremiah. Study on a topic like that which I have set out to investigate cannot prescind, in fact, from the question of the placement of pertinent texts within the complex geography of the Jeremianic corpus.

2.4.3. Semiotic arcatas and narrative analysis

As I observed in the beginning, many scholars have addressed the problem of the organisation of the book of Jeremiah. Their findings are conflicting, ranging from declarations of impractibility to suggestions of possible meanings for the arrangement. In the vein of this second perspective, and after having presented L. Stulman's proposition, I will now, for critical confrontation, touch upon another working theory.

In the places where the text proceeds by joining the words of the prophet to a succession of facts that concern him directly, solutions have been proposed, amongst others, that derive from narrative analysis. The study done by Elena Di Pede with regard to chs. 32–45[95] comes to mind. She argues in favour of a "logique du récit" that takes into account the sudden spatial-temporal disorientations of the Jeremianic text. Rightly so, the author also emphasises phenomena typical of Semitic rhetoric and seeks to present a structuring of the narrative section chosen as the object of her study. In my opinion however, it need be noted that while the two perspectives are, in a certain sense, complementary, a true and proper overall logic can be more suitably observed and demonstrated through the perspective suggested by the second approach alone, that of a rhetorical-structural nature.

The search for a "cohérence narrative" based entirely on narrative analyses does not seem to me to be exempt, in this case, from serious underlying methodological problems, because it is not adaptable to the specific nature of the Jeremianic corpus. The book of Jeremiah, with its disorienting alternation of communicative registers, is by no means reducible to the diachronic continuum of a narrative. Mind you: that the result of such an approach be the enucleation of a text's meaning (with respect to a given level of communicative strategy) is not only evident, but also appreciable. This is apparent at least on the local level, where more or less brief streams of narratives,

---

95   See the already cited contribution of E. Di Pede, *Au-de là du refus*.

Overall literary organisation of the book of Jeremiah and hermeneutical notes   109

even dischronic ones, can be found. Precisely this, however, is at the same time both the value and the intrinsic limit of the approach in question.

Given the vast array of possible configurations for any single narrative, one could almost say that every sequence of narrated events, *independent of its plot*, can be subject to any attribution of meaning on the part of the author and/or reader.[96] Raymond Queneau, in his "Exercices de style",[97] shows how the same story (*fabula*), and a fairly banal one at that, can be retold in different styles, on as many as ninety-nine different stylistic levels, with a narrative organisation of the facts (*plot*) that at times shuffles even this around entirely.[98] This, to say that in and of itself, meaning can be detected in any expressive form and (almost) any sort of plot. But not every plot can present a reasonable or coherent *structural organisation* of textual elements. This is especially true when, as in the case of the organic totality of the book of Jeremiah, narrative texts are interspersed amongst oracular forms of a different literary nature. Thus the analogical references proposed by the author when, in citing films and novels,[99] she recalls homogeneous narrative textualities that are, in fact, not comparable with the book of Jeremiah on a global level, do not appear to me to have a convincing heuristic force.

If an analogy were to be sought, it would be more opportune to look towards the *field of music*. Here, the notion of a "semiotic *arcata*" thrives. The general structure of meaning that we have before us when we read Jeremiah is, as has been observed, that of a linearity that at the same time goes hand in hand with the synchrony of particular consonances between specific textual units. These function as chords, combinations (or superimpositions) of two or more harmonic intervals or notes. While each alone expresses its corresponding sound, it is only by being played simultaneously that harmony, or specifically a chord, is generated. This, mind you, cannot come about by placing the notes in just any order. The book of Jeremiah generates cacophony only if its complex notational system is neither grasped nor respected.

On a different note, the same holds true in a *building* analogy. Single architectonic elements can be assembled in a variety of ways, but only some of them *structure*. That

---

96   Even if for some authors there are anthropological limits that nonetheless necessarily oblige a limited series, however extensive, of expressive outcomes (see, in this respect, J. BRUNER, *Actual Minds, Possible Worlds*, Cambridge [MA] 1986, 16).

97   R. QUENEAU, *Exercices de style*, Paris 1947; cf. amongst others, in Italian language, these two eds. by Einaudi: the translation-elaboration by U. Eco [R. QUENEAU, *Esercizi di stile*, Struzzi 282, Torino 1983] and that edited by S. Bartezzaghi [R. QUENEAU, *Esercizi di stile*, Tascabili 849, Torino 2001]).

98   The introduction of the distinction between *fabula* and *plot* (*sjužet*) is thanks to the Russian formalists (beginning with Vladimir Propp). By *fabula*, one means the "story" (real or imaginary), to wit, the concatenation both logical (first the causes, then their effects) and temporal (according to a "first" and "after") of the events object of narration. The *plot* on the other hand, is the reorganisation of the same events of the *fabula* ("story") operated by a precise choice of the author of the text. This process generates the construction of a *story*. One can also choose for the plot (storyline) to coincide with the *fabula* ("story"). In the version denominated "Notations", e.g. *fabula* and plot coincide, respecting the logical and chronological order of events, while in the "Rétrograde" version, the order of events is completely inverted with respect to the chronology of the story (the *fabula* remains the same, but the plot does not).

99   Cf. E. DI PEDE, *Au-de là du refus*, 155–158.

is, only some have a capacity for bearing other minor (otherwise disarticulated) elements in order to configure a reasonable and coherent whole. This is why, in the case of the book of Jeremiah (and not only), narrative analysis can work only on a (more or less broad) local level, but not on the level of the overall text.

From this critical confrontation with narrative analysis, yet another hermeneutical insight related to the complementarity of the two approaches can be enucleated. Both levels of analysis, in fact, also correspond to the two different complementary viewpoints of *temporality* that, in the exegetic field, are commonly indicated as "diachrony"[100] and "synchrony". Time is relationship. It is a relationship between phenomena that can be either successive or simultaneous (or even successive in their simultaneity, when there is permanency).

The narrative method endeavours to discover the logic of the narrative, that is, its *télos*.[101] The "achievement" of this has to do with a *diachronic-narrative temporality* that generates, in its own image, a *narrative paradigm*. A story, or plot interweaving several storylines, can be presented in this sense as a hermeneutical key to the history presently taking place. The dynamic of human learning is generally favoured by this cognitive device. And it is not surprising that precisely the prophets, and the very book of Jeremiah, make great use of it, since they are interpreters of the meaning of history as revealed by God.

On the contrary, structural study of the text from a perspective of rhetorical analysis is, in my opinion, even more effective if it refers to the more agile notion of the "semiotic *arcata*". Its implementation can shed some light on another understanding of time, and another sort of paradigm: *synchronic-paradigmatic temporality.* If the narrative paradigm is played out in linear concatenation (whether inverted or dischronic) between a first time and a later time, the structural paradigm can be grasped in the *simultaneity* of forms in reciprocal relation. This consents an attribution of semantic unity even between texts that are different or distant from one another. The first paradigm takes shape in the *flowing* from one element to the next, while the second paradigm becomes manifest in the *order* (or reasonable disorder) of a structure.

In other words, confronted with the problem presented by the organisation of the book of Jeremiah, we can ask ourselves if all that which appears to be contradictory or senseless truly be so, or if it is not instead perhaps a question of managing to grasp a logic that is different from our own. In constructive polemic against certain abuses of the historical-critical method, it would always be useful to ask oneself if the textual tensions that we observe truly are always and only attributable to the jagged history of the text, or if they do not perhaps instead conceal a communicative intentionality peculiar unto itself. My study of the theme of the surrender to Babylon assumes this hermeneutical perspective as its working hypothesis.

---

100   Obviously, the "diachrony" with which the historical-critical method deals is entirely different from the intrinsic diachrony of every narrative text.

101   Cf. M. STERNBERG, «Telling in Time (II)», 512.

3. The texts relevant to the theme of the surrender to the king of Babylon

3.1. Criteria for the textual "decoupage"

Identifying the theme (or *topic*) of a complex text (topicalisation) or intercepting a textual articulation within it that can be linked to a common topic is always a more complicated operation than it might seem. From a semiotic viewpoint,[102] this means circumscribing a specific semantic content, both on the basis of possible metasignals of the paratextual sort[103] (colophones, titles, and other indications of a rhetorical nature) and, even in their absence, taking stock of the specific encyclopaedic competence of the reader. In other words, precisely that set of data acquired about the world of the text (and its authors) can be decisive for the level of descriptive accuracy of the *topic* and exact delimitation of its textual perimeter.

It should thus be noted that, at least in an initial approach, the linking of texts to a theme is, per se, a *pragmatic* operation.[104] It means formulating a hypothesis of meaning that is at times not immediately recognisable. If the degree of coherence proposed does not want to remain on a purely extrinsic level (it could, in fact, in and of itself be traced in reference to an entirely extratextual criterion) or be considered arbitrary, then it is necessary to find, subsequently, confirmation within a semantic structure (isotopy)[105] inherent to the text itself. For these reasons, remaining on an introductory level, I must for now limit myself to selecting and presenting a sequence of texts (excerpts from the textual flow of the book of Jeremiah) that still have, inevitably, a rather empirical character. Only the exegetical analysis of the individual pericopes will be able to fully account for their choice. Their degree of pertinence is, in any case, already more calibrated here than in the first textual series mentioned in the General Introduction (§ 3.2), which highlighted the provisional relevance (by default) of Jer 21:1–10, 27–28; 38:14–28a.

The criteria for the selection I denote are based on the focalisation of two fundamental, interdependent semantic structures: 1) the contextual presence of the figure

---

102 I continue here, in a more technical way, what was introduced in the preceding paragraph with regard to the delimitation of the theme in its structural elements and the definition of the methodological approaches adopted.

103 These are devices that serve to suggest to the reader how to cut up the text (a process also called *découpage*, a term borrowed from cinema studies) and according to what modality it should be read. In the case of biblical text, we have *peritexts*, that is, indicators contained in the text itself and not placed outside of it (as might be epitextual elements such as reviews, interviews, etc.).

104 It should be pointed out, in fact, that contrary to what is commonly thought in the exegetic field, the presence of a *topic* is defined neither previously nor exclusively by the semantics of the text. As explained by U. VOLLI, *Semiotica*, 66: "the topicalisation of a text is the operation of *bringing a text itself into focus* on the basis of a certain *hypothesis* of meaning, and this therefore depends both on the initiative of the reader as well as their *encyclopaedic competence*" (my translation).

105 U. Eco, examining A.J. Greimas' concept of "redundant semantic categories", refers to the isotopy as "an umbrella term covering diverse semiotic phenomena generically definable as *coherence* at the various textual levels" (cf. ID., *Lector in fabula*, 93, my translation).

of the (Babylonian) *enemy,* and 2) the Jeremianic request for *submission* to its power. On the basis of a first reading, some of the texts I propose may not immediately appear to be linked to my theme. The identification of these texts is, however, already the (verified) pragmatic result of a hypothesis of isotopic meaning, confirmed by the presence of the pertinent semantic field. I will subsequently study with utmost rigour the configuration and significance of meaning that the complex relationship between the two semantic dimensions highlighted assumes.

3.2. Selected texts

Following are the texts related to my theme, identified according to the criteria set out above. The references in square brackets indicate the texts for which I will be unable to reserve detailed analysis herein:

[6:1–8, 22–30]   I consider it important to include these oracles in the textual series that I wish to highlight. In my opinion, they can serve as an introduction to the subsequent texts by providing a suitable key for their interpretation. Indeed, while there is no formal connection between the threat from the North and Babylon in them, these oracles present elements of significant interest to my theme, such as, for example, the dramatic representation of the siege, the proclamation of a "holy war" against the "daughter of Zion", the invitation to find a way to escape from Jerusalem, and the threat of the end. Another interesting aspect not to be underestimated is the fact that these are textual units that scholars unanimously trace back to the most "original" core of the book. While mine is not a work of literary criticism, this fact will allow me to demonstrate that the theme of the surrender, while it may be explicitly evidenced in other texts that are more controversial from the point of view of Jeremianic originality, is not to be considered an extraneous body inserted from the *outside,* but rather belongs to the constitutive fabric of the book and to the message of Jeremiah. It is from this general context, therefore, that the probability of its proper exegetic comprehension can be derived.

21:1–10   According to the present arrangement of the book, this is the *first text* in which the theme of the surrender emerges clearly, joined to the announcement of the end. Given, however, that the context is that of an oracular response by Jeremiah delivered to a delegation sent by the king Zedekiah modelled after what is narrated in another section of the book (34:1–7; 37:3–10, 17–21; 38:1–3, 14–28a), and that the historical period most likely coincides with the last stage of the siege on Jerusalem by the Babylonians, the problem of the text's bizarre positioning arises. In fact, it anticipates a theme introduced in the prophet's preaching only within the historical circumstances attested later, in chs. 27–28.

The texts relevant to the theme of the surrender to the king of Babylon 113

[25][106]   The need for *universal submission* to God's punishment is expressed plastically (25:15–38) through use of the metaphoric image of the cup of wine of the Lord's wrath, which the prophet must make the nations gulp down. The punitive instrument is shown as being the figure of the king of Babylon (25:1–14).

27–28   At a strategic colloquy with anti-Babylonian political valence held before Zedekiah in Jerusalem with the ambassadors of the neighbouring states, Jeremiah publicly proclaims for the *first time*, through the symbolic gesture of the yoke, the *universal* necessity of submission to the power of Nebuchadnezzar. YHWH has decided to confer sovereignty over the entire world to him. It is evident from the text that the very same message, directed specifically at the king Zedekiah, the priests, and all the people (27:12–16), had already been announced previously. Nevertheless, ch. 27 remains the first and most "ancient" literary attestation of this prophetic word. Chapter 28 develops the same theme, retaining the same universal importance (because it concerns Babylon's influence on "all the nations"), in the context of the controversial confrontation with the (false) prophet Hananiah and his antagonistic proclamation.

[29]   This is the text of the "letter" that Jeremiah writes to the exiles of the first deportation (597) inviting them to not harbour false hopes of returning to their homeland as soon as some (false) prophets have suggested to them. This too means *surrendering*. It is time to fully accept living in a foreign land for a long time, *subjugated* to another people, praying for Babylon and invoking peace upon it, pending the completion of YHWH's designs.

[37]   Chronologically, this situation falls after chs. 27–28. Jeremiah is arrested while leaving Jerusalem on charges of having *defected to the enemy*. The prophet denies this, but his position on the matter is well known. For this reason, his self-defence is not believed. He had formerly announced the inevitable defeat to Zedekiah, despite the fact that the pharaoh's army had forced the Babylonians to suspend their assault. The king consults Jeremiah a second time while he is in prison. But the tenor of Jeremiah's message remains the same: Zedekiah will definitely be delivered into the hands of the king of Babylon.

---

106   I will, in any case, look at this text during my exegetic study of chs. 27–28 for reasons that I will clarify at that point.

38:[1–13], 14–28a	This is the last explicit declaration of the prophetic call to surrender before the "end". It earns Jeremiah his being thrown into the cistern (38:1–13), where he looks death in the face. He is, however, saved *in extremis* by the intervention of a foreign eunuch in service of the court (Ebed-melech). Jeremiah thus becomes the embodiment of his message, the paradigmatic icon of the human being "consigned" and thus saved (as was already pointed out in ch. 26). This word of salvation that passes through "consigning oneself" is repeated (in vain) in the final, decisive exchange between the king Zedekiah and Jeremiah on the verge of the impending intrusion of the Babylonian armies and consequent fall of Jerusalem (38:14–28a).
[42–43:7]	Even after the end of Jerusalem, the theme finds its dramatic reproposal. Having conquered the city, the Babylonians constitute Gedaliah as governor of the country. He gets killed by Ismael, a rebel of royal blood. For fear of retaliation, Johanan, along with other surviving military leaders, assembles the people and prepares to flee to Egypt. Before they do so, Jeremiah is consulted. But the prophet essentially repeats the same message: *do not fear* the king of Babylon (for God will induce him to have feelings of mercy; cf. 42:12), *submit* to him and do not go to Egypt but stay in the territory of Judah (42). The leaders and the people are not willing to risk it and do not listen to him. They prefer to flee to Egypt, dragging with them both the prophet and Baruch, who is accused of having manipulating Jeremiah's prophetic message (43:1–7).

4. The framing of the texts within the literary organisation and thematic interweaving of the book of Jeremiah

4.1. The textual portions 6:1–8, 22–30; 21:1–10, and 25 within the first part (1–25)

4.1.1. Overview

The first part of the book of Jeremiah is dominated by the motif of the threat of YHWH's punishment caused by the invincible deep rooting of sin in Israel's history. Opposite this thematic horizon, which is as unitary as it is generic, is a corresponding, complex composition, a confluence of several literary genres and a great deal of factual content. For these reasons, proposals regarding the literary organisation of this section differ greatly, depending on the commentators. From amongst the various proposals put forth, I will steer us towards the following subdivision, which some important scholar share. I will propose it first of all in schematic form, and then explain it in detail[107]:

---

107 Anticipating, in a certain sense, the conclusions of this chapter, I have highlighted in bold type those chapters (and where appropriate, also those verses) which include text related to my theme, in order to already demonstrate, over the course of the present analysis, the relevance of their positioning in the composition of the book of Jeremiah.

The framing of the texts within the literary organisation and thematic interweaving 115

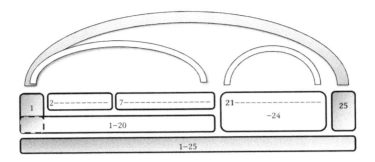

A first big delimitation is drawn between chs. 1–20 and **21–24**. Section 1–20 is identified by several authors on the grounds of the inclusion between 1:5 and 20:18, along with other important links.[108] A smaller section follows (**21–24**) with a collection of oracles directed against the kings of Judah (21:1–23,8) and the false prophets (23:8–40). The whole unit ends with ch. **25**, a text of great importance to the structure of the book.[109] It makes an (negative) assessment of the results of Jeremiah's prophetic ministry up to that point, due to the rejection of the prophetic word (**25:1–7**), and the punishment of Judah and the nations resulting from it is announced (**25:8–38**). In any case, it should be noted that precisely because several semiotic *arcata*s, themselves leading in turn to many more textual units significant for the structure of the whole book, can be traced as leading from the textual "pillar" of Jer 1, that first chapter (just like Jer 25) serves several functions simultaneously: it can be considered an integral part of section 1–20, but also looked at as a separate element. Thus, after setting aside the extremities of chs. 1 and 25, the subdivision would be: 2–6; 7–20; **21–24**; or, more simply: 2–20; **21–24**. I prefer the first option.

4.1.2. Articulation of the structuring elements

Wishing to further detail the composition of the first large subsection (1–20), I can isolate the following units:

Chapter 1 forms a literary unit in its own right. A programmatic introduction of a "redactional" nature for the entire book of Jeremiah, it anticipates its fundamental

---

108 Cf. J.R. LUNDBOM, *Jeremiah: A Study*, 42–44, who indicates the inclusion between Jer 1:5 ([...] תֵּצֵא מֵרֶחֶם [...]) and 20:18 ([...] מֵרֶחֶם יָצָאתִי [...]) as a decisive literary clue. As does W.L. HOLLADAY, *The Architecture of Jeremiah 1–20*, Lewisburg – London 1976, 20.

109 See, in this regard, M. KESSLER, «Jeremiah 25,1–29: Text and Context. A Synchronic Study», *ZAW* 109 (1997) 44–70. The same author has shown the final function of ch. 25, also in relation to chs. 50–51 (cf. ID., «The Function of Chapters 25 and 50–51 in the Book of Jeremiah», in: *Troubling Jeremiah*, eds. A.R.P. DIAMOND – K. O'CONNOR – L. STULMAN, JSOT.S 260, Sheffield 1999, 64–72). Cf. also A. AEJMELAEUS, «Jeremiah at the Turning-Point of History: The Function of Jer. XXV 1–14 in the Book of Jeremiah», *VT* 52 (2002) 459–482, on the hypothesis of 25:1–14 being the original introduction to the oracles against the nations.

116 Orientative literary-hermeneutical coordinates

elements. Attention is obviously drawn to the structuring relationship it has with ch. **25**, with which it forms a literary frame comprising of the entire first section of the book.[110]

Chapters **2–6** constitute a highly important textual portion. These collect the main grounds for all of Jeremiah's prophetic preaching in a nutshell.[111] Two distinct units are easily recognised: (1) chs. 2:1–4:4 are a series of oracles probably originally addressed to the North, with denunciation of sin and calls for conversion; (2) chs. 4:5–**6:30** are oracles directed at the kingdom of the South and Jerusalem, with the announcement of the enemy's invasion from the North and the end of the kingdom of Judah.

Chapters 7–20, rather heterogeneous in nature (a unit that can be further sub-divided into 7–10 and 11–20),[112] contain both threat oracles and stories of symbolic gestures and their related commentary in prose. Also found herein are the famous *Confessions* (11:18–12:6, 15:10–21, 17:14–18, 18:18–23, 20:7–18). These are dramatic testimonies of the personal implications caused by the difficulties of prophetic ministry narrated in third person in the following section (26–45).

The delimitation proposed by L. Stulman, while overlapping what I have high-lighted, identifies still further sub-units within 7–20. It is good, however, to briefly detail the criteria that allow him to present his hypothesis of a structuring function (with a "redactionally" produced theological intent) of the most prominent prose discourses scattered throughout 1–25.

The key clue for a correct demarcation of 1–25 is identified by L. Stulman in 7:1, 11:1, 18:1, **21:1**, where the well-known *Wortereignisformel* (הַדָּבָר אֲשֶׁר־הָיָה אֶל־יִרְמְיָהוּ מֵאֵת יְהוָה) recurs as the *incipit* of the prose texts having the same literary scheme.[113] These were traced by S. Mowinckel back to the C "source" since they are characterised by a style very similar to that of the Deuteronomic style. In the "chaos" caused by the unpredictability of poetic evocations, the speeches in prose highlighted (7:1–8:3; 11:1–17; 18:1–12; **21:1–10**) permit L. Stulman to isolate five "structural macro-units"[114]

---

110 According to L. Stulman, *Order Amid Chaos*, 36–38, there are various elements that cross-reference each other: the dating (cf. 1:2; 25:3); the prophecy-fulfilment pattern (threat in ch. 1; fulfilment of the punishment in ch. 25); the theme of the resisted and rejected prophetic word (cf. 1:8, 17–19; 25:3–7); the taking shape of the instrument of punishment (the enemy from the North in ch. 1 is identified with the king of Babylon in ch. 25); the dynamism of the announced word becoming written word (cf. 1:7, 9; 25:13); Jeremiah as "prophet to the nations" (in 1:5, he is "consecrated" as such, and 25:9, 11–15, 17 summarises the prophetic ministry developed in 46–51); the reason for the wrath of YHWH: Jerusalem and "all the cities of Judah" (cf. 1:3, 15–16; 25:2, 9, 11a, 18); and the reason for the punishment: idolatry (cf. 1:16; 25:4–7). For other corresponding elements (of a lexical nature), cf. *ibid.*, 38.

111 For a specific study (of a redactional nature) of this section, see R. Liwak, *Der Prophet und die Geschichte*. Eine literar-historische Untersuchung zum Jeremiabuch, BWANT 121, Stuttgart 1987 and C. Hardmeier, «Die Redekomposition Jer 2–6. Eine ultimative Verwarnung Jerusalems im Kontext des Zidkijaaufstandes», WuD 21 (1991) 11–42.

112 As, e.g. G. Fischer, *Jeremia 1–25*, 84.

113 L. Stulman, *Order Amid Chaos*, 32, n. 37, highlights the following elements: 1) an introductory word by YHWH (7:1; 11:1; 18:1; 21:1); 2) an imperative addressed to the prophet to act or speak (7:2; 11:2; 18:2; 21:2); and 3) the content of the action or message communicated (7:3–15; 11:3–13; 18:5–11; 21:3–7).

114 Cf. *ibid.*, 39–55.

The framing of the texts within the literary organisation and thematic interweaving 117

(2–6; 7–10; 11–17; 18–20; 21–24) that underscore a certain theological "order". This is summarised in the concept of the systematic "dismantling" of the socio-religious pillars upon which the false security of Judah has been set.[115] These pillars are: the temple and the "myth" of its eternal stability (ch. 7); the covenant itself, declared culpably broken (ch. 11) and implicitly overcome (cf. 31:31–34); the integration of Israel in a divine design on history that does not differ from that of all other peoples (ch. 18); the unreliability and rejection of the theology of the impregnability of Zion and of the Davidic monarchy itself (ch. 21).[116]

In short, the narrative structure offered by the texts attributable to the C "source" would highlight three fundamental themes: (a) Judah's refusal of the prophetic word; (b) the consequent punitive judgment of God; and (c) the announcement of a possible new world.[117]

This is undoubtedly an interesting path of interpretation. But at least two fundamental limitations catch my attention: (1) The considerations upon which the relations between the texts in prose and their following context are established are almost exclusively content-based in nature. They lack the contribution of serious analysis founded in study of the lexicon and – as I have already observed – use of the methodology offered by rhetorical analysis.[118] For a sufficiently rigorous identification of clues of a formal nature (objective literary signs) that allow for the recognition of precise textual structures, the use of these would be, in my opinion, more appropriate; (2) I do consider it appropriate to attribute a structuring function to the texts proposed by L. Stulman (on precisely the basis of a significant formal aspect: the recurrence of the "word-event formula"). However, the presence of the other passages in prose in this part cannot be ignored. And yet, in the proposal our author makes for the composition, these simply disappear, with no attempt made to provide framing for them.[119] The general impression that emerges is unfortunately therefore one of a marked approximation.

---

115   Cf. *ibid.*, 31–32, where further details on his above-mentioned proposal regarding the composition are provided: 1–25 (The Dismantling of Judah's "First Principles"); 1:1–19 (The Functional Introduction: God's Sovereign Plan Regarding Judah's Newly Defined Place Among the Nations); 2:1–6:30 (Macro-Unit One. Judah's Departure From Yahweh: The Basis for Guilt and Penality Death); 7:1–10:1–16[*sic!*] (Macro-Unit Two. Dismantling of Temple Ideology); 11:1–17:27 (Macro-Unit Three. Dismantling of Covenant Ideology); 18:1–20:18 (Macro-Unit Four. Dismantling of Insider-Outsider Understandings); 21:1–24:10 (Macro-Unit Five. Dismantling of Royal Ideology); 25:1–38 (The Functional Closure: The Fulfillment of God's Sovereign Plan Regarding Judah's Newly Defined Place Among the Nations).

116   Cf. *ibid.*, 54.

117   Cf. *ibid.*, 53–54.

118   I refer in particular to the guidelines set by R. MEYNET, *Traité de rhétorique biblique* (a study that replaces the previous work done on the argument; cf. ID., *L'analyse rhétorique*).

119   In particular, not taken into account are: 3:6–12(13), 14–18 (vv. 12b-13 are an oracle in poetry); 12:14–17 (an oracle of warning and promise addressed to the neighbouring peoples); 13:1–11 (the symbol of the loincloth), 12–14 (the metaphor of the wineflask); 14:11–16 (the prohibition to intercede on behalf of the people).15:1-3; 16:1–13 (the symbolic gesture of celibacy that announces the end), 14–18 (a new oath

118   Orientative literary-hermeneutical coordinates

Apart from these observations, one need regardless consider that the texts in prose not cited, from the point of view of their content, fall within the horizon previously highlighted, that of the *eradication* of the supporting pillars of a socio-religious system already on the verge of collapse.[120] For me, it suffices to have pointed out the bearing that the texts identified for my theme assume, having been placed in particularly significant points.

It is interesting to note, in fact, that the oracles contained in **6:1–8**, 22–30, while not fully explicating the theme of submission to Babylon developed in the complex narrative framework of the second part of the book, still attest full conceptual compatibility with the part which, in the unanimous opinion of critics, represents the oldest and most "authentic" part of Jeremiah (chs. 2–6). The invitation to flee from Jerusalem is, in fact, an invitation to acknowledge, as the prophetic word affirms, that disaster is imminent and ineluctable (cf. 6:2–3). The Holy City is now subject to "holy war" (cf. 6:4), which is forewarned to be a siege by ruthless, tireless enemies in exclusive service of the Lord of hosts (cf. 6:6, 22–30).

The anonymous enemy in 6:1–8, 22–30, characterised by its origin in the North, is actually identified beforehand in 20:1–6 and directly after in **21:1–10** as the king of Babylon. Here, the twofold theme of the end and the surrender is made fully explicit. The positioning of **21:1–10**, which opens the unit of **21–24** and seems to have been deliberately extrapolated from the second part of the book, cannot go unnoticed and will therefore be the object of a dedicated study.

Finally, in ch. 25, we find, in another highly strategic point, the twofold motif of the submission to Babylon and God's punishment. This time, not only Israel is included, but all the (bordering) nations as well. The imperative to drink the cup of the wine of the Lord's wrath is given (25, 28) to all. This incisive metaphor expresses the necessity of accepting God's design on history.

---

formula); 17:19–27 (the observance of the Sabbath); 19 (the symbolic gesture of the broken flask); 20:1–6 (the clash with Pashhur).

120   One might add, in fact, that: 1) the rebel Israel is more righteous than is her perfidious sister Judah (3:6–11); 2) there will be no need for the Ark of the Covenant, it will not be sought and another one will not be made (3:14–18); 3) the Lord's compassion is also for other peoples, called to swear by YHWH (12:14–17); 4) Israel, chosen to "adhere" tightly to the Lord is now like a useless loincloth (13:1–11), and the kings, priests, prophets, and all the inhabitants of Jerusalem will be smashed one against the other (13:12–14); 5) Jeremiah is even forbidden to intercede for the people (14:11–16); 6) an uncommon symbolic gesture, celibacy, announces the end (16:1–13); 7) a new oath formula tied to a new Exodus (16:14–18); 8) the non-observance of the Sabbath will lead to the destruction of Jerusalem (17:19–27); 9) with another symbolic gesture – the broken flask – the end is threatened; 10) that which is threatened for all the people strikes Pashhur, emblem of the rejection of the prophetic word and the resulting punishment (20:1–6).

The framing of the texts within the literary organisation and thematic interweaving 119

4.2. The textual portions 27–28; 29; 38; 42–43:7 within the second part (26–45)

4.2.1. Overview

For the section including chs. 26–45, from amongst the various proposals,[121] I find the following further division into two subsections to be the most plausible:

I. 26^{122}–35

II. 36–45

It seems to me appropriate to point out, once again, the significative "redactional" arrangement that has produced by that which J.M. Abrego de Lacy calls "sensato desorden", making particular reference to the part of the text that is the object of his own study (36–45).[123] Through repetitions, anticipations, and sudden chronological jumps, the "redactor"[124] delivers a message for us to decipher, an authoritative interpretation of the global meaning of the Jeremianic prophecy. Section 26–45 is primarily narrative in nature, and it is precisely the impossibility of detecting the evident criteria by which a logically constructed story should be developed that leaves the reader disoriented.[125]

---

121   The opinions of scholars in this regard are far from unanimous. In particular, they propose a subdivision in 26–36 and 37–45: M. KESSLER, «Jeremiah, Chapters 26–45 Reconsidered», *JNES* 27 (1968) 81–88 and R.P. CARROLL, *Jeremiah*, 510. The latter is based on explicit dating at the beginning of chapters (26:1 and 36:1: at the time of Jehoiakim; 37:1: at the time of Zedekiah). Chapter 36 would serve as a summary-conclusion of the whole section (the conversion requested in ch. 26 is refused in ch. 36). I instead consider chs. 26 and 36 to be *initial* chapters having a proleptic function in relation to the contents of their respective subsections. The most evident clue of a formal nature proves to be the double mention, in the opening (with ch. 36) and in the closing (with ch. 45), of the figure of Baruch. I thus share in the analysis of J.M. ABREGO, *Jeremías*, 62, nn. 78 and 185, and the position of P. BOVATI, *Jeremiah 30–31.* Dispense PIB, Rome 2001, 21–29.

122   The introductive function of ch. 26 in relation to chs. 27–52, observed in various commentaries, was illustrated in particular by K.M. O'CONNOR, «Do Not Trim a Word: The Contribution of Chapter 26 to the Book of Jeremiah», *CBQ* 51 (1989) 617–630.

123   Cf. J.M. ABREGO, *Jeremías*, 185.

124   I use the term "redactor" here in a conventional (or, more precisely, "analogical") way, referring without further specification to the multiple and subsequent redactional interventions, attributable to one or more hands, which led to the current compilation of the book of Jeremiah (MT). On the problematic of terms such as "author", "redactor", "editor", and "compiler" applied to the biblical texts, see the (contrasting) positions of J. VAN SETERS, «The Redactor in Biblical Studies: A Nineteenth Century Anachronism", *JNSL* 29 (2003) 1–19; ID., «An Ironic Circle: Wellhausen and the Rise of Redaction Criticism», *ZAW* 115 (2003) 487–500; ID., *The Edited Bible.* The Curious History of the "Editor" in Biblical Criticism, Winona Lake 2006, and of J. SKA, «A Flea on Behalf of the Biblical Redactors», *StTh* 59 (2005) 4–18.

125   Precisely not trying to account for this problem, I think, demonstrates another clear limit of L. Stulman's interpretative proposition, which, while struggling to develop

I am, however, convinced that this fact is anything but accidental. Indeed, it is a phenomenon that hides a great wealth of meaning. Trying my hand in the arena where the MT's redactional design launches its challenge of confrontation, and without shielding myself behind a too simplistic judgment of "randomness", I will directly interrogate the aim of its design. I will examine the exact meaning that wants to be conveyed by intentionally producing an apparent short-circuit between stories that result always dateable (albeit sometimes indirectly)[126] and the absence of a well-paced linear temporal evolution, as our logic would expect from a coherent historical narrative.[127]

For both sections, based on the different dating of the texts, I believe that from the viewpoint of rhetorical analysis, an interesting concentric structure can be seen. Since I will return to the question in greater depth in ch. V of this dissertation (§ 2.5), where I will deal with the specific positioning of 38:14–28a, I will limit myself at present to a schematisation of the key elements.

---

a symbolic interpretation of the arrangement of the various text blocks, actually reduces itself to an analysis that is too approximative, once again based not on formal data, but prevalently on considerations that concern the contents of the "macro-units" he has highlighted: 1. The New Script for the Reimaged Community: (26) 27–35 (36); 2. The Narratized Act of Dismantling with Cracks of Hope: (36) 37–45; 3. The Oracles Against the Foreign Nations; 46–51; cf. L. STULMAN, *Order Amid Chaos*, 72–98.

126 It seems quite pertinent to me that the historical placement of the individual stories be taken into account in order to configure a proposal for the composition of the second part of the book of Jeremiah, given the use of the narrative register that makes chs. 26–45 essentially homogeneous from this point of view (apart from, of course, chs. 30–31). In this regard, some brief notes: the attribution of ch. 33 to the time of Zedekiah (who it does not actually mention) does not create a problem, since 33:1 speaks of the word of the Lord addressed to Jeremiah *a second time* (שֵׁנִית), thus referencing back to ch. 32. Chapter 32 can be clearly dated to the time of Zedekiah (cf. v. 1), to which the imprisoning of the prophet in the "court of the guard" also leads back (cf. 33:1; 37:21). Note also the (formally) erroneous information provided in 27:1 (MT, repeated by Vg and Tg), scribal repetition of 26:1 (for more details on the question, refer to ch. IV, § 2.1, n. 6).

127 An attempt to reconstruct this "logic" can be seen in H. MIGSCH, *Gottes Wort über das Ende Jerusalems. Eine literar-, stil- und gattungskritische Untersuchung des Berichtes Jeremias 34,1–7; 32,2–5; 37,3–38,28*, ÖBS 2, Klosterneuburg 1981.

The framing of the texts within the literary organisation and thematic interweaving 121

26–45	
First subsection *(26–35)*	Second subsection *(36–45)*

	First subsection	Second subsection
	26: at the time of *Jehoiakim*	36: at the time of *Jehoiakim*
THE TIME OF THE END	27–29: at the time of **Zedekiah**	37–38: at the time of **Zedekiah**
	30–31: without dating THE NEW COVENANT	39: at the time of **Zedekiah** THE END OF JERUSALEM
	+32–33: at the time of Zedekiah PROMISES OF LIFE	"END" OF ZEDEKIAH LIBERATION OF JEREMIAH
	34: at the time of **Zedekiah**	40–44: after **Zedekiah**
	35: at the time of *Jehoiakim*	45: at the time of *Jehoiakim*

As can be easily noted from the diagram, according to chronological criterion, it is the epoch of the king Jehoiakim that frames and identifies the two subsections. I will also briefly mention, in a way that is for now necessarily concise, another element that also invites us to distinguish the epochs relating to the kings Jehoiakim and Zedekiah, respectively. Beginning with the first subsection (26–35), it seems interesting to note, as a matter of fact, that although the prophetic word assumes, in the time of the king Jehoiakim, a prevalently negative tone, always loaded with grave threats due to Israel's sin, Jeremiah's proclamation still seems to be articulated with the possibility of conversion, thus suggesting that there be a positive openness. On the contrary, the days of the king Zedekiah see a radical change in perspective. The end of Jerusalem seems to be an inevitable fact by now, while the only chance for salvation is indicated as that of submission to the king of Babylon. The consolation message of chs. 30–31 (32–33) is situated precisely within this specific context.

I can say something similar for the 36–45 subsection as well.[128] In the days of Jehoiakim, in ch. 36, Jeremiah is ordered to write a scroll containing threatening words against Judah, Israel, and the nations. YHWH himself explains the meaning of this gesture:

---

128   I bear in mind, in particular, the study of the structuring of this section proposed by J.M. ABREGO, *Jeremías*.

Perhaps, if the house of Judah hears all the evil I have in mind to do to them, so that all of them turn from their evil way, then I can forgive their wickedness and their sin (v. 3).

Here too, then, it would still seem possible to avoid the worst.

In ch. 45, even if the possibility of a change of mind on YHWH's part is not clearly developed (but then, we are still at the time of Jehoiakim), the positive opening takes on the form of an oracle of consolation. And salvation is reserved for a single man: Baruch. To him, "life as war booty" is promised. The same character, moreover, is present in both of the chapters that serve as a frame,[129] thus confirming the proposed structure.

I believe that the section (i.e. chs. 37–44) that can be found between the two extremities (36 and 45), could correspond to the central one of the first subsection, chs. 27–34 (except for, obviously, the fulcrum composed of 30–31). These are still "the days of Zedekiah" and those immediately following. That is, respectively speaking, these are the days in which the *end* is no longer threatened but simply foretold (37–38) and then realised (39–44).

This double concentric figure, identifiable on a general level, invites me to set the two textual units side by side to observe the presence of a significant correspondence between them. This correspondence is on the one hand *specular*, while on the other, *complementary*. It is specular from the formal point of view, there being two concentric structures. And it is complementary from the point of view of content since the two central elements, once matched up, assume the function of two poles of opposite sign.

The first subsection, in fact, definitely has its own, well-defined centre. It is comprised of the (undated) book of the New Covenant (the oracles in chs. 30–31), inserted into the days of Zedekiah, that is, in the time of the (announced) end. Chapters 32–33 could also be associated with these for their openness to hope. Upon a closer look, the structure of the second subsection seems to reinforce this paradoxical matching up (end – new beginning), precisely because the end (this time, fulfilled) is placed at its centre (ch. 39).

In short, I think that the *end – new beginning* relationship is not only articulated within the first section, but that it also crosses through and expresses the meaning of the mutual relationship between the two subsections that make up this part of the book of Jeremiah.[130] The two central parts that I have identified (the New Covenant – chs. 30–31 – and the end of Jerusalem – ch. 39) appear, in fact, so intimately connected that they suggest even more strongly how this striking relationship between the act of eradicating (or demolishing) and that of planting (or building) may actually be the cornerstone of the entire prophetic message of the book of Jeremiah.[131]

---

129   In ch. 36, Baruch appears as a bearer of Jeremiah's oracles, while in ch. 45, as a recipient of his prophetic message.

130   Thus tying back to the programmatic message of ch. 1, in which verbs of opposite meaning are placed together: eradicate, demolish – build, plant.

131   Borrowing the words of P. Beauchamp, «Propositions sur l'alliance de l'Ancien Testament comme structure centrale», RSR 58 (1970) 161–194 (=Id., Pages exégètiques, LeDiv 202, Paris 2005, 55–86), we might acknowledge that "[...] il est, à la

The framing of the texts within the literary organisation and thematic interweaving 123

4.2.2. Articulation of the structuring elements

From the point of view of its content, subsection 26–35 is articulated thus:

Ch. 26. This opens the truly narrative part of the book by developing the context of Jeremiah's speech at the temple, already introduced in 7:1–15. There is significant emphasis on the trial the prophet undergoes. During this trial, he does not desist from his testimony and announcement of the end. The plot of the story shows how his not retreating in the face of death but rather *delivering himself* into the hands of human beings in obedience to God fulfils in the prophetic body the promise of salvation that had been anticipated in the story of his vocation in ch. 1. In this way, the story of the prophet himself, transmitted in written form, becomes detached from the level of pure chronicle and assumes the contours of a real, proper prophetic message. And this is ultimately the theological nucleus that substantiates, as we shall see, the call to surrender to the king of Babylon addressed to all of Jerusalem.

Chs. 27–29. Although a tighter relational unity (of both a narrative and thematic type) is easily recognisable between chs. 27–28, the *fil rouge* joining these three chapters seems to be the opposition between Jeremiah and the false prophets (and their reassuring oracles).[132] The sparing of life is not granted until after submission is accepted (cf. 27:11–12, 17), while those who promise unconditional salvation and consolation lead only to disaster and death (cf. 27:8, 10, 13, 15, 17). The theme of the submission is not only announced with a symbolic gesture as a "universal" necessity for the historical time of Jeremiah's contemporaries, but also becomes both the motive for the clash between Jeremiah and Hananiah (ch. 28) and the key theme of the letter sent to those deported in 597 (ch. 29). They too, in fact, as we shall see, are invited to accept surrender as the existential cipher and key to understanding their exile in a foreign land.

Chs. 32–33. As I have already mentioned, these chapters also share the same positive outlook of 30–31. We are, nevertheless, back in the time of Zedekiah, that is, before the horizon of the unavoidable disaster. The *end – new beginning* relationship is replicated within this dyad because the prophetic word of hope is pronounced within the

---

fin du texte, l'acte de grâce qui déclenche tout (cfr. Ezek 16,63). Avant lui encore était venue la mort, le châtiment (Ezek 37). Avant lui le péché et la loi. C'est quand tout cela est fini (Isa 40,2) que tout commence" (p. 193). If this is true, then one can overcome the impression that chs. 30–31 (including the horizon of meaning of chs. 30–34) "wander as foreigners through the smoking ruins of Jeremianic judgment rhetoric", to use the expression of C.J. SHARP, «Jeremiah in the Land of Aporia», in: *Jeremiah (Dis)placed.* New Directions in Writing/Reading Jeremiah, *eds.* A.R.P. DIAMOND – L. STULMAN, LHBOTS 529, London – New York 2011, 35–46, here, p. 44 in ref. to chs. 30–31).

132 The unity and articulation of this block has already been highlighted (and subject to literary criticism) in particular by T. SEIDL, *Texte und Einheiten in Jeremia 27–29.* Literaturwissenschaftliche Studie. 1. Teil, ATSAT 2, St. Ottilien, 1977; ID., *Formen und Formeln in Jeremia 27–29.* Literaturwissenschaftliche Studie. 2. Teil, ATSAT 5, St. Ottilien, 1978. According to the antithetical perspective (true and false prophecy), we can understand the literary unit of chs. 27–28 to be a thematic core that could be extended concentrically to chs. 26–29, where the same clash appears, according to A. OSUJI, «True and False Prophecy in Jer 26–29 (MT). Thematic and Lexical Landmarks», *ETL* 82 (2006) 437–452.

124   Orientative literary-hermeneutical coordinates

dark scenario of the imminent fall of Jerusalem. Both chapters refer to the time when Jeremiah was imprisoned in the courtyard of the guard. In Jer 32, the redemption of the future is announced through the complex symbolic gesture of the purchase of the field. This is followed by a prayer of Jeremiah and YHWH's response, while ch. 33 contains a series of oracular pronouncements.

Ch. 34. We are still in the time of Zedekiah, and it is precisely to this sovereign that it be declared with certainty that YHWH will deliver both him and Jerusalem into the hands of the Babylonian king. The farcical case of the release of the slaves, whose respective Jewish masters had solemnly sworn an oath to YHWH before breaking it immediately after, the moment the dangerous conditions that had inspired them seemed to cease, is mentioned almost as confirmation of their punishment for this.

Ch. 35. The episode of the Rechabites is of a deliberately opposed tenor. Put to the test by the Jeremianic injunction to drink wine in the temple area, they decidedly refuse to do so by virtue of their fidelity to the traditions of their fathers. For this reason, they are made a promise of good things and are referred to as a paradigm of obedience. This is precisely the attitude that could save the people of YHWH, but which lacks entirely.

Let me also mention the articulation of the content of the following subsection (36–45):

Chapter 36. The scroll written by Jeremiah and then burned by the king is a sign of the "passion" of the word of God refused by the act of non-listening which, for precisely this, is then increased and manifested as indestructible by means of the rewriting (of a new scroll). This allows for the perpetuation of the prophetic word, even by way of the figure of the disciple (Baruch). Here, that which is to be said of the "prophetic body" in the following chapters is anticipated in the "literary body": the word of God is *delivered* into the hands of human beings, passes through death (in a symbolic way), and is then re-established and strengthened.

Chs. 37–44 (a section further subdivided into 37–39 and 40–44). In the same manner, Jeremiah is subjected to the whim of the king and his ministers for his obedience to his mission. He is first imprisoned (37) and then thrown into a cistern to be tacitly killed (38:1–13). From here, the foreign eunuch Ebed-melech saves him. In fact, this is the same path of descent and ascension, death and salvation, that Jeremiah then recommends to the king Zedekiah when he asks him to go out towards the king of Babylon to save his life (38:14–28a).

After the narration of the fall of Jerusalem (39), which coincides with Jeremiah's liberation by a foreigner (Nebuzaradan [נְבוּזַרְאֲדָן]), chief of the guard of Nebuchadnezzar [נְבוּכַדְרֶאצַּר][133]), Jeremiah choses to share the fate of the rest of the people left behind in the land of Judah. As a result of the murder of Gedaliah, the governor installed by the Babylonians, at the hand of the rebels (41), the situation precipitates. Jeremiah gets consulted on what to do. He repeats his pre-catastrophe message, applying it to the new situation. He tells them to not be afraid of the king of Babylon and to consign themselves to him, without seeking alternative solutions like flight to Egypt. Nevertheless, the leaders of the rebels reject the oracle that they themselves

---

133   This is one of the graphic variants with which the name itself of the Babylonian king is reproduced in the MT (here, Jer 39:1). I will return to the question in the historical part (ch. II, § 2.1.3).

had demanded and accuse Baruch of manipulating the prophet. And so for fear of a Babylonian retaliation, they flee to Egypt along with the residual population remaining, dragging Jeremiah along with them. He nonetheless does not cease to denounce the sin of the people and predict doom for those who did not wish to submit to the king of Babylon, deluding themselves that they could save themselves by their own hands (42–44).

Chapter 45. As already mentioned, in an almost eschatological context, this is an oracle of consolation and salvation for Baruch. Even the placement of this chapter is strategic. It is one of the three conclusions of the book of Jeremiah (cf. 45 with 51 and 52) and its dating brings us unexpectedly (but not coincidentally) to the time of Jehoiakim. Actually, more precisely, it brings us to the "fourth year of Jehoiakim", a recurrent "axial" date that also symbolically recalls the time of punishment decreed by YHWH (cf. 25:1, 36:1, 46:1). So once again, in this case, the reader is called upon to reflect and penetrate beyond the textual surface.[134]

Having seen the general structure of section 26–45 also on the level of content, I can now better highlight, even if only as a starting point, the particular position assumed by the presence of the theme of my study within the two subsections (26–35 and 36–45). Both chs. 27–28 and ch. 38 are set within *immediate proximity* of the "centre" of their respective subsections. The first is dedicated to the announcement of the New Covenant and the other focuses on the event of the "end", provoking the reader's hermeneutical act. As I will be able to examine in depth over the course of my study, the mysterious relationship between the *end* and the *new beginning* that is the meaning of the totality of the Jeremianic corpus is reflected even in its textual organisation. After all, that the theme of the surrender to Babylon be a cipher of all of Jeremiah's prophecy and not simply an episodic theme is perceivable by now, considering the reproposal of it given in 42–43:1–7, that is, following the destruction of Jerusalem itself.

5. General composition and thematic insertion: First hermeneutical observations

5.1. The necessity of surrender to Babylon: A far from marginal theme

In order to summarise the most relevant elements that emerge from a first survey of the complex literary panorama of the book of Jeremiah, I can indicate the following orientative coordinates as being attributable to the fundamental object of my inquiry and propaedeutic to the more in-depth analysis that I will present in the following chapters.

First of all, it should be duly noted that the theme of "submission to the enemy" (or of the "surrender"), however neglected by specialised exegetical scholars, is by no means marginal in the overall economy of the corpus. The texts that express its fundamental components of meaning are, in fact, localised in *strategic positions*. It seems opportune to emphasise this.

---

134 I will study the function of this conclusive text in further depth in ch. V, § 2.5 of the present dissertation.

126   Orientative literary-hermeneutical coordinates

The second part of the book, made up of chs. 26–45, is certainly the context in which the prevalence of the narrative module provides the most suitable scenario for a demand, that of Jeremiah. And while this may be modulated in an oracular response, it intersects directly with the precise, dramatic, historical events concerning the end of the kingdom of Judah mentioned therein. This fact perhaps unconsciously led many exegetes to suppose that the theme of "surrender" be decentralised with respect to the more "original" core of the book (as seen briefly in the first part).[135] It does not, however, seem irrelevant to ascertain instead that: (1) the "redactor" chose to place a significant text in prose like 21:1–10 right within the literary perimeter of section 1–25 (in which the poetic module prevails), where it provides a narrative frame (cf. 21:1) and is inserted, not without a precise symbolic intent, at the beginning of the 21–24 unit (containing mostly oracles in poetry); and that (2) texts such as 6:1–8, 22–30 do not allow my theme to be considered an exclusively second-hand theological production.[136]

5.2. A scribal explication of the prophetic preaching

That this be the explication of a motif pertaining to the preaching of the prophet itself (even if this be merely hinted in rapid imagery), rather than simply a sort of scribal-redactional *creatio ex nihilo*, can be deduced by tracing back through the chapters of the book in reverse order, following the *Leitmotiv* of the threat coming from the Northern country which is announced from ch. 1.

Within the section of the oracles contained in 2–6, generally considered to be more "original", the roaring of a fearsome enemy is announced (particularly in 4–6). Only later will this roaring be identified with Babylon. With vivid, anguishing images, YHWH himself announces the prospect of the outbreak of a "holy war". The ruthless determination of the invaders and the various stages of an exhausting, irrevocable siege are described. This justifies the prophetic injunction to leave Jerusalem (6:1–8), the infidel city destined to end. This is a scenario which, while not yet fully defined,[137] turns out to be perfectly compatible with that announced in the oracle response of

---

135   With regard to the passages in prose of 26–45, it should be said that there is no lack of defenders of their Jeremianic paternity, or in any case, of their having a Jeremianic base developed subsequently in view of particular new situations. Cf. e.g. W.L. HOLLADAY, «Prototypes and Copies: A New Approach to the Poetry – Prose Problem in the Book of Jeremiah», *JBL* 79 (1960) 351–367; ID., «The Recovery of Poetic Passages of Jeremiah», *JBL* 85 (1966) 401–435; E.W. NICHOLSON, *Preaching to the Exiles*; H. WEIPPERT, *Prosareden*; W.L. HOLLADAY, «A Fresh Look at "Source B" and "Source C" in Jeremiah», *VT* 25 (1975) 394–412.

136   According to the position expressed e.g. by Y. HOFFMAN, «Reflections», 95.

137   This understandable vagueness probably adheres to an archaic stage of Jeremianic preaching. This induces passages like 4:5–6; 6:25 to be interpreted not so much as incitement to resistance, but rather as rhetorical attitudes adopted by the prophetic discourse. These would dramatically anticipate (in the form of a threat) what would actually happen in Israel in the face of the spread of enemy power. Moreover, an invitation to seek shelter in the "fortified cities" would be incomprehensible if, at the same time, the destruction of the entire country and the cities of Judah (4:7) were prophesied. Indeed, these will fall, one after the other, despite every system of defence.

General composition and thematic insertion 127

21:1–10 as well as with the attestations contained in the other pericopes I indicated as pertinent for my research.

As far as the structure of the second part of the book is concerned, beginning with study of the composition of the major textual units, I have been able to highlight the relationship created between the announcement of the *end* and the promise of a *new beginning* (a relationship that is, moreover, anticipated – as we shall see – in 21:1–10 with its structural reference in ch. 24). In my opinion, this relationship is intentional. The centrality of the theme in question, described on a general level, cannot allow the dynamics developed in the texts I have identified to go unheeded. In these, the call for submission to Babylon is set in relation to the possibility that the history of Israel could continue. Indeed, it could begin again. And all this, it must be emphasised, assumes a dimension of *universal validity* through the programmatical reference to the nations contained in 1:10, the significant recurrence lying precisely within the symbolic gesture of the taking up of the yoke with which obedience to YHWH's design of history is requested, and the series of oracles in the third part of the book (46–51), which should be considered in light of the previous references.

One last point to emphasise is that Jeremiah's prophetic message regarding the surrender appears – already from this introductory analysis – to be much more than an intelligent political expedient suggested in order to escape the (contingent) catastrophe of war. In fact, the call to "surrender" goes beyond the historical context of the first deportation (cf. ch. 29) to address the exiles in Babylon, and then even surpasses the scenario of the capitulation of the Holy City itself (cf. chs. 42–43:7), since it is then a message repeated to the survivors of 587 remaining in the territory of Judah. Recognising this, I am thereby induced to regard that call as a cipher for global interpretation, a *prophetic choice* that expresses full acceptance of a paradoxical design of God.

CHAPTER II
Facing the might of the Babylonian empire. Historical international emergencies as the pragmatic context of the call to surrender

Si potrebbe dunque con qualche ragione sostenere che il ruolo della storiografia "drammatica" è quello di impedire che si raffreddino i fatti storici: un freno all'acre piacere di ridimensionare i fatti. È dunque il principale freno al "revisionismo" storiografico. La storiografia pragmatica, invece, incarna nel mondo antico, ciò che noi oggi definiamo – certo in modo vasto e indefinito – revisionismo storiografico. I morti sono annullati, nella storiografia pragmatica, le stragi, il dolore umano diventano insignificanti.[1]

1. The historical-literary context as the pragmatic-cognitive context of the surrender

1.1. Preliminary notes on the epistemology of history

When Titus Livius (Livy) finishes telling the story of the dramatic events of the Punic War, he pens a confession that succinctly expresses an entire historiographic programme:

> I also am relieved, just as if I myself had shared the labour and the peril, that I have come to the end of the Punic War.[2]

The desire to understand one's roots, a fascination with the past, and the need to question the meaning of the events, phenomena, and evolutions that determine the present and orient the future are all fundamental anthropological imperatives. One receives answers to these questions bit by bit, and in different ways, insomuch that a history of these reconstructions and interpretations could itself, in turn, be delineated. In the case of this work by Livy (and of Latin historiography in general), there is a distinct preference for psychagogic aspects. Indeed, the reader's fascination follows along with

---

1   "One could hence argue, somewhat justifiably, that the role of 'dramatic' historiography be that of preventing historical facts from cooling down: putting the brake on the acrid pleasure of resizing the facts. It is, thus, the principal brake on historiographical 'revisionism'. Pragmatic historiography, however, in the ancient world, embodies what we define today – in a vast, undefined way – as historiographic revisionism. The dead are nullified in pragmatic historiography; massacres and human pain become insignificant" (translated from L. CANFORA, *Storiografia greca*, Milano 1999, 58–59).

2   *Me quoque iuvat, velut ipse in parte laboris ac periculi fuerim, ad finem belli Punici pervenisse* (*Ab Urbe Condita History of Rome*, XXXI,1,1). I use the translation published in LIVY, *Livy. With an English Translation in Fourteen Volumes*, IX, Books XXXI–XXXIV, Translated by E.T. SAGE, LCL 295, Cambridge (MA) – London 1935, ²1985, 3 (cf. TITO LIVIO, *Storie. Libri XXXI–XXXV*. A cura di Piero Pecchiura, Classici UTET.CG, Torino 1970, 31).

130 Facing the might of the Babylonian empire

that of the historian, and the facts of the past are reactualised in a "mimetic" narration that resembles precisely that of a drama. Through this, the author endeavours to engage the listeners/readers in the emotional charge emanating from the intrigue of these human events.[3]

In contrast with this orientation in certain respects is the "pragmatic" one (improperly attributed to Thucydides[4]), by which the purpose of historiography is its usefulness. Indeed, this rejects the fableistic and delectable element that typifies Herodotus, and addresses its attention entirely to constructing a critical assessment of the "facts" ($\pi\rho\acute{\alpha}\gamma\mu\alpha\tau\alpha$). And it is over the course of this trajectory, beginning with the Enlightenment, that in an attempt to pursue an impossible scientific objectivity following the model of the "exact sciences", modern historiography was reduced at a certain point to mere historical Positivism (or Neo-positivism). Having been (apparently) purged of their every subjectivism in order to be restored to their naked "truth", the facts lost the charge of global signification that stemmed from their inescapable interrelationships (social, religious, emotional, etc.). But it had been these significations to engage the direct protagonists and the manner in which they understood the events experienced. So what derived from it instead was an impersonal truth, impaired and ingenuously separated from the indispensable precomprehensions of the interpreter generating them. There has, however, been no lack of reactions to this perspective. Indeed, we have come to realise that the telling of a story, any story, *always* involves a transformation of time into human temporality[5] and an interrogation of facts that begins from their own hypotheses.[6] In particular, the overcoming of the "scientific" conception of a positivist matrix by the exponents of the *Ecole des Annales*[7] of Paris saw, as an appealing backlash, the development of diachronic panoramas that were

---

3   It is, however, worth noting that in his *Annales* (IV,34), Tacitus appears to indirectly recognise Livy's credibility, putting these words in the mouth of another Roman historian, Cremutius Cordus: *Titus Livius, eloquentiae ac fidei praeclarus in primis* [...] ("Titus Livius, quite brilliant as he is for eloquence and credibility [...]"; TACITUS, *Tacitus*. In Five Volumes, IV, The Annals, Books IV-VI, XI-XII, with an English Translation by J. JACKSON, LCL 312, Cambridge (MA) – London 1937, 60; I use the translation published in TACITUS, *The Annals*. Translated, with Introduction and Notes, by A.J. WOODMAN, Indianapolis – Cambridge 2004, 138). This expresses awareness that being scrupulous historians and careful examiners of available sources does not mean pursuing (or flaunting) an aseptic and impossible objectivity.
4   Cf. the notation that introduces the historical reconstruction of the Great Peloponnesian War (in *Historiae*, I,23).
5   "[...] Il existe entre l'activité de raconter une histoire et le caractère temporel de l'expérience humaine une corrélation qui n'est pas purement accidentelle, mais présente une forme de nécessité transculturelle. Ou, pour le dire autrement: *que le temps devient temps humain dans la mesure où il est articulé sur le mode narratif, et que le récit atteint sa signification plénière quand il devient une condition de l'existence temporelle*" (P. RICŒUR, *Temps et récit*. Tome I, Paris 1983, 85).
6   In this regard, note P. RICŒUR, *La mémoire, l'histoire, l'oubli*, Paris 2000, 225 (taking up the observations of A. PROST, *Douze leçons sur l'histoire*, Paris 1996; P. LACOMBE, *De l'histoire considérée comme science*, Paris 1994): "Les documents ne parlent que si on leur demande de vérifier, c'est-à-dire de rendre vraie, telle hypothèse."
7   Marc Bloch and Lucien Febvre, Henri Pirenne, Jacques Le Goff, Michel Nora, and Michel Vovelle come to mind.

The historical-literary context

131

more interdisciplinary and, at least in principle, not invalidated by univocal keys of interpretation.[8]

The epistemology upon which the historiography of the ancient Near East is based would merit a specific, in-depth analysis of its own.[9] And this is particularly true for biblical epistemology, given the peculiarity of its object of study and the long-standing problematicity of this.[10] But I can at least point out that in this field as well, scholars' approaches have undergone a considerable evolution, one that is on-going. From the use of archaeological findings and epigraphs as elements used to either confirm or contradict the "revealed text" (in its literality), scholars' attention has shifted to a critical sifting of biblical stories and their respective communicative intentionality. The prophetic books come to mind in particular. Having initially conceived these as literary productions, fruit of a complex history of composition, tradition, and inter-pretive rewriting, scholars subsequently realised the intrinsic difficulty of tracing the "authentic" prophetic words and the biographical profiles of the prophets and their interlocutors themselves. Revaluating the textuality precisely as such, the question of the relationship between story, narrativity, fiction, and ideology (and/or theology) was also posed. This interdependence, in reality, concerns the very nature of histori-ography.[11] The boundary between (narrative) fiction and an "objective" reconstruction (by the historian) therefore seems ever more blurred.[12] Even raw archaeological data,

---

8 "On the whole, there can be little doubt that a weakening of the notion of 'event' has taken place. This, however, is not a bad thing. The question is how we can best compensate for the loss of our positivistic innocence, and learn to live with our frus-trations. The future belongs to true interdisciplinary approaches, something which, unfortunately, is not yet sufficiently developed within biblical studies" (H.M. BARSTAD, «History and Memory: Some Reflections on the "Memory Debate" in Relation to the Hebrew Bible», in: *The Historian and the Bible*. Essays in Honour of Lester L. Grabbe, eds. P.R. DAVIES – D.V. EDELMAN, LHBOTS 530, London – New York 2010, 1–10, here, p. 8).

9 It must be kept in mind that, first of all, "there was no proper historiography in the Near East in the way we understand it today. Royal inscriptions and annals were political texts aimed at celebrating specific individuals. Thus, they were part of a propagandic plan, rather than an accurate account of events" (M. LIVERANI, *The Ancient Near East*, 31).

10 For an initial orientation, see the considerations relating to the "case of Israel" *Ibid.*, 566–567.

11 For the differences between Geschichte (history), Vergangenheit (past), and Geschichtsschreibung (historiography), I refer to H.M. NIEMANN, «Von Oberflächen, Schichten und Strukturen. Was leistet die Archäologie für die Erforschung der Geschichte Israels und Judas?», in: *Steine – Bilder – Texte*. Historische Evidenz außer-biblischer und biblischer Quellen, ed. C. HARDMEIER, ABIG 5, Leipzig 2001, 79–121 (esp. pp. 86–89).

12 "Perhaps some useful distinction might be made in terms of 'imaginative' genres (saga, legend, novella, etc.) and 'recording' genres (anecdote, annalistic extract, memoirs, history writing, etc.). In practice, however, such distinctions are not easily sustained. The difference between fiction and non-fiction, for example, is not always clear, even when dealing with modern genres of 'history' or 'biography'. All history writing involves defining and selecting 'events' and interpreting their relationships, which means constructing a plot and positing the motivation of the participating characters. All authors and editors serve ideological agendas, expressed or unexpressed, and

132   Facing the might of the Babylonian empire

in order to become truly meaningful, require interpretations, and these can diverge and even contradict each other.[13]

1.2. Towards a focalisation of the pragmatic context underlying the Jeremianic message

In the same vein, as far as the question of the historicity of the prophet Jeremiah in particular is concerned, as I have already mentioned,[14] a shift of the hermeneutical paradigm has been established moving scholars' interest from an attempt to identify the figure of the "historical Jeremiah" (with his oracles) to consideration of the Jeremianic work as a literary production. Let me therefore further specify the aim to which the interpretive operation of the present chapter of my dissertation will be dedicated, as I disclosed in the General Introduction (in § 4.2).

Clearly, my starting point as well cannot but be the text of the book of Jeremiah. It is precisely from this point, however, that the specific importance of the historical question it poses emerges, at least on two levels: regarding the well-known problem of the *history of the composition* of the text (MT/LXX), and in relation to the *historicity* of the "possible world" described in the Jeremianic work. Of upmost interest to us now is this second level. The issue is that of questioning in this regard not only the overall solidity of the narrative system/structure (founded, above all, on spatial-temporal coordinates that are usually verifiable), but also the plentiful detail and historical information provided to the reader for no apparent reason.[15]

---

  shape their account accordingly. In practice, then, there must always be a distance between the narrative world and the world of 'what actually happened'. Indeed, we could argue that there is no such thing as 'what actually happened'; there are only stories (or histories) of what happened, always relative to the perspective of the story-teller (historian)" (D.M. GUNN – D. FEWELL, *Narrative in the Hebrew Bible*, 7). See also K. BIEBERSTEIN, «Geschichten sind immer fiktiv – mehr oder minder. Warum das Alte Testament fiktional erzählt und erzählen muss», *BiLi* 75 (2002) 4–13.

13 In this regard, see N. NA'AMAN, «Does Archaeology Really Deserve the Status of a «High Court» in Biblical Historical Research?», in: *Between Evidence and Ideology*. Essays on the History of Ancient Israel Read at the Joint Meeting of the Society for Old Testament Study and the Oud Testamentisch Werkgezelschap Lincoln, July 2009, *eds.* B. BECKING – L.L. GRABBE, OTS 59, Leiden 2011, 165–184, and also the reaction of I. FINKELSTEIN, «Archaeology as High Court in Ancient Israelite History: A Reply to NadavNa'aman», *JHS* 10 (2010) 1–8 (which, while giving priority to the authority of archaeological evidence regarding biblical texts, also admits the possibility of their misinterpretation).

14 Cf. General Introduction, n. 66.

15 For example, one of the episodes of particular interest to us comes to mind: the lowering of the prophet into the muddy cistern, his subsequent liberation (38:1–13), and also the place where the final encounter with Zedekiah takes place (38:14). On the relation between the book of Jeremiah and archaeological data, see P.J. KING, *Jeremiah. An Archaeological Companion*, Louisville 1993; D.A. GLATT-GILAD, «The Personal Names in Jeremiah as a Source for the History of the Period», *HebStud* 41 (2000) 31–45; H.M. BARSTAD, «Jeremiah the Historian: The Book of Jeremiah as a Source for the History of the Near East in the Time of Nebuchadnezzar», in: *Studies on the Text and Versions of the Hebrew Bible in Honour of Robert Gordon, eds.* G. KHAN – D. LIPTON, VT.S 149, Leiden – Boston 2012, 87–98.

The historical-literary context   133

While historical dating can also have or certainly has value that is symbolic (and the two need not be mutually exclusive),[16] these clues of historical verisimilitude have led to the notion that there be a direct eyewitness of the facts narrated. It is not my intention to address this problem, which is practically unsolvable in principle if one considers that the expressive potential of "fiction" is substantiated by precisely the use of specific historical data.[17] Between an attempt to draw an outline of the "historical Jeremiah" and a reduction of this to a solely literary phenomenon, my study, in this phase, chooses to place itself instead on yet another level, and to question the *historicity of the prophetic request* attributed to Jeremiah, focalising the *pragmatic context* of the Jeremianic message that calls for surrender to the king of Babylon. Let me specify the nature of this approach.

As I highlighted in the General Introduction, it is precisely the assumption of the book of Jeremiah as an event of communication that calls to account the *pragmatic dimension* of its language in its constitutive configuration of dynamic interactions between words and the world, along with the *cooperative dimension* of the interpretive act to which the reader is continually called.[18] The contextualist approach (and, in particular, that of the Relevance Theory) shows that the determination of lexical meaning is fruit of an abductive inference process dependent upon the real context of use in which the event of communication occurs. Hence, for my research, the extratextual factors become not only the object of a reconnaissance animated by mere historical interest, but also valuable clues for attempting to rebuild, insofar as possible, the relevant *cognitive horizon* within which the Jeremianic message is to be read.

Certainly, it should be kept in mind that we are not in the presence of oral communication, in which these extralinguistic factors are more easily detectable. By nature, a written text[19] is endowed with a certain semantic autonomy that sets it apart from the event of its production. And this autonomy is transformed in reality into potential semantic relativism. The text remains (in principle) the same, but as it goes through time, it becomes available to generations of readers who may not share the encyclopaedic world of its author any longer, as P. Ricœur also emphasised in other terms.[20] It is nevertheless my opinion that my research can be guided by precisely this awareness

---

16   As, e.g. G. Fischer, *Jeremia*, 121–122 seems to have done, tending to declassify the historicity of the dating of the book of Jeremiah as being symbolic (i.e. invented) elements. An in-depth investigation of the phenomenon of symbolic communication can clearly demonstrate that "symbolic" does not necessarily mean "non-historical". On the contrary, symbolic language by nature is based precisely on the factual concreteness of material data.

17   On the relationship between fiction, other communicative registers, and the representation of the world, see O. Dyma, «Wahre Geschichten: Zwischen Fiktionalitat, Gattung, Weltbild und Geltungsanspruch», in: *Methodik im Diskurs. Neue Perspektiven für die Alttestamentliche Exegese*, BThS 156, Neukirchen-Vluyn 2015, 32–51.

18   See esp. the General Introduction, from § 3.3.4 to § 3.3.6.

19   Cf J. Hill, «The Dynamics of Written Discourse and the Book of Jeremiah MT», in: *Jeremiah (Dis)Placed*, 104–111.

20   Cf P. Ricœur, «Qu'est-ce qu'un texte? Expliquer et comprendre», in: *Hermeneutik und Dialektik. Aufsätze II*, *eds.* R. Bubner – K. Cramer – R. Wiehl, Tübingen 1970, 181–200; Id., «The Hermeneutical Function of Distanciation», *Philosophy Today* 17 (1973) 129–141.

134   Facing the might of the Babylonian empire

in order to reconstruct a plausible *cognitive horizon* within which the theo-politcal message of the surrender attributed to the figure of Jeremiah was placed.

Keeping to the Jeremianic story, the prophetic request is set within a precise historical-political and religious context. But besides the question of the prophet's historicity, and before hypothesising an *ex-nihilo* literary creation completed centuries after the narrative scenario, it seems appropriate that Jeremiah's message be placed in relation to its explicit *pragmatic anchoring*. This is necessary precisely because the context of use of the language remains a decisive one. And this can be seen even in the adjective "pragmatic" itself, which can have, as one will note, beginning with a reading of the exergue that opens this chapter and by the diverse meanings I assign to this adjective in my methodological system, (at least) two completely opposing, semantic references. *Disambiguation* is, in effect, the watchword for every process of pertinisation. The "pragmatic" historiography of the Greek matrix to which I referred in the beginning holds the intention of limiting itself to the "facts". For this reason, it dismisses mimetic-dramatic elements as being subjective (and therefore unreliable or irrelevant), when instead, in other perspectives, these are essential. The "pragmatic" approach to language, on the other hand, considers mere "factual" linguistic elements to be altogether insufficient. There are whole series of extralinguistic factors that bear a powerful contextual salience (or relevance), to which one need turn in order to understand the meaning of a communicative act. Not the least of these are the elusive colours of the emotional world, to not mention virtually every anthropological fact. My contribution therefore places itself along the lines of those new attempts to approach the historical question with the intent of not reducing historiography to merely a recognition of impersonal economic, social, political, and ideological factors.[21]

In other words, returning to the L. Canfora quotation placed as exergue to this chapter and paraphrasing it, we could say that if one were to disregard extralinguistic factors (ranging from archaeological, epigraphical, and iconographical data to those of an anthropological-cognitive nature, etc.), the "facts" would remain coldly to the letter. However challenging a reconstruction may be, since we do not share the context of use within which the Jeremianic message is placed, we must nevertheless attempt this important operation of disambiguation and pertinisation in order to focalise the cognitive frames that underlie the communicative dynamics of the book of Jeremiah. Only in this manner will it be possible to lay down more solid foundations for an interpretive act that does not reduce the act of "surrender to the king of Babylon" to a merely anecdotal and/or ideologico-political level. In this way, the human suffering, the siege, the massacres, the fear of succumbing, and the drama of the surrender that set the scene, which every reader is invited to enter in first person, become elements that are far from *insignificant*. And this is true not only in a pathematic sense, but also in the most radically historical-critical sense, which, in my opinion, should not disregard reference to the pragmatic-cognitive context of communication. Perhaps then the perspective already drawn by an enthusiast of human history like Livy can be discovered as still having something to say to modern historiography and, why not, even to scholars of biblical *lógos* in particular. After all, today, what historiography is or what it should be is up for discussion.

---

21   According to the perspective highlighted, e.g. in I. KALIMI – S. RICHARDSON, «Sennacherib at the Gates of Jerusalem–Story, History and Historiography: An Introduction», in: *Sennacherib at the Gates of Jerusalem. Story, History and Historiography, eds.* I. KALIMI – S. RICHARDSON, CHANE 71, Leiden – Boston 2014, 1–7 (here, p. 4).

The question of what historiography actually is or, even more difficult to determine, what it should be, remains unresolved. Is it a tool for keeping memory alive or a means of comprehension/justification (that is, a training ground for the wisdom of posterity)? Perhaps it is already enough for it to help us understand what people and their hearts were like *in that moment*, without meaning by this to say that what they chose to do was inevitable.[22]

2. Babylon is victorious (605 B.C.) and becomes the new global threat. A general historical contextualisation

2.1. How a geopolitical scenario changes

2.1.1. Prophecy and history in the shadow of the great empires

According to the attestation in Jer 27, the temporal horizon within which the message of submission to the king of Babylon is explicitly proclaimed for the first time coincides with the beginning of the reign of Zedekiah (597–587).[23] His ascent to the throne is part of a historic period that is of great political importance on an international level. It is marked by clashes and war between the major powers of the ancient Near East in the seventh-sixth centuries: Egypt, Assyria (no longer on the scene by Zedekiah's time), and Babylonia.

Even if, within this grand scenario, the events of the small reign of Judah appear to scholars to be entirely subordinate to more complex dynamics, and if even its end appears to be simply a collateral effect of broader political manoeuvres or exemplary manifestation of well-known politico-cultural transition processes,[24] the fall

---

22 Translated from L. CANFORA, *Storiografia greca*, 59–60: "È insoluta la questione di che cosa propriamente sia, o, cosa ancor più difficile da stabilirsi, che cosa debba essere la storiografia. Lo strumento per mantenere vivo il ricordo o il veicolo della comprensione/giustificazione (cioè la palestra della saggezza dei posteri)? Forse è già molto se essa saprà aiutarci a capire come erano gli uomini e gli animi *in quel momento*, senza con ciò voler dire che era inevitabile che facessero quel che hanno scelto di fare."

23 H. LESÊTRE, «Sédécias», *DB(V)* V, 1556–1559; R. ALTHANN, «Zedekiah», *ABD* VI, 1068–1071; G. GALIL, *The Chronology of the Kings of Israel and Judah*, SHCANE 9, Leiden – New York – Köln 1996, 108–126; J.B. JOB, *Jeremiah's Kings. A Study of the Monarchy in Jeremiah*, MSSOTS, Aldershot 2006, 99–119.

24 I refer once again to L. TATUM, «Jerusalem in Conflict», 291–294, who, taking up the working hypothesis of the archaeologist Colin Renfrew (ID., «Transformations», in: *Transformations*. Mathematical Approaches to Culture Change, *eds.* C. RENFREW – K.L. COOKE, New York 1979, 3–44 [cf. esp., pp. 16–17]) interprets the end of the kingdom of Judah as a phenomenon that can be traced back to an intercultural transition model ("allactic form") common to many state entities whose final collapse is interpreted as being the outcome of a previous process of decline lasting at least one century. According to this perspective (defined by L. Tatum as "secondary state collapse"), the destruction of the kingdom of Israel first, and then of Judah, would not be directly attributable to external invasions (Assyrian and Babylonian). This assertion is, in my opinion, very problematic. While this type of research does indeed demonstrate a (moreover predictable) resemblance to the post-catastrophe conditions of collapsed social systems (cf. pp. 292–293), it does not, however, present sufficient evidence to explain the

136   Facing the might of the Babylonian empire

of Jerusalem, destruction of the temple, and subsequent (second) Babylonian exile will remain uncancellable in the historical memory of Israel attested by the biblical tradition.[25] It is an event that calls into question a theological vision of history, both to contest it and to draw hope and meaning from it.

The prophetic ministry of Jeremiah, deeply embedded in the complex fabric of these decisive events, becomes particularly interesting in this conjuncture. If prophecy and history are indeed intimately interconnected realities in the biblical world, this can especially be seen here in the Jeremianic message that is the object of my study, where the political implications of it are immediately evident. It is certainly entirely logical from a methodological point of view, based on merely literary or thematic interests, to limit study of the Jeremianic message about submission to Babylon to the limited set of textual data offered by the book of Jeremiah itself, considering this data to be the binding hermeneutical context of the message. However, it is instead opportune at this turn in the historical framing to turn to an interdisciplinary approach that can place biblical and extrabiblical sources in a critically plausible relationship (cf. fig. 11)

Therefore, to adequately comprehend the prophetic reverberation of the option to "surrender" and to verify its precise historical anchoring, it is opportune to take a few steps back and to attempt, on the basis of sources available, a rapid reconstruction of the unfolding of the principal events that mark this travailed epoch.[26] The period is that in which Babylonia, having raised itself back up from the destruction inflicted by the Assyrian king Sennacherib in 689, becomes the main (and feared) protagonist.

---

eventual "necessity" of the phenomenon itself, aside from the fact that it underlines the presence of concurrent factors, as is obvious. And it is not clear how the fact can be affirmed that the kingdom of Judah, specifically, would have collapsed in any case, even without the Babylonian invasion. That there be uniformity or analogous aspects of the destinies of historical subjects that resemble each other (and which sapiential reflection indeed investigates; cf. Eccl 1:9–10) cannot obscure the fact that history is also, or even structurally, made through events that are unique and unrepeatable. And it is precisely within this dimension that prophecy purports to utter a decisive revelatory word.

25   Amongst the most painful events in the history of Israel, Jewish tradition still specifically remembers the destruction of the first temple on a particular day of mourning, the Tishah be-Av (cf. *Tosefta Taanit* IV,6; M. YDIT, «Av, The Ninth of», in: *EJ.SE* II, 714–716). It is worth remarking that the public reading done on this occasion is not a chronicled narration of the events but rather a reading of verses from the book of Lamentations. "It appears therefore that the rational, informative and documentary account is less effective than the poetic imaginative poem" (Y. GITAY, «The Poetics of Exile», 203).

26   For an *overall panorama* of the events affecting the final phase of the kingdom of Judah through to the Babylonian exile, from amongst the many contributions, I mention esp.: J. BRIGHT, *A History of Israel*, London 1960, Louisville ⁴2000, 324–339; A. MALAMAT, «The Twilight of Judah: in the Egyptian-Babylonian Maelstrom», in: *Congress Volume*. Edinburgh 1974, eds. G.W. ANDERSON *et al.*, VT.S 28, Leiden 1975, 123–145; H. CAZELLES, *Histoire politique d'Israël. Des origines à Alexandre le Grand*, PBSB 1, Paris 1982, 185–191; J.M. MILLER – J.H. HAYES, *A History of Ancient Israel and Judah*, Philadelphia 1986, Louisville ²2006, 439–497; J. OATES, «The Fall of Assyria (635–609 B.C.)», in: *The Cambridge Ancient History. The Assyrian and Babylonian Empires and Other States of the Near East, from the Eighth to the Sixth Centuries B.C.*, vol. III/2, eds. J. BOARDMAN *et al.*, Cambridge 1991, 162–193; D.J. WISEMAN, «Babylonia 605–539 B.C.», *ibid.*, 229–251; T.C. MITCHELL, «Judah

until the Fall of Jerusalem (*c.* 700–586 B.C.)», *ibid.*, 371–409; R. ALBERTZ, *Religionsgeschichte Israels* (on the relationship between religion and politics, esp. pp. 304–310); G.W. AHLSTRÖM, *The History of Ancient Palestine from the Palaeolithic Period to Alexander's Conquest.* With a contribution by G.O. Rollefson, *ed.* D. EDELMAN, JSOT.S 146, Sheffield 1993, 754–811; A. MALAMAT, «The Kingdom of Judah between Egypt and Babylon: A Small State within a Great Power Confrontation», in: ID., *History of Biblical Israel.* Major Problems and Minor Issues, CHANE 7, Leiden 2001, 322–337; A. SOGGIN, *Storia d'Israele.* Introduzione alla storia d'Israele e Giuda dalle origini alla rivolta di Bar Kochbà, BCR 44, Brescia 2002, 300–331; O. LIPSCHITS – J. BLENKINSOPP, eds., *Judah and the Judeans in the Neo-Babylonian Period,* Winona Lake 2003; M. LIVERANI, *Oltre la Bibbia.* Storia antica di Israele, Bari 2003; O. LIPSCHITS, *The Fall and Rise of Jerusalem.* Judah under Babylonian Rule, Winona Lake 2005; B.A. LEVINE, «The View from Jerusalem. Biblical Responses to the Babylonian Presence», in: *The Babylonian World, ed.* G. LEICK, Abingdon 2007, 541–561; L.L. GRABBE, *Ancient Israel.* What Do We Know and How Do We Know It?, London 2007, ²2017, 210–259. Amongst the *principal sources* for a reconstruction of the salient events of this historic period, besides the (secondary) testimonies of Flavius Josephus (cf. the *Antiquitates iudaicae*) and Berossus (cf. the remaining fragments of his *Babyloniaca*), I refer above all to the literary work, the "Babylonian chronicles" (I will make reference to other epigraphic and iconographic sources at the points most opportune, but for the chronicles, I rely on D.J. WISEMAN, *Chronicles of Chaldean Kings [626–556 B.C.] in the British Museum,* London 1956; A.K. GRAYSON, *Assyrian and Babylonian Chronicles,* Locust Valley 1975; J. BRIEND – M.-J. SEUX, *Textes du Proche-Orient Ancien et Histoire d'Israël,* Paris 1977; J.-J. GLASSNER, *Mesopotamian Chronicles,* SBLWAW 19, Atlanta 2004; B.T. ARNOLD – P. MICHALOWSKI, «Achaemenid Period Historical Texts Concerning Mesopotamia», in: *The Ancient Near East.* Historical Sources in Translation, *ed.* M.W. CHAVALAS, Malden 2006, 415–417; M. COGAN, *The Raging Torrent.* Historical Inscriptions from Assyria and Babylonia Relating to Ancient Israel, Jerusalem 2008, 176–223), together and in comparison with the data obtained from the books of Kings and Chronicles and from the book of Jeremiah itself (for the relationship between the latter and the data obtained from archaeological research, see L.L. GRABBE, «The Kingdom of Judah from Sennacherib's Invasion to the Fall of Jerusalem: If We Had Only the Bible...», in: *Good Kings and Bad Kings, ed.* L.L. GRABBE, LHBOTS 393, London – New York 2005, 78–122; ID., «"The Lying Pen of the Scribes?". Jeremiah and History», in: *Essays on Ancient Israel in Its Near Eastern Context.* A Tribute to Nadav Na'aman, eds. Y. AMIT – E. BEN ZVI – I. FINKELSTEIN – O. LIPSCHITS, Winona Lake 2006, 189–204). Amongst the *epigraphic material,* the well-known "Lachish Letters" are of note (the *ostraca* found in the excavations of the homonymous city that was definitively destroyed by the Babylonians), for which one can refer (from amongst the many contributions) to H. TORCZYNER *et al.* eds., *Lachish I (Tell ed-Duweir).* The Lachish Letters, WARENEP 1, London 1938 (the first editor of the "letters", to which I refer for their numbering); A. LEMAIRE, *Inscriptions hébraïques.* Tome I: Les ostraca, LAPO 9, Paris 1977, 83–143; J. RENZ, *Die althebräischen Inschriften.* Teil 1. Text und Kommentar, HAE 1, Darmstadt 1995, 419–438; B. STUDEVENT-HICKMAN – S.C. MELVILLE – S. NOEGEL, «Neo-Babylonian Period Texts from Babylonia and Syro-Palestine», in: *The Ancient Near East,* 400–406; W.W. HALLO – K.L. YOUNGER, Jr., eds., *The Context of Scripture.* Archival Documents from the Biblical World, vol. III, Leiden 2002, 78–81; J.M. LINDENBERGER, *Ancient Aramaic and Hebrew Letters,* SBLWAW 14, Atlanta 1994, ²2003, 113–131 (also for the "Arad letters"); F.W. DOBBS-ALLSOPP *et al.*, *Hebrew Inscriptions.* Texts from the Biblical Period of the Monarchy with Concordances, New Haven – London 2005, 299–347; S. AHITUV, *Echoes from the Past.* Hebrew and Cognate Inscriptions from the Biblical Period, Jerusalem 2008, 56–91. As for the (scarce) *Egyptian sources* available to us, see D.B. REDFORD, «New Light on Egypt's Stance towards Asia, 610–586 BCE», in: *Rethinking the Foundations.* Historiography in the Ancient World and in the Bible. Essays in Honor of John Van Seters, eds. S.L. MCKENZIE – T. RÖMER, Berlin 2000, 183–195.

Fig. 11. A portion of the Babylonian Chronicles (BM 21946), which report important events occurring between 605 and 594, such as the battle of Carchemish, the ascent to the throne of Nebuchadnezzar II and the taking of Jerusalem in 597 (Photograph © Trustees of the British Museum).

2.1.2. Babylon resurgens, *the disappearance of the Neo-Assyrian empire, and the Egyptian manoeuvres*

Beginning from the second half of the seventh century, the Neo-Babylonian empire[27] assumes an ever more preponderant role in the middle-eastern theatre. This occurs not only with respect to Assyria, which passed from its apogee to its twilight over the course of just a few years,[28] but also and above all with respect to Egypt, the only great power of the ancient Near East capable of counterbalancing the Mesopotamian empires in Syria-Palestine.

Following the fall of the capital city-fortress Nineveh (612), Babylonia (and its king Nabopolassar), with the decisive help of the Medes, progressively and inexorably devoured what remained of the Assyrian empire. Then, in an ironic turn of fate, as it advanced north-east, it found itself having to confront the very same Egypt that not so many years earlier had fallen into the hands of the Assyrians.[29] Only now, Egypt seemed to rush to the aid of its enemies of yesteryear. More realistically,

---

27 By the term "Neo-Babylonian", I refer to the era of the dynasty (begun by Nabopolassar) that governed in Babylon from 626 to 539 (the year of the taking of the city by Cyrus the Great). In another sense, one that is chronological rather than linguistic in nature, the same adjective indicates the Akkadian dialect typical of the Babylonian region during the period from the end of the second millennium to the middle of the sixth century B.C. (cf. D.S. VANDERHOOFT, *The Neo-Babylonian Empire*, 9, n. 1).

28 In 612, Nineveh falls at the hands of the Medes of Cyaxares (625–585) and the Babylonians of Nabopolassar (626–605).

29 During its period of maximum expansion, under the reign of Esarhaddon (680–669) and then Ashurbanipal (668–631), Assyria had managed to subjugate even Egypt.

Babylon is victorious (605 b.c.) and becomes the new global threat 139

what compelled the pharaoh Necho (609/610–594/595)[30] and his army to lend man-power to the Assyrians even as far as the banks of the Euphrates was a conscious political calculation in defence of his own interests. For some years, since the time of Ashurbanipal, they had shared a relationship of non-belligerence, if not actual alliance. Theirs was basically a division of the spoils of the great Assyrian empire, which was now in agony, ever since Ashur-uballit, its final sovereign, had established himself at Haran, setting up a sort of provisional government in exile there with the support of residual army forces.

Necho, in his ascent north along the Syrian-Palestine corridor, had been slowed down by the king Josiah, determined to bar the road in the valley of Megiddo. At least, this is the version of the facts explicated in 2 Chr 35:20–22 (the story in 2 Kgs 23:29 is more elliptical). According to this succinct (and ambiguous) biblical account, this (historically problematic) attempt also proved to be entirely unrealistic (cf. 2 Kgs 23:29–30; 2 Chr 35:23–27). However things may have actually gone,[31] the unexpected death of the king of Judah (609),[32] described as a faithful reformer of the Yahwist cult, probably had a strong destabilising impact on Deuteronomistic convictions (cf. e.g. Deut 20:1).[33] In fact, Josiah's traumatic exit from the scene is followed by a socio-politico-religious crisis that will grow deeper and deeper, until the final collapse.[34] If one keeps to the biblical text,[35] this marks the end of the brief period of independence

---

30 Necho II, to be precise.
31 According to N. Na'aman, «Josiah and the Kingdom of Judah», in: *Good Kings and Bad Kings*, ed. L.L. Grabbe, LHBOTS 393, London 2005, 226–229, the most likely hypothesis (keeping in mind the "reticence" of the version of the facts in 2 Kgs 23:29), would be that which considers the death of Josiah a genuine "execution" decreed by Necho for his suspected (or ascertained) infidelity.
32 This is the commonly accepted date. Some scholars, more recently, argue that the death of Josiah would instead be placed in the year 610 (cf. P.K. Hooker – J.H. Hayes, «The Year of Josiah's Death: 609 or 610 BCE?», in: *The Land That I Will Show You. Essays on the History and Archaeology of the Ancient Near East in Honour of J.M. Miller*, eds. J.A. Dearman – M.P. Graham, JSOT.S 343, Sheffield 2001, 96–103).
33 By their embarrassed reticence, biblical sources suggest the extent of the dismay itself. The loss of the king Josiah was commemorated for generations (cf. 2 Chr 35:25; Flavius Josephus, *Antiquitates iudaicae*, X,78).
34 Cf. R. Albertz, *Religionsgeschichte*, 361–366.
35 From the historiographic point of view, apart from the biblical data, the figure of Josiah is a rather problematic one, since we have no explicit evidence even of his existence (in the nineties, this king was thought to have been identified in the name of the sovereign appearing in one of the two ostraca, by the same hand but with different content, in the Moussaïeff collection, published in P. Bordreuil – F. Israel – D. Pardee, «Deux ostraca paléo-hébreux de la collection Sh. Moussaïeff», *Semitica* 46 [1996] 49–76; Eng. tr.: Id., «King's Command and Widow's Plea: Two New Hebrew Ostraca of the Biblical Period», *NEA* 61 [1998] 2–13; following an initial confirmation of their authenticity, more recent and in-depth laboratory analyses instead suggest that they be sophisticated fakes). Obviously, the period of state independence and territorial expansion described in the Bible is also in question (since "David's Empire"; cf. e.g. G. Garbini, *Storia e ideologia nell'Israele antico*, Brescia 1986, 21–32). In particular, some scholars believe that Josiah was actually left with a permanent *status* of vassalage, first to Assyria and then to Egypt. See, e.g. L.L. Grabbe, *Ancient Israel*, 204–207.

140 Facing the might of the Babylonian empire

of the kingdom of Judah, which initially falls under Egyptian control, only to then be swept up in the wave of Babylonia.

According to 2 Kgs 23:30, the "people of the land" (in this case, perhaps the landed gentry of anti-Egyptian orientation)[36] put Josiah's youngest son, the third-born Yehoahaz[37] (יְהוֹאָחָז) on the throne. This was most likely done because a possible continuity with the Josiahanic policies could be seen in him.[38] But as soon as the pharaoh was able to address the issue, he proved to be entirely dissatisfied with the solution. After only three months of Yehoahaz's reign, the pharaoh gave orders for his removal. He deported him to Egypt (where he died) and *opportunistically* re-established the right of succession to his older brother (by a different mother) Jehoiakim (Eliakim [אֶלְיָקִים]; cf. 2 Kgs 23:34; 2 Chr 36:4), upon whom the pharaoh imposed a tribute in gold and silver as punishment. And, in turn, the new king, according to 2 Kgs 23:35, made this tribute fall, moreover, directly on the "people of the land".

With Jehoiakim (609–598) and his supporters, the "reform" is substantially abandoned.[39] The idolatrous cults regain their strength, the government becomes particularly despotic, social and moral life deteriorates, and all this is concealed behind the false security placed in the Covenant and the temple. This attitude is strongly denounced by the prophet Jeremiah. In a renowned (and subversive) discourse, he

---

36 For the identification of the expression עַם־הָאָרֶץ ("the people of the land") proposed in this context, for which an ambiguous semantic oscillation subject to much discussion amongst scholars need be recognised, I refer to R. ALBERTZ, *Religionsgeschichte*, 364 and A. SOGGIN, *Storia d'Israele*, 323–324. Elsewhere, especially after the fall of Jerusalem in 587, the same locution instead indicates the less affluent social class left in the country (cf. 2 Kgs 24:14; 25:3, 19; Jer 34:19; 37:2; 44:21; 52:25; Ezek 7:27; etc.). A discussion on the various possible interpretations can be found in the *excursus* by C.R. SEITZ, *Theology in Conflict*, 42–51. For a more recent contribution, see W.M. SCHNIEDEWIND, *Society and the Promise to David*. The Reception History of 2 Sam 7:1–17, New York 1999, 77–80, and above all, J.T. THAMES, Jr., «A New Discussion of the Meaning of the Phrase *'am hā'āreṣ* in the Hebrew Bible», *JBL* 130 (2011) 109–125, according to which, based on the biblical attestations, the term would have no technical meaning and would most coherently be simply an idiomatic expression "used to communicate something very ordinary, such as 'everyone in a particular locality who is relevant to a particular set of circumstances', but with the deliberate intent to efface or obfuscate the exact actor(s)" (p. 120). For my part, I believe that it be possible (and opportune) to delineate or infer a less generic definition of the expression on a case-by-case basis depending on the context of reference.

37 Also called Shallum (שַׁלֻּם) in Jer 22:11.

38 And not necessarily for anti-Babylonian political use, as claimed by J.A. WILCOXEN, «The Political Background of Jeremiah's Temple Sermon», in: *Scripture in History & Theology*. Essays in Honor of J. Coert Rylaarsdam, eds. A.L. MERRILL – T.W. OVERHOLT, Pittsburgh 1977, 151–165 (here, p. 159).

39 Assuming it had ever been achieved, some minimalists would say (cf. C. UEHLINGER, «Gab es eine joschijanische Kultreform? Plädoyer für ein begründetes Minimum», in: *Jeremia und die "deuteronomistische Bewegung"*, ed. B. GROSS, BBB 98, Weinheim 1995, 57–89). I prefer to phrase it somewhat differently: assuming that (as usually happens, after all, with every attempt to reform) it had the strength to impose itself in the manner described in the Bible.

Babylon is victorious (605 b.c.) and becomes the new global threat 141

links the threat of destruction by YHWH of that very temple to the absence of proper conversion (cf. Jer 7:1–15; 26).

The king of Judah remains a faithful vassal of Necho, at least as long as the Egyptian protectorate endures. Meanwhile, in the years ranging from 609 to 605, the Egyptian and Babylonian armies face-off between Haran and the Euphrates several times. Their alternating victories and defeats are always provisional. Then, in 607, the young crown prince Nebuchadnezzar appears on the scene (in Akkadian: *Nabû-kudurrī-uṣur*[40]). He is the son of Nabopolassar and a general. A skilful and unscrupulous strategist, it will be under him that the international balance definitively overturns, allowing a new empire to impose its dominion across the ancient Near East.

2.1.3. Nebuchadnezzar and the collapse of the Egyptian hegemony over Palestine

The Battle of Carchemish in 605, one of the greatest war conflicts of antiquity,[41] is the turning point. This city, situated in a strategic position in the north of Syria on the right

---

40 This was believed to mean "*Nabu* est *deorum princeps*" (cf. GESENIUS[T], 840), or "O Nabû, protect the border" (cf. *BDB*, 613), but more recently, this reading was corrected to be: "Nabû protect my son/my heir!" (cf. GESENIUS, 771; H.D. BAKER – J.A. BRINKMAN, «*Nabû-kudurrī-uṣur*», *PNA* 2/II, 841–842). The conventional and Italianised form (Nabucodonosor) derives from the late (and imprecise) transcriptions in Greek (Naboucodonosor) and Latin (*Nabuchodonosor*) of the Babylonian name. Some modern English versions use the spelling Nebukadnezzar or Nebukadrezzar, transliterating the name from the two variants most attested in the HB, that is, נְבוּכַדְרֶאצַּר (33x) or נְבוּכַדְנֶאצַּר (27x), the latter considered by some to be degrading or derisive, used particularly in Jeremiah and Ezekiel (this lexical uncertainty, according to A.D. HORNKOHL, *Ancient Hebrew Periodization and the Language of the Book of Jeremiah. The Case for a Sixth-Century Date of Composition*, StSLL 74, Leiden – Boston 2014, 99–103, is actually only a phonetic phenomenon typical to any borrowed term or foreignism, and reveals a linguistic transitional phase between classical and post-exilic Hebrew in Jeremiah). The reference is precisely to Nebuchadnezzar II (successor of his father, Nabopolassar), whose reign, according to the surviving Babylonian sources (cf. R.A. PARKER – W.H. DUBBERSTEIN, *Babylonian Chronology 626 B.C. – A.D. 75*, Providence 1956, 12), lasted from 605 to 562. Despite the many inscriptions remaining, the events of his reign are not reconstructible in great detail. For an overview with references to sources, see R. DA RIVA, *The Neo-Babylonian Royal Inscriptions. An Introduction*, GMTR 4, Münster 2008, 8–14. Amongst the numerous sources, we especially note D.J. WISEMAN, *Nebuchadrezzar and Babylon*, SchL 1983, Oxford 1985; M. LEIBOVICI, «Nabuchodonosor», *DBS* VI, 286–291; R.H. SACK, «Nebuchadnezzar», *ABD* IV, 1058–1059; D.S. VANDERHOOFT, *The Neo-Babylonian Empire*; M.P. STRECK, «Nebukadnezzar II. A. Historisch. Konig von Babylon (604–562)», *RLA* IX, 194–201; R.M. CZICHON, «Nebukadnezzar II. B. Archäologisch», *RLA* IX, 201–206; R.H. SACK, «Nebuchadnezzar II and the Old Testament: History versus Ideology», in: *Judah and the Judeans*, 221–233; I. EPH'AL, «Nebuchadnezzar the Warrior: Remarks on his Military Achievements», *IEJ* 53 (2003) 178–195; D. ARNAUD, *Nabuchodonosor II roi de Babylone*, Paris 2004.

41 This is the conviction of, e.g. J. OATES, «The Fall of Assyria», 182–183. A. Neher, on the other hand, defines the year 605 as a "Hegelian" year, that is, the moment in which "le *Weltgeist* y est à l'œuvre, distillant et suscitant des événements dont le caractère le plus frappant est d'être universel" (cf. ID., *Jérémie*, Paris 1960, 55).

142 Facing the might of the Babylonian empire

bank of the Euphrates, had long become an international trade centre. The Egyptians had placed their headquarters here, making it a solid stronghold and a tactically decisive outpost that was, at least on paper, difficult to conquer. The pharaoh probably counted on protecting his interests in Syria and Palestine from here by maintaining a defensive garrison or, more actively, by conducting every eventual military operation necessary to prevent the nightmare of a new and terrible empire from taking shape in Mesopotamia. It was preferable for that vast region to remain divided (and thus weakened) between the Assyrians, Medes, and Babylonians.[42] The potential threat that they posed could predictably, as it had during the Assyrian empire, transform into a direct attack on Egypt sooner or later.

Against all odds, however, with a surprise attack and gory battle,[43] Nebuchadnezzar gets the upper hand and conquers Carchemish (cf. Jer 46:2–12). He then annihilates the surviving Egyptian forces in Hamat. With emphatic imperial auto-celebration, in a lapidary and sinister way, the Babylonian chronicles record that

[...] Not one man [returned] to his country.[44]

This is the collapse of the pharaoh's power over the region and history's final word on the Assyrian empire. However, Nebuchadnezzar finds himself unable to invade Palestine immediately. Surprised by news of his father's death, he is forced to return to the capital in haste to secure his succession to the throne. But from this moment, Babylonia becomes the official heir of the Neo-Assyrian empire and in a short time, its advance effectively forces the Egyptian hegemony out of Palestine with a series of effective military campaigns (cf. 2 Kgs 24:7).[45] The campaigns are not enough to completely "pacify" these territories (denominated by the Babylonian sources as the "Land of Ḫatti"), however. In fact, the area will remain turbulent. As the Babylonian chronicles attest, almost every year, Nebuchadnezzar will be forced to undertake an

---

42 According to Flavius Josephus (*Antiquitates iudaicae*, X,74), Necho "had a strong desire to dominate Asia" ([...] τῆς γὰρ Ἀσίας βασιλεῦσαι πόθον εἶχε); cf. B. NIESE, *ed.*, *Flavii Iosephi Opera*. Edidit et apparatu critico instruxit Benedictus Niese, vol. II, Antiquitatum Iudaicarum Libri VI–X, Berolini 1885, 346.

43 The violence of the clash within the city itself was emphasised by the excavations of C.L. Woolley (complete reports are contained in D.G. HOGARTH, *Charchemish*. Part I: Introductory, London 1914; C.L. WOOLLEY, *Charchemish*. Part II: The Town Defenses, London 1921; C.L. WOOLLEY – R.D. BARNETT, *Charchemish*. Part III: The Excavations in the Inner Town, and the Hittite Inscriptions, London 1952).

44 Cf. J.-J. GLASSNER, *Mesopotamian Chronicles*, 226–229.

45 See, in particular, D.J. WISEMAN, *Nebuchadrezzar and Babylon*, 1–41; O. LIPSCHITS, «Nebuchadrezzar's Policy in "Hattu-Land" and the Fate of the Kingdom of Judah», *UF* 30 (1998) 467–487; I. EPH'AL, «Nebuchadrezzar the Warrior», 178–195. According to the interpretation of N. NA'AMAN, «Nebuchadrezzar's Campaign in the Year 603 BCE», *BN* 62 (1992) 41–44 (= in: ID., *Ancient Israel and Its Neighbors*. Interaction and Counteraction. Collected Essays. Vol. I, Winona Lake 2005, 399–402), regarding the missing part of the Babylonian chronicles for the year 603 (about a good 12 lines), Nabuchadnezzar headed this year's military campaign not in Syria-Palestine, whose kingdoms had already been subjugated in the two years preceding, but in the North, in the land of Kimuhu and other regions of Anatolia with whom Babylon had a score to settle since 607.

Babylon is victorious (605 b.c.) and becomes the new global threat   143

expedition or keep his armies engaged. And this will go on at least throughout the last period of reign that is reported in the chronicles (from the year of his ascent to the throne until the eleventh year).[46]

It is in the context of this radical mutation of the geopolitical scenario that YHWH orders Jeremiah (cf. Jer 36) to write a synthesis of the entire prophetic preaching of the preceding years "concerning Jerusalem, Judah, and all the nations" on a scroll (cf. v. 2) and to hold a public reading of it in the temple of the Lord by means of Baruch (בָּרוּך). In fact, Jehoiakim has the text read aloud. But then, mocking its extreme appeal for conversion, he slices the scroll bit by bit with a penknife and tosses it, piece after piece, into the fire. When he has finished, he gives the order for both Jeremiah and Baruch to be arrested. In this situation, this extreme act of rejection of the prophetic word inviting conversion takes on a tone of dramatic finality. The symbolic expression of the killing of the "literary body" of the prophecy marks, I believe, the *point of no return*. This, in the book of Jeremiah, distinguishes the oracles that unite a threat of punishment with a demand for (still possible) conversion, from those thereafter, which become the simple, tragic proclamation of an end that is already decreed and inevitable.

In fact, the episode of the scroll in ch. 36 carries the same date (the fourth year of Jehoiakim) as does 25:1–14, a text that, after having made a negative appraisal of a good twenty-three years of prophetic appeals, acknowledges their refusal and announces the catastrophic outcome.[47] This is not just an insightful judgement of international politics, as I will seek to demonstrate, but a prophetic verification of the impossibility of conversion and inevitability of the end. The fourth year of Jehoiakim, in fact, significantly coincides with the first year of Nebuchadnezzar, as if to say that, at this point, the rejection of the Covenant now triggers the historical manifestation of the disastrous failure that this refusal signified. This manifestation means the ruin of an entire nation born of the Alliance and for the Alliance. The time for patience is thus over. And it is over because, in the person of the king, disobedience to the word of YHWH by a whole people has been sanctioned.

These considerations concerning the theology of history emerge from the pages of the book of Jeremiah. The same vicissitudes, however, reconstructed from extra-biblical sources, do not portray a less bleak scenario. I will proceed by retracing the salient stages.

The first clear signal of what Nebuchadnezzar had in mind for these small states along the Syrian-Palestinian strip that had not immediately opened their gates to his troops in surrender was a shocking act of unforgiving force. Probably already towards

---

46   What has remained of the Babylonian chronicles regarding the reign of Nebuchadnezzar refers above all to this series of military campaigns undertaken in the West (cf. J.-J. GLASSNER, *Mesopotamian Chronicles*, 226–231).

47   Cf. 25:3, 8–9: "[3] Since the thirteenth year of Josiah son of Amon, king of Judah, to this day, that is, twenty-three years, the word of the Lord has come to me and I spoke to you untiringly, but you would not listen. [...] [8] Hence, thus says the Lord of hosts: Since you would not listen to my words, [9] I am about to send for and fetch all the tribes from the North, oracle of the Lord, and I will send for Nebuchadnezzar, king of Babylon, my servant; I will bring them against this land, its inhabitants, and all these neighbouring nations. I will doom them, making them an object of horror, of hissing, of everlasting reproach."

the end of 604,[48] right in the middle of the winter season, the Philistine Plain is invaded and Ashkelon, an important port city loyal to Egypt is besieged, taken, and razed to the ground with unprecedented violence[49] (cf. Fig. 12; Jer 47:5-7). Its king and the most influential people amongst the survivors are deported to Babylon[50] along with the plundered spoils of war. Vividly, and in the usual lapidary style, the Babylonian chronicles thus report:

> (Nabuchadnezzar) marched on Ašeklôn; he took it in the month of Kislev (November/December); seized its king, pillaged and [plu]ndered it. He reduced the city to a heap of rubble (lit. in Akkadian: *ana tīli*; "to a *tell*.")[51]

Fig. 12. One of the more disturbing signs of the ferocity of the Babylonian destruction brought to light by the Ashkelon excavations: the skeleton of a woman about 35 years old who had probably sought refuge in a jar shop, in the position of protecting her head. Scholars have found that the woman was killed from a blow to the head by a blunt object (photo from L.E. STAGER, «The Fury of Babylon», 76).

Thereby, after the victory at Carchemish, sources once again present Nebuchadnezzar as a leader who is ruthless towards his enemies and a bold and daring strategist, unafraid of endangering soldiers, chariots and mounts, or the very success of his military

---

48   Cf. J. BRIGHT, *History*, 326-327; J.M. MILLER – J.H. HAYES, *History*, 466.
49   Archaeological evidence does not leave much doubt about it; cf. L.E. STAGER, «The Fury of Babylon: Ashkelon and the Archaeology of Destruction», *BArR* 22 (1996) 56-69, 76-77; T.C. MITCHELL, «Judah», 396. According to some reconstructions, the brother of the Greek poet Alcaeus, a mercenary on the behalf of the Babylonians, may have participated in precisely this battle; cf. J.D. QUINN, «Alcaeus 48 (B 16) and the Fall of Ascalon (604 B.C.)», *BASOR* 164 (1961) 19-20.
50   The fragment of a letter coming from Ashkelon (according to J. BRIGHT, *History*, 326-327) or rather from Ekron (according to M. LIVERANI, *Oltre la Bibbia*, 206-207) seems to refer to this historical context. Written in Aramaic and found at Saqqara in Egypt, it contains a (futile) appeal to the pharaoh for urgent assistance.
51   Cf. J.-J. GLASSNER, *Mesopotamian Chronicles*, 228-229.

Babylon is victorious (605 b.c.) and becomes the new global threat 145

manoeuvres in order to pursue his goals. Armies of antiquity (and not these alone) had one of their most feared enemies in potential torrential rainstorms and related rigidity of the winter climate (and the consequent scarcity of supplies). The Bible, however, specifically attest as common knowledge the fact that it was actually springtime "[...] the time when kings *go* [*to war*] (הַמַּלְאכִים צֵאת לְעֵת)" (lit.: "*go out*"; cf. 2 Sam 11:1).[52] The Babylonian chronicles,[53] on the other hand, not only specify that war operations against Ashkelon lasted into the winter season (i.e. until the month of Kislev, which corresponds to our own November/December), but also claim that Nebuchadnezzar could afford to conduct a whole series of military campaigns in Palestine right in the middle of winter (just as the great Assyrian conqueror Sennacherib had done previously). This would demonstrate not only a considerable strategic ability on his part, but also the efficiency and impressive strength of his military apparatus. The motif was already a familiar one in Assyrian sources as a subject of pride.

Within the general context thus outlined, the treatment reserved for Ashkelon was meant to be seen as a warning of what could possibly happen to Jerusalem, along with other cities. In addition to the obvious propagandistic motives deducible from the account in the Babylonian chronicles, this heinous military act also fulfilled an important strategic objective. It definitively eliminated the last substantial Egyptian garrison in Palestine, the stronghold from which designated fierce mercenaries of Greek origin could threaten the consolidation of Babylonian power in the region.[54] This fact is to be taken into account because it clarifies the decision, made later on, to do away with Jerusalem as well, seeing as its political inclination very clearly tended towards Egypt. Given these premises as a pragmatic context of reference, can the Jeremianic message calling for surrender to Babylon be understood merely as a realistic option for salvaging the salvageable? This is seriously doubtful. But we will see this better in § 3.3.

Needless to say, such a severe punitive campaign, undertaken in the first regnal year of Nebuchadnezzar, sent a powerful message to the other kingdoms in the region. Apparently, however, the lesson was not learned, and soon a number of additional kingdoms and their sovereigns would share the fate of Ashkelon under Babylonian rule.[55]

---

52 This testimony is also considered to be that of Herodotus, who puts these words on the lips of Xerxes, intent on marching with an immense army against Greece: "We, then, will do as they did; we are using the fairest season of the year to journey in, and we will return home the conquerors of all Europe, having nowhere suffered famine or any other harm" (*Historiae*, VII,50; we quote from HERODOTUS, *The Persian Wars*. With an English Translation by A.D. Godley, III, Books V–VII, LCL 119, London – Cambridge (MA) 1938, 365–366; cf. ERODOTO, *Le Storie*. A cura di Aristide Colonna e Fiorenza Bevilacqua, Vol. II, Libri V–IX, Classici UTET.CL, Torino 1996, 319).

53 Cf J.-J. GLASSNER, *Mesopotamian Chronicles*, 229–231.

54 In this regard, I take from the result of the study done by A. FANTALKIN, «Why Did Nebuchadnezzar II Destroy Ashkelon in Kislev 604?», in: *The Fire Signals of Lachish. Studies in the Archaeology and History of Israel in the Late Bronze Age, Iron Age, and Persian Period in Honor of David Ussishkin, eds.* I. FINKELSTEIN – N. NA'AMAN, Winona Lake 2011, 87–111.

55 *Ibid.*, 103.

146   Facing the might of the Babylonian empire

Despite the hotbeds of rebellion that would not have been slow to ignite (with the relative consequences), the immediate (anticipated) effect of this and of other similar military operations conducted almost every year in Palestine (some of which, once again, in the thick of winter) had to be that of general concern in the region. This is most likely confirmed by the call for a public fasting in Jerusalem "in the fifth year of Jehoiakim", that is, in relation to this new political scenario (cf. 36:9),[56] referred to in 2 Kgs 24:7:

> The king of Egypt did not again leave his own land, for the king of Babylon had taken all that belonged to the king of Egypt from the wadi of Egypt to the Euphrates River.

It would seem that a direct invasion of the kingdom of Judah was not necessary, since we know that in this historical context, Jehoiakim separates from Egypt and submits to Babylon (cf. 2 Kgs 24:1).[57] Nebuchadnezzar leaves him on the throne, despite his having been placed there by the pharaoh Necho, but not without a precise political calculation. He does so both to maintain stability in Judah and to secure the new vassal's loyalty to the new empire also by means of indebted gratitude,[58] which should have been expressed through time (and with expected annual tributes). For their part, the Babylonian chronicles, distancing themselves from the historiographic style of the Assyrian annals, which almost complacently indulged in describing the destruction carried out during military campaigns (with a clearly intimidatory, propagandistic aim), usually do not mention the bloody interventions of war (apart from the case of Ashkelon). They limit themselves to reporting here that Nebuchadnezzar "travelled [...] victoriously" in the region, and that

> [...] All the kings of Ḫatti came into his presence, and he received their massive tribute.[59]

This low profile sustained by the Babylonian sources seems to be in line with the rest of the new power's imperialist propaganda. While its brutality was not inferior to that customary of the Assyrians (contrary to what is commonly thought),[60] and while absolutely not failing to exploit the dissuading impact of its destructive military operations, it preferred to exalt the "liberating" value of its achievements.[61] This "liberation" (with heavy taxation, substantial annual tributes, and probably various forms of corvée, such as the obligation to provide military contingents for imperial campaigns or contributions to the labour force for the construction of the ziggurat) was probably one that the Syrian-Palestina kingdoms would have gladly done without, as chs. 27–28 of the book of Jeremiah and the history that followed reveal.

---

56   The sense of dismay and terror aroused by the invasion of the Babylonian (or Chaldean) army in the region is also well attested in Hab 1:6–10.
57   Historians do not agree in their designation of the precise year in which Judah fell subject to Babylonian power, and they propose dates that oscillate within a timespan ranging from 605 to 601. For an in-depth study of the various hypotheses, see A. MALAMAT, «The Twilight of Judah», 123–145.
58   As is justly pointed out by O. LIPSCHITS, *The Fall*, 48.
59   Cf. J.-J. GLASSNER, *Mesopotamian Chronicles*, 229–231; T.C. MITCHELL, «Judah», 396.
60   Cf. M. LIVERANI, *The Ancient Near East*, 541; ID., *Oltre la Bibbia*, 203–204.
61   Cf. D.S. VANDERHOOFT, *The Neo-Babylonian Empire*, 41–46.

2.2. Winds of rebellion

2.2.1. *The capitulation and trauma of 597: On the brink of the abyss*

Jehoiakim, seeing no room for manoeuvre, remains a tributary of Nebuchadnezzar for about three years. But in 601, due to an incursion in southern Palestine by Necho or following a direct attack on Egypt by Nebuchadnezzar, the two powers collide once again, this time in an open field near the Egyptian border.[62] There were heavy casualties on both sides.[63] And even if the Egyptian victory was not exactly a resounding one, the pharaoh does seem to have got the better of it, thereby demonstrating to still have considerable military strength. What is certain is that Egypt was not invaded and, indeed, seems to have reclaimed Gaza (cf. Jer 47:1). It appears, in a certain sense, to have relaunched its influence in Palestine,[64] while Nebuchadnezzar had to spend at least the entire following year reorganising and replenishing his army ranks in Babylon.

It is this first sign of Babylonia's weakness and, consequently, the concrete possibility of remaking Egyptian hegemony over the region (which many perhaps secretly hoped) that induces or compels Jehoiakim to discontinue payment of his annual tribute. The political significance of his gesture is clear.[65] Perhaps having no other possible choice,[66] or being that a long-awaited circumstance presented itself, he decides to take an action that will later prove to be a fatal error. In a move that probably seemed to ensure greater (however relative) independence of government, he breaks the bond of vassalage with Babylon and returns to his ancient ally.

---

62 This military offensive was also carried out in the middle of the winter season (cf. E. LIPIŃSKI, «The Egypto-Babylonian War of the Winter of 601–600 B.C.», *AION* 32 [1972] 235–241).

63 As the Babylonian chronicles clearly tell us (cf. J.-J. GLASSNER, *Mesopotamian Chronicles*, 229).

64 A historical reconstruction which, in the view of O. LIPSCHITS, *The Fall*, 50, seems to be congruent with the testimony of Herodotus (*Historiae*, II,159; cf. HERODOTUS, *The Persian Wars*. With an English Translation by A.D. Godley, I, Books I–II, LCL 117, London – Cambridge (MA) 1920, ²1981, 472–473; *Herodoti Historiae*. Vol. I Libros I–IV continens, *ed.* H.B. ROSÉN, Leipzig 1987, 240). Sharing this view is G.W. AHLSTRÖM, *History*, 782.

65 Talking about the relations between Assyria and the vassal states, J.P. POSTGATE «The Land of Assur and the Yoke of Assur», *WAr* 23 (1992) 247–263, explains: "Even before any form of overlordship was formally acknowledged, prudence will often have dictated a visit bearing gifts, or bribes, to deflect the marauding armies. Tribute from the client king is an institutionalized form of the same statement: the exact level of annual contribution would be fixed, and failure to make it would be construed as a political statement" (p. 254).

66 This is the (plausible, though not demonstrable) opinion of O. LIPSCHITS, *The Fall*, 51, founded on an interpretation of that highlighted by Flavius Josephus in *Antiquitates iudaicae*, X,88: "But in the third [year], after hearing that the Egyptians were marching against the Babylonian and not having given his tribute […]"; FLAVIUS JOSEPHUS, *Judean Antiquities 8–10*. Translation and Commentary by Christopher T. BEGG – P. SPILSBURY, FJTC 5, Leiden – Boston 2005, 234.

148 Facing the might of the Babylonian empire

Unable to intervene directly, at first Nebuchadnezzar makes use of some of his contingents present in the area, alongside auxiliary forces composed of bands of Aramean, Moabian, and Ammonite raiders. They launch rapid, devastating incursions, especially at the expense of the rural areas (cf. 2 Kgs 24:2; Jer 35:11).[67] But then in December of 598, he decrees the siege on Jerusalem. According to 2 Kgs 24:6, Jehoiakim exits the scene at this point (about two months before the arrival of the Babylonians, possibly assassinated by his own court in the hope of mitigating the consequences of his rebellion).[68] In his place, he is succeeded, if only briefly, by his eighteen-year-old son, Jehoiachin.

After only three months of his reign, according to 2 Kgs 24:11, Nebuchadnezzar arrives to conduct operations personally. "Jehoiachin, king of Judah, together with his mother, his ministers, officers, and functionaries, surrendered to the king of Babylon" (v. 12). Though the price was quite high, this gesture saved the city. The surrender was followed by the deportation[69] of the king, together with the queen mother, officers, and prominent citizens, along with the professional soldiers and skilled labourers.[70] A large part of the riches of the temple (sacred vases and other furnishings) were removed, and there were considerable spoils of war, very likely well above the sum of the annual tributes left unpaid to the empire coffers. The Babylonian chronicles recount the event thus[71]:

> The seventh year (of Nebuchadnezzar)[72], in the month of Kislev[73], the king of Akkad (Nebuchadnezzar) gathered his troops, marched on Ḫatti (Syria-Palestina), and set up his quarters facing the city of Yeḫud (Judah). In the month of Adar, the second day[74], he took the city and captured the king (Jehoiachin). He installed there a king (Zedekiah) of his choice (lit.: *ša libbišu*, "in accordance with his heart"). He colle[cted] its massive tribute and went back to Babylon.

---

67 This type of raid, necessary in border areas not immediately reachable by the imperial armies, is also attested at the time of Ashurbanipal (cf. I. EPH'AL, «On Warfare and Military Control in the Ancient Near Eastern Empires: A Research Outline», in: *History, Historiography and Interpretation*. Studies in Biblical and Cuneiform Literatures, *eds.* H. TADMOR – M. WEINFELD, Jerusalem 1983, 95).

68 On the uncertain fate of Jehoiakim, with regard to the problematic nature of biblical dating, see A. GREEN, «The Fate of Jehoiakim», *AUSS* 20 (1982) 103–109.

69 The number of deportees varies according to the traditions. In all, it seems there were about 10,000 men (without counting women and children who, in antiquity, were not counted), as in 2 Kgs 24:14, which, however, in v. 16, instead provides the figure of 8,000. For Jer 52:28, they were 3,023.

70 These are mostly blacksmiths and other master tradesmen who were also (and above all) able to build weapons. An understandable countermeasure to prevent a dangerous (more or less clandestine) rearmament. According to 1 Sam 13:19–22, the same provision, once again against the Israelites, was adopted by the Philistines at the time of Saul.

71 For the translation, I rely again on J.-J. GLASSNER, *Mesopotamian Chronicles*, 231, whilst for the dating provided in the following notes, J. BRIEND – M.-J. SEUX, *Textes*, 140.

72 The year is 599.

73 Between 18 December 598 and 15 January 597.

74 On 16 March.

The kingdom of Judah reaches the brink of the abyss. Even though the city was not destroyed and the Davidic dynasty left to govern (in a tight relationship of vassalage, obviously), the blow was doubtlessly a terrible one. And it was one that most probably would have left no room, in the case of a new rebellion, for anything but the final catastrophe.[75]

2.2.2. Political instability and international plots in Jerusalem (594)

When the revolt was extinguished and deportation of the most influential strata of the population of Jerusalem along with the king Jehoiachin decided, Nebuchadnezzar appointed the latter's uncle, Mattaniah (cf. 2 Kgs 24:17), one of the sons of Josiah, as king. The symbolic significance of the imposition of his new name (from Mattaniah, "the gift of YHWH", to Zedekiah, "the justice of YHWH", or "my justice is YHWH") expressed his direct appointment by Babylon.[76] While this name may be of a theophoric ("orthodox") nature and thus formally respectful of the faith of Israel, the intent of it is to make the ruler of Judah a perfect vassal. A puppet monarch, he must carry within his name, that is, in that which most intimately identifies him, reference to the Babylonian power as the origin of his regal authority.

Furthermore, to seal this intention, according to what is apparent from Ezek 17:11–21; 2 Chr 36:13, and in line with the use attested in Assyrian and Babylonian extrabiblical sources, Zedekiah is expressly required to swear solemn allegiance to the king of Babylon *in the name of YHWH himself*, and not only in the name of the deities of the victorious power (as had been the differing Assyrian custom).[77] From the theological point of view, this element is important, both to better understand Jeremiah's position and to explain that which, even more explicitly unfavourable towards Zedekiah, is attested in the book of Ezekiel.

The situation that arises in the kingdom of Judah under its final king is particularly problematic and fraught with incertitude. Jehoiachin is held hostage, and his royal title appears to continue to be recognised by the Babylonians themselves.[78] This is

---

75   I will try to justify this interpretive hypothesis in § 3.3, dedicated to the so-called "political realism" of the Jeremianic option indicating surrender as the only way out.

76   The pharaoh Necho, after the battle of Megiddo (and consequent death of the king Josiah), had done the same, replacing Jehoahaz with his brother Eliakim, on whom he imposed the name Jehoiakim.

77   For Ezek 17:11–21, see W. ZIMMERLI, *Ezechiel*, I. Teilband, BKAT 13/1, Neukirchen-Vluyn 1968, 384–388. The author makes note of the fact that according to the documented common practice of the Hittites, the stipulation of an alliance (of "vassalage") would be sanctioned by the contractors making an oath in the name of their respective deities. While the Assyrians imposed an oath sworn only to their gods, ignoring those of the vassal, the Babylonians, on the other hand, required that the latter also call upon their own national god (or gods) as witness to the pact (cf. p. 386, with relative bibliographical references).

78   Indeed, Zedekiah would simply be a regent, given that the legitimate king was alive, even if his functions were being impeded (by his being a deported prisoner). Some texts of an administrative nature discovered in Babylon regarding the food rations designated for the royal family in exile ascribe to Jehoiachin the title of "king of Judah" and confirm his *status* as prisoner at the court of Nebuchadnezzar (cf. Y. AVISHUR – M. HELTZER, «Jehoiakin, King of Judah in Light of Biblical and

150 Facing the might of the Babylonian empire

probably done intentionally as a prudent political calculation aimed to prevent the coagulation of a new and dangerous national unity in Jerusalem on the one hand,[79] and simultaneously, on the other, to favour a separation of the new government they themselves established in the kingdom of Judah from the exiles of 597. The latter may have felt themselves best represented by Jehoiachin instead.[80] But at this point, he was made harmless and placed under the direct control of Babylon's central authority.

One need also consider that Zedekiah is young and, in many respects, weak and insecure. In fact, when placed on the throne, he is no more than 21 years of age (cf. 52:1)[81] and must contend not only with his own personal lack of experience and indecisive character,[82] but also with what remains of the ruling class left behind by Nebuchadnezzar. These officials (the שָׂרִים in ch. 38) are presumably not up to par with the situation, but undoubtedly have considerable pro-Egyptian or otherwise anti-Babylonian political clout. And they are endowed with a strong power of influence over the new king, at least according to the book of Jeremiah (cf. 38:5, 24–27). Supported or stirred up by the propagandistic activity of the (false) prophets, the new prominent members of Jerusalem awaited an auspicious moment for a new revolt. They believed that the return from exile of Jehoiachin (very probably still considered by most to be the legitimate successor of Jehoiakim; cf. 28:4)[83] and the end of the Babylonian hegemony over the region were imminent.

Extra-Biblical Sources: His Exile and Release According to Events in the Neo-Babylonian Kingdom and the Babylonian Diaspora», *TrEu* 34 [2007] 17–36).

79 The unearthing of some seal imprints on jar handles with the paleo-Hebrew inscription *l'lyqm n'r ywkn*, considered for many years to be "property of Eliakim, steward of King Jehoiachin" (since W.F. ALBRIGHT, «The Seal of Eliakim and the Latest Preëxilic History of Judah, with Some Observations on Ezekiel», *JBL* 51 [1932] 77–106), led W.F. Albright to believe that Zedekiah had not been able to take possession of the property of his nephew Jehoiachin. This would have instead been safeguarded by an administrator of his, despite his condition of forced domicile in Babylon (see W.F. ALBRIGHT, «King Joiachin in Exile», *BA* 5 [1942] 49–55, esp. pp. 50–51). In fact, it has now been established that these imprints are older and cannot be linked to Jehoiachin (see Y. GARFINKEL, «The Eliakim Na'ar Yokan Seal Impressions. Sixty Years of Confusion in Biblical Archaeological Research», *BA* 53 [1990] 74–79).

80 Commenting on this, W.F. ALBRIGHT, «King Joiachin in Exile», 51: "Presumably the Chaldeans themselves blew hot and cold, favouring Zedekiah one year and his nephew the next."

81 Hence, it is not accurate to say that in Jerusalem "the old Zedekiah" reigned, as in L. ALONSO SCHÖKEL – J.L. SICRE DIAZ, *Profetas I*, Madrid 1980, 587.

82 At least, this is the impression evoked in the reader by what is narrated in chs. 37–38.

83 This expectation was historically founded, insofar as some cases are known to us in extrabiblical sources in which the Assyrians had reinstalled on the throne kings who had been conquered and deported (or who had escaped). I will cite at least one such example, reported in the Assyrian inscriptions regarding the Tiglath-Pileser III campaign of 734 against Philistea: the case of Ḥanunū, king of Gaza. Having escaped to Egypt because of the advancing Assyrian army, upon his return, he was reinstalled on the throne of the city, by now conquered, and a heavy tribute was imposed upon him (RINAP 1, 105–106 [ll. 8'b-15'a]; 127 [ll. 14'b-19a]; 132 [ll. 13–16, *verso*]). But this is also seen in the HB when, in 2 Chr 33:11–13, it is attested about Manasseh.

Babylon is victorious (605 b.c.) and becomes the new global threat 151

The episode mentioned in Jer 27 (as well as the facts recounted in the subsequent ch. 28 and events underlying ch. 29)[84] refers to this phase of precarious political equilibrium. The situation is such that the circles of politico-religious power are in a state of anxiety as Nebuchadnezzar, suddenly and in a short period of time, is faced with two different critical situations that seem to compromise the stability of his supremacy.[85] According to the Babylonian chronicles,[86] between 596 and 595, the empire was under threat of an attack by the Elamites.[87] And immediately following, between the end of 595 and the beginning of 594, a serious insurrection erupts in Babylon against Nebuchadnezzar, lasting two months.[88] During the uprising, authoritative members of the army are implicated. It is probable, as many commentators sustain, that some prophets of the Jewish community that had been deported there were put to death as insurgents, as is attested in Jer 29:21–23:

> [21] This is what the Lord of hosts, the God of Israel, says about Ahab son of Kolaiah, and Zedekiah son of Maaseiah, who prophesy lies to you in my name: I am handing them over to Nebuchadnezzar, king of Babylon, who will kill them before your eyes. [22] And because of them this curse will be used by all the exiles of Judah in Babylon: "May the Lord make you like Zedekiah and Ahab, whom the king of Babylon roasted in fire,"[23] because they have committed an outrage in Israel, committing adultery with their neighbours' wives, and alleging in my name things I did not command. I know, I am witness – oracle of the Lord.

The sedition was stifled in blood, but it must have nourished aspirations of independence in the Palestinian area all the same[89] if, within a year (594/593), the ambassadors

---

84 Cf. H. SCHMIDT, «Das Datum der Ereignisse von Jer 27 und 28», *ZAW* 39 (1921) 138–144.
85 Cf. I. EPH'AL, «Nebuchadnezzar the Warrior», 181–183.
86 The Babylonian chronicles provide us with testimony regarding both these events (cf. D.J. WISEMAN, *Chronicles*, 72–73; J.-J. GLASSNER, *Mesopotamian Chronicles*, 231).
87 Often cited in this regard is the oracle against Elam in Jer 49:34–39, dated precisely at the beginning of the reign of Zedekiah (v. 34: בְּרֵאשִׁית מַלְכוּת צִדְקִיָּה מֶלֶךְ־יְהוּדָה). Actually, the magnitude of the defeat described by the Jeremianic prophecy does not match the version in the Babylonian chronicles, which instead narrate an Elamite enemy army that initially appears threateningly on the shores of the Tigris river but then, gripped by panic, rapidly flees upon the arrival of Nebuchadnezzar's army.
88 From the month of Kislev to the month of Tevet of his tenth year of reign, that is, from December of 595 to January of 594.
89 Moreover, according to N. NA'AMAN, «The King Leading Cult Reforms in His Kingdom: Josiah and Other Kings in the Ancient Near East», *ZABR* 12 (2006) 131–168 (esp. pp. 140–141), Josiah also undertook the reformist measures centred on loyalty to YHWH (including the elimination of spurious cultural elements) when Assyria didn't manage to quell the Babylonian uprising that gave way to the fall of its hegemony over the entire ancient Near East. On the strategy of the anti-imperial coalitions during the Assyrian epoch, which validate the historicity of what is attested in the book of Jeremiah, see C.S. EHRLICH, «Coalition Politics in Eighth Century B.C.E. Palestine: The Philistines and the Syro-Ephraimite War», *ZDPV* 107 (1991) 48–58; P.E. DION, «Syro-Palestinian Resistance to Shalmaneser III in the Light of New Documents», *ZAW* 107 (1995) 482–489; S. YAMADA, *The Construction of the Assyrian Empire. A Historical Study of the Inscriptions of Shalmanesar III (859–824 b.c.) Relating to His Campaigns to the West*, CHANE 3, Leiden 2000, 143–163.

152   Facing the might of the Babylonian empire

of Edom, Moab, Ammon, Tyre, and Sidon[90] – as is reported in 27:3[91] – converge in Jerusalem before Zedekiah with clearly rebellious intentions against the Babylonian domination.

> [1] In the beginning of the reign of Zedekiah son of Josiah, king of Judah, this word came to Jeremiah from the Lord: [2] The Lord said to me: Make for yourself thongs and yoke bars and put them on your shoulders. [3] Send them to the kings of Edom, Moab, the Ammonites, Tyre, and Sidon, through the ambassadors who have come to Jerusalem to Zedekiah, king of Judah [...].

It can be assumed with some degree of certainty that this was done to organise a rebellion. And it is also legitimate to assume that behind this attempt to form an anti-Babylonian alliance was the occult hand of Egypt and a guarantee of its military support.[92] All this fused with the strong perception that, with the new pharaoh Psammetichus II (595–589), Egypt was on the verge of newly overturning the political balance of the region in its favour.[93]

While this reconstruction of the sequence and logic of the events taking place at this historical juncture may be that most shared by commentators, it is not the only one possible. I note in particular the proposal put forth by Nahum Sarna,[94] which seems to have a considerable degree of plausibility, also considering its solution and consequent harmonisation of some textual difficulties regarding the chronology attested in Jer 27:1 and 28:1. Here below, I re-elaborate (with some further explanatory annotations and integrations of my own) the schematisation that the author himself includes in his research conclusions:

---

90   The absence of representatives from the Philistean cities would be due to the destructions these urban cities suffered over the course of the Egyptian-Babylonian war conflict. On the lack of representatives from Egypt, one can consider this to be a prudential measure, one easily comprehensible given the instability of the political situation, the possibility of guaranteeing a surprise effect, and an awareness that it be unlikely that an official Egyptian representative pass unnoticed by the Babylonians, who were certainly not lacking an efficient system of espionage (cf. the following n. 99).

91   For detailed commentary on the text, I defer to ch. IV (for textual questions in particular, see § 2.1).

92   See e.g. Ezek 17:15 and Ostracon III of the "Lachish Letters" (J. RENZ, *Die althebräischen Inschriften*, 412–419), which demonstrates the existence of collaborative military relations with Egypt.

93   In 593, Psammetichus II successfully conducts a military campaign in Nubia and, following, a visit of a religious and propagandistic nature in Philistia, thus abandoning the policy of non-intervention in Asia that had characterised the last five years of his father's reign (cf. O. LIPSCHITS, *The Fall*, 63, n. 97). For more on his foreign policy, see R.B. GOZZOLI, *Psammetichus II. Reign, Documents and Officials*, GHP Egyptology 25, London 2017, 45–76, especially pp. 72–76, which refer to our historical context. With regard to the pharaoh's expedition to Nubia and subsequent trip to Khor (Palestine), that is, territories formally subject to Babylonian control, the author notes that "the Nubian victory was exploited with the idea of shifting Babylonian vassals to the Egyptian side" (pp. 74–75).

94   Cf. N. SARNA, «The Abortive Insurrection in Zedekiah's Day (Jer. 27–29)», in: *Studies in Biblical Interpretation*, ed. N. SARNA, Philadelphia 2000, 281–294 (= in: *Eris* 14 [1978] *89–*96 [Hebrew]).

602–601	(Tishri-Elul)	SABBATICAL YEAR	
597	(Nisan-Elul)	Year of the enthronement of Zedekiah = IV year [*of the sabbatical cycle*] (27:1; 28:1). International meeting in Jerusalem to organise the rebellion (27:3)	
	(Ab)	Prediction of Hananiah on the end of the yoke of Babylon and of the exile	"WITHIN TWO YEARS" (28:3,11)
		First delegation of Zedekiah in Babylon (29:3)	
596–595		Elamite attack against Babylon[95] (cf. 49:34–39)	
595–594	(Kislev-Tebet)	SABBATICAL YEAR REVOLT IN BABYLON (cf. 29:21–23)	
594–593		Second delegation of Zedekiah in Babylon (51:59) IV year *of the reign of Zedekiah* (cf. 28:1)	
588–587	(Before Kislev 588)	SABBATICAL YEAR Liberation of slaves (cf. 34:8–22 and Deut 15)	

According to N. Sarna, who in any case interprets the coming of the ambassadors to Jerusalem as a clear sign of conspiracy against Babylon, the chronology of events would thus be as follows: The meeting in Jerusalem would actually be placed right at the beginning of the reign of Zedekiah (according to 27:1), that is, in 597, but within the frame of an insurrection coordinated on a much larger scale, one of a truly international nature. This revolt would encompass forces within the Babylonian capital itself (that attested in the Babylonian chronicles, which explodes right at this time), the forces of Elam, and a group of allies in the west (mentioned in 27:3). Thereby, taking into account the data (and relative problems of chronology) contained in the book of Jeremiah, at the textual level this would explain:

a) the apparent contradiction between the two chronological references that can be detected in 28:1[96]: "in the beginning of the reign of Zedekiah" (בְּרֵאשִׁית מַמְלֶכֶת צִדְקִיָּה) and "in the fourth year" (בַּשָּׁנָה הָרְבִעִית). This last notation, provided without any other specification, would therefore refer to the computation of the years of the sabbatical cycle.[97] The year of Zedekiah's enthronement would thus coincide with the fourth year of that cycle.

---

[95] N. Sarna makes no mention of it, but this event would fall within the deadline set by the prophet Hananiah as well.
[96] 'In that same year, at the beginning of the reign of Zedekiah, king of Judah, in the fifth month of the fourth year, Hananiah the prophet, son of Azzur, from Gibeon, said to me [...]"
[97] For an attempt to demonstrate this hypothesis, upon which I cannot dwell herein, I refer to N. SARNA, «The Abortive Insurrection», 289–290.

154   Facing the might of the Babylonian empire

b) the peremptory term of "two years" (שְׁנָתַיִם יָמִים) established by Hananiah in 28:3, 11 for the fulfilment of his prophesy regarding the removal of the yoke of Babylon from the neck of all the nations and the return of the exiles. This cut-off date, to be placed in relation to the expression "very soon", "shortly" (עַתָּה מְהֵרָה) in 27:16, is rather unusual for its accuracy. According to N. Sarna's reconstruction, these "two years" would be the lapse of time between the enthronement of Zedekiah on one end and the following sabbatical year on the other. That year was, as a matter of fact, internationally marked by the Elamites' attack against the Babylonian empire and the insurrection that erupted in Babylon (which ought to have been accompanied by the revolt of the Palestinian states mentioned in 27:3).

The difficulties involved in a precise logical-chronological reconstruction of the events aside, the motive for the choice of meeting place must be considered. The capital of the kingdom of Judah lent itself as a venue for this colloquy not only for its strategic location, but also for the political position of Zedekiah, who was far from assuming a leading role in the conspiracy. The attempt of the court dignitaries having a staunch anti-Babylonian tendency, like that of the neighbouring states, would have thus been to place further pressure on the (understandably) reluctant sovereign to get involved in the envisaged rebellion. A rebellion of which – we can reasonably presume – Zedekiah sensed the enormous risk, given his position as a newly enthroned vassal, and from which he personally had nothing to gain and everything to lose.[98]

This is the framework within which fit Jeremiah's intervention and the symbolic gesture of the yoke with which the prophet asks for submission to the king of Babylon in the name of YHWH and his design on history. We cannot know what the motivations of Zedekiah and the other states involved actually were historically. Support from the Egyptians may have been lacking, or agreement between the various parties may not have been found (or they had heard the Jeremianic message). The fact is, we are not aware of any concrete anti-Babylonian stance having been taken. Indeed, the king of Judah had to hastily renew his declaration of allegiance to Nebuchadnezzar by sending assurances to this effect by means of envoys (cf. 29:3) or by subsequently going to Babylon personally (according to 51:59) to avoid an accusation of treason and consequent condemnation.[99] The following year (in November

---

98 At least, this is the reconstruction, in my view plausible, of N.K. GOTTWALD, *All the Kingdoms of the Earth*. Israelite Prophecy and International Relations in the Ancient Near East, New York 1964, 258–259. Of the same opinion, N. SARNA, «The Abortive Insurrection», 288, who specifies, in reference to the dating of 597 of the attempted conspiracy: "It would be just at the beginning – when he [Zedekiah] would still enjoy the confidence of the Babylonians, but before he would have had time to consolidate his power internally – that the anti-Babylonian party would find it most convenient to plot rebellion. Since he would certainly have lost his throne, and probably his life as well, had Jehoiachin returned, it must be assumed that Zedekiah was coerced into the insurrectionary conclave against his will and better judgment." This sort of behaviour on the part of Zedekiah, motivated by his weak position, emerges clearly in Jer 38:14–28a.

99 Knowing that the Assyrians had already developed an efficient network of informants of their own to monitor their vassals and their loyalty, it is fairly easy to think that a political manoeuvre of the sort, and its very hostile nature, had absolutely not gone unnoticed by the Babylonian regime (for the Assyrian world, there is documentation

of 594), Nebuchadnezzar returns to Syria-Palestine once more to demand his tribute from the vassal states. We do not know what consequences this held for the various kingdoms who had conspired, but indubitably, his clear intent was that of intimidation. This does not, however, evolve into military action taken against the kingdom of Judah.

Confirming the politically instable climate of this period, ch. 28 clearly demonstrates, through the person and message of Hananiah, what were the hopes of many (or, the majority): that they soon be released from Babylonian domination and that the deportees of 597 be able to return, bringing with them the precious temple furnishings that had been stolen by Nebuchadnezzar. Based on the "letter from Jeremiah" contained in Jer 29 (cf. also that which follows in vv. 24–32) sent with Zedekiah's envoys to the Babylonian sovereign, we gather that these same ideas also circulated amongst the deportees (who maintained tight epistolary contact with the motherland) and were supported or nurtured by the prophecies of some (false) prophets. The Jeremianic message, on the other hand, continues to maintain its same register: accept submission to Babylon, and thus fully accept the meaning of history revealed through the punitive action of God pending something entirely new. The oracles of Jeremiah against such agitators and propagators of false hopes (vv. 21–23, 30–32), foretelling the ignoble end at the hands of the imperial authority, correspond well with the historical context that can be deduced from the Babylonian chronicles regarding the suppression of the intestine revolt of 595/594.

On the other hand, a different sort of position seems to emerge from the text of ch. 24, one that is perhaps even more illusory. In fact, the prophetic vision of the two baskets of figs, indicating the deportees as the good figs and the survivors as the bad figs, quite clearly overturns an equally widespread certainty. This certainty was probably diffused in the new class of notables who had been brought to the fore by the deportation of their predecessors, who considered themselves to be the true heirs of the land and promises (cf. Ezek 11:15; 33:24). From this point of view, Nebuchadnezzar's punitive action had fulfilled (and exhausted) Jeremiah's prophetic threats: YHWH had punished his people for their sins, but without abandoning them to destruction. Identifying the deportees as the culprits and the survivors as those pardoned (custodians of the promises and of YHWH's unfailing rescue) had to have been an equation that was just as reassuring as it was misleading. Indeed, it was an interpretive model of history that was actually only capable of inducing an aberrant spiritual attitude and decidedly fatal consequent political moves.

---

of a genuine system of *intelligence*. See, in this regard, the study by P. DUBOVSKÝ, *Hezekiah and the Assyrian Spies*. Reconstruction of the Neo-Assyrian Intelligence Services and its Significance for 2 Kings 18–19, BibOr 49, Roma 2006; and also T. DEZSŐ, «Neo-Assyrian Military Intelligence», in: *Krieg und Frieden im Alten Vorderasien*. 52e Recontre Assyriologique Internationale. International Congress of Assyriology and Near Eastern Archaeology, Münster 17.–21. Juli 2006, eds. H. NEUMANN *et al.*, AOAT 401, Münster 2014, 221–235 (cf. in particular the complex structuralisation of the "intelligence pyramid" on p. 234). See instead H.J. CURZER, «Spies and Lies: Faithful, Courageous Israelites and Truthful Spies», *JSOT* 35 (2010) 187–195, for a rereading of the famous episode in Num 13–14 about the spies sent by Moses to explore the lands of Canaan.

2.3. The fall of Jerusalem and disappearance of the kingdom of Judah

2.3.1. The situation precipitates: It is the end

No more than five years passed before the policy of nationalism and sedition regained strength and eventually prevailed,[100] most certainly counting on the (rash) support of the new pharaoh Apries (589–570)[101] and his revival of an interventional policy in the Asian sphere. The rebellion does not, however, seem to have spread throughout

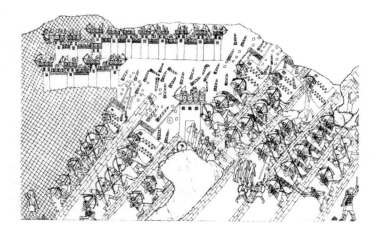

Fig. 13. *The fate of Jerusalem, scenes of battles and violence, executions of commanders, raids, exiles, etc. cannot have amounted to a drama much different from that undergone by the city of Lachish at the hand of the Assyrians in 701. The event is immortalised in the renowned sequence in bas-relief discovered in room 36 of the royal palace of Sennacherib in Ninive (here, a drawing of one segment, from D. USSISHKIN,* The Conquest of Lachish by Sennacherib, *Tel Aviv 1982, 74, pl. 63).*

---

100   This portion of the Babylonian chronicles is damaged and the information that relates to the years from 594/593 to 557/556 is lacking. In compensation, the book of Jeremiah documents the events of the last stage of the reign of Judah (revolt, siege, conquest, and destruction of Jerusalem, exile and establishment of Mizpah as the new administrative centre of the small portion of the territory, limited to the area of Benjamin, spared from the devastation) in a fairly detailed way. Some interesting data derived from the "Lachish Letters" correspond to the historical context that immediately precedes the Babylonian invasion and confirm this scenario. For a summary of the excavations carried out to date on the site identified as the city of Lachish (*Tell ed-Duweir*), see the recent work of D. USSISHKIN, *Biblical Lachish. A Tale of Construction, Destruction, Excavation and Restoration*, Jerusalem 2014.
101   Mentioned by the name "Hophra" (חָפְרַע) in 44:30, he had succeeded Psammetichus II at a young age, without, however, inheriting his political acumen and charismatic role, in foreign policy above all.

all of Palestine. Besides Judah, it may have involved only Tyre (placed under siege immediately following the fall of Jerusalem) and Ammon (as can be deduced from Jer 40:14; 41:15; Ezek 21:23–27).[102]

As soon as payment of the tribute to Babylon is refused, Nebuchadnezzar's powerful war machine is set in motion with inexorable determination. In the heart of winter, on the tenth day of the month of Tebet, in the ninth year of Zedekiah (January 589), the final siege of Jerusalem begins (cf. 2 Kgs 25:1; Jer 39:1; 52:4; Ezek 24:1–2; Fig. 13). The capital is surrounded and simultaneously all the other cities and fortresses of Judah are attacked and taken, one by one,[103] until only Lachish and Azekah remain standing. These are the last to fall.[104] The marching out of the pharaoh's troops from Egypt, of which we receive news only in Jer 37:5, proves to be purely an illusion. The siege is lifted for a brief time, but only so the concentration of Babylonian forces can scare away the Egyptian army, quite possibly even without a fight. The events recounted in 37:1–16[105] are set in this brief time span.

---

102 Even Edom sided with the Babylonians and participated in the pillaging of Jerusalem (a fact bitterly condemned by the later biblical tradition; cf. e.g. Obad 10–16; Ps 137:7; Lam 4:21–22).

103 Both archaeological data and the version of the facts reported in the book of Jeremiah show how some cities of the area of Benjamin were not hit by "the fury of Babylon". In particular, the urban centre of Mizpah (Tell en-Naṣbeh) became the seat of the post-war administration. This was probably due either to their prompt submission or to a Babylonian desire to guarantee at least a minimal nucleus of political-administrative polarity, in anticipation of the destruction of the capital and other major city-fortresses in the kingdom of Judah.

104 This phase of the war (on this topic, see A.F. RAINEY, «The Fate of Lachish during the Campaigns of Sennacherib and Nebuchadrezzar», in: *Investigations at Lachish*. The Sanctuary and the Residency (Lachish V), *ed.* Y. AHARONI, PIATA 4, Tel Aviv 1975, 47–60), alluded to in 34:7, is also testimonied to, in all its drama, by the archaeological excavations carried out between 1932 and 1938 at Tell ed-Duweir (almost certainly the ancient city of Lachish). In Layer 2 of this excavation, in a room that was part of the city gate, a series of ostraca (of a heterogeneous nature), amongst which the so-called "Lachish Letters" to which I have referred, were brought to the light. According to the reconstructions that I consider most reliable, in this precious epigraphic material, the brief replies of an officer in charge of a strategic outpost to the dispatches of his military commander in defence of Lachish can be identified. Worth noting is Ostracon IV [KAI 194], in which the officer, in ll. 10–13 writes: "[...] we are paying attention to the signals [of smoke or of fire] coming from Lachish, following the indications that my lord gave, but we cannot (anymore?) see (those of) Azekah" (my translation); cf. A.F. RAINEY, «Watching out for the Signal Fires of Lachish», *PEQ* 119 (1987) 149–151. The match to what is reported in Jer 34:7 is striking: "While the army of the king of Babylon was attacking Jerusalem and the remaining cities of Judah, Lachish, and Azekah. Only these fortified cities were left standing out of all the cities of Judah." This fits perfectly with Ost. IV,10–13 according to Z.B. BEGIN, «Does Lachish Letter IV Contradict Jeremiah XXXIV 7?», *VT* 52 (2002) 166–174.

105 Cf. M. GÖRG, «Jeremia zwischen Ost und West (Jer 38,1–6). Zur Krisensituation in Jerusalem am Vorabend des Babylonischen Exils», in: *Künder des Wortes*. Beiträge zur Theologie der Propheten, *eds.* L. RUPPERT – P. WEIMAR – E. ZENGER, Würzburg 1982, 121–136.

158 Facing the might of the Babylonian empire

The military grip resumed, upon reaching the eighteenth[106] month of strenuous resistance, amidst hunger and other effects of the seize (cf. Lam 4:2–10), the Babylonians manage to breach the walls and rush the city. It is the fourth month (Tammuz) of the eleventh year of Zedekiah (July 587).[107] Jerusalem falls. Cloaked in the darkness of night, the king attempts to escape towards Ammon with members of his family and some of his choice soldiers, but he is chased and finally caught in the steppe of Jericho. Abandoned by his people, he is captured and led to Riblah. The Babylonian headquarters had been placed in this city, which had already been strategic during the Egyptian hegemony.[108] Here, Nebuchadnezzar issues his judgement condemning the unfaithful vassal. He has all of his children slaughtered in front of their father, and then blinds him[109] (cf. Fig. 14) and leads him in chains to Babylon, where he will remain prisoner to the end of his days. Nothing more is ever known of him.

Jerusalem does not receive any better treatment. The sinister warning of the fate of Ashkelon finally takes shape for the capital of the kingdom of Judah, the Holy City, as well. A month after its conquest, after the plundering and violence tolerated or predetermined under such circumstances, the time necessary to collect the loot, identify and massacre those mainly responsible for the revolt, organise the deportation[110] of survivors, defectors, and the most influential part of the population, the general Nebuzaradan carries out his systematic devastation and destruction (cf. 2 Kgs 25:8–10; Jer 52:12–14). What ensued was probably not unlike that which, about a century and a half earlier, had been endured by the town of Lachish, the second city-fortress of the kingdom after Jerusalem (cf. Fig. 13): the walls got demolished, the temple, palace, and "houses of the people" burned and destroyed (cf. 21:10; 39:8; 52:13). Only rubble or little more would remain, along with some of the poorest people, left behind in the region to care for the grapevines and till the soil (cf. 2 Kgs 25:12; Jer 52:16). The attempts of some scholars to downplay the historical reality of the consequences of this catastrophe, limiting it to a quantitative issue, seem implausible. If the land had

---

106 Cf. Jer 39:1–2; 52:4–7 and also 2 Kgs 25:1–4. According to other calculations, the siege lasted thirty months. In this regard, see A. MALAMAT, «The Last Kings of Judah and the Fall of Jerusalem. An Historical-Chronological Study», *IEJ* 18 (1968) 137–156 (here, p. 150).

107 Scholars oscillate between 586 and 587. For the chronology adopted, see R.C. YOUNG, «When Did Jerusalem Fall?», *JETS* 47 (2004) 21–38.

108 A military contingent positioned near the town of Riblah in Syria (בְּאֶרֶץ חֲמָת, "in the land of Hamath"; cf. 2 Kgs 23:33; 25:21; Jer 39:5; 52:9, 27) could have access to water and other supplies and, above all, control an important communication route for both military and caravans that linked Egypt (from South to North) with the area north of the Euphrates. For this reason, it was an important base for the pharaoh Necho as well (cf. 2 Re 23:29–34). From here, Nebuchadnezzar could simultaneously conduct military operations in Jerusalem, keep Damascus under control, and quickly return to Babylon when necessary.

109 This type of punishment was often imposed by Assyrian kings on their vassals guilty of disloyalty (cf. Fig. 15 and A. PARROT, *Samarie, capitale du royaume d'Israël*, CAB 7, Paris-Neuchâtel 1955, 62, Fig. 23).

110 As in 597, this was for the elite of the population. According to Jer 52:29, there were 832 men (women and children are not counted), to which 754 were added in 582.

not remained entirely "empty",[111] as for that matter the book of Jeremiah itself confirms, the fall of the City of the Davidic reign couldn't but create not only a void, but a virtual abyss in the human and religious experience of the survivors.

Fig. 14. Sargon II (721–705) with a spear, carves out the eyes of a defeated rebel vassal. Sketch from a bas-relief from Dur-Sharrukin (Horsabad) (photo from W. ORTHMANN, Der alte Orient, PKG 14, Berlin 1975, Fig. 226).

2.3.2. Amidst the rubble of the Davidic kingdom: New disobedience of the prophetic word, flight to Egypt, a new germ of hope

The destruction of Jerusalem ought not to be considered an act dictated by a momentary impulse, since it clearly reveals the will of the king of Babylon to extinguish, once and for all, the outbreak of rebellion, putting an end to the Davidic dynasty, erasing the religious centre, and moving the administrative fulcrum of the region to Mizpah

---

111   Here, I do not enter into the thorny question regarding criticism of the myth "of the Empty Land", which many scholars hold as being anything but an unfounded exaggeration (as the minimalists instead assert). A position midway seems the most plausible. I believe that what is important is to grasp the symbolic significance of the incident, where "symbolic" is intended not as non-historic but as being packed with theological significance.

(currently Tell en-Naṣbeh). And installed here as governor of what remains of the kingdom of Judah,[112] is Gedaliah (גְּדַלְיָהוּ)[113] son of Ahikam (אֲחִיקָם).

According to what is narrated in the book of Jeremiah, the prophet receives favourable treatment. He is taken directly from the prison courtyard and entrusted to Gedaliah (cf. 39:11–14) or identified by the occupiers to Rama from amongst the enchained prisoners destined for deportation (cf. 40:1–6)[114] and freed. Given the right to choose whether to remain in Judah or go to Babylon where he will be looked after with care, Jeremiah opts to settle amongst the survivors left behind in the country.

But the story, as we well know, does not end here. In every sense. Following along the narrative plot of the book of Jeremiah (cf. 40:7–44), we see that Gedaliah, while trying to restore a certain normality, is assassinated along with the Babylonian garrison stationed in the city by Ishmael (יִשְׁמָעֵאל). Ishmael is a member of the royal household who belongs to an anti-Babylonian faction and who had returned from Ammon, where he had fled to carry on the resistance. He manages to flee here once more, albeit with Gedaliah's men on the hunt. For the few remaining, the situation turns dramatic once again. Yet another Babylonian repression is feared. And after everything that has happened, it is not difficult to imagine that it would be a ruthless one.[115]

Fig. 15. Tablet with reference to the food supplies reserved for Jehoiachin and his children, found alongside other 300 cuneiform texts of an administrative nature, in what must have been an important public building (and storage), currently located at the Pergamum Museum of Berlin (VAT 16378; photo by Olaf M. Teßmer, courtesy of the Staatliche Museen zu Berlin, Vorderasiatisches Museum; cf. D.J. WISEMAN, Illustrations from Biblical Archaeology, London 1958, 73).

---

112 According to B. ODED, «Where Is the "Myth of the Empty Land" to Be Found?», in: *Judah and the Judeans*, 68, we have no proof that would permit us to speak about the establishment of a "province of Judah (Yehud)" in this period. It is attested clearly only in the Persian period.

113 Cf. F. BIANCHI, «Godolia contro Ismaele. La lotta per il potere politico in Giudea all'inizio della dominazione neobabilonese (Ger 40–41 e 2Re 25,22–26)», *RivBib* 53 (2005) 257–275; J. WEINBERG, «Gedaliah, the Son of Ahikam in Mizpah: His Status and Role, Supporters and Opponents», *ZAW* 119 (2007) 356–368.

114 There is not great consonance in the relation between the two versions of the liberation.

115 In fact, even though this particular circumstance cannot be attributed to it with any certainty, a third deportation dating 582 is recorded in 52:30.

Jeremiah is consulted once more. After ten significant days of silence and waiting for the word of YHWH, he puts his message forth anew: to not fear the king of Babylon, remain in the land, and submit to him. Once again, the prophet from Anathoth is not believed. He is accused of being steered by Baruch, his scribe and aide, and flight to Egypt is preferred. Dragged there[116] along with Baruch, the prophet remains sympathetic with his people to the end, even though the most extreme consequences of their insipience, which continues even in the foreign land through their idolatrous cults, which are harshly condemned by the prophet (cf. Jer 44). Then in Egypt, while the control of Judea is being transferred to the administration of the province of Samaria, all trace of him is lost.

What had been foretold with the incident of the prophetic scroll in Jer 36 *becomes fulfilled*. The end comes. And yet, the book of Jeremiah closes with a sign of hope. Jehoiachin, the very king who surrendered to the Babylonians, losing everything and being forced to live the remainder of his days as a "captive" (אָסִר; cf. 1 Chr 3:17) in exile, gets rehabilitated (2 Kgs 25:27–30; Jer 52:31–34). An archaeological finding as precious as it is significative, discovered in the ruins of a vaulted building located near the famous Ishtar Gate of Babylon, documents for us some of the food commissions regularly supplied specifically to Jehoiachin and his children, thus illustrating the respect that the royal family enjoyed in exile (cf. Fig. 15).[117] We know, however, that the monarchy never re-established itself again. But we also know that the messianic prophecies and the hope that accompanied them were never erased.

On the one side, the history of the Davidic dynasty comes to a close with Zedekiah. The last descendant of David to actually reign in Jerusalem, he was placed before the necessity of surrender and erased from history for having refused to go out to meet the generals of the king of Babylon. On the other, it closes with Jehoiachin, a ruler in exile who precisely because he had surrendered, becomes, in a certain sense, rehabilitated.

3. The City and its destiny, between resistance and surrender. A particular historical-theological contextualisation

3.1. History, narration, and theology

After having attempted to trace a plausible historical path through the fundamental turning points of the vicissitudes of the final years of the kingdom of Judah, a

---

116   Contrary to what is believed by H.-J. STIPP, «Legenden der Jeremia-Exegese (II): Die Verschleppung Jeremias nach Ägypten», *VT* 64 (2014) 654–663, whose argumentation seems fairly weak to me, insofar as it is anchored in a literal reading of the texts and has a concept of historical plausibility that is detached from the pragmatic context implied in the Jeremianic text.

117   Cf. E.F. WEIDNER, «Jojachin, König von Juda, in babylonischen Keilschrifttexten», in: *Mélanges syriens offerts à Monsieur René Dussaud*, eds. F. CUMONT *et al.*, vol. II, BAH 30, Paris 1939, 923–935; W.F. ALBRIGHT, «King Joiachin in Exile», 51–53; I. CARDELLINI, «L'esilio. Un normale evento storico riletto con innovativa forza ideale», in: *Studi sul Vicino Oriente Antico*. Dedicati alla memoria di Luigi Cagni, *ed.* S. GRAZIANI, vol. III, IUO.SAMi 61, Napoli 2000, 1340–1343; P. KASWALDER «Re Ioiachin, una speranza perduta (2Re 25,27–30)», *LASBF* 54 (2004) 9–24.

162 Facing the might of the Babylonian empire

reconstruction that I have proposed within the framework of the great power struggles of the ancient Near East based on the most relevant documents and specialised studies, I think it now opportune to focalise more precisely and directly on the context within which Jeremiah's message in particular is historically and literarily set. In this transitional stage, one that is essential from the hermeneutical point of view, I will therefore focus on the question of the discernment of the most opportune stance to take in the face of the advancing Babylonian empire, a *theo-political controversy* that must have inflamed the discussions of the authorities and governing bodies of Jerusalem considerably.

Hence, the "City",[118] symbol of an entire people and a rich and complex religious tradition, and its *destiny*: the book of Jeremiah creates a tight interconnection between these two thematic polarities and thus calls for a devoted study. This inquiry can isolate and identify with a reasonable level of clarity, all the elements that will prove useful during the present dissertation's development to further contextualise the message of Jeremiah. In this way, it will be possible to grasp the diverse implications of the laboured decision that had to be confronted by the people of his time, from the king and his court down to anyone else in the position of deciding their own destiny (or of simply creating "public opinion") by choosing to resist or, instead, consign themselves into the hands of the king of Babylon. As one will have easily noted from the historical framework I have presented, the question is not a contingent one tied exclusively to the final moments of the siege of 589–587, but is rather an alternative upon which one was obliged to reason — willingly or not — from when Nebuchadnezzar first burst onto the Syro-Palestinian geopolitical scene in 605 at the expense of Egypt, up through the events that followed the fall of the capital.

It is within this context that at a certain point, and *only at a certain* point, that is, under the reign of Zedekiah, Jeremiah modulates his prophetic message about the impelling call for submission and then for surrender to the king of Babylon, lending political impact to his words that is even more vigorous and subversive. But it is precisely in this historical-political "concentration" that the specificity of biblical prophecy is most revealed. Without reducing itself in the least to subjective or debatable options of governance, it presents itself instead as a reading, interpretation, and questioning of history. An insertion of the God of Israel's vertical perspective into the horizontal timeline of humanity, it is an appeal for freedom and originating creative power.

---

118 With this term in Ostracon IV,7 from Lachish, reference is made quintessentially to Jerusalem as capital of the kingdom of Judah (a use that can also be observed in the HB, e.g. in Isa 6:66; Ezek 7:23; 9:9; Zeph 3:1).

3.2. Surrender or resist? People and opposing politico-theological orientations in the turmoil of history

Setting aside the hypothesis of the *escape* of the sovereign and his closest relatives along with some dignitaries and a chosen handful of soldiers (a possible but extreme option[119] attested by both extrabiblical sources[120] and the Jeremianic narration itself; cf. 39,4; 52:7–8), the choices affecting the destiny of the nation as a whole are reduced to two.

Hand themselves over or resist? Submit to the new empire of Babylon and its "annual extortions" (heavy tributes) or count instead once again, as in the past, on the help of the pharaoh, considering power and geographic proximity as advantages alongside the perilous disadvantages? Should they pragmatically attempt to salvage the salvageable, or continue to nurture desires of glory and relative independence, attempting to maximise the possible benefits (either hoped or believed viable), but with the (almost unconfessable) risk of losing everything?

And from a markedly theological point of view, precisely the perspective of the book of Jeremiah: Should they give credit to the unusual words of the prophet from Anathoth, by which YHWH himself would be asking for submission to Babylon, or should they trust the stable theological certainties handed down through the tradition of Zion and forcefully repeated by all of the other prophets, according to whom Jerusalem, the City chosen as abode of the Name, would never be abandoned by YHWH, who had already miraculously saved it from the Assyrians at the time of Hezekiah?

Resist or surrender? This, then – synthesising and simplifying – is the fundamental alternative the political-religious establishment of Jerusalem had to face,[121] even if, as I previously mentioned, the semantically broad prophetic call for "submission" programmatically expressed[122] in Jer 27–28 was modelled on the basis of the temporal articulation in which the Jeremianic message resounded according to at least *four*

---

119 The option seems to regard only the self-preservation of the life of the king who, having fallen short of his role as leader and protector of the nation, in the face of the advancing enemy forces, abandons the state and its people to their destiny.

120 There are numerous cases where mention is made of the (also quite adventuresome) escape of rebel sovereigns in the face of overpowering advancing enemy armies. See e.g. that attested in the Assyrian Annals in the context of the military campaigns of Sennacherib (amongst which, that of 701 in Syria-Palestine) in D.D. LUCKENBILL, *The Annals of Sennacherib*, OIP 2, Chicago 1924, 68–71, etc. (and in the more current edition of the Annals prepared by A.K. GRAYSON – J. NOVOTNY, eds., *The Royal Inscriptions of Sennacherib, King of Assyria (704–681 BC), Part 2*, RINAP 3/2, Winona Lake 2014, 79–81, etc.).

121 It seems inaccurate to me to speak of a clash of factions divided between "'autonomist' or 'co-existence' political action", as does B.O. LONG, «Social Dimensions», 49, given that the situation was not one of peaceful "co-existence" but rather of genuine submission, complete with a huge annual tribute (and finally, desperate surrender).

122 Historically but not *literarily* programmatic, given that this is already introduced in 21:1–10. I will highlight this conceptual distinction adequately in the chapter dedicated specifically to this important pericope, where I will attempt to account for its apparently bizarre insertion in the text.

164   Facing the might of the Babylonian empire

specific denotations, whilst still remaining the lowest common denominator of all the variants.

In fact, depending on the different historical moments, the question remains primarily and precisely that of comprehending, requesting, and expressing submission (and all that this can signify): (1) as *universal political acceptance of the Babylonian sovereignty* and *particular* respect for the oath of loyalty granted to Nebuchadnezzar by Zedekiah after the capitulation and deportation of 597 (cf. chs. 27–28); (2) as a concrete embracing on the part of the deportees of an existential project consisting in *living for a long time in exile,* renouncing the dream of an imminent return to the homeland (cf. ch. 29); 3) as a specific act of *surrender*[123] under the grip of the final siege (cf. 21:1–10; 38); 4) as an act of courage and faith in the prophetic word to be expressed by *remaining in the land* at the mercy of the dreaded Babylonian reaction following the assassination of Gedaliah, without fleeing to Egypt (cf. chs. 42–43:1–7).

In reference to the only two feasible political-religious options overall, from the turning point of 605, which consisted in turning either to Egypt or to Babylon, the only powers that could contend for dominance over the Syrian-Palestinian region, it is easy to note how virtually all the commentators always speak (and in a manner that is perhaps hasty and assumptive, in my opinion) comparing a pro-Egyptian "party" with a pro-Babylonian "party", citing only a few names obtained from the book of Jeremiah[124] and giving the impression of a sort of political "bipolarism" that consists of two *equally influential* positions supported by opposing milieu of the court.[125]

That there would have been factions and discordant opinions is entirely plausible to suppose and is, moreover, clear from the clues at our disposal.[126] But as far as the approach (and relative terminology) that seems to suggest that the two positions be equivalent is concerned, represented primarily by R. Albertz,[127] it is worth running a

---

123   I believe, in any regard, that it be possible to use the same term "surrender" in a broad sense (i.e. to include the meanings of "submission", "acceptance of the exile", "the choice to not escape in the face of the possibility of a Babylonian retaliation after the killing of Gedaliah") because it refers to the most dramatic moment of the controversy over what political stance to take before the might of Babylon, arrayed against Jerusalem to achieve the "final solution" over the kingdom of Judah. It need furthermore be recognised that the antonymic pair "resist and surrender" has been made famous by now by the edition of Dietrich Bonhoeffer's letters written from prison, edited by Eberhard Bethge (*Widerstand und Ergebung.* Briefe und Aufzeichnungen aus der Haft, München 1951) in which, amongst other things, the problem of the position of Christians before making "necessary decisions" is thematised.

124   E.g. M. Smith, *Palestinian Parties and Politics That Shaped the Old Testament,* New York 1971, 46 limits himself to this.

125   See, as an example, A. Soggin, *Storia d'Israele,* 375.

126   As far as extrabiblical testimony is concerned, mention can be given at least to the case of Ashdod, as recalled by J. Høgenhaven, «Prophecy and Propaganda», 130, n. 15.

127   See the presentation of the internal political controversy in the kingdom of Judah prior to 587 in R. Albertz, *Religionsgeschichte,* 366–372. The same configuration can be seen already in B. Lang, *Kein Aufstand in Jerusalem.* Die Politik des Propheten Ezechiel, SBB, Stuttgart 1978, 135–146. For his part, M. Smith, *Palestinian Parties,* 46 notes instead, though *en passant,* that the sustainers of Jeremiah must have only been a minority.

The City and its destiny, between resistance and surrender 165

query that can critically evaluate the consistency. I will therefore try to define a more precise picture of the relationship between the figure of the prophet Jeremiah and the political-religious (but also basically human) struggle that Jerusalem and the kingdom of Judah on the whole faced during this historical phase that was so decisive for its future and its very existence.

3.2.1 *Jeremiah and the option to* surrender: *Supporters and motivations*

Whilst not aspiring to complete an exhaustive reconstruction of the complexity of the balances and relations at stake between the powers that be, which would require a monographic treatment, I will evaluate, foremost, based first on the elements offered by the book of Jeremiah, and subsequently by what can be reasonably deduced from other extrabiblical data (obtained from the *ostraca* of Lachish), not so much the existence, but rather the magnitude of the pro-Babylonian "party" that is presumed to have sympathised with the prophet *and his message.*

I will point out, however, that these two main sources, namely the book of Jeremiah and the ostraca of Lachish, should be either considered jointly or separately on the basis of the methodological approach that one decides to adopt (and not simply because they are of a different nature). In fact, a purely historical-archaeological reconstruction requires a critical examination of all data available, taking their reciprocal relationship into consideration, as I have done up to this point. Likewise, it would appear entirely legitimate for a study stemming instead from a specifically literary interest to limit itself to the thematic space circumscribed by the textual boundaries of the book of Jeremiah (and extend, potentially, to other literary intertextual relationships with other portions of the HB).

Thus, logically keeping these perspectives distinct, I will proceed first with an analysis based directly on the textual elements found in our prophetic book. And then secondly, I will confront this with the results obtained with the data collected from the Lachish Letters, historical-archaeological testimony that is unfortunately fragmentary but regardless valuable about the final phase of the kingdom of Judah.

3.2.1 1. *Supporters*

Jeremiah called for submission and surrender to Babylon in the name of YHWH. That is clear. It would likewise seem evident that those who defended him, for one reason or another, tended to be pro-Babylonian. The question would hence be that of looking at who defended Jeremiah. Let us try, for the moment, to follow this logic, which appears to be the most obvious. One could thus list the names of a number of prominent figures who, under different circumstances, showed respect towards the prophet and his message.

A) On Jeremiah's side

Individuals of a certain notoriety should be counted, such as *Baruch* himself, "the scribe" (הַסֹּפֵר), son of Neriah, faithful "secretary" of the prophet; his brother *Seraiah* (שְׂרָיָה), "chief quartermaster" or "great chamberlain" (שַׂר מְנוּחָה), who will be saddled with the task of reading to Babylon the scroll containing this city's prophesies (cf. 51:59–64); the court eunuch of Ethiopian origin *Ebed-melech* (עֶבֶד־מֶלֶךְ), who manages at the last moment to save Jeremiah from the cistern by interceding directly with

166   Facing the might of the Babylonian empire

the king[128]; and perhaps, in some respects, even the priest *Zephaniah* (צְפַנְיָה) son of Maaseiah (מַעֲשֵׂיָה), though in 29:25 he is presented as the principal interlocutor of the exiled nationalists (who ask for a halting of Jeremiah's action).[129]

A remarkable group of "supporters" is highlighted in ch. 36. These are the "leaders" (שָׂרִים) cited in v. 12, of which five proper names are given: ("*Elishama* [אֱלִישָׁמָע] the scribe, and *Delaiah* [דְּלָיָהוּ] son of Shemaiah [שְׁמַעְיָהוּ], *Elnathan* [אֶלְנָתָן] son of Achbor [עַכְבּוֹר], *Gemariah* [גְּמַרְיָהוּ] son of Shaphan [שָׁפָן], and *Zedekiah* [צִדְקִיָּהוּ] son of Hananiah [חֲנַנְיָהוּ]"). In particular, in 36:19, it is noted that these שָׂרִים (considered as a single entity), after having heard the words of the scroll, advise Baruch and Jeremiah to hide to protect themselves from the foreseeable reaction of King Jehoiakim. Of the five dignitaries cited, three plead the sovereign to not burn the scroll (36:25).

Apart from this heterogeneous group, an influential core pro-Babylonian faction could be identified in the family headed by Shaphan (שָׁפָן).[130] Several of its members are cited in the book of Jeremiah in relation to the prophet in a positive way. *Ahikam* son of Shaphan, saves Jeremiah from the hands of those who want him put to death (cf. 26:24); *Elasah* (אֶלְעָשָׂה), also a son of Shaphan, takes Jeremiah's letter to the exiles (cf. 29:3); and a grandson of the same Shaphan, *Gedaliah* (גְּדַלְיָהוּ; cf. 39:14; 40:5, 9, 11; 41:2; 43:6), is chosen by the Babylonians as governor after the destruction of Jerusalem. Jeremiah will be entrusted to him after the catastrophe, a clue that would show the Shaphanide family to be substantially favourable to the policy of submission to Babylon.

Some scholars trace this family's pro-Babylonian orientation back to the time of its progenitor Shaphan, a key figure in the court of Josiah. This is because the disappearance of the reformer king is interpreted as being an effect of a simultaneously anti-Egyptian and anti-Assyrian act of war, with a subsequent pro-Babylonian backlash, since the Chaldeans represented the emerging power that had destroyed Nineveh. In this sense, official contact with Babylon attested at the time of Isaiah and Hezekiah (cf. 2 Kgs 20:12–19) is emphasised.

It seems, however, rather hasty to attribute a clear pro-Babylonian stance to Shaphan or some of his court based on these elements. The picture remains too uncertain, also considering that at this historical stage, in fact, as a commander, Nabopolassar appears

---

128   Cf. 38:7–13 and the oracle of salvation that concerns him directly in 39:15–18.

129   Keep in mind, however, that it is Zephaniah himself who reads the letter from Shemaiah in the presence of Jeremiah. Not only does he not seem to implement what is requested but, on the contrary, it is he who receives the order from Jeremiah to send back a harsh oracle in response (cf. 29:29–32).

130   This is implicitly acknowledged by R. ALBERTZ, *Religionsgeschichte*, 368. Shaphan "the scribe" (הַסֹּפֵר) almost always appears with this title in the second book of Kgs in relation to the organisation of the restoration of the temple in 621 and the subsequent reform of Josiah founded on the finding of the book of the Law (cf. 2 Kgs 22:8). After the tragic end of Josiah and substantial failure of the reformist movement, we still find some of his sons (and grandsons) cited in the book of Jeremiah. These seem to have friendly relations with the prophet and, in any case, consider his message worthy of attention, even if it is not said whether this was only for purely political or even religious motives (albeit that a clear distinction between the two spheres is unfathomable in the ancient Near East). For a more detailed presentation of this figure, one can see J.M. KENNEDY, «Shaphan», *ABD* V, 1159.

The City and its destiny, between resistance and surrender   167

to be more fortunate than skilful, and credit for the Assyrian defeat would have been mainly attributed to the Medes of Cyaxares. If Josiah's death were truly attributable to an anti-Egyptian political line, which remains to be demonstrated, the complacent gaze before the desirable prospect of the end of the Assyrian empire could simply have been limited to a positive assessment of the existence of the forces (Babylonian, Medes, etc.) that were producing it, without this materialising in direct, explicit alliances (which, imaginably, would have regardless been problematic in the context of a rigorously Yahwist reformist movement).

B) The time of Jehoiakim and that of Zedekiah: What changes, decisively

From the data just highlighted, one could generically deduce that, despite all, Jeremiah could count on a good number of authoritative supporters and that consequently, many were oriented in a pro-Babylonian direction. In reality, this impression must be subjected to a more accurate assessment. In my opinion, a fundamental discriminating factor (already introduced in ch. I, § 4.2.1) needs to be reconsidered. This consists in distinguishing two distinct moments (aside from the period of Josiah) in the prophetic ministry of Jeremiah: *the time of Jehoiakim and that of Zedekiah*. Only at the time of Zedekiah, in fact, can Jeremiah's message be read *clearly* in a pro-Babylonian sense.[131] At the time of Jehoiakim, on the other hand, Jeremiah does not at all ask for a political act to be committed: he threatens the end and calls for (ethical) conversion.[132]

Obviously, as with any prophetic intervention, this appeal is neither conceived nor presented devoid of direct implications and precise perceivable consequences in the historical horizon. Just as the act of conversion, in fact, means "to thoroughly reform your ways and your deeds" (cf. e.g. 7:5) and thus also to perform certain specified acts that are external and historical, likewise not performing these means concretely attracting the ruin of the state and expulsion from the presence of YHWH (cf. e.g. 7:15), precisely through the king of Babylon and his devastating function, to which Jeremiah, in any case, already makes explicit reference at the time of Jehoiakim (cf. 36:29). In this perspective, those who were shifting towards a pro-Babylonian orientation (like the members of the Shaphan family)[133] might have, since the time of Jehoiakim, considered Jeremiah's message seriously, given that it could have been utilised to support a possible pro-Babylonian political line, even regardless of its peculiar act of prophetic reading of history. Let us look at how this hermeneutical key can orient a reconsideration of the various textual data, especially those that can be deduced from chs. 26 and 36.

---

131 Although, as I will attempt to demonstrate in the present dissertation, this message can be adequately understood only by respecting its explicit prophetic connotation.

132 In 26:20–23, another prophet is mentioned. This is Uria (אוּרִיָּהוּ), who had spoken in a way that was similar to Jeremiah (v. 20) but did so at the time of Jehoiakim (by whom he is then suppressed) and against "this land and this city", without any mention of need for submission to Babylon.

133 This would seem to be confirmed by the mention of Gedaliah, grandson of Shaphan, as governor installed by Babylon after the destruction of Jerusalem (cf. 2 Kgs 25:22; Jer 40:5).

168 Facing the might of the Babylonian empire

When it is narrated in ch. 26 that Jeremiah is sent by YHWH to the temple to threaten its destruction if there is a lack of adequate conversion, it is Achikàm[134] son of Shaphan, who manages *in extremis,* in the course of the trial brought against the prophet for his subversive speech, to slip him from the "hands of the people", and thus from certain death (cf. 26:24). To understand the political relevance of this decisive gesture, two clarifications should be made here:

1) It should be noted that while this intervention demonstrates a certain authority (expressed, however, by a single individual on a personal basis),[135] the significance of this is not to be blown out of proportion. Over the course of the events narrated in the chapters following, aside from what is said in 36:19, 25 (which refers, in any case, to the time of Jehoiakim), there is no trace of any other similar public gesture towards Jeremiah during the final eleven years of the kingdom of Judah, that is, under the king Zedekiah. And yet, a gesture of the sort might have been expected both from a political party (or political lobby) worthy of this name towards its so authoritative (or only) "spokesman",[136] or from a ("Shaphanide" Deuteronomist, or in any case, pro-Babylonian) "redactor" who, during the exile or post-exile epoch would have wanted to ideologically reorientate the text for propagandistic ends, to the advantage of the exiles or returnees. Bearing in mind, amongst other things, that despite a member of the Shaphan family (Gedaliah) being named governor, the Jews who had defected or "fallen away to the Chaldeans" (cf. 38:19) during military operations also got deported to Babylon (cf. 39:9).

2) Moreover, and even more importantly, it should be pointed out that defending Jeremiah (or not) in a circumstance of the sort could not have corresponded yet directly to the concession (or not) of a *precise* party line. We are, in fact, still in the time of Jehoiakim and on the part of Jeremiah, as I have pointed out, *the subject of submission (surrender) to the king of Babylon is not yet in question.* This option will be explicitly asked of the weak and wavering Zedekiah. He will be the only one, in any event – still, according to the book of Jeremiah – to be counted explicitly amongst those who, in the end, seem to take this possibility seriously (cf. 38:19).

No text clearly shows the contrary. And even if one could retrace and demonstrate the pertinence of some allusions contained in the poetic texts in the first part of the book of Jeremiah (cf. above all 6:1–8, 22–30) in this sense, it does not seem justifiable by any means to assert, as does R. Albertz in his reconstruction, that before the deportation of 597 Jeremiah had already invited the authorities *to consign the city,*[137]

---

134 Again in 2 Kgs 22:12 (2 Cr 34:20), an "Ahikam son of Shaphan" is named. But in this case, it is disputable if the Shaphan is one and the same, given that in the same verse, this name seems to be distinguished from that of Shaphan "the scribe".

135 I highlight this because, despite the wavering behaviour of the various groups present, it does not seem relevant to see a clear manifestation of equally powerful but contrasting socio-political factions present at court in this episode, as is suggested by P. DUTCHER-WALLS, «The Social Location of the Deuteronomists: A Sociological Study of Factional Politics in Late Pre-Exilic Judah», *JSOT* 52 (1991) 86.

136 It is R. ALBERTZ, *Religionsgeschichte,* 368, who presents, above all, in my opinion unfitly, the clash between Jeremiah and Hananiah as a clash between the spokespersons of two respective "parties".

137 Cf. R. ALBERTZ, *Religionsgeschichte,* 367.

The City and its destiny, between resistance and surrender   169

that is, to surrender, supporting this by 13:18–19 alone.[138] The text in question, in fact, though referring to the immediate successor of Jehoiakim (i.e. Jehoiachin), does not prove anything to this effect, since it consists of prophesies that present, through the so-called "prophetic perfect" and according to stereotypical poetic registers (cf. e.g. 48:18[139]; 49:3 and Isa 47:1; Ezek 26:16; Job 2:8), the end as *already underway* (still, however, in the form of a threat) and the king and the queen as *already dethroned*.[140] It is, therefore, not possible to interpret this fleeting allusion as a chroniclistic attestation of a precise political orientation,[141] since using the same criteria, one would then need to say that in 4:5 and 6:25 Jeremiah calls for the exact opposite, that is, for *resistance*.[142] This would seem somewhat forced. In the context of ch. 26, what is called for is "simply" conversion, and the end is threatened. The destruction of Jerusalem and of the temple is obviously a state matter and not only a moral question, but in the Jeremianic appeal there is still no indication of a relevant precise political alternative. His request remains one of an exclusively *ethical* sort (as we will better see in the commentary on 21 1–10), even if it is, as one would logically expect, presented as having crucial political repercussions. Let us proceed.

After the speech at the temple, the different orientations of the court emerge in another likewise provocative and dramatic circumstance, which can again be dated in the time of Jehoiakim. We are in ch. 36, which I have already cited. The proclamation of the prophecies of menace dictated by Jeremiah to Baruch on a scroll arouse concern amongst the court dignitaries. Here too, however, it should be pointed out that Jeremiah *still does not call for surrender to Babylon*. His appeal definitely appears

---

138   "Say to the king and to the queen mother: humble yourself, take a lowly seat, for your beautiful crown has come down from your heads. The cities of the Negeb are shut, with no one to open them, Judah is taken into exile, in total exile."

139   "Come down from glory, sit on the parched ground, oh people of Dibon; for the destroyer of Moab has fallen upon you, shattered your strongholds."

140   A further note in this regard. Verse 13:19a says: "The cities of the Negeb are shut (סֻגְּרוּ)." This expression could also be read as a specific reference both to the events preceding the capitulation of 597, when Nebuchadnezzar, intent on reorganising his army, makes use of military forces composed of local ethnicities (cf. 2 Kgs 24:2; W.L. HOLLADAY, *Jeremiah 1*, 409), and to the final phase of war operations against the kingdom of Judah, alluded to in an important text: 34:7. The immediate context, however, does not permit an unequivocal interpretation, since the poetic genre of the oracle condenses on a single plane elements for which, from a historical point of view, it is difficult to designate a precise historical moment. It says emphatically that the sovereign and queen mother must humiliate themselves, for the fact that the sign of their kingship has already fallen. It says that the cities are besieged, at a standstill (an image that seems to more appropriately describe the war operations scenario of 589–587 than those of 597, which were brought to a quick conclusion). It announces a complete deportation as having already come to pass, while Jeremiah, at least in 27:11, ties the act of submission to a guarantee of remaining in the land.

141   I hold that the same can be said for Ezek 21:31 (as agrees B. LANG, *Kein Aufstand*, 118, n. 12, contrary to the opinion of K. SEYBOLD, *Das davidische Königtum im Zeugnis der Propheten*, FRLANT 107, Göttingen 1972, 142), even if the gesture of removing the turban and laying down the crown has a strong symbolic importance for the purpose of an accurate analysis of the semantic axes of the act of surrender.

142   Cf. 4:5: "Proclaim it in Judah, in Jerusalem announce it; Blow the trumpet throughout the land, call out, '*Fill the ranks!*' Say, '*Assemble, let us march to the fortified cities!*'";

170 Facing the might of the Babylonian empire

to be final, an ultimate possibility (cf. 36:1–3, 7). It is the synthesis of Jeremiah's entire prophetic ministry up to that point: YHWH calls for conversion and threatens the end, whilst specifying that the punitive instrument will be the king of Babylon himself (cf. 36:29).

The reading takes place in a room made available by *Ghemaria*, a son of Shaphan. Ghemaria, however, is not present. It is his son *Michea* (מִכָיְהוּ), a grandson of Shaphan, who then goes to personally bring word of what he has heard, interrupting an important session. All of the prominent members of the court are present, the "princes" or "leaders" (שָׂרִים). Some names are given, amongst which that of Ghemaria himself, and it is once more made clear that "the leaders" are all there. They are, it says, fear struck. What is described is a reaction grounded in a religious sensibility (or perhaps, more simply, in superstition). This expresses the credit given to the prophetic word in general[143] and to Jeremiah in particular, at least on this occasion and in this context of assemblage in which, according to the mentality of the time, religion and politics are mixed and blended together. The matter at stake, in any case, is not one that we could qualify today as being merely tactical or strategic in nature, on an entirely human plane. To fear the prophet, protect him, and attempt to save the prophetic scroll does not automatically mean opting for submission to the king of Babylon.

C) The prophet alone, with his message and his mission

In conclusion, the most evident fact that emerges from a focused analysis of the text of the book of Jeremiah is that the prophet, despite finding himself amidst interwoven personal relationships and even influential parental relations[144] from which he must have received some support (during the time of Jehoiakim), gets left practically *alone* at the mercy of his adversaries (when not openly opposed and persecuted, even by his own family members; cf. 12:6[145]) in the final phase of the story of the kingdom of Judah, that is, at the time of Zedekiah, a time frame in which the prophet explicitly calls first for submission and then for surrender to the king of Babylon. Jeremiah is presented as having a single faithful collaborator, Baruch. And unlike Isaiah (cf. Isa 8:16, 18), he has no circle of disciples upon whom to rely, let alone consideration as an *official* "spokesman" of a given political faction[146] (although some people, such as the

---

6:25: "*Do not go out into the field, do not step into the street*, For the enemy has a sword; terror on every side!"

143 This is also clearly confirmed by the reference in Ost. III,3 to an unidentified "prophet" (who is mentioned, however, as being well known, that is, as "*the*" prophet, הנבא) and his message (synthesised in the expression on l. 21 [*verso*]: השמר "Beware!"), in the context of the military dispatches of the "Lachish Letters".

144 See the analyses (accompanied by suggestive conjectures) of B.O. LONG, «Social Dimensions», 45–47, from which more or less probable relationships emerge, both familial and in friendship, with high-ranking exponents in the court, priestly, and administrative realms, often with ties to Josiah's reform movement.

145 A fairly bleak picture emerges: "[...] your kindred and you father's house, even they betray you; they have recruited a force against you. Do not believe them, even when they speak fair words to you".

146 Contrary to what is thought by, e.g. J.M. MILLER – J.H. HAYES, *History*, 462, as well as the aforementioned R. ALBERTZ, *Religionsgeschichte*, 368, and others.

The City and its destiny, between resistance and surrender 171

members of the family of Shaphan, for various reasons, may have shared or exploited the political aspect of his message).

These facts are also striking since no clear pro-Babylonian faction coagulates around the prophet's sympathisers, contrary to what one might expect after the elite pro-Egyptians were removed from the picture in 597 and the power was conferred to another class of notables. On the contrary: the remaining dignitaries (and/or the new ones) seem even more resolutely orientated towards Egypt than those preceding, and eager to shake off the yoke of Babylon. This would lead to a significant scaling down of the notion of a powerful pro-Babylonian "party" active in Jerusalem up until the city's conquest.

It is true that in 38:19, Zedekiah claims to fear being consigned into the hands of the Jews "who have deserted to the Chaldeans" (אֲשֶׁר נָפְלוּ אֶל־הַכַּשְׂדִּים) in the case of surrender. This almost gives the impression that there be a compact, influential pro-Babylonian faction present who, in turn, not seeing space for political manoeuvring within the court, had decided to hand itself over to the Babylonians. But this is very doubtful and seems to correspond more to the king's fears than to reality itself.[147] In fact, not only does Jeremiah deem this fear unfounded, but from 52:15–16 we learn that *all the deserters* are deported to Babylon and that only the poorest people in the country are left in Judah (v. 16: מִדַּלּוֹת[148]הָאָרֶץ). They are left under a Shaphanid leader, without further clarification or reference to any other Jewish authoritative political "pro-Babylonian" exponents.

All this leads us to think that in 38:19, reference is being made to a heterogeneous set of defectors, common people, soldiers, or nobility, without a univocal, identifying political programme or particularly privileged relations with the Babylonian government and military apparatus. In 52:15, the deserters and survivors of the siege and subsequent military operations (the rest of the people, the craftsmen remaining) form a single set of prisoners destined for exile. The only proper names given along with the notable figures are those led before Nebuchadnezzar (52:24–27), to be executed:

> [24] The captain of the guard also took prisoner Seraiah, the high priest, and Zephaniah, the second priest, along with the three keepers of the entrance. [25] From the city, he took prisoner one eunuch, who was a commander of soldiers, and seven privy counselors to the king still in the city, the scribe of the army commander, who was in charge of mustering the people of the land, and sixty of the common people remaining in the city. [26] The captain of the guards, Nebuzaradan, arrested them and brought them to the king of Babylon at Riblah. [27] The king of Babylon had them struck down and put to death in Riblah, in the land of Hamath. Thus Judah was exiled from its land.

---

147 Though I believe it legitimate to hypothesise that amongst the "Jews gone over to the Chaldeans", there may have also been a number of prominent proponents of that orientation who had handed themselves over to the Chaldeans at the right time (so as not to be executed). Amongst these was perhaps Gedaliah himself, the grandson of Shaphan who would then be made governor.

148 The f. noun דְּלָה is usually taken as being a collective name. The parallel passage in 2 Kgs 25:12, in fact, confirms the sing. (וּמִדַּלַּת הָאָרֶץ). The pl. forms מִדַּלּוֹת in vv. 15 and 16 of Jeremiah are thus surprising. According to W.L. HOLLADAY, *Jeremiah 2*, 437, it could be hypothesised that the vocalisation of the MT attests an attempt to (lead to) understand the expression as an f. pl. of דַּל ("the poor women").

D) Extrabiblical evidence: Confirmation or complication? The Lachish Letters and Ostracon VI

This assessment, on the other hand, founded on elements of a literary nature drawn from the book of Jeremiah alone, must be placed in relation to what can be drawn from an important extrabiblical source, namely, the aforementioned "Lachish Letters",[149] and in particular Ostracon VI ([KAI 196] cf. Fig. 16). This document fits perfectly within the context of the political upheaval in the final phase of the kingdom of Judah attested in the book of Jeremiah.[150]

Fig. 16. Ostracon 6 from Lachish (recto), *sketch (S. Aḥituv, Echoes from the Past, 81–82; J. Renz, Texte und Tafeln, pl. LII).*

---

149 The group of ostraca of greatest interest is usually dated between 589 and the beginning of 588, thus a short time before the Babylonian invasion. The atmosphere one senses substantially conforms to the scenario of the situation that can be derived from the book of Jeremiah. Despite the fact that the enemy is never explicitly named and that it still be possible to communicate with the capital (Ost. IV,7; VI,8–11) and even to harvest the grain (Ost. V,7–10), reference is made to the function and message of the prophets (Ost. III,19–21; 16,5), to the army commander's journey to Egypt (most probably to secure military support; Ost. III,13–16), there is tension in the air, suspision and accusations (Ost. IV,8), the tone is anxious (Ost. II,5; III,4–13; VI,5–15), war preparations are underway (Ost. IV,10–13; XIII?). It is as if the enemy could invade the region at any given moment.

150 Cf. D. Pardee, *A Handbook of Ancient Hebrew Letters*. A Study Edition, SBLSBS 15, Chico 1982, 103.

The City and its destiny, between resistance and surrender

In fact, the author of the message, who would appear to be an officer overseeing a not so distant military outpost[151] (perhaps Maresha), addresses his superior, Ya'uš (יאוש) in astonishment. Ya'uš was probably the commander-in-chief of Lachish itself and owner of the archive. He had sent the officer to have a look (thus requesting *feedback*) at extremely confidential and shocking documents[152]: a personal letter from the king and the letters of his officers, the "leaders" (שָׂרִים). In these letters are words judged by the author of the missive sent in reply as being "not good" (לא טבם), words that (clearly, in a critical context of war mobilisation) get perceived, in an anti-nationalist sense (detrimental to the royal authority itself), as being capable of weakening the morale of the troops engaged against the enemy. Looking at the text, according to one of the reconstructions finding the greatest consensus amongst scholars[153]:

אל אדני יאוש. ירא. יהוה א	1	*To my lord Ya'uš. May YHWH show*
ת. אדני את העת הזה. שלם מי	2	*my lord this time (in) peace. What can ever be considered*
עבדך כלב כי. שלח. אדני א[ת ספ]	3	*your servant (if not) a dog? And yet my lord sent him t[he*
ר המלך [ו]אֹת ספרי השר[ם לאמ]	4	*lette]r of the king [and] the letters of the leader[s saying]:*
ר קרא נא והנה. דברי. ה[שרם]	5	*"read please!". And behold the words of t[he (?)leaders]*
לא טבם לרפת ידיך [ולהש]	6	*are not good: these in fact slacken your hands [and render*
קט. ידי הא[נשם] הֹגֹּיֹדע[ם]	7	*w]eak the hands of the m[en] [...] (?) who kn[ow].*
[--] ועת] אֹדֹנֹי הלא תב	8	*[...(?) and now] my lord, should you not wri-*
תב אל[יהם] לא[מ]ר למ]ה תעשו	9	*te to t[hem] say[ing: wh]y do you act*
כזאת ו[ביר]שֹלם ה[נ]ה ל	10	*this way (?) and (right) [in Jeru]salem? B[eh]old: to*
מלך [ולביתה. ת[עֹשֹו הֹרֹבֹ	11	*the king [(?) and to his house you d]o (?) this.*
ר חֹיֹֹה חי. יהוה אלה	12	*Living is YHWH your God:*
יך כ]י מ]אז קרא עב	13	*Tru[ly sin]ce your servant read*
דך אֹת הספרם לא הֹיֹה	14	*the letters, there has not been*
[--- לעב]דך	15	*for [your] serv[ant] [(?) a moment of peace].*

---

151   According to some scholars, he could be identifiable as Hoša'yahu (הושעיהו) of Ost. III,1, who appeals to the same Ya'uš (l. 2), also because five other ostraca (II, VI, VII, VIII, XVIII) appear to be fragments of the same vase from which Ostracon III comes. But this interpretation is, regardless, dubious (or completely discounted; see e.g. A. Lemaire, *Inscriptions hébraïques*, 140–141). Besides the fact that as author of the missive, Hoša'yahu appears only in Ostracon III, there are also literary palaeographic motifs (I refer, in this regard, to S. Birnbaum, «The Lachish Ostraca I», *PEQ* 71 (1939) 20–28, 91–110 [here, pp. 20–23]; R. de Vaux, «Les ostraka de Lachis», *RB* 48 [1939] 181–206 [here, p. 205]).

152   Ostraca II, III, and VI are explicitly addressed to him.

153   The ostracon was discovered broken into three parts (cf. Fig. 16) and the text is not legible in its entirety, since complete words and single letters are no longer visible in certain points, while there is some doubt concerning the interpretation of others (hence the varied transliterations of different scholars). For my translation (as literal as possible), I have adhered to the reconstruction of the text by J. Renz, *Die althebräischen Inschriften*, 425–427, on which other scholars likewise substantially converge.

174   Facing the might of the Babylonian empire

The phraseology used to describe the subversive potential of the message contained in the correspondence received is immediately striking. In the writer's opinion, it contains words that can "slacken the hands" (לרפת inf. constr. pi. of √רפה preceded by ל)[154] of the commander (line 6) and "[render w]eak" (ק[ש[ולה] inf. constr. hi. of √שקט preceded by ל; the regent verb is a conjecture) those of the soldiers (ll. 6–7). To undermine the morale of the troops, to lead to collapse, and to express words that are "not good" (לא טבם): this is precisely the accusation that the leaders direct towards the king in 38:4 against Jeremiah. The syntagmatic construct used (√רפה pi. + ידי) is identical (cf. also Job 12:21; Ezra 4:4) and the negative synthetic assessment strikingly similar:

> Then the leaders said to the king: "This man ought to be put to death for he is *weakening* (מְרַפֵּא) the hands of the soldiers left in this city, and the hands of all the people, by saying such things to them. This man is not *seeking the welfare* (אֵינֶנּוּ דֹרֵשׁ לְשָׁלוֹם) of these people, but their ruin."

However, this clear reference only underscores an intriguing hermeneutical question, one based on an equally clear (at least apparently) dissimilarity: According to the reconstruction of the ostracon that I have presented, it would be not Jeremiah (or some other prophet) who was supporting this dangerous political option, but rather the "leaders" themselves from whom the letters were received (cf. line 5). For this reason, in a way that takes too much for granted, many scholars hasten to comment on this ostracon, making reference instead to the struggle between the opposing factions active *in the capital*[155] under Zedekiah. Certainly, if they were right, it should at least be acknowledged that this version of the facts does not seem to correspond absolutely to the scenario I have attempted to reconstruct based exclusively on the Jeremianic texts. Indeed, an active, powerful pro-Babylonian "party" *in Jerusalem* during the last phase of the history of the kingdom of Judah[156] cannot be identified therein.

But things are not so simple, in my opinion, nor can we stop at such a (hypothetical) finding. In fact, this interpretation is based solely on the conjectural reconstruction of the text of line 5 which, at the point where the writer explicitly attributes the authorship of the words "not good", is illegible. Due almost exclusively to considerations of internal criteria,[157] many read here (or rather, insert here) the term שרם, as in the previous line. Thus, the words upsetting the officer would be those of the "leaders" (שָׂרִים). But this affirmation presents more problems than it solves. Indeed, if we were to ask ourselves what the specific content of the king's letter might be, and about the correlation between that missive and what his ministers write, some questions arise.

---

154   Cf. GK §114o.
155   See e.g. K.A.D. Smelik, *Writings from Ancient Israel.* A Handbook of Historical and Religious Documents, Edinburgh 1991, 116–131, here, p. 130 (original Dutch: Id., *Behouden Schrift: historische documentation uit het oude Israël,* Baarn 1984) and B. Studevent-Hickman – S.C. Melville – S. Noegel, «Neo-Babylonian Period Texts», 402.
156   It is, instead, clear from 38:19 that there were prominent figures who "have deserted to the Chaldeans".
157   R. Dussaud, «Le prophète Jérémie et les lettres de Lakish», *Syr.* 19 (1938) 256–271, asserts (on p. 262, n. 5) that the vestiges of the first letter best conform to the letter *nun*, while there is no trace of either *resh* or *shin*.

The City and its destiny, between resistance and surrender   175

And if one wishes to remain within the confines of the commonly proposed solution, these do not have entirely satisfactory answers.

Quite possibly, the king and his ministers are in fact saying the same thing (which is probable, regardless of the tenor of the message),[158] ventilating the hypothesis of surrender, and the officer, out of respect, takes issue only with the ministers for their poor advice. In this case, however, the sovereign would then seem to be entirely at the mercy of a *pro-Babylonian* faction (which is difficult to even conceive, considering the final outcome of the story of the kingdom of Judah). Or instead, the messages say opposing things (unlikely), in which case it is not clear how the letters of the king and his ministers could have reached Ya'uš together (as it seems) and then (as is attested) be sent to his subordinate, without there being any reference to "high treason" but rather only to "not good" words that discourage (the troops). It is hence far-fetched to claim that the resentful, indignant tone and the reproach the officer asks to have forwarded to the highest authorities of the capital (as what is said in ll. 8–11 is usually interpreted as saying) should have the king's ministers as its direct object. It does not seem permissible that a man who calls himself "a dog" (cf. line 3: כלב), that is, an officer of a modest outpost (or even simply a political counsellor) would address (or request to address) superiors on that level in similar terms.

In short, something does not seem to square up with the interpretation that is, in fact, most commonly shared. In my opinion, the path already suggested at the time of the ostracon's discovery by the text's first editor ought to be reconsidered. In fact, H. Torczyner, driven perhaps, according to some, by his enthusiasm of the discovery (though this does not necessarily mean that it should therefore be wrong) had proposed integrating after the article ה the term נבא ("prophet" without *mater lectionis*,[159] which could fit in the space cancelled out just as well as the term שרם). He intended this to be a reference not to Jeremiah, however, but to the prophet Uria (אוריהו), cited in 26:20–23 and identified (arguably) by H. Torczyner himself as "the prophet" (הנבא) in Ostracon XVI,5, whose name is legible only in the last part (הו-), which is, in truth, and ending common to many theophoric names.[160] Lines 5–6 should thus read: "And

---

158 It can also be seen in the book of Jeremiah that Zedekiah, perhaps because he was kept in check by the "leaders", does not ever act in an official way without them (except, in fact, in singular events such as the secret consultations with Jeremiah and his liberation from the cistern, an event that was however suggested by another court dignitary and not actualised by an independent initiative of the king). That the king Zedechiah would have sent official communication to his generals without or against the views of his ministers (who would then have written independently, presenting themselves as being against the directives or lines of the king) seems, in my opinion, entirely implausible.

159 This *forma defectiva* is attested in the only two clear occurrences of the term in the body of the "letters" (cf. Ost. III,20; XVI,5) even if, from the sixth century, use of the consonant *yod* as an internal *mater lectionis* is generally more frequent in the orthography of Hebrew epigraphy (cf. S.L. GOGEL, *A Grammar of Epigraphic Hebrew*, SBLRBS 23, Atlanta 1998, 73, 353).

160 Cf. H. TORCZYNER, *The Lachish Letters*, 117–119; 172–173; U. RÜTERSWÖRDEN, «Der Prophet in den Lachish-Ostraka», in: *Steine – Bilder – Texte*, 179–192.

176   Facing the might of the Babylonian empire

behold: the words *of the [prophet]* are not good."[161] This reconstruction is also accepted by other scholars, amongst whom J.C.L. Gibson and S.B. Parker.[162]

It is obvious that if the prophet were actually Jeremiah,[163] this hypothesis would accord perfectly with 38:4, as well as with the picture of the situation that emerges from the whole of the other pertinent Jeremianic texts. But that is not all. Even in the case that the correct reading be [שרם]ה and not [נאב]ה, to suppose that the subject of the problematic content of the letters of the officials and the king be not their own personal orientation, but rather a reference to the highly delicate oracle of a prophet requested by the king Zedekiah himself would seem to be in greater harmony with both the explicit and implicit elements of the ostracon in question.

In other words, I believe it is necessary to keep in the background what the book of Jeremiah refers to in various ways and on multiple occasions with regard not only to Zedekiah's (repeated or literarily duplicated) consultation with the prophet through his ministers,[164] in a context of a potential or concrete Babylonian threat (cf. 21:1–10; 27:12–15; 37:3–10), but also to what Jeremiah himself, since the first year of Zedekiah, proclaims and requests of the priests and all the people (cf. 27:16–17; 38:1–3). The king is and remains uncertain to the end (cf. 38:19), while his ministers do not appear to look well upon Jeremiah's words (cf. 37:11–16; 38:1, 4, 24–27). The fact remains that, given the officiality of the colloquy to which the words "not good" could refer, and considering the credit that Jeremiah had earned, despite all, due to the evidence of the facts (cf. 37:19), a certain number of defections (cf. 38:19; 39:9; 52:15), and the doubts of others (of the soldiers, above all; cf. 38:4), the king felt obliged to inform his closest collaborators in the field of what the last credible (however disturbing) prophetic word had proclaimed about the destiny of the city and of what YHWH was requesting (surrender).

There is another clue that leads me to propose this interpretation: the fact that some significant data that can be deduced from the ostracon can be related, according to my interpretation, not only to 38:4, but also to another quite similar circumstance attested in the book of Jeremiah. This is the reaction that the prophet's letter arouses amongst some *leaders* of the deportees in Babylon from 597 (cf. ch. 29). Here too, we have: (1) a message that is considered dangerous and subversive (29:28); (2) the fact that it is the message of a prophet (29:27) and that (3) this message has found a certain

---

161   Lines 5–6: [...] והנה. דברי . הנ[בא]ן/לא טבם.
162   Cf. J.C.L. Gibson, *Hebrew and Moabite Inscriptions,* TSSI 1, Oxford 1971, ²1973, 35–36.45; S.B. Parker «The Lachish Letters and Official Reactions to Prophecies», in: *Uncovering Ancient Stones.* Essays in Memory of H. Neil Richardson, *ed.* L.M. Hopfe, Winona Lake 1994, 76–78.
163   Whilst remaining, for the time being, an unverifiable conjecture (given the considerable number of Yahwist theophoric names ending the same way), this can still be posed, as is pointed out by e.g. R. Dussaud, «Le prophète Jérémie», 263, 269 (who actually practically takes the possibility as a given, observing how, in that historical context, only a prophet of the calibre of Jeremiah could have such a striking effect on the people and highest ranking authorities of the kingdom of Judah; cf. nevertheless Bar 2:20–23, which refers to "prophets") and A. Lemaire, «Prophètes et rois dans les inscriptions ouest-sémitiques (IXᵉ–VIᵉ siècle av. J.-C.)», in: *Prophètes et rois,* 113–114.
164   Very frequently in the book of Jeremiah, the figure of the king is associated with that of the "leaders"; cf. e.g. 1:18; 2:26; 4:9; 8:1; etc.

The City and its destiny, between resistance and surrender   177

degree of consideration amongst court circles, since it is brought and communicated to the exiles by the king's ministers themselves, and certainly not without his consent (29:1–3); (4) a reaction of disdain that is made explicit by the sending of harsh letters of protest (29:25b) to the competent authorities (in this case, the high priest, since it is not permissible to accuse the king directly[165]) with (5) a formal request that credit not be given to that line of thinking and that the "madman" prophet be silenced (29:26–27).

Similarly, in the case referred to in Ostracon VI, these could be the letters of the king and his ministers, in which the most important people in charge of the defence of the kingdom are informed both of Jeremiah's oracle and of the effects this was causing in Jerusalem (especially amongst the soldiers), and an opinion about this is requested, even if perhaps unwillingly on the part of the leaders, just as evidently unwillingly Pashhur son of Malchiah must have obeyed Zedekiah's order to go and consult Jeremiah on the king's behalf.[166]

Certainly, the king consults Jeremiah several times in secret (cf. 38:16, 24–27), interested in his own personal fate more than anything else. But without a doubt, everyone in Jerusalem would have known the prophet's message. It seems therefore probable, as J.C.L. Gibson argued,[167] that the reproach the officer requested be forwarded to the capital (cf. ll. 8–11) regard not so much the king's ministers (which is not very plausible) but rather the soldiers posted in the capital. These are the same soldiers who, just previously (in l. 7), are said to be becoming aware of the (deleterious) message in question and losing their courage and desire to fight. If, on the other hand, the attestation of the book of Jeremiah is to be considered reliable then, according to this, an exchange of correspondence between Jerusalem and the exiles in Babylon existed. In particular, some prominent figures in exile thousands of miles from Jerusalem were able to lodge formal complaints against the authorities of the capital. So then, it does not appear at all unlikely that a commander of Ya'uš's stature, responsible for the most important fortress after Jerusalem, and thus a fundamental bastion of the resistance against the enemy, could "scold" other branches of the army, inciting them to be disciplined and faithful to the king and nation.

E) A given fact

Aside from these interpretations of the clues at our disposal, which may have a variable degree of historical plausibility and can thus be more of less agreed upon (short of absolute and certain confirmation), it should be noted that at least one factor stands out as incontestable in any case, and it is good to keep it in mind for the study of my topic. In the few but precious fragments of military correspondence discovered at Lachish, the figure of a *prophet* is named with certainty at least twice. He is cited, moreover, using the definite article: "*the* prophet" (הנבא). That is, he is a figure who is well known to the interlocutors (cf. Ost. III,20; XVI,5). This attests the strict interaction

---

165   Which Ezekiel, on the other hand, does, and with unprecedented words (cf. Ezek 21:30–31), even if for entirely other reasons and apparently without there being any particular risks for his safety.

166   As is apparent from the fact that the same figure, in 38:1–4, after hearing the words of Jeremiah, asks along with the other dignitaries that he be condemned to death.

167   Cf. J.C.L. GIBSON, *Hebrew and Moabite Inscriptions*, 46, n. 9.

178 Facing the might of the Babylonian empire

he had with the military establishment and the royal institution, not only orally but also mediated through the channel of *written* communication.[168] So we find that what emerges clearly from the book of Jeremiah is confirmed without a shadow of a doubt by important (since contemporary and contextual) extrabiblical sources: for its diffusion, prophecy could make use of high-ranking intermediaries (and indeed, a network of Palatine officials involved in the monitoring of oracles concerning politico-military questions did exist).[169] And, for better or for worse, the word of the prophets played an *important role* in the court and highest state positions, carrying considerable political impact on the level of *military strategy* as well,[170] especially in the historical juncture leading to the end of the kingdom of Judah.[171]

This is a factor that, at least in this respect, moreover aligns biblical prophecy with the prophetic phenomenology attested even beyond the borders of Israel. The major political relevance attributed to the prophetic oracles by the officers and ministers of the king of the kingdom of Judah, in fact, finds a particular equivalence (and thus, confirmation) in the extrabiblical sphere. This can be seen especially in the Amorrean prophecies of the eighteenth century B.C. documented in the "Mari Letters",[172] in the Neo-Assyrian prophetism[173] of the seventh century, and in the inscriptions discovered in the Western-Semitic area[174] dating from a period that runs from the ninth to sixth centuries B.C. (the Moabite "Mesha Stele" from the second half of the ninth century B.C. comes to mind in particular). The same tendency was thus presumably common throughout the whole ancient Near East, as was pointed out by A. Lemaire[175]:

---

168 On the importance of letters as a form of (especially military) communication between the capital of Jerusalem and other areas of the kingdom of Judah, see N. Na'aman, «The Distribution of Messages in the Kingdom of Judah in Light of the Lachish Ostraca», *VT* 53 (2003) 169–180.

169 As is clearly emphasised by P. Merlo, «Il profetismo nel Vicino Oriente antico: panoramica di un fenomeno e difficoltà comparative», in: *Religione biblica e religione storica dell'antico Israele: un monopolio interpretativo nella continuità culturale*. Atti del XV Convegno di Studi Veterotestamentari (Fara Sabina, 10–12 Settembre 2007), *ed.* G.L. Prato, RStB 21, Bologna 2009, 81–82, also in reference to the shared context of other kingdoms of the ancient Near East.

170 While it may not be stated with certainty, prophets probably accompanied kings on their military expeditions as qualified members of their "divinatory staff" (cf. 1 Kgs 22:5–12).

171 Think of the propagation dynamics of the Jeremianic prophecy described in ch. 36.

172 Cf. A. Malamat, «Mari and the Bible: Some Patterns of Tribal Organization and Institutions», *JAOS* 82 (1962), 143–150; B. Parker, «Official Attitudes towards Prophecy at Mari and in Israel», *VT* 43 (1993) 50–68 (esp. p. 68); A. Malamat, *Mari and the Bible,* SHCANE 12, Leiden 1998; D. Charpin, «Prophètes et rois dans le Proche-Orient Amorrite», in: *Prophètes et rois,* 21–53; P. Merlo, «Il profetismo», 55–83 (above all, pp. 77–79.81–82).

173 Cf. P. Villard, «Les prophéties à l'époque Néo-Assyrienne», in: *Prophètes et rois,* 55–84.

174 Cf. A. Lemaire, «Prophètes et rois», 85–115.

175 A. Lemaire, *ed., Prophètes et rois,* 16.

The City and its destiny, between resistance and surrender   179

Le rapport prophète-roi est au cœur de la documentation extra-biblique actuellement disponible et celle-ci peut donc nous aider à jeter un regard neuf sur les relations des prophètes bibliques avec les rois d'Israël et de Juda.

3.2.1.2. Motivations

Much less complex than the study of the identity and political consistency of the supporters of Jeremiah and the option to "surrender" is the enucleation of the motives and convictions that might have been the foundations of a pro-Babylonian orientation. These elements can also easily be deduced from the historical framework that I have already illustrated. If we prescind from the reception of the motivations of an eminently theological-prophetic nature upon which Jeremiah's message is based, which we will have the opportunity to study in-depth later, we can trace the foundation of the pro-Babylonian option back to some simple but important factors:

1) the belief that from 605, the geopolitical scenario in the area had actually been transformed, in a way that was stable, in favour of the Babylonians;
2) a negative assessment of the staying power of its own military defence against the deployment of enemy forces;
3) distrust of the aid that was expected to come from Egypt. And, based on this,
4) an awareness that, once the pact of "vassalage" had been betrayed and the consequent military retaliation and siege of the capital had ensued, in order to minimise damages and avoid catastrophe, the only practicable choice was to either remain subjugated to Babylon or to surrender as soon as possible (as King Jehoiachin had already done in his time, in 597).

I will reserve an assessment of whether or not a pro-Babylonian orientation of the sort were opportune and its actual practicability for paragraph 3.3, which will be dedicated specifically to this question. What will be fundamental is the question of what relation this would have had to the real motivations underlying Jeremiah's request which, in my opinion, do not coincide in the least with those just listed, but which are instead of an entirely different nature.

3.2.2. The resistance option and its "prophets": Motivations and supporters

3.2.2.1. Motivations

For the "resistance" option, I will invert the perspective, placing a study of its possible motivations before an individuation of its propagators. In fact, before identifying the people or socio-politico-religious groups who, driven by a will to cast off the Babylonian yoke, become the promoters of a nationalistic, opportunistic pro-Egyptian government policy, it is necessary, in my view, to first bring into focus the characterising elements of the *flow of theo-political tradition* that had been inherited from the past and had crystallised into a whole series of widely diffused convictions (or manipulations?). During the time of Jeremiah, these led to generate deeply rooted, shared convictions, certainties that contributed to the perception that the Jeremianic proposal was inadmissible, and steered instead towards choices that would reveal to be dramatically wrong. After having retraced the history of the final years of the kingdom of Judah, the purely political motivations of the resistance seem evident to me. And I will subsequently recall these when I address the question of the "realism"

180 Facing the might of the Babylonian empire

of the Jeremianic proposal (§ 3.3). Of present interest is to make sense of what cannot be adequately expressed by a synthetic historical account, since it can only be derived from a careful reading of the texts.

A) "You must not serve the king of Babylon!" Opposing perspectives of שָׁלוֹם

The option advocated by Jeremiah, which, in precisely the eyes of the priests and prophets, seems particularly subversive (cf. 26:8, 11), since it lacks solid (or rather: evident) theological-traditional anchoring and is thus clearly contrary to the good of the state and the common sentiment of his fellow countrymen. These supporters of the opposition, dissimilarly, appear to be (or present themselves as being) in line with firmly established theological traditions. I will now try to demonstrate this by *drawing from facts provided in the book of Jeremiah*. I will also, however, integrate these in the final part with some interesting elements offered by the *book of Ezekiel* (cf. Ezek 8; 11). Threatening and announcing misfortune (the end of the kingdom, Jerusalem, and the temple), asking to look this straight-on and to submit to the foreign invader, while recognising the action of YHWH in all of this, in fact, results as being entirely incompatible with the optimistic prospects of national well-being, peace, prosperity, and political independence, of which the prophet's adversaries become propagators.

These perspectives find their synthetic expression in a term: שָׁלוֹם.[176] This refers to a concept that is central to the book of Jeremiah,[177] and around which decisive themes

---

176 It is impossible to convey the semantic amplitude of the term שָׁלוֹם in a single English vocabulary word, which must be rendered specifically on each use, depending on the different contexts of use. It nonetheless continues to remain somewhat elusive, even if only its fundamental basic semantic traits are considered, that is: well-being, peace, prosperity, etc. See e.g. the following lessicographical studies: G. VON RAD, «שָׁלוֹם im AT», *ThWNT* II, 400–405; G. GERLEMAN, «שלם», *THAT* II, 919–935; F.J. STENDEBACH, «שָׁלוֹם», *ThWAT* VIII, 12–46. In our own context, from the numerous textual areas of reference possible, it seems particularly pertinent to make reference to Lev 26:6, where by שָׁלוֹם, reference is made to the peace promised by YHWH to his people in the Promised Land, peace as safety from enemies and from every sort of threat (even natural ones), a condition of well-being and prosperity. Indeed, the prophets of שָׁלוֹם seem to clearly allude to a concrete state of political peace, a semantic accent that is common in Deuteronomy, in Deuteronomistic history, and in the work of the Chronicler. In any case, it should be kept in mind that the term שָׁלוֹם is tied to the idea of covenant and condition of stable peace that in a variety of contexts follows, and thus to an important term with which this concept is often lexicalised, that is, בְּרִית (see e.g. the expression בְּרִית שָׁלוֹם in Ezek 34:25; 37:26). שָׁלוֹם, therefore, as effect and consequence of a relationship of alliance with YHWH. But, as I have already said, on the lips of the false prophets, this alliance seems to subsist only as a unilateral guarantee of aid and not as an appeal to the freedom to remain within the confines of a concrete fidelity (observance of the commandments).

177 As notes G. FISCHER, *Jeremia 1–25*, 216, from amongst the books of the OT, it is precisely the book of Jeremiah that records the greatest number of reoccurrences of the term שָׁלוֹם (which is not to be identified, however, *tout-court* with the concept that it lexicalises): a good 31x in a total of 237 overall occurrences in the HB. It is also interesting to note that immediately following Jeremiah are Isaiah with 29x and the Psalter with 27x, that is, the books that attest more clearly than others the key pillars of that same theological current from which Jeremiah's adversaries take their inspiration.

The City and its destiny, between resistance and surrender 181

and counterposed hermeneutic paradigms revolve. In truth, Jeremiah also announces "peace" and "well-being" (שָׁלוֹם), but his is a "peace" that will come forth mysteriously from the womb of "misfortune" (רָעָה)[178] or from the "deadly" narrow passage of self-surrender to the enemy (cf. e.g.: 21:8–9; 29:11; 33:6, 9, 14; 46:27). And while his message poses the problem of apt discernment of what is truly the path of life and what is, instead, the path of death (cf. 21:8–10), his opponents alternatively promise שָׁלוֹם not as the effect of a choice of obedience and conversion, but as a unilateral gift of YHWH, independent of the concrete demands of Israel's faithfulness to the Covenant.[179]

Chapters 27–28 are emblematic in this respect, since they clearly highlight a frontal juxtaposition of the two positions[180]: that of Jeremiah versus that of Hananiah and the other (false) prophets (placed of the same level as other problematic mediating figures, such as dreamers, magicians, and sorcerers). The latter make themselves guarantors, in the name of YHWH, of an imminent and far too easy freedom:

> [9] So do not listen to your prophets, your diviners, your dreamers, your fortune-tellers, or to your sorcerers, who are telling you: 'You must not serve the king of Babylon!'. [...] [14] Do not listen to the words of the prophets who are telling you: 'You shall not serve the king of Babylon!'. It is a lie that they are prophesying to you! (27:9, 14).
> [1] That same year [...], Hananiah the prophet, son of Azzur, from Gibeon, said to me in the house of the Lord, in the sight of the priests and all the people: [2] "Thus says the Lord of Hosts, the God of Israel: 'I have broken the yoke of the king of Babylon! [3] Within two years I will restore to this place all the vessels of the house of the Lord which Nebuchadnezzar, king of Babylon, took from this place and carried away to Babylon.' [...]" (28:1–3; cf. vv. 4, 11).

B) "I will give you lasting peace (שָׁלוֹם אֱמֶת) in this place!" (14:13): Peace, temple, and palace in the unconditional safekeeping of YHWH?

These promises of freedom and liberation, which, during the reign of Zedekiah, seem to be directed *precisely* against Babylon (see also 37:19) and appear to exalt, in a completely "orthodox" way, the benevolence of YHWH towards his people, are actually the explicitation or actualisation of *more general promises of peace and prosperity*. These constitute the *Leitmotiv* of the same prophets (and not only) *at the time of Jehoiakim* (or Josiah) *as well*, that is, when Babylon had not yet even appeared upon the Syrian-Palestinian political scene.[181] This can be easily deduced from texts like the following:

---

178 See e.g. 29:10–14.
179 The most immediately relevant texts for reflection on the topic are: 4:10; 6:14(//8:11); 14:13, 15, 19; 23:17; 27:9, 14; 28:2–4, 11; 30:5.
180 Cf. ch. I, § 4.2.2, n. 132.
181 I interpret thus the literary motif of the "enemy from the North", as opposed to B CHILDS, «The Enemy from the North and the Chaos Tradition», *JBL* 78 (1959) 187–198 (= in: *A Prophet to the Nations. Essays in Jeremiah Studies*, eds. L.G. PERDUE – B W. KOVACS, Winona Lake 1984, 151–161), who considers the oracles in chs. 4–6 as having an exilic provenience.

182 Facing the might of the Babylonian empire

[13] Small and great alike, they are all greedy for unjust gain; from prophet to priest, all act falsely. [14] With palliative measures,[182] they have treated the wound of my people carelessly, saying: "Peace, peace!" (שָׁלוֹם שָׁלוֹם), though there is no peace (וְאֵין שָׁלוֹם) (6:13–14;//8:11; cf. also 30:5 and Ezek 13:10, 16).

Then I said, "Ah! Lord God, here are the prophets saying to them continually, 'You shall not see the sword; famine shall not befall you, for I will give you lasting peace (שְׁלוֹם אֱמֶת) in this place (בַּמָּקוֹם הַזֶּה) [...].' " (14:13).

They say continually to those who despise the word of the Lord, "Peace (שָׁלוֹם) shall be yours"; And to everyone who walks in the hardness of heart, they insist, "No evil shall come upon you" (23:17).

Based precisely on the elements highlighted thus far, I can propose a clear identification of the traditional theological vein into which these expectations were principally grafted. These elements represent important clues that suggest we turn our attention towards an important factor: the connection between the proclamation of שָׁלוֹם and the *cultic world*,[183] in turn connected to the *Davidic monarchical institution*.

C) Zion: The inviolable city, prey to a deceptive theology

While an allusion to it can probably already be recognised in 14:13,[184] it is in the emblematic expression in 7:4b (in reference to the literary and thematic contexts of 7:1–15 and ch. 26) that the ideology with which the Jeremianic message so strongly collides emerges[185]:

The temple of the Lord (הֵיכַל יְהוָה), the temple of the Lord (הֵיכַל יְהוָה); this is the temple of the Lord! ([186]הֵיכַל יְהוָה הֵמָּה).

---

182   I render the adverbial form of the MT עַל־נְקַלָּה; thus, interpreting it more liberally, so it functions within the context. Literally, it would sound: "lightly".

183   In this regard, see J.P. SISSON, «Jeremiah and the Jerusalem Conception of Peace», *JBL* 105 (1986) 429–442.

184   Consider the expression בַּמָּקוֹם הַזֶּה ("in this place"). Although the term מָקוֹם seems to undergo a semantic dilatation in the book of Jeremiah with respect to the Deuteronomistic literature committed to valorising a single Jerusalemite place of worship (see M. LEUCHTER, «The Temple Sermon and the Term מקום in the Jeremianic Corpus», *JSOT* 30 [2005] 93–109), it is not to be ruled out that in the last part of v. 13 there be a tie between the proclamation of שָׁלוֹם and the religious dimension evoked by the temple (בַּמָּקוֹם הַזֶּה) and then extended to the whole "country" (אֶרֶץ) of Judah as land given by YHWH to the fathers by virtue of the promise (cf. 7:3, 7).

185   Whilst the term שָׁלוֹם does not appear, it is clear that it (and the concept to which it refers) remains in the background, given that Jeremiah counters this announcement precisely with the destruction of the temple, and thus the end of the שָׁלוֹם strictly tied to the temple of Solomon and promises concerning his dynasty (cf. 1 Chr 22:9–10).

186   The unusual use of the plural הֵמָּה could refer to the different elements of the temple structure (with a particular allusion perhaps not only to the chambers and other rooms in the temple complex, but to the three principal parts of which it was composed), or rather, according to A.D. CORRÉ, « *'elle, hemma* = sic», *Bib.* 54 (1973) 263–264, it would be no more than the Hebrew equivalent of the Latin *sic*, indicative that the foregoing is not an error of the copyist, but a faithful reproduction of the original (in this case, the triple repetition may have appeared to be an dittographical error).

The attempt Jeremiah's prophetic word insists on making to reveal the lie and false securities (cf. the use of the root בטח in 7:13) seems to reach one of its culminations, on both a communicative and dramatic level, in the famous speech at the temple. The clash is, in fact, a frontal one, and its perversion is of the most devious and nefarious nature – that which camouflages itself in worship and feeds on the sacred. The priests and prophets, above all, obsessively repeat this slogan (or formula),[187] undoubtedly exercising an important mediating function "in favour" of the people and, subsequently, providing a solid ideological foundation for the monarchical institution. The evident reference is to the two fundamental pillars of the Yahwist faith of the kingdom of Judah[188]: the *election of Zion* and the *Davidic dynasty*. This is demonstrated explicitly in 8:19b, an eloquent text to this effect, which permits a retrospective look at the pre-exilic convictions on the matter (probably in reference to the traumatic experience of 597)[189]:

> Listen! The cry of the daughter of my people, far and wide in the land! "Is the Lord no longer in Zion, is her King no longer in her midst?" [...] (cf. also 14:8–9).

The abode of YHWH in Zion, the Davidic king as its eternal representative: It is from this sacralising matrix that the so-called *theology of the inviolability of Zion*[190] takes shape. Otherwise attested and developed by more than a few texts of the prophet Isaiah (cf. e.g. 8:9–10; 14:28–32; 17:12–14; 29:1–8; 31:4–5) and of the book of Psalms,[191] it was surely corroborated by the narrow escape from the Assyrian threat in 701 under

---

    For other hypothetical solutions, see A. Aguilera, «La fórmula "Templo de Yahvé, Templo de Yahvé, Templo de Yahvé" en Jer 7,4», *EstBib* 47 (1989) 324–325.

187   As this text is usually regarded; cf. W. McKane, *Jeremiah*, I, 160.

188   Not dissimilar in its underlying elements from monarchical theology typical of the ancient Near East.

189   Cf. T.A. Rudnig, «"Ist denn Jahwe nicht auf dem Zion?" (Jer 8,19). Gottes Gegenwart im Heiligtum», *ZThK* 104 (2007) 267–286.

190   On this subject, from amongst the many contributions, see esp.: J.H. Hayes, «The Tradition of Zion's Inviolability», *JBL* 82 (1963) 419–426; R.E. Clements, *Isaiah and the Deliverance of Jerusalem*. A Study of the Interpretation of Prophecy in the Old Testament, JSOT.S 13, Sheffield 1980, 72–89; J.J.M. Roberts, «Zion in the Theology of the Davidic-Solomonic Empire», in: *Studies in the Period of David and Solomon and Other Essays*. Papers Read at the International Symposium for Biblical Studies, Tokyo, 5–7 december, 1979, *ed.* T. Ishida, Tokio 1982, 93–108; M. Weinfeld, «Zion and Jerusalem as Religious and Political Capital: Ideology and Utopia», in: *The Poet and The Historian*. Essays in Literary and Historical Biblical Criticism, *ed.* R.E. Friedman, HSS 26, Chico 1983, 75–115; Ben C. Ollenburger, *Zion, the City of the Great King*. A Theological Symbol of the Jerusalem Cult, JSOT.S 41, Sheffield 1987; B. Ockinga, «The Inviolability of Zion – a Pre-Israelite Tradition?», *BN* 44 (1988) 54–60; W.M. Schniedewind, *Society* (above all, pp. 104–105); L.J. Hoppe, *The Holy City*. Jerusalem in the Theology of the Old Testament, Collegeville 2000, 37–38; J.J.M. Roberts, «Solomon's Jerusalem and the Zion Tradition», in: *Jerusalem in Bible and Archaeology*. The First Temple Period, *eds.* A.G. Vaughn – A.E. Killebrew, SBLSymS 18, Atlanta 2003, 163–170; W.J. Wessels, «Zion, Beautiful City of God. Zion Theology in the Book of Jeremiah», *VerEcc* 27 (2006) 729–748.

191   Cf. B. Uffenheimer, «The Religious Experience of the Psalmists and the Prophetic Mind», *Immanuel* 21 (1987) 7–27.

184 Facing the might of the Babylonian empire

Hezekiah (handed down as a prodigious fact in 2 Kgs 18:13–20, 19; Isa 36–39)[192] and by the undeniable fact that, unlike the other large and powerful cities of the Syrian-Palestinian strip, it was universally evident that Jerusalem, all said and done, had never suffered devastation[193] since the time of its founding as capital of the kingdom (which, in reference to the destruction of Samaria and the promises made to David, Deuteronomistic historiography does not miss the opportunity to note; cf. 1 Kgs 11:13, 36; 15:4; 2 Kgs 8:19; 19:34; 21:4).[194]

One can consider, more generally speaking, that trust in a deity actually means trust in their temple. Even in Amos 9:10, the certainty of not being affected by misfortune is to be tied to the sanctuary (cf. Amos 9:1) as a place of refuge. In this case, the sanctuary would be that of Bethel, but it should be remembered that throughout the ancient Near East, the destruction of a temple or statue of the deity that dwelt there (or even its deportation) was recognised as the defeat of that deity itself by a more powerful god.[195]

At the time of Jeremiah, a sort of "crazed theology", most likely emphasised by the reform of Josiah, had derived from this complex political-religious amalgamation. And it had become a shield amongst those who were most resistant to the appeals for conversion pronounced in the name of that God himself who was supposed to *unilaterally* guarantee the certainties of this powerful (albeit fragile) ideological structure.

It seems appropriate to make a brief note in this regard. Once the Jebusite Jerusalem is conquered, its fortress (Zion) becomes the "city of David" (2 Sam 5:6–10). From that point on, Jerusalem (Zion) and its sovereign are firmly associated with the presence of YHWH, the great king (not only of Israel, but of the nations as well), and his

---

192 Herodotus himself (*Historiae*, II,141; HERODOTUS, *The Persian Wars*, I, 446–449) seems to invoke at least an echo of this tradition (though in relation to another context, which is the failure of an Assyrian attack against the Egyptians due to a nocturnal invasion of rodents in their field).

193 In relation to the period of destructive military campaigns by the Assyrians, M.L. STEINER, «Expanding Borders: The Development of Jerusalem in the Iron Age», in: *Jerusalem in Ancient History and Tradition*, ed. T.L. THOMPSON, JSOT.S 381, London – New York 2003, 68–79, notes that Jerusalem: "[...] was the only town in the wide region that had not been taken by the mighty Assyrians. It had grown to huge dimensions, mainly because of the many refugees fleeing to this 'safe haven'. All economic and political power of the country was concentrated within its walls. This 'special status', in so many respects, could have given rise to a change in religious significance and importance as well" (here, p. 79).

194 It is interesting to observe that according to Thucydides (*Historiae*, V,112.2), a similar motivation (similar also in its expectation of outside aid) drives the inhabitants of Melos to refuse the calls to surrender put forth by the Athenians, and spurs them towards opting to resist their siege to the bitter end: "Athenians, we see no reason to change our original decision. Nor in a few short minutes are we about to deprive of its freedom a city that has now been inhabited for 700 years. Instead, we will put our trust in the good fortune we owe to the gods, which has protected our city thus far, and in the help of our fellow men, particularly the Spartans, and so seek our salvation"; translation by J. Mynott (THUCYDIDES, *The War of the Peloponnesians and the Athenians*. Edited and Translated by J. MYNOTT, CTHPT, Cambridge 2013, 384). I will return to the case of the siege of Melos in § 3.3.2.5.

195 I will take the matter back up in ch. VI § 4.3.4, n. 126 and 127 (with bibliography).

The City and its destiny, between resistance and surrender   185

gratuitous election. More than a few texts aim to legitimise the Davidic tradition (cf. 1 Sam 16:14–2 Sam 5:12), but the essential element remains the transportation of the Ark (2 Sam 6) and subsequent conception and construction of the temple on the area that had become, for this very reason, "holy mount Zion" (cf. e.g. Ps 2:6; 78:68; 87:1; etc.), together with the unconditional promises concerning the eternal stability of the house of David (cf. 2 Sam 7).

Perhaps drawing on local Canaanite traditions related to the god 'El[196] (cf. e.g. Ps 46; 48; 76) or in any case, a theological motif common in the ancient Near East,[197] Zion comes to assume a symbolic meaning of cosmic proportions. This identifies it as a stable residence of the divine (cf. Ps 9:12; 74:2) having invincible power over all enemy forces (both those of Chaos and those earthly), of which even the Davidic king benefits, becoming (at least theoretically) the visible sign of YHWH's benevolence and right-eousness towards his people. The mythical literary motif of YHWH's victory over the indistinct forces of primordial Chaos, this also having extrabiblical parallels,[198] could be found in the preaching of Isaiah,[199] but within the context of precise entities and international political manoeuvres (cf. e.g. Isa 14:24–32; 17:12–14; 28:14–22; 29:1–8; 30:27–33; 31:1–8; 33:20–24). It is precisely through the prism of this tradition, adopted and distorted by personal interests and convictions,[200] that the theological paradigm dominating the days of Jeremiah seems to establish itself. This paradigm had already been attested and fought by Micah (Mic 3, 5:11–12), whose antagonistic message (Mic 3:12) is also recalled in 26:18 and placed alongside that of the prophet from Anathoth.

This powerful ideological base must be placed in relation to the awareness that, once the rebellion was decided upon and the foreseeable Babylonian reaction trig-gered, in the event of defeat (thought to be "impossible"), the least to be expected

---

196 This is a theory of F.M. CROSS, *Canaanite Myth and Hebrew Epic. Essays in the History of the Religion of Israel*, Cambridge (MA) 1973, ⁹1997.

197 For the well-known parallels of this motif, see e.g. R.J. CLIFFORD, *The Cosmic Mountain in Canaan and the Old Testament*, HSM 4, Cambridge (MA) 1972; K. KOCH, «Ḥazzi-Ṣafôn-Kasion: Die Geschichte eines Berges und seiner Gottheiten», in: *Religionsgeschichtliche Beziehungen zwischen Kleinasien, Nordsyrien und dem Alten Testament*. Internationales Symposion, Hamburg, 17.-21. März 1990, eds. E. JANOWSKI – K. KOCH – G. WILHELM, OBO 129, Freiburg – Göttingen 1993, 171–223.

198 Also in the context of the ancient Near East; cf. J. DAY, *God's Conflict with the Dragon and the Sea. Echoes of a Canaanite Myth in the Old Testament*, Cambridge 1985.

199 For the importance of the "theology of Zion" in Isaiah, see G. VON RAD, *Theologie des Alten Testaments*. Band II: Die Theologie der prophetischen Überlieferungen Israels, München 1960, ⁷1980, 162–175 and also C.R. SEITZ, *Zion's Final Destiny. The Development of the Book of Isaiah. A Reassessment of Isaiah 36–39*, Minneapolis 1991, about which, along the lines of the relevant observations by J.J.M. ROBERTS, «Solomon's Jerusalem», 164–166, with regard to the evident pre-existence of fun-damental elements of the theology of Zion with respect to its Isaianic use, it seems unfounded to me to believe that this be born only following the Assyrian withdrawal in 701, as C.R. Seitz instead sustains on p. 146.

200 In fact, it is incorrect to assert, as does W.L. HOLLADAY, *Isaiah: A Scroll of a Prophetic Heritage*, Grand Rapids 1978, 121, that the message of Jeremiah presents itself as directly antithetical to that of Isaiah (which is actually ultimately informed by an authentic relationship with YHWH founded on obedient trust; cf. e.g. Isa 7,9b), as if the two positions were diametrically opposed.

186   Facing the might of the Babylonian empire

would have been that of another massive and possibly definitive deportation. For the nationalist conscience of Israel (in this respect, the same as other states of the ancient Near East, that is, one founded on the indivisibility between national God, the people, and the land[201] and, I would add, the Davidic dynasty), this would have meant the dissolution of its national identity and end of its traditions.

D) Where the desire for good meets the power of seduction.
    The prophet's lamentation

From at least one other text, we can deduce that these repeated, persistent proclamations and their "prophets" had a *profoundly pervasive and persuasive power* precisely because they were rooted in a widely accepted theological tradition (or widely confused one, even under the name of Isaiah[202]). In this text, Jeremiah himself, according to my interpretation, seems shocked at how much freedom of action even YHWH seems to have granted them, as if falling into the seduction's deception were almost inevitable for anyone:

> Then I said[203]: "Ah! Lord God, how utterly have you deceived these people and Jerusalem when you said: 'Peace (שָׁלֹם) be with you', while the sword was coming for our throats?" (4:10).

The prophet shows solidarity with his people (see also 8:21–23) to such an extent that we can sense the presence of a painful scission within his own soul, a laceration produced by two opposing poles of attraction: on the one hand, the compelling duty to remain faithful to his solitary mission, felt to be an inescapable necessity urging him, against everyone, to proclaim the misfortune threatened by YHWH (cf. 15:16–17; 20:9); on the other, his deep desires that seem to induce him, on what we could call an unconscious or subconscious level, to accede to the hope announced by the other prophets in the name of the same YHWH. It is as if, deep down, he would prefer to believe that YHWH's true word could be found on the lips of the other prophets rather than on his own. Indeed, the pronouncement of the end/disaster seems to essentially contradict the divine promise. And yet, those hopes of שָׁלֹם, almost heard by Jeremiah himself as coming from YHWH, would turn out to be nothing but cruel deceptions.

---

201   For study on this topic, see D.I. BLOCK, *The Gods of the Nations*. Studies in Ancient Near Eastern National Theology, ETSMS 2, Jackson 1988.

202   About the different positions of Isaiah and Jeremiah on the role of Jerusalem and Zion, see the note by G. FISCHER, «Partner oder Gegner? Zum Verhältnis von Jesaja und Jeremia», in: ID., *Der Prophet wie Mose*. Studien zum Jeremiabuch, BZAR 15, Wiesbaden 2011, 188–199 (= in: F. HARTENSTEIN – M. PIETSCH, eds., *"Sieben Augen auf einem Stein" [Sach 3,9]*. Festschrift für Ina Willi-Plein zum 65. Geburtstag, Neukirchen 2007, 69–79), on p. 198.

203   W. Rudolph, curator of the BHS's critical apparatus for the book of Jeremiah, leaning on the LXX of the Codex Alexandrinus (which has καὶ εἶπαν instead of καὶ εἶπα) and to the Arabic version, suggests amending the verb וָאֹמַר (I said) to be וְאָמְרוּ ("they will say", or "they say"). This would attribute the phrase, as *would seem* more logical, not to Jeremiah but to the false prophets. Along with the majority of the modern versions and the commentators (e.g. W.L. HOLLADAY, *Jeremiah 1*, 155; G. FISCHER, *Jeremia 1–25*, 216), I believe this amendment to be unjustifiable and prefer to opt for the MT, insofar as it be *lectio difficilior* supported by all the other versions.

The City and its destiny, between resistance and surrender 187

This all seems strictly tied to the theme of denied intercession (cf. 14:1–15:9).[204] Indeed, if the text of 14:19 were to express a thought of Jeremiah's as well,[205] this would do none other than repeat, for the purpose of intercession, those very same words that in 8:15 seem to express the painful lamentation of the people,[206] whose bitterness is directly proportional to the credit bestowed on the pronouncements of peace and healing inherited from the memory of those who had heard the ancient and *true* prophets:

> We hoped for peace (שָׁלוֹם), but no good (טוֹב) has come; for a time of healing (עֵת מַרְפֵּה), but terror is here instead! (8:15; cf. also 13:16).
> Have you rejected Judah completely? Is Zion loathsome to you? Why have you struck us a blow that cannot be healed? We hoped for peace, but no good has come; for a time of healing, but terror is here instead! (14:19).

Here, the concept of the time (or moment) of "healing" (מַרְפֵּא/מַרְפֵּה)[207] alludes to the "personification of the recipient nation of plagues, wounds, beatings, infirmities, which, taken figuratively, are the wars and what they involve: devastation, desolation, and extermination, together with the great affliction, material and moral, of all the inhabitants".[208] Probably echoing behind this concept are promises transmitted from other traditions and ancient texts, e.g. Isa 30:26 and especially Hos 6:1–2 (in relation to Hos 5:13), as well as Hos 7:1; 11:3; 14:5, in which the "healing" intervention of YHWH in favour of the people is promised. Jeremiah takes up the same concept, but reference is being made to a healing that takes place, in this case as well, through the crucible of misfortune and an effective re-establishment of justice carried out through the recognition and forgiveness of sins (cf. 30:17; 33:6–8).

---

204 On this theme, see B. ROSSI, *L'intercessione nel tempo della fine*. Studio dell'intercessione profetica nel libro di Geremia, AnBib 204, Roma 2013.

205 But the attribution here is dubious, as it could be simply the voice of the people or that of their mediators before YHWH, that is, of the "prophet and priest" who, in the context immediately preceding v. 18c, are presented as being prey to a state of confusion, consequence of their incomprehension of the logic underlying the historical action of YHWH.

206 According to the suggestive interpretation of S. MANFREDI, «Il tempo della guarigione. Studio della radice RP' "curare, guarire" in *Ier* 8,11.15.22», *Ho Theologos* 3 (1985) 214–220, also the text of 8:14–15 which, on first impression seems to refer to the people (cf. אֲנַחְנוּ of v. 14a), would express the deep solidarity of Jeremiah with his people. His extreme attempt at intercession as "vicarious" recognition of sin (cf. כִּי חָטָאנוּ לַיהוָה at the end of v. 14) gets repudiated, however, by YHWH, since it lacks analogous, corresponding behaviour on the part of the people (v. 15).

207 Due to its being attributable to two distinct verbal roots, the substantive מַרְפֵּא/מַרְפֵּה can have two different meanings. Translating it as "healing", I believe it derives from √רפא (as suggested by W.L. HOLLADAY, *Jeremiah 1*, 292), and considering the immediate context (cf. vv. 17.22), this seems to be the most pertinent. The second possibility is not extraneous to that semantic horizon, however, since in other contexts, the term in question seems to signify "calm, rest, quiet", deriving from √רפה (in this direction, ZORRELL, 475 [*remissio = lenitas, mansuetudo*] and *HALAT*, 345, in reference to Prov 14:30; 15:4; Eccl 10:4).

208 Translated from S. MANFREDI, «Il tempo», 209.

188 Facing the might of the Babylonian empire

E) "Ask the pathways of old!" (6:16): Taking on history in a way that is prophetic so that there can continue to be a history

It is thus undoubtedly from this theological horizon having strong roots in tradition that Jeremiah's adversaries draw the lifeblood of their convictions and consequent anti-Babylonian propagandistic activities. So it might seem surprising that Jeremiah himself, in the context of his act of prophetic accusation in 6:16, specifically demands to stand by the roads (cf. 48:19) and to inquire (cf. 30:6) about "the pathways of *old*" (וְשַׁאֲלוּ לִנְתִבוֹת עוֹלָם),[209] in order to take the right road that will lead to "rest" (מַרְגּוֹעַ).[210] That same idolatrous practice can indeed boast a long history, as can be clearly recognised in 18:15, which likewise speaks of "ancient ways" (שְׁבִילֵי עוֹלָם). Jeremiah could actually also be posing an ironic question, like those expressed in 2:10 and 30:6. The invitation to read up on something universally known (the infidelity of the fathers and the disastrous consequences of this) or, on the contrary, something impossible, suggests a specific literary modality (cf. also Deut 4:32; Amos 3:9; Lam 1:12). I believe that regardless, an interpretation that reads a positive perspective on the past into the Jeremianic words be preferable, along the same lines upon which the great *rîb* of Jer 2 opens. Here, the present crisis of the relationship between YHWH and his people is stigmatised in light of the love in the beginnings.

So to read up on the pathways of old is an invitation to conduct an act of reading of tradition that is quite different from that which is most common (cf. also Job 8:8) and reassuring. It is a way that is, no doubt, *prophetic*. For Jeremiah, in fact, it is not possible to speak of שָׁלוֹם irrespective of the requirements of fidelity to the Covenant (cf. 22:15). Indeed, neither well-being nor peace (שָׁלוֹם; טוֹב) can be expected without justice and righteousness (מִשְׁפָּט וּצְדָקָה). But this, in reality, was also true for Isaiah (cf. e.g. 9:5–6), on whom the prophets of שָׁלוֹם seem to draw in a way that is only partial and selective (cf. Isa 26:1–12).

Some commentators[211] see the vicissitudes of the people of YHWH as having two "stories" or traditional visions of the world running through them: the originating one of the kingdom of the North based on the centrality of the Mosaic Covenant and

---

209 Depending on its context of use, the term עוֹלָם can refer to the past (cf. e.g. 5:15) or even to a future time (and in this case, it is expressed in English as "everlasting, eternal, eternity"; cf. e.g. 32:40). In our case, as aptly noted by J.R. LUNDBOM, *Jeremiah 1–20*, 435, it clearly seems to refer to the ancient path of liberation of the Exodus (cf. 2:2) and consequently, to the norms of the Mosaic Covenant as the path to benediction (G. FISCHER, *Jeremia 1–25*, 273, prefers to translate it instead as "Pfade der Ewigkeit", as was similarly already done by B. DUHM, *Jeremia*, 70). Turning to the past in view of the present has a clear sapiential function also in Deut 4:32; 32:7 (and in this sense, it is clearly a past that has an "eternal" value). See also the discussion in J. BOU RAAD, *Malheur annoncé, malheur dénoncé. Étude rhétorique de Jérémie 6*, Amchit [Lebanon] 2008, 225–228.

210 This term is a *hapax legomenon* in the HB, but on the basis of the analogous מַרְגֵּעָה in Isa 28:12 (cf. also לְהַרְגִּיעַ in Jer 31:2), the most probable meaning in the context, according to W.L. HOLLADAY, *Jeremiah 1*, 221, is that of "national security" with respect to potential external threats.

211 See e.g. W.L. HUMPHREYS, *Crisis and Story. An Introduction to the Old Testament*, Mountain View 1990; W. BRUEGGEMANN, *Old Testament Theology. Essays on Structure, Theme, and Text*, ed. P.D. MILLER, Minneapolis 1992, 273–278.

The City and its destiny, between resistance and surrender 189

its demands for justice and fidelity, and that of the kingdom of the South, centred around the election of the Davidic dynasty and Zion as determinative factors of order and institutional cohesion. If this is so, then we can say that in the book of Jeremiah, these two hermeneutical perspectives of the history of Israel slam into each other in a certain sense, in a violent collision. Not to eliminate each other, but to fuse together and be purified. To be fully valorised as completely new, a novelty requiring that something end, and in the most radical way. Zion and its temple will be destroyed (cf. 6:1–8; 8:14–23; 21:10; etc.), the Davidic dynasty will end (cf. 22:30), and the Covenant written on tablets of stone guarded in the holy Ark will also give way (cf. 3:16) to an unusual "new Covenant" (cf. 31:31–34), something entirely new.

F) Recalibrating the balance of the hermeneutic framing based on Ezek 8

As I programmatically pointed out at the beginning of the paragraph, my reconstruction has been based primarily on the study of elements presented in the book of Jeremiah and subsequently in other related texts of direct interest to achieve a plausible identification of the theological-traditional grounding of the prophet's opponents. The completion of this overall picture, however, requires another series of data inferable from ch. 8 of the book of Ezekiel.[212] Indeed, looking closely at this text, some valuable indications emerge. These lead to the discovery and radicalisation of a question that, whilst per se already evident in the Jeremianic corpus, would otherwise be destined to remain if not obscured then certainly underestimated, at least in regard to my theme. The question is that of idolatry.

In fact, if we unequivocally identify the theology of the inviolability of Zion as the most fitting hermeneutical key to account for the prevailing anti-Babylonian orientation, then we risk, while hardly noticing it except consequentially, drawing a sketch of the Yahwist faith (in the kingdom of Judah under the reign of Zedekiah) that is exaggeratedly orthodox (albeit only from a formal point of view, as we have seen) and substantially incompatible with the picture provided instead by the prophetic preaching of Jeremiah, in which accusations of idolatry have a decidedly fundamental importance. The question is thus a simple one: if the theology of Zion founded on the faith in YHWH had such an important role, then what about all those fully-fledged idolatrous cults (and their socio-political implications) that endured or reflourished after the failure of the reform of Josiah and which the prophet explicitly and vehemently condemned? How are hopes of a Yahwist matrix (albeit false or more or less deliberately misunderstood) to be reconciled with the practice of idolatrous cults that were prevalent across all strata of the population?

An attempt at a response that recalibrates or completes this analysis is possible on precisely the basis of Ezek 8. Following the prophet Ezekiel through his visions, which, in four successive moments, reveal the harsh truth about the sin of the "House of Judah" (Ezek 8:17), we witness a ruthless description of the prevailing religious syncretism, well known to Jeremiah, rooted right in the heart of Yahwist worship, the

---

212 Cf. H. LEENE, «Blowing the Same Shofar: An Intertextual Comparison of Representations of the Prophetic Role in Jeremiah and Ezekiel», in: *The Elusive Prophets*. The Prophet as Historical Person, Literary Character and Anonymous Artist, *ed.* J.C. DE MOOR, OTS 45, Leiden 2001, 175–198.

190 Facing the might of the Babylonian empire

Holy City, and the temple of Jerusalem[213] (as had already been denounced by Jeremiah; cf. e.g. 1:16; 7:9; 8:30; etc.).

Directly at the entrance to the inner courtyard of the sanctuary[214] of YHWH, the prophet Ezekiel is shown the first abominable scene, cause for the Lord's departure from his elected residence: the "idol of jealousy" (סֵמֶל הַקִּנְאָה), identifiable most probably with the goddess Asherah (cf. 2 Kgs 21:7;//2 Cr 33:7),[215] and therefore, according to some scholars, with the "Queen of Heaven" (מְלֶכֶת הַשָּׁמַיִם)[216] in Jer 7:18; 44:17, 18, 19, 25, the fertility cults of Canaan (Ezek 8:3, 5), and the re-established "peaceful" cohabitation within the Yahwist faith (cf. 2 Kgs 23:6). Continuing on, we are led to a secret room of the Templar complex decorated with therianthropic figures, where seventy men are seen dedicating themselves to cultual practices probably of Egyptian derivation. Amongst them, standing upright, almost as if presiding over the liturgy, is Jaazaniah, a son of Shaphan. He is a symbol of the failure of Josiah's reform, since Shaphan and his family had specifically assumed responsibility for its demands for purity. Upon entering the temple courtyard, instead, there is a natural cult, clearly of Sumerian-Assyrian-Babylonian origin: women who "mourn Tammuz" (a Mesopotamian deity linked to the seasonal cycles). Meanwhile, in the innermost part of the sanctuary, twenty-five men can be seen with their backs turned to the Holy of Holies, adoring the sun (which is rising). Scholars discuss whether a solar cult of Egyptian origin is to be seen represented here, if it is a reference to the Babylonian god Shamash, or if it is, instead, a "solarisation" of the cult of YHWH. In any case, it is important to observe that the spread of violence and abuse in Jerusalem is shown as being closely linked to these cultual acts.

This striking syncretistic religious scenario and the degeneration of the social fabric founded on relations of fairness and justice accord well with Jeremiah's oracles of accusation and lead us to consider the theology of the inviolability of Zion, though derived from authentic Yahwist faith, as *one of the various ingredients* (while, in all probability, the most important) of this magma of multiform religiosity, also characterised by contradictory elements. Indeed, it is very interesting to highlight what is put on the lips of the "elders of the house of Israel" in Ezek 8:12 at a time when the scene, in the flux of the moveable laws of dreamlike representations, seems to pass from the single great hall into the symbolic secret room of the idolatrous heart of each of the elders of Israel:

---

213 Cf. W. Eichrodt, *Der Prophet Hesekiel*, ATD 22, Göttingen 1966, 58–64; W. Zimmerli, *Ezechiel*, I; 215–222; 230–246; M. Greenberg, *Ezekiel 1–20*, AncB 22, Garden City 1983, 164–173; D.I. Block, *The Book of Ezekiel*. Chapters 1–24, NICOT, Grand Rapids 1997, 276–300.

214 Or at the city gate entrance, as intended by W. Zimmerli, *Ezechiel*, I, 238.

215 Cf. W. Eichrodt, *Hesekiel*, 58–59.

216 According to W.L. Holladay, on the other hand, considering the kind of food offering talked about in Jer 7:18 and 44:19 (the כַּוָּנִים, i.e. the "sacrificial cakes"), this can be identified with that used in the cult of the Assyrian-Babylonian goddess Ishtar/Astarte, and this would be her Palestinian manifestation. But other identifications are possible (cf. W.L. Holladay, *Jeremiah 1*, 254–255).

The City and its destiny, between resistance and surrender   191

Have you seen, son of man, what the elders of the house of Israel are doing in the dark, each in the secret chamber of his idol? They say: "The Lord cannot see us,[217] the Lord has forsaken the land".

Here, we are in direct opposition to the ideology of Zion's inviolability. These words and their cynical bent could perhaps be explained as mistrust generated by the events of 597 (cf. Jer 8:19–20; Ezek 9:9). A potentially Egyptian origin of the cults cited by Ezekiel might then, at first glance, suggest an anti-Babylonian tendency in this class of public figures clearly having political influence. It is as if the defence of Zion, once the national deity's failure had been established, had been devolved to the powerful deities of Egypt. But this is only an indemonstrable theory, since such practices, like the cults of Mesopotamian extraction themselves could, more than defer to specific power groups that were politically orientated in one sense or another (pro-Egypt or pro-Babylon), simply be the legacy of previous cultual (and cultural) contaminations, and have no particular contingent political significance whatsoever.[218]

---

217   Cf. instead Jer 7:11: "Has this house which bears my name become in your eyes a den of thieves? *I have seen it for myself!* (רָאִיתִי הִנֵּה אָנֹכִי גַּם). Oracle of the Lord."

218   Along these same lines, the interpretation proposed by W. EICHRODT, *Hesekiel*, 67–69, does not seem to be credible. He holds that a politically significant relationship can be identified between the cultural matrix of idolatric practices and the political orientation of their followers. According to this reading, the group devoted to the cults of Egyptian origin (cf. Ezek 8:11) would thus be ascribable to the anti-Babylonian faction. The evidence would consist in the secrecy of the liturgy officiated in the "darkness" (cf. Ezek 8:12: בַּחֹשֶׁךְ), that is, within a context presumably controlled by the opposing faction. Meanwhile, the group consecrated to the public Mesopotamian cult (cf. Ezek 8:16) would be formed of governing authorities in the new, post-587 political class, that is, servile slaves of the foreign power engaged in the murderous repression of dissidence (cf. Ezek 8:17; 11:6). As suggestive as this may be, such a reading is founded on rather fragile arguments: to understand the secrecy of the cult as being a realistic datum is truthfully hardly plausible, if all the elements in Ezekiel's vision are taken literally: that as many as seventy elders of the people habitually meet right inside the temple complex (which would be in the hands of the leaders of the opponents) officiating solemn liturgies in utter secrecy seems, to say the least, unlikely. The element of "secrecy" or better yet of "darkness" must allude to the private cult or have a symbolic meaning, probably in reference to that said immediately following ("The Lord does not see us..."), and thus idolatry understood as adultery (cf. Ezek 23:30, 37–38). With regard to the faction that W. Eichrodt considers pro-Babylonian (of which I have already proven the invalidity under the reign of Zedekiah) because of its dedication to the cults of Mesopotamian origin, one need think on the basis of the immediate context of the opposition, that is, of the *anti-Babylonian* group, instead. In fact, the literary context of the proverbial saying about the "pot", then overturned, first identifies them as having a grip on the political situation, and then it makes them object of bitter punishment (and one cannot but think of the end of Jerusalem and of the exile). Furthermore, the "bad advice" given in times of crisis, rather than refer to conspiracies to eliminate the adversary, instead invoke the decision to rebel against Babylon, betraying the oath of loyalty, and the choice of resistance to the bitter end, confiding in military aid from Egypt.

192   Facing the might of the Babylonian empire

Instead, it would be fitting to recall, in this context, a verse from the book of Jeremiah that presents interesting similarities. I deliberately omitted it earlier, in order to better gather its significance fully in the light of the context just highlighted:

> [12] They denied the Lord, saying: "He is nothing! No evil shall come upon us, neither sword nor famine shall we see".[13] The prophets have become wind, the word [of the Lord] is not with them. Let it [the disaster] befall them! (5:12–13).

"He is nothing"; or: "It is not he": it is not YHWH *who takes action, who counts, who intervenes in history*, we could add. I will note that, in this case as well, the expectation of שָׁלוֹם, despite seeming to be antecedent to the facts of 597, is not in the least founded on trust in YHWH (and neither, therefore, on the theology of Zion or the Davidic election). It is rather, paradoxically, founded precisely on the idolatric denial of his real ability to intervene (even punitively) in history. Evidently, it was believed that national well-being and security was better guaranteed by other deities and cultual homages (indeed, see the preceding v. 11: "For they have brazenly rebelled against me, the house of Israel and the house of Judah. Oracle of the Lord"). After all, we find this conviction still strong (if not actually strengthened) amongst those who escaped the disaster of 587 as well (cf. 44:17–19).

I can therefore conclude that, while certainly having a *preponderant force*, as is evident on the basis of the other aforementioned Jeremianic texts, as well as on the basis of the book of Ezekiel itself (i.e. Ezek 13:1–16), the theology of Zion's inviolability cannot be considered an all-encompassing monolithic ideology. Nor can it be considered the only theological basis of the anti-Babylonian orientation. Comparing the data scattered amongst the textual folds of the books of the two exilic prophets, what we become aware of is a complex picture distinctly marked by a multivalent and ambiguous religious syncretism.

3.2.2.2. Supporters

It is already obvious during the reign of Jehoiakim that in the kingdom of Judah, thanks precisely to the dominant theological-political *milieu*, an anti-Babylonian faction formed very early and that this had a prevailing influence in the political orientation of the Davidic monarchy. Originally installed on the throne in place of his brother Jehoahaz directly by the Pharaoh, it is Jehoiakim himself, in fact, who decides to rebel against Babylon. And he most definitely does not do so without the support of the court and of the people, let alone – one can only believe – of the prophetic and priestly world.[219] This political line emerges explicitly in the narrative fabric of the book of Jeremiah, however, only in chs. 27–28.

Though the prophet of Anathoth addresses not only Zedekiah (27:12), but practically the entire population (27:13.16), in the text that I will scrutinise (chs. 27–28), it is once again the king who has an anti-Babylonian orientation and the figure of the prophet of Gabaon, Hananiah son of Azzur, who reveals the strongly national-religious connotation of this position. As opposed to Jeremiah, who appears to be

---

219   The land aristocracy of the "people of the land", who get penalised by the pharaoh with the removal of Jehoacaz in favour of Jehoiakim, seemed to be united more by an attempt to promote a continuation of Josiah's internal politics than by a foreign policy oriented either for or against Babylon.

The City and its destiny, between resistance and surrender   193

the only prophet calling for submission to Babylon (but cf. Bar 2:20–23), Hananiah is by no means isolated, far from it. In 27:16, mention of "your prophets" (נְבִיאֵיכֶם) is made in reference to the priests and all the people, as if to a group that included the entire category of those who were active in Jerusalem. These prophesise the end of the Babylonian hegemony, symbolically guaranteeing the imminent return of the temple furnishings.

It is interesting to note that in Ezek 11:1, a certain Jaazaniah, also a son of Azzur (together with Pelatiah son of Benaiah), is cited as being one of the leaders of the people who "hand down evil and give bad advice" to Jerusalem, along with twenty-five other men who are not further identified (though their considerable political influence is clearly perceived, and which must have been common knowledge amongst the exiles as well).[220] The proverb put on their lips to identify their position (Ezek 11:3: "The time is not near to build houses. This city is the pot and we are the meat"), despite that fact that the first part (v. 3a) gets interpreted and translated in numerous different ways (a possible alternative: "It is not the time to build houses"), corresponds quite well with the sense of false security that inspired the court's anti-Babylonian (and pro-Egyptian) orientation and fierce will of resistance during the siege.[221] In v. 11 (cf. also Ezek 24:1–14), the prophet overthrows this security on the basis of the very same proverbial saying, interpreting it, however, differently.

The presence of other prophets amongst the deportees of 597 urging in the same direction is well known: Ahab son of Kolaia, Zedekiah son of Maasa (29:21–23), and also Semaia the Nechelamita (29:24–32). The latter addresses a letter to the priest superintendent Zephaniah son of Maasia (called כֹּהֵן הַמִּשְׁנֶה, "second priest" in 52.24), all the people, and all the other priests (according to what we read in 29:24–29) calling for Jeremiah be silenced. In this letter, Jeremiah is practically equated to a *madman* (cf. 29:26: אִישׁ מְשֻׁגָּע) explicitly in reference to his subversive arguments against their (traditional) theological vision, since his arguments regarded peace and blessings that would come to Israel in a foreign land, flowing back through precisely the despised Babylonians themselves, for whose well-being the exiles ought to have prayed. Even Ezekiel lashes out against anonymous prophets (and prophetesses) of deceitful peace (cf. Ezek 13) that distort the reality of things with their lies passed off as oracles of YHWH.

The clergy of the temple, headed and represented by the "high priest" (כֹּהֵן הָרֹאשׁ) Seraiah (cf. 52:24; // 2 Kgs 25:18), and by Zephaniah, thus seem to be in a rather *ambiguous* position. He is the direct interlocutor of the prophets and the anti-Babylonian faction in exile, but is accused of not suppressing the message and person of Jeremiah.[222]

---

220 Based on Ezek 8,11.16, as we have seen, it is possible to trace, amongst other things, a link between the political policy of these men (although in Ezek 8:16, their number does not exactly correspond to twenty-five) and the sin of idolatry.

221 I am inclined to understand the two phrases as two independent proverbs linked together by the meaning conferred on them by the historical context of the (imminent or full-blown) rebellion against the Babylonian power, in which the predetermined objective (full autonomy) is to be pursued with patience (as the edification of a house requires time and constant commitment), and with an awareness of being in any case safe (like chosen meat in a pot).

222 Surprising information, regardless, if one considers two significant facts mentioned elsewhere: (1) in 20:1–2, it is precisely a priest, Pascur, chief superintendent of the

194 Facing the might of the Babylonian empire

This ambiguity must not have been a particular source of doubt for the those directly involved (the invaders) who, heirs of the various military techniques of the Assyrians, surely did not lack an adequate information service.[223] Indeed, when the Babylonians, once victorious, sweep up the survivors, organise the deportation, and inflict "ritual" capital punishments, both Seraiah and Zephaniah are counted amongst the enemies of Nebuchadnezzar. And for this reason, they are led before the king at the headquarters in Riblah and executed along with other prominent figures (cf. 52:24–26;/2 Kgs 25:18–21).

The presence and power of the anti-Babylonian faction emerges once again in ch. 37, when, the siege momentarily suspended due to the advance of the Egyptian army, Jeremiah decides to leave Jerusalem "[...] to go to the territory of Benjamin to take possession of a property amongst his people" (37:12; cf. ch. 32). He has not even have time to cross the threshold of the city gate from which he had wished to leave before he is instantly arrested as a *defector* by an officer on guard (Irijah, a son of Shelemiah) and locked up in the house of the scribe Jonathan, which had been transformed into a prison.[224]

We can reasonably deduce at least three things from this fact: (1) the existence of a certain number of people who had decided to surrender to the Babylonians and were attempting to do so; (2) the fact that the dominant political power was undoubtedly that of the anti-Babylonian faction, since it had military control over the entrances to the city; and that (3) these had the firm will to prevent (at least the most prominent figures from) dangerous anti-nationalistic gestures liable to indictment of "high treason", such as abandonment of the capital and/or surrender to the enemy, and the leak of information on the weak points of the defensive apparatus that could get out this way. In fact, as we have already noted, in 38:19, the presence of a group of defectors destined for deportation is attested (cf. 39:9), and Jeremiah himself is arrested under allegations so serious as to merit a death sentence.[225]

---

temple, who has the prophet flogged; (2) in ch. 36 (at the time of Jehoiakim), it is precisely the priests (along with the prophets) who ask for Jeremiah to be condemned to death.

223 As I have already been able to highlight (cf. n. 99 of the present chapter).

224 I do not believe that reference to another prominent figure, an opponent of Jeremiah's, can be immediately deduced from this annotation (as is instead asserted by J. HILL, «Writing the Prophetic Word. The Production of the Book of Jeremiah», *ABR* 57 [2009] 26). On the contrary, the fact that the home of a leading figure had been turned into a prison (כִּי־אֹתוֹ עָשׂוּ לְבֵית הַכֶּלֶא) would easily bring to mind measures of expropriation (cf. 1 Kgs 21:2: [...] וִיהִי־לִי לְגַן־יָרָק [...]), and the expression "house of Jonathan the scribe" (בֵּית יְהוֹנָתָן הַסֹּפֵר) would seem to be a conventional allusion to its ex-owner (who, in light of the context, could be dead or alive, and this is unclear; but see the case in 1 Kgs 21:15 that speaks of the "vineyard of Naboth" even after its owner is assassinated).

225 In one of the most important texts from Qumran, the "Temple Scroll" (11QT=11Q19–21, 4Q365a, 4Q524; cf. J. MAIER, *The Temple Scroll*. An Introduction, Translation and Commentary, JSOT.S 34, Sheffield 1985), we find the penalty for the crime of high treason, configured from the indications in Deut 21:22–23: "[7] There is a person who is an informer among my people, and delivers up my people to foreign nations, and does evil to my people, [8] you shall hang him upon a tree, and he shall die. On the testimony of two witnesses or on the testimony of three witnesses, [9] he shall be put to death, and they shall hang him (on) the tree. (VACAT) If a person is (guilty of) a sin

The City and its destiny, between resistance and surrender   195

Based again on the data obtained from the book of Jeremiah, we have confirmation that at this stage, government authorities were massively oriented in an anti-Babylonian sense from the fact that Jeremiah is led to the "leaders" (שָׂרִים). This term, carrying no further specification, identifies all of the most authoritative members of the government aside from the king. These inflict harsh corporal punishment on the prophet and imprison him, while the king is unable to object to anything. He only, after consulting Jeremiah, mitigates his state of imprisonment.

Other men of authority in the court who were promoting the same anti-Babylonian policy are explicitly named (and again called שָׂרִים) in 38:1[226] as the direct promoters of the attempt to stifle, once and for all, the message and life of the prophet Jeremiah (38:4–6), accused of favouring the enemy cause (but see also 21:1). This text also clearly highlights that during the scenario of the last years of the kingdom of Judah, the law in Jerusalem is dictated exclusively by this political group. And it is only with difficulty and following the impulse of a foreigner in the service of the court (the Ethiopian eunuch Ebed-melech) that the king prevents the prophet from being killed. It seems that in particular, through some of their members, two important, prominent families can be distinguished: the families of Malkijah (21:1; 38:1, 6) and Shelemiah (36:26; 37:3, 13, 38:1).

This is precisely the political picture that the "redactor" of the book of Jeremiah wants to communicate when this all too explicit declaration of impotence (which, in any case, we believe reflects the political reality of the situation) is put in the mouth of the king Zedekiah:

> So the king Zedekiah said: "Behold he is in your hands, *for the king can do nothing against you*" (38:5).

With the end imminent, the situation is confirmed: the king feels that he is controlled by these court dignitaries (cf. 38:25, 27; specifically, "all the leaders", with no exclusions: כָּל־הַשָּׂרִים), and he is forced to consult Jeremiah secretly, even ordering him to dissimulate the content of their dialogue to avoid problems (cf. 38:24–28a).

3.2.3. For a synthetic assessment

Rebellion and resistance, or submission and surrender? As I have documented, in the context of the last years of the kingdom of Judah, these are the only possible options.[227] It is, however, necessary to clarify and revise the classic counterposed

---

(with) a judgment of death, and he flees into [10] the midst of the nations and curses my people, the sons of Israel, then you shall also hang him upon the tree, [11] and he shall die [...]" (64,7–11; for the edition of the Hebrew text and the translation, I refer to J.H. CHARLESWORTH, *The Dead Sea Scrolls*. Hebrew, Aramaic, and Greek Texts with English Translations. Vol. 7: Temple Scroll and Related Documents, Tübingen 2011, 166–167).

226   These would be Shephatiah son of Mattan, Gedaliah son of Pashhur, Jucal son of Shelemiah, and Pashhur son of Malchiah.

227   At least on the level of a general political position. As a single individual, the sovereign could also consider the option of escaping (with a small contingent), as is repeatedly attested in the context of the ancient Near East and as Zedekiah himself will choose to do along with his closest relatives and collaborators (39:1–7; 52:6–11;

196 Facing the might of the Babylonian empire

stances repeated by the majority of commentators: a supposed pro-Egyptian "party" and a pro-Babylonian faction that would have dominated the political scene of the kingdom of Judah during its impact with the incursion of the might of Babylon. To orient to a more accurate reconstruction based on the literary data of the book of Jeremiah, the fundamental determinant lies in the clear distinction between the two most important historic periods: *the time of Jehoiakim* and *the time of Zedekiah*. During the time of Jehoiakim, Jeremiah makes no mention of submission to Babylon. So those who support him in one way or another can by no means be counted amongst the members of a pro-Babylonian "party".

Under Jehoiakim, the choice was as clear as it was disastrous: Nebuchadnezzar had left this sovereign on the throne, relying on his gratitude and loyalty, but at the first sign of weakness in the Babylonian empire, the king had revolted regardless. At this point, however, as far as the orientation of the courts is concerned, nothing can be affirmed with certainty. Jehoiakim dies in unclear circumstances before the besieging army arrives and his son surrenders instantly.

It is quite probable that the Babylonians took great care in purging the ruling class, deporting all of the most influential and prominent notables, particularly those clearly anti-Babylonian, just as had happened after Jerusalem was taken the second time. If a pro-Babylonian party were to be found, it would thus be easier to find it in court after 597, in the time of Zedekiah, amongst the (new) prominent figures left in Jerusalem. But, sticking to the book of Jeremiah, precisely the opposite appears to be true. Even under Zedekiah, the pro-Egyptian and anti-Babylonian orientation dictates the law and provokes the final catastrophe, while of a pro-Babylonian "party", there is no trace.

These are the literary data. And they are striking when considered in the context of the numerous contributions of scholars that see the book of Jeremiah as a sort of enclave in which opposing factions would have intervened at will to legitimise themselves by force of redactional insertions or manipulations. Indeed, why is there no mention of a pro-Babylonian party if this is precisely the group of exiles who have the last word on the text of Jeremiah, thus sealing its tendentious (pro-*gôlâ*) orientation? When a few simple hints or the mere interpolation of a verse would have sufficed to place a huge potential for self-recognition and political-religious vindication before the present and future generations of the people of Israel, instead, there is not a single name, note of merit, or even simple presence.

The Lachish Letters, and Ostracon VI in particular, by my interpretation, would confirm this picture, dominated by an anti-Babylonian orientation and Egyptian party line. However, this is not an indisputable assertion. In any case, these confirm the political impact that Jeremiah's message must certainly have had. Obviously, what they do not confirm is that its *nature* be purely political. And this, we will look at starting from the path traced thus far.

As far as the motives behind the rejection of the Jeremianic option are concerned, as we have seen, one can basically speak of a unilaterally conceived and politically exploited flow of tradition coagulating around a so-called theology of the inviolability of Zion. This, however, need be inserted within a complex framework, marked by syncretist idolatrous ideologies, if not even at times anti-Yahwist ones. And considerations

---

cf. 2 Kgs 25:1–7; Ezek 12:12–14). I will return to this topic in ch. V, § 3.1.6 and ch. VI, § 3.4 of the present dissertation.

The City and its destiny, between resistance and surrender   197

of an economic-political-military nature focusing hopes and expectations on the role of Egyptian power, which until a few years prior had dominated the entire Syro-Palestinian strip, certainly played an important role in this.

3.3. Surrender: The solution of a "realist"?

3.3.1. Isaiah and Jeremiah, between utopia and realism. The emblematic interpretation of F.J. Gonçalves

Commenting on the political-religious option tenaciously sustained by Jeremiah, more than a few authors speak in terms of its "realism" (or pragmatism). That is, they consider his to be a position which would have had, based on a correct assessment of the political landscape of the moment, guarantees of success more than any other. In the context of the siege on Jerusalem, that success could not aspire to materialisation beyond that of "salvaging the salvagable", that is, preventing total destruction of the kingdom of Judah and the annulment of the very elements constituting the national identity.

Jeremiah is thus considered a *realist* because he seems (at least *a posteriori*) to discern and indicate the best political option, fully ensuring "life *as* war booty [לְשָׁלָל]" (an expression that actually deserves specific, in-depth study).[228] But light can be shed on this inclination of his, particularly by comparing his message with that of Isaiah,[229] whose message, on the contrary, is defined by more than a few authors as absolutely *utopian* or removed from reality, insofar as it would be marred by a theological vision quite difficult to reconcile with diplomatic motives and *Realpolitik*.[230]

---

228   In fact, I will study this in ch. III, § 4.2.2, above all.

229   The reference, in more specific terms, is to the so-called "first"-Isaiah. The majority of authors recognise the material in this section of the book as being attributable to the Isaianic tradition of the eighth century (at the time of the Assyrian domination). See, in particular, the already cited contribution of M.J. DE JONG, *Isaiah*. This author believes that it be possible to identify three groups of texts from this period (1: Isa 6:1–9, 6*; 2: Isa 10:5–11:5; 3: Isa 28–32*), corresponding to the three most historically critical moments in which the kingdom of Judah had to deal with Assyrian imperialism (cf. pp. 449–452). These would be in 734–732 (we are in the context of the Syro-Ephraimite crisis), in 723–720 (Sargon subjugates the kingdom of Judah), and in 705–701 (the military campaign of Sennacherib against Judah). For a general overview of the relationships between the books of Jeremiah and Isaiah, see also G. FISCHER, «Partner oder Gegner?», and also the more focused M.A. SWEENEY, «Jeremiah's Reflection on the Isaian Royal Promise: Jeremiah 23:1–8 in Context», in: *Uprooting and Planting*. Essays on Jeremiah for Leslie Allen, *ed.* J. GOLDINGAY, LHBOTS 459, London – New York 2007, 308–321 (esp. pp. 84–88).

230   This, beginning with E. TRÖLTSCH, «Das Ethos der hebräischen Propheten», *Logos* 6 (1916–1917) 1–28; ID., *Gesammelte Schriften*, vol. IV, Tübingen 1925, 36 and F. WEINRICH, *Der religiös-utopische Charakter der "prophetischen Politik"*, Giessen 1932. In truth, I have the impression that judgements made regarding the presumed (or not) "utopian" reach of the prophetic messages be linked, on the one hand, to the conception – perhaps not yet entirely truly overcome – of biblical prophecy as having, in a unique way, to do with the prediction of future events which, not yet verified or verifiable, would denounce the utopia of the prophets, and on the

198 Facing the might of the Babylonian empire

I refer, in this regard, to the position taken by F.J. Gonçalves (which can be joined to that already mentioned of H. Rouillard-Bonraisin),[231] which is the most emblematic representative of the sort of hermeneutics with which I place ourselves in critical dialogue.[232] In his article dedicated to the study of the relationship between the two prophets and the international politics of Judah,[233] assuming an exclusively "historical" perspective, he reaches his conclusion defining the position of Isaiah as "pure idéologie" and "irréalisme absolu", while the Jeremianic option, shared by the (presumed) pro-Babylonian party, as "par simple réalisme politique", to wit, simply being *realistic*.

The motive for this radical perspectival difference would be attributable to the different religious experiences that would have generated their prophetic ministries (at least, according to that attested in the current textual form consolidated by tradition). Isaiah, gripped by an intuition of holiness and the limitless sovereignty of the God of Israel, would have "relentlessly" marked every politically relevant oracle of his (think of the Syro-Ephraimite crisis or the Assyrian invasion at the time of Hezekiah) with a theology that was detached from the real. That is, one that would imply naked faith in YHWH's resolutive intervention, to the complete detriment of the inevitable logic of the strategic equilibrium and indispensable international alliances.

Jeremiah, on the other hand, as if the literary motif of his being consecrated from the maternal womb and his being established prophet of the nations by a God whose absolute dominion over creation and history is explicitly recognised did not hold a likewise "transcendent" value, would be more unfettered by that kind of theological precomprehension and hence freer to "objectively" evaluate the political situation and indicate the best path for the preservation of the kingdom and its institutions. Nevertheless, even while admitting that Jeremiah's basic perspective be less linked

---

other, with the undeclared precomprehension (tending towards prejudice) by which research claiming to be rigorously "scientific" must be founded exclusively on the axioma of the unobtainability (or negation) of the interaction between the divine and human worlds. Thus, if the prophets call on the people for an act of faith in God's concrete action on the historical plane, they are thinking in a utopian way, while if, on the contrary, fulfilment of a prophetic world is attested, then one must indubitably conclude to be before *ex eventu* prophesies. The limit of this approach seems evident to me, above all when its *a priori* are not made explicit. For while a rational argument stemming from certain premises may also be *coherent*, it cannot, however, be accepted *ipso facto* as a "true" description of the real for this reason.

231 See the General Introduction, § 1.4.1.
232 See F.J. Gonçalves, «Isaïe, Jérémie», 282–298. But also see e.g. the contribution of R. Irudaya, «A Prophetic Call against War. A Political-Theological Study of Jeremiah 21:1–14», *VJTR* 66 (2002) 796–808, who, with a more theological and "actualising" slant, seems regardless to conceive the Jeremianic message only as a winning military "strategy" that would reveal that the will of YHWH be for his people to avoid disaster in a context in which they needed to *realistically* acknowledge that at this point, Babylon was imposing itself as a new superpower of the ancient Near East (cf. pp. 800–801). It is needless to emphasise that my interpretive perspective is quite different. The theme of biblical prophecy and its relationship to the political world of the time has been subject to studies based on opposing perspectives; cf. B. Albrektson, «Prophecy and Politics in the Old Testament», in: *The Myth of the State*, ed. H. Biezais, SIDA VI, Stockholm 1972, 45–56.
233 Cf. F.J. Gonçalves, «Isaïe, Jérémie», 296–298.

The City and its destiny, between resistance and surrender   199

to the Temple and centrality of Zion, one might wonder how it could be considered plausible that the entire political class ruling in the time of Zedekiah be so close to the absolute (and, I would also add, presumed) utopia of Isaiah that they would have had no realistic analytical capability whatsoever regarding the unravelling of the historical-political events of his time. Or in other words, is it conceivable that Jeremiah would have been the only one capable of "clairvoyant political reflection"[234] in seeing the inevitability of surrender to Babylon? One can *realistically* doubt this to be so. And we will see why.

3.3.2. Some critical notes: Redefining the category of "realism" in light of the historic context

3.3.2.1. Then, now

So then, Isaiah was a utopian and Jeremiah a realist?

At first glance, this would seem to be an acceptable distinction posed by a hermeneutic of the texts. Even if, and this is the doubt that stimulates my inquiry, the excessive clarity of this distinction, a far stretch from the usual complexity of biblical questions, suggests that it be a simplification dictated more from "hindsight" (in the case of Jeremiah) or from a too "external" and modern vision of the facts rather than from a precise evaluation of the historical context and various elements in play. By retracing the various stages of the kingdom of Judah, I have already been able to rapidly allude to the question, but it is now time to return to it and take an in-depth look at it.

In order to aptly adjudicate whether the message of Jeremiah is *realistic* or not, it is necessary, from the methodological point of view, to first distinguish and then integrate two different perspectives: (1) what we can *now* reasonably reconstruct of the international political context of the time, based on a historical-critical study of the available elements; (2) what, of this same context and same dynamics, could have been perceived *then* by the governing bodies of Jerusalem. It is, in fact, evident that a political approach that moderns might consider far-sighted could, on the contrary, have been reputed detached from reality or actually impracticable from the perspective of the direct protagonists. These may have had different priorities or have based themselves on a vastly different array of knowledge (whether more limited or more relevant, as the case may be).

3.3.2.2. Submission

When, for the first time, at the beginning of the reign of Zedekiah, Jeremiah clearly proclaims the necessity of submission to the king of Babylon,[235] his *position can hardly*

---

234 As in H. ROUILLARD-BONRAISIN, «Ésaïe, Jérémie», 222.

235 The ch. 27 episode takes place precisely in the fourth year, that is, towards 595/594, even if from 27:12, 16 (דִּבַּרְתִּי), it can be deduced that the message had already been personally delivered to the king, the priests, and all the people. In any case, its proclamation always comes about within the first four years of the reign of Zedekiah, and not before. All this is obviously according to what is attested in the book of Jeremiah, which remains the only source on the matter, and which is my essential hermeneutical context of reference for the study of the prophetic theme of "surrender" to Babylon.

200 Facing the might of the Babylonian empire

be defined as an absolutely realistic one, if not in hindsight. The new power, in fact, once the Egyptian influence had at first (though not definitively) been driven out of Syria-Palestine, showed signs of fragility and may have *appeared* to be already undermined from within.

Indeed, between 596 and 595, Nebuchadnezzar had been forced to conduct a military campaign against the king of Elam. This was a sign that the political situation was unstable even at the eastern borders of the empire.[236] But the situation within was no better, as I highlighted by retracing the salient historic phases of this period. A serious and prolonged uprising in the heart of the capital, right amongst the high ranks of the army (a strength crucial for conquests, control of the territory and, ultimately, for maintaining the power itself) had completely preoccupied Nebuchadnezzar.

Even on the Egyptian front, the scenario was not encouraging. Psammetichus II had brought his campaign in Nubia to a close with great success in 593, and had proven to be a reliable force on the sea as well.[237] His appearance the following year on the Phoenician coast aroused great awe of his might amongst the states of the region who had become subjugated to Nebuchadnezzar not long before, refuelling the expectation that Egyptian power could be re-established, to the detriment of Babylonia,[238] as well as hopes of rescue that had only recently been muted. These hopes, *from the point of view of these small states,* might have seemed like realistic, concrete prospects for independence, founded on the probability of being able to count on the decisive aid of Egypt. The vassalage conditions that this would certainly come with were more favourable than those under of the Babylonian yoke. Indeed, the most plausible motive behind the international colloquy held in Jerusalem before Zedekiah would seem to be this.

The question of Jeremiah's realism thus concerns not so much the message regarding generic submission to Babylon (an option of great importance in other respects, presented in 27–28 as having "universal" significance), but rather the final events, final siege, and months preceding the final catastrophe. It regards, to be precise, the call to "surrender".

3.3.2.3. Surrender

Beginning from consideration of the international emergency scenario that I highlighted previously (cf. § 2), the first substantial criticism of the hermeneutic perspective framing the Jeremianic option within the canons of some kind of *Realpolitik* that can be put forth is that it seems misleading to speak of the surrender-option decontextualising it, that is, bearing in mind only the final stage of the siege of Jerusalem, without regard for the complex chain of events that bring about the decisive crisis of 589–587.

The rebellion of Zedekiah and consequent Babylonian reaction are, in fact, simply the last link in a chain of reiterated attempts at liberation from the yoke of Babylon that lead the story to its extreme. And it is a decision to which, in all probability, as I noted, Nebuchadnezzar could have only reacted by pushing his repression to its

---

236 Cf. O. Lipschits, *The Fall,* 62.
237 This is written about very effectively by A. Neher, *Jérémie,* 76: «La mobilité des opérations sur mer permet aux Égyptiens d'apparaître soudain comme une promesse, puis de s'évanouir tel un fantôme. Yoyaquim sera victime de ce mirage».
238 Cf. O. Lipschits, *The Fall,* 63.

The City and its destiny, between resistance and surrender — 201

ultimate consequences. The situation had already reached the brink of catastrophe in 597 and, despite the sudden death of the unfaithful Jehoiakim and immediate surrender of his successor Jehoiachin, the blow dealt had been a harsh one. Jerusalem had not been destroyed but, as O. Lipschits noted in this respect, they had had a brush with the end:

> Considering the fact that it was not Jehoiakin who revolted, we can understand why the Babylonians did not demolish Jerusalem and allowed Judah to remain as a subject kingdom, with a Davidic dynast on the throne.[239]

On the other hand, in the context of Zedekiah's rebellion, the last in a long-standing history of uprisings, one can immediately see that speaking of the option of "surrender" as realism no longer appears so convincing. It would have also been realistic to carry out an attempt to resist to the bitter end, trusting in the help of Egypt and its defensive apparatus.[240] Moreover, in view of the pragmatic-cognitive context underlying the facts narrated in the book of Jeremiah, it should be noted that from the sources regarding the ancient Near East, it was by no means self-evident that the outcome of a siege would be capitulation and surrender. Under certain conditions, resistance could always be considered the best option, as is clearly evidenced by the study of I. Eph'al:

> [...] the rationale motivating defenders to prefer siege above surrender, from the onset or during the course of battle, was the evaluation of the difficulties that confronted the besiegers, in light of the limitations of time and space that restricted the operation of imperial armies against cities of the ancient Near East, and in light of the knowledge that not every siege ended in conquest.[241]

3.3.2.4. Escalation

In other words, in my opinion, a correct assessment of the "surrender" as a more or less opportune political-military choice is obtainable if it is placed within the category of *escalation*. That is, it should be considered within a progressive and studied dramatisation of the conflict that seems to clearly determine the balance of power between – first

---

239 Cf. O. Lipschits, *The Fall*, 54–55.

240 In Ezek 17:15, reference is made to the request sent by Zedechiah to the pharaoh to ensure the availability of massive troupes and warhorses, while in Ost. III,14–16 there is talk of a journey taken by the head commander of the Judean army, Coniah son of Elnathan, to see the pharaoh, apparently for the same motive. In 37:5–11, explicit mention is made of an Egyptian military intervention that forces the Babylonians to momentarily disengage their military from the siege of Jerusalem (cf. O. Lipschits, *The Fall*, 64). Aside from the arduous siege of Tyre, which lasted a good thirteen years due to its unusual geographical position (only Alexander the Great in 332 will prove to be right in having his engineers construct an embankment to reach the portion of the city that stood on an island 750 metres off the coast), it is no small matter for Jerusalem to have resisted the Babylonian army, expert in siege craft, for a good eighteen months. One should consider that the great Assyrian city of Nineveh, protected by three city walls, had resisted the same troupes, who fought together with the Medes, for only three months.

241 I. Eph'al, *The City Besieged. Siege and Its Manifestations in the Ancient Near East*, CHANE 36, Leiden 2009, 113.

202   Facing the might of the Babylonian empire

the Assyrians, then the Babylonians – and the peripheral state entities either affected by the progressive expansionist drive of these great empires or already subject to their influence through relationships of strict vassalage and control. A close look shows this to be more than a mere model of representation verifiable with today's instruments of the historical sciences. Since it is a political dynamic that manifested repeatedly over a long span of time, it is one that could also be clearly perceived, and its foreseeable consequences taken into account throughout the whole context of the ancient Near East (at least during the historical phase which we are dealing).

This interpretative hypothesis, which leads to a critical relativisation of the "realism" of Jeremiah, can be partially founded, in my opinion, on a study of the political-military strategy typical of the imperialist model implemented by the Assyrian hegemonic policy (especially by Tiglath-Pilezer III; ca. 745–727,[242] though already from the Middle Assyrian imperial state; ca. 1,350–1,000[243]). While differentiating themselves in various respects (especially those of an administrative nature), the Babylonians essentially prove to have reaped the legacy of this policy.[244] And this

---

242   See R. LAMPRICHS, *Die Westexpansion des neuassyrischen Reiches.* Eine Strukturanalyse, AOAT 239, Neukirchen 1995; A. FUCHS, «Assyria at War: Strategy and Conduct», in: *The Oxford Handbook of Cuneiform Culture, eds.* K. RADNER – E. ROBSON, Oxford 2011, 380–401; K. KESSLER, *Das neuassyrische Reich der Sargoniden (720–612 v. Chr.) und das neubabylonische Reich (612–539 v. Chr.),* TAVO Karte B IV 13, Wiesbaden 1991 (interesting historical maps from the period of great interest to us); S. YAMADA, *Assyrian Empire*; G.G. FAGAN, «"I Fell upon Him Like a Furious Arrow": Toward a Reconstruction of the Assyrian Tactical System», in: *New Perspectives on Ancient Warfare, eds.* G.G. FAGAN – M. TRUNDLE, HW 59, Leiden – Boston 2010, 81–100. For the particular vicissitudes of the Aramean states of Syria in relation to Assyrian expansionism, see H. SADER, *Les états araméens de Syrie depuis leur fondation jusqu'à leur transformation en provinces assyriennes*, BeTS(W) 36, Wiesbaden 1987. With regard to the Assyrian expansionism that began with Tiglath-Pilezer III, G.B. LANFRANCHI writes, «The Assyrian Expansion in the Zagros and the Local Ruling Elites», in: *Continuity of Empire (?).* Assyria, Media, Persia, *eds.* G.B. LANFRANCHI – M. ROAF – R. ROLLINGER, HANE.M 5, Padova 2003, 79–118: "This is the period in which Assyria started and carried out in every direction an impressive series of systematic annexations accompanied by the elimination of local dynasties, aiming at creating a true territorial empire of a type which had never existed before. In this complicated process, the elites of the polities peripheral to the core of Assyrian territory – either because they had been recently annexed to the provincial system or because they still retained their tributary status – were progressively drawn into the imperial mechanisms, as it is attested by the increasing importance of the western social element within the Assyrian governmental elite" (p. 80).

243   As in B.S. DÜRING, «At the Root of the Matter. The Middle Assyrian Prelude to Empire», in: *Imperial Peripheries in the Neo-Assyrian Period, eds.* C.W. TYSON – V.R. HERRMANN, Louisville 2018, 41–64. The author notes moreover that it is precisely the progressive annexation of neighbouring territories and their transformation into provinces that distinguished the Assyrian state from other contemporary political entities: "The Assyrians stand out [...] for how they dealt with conquered territories and how they transformed provinces and peripheries" (here, p. 44).

244   This applies, to some extent, to the various, successive transfers of power in this area: "[...] the Neo-Babylonian period, more than a new empire, appears to be the last manifestation of ancient Mesopotamia, in which power is held simultaneously

The City and its destiny, between resistance and surrender 203

pragmatic context has significant hermeneutic effects that concern the accurate historical focalisation of my topic.[245] The implementation of a precise political design would greatly depend on individual sovereigns' plans as well as variables that are not always foreseeable (and which, in fact, generated exceptions).[246] Nonetheless,

---

or successively by various dynasties [...]" (translated from G. RINALDI, *Le letterature antiche del Vicino Oriente: sumerica, assira, babilonese, ugaritica, ittita, fenicia, aramaica, nord e sud-arabica*, LettM 29, Firenze 1968, 224). For specifics in this regard, see H.W.F. SAGGS, *The Greatness that Was Babylon*. A Survey of the Ancient Civilization of the Tigris-Euphrates Valley, New York 1962, London [2]1988, 229; S. DALLEY, «The Transition from Neo-Assyrians to Neo-Babylonians: Break or Continuity?», in: *Hayim and Miriam Tadmor Volume*, eds. I. EPH'AL – A. BEN-TOR – P. MACHINIST, ErIsr 27, Jerusalem 2003, 25*-28*. Along the same lines, R.H. SACK, *Images of Nebuchadnezzar. The Emergence of a Legend*, Selinsgrove 1991, [2]2004, 89 (contrary to the opinion of D.S. VANDERHOOFT, *The Neo-Babylonian Empire*, 98) and the recent contribution by R. DA RIVA, «Assyrians and Assyrian Influence in Babylonia (626–539 BCE)», in: *From Source to History*. Studies on Ancient Near Eastern Worlds and Beyond, *eds*. S. GASPA *et al.*, AOAT 412, Münster 2014, 99–125, who concludes by stating: "The connections and mutual influence between the two cultures were numerous and multifaceted: in political institutions, in administrative procedures, in literature and religion. In many respects, the Babylonian culture and past were a model for Assyria, but many Assyrian elements functioned as templates for the Neo-Babylonian state as well" (p. 120). My own methodological choice, which leads me to confer a paradigmatic or heuristic significance on the Assyrian strategic model, is thus not only in a certain sense constrained by the scarcity of documentation regarding the Neo-Babylonian period, but in my view also legitimatised due to the tight relationship (or contamination) that exists between the two cultures. In specific reference to their respective military strategies, N. STILLMAN – N. TALLIS, *Armies of the Ancient Near East 3,000 BC to 539 BC*, Worthing 1984, 62, expresses it thus: "Very little is known about the tactics employed during the Neo-Babylonian Empire, but they were probably similar to those used by the Assyrians." It is important to emphasise that we are talking about a substantial cultural affinity (and in this, Assyria was indebted to the more refined Babylonian culture) and its specific reflection (the political-military practices with which imperial expansionism took shape), and not a perpetuation of the same system of administrative government, which was not structured (especially in the West) on the model of the province according to the previous Assyrian organisation. For a comparison, see D.S. VANDERHOOFT, *The Neo-Babylonian Empire*, 90–114. On the different administrative politics concerning the East, see ID., «Babylonian Strategies of Imperial Control in the West: Royal Practice and Rhetoric», in: *Judah and the Judeans*, 235–262 (see esp. pp. 248–250).

245 "In sum, it is in the context of Assyrian practices that we more fully understand the events that led to the Neo-Babylonian conquest of Judah, the placing of chosen rulers on the throne, and the significance of deportation" (this, according to the study perspective of D.L. SMITH, *The Religion of the Landless*. The Social Context of the Babylonian Exile, Bloomington 1989, 29).

246 E.g. M. COGAN, «Judah under Assyrian Hegemony: A Reexamination of Imperialism and Religion», *JBL* 112 (1993) 406–408, makes note, citing the case of Gaza and Ashdod, that *ad hoc* solutions could also come about, depending on the different circumstances. For this reason, the usual terms of "vassal" (or "client") and "province" should not refer to standardised criterions, as they are categories that do not exhaust all the forms of submission of which we are aware.

204 Facing the might of the Babylonian empire

one can generally recognise a multileveled differentiation in the relations between the *expanding* Assyrian empire and the various, more or less large or modest states (or cities) that suffered the consequences.[247] In this *policy*, three (usually progressive) stages, or three forms of dependence, can be identified.[248]

The *first stage*, which is only apparently the most "bland", was created when, under direct Assyrian pressure or due to other forms of external threats demanding powerful "protection", a state would voluntarily subject itself. The state would begin to pay an annual tribute and thus accept – *de facto* – a statute of vassalage, together with its advantages and its collateral effects.[249] In reality, the stipulation of such a treaty with the Assyrian sovereign did not portend that this relationship would be temporary, nor did it the possibility of unilateral termination. On the contrary, the condition of subordination ordinarily layed down was destined to evolve into more stringent forms of control. Indeed, even an eventual breaking of the pact by the vassal state would bring about advantage for the empire, for in the event of an absent tax payment, the Assyrian state would not remain inert but would set off

---

247 Cf. H. Donner, *Israel unter den Völkern*. Die Stellung der klassischen Propheten des 8. Jahrhunderts v. Chr. zur Aussenpolitik der Könige von Israel und Juda, VT.S 11, Leiden 1964, 1–3; H.W.F. Saggs, *Babylon*, 215–220; Id., *The Might that Was Assyria*, London 1984, 86–87; A. Soggin, *Storia d'Israele*, 338; S. Parpola, «International Law in the First Millennium», in: *A History of Ancient Near Easter Law*, ed. R. Westbrook, HdO 72, I, Leiden – Boston 2003, 1051: "Broken treaties resulted in the incorporation of the rebel country into the Assyrian provincial system with the imposition of regular taxation, military service and corvée, a single imperial language (Aramaic), and in the long run, a uniform imperial culture."

248 This "oil-stain" model was criticised by M. Liverani, «The Growth of the Assyrian Empire in the Habur/Middle Euphrates Area: A New Paradigm», *SAAB* 2 (1988) 81–98, who proposed a different paradigm, based on the notion that the Assyrian empire (in the ninth century, above all) is not to be conceived as "a spread of land but a network of communications over which material goods are carried" (p. 86). A system of exploitation of a network of resources (or "islands"), therefore, based on the consolidation and reinforcement of pre-existing networks and others created stemming from these. This paradigm was likewise criticised and recalibrated, in my view rightfully, by J.P. Postgate «The Land of Assur», 247–263 (see, in particular, pp. 255–257) and S. Yamada, *Assyrian Empire*, 308. In any case, what I am interested in emphasising is the existence of different models of (progressive) dependence ("transitional cases") in the face of the Assyrian hegemony in expansion. In this sense, also P.R. Bedford, «The Neo-Assyrian Empire», in: *The Dynamics of Ancient Empires*. State Power from Assyria to Byzantium, eds. I. Morris – W. Scheidel, Oxford 2009, 30–65 (cf. above all, pp. 44– 47, where, with regard to policy towards bordering states, it talks about the transition from a system of clientelistic dependency to a reduction in provinces directly administered by central Assyrian power).

249 A clear example of this first level is the request for help and concomitant voluntary request to assume a vassal status made by Acaz to Tiglath-Pilezer III (attested in 2 Kg 16:7–9), in the context of the Syro-Ephramite war (for more in-depth study regarding this, see A. Soggin, *Storia d'Israele*, 339–345). Syncretistic contamination is one of the effects of this policy (cf. 2 Kgs 16:10–18).

The City and its destiny, between resistance and surrender 205

countermeasures, as soon as possible,[250] and these would exacerbate the recalcitrant vassal state's *status* of submission.[251]

And so we move to the *second stage*: having recognised the hostile significance of the act, the option of direct military action would be triggered. This would consist in the field deployment of forces that, while not enormous, would still impose an annexing of large portions of the defiant kingdom's territory to the empire. In addition, this would generate massive intervention in domestic political policy in order to bow it to Assyrian wishes by removing the rulers who had promoted the attempt to pull out. These rulers would be substituted with sovereigns who would ensure future loyalty without hesitation.[252] Sometimes, as a sign of great magnanimity, and thusly asserting the need for absolute fidelity, the Assyrians might even reinstall infidel vassals on the throne. The new king would be obliged to make a solemn oath of loyalty, pronounced in front of and in the name of the great Assyrian gods. In this way, conditions were put into place so that any possible new rebellion could be considered a serious offence not only towards the Assyrian king but also, and above all, towards the gods before whom they had committed themselves.[253] Thus, that which would be obtained by law (almost *formally*) was not so much an act of vengeance or repression that would serve as a warning to other vassals, but rather *necessary* atonement[254] since, in its absence,

---

250 In fact, it could happen that the army be busy in other parts of the empire quelling rebellions or carrying forth other expansion (or defence) campaigns. Indeed, it should be said that precisely these facts could favour attempts at emancipation on the part of peripheral states, such as those in the Palestinian area.

251 "By signing a treaty with the Assyrian emperor, these rulers traded off their national independence for Assyrian vassalage. And once Assyria's overlordship had been formally established, there was no escaping from it. Broken treaties were severely punished; sooner or later Assyrian poured in the rebel country, which was utterly destroyed and annexed to Assyria" (S. PARPOLA – K. WATANABE, *Neo-Assyrian Treaties and Loyalty Oaths,* SAA 2, Helsinki 1988, xxiii; with various examples given on pp. xxii-xxiii to be compared with the damnations provided for in the treaty between Aššur-nerari V and Mati'-ilu, king of Arpad [SAA 2 2]).

252 As a further security measure, it was possible for an Assyrian official (with his respective garrison) to establish himself in a role of power within the territory of the vassal kingdom. Architectural details providing testimony to this are the foundations of well-known Assyrian palaces uncovered on several sites.

253 Cf. M. LIVERANI, *The Ancient Near East,* 517; B. ODED, *War, Peace and Empire. Justifications for War in Assyrian Royal Inscriptions,* Wiesbaden 1992, 83–99. It should be highlighted that the Babylonians, taking up this practice, would make the vassal (also) take his oath in the name of his own national deities, and thus, as in the case of the kingdom of Judah, in the name of YHWH. Ezekiel's fierce criticism of Zedekiah, accused of having violated the pact with Nebuchadnezzar sworn in the name of YHWH, in fact, comes to mind (cf. Ezek 17:13–16). In this regard, see G. FURLANI, «Le guerre quali giudizi di Dio presso i Babilonesi e Assiri», in: *Miscellanea G. Galbiati,* FAmb 27, Milano 1951, 39–47.

254 It is in this (self-imprecatory) context prescribed by the oath of loyalty that, according to H.W.F. SAGGS, *Babylon,* 216–218, all of those atrocious practices for which the Assyrians are often remembered should be taken: kings could be tortured, flayed, maimed in the tongue, walled-in alive, set ablaze, impaled, etc. Despite this, the Assyrian bas-reliefs *jointly* demonstrate with document scenes of violence (cf. e.g.

206 Facing the might of the Babylonian empire

divine wrath would be unleashed on the entire territory of the empire through sword, hunger, plague, etc. (cf. e.g. 21:1–10).

The *third stage* would mean, *de facto*, the *end* of the rebellious kingdom.[255] In the event of reiterated rebellion, its fundamental socio-political structures would be dismantled through the notorious use of mass deportations.[256] This practice had been infamous for some time in Mesopotamia (and also amongst the Egyptians and Hittites),[257] but with the Neo-Assyrian empire of Tiglath-Pilezer III (and his successors, Sargon II and Sennacherib), it became an effective and systematic (however traumatic) instrument for consolidating dominion over its vast territory. The local population[258] would be transferred to other parts of the empire. And the country, now transformed into provinces and subject to direct imperial administration (for the exploitation of local

---

Ibid., pls 33a; 34; 46a) also a certain "human sensitivity". After all, the great kings of Mesopotamia not only assigned themselves the title of "king of the world", but also sought to present themselves as or believed themselves to be "pious shepherds" and defenders of the weak. This is, at least, the opinion of S. REED, «Blurring the Edges: A Reconsideration of the Treatment of Enemies in Ashurbanipal's Reliefs», in: *Ancient Near Eastern Art in Context*. Studies in Honor of Irene J. Winter by Her Students, *eds.* J. CHENG – M.H. FELDMAN, Leiden 2007, 101–130; but see also L. BERSANI – U. DUTOIT, *The Forms of Violence*. Narrative in Assyrian Art and Modern Culture, New York 1985. Consider, however, the following words of Nebuchadnezzar that open and close the two long, significant twin inscriptions in Wadi Brisa (edited by R. DA RIVA, *The Twin Inscriptions of Nebuchadnezzar at Brisa [Wadi Esh-Sharbin, Lebanon]*. A Historical and Philological Study, AfO.B 32, Wien 2012, 42–43, 63). On the first line: "I am Nebuchadnezzar, king of Babylon, the loyal shepherd, the favourite of Marduk, the august city-ruler [...]" (WBA I 1–3 = WBC Ia 1–3). "He (Marduk) handed over to me the shepherd-staff which keeps people safe [...]" (WBA II 1–2). At the end, right before the final admonitions (and damnations): "I let the inhabitants of the Lebanon live in safe pastures, I did not permit anyone to harass them. So that nobody will oppress them, I (installed) an eternal image of myself as king to (protect them)" (WBC IX 47–53). Other similar expressions are repeated within the body of the text.

255 "Literary sources, reliefs and archaeological excavations agree that the conquest of non-submissive cities by Assyrian was always an extremely destructive event" (N. NA'AMAN, «The Historical Background to the Conquest of Samaria [720 BCE]», *Bib.* 71 [1990] 206–225; here, p. 208).

256 Cf. B. ODED, *Mass Deportations and Deportees in the Neo-Assyrian Empire*, Wiesbaden 1979, 41–43. According to the calculations done by this scholar, over the arc of approximately three centuries, the sum of the deportees would have reached the considerable figure of four and a half million people (*Ibid.*, p. 20). The Babylonians also use this political-military tool, but make more moderate use of it.

257 See e.g. L. ROVIRA, «"Share Them Out...". On the Mass Deportation of People according to the Texts of Mari (18th Century BC)», in: *The Other Face of the Battle*. The Impact of War on Civilians in the Ancient Near East, *eds.* D. NADALI – J. VIDAL, AOAT 413, Münster 2014, 25–36.

258 Despite the emphasis of royal inscriptions often boasting the complete deportation of conquered peoples, to overturn the state structure and stamp out the threat of further revolts, quite often a compulsory transfer of the most affluent part of the population would suffice: notables, officers, skilled labourers (artisans, blacksmith, etc.). See B. ODED, *Mass Deportations*, 44. This is what Nebuchadnezzar will do initially with Jerusalem in 597.

The City and its destiny, between resistance and surrender   207

resources), would be repopulated with other peoples who had suffered a similar fate elsewhere[259] or even with colonies of Assyrian citizens or soldiers.

Thanks also to the remarkable intimidation propaganda,[260] this strategy of governance and expansion was indubitably universally known, at least in the concrete, immediate effects obtained by the complex and efficient devastating Assyrian war machine.[261] And it was likewise obvious that the Babylonian empire (also an enemy coming from the "North") be considered the direct heir of this policy of aggression and conquest.[262] In fact, from the surviving documentation, Babylon itself shows that it considers itself such. As R. Da Riva, for example, comments about what is made apparent from the important neo-Babylonian inscription of Wadi Brisa:

> The Brisa Inscription is the best symbol of Nebuchadnezzar's aggressive military campaigns in the West, which are a continuation of Neo-Assyrian policies. The geographical location and intended audience of the monument demonstrate that the Babylonians believed themselves to be the heirs of the Assyrians in the area of the North Biqa'.[263]

---

259   An eloquent example of the fate that might await a vassal state (and its population) in case of rebellion against the empire (having the value of a pragmatic context for my topic, given that it be part of the relatively recent history of the kingdom of Judah), can be admired in the renowned bas-relief description of the destruction of Lachish at the hands of Sennacherib carried out in 701 (with accompanying torture, impalements, and other intimidatory executions); cf. ANEP, 129–132; C. UEHLINGER, «Clio in a World of Pictures – Another Look at the Lachish Reliefs from Sennacherib's Southwest Palace at Nineveh», in: *Like a Bird in a Cage*. The Invasion of Sennacherib in 701 BCE, *ed.* L.L. GRABBE, JSOT.S 363, Sheffield 2003, 221–305.

260   On which one can see W. MAYER, *Politik und Kriegskunst der Assyrer,* ALASP 9, Münster 1995, 478–482.

261   As concludes the study by G.G. FAGAN, «"I Fell upon Him Like a Furious Arrow"», 100: "Finally, Assyrian tactical arrangements as reconstructed here would require the rejection of arguments that ancient Near Eastern armies shunned head-on battles and preferred ruse, ambush, negotiation, or raiding to achieve victory. The opponents of Assyria knew otherwise."

262   Also from a military point of view its influences are undeniable, and extend well beyond the Neo-Babylonian period (cf. J. KEEGAN, *A History of Warfare,* New York 1993, 169: "At the height of its powers, say in the eighth century B.C., the Assyrian army revealed features on which many of those of successor armies in other empires were to be modelled; some of them have come down to our own day. Foremost amongst them were its logistic arrangements: supply depots, transport columns, bridging-trains. The Assyrian was the first true long-range army, able to campaign as far as 300 miles from base and to move at speeds of advance that would not be exceeded until the coming of the internal combustion engine").

263   R. DA RIVA, *The Twin Inscriptions,* 96. In the initial part of her study, the author had already noted that, beyond the typical Neo-Babylonian imperialist rhetoric, the empire of Nabuchadnezzar had taken up substantial elements of the Assyrian empire: "Babylonian rule in the West and elsewhere was as violent and 'imperialistic' as the Neo-Assyrian regime had been, the kings simply do not boast of it. The Neo-Babylonian empire inherited many elements of the previous Neo-Assyrian empire (notably, administrative and military procedures), but not the idea of kingship. Neo-Babylonian imperial rhetoric is Babylonian in language, concepts and

208 Facing the might of the Babylonian empire

To surrender, once the Babylonian king's war machine was activated and his army engaged in the costly siege of Jerusalem, could not in all likelihood have guaranteed certain physical security, nor a less harsh retaliation. And this was precisely because it was by no means their first and only act of insubordination. In 597, at the time of Jehoiakim and Jehoiachin, it would certainly not have had the same significance. Oded Lipschits also agrees, convinced that the destruction of Jerusalem brought on by Nebuchadnezzar was neither impulsive revenge nor mere punishment for a single rebellion, but rather a carefully premeditated act with precise political ends, namely:

> [...] to remove the House of David from government after they had proven disloyal, and to destroy Jerusalem which had proven again and again to be the center of resistance to Babylonian rule.[264]

As far as Jehoiakim is concerned, it should be noted that according to the late version in 2 Chr 36:6–7 (as compared to the prophecies of Jeremiah on his ignominious end in Jer 22:18–19), he does not die before the siege of 597, but was rather led to Babylon as a prisoner. The version of the facts presented by Flavius Josephus (*Antiquitates iudaicae*, X,96–97) is interesting for my thematic, despite its lack of historical evidence. If nothing else, this version suggests a pertinent pragmatic contextualisation: that is, that it was by no means assumed that the option of "surrender" would automatically guarantee salvation. And this becomes even more significant when said by he who, during the Roman siege of Jerusalem in 68–70, had tried in every way possible to persuade his compatriots to surrender to the Romans, exalting clemency and respect for the sacred places of the enemies:

> When, not long aferwards, the king of the Babylonians campaigned against him, Jehoiakim, in his fright at the things predicted by this prophet, admitted him. [He did this], thinking that he would suffer nothing terrible, seeing that he was neither shutting out nor making war on [the invader]. But when he set out to him, the Babylonian did not keep his pledges. Rather, he killed those of the Hierosolymites who were most fit and outstandingly handsome, along with King Jehoiachin, whom he commanded to be tossed out unburied in front of the walls. He designated his son Joakeim king of the country and of the city.[265]

On the unreliability and cruelty of Nebuchadnezzar (once again, according to Flavius Josephus), see also the following episode portrayed in the *Antiquitates iudaicae*, X,100–101, in which the king of Babylon breaks his oath concerning his benevolent intentions towards the relatives of Jehoiachin (who had handed the latter over to Nebuchadnezzar as a sign of surrender) and towards Jerusalem itself.

---

essence, carefully avoiding Neo-Assyrian patterns" (p. 19). The same observation is basically reiterated in R. Da Riva, *The Inscriptions of Nabopolassar, Amēl-Marduk and Neriglissar*, SANER 3, Göttingen 2013, 4: "[...] recent studies have demonstrated that Neo-Babylonian political institutions followed Neo-Assyrian models, and many imperial officials bear titles of Assyrian origin. Paradoxically, then, despite expelling the Assyrians, the Babylonian kings were establishing the foundations of their administration based on Assyrian institutions and patterns."

264 O. Lipschits, «Nebuchadrezzar's Policy», 473, 480.
265 Flavius Josephus, *Judean Antiquities 8–10*, 237–238.

The City and its destiny, between resistance and surrender   209

3.3.2.5. Emblematic examples

To corroborate the far from remote possibility of the failed outcome of hypothetical negotiations for surrender and the catastrophic inevitability of the Babylonian reaction against the umpteenth rebellion of the kingdom of Judah, at least two interesting cases can be cited (in addition to the forceful military campaigns in the Syrian-Palestinian strip by Nebuchadnezzar himself, which I will highlight later on). These cases both regard well-documented Assyrian war operations that are not temporally distant from the historical framework referred to in the book of Jeremiah: the destruction of Lachish (of primary interest also for its geographical-cultural proximity to the events of Jerusalem) and of Uppume, capital of the kingdom of Shubria, located in the mountainous area of north-western Assyria.

The campaign of Sennacherib in Philistia and Judah in 701, according to the study by D. Ussishkin[266] of the fortunes of the cities of Ekron, Lachish, and Jerusalem (all endowed with powerful fortifications and considerable defensive apparatuses), would suggest the application of a precise, predetermined political-military strategy, carried out *regardless* of any negotiation attempts undertaken by the cities designated as priority targets. This is the case of the strongholds of Ekron and in particular Lachish, a city-fortress of highly strategic importance for the kingdom of Judah.

Ekron, a Philistine city, was the first to be besieged by the Assyrian army. It was conquered but not destroyed. It is unknown whether this relatively favourable treatment depended on its capitulation having been tempestive. While this is certainly possible, it is not demonstrable. In any case, a certain differentiation regarding the fate reserved for the rebels seems to be apparent one, dependent upon the perceived degree of future threat that they could constitute towards the imperial authority. Indeed, once Ekron was taken, Sennacherib had the rulers and nobles who had stirred up its rebellion butchered. He hung their bodies on poles around the city, while showing clemency with the remaining citizens.[267] The same discriminating factor is suggested by another fragmentary text, in which the (unknown) author of a missive writes to Sennacherib on behalf of repentant rebels (of Borsippa), stressing that his guilt must not be deemed grave (i.e. he should not be considered a future threat) and that he wishes to be considered to be amongst the servants of the sovereign.[268]

---

266 Cf. D. Ussishkin, «Sennacherib's Campaign to Philistia and Judah: Ekron, Lachish, and Jerusalem», in: *Essays on Ancient Israel in Its Near Eastern Context*. A Tribute to Nadav Na'aman, *eds.* Y. Amit – E. Ben Zvi – I. Finkelstein – O. Lipschits, Winona Lake 2006, 339–357.

267 "I drew near to Ekron and slew the governors and nobles who had committed sin (that is, rebelled), and hung their bodies on stakes around the city. The citizens who sinned and treated (Assyria) lightly, I counted as spoil. The rest of them, who were not guilty (carriers) of sin and contempt, for whom there was no punishment, – I spoke their pardon" (D.D. Luckenbill, *The Annals of Sennacherib*, 32, col. III: 8–14; cf. RINAP 3/1, no. 22, p. 176).

268 "(2) The king, my lord, should examine the cri[mes ... of a]ll [...s], have [compassio]n on those whose crimes are lig[ht like breath], count (them) among [his servants], and [appoint them] to the ro[yal] service. [...] (8) The Borsippeans [...] – since he pardoned the offence of the protégé [who ..., he will bless him] for as long as he lives and not [commit] a further misdemeanour anymore" (SAA 17 83, ll. 2–11, p. 74). As one can see, the appeal for clemency by the repentant insurgents seems to be founded on an

210 Facing the might of the Babylonian empire

In comparison to that of Ekron, the case of Lachish appears to be quite different. That its fate was sealed anyway, regardless of an inevitable or not act of surrender, is much more probable. In fact, Sennacherib's intention seems from the outset to have been not that of directly attacking Jerusalem, but rather of forcing Hezekiah, who had long been prepared for war and resistance, to negotiate a capitulation, without moving forward with the costly siege of a city even more fortified than the forty-six settlements and fortresses that the Assyrian ruler prided himself on having conquered.[269] To do so, he concentrated his war efforts against Lachish, the most important city-fortress after the capital. Presumably, he had two very precise motives: to drastically reduce the military potential of Hezekiah, and to demonstrate the overwhelming scale of his unequalled power in the battlefield.[270] That is why Lachish *had* to be annihilated. And so it came to pass. The city was conquered by force and burnt to the ground, the enemy officers executed and surviving population led into exile. At this point, for Hezekiah, every humanly practicable option of resistance vanished and he hastened to submit to the hefty tribute.

The second case is equally noteworthy regardless, in other respects, for at least two reasons: it took place only a few decades before the historical conjuncture that we are directly dealing with and, as is pointed out by G.B. Lanfranchi,[271] it is attested in a self-accusing record of correspondence of a foreign king (in which mention is made, in detail, of the events that determined his behaviour) that has no equal in the entire corpus of the surviving royal Assyrian inscriptions. Let us have a look.

The Assyrian king Esarhaddon,[272] son of the great Sennacherib, according to what is attested in his "Letter to God",[273] had officially intimated to Ik-Teshub, sovereign of

---

     attempt to persuade Sennacherib that they do not, in any way, represent a possible threat to the empire. The pragmatic context presupposed would thus be the notorious fact by which the most severe punitive measures would mainly regard those deemed to be threats for future and probable new destabilisations and rebellions.

269   Cf. D.D. LUCKENBILL, *The Annals of Sennacherib*, 32, col. III: 19; 70, l. 28; RINAP 3/2, 80, no. 46, ll. 27b-28a; 185, no. 140, ll. 13–15 (*verso*), etc. Also according to E. Frahm, Sennacherib's decision would not be due to an act of clemency, but rather a calculation of the costs/benefits of such an undertaking: "[...] the effort to capture and destroy the well-protected city would have been so great that it made more sense for Sennacherib to leave its king in office as a loyal vassal of Assyria, following long-standing Assyrian policy" (ID., «Family Matters: Psychohistorical Reflections on Sennacherib and His Times», in: *Sennacherib*, 163–222, here p. 207).

270   As emphasised by D. USSISHKIN, «Sennacherib's Campaign», 353.

271   See G.B. LANFRANCHI, «Ideological Implications of the Problem of Royal Responsibility in the Neo-Assyrian Period», in: *Hayim and Miriam Tadmor Volume*, 100*-110* (here, p. 100*).

272   His reign is to be placed between 681 and 669.

273   See R. BORGER, *Die Inschriften Asarhaddons Königs von Assyrien*, AfO 9, Graz 1956, § 68; E. LEICHTY, «Esarhaddon's "Letters to the Gods"», in: *Ah, Assyria... Studies in Assyrian History and Ancient Near Eastern Historiography Presented to Hayim Tadmor, eds.* M. COGAN – I. EPH'AL, ScrHie 33, Jerusalem 1991, 52–57; I. EPH'AL – H. TADMOR, «Observations on Two Inscriptions of Esarhaddon: Prism Niniveh A and the Letter to the God», in: *Essays on Ancient Israel in Its Near Eastern Context. A Tribute to Nadav Na'aman, eds.* Y. AMIT – E. BEN ZVI – I. FINKELSTEIN – O. LIPSCHITS, Winona Lake 2006, 163–168. The most recent critical edition can be found in RINAP 4, 79–86, no. 33.

The City and its destiny, between resistance and surrender 211

the neighbouring small kingdom of Shubria, the extradition of some important political refugees (i.e. prominent members of his government entourage who had rebelled against him and fled, in search of asylum). After putting up with a third consecutive insulting refusal,[274] in the year 673 Esarhaddon undertook a punitive expedition against this state and laid siege to the Uppume capital with definite, irrevocable intentions.

The nature of these intentions appeared dramatically clear to Ik-Teshub the moment of the Assyrian army's arrival. Putting forth an explicit, immediate act of surrender and submission, by which he handed over himself and his kingdom, Ik-Teshub blatantly declared to accept the *yoke* of Esarhaddon unconditionally, thus hoping to avoid the worst. The refusal he received was dry and contemptuous. The exact words attributed to the king are:

> Let the land Šubria, the land that sinned against you, serve you in its entirety. Place your official over them and *let them pull your yoke*! Lay tribute (and) payment upon them, yearly, without ceasing! [...] May the anger of your heart be appeased. Have mercy on me and remove my punishment![275]

Though the outcome is the opposite, his speech closely resembles the plea for mercy made successfully by Hezekiah to Sennacherib following his own rebellion and the consequent threat of destruction: "Hezekiah, king of Judah, sent (this message) to the king of Assyria at Lachish: 'I have done wrong! Withdraw from me, and I will bear all that you impose on me.' The king of Assyria exacted three hundred talents of silver and thirty talents of gold from Hezekiah, king of Judah" (2 Kgs 18:14). As I emphasised with the use of italics, in the words of the king of Shubria ("Let them *bear your yoke*"), we find the emblematic image of the *yoke* imposed on the neck of the beasts of burden widely attested in the book of Jeremiah (and in the ancient Near East), which metaphorises the concept of submission or surrender to a higher power.

It is interesting to note the official justification given for having refused an act of clemency (which I already mentioned with regard to the clauses of vassalage treaties in the event of a breach of pact): the Assyrian king simply declared his legal function as executor of the judgment delivered by the gods against the sacrilegious violator of the oath of loyalty. And thus, the capital (cf. Fig. 17) and the most important cities were mercilessly destroyed.[276]

Aside from this official justification, a clear propagandistic intent can be read[277] in the entire operation and its scribal documentation, given that with this show of

---

274 Significantly, Esarhaddon, once again in his "Letter to god", specifies that for a sovereign of his rank, it would have been unthinkable to receive even a single denial: "Did you ever hear a mighty king (give his) order twice?" (RINAP 4, 82, no. 33, col. I: 29; cf. R. Borger, *Die Inschriften Asarhaddons*, § 68, Gbr. II, col. I: 29).

275 RINAP 4, 81, no. 33, col. I: 12–14.24 (cf. R. Borger, *Die Inschriften Asarhaddons*, § 68, Gbr. II, col. I: 12–14.24).

276 And in the "Letter to god", as if to further emphasise full conformity to the (politico-religious) right of this military option, the divine favour (of Marduk) is explicitly underscored, manifested quite clearly during the most delicate and decisive siege operations (cf. R. Borger, *Die Inschriften Asarhaddons*, § 68, Gbr. II, col. II: 1–13; RINAP 4, 82–83, no. 33, col. II: 1–13).

277 This aspect is emphasised by A.L. Oppenheim, «Neo-Assyrian and Neo-Babylonian Empires», in: *The Symbolic Instrument in Early Times*, vol. I: *Propaganda and*

strength, only a few months after the scalding defeat suffered in Egypt (in the winter of 673), Esarhaddon could demonstrate that the Assyrian power was still intact. Such exemplary punishment thus acquired a doubly intimidating importance: on the domestic front, it discouraged eventual uprisings and, on the external one, it demonstrated just what those vassals who dared to rebel against his dominion should expect. A few months later, he also invaded Egypt again, and this time successfully.

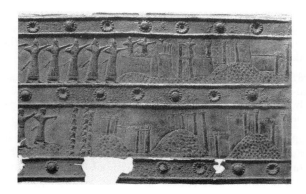

Fig. 17. *The city of Uppume as depicted on bronze panel VIII (top right) of the Balawat Gates of Shalmaneser III (858–824), identified by the caption that reads: "I conquered the city of Uppume, belonging to Anhitte of Šubria". In the lower register, another city can be seen, perhaps from the same kingdom of Šubria (from L.W.* KING, Bronze Reliefs from the Gates of Shalmaneser King of Assyria, London 1915, pl. XLIV).

In addition to these two examples, which are highly significant for my research, I can briefly mention at least a few others. These also come from the ancient world, but they relate to the Greco-Roman realm.[278] I will consider three cases from Greek history and touch upon the Latin world. However distanced their historical-temporal context may be, in my opinion, these references are not less interesting or emblematic, also because they demonstrate that the "escalation" factor is a constant that can be applied in a similar manner to comparable events situated in different segments of universal history.

Let us look at the first two cases, preserved as never-to-be-forgotten in the historiographic accounts of the time. These regard the siege of Plataea led by the Peloponnesians, which lasted from 429 to 427, and the small island of Melos, the Spartan colony destroyed by the Athenians in 416 despite its distinctly neutral stance. We are in the context of the famous thirty-year Peloponnesian war (431–404) that set

---

     Communication in World History, eds. H.D. LASSWELL – D. LERNER – H. SPEIER, Honolulu 1979, 111–144, and above all by I. EPH'AL, «Esarhaddon, Egypt, and Shubria: Politics and Propaganda», *JCS* 57 (2005) 99–102.

278 These are exemplifications that increase in number in proportion to the greater availability of historiographic evidence, especially concerning Roman history.

The City and its destiny, between resistance and surrender   213

Athens (and the The Delian League) against Sparta (with the Peloponnesian League). And, in fact, their opposing hegemonic ambitions[279] led them to pummel the entire world in the bloodiest war event that history had ever seen.

In the case of Plataea, while reading the detailed and dramatic account of Thucydides' *History of the Peloponnesian War* (which unfolds in the events reported in books II and III), the reader finds themself partaking in the thrill of a gruelling siege. They experience ceaseless attempts at assault and defence characterised by chequered fortunes, with tremendous use of ingenuity and energy to cope with the developments of an ever-precarious, evolving situation. For my topic, it is interesting to highlight the story's epilogue by setting it in relation, as does Thucydides himself, with a close pragmatic context: that is, the negotiations that had previously taken place, in several stages (cf. II, 2; 4–6; 12; 71–74; etc.), as the enemies had vainly attempted to persuade the Plataeans to secede from Athens and join the Lacedaemonians. Just as in the case of Jerusalem in the face of the Babylonian empire, here too, what is staged is an imperialism (the Spartan one) attacking a minor state entity that does not intend to give in to its various requests for submission. For the city of Plataea, the cost of their repeated refusal was brute annihilation. Exhausted by the siege and seeing their hopes of getting help from Athens collapse, after bartering a negotiation, the Plataeans ultimately surrendered, and gains and losses were quickly drawn. The besiegers had carried on a tremendous effort for a long time, depleting themselves significantly to get the better of a garrison of, in the final stages of the war, a mere 250 men (or little more, since another 200, at least, had managed to flee). These, with their fierce resistance, had increasingly exacerbated the spirits of the assailants. Not to mention that at the end of an Athenian siege of Potidea, which during the same years had been in counterposition to those attacking Plataea, the winners' treatment of the defeated had aroused indignation. While the Athenians had not killed the Potideans, they had reduced them to starvation and released them with no more than the mere necessities for immediate survival. Holding this in consideration, the victors at Plataea staged a farcical trial that concluded in the brutal butchering of all the survivors, despite their having surrendered to given conditions. It is therefore easy to observe how, in these circumstances as well, the "escalation" factor proved decisive for the final outcome.

I now turn to the case of Melos. The Athenians had sent a diplomatic mission to the island to negotiate and impose submission. The Melians, however, had reiterated their wish to remain neutral, offering their friendship in any case. This was not considered sufficient by the aggressors and it came to a fight, one in which the preponderant military force of Athens had a clearly disproportionate advantage. In Thucydides' famous account, one can see the dramatic outcome of a resistance to the bitter end, carried out beyond any "reasonable" motive (this, obviously, according to the imperialistic perspective of the assailants, which the Greek historian stigmatises).[280] And so once again, in this case, the phenomenon of *escalation* returns. The conflict is exasperated to the point where,

---

279   For the obsidional techniques used in this period, it is also useful to look at M. BETTALLI, «Il controllo di città e piazzeforti in Tucidide: l'arte degli assedi nel V secolo a.C.», ASNSP.L Serie III 23 (1993) 825–845.

280   In this regard, see the text extracted from the *Historiae* of Thucydides for its literary peculiarities and narrative autonomy, translated into Italian and commented with

214   Facing the might of the Babylonian empire

nearly on the brink of the collapse, the inhabitants of Melos decide to surrender. They *hand themselves over* to the Athenians and their will. The siege concludes, nonetheless, with a full-blown slaughter: the city was destroyed, all the adult males butchered, and women and children deported and sold as slaves.

> At about the same time the Melians seized another part of the Athenians' encircling wall, which was only lightly guarded. But as a result of this passage of events another force was subsequently dispatched from Athens, under the command of Philocrates son of Demeas. The Melians were now under heavy siege and there was also some treachery from within, so they surrendered to the Athenians, to be dealt with as they wished. The Athenians killed all the adult males they had taken and enslaved the women and children. The place itself they occupied with their own people, sending out 500 colonists at some later time.[281]

A third case worthy of note, in the Greek world, is that of Mantineia, laid to siege and then destroyed (in 226) by the Macedonian Antigonus Doson, ally of the Achaeans. I will briefly mention this case as seen through the eyes of the historian Polybius (*Historiae*, II, 54, 57),[282] who places himself in critical dialogue with the Athenian Phylarchus (of whose body of work only fragments remain). The killing of all adult males and sale of the rest of the population as slaves despite a surrender treaty is justified by Polybius, a supporter of Antigonus, as a consequence of the betrayal which had tarnished the inhabitants of Mantineia four years previous. Subjugated by Aratus, they had received treatment of great lenity which, however, they had later repaid by betraying the stipulated alliance in order to turn to the Spartans, slaughtering all the Achaeans stationed in the city. Here the category of *escalation* conflates more than elsewhere with that of *revenge*.[283] But the underlying question does not change. This example also clearly demonstrates that negotiations for surrender and a consequent voluntary submission to the besiegers were not means sufficient to guarantee a more favourable fate than that met by the inhabitants of Plataea or Melos.

As for Roman world, which is rich with testimonies of this sort,[284] it may suffice to highlight the implications deriving from the idea of "peace" that oriented all

---

      acute reflections by Luciano Canfora (TUCIDIDE, *Il dialogo dei Melii e degli Ateniesi. A cura di Luciano Canfora con testo a fronte*, Venezia 1991).

281   THUCYDIDES, *Historiae*, V,112–116 (I cite from § 116,2–4, referring again to the translation by J. Mynott (THUCYDIDES, *The War*, 385–386).

282   Plutarch also gives news of this in *Aratus*, 45,6–9.

283   In this regard, see D. KONSTAN, *Pity Transformed*, London 2001, 85–88.

284   Amongst the many examples that could be cited, think of the emblematic outcome of the Punic Wars, which terminated with the total destruction of Carthage in 146 B.C. on the part of Scipio Aemilianus, despite the unconditional surrender offered by the Carthaginians ("For the Carthaginians had been guilty of no immediate offence to Rome, but the Romans had treated them with irremediable severity, although they had accepted all their conditions and consented to obey all their orders"; cf. POLYBIUS, *Historiae* XXXVI,9.5–8; translation from POLYBIUS, *The Histories*. With an English Translation by W.R. Paton, VI, LCL 161, Cambridge [MA] – London 1968, 369), or the campaigns of the emperor Aurelian against Palmyra (and its queen Zenobia), which came to a conclusion in A.D. 273 with the decision to raze the city to the ground ("[...] which he took and razed without a struggle"; ZOSIMUS, *Historia*

The City and its destiny, between resistance and surrender

interrational politics[285] at the time of the Republic. The notion of *pax*, contrary to our modern preconceptions, was not conceived so much as a state of well-being or alliance (a meaning reserved, more than anything, for the "domestic" sphere), but as a series of restrictions imposed from above (whether *pax deorum* or that of the victorious generals) in response to the pleas of those defeated.

The semantic field of *pax* was interwoven with the concept of a necessary *deditio*, that is, a total and absolute surrender (which I will return to discuss in the next chapter in reference to the Jeremianic request), tied to *deprecatio* (supplication) and a spirit that was *fractus*, devoid of any arrogance or claim to mercy. The conquerors could be merciful, or not be so at all. But this was always seen on a case to case basis, as deemed best for the implementation of the conqueror's notion of *pax*. Hence, it is not directly of *escalation* that one speaks here, but rather of a concept lying even further upstream: surrender neither implied nor provided for the stipulation of a treaty, but rather a complete handing over of oneself to the unforeseeable will of those representing the power of Rome. In that regard, this is Polybius' attestation about what was meant by the act of surrender (expressed in Greek on the basis of the Latin locution *dedere se in fidem*), at least at the time of the Third Punic War:

> I have previously stated what this phrase (*dedere se in fidem*) means, but it is here necessary to remind my readers briefly of its significance. *Those who thus commit themselves to the faith of Rome* [οἱ γὰρ διδόντες αὑτοὺς εἰς τὴν Ῥωμαίων ἐπιτροπήν] surrender in the first place the whole of their territory and the cities in it, next all the inhabitants of the land and the towns, male and female, likewise all rivers, harbours, temples, tombs, so that the result is that the Romans enter into possession of everything and those who surrender remain in possession of absolutely nothing.[286]

There is a literary example that can help us grasp the meaning of the many other actual cases that I will not be exploring herein. In the *Aeneid*, Virgil would seem to render the said programmatic *parcere subiectis et debellare superbos* (6, 853) incarnate in the protagonist. And yet, when Aeneas imagines the defeated Turnus imploring mercy, prostrated on his knees in front of him before the eyes of all the people, he shows him no mercy and kills him (12, 930–931; 936–937). Surrendering to the Romans could, in any case, mean this. And a dramatisation of the conflict could only render this possibility even more probable.

Nova, I, 54–61, here no. 61; translation from Zosimus, *New History. A Translation with Commentary by Ronald T. Ridley*, AABS 2, Camberra 1982, 19) and to exterminate almost all of its inhabitants ("We have not spared the women, we have slain the children, we have butchered the old men, we have destroyed the peasants [...]"; cf. Scriptores Historiae Augustae, *Divus Aurelianus*, 31,5–6; translation from Scriptores Historiae Augustae, *The Scriptores Historiae Augustae. With an English Translation by D. Magie*, III, LCL 263, Cambridge (MA) – London 1932, 255), as a result of its repeated rebellions.

285 For further study on the topic, I refer in particular to C.A. Barton, «The Price of Peace in Ancient Rome», in: *War and Peace in the Ancient World*, ed. K.A. Raaflaub, Malden – Oxford 2007, 244–255.

286 Polybius, *Historiae* XXXVI,4,1–3; translation from Polybius, *The Histories*, VI, 359.

216 Facing the might of the Babylonian empire

An historical example from the Roman era, which is in any case worth mentioning for its suggestive analogy with the facts with which we are dealing, illustrate the concept. We can draw this from the final events regarding the fall of Jerusalem in A.D. 70, as recounted by Flavius Josephus in his *Judean War*. In the decisive stages of the gruelling siege lead by Titus, in which the diehard rebels put the Roman army up to a stiff challenge, the priests who survive decide to surrender and plead with the Roman general to spare their lives. Titus, however, who had even shown himself as merciful, considerate towards the fate of the temple and ready to forgive, presents himself as utterly unbending:

> But he told them that the time for pardon had for them gone by, that the one thing for whose sake he might with propriety have spared them was gone [the Temple], and that it behoved priests to perish with their temple, and so ordered them to execution.[287]

Despite this, Titus proves still willing to resume negotiations and puts surrender back on the table, guaranteeing the insurgents salvation. So Flavius Josephus places a speech on Titus' lips that is very meaningful for my topic, since it is thoroughly dominated by the category of *escalation*,[288] the motivation that determines the dramatic final destiny of Jerusalem and its inhabitants. The Roman commander, addressing the rebels, retraces all the historical stages that led them to that decisive moment, a story studded with countless acts of tolerance, patience, and clemency on the part of the Romans towards the Jews, who had instead responded with continual, senseless rebellions. Even during the siege, Titus claims to have shown himself to be exceedingly lenient, to the point where he has surpassed all limits. His reaction is presented as a comprehensible one: "And after all this, most abominable wretches, do you now invite me to a parley?"[289] And yet, he would still be willing to grant them their lives, reserve punishment for the incorrigible and dispose of the others according to his will (along precisely the lines referred to by Jeremiah with life saved "as war booty"). The conditions the Jews pose are, however, unacceptable, since they do not seem to configure in the least to a real act of surrender. And it is only at this point that Titus, overtaken with rage, decides to spare no one.[290]

What emerges from all this data and the respective historical reconstructions is that the outcome of a war launched by a besieging power resulting from an exasperation of the conflict or a willingness to definitively and drastically resolve a problematic political-military scenario, could, without a doubt, also take no account of negotiations or treaties of surrender aimed to offer special guarantees to those defeated.

---

287 *Bellum iudaicum*, VI,6,321–322; translation from FLAVIUS JOSEPHUS, *Josephus.* The Jewish War, Books IV–VII, With an English Translation by H. St. J. Thackeray, III, LCL 210, London – New York 1928, 471.

288 Cf. *Bellum iudaicum*, VI,6,323–355.

289 *Ibid.*, VI,6,347; FLAVIUS JOSEPHUS, *Josephus*, III, 477.

290 "Thereupon Titus, indignant that men in the position of captives should proffer proposal to him as victors, ordered proclamation to be made to them neither to desert nor to hope for terms any longer, for he would spare none; but to fight with all their might and save themselves as best they could, because all his actions henceforth would be governed by the laws of war (*Bellum iudaicum*, VI,6,352; FLAVIUS JOSEPHUS, *Josephus*, III, 479). But he then changed his mind and even the soldiers, tired of killing, used clemency (cf. *Ibid.*, VI,8,378–383).

The City and its destiny, between resistance and surrender · 217

But let me now return to our own specific historical frame of reference and try to focalise the political scenario that we are reading in light of the category of *escalation*. Nebuchadnezzar had actually already shown himself as being too benevolent when, tyrannically entering the Syrian-Palestinian strip after the victory of Carchemish of 605, he had accepted the oath of allegiance of Jehoiakim, a former vassal of Egypt, without replacing him with another ruler of his choice. Just three years later, this action was followed by an about-face by Jehoiakim and a consequent Babylonian military intervention, which, with a heavy hand, had intended to resolve the issue in a radical way. It was the Babylonian ruler's intention that the question be closed with the depredation of the riches of the temple and other raids, and above all with the deportation of the successor to the throne (Jehoiachin) along with the most influential part of the population. Nebuchadnezzar still trusted the Davidic dynasty with Zedekiah. But the latter, soon suspected of secessionist plots for which he very likely had to respond to Babylon personally, also eventually rebelled.

Aside from this progressive deterioration of international relations between Babylon and Jerusalem, the political situation of Nebuchadnezzar could be placed in parallel with precisely that of Esarhaddon. The latter, after experiencing defeat in Egypt, knew how to react promptly through an effective campaign of deterrence towards internal and external rebellions. Likewise, Nebuchadnezzar, after his unsuccessful Egyptian expedition, found himself in a situation that was similar, if not worse. He could not, in fact, avoid the risk of internal destabilisation, and found himself engaged in the violent repression of a dangerous sedition at court. If, as is probable, precisely this sign of weakness gave rise to Zedekiah's rebellion, then even Nebuchadnezzar had to have found himself – *a fortiori* – in need of presenting a show of force like that Esarhaddon had presented against the kingdom of Shubria.

And here, my initial question proves even more relevant: would it have been realistic on the basis of this political context, which could have been well known and assessed (perhaps better than now), to expect the same positive result from the act of surrender that had derived from it at the time of Jehoiachin in 597, when the city had been saved, almost *in extremis* from destruction? To respond negatively with utter confidence would most definitely not be prudent. But we can, at this point, by all means avoid qualifying the Jeremianic proposal as the *only* truly "realist" one, practically believing that all his adversaries were completely blinded by an ideology electing for collective suicide and incapable of a political assessment oriented towards an alternative, acceptable, and above all, feasible solution to the crisis.[291]

---

291   In this sense, the position taken by C.R. SEITZ, *Theology in Conflict*, 206–208, also seems rather simplistic to me. According to this, Jeremiah's stance would "obviously" derive from the experience of 597: given that the surrender of Jehoiachin had saved Jerusalem and that only a part of its inhabitants had been deported, in the case of the rebellion of Zedekiah as well, if they were to surrender, things ought to have gone the same way. Even this perspective, which implicitly makes Jeremiah out to be a realist and the majority of his contemporaries clueless (keeping in mind the scenario that can be derived from the book of Jeremiah), does not take into consideration in the least bit either the evolution of the complex politico-military aspects of the situation or the *escalation* factor and exasperated intensification of the conflict.

218   Facing the might of the Babylonian empire

3.3.2.6. Scorched earth

To further confirm the plausibility of this interpretation, attention need also be drawn to another important element. The Assyrians, despite their notorious "decisiveness" in the suppression of riots, destruction of rebel cities, and mass deportations, had always shown considerable interest in the economic development of the border provinces and paid particular attention to the cities of the Philistine plain.[292] The Babylonian policy on these territories, on the other hand, seems to assume the physiognomy of a "scorched earth" strategy.[293] Their primary interest was turning out not to be the systematic economic exploitation of those regions (apart from the drain of annual tributes, of course), but rather the eradication of the dangerous Egyptian influence and zeroing of the state structures gravitating in its orbit, real or potential allies on whom the pharaoh could count for a possible reconquering of Palestine.[294]

As a matter of fact, the Babylonian Empire had a strongly centralised system of government that was fundamentally concerned with the prosperity of the capital and its adjacent Mesopotamian territories. For this reason, the cities and states that dared rebel against it were more likely to risk total destruction, given its fundamental lack of any desire tending towards any long-term systematic exploitation of territorial resources, or reorganization of any efficient government structure. The Assyrians, on the other hand, had invested a great deal in this, in terms of urbanisation and deployment of military and bureaucratic personnel. In short, if annual tributes failed to be delivered to the Babylonians, the stripping and depredation of the rebel cities and their reduction to military provinces or outposts was not in the least inconceivable as a possibility. This was especially true along the Syrian-Palestinian strip, considered to be a strategic buffer zone from Egypt. It made more sense to depower this area than to entrust its management to vassal states upon whose loyalty one could not necessarily count.[295] The result of this orientation turned out to be devastating for all of Palestine, even for the years to come, up to the Persian period.[296]

---

292   As is clearly shown by D.S. VANDERHOOFT, *The Neo-Babylonian Empire*, 82–83.
293   As does, again, D.S. Vanderhooft (*Ibid.*, 82 and 111), who speaks of a "scorched earth policy".
294   Cf. *Ibid.*, 112.
295   Cf. O. LIPSCHITS, *The Fall*, 66.
296   My reconstruction of this is based predominantly on E. STERN, *Archaeology of the Land of the Bible*. Vol. II. The Assyrian, Babylonian, and Persian Periods 732–332 B.C.E., New York 2001, 307–311 and on the contribution by E. GASS, «Nebukadnezzar ante portas – Zu den babylonischen Interessen in der südlichen Levante», *ZAW* 128 (2016) 247–266, which demonstrates how there are serious elements of an archaeological nature (above all, the absence of pottery from the Babylonian period), both to validate the confirmation of their being a destructive "scorched earth policy" on the part of the Babylonians, and to maintain that the so-called "empty land" myth not be a myth at all: "Alles in allem gilt: Der Keramikbefund und die Glyptik zeigen deutlich, dass die Babylonier kaum an einer wirtschaftlichen Blüte der südlichen Levante interessiert gewesen sind" (p. 258); "Zu Beginn der babylonischen Zeit kam es offenbar zu einem Kollaps, von dem sich Juda erst nach zwei Jahrhunderten persischer Zeit erholen konnte. Somit war die Zerstörung des judäischen Berglandes durch die Babylonier größer, als dies oft zugegeben wird. Hinzu kommt, dass es nur im Norden zu einer nachweisbaren Zunahme von neuen Siedlungen kam, während eine

The City and its destiny, between resistance and surrender   219

The systematic destruction of Ashkelon, Ekron, Ashdod, Tel Batash-Timnah, and other Philistine cities (and not only) by Nebuchadnezzar[297] would have most likely delivered a clear sign of this policy, readable not only to us, external observers judging from documents that attest so *faits accomplis*. Indeed, it is not hard to conceive that these signs would have also fairly clearly rendered to the kingdom of Judah the probability that the Babylonians would have had no particular scruples about reducing even Jerusalem to a "heap of rubble" (according to the term used in the Babylonian chronicles to refer to the fate inflicted on the city of Ashkelon),[298] notwithstanding a possible surrender *in extremis*, seeing as they did not, in fact, have any particular interest in the development of that peripheral region which was, moreover, the seat of an obstinately rebellious state.[299]

The end of Jerusalem, as was already observed, does not, in fact, appear to be an act dictated by a chance vindictive impulse. Its end seems rather to have been a well-calculated decision aiming to: (1) remove the Davidic dynasty from the throne, since it had proven again and again to be rebellious and unreliable; (2) erase Jerusalem's key role, and to replace it with another local administrative centre (Mispa) placed under direct Babylonian control.[300] This, I would add, should be linked to the Chaldean ruler's never-abandoned ambition to match the achievements of the great Ashurbanipal: to subjugate, once and for all, Egypt, its eternal rival and sole obstacle to Babylon's dominion over the entire Orient. In this light, ensuring absolute control of the border territories by definitively eliminating all small rebel kingdoms had to be a central objective, one long overdue.

---

     merkliche Wiederbesiedlung im Süden ausblieb. Die babylonische Eroberung führte folglich zu einem demographischen und wirtschaftlichen Kollaps Judas" (p. 262).

297   Cf. D.S. Vanderhooft, *The Neo-Babylonian Empire*, 82–83. Considering the extent of the period of Babylonian hegemony overall, the list is obviously much longer and truly impressive, confirmation of the interpretive method that I have called *escalation*: "The evidence for Babylonian destructions of cities and towns in Judah and adjacent regions is overwhelming: Jerusalem, Ramat Rahiel, Lachish, Gezer, Beth-Shemesh, Ein Gedi, Arad, Kadesh Barnea, Meṣad Hashavyahu, Tell Keisan (IV), Megiddo (II), Dor, Akko, Tell 'Erani, Tell el-Hesi, Tell Jemmeh, Tell Malhata, and Tell er-Ruqeish [...] are among the cities destroyed in the early sixth century" (p. 106). See also A. Mazar, *Archaeology of the Land of the Bible: 10,000–586 B.C.E.,* New York 1990, 458–461. On the other hand, H.B. Barstad, «Who Destroyed Ashkelon? On Some Problems in Relating Text to Archaeology», in: *Let Us Go up to Zion*. Essays in Honour of H.G.M. Williamson on the Occasion of His Sixty-Fifth Birthday, *eds.* I. Provan – M.J. Boda, Leiden – Boston 2012, 345–357, disputes the identification (made by A.K. Grayson) of Ashkelon as the city about which Nebuchadnezzar boasts in the Babylonian chronicles of having entirely destroyed (attested by *in situ* excavations), and holds the Assyrians responsible.

298   Cf. J.-J. Glassner, *Mesopotamian Chronicles*, 229.

299   And, in fact, the archaeological data show that the Babylonians spared only a small strip of the kingdom of Judah, in particular, the area of Benjamin and the city of Mizpah, which was chosen as the seat for the governor installed by them (Gedaliah) after the destruction of Jerusalem.

300   Cf. O. Lipschits, *The Fall*, 68.

220 Facing the might of the Babylonian empire

3.3.2.7. Reasons

In conclusion: I believe it is incorrect to consider Jeremiah's position as being more realistic than that of his opponents. The factual data does not confirm this interpretation. Even considering the question from a modern point of view, that is, by setting aside the more markedly religious motivations that I have highlighted, both positions had a fairly solid basis, politically speaking. It seems, therefore, too simple to divide the actors of this drama into realists on the one hand, and nationalist, religious fanatics on the other. Both could have had their own, well-founded reasons.[301]

From the historical context we have illustrated, it follows that the act of surrender, repeatedly called for by Jeremiah in the final phase of the kingdom of Judah, is not to be considered the suggestion of an *exit-strategy* with an absolutely guaranteed positive outcome (indeed, almost the contrary would appear so). Nor, on the other hand, can the decision to rebel against Babylon and resist to the bitter end be considered senseless, in the belief that perhaps the future fate of the kingdom was, in fact, definitively sealed regardless. And in any event, it is obvious that any choice, however politically far-sighted, can never take into account all the variables at stake and be immune from the unforeseen.

If Jeremiah is not exactly a "realist", then is Isaiah, on the other hand, hopelessly destined to be considered a "utopian"? Addressing this issue now would carry me beyond my present scope, but I can state that this conception as well calls for a serious revisitation, as has already been emphasised for some time.[302]

3.3.3. Towards an alternative solution: Surrender as a "prophetic act"

The attribution of a special "political clairvoyance" or "realism" in reference to Jeremiah's position and based on an oppositional comparison with Isaiah is, as we have seen, in and of itself, rather fragile, especially if set in relation to a thorough assessment of the historical-political context of the time. For this reason, this hermeneutical perspective appears to not be capable of adequately accounting for the peculiarity of the Jeremianic message. This does not, however, mean affirming that at the time of Jeremiah, even according to a *Weltanshauung* that inextricably intertwined the religious and political dimensions,[303] the prophetic messages could not have been understood by activating communicative-receptive channels that were inadequate and misleading all the same. In a certain sense, likewise according to *ante litteram* "realistic" perspectives.

---

301 Those of Jeremiah are well known and clearly expressed in his prophetic oracles, but I will study them more in-depth later on.

302 For Isaiah, in fact, contrary to what is often asserted, faith does not mean mere passivity and does not oppose the use of human resources. Nor can it be said to be the expression of a utopian a-political position. Along these lines, see e.g. B. UFFENHEIMER, «Isaiah's and Micah's Approaches to Policy and History», in: *Politics and Theopolitics*, 176–188 (here, p. 183); G.C.I. WONG, «The Nature of Faith in Isaiah of Jerusalem», *TynB* 47 (1996) 188–190; ID., «Faith in the Present Form of Isaiah VII 1–17», *VT* 51 (2001) 535–547; H. ROUILLARD-BONRAISIN, «Ésaïe, Jérémie», 197–198.

303 While not sharing the extremist position of S.M. PAUL, *Studies in the Book of the Covenant in the Light of Cuneiform and Biblical Law*, VT.S 18, Leiden 1970, 37 (according to which, the distinction typical of Roman law between *jus* and *fas* would be

The City and its destiny, between resistance and surrender   221

Following a broad definition of the term, the message to surrender could have been perceived as more or less "realistic" to the extent that it may have been found to correspond to prudent political calculations ("the king's affairs"). Meanwhile, the more properly religious aspects ("the things of God") may have also been devolved to specialists in the sector[304]: priests, Levites, prophets, or anyone who could not do without that templar institution that guaranteed their permanence and social recognition. These institutional figures needed favourable oracles, a call to tradition, and a healthy dose of irrationality and popular fury. For them, Jeremiah's message was neither utopian nor realistic. It was simply *outrageous*.

The rulers (שָׂרִים), on the other hand, could favour a more pragmatic approach (cf. ch. 26) and then, as now, things could be seen in a different way, that is, in a privileged relationship with their own interests and reasons of state. And this is just how then, as now, Jeremiah's position could be reduced, perhaps unknowingly, to merely a *debatable political stance*. Fatal for some, instrumentally advantageous for others. The point however is precisely this: the call to surrender, according to my hermeneutical act, in the twofold context of the book of Jeremiah (historical and/or solely literary) cannot be reduced to one perspective or the other. It is, first and foremost, *prophecy*. And it demands to be understood and studied on precisely this eminently theological level.

Some authors admit this, even if they do so *en passant*.[305] F.J. Gonçalves himself, while stating with regard to the "realistic" position of Jeremiah that "en l'occurrence, le réalisme coïncidait avec ce que Jérémie croyait être la volonté de Yahvé",[306] recognises that the underlying motivations of both prophets, though only insofar as these regarded a condemnation of the alliances with Egypt and Assyria, are to be understood exclusively as "d'ordre religieux".[307] But if it is true that Jeremiah's message about the need for surrender is also conceived within this theological (or theo-political) program, then its significance cannot be adequately comprehended by limiting oneself to an analysis carried out solely on the level of historical factuality considered merely from a political viewpoint. Indeed, we have seen that the call to "surrender to the king of Babylon" cannot be considered in and of itself the suggestion of a strategic choice with known or evident probabilities of success.

According to a hermeneutic respectful of the revelatory significance of the biblical text, judging these prophetic messages on the merit of their being realistic or not

---

entirely abolished by the law expressed by the Bible), it can however be said that too rigid a separation between these two dimensions is unknown in the ancient Near East and in biblical Israel, as is pointed out e.g. by Z.W. FALK, «Religion and State», 49; M. DANDAMAYEV, «State Gods and Private Religion in the Near East in the First Millennium B.C.E.», in: *Religion and Politics in the Ancient Near East, ed.* A. BERLIN, Bethesda 1996, 35–45.; N.K. GOTTWALD, *The Politics of Ancient Israel,* Louisville 2001, 3,10,14–15.

304 Cf Z.W. FALK, «Religion and State», 50.
305 E.g. J.A. WILCOXEN, «Political Background», 160, states that the pro-Babylonian position of Jeremiah "may have been colored by non-political factors". In my opinion, on the other hand, the ultimate meaning of the Jeremianic message is to be sought in precisely this direction.
306 Cf. F.J. GONÇALVES, «Isaïe, Jérémie», 298.
307 Cf. *Ibid.*, 296.

proves to be quite gratuitous. It would seem more pertinent to study them as they are presented and have been transmitted, that is, as "prophecies". In this sense, they are comprehensible only by starting from the symbolic and literary coordinates (of pragmatic significance) of exactly the world in which they are grounded. The world of the text and the world to which the text refers. This is the fundamental hermeneutical context. And a structurative part of this context, as we will see, is its *symbolic-semiotic dimension.*

Grounded in factuality but projected towards a germination of meaning that moves past it and opens onto a "beyond", what occurs in the *hic et nunc* of the text, read and transmitted prophetically, reaches not only its contemporaries with a precise and authoritative prophetic injunction, but also an indefinite number of potential readers, and thus, it can define the paradigmatic meaning of other existential horizons. The call for submission to Babylon and, specifically and above all, the call to an act of surrender, therefore waits for a reception and assessment that is to be carried out on an eminently *prophetic* plane. And this is precisely because the message of Jeremiah, in the context of its literary microcosm, is first and foremost a *proclamation* and *prophetic call.* In other words, it is an act of reading history considered from the point of view of YHWH.

Let me now, therefore, enter into the merits of a study of the message of Jeremiah that takes account of this horizon given by the text and its symbolic-semiotic paradigms. An analysis of their articulated and complex communicative potential will be the key to understanding that what Jeremiah asked of the people of his time (at least, according to the semiotic architecture of the text that we are given to read today) was not simply to surrender, but to surrender *prophetically.* To make a choice, yes, but a "prophetic choice". And in order to properly focalise this interpretative category, we must continue our journey through the book of Jeremiah.

PART II

"Bow your necks beneath the yoke of the king of Babylon!"

TEXTS
WORDS – ACTIONS – SIGNIFICATIONS

The Lord said to me:
Make yourself (yoke) halters and pegs
and place them across your neck [...]

(Jer 27:2)

Chapter III
Jer 21:1–10.
The surrender as acceptance of the end:
A symbolic-narrative prolepsis
and hermeneutical key to an entire history

φωνὴ ἀπ᾽ ἀνατολῆς, φωνὴ ἀπὸ δύσεως, φωνὴ ἀπὸ τῶν τεσσάρων ἀνέμων, φωνὴ ἐπὶ Ἱεροσόλυμα καὶ τὸν ναόν, φωνὴ ἐπὶ νυμφίους καὶ νύμφας, φωνὴ ἐπὶ τὸν λαὸν πάντα.[1]

1. Introduction: Orientative coordinates

1.1. Literary context and intertextual references as devices for meaning

One can certainly study a particular theme that is not exclusively ascribable to an isolated text and purport to have obtained scientific results by having performed a detailed analysis of all the attestations in which the theme of interest emerges. If a study of this sort lacks a general hermeneutic, however, it risks remaining devoid of a wider-ranging scope. It could, in other words, be in jeopardy of limiting itself to merely highlighting the same elements in several texts and producing an expositive repetitiveness unsuitable for penetrating the argument according to its variegated characteristic features. In the end, these traits would wind up somehow dispersed throughout the various texts (and in the relative chapters of the dissertation), without being adequately organised within a convincing interpretive schema.

I am instead persuaded that the very nature of the scientific method be not only that of meticulously investigating minute individual data, but also – and above all – that of proposing, testing, and verifying the plausibility of a hermeneutical key adequate for providing an explanation of the phenomenon in the light of broader contexts. I will thus, henceforth, attempt to adopt this twofold analytical-interpretive approach. While it will be the third part of the present dissertation that is consecrated, above all, to the hermeneutical dimension, in this second part, this perspective will already consent me to render an account of the peculiar specificity of the various texts I have selected as those most significant with respect to the attestation of the theme of the surrender.

---

1   "*A voice from the east, a voice from the west, a voice from the four winds; a voice against Jerusalem and the sanctuary, a voice against the bridegroom and the bride, a voice against all the people*" (*Bellum iudaicum*, VI,5,301; FLAVIUS JOSEPHUS, *Josephus*, III, 462–465). Flavius Josephus prefixes his narration of the destruction of the temple of Jerusalem (70 B.C.) with an articulated prolepsis in which several warning signs are reported. Amongst these, we see presented the figure and words of a certain Jesus son of Ananias, who, in the seven years preceding the Roman siege, announces the impending end in every way possible.

226   Jer 21:1-10. The surrender as acceptance of the end

As a case in point, Jer 21:1–10, for the problems tied to its placement within the book of Jeremiah and the complex symbolic plot it gives us a glimpse into, allows me to focus my inquiry on two fairly circumscribed areas that are, in any case, mutually interdependent. On the one hand, we have the question regarding the *insertion of the theme* of surrender given within a literary context strangely distant from the narrative section of the book of Jeremiah dedicated to the facts pertaining to the prophet's biography and the final days of Jerusalem (chs. 26–45; not counting 30–31). On the other, I have the sense that it be precisely the succinctness of the historical framing of the account, almost a pretext for introducing the Jeremianic oracle about the end and the surrender according to a precise perspective,[2] that gives emphasis to a *dense interweaving of references* to highly significant biblical motifs. It is together that these contribute to confer a *symbolic-prophetic* dimension (and not so much a cautionary or anecdotal one) on the need to surrender to the king of Babylon.

1.2. Specific objectives and articulation of the study of Jer 21:1–10

In this phase of my research, building upon the hermeneutical implications resulting from the particular redactional positioning of 21:1–10 and based on specific textual evidence, I propose to demonstrate that the political act of surrender is adopted by the prophetic word to *symbolically-prophetically* signify and solicit acceptance of the end (YHWH's righteous judgement on Jerusalem) as a paradoxical condition for remaining alive (and thus gaining access to a new Covenant). Invoking the symbolic dimension means referencing a complex world. To begin, I will refer to the dynamic of signification that extends beyond literality while still being grounded within it, and will postpone more in-depth study of the categorisation that I propose to chapters VI and VII of the present dissertation.

Following the initial approach to the textual data (§ 2), I will seek to demonstrate the plausibility of this interpretation by articulating my study in two phases:

1. An analysis of the particular relationship that Jer 21:1–10 has with the *context* of the proximal chapters (§ 3) will provide us with important *clues*[3] to the symbolic relevance that the "redactor" wished to bestow upon the gesture of "surrender to the king of Babylon" under a twofold articulation: to the theme of the end, and to that of a new beginning. The final judgement on Jerusalem is, in fact, established as a key of interpretation for all that follows (from 21:11–14 to ch. 24), in the same way that the call to surrender coincides with the possibility of entering into the design of that God who operates mysteriously for the good of his people in view of a new beginning.

2. Once these two fundamental thematic poles (end – new beginning) have been identified, we will study the oracle of Jeremiah in the light of some Covenant motifs (§ 4). I will demonstrate how 21:1–10 recalls and remodulates *ad hoc* the literary traditions of the origins[4] not simply by inverting them, but by reutilising them to

---

2   Cf. 21:2: As we shall see, this regards the perspective that recalls fundamental originary motifs of the history of Israel.

3   It should be remembered that according to the inferential model of communication I have adopted (cf. General Introduction, § 3.3.4), to communicate corresponds to the production and interpretation of *clues* (cf. C. BIANCHI, *Pragmatica del linguaggio*, 106).

4   Moreover, as was clearly pointed out by G. Fischer (in his already cited article «Il libro di Geremia»), the text we have before us reveals a broad knowledge of much

A first approach to the textual data

indicate, within the drama of a radical and now inevitable punitive judgement, the powerful presence of the *same* liberator and saviour God who is protagonist of the Exodus (§ 4.1). The question will thus not be simply that of recognising the narrative threads of an "anti-Exodus" (as an end in itself) within the textual drama, but rather the *emergence* of a genuine "new Exodus" of salvation initiated not only *after* the punishment (as a return from the country of the North; cf. 23:8), but already from *within* it (§ 4.2). It is like a new time of origin inaugurated by YHWH in the history of Israel by way of a call to voluntarily accept punishment (and death) as a *transition* toward a new life ("given as war booty"), for a new Covenant.

The methodological procedures, prevalently of a lexicographic nature, that will follow will thus have the function of underscoring in particular those aspects of the text that can steer comprehension of the message of Jeremiah towards its eminently prophetic dimension.

2. A first approach to the textual data

2.1. Hebrew text, translation, and philological-exegetical notes[5] on Jer 21:1–10

הַדָּבָר אֲשֶׁר־הָיָה אֶל־יִרְמְיָהוּ   **1**   [This is] the word that came to Jeremiah
מֵאֵת יְהוָה בִּשְׁלֹחַ אֵלָיו הַמֶּלֶךְ צִדְקִיָּהוּ   from the Lord, when King Zedekiah sent him
אֶת־פַּשְׁחוּר בֶּן־מַלְכִּיָּה וְאֶת־צְפַנְיָה   Pashhur son of Malchiah and Zephaniah,
בֶן־מַעֲשֵׂיָה הַכֹּהֵן לֵאמֹר   son of Maaseiah, the priest to tell him:

דְּרָשׁ־נָא בַעֲדֵנוּ אֶת־יְהוָה כִּי נְבוּכַדְרֶאצַר   **2**   "*Consult the Lord for us, because Nebuchadnezzar,*
מֶלֶךְ־בָּבֶל נִלְחָם עָלֵינוּ   *king of Babylon, is making war against us.*
אוּלַי יַעֲשֶׂה יְהוָה אוֹתָנוּ   *Perhaps the Lord <u>will repeat for us</u>*
כְּכָל־נִפְלְאֹתָיו[ ]   *<u>one of his many wonders,</u>[6]*
וְיַעֲלֶה מֵעָלֵינוּ[ ]   *and he will be forced to <u>withdraw</u>[7]*".

---

      of the most ancient biblical literature as well as a complex, refined capacity for re-elaboration, along with an acute reflective ability that is theological in nature.

5   Given that the most interesting texts for my research don't generally present conspicuous *critica textus* difficulties, I will not treat questions of this sort in a specific paragraph. I will limit myself to bringing up some specific aspects for exegetical purposes (which will already be mentioned in the following philological notes) when these serve the topics being covered. In translation, here and elsewhere, I will use cursive to highlight direct speech (to which I will be paying preferential attention).

6   Lit.: "will do for us *as* (according) all of his wonders". I prefer to omit the comparative (כְּכָל־נִפְלְאֹתָיו) in the translation, seeking to render the syntagm יַעֲשֶׂה יְהוָה אוֹתָנוּ in such a way as to express the expectation expressed by the ministers sent by the king. In other words: that God manifest himself yet again in the history of his people *repeating* one of his salvific wonders (cf. Vaccari, "se mai il Signore vuol fare con noi alcuno dei suoi tanti prodigi"; NRSV: "perhaps the LORD will perform a wonderful deed for us, as he has often done").

7   More lit.: "and he will go up away (he will retreat) from us". To not encumber the English translation, I omit the translation of מֵעָלֵינוּ ("from us") at the end of the

228   Jer 21:1-10. The surrender as acceptance of the end

וַיֹּאמֶר יִרְמְיָהוּ אֲלֵיהֶם
כֹּה תֹאמְרֻן אֶל־צִדְקִיָּהוּ

3 Then Jeremiah said to them:
"*Thus you shall say to Zedekiah:*

כֹּה־אָמַר יְהוָה אֱלֹהֵי יִשְׂרָאֵל
הִנְנִי מֵסֵב אֶת־כְּלֵי הַמִּלְחָמָה
אֲשֶׁר בְּיֶדְכֶם אֲשֶׁר אַתֶּם נִלְחָמִים בָּם
אֶת־מֶלֶךְ בָּבֶל וְאֶת־הַכַּשְׂדִּים
הַצָּרִים עֲלֵיכֶם מִחוּץ לַחוֹמָה
וְאָסַפְתִּי אוֹתָם
אֶל־תּוֹךְ הָעִיר הַזֹּאת

4 *Thus says the Lord, God of Israel:*
Behold, I will turn back the weapons
that are in your hands, with which you fight <u>outside</u>
<u>the walls</u>[8] the king of Babylon and the Chaldeans
who are besieging you
and I will gather them <u>to hurl them</u>[9]
against the very heart <u>of this city</u>.[10]

וְנִלְחַמְתִּי אֲנִי אִתְּכֶם
בְּיָד נְטוּיָה וּבִזְרוֹעַ חֲזָקָה
וּבְאַף וּבְחֵמָה וּבְקֶצֶף גָּדוֹל

5 *I myself will then fight against you*
with outstretched hand and with strong arm,
with anger, with fury, and with great indignation,

וְהִכֵּיתִי אֶת־יוֹשְׁבֵי הָעִיר הַזֹּאת וְאֶת־הָאָדָם
וְאֶת־הַבְּהֵמָה בְּדֶבֶר גָּדוֹל יָמֻתוּ

6 *and I will strike the inhabitants of this city, both man*
and beast: they will die of a great plague.

וְאַחֲרֵי־כֵן נְאֻם־יְהוָה אֶתֵּן
אֶת־צִדְקִיָּהוּ מֶלֶךְ־יְהוּדָה וְאֶת־עֲבָדָיו וְאֶת־הָעָם
וְאֶת־הַנִּשְׁאָרִים בָּעִיר הַזֹּאת
מִן־הַדֶּבֶר מִן־הַחֶרֶב וּמִן־הָרָעָב בְּיַד
נְבוּכַדְרֶאצַּר מֶלֶךְ־בָּבֶל
וּבְיַד אֹיְבֵיהֶם וּבְיַד
מְבַקְשֵׁי נַפְשָׁם וְהִכָּם
לְפִי־חֶרֶב לֹא־יָחוּס עֲלֵיהֶם
וְלֹא יַחְמֹל וְלֹא יְרַחֵם

7 *And afterward, oracle of the Lord, <u>I will consign</u>[11]*
Zedekiah, king of Judah, his servants, the people
and those in this city who will have survived
the plague, the sword and famine, into the hands of
Nebuchadnezzar, king of Babylon,
into the hands of their enemies and into the hands of those
who seek their lives, and he shall strike them down with
the edge of the sword without sparing them,
without mercy, without pity.

וְאֶל־הָעָם הַזֶּה תֹּאמַר כֹּה אָמַר יְהוָה
הִנְנִי נֹתֵן לִפְנֵיכֶם אֶת־דֶּרֶךְ הַחַיִּים
וְאֶת־דֶּרֶךְ הַמָּוֶת

8 *And to this people you shall say: Thus says the Lord:*
Behold, I set before you the way of life
and the way of death.

הַיֹּשֵׁב בָּעִיר הַזֹּאת יָמוּת בַּחֶרֶב
וּבָרָעָב וּבַדָּבֶר וְהַיּוֹצֵא
וְנָפַל עַל־הַכַּשְׂדִּים

9 *Whoever remains in this city shall die by the sword, by*
famine and by plague; but whoever goes out
<u>and consigns himself</u>[12] to the Chaldeans

---

sentence, which represents the fourth repetition in a single verse of the pronominal suffix נוּ‎ ("us"). My translation also makes the "coercive" significance of the intervention expected of God against the king of Babylon explicit.

8 מִחוּץ לַחוֹמָה‎: "outside the walls" can syntactically refer either to the participle נִלְחָמִים‎ (cf. EÜ) or to הַצָּרִים‎ (cf. NAB; TOB). I opt for the first possibility for exegetical reasons (cf. n. 67).

9 Or more succinctly: "and I will hurl them". I thus render in English the syntagm √אסף‎ + אֶל‎, (lit.: "gather against", for war; cf. *BDB*, 40, no. 4, for the hostile sense of אֶל‎, "towards") since it is a technical expression pertaining to the semantic field of military operations (for further clarification, see § 4.1.3).

10 Lit.: "against the centre (inner part) of this city".

11 From here on, I will express the meaning of the syntagm √נתן‎ + dir. obj. + בְּיַד‎ (lit.: "give someone into the hand of") with the verb "to consign" or "to hand over", interchangeably.

12 Lit.: "and will fall/pass over" (√נָפַל‎).

הַצָּרִים עֲלֵיכֶם יִחְיֶה¹³	*who are besieging you __shall live__,*[13]
וְהָיְתָה־לּוֹ נַפְשׁוֹ¹⁴ לְשָׁלָל	*and shall have his own life*[14] *as war booty.*
כִּי שַׂמְתִּי פָנַי בָּעִיר הַזֹּאת **10**	**10** *For I have set my face against this city*
לְרָעָה וְלֹא לְטוֹבָה נְאֻם־יְהוָה	*for disaster and not for good, oracle of the Lord.*
בְּיַד־מֶלֶךְ בָּבֶל תִּנָּתֵן	*It shall be consigned into the hands of the king of Babylon*
וּשְׂרָפָהּ בָּאֵשׁ¹⁵	*who shall burn it __with fire__*[15]*".*

2.2. Contextual insertion and demarcation of the communicative unit

Jer 21:1–10 is separated from the text that precedes it (the last passage of the "confessions' which, in turn, closes the unit constituted by chs. 1–20[16]) for obvious stylistic and thematic reasons. Whether our pericope should end at v. 10 or v. 12 (or v. 14), however, remains to be established. This is due to the current formulation of v. 11a ([...] מֶלֶךְ יְהוּדָה וּלְבֵית, "and to the house of the king of Judah [...]"), which seeks to formally connect the oracle of vv. 11–14 (or 11–12) with v. 8aα (וְאֶל־הָעָם הַזֶּה תֹּאמַר, "and to this people you shall say").

The redactional attempt to render less abrupt the passage from 21:1–10 to the literary unit that follows is undeniable. According to the LXX, 21:11 begins only with ὁ οἶκος βασιλέως Ἰουδα, while the MT has it preceded by a *waw* followed by a *datival lamed* (יְהוּדָה וּלְבֵית מֶלֶךְ).[17] The effect that derives from this could be that of structuring the oracular response of Jeremiah into three brief discourses. These would regard, firstly, God's rule over his people and the king Zedekiah (vv. 4–7), then, the alternative between life and death offered to the people (vv. 8–10), and finally, an oracle generically addressed "to the house of the king of Judah" (vv. 11–14 or 11–12[18]).

Given, however, that the whole unit of 21:1–23:8 + 23:9–40 is the result of a stitching together of separate passages[19] and that the introductory formula in 21:8 already

---

13 Case of Q (וְחָיָה) / K (יִחְיֶה). It is preferable to follow the K (= LXX, Syr, Vg).

14 As I have already done in v. 7, here as well, I translate as "life" a Hebrew term (נֶפֶשׁ) that is different from that which appears in v. 8 (הַחַיִּים).

15 This expression, which sounds pleonastic even in Hebrew (although this is frequent in analogous royal Assyrian inscriptions as well; cf. e.g. RINAP 3/2, 74–82, no. 46,10b-11a; 12b-15a; 33–34a; 41b-42a; etc.), seems to derive from a cultic use of √שׂרף with the most generic meaning of "to destroy", referring to the annihilation of metal or stone objects that, in themselves, could not be burnt (cf. U. RÜTERSWÖRDEN, «שָׂרַף», *ThWAT* VII, 883–891, esp. p. 881).

16 In this regard, I refer to what was already observed in ch. I, § 4.1.1 of the present dissertation.

17 The linking function of this ו with that which precedes it had already been observed by Jerome (*In Hieremiam prophetam libri VI,* CCLS 74, Turnholti 1960, 198) and Kimchi. Regardless, the fact remains that the connection with v. 8a is dubious, due to the different preposition (לְ/אֶל) and the syntactic distance between them.

18 According to W. MCKANE, «The Construction of Jeremiah XXI», *VT* 22 (1982) 59–73 (esp. pp. 69–73), there would be no connection whatsoever between v. 11 and v. 13.

19 Cf. e.g. J. FRANZKOWIAK, *Der Königszyklus Jer 21,1–23,8. Das vordeuteronomistische Traditionsgut und seine redaktionelle Bearbeitung,* Diss., Stuttgart 1989;

230   Jer 21:1-10. The surrender as acceptance of the end

creates some narrative incoherencies with the preceding vv. 1–7 (cf. n. 23), a comparison with the LXX makes it clear that 21:11 is an adaptation of what was intended to read like the title of an autonomous literary unit.[20] It is in this respect that I indicate the (interrelated) terms דָּבָר; וִיהוָה; מֶלֶךְ as *initial terms* marking the beginning of the two pericopes 21:1–10 and 21:11–12 (14).[21]

For these motives, I can establish v. 10 as the end of our pericope.

2.3. Composition

While some authors affirm the unity[22] of 21:1–10, still others deny it, believing the connection between vv. 1–6 and 7; 1–7 and 8–10 to be a problematic one.[23] Though my intent is not that of responding to the observations of literary criticism regarding the internal cohesion of 21:1–10 with an analysis of the pericope's composition, I will however note that the structure emerging from the final text is a homogeneous and balanced one, and that its thematic development is indeed coherent. With the study that follows, I can confirm the substantial unity of 21:1–10 even on a literary level.

Bearing this purpose in mind, I propose the following structuring of the text, in which I have highlighted the most significative rhetorical phenomena.[24]

H.-J. HERMISSON, «Die "Königsspruch"-Sammlung im Jeremiabuch – von der Anfangs – zur Endgestalt», in: *Die Hebräische Bibel und ihre zweifache Nachgeschichte. Festschrift für Rolf Rendtorff zum 65. Geburtstag, eds.* E. BLUM – C. MACHOLZ – E.W. STEGEMANN, Neukirchen 1990, 277–299; M. ERNY, *Jeremias Königslogien. Königstexte im Jeremiabuch*, Diss. Univ. Basel [Locarno 2004], 27–32.

20 This is even more evident with the oracle in 23:9–40, the "title" of which (לַנְּבִאִים, "to/ against the prophets") has not undergone modification. This identifies the passage as being an oracle that is independent as such. Analogous titling can be seen composed by לְ + substantive (particularly frequent in the section regarding the oracles against the nations), such as, e.g. 35:18; 46:1–2; 48:1; 49:1, 7, 23, 28.

21 Cf. 21:11: "And to the house of the king (מֶלֶךְ) of Judah say: 'Hear the word of the Lord (דְּבַר־יְהוָה)'."

22 Cf. e.g. K.-F. POHLMANN, *Studien*, 39–41; J.R. LUNDBOM, *Jeremiah 21–36*, 93–97.

23 Cf. e.g. W.L. HOLLADAY, *Jeremiah 1*, 569, and esp. M. ERNY, *Jeremias Königslogien*, 61, who considers v. 7 to be an addition (essentially, only for content motives) by the same hand to which he ascribes vv. 1–3. He also emphasises the difficulty of connecting vv. 1–6, 7 with vv. 8–10 for the fact that 21:3 introduces the oracle that follows in a way that differs from the introduction to v. 8. In this second case, in fact, it is the Lord who commands Jeremiah to speak ([...] וְאֶל־הָעָם הַזֶּה תֹאמַר, "And to this people you [Jeremiah] shall say [...]"), while in v. 3b, Jeremiah speaks in the 1st person, even whilst giving a voice to the Lord ([...] כֹּה תֹאמְרוּן אֶל־צִדְקִיָּהוּ, "Thus you shall say to Zedekiah [...]"). Taking up the proposal of K.-F. POHLMANN, *Studien*, 38, n. 110, Erny speculates that the 2nd at apex per. sing. of the currently found תֹאמַר could be due to the accidental dropping of an original ו (תֹאמְרוּ = "and to this people *you* [*pl.*] *shall say*").

24 To render more evident the phenomena of the text's composition, generated by the strategic repetition of lexemes, syntagms and phrases, I will now adopt the use of a translation that is as literal as possible (also indicating, for the same motive, but only herein, the omissions of the LXX by setting them in brackets). As I established in ch. I (§ 2.4.1, n. 67), for the present stage of my study of the text, I take my inspiration from along the fundamental lines of the methodological approach proposed by R. Meynet.

A first approach to the textual data

231

I	**1** (This is) the word that came to JEREMIAH from the Lord, when King ZEDEKIAH sent him Pashhur son of Malkijah and Zephaniah, son of Maaseiah, the priest to tell him: **2** "Consult the Lord for *us* (נו-), because [NEBUCHADNEZZAR], **KING OF BABYLON**, makes war against *us* (נו-). Perhaps the Lord will act for *us* (נו-) according to all his wondrous works, and he will withdraw from *us* (נו-)."

IIa	**3** JEREMIAH said to them: "Thus you shall say to ZEDEKIAH: **4** *THUS SAYS THE LORD*, [God of Israel]: Behold, I am turning back (הִנְנִי + part.) the instruments of war [that are in your hands], with which you fight against [the **KING OF BABYLON** and] against the **CHALDEANS WHO ARE BESIEGING YOU** outside the walls [and I will gather them] against (the inner part of) *this city*. **5** I myself will then fight against you with outstretched hand and with strong arm, with anger, with fury, and with great indignation, **6** and I WILL STRIKE (√נכה hi.) the inhabitants of *this city*, both man and beast: they will die of a great **plague**.
IIb	**7** And afterward, ORACLE OF THE LORD, *I WILL PLACE* (נתן√) ZEDEKIAH, king of Judah, his servants, the **PEOPLE** [and those] in *this city* who will have survived the **plague**, the **sword**, and **famine**, [into the hand of NEBUCHADNEZZAR, **KING OF BABYLON**], into the hand of their enemies, [and into the hand of those] who seek their lives, and he SHALL STRIKE THEM DOWN (√נכה hi.) with the edge of the **sword**: he shall not spare them [and shall not have mercy] and shall not have compassion.

III	**8** And to this **PEOPLE** you shall say: *THUS SAYS THE LORD*: Behold, I am *placing* (הִנְנִי + part.) (נתן√) before you the way of the life and the way of the death. **9** Whoever remains in *this city* shall die by **sword**, by **famine** [and by **plague**]; but whoever goes out and consigns himself to the **CHALDEANS WHO ARE BESIEGING YOU** shall live, and shall have his own life as war booty. **10** For I have set my face against *this city* for disaster and not for good, ORACLE OF THE LORD. *IT SHALL BE PLACED* (נתן√) into the hand of the **KING OF BABYLON**, and he shall burn it with fire".

A series of *initial terms* allow for the passage to be divided into three parts: (I) vv. 1–2; (II) 3–7; and (III) 8–10. The proper names "Zedekiah" (צִדְקִיָּהוּ) and "Jeremiah" (יִרְמְיָהוּ) paired together mark the beginning of I and II, while the messenger formula "thus says the Lord" (כֹּה־אָמַר יְהוָה) marks the beginning of II and III (note also that the repetition of the particle הִנְנִי + participle in vv. 3 and 8 has the same function). I will also point out the use of the formula "oracle of the Lord" (נְאֻם־יְהוָה), which in v. 7 (IIb) functions as an *initial term* (or *middle*, if one considers IIa+IIb unitarily), while in v. 10 (III), it has a conclusive function.[25]

+ The I part, thematically well defined, is also characterised by the (4x) repetition of the pronominal suffix נו-.

---

25 This may be a redactional device to further unify IIa with IIb and, at the same time, IIb with III.

232   Jer 21:1-10. The surrender as acceptance of the end

+ The II part (having the theme of the fate of Zedekiah and the inhabitants of Jerusalem) is subdivided, for formal (and thematic) reasons,[26] into two sub-units: IIa) vv. 3–6, and IIb) v. 7.

In both IIa and IIb, in fact, the term "Zedekiah" (צִדְקִיָּהוּ) functions as the *initial term* (v. 3 and v. 7a), while the verb "to strike" (נכה√ hi.) functions as the *final term* (v. 6a and 7b).

+ The III part is also delimited by the repetition (forming an inclusion) of the verb "to give/to put/to place" (נתן√) as the *initial term* (v. 8b) and the *final term* (v. 10b).

The close connection between parts IIab (vv. 3–7) and III (vv. 8–10) is indicated by the use of structuring expressions like "the Chaldeans who are besieging you" (הַכַּשְׂדִּים הַצָּרִים) and by some *middle terms (catchwords or Stichworte)*. I will point out, in particular, the triad "sword", "famine", and "plague" (חֶרֶב; רָעָב; דֶּבֶר; v. 7a and v. 9a), even if, considered individually, these same elements could also perform the functions of final terms for their respective parts: "plague" (v. 6); "sword" (v. 7b); and "fire" (v. 10). Also to be noted is the frequent recurrence in IIab and III of the terms "this city" (הָעִיר הַזֹּאת or בָּעִיר הַזֹּאת) in vv. 4b; 6a; 7a (IIab) and 9a (III); of "hand" (יָד) in vv. 4a; 5; 7a (IIab) and 10b (III); and of "to give/to put/to place" (נתן√) in v. 7a (IIb) and 8b (III) as initial terms (in the condemnatory "judgement").

Particularly significant, then, is the strategic positioning and alternation of the expressions "Nebuchadnezzar king of Babylon" (נְבוּכַדְרֶאצַּר מֶלֶךְ־בָּבֶל; v. 1, part I; v. 7, part IIb) and "king of Babylon" (מֶלֶךְ־בָּבֶל; v. 4, part IIa; v. 10b, part III), which give unity to the entire composition of the MT. This clearly redactional device is confirmed by their significant omissions in the LXX (herein, placed in brackets).[27]

In terms of content, the following development thus becomes apparent:

I:	(vv. 1–2)	Request to Jeremiah by the king's emissaries for an oracle
IIab:	(vv. 3–7)	The announcement of the end
III:	(vv. 8–10)	Presentation of the alternative (to leave=life/to stay=death)

The following study will seek to clarify the relationship between the announcement of the end and the salvific prospect presented in the final part of the text.

---

26 To be precise, this is due to the logical-temporal articulation of the action described. While in vv. 3–6, God strikes Jerusalem, he *then* (וְאַחֲרֵי־כֵן), in the following v. 7, delivers the city (and Zedekiah, etc.) into the hands of Nebuchadnezzar for the completement of the destruction.

27 The expressions that are present in the MT would instead seem to be very late insertions, as is pointed out in the study by R.D. WELLS Jr., «Indications of Late Reinterpretation of the Jeremianic Tradition from the LXX of Jer 21 1 – 23 8», *ZAW* 96 (1984) 405–420.

3. The broad context: The necessity of surrender as the "first" word of Jeremiah

3.1. The problem of the literary context: An altogether unusual positioning

It is evident that 21:1–10 is not the first time that the word of "judgement" (or better yet, punishment) upon Jerusalem appears. Indeed, it is present both in the form of a poetic oracle and programmatically from the first chapter of the book, when it is announced that "from the North disaster will pour out over all the inhabitants of the land" (cf. 1:14–16, 18). This constitutive aspect of the prophetic message of Jeremiah (though not it alone) is expressed repeatedly in oracular form throughout the first part (chs. 1–25). Chapter after chapter, the instrument of divine castigation is evoked through threatening images that appear as shadows that instantly fade, only to reappear and assume, bit by bit, new configurations,[28] always remaining, however, without precise identification. It is not until ch. 20 that Babylon and its king (20:4) are explicitly mentioned for the first time. Then, unexpectedly, with 21:1–10, a brief narrative preamble introduces a text in prose laden with the drama of the crucial moment when Nebuchadnezzar lays siege on Jerusalem.

3.1.1. Disorientations

Let us now look more closely at why 21:1–10 presents itself as a text (or, one of several texts) that, more than others, disorientates a reading eager to be anchored in clear schemas of textual arrangement, potentially ones based on well-ordered chronological references.[29]

---

28 It is a catastrophe that comes from the North (4:6, 16; 6:1, 22; 8:16; 10:22; 13:20; 16:15); a cruel people, a great and terrible nation that comes from the farthest parts of the earth, from a nation far away (5:15; 6:22–25); it is like a lion that comes out of its thicket (4:7) to destroy the nations (6:26; 7:26; 15:8); like a scorching wind from the desert (4:11); advances like a cloud, and the roar of his chariots is like that of a whirlwind, his horses swifter than eagles (4:13); they cry out against the cities of Judah (4:16) and hem her in (for the siege) like men guarding a field (4:17); they are despising lovers who want to kill (4:30), they are murderers (4:31); and then a lion from the forest; a wolf from the arid plains, a leopard lying in wait around their cities (5:6); again a mighty nation with an incomprehensible language, whose quiver is like an open sepulchre that will devour everything (5:15–17); shepherds who will lead their flocks into Jerusalem and pitch their tents around her (6:3; 12:10) for the siege; it is a warrior people without mercy, terrifying (6:23–25), whose horses make the whole land quake (8:16); they are poisonous snakes who bite (8:17); a great commotion is announced (10:22), it is a disaster from which they cannot escape (11:11); birds of prey who circle around, beasts of the field who gather to devour (12:9); Jerusalem has tried to cultivate them as friends but in vain, for they will be its rulers (13:21).
29 This is a challenge that permeates Jeremiah overall, and that Jerome had already pointed out, implicitly suggesting that other interpretive paths need be sought: "Non enim curae erat, ut ante iam dixi, prophetiae tempora conservare, quae historiae leges desiderant; sed scribere, utcumque audientibus atque lecturis utile noverant; unde et in Psalterio male quidam iuxta textum historiae psalmorum requirunt ordinem,

234 Jer 21:1-10. The surrender as acceptance of the end

Within the first part of the book (1–25) and following the section composed of chs. 1–20, which closes with the last passage of the "confessions", ch. 21 opens, in a way that is unique, the final literary unit.[30] This unit is dedicated to the kings (21:1–23:8) and prophets (23:9–40). The formally "initial" character of 21:1–10 in relation to the pericopes that follow (and especially in relation to 21:1–23:8) seems to be immediately rebutted by a series of facts:

a) the explicit dating of this text (in "prose") takes us to the time of Zedekiah (21:1). But then, unexpectedly, it is followed by a series of oracles (almost all in "poetry") that mention, in ordered succession, the names of the kings who preceded him: Shallum (22:11; i.e. Jehoahaz; cf. 2 Kgs 23:30), Jehoiakim (22:18), and Coniah (22:24, 28; another name for Jehoiachin; cf. 2 Kgs 24:8);

b) in particular, from a thematic point of view, 21:1–10 presents the end of Jerusalem as a now certain and irreversible fact, while the subsequent oracles remain within the horizon of the threat having (still possible) conversion as its aim[31];

---

quod in lyrico carmine non observatur"; cf. HIERONYMUS, *In Hieremiam prophetam libri VI*, ed. S. REITER, CChr.SL 74, Turnholti 1960, 236–237. Recently, the problem was reproposed by E. DI PEDE, *Au-de là du refus*. Hers is a study based on the principles of narrative analysis that relate to only a particular section (32–45) in which, moreover, 21:1–10 could find its ideal positioning as well. The author does not, however, raise the question.

30 When ch. 24 is not included as well (as I will instead do in the present work), one can regardless see an independent literary unit (even if a composite) in 21:1–23:40. In it, a certain thematic coherence given by those being addressed (the "audience") in the oracles (king and prophets) can be recognised. Cf. e.g. J.R. LUNDBOM, *Jeremiah 21–36*, 93 ("On Kings and Prophets").

31 Contrary to what is thought by D.E. GOWAN, *Theology of the Prophetic Books*. The Death and Resurrection of Israel, Louisville 1998, 105–106, according to whom the appeals to conversion would be not real possibilities of salvation but rather reflections of the optimism of Deuteronomy "in sharp contrast with everything in the oracles", this distinction is real and regards the diversity in tenor between Jeremiah's message proclaimed at the temple of Jehoiakim, and that in the time of Zedekiah (cf. n. 44 and ch. II, § 3.2.3). Concordant with this change in perspective are e.g. W.L. HOLLADAY, «A Fresh Look», 408–410; T.M. RAITT, *Theology of Exile*. Judgment, Deliverance in Jeremiah and Ezekiel, Philadelphia 1977, 37; J. UNTERMANN, *From Repentance to Redemption*. Jeremiah's Thought in Transition, JSOT.S 54, Sheffield 1987, 176. In the case cited, I notice how, in contrast to 21:1–10, which does not contain any imperative form amongst the verbs placed on the lips of Jeremiah (without counting, obviously, v. 3b: כֹּה תֹאמְרֻן אֶל־צִדְקִיָּהוּ) but only epistemic modal verbs that simply announce facts (the announcement of the disaster), instead, the threat of the end is articulated in the following oracles generically addressed to the "house of the king of Judah" or to explicitly named kings with the possibility of repentance (and a wavering of punishment). This is expressed by way of the use of numerous imperatives (deontic modality) that configure just as many appeals to conversion (cf. 21:11: שִׁמְעוּ דְּבַר־יְהוָה, "hear the word of the Lord!"; 21:12a: דִּינוּ לַבֹּקֶר מִשְׁפָּט, "administer justice fairly every morning!"; 21:12b: מִיַּד עוֹשֵׁק וְהַצִּילוּ גָזוּל, "rescue the one who has been robbed from the hand of the extortionist!"; 22:2: שְׁמַע דְּבַר־יְהוָה, "listen to the word of the Lord!"; 22:3a: עֲשׂוּ מִשְׁפָּט וּצְדָקָה, "execute justice and righteousness!"; 22:3b: וְהַצִּילוּ גָזוּל מִיַּד עָשׁוֹק, "rescue the oppressed from the hand of the oppressor!"; 22:3c: אַל־תֹּנוּ, "do not brutalise!"; 22:3d: אַל־תַּחְמֹסוּ; "do

The broad context: The necessity of surrender as the "first" word of Jeremiah   235

c) finally, it should be noted that the natural context in which one might expect the king to consult the prophet is not at all the first part of the book of Jeremiah,[32] but rather the second, and in particular, the section of chs. 36–45, which hosts the account of the events that befall the prophet in the final stages of the kingdom of Judah (from the speech at the temple until the deportation to Egypt after the assassination of Gedaliah) and his "passion".

It is thus not the least bit clear why the account of what appears to be Zedekiah's first consultation of Jeremiah found itself placed out of the context within which it would have been naturally inserted, namely, the variations on the same theme provided in 34:1–7; 37:3–10, 17–21; 38:1–3, and 14–28a. If we were being faced with a fictional narrative, a servile respect of temporal consequentiality would most likely cause problems.[33] But the Jeremianic text cannot be reduced to this literary register. Faced with problems of a similar nature, a number of commentators[34] have matured the conviction that the current redactional layout of the book of Jeremiah be fundamentally devoid of logic and hence chaotic. Consequently, in their commentaries, they have taken care to offer the reader rearrangements of the oracles and narrative portions modelled on (hypothetical) chronological orderings.[35]

I am, however, convinced otherwise. I prefer to not renounce the possibility of the identification of other criteria of literary arrangement, without however wishing to

---

not oppress! [the foreigner...]"; 22:3e: וְדָם נָקִי אַל־תִּשְׁפְּכוּ, "do not shed innocent blood!"). The possibility of conversion is expressed, furthermore, through the alternative in 22:4–5 (v. 4a: כִּי אִם־עָשׂוֹ תַעֲשׂוּ, "if you truly carry out [this word]"; v. 5a: וְאִם לֹא תִשְׁמְעוּ, "but if you do not obey [this word]"), which even more clearly shows the judgement as only a threat and not an ineluctable necessity. On the concept of modality (deontic and epistemic) in relation to biblical Hebrew, cf. A. GIANTO, «Mood and Modality in Classical Hebrew», *IOS* 18 (1998) 183–198.

32 As notes A. WEISER, *Das Buch Jeremia*. I, there would be a jump of about 10 years between the situation described in 21:1–10 and that in ch. 20 (which dates back to the epoch of Jehoiakim). Also W. THIEL, *Jeremia 1–25*, 231, highlights that a reference to the siege of Jerusalem at this point in the book results as being entirely out of place. The similitude with 37:3–10 has prompted a wide debate amongst those who, on the one hand, consider 21:1–7(8–10) to be a re-elaboration by the Deuteronomistic redactor of the events of 37:3–10, such as e.g. B. DUHM, *Jeremia*, 168; G. WANKE, *Untersuchungen zur sogenannten Baruchschrift*, BZAW 122, Berlin 1971, 96; and those who, on the other hand, rigorously defend their mutual independence, like J. BRIGHT, *Jeremiah*, 217; H. WEIPPERT, *Die Prosareden*, 68; given, in fact, the different temporal context and different figures who make up the delegation sent to consult the prophet.

33 Cf. M. STERNBERG, «Telling in Time (I): Chronology and Narrative Theory», *Poetics Today* 11 (1990) 901–948 (esp. pp. 901–907).

34 I refer to what is highlighted in ch. I, § 2.2.2.

35 A formulation with disputable hermeneutical presuppositions, in my opinion, given that it in fact tends to present the text reconstructed by the exegete as more authoritative than that which the Tradition presents as "inspired" and a source of authentic revelation. For a list of some representative authors and a synopsis of the reconstructions elaborated by C.H. Cornill, J. Steinmann, and J. Bright (with particular reference to chs. 32–45), cf. E. DI PEDE, *Au-de là du refus*, 136–154 (the chapter is the one dedicated to "Solutions «classiques» au problème chronologique").

externally impose a pre-construed schema of my own. To study 21:1–10 from this perspective means, in other words, giving the current (canonic) arrangement of the MT more credit. And it means taking up the challenge of a text whose unexpected positioning astonishes and provokes the reader, placing them in abrupt contact with the narrative development of a theme that is crucial to the book and provided in advance: the end of Jerusalem.

I believe it be important to highlight, in fact, that 21:1–10 is redactionally, and therefore *intentionally*, placed at the *beginning* of the new literary unit. And thus, the question I do not want to elude is: why? The problem is in putting forth reasonable arguments that can make plausible sense of this "forced contextualisation", the impact of which calls for interpretation, regardless of whether 21:1–10 be considered an abrupt extrapolation of a text from its natural, original literary setting or, as some scholars assert, a composition produced by the elaboration of one or more pre-existing texts.[36]

3.1.2. Proposals for a solution

Depending on whether their attention is concentrated on that which precedes or that which follows, authors essentially put forth two types of solutions. For some (by now a minority), the current textual placement of 21:1–10 would be due to the repetition of the name "Pashhur (son of Immer)" in 20:1–6 and "Pashhur (son of Malkijah)" in 21:1.[37] Others, instead, explain it as an introduction to the entire subsection of chs. 21:11–23:40 (24),[38] which contains oracles against the royal house (22:11–23:8) and false prophets (23:9–40). In particular, W. Thiel[39] sees in 21:1–10 a preamble to the

---

36 Cf. B. Duhm, *Jeremia*, 168; W. Rudolph, *Jeremiah*, 135; W. Thiel, *Jeremia 1–25*, 231.

37 The first to draw attention to this point was J.D. Michaelis, *Observationes philologicae et criticae in Ieremiae Vaticinia et Threnos*, Goettingae 1793, 137. According to W. Rudolph, *Jeremia*, 134–135 (who maintains that the pericope belongs to the traditional "source C"), the name Pashhur, whilst still designating two distinct people, would have served to create a connection to emphasise a certain antithesis of content between the two passages. In other words, whilst in 20:1–6, the prophet is beaten and taken into prison custody by the priest and chief inspector of the temple (Pashhur son of Immer), in 21:1–10, the king Zedekiah sends a priest (Zephaniah) and one of his officials (Pashhur son of Malkijah), implicitly underlining that, in this way, Jeremiah can see "den Triumph, daß der König selbst zu ihm schickt, um ein Jahwewort zu empfangen".

38 Many authors identify an independent literary complex in chs. 21–24, accentuated in 21:1a by the *Wortereignisformel* ("word-event formula"), which then recurs in 25:1 with the function of "initial term" of the following textual unit; cf. e.g. W. Rudolph, *Jeremia*, XVIII-XX; C. Rietzschel, *Der Problem der Urrolle*. Ein Beitrag zur Redaktionsgeschichte des Jeremiabuches, Gütersloh 1966, 125; W. Thiel, *Jeremia 1–25*, 230; R.P. Carroll, *Jeremiah*, 38; K. Seybold, *Der Prophet Jeremia*, 97; G. Wanke, *Jeremia 1*, 188–189; G. Fischer, *Jeremia 1–25*, 628. In particular, K.-F. Pohlmann, *Studien*, 19–47, more explicitly lays out the relationship (which I will address) between 21:1–10 and ch. 24.

39 Cf. W. Thiel, *Jeremia 1–25*, 230–231, 237; R.P. Carroll, *Jeremiah*, 407. In any case, W. Thiel points out as well – albeit as a secondary consideration – the opposition (*Kontrastwirkung*) highlighted by Rudolph. I will mention incidentally that

The broad context: The necessity of surrender as the "first" word of Jeremiah   237

oracles that follow, composed by a Deuteronomist hand and having the function of reconnecting these to the motif of God's condemnation of (or threat against?) the "leaders" (*"die Führenden"*).

To me, both of these proposals seem insufficient. And the motives for this follow.

The attribution of an oppositional intentionality between the two episodes (20:1–6 and 21:1–10) on the basis of the recurrence of the name "Pashhur" seems forced,[40] because it does not take into account for the intermediate unit constituted by 20:7–18 (the final passage of the "confessions"), but also because it is not even thematically convincing.[41]

To speak of 21:1–10 as having an "introductive" function with respect to the oracles (and other passages in prose) against the king (21:11–23:8)[42] and the prophets (23:9–40) seems, instead, to be substantially correct to me, just too reductive. What, in fact, remains to be explained is *the motive* for choosing as an introduction to 21:11–23:8 precisely a passage that wedges the narrative form into a prevalently oracular context that (even more surprisingly) regards the *final* (reigning) king of Judah, and places him – with no respect for chronology – before a series of kings cited (in the oracles that relate to them) according to a chronologically ordered succession: Shallum (22:11), Jehoiakim (22:18), and finally Jehoiachin – "Coniah" (22:24).[43] Jeremiah's message, moreover, appears altogether out of context since it is the one concomitant to the final days before the end of Jerusalem (cf. 38:24–28a), and of a tenor quite different from that proclaimed at the time of Jehoiakim.[44]

---

commentators generally consider 21:1–10 to be "secondary". Its attribution to a Deuteronomistic editor (identifed as the so-called *"Quelle* C") dates back to S. MOWINCKEL, *Jeremia*, 31. For an overview of the history of the research on this "source", cf. L. STULMAN, *The Prose Sermons of the Book of Jeremiah. Redescription of the Correspondences with the Deuteronomistic Literature in the Light of Recent Text-critical Research*, SBLDS 83, Atlanta 1986, 7–32.

40   The same can be said for the – rather weak – proposal of W.L. HOLLADAY, *Jeremiah 1*, 568–569, whereby the proximity between √בבס *hi.* in v. 4 and √קדח in 20:16 (belonging to the same semantic field) would be enough to justify the current (at first glance puzzling) redactional layout of 21:1–10.

41   It seems unlikely that such power of "attraction" be attributed to the repetition of a proper name (which, moreover, recurs frequently in Jeremiah). In fact, the impression of there being an incongruence in the arrangement of the textual material continues to be much stronger than that of there being some sort of immediately perceptible hermeneutical benefit for the reader. Obviously, the concept of "hermeneutical benefit" presupposes that the redaction of the book of Jeremiah corresponds to some "logical" (however difficult to determine) criterion, and that it not be merely a clumsy stitching together of disparate passages.

42   According to W.J. WESSELS, «Setting the Stage for the Future of the Kingship: An Ideological-Critical Reading of Jeremia 21:1–10», *OTEs* 17 (2004) 470–483, the placing of 21:1–10 serves "to communicate to the people of Zedekia's time that they should not entertain any hope in his kingship" (p. 477). In my opinion, this is only one of its possible meanings, to be contextualised within a broader vision having its nodal point in the call for the act of surrender.

43   One would, in fact, have expected its placement to follow 22:22–29 (which has Jehoiachin as its subject).

44   Since the end is contingent on the call for conversion, at the time of Jehoiakim, this is chiefly threatened. At the time of Zedekiah, however, it is simply announced,

3.1.3. New indications of meaning

In order to comprehend the meaning that the "redactor" wanted to give the textual positioning of 21:1–10, in my opinion, the decisive criteria are:

a) the reference to the concluding portion of the unit 21:1–23:8, dedicated to the future "king-shepherd" (23:1–8)[45];
b) the relationship 21:1–10 has to the unit regarding the oracles against the prophets (23:9–40);
c) and, above all, the relationship 21:1–10 has to ch. 24 (the vision of the baskets of figs).

A more thorough analytical examination of the textual data will carry us beyond a generic assertion, allowing me to establish, on the basis of multiple elements, the *introductory function* of our pericope, and not only. The concept can also be further clarified by conjoining it with the rhetorical category of *hysteron proteron*,[46] or with (considered from a more narratological point of view) *prolepsis*.[47] Indeed, through its unusual textual positioning, Jer 21:1–10 assumes a strong proleptic significance, not only by mentioning many motifs that will be taken up in the following units but also, and above all, by conferring a veritable programmatic value to the gesture of surrender. This final message of Jeremiah (proclaimed only at the time of Zedekiah) is flagged as being his "first" word (at least, in relation to all that follows 21:1–10), not in a chronological sense but rather as that entrusted to express the totality. In other words, it is intended to make the meaning of all the rest comprehensible (be it the condemnation of the various kings [21:11–23:8] and the identification of "good" with the deportation to Babylon [ch. 24]).[48] Hereinafter, I will look at the arguments that demonstrate the importance of these aspects and the mutual relationships between them.

---

and the ethical instance gives way to a "religious" duty of submission to the king of Babylon (the announcement of the end is a peculiar characteristic of the word of Jeremiah; cf. G.C. MACHOLZ, «Jeremia in der Kontinuität der Prophetie», in: *Probleme biblischer Theologie.* Gehrard von Rad zum 70. Geburtstag, *ed.* H.W. WOLFF, München 1971, 306–334). This contrast can be noted not only when comparing 21:1–10 with the following vv. 11–12, but also e.g. 26:2–6; 35:13–17 (for the time of Jehoiakim) and 27:12–13; 28:14; 32:3–5, 24–25; 34:2–5; 37:9–10, 17 (for the time of Zedekiah). Cf. in this regard C.R. SEITZ, *Theology*, 205–207, who makes note of the appearance (after 597) of the theme of submission to the king of Babylon, placing it in relation only to a "prudential" attitude to take, and not to the definitive announcement of the end that instead characterises the prophetic activity of Jeremiah at the time of Zedekiah.

45 Subdividable, in turn, into three sub-units (vv. 1–4, 5–6, 7–8).

46 This rhetorical device consists in the inversion of the chronological (and logical) order of a succession of events (that which took place last is given first), in order to place emphasis on the date of greatest importance and/or to obtain a particular emotional effect (cf. the definition by B. MORTARA GARAVELLI, *Manuale di retorica*, Milano 1988, 256–257, who in my opinion underestimates on the narrative level the importance that the "how" thus acquires in determining the final result). In our present case, this is applied not on a phrasal level but on a macrostructural level.

47 I will look at the question in greater depth in § 3.2.5.

48 In this sense, my perspective is contrary to that of W. THIEL, *Jeremia 1–25*, 230.237, for whom the relationship of 21:1–10 with what follows is tantamount to the relationship between the threat of punishment and its grounding (*Begründung*).

3.2. Introductive and proleptic function of Jer 21:1–10

3.2.1. *Entering into a story. The figure of the king (מֶלֶךְ) and destiny of the nation*

As far as the introductive function is concerned, I will note, first of all, how in 21:1–10, the figure of the *king* (Zedekiah and Nebuchadnezzar) upon whom the fate of the people and the *city* (delivered to *fire* by the hand of the king of Babylon) depend emerges. In 21:11–23:8, the thematic and lexical articulation is largely determined by this institutional figure, expressed by the recurring term מֶלֶךְ and other synonymous expressions.

In the following diagram, I also report the recurrence of the correlated themes of "fire" (as divine punishment), "city" (whose fate depends on the behaviour of the king), and the re-emergence of the "deliverance formula" (the king, of Judah – delivered into the hands of another king – foreigner and enemy).

21:1–10	The figure of the king		The city	The fire	The deliverance formula
21:1	הַמֶּלֶךְ צִדְקִיָּהוּ	the king Zedekiah			
21:2	נְבוּכַדְרֶאצַּר מֶלֶךְ־בָּבֶל	**Nebuchadnezzar, king of Babylon**			
21:3	צִדְקִיָּהוּ	Zedekiah			
21:4	מֶלֶךְ־בָּבֶל	**king of Babylonia**	הָעִיר הַזֹּאת		
21:6			הָעִיר הַזֹּאת		
21:7	צִדְקִיָּהוּ מֶלֶךְ־יְהוּדָה	Zedekiah, king of Judah	בָּעִיר הַזֹּאת		בְּיַד + נתן√
»	נְבוּכַדְרֶאצַּר מֶלֶךְ־בָּבֶל	**Nebuchadnezzar, king of Babylon**			
»	[מֶלֶךְ־בָּבֶל]	**[king of Babylon]** subj. of וְהִכָּם			
21:9			בָּעִיר הַזֹּאת		
21:10			בָּעִיר הַזֹּאת	בָּאֵשׁ וּשְׂרָפָהּ	בְּיַד + נתן√
Jer 21:11 23:40					
21 11	לְבֵית מֶלֶךְ יְהוּדָה	to the house of the king of Judah			
21:12	בֵּית דָּוִד	house of David		אֵשׁ	
21:14				וְהִצַּתִּי אֵשׁ	

21:1–10	The figure of the king		The city	The fire	The deliverance formula
22:1	בֵּית־מֶלֶךְ יְהוּדָה	house of the king of Judah			
22:2	מֶלֶךְ יְהוּדָה	king of Judah			
»	כִּסֵּא דָוִד	throne of David			
22:4	מְלָכִים	the kings			
»	דָוִד	David			
22:6	בֵּית־מֶלֶךְ יְהוּדָה	house of the king of Judah	עָרִים		
22:7				עַל־הָאֵשׁ	
22:8			הָעִיר הַזֹּאת		
22:11	שַׁלֻּם	Shallum, son of Josiah, king of Judah			
»	יֹאשִׁיָּהוּ	Josiah (2x)			
»	מֶלֶךְ יְהוּדָה	king (2x) of Judah			
22:15	מֶלֶךְ	king			
»	אָבִיךָ	your father			
22:18	יְהוֹיָקִים	Jehoiakim			
»	יֹאשִׁיָּהוּ מֶלֶךְ יְהוּדָה	Josiah, king of Judah			
»	אָדוֹן	lord			
»	הֹדֹה	majesty			
22:19			יְרוּשָׁלַ͏ִם		
22:22	רֹעִים	shepherds			
22:24	כָּנְיָהוּ	Coniah			
»	יְהוֹיָקִים	Jehoiakim			
»	מֶלֶךְ יְהוּדָה	king of Judah			
22:25	נְבוּכַדְרֶאצַּר מֶלֶךְ־בָּבֶל	**Nebuchadnezzar, king of Babylon**			נתן + בְּיַד√
22:28	כָּנְיָהוּ	Coniah			
22:30	הָאִישׁ הַזֶּה	this man			
»	מִזַּרְעוֹ אִישׁ	n[one] of his descendents			
»	כִּסֵּא דָוִד	throne of David			
23:1	רֹעִים	shepherds			
23:2	רֹעִים	shepherds			
23:4	רֹעִים	shepherds			
23:5	דָוִד	David			
»	מֶלֶךְ	king			

The broad context: The necessity of surrender as the "first" word of Jeremiah   241

3.2.2. *Saying it both before and after: Semiotic* arcatas *(starting from Jer 23:1–8)*

I will now present the arguments that justify not only the introductive function of 21:1–10, but also its proleptic function whereby key fundamental themes are unexpectedly revealed in advance. The structure of the signification is presented, in other words, in the form of semiotic *arcatas* of variable radii (easily identifiable on a schematic level; cf. § 3.3), marked by textual elements that correspond over varied distances, from the most extreme points to those closest.

The first element that should be highlighted is an important oppositive correspondence between 21:1–10 and 23:1–8. This is based on the mutual evocation[49] between the meaning (and sonority) of the (theophoric) name of the king "Zedekiah" (צִדְקִיָּהוּ)= "(my) justice (is) YHW(H)"[50] and the appellative solemnly attributed to the promised king, "YHWH (is) our justice" (יְהוָה צִדְקֵנוּ)[51]. It is highly probable that the intention was to form an inclusion this way.[52] This connection is reinforced by two other occurrences of the root צדק in 23:5,[53] as well as by the synonymic מִשְׁפָּט ("justice") coupled with צְדָקָה ("right.")[54]

The relation (repetition) is not, as in the case of the name Pashhur (20:1 and 21:1), one that is merely accidental. The correspondence appears instead to be intentional, it being semantically significant. What is highlighted, in fact, through connotations that are all linked to the semantic field of "justice", is the antithetical relationship between the (perverted) צְדָקָה of the kings of Judah (Zedekiah is the last of a series reigning on the throne of David) and the king promised and raised up (√קום)[55] directly by YHWH,

---

49   Already pointed out by J.R. LUNDBOM, *Jeremiah: A Study*, 45–47.

50   There are two possible readings of the name (cf. M. NOTH, *Die israelitischen Personennamen im Rahmen der gemeinsemitischen Namengebung*, Stuttgart 1928, 36, 161–162): 1) as a noun phrase *tout court*: "YHWH is (my) justice" (this sounds better in English, even if the usual order of theophoric Hebrew names is predicate + subject, and not vice versa; cf. *BDB*, 843; J.D. FOWLER, *Theophoric Personal Names in Ancient Hebrew. A Comparative Study*, JSOT.S 49, Sheffield 1988, 75, 358), or 2) as a verbal phrase (with A. LEMAIRE, *Inscriptions hébraïques*, 128–129, cf. pp. 239 and 241): "my justice is YHWH" = "YHWH is he who did me justice/who saved me" (cf. *HALAT*, 944–945).

51   Also note the chiastic inversion of the terms: first "justice – YHW(H)", then "YHWH – justice".

52   Thus e.g. also H-J. HERMISSON, «Königsspruch», 291; J.R. LUNDBOM, *Jeremiah 21–36*, 94–95.

53   "[...] I will raise up for David a righteous branch (צֶמַח צַדִּיק) who will reign as (true) king, be wise and administer justice and righteousness (צְדָקָה) in the land."

54   Since the thematic of the administration of justice is strictly tied to the monarchical institution, it is not surprising to find lexical references of the same sort in the remaining units concerning other kings of Judah as well; cf. J.L. SICRE, «La monarquía y la justicia. La práctica de la justicia como elemento aglutinante en la redacción de Jr 21,11–23-8», in: *El misterio de la palabra. Homenaje de sus alumnos al profesor D. Luis Alonso Schökel al cumplir veinticinco años de magisterio en el Instituto Bíblico Pontificio*, eds. V. COLLADO – E. ZURRO, Madrid 1983, 193–206.

55   It is significant that this root recurs only in reference to the *first* succession to the throne of David, that of Solomon (cf. 1 Kgs 8:20; 2 Chr 6:10), and at the time of another promise of messianic restoration, in Amos 9:11.

i.e. the "righteous sprout" (צֶמַח צַדִּיק) who will finally reign as (true) king (מֶלֶךְ מָלַךְ): he will act wisely (הִשְׂכִּיל) and practice law and justice in the land (עָשָׂה מִשְׁפָּט וּצְדָקָה), and for this, he will be called "YHWH our justice" (יְהוָה צִדְקֵנוּ).

Then, in 23:1–8, there are a series of themes, like those of "gathering" (v. 3a: √קבץ), "bringing back" (v. 3b: √שׁוב hi.), "being saved" (v. 6a: √ישׁע), "dwelling in security" (v. 6b: √שׁכן + לְבֶטַח), "bringing up = leading back" (v. 7b.8a: √עלה hi.) from Egypt, and "dwelling" (v. 8b: √ישׁב), etc., which find antithetical references not only in 21:1–10, but also in the successive oracles of justice pronounced either generically against the house of Judah or against specific kings. Accordingly, I record herewith the verbal roots I believe most pertinent, grouping them together into two separate semantic fields of a general nature, delimited by the relevance or not of the ADVANTAGE/DISAD-VANTAGE derived with respect to the terms "people" and "king"[56]:

Roots involving ADVANTAGE for the people or the kings			Roots implying DISADVANTAGE for the people or the kings
23:3a	√קבץ	to gather together	**21:4:** √אסף + אֶל, to gather against (to fight)
23:3b	√שׁוב hi.	to bring back	22:10: √הלך, to go (depart); לא + √שׁוב, to not return (= v. 11); ראה + לא, to not see (his native land again) (= v. 12); 22:11: √יצא, to go out; 22:12: גלה hi., to deport; 22:27: לא + √שׁוב, to not return; 22:28: √שׁול ho., to be rejected; שׁלך ho., to be cast out
23:7b,8a	√עלה hi.	to bring up	
23:8b	√ישׁב	to dwell	**21:10:** √שׂרף, to burn (the city); 21:14: √יצת hi., to kindle (a fire); 22:5: לְחָרְבָּה + √היה, to become a ruin; 22:6: √שׁית + מִדְבָּר, to turn into a desert; 22:7: √כרת + √נפל + עֵץ־הָאָשׁ, to cut and burn (the cedars); 22:10: √בכה, to weep; 22:23: √אנח ni., to groan; √בוא inf. constr. + חֲבָלִים + חִיל, to come (birth pangs)
23:6b	√שׁכן + לְבֶטַח	to live safely	
23:6a	√ישׁע ni.	to be saved	21:14: √פקד, to punish; 22:12: √מות, to die; **21:5:** √לחם, to fight; √נכה, to stike; **21:6:** √מות, to die; **21:7b:** √נכה + לְפִי־חֶרֶב, to strike (without mercy) with the edge of the sword
23:3b	√פרה	to be fruitful	
»	√רבה	to multiply	
23:4	פקד + לא ni.	to not be missing ("sheep"?)	

---

56 I have organised the lexical material in such a way as to point out the counterposition-ing between different semantic fields. Obviously, the schema proposed serves only to provide guidelines, without pretending to be exhaustive, given the complexity and polyvalence of those relationships (e.g. √שׁול hi., "cast away" of 22:26 counterposes both √קום hi. of 23:4 (having a king as object), and the group √קבץ; √שׁוב hi.; √עלה hi. (semantic field of the return).

The broad context: The necessity of surrender as the "first" word of Jeremiah   243

Roots involving ADVANTAGE for the people or the kings			Roots implying DISADVANTAGE for the people or the kings
23:4	√קום hi.	to appoint ("shepherds")	22:19: √קבר ni. + √סחב inf. absol. + √שלך hi., to bury (like an ass), drag away and throw outside; 22:22: √רעה, to herd (or to devour; subj.: the wind); 22:24: נתק, to tear off; 22:25: √נתן + בְּיַד, to hand over to; 22:26: √טול hi., throw away; √מות, to die; 22:30: לא + √צלח, to not prosper (2x); לא + √ישב, to not sit (on the throne); לא + √משל, to not rule (ever again)
»	+ לא		
»	√פקד ni.	to not be missing ("shepherds"?)	
23:5	√מלך	to reign	
»	√שכל hi.	to prosper/to be wise	
»			

Starting from the above-mentioned elements, the hypothesis could be formulated that, by way of the placement of the textual units of this section, there be a veritable (redactional/authorial) "semiotic intentionality" in act: the name "Zedekiah" (as the last reigning representative of the Davidic dynasty) would seem to have been chosen as a *symbol* of the expectations (of justice) that had been betrayed by the kings of Judah. On the basis of this function, one could thus explain why a prophetic word regarding him would be placed, achronistically, beforehand with respect to those having Shallum, Jehoiakim, and Jehoiachin as their recipients, names that are instead given in ordered chronological succession.

Thus, the redaction of this literary unit does not lack a chronological criterion (nor do the other sections of the book of Jeremiah),[57] but rather chooses to subordinate it when necessary (and i.e. in our opinion, quite often)[58] to a textual interweaving that delineates a structural organisation with semiotic significance designed to carry a particular theological message.[59]

---

57 I am referring to the succession of events narrated in chs. 40–44. For a recent study of a critico-narrative sort on the section, see K. BODNER, *After the Invasion. A Reading of Jeremiah 40–44*, Oxford 2015.

58 We find this type of construction (problematic for exegetes because it does not respect the chronology) again in 26–35 (with the question of chs. 30–31) and also in 36–45.

59 As I highlighted in ch. I, § 2.4, this approach of structural semiosis, which introduces a perspective on the question of the positioning of 21:1–10, has been, in my opinion, until now highly underestimated by scholars. I instead believe that it can be applied advantageously to the study of the structure of the entire book of Jeremiah. In this, I distance myself, however, from the hermeneutic of an enthusiast of *Rhetorical Criticism* who has already been mentioned (and who highlighted in great detail the rhetorical structure of the section with which I am dealing; cf. ID., *Jeremiah*, 133–136), J.R. Lundbom. In my view, in other words, it is not *only* mnemonic demands for stylistic balancing of the textual units that determine the final form of the text, but rather – and primarily – the intent to inform the final structure with a theological meaning that is inferred (but also pushed "beyond") by the various materials available. This could be demonstrated by highlighting the relevant and convincing catchwords.

3.2.3. *The intermediary semiotic* arcata *of Jer 21:1–10 and Jer 23:9–40: The opposition between true and false prophecy*

Jer 21:1–10 also maintains a relationship of structural opposition with the passage devoted to the false prophets (23:9–40). Reading the two units in parallel, the contraposition between true and false prophecy appears to be a radical one. I will schematically outline these two fundamental points in particular:

a) Jeremiah's claim to be speaking in the name of the Lord, in contrast with the visions/dreams/lies of the false prophets;
b) the opposite content of the message: Jeremiah announces destruction, while the false prophets, "peace".

It should then also be noted that the motif of the condemnation of the "city" (Jerusalem) reappears in section 23:9–40 with a conclusive function (cf. vv. 39–40), as in 21:10.

Jer 21:1–10		Jer 23:9–40	
Origin of the prophetic word			
21:1	Jeremiah proclaims *the word* (הַדָּבָר)	23:13	The prophets of Samaria prophesy *by Baal* (בַּבַּעַל)[60]
	received *from the Lord* (אֲשֶׁר־הָיָה אֶל־יִרְמְיָהוּ מֵאֵת יְהוָה)	23:16	Those from Jerusalem announce *words* (דְּבָרִים)
			fruit of the *visions of their own heart* (חֲזוֹן לִבָּם)
21:8b	He is the messenger of God (כֹּה אָמַר יְהוָה)[61]		that *do not come from the Lord* (יְדַבְּרוּ לֹא מִפִּי יְהוָה)[62]
		23:21	The prophesied without having been sent or
			spoken to by God
		23:25	They speak *lies* (שֶׁקֶר) fruit of their *dreaming* (√חלם)
		23:30	They steal the words ("of God") from each other
		23:32	They have not been sent or ordered to go

---

60 That is, "in the name of Baal".
61 Obviously, what identifies a true prophet is not the use of the "messenger formula". But placing the two pericopes in comparison, the judgement of the redactor is implicit. On the one hand, he has Jeremiah say "thus says the Lord", while on the other, he has YHWH say of the false prophets (cf. 32:25): "[...] they prophesy falsehood (שֶׁקֶר) in my name (בִּשְׁמִי)".
62 Regarding this, cf. also 23:18, 21–22.

		Content of the prophetic word	
21:10	Jeremiah prophesies *disaster* (לְרָעָה)	23:17	They announce *peace* (שָׁלוֹם) and say that
	and not good (וְלֹא לְטוֹבָה)		*no disaster will come* (לֹא־תָבוֹא [...] רָעָה)
		23:12	But *disaster* (רָעָה) will come and strike them too
21:2	The word of Jeremiah that announces the catastrophe is already in the process of *completion* (נְבוּכַדְרֶאצַּר מֶלֶךְ־בָּבֶל נִלְחָם עָלֵינוּ)	23:25	They prophesy (saying they have *dreamed*; √חלם) the *lies* (שֶׁקֶר) in the name of the Lord
		23:26	Their word is not fulfilled because they prophesy *falsehood* (הַשֶּׁקֶר), the *deceit of their own hearts* (תַּרְמִת לִבָּם)
		23:32	They are prophets of *deceitful dreams* (חֲלֹמוֹת שֶׁקֶר)

Understood in dialectical relation to 23:9–40, the pericope of 21:1–10 thereby anticipates a central theme of the book of Jeremiah: the opposition between true and false prophecy. This *proleptic function* is carried out through a synthesis and anticipation of the fundamental aspects of the problem that will be developed throughout the rest of the book: the origin, content, and completion of the prophetic proclamation in relation to the fate of Jerusalem.[63] In this sense, 21:1–10 is not to be understood merely as an introduction to the following units, but rather as a connective bridge to the second section of the book (chs. 26–45), in which, in narrative form, the question of true-false prophecy is taken up once again, in its spatial-temporal development: from the speech at the temple (at the beginning of the reign of Jehoiakim; cf. ch. 26, which, unlike ch. 7 develops precisely the problem of the origin of the prophetic mission), through the dispute with the prophet Hananiah (at the beginning of the reign of Zedekiah; cf. 27–29: the opposing words regarding the "yoke" of the king of Babylon), up to the fulfilment of Jeremiah's word about the end of the kingdom of Judah (at the end of and following the reign of Zedekiah; cf. 36–45).

---

63 In relation to the thematic of the "fulfilment" of the prophetic word, I could point out that in 21:2, the veracity of Jeremiah's message (נְבוּכַדְרֶאצַּר מֶלֶךְ־בָּבֶל נִלְחָם עָלֵינוּ) announcing the catastrophe is implicitly affirmed, while with their dreams, the false prophets (cf. 23:35) pronounce only falsity (שֶׁקֶר). Another difference to highlight regards the "salvific mediation" of the prophetic function. While in 21:8–9, Jeremiah (despite everything) points out to the people in obedience to YHWH (v. 8b: כֹּה אָמַר יְהוָה) "the way to life" (v. 8c: אֶת־דֶּרֶךְ הַחַיִּים) for their good, of the false prophets it is said (cf. 23:32, but also vv. 22, 27) that with their "deceiptful dreams" (v. 23:32a: חֲלֹמוֹת שֶׁקֶר) and "their lies and bragging" (v. 23:32b: בְּשִׁקְרֵיהֶם וּבְפַחֲזוּתָם), they lead astray (v. 32b: √תעה hi.) the people and are of no use to them (v. 32b: √יעל hi. inf. ass. + לֹא + √יעל hi.).

246   Jer 21:1-10. The surrender as acceptance of the end

3.2.4. The most extreme semiotic arcata of Jer 21:1–10 and Jer 24: New elements and other connections

By extending our attention to ch. 24,[64] I can highlight some other, even more significative, relationships. Some elements that strictly correlate to 21:1–10, in fact, demonstrate the redactional desire to put forth chs. 21–24 as a section that, while complex, is endowed with unitary meaning. The most evident correspondences are:

a) the structuration of the literary entirety with texts that are chronologically homogenous placed at the extremities, given that unexpectedly, after the ordered series of the kings, we are brought once again to the time of King Zedekiah (v. 8);

b) and, above all, the identification of "good" with the deportation to Babylon.

More precisely: in 21:8–9, the life-death alternative takes the shape of the option to commit the act of surrender (and live) or to remain in the city (and die there), identifying the path decided by YHWH for the "good" of his people as that of submission to the king of Babylon (cf. 24:6). The two baskets of figs (just-ripened/rotten)[65] in ch. 24 correspond to this: the first, chosen to indicate (surprisingly) those deported to Babylon in 597, upon whom YHWH's benevolence and promise of life are turned (24:5–7), and the second, identified as "Zedekiah king of Judah, his princes, and the rest of Jerusalem" (24:8) left in the country (plus those who escaped to Egypt),[66] destined to be exterminated by way of "sword, famine, and pestilence" (cf. 24:10 with 21:7, 9).

Other lexical recurrences between 21:10 and 24:6 can be easily noted. In 21:10, it is said that YHWH has set (שׂים√) his face against Jerusalem (and, above all, against those who decide to remain there without handing themselves over to the king of Babylon) for harm (לְרָעָה) and not for good (וְלֹא לְטוֹבָה), while in Jer 24:6, YHWH sets (שׂים√) his eyes towards the exiles for their good (לְטוֹבָה). We then find a precise textual echo of the expression of 21:7 in 24:8: the beginning of the phrase is identical (אֶת־צִדְקִיָּהוּ מֶלֶךְ־יְהוּדָה, "I will hand over Zedekiah, king of Judah"). In 21:7, however, this continues with the "servants" (וְאֶת־עֲבָדָיו), followed by the binominal "the people and those who survived" (וְאֶת־הָעָם וְאֶת־הַנִּשְׁאָרִים) or "the people surviving" (וְאֶת־הָעָם הַנִּשְׁאָרִים)[67],

---

64   It should be noted that the positioning of this chapter also raises problems amongst scholars. According to W.L. HOLLADAY, *Jeremiah 1*, 656, e.g. it ought to be placed after Jer 22:30. For his part, H.-J. HERMISSON, «Die "Königsspruch"», 277–299, considers only 21:1–23, 8 to be a literary unit, maintaining (too hastily, see p. 278) that the "Rahmenfunktion" of ch. 24 be too fragile (only because he is unable to fathom a reason why elements of the subsection against the prophets in 23:9–40 are not also taken up in ch. 24).

65   On this theme, see the monograph by R.J.R. PLANT, *Good Figs, Bad Figs*. Judicial Differentiation in the Book of Jeremiah, LHBOTS 481, New York – London 2008.

66   This is another indication of proleptic positioning: associated to Zedekiah and the people remaining after the first deportation are (under the sign of a single disobedience to the same divine command) those who, once again, refuse the word of Jeremiah (still about submission to the king of Babylon) even after the disaster of 587 and escape to Egypt (cf. 42–43) to remain there (cf. 24:8: שׂים√), fearing a reprisal by Nebuchadnezzar for the murder of Gedaliah.

67   The direct object marker (וְאֵת) is absent from some mss, the LXX, the Syr, and the Tg. Several modern translations omit it as well, believing it to be a dittography (cf. RSV;

The broad context: The necessity of surrender as the "first" word of Jeremiah   247

while in 24:8, what appears is the "leaders/princes" (וְאֶת־שָׂרָיו)[68] + "the rest of Jerusalem" (שְׁאֵרִית יְרוּשָׁלַ͏ִם), "those who survive" (הַנִּשְׁאָרִים).

Lastly, I will mention a final element (though not of secondary importance) that I will better clarify further on (cf. § 4.2.1): if we consider that the alternative of choosing between two paths (obedience-disobedience) with its consequences of blessing-curse is, in and of itself, a theme typical of the stipulation of the Covenant that recurs in Deut 11:26–29; 28; 30:15–20 (blessing-curse; life-death), we can also reconnect 21:8–9 with 24:7, which clearly foreruns the vocabulary of the new Covenant in 31:33–34.[69]

NAB: "and the people in this city who survive pestilence"; TOB: "et les gens qui, dans cette ville, auront survécu à la peste"; EÜ: "und das Volk, das in dieser Stadt der Pest... entronnen ist"). Amongst the commentators holding this same view as well are W. RUDOLPH, *Jeremia*, 134; W. McKANE, *Jeremiah*, I, 501; R.P. CARROLL, *Jeremiah*, 405; P.C. CRAIGIE – P.G. KELLEY – J.F. DRINKARD, *Jeremiah 1–25*, 282–283; and A. WEISER, *Jeremia 1–25*, 176. Following the opinion of D. BARTHÉLEMY, *Critique textuelle de l'Ancien Testament. 2. Isaie, Jérémie, Lamentations*, OBO 50/2, Fribourg – Göttingen 1986, 635–636, I believe that the omission of וְאֵ be explainable as a syntactic facilitation, and that the reading of the MT (followed by the Vg and some modern versions like BJ; LND; EP) should be maintained. Perhaps the apparent incongruence of the MT, which distinguishes "the people" from "those left in the city" could realistically allude to a portion of the population of the kingdom of Judah distinct from that which will resist inside the city until the end. The fortresses of Lachish and Azekah, e.g. when Jerusalem is in the initial phase of the siege, have still not fallen into the hands of the Babylonians (cf. Jer 34:6 and, for a comparison with the "letters of Lachish", S. HERRMANN, *Geschichte Israels in alttestamentlicher Zeit*, München 1973, 345–346; in support of this position, cf. also Jer 39:9; 52:15, where the same distinction is attested between the people left in the city – the rest of the population). One may think, moreover, of defensive operations (unexpected sorties) that can still be carried out from "outside the walls" (cf. 21:4: מִחוּץ לַחוֹמָה) that result in weapons, nevertheless, being turned back (cf. H. WEIPPERT, *Jahwekrieg*, 398, n. 11; A. WEISER, *Jeremia 1–25*, 178; G. FISCHER, *Jeremia 1–25*, 636) until the last battle in the heart of the city (cf. Jer 9:20). See the description of similar military manoeuvres attested during the siege of Rabbah in 2 Sam 11:16–24, or also in 2 Kgs 3:26 and 1 Mac 6:31 (on siege dynamics in general and on this military operation – sorties – particularly possible for the besieged, see the excellent study by I. EPH'AL, *The City Besieged*, 106–108; and also W.J. HAMBLIN, *Warfare in the Ancient Near East to 1600 BC. Holy Warriors at the Dawn of History*, W&H, London 2006, 220). This eventuality was, moreover, far from underestimated by masters of siegecraft, as were the Assyrians (and the Babylonians themselves); cf. W. MAYER, *Politik*, 471.

68   This allows me, moreover, to specify that in 21:7, by use of the generic term "servants", the "ministers" of the king is intended.

69   For all of these reasons, I do not share the stance taken by J.R. Lundbom, who (without providing arguments) organises his commentary detaching ch. 24 from 21–23, 40 to make it the beginning of a literary unit that would thus terminate with ch. 29:32.

Let me review the highlighted elements in a schematic synthesis:

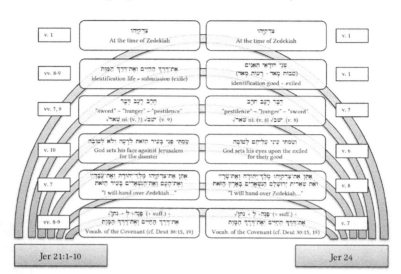

3.2.5. *The negation of suspense. In search of the meaning and strength of the pragmatic context of an already familiar story*

There is another fact that should be emphasised. Considering the phenomenon from the perspective of narrative analysis, the use of alteration (interweaving) in the logical and chronological order of events (of the story, namely the *fabula*)[70] through the use of prolepsis (or *flash-forward*) seems, upon a first look, to mortify the very spirit of narrativity itself, since this is generally constituted by its ability to generate *suspense*, curiosity, and surprise.[71] In fact, modern readers rarely use this device, precisely to avoid demotivating the reader (or spectator).[72] And yet, when the outcome of a story is known (and made known), the interpretive tension is not nullified but simply reoriented. If the ending, or the "thing that happened", is revealed in advance, this is done in order to channel the interest and hermeneutical solicitation towards the "how"

---

70 See ch. I, § 2.4.3, n. 98.
71 These are three true and proper "narrative universals" characteristic of the art of narration (cf. M. STERNBERG, *The Poetics of Biblical Narrative*, 264–320).
72 Cf. J.-L. SKA, *"Our Fathers Have Told Us"*. Introduction to the Analysis of Hebrew Narratives, SubBi 13, Roma 1990, ²2000, 8. Thus, D.M. GUNN – D. FEWELL, *Narrative in the Hebrew Bible*, 105: "Recent theoretical work on plot has drawn an analogy between readers' experience of this classic plot pattern and Freud's pleasure principle. The implication of this model is that plots, and the reading of plots, are goal-oriented: we read to get to the end because the end will make sense of what has gone before [...]. The end represents meaning, fulfilment, completion, and closure."

and "why" things ended up that way.[73] This means, in other words, that attention is to be paid to the concatenation of causes and effects that brought about the already known outcome,[74] to reconsider what is effectively at stake and become aware of the modalities of human-divine interaction.

This is, for example, the nature of the incipit of the well-known (and controversial) work by Victor Davis Hanson on the Peloponnesian War,[75] "a war like no other", in which the prologue immediately describes the tragic epilogue for the city of Athens. Right off, the reader is informed of the precise "end time" (the year 404) that coincides with the capitulation of the city, on its last legs at this point. And, practically with their own eyes, the reader can see the scene where the Spartan Admiral Lysander leads his immense fleet of 30,000 festive sailors crammed into ships as they arrive victoriously in the Athenian port of Piraeus. The author confirms that this event marked the end of Sparta's thirty-year war against Athens, an ending that, thirty years earlier, was entirely inconceivable. The question is posed explicitly, but it has already been aroused in the reader: *how* is it possible that such an incredible event could have come to be? The intent of the author is then clarified definitively, still in the prologue:

> This book does not answer that question through a strategic account of the conflict's various campaigns. Much less is it a political study of the reasons that caused the Spartans to fight against Athens. [...]. Instead, *how* did the Athenians battle the Spartans on land, in the cities, at sea, and out in the Greek countryside? What was it like for those who killed and died in this horrific war, this nightmare about which there has been little written of how many Greeks fought, how many perished, or even how all of it was conducted? My aim, therefore, after a brief introduction to the general events of the Peloponnesian War, is to flesh out this three-decade fight of some twenty-four hundred years past as something very human and thus to allow the war to become more than a far-off struggle of a distant age.

But let us return to the book of Jeremiah. If V.D. Hanson seeks, in other words, to have the pragmatic force of the context emerge, while other, perhaps more accurate reconstructions would leave this implied or entirely unexpressed, it should be made clear that in our case, the "how" specifically regards the *motivations* that have led to the end, though certainly not these alone. Here as well, the experience lived by the protagonists is also strongly emphasised, and that of Jeremiah *in primis*, rendering the reader participant in the emotional backlash of the events taking place and in which he himself is involved. In a certain sense, if we were to limit ourselves to considering

---

73   In this sense, it can be understood as a *revelatory plot*, since the issue is not so much that of reaching the resolution of a crisis that has, after all, already come about (*plot resolution*), but rather that of passing from a not-knowing (why) to a deeper awareness of the motives for the already well-known catastrophe.

74   A film critic would be interested in observing the performance of the actors in detail. The truth is, knowing the end is not tantamount to already knowing the whole story. And in fact, the *suspense* is rebuilt on a local level, within the various scenes of a story. That Jerusalem came to an end is a well-known fact. But the episodes to be recounted, the destinies that intertwine, and the choices that the different people make through the course of events leading to that outcome are many.

75   V.D. HANSON, *A War Like no Other. How the Athenians and Spartans Fought the Peloponnesian War*, New York 2005, xiv.

Jer 21:1–10 out of context, the *suspense* could not be said to be entirely nullified here either, given that the end of Jerusalem is not narrated. And yet, it is clear that the catastrophe befalling the Holy City and the consequent experience of the exile is the fact that dominates the entire narrative horizon of the book of Jeremiah. The "title" of the work is explicit in this regard (cf. 1:1–3). After all, for the author (or authors), as well as for listeners or readers, it would have made no sense to conceal the final outcome of the story, for this outcome is hot-branded on the conscience of faith of an entire people. The interest was, and continues to be, in the *rereading* of this story. It is a search for the "why", for the ultimate meaning, theologically speaking, that lies beyond the contingent causes tied to the historical-political dynamics that typify all ages.

3.3. A hermeneutical key for entering into the logic of God's judgement

Putting together the principal elements exposed thus far, I can compose the following recapitulatory diagram[76] and draw some conclusions.[77]

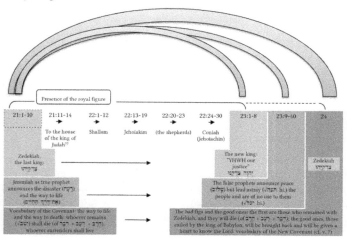

According to K.-F. Pohlmann,[78] the redactor who handled the arrangement of chs. 21–24 intends to respond to the question that he himself implicitly left hanging with the antecedent placement of 21:1–10 (and then resumed in the units following, until ch. 24) regarding the significance of the condemnation of Jerusalem and the destiny of the exiles. This scholar also maintains that the redactional arrangement of the unit comprised of chs. 21–24 would serve to highlight a "literary" message (which I would

---

76 The subdivision of the units from 21:11 to 22:30 takes into account only the most relevant textual delimitations.
77 Though the name of no king is cited expressly, in all probability, this pericope should be placed chronologically before the reign of Zedekiah (cf. n. 31).
78 Cf. K.-F. POHLMANN, *Studien*, 41–43.

The broad context: The necessity of surrender as the "first" word of Jeremiah   251

call theological or "semiotic-prophetic") drawing a distinction between a "zum Guten" judgement and a "zum Bösen" one. Only, in his opinion, the redactor had wanted to identify (and redactionally distinguish) the first with the event of 597 at the time of Jehoiakim, and the second with the catastrophe of 587.

My perspective, nevertheless, differs. Beginning with the meaning conferred by the prophetic word upon the gesture of surrender (and upon the whole divine action towards Jerusalem in its entirety, as we shall see), I recognise, even in the second "judgement" of God, a parallel salvific scope (though in a specific, definitive sense) with respect to that of 597. The current redactional positioning of 21:1–10 would therefore not have the scope of distinguishing between two judgements of God having opposite meaning,[79] but would rather provide a reading of what may have very well seemed to be the absolute, definitive condemnation of Jerusalem as the manifestation of a paradoxical *salvific will.* In this sense, ch. 24, with its positive vision of the conditions of the exiled of 597, is not to be set in oppositional relation to 21:1–10, but to be understood instead as *confirmation* of the design of God proleptically announced in 21:1–10 (and above all, in vv. 8–10) through the promise of life "as war booty" for those who accept to surrender to Nebuchadnezzar in obedience to the word of God. Those exiles who are represented by the basket of good figs in 24:5 are, in fact, (like those spoken about in ch. 29) those who had already *surrendered* to the king of Babylon with Jeconiah/Jehoiachin (cf. 24:1 and 2 Kgs 24:12).

The last word of Jeremiah pronounced before the imminent end thus becomes the "first", insofar as it is entrusted to reveal the meaning of the "judgement" of God brought about in a precise historical moment. And as such, it is placed antecedent to the very oracles against the royal house articulating the call for conversion. Nuances fade and the ineluctability of the end emerges. With it, on the one hand, the irreducible, obstinate disobedience of the people of the Covenant is revealed. While on the other, so is the unexpected opening, within the same misfortune, onto a new beginning: a "path of life" which, through acceptance of the end (surrender), will bring – solely through YHWH's action – a radical pardoning via the creation of a new heart upon which the new Covenant may be written (cf. 24:7; 31:31–34). A more detailed analysis will confirm this interpretation.

3.4. A content-related synthesis and focalisation of thematic saliencies

Let us now return to the *content* of the text of 21:1–10 with a brief *synthesis* of its fundamental elements in order to focalise the points I shall discuss.

The passage opens placing a new *word event* in the foreground, a new communication addressed to Jeremiah by YHWH (v. 1). The reader is presented with the historical-existential circumstance of this Jeremianic pronunciation: it is a *response of the prophet* to a delegation sent by King Zedekiah for a consultation. The situation in the kingdom of Judah is a dramatic one: It is under the king of Babylon's devastating attack. Jeremiah is asked for an *intercessory intervention,* and thus a word of YHWH that will guarantee the *salvation* of Jerusalem by way of the *great works of God* of the past (vv. 2–3).

---

79   *Ibid.,* 43.

252   Jer 21:1-10. The surrender as acceptance of the end

Jeremiah responds in a way that is disconcerting: YHWH himself will turn the weapons of the soldiers defending the City from the Babylonian siege back upon them. He himself *will combat* contrariwise against Jerusalem with *pestilence, famine,* and the *sword.* And the survivors will then be placed in the hands of the king of Babylon, who will show no mercy (vv. 4–7). In a certain sense, the great divine works of the past will repeat themselves, only this time, they will be against the people of God.

Not all is lost, though. The path of *life* is still viable. Jeremiah proposes two options in the name of YHWH: *to choose death,* remaining within the walls of Jerusalem in obstinate *resistance,* or *to accept the* end, going out to meet the generals of the king of Babylon and making an *act of surrender.* Only in this way can they at least conserve the bare possession of life (vv. 8–10), a return to the originary condition, in which God can once again manifest his creative force.

4. Study of the fundamental themes: Surrender, the inevitable end, and possible life

4.1. The announcement of the end through reuse of the symbolic coordinates of the origins

4.1.1. The communicative and political-religious context of the pericope

Thus far, I have dealt with the broader context, and this has already provided specific arguments for better focalising the meaning of the Jeremianic message about the surrender to Babylon. I will now concentrate on the immediate context, one that highlights how the topic that we are studying – which, in itself, appears to be almost exclusively political in nature – is presented in the book of Jeremiah by way of an essentially religious perspective. Certainly, in the ancient Near East, and above all in the Old Testament biblical world, religion and politics tend to overlap. They are not conceptually separable, at least not according to the modern schemas typical of Western culture. I already emphasised this in the General Introduction (cf. § 1.4.1). The figure of the king, just as that of the prophet, belong to a universe that is subject to divine sovereignty and their functions draw their very authority and reason for existence from this constituting relation.[80]

Nevertheless, there is no need to take these assumptions to the extreme.[81] Limiting ourselves to consider the section of the Scripture the Jewish canon denominates נְבִיאִם (early prophets: Josh; Judg; 1–2 Sam; 1–2 Kgs; later prophets: Isa; Jer; Ezek; and the Book of the Twelve), it should be noted that there is a certain oscillation in the way

---

80   Cf. N.K. GOTTWALD, *The Politics,* 3: "When we evaluate the politics of ancient Israel, we are inevitably evaluating its religious component as reported by the Hebrew Bible. To question the politics is necessarily to question the religion."

81   At least in the Neo-Babylonian epoch, what seems to be attested is the conceptualisation of a division between the religious sphere and worldly sphere. See, in this respect, P.-A. BEAULIEU, «נבופלאסר וקדמוניות בבל/Nabopolassar and the Antiquity of Babylon», in: *Hayim and Miriam Tadmor Volume,* 9*-1*, which concludes asserting: "Neo-Babylonian civilization appears to have fully conceptualized the separation between transcendental and mundane which is usually deemed the hallmark of «Axial-Age» civilizations" (p. 7*).

Study of the fundamental themes: Surrender, the inevitable end, and possible life   253

"historical"-political events are presented or to which they are alluded. Although the entire history of Israel is present as being, in a certain sense, "sacred"[82] (insofar as it is the place within which the election is manifested), and attestations of frequent contact between the figure of the king and that of the prophet (cf. e.g. 1 Kgs 22:1–28) or other divinatory means abound, such as dreams, 'ēfôd, 'ûrîm and tummîm (cf. e.g. 1 Sam 23:9–12; 28:26), there is also no shortage of episodes concerning important decisions for the life of the state in which reference to consultation of YHWH (and at times, to the religious dimension in general) is almost entirely lacking, at least in the *dynamic of the narrative* and its immediate context.[83] Reading 21:1–10, on the other hand, one instantly notes that the theme of "surrender" is explicitly placed within the religious sphere through a request for an oracle/intercession by the king's emissaries. This request, moreover, appears to be mentioned simply as the *circumstance* that provides the prophet with a way to manifest a decisive "word" upon which the attention of the pericope is then, in fact, concentrated.

Through his emissaries, the king speaks as representative of the entire community.[84] The expression used by his delegation is דרשׁ√ + direct object (אֶת־יְהוָה) + complement of advantage (בַּעֲדֵנוּ)[85] And according to R.I. Thelle,[86] it does not appear possible to restrict

---

82   Though it is simply not true that all the events in the Bible, particularly those that are inauspicious in nature, are automatically correlated to the divine, as the emblematic case of 1 Sam 6:9 demonstrates. Here, in fact, the biblical narrator presents the Philistines who discuss the *possibility* of "chance/fate" or of an "accident" (מִקְרֶה) taking place for no precise motive, unattributable to direct intervention by the deity.

83   Cf. e.g. 1 Sam 13:1–4; 22:6–23; 2 Sam 5:6–9; 11:1; 12:26–31; 15:1–29; 18:1–8; 21:15–22; 1 Kgs 12:1–20; 2 Kgs 14:7–12; etc. In the book of Jeremiah itself, the heavy silence about the fate of the pious king Josiah is striking. While he is certainly remembered for his justice (22:15), this is done without even minimal mention being made of his decision to go out to battle against the pharaoh Necho (2 Kgs 23:29–30), nor is a religious interpretation of his dramatic, premature death provided (but cf. 2 Chr 35:20–27), as opposed to promises of life in the Law (cf. e.g. Deut 4:1). And again, from the point of view of the biblical story, though it may have been normal to consult the prophets about political decisions, the (guilty) absence of prior consultations of the (true) prophetic word is underscored in Isa 30:1–2; 31:1 in the case of the alliance with Egypt. Likewise, neither the capitulation of Jehoiachin (2 Kgs 24:10–12; 2 Chr 36:10) nor the flight of Zedekiah (2 Kgs 25:1–7; Jer 52:1–11) is placed in direct correlation with the religious sphere.

84   As is rightly noted by L.C. ALLEN, *Jeremiah*. A Commentary, OTL, Louisville 2008, 241.

85   The same construction (having the typical significance of consulting God or the dead to obtain a word) can be found in 2 Kgs 22:13 and in the parallel passage in 2 Chron 34:21 (the king sends a delegation to the prophetess Huldah to get a word of the Lord – for himself, for the people, and for all of Judah – about the book of the Law found in the temple); Isa 8:9 (regarding the practice – prohibited by Law – of consulting the dead for the benefit of the living).

86   Cf. R.I. THELLE, «דרשׁ אֶת־יהוה. The Prophetic Act of Consulting Yhwh in Jeremiah 21,2 and 37,7», *SJOT* 12 (1998) 249–255; ID., *Ask God*. Divine Consultation in the Literature of the Hebrew Bible, BET 30, Frankfurt am Main 2002, 83–86. Along this line of thinking, see the earlier C. WESTERMANN, «Die Begriffe für Fragen und Suchen im Alten Testament», *KuD* 6 (1960) 2–30 (here, pp. 20–22), as well as H. LALLEMAN-DE WINKEL, *Jeremiah in Prophetic Tradition*. An Examination of the Book of Jeremiah in the Light of Israel's Prophetic Traditions, CBET 26, Leuven 2000, 219–220.

254   Jer 21:1-10. The surrender as acceptance of the end

the meaning of this in Jer 21:2 to technically that of "consulting the divinity to obtain an oracle".[87] In fact, in 37:3–10, which reports another consultation of Zedekiah's emissaries with the prophet, the same verb (v. 7a) is utilised as a synonym of פלל√ hitp. (v. 3). In construction with בְּעַד, this has the primary meaning of "to intercede"[88] (the locution בַּעֲדֵנוּ אֶל־יְהוָה is very similar to that in 21:2: the only difference is the use of אֶל instead of אֵת before (יְהוָה)[89]. The question would therefore not only be that of knowing in advance what destiny had been reserved by God for the kingdom of Judah, but of exercising on Him – through he who is implicitly recognised as a true prophet[90] – a sort of pressure that might alter the dramatic course of events.[91] We are therefore within the same perspective as a similar consultation, in an analogous context, attested in 2 Kgs 19:1–4, where the king Hezekiah sends his dignitaries to the prophet Isaiah to solicit his intercession[92] for the salvation of Jerusalem, laid siege by the Assyrian army of Sennacherib. Here as well, through a linguistic act, hope of fulfilment is expressed. While it is more explicit and articulated than Jer 21:2, it is introduced by the same lexeme אוּלַי ("perhaps"; cf. 2 Kgs 19:4).

In any case, if we limit ourselves to the book of Jeremiah, the interpretation of the king's request that I am highlighting derives, in my opinion, more from a contextual reading of the verb דרשׁ√ in 21:2 (Jerusalem under siege) than from its comparison with 37:3. Observing, in fact, the use of פלל√ hitp. in a similar context, that of 42:2, 4, 20, we notice that the intent of the intercession requested by the people is to obtain an

---

87   Collocated along this line of thinking instead would seem to be the texts suggested as terms of comparison by G. FISCHER, *Jeremia 1–25*, 633 (1 Kgs 22:5 and 2 Kgs 22:13), in which the expression דְּרָשׁ־נָא recurs. The authors who, in this context, understand the phraseology as a request for oracular response include: E.F.C. ROSENMÜLLER, *Scholia in Vetus Testamentum,* VIII: Ieremiae vaticinia et Threnos, vol. I, Lipsiae 1826, 506; F. HESSE, *Die Fürbitte im Alten Testament.* Inaugural-Dissertation zur Erlangung der Doktorwürde der hohen Theologischen Fakultät der Friedrich-Alexander-Universität, Erlangen 1951, 51; W. RUDOLPH, *Jeremia*, 135; M.E. BIDDLE, *Polyphony*, 56; W. WERNER, *Das Buch Jeremia.* Kapitel 1–25, NSK.AT 19/1, Stuttgart 1997, 190.

88   Cf. ZORELL, 651: "1. *se prebuit arbitrum, mediatorem, deprecatorem;* 2. *oravit, preces ad Deum fudit*"; *HALAT*, 882: "Fürbitte tun für, fürbittend eintreten für".

89   Cf. also 7:16 (בְּעַד הָעָם הַזֶּה); 11:14 (בְּעַד־הָעָם הַזֶּה); 14:11 (בְּעַד־הָעָם הַזֶּה); 29:7 (בַּעֲדָהּ אֶל־יְהוָה); 42:2, 20 (בַּעֲדֵנוּ אֶל־יְהוָה).

90   If Jeremiah is directly and repeatedly consulted by the king, it is because the facts are distinctly proving him right, and not the others – like Hananiah – who announced false prospects of peace and liberation.

91   An analogous situation could be seen in the episode in 1 Sam 28, where Saul consults the necromancer of Endor hoping, deep down, that even at the last minute, the spectre of Samuel will communicate a favourable reversal of fate to him. In the case of Jer 21:2, it is not clear from the context if the direct (and abrupt) insertion of the prophetic response confirming the irreversible punishment of YHWH is the result of an "intercession" or if, instead, it is in line with the insistence of the prohibition to intercede (cf. 7:16; 11:14; 14:11; 15:1), as is held to be true by C.R. SEITZ, «The Prophet Moses», 11–12; ID., «Mose als Prophet. Redaktionsthemen und Gesamtstruktur des Jeremiabuches», *BZ* 34 (1990) 234–245 (here, p. 241). Cf. also B. ROSSI, *L'intercessione nel tempo della fine*, 314–320.

92   The terminology employed here is: נשׂא√ ("lift up/offer") + תְּפִלָּה ("a prayer" [implied: to YHWH]) + בְּעַד ("in favour" [of the people: i.e. הַשְּׁאֵרִית הַנִּמְצָאָה; "for the remnant that is left"]).

Study of the fundamental themes: Surrender, the inevitable end, and possible life   255

"informative oracle" (what to do) and not a "particular grace" (change in the situation). It is ـn this same sense that √פלל hitp. is also used in 37:3, when the scenario appears to be much less dramatic than that in 21:1 (the Babylonian army has just retreated) and the desire is solely that of *knowing* if the turn that events are taking is actually positive.

4.1.2. The wonders of the Exodus

The historical context is presumably that of the first phase of the siege of Jerusalem[93] described in 34:6–7 (the siege begins in the month of Tebeth 587, the ninth year of the reign of Zedekiah).[94] The same verb לחם ni. part. + עַל ("fighting against"; vv. 1 and 7) recurs, and some cities other than Jerusalem, not yet fallen into the hands of the Babylonians, are expressly mentioned. It is difficult to establish a precise orders of precedence amongst the stages of the war that frame 21:1–10 and 34:1–7. Certainly, from the use of √צור part. ("besiege"; which is instead absent in 34:1–7) in 21:4, 9, it can be deduced that the siege of the capital has already begun and that the situation appears grave enough to impel the king to set aside the advice of his wise court advisors (including the prophets) and send a delegation to Jeremiah in the hope that the Lord might act "according to all of his wonders" (כְּכָל־נִפְלְאֹתָיו) and cause the king of Babylon to retreat.

4.1.2.1. Now is not the time. An invitation to "surrender" for Baruch as well

In the entire book of Jeremiah, the term נִפְלָאוֹת ("wonders"; elsewhere also in the defective form נִפְלָאֹת), which is an ni. part. pl. f. substantivised from √פלא ni. "to be extraordinary/wonderful",[95] is attested only here.[96] The basic reference is to the great salvific acts of intervention made by the Lord of history in favour of his people, celebrated in the cult[97] and represented as model and hope for new acts of salvation for every present and future necessity, for both the individual and the entire nation (cf. e.g. Ps 107:8, 15, 21; Judg 6,13; Isa 63,15; Hab 3,2; etc.). There is no doubt that, in the consciousness of Israel, the event

---

93   Cf. e.g. M. Avioz, «The Historical Setting of Jeremiah 21:1–10», *AUSS* 44 (2006) 213–219. Amongst scholars, only C.H. Cornill, *Das Buch Jeremia*, 242–243 places the consultation of Jeremiah described in Jer 21:1–10 before the siege.

94   As in G. Galil, *The Chronology*, 118, although different opinions exist on the precision of this date, just as they do on the fall of Jerusalem; cf. e.g. H. Cazelles, «La vie di Jérémie dans son contexte national et international», in: *Le livre de Jérémie. Le prophète et son milieu. Les oracles et leur transmission*, *ed.* P.-M. Bogaert, BEThL 54, Louvain 1981, 37.

95   In the infin. constr. pi., √פלא instead assumes the meaning "fulfill a vow" (as e.g. in Lev 22:21; Num 15:3; 15:8); cf. *BDB*, 811.

96   The same root appears in 32:17, 27. The two citations unify the power of God manifested in creation (v. 17) and what shall be revealed (v. 27; cf. also Gen 18:14) in the reconstitution of the people of the Covenant (vv. 36–44) in a single context. Other synonyms are detectable in 32:20–21, with an explicit reference to the liberation of the Exodus (אֹתוֹת וּמֹפְתִים; "signs and wonders").

97   As is pointed out by R. Albertz, «פלא», *THAT* II, 414, most of the recurrences of פלה/√פלא are found in the liturgical-celebrative context of the Psalter (41x out of 78x). In Job (5x), the privileged reference is to the creationary action of YHWH.

256   Jer 21:1-10. The surrender as acceptance of the end

of the Exodus constitutes the archetypal example to which explicit reference is most frequently made.[98]

I will present some of the most significant recurrences in this respect.[99]

Exod 3:20   *I will stretch out my hand (שלח√) and I will strike (נכה√ hi.) Egypt with all my wonders (בְּכֹל נִפְלְאֹתַי) which I shall do in the midst of it [...].*
Note also the reuse of שלח√ in Jer 21:5 and of נכה√ hi. in Jer 21:7.

Exod 15:11   *[...] Who is equal to you, glorious in holiness, awesome in praiseworthy actions, worker of wonders (פֶלֶא)[100]?*
These wonders are those in Exodus celebrated in the song of Moses (ch. 15).

Exod 34:10   *The Lord said: behold I make a covenant (כֹּרֵת בְּרִית) before all the people: I will do wonders (נִפְלָאֹת) [...].*
In this last citation, the working of wonders on the part of God is clearly placed in relation to the Covenant.

Josh 3:5   *And Joshua said to the people: Sanctify yourselves, because tomorrow the Lord will do wonders (נִפְלָאֹות) in your midst.*
These "wonders" are carried out through the passage of the Jordan that renews the wonders of the Exodus, as is explicitly stated in Josh 4:23.

---

98   Cf. F. STOLZ, «Zeichen und Wunder. Die prophetische Legitimation und ihre Geschichte», *ZThK* 69 (1972) 138; J. CONRAD, «פָּלָא», *ThWAT* VI, 569–583 (here, col. 576).

99   It should be noted that out of a total of 42x (without counting Job 42:3; Ps 131:1, in which it recurs as an adjective; cf. *Ibid.*, 569) the term נִפְלָאֹות *explicitly* refers to the wonders of the Exodus distributed as follows: 2x out of 2x in the book of Exodus; 1x out of 1x in Judg; 1x out of 1x in Mic; 1x out of 1x in Neh; and 8x out of 27x in Ps. Considering a couple of more indirect references as well, the occurrences are almost a third of the total number. To recapitulate, we have 11x in which the reference to the Exodus (and to YHWH as creator of the נִפְלָאֹות) is clear from the context: Exod 3:20; 34:10; Judg 6:13; Mic 7:15; Neh 9:17; Ps 78:11, 32; 105:2, 5; 106:7, 22; 2x with a more indirect reference: Josh 3:5 (cf. Josh 4:23); Ps 111:4 (cf. v. 5); 17x with reference to "wonders" in a more generic sense: Ps 9:2; 26:7; 40:6; 71:17; 72:18; 75:2; 86:10; 96:3; 98:1; 107:8, 15, 21, 24, 31; 119:18, 27; 145:5; 1 Chr 16:9, 12 (which is, in any case, a citation of Ps 105:5), 24; 4x in reference to YHWH's creative work: Job 5:9; 9:10; 37:5, 14; 2x it means "astounding things" (Dan 8:24; 11:36) but not referring to God. Out of a total of 30x occurrences in which נִפְלָאֹות regards an intervention of God in history, almost half make reference to the Exodus (13x) and those remaining belong to the literary genre of psalmic prayer (also used in 1 Chr).

100   I cite this example (without calculating it amongst the occurrences of נִפְלָאֹות) because the substantive פֶלֶא has fundamentally the same meaning as נִפְלָאֹות and this too refers, above all, to the context of the Exodus (Exod 15:11; Ps 78:12; 77:15). Cf. J. CONRAD, «פָּלָא», 580.

Study of the fundamental themes: Surrender, the inevitable end, and possible life   257

Judg 6:13   [...] *Where are all his wonderous works* (כָּל־נִפְלְאֹתָיו) *that our fathers recounted to us, saying: Did not the Lord bring us up from Egypt? But now the Lord has has forsaken us and has delivered us into the hands of Midian.*

The words of Gideon express that not seeing "all of his wonders" narrated by the fathers (who coincide with the exit from Egypt) in the historical present results in a perception of abandonment (√עזב hi. + suff. 1st pl.) on God's part. Note the antithetical reference to Jer 21:2: here the "wonders" of God are invoked so that the king of Babylon will withdraw from the city (√עלה qal + מֵעָלֵינוּ). Judg 6:13 and Jer 21:2 then have in common the idea of "totality" expressed by the locution כָּל־נִפְלְאֹתָיו.

Mic 7:15   *As in the days when you came out from the land of Egypt, I will show them marvellous things* (נִפְלָאוֹת).

Neh 9:17   *They refused to obey and no longer remembered the wonders* (נִפְלְאֹתֶיךָ) *that you had performed amongst them* [...].

These are the wonders of the Exodus (cf. vv. 9–12).

Ps 78:11(32) [...] *they forgot his deeds and his wonders* (וְנִפְלְאוֹתָיו) *that he had shown them.*

These are the wonders of the Exodus (cf. vv. 12–16).

Ps 105:2(5)   *Sing to him, sing praise to him, meditate on all his wonders* (בְּכָל־נִפְלְאוֹתָיו).

These are, above all, the wonders of the Exodus (cf. vv. 23–55).

Ps 106:7(22) *Our fathers in Egypt did not understand your wonderful works* (נִפְלְאוֹתֶיךָ), *they did not remember your many acts of mercy and they rebelled by the sea, by the Red Sea.*

As their underlying motive, the "wonders" performed by the Lord for his people have the gratuity of election and consequent stipulation of the Covenant (cf. e.g. Ps 111:4–5, 9 for the connection between נִפְלָאֹת and בְּרִית). In the context of our pericope, I believe that an allusion should also be seen to the episode portrayed in 2 Kgs 19:35–37 (//Isa 37:36–38), where YHWH frees Jerusalem in an extraordinary way from the siege of Sennacherib.[101] This would thus also be an implicit reference to the theology of the impregnability of Zion acritically revived by the false prophets at the time of Jeremiah.[102]

---

101 This allusion (reinforced by use of the same locution [...]־אֶל כֹּה תֹאמְרוּן with the archaic form of √אמר 2nd pers. pl.; cf. תֹאמְרָן in v. 3 and תֹאמְרוּן in 2 Kgs 19:10 and Isa 37:10) is pointed out by various commentators, such as, e.g. B. DUHM, *Jeremia*, 169; W. RUDOLPH, *Jeremia*, 135; K.-F. POHLMANN, *Studien*, 33; W. McKANE *Jeremiah*, 496. The question of the historicity or not of the biblical accounts relating to the Assyrian siege of 701 remains disputed (cf. M. COGAN, «Judah», 406, which is based on H. TADMOR, «Sennacherib's Campaign to Judah: Historical and Historiographical Considerations», *Zion* 50 [1985] 65–80 [Hebrew]).

102 Cf. e.g. R. DE VAUX, «Jerusalem and the Prophets», in: *Interpreting the Prophetic Tradition*, ed. H.M. ORLINSKY, New York 1969, 277–300; J. BRIGHT, *Covenant and Promise*, London 1977; J.P. SISSON, «Jeremiah», 429–442; J. FERRY, *Illusions et salut dans la prédication prophetique de Jérémie*, BZAW 269, Berlin – New York 1999, 94–97;

258   Jer 21:1-10. The surrender as acceptance of the end

These references, in turn, call into question yet another one, all within the book of Jeremiah. The desire for salvation expressed by sending notables to consult the prophet (21:1–2) is not all that different from the longings of Baruch, the faithful friend. In ch. 45, a text that is key to the textual organisation of the Jeremianic work, there is an oracle that also responds to the worries and hopes of this companion in many painful experiences (cf. 45:3), precisely when he must write down (and then read in public) a synthesis of all of Jeremiah's threatening oracles on the pivotal date of the "fourth year of Jehoiakim" (605/604).[103] The response of the prophet, though promising that this time of disaster will need to be endured, is an invitation to not expect "great things" (גְדֹלוֹת)[104]. Because now is the moment for YHWH to set his hand to the destruction of all that he himself admirably built, and if he is asking for all of Jerusalem to surrender, then Baruch is also being invited to *consign himself* to the (theological) meaning of the moment underway:

כֹּה תֹאמַר אֵלָיו [105] כֹּה אָמַר יְהוָה	**4**	Thus you shall say to him[105]: thus says the Lord:
הִנֵּה אֲשֶׁר־בָּנִיתִי אֲנִי הֹרֵס		Behold, that which I have built I will tear down,
וְאֵת אֲשֶׁר־נָטַעְתִּי אֲנִי נֹתֵשׁ		and what I planted I will uproot,
וְאֶת־כָּל־הָאָרֶץ הִיא		and this through the whole land.
וְאַתָּה תְּבַקֶּשׁ־לְךָ גְדֹלוֹת	**5**	And you are looking for *great things* for yourself?
אַל־תְּבַקֵּשׁ כִּי הִנְנִי מֵבִיא		Seek them not. For behold: I will bring
רָעָה עַל־כָּל־בָּשָׂר נְאֻם־יְהוָה		disaster upon all flesh, oracle of the Lord.
וְנָתַתִּי לְךָ אֶת־נַפְשְׁךָ לְשָׁלָל		But I will give you your life as war booty,
עַל כָּל־הַמְּקֹמוֹת אֲשֶׁר תֵּלֶךְ־שָׁם		in all the places where you go.

In the book of Jeremiah, we find the term גְדֹלוֹת as an adjectival noun again only in 33:3. This attestation provides us, in any case, with important clues for grasping its meaning in the context of the oracle to Baruch. After the symbolic gesture of the acquisition of the field (32:6–15), Jeremiah's subsequent invocation of astonishment (32:16–25)[106]

A. BARUCHI-UNNA, «The Story of Hezekiah's Prayer (2 Kings 19) and Jeremiah's Polemic concerning the Inviolability of Jerusalem», *JSOT* 39 (2015) 281–297.

103   This can be deduced from the redactional notation in v. 1. But one could also think of a reference to the "passion of Jeremiah" narrated in chs. 37–38. In the story logic, these events clearly determine serious repercussions for the trusted collaborator Baruch.

104   Cf. J.M. ABREGO, *Jeremías*, 136–138.

105   This phrase, given the communicative context, creates difficulty, and for this reason, many commentators and modern versions omit it, though without solid textual motives. It is as though something has been lost over the course of the transmission of the text which, in this way, remains elliptical and leads the reader to presuppose a previous dialogue between Jeremiah and YHWH concerning Baruch, his lamentation and his destiny. For an explicative theory, see J.R. LUNDBOM, *Jeremiah 37–52*, 175–176.

106   According to the clues that can be obtained from 32:1 and 33:1, a relationship of chronological order can be established between the two episodes (cf. K. SCHMID, *Buchgestalten des Jeremiabuches. Untersuchungen zur Redaktions- und Rezeptionsgeschichte von Jer 30–33 im Kontext des Buches*, WMANT 72,

and the response of YHWH (36:26–44), chapter 33[107] also invites looking beyond the horizon of the catastrophe to where only divine power can operate: "Call to me and I will answer you; I will tell you *great things* (נְדֹלוֹת), hidden things (וּבְצֻרוֹת), which you do not known (לֹא יְדַעְתָּם)".

This text can be placed initially with the נִדְלוֹת spoken about in the book of Job, to wit, the wonders that YHWH works in nature and history (cf. Job 5:9; //9:10 in parallel with נִפְלָאֹת; 37:5). The נִדְלוֹת for which YHWH is praised in Ps 71:19 are tied to his "justice" (צְדָקָה) and to the hope of the person praying to rise again "from the depths of the earth" (מִתְּהֹמוֹת הָאָרֶץ).[108] Nevertheless, in Ps 136:4, where the "great works" are still both those of a creative-natural sort and interventions in the human story, as in Job, an explicit reference to the events of the Exodus is specified. This meaning of נִדְלוֹת becomes direct and unequivocal in Ps 106:21: "They forgot God, their Saviour, who had done *great things* (נִדְלוֹת) in Egypt" (also seen, again from √גדל, in Deut 11:7; 1 Sam 12:24, and the homologous term נְדֻלּוֹת in Ps 145:6; 1 Chron 17:21; etc.).

Returning to Jer 33:3, from here to 45:5, and thus, once again, to the "wonders" (נִפְלָאֹת) of 21:2, we can more clearly see a unifying common thread between these attestations established by a shared originary reference. In 33:3, what no one is humanly capable of imagining or hoping while experiencing death is precisely what is revealed and promised by YHWH: the re-establishment of the fortunes of Judah, return of the dispersed, a reflourishing of life and the Davidic dynasty, a pardoning, and a persisting of an infrangible covenant (cf. 33:4–26). And in the language used here, it is easy to see the reference, which is an archetypal model, to the originary event by which YHWH gave his people life and liberty, extracting them from Egypt and leading them to the Promised Land.

In the context of the oracle in 45:2–5, the imminent actions of YHWH announced by Jeremiah, poised to raze what had been built and uproot what had previously been planted (v. 4), recall various (also Jeremianic) texts in which √בנה ("to build")[109] and above all √נטע ("to plant"),[110] having YHWH as subject and also in conjunction with each other, express in different ways (and according to the twofold metaphor of construction and agriculture) the "generative" intention of the Lord towards the house of David and the people that he chose to make prosper in the land of Canaan.[111] Hence,

---

Neukirchen-Vluyn 1996, 98; J. FERRY, «"Je restaurerai Israël" (Jr 33,7.9.26). L'écriture de Jérémie 33», *TrEu* 15 (1998) 69–82, here, p. 71).

107   On the numerous connections between the two chs., see E. DI PEDE, *Au-de là du refus*, 207–211.

108   And think of Jeremiah pulled out alive from the cistern/sepulchre of death (cf. 33:1–13).

109   Cf. 1 Sam 2:35; 2 Sam 7:27; 1 Kgs 11:38; Ps 89:4; 1 Chr 17:10, 25: in reference to the Davidic lineage; Isa 5:2: the tower of protection for the vineyard, metaphor for Israel; Jer 18:9: a nation; Ps 78:69: the temple.

110   Cf. Gen 2:8: the garden of Eden; Exod 15:17; 2 Sam 7:10; //1 Chr 17:9; Ps 44:3; 80:9, 16: Israel (in Num 24:6; Isa 5:2; Jer 2:21; 11:17; the same reference is mediated by the plant metaphor, already implied, for that matter, by the verb itself); Jer 12:2 (the wicked); 18:9: a nation.

111   I will omit the attestations that refer not to the originary event but to the future restoration.

260   Jer 21:1-10. The surrender as acceptance of the end

if now YHWH has decided to tear down and uproot, it is clear (at least on a linguistic level) that we are in the context of a deconstruction of the originary event.[112]

More than allude to the wonder of a reconstruction,[113] which does not appear to be a pertinent theme in the temporal context where the oracle to Baruch is positioned, and much more than merely be of personal advantage, in all probability, the "great things" (גְדֹלוֹת) referred to are therefore none other than a desire for the great wonders of salvation typical of the season of the Exodus to be repeated. After all, it is a right of every Israelite who, every year, through the paschal memorial, crosses the sea of rushes with the Fathers (cf. Exod 12:25–27; 13:3–10; Deut 4:37, 5:3; 16:1–3; etc.) to expect that the same God can at any moment re-enact the great wonders of the past in the present time and in unforeseen forms. In truth, Jeremiah does not in the least negate this possibility, because precisely divine intervention, which now eradicates and destroys, will indeed be the definitive response to the desire for good to which Baruch aspires (cf. 31:28: all will be rebuilt and planted anew). This response is even more marvellous than the originary salvation, inasmuch as it corresponds to a condition even more grave than the ancient one. But the point *now* is that Baruch must also fulfil his own symbolic-prophetic act to personally interpret what Jeremiah is asking of everyone. And it is an act that addresses the very root of every other human resolve, because it touches that vital fountainhead that is the heart's desires: it is about renouncing the very desire for "great things" to occur.

In the oracle addressed to Baruch, one can thus intuit the motives that urge him to seek (√בקשׁ pi.) "great things" for himself, even if these remain unexpressed. Instead, the words of the delegation sent to Jeremiah seem more clearly founded on the relational implications of the Covenant between YHWH and his people, and in particular, on the hope of its salvific implications (cf. v. 2b: אוּלַי; "perhaps"),[114] That they still not be "seeking" YHWH "wholeheartedly" (√בקשׁ pi.; cf. 29:13) can be understood nonetheless from the fact that this reference does not in the least pose the problem of fidelity, either of the king or the people. A serious omission, because all of God's threats referred by Jeremiah himself also implied a hope (אוּלַי): that Israel would want to convert and thereby avoid punishment.[115]

Jeremiah's oracular response is placed on the same symbolic horizon that is evoked in the question, and it takes up other elements endowed with great allusive strength. Assumed and remodelled by the prophetic word, these become part of a staggering

---

112   As, on the contrary, the promises of salvation in 24:6 and 42:10 relaunch a reactualisation of the selfsame originary event toward times to come.

113   J.M. ABREGO, *Jeremías*, 136–137.

114   In 32:27, we find a link between an interrogative clause (introduced by הֲ) and the root פלא: "Behold, I am the Lord, the God of all flesh: is there perhaps anything (too) wondrous (√פלא ni.; = "impossible") for me?". The "wonder" that YHWH will perform will not, however, be the one Zedekiah requests, but rather the reconstruction of Israel after its (now inevitable) destruction.

115   Cf. 26:3: "Perhaps (אוּלַי) they will listen and each will turn from their evil ways and I will repent of the evil I plan to inflict on them for the evil they have done"; 36:3: "Perhaps (אוּלַי) the house of Judah will listen to all the disaster I plan to do to them and each will turn from their evil way, and so I will forgive their iniquity and their sin"; 36:7: "Perhaps (אוּלַי) they will present their supplication before the Lord and they shall turn each one from his evil way, for great is the anger and wrath that the Lord has pronounced against this people."

Study of the fundamental themes: Surrender, the inevitable end, and possible life   261

new revelation of YHWH's action in history.[116] The relevancy of these references should not be considered on the basis of analyses of the single expressions themselves alone. As is evident, after all, these cannot recur exclusively within the context of the traditions of the Exodus, but are attested elsewhere as well. It is rather due to the *concentration* and *reciprocal relation* of terms that are all significative in that sense and given the general context of the pericope[117] that they cannot fail to evoke in a reader familiar with the great pillars of the biblical history of Israel the grand motif of the miraculous exit from Egypt. Besides, as G. Fischer has pointed out as well,[118] the intensive use of Exodus traditions that can be found in Jeremiah cannot be found in the other important prophetic books like Isaiah and Ezekiel. This attests to both the authority enjoyed by the *Tôrâ* at the time of its composition as well as the creative, modernising remodelling of these traditions.[119]

With regard to this theologically oriented reworking of the themes of the Exodus, to which the term נִפְלָאוֹת directed us immediately, the following should also be highlighted:

a) the expression in v. 5: לחם √ ni. ("to fight") + בְּיָד נְטוּיָה וּבִזְרוֹעַ חֲזָקָה ("with outstretched hand and mighty arm") + וּבְאַף וּבְחֵמָה וּבְקֶצֶף גָּדוֹל ("with anger, with fury, and with great indignation");
b) the scourge of the plague (דֶּבֶר) in vv. 67, 9a (linked to מות √ and נכה √ hi.);
c) the use of the verb יצא √ in v. 9b.

---

116   The reutilisation of and allusion to historic and/or prophetic traditions that were antecedent and hence well known to the interlocutors, readapted for new situations and contexts, is a continual characteristic of biblical prophetism and the art of its rhetoric, which aims to communicate the word of God in the most incisive manner possible. Cf. e.g. G. von Rad, *Theologie,* II; H.G.M. Williamson, *The Book Called Isaiah.* Deutero-Isaiah's Role in Composition and Redaction, Oxford 1994; B.D. Sommer, *A Prophet Reads Scripture.* Allusion in Isaiah 40–66, Stanford 1998; R.L. Schultz, *The Search for Quotation.* Verbal Parallels in the Prophets, JSOT.S 180, Sheffield 1999, 335–336; R. Nurmela, *The Mouth of the Lord Has Spoken.* Inner-Biblical Allusions in Second and Third Isaiah, SJ(L), Lanham 2006.

117   The general context, which will be further explicated over the course of the present chapter, regards a crucial moment for Israel. During this time, what are up for discussion, and radically so, are precisely those fundamental good things that can be traced back to the founding event: the identity of Israel as a people liberated by YHWH and its legitimate dwelling in the Promised Land.

118   G. Fischer, «Zurück nach Ägypten? Exodusmotivik im Jeremiabuch», in: *A Pillar of Cloud to Guide.* Text-Critical, Redactional, and Linguistic Perspectives on the Old Testament in Honour of Marc Vervenne, eds. H. Ausloos – B. Lemmelijn, Leuven – Paris – Walpole 2014, 73–92. See also M.P. Maier, *Ägypten – Israels Herkunft und Geschick.* Studien über einen theo-politischen Zentralbegriff im hebräischen Jeremiabuch, OBS 21, Frankfurt am Main 2002.

119   Cf. *Ibid.,* 92: "Die engen Beziehungen zwischen Exod und Jer sind uberdies ein Beispiel dafür, wie prophetische Schriften in späterer Zeit mit der Tora umgehen. Dabei werden klar zwei Momente sichtbar. Einerseits hat die Tora Autorität und gilt als Basis. Doch anderseits werden diese alten Traditionen des Glaubens nicht einfach wiederholt, sondern variiert, weitergeführt und diskutiert. Sie zeigen in dieser je neuen Lebendigkeit ihre Kraft und Bedeutung."

262   Jer 21:1-10. The surrender as acceptance of the end

I will address the first two points directly and postpone discussion of the third until § 4.2.1, where I will take on the question of the "anti-Exodus" and the "new Exodus".

4.1.2.2. With outstretched hand and mighty arm, but against Jerusalem!

The image of YHWH who *fights* (√לחם ni.) in favour of his people to liberate them from the slavery of Egypt typifies the traditions of the Exodus (cf. § 4.1.3). The modality of this liberation is described using stereotyped phraseology, including the characteristic expression בְּיָד חֲזָקָה וּבִזְרוֹעַ נְטוּיָה ("with mighty hand and outstretched arm")[120] that represents a fixed formula (evidently "original" compared to 21:5)[121] and recurs in this complete form 11x in the HB.[122] In the book of Jeremiah, a similar expression recurs 2x in reference to the creative power of YHWH, a theme that I will address in my study of chapters 27–28 (in ch. IV of the present dissertation).

> It was I who made the earth, human beings, and beasts that are on the face of the earth, *with my great power and with my outstretched arm* (בְּכֹחִי הַגָּדוֹל וּבִזְרוֹעִי הַנְּטוּיָה) [...] (Jer 27:5).

> Oh, Lord God, behold, you have made the heavens and the earth *with your great power and your outstretched arm* (בְּכֹחֲךָ הַגָּדוֹל וּבִזְרֹעֲךָ הַנְּטוּיָה); nothing is too hard for you! (Jer 32:17).

The fact that in the entire HB,[123] only 21:5 presents an inversion of the attributes (נְטוּיָה is an attribute of יָד, while חֲזָקָה is one of זְרוֹעַ: "with outstretched hand and mighty arm") is almost certainly intentional. One need simply pay attention within the book of Jeremiah itself. In 32:21[124] (cf. also 27:5; 32:17),[125] in fact, we find the same locution,

---

120   For the study of this formula, see S. Kreuzer, «Die Mächtigkeitsformel im Deuteronomium. Gestaltung, Vorgeschichte und Entwicklung», *ZAW* 109 (1997) 188–207; Id., «Die Verwendung der Mächtigkeitsformel außerhalb des Deuteronomiums. Literarische und theologische Linien zu Jer, Ez, dtrG und P», *ibid.*, 369–384. By the name *Mächtigkeitsformel,* this author intends not only the expression "mighty hand and outstretched arm", but also other elements (which he denotes as "Abwandlungen" ["variations"]), such as the binominal "signs and wonders". The biblical passages (32) have been collected together based on their least mention of the combination of two elements (considering also synonymic expressions) and inserted into an outline that does not, however, indicate the verbal root upon which they depend. An observation: while on the one hand, it is right for the study of a formula to analyse all the passages in which related elements recur, on the other, it does seem risky that every single element, wherever attested and irrespective of its contextual linguistic use, be enclosed within the category of *Mächtigkeitsformel.* Ultimately, the very meaning of the "formula" depends on its context of reference.

121   Of the same opinion, W.L. Holladay, «Elusive Deuteronomists, Jeremiah, and Proto-Deuteronomy», *CBQ* 66 (2004) 58–60.

122   There are other passages in which the formula is present as a single element.

123   Amongst the prophets, only Ezekiel takes up the expression, though he does so according to its traditional form; cf. Ezek 20:33–34.

124   "You brought your people Israel out of the land of Egypt with signs and wonders, with a mighty hand and outstretched arm (בְּיָד חֲזָקָה וּבְאֶזְרוֹעַ נְטוּיָה) and with great terror."

125   Both of the texts make reference to the creative force of YHWH according to a use that characterises the book of Jeremiah (K. Martens, «"With a Strong Hand and an Outstretched Arm". The Meaning of the Expression ביד חזקה ובזרוע נטויה», *SJOT*

Study of the fundamental themes: Surrender, the inevitable end, and possible life   263

explicitly placed in relation to the event of the Exodus, with the placement of the attributes that reflects the originary formulation. To reinforce the relevance of this interpretation, I would add the observation that the case is not an isolated one, but rather one of many examples of a creative reutilization of well-known formulations[126] or an intentional adoption (at times also in the inversed sense) of other biblical texts that constitute one of the specific peculiarities of the book.[127]

We are, therefore, in the presence of a category of *citations*, with all the hermeneutical implications that this complex communicative practice can have.[128] In the case at hand, the tendency highlighted is ascribable, in my opinion, to the literary phenomenon identified back by M. Seidel (hence the term "Seidel's law")[129] and studied with even greater rigour in particular by P.C. Beentjes, who holds it to be a (generally neglected) stylistic model founded on intentionally "inverted quotations".[130] The latter

---

15 (2001) 123–141). In 21:5, one can thus discern an underlying allusion to the same theme, though in this case as well, it is used in an *oppositive* sense. It is in fact a "de-creation", in conformity with the literary motif developed in 4:23–28. As highlighted by S. Paas, *Creation and Judgement. Creation Texts in Some Eighth Century Prophets*, Leiden 2003, 315, 323, 325, 434–436, the theme of God the creator also establishes "the darker side of God's creative power", that is, his punitive action in history, which can "overturn the historical order of things and turn himself against his own people".

126   Cf. e.g. R. Bach, *Die Aufforderung zur Flucht und zum Kampf im alttestamentlichen Prophetenspruch*, WMANT 9, Neukirchen 1962, 26–28 and 33, 73.

127   As we are rightfully invited to observe by G. Fischer, *Jeremia 1–25*, 64–65. Think, e.g. of the relationship between Deut 13:14, 17, Jer 30:18, 21 (on this, see esp. G. Fischer, *Das Trostbüchlein*. Text, Komposition und Theologie von Jer 30–31, SBB 26, Stuttgart 1993, 207–208), and 31:37; between Deut 32:20 and Jer 12:4; between the text of the creation in Gen 1 and the return to the primordial וָבֹהוּ תֹהוּ evoked in Jer 4:23–26.

128   See, in this regard, M. Sternberg, «Proteus in Quotation-Land: Mimesis and the Forms of Reported Discourse», *Poetics Today* 3 (1982) 107–156, who underscores how any text subject to citation, even literal, inevitably encounters semantic variations. These variations, determined by the new context of reference, can even be radical: "[...] even if the original could be copied down to the last detail, its transplanting and framing in a new environment would impose on it a new mode of existence. What this new mode of existence involves is not just formal restructuring but manifold shifts, if not reversals, of the original meaning and significance" (p. 108); "[...] substitution, addition and recontextualisation, for instance, may all result in comparable shifts of meaning. [...] the consequences of lexical substitution, say, range from the semantic to the stylistic, from shift in referent to shift in referring expression, from preservation to reversal of meaning" (p. 129).

129   Cf. M. Seidel, «Parallels between Isaiah and Psalms», *Sinai* 38 (1955–1956) 149–172, 229–240, 272–280, 335–355 (here, p. 150).

130   Cf. P.C. Beentjes, «Inverted Quotations in the Bible: A Neglected Stylistic Pattern», *Bib.* 63 (1982) 506–523. Unlike L. Dorn, «The Unexpected as a Speech Device: Shifts of Thematic Expectancy in Jeremiah», *BiTr* 37 (1986) 220, who flags the rhetorical function of the expression, P.C. Beentjes makes no note of Jer 21:5 amongst the various cases presented, nor does he dwell on the possible interpretive implications of this special rhetorical figure, while he does, however, express hope that more in-depth study on the subject will be done (cf. p. 523). The problem that presents itself most frequently is instead that of the "originality" of the expression. The historical

264   Jer 21:1-10. The surrender as acceptance of the end

scholar, followed in turn by others,[131] emphasised how throughout the Scripture (OT and NT), there is a detectable presence of brief locutions or clauses (ordinarily, no more than a single verse) that present anew *already known* texts in which the fundamental elements are *deliberately* inverted.[132]

The use of this rhetorical device, which fits well within the framework of a frequent use of wordplay[133] attested in the prophetic traditions, confirms the overall meaning of the oracle in 21:3–10. This – as I am attempting to demonstrate – draws its expressive and revelative strength from the taking up and flipping of perspective of phraseologies and themes anchored in highly specific traditions and known to the listeners. In 21:5, the inversion is also a formal one, according to a literary procedure that tells the "end" by repeating literary forms typical of the "origin". In this manner, tension is generated between two opposite poles that triggers a fruitful hermeneutical circle for understanding both the meaning of the end and the decisive importance of that which anchors originarily the YHWH – Israel relationship.

The particular linguistic application of the formula in question reveals, moreover, how it should be placed in relation not only with the military action of YHWH against Jerusalem, but also with the prophetic request to "go out towards the Chaldeans". I will present the eleven recurrences present in the HB schematically, arranging them according to the context and type of action designated by the main clause verbal root:

---

precedence to be attributed to the various occurrences depends on this. In our case, since we are in the presence of a manifold attestation of a stereotypical formula (that is: בְּיָד חֲזָקָה וּבִזְרוֹעַ נְטוּיָה), it is evident that in Jeremiah, use is being made of a prior, already well established, literary expression.

131   See e.g. the contributions of S. TALMON, «The Textual Study of the Bible – A New Outlook», in: *Qumran and the History of the Biblical Text*, eds. F.M. CROSS – S. TALMON, Cambridge 1975, 358–378; B.M. LEVINSON, *Deuteronomy and the Hermeneutics of Legal Innovation*, New York – Oxford 1997, 18–20, 35; I. KALIMI, *The Reshaping of Ancient Israelite History in Chronicles*, Winona Lake 2005, 232–274.

132   For the OT, the following correspondences are analysed: Eccles 46:13–20 and 1 Sam 12:3; Ezek 8:12 and 9:9; Gen 27:29 and Num 24:9; Lev 26:4b and Ezek 34:27a; Lev 26:42 (presenting the traditional order in which patriarchs are cited, that is Abraham – Isaac – Jacob, in inverted order); Ps 23:6 and 27:4; Hag 1:10 and Zech 8:12; Ps 83:14–16 and Isa 17:13–14. Aside from these, refer to: Deut 32:1 and Isa 1:2; Ps 35:9 and Isa 61:10; Eccles 9:5a and Job 31:1b; Eccles 18:32 and Prov 23:20–21; Eccles 20:4 and Prov 17:28; Eccles 32(35):23 and Prov 19:16; Eccles 45:15b and Exod 28:41; Eccles 48:1 and Mal 3:19; Josh 2:2 and Ps 120:1.

133   These are communication techniques that intend to expose truths the interlocutor does not want to see, and not without the aid of a certain irony that derives from devising the discourse in this fashion.

Study of the fundamental themes: Surrender, the inevitable end, and possible life   265

Context	Main clause verbal root		Expression		Other elements (inserted before or after)	
(Exodus)						
Deut 5:15	יצא hi.	to bring out	בְּיָד חֲזָקָה	with mighty hand		
			וּבִזְרֹעַ נְטוּיָה	and outstretched arm		
Deut 26:8	יצא hi.	to bring out	בְּיָד חֲזָקָה	with mighty hand	וּבְמֹרָא גָּדֹל	and with great terror
			וּבִזְרֹעַ נְטוּיָה	and outstretched arm	וּבְאֹתוֹת וּבְמֹפְתִים	and with signs and wonders
Jer 32:21	יצא hi.	to bring out	וּבְיָד חֲזָקָה	and with mighty hand	בְּאֹתוֹת וּבְמוֹפְתִים	with signs and wonders
			וּבְאֶזְרוֹעַ נְטוּיָה	and with outstretched arm	וּבְמוֹרָא גָּדוֹל	and with great terror
Ps 136:11–12	יצא hi.	to bring out	וּבְיָד חֲזָקָה	and with mighty hand		
			וּבִזְרוֹעַ נְטוּיָה	and outstretched arm		
Deut 4:34	לקח	to take	וּבְיָד חֲזָקָה	and with mighty hand	בְּמַסֹּת בְּאֹתֹת	with trials, signs
			וּבִזְרוֹעַ נְטוּיָה	and outstretched arm	וּבְמוֹפְתִים	and wonders
					וּבְמִלְחָמָה	and war
					וּבְמוֹרָאִים גְּדֹלִים	and great terrors
Deut 11:2–3	ידע ראה	to know to see	אֶת־יָדוֹ הַחֲזָקָה	his mighty hand	וְאֶת־אֹתֹתָיו	his signs
			וּזְרֹעוֹ הַנְּטוּיָה	and his outstretched arm	וְאֶת־מַעֲשָׂיו	and his deeds
Deut 7:19	זכר	to remember	וְהַיָּד הַחֲזָקָה	the mighty hand	הַמַּסֹּת הַגְּדֹלֹת	the great trials
			וְהַזְּרֹעַ הַנְּטוּיָה	and the outstretched arm	וְהָאֹתֹת וְהַמֹּפְתִים	the signs and the wonders
(Other)						
Ezek 20:33	מלך	to rule over	בְּיָד חֲזָקָה	with mighty hand	וּבְחֵמָה שְׁפוּכָה	and with overflowing fury
			וּבִזְרוֹעַ נְטוּיָה	and outstretched arm		

Context	Main clause verbal root	Expression		Other elements (inserted before or after)	
Ezek 20:34	יצא hi.	to bring out	בְּיָד חֲזָקָה	with mighty hand	וּבְחֵמָה שְׁפוּכָה	and with overflowing fury
	קבץ pi.	to gather	וּבִזְרוֹעַ נְטוּיָה	and outstretched arm		
2 Chron 6:32	בוא + מִן	to come from (far away because of)	וְיָדְךָ הַחֲזָקָה	and of your mighty hand	שִׁמְךָ הַגָּדוֹל	and of you great name
			וּזְרוֹעֲךָ הַנְּטוּיָה	and of your outstretched arm		
1 Kgs 8:42	שמע	to hear	וְאֶת־יָדְךָ הַחֲזָקָה	of your mighty hand		
			וּזְרֹעֲךָ הַנְּטוּיָה	and of your outstretched arm		

When used in reference to the event of the Exodus (the majority of the attestations), the expression (which appears to be Deuteronomistic in origin[134]) is more frequently found inserted in contexts expressing the *movement of going out* (from Egypt) caused by the powerful action of YHWH: 4x, √יצא hi. ("bring out") is used, and 1x, √לקח ("take")[135] is used as its synonym. The other two attestations present two verbs pertaining to another semantic field ("knowledge-memory").

In other contexts, the prevalence of verbs of *motion* is still recorded over others. In 2 Chron 6:32, the act of "coming" is predicated of the "foreigner" in relation to the fame of the temple of Jerusalem and their desire for prayer. A verb tied to the sphere of awareness is implicit here (cf. the parallel passage in 1 Kgs 8:41), but this does not prove very relevant to our subject matter. In 1 Kgs 8:42, the reference is to the story of the origin of Israel.

Jer 21:5 is the only case in which the locution in question is tied explicitly to the verb √לחם ni. with subj. YHWH and obj. Israel. It should be noted, however, that this root, with its military connotation, is clearly attested in the founding event of the Exodus in Exod 14:14, 25. We thus have a twofold semantic articulation: the "power of YHWH" (expressed with the *Mächtigkeitsformel*) is coordinated explicitly with the exit of Israel (√יצא hi.) and implicitly to the military action (√לחם ni.) against the Egyptians. We find this relationship in Jer 21:1–10 as well, only apparently inverted[136]: YHWH

---

134   More precisely, "spätdeuteronomisch", according to S. Kreuzer, «Die Mächtigkeitsformel», 207; Id., «Die Verwendung», 383.

135   The overall formulation of Deut 4:34a puts even greater accent on "movement": "Or has any god ever attempted to go and take a nation for himself (אוֹ הֲנִסָּה אֱלֹהִים לָבוֹא לָקַחַת לוֹ גוֹי) [...]".

136   The inversion of the emphasis is a curious one. While in the contexts that make direct reference to the event of the Exodus, the formula is placed primarily in relation to the act of "bringing out" (√יצא hi.) the people, leaving implicit that this entails a military action of YHWH against the Egyptians, instead, in our pericope, it is the military action of God that is brought to the forefront, later on becoming the implicit motive for the call given to the people to "go out" (√יצא) from the city.

Study of the fundamental themes: Surrender, the inevitable end, and possible life   267

"fights" Jerusalem itself "with outstretched hand [...]" (v. 5) but always as the same God of the Exodus who intends to "bring out" his people (v. 9). The difference is that the causative form is not used, but rather √יצא qal part. (with subj. the people, or the single Israelite). This is a sign that it concerns the implementation of a decision, underscored by the literary form of the choice between life and death typical of the stipulation of the Covenant according to Deut 31:15–20 (cf. § 4.2.1).

The second part of the expression contained in Jer 21:5 (וּבְאַף וּבְחֵמָה וּבְקֶצֶף גָּדוֹל) recurs, with the terms unvaried and in a similar context, in both 32:37 (governed by the verb √נדח hi. "to scatter")[137] and Deut 29:27.[138] In this latter case, in which it is said that the Lord uproots (√נתש) his people from the land in his anger (בְּאַף וּבְחֵמָה וּבְקֶצֶף גָּדוֹל), in v. 24, the motive is expressly mentioned. And this consists in their having voluntarily abandoned the Covenant (אֶת־בְּרִית יְהוָה +עזב√) established with the fathers when the Lord had them leave the land of Egypt (בְּהוֹצִיאוֹ אֹתָם מֵאֶרֶץ מִצְרָיִם).

4.1.2.3. The scourge of the plague (דֶּבֶר) is no longer for Egypt

Normally, the term דֶּבֶר[139] appears not alone but inserted in a series (or, at least, in a parallelism) with elements belonging to the semantic field of "calamities" that God can send upon human or animals. The sequence דֶּבֶר + רָעָב + חֶרֶב ("sword, starvation, disease"; cf. 14:12; 21:7, 9; 24:10; 27:8, 13; 29:17, 18: 32:24, 36; 34:17; 38:2; 42:17, 22; 44:13) is typical in Jeremiah. Bearing in mind this triad, one can infer that the term מָוֶת is used as a synonym of דֶּבֶר to make reference to a fatal epidemic outbreak in 15:2 (cf. 43:11). On the basis of the biblical data, it is not possible to identify what disease it refers to precisely, though it is definitely some sort of fatal epidemic (cf. the LXX which, when it does not omit the term, always translates it with θάνατος, except in Hab 3:5).

With I. Eph'al,[140] it should be emphasised that while ancient Near Eastern sources concerning the event of the siege often speak of "hunger" and "sword" as elements that facilitate the conquering of a city, they very rarely speak of "plague". Since, as opposed to the induction of starvation or violent attack, it was not at all in the direct power of human beings to control the spread of diseases or not, it never appears amongst the consultations made to the deity to know how to proceed in polyorcetic activities. Plagues and pestilences are considered either punitive means that can be invoked[141] or deadly instruments dependent upon the whim of the gods that could strike the besieged and the besiegers indistinctively.[142]

---

137   "Behold, I will gather them out of all the countries to which I scattered them (√נדח hi.) in my anger, in my rage, in my great indignation (בְּאַפִּי וּבַחֲמָתִי וּבְקֶצֶף גָּדוֹל) [...]."
138   According to Kreuzer, «Die Verwendung», 376, the "original" expression would be that in Deut 29:27.
139   Cf. G. Mayer, «דֶּבֶר», ThWAT II, 133–135.
140   I. Eph'al, The City Besieged, 66–68.
141   This is how, e.g. Tiglath-Pileser I (1114–1076) addresses the god Adad, with an imprecatory prayer against an enemy: "May the god Adad strike his land with terrible lightning (and) inflict his land with distress, famine, want, (and) plague" (RIMA 2,31,83–86).
142   On the "plague" as a weapon in the hands of the gods, see again I. Eph'al, The City Besieged, 67, n. 88. It is regardless comprehensible that military action (sword) provoked destruction and raids (hunger) and consequently, unfavourable hygienic

268   Jer 21:1-10. The surrender as acceptance of the end

As far as the HB is concerned, the recurrences of דֶּבֶר in the founding stories are not many (6x: Exod 5:3; 9:3, 15; Lev 26:25; Num 14:12; Deut 28:21). They are, however, placed in contexts that have paradigmatic value for all the other traditions, especially the prophetic ones. I note, incidentally, that the highest recurrence of the term (47x in the whole MT) can be observed precisely in the book of Jeremiah (17x), followed by that of Ezekiel (11x). As early as Exod 5:3, with דֶּבֶר, a scourge is indicated that depends on YHWH (presented as a threat to Israel itself) and is tied to the concept of disobedience. But it is with Exod 9:3, 15 that the term becomes part of the series typical of the portents unleashed by YHWH against Egypt to manifest his glory (cf. the recurrence in Ps 78:50). This is the fifth scourge that strikes and causes the death of all the livestock of the Egyptians. In Exod 9:3, we once again find the image of the hand of the Lord (יַד־יְהוָה הוֹיָה בְּמִקְנְךָ), and in Exod 9:15, √שׁלח is added to it (recalling the concept of "outstretched hand" seen previously). It is also worth mentioning Amos 4:10 (cf. דֶּבֶר and חֶרֶב), where the plague sent against Israel as a punitive act is expressly set in an analogical relation with that through which YHWH had once struck Egypt.

The syntactic construction of דֶּבֶר in Exod 9:15 is √נכה hi. (with subj. YHWH) + compl. obj. + בְּ + דֶּבֶר and it recurs as such only in Num 14:12. In itself, in Jer 21:6, the governing verb is instead √מות + בְּ + דֶּבֶר ("die of the plague") but immediately preceding, the same √נכה hi. appears with a clear reference to the plague.[143] The LXX, uniting בְּדֶבֶר גָּדוֹל with וְהִכֵּיתִי in a single clause ("I will strike... with a great plague"), translates יָמֻתוּ of the MT with καὶ ἀποθανοῦνται ("and they will die"), seeming to suppose a different *Vorlage* (BHS: וָמֵתוּ). The resulting text flows more smoothly and recalls the construction in Exod 9:15 exactly. Given then that the syntagm √מות + בְּ + the ternary sequence דֶּבֶר + רָעָב + חֶרֶב (cf. Jer 21:9; 27:13; 38:2; 42:17, 22) is common in Jeremiah, while it does not recur elsewhere in the MT except in Ezekiel (cf. Ezek 5:12; 6:11–12; 7:15; 33:27),[144] it is probable that the actual form of 21:6 (MT) is due to a harmonisation with the other recurrences. The literary contact with Exod 9:15 seems, therefore, quite probable.

It is interesting to note that in Exod 9:14–16, the Lord says he had wished to spare the Pharaoh (and his people) from the plague in order to make him a witness (in spite of himself) of his strength and so he could make his name resound

---

conditions with a spread of infections and epidemics (plague). Just as what happened, for example, with the pestilence Alessandro Manzoni speaks of in *I Promessi Sposi* (The Betrothed).

143   The verb נכה hi. with the subject God recurs in the MT 68x. With the object the enemies (of Israel), it is attested 36x, of which a good 17x in direct reference to Egypt: Exod 3:20; 7:17, 25; 9:15; 12:12, 13, 29; Num 3:13; 8:17; 33:4; 1 Sam 4:8; Ps 78:51; 105:33, 36; 135:8, 10; Ezek 32:10 (in particular, 9x it has as obj. the firstborn).

144   On the relationship between Jeremiah and Ezekiel, see the study by D. Rom-Shiloni, «Ezechiel and Jeremiah. What Might Stand behind the Silence?», *HeBAI* 1 (2012) 203–220, according to whom "the great majority of the presumed parallels between the prophets may only be classified as influence or echo at best, leaving but very few passages which may actually be defined as implicit allusions". He maintains that such similarities should be ascribed to the independent use of common sources (p. 219), while the direction of the existing literary influences would be traced regardless from Jeremiah towards Ezekiel, and not vice versa (p. 228).

Study of the fundamental themes: Surrender, the inevitable end, and possible life   269

throughout the earth (v. 16). In the context of Jer 21:1–10, the scourge of the plague thus assumes a destructive significance that is more radical than that in the book of the Exodus, since it is not directed only at the livestock but against mankind as well (cf. also Jer 7:20). The other three citations (Lev 26:25; Num 14:12[145]; Deut 28:21)[146] clearly shift their mark and begin the series of references in which the plague is understood as punishment aimed at Israel itself for its infidelity.

As a concluding observation, I can affirm that the taking up of Exodus motifs is functional for emphasising that the God now operating in the history of his people is the same God who brought Israel out of Egypt in a marvellous way, that same God who, even when he punishes, has salvation (to manifest his glory and set free from slavery) as his end purpose.

Let us now look at how the themes of "punishment" and "salvation" are configured.

4.1.3. The (inverted) symbolic coordinates of the "holy war" and the ḥerem

Responding to the king's delegation, Jeremiah does not threaten the *end* of Jerusalem but simply predicts it. With his discourse, he makes it understood that YHWH will intervene in history as an enemy via the attack of the king of Babylon, on precisely the basis of the provisions of that (violated) pact. The king of Babylon thus assumes the role of the executor of righteous punishment.[147] The surrender – which is desired by YHWH – is therefore to be understood according to this prophetic vision of history, in which the superpowers of the time must submit to the Lord of history and his special relationship with Israel (both acting as instruments of punishment and mediators of salvation).[148]

---

145   We find the syntagm נכה hi. + compl. obj. + בְּ + דֶּבֶר once again.

146   I will return to Lev 26:25 and Deut 28:21 once again further on, as they are of great interest for the question regarding the relationship between Jer 21:1–10 and the curses of the Covenant.

147   It seems too approximate to me to speak simply of *identification* between YHWH and the king of Babylon, as does repeatedly J. Hill, *Friend or Foe? The Figure of Babylon in the Book of Jeremiah MT*, BiblInterp 40, Leiden – Boston – Köln 1999, 80, 82, 88. In my opinion, it is more correct and clarifying to refer to the figure of the "executor of the sentence" (if the judiciary metaphor of the *mišpaṭ* is adopted as the key to interpretation), with YHWH who intervenes to condemn the oppressors leaving open a path to salvation for the oppressed in the surrender), or to that of the "punitive instrument" (in the context of the metaphor of the *rîb* or legal dispute that sets YHWH in opposition to his people as a betrayed partner who seeks to save the relation even with extreme measures). For in-depth study of the juridical figure cf the "executioner", see P. Bovati, *Ristabilire la giustizia*. Procedure, vocabolario, orientamenti, AnBib 110, Roma 1986, ²1997, 351–352; on the instrumental function of sanction within the dynamic of the *rîb*, cf. instead pp. 70–77 (Eng. tr.: P. Bovati, *Re-Establishing Justice*. Legal Terms, Concepts and Procedures in the Hebrew Bible, JSST.SS 105, Sheffield 1994).

148   In this regard, see J. Goldingay, «Jeremiah and the Superpower», in: *Uprooting and Planting*, 59–77.

270   Jer 21:1-10. The surrender as acceptance of the end

As we have already seen,[149] according to F.J. Gonçalves,[150] whoever affirms this[151] is giving "une réponse que les textes n'étayent pas", since no text would affirm that submission to Babylon would be a "châtiment de la rupture de son [of Judah] alliance avec Yahvé, voire d'une quelconque autre faute de Juda". This is, on the contrary, a fact that regards all peoples (he cites 27:11) and to accept it is, for the kingdom of Judah, "la condition de la paix et du bien-être". "En un mot, la soumission à Babylone est" the same author concludes, "d'après Jérémie, une décision souveraine de Yahvé dont il ne donne aucune raison".

Ultimately, the call for submission would be an expression of pure divine whim. And this book is all the more surprising insofar as it is not limited to a formal finding regarding the discourse of Jeremiah in chapters 27–28, but rather extends judgement to the entire theme of surrender to Nebuchadnezzar, a theme attested repeatedly and to different recipients at strategic points of the Jeremianic literary perimeter. This interpretation[152] seems to be the emblematic fruit of a hermeneutic that is unfortunately still very widespread in the exegetic field, which due to a misunderstood conception of scientific methodology believes that it be possible (and proposes) to base its deductions exclusively on a *formal* verification of a given (technical) vocabulary, one rigorously limited to the boundaries (?) of the text subject to analysis.

Instead, I will show the arguments that sustain my own hermeneutical perspective[153] by applying one of the basic principles of modern theories of communication and of lexicographic study to the single textual unit of 21:1–10, by which, in order to understand the meaning of a lemma or event of communication (verbal or non-verbal), it is necessary to take account of the immediate or remote context into which it fits and with which it naturally interacts,[154] in other words, its communicative context (also, or above all, of a pragmatic nature).

Formally, it is true that within the perimeter of 21:1–10, there is no clause dedicated to rendering explicit the motives for which the prophet calls for the act of the surrender. And yet it would suffice to consider that Zedekiah is, in fact, *the last king* and that, from 21:11 to 22:30, it is said that the kings of Judah have not done what YHWH commanded (justice). This is why the end is (already) announced. If the self-evident recurrence of the communicative context established by the literary unit offered by the book of Jeremiah itself (in which all the geopolitical upheavals are explicitly traced

---

149   Cf. General Introduction, § 1.4.1 and ch. II, § 3.3.1.

150   Cf. F.J. GONÇALVES, «Isaïe, Jérémie», 295–296.

151   Cf. e.g.: J. BRIGHT, *Jeremiah*, ci and cix; R. MARTIN-ACHARD, «Ésaïe et Jérémie aux prises avec les problèmes politiques. Contribution à l'étude du thème: Prophétie et politique», *RHPR* 47 (1967) 208–224 (here, p. 222); R.E. CLEMENTS, *Jeremiah*, Interpretation, Atlanta 1988, 163.204.

152   Probably derived from H.-J. STIPP, *Jeremia im Parteienstreit*, 223–224.

153   Specific development of this question in relation to chs. 27–28 will be reserved for ch. IV (§ 4.3) of the present dissertation.

154   The delimitation of the text is therefore an exegetic operation that is most certainly useful and necessary in some respects, but which calls for careful vigilance. It cannot, in fact, lead to an unnatural isolation of the text from its network of intertextual relations established by its distinct communicative event (of a textual nature) and of which it plays an inseparable part. The repercussions on the hermeneutical act would be quite serious.

Study of the fundamental themes: Surrender, the inevitable end, and possible life   271

back within the theological framework of the relationship between YHWH and his people) were not clear enough, then the symbolic coordinates laid down in vv. 4–7 are instead quite clear. As H. Weippert already highlighted in a contribution of her several years ago,[155] the terminology deployed in these verses does nothing but recall the concept of "holy war" (or "war of YHWH"),[156] overturning the perspective.[157] God has declared this war not against foreign peoples but against his own people. And the *motive* is infidelity to the Covenant, continually reiterated along the whole textual axis

---

155   Cf. H. Weippert, «Jahwekrieg und Bundesfluch in Jer 21 1–7», *ZAW* 82 (1970) 369–409, a work that builds upon the article by J.A. Soggin, «Der prophetische Gedanke über den heiligen Krieg, als Gericht gegen Israel», *VT* 10 (1960) 79–83. Cf. also H. Weippert, *Die Prosareden*, 83–86.

156   This expression (*Jahwekrieg*; cfr. R. Smend, *Jahwekrieg und Stämmebund*. Erwägungen zur ältesten Geschichte Israels, FRLANT 84, Göttingen 1963), more precise than that used in the classic study by G. von Rad, *Der heilige Krieg im alten Israel*, AThANT 20, Zürich 1951, Göttingen ³1958, corresponds to the Hebrew locution attested (in plural form) in 1 Sam 18:17; 25:28; Num 21:14 (without *mater lectionis*): מִלְחֲמוֹת יְהוָה. While there is never talk of "holy war" in the MT, I will continue to use this expression, which has by now become a *topos*, beginning from the work of F. Schwally, *Der heilige Krieg im alten Israel*, Leipzig 1901. On the topic of "holy war", I will indicate the following contributions as well: P.D. Miller, *The Divine Warrior in Early Israel*, HSM 5, Cambridge (MA) 1973; D.L. Christensen, *Transformations of the War Oracle in Old Testament Prophecy*. Studies in the Oracles against the Nations, HTR 3, Missoula 1975, 184–208; M.C. Lind, *Jahweh is a Warrior*. The Theology of Warfare in Ancient Israel, Scottdale 1980; A. de Pury, «La guerre sainte israélite», *ETR* 56 (1981) 5–38; G. Galbiati, «La guerra santa israelitica», *RBR* 18 (1983) 11–41; M. Weinfeld, «Divine Intervention in War in Ancient Israel and in Ancient Near East», in: *History, Historiography and Interpretation*. Studies in Biblical and Cuneiform Literatures, eds. H. Tadmor – M. Weinfeld, Jerusalem 1983, 121–147; R.M. Good, «The Just War in Ancient Israel», *JBL* 104 (1985) 385–400; S.-M. Kang, *Divine War in the Old Testament and in the Ancient Near East*, BZAW 177, Berlin 1989; G.H. Jones, «The Concept of Holy War», in: *The World of Ancient Israel*. Sociological, Anthropological and Political Perspectives, ed. R.E. Clements, Cambridge 1989, 299–321; B. Oded, *War*, 13–18; Longman, T. – Reid, D.G., *God is a Warrior*, StOTBT, Grand Rapids 1995; M. Walzer, *In God's Shadow*. Politics in the Hebrew Bible, New Haven – London 2012, 34–49.

157   This was already noted with regard to 21:5–6 by W.L. Moran, «The End of the Unholy War and the Anti-Exodus», *Bib.* 44 (1963) 338. For my part, I will highlight a further aspect, which regards the field of literary criticism: the fact that this "reversal" of perspective, as well as the invitation to "go out of" Jerusalem itself, does not seem solely attributable to the so-called "source C" (cf. W. Rudolph, *Jeremia*, 135) of the book of Jeremiah (secondary rearrangements in prose completed by various authors, usually identified as the Deuteronomistic "redactor"). In the same section considered by most commentators to be the most "original" (containing, above all, oracles in poetry, and to be placed in relation perhaps with the famous scroll in ch. 36), we find the same themes attested. I refer to 6:1–6, and in particular to vv. 1, 4: v. 1: "O children of Benjamin, *run away, take shelter from Jerusalem*. Blow the trumpet in Tekoa and raise a smoke signal over Beth-Haccherem, for evil looks down from the North, mighty destruction"; v. 4: "*sanctify war against her* [Jerusalem] (קַדְּשׁוּ עָלֶיהָ מִלְחָמָה)" (as such, the modern versions BJ; TOB; EP; EÜ [the 1980 edition only]). Cf. n. 170.

272   Jer 21:1-10. The surrender as acceptance of the end

of the book. Therefore, to surrender means recognising one's own sin and accepting just punishment. But at the same time, it means opening up to an unprecedented possibility of salvation. Let me demonstrate this in detail.

In v. 5, YHWH is the subject of √לחם ni. (reinforced by the pron. אֲנִי, "I myself") and figures as such also in Exod 14:14, 25; Deut 1:30; 3:22; 20:4; Josh 10:14, 42; 23:3, 10; Isa 30:32; 63:10; Zech 14:3; Neh 4:14; and 2 Chron 20:29; 32:8. The war that God ("he himself") fights in favour of his people against his enemies is talked about in these contexts (with the exception of Isa 63:10).[158] Note also the construction of √לחם ni. + לְ + compl. of advantage in the following schematic outline.

Ex 14:14a	יְהוָה יִלָּחֵם	YHWH will fight	לָכֶם	for you	
Exod 14:25b	יְהוָה נִלְחָם	YHWH is fighting	לָהֶם	for them (Isr.)	בְּמִצְרַיִם against Egypt
Deut 1:30	הוּא יִלָּחֵם	He himself will fight	לָכֶם	for you	
Deut 3:22	הוּא הַנִּלְחָם	It is he himself who fights	לָכֶם	for you	
Deut 20:4	לְהִלָּחֵם	to fight	לָכֶם	for you	עַם־אֹיְבֵיכֶם against your enemies
Josh 10:14	יְהוָה נִלְחָם	YHWH fought	לְיִשְׂרָאֵל	for Israel	
Josh 10:42	[...] יְהוָה נִלְחָם	YHWH [...] fought	לְיִשְׂרָאֵל	for Israel	
Josh 23:3, 10	הוּא הַנִּלְחָם	It is he himself who has fought	לָכֶם	for you	
Isa 30:32	נִלְחַם	He will fight			וּבָם Q (בָּהּ) K against them
[Isa 63:10]	הוּא נִלְחַם	He himself fought			בָּם against them (Isr.)
Zech 14:3	יְהוָה [...] וְנִלְחַם	YHWH [...] and he will fight			בַּגּוֹיִם הָהֵם against those nations
Neh 4:14	אֱלֹהֵינוּ יִלָּחֶם	Our God will fight	לָנוּ	for us	
2 Chron 20:29	נִלְחָם יְהוָה	YHWH had fought			אוֹיְבֵי יִשְׂרָאֵל עַם against the enemies of Israel
2 Chron 32:8	וּלְהִלָּחֵם	and to fight			מִלְחֲמֹתֵנוּ our battles

---

158 The classic attribution of Exod 14 to the story genre of "holy war (or war of YHWH)" (cf. e.g. G. VON RAD, *Der heilige Krieg*, 45–47, who made note, however, of some anomalies) was justly criticised by J.-L. SKA, «Exode xiv contient-il un récit de "guerre sainte" de style deutéronomistique?», *VT* 33 (1983) 454–467; ID., *Le passage de la mer. Étude de la construction, du style et de la symbolique d'Exod 14,1–31,* AnBib 109, Rome 1986, 47–53, 147–175, 177–178. Nevertheless, it seems opportune that I make mention of it (vv. 14 and 25) since, for my argumentation, it is determinative not that Exod 14 not be specifically "récit de bataille", but rather that it contains many precise terms of the "guerre de YHWH" sort (p. 148, n. 2). This demonstrates, in fact, how the oracle of Jeremiah draws upon themes attested by fundamental biblical traditions. In this case, the warlike action of God against the Egyptians belongs more to the sphere of the "wonders" worked for the people (which, in Jer 21:1–10, are turned against Jerusalem).

Study of the fundamental themes: Surrender, the inevitable end, and possible life   273

In Jer 21:5 (and Isa 63:10), however, the terms are inverted. God himself (אֲנִי) is the subject of the military action (וְנִלְחַמְתִּי) that has the Israelites as its object (אֶתְכֶם). Even the verbs that express the decisive offensive against Jerusalem (v. 4: הִנְנִי + סבב hi. part. "to make turn back"; √אסף "assemble"; v. 6: √נכה hi. "strike"; v. 7a: √נתן + בְּיַד "give into the hands of") all have God as their subject.[159] For Nebuchadnezzar (consistent with the "holy war" schema), meanwhile, a subordinate, conclusive role is reserved (cf. v. 7b: √נכה hi. + לְפִי־חָרֶב "strike with the edge of the sword"; v. 10b: √שׂרף + בָּאֵשׁ "burn [Jerusalem] with fire").

To speak comprehensively about symbolic coordinates drawn from the "holy war" vocabulary,[160] however, it is necessary to go still one step further and refer to terminology of a more technical nature.[161] A typical formula in this sense (the so-called *Übergabeformel*),[162] according to the schema outlined by G. von Rad, is given with the use of √נתן ("deliver") having YHWH as subj. + compl. obj. ("someone") + בְּיַד ("to the hands of").[163] This can be found again in v. 7a, having the king Zedekiah, his servants,

---

159   Cf. KANG, *Divine War*, 108: "The basic concept of divine war is that god is a warrior who fights against the enemy. This concept was strongly attested in the Hittite and Mesopotamian context, but not in the Egyptian context."

160   As pointed out by M. WEIPPERT, «"Heiliger Krieg" in Israel und Assyrien. Kritische Anmerkungen zu Gerhard von Rads Konzept des "heiligen Krieges" im alten Israel», *ZAW* 84 (1972) 460–493, in the ancient Near East, one could actually not make a distinction between a "holy" or "profane" war. Every incident of war calls the divinities of the respective peoples into question, so one should not conceive of a sacred institution or an ideology characteristic of Israel alone (contrary to G. von Rad). The fact remains that in the HB, precise literary forms exist that explicate the warlike intervention of God in favour of his people and not of others. According to this perspective, F. STOLZ, *Jahwes und Israels Kriege*. Kriegstheorien und Kriegserfahrungen im Glauben des alten Israel, AThANT 60, Zürich 1972, concludes that the literary schema of the "holy war" be a product of Deuteronomistic theology, that is, of a (late) literary creation embodying ancient (and real) experiences of the "war of YHWH" that are not, however, traceable to a homogeneous institutional, ritualistic, or terminological patrimony common to all the ancient Israeli tribes (cf. e.g. the adaptation to that effect of Num 21:21–26 in Deut 2:26–37).

161   Cf. G. VON RAD, *Der heilige Krieg*, 6–14. The elements identified as characteristic are: 1. a call to holy war by means of a sounding trumpet; 2. rites of consecration of the combatant corps; 3. an oracle of YHWH and formula with which it is expressed that the enemy has already been delivered into the hands of his people; 4. YHWH marches ahead of his army; 5. an appeal for faith in YHWH; 6. YHWH is the only true performer of the victory; 7. the enemy loses courage and YHWH provokes divine terror in them; 8. a prescription of the *herem*; and 9. a dissolution of the militia. It should be noted very clearly that amongst the texts cited by the author, not a single one contains all of the above listed elements.

162   Cf. Josh 2:24; 6:2; 6:16; 8:1, 18; 10:8, 19; Judg 3:28; 4:7, 14; 7:9, 15; 18:10; 20:28; 1 Sam 14:12; 17:46; 23:4; 24:4; 26:8; 1 Kgs 20:28. The same *Übergabeformel* is very attested in extrabiblical contexts of "holy war" (in Mesopotamia, above all); cf. J.G. HEINTZ, «Oracles prophétiques et "guerre sainte" selon les archives royales de Mari et l'Ancien Testament», in: *Congress Volume*. Rome 1968, eds. G.W. ANDERSON et al., VT.S 17, Leiden 1969, 126–127; S.-M. KANG, *Divine War*, 43–44.

163   The absence of this formulation would lead to the exclusion of the case of Isa 63:10.

274   Jer 21:1-10. The surrender as acceptance of the end

the people, and those who escaped the scourge of the siege as its object. These are "delivered" (נתן√) by God into the hands of the king of Babylon, in whose favour the entire "divine" action of war seems to unfold.[164] In this regard, it is appropriate to also take note of the juridical connotation of this phraseology (cf. Lev 26:25; Deut 7:24; 19:12; 2 Sam 21:8–9; 1 Kgs 18:9; Jer 26:24; 38:16; etc.),[165] which has God take on the connotations of the (righteous) judge and Nebuchadnezzar – as we will later see – those of the executor appointed to enforce the sentence.

Another important clue is the expression in v. 7b that literally reads: "He (Nebuchadnezzar) shall strike them down with the edge of the sword (וְהִכָּם לְפִי־חֶרֶב): he will not spare them (לֹא־יָחוּס עֲלֵיהֶם) and will have no pity (וְלֹא יַחְמֹל) and will have no compassion (וְלֹא יְרַחֵם)." It does not seem excessive to see an allusion to the prescription of the *ḥerem*[166] (this, too, inverted) in the context, also considering the final outcome described in v. 10b by the phrase וּשְׂרָפָהּ בָּאֵשׁ ("and he will burn it [Jerusalem] with fire"). This terminology[167] is very close to that used in some classic stories about the vow of

---

164   The syntagm נתן + (compl. obj. +) בְּיַד is attested 27x in Jeremiah and has the Lord as subject 23x (including the cases of 32:4, 24, 25, 36, 43; 38:3, 18; 46:24 ni. understood as the "theological passive") and as object Judah and its leaders (or the nations), destined to be delivered into the hands of the enemy: cf. 20:4, 5; 21:7; 22:25; 27:6; 29:21; 32:3, 4, 24, 25, 28, 36, 43; 34:2, 20, 21; 38:3, 18, 19; 44:30(2x); 46:24, 26. In 26:24; 38:16, it is in reference to the prophet (and his escape from the hands of his persecutors); in 39:17, the Lord promises that the life of Ebed-Melech will be saved; in 43:3, it is Baruch who is accused of wanting to betray the people by putting pressure on Jeremiah.

165   Cf. P. BOVATI, *Ristabilire la giustizia*, 351–352.

166   In this regard, see G. VON RAD, *Der heilige Krieg*, 13–14; P.D. STERN, *The Biblical Ḥerem. A Window on Israel's Religious Experience*, BJSt 211, Atlanta 1991; C.L. CROUCH, *War and Ethics in the Ancient Near East*. Military Violence in Light of Cosmology and History, BZAW 407, Berlin – New York 2009, 174–189, who defines this practice as "an extreme form of the military response to the chaotic threat of the enemy, but is not outside the range of what is observable in other Judahite and Assyrian texts, even if the latter did not develop a special language with which to refer to it" (p. 189). For other, more recent studies, cf. L.A.S. MONROE, *Josiah's Reform and the Dynamics of Defilement*. Israelite Rites of Violence and the Making of a Biblical Text, Oxford 2011, 45–76 (the section on "*Ḥērem* Ideology and the Politics of Destruction"); K.L. YOUNGER, Jr., «Some Recent Discussion on the ḤĒREM», in: *Far from Minimal*. Celebrating the Work and Influence of Philip R. Davies, eds. D. BURNS .J.W. ROGERSON, LHBOTS 484, London, New York 2012, 505–522 (with an ample updated bibliography); P. BOVATI, «"Sterminerai ogni essere vivente (Gs 10,39)". La conquista della terra di Canaan», in: *Il Dio violento della Bibbia*, SusBi 116, Reggio Emilia 2012, 25–53; A. VERSLUIS, «Devotion and/or Destruction? The Meaning and Function of חרם in the Old Testament», ZAW 128 (2016) 233–246.

167   Cf. e.g. Deut 7:2 ("show no mercy", חנן√); 7:16 ("your eye shall not pity them", חוס√); 13:16 ("you shall put the inhabitants of that city to the sword", נכה√ hi. + לְפִי־חֶרֶב; but cf. also v. 9); 20:13 ("put every male in it to the sword", נכה√ hi. + לְפִי־חֶרֶב); Jos 6:21 ("they utterly destroyed [...] with the edge of the sword", חרם√ hi. + לְפִי־חֶרֶב); 6:24 ("and they burnt the city with fire", שָׂרְפוּ בָאֵשׁ); 7:15 ("he who is taken in the *ḥerem* will be burned with fire", יִשָּׂרֵף בָּאֵשׁ); 8:24 ("they had all fallen by the edge of the sword", נפל√ hi. + לְפִי־חֶרֶב; "struck it down with the edge of the sword", חרם√ hi. + לְפִי־חֶרֶב); 8:28 ("so Joshua burned Ai", שׂרף√); 10:20 ("after having finished inflicting a terrible slaughter

extermination (the more rare frequency of √חוכ, √חמל and √רחמ pi., verbs introduced by the negation לא – not devoid of juridical value[168] –, is to be placed in relation to their peculiar function of marking and explicating, in our context, the meaning of the expression "strike them down with the edge of the sword").[169]

In any case, confirmation comes from Jer 25:8–9,[170] to which our text is placed in a relation of "fulfilment" (even if, in the canonical disposition, it comes first). Here, it is clearly stated that specifically due to infidelity to the Covenant (v. 8: have not listened to the words of God; cf. Lev 26:14ss), the Lord will elect to exterminate (v. 9: חרמ hi.) his own people by means of Nebuchadnezzar. The role that the latter assumes in vv. 4–7 is comparable to that (paradigmatic role) of Israel in the contexts of "holy war" associated with *herem*.[171]

---

on them until they were consumed", √חרמ hi. and √תממ); 10:28 ("took Makkedah and struck it down with the edge of the sword", √נכה hi. + לְפִי־חֶרֶב); 11:11 ("he struck down all those found there with the edge of the sword", √נכה hi. + לְפִי־חֶרֶב; "then he burned Azor with fire", שָׂרַף בָּאֵשׁ); 1 Sam 15:3 ("strike Amalek and utterly destroy all that he has and do not (spare him) have pity on him", √נכה hi.; √חרמ hi.; לֹא + √חמל); etc.

168 Cf. P. Bovati, *Re-Establishing Justice*, 382–387: "[...] in the Old Testament tradition, we have not just a body of legislative warnings, but also severe prescriptions that bind authorities to carrying out the dictates of the law, without leaving room for considerations or feelings that might seem to us more humanitarian; it should be enough to quote Deut. 13.9–11."

169 It is interesting to note that the same verbs appear in sequence (even if in a different order) in Jer 13:14 with God as their subject. By placing the two passages side by side, it is even more evident how Nebuchadnezzar incarnates the (punitive) sentiments of God and actuates the concrete implications against Jerusalem in history. Cf. also √רחמ pi. in Isa 9:16; 13:18; 27:11; Jer 6:23; 50:42; Hos 2:4; √חוכ in Ezek 5:11; 7:4, 9; 8:18; 9:5, 10; 24:14; √חמל in Isa 30:14; Jer 51:3; Zech 11:6; and, also using other terminology, cf. Lam 2:2, 17, 21; 3:43; Ezek 5:11; 7:4, 9; 8:18; 9:5, 10.

170 "Therefore thus says the Lord of hosts: because you have not listened to my words, behold, I will send for and fetch all the nations of the North, declares the Lord, and Nebuchadnezzar, king of Babylon, my servant, and I will have bring them against this land and against its inhabitants and against all these surrounding nations and I will devote them to destruction (וְהַחֲרַמְתִּים) and I will make them an object of horror, of scorn, and an everlasting ruin." The expression קָדְשׁוּ עָלֶיהָ מִלְחָמָה (cf. 22:7; 51:27, but without מִלְחָמָה) in 6:4 should also be mentioned. Cf. also Mic 3:5 and Joel 4:9.

171 Without hesitation, some important scholars consider v. 7 to be lacking coherence with the preceding verses, judging it as "otiose" or "superfluous" (cf. R.P. Carroll, *Jeremiah*, 409; and more recently, M. Erny, *Jeremias Königslogien*, 61), "a subsequent expansion founded on a misreading of vv. 1–6" (cf. W. McKane, «The Construction», 67; Id., *Jeremiah*, 500), because it would appear an unnecessary addition after the completeness of the destruction described in v. 6. It does not seem – and this comment is my own – that the intuition that 21:1–7 (and, I would add, also v. 10b) has something to do with an inversion of the "holy war" motif was actually taken seriously. Indeed, even while citing and accepting all the results of the work of H. Weippert, scholars do not derive logical consequences from them. That is to say: inserted within the perspective of the schema of the "holy war", v. 7 does not appear useless in the least, on the contrary. It carries forth the warfare just as it is configured, by which, after the *decisive* action of God that spreads panic amongst the Israelites, making them turn back their weapons (v. 4), and definitively breaks

276   Jer 21:1-10. The surrender as acceptance of the end

In some cases, in fact, it can be clearly seen that the military action of Israel
consists in taking possession (with *herem* as its objective) of the cities that God has
already put in its hands (cf. e.g. Josh 2:24; 6:2, 16; 8:1).[172] In the same manner, in v. 7b,
Nebuchadnezzar is not the principal agent of the victory, but simply the executor[173]
of the justice of God on the enemy city (for it too is guilty; cf. e.g. Exod 22:19; Lev
18:28; Deut 4:25–26; 7:26; 8:17–20), actually already won by God by means of general
confusion (vv. 4–5) and plague (which is not presented as a natural consequence of
the siege, but as a plague sent by God; cf. v. 6: וְהִכֵּיתִי; "I will strike.")[174]

---

their resistance by striking them with the plague (v. 5–6), *then* (v. 7) he delivers the
city into the hands of the king of Babylon (according to the famous "deliverance
formula": נתן √ + בְּיַד), designated to carry out a sort of *herem* putting to death all the
survivors (לְפִי־חֶרֶב, "by the edge of the sword") without remission, and burning the
entire city with fire (v. 10b). In this sense, the temporal locution (וְאַחֲרֵי־כֵן, "and after
this") should not at all be understood as a (clumsy) attempt to reproduce an outline
of the historical events corresponding to the phases of the capitulation described in 2
Kgs 25:1–12 (Jer 52:4–16; 39:1–10), as was said by W. McKANE, «The Construction»,
67–68; ID., *Jeremiah*, 500 and R.P. CARROLL, *Jeremiah*, 408. It should be understood
instead as a transition to a subsequent aspect of the progressive phases that were
traditionally part of "holy war" stories.

172   For the same use of the syntagm נתן √ (with subj. YHWH and the value of the per-
      fect) + בְּיַד but not applied to city, cf. Josh 10:8, 19; Judg 3:28; 4:14; 7:9, 15; 18:10; and
      1 Sam 14:12.

173   Remember that three times in the book of Jeremiah (cf. 25:9; 27:6; 43:10), the title
      of עַבְדִּי ("my servant") is given to Nebuchadnezzar. There is debate, however, over
      whether this expression (which lacks in the LXX) ought not be translated instead
      as "my vassal". Cf. W.M. LEMKE, «Nebuchadrezzar My Servant», *CBQ* 28 (1966)
      45–59; T.W. OVERHOLT, «King Nebuchadrezzar in the Jeremiah Tradition», *CBQ* 30
      (1968) 39–48; Z. ZEVIT, «The use of *'bd* as a Diplomatic Term in Jeremiah», *JBL* 88
      (1969) 74–77 (this is the author who poses the question of Nabukadnezzar as "vas-
      sal" of YHWH); A. SCHENKER, «Nebukadnezzars Metamorphose – Vom Unterjocker
      zum Gottesknecht», *RB* 89 (1982) 498–527; W. McKANE, «Jeremia 27,5–8, Especially
      "Nebuchadnezzar, My Servant"», in: *Prophet und Prophetenbuch*. Festschrift für
      Otto Kaiser zum 65. Geburtstag, *eds.* V. FRITZ – K.-F. POHLMANN – H.-C. SCHMITT,
      BZAW 185, Berlin – New York 1989, 98–110; R. DE HOOP, «Perspective after the
      Exile: The King, עבדי, "My Servant" in Jeremiah – Some Reflections on MT and
      LXX», in: *Exile and Suffering*, 105–121; A. AEJMELAEUS, «"Nebuchadnezzar, My
      Servant": Redaction History and Textual Development in Jer 27», in: *Interpreting
      Translation*. Studies on the LXX and Ezekiel in Honour of Joahn Lust, *eds.* F. GARCÍA
      MARTÍNEZ – M. VERVENNE, BEThL 192, Leuven 2005, 1–18; G. FISCHER, «"Mein
      Diener Nebukadnezzar". Zur Rolle von Fremden im AT», in: ID., *Der Prophet wie
      Mose*, 334–336 (= in: *WWeg* 293 [2004] 6–9).

174   Just as in the *herem* (at least, in its most extreme form; cf. e.g. Josh 6:21), thus also
      in vv. 6 and 7b, the nature of the destruction inflicted on the city and its inhabitants
      is found to be exhaustive: though men and beasts (cf. the merism of v. 6: וְאֶת־הָאָדָם
      וְאֶת־הַבְּהֵמָה) are struck directly and especially by the action of God, what is reserved
      for all survivors is death by the hand of the king of Babylon (v. 7b) – servant of the
      Lord! In v. 10b, he brings the divine action against the city to completion, delivering
      all of it to fire (and note that the text, wanting to remain within these coordinates,
      does not make the least reference here to precise historical events such as raids or
      subsequent deportations).

Study of the fundamental themes: Surrender, the inevitable end, and possible life   277

As is pointed out by G. von Rad,[175] this divine action is often manifested as general terror (√המם) spread amongst the enemies. This, as a rule, leads them to total paralysis, to escape, or (in some cases; cf. Judg 7:22; 1 Sam 14:20) to turn their weapons against their own companions to the point of self-destruction. According to H. Weippert,[176] who cites contexts of war of YHWH in which this motif appears (Judg 7:22; 2 Chron 20:23, and Zech 14:13), what is alluded to in v. 4 could be this, by √סבב hi. ("to turn back, towards a new direction")[177] and the syntagm אסף + אל (understood as "assemble against", to venture into battle),[178] which also have God as their subject. In support of her thesis, the author presents a comparison with some curse formulas provided for in the treatises of the ancient Near East, citing an Hittite text[179] from 1300–1250 and an Assyrian one[180] precisely dated May 672. In these, the motif of "the turning back of arms" against themselves or their own companions as a prescribed form of divine punishment (amongst others) in case of infidelity to a sacred pact emerges clearly (and with very similar terminology). Verse 4 would therefore be understood as: "I will turn back (√סבב hi. part.) the instruments of war that are in your hands [...] and I will gather them (√אסף) against (the inner part of) this city (אֶל־תּוֹךְ הָעִיר הַזֹּאת)." I share the opinion of the author and underscore, furthermore, that this interpretation gives greater coherence to the relationship between v. 4 and v. 5, highlighting how not only will the hoped-for aid not come, but their *own* weapons (אֶת־כְּלֵי הַמִּלְחָמָה אֲשֶׁר בְּיֶדְכֶם) and their *own* God (וְנִלְחַמְתִּי אֲנִי) will themselves be their foremost enemies.

For my research, it is important to emphasise that the handing over of the land of Canaan to the Israelites (by way of "holy war") coincides, in fact, with a punitive

---

175   Cf. G. von Rad, *Der heilige Krieg*, 12–13. It is underscored by S.-M. Kang, *Divine War*, 80–84, that this practice is only part of wars of attack and not those of defence, and seems to be unattested (the study by C.H.W. Brekelmans, *Ḥerem in het Oude Testament*, Nijmegen 1959, 128–145 is cited) in Hittite, Egyptian, or Mesopotamian customs (including Mari), as well as those Roman, Celtic, Gallic, or Germanic. However, it is attested in the Bible, and here in the case of King Mesha of Moab and the god Chemosh, described in the "Mesha Stele". It would thus be a technical use of a root (חרם) diffused in almost all the Semitic languages (cf. C.H.W. Brekelmans, «חרם», *THAT* I, 635). In reality, since more recent studies highlight how the ideological instance of total annihilation of the enemy was well known in the ancient Near East, it should at least be specified, along with C.L. Crouch, *War and Ethics*, 182, in special reference to the Assyrian texts, "What we are lacking elsewhere, therefore, is not so much the phenomenon of total destruction, but the articulation of the phenomenon as an imperative."

176   Cf. H. Weippert, «Jahwekrieg», 401–402.

177   Cf. Zorell, 544: "*circumvertit, retro vertit* faciem" (cf. Judg 18:23; 1 Kgs 8:14; 2 Chr 6:3); *HALAT*, 698: "Bewegungsrichtung ändern"; *BDB*, 685: "*turn* (in a new direction)". The form מֵסֵב does not recur elsewhere in the MT.

178   The verb √אסף is often used as a technical military term for the rallying of troops (cf. Jer 4:5). The preposition אל specifically indicates the objective towards which the military manoeuvre is launched. See the lexicographic explanation by H. Weippert, «Jahwekrieg», 407–408, which I take as generally-accepted.

179   Cf. H. Otten, «Die inschriftlichen Funde», in: *Bericht über die Ausgrabungen in Boğazköy im Jahre 1954, MDOG* 88 (1955) 35–36; E. von Schuler, *Die Kaškäer. Ein Beitrag zur Ethnographie des alten Kleinasien*, UAVA 3, Berlin 1956, 111.

180   Cf. D.J. Wiseman, *The Vassal-Treaties of Esarhaddon*, London 1958, 71–72.

278   Jer 21:1-10. The surrender as acceptance of the end

judgement of God on the enemy peoples (cf. Lev 18:24–27; Deut 9:4–5). These are guilty of having contaminated themselves (Lev 18:24: √טמא ni., and the land that now vomits them out; cf. v. 25), of having committed "abominations" (cf. Lev 18:26–27, 29, [30]: תּוֹעֵבַת), and of "wickedness" (cf. Deut 9,4–5: רִשְׁעָה). In the cities doomed for destruction, only a few people are saved, namely those who, in one way or another, "surrender" themselves to the power and design of the God of Israel: Rahab and his family in Jericho (cf. Josh 2:9–13) and the inhabitants of Gibeon (cf. Josh 9:3–15, 24–27).[181] It should be emphasised that according to Deut 20:10–18, a ("holy") war of conquest of land involved the obligation to exterminate the local population, while it permitted possibly asking "cities that are very far" to surrender (cf. also Josh 11:19–20, in which the refusal to surrender on the part of the various populations is instead the result of a hardening of the heart desired by God for their extermination).

The prophetic use of the symbolic coordinates of "holy war" leads to the identification of the implementation of an irrevocable plan of God in the Babylonian offensive. This corresponds, in a certain sense, to the "definitive" nature of the sin of Judah, highlighted by the repeated, provocatory command given to Jeremiah to not intercede for the salvation of the people (7:16; 14:11; 15:1). In the hyperbolic language of 5:1, there is not even one righteous man in Jerusalem.[182] This righteousness is intended not so much in the sense of nonguilt, but in the dynamic acceptation of people who can be a *principle* (inception) *of justice*. And given that with its wicked deeds and "abominations" (תּוֹעֵבָת; cf. 2:7; 6:15; 7:10; 8:12; 16:18; 32:35; 44:4, 22), Jerusalem profaned the land (cf. 16:18), this shall *in fact* be equated to the Canaanite cities of the past, from which it had not managed to really separate itself and the fate of which it must now suffer, since it is soaked in the same iniquity.[183]

The textual isotopy of the urban centre completely scarred by iniquity renders the reference to the fate of Sodom and Gomorrah (cf. Gen 13:13; 18:16–33; 19:23–25) particularly pertinent, reinforced by the fact that it comes from within the same book of Jeremiah. Their destruction is recalled in 49:18 and 50:40 to announce one similar for Edom and Babylon. But in 23:13–14, once again in a context where idolatry and perversions typical of the Canaanites are recalled, an analogy to the situation of Jerusalem is presented:

> [13] Among Samaria's prophets I saw something unseemly: They prophesied by Baal and led my people Israel astray. [14] But among Jerusalem's prophets I saw something more shocking: they commit adultery, walk in deception, strengthen the power of the wicked, so that no one turns from evil. To me they are all *like Sodom* (כִּסְדֹם) and [Jerusalem's] inhabitants *like Gomorrah* (כַּעֲמֹרָה)."

---

181   It should be specified that what can be derived from the text is that the survival of the various characters is guaranteed not by their "surrender", but by their having recognised and accepted a design of God that is humanly indisputable. This is why Rahab hosts the explorers, asking for his life and the lives of his family in exchange. This is why the Gibeonites resort to a stratagem to stipulate an alliance of peace with the Israelites. Thus, in Jer 21:1–10, within the symbolic framework of the "holy war", to call for surrender *does not mean suggesting a practice that takes for granted that the outcome will be positive.*

182   Cf. Ps 14:1–3 and the Pauline perspective in Rom 13 (cf. 3:10–18).

183   Cf. Jer 2:8, 23; 6:27–30; 7:9, 29; 9:13; etc.

Study of the fundamental themes: Surrender, the inevitable end, and possible life   279

Consider, therefore, also the modality by which Lot is saved (Gen 19:12–26), invited (and then pushed) to *leave* (√יצא) the city that YHWH has irremediably condemned to destruction at this point, since it is thoroughly corrupted by evil. So it is clear, in synthesis, why the gesture of the surrender, inserted in this rich symbolic framework, acquires the prophetic meaning of obedient recognition of God's just punishment (the end) and why, for this very reason, it is indicated as the only, extreme possible path to salvation (for a new beginning).

4.1.4. The curses of the Covenant

It is not hard to demonstrate that for Jeremiah, the disaster announced is the consequence of infidelity to the Law by the people and its leaders.[184] Some (certainly not random) relationships between our passage and the (negative) clauses of the Covenant should, however, be clearly put into perspective. That this connection be pertinent is attested in Jer 11:1–13,[185] where punishment and the implementation of the curses threatened and provided for in case of non-compliance are set explicitly in relation (cf. Lev 26:14–46; Deut 11:26–29; 27:12–26; 28:15–69; 29:18–28; Josh 8:33–34; 24:20). These, to which the treaties of the ancient Near East also provide testimony,[186] show the possible dramatic outcome of the בְּרִית: if one of the two contracting parties sunders the relationship (Israel), also the other (YHWH) acts in consequence.[187] With regard to Jer 21:1–10, the following motifs confirming a reading of "surrender" as recognition and acceptance of the punitive act of YHWH provided for by the Covenant and

---

184 Cf. e.g. 16:10–12: "And it shall come to pass that when you will tell this people all these things, they will say to you: Why has the Lord pronounced all this great disaster against us? What is our crime? What sin have we committed against the Lord our God? You are then to answer them: Because your fathers abandoned me (√עזב), oracle of the Lord, they followed (√הלך) other gods, they served them (√עבד) and they bowed down (√חוה histhth.) before them, they abandoned (√עזב) me and have not obeyed (√שמע) my law. And you have done worse than your fathers, for behold, each one walks (√הלך) following the stubborness (שְׁרִרוּת אַחֲרֵי) of his evil heart and refuses to listen to me (√שמע)." Cf. also 32:28–35; 33:4–5; 34:13–22; 36:29–31; 37:2; 40:2–3; 44:2–6, 20–23.

185 Cf. esp. 11:3: "Say to them: Thus says the Lord, God of Israel: *Cursed be* (אָרוּר) the man who does not observe *the words of this covenant* (אֶת־דִּבְרֵי הַבְּרִית הַזֹּאת)"; v. 8b: "So I will bring upon them *all the words of this covenant* (אֶת־כָּל־דִּבְרֵי הַבְּרִית־הַזֹּאת) which I commanded them to do and they did not do it."

186 Cf. F.C. Fensham, «Malediction and Benediction in Ancient Near Eastern Vassal-Treaties and the OT», *ZAW* 74 (1962) 1–9; Id., «Common Trends in Curses of the Near Eastern Treaties and *Kudurru*-Inscriptions Compared with Malediction of Amos and Isaiah», *ZAW* 75 (1963) 155–175; D.R. Hillers, *Treaty Curses and the Old Testament Prophets*, BibOr 16, Rome 1964; K. Baltzer, *Das Bundesformular*, WMANT 4, Neukirchen-Vluyn 1960, ²1964; D.J. McCarthy, *Treaty and Covenant. A Study in Form in the Ancient Oriental Documents and in the Old Testament*, AnBib 21, Rome 1963, ²1978; S. Parpola, «Neo-Assyrian Treaties from the Royal Archives of Niniveh», *JCS* 39 (1987) 161–189; D.I. Block, *The Gods of the Nations*, 98–124.

187 Cf. Josh 24:20: "He will turn, and, after he has been good to you, he will do you harm and destroy you."

280   Jer 21:1-10. The surrender as acceptance of the end

against which it is senseless to hope to obtain "a prodigy" (cf. Jer 21:2), should be highlighted[188]:

Lev 26:17	"I will set my face against you" (בְּ + פָּנֶה + נתן\√)	Jer 21:10	"I have set my face against (בְּ + פָּנֶה + שׂים\√)"
	to be defeated by your enemies; to escape	Jer 21:4–7, 8	*similar expressions*
Lev 26:24	"I will strike (וְהִכֵּיתִי) you"	Jer 21:6	"I will strike (וְהִכֵּיתִי) the inhabitants of this city"
Lev 26:25	"And I will bring a sword against you (חֶרֶב) that shall execute vengence for the covenant; you will be gathered together (אסף\√) in your cities, but I will send pestilence among you (דֶּבֶר) and you shall be delivered into the hand (בְּיַד + .ni נתן\√) of the enemy"	Jer 21:2 Jer 21:7, 9a Jer 21:4b, 9b Jer 21:6–7a, 9a Jer 21:7a, 10b	attack of Nebuchadnezzar sword (חֶרֶב) + (אסף\√) being under siege pestilence (דֶּבֶר) deliverance formula (נתן\√ + compl. obj. + בְּיַד)
Lev 26:28	"I myself (אַף־אֲנִי) will oppose you with vicious rage (בַּחֲמַת־קֶרִי) and I will punish you sevenfold for your sins"	Jer 21:5	"I myself (אֲנִי) will then fight against you [...], with anger and fury (וּבְאַף וּבְחֵמָה) and with great indignation"
Lev 26:33	"[...] I will unsheathe the sword (חֶרֶב) against you; your land shall become desolate and your cities left in ruins"	Jer 21:7, 9a Jer 21:6–7, 9–10b	sword (חֶרֶב) destruction of the inhabitants and city burned with fire
Deut 28:20	be destroyed (שׁמד\√ ni.); perish (אבד\√)	Jer 21:5–7, 10b	*similar expressions*
Deut 28:21	"The Lord will make the plague (דֶּבֶר) cling to you, until he has consumed you in the land that you are entering to possess"	Jer 21:6–7a, 9a	pestilence (דֶּבֶר) and to die (מות\√)
Deut 28:25	"The Lord will put (נתן\√) you to defeat before your enemies; you will go out against them in one direction and flee before them in seven [...]"	Jer 21:4–10	*similar expressions*

---

188   In the chart, I report in Hebrew only those lemmas or syntagmas that can be immediately matched to the terminology used in our pericope. The subject of the verbs is always YHWH and the action described always has Israel as its object.

Lev 26:17	"I will set my face against you" (בְּ + פָּנֶה + נתן√)	Jer 21:10	"I have set my face against (בְּ + פָּנֶה + שׂים√)"
Deut 28:27	"The Lord will strike you (נכה√ hi.) with the boils of Egypt, with boils, scurvy, and rashes from which you cannot be healed"	Jer 21:6 Jer 21:7b	to strike (נכה√ hi.) + to die (מות√) + plague he (Nebuchadnezzar) shall strike them down (נכה√ hi.) with the edge of the sword
Deut 28:32	"Your sons and your daughters will be given to (לְ + נתן√) another people [...]"	Jer 21:7a, 10b	cf. deliverance formula (נתן√ + compl. obj. + בְּיַד)
Deut 28:48	"you will serve the enemies whom the Lord will send against you, in hunger (רָעָב), in thirst, in nakedness and in the lack of all things. He will put an iron yoke (cf. Jer 28:14!) on your neck, until he has destroyed you"	Jer 21:7a, 9a	siege; famine (רָעָב)
Deut 28:49–50	God will raise up a nation against you from far away "that will show no respect for the elderly or mercy (חנן√) for the young"	Jer 21:7b	(Nebuchadnezzar) will not spare them nor have pity nor compassion
Deut 28:51	To be destroyed (שמד√ ni.)	Jer 21:5–7, 10b	*similar expressions*
Deut 28:52–53	"he will besiege you in all of your cities [...]"; (2x, צרר hi.) + "siege" (מָצוֹר) + hunger (רָעָב)	Jer 21:4b, 9b Jer 21:7a, 9a	to besiege (צור√) famine (רָעָב)
Deut 28:59–60	God will bring back all the plagues of Egypt	Jer 21:5–7a, 9a	*Mächtigkeitsformel* + plague
Deut 28:63	God will take delight in ruining and destroying	Jer 21:5–7, 10b	*similar expressions*
Deut 29:21	Calamities and diseases	Jer 21:6–7a, 9a	*similar expressions*
Deut 29:27	"The Lord uprooted them from their land in anger, *with fury and great wrath* (בְּאַף וּבְחֵמָה וּבְקֶצֶף גָּדוֹל) [...]".	Jer 21:5	"I myself will fight against you in anger, *with fury and great wrath* (בְּאַף וּבְחֵמָה וּבְקֶצֶף גָּדוֹל)".

From amongst the curses presented in the cited texts as a *threat* conditioned by the eventuality of non-fulfilment of the obligations arising from the Covenant ([...] וְאִם־לֹא); cf. Lev 26:14, 15, 18, 21, 23, 27; [...] אִם־לֹא; cf. Deut 28:15), Jer 21:1–10 takes up many of the more significant elements and announces their *actualisation*. In particular, the disasters chosen are those that, according to the *escalation* in Lev 26:14–46 (cf.

282   Jer 21:1-10. The surrender as acceptance of the end

the last two "[...] וְאִם" in vv. 23, 27), are reserved for the highest level of hardening of the heart. These are the intervention of the Lord in first person, who "strikes" (v. 24; cf. Jer 21:5, 6) and has "the sword" come for revenge (v. 25, 33; cf. Jer 21:7, 9a), followed by the gathering together of the people in the cities (siege: v. 25b; cf. Jer 4b, 9b), "the plague" (v. 25c; cf. Jer 21:6–7, 9a), "being delivered" into the hands of the enemy (v. 25d; cf. Jer 21:7a, 10b), and devastation of the city and the whole country (v. 33; cf. Jer 21:6–7, 9, 10b).

In the references drawn from Deut 28:15–69; 29:21–27 (which present a list of curses in a less logical order),[189] the following expressions should be noted: the "nation from afar" that "will show no mercy" (28:49–50; cf. Jer 21:7b); the "siege" (vv. 48a, 52–53; cf. Jer 4b, 9b); the scourge typical of the "plague" (v. 21; which is clearly tied in vv. 28.59–60, along with other diseases, to the pains of Egypt; cf. Jer 21:6–7, 9a); the "being delivered" to the enemy (vv. 25, 32; cf. Jer 21:7a, 10b); the "total destruction" (vv. 48b, 51, 63; cf. Jer 21:5–7, 10b); and the punitive intervention of God (cf. Jer 21:5b) actualised with "anger, fury, and great wrath" (29:27).

All these elements of resemblance, with particular reference to Deuteronomy (above all, Deut 28),[190] demonstrate that the disasters announced by the oracle of Jeremiah are to be understood in the light of the *fulfilment* of the *curse*, that is, of the punishment threatened by YHWH in case of a breaking of the Covenant. Nevertheless, the prospect is not one with no way out, as the Deuteronomic curses instead appear to be. Already, the fact that one of the formulations indicated (Deut 28:63) is taken up and inverted (in the typical Jeremianic style that I spoke about) indicates the possibility of future salvation beyond the disaster. But specifically, it is the call to surrender that opens that horizon in the precise moment that the end comes about. And it is opened not as an automatic fact, but as an event in which human free will can find an extreme opportunity for redemption.

4.2. Anti-Exodus, new Exodus, and new Covenant. A new prospect for salvation

4.2.1. The two paths: The ethical option (Deut) and the "prophetic choice"

The gesture of the "surrender" is proposed in vv. 8–9, expressed by the syntagm יצא ("to go out") + עַל + נפל ("to fall upon", "to hand oneself over", "to consign oneself"). While deferring a detailed analysis of the terminology of the "consign oneself" to chapter V of the present dissertation, I can nevertheless anticipate that in the HB, the particular use of the roots just cited (in the syntagms יצא + אֶל and נפל + עַל) would seem to be of a technical sort, at least when placed within a military context. This is perhaps the strongest argument that would lead me to consider an immediate correlation between the root יצא in 21:9 and the event of the Exodus unsuitable, besides the fact that the

---

189   See, in this regard, M. ZEHNDER, «Fluch und Segen in Buch Deuteronomium. Beobachtungen und Fragen», in: *Deuteronomium – Torah für eine neue Generation*, eds. G. FISCHER – D. MARKL – S. PAGANINI, BZAR 17, Wiesbaden 2011, 193–211.

190   See, in particular, the observations of G. FISCHER, «Fulfiment and Reversal: the Curses of Deuteronomy 28 as a Foil for the Book of Jeremiah», *SemClas* 5 (2012) 43–49.

Study of the fundamental themes: Surrender, the inevitable end, and possible life   283

causative form hi. (with subj. YHWH) plus the preposition מִן is used to speak of the exit of Israel from Egypt instead.[191]

It should be noted, however, that the use of √יצא does recur in a significant passage that adopts a military vocabulary, Exod 12:41: "[...] on that very day, *all the armies* (כָּל־צִבְאוֹת) of the Lord *went out* (√יצא qal) of the land of Egypt". The syntactic construction underscores, in this case as well, a motion from a place, as a distancing from the place of slavery (מֵאֶרֶץ מִצְרַיִם), but one must recall that it is likewise evident how the movement to exit is attributed to an "army" (more than to a defenceless fugitive population) and in function of a direction and a very precise point of arrival (the mountain, the promised land, the service of the Lord, √עבד), for which other passages use the preposition אֶל.[192]

The distinct literary relationships recognised (and debated) between the books of Jeremiah and Deuteronomy[193] then bestow a particular importance to the frequency with which the verb יצא is used in the latter in reference to the exit from Egypt,[194] which seems to appear only beginning with Jeremiah.[195] In the "Deutero-Isaiah", the (less frequent) form qal is used instead, precisely to indicate the new Exodus (cf. Isa 48:20 [imp.]; 52:11 [2x, imp.], 12; 55:12).

Certainly, the act of surrender, presented as "to go out" and "to serve" the Babylonians (√עבד; cf. e.g. Jer 27:12, 17) seems, at a first glance, to be diametrically opposed to the going out of Egypt, which is also linked to "to serve" (√עבד; cf. e.g. Exod 3:12; 4:23), but the Lord. For my part, I will reiterate that, even if a technical meaning can be recognised in the vocabulary used in Jer 21:1–10, it should be considered within the complex symbolic interweaving that I have highlighted thus far. According to this picture, Jerusalem appears to be a doomed city at this point, since it wanted to *serve* not the Lord (cf. Jer 2:20; √עבד) but the idols (cf. Jer 5:19; 8:2; 11:10; 13:10; 16:11; 22:9; 25:6; 35:15; 44:3; √עבד); identified even with the (Canaanite) abomination that YHWH intends to destroy, and thus also with Babylon itself (!), the city destined to destruction and from which the prophet says to leave (cf. Jer 51:6; √נוס imp.; 51:45: √יצא imp.). So they are to leave the new slavery, that of idols, to serve not just any foreign king, but the one defined as the Lord's servant ("my servant"; cf. 25:9; 27:6; 43:10). So one must go out to serve YHWH and his design (of paradoxical salvation), just as in the event of the Exodus.

For this very reason, in my way of seeing it, the prophetic request presented by Jeremiah does not at all intend to nullify the existence of the people of God, almost

---

191   Cf. E. JENNI, «יצא», *THAT* I, 755–761; H.D. PREUSS, «יָצָא», *ThWAT* III, 809–821.

192   Cf. e.g. Exod 3:8: "I have come down to deliver them out of the hand of the Egyptians and to bring them up out of that land towards (אֶל) a good and spacious land, towards (אֶל) a land flowing with milk and honey, towards (אֶל) the place of the Canaanites [...]"; 32:34: "Now go, lead my people towards (אֶל) the place I have spoken to you about [...]"; etc.

193   Cf. e.g. L.S. SCHEARING – S.L. MCKENZIE, eds., *Those Elusive Deuteronomists*. See, in particular, G. FISCHER, «Der Einfluss des Deuteronomiums auf das Jeremiabuch», in: *Deuteronomium*, 247–269 (above all, pp. 250–251).

194   Cf. Deut 1:27; 4:20, 37, 45, 46; 5:6, 15; 6:12, 21, 23; 7:8, 19; 8:14; 9:12, 7, 26, 28[2x], 29; 11:10; 13:6, 11; 16:1, 3[2x], 6; 23:35; 24:29; 25:17; 26:8; 29:24.

195   Cf. E. JENNI, «יצא», 760.

as if it were an "anti-Exodus".[196] Certainly, the word that still offers salvation does not do so by promising a miraculous re-establishment of the city but, on the contrary, by ratifying the *end*. The paradox is, however, that the end is spoken about with the evocation of a *beginning* formula.[197] And this formulation precisely recalls texts that closely relate to the stipulation of the Covenant, such as Deut 11:26–28; 30:15–20 (but cf. also the sapiential echo of Prov 4:10–19; Eccles 15:16–17; etc.), in which Israel is urged to issue a decision of vital importance.[198]

The word is addressed to the *people* in the name of YHWH (cf. Jer 21:8a) and imposes the obligation of a *choice*. The question is that of deciding on a new relationship with God, whether to surrender oneself to Him based on a bond of trust and obedience, or not. It is, in other words, a question of choosing between the path of *life* and that of *death*. Let us compare the texts:

---

196 It is S. Kreuzer, «Die Verwendung», 376, who speaks about "Anti-Exodusaussage" with regard to the "Mächtigkeitsformel" of Jer 21:5. For his part, L. Alonso Schökel, «Jeremías como anti-Moisés», in: *De la Tôrah au Messie*. Hom. à H. Cazelles, *eds*. M. Carrez – J. Doré – P. Grelot, Paris 1981, 245–254, considers the figure of Jeremiah like an "anti-Moses". This is, however, mainly in reference to the events narrated in Jer 42 (and I will take up the question in ch. V, § 3.1.7). Actually, what can be deduced from this text is that the true anti-Exodus is not provoked by YHWH, but is consciously chosen by the people and its leaders.

197 Another paradox: God forbids Jeremiah to intercede (a sign that the end is inevitable), but makes him the mediator of a message of salvation (a sign that the Exodus continues). Indeed, this is quite comprehensible in the dynamic of the *rîb*, which, by metaphorising the juridic procedure of bilateral controversy, allows for a proper interpretation of the action of God in the history of Israel. The scope of the threat of punishment and infliction of the punishment itself, however severe, is always that of recuperating the partner of the Covenant in a relationship of communion in truth and love. Cf. P. Bovati, *Ristabilire la giustizia*, 70–77. The observations of the authors who insist on presenting Jeremiah as a warrior chosen to fight in the name of God against his own people should be relocated within this horizon; cf. e.g. the *excursus* on "Geremia e la 'guerra santa'" in M. Ceccarelli, *Il profeta rifiutato*. Studio tematico del rifiuto del profeta nel libro di Geremia, Roma 2003, [2]2014, 100–106, and in particular E.D. Lewin, «Arguing for Authority. A Rhetorical Study of Jeremiah 1.4–19 and 20.7–18», *JSOT* 32 (1985) 105–119 (here, p. 110); E.W. Conrad, *Fear not Warrior. A Study of 'al tîrā'* Pericopes in the Hebrew Scriptures, BJSt 75, Chico 1985, 47; J.H. Smit, «War-related Terminology and Imagery in Jeremiah 15:10–21», *OTEs* 11 (1998) 110. Likewise, all those (diffused) interpretations that tend to present the punishment of Jerusalem in terms of "forensic judgement", not fully grasping the structural difference of the final objectives of *rîb* and of the *mišpāt*, ought to be reconsidered (cf. P. Bovati, *Ristabilire la giustizia*, 358–362).

198 This would be another interesting relation to the founding event of the Exodus: just as the exit from Egypt is made in view of the Covenant, so also does the exit from Jerusalem fit into freely entering that divine will to create a *new* Covenant.

Deut 11:26–28

רְאֵה	**26**	See,
אָנֹכִי נֹתֵן לִפְנֵיכֶם הַיּוֹם		I am setting before you today
בְּרָכָה וּקְלָלָה		a blessing and a curse:
אֶת־הַבְּרָכָה אֲשֶׁר תִּשְׁמְעוּ אֶל־מִצְוֹת יְהוָה	**27**	the blessing if you obey the commandments of the Lord
אֱלֹהֵיכֶם אֲשֶׁר אָנֹכִי מְצַוֶּה אֶתְכֶם הַיּוֹם		your God which I command you today;
וְהַקְּלָלָה אִם־לֹא תִשְׁמְעוּ אֶל־מִצְוֹת	**28**	the curse, if you do not obey the commandments
יְהוָה אֱלֹהֵיכֶם		of the Lord your God.

Deut 30:15–20

רְאֵה	**15**	See,
נָתַתִּי לְפָנֶיךָ הַיּוֹם		I set before you today
אֶת־הַחַיִּים וְאֶת־הַטּוֹב וְאֶת־הַמָּוֶת וְאֶת־הָרָע		Life and what is good, death and what is evil

אֲשֶׁר אָנֹכִי מְצַוְּךָ הַיּוֹם לְאַהֲבָה אֶת־יְהוָה אֱלֹהֶיךָ	**16**	for I command you today to love the Lord your God
לָלֶכֶת בִּדְרָכָיו וְלִשְׁמֹר מִצְוֹתָיו וְחֻקֹּתָיו		to walk in his ways, to observe his commands, his statutes
וּמִשְׁפָּטָיו וְחָיִיתָ וְרָבִיתָ		and his judgements, so that you shal live and multiply
וּבֵרַכְךָ יְהוָה אֱלֹהֶיךָ בָּאָרֶץ אֲשֶׁר־אַתָּה		and the Lord your God will bless you in the land which
בָא־שָׁמָּה לְרִשְׁתָּהּ		you are about to enter and possess.
וְאִם־יִפְנֶה לְבָבְךָ וְלֹא תִשְׁמָע	**17**	But if your heart turns away and you do not obey
וְנִדַּחְתָּ וְהִשְׁתַּחֲוִיתָ		and you let yourself be drawn away to bow down
לֵאלֹהִים אֲחֵרִים וַעֲבַדְתָּם		before other gods and serve them
הִגַּדְתִּי לָכֶם הַיּוֹם כִּי אָבֹד תֹּאבֵדוּן	**18**	I declare to you today that you shall surely perish,
לֹא־תַאֲרִיכֻן יָמִים עַל־הָאֲדָמָה אֲשֶׁר		you shall not prolong your days upon the land to which
אַתָּה עֹבֵר אֶת־הַיַּרְדֵּן לָבֹא שָׁמָּה לְרִשְׁתָּהּ		you are headed to possess it, crossing the Jordan.
הַעִידֹתִי בָכֶם הַיּוֹם אֶת־הַשָּׁמַיִם וְאֶת־הָאָרֶץ	**19**	Today I call heaven and earth against you (as testimony):
הַחַיִּים וְהַמָּוֶת		life and death
נָתַתִּי לְפָנֶיךָ		I place before you,
הַבְּרָכָה וְהַקְּלָלָה		the blessing and the curse;
וּבָחַרְתָּ בַּחַיִּים לְמַעַן תִּחְיֶה אַתָּה וְזַרְעֶךָ		therefore choose life, that you and your descendants live
לְאַהֲבָה אֶת־יְהוָה אֱלֹהֶיךָ לִשְׁמֹעַ בְּקֹלוֹ	**20**	and you may love the Lord your God, obey his voice
וּלְדָבְקָה־בוֹ כִּי הוּא חַיֶּיךָ וְאֹרֶךְ		and adhere to Him, for He is your life and the length
יָמֶיךָ לָשֶׁבֶת עַל־הָאֲדָמָה אֲשֶׁר		of your days, so that you may dwell in the land that
נִשְׁבַּע יְהוָה לַאֲבֹתֶיךָ		the Lord swore to give to your fathers,
לְאַבְרָהָם לְיִצְחָק וּלְיַעֲקֹב לָתֵת לָהֶם		to Abraham, Isaac, Jacob.

Jer 21:8–9

וְאֶל־הָעָם הַזֶּה תֹּאמַר כֹּה אָמַר יְהוָה	**8**	And to this people you shall say: Thus says the Lord:

הִנְנִי		Behold,
נֹתֵן לִפְנֵיכֶם		I set before you
אֶת־דֶּרֶךְ הַחַיִּים וְאֶת־דֶּרֶךְ הַמָּוֶת		the way of life and the way of death:

הַיֹּשֵׁב בָּעִיר הַזֹּאת יָמוּת בַּחֶרֶב וּבָרָעָב	**9**	Whoever remains in this city shall die by the sword, by
וּבַדָּבֶר וְהַיּוֹצֵא וְנָפַל		famine and by plague; but whoever goes out and consigns
עַל־הַכַּשְׂדִּים הַצָּרִים עֲלֵיכֶם יִחְיֶה		himself to the Chaldeans who are besieging you shall live,
וְהָיְתָה־לּוֹ נַפְשׁוֹ לְשָׁלָל		and shall have his own life as war booty.

286   Jer 21:1-10. The surrender as acceptance of the end

The correspondences are evident, and the differences interesting:

1. The speaker does so in the name of God according to a prophetic function.[199]
2. The recipient is the people of Israel, in a decisive moment in its history (beginning – end/new beginning).
3. On the level of general structure,[200] two parts in every passage can be highlighted: a synthetic presentation of the alternative blessing/curse – life/death (cf. Deut 11:26; 30:15; Jer 21:8b) followed by an explication of this relation of opposition tied to correspondent acts to either do or avoid doing (cf. Deut 11:27–28; 30:16–18; Jer 21:9).
4. On the micro level (synthetic presentation), I make note of the selfsame wording:
   a) it begins with a term that has the function of introducing the alternative by highlighting its decisive importance: רְאֵה ("see"; cf. Deut 11:26; 30:15) and הִנְנִי ("behold"; cf. Jer 21:8b)[201];
   b) the question of the choice is posed according to a vocabulary typical of the stipulation of covenant: the same verb נתן is used, followed by לְ + פָּנֶה + suff. 2nd pers. sing./plu. This syntagm, used to indicate the act with which YHWH bestows the Law upon Israel,[202] is elsewhere found *only* in Deut 4:8; 11:32, and in Jer 9:12; 26:4, 44:10 (+ Dan 9:10);
   c) terms opposing each other follow: the blessing/curse pair, or the synonymic terms life-good/death-bad.

---

199   It is precisely Deuteronomy that attributes the title of "prophet" to Moses (cf. Deut 18:15, 18), and even speaks about him as the prophet (נָבִיא) who is the greatest (cf. Deut 34:10). From Deut 18:15–21, which announces the coming of a prophet "like Moses", the characteristics of his prophetic function can be indirectly deduced, as in a reflection: He is the man chosen from amongst his brothers (cf. Dt 18:15a, 18a) as a mediator between God and the people (vv. 16–17) in the favour of the latter (v. 15a.18a), into the mouth of whom God placed his words (v. 18b), words that come to pass (v. 22), and to which he must listen and obey (v. 15b, 19). There are a number of indications in the first chapter of the book of Jeremiah (and not only) that lead one to think specifically of Jeremiah as the prophet announced by Moses. I will point out only those most evident: v. 5: "before I formed you in the womb I knew you (√ידע)" can be matched to Deut 34:10b, in which it says that the Lord "knew (√ידע) Moses face to face"; v. 6 "Ah, Lord God! Behold, I cannot speak, for I am a youth", in a certain sense, recalls Moses' speech defect expressed in Exod 4:10; v. 9b: "Behold I have put my words in your mouth (נָתַתִּי דְבָרַי בְּפִיךָ)" to the above-mentioned Deut 18:18b (וְנָתַתִּי דְבָרַי בְּפִיו); v. 17c: "tell them all that I command you" (וְדִבַּרְתָּ אֲלֵיהֶם אֵת כָּל־אֲשֶׁר אָנֹכִי אֲצַוֶּךָ) would correspond to Deut 18:18c (וְדִבֶּר אֲלֵיהֶם אֵת כָּל־אֲשֶׁר אֲצַוֶּנּוּ). See, in this regard, B. ROSSI, «Reshaping Jeremiah: Scribal strategies and the *prophet like Moses*», *JSOT* 44 (2020) 575–593.
200   Cf. T.A. LENCHAK, *"Choose Life!"*. A Rhetorical-Critical Investigation of Deuteronomy 28,69–30,20, AnBib 129, Roma 1993, 179, 201–202.
201   According to the commentary in the new critical apparatus of the BHQ, the semantic value of the sing. imp. רְאֵה corresponds, in the case of Deut 11:26 (but cf. also Deut 1:21; 4:5), to the exclamative force of the particle הִנֵּה. This reinforces the connection with Jer 21:8b. Cf. C. McCARTHY, *ed.*, *Deuteronomy*, BHQ 5, Stuttgart 2007, 38, 49*.
202   In Ezek 23:24c, I note that it also has juridical value (וְנָתַתִּי לִפְנֵיהֶם מִשְׁפָּט וּשְׁפָטוּךָ בְּמִשְׁפְּטֵיהֶם); cf. P. BOVATI, *Ristabilire la giustizia*, 320–321: here, the semantic field is that of the "judicial decision".

Study of the fundamental themes: Surrender, the inevitable end, and possible life   287

5. *Promised* as a consequence of obedience to the word of God is "life" (הַחַיִּים, Deut 30:15, 19c; Jer 21:8b; נֶפֶשׁ, Jer 21:9b), "good" (הַטּוֹב, Deut 30:15), or "blessing" (בְּרָכָה, Deut 11:26–27; 30:19b). In Deut 30:19c, a specification (לְמַעַן תִּחְיֶה אַתָּה וְזַרְעֶךָ, "so that you and your descendants may live") is offered, which greatly resembles Jer 38:17c: וְחָיְתָה אַתָּה וּבֵיתֶךָ ("you and your household shall live"). It is interesting to note, furthermore, that the benefic objective deriving from the observance of the Law explicitly foresees being blessed *in the land* given in possession (cf. Deut 11:21; 30:20), while from the point of view of the book of Jeremiah, the land within which an unhoped-for but real blessing is received is the land of exile (cf. Jer 24). It should be specified that this blessing is regardless, in a certain sense, "temporary", for the point of arrival indicated in the divine promise is that of a return to the land of Israel (cf. Jer 30,31).

6. Then there is a difference of fundamental importance that accentuates and "consecrates" the symbolic value of deliverance to the king of Babylon": the fact that in Deuteronomy, the choice of life coincides with obedience to an imperative of an ethical nature,[203] namely, observance of the Law (understood as "his command-ments", מִצְוֹתָיו; "his ways", דְּרָכָיו; "his orders", חֻקֹּתָיו; "his decrees"; מִשְׁפָּטָיו), while in Jeremiah (a singular case), this *ethical demand* (present also in Isa 1:19–20) gives way to a word commanding a concrete (political) act upon which the symbolic significance of the totality of the obedience to the Law is conferred, given that the promise of "life" is also tied to it. The structural correlation to chapter 24 makes explicit this positive significance of an end/punishment (lived in obedience) that leads to life, understood not as simple survival but as entrance into a new Covenant, for a renewed relationship with God.[204]

The alternative of an ethical nature between the path of good that leads to life and that of evil that leads to death usually assumes the conditional form, of the type "if *x*" (protasis), "then *y*" (apodosis). This is the case in many significant Jeremianic texts as well (Jer 4:1–2; 7:5–7; 12:16–17; 15:19; 17:24–25; 22:4–9; 26:4–6; cf. also Isa 1:18–20; 58:9b-14; Ezek 2:5–7; Zech 3:7; Mal 2:2). The numerous extrabiblical parallels from the area of Mesopotamia attest that this was a well-known communicative register (called "Sittenkanon" by scholars).[205] In fact, the theme of surrender, presented in 21:8–9 as the choice of life as opposed to the prospect of death, is also formally expressed according to the modality of this "ethical canon" in 38:17–18. But it is clear that in the horizon of the end of Jerusalem, the Jeremianic proposal is configuring a path of life unbound

---

203   On the relationship between theology and ethics in Deut, see J.G. MILLAR, *Now Choose Life. Theology and Ethics in Deuteronomy*, NSBT 6, Leicester 1998; E. EHRENREICH, *Wähle das Leben!* Deuteronomium 30 als hermeneutischer Schlüssel zur Tora, BZAR 14, Wiesbaden 2011.

204   After what I have highlighted about the symbolic coordinates implied in 21:1–10, it seems obvious that the case is not in the least that of counterposing just "simple prudence" to an ethical imperative (Deut), as is affirmed by W.L. HOLLADAY, *Jeremiah 1*, 547.

205   See, in this regard, R.C. BAILEY, «Prophetic Use of Omen Motifs: A Preliminary Study», in: *The Biblical Canon in Comparative Perspective*. Scripture in Context IV, eds. K.L. YOUNGER, Jr. – W.W. HALLO – B.F. BATTO, ANETS 11, Lewiston – Queenston – Lampeter 1991, 195–215 (above all, pp. 195–203).

288   Jer 21:1-10. The surrender as acceptance of the end

to the ethical-moral plane, at this point entirely impracticable, given the incorrigible obstination of the people of God in their infidelity to the Covenant. This variation of perspective is attested, above all, in the mutation of the meaning of the term דֶּרֶךְ.[206] While throughout Deuteronomy (and not only, cf. e.g. Ps 1; 25:8, 12; 32:8), the choice to be made refers to the "way of the commandments", in Jer 21:8, the "way" to be taken is that which leads towards the enemy, disarmed, beyond the walls of Jerusalem, and coincides with the act of accepting punishment.

Indeed, a detailed look shows that these observations are definitely also of interest for the problem of the literary and theological relationship between Deuteronomy and the book of Jeremiah. While specific treatment of this question[207] does not lie within the principle intention of my research, I will regardless note that the shift from the ethical dimension of the choice[208] to a symbolic-prophetic one that expresses itself as a political act appears to be a characteristic of Jeremiah that is *original*, not attributable to Deuteronomistic literary influences.

Regardless, this does not mean dismissing that Deuteronomy itself attests a unifying process of symbolisation, in the sense that, while reaffirming the necessity to obey *all the prescriptions* (cf. e.g. Deut 4:6, 8; 6:2, 24–25; 8:1; 11:8), it goes so far as to identify, with respect to each context, *a commandment* to which it attributes, for its particular nature, a value of complete observance, in other words, a single imperative that expresses – in synthesis – the entire meaning of the *Tôrâ* and consequently, perfect obedience to YHWH.[209]

Even in the book of Jeremiah, some textual articulations can be found where a sort of "ethical-symbolic" concentration is recorded, identifying, depending on the historical circumstances (and not without the participation of prophetic charism), some focal

---

206   Cf. E.H. MERRILL, «דֶּרֶךְ», *NIDOTTE* I, 989–993, but in particular, M. ZEHNDER, *Wegmetaphorik im Alten Testament. Eine semantische Untersuchung der alttestamentlichen und altorientalischen Weg-Lexeme mit besonderer Berücksichtigung ihrer metaphorischen Verwendung*, BZAW 268, Berlin 1999, 593–594.

207   The fact that there are terms that recur in both Deuteronomy and Jeremiah does not mean that one finds oneself in the presence of the same content or even the same author (or redactor), as is justly observed by H. WEIPPERT, *Die Prosareden*, 24. The context remains decisive. In this specific case, I agree with J.M. BERRIDGE, *Prophet, People, and the Word of Yahweh. An Examination of Form and Content in the Proclamation of the Prophet Jeremiah*, BST 4, Zürich 1970, 205 in his saying that "[...] there would appear to be no reason to doubt that these verses faithfully render the either-or spoken by Jeremiah himself".

208   On the theme of the choice, cf. also Josh 24:15; 1 Kgs 18:21; Ezek 21:26.

209   As has already been pointed out by P. BOVATI, *Il libro del Deuteronomio (1–11)*, GSAT, Roma 1994, 149–154, who speaks of three modalities whereby Deuteronomy confers a unitary meaning to the *Tôrâ*: the "principal" commandment (or the "first commandment" from which all others arise: cf. e.g. Deut 6:5 and 10:12, 15; 11:13, 15, 22; 13:4); the "tautological" commandment (the so-called "paraenetic schema", i.e. the imperative that has as direct object very necessity of observing the *Tôrâ*: cf. e.g. 4:6; 5:1; 6:24; 7:11; 10:12); the commandment "sign" of all the "Law" (a commandment that expresses perfect obedience to God; cf. e.g. the absolute prohibition of making an image of YHWH in Deut 4:15–19, 23–26; the law of the *ḥerem* in ch. 7; the norm of love for the foreigner in 10:19, placed in the solemn context of the whole of ch. 10). I will return to the argument in further depth in ch. VII, § 3.3.7.

Study of the fundamental themes: Surrender, the inevitable end, and possible life   289

points of the Law upon which global fidelity to the God of Israel is determined.[210] In my opinion, there are at least two elements to highlight in this sense. The first is the pressing call of fidelity to the one and only Lord (YHWH) against idolatry, something moreover common in the prophetism of Israel. The other, which is more meaningful for our discourse, is the case of the predication of the commandment concerning the sanctification of the Sabbath in 17:19–27, solemnly addressed as "word of the Lord" to the kings of Judah, all the land, and all of Jerusalem, from all the gates of the city (17:19–20).[211]

Both the special promises[212] contingent on obedience (17:24–26) and the drastic threats prognosticated in case of disobedience (17:27), are presented as consequences of such importance that, in one sense or another, they lead one to consider the commandment about the Sabbath as the norm that, in a particular moment in history, is held up as "sign" of the entirety of the Law.

The book of Jeremiah pushes, in any case, beyond this for that matter interesting perspective, which remains prevalently in the orbit of the moral and religious

---

210   Regarding the relationship between Jeremiah and the *Tôrâ*, see: C. M. MAIER, *Jeremia als Lehrer der Tora*. Soziale Gebote des Deuteronomiums in Fortschreibungen des Jeremiabuches, FRLANT 196, Göttingen 2002; G. FISCHER, G., «ותפשי התורה לא ידעוני» The Relationship of the Book of Jeremiah to the Torah», in: *The Formation of the Pentateuch*. Bridging the Academic Cultures of Europe, Israel, and North America, *eds*. J.C. GERTZ *et al.*, FAT 111, Tübingen 2016, 891–911; R. KESSLER, *Der Weg zum Leben*. Ethik des Alten Testament, München 2017, 388–393.
211   A separate situation, though one not so far from along these same lines, is represented by the episode regarding the emancipation of slaves reported in 34:8–22. The same Law that foresaw the institution of slavery also for the Jews in certain circumstances established that they be freed in the seventh year (or in the jubilee year) for religious motives (cf. Exod 21:2–6; Lev 25:44–55; Deut 15:12–18). Zedekiah, during the siege of Jerusalem, perhaps due to the dramatic nature of the moment, or for other motives upon which I will not now dwell (cf. W.L. HOLLADAY, *Jeremiah 2*, 239), had made himself mediator of a pact on behalf of the people (consummated "before the Lord"; cf. 34:18) that pledged to liberate these slaves. When the Babylonian army retreated momentarily for the Egyptian intervention (probably alluded to in 34:22), the pledge was violated and everyone took back their slaves. This is the motive for Jeremiah's invective, which denounces the graveness of the act taken and the drastic punishments that would follow (cf. 34:17–22). As is apparent in 34:13–15, it was a rule that had not been observed for a long time. And it was evidently one of many, seeing as it had not been expressly cited previously amongst the Jeremianic accusations. I do not believe that, in this case, one can fully speak of a commandment being a "sign" of the entire Law, given that the aim of the prophet's speech seems to be more concentrated on the blatant infidelity to the oath that had just been made to YHWH than on the norm itself. The norm had long been unfulfilled and not explicitly indicated by the prophet himself as a decisive precept in that historical moment (as instead occurs in the case of the Sabbath in 17:19–27).
212   Within the thematic horizon of the prophetic message of Jeremiah, marked by the threat and announcement of the "end", it does seem truly significative that the persistence of all that which will historically come to an end (the Davidic dynasty, the possession of the land and the temple) is, in fact, cited in this pericope (cf. 27:25–26) and made conditional exclusively upon the observance of a single precept of the Law.

290 Jer 21:1-10. The surrender as acceptance of the end

dimension, managing to offer the same possibility of a radical, synthetic choice just precisely beyond the failure of the ethical horizon, by now irretrievable place of salvation, given the radicality of the sin.[213]

The option indicated as absolutely decisive, insofar as it is an expression of an extreme possibility of free, conscious reintegration in the design of God and of the vital dynamism of the Covenant, ends up paradoxically coinciding with what is objectively (or apparently) simply a *political act.*

As a minimum common denominator between these different perspectives (Deut and Jer), the repeated focalisation on the centrality of obedience to the word of God remains regardless. In Deuteronomy, it is expressed in a way that is legal and "sapiential" (cf. Deut 4:6: חֲכְמַתְכֶם וּבִינַתְכֶם). In Jeremiah, it is expressed in a way that is "prophetic". Sapience treats that which is always of value, while prophecy tells the meaning of the present.[214] And in fact, on the one hand, obedience coincides with the observance of a *corpus* of established norms, valid for all, *in every* age and in every circumstance,[215] while on the other, everything is concentrated in a single, specific act to be fulfilled *at a given historic moment* (cf. also Jer 38:17–18; 42:9–22).

Alongside these considerations, it appears fairly clear how difficult it is to share the opinion of S. Mowinckel when he attributes 21:1–10 to "source" C. Here, Jeremiah would be presented as an avid preacher of the Law with a concept of religion of a moralistic and dogmatic mould having a clear Deuteronomistic imprint. This is far removed from the brilliant prophetic figure sketched in sources A and B.[216]

4.2.2. *The gesture of surrender as "life as war booty"*

As I highlighted in ch. II, § 3.3.2, the act of surrender cannot be arbitrarily placed in relation with a pre-established outcome. The ability or not to obtain special guarantees from the winners always depends on the specific situation. Considering, however, the dynamic typical of the *escalation* of conflict (and taking into account, insofar as

---

213   In this sense, I think it necessary to go beyond the vision of E.W. NICHOLSON, *Preaching to the Exiles*, 71–93, who maintains that the part of the book of Jeremiah in prose be centred around the announcement of hope for the people who repent and obey the Law.

214   Cf. P. BEAUCHAMP, *L'un et l'autre Testament*, 74–135.

215   It must be said, however, that Jeremiah's perspective is prepared by the fundamental conviction expressed by Deuteronomy that, in essence, the most important commandment consists in loving God and obeying His word (even if this is expressed in multiple precepts). And in fact, if it is this Word that asks, at a certain point, for a "prophetic choice" (and not an ethical one) to be implemented, then it does not fall within the insignificance of an arbitrary act, but remains anchored in the realm of meaning that expresses total observance of the Law.

216   Cf. S. MOWINCKEL, *Zur Komposition*, 39. In my opinion, R. IRUDAYA, «Prophetic Call», 806, does not hit the mark either. According to him, the positioning of 21:11–14 after 21:1–10 would serve to convey that it would be not so much the surrender that saves Jerusalem as the implementation of justice and liberation of the oppressed. In fact, before the now certain end (to whatever extent that may be), the ethical dimension becomes secondary, like a level that is, at this point, no longer recoupable. At the time of Zedekiah, obedience to YHWH can only mean the acceptance of just punishment for the crimes committed.

Study of the fundamental themes: Surrender, the inevitable end, and possible life   291

possible, the intentions of the attackers), several examples attested in ancient sources demonstrate that in not a few cases, surrender meant exposing oneself to *mortal danger* and allowing that one's own destiny be decided by the uncontrollable, indecipherable will of the strongest.

It can be interesting to observe that, in a certain sense, this pragmatic context corresponds to the concept of the *deditio,* a term the Romans used to express their concept of surrender.[217] While this hypothesis was entirely prohibited and dishonourable for them, it was inevitable for many of their enemies. As we have already outlined (cf. ch. II § 3.3.2.5), according to this Roman notion, surrender had to coincide with total, absolute yielding to their will. And it foresaw no promises for the defeated, nor any guarantee of tutelary: not for their life, let alone for maintaining possession of any property.

The surrender that Jeremiah presents, however complete this too must be, does not, on the other hand, implicate the consignment of oneself into the hands of an arbitrary, inexorable divine whim. In fact, just as the Law of Moses, received within the stipulation of the Covenant, promises the gift of "life" (according to an articulated terminology), likewise, acceptance of the prophetic word of Jeremiah (which asks for surrender to the king of Babylon, reintroducing a typical formula of the Covenant) corresponds to a promise of life "as war booty" (לְשָׁלָל).

In the whole of the MT, the expression וְהָיְתָה־לּוֹ נַפְשׁוֹ לְשָׁלָל is attested only in Jeremiah (4x with minimal syntactic variants: 21:9; 38:2; 39:18; 45:5[218]). According to Holladay, the question is a fairly simple one: "more recently, it has become clear that it is an ironic soldier's joke: when a soldier is defeated and escapes, having barely saved his life, he has at least that as 'booty'".[219] In truth, there are no arguments to sustain this opinion, given that the recurrences are all found in Jeremiah (in different passages, but within the same context) and the very authors cited[220] consider this interpretation to be entirely hypothetical.

The path to be taken, in my opinion, need give greater consideration to the textual data we have available.[221] The first and most evident is that in the pragmatic context

---

217   In this regard, see again C.A. BARTON, «The Price of Peace», 249–250.

218   Moreover, this ch., according to G. WANKE, *Baruchschrift*, 135–136.144, should contain authentic words of the prophet Jeremiah.

219   Cf. W.L. HOLLADAY, *Jeremiah 1*, 574. Also speaking of "irony" are R.P CARROLL, *Jeremiah*, 411; M. ERNY, *Jeremias Königslogien*, 69; C.M. MAIER, Jeremia 1-25, IEKAT, Stuttgart 2022, 371.

220   Cf. P. VOLZ, *Der Prophet Jeremia,* KAT 10, Leipzig 1922, 216; J. BRIGHT, *Jeremiah,* 184–185.

221   It is probable that a wide range of sayings, proverbs, and idiomatic (and metaphoric) expressions common in the military sphere existed. Of these, only some fragments reach us, inserted in specific contexts. Think, e.g. of the polemic confrontation between Ahab and Ben-Hadad in 1 Kgs 20:10–11. Faced with Ahab's refusal, the king of Aram swears: "May the gods deal with me, be it ever so severely, if enough dust remains in Samaria to give each of my men a handful!" (v. 10). To such hyperbolic threats, Ahab retorts: "One who puts on his armour should not boast like one who takes it off" (1 Kgs 20:11). Apart from the originary context of these images, which is regardless not hard to imagine, even for these expressions, the actual pragmatic context remains fundamental.

of the book of Jeremiah, this expression *is not ironic in the least*. It suffices to look at 39:18 (but also 45:5): from this extremely serious oracle, it appears clear that "life as war booty" is promised as a prize to Ebed-Melech for having had faith in YHWH (כִּי־בָטַחְתָּ בִּי).

Studying the recurrence of the lexeme שָׁלָל ("war booty", "prey") in the rest of the MT (73x), and leaving out the self-evident observation that the reference is always to something precious, an object of partition and sign of a victory obtained[222] (linked as well to the idea of "joy"; cf. Ps 119:162), one can note its considerable frequency in contexts tied, particularly, to the theme of "holy war" (cf. Num 31:11, 12; Deut 2:35; 3:7; 13:17[2x]; 20:14[2x]; Josh 7:21; 8:2, 27; 11:14; 22:8; Judg 8:24, 25; 1 Sam 14:30, 32; 15:19, 21; 2 Chron 14:12; 15:1; 20:25[2x]). Following the analysis that I carried out previously, this observation cannot be underrated. Now, while the prescription of the *herem* may, on a case-by-case basis, provide for the saving of material goods or livestock for oneself, it strictly excludes, on the other hand, consideration of the conquered population (Canaanite) as war booty: this is to be "put to the sword" entirely.[223]

Considering that, according to the symbolic coordinates of 21:4–7, 10b, Jerusalem itself and its inhabitants are presented as object of *herem*, the promise of being able to save one's life as שָׁלָל to be subtracted from the foreseen extermination constitutes an altogether extraordinary privilege. This is underscored by two elements:

a) Even though survivors and deserters would become, to all effects, prisoners of war *of the Babylonians*, Jeremiah's expression paradoxically highlights that the "war booty" (life) will be the property (וְהָיְתָה־לּוֹ) not of the enemy, but of those who obey the word of YHWH and leave the city to hand themselves over to the Chaldeans.[224]

b) In case of undergoing a siege (defensive war), the victory, that is, the maximum result possible (apart from exceptional cases) coincides precisely with the preservation of possessed goods, the first of all being that of "life" itself. It is interesting to note that the term נֶפֶשׁ ("breath of life", "soul", "life", "person")[225] with which this "war booty" is indicated, is quite often used in Jeremiah as the object of √בקשׁ pi. ("to seek", "to persecute"; cf. Jer 4:30; 11:21; 19:7, 9; 21:7; 22:25; 34:20, 21; 38:16; 44:30[2x]; 46:26; 49:37)[226] to indicate not only the primary object craved by the

---

222   Through metonymy, war bounty and the partitioning of it can indicate the event of the victory itself (cf. Isa 8:1, 4; Zech 14:1). On this topic, see D. ELGAVISH, «The Division of the Spoils of War in the Bible and in the Ancient Near East», *ZAR* 8 (2002) 242–273.

223   Num 31:11–12 is a special case, but it seems to be the classic exception that confirms the rule: Moses is resentful about the women and children having been spared and orders rituals of purification. The inhabitants can be spared only in the case of "distant cities" (cf. Deut 20:11–18) that are not Canaanite.

224   Leaving the city, one leaves the sacred space of the *herem* where the war booty gets burned (cf. Deut 13:16), going only with one's own life, and this alone is spared.

225   Cf. ZORELL, 525–527.

226   In the passages cited, the enemies of Jerusalem are defined as those "who seek the life" (√בקשׁ pi. + נֶפֶשׁ [compl. obj.]+ suff.) of the Israelites. This expression is typical of Jeremiah. Its other recurrences are: Exod 4:19; 1 Sam 20:1; 22:23[2x]; 23:15; 25:29; 2 Sam 4:8; 16:11; 1 Kgs 19:10, 14; Lam 1:19; Ps 35:4; 38:13; 40:15; 54:5; 63:10; 70:3; 71:13; 86:14; Prov 29:10 (here, in a positive sense).

Study of the fundamental themes: Surrender, the inevitable end, and possible life   293

enemy, but to define the adversary as such: he is "the one who seeks life", who essentially wants the death of his antagonist.

It is important to reiterate also from a literary point of view what I already clarified from a historical point of view in ch. II: *by surrender, the message of Jeremiah does not intend to suggest a military tactic usually giving positive results,* also because – as we have seen – it announces the actualisation of the damnation that foretells the arrival of "a nation from afar [...] that shows neither respect for the aged nor mercy for the young" (cf. Deut 28:49–50), and Nebuchadnezzar himself in 21:7b is clearly presented as a ruthless instrument of the justice of God, the executor of a just sentence that intends to spare no one[227] (cf. also 2 Chron 36:17).

This is why having one's life saved, in case one falls into his hands, necessarily implies that there be a special intervention of God who can change hearts and render such a murderous desire ineffective, as is moreover clearly affirmed in 42:11–12.[228] But this is not for the fact that the "punishment" or "sentence" become (unjustly) annulled. It is instead because, since the act of surrender signifies the admission of one's guilt, the punishment itself (to which one must necessarily submit) can reveal its salvific purpose fully.

I will then add that the exceptions found in contexts of "holy war" (whether permitted or not) are, in a certain sense, inverted. Rather than livestock or precious objects being spared, in Jer 21:1–10, these "goods" (which are then identifiable with the Temple, the royal palace, Jerusalem as the capital of the kingdom of Judah, etc.) are considered irretrievably lost regardless, given that the entire city must be delivered to fire. What is identified as "war booty" or, in other words, as a precious reality and inconceivable exception, coincides in reality with the *bare* possession of life (נֶפֶשׁ).

In this respect, this "privilege" cannot fail to be understood as a paradoxical gift, in that it implies, in any case, the experience of some form of "death",[229] the willingness to

---

227 This attitude corresponds to that which animates "the people who come from the North" according to the oracle of 6:22–23: "Thus says the Lord: 'Behold, a people comes from the land of the North and a great nation shall be raised from the remote parts of the earth. They have taken up their bows and swords; they are cruel and merciless (√רחם) [...]'."

228 "Do not fear the king of Babylon, of whom you are afraid; do not fear him, says the Lord, for I am with you to save you and to deliver you from his hand. I will show you compassion so that he will have compassion (√רחם) on you and let you return to your own land." On this thematic, I once again refer to W. BRUEGGEMANN, «At the Mercy of Babylon».

229 It would be wrong, in fact, to think to be able to identify the pure, biological fact of living as the full realisation of the concept of "life". That which constitutes life in a human being cannot be reduced to this (even if it obviously makes up its essential foundation) because it includes more complex and specifically human values, all founded on a person's fundamental relational nature of dignity, identity, love, etc. The confirmation of this is given by the fact that when these constitutive elements are radically lost by the person and all of their most significative relationships vanish, often also pure survival is perceived as useless and even a source of still greater pain. See e.g. the case of Saul who, feeling rejected by YHWH and seeing himself as defeated at that point, chooses suicide in order to conserve that shred of dignity that the mockery and insults of the Philistines might have torn from him (1 Sam

294   Jer 21:1-10. The surrender as acceptance of the end

risk losing everything to become the "true winners". By saying this, I am not forcing the message of Jeremiah by making an abstraction in general categories: it is, rather, precisely the last recurrence (45:5) of the expression "life as war booty" (נֶפֶשׁ לְשָׁלָל) that deepens and dilates the meaning of "surrender to the king of Babylon".

Jer 45 draws our attention both because it closes the second part of the book of Jeremiah (followed only by that dedicated to the oracles against the nations) and because it as well seems entirely out of place.[230] Here, the dimension of the "disaster" (רָעָה) goes beyond the ("reassuring"?) limits[231] of guilt, both individual and collective, and assumes universal importance. Indeed, it is destined by YHWH to strike "all the land" (כָּל־הָאָרֶץ) and fall upon "all flesh" (כָּל־בָּשָׂר).

Thus, not only the unjust, the idolater, but also the faithful disciple Baruch and the prophet Jeremiah himself are called to carry out the symbolic act of surrender[232]: to whomever obeys the word of God, which asks that they not retreat in the face of "death" (whether punishment *or* disaster),[233] "life as war bounty" is thus promised. It is a gift that expresses the ratification of the end (of that which must necessarily be left behind: cf. 45:5c: "in all the places where *you will go*", עַל כָּל־הַמְּקֹמוֹת אֲשֶׁר תֵּלֶךְ־שָׁם). And contemporaneously, it becomes the sign of an (new) absolute beginning (life itself rediscovered as "grace" that is granted). In particular, as we have seen from the literary articulation of 21:1–10 with ch. 24, what follows the word of destruction is "good" (טוֹבָה), a "planting" (√נטע) and "building/establishing" (√בנה) in a new and definitive way (cf. 24:6), a new relationship (√ידע) with God (v. 7).

    31:4; 2 Sam 1:9); or the drama of Ahithophel (cf. 2 Sam 17:23), the great advisor first of David and then of Absalom (2 Sam 16:23) who, seeing for the first time that not his opinion but instead that of another is listened to, loses his meaning for life, and decides to return home and take his life. Jeremiah himself desires to die (to have died in the maternal womb) when he perceives his existence as being marked by failure (cf. Jer 20:14–18).

230   Cf. M.A. Taylor, «Jeremiah 45: the Problem of Placement», *JSOT* 37 (1987) 79–98.

231   The mentality that attributes a causal link between the sin of humanity and "catastrophe", in a certain sense sheltering God from the accusation of being an unjust judge, is attested as being common thought up until the NT (cf. John 9:2), even if, already in the OT, with the book of Job, profound criticism of this unidirectional theological position (to which, in any case, the Mosaic Law itself offers pretexts that are far too simple, as we saw e.g. in Deut 11:26–28; 30:15–20) is already familiar.

232   One can also believe that the prophet and his disciple had been called to experience the surrender as an act of solidarity with the people (cf. the example of Moses; cf. Exod 32:32). In this sense, accepting to surrender means signifying love for a people marked by sin that is not even recognised. In fact, Jeremiah (accompanied once again by Baruch) will share the fate of the survivors of the destruction of Jerusalem (cf. Jer 39:11–14; 40:1–6), even when, disobedient to his prophetic word (cf. Jer 43:5–6), they decide to escape to Egypt.

233   It seems clear that the concept of "catastrophe" is now no longer linked to the connotation that elsewhere links it to the idea of "punishment".

5. Conclusions: Surrender as a "prophetic choice" on the basis of semiotic-literary coordinates

5.1. Accepting the end of one (hi)story so there can still be any (hi)story. Principal acquisitions

As we come to the end of this stage of our path of inquiry, it seems opportune that I briefly retrace the passages that are fundamental to show their articulation in an initial synthesis and highlight the most relevant results that I believe have been achieved.

As I specified in the General Introduction, an interest in the theme of "surrender", an original message of Jeremiah, was the stimulus for embarking on a detailed study of the question. And upon a first reading, the hermeneutical approaches that tend to conduce the problem to a merely political, politico-redactional, or ethical plane seemed insufficient.[234] The research conducted in ch. II of my dissertation reinforced this perception, establishing the need for alternative paths to be researched. The thesis from which the present stage of my study, more intensely focused on certain Jeremianic texts, took shape was therefore that of considering the *act* that Jeremiah requests in 21:1–10 (inserted within the broader theme of submission to the king of Babylon) as a specific "prophetic choice", namely, a concrete gesture designated by the prophet's word to transmit the significance of a specific historical moment (the final siege of Jerusalem and end of the kingdom of Judah).

A study of the particular redactional positioning of the pericope allowed for the establishment of its key function, *proleptic* in nature, in relation to the texts following (21:11–23:8; 23:9–40; and above all, ch. 24). In fact, already on this level of analysis, which I defined as "semiotic-literary", the request to "surrender" revealed its eminently "prophetic" (and not only political) nature, demonstrating to be the decisive word, the one announced "first" precisely in order to decipher the meaning of the entirety. In other words: only by way of *accepting the inevitable punishment of YHWH* can one open up onto the inconceivable possibility of a new beginning, of a new Covenant (ch. 24).

The twofold articulation thus highlighted (end – new beginning), studied according to detailed analyses of fundamental terms and expressions in 21:1–10, allowed for the emergence of a complex symbolic framework. This was constructed beginning from literary coordinates drawn from important traditions of the origins: the event of the Exodus, the "holy war" and prescription of the *ḥerem*, and the curses of the Covenant. Moreover, as was already suggested by G. Fischer,[235] the book of Jeremiah demonstrates a significant reconstruction of biblical literature, reutilising well-known texts and themes in a creative, ingenious way. For this very reason, the Jeremianic corpus can only be comprehended in reference to these evocations and allusive re-elaborations. In our case, the question is that of a reorientation of motifs aimed at the announcement of two complementary themes: on the one hand, the radical guilt of Jerusalem, destined to be punished definitively (the "end"), and on the other, the action of the selfsame God of the time of founding, whose scope is always the good of his people (a "new beginning").

---

234 Cf. General Introduction, § 1.4.
235 See G. FISCHER, *Jeremia*, 134 and, above all, ID., «Il libro di Geremia».

296   Jer 21:1-10. The surrender as acceptance of the end

This design of salvation directed toward the new Covenant (mentioned in Jer 24 and announced in 31:31) is not, however, an automatism that strips human free will (as it may seem from certain texts and as some authors seem to insinuate). Far from it. It is precisely when the end is proclaimed and, indeed, in the gloomiest hues, that the vocabulary of the stipulation of the Covenant appears. And what is requested by this (contrary to what S. Mowinckel believes about "source" C), is no longer an act of an *ethical* nature (Deut), but rather a gesture of a *political* one, taken on, however, by the word of the prophet to "*prophetically*" indicate acceptance of the "end" as a paradoxical condition necessary for retaining life itself. It is life "as war booty", life in its "initial" state: having blossomed forth from death by the power of God, a new hope and new Covenant can come to be.

5.2. Holy wars and side effects. Some secondary conclusions

The decipherment of the semiotic-symbolic coordinates innervated in our text author- ises me, I believe, to speak about surrender as a "prophetic choice", thus introducing some fundamental semantic axes of a new hermeneutical category, which, by the end of our course of study, should result as clearer, better defined, and more convincing. At any rate, its heuristic value has immediate hermeneutical repercussions on the assessment of some interpretations coming from literary criticism, which I will not avoid confronting, even though these solutions base themselves on a perspective that questions the text in a way that is quite different from the approach I have adopted.

The significance of the fate reserved for Zedekiah (and for the people) in v. 7, for example, proves to be more comprehensible. Almost all commentators point out the irreconcilability between the two oracles (21:7 and 34:1–5[236]) that concern the des- tiny of Zedekiah (and there are those who, in regard to it, speak of an improbable "redactional debate", as I have had the opportunity to note elsewhere).[237] In fact, the perspectives do seem to be diametrically opposed: the prediction of complete exter- mination, and of "death in peace".[238]

---

236   Cf. R.P. CARROLL, *Jeremiah*, 410: "[...] the fate of kings is a theme full of discrepan- cies, contradictions and problems for the exegete."
237   Cf. J. APPLEGATE, «The Fate of Zedekiah». The historicity of the account in 2 Kgs 24:18–25,7 has been called into question (against most of the commentators and, in my opinion, with fairly fragile arguments) by J. PAKKALA, «Zedekiah's Fate and the Dynastic Succession», *JBL* 125 (2006) 443–452.
238   Cf. J. APPLEGATE, «The Fate of Zedekiah», 151, which bears this example, or textual evidence of contradiction, precisely to affirm the existence of a "debate". He points out that, unlike the MT, the LXX does not have the phrase "you will not die by the sword" (34:4), as if the MT had wanted to accentuate the difference with 21:7. The fact does not seem conclusive to me at all. First of all, it should be considered that Zedekiah, in 21:7, is an integral part of a broader group of people. The disastrous fate is announced for an entire social body, not only for the king. In 21:7 then, there are other elements that concern the fate of Zedekiah and it seems strange that in 34:1–5, only mention of the "sword" recur in oppositive function. Even if the motive were the fact that the term חֶרֶב recurs twice in the same v. 7, the fact remains that the additional "you shall not die of the sword" is only explicative and does not really add anything that is not already contained in that "you shall die in peace", prophecy that alone already contradicts the letter of all 21:7 and not just one of its elements (the sword).

Indeed, if a reading of 21:7 cannot be disassociated from the "holy war" framework that I have highlighted (just as the tendency of the biblical communicative style to make absolute affirmations that are then later toned down or renegotiated need be kept in mind),[239] then from this point of view, it is logical to read the oracle about Zedekiah not as a precise prediction of the modalities of his death, but rather as an insertion of the figure of the king (or of whoever does not want to perform the gesture of surrender) within the symbolic coordinates of the *ḥerem*. According to this line of interpretation, which dissolves the irreconcilable tensions recognised by commentators, v. 10 as well does not intend to adjudicate on the possibility of still living in the land (of Judah) or not, but rather to provide an explanation of the *meaning* of a dramatic event (that Jerusalem be equivalent to the idolatrous cities, and thus punished). In this sense, the opinion of C.R. Seitz[240] would thus also be inadequate. According to this, v. 10 (attributed to the "Golah redactors" and thus tendentious) would only serve to pose the question of whether life in the land is still possible and to respond with a definitive (and emphatic) no, to the benefit of the exiles of the first deportation.

Within these same coordinates, the theme of the "turning back of weapons", scourge of the plague, and extermination of survivors can be comprehended. The intention of the prophecy, in other words, is not that of describing with precision how the Israelites themselves will fight and decimate each other within the city, and neither should the value given to the plague be primarily factual (though it is, along with hunger, a natural consequence of a siege).

Even the so-called "pro-*gôlâ Tendenz*" that would be so evident[241] in chapter 24 seems to dissolve in the light of the precise interweaving of textual relations in unit 21–24. In other words, it is no longer necessary to see the distinction between good figs and bad figs as a surreptitious self-legitimisation of the exilic community to which the insertion of this text would be ascribed *in toto*. This surprising distinction corresponds precisely, in fact, to the line of demarcation traced in 21:8–9: only those who – by surrendering themselves – accept the righteous judgement of YHWH can hope for a future. Those who, instead, do not accept the prophetic message, deliver themselves to death. This is therefore not primarily a political message, but rather a *theological* one. So much so, that whoever decides to not surrender is overcome by the disaster precisely for having not trusted YHWH, and for no other reason (cf. the choice of the two paths). Whilst on the other hand, the exiles of 597 themselves are called, according to ch. 29 against their intentions, to accept a symbolic form of surrender, namely, to lay down their hope of a quick, easy return to the homeland, it is not, in other words, the physical condition of the exile that guarantees some statute of pre-eminence, but rather, once again, the concrete – "prophetic" – acceptance of the theological function of Babylonia. Only thus can one play an *active* role in the design of God.

Therefore, in synthesis, the semiotic-symbolic interweaving of 21:1–10 (and its relationship to ch. 24, as well) does nothing but announce these fundamental theological-prophetic polarities. For Jerusalem, the time of the end has come. That end is due to

---

239 Cf. *Ibid.*, 151–152. Also to Josiah, among other things, it is announced by the (true) prophetess Huldah a death "in peace", which the biblical story seems to belie (cf. 2 Kgs 22:18–20).

240 Cf. C.R. SEITZ, «The Crisis of Interpretation», 78–97 (esp. p. 82).

241 Cf. C.J. SHARP, *Prophecy*, 159 ("so manifest").

transgression. And the executor of the sentence or righteous divine punishment is the king of Babylon. To not recognise this, however unusual it may seem, means taking on *de facto* the role of the foreign idolatric cities that YHWH had once handed over to his people for complete destruction. On the contrary, surrendering oneself to the king of Babylon, in this historic moment and in obedience to the prophetic word, becomes a prophetic gesture that expresses acceptance of just punishment and radical trust in the Lord of life for a new and inconceivable beginning.

Chapter IV
Jer 27–28.
The world beneath the yoke of the king of Babylon:
The multi-levelled *ante factum* of the prophetic call to surrender

Pour ceux qui reconnaissent ces actes comme signes de l'action créatrice de Dieu, ils sont comme des viatiques pour traverser les silences, les doutes, le rejet et la mort. Pour les traverser, non pour les éviter.[1]

1. Introduction

Setting aside the threatening, albeit still historically indeterminate, references to an invasion from the North,[2] the anguished scenes of a besieged Jerusalem, and terrifying events envisaged in Jer 6 (particularly in vv. 1–8, 22–30), the Jeremianic message demanding unconditioned surrender to Babylon is presented explicitly to the reader upon the stage of history that "emerges" from the book of Jeremiah only in 21:1–10.

For the reasons that I have attempted to identify (cf. ch. III, § 3), this comes about, moreover, in a way that is altogether unexpected, both with regard to the logical and chronological concatenation of the events (*fabula*) object to narration (*plot*), as well as to the reader, who expects to find an evident criterion of structuralisation for the various textual units. In fact, one finds oneself projected quite suddenly into the geopolitical scenario concerning the final stages of the story of the kingdom of Judah. And it is only later, in ch. 25, and above all in chs. 27–28, that this thematic will find a contextualisation referable to a historical-narrative framework some years antecedent to both the temporal (and theological) context presupposed by 21:1–10 and, *a fortiori*, to the final colloquy between Zedekiah and Jeremiah, that is, in the imminence of the fall of Jerusalem (38:14–28a).

---

1 D. CLERC, «Des actes pour parler», in: *Jérémie*. Un prophète en temps de crise, *eds.* R. BLANCHET *et al.*, EssBib 10, Genève 1985, 107–147 (here, p. 112).

2 The term צָפוֹן in 1:14 (cf. vv. 13 and 15) could be translated as the "North" or as "northern" (adj.). In line with a tradition prevalent in the ancient Near East, it identifies the place of origin of disaster and "judgment", rather than the precise historical instrument of the punishment decreed by YHWH. More than a geographical point traceable on a "horizontal" plane, according to some scholars, it indicates a "vertical" dimension of a mythical nature (a peak, a holy mountain, if not the dwelling place of the divine itself). In the Ugaritic tradition, the reference seems to be to a specific mountain, seat of Baal and other deities, placed on the northern border of the Syrian-Palestinian strip. See in this regard D.J. REIMER, «The "Foe" and the "North" in Jeremiah», *ZAW* 101 (1989) 223–232, in particular pp. 229, 231–232.

Taking a cue from these preliminary points, I will define Jer 27–28 as an *ante factum* dense with signification, while specifying nevertheless that I will take on the category of *anticipation* according to *multiple levels of meaning*. The task of the present stage of research will be that of illustrating and adequately justifying the bearing of this programmatic premise and the heuristic function of the notion of "ante factum", which I will adopt as an "umbrella" term.[3] I will specify straightaway that, as we have just observed, Jer 27–28 is to be understood on a *first level*, with reference to the conceptual instrumentation proper to narrative analysis, as an *analepsis (flashback or retrospection)* with respect to the episode in 21:1–10. And within this same perspective, Jer 27–28 is, at the same time, a fundamental *ante factum*, "relatively" speaking, obviously,[4] with respect to the prophetic call to surrender addressed to King Zedekiah in 38:14–28a.

Having established that the *factum* of reference can be both 21:1–10 and 38:14–28a, the textual unit that I will now give consideration expresses a value of *anteriority* that does not exhaust itself on the level of strategic anachronies that typify well-constructed tales, despite its being founded, on the level of expression, on a narrative structure. Indeed, the peculiar textual displacement of chs. 27–28 within the book of Jeremiah needs to be understood in relation to the *historical-theological motivations* and *communicative-pragmatic dynamics* codified and expressed within it as well. We are dealing with an important *founding level* that enables, on the one hand, a rereading of 21:1–10 that can deepen its understanding, while on the other, the configuration of a *paradigmatic anticipation* (through, above all, the mimetic gesture of the yoke) of all that which will enter onto the scene of the text in 38:14–28a, where the theme of the alternative between resistance and surrender to the king of Babylon will assume its dramatic (though not thematic, given that the textual isotopy will re-emerge in 42–43:7) culmination.

Continuing to follow the provocation of this unusual narrative (*interweaving*) flow, I will thus only now turn my focus to chs. 27–28, selecting and analysing the elements and *different levels of meaning* that are, by my judgement, those most pertinent to my research. As an initial approach to the textual data (§ 2), I will execute some basic operations, like a translation of the Hebrew text, accompanied by some philological-exegetic notes (§ 2.1 and 2.2) and a study of the textual delimitation of the unit under scrutiny (§ 2.3). I will then bring into focus the compositive structure of Jer 27–28 and look at some significative implications thereof (§ 2.4). Considering that I have

---

3   In the Echian sense, that is, as a term (or locution: the *ante factum*) that covers several semiotic phenomena.

4   "Relative" in the sense that the *ante factum*, in and of itself, precedes the actual *fabula*, and in the absolute sense, the *ante factum* for the "total" biblical narrative should be sought in the pages of the Genesis that narrate the mystery of the origins (of the world and of Israel). Nevertheless, the book of Jeremiah, which on the whole attests to an (albeit decisive) segment of this broader story of the relation between YHWH and his people, can be considered a communicative unit in its own right that contains its own narrative development (with its own particular *ante factum*, like the prophetic vocation in ch. 1). This *fabula*, of a particular nature because it is rearranged to form a plot that is *sui generis* and is mixed, moreover, with texts of a "poetic" genre, contains several narrative sequences within it that can then, in turn, each be studied in an isolated way. Choosing to focus on the thematisation of the surrender to Babylon contained, above all, in 21:1–10 and 38:14–28a, the most significative *ante factum* can undoubtedly be considered chs. 27–28.

Introduction   301

already dedicated in-depth study to the historical aspect in ch. II, from which herein, I will only pick back up some useful data, once I have laid forth these fundamental premises, I will then focus my attention on the following thematic poles in particular:

I. The specific *communicative device* implemented, namely, the symbolic gesture of the yoke. The question will be that of grasping, at least on an initial level, the profound hermeneutical implications inherent to the assumption of this type of *non-verbal* communication, considered within the context of the communicative dynamics that characterise biblical prophetism in general and Jeremianic prophetism in particular (§ 3). This will allow us to see how the theme of the surrender to Babylon involves not only (theological-literary) *conceptual aspects*, but also the profundity of the *relational dimension*, and this extends far beyond the rhetorical finalities to which the symbolic gestures of prophets are commonly reduced.

II. The *universal slant* assumed by the Jeremianic message in Jer 27–28 (§ 4), which is expressed through a communicative synergy between the gesture of the yoke and a characteristic phraseology through which the interlocutors are asked to actualise its symbolic significance on the concrete level of a political decision. This is the topic that I will deal with most of all. First, I will study its semantic-pragmatic significance (§ 4.1). Once the configuration of the *non-verbal* communication has been introduced, the text then prompts, on a *verbal* level, the *prophetic* injunction to submit to the Babylonian power with a preliminary reference of a *sapiential* sort to the sovereign *lordship of YHWH over creation and history*. The submission to Babylon is presented in this way, intermediating however between *wisdom* and *prophecy*, between the *universal* and the *particular*, like a historical-theological necessity in a given historical moment, destined to call into question not only the fate of the kingdom of Judah, but also that of "all nations" (§ 4.2). So will then need to ask if other motives do not also underlie the prophetic request besides that of the inscrutable design of God, which seems to be placed as the fundamental axiom of the thematic development of the Jeremianic call. The fact that "the nations" are the subject of a key chapter like Jer 25 and the entire third part of the book (chs. 46–51) certainly invites us to proceed with a complementary intertextual investigation (§ 4.3).

III. Not least, the question regarding the discernment between true and false prophecy (§ 5). A complex problem, one that exceeds the textual limits of the Jeremianic work (and of the present dissertation), but which is connoted, precisely herein, by decisive importance (§ 5.1). I will therefore only take some well-aimed exegetic stabs at it, ones pertinent to my study, starting from a contribution by M.J. de Jong[5] that seems to call into question the very legitimacy of the conventional oppositional categorisation between true and false prophecy (§ 5.2). While the theme is already introduced in ch. 27 (and even earlier still, in 23:9–40), it will nevertheless be the data offered in ch. 28, above all, that allows me to focalise interesting reading perspectives exploring the theme of "surrender" in-depth (§ 5.3). Then, on the basis of the insights gained, in the next chapter, dedicated to the study of Jer 38:14–28a, we will be able to grasp the dramatic implications, both personal and universal, of recognition of the word of God in the word of the human being-prophet (ch. V).

---

5   M.J. DE JONG, «The Fallacy of "True and False" in Prophecy Illustrated by Jer 28:8–9» *JHS* 12 (2012) 1–29 [DOI: 10.5508/jhs.2012.v12.a10].

302   Jer 27–28. The world beneath the yoke of the king of Babylon

2. Jer 27–28: A first approach to the textual data

2.1. Jer 27: Hebrew text, translation, and philological-exegetical notes

Ch. 27

בְּרֵאשִׁית מַמְלֶכֶת יְהוֹיָקִם⁶   **1** In the beginning of the reign of <u>Jehoiakim</u>⁶
בֶּן־יֹאשִׁיָּהוּ מֶלֶךְ יְהוּדָה הָיָה   [Zedekiah,] son of Josiah, king of Judah,
הַדָּבָר הַזֶּה אֶל־יִרְמְיָה מֵאֵת יְהוָה לֵאמֹר   this word came to Jeremiah from the Lord:

---

6   Almost all the recent commentators, based on some mss and the Syriac and Arabic version, propose emending the phrase בְּרֵאשִׁית מַמְלֶכֶת יְהוֹיָקִם בֶּן־יֹאשִׁיָּהוּ מֶלֶךְ יְהוּדָה (omitted entirely from the LXX), to substitute the name of Jehoiakim (according to many, erroneously copied from 26:1, to which אֶל־יִרְמְיָה is added, but which was used again in the Vg and Tg) with that of Zedekiah. Indeed, the narration that follows explicitly refers to Zedekiah several times (27:3, 12) and to the first deportation (27:16, which took place at the time of Coniah (Jehoiachin), son of Jehoiakim (27:20). Further confirmation to that effect comes from the beginning of the following ch. (28:1: "And that same year, in the beginning of the reign of Zedekiah, [...], in the fourth year [...]"), where an episode is introduced that is in clear temporal and thematic continuity with ch. 27, set during the reign of Zedekiah. For J.D. MICHAELIS, *Observationes*, 220–221, there should be no doubt about the necessity of this correction. It is, however, possible to understand the literally erroneous mention of the name of Jehoiakim in a sense that is symbolic-metaphorical, and thus intentional (this is e.g. how it is intended by G. FISCHER, *Jeremia 26–52*, 50, who does not amend the MT). In this sense, the text would use the name of Jehoiakim as a symbolic cypher, wanting to underscore that under Zedekiah, the same nefarious influence of the Davidic post-Josiahian dynasty continues on the history of Israel (of which the most emblematic representative in a negative sense is Jehoiakim himself). In my opinion, as far as the symbolic significance is concerned, it seems more plausible that what can be seen put into effect is the intention of demonstrating the precise fulfilment of the Jeremianic prophecy of 70 years of exile (from the beginning of the reign of Jehoiakim, the year 609 [which also coincides with the death of Josiah, an event of great symbolic value as well] to the fall of the Babylonian empire at the hands of Cyrus the Great in 539, there are exactly 70 years, while if v. 1 were to refer to the first [597] or fourth year of Zedekiah [594/593], there would only be 58 or even fewer, respectively). In any case, I believe that it be appropriate to leave both interpretive possibilities open (symbolic intentionality/scribal error), putting the name of Zedekiah in parenthesis beside that of Jehoiakim. It should be noted, in any case, that all of v. 1 appears to be a late addition (cf. T. SEIDL, «Datierung und Wortereignis: Beobachtungen zum Horizont von Jer 27,1», *BZ* 21 [1977] 23–44, 184–199; D. BARTHÉLEMY, *Critique textuelle*, 665–666). This could support the symbolic-metaphorical value of the current arrangement of the MT (result of a scribal/redactional rereading), also since the emendation of the name "Jehoiakim" would not, in any case, help in precisely identifying the historical context (as was already noted by E.F.C. ROSENMÜLLER, *Scholia in Vetus Testamentum*, VIII: Ieremiae vaticinia et Threnos, vol. II, Lipsiae 1827, 5–6). In fact, the expression בְּרֵאשִׁית מַמְלֶכֶת (equivalent of the Akkadian formula *rēš šarrūti*, which usually indicates the interval between the acceptance of the throne by a sovereign and his official coronation, which would take place the following calendar year), should be understood differently than 26:1, that is, as referring to the fourth year of the reign of Zedekiah (cf. 28:1) and not to that of his enthronement. But see the sequence of events as proposed instead by N. SARNA, «The Abortive Insurrection», 287–290 (cf. ch. II, § 2.2.2).

Jer 27–28: A first approach to the textual data

כֹּה־אָמַר יְהוָה אֵלַי[7]	2	*"This is what the Lord said to me*[7]:
עֲשֵׂה לְךָ מוֹסֵרוֹת וּמֹטוֹת וּנְתַתָּם[8] עַל־צַוָּארֶךָ		*Make straps and poles and put them*[8] *on your neck;*
וְשִׁלַּחְתָּם[9] אֶל־מֶלֶךְ אֱדוֹם	3	*then send them*[9] *to the king of Edom,*
וְאֶל־מֶלֶךְ מוֹאָב וְאֶל־מֶלֶךְ בְּנֵי		*to the king of Moab, to the king of the sons of*
עַמּוֹן וְאֶל־מֶלֶךְ צֹר וְאֶל־מֶלֶךְ צִידוֹן		*Ammon, to the king of Tyre, and to the king of Sidon,*
בְּיַד מַלְאָכִים[10] הַבָּאִים		*through the ambassadors*[10] *who are coming*
יְרוּשָׁלַםִ אֶל־צִדְקִיָּהוּ מֶלֶךְ יְהוּדָה		*to Jerusalem to Zedekiah, king of Judah,*

---

7 For the rendering of the well-known messenger formula in the past tense, which here, is not to be understood in the performative, given that the narrator has Jeremiah refer to a prophetic communication received previously in respect to the message that he is conveying, see J. KRISPENZ, «Grammatik und Theologie in der Botenformel», *ZAH* 11 (1998) 133–139, who on p. 137 calls attention to analogous cases (with אֵלַי): Isa 8:11; 18:4; 31:4; Jer 13:1; 17:19; 25:15.

8 The suffix of the 3rd pers. m. pl. of וּנְתַתָּם (and also of the following וְשִׁלַּחְתָּם) does not correspond to the f. pl. substantives מוֹסֵרוֹת and מֹטוֹת (a phenomenon that is not rare in the MT; cf. GK §135o and G.A. RENDSBURG, *Diglossia in Ancient Hebrew*, AOS 72, New Haven 1990, 49; and, esp. O. GLANZ, *Understanding Particpant-Reference Shifts in the Book of Jeremiah. A Study of Exegetical Method and Its Consequences for the Interpretation of Referential Incoherence*, SSN 60, Leiden 2013). Cf. also 28:10.

9 As I will explain later on (cf. n. 30), the textual elements lead to believe that what is requested of Jeremiah not be the fabrication of a complete yoke, but of a yoke "collar" (made up of poles or planks of wood to be fixed to the horizontal axis of a yoke, which, together with the cords, would clamp the neck of the beast). It is not clear if this refers to the actual sending of five different samples of this collar to the respective kingdoms represented in Jerusalem, and for this reason, my translation also seeks to conserve the ambiguity of the MT. Some have considered that it be a symbolic imperative along the lines of 25:15 (cf. e.g. already E.F.C. ROSENMÜLLER, *Scholia*, II, 7–8, who speaks of a "*phraseologia allegorica*"; but see also 1 Sam 11:7, where an analogous symbolic communication is actually played out: Saul, disdained, chops up a pair of oxen and sends them all across Israel threatening a similar fate for the oxen belonging to those who had not responded to his call to war against Nacas, the Ammonite). In any case, the reading וְשִׁלַּחְתָּם (that cannot be in reference to the dispersion of the various elements of the collar, since the strength of the sign would be lost) is well attested (cf. 4Q72[Jerᶜ] in: DJD XV, 194, col. XVIII, l. 2 [Jer 27:3], pl. XXXIII [= E. ULRICH, *The Biblical Qumran Scrolls*. Transcriptions and Textual Variants. Vol. 2: Isaia–Twelve Minor Prophets, Leiden – Boston 2013, 574]; LXX; Vg; Tg) and does not prevent us in the least from understanding the meaning of the prophetic discourse (as e.g. D. BARTHÉLEMY, *Critique textuelle*, 666–667 and W. MCKANE, *Jeremiah*, II, 686). It should be noted, however, that several modern versions, following the opinion of many commentators, omit in translation the pron. suff. (which, by the way, like that of the preceding verb וּנְתַתָּם is m. pl. instead of f.; cf. JM §149b) and interpret the act of sending as a reference to Jeremiah's message (e.g.: NRSV: "send word"; EÜ: "schick eine Botschaft"; LB: "schicke Botschaft"; CEI: "manda un messaggio"). This option refers back to an elliptical construction of the verb שָׁלַח that is well attested (√שלח + [implied: a message or a messenger] + אֶל/עַל + name of the recipient): see e.g. Num 22:10, 37; Josh 11:1; 1 Sam 20:12; 2 Sam 12:25; 11:6 and Jer 23:38; 29:28, 31. It should be noted, in any case, that in addition to ignoring the clear indication coming from the ancient versions, a revocalisation as qal should be done, because √שלח does not ever appear as piel in this syntagmatic construction, unless it is read as a *hapax* with an intensive meaning, in a way analogous to Mal 2,4 (שִׁלַּחְתִּי אֲלֵיכֶם אֵת הַמִּצְוָה הַזֹּאת [...]).

10 The LXX has "their ambassadors" (ἀγγέλων αὐτῶν). According to S. WHITE CRAWFORD – J. JOOSTEN – E. ULRICH, «Sample Edition of the Oxford Hebrew

304   Jer 27–28. The world beneath the yoke of the king of Babylon

וְצִוִּיתָ אֹתָם אֶל־אֲדֹנֵיהֶם לֵאמֹר
כֹּה־אָמַר יְהוָה צְבָאוֹת אֱלֹהֵי יִשְׂרָאֵל
כֹּה תֹאמְרוּ אֶל־אֲדֹנֵיכֶם

4   *and command them for their masters:*
Thus says the Lord of hosts, the God of Israel:
Thus you shall say to your masters:

אָנֹכִי עָשִׂיתִי אֶת־הָאָרֶץ אֶת־הָאָדָם
וְאֶת־הַבְּהֵמָה אֲשֶׁר עַל־פְּנֵי הָאָרֶץ
בְּכֹחִי הַגָּדוֹל וּבִזְרוֹעִי הַנְּטוּיָה
וּנְתַתִּיהָ¹¹ לַאֲשֶׁר יָשַׁר בְּעֵינָי

5   *I made the earth, humankind*
and the animals that are on the face of the earth,
by my great power and by my outstretched arm,
<u>and I give it</u>¹¹ to whomever seems right in my eyes.

וְעַתָּה אָנֹכִי נָתַתִּי¹² אֶת־כָּל־הָאֲרָצוֹת הָאֵלֶּה
בְּיַד נְבוּכַדְנֶאצַּר ¹³ מֶלֶךְ־בָּבֶל
עַבְדִּי וְגַם אֶת־חַיַּת הַשָּׂדֶה
נָתַתִּי לוֹ לְעָבְדוֹ

6   *<u>And now I have given</u>¹² all these lands*
into the hand of <u>Nebuchadnezzar,</u>¹³ king of Babylon,
my servant; even the beasts of the field
I have given to him, to serve him.

וְעָבְדוּ אֹתוֹ כָּל־הַגּוֹיִם וְאֶת־בְּנוֹ
וְאֶת־בֶּן־בְּנוֹ עַד בֹּא־עֵת
אַרְצוֹ גַּם־הוּא

7   *And so all the nations shall serve him, his son*
and his son's son, until the time comes
for him and his own land as well!

Bible: Deuteronomy 32:1–9, 1 Kings 11:1–8, and Jeremiah 27:1–10 (34 G)», *VT* 58 (2008) 352–366 (here, p. 365), the MT would be corrupt, and should be read according to the lesson attested in the LXX, that is, מַלְאֲכֵיהֶם.

11   The MT with the suffix in 3ʳᵈ pers. f. of √נתן refers to the land (אֶרֶץ) named previously, as an all-encompassing term for the great majority of the realities created (Gen 1:1, 2, 10; etc.). The LXX does the same, omitting, however, the reference to human beings and animals (according to some, for haplography, but it is more probable that it be the MT that presents an elaboration of the text) and thus coordinating the creation of the earth and its destination (ἐγὼ ἐποίησα τὴν γῆν [...] καὶ δώσω αὐτὴν) in a way that is clearer and more straightforward. Cf. Gen 1:26, 28, and particularly v. 29: [...] נָאַמֶר אֱלֹהִים הִנֵּה נָתַתִּי לָכֶם. Some modern versions underscore the universal dimension of this conferment of vicarial authority (made explicit, in any case, in v. 6 where the verb נָתַן is repeated 2x with a performative value) including the reference to human beings and beasts mentioned by the MT through the introduction of a pl. pronoun (cf. e.g. NAB: "and I can give them"; BJ: "et je les donne"; CEI: "e li do").

12   On the temporal conjugation and semantic of the various occurrences of √נתן here and in 28:14, see the exegetical comment in § 4.2.7.

13   The name of the Babylonian sovereign is attested in the MT according to several variants (no less than eight). In the book of Jeremiah, the same form (more original and official) is always repeated with ר (נְבוּכַדְרֶאצַּר), except in 27:6–29:3, where we find, as in the present case, the second most attested variant, with נ (נְבוּכַדְנֶאצַּר). This is done 8x, while in 29:21, the spelling with ר returns (cf. what was already observed in ch. II, § 2.1.2, n. 40). If we take into account that this proper name is absent from the corresponding text of the LXX, we might find ourselves before an additional clue to the substantially unitary literary development of chs. 27–29 (cf. § 2.3), provided it is not only a random phenomenon of scribal error in transcription. Curiously, in any case (as notes W.L. HOLLADAY, *Jeremiah 2*, 114), the name of Jeremiah itself, rather than its usual spelling (יִרְמְיָהוּ), presents an unusual form without the final ו (יִרְמְיָה) only in this section, in this case again 8x (cf. 27:1; 28:5, 6, 10, 11, 12, 15; 29:1, and also Ezra 1:1; Dan 9:2). For additional information and for the probable etymological differences ascribable to the two principal variants of the proper name of the king of Babylon, see A. VAN SELMS, «The Name Nebuchadnezzar», in: *Travels in the World of the Old Testament. Studies Presented to Professor M.A. Beek on the Occasion of his 65th Birthday*, eds. M.S.H.G. HEERMA VAN VOSS *et al.*, Assen 1974, 223–229; see also H.-J. STIPP, *Jeremia 25–52*, HAT I/12,2, Tübingen 2019, 113–114.

Jer 27–28: A first approach to the textual data

וְעָבְדוּ בוֹ[14] גּוֹיִם רַבִּים[15]
וּמְלָכִים גְּדֹלִים

Then he will be made a slave[14] *by great nations*[15] *and powerful kings.*

וְהָיָה הַגּוֹי וְהַמַּמְלָכָה
אֲשֶׁר לֹא־יַעַבְדוּ אֹתוֹ אֶת־נְבוּכַדְנֶאצַּר

8 *And it shall come to pass that the nation or kingdom that will not want to serve him, Nebuchadnezzar,*

---

14 It should be noted that, with most commentators, √עבד qal in syntagmatic relationship with בְּ + suff. (which creates a word game with the preceding אֹתוֹ וְעָבְדוּ at the beginning of the same v.; and cf. also the additional semantic variation of √עבד in v. 11: "to till the land") assumes a causal value in the context ("to make serve, reduce [someone] to servitude"; as e.g. also in Exod 1:14; Lev 25:39; etc., and Jer 22:13; 25:14; 30:8; 34:9). The LXX omits the v., while instead the Vg (wrongly) does not recognise any semantic difference between √עבד qal + direct obj. and √עבד qal + בְּ, and translates: "[...] *et servient ei gentes multae et reges magni*".

15 The same expression recurs in 25:14. Given the potential semantic ambivalence of the adjective רַב (cf. H.-J. FABRY – E. BLUM – H. RINGGREN, «רַב», *ThWAT* VII, 294–320) which, depending on the context, can more or less distinguish the aspect of "numeric greatness" (cf. 22:8, where the same expression גּוֹיִם רַבִּים recurs in this sense; Isa 54:1; Ezek 38:23; 39:27; Mic 4:2; Neh 13:26; Ps 135:10; etc., also being understood as an inclusive plural indicating a *totality*) or that of "generic eminence or importance" (cf. 50:41, where the kings can be understood as sovereigns – more *powerful* than many – who succeed each other as the head of the only named nation; cf. also, e.g. Gen 25:23; Num 26:54, 56; 33:54; 35:8 in reference to the most powerful tribes, because they are numerous; Ezek 31:6; Ps 135:10), could also be translated as "*numerous* nations". In most of the occurrences in which רַב is placed close to one or more collective subjects, it seems to convey, above all, or at least *in the first logical instance*, the idea of "relevant numerical entity" (cf. e.g. Exod 1:7 [√רבה]; 23:2; Num 21:6; 22:15; Deut 7:1: an interesting case, because the expression גּוֹיִם רַבִּים is used before with the idea of "numerous nations" [the list of which follows] and immediately after with that of "great, powerful nations" [that only the Lord can win over]), from which then follows also that of "importance" on a broader level (cf. e.g. Num 22:3; Josh 11:4; 17:14; etc., in the sing. and Deut 7:17; 15:6; 28:12; etc., in the pl.). When wanting to highlight the concept of eminence or relevance, even in the political-military sense, the adjectives עָצוּם are usually used (cf. Exod 1:9; Deut 7:1; 9:14; 26:5), הֶחָזָק (cf. Num 13:18) or גָּדוֹל (cf. Gen 12:2; 17:20; Exod 32:10; Deut 2:10, 21; 4:6; etc.), also in connection with רַב (cf. e.g. Deut 9:14; 26:5), which seems, in this series, to distinguish rather the quantitive or numerical basis of this importance. The entire v. is lacking in the LXX, while the modern versions are divided between the two options ("*important* nations" [NAB; EÜ; BJ; CEI; etc.] or "*many* nations" [LND; NRSV; LUT; TOB; etc.]). For exegetical-contextual reasons, I opt for the idea of power and greatness, considering the parallel syntagm מְלָכִים גְּדֹלִים ("powerful kings"), given the fact that historically, Babylon fell at the hands of the Persians alone, and that it refers to the absolute power of YHWH (vv. 5–6), who can decide as he pleases to share it with single human entities in limited or transitional forms (in this case, socio-political). Regardless, the notion of a conquest caused by *multiple* nations remains unvaried in both cases.

306 Jer 27–28. The world beneath the yoke of the king of Babylon

מֶלֶךְ־בָּבֶל וְאֵת אֲשֶׁר¹⁶ לֹא־יִתֵּן		*king of Babylon, and that*[16] *will not want to place*
אֶת־צַוָּארוֹ בְּעֹל מֶלֶךְ בָּבֶל		*its neck under the yoke of the king of Babylon,*
בַּחֶרֶב וּבָרָעָב וּבַדֶּבֶר אֶפְקֹד		*by sword, famine and plague will I punish*
עַל־הַגּוֹי הַהוּא נְאֻם־יְהוָה עַד־תֻּמִּי¹⁷		*that nation, oracle of the Lord, until I have completely*
אֹתָם בְּיָדוֹ		*destroyed*[17] *them by his hand.*
וְאַתֶּם אַל־תִּשְׁמְעוּ אֶל־נְבִיאֵיכֶם	**9**	*So you must not listen to your prophets,*
וְאֶל־קֹסְמֵיכֶם וְאֶל חֲלֹמֹתֵיכֶם¹⁸		*nor to your diviners, nor your dreamers,*[18]
וְאֶל־עֹנְנֵיכֶם וְאֶל־כַּשָּׁפֵיכֶם		*nor your enchanters, nor your sorcerers,*
אֲשֶׁר־הֵם אֹמְרִים אֲלֵיכֶם לֵאמֹר		*who say to you:*
לֹא תַעַבְדוּ אֶת־מֶלֶךְ בָּבֶל		*'You must not serve the king of Babylon!'.*
כִּי שֶׁקֶר הֵם נִבְּאִים לָכֶם	**10**	*For they are prophesying lies to you,*
לְמַעַן הַרְחִיק אֶתְכֶם מֵעַל אַדְמַתְכֶם		*so you will be driven out of your land,*
וְהִדַּחְתִּי אֶתְכֶם וַאֲבַדְתֶּם		*for I cast you out and you shall perish.*
וְהַגּוֹי אֲשֶׁר יָבִיא אֶת־צַוָּארוֹ בְּעֹל	**11**	*But the nation that will place its neck under the yoke*
מֶלֶךְ־בָּבֶל וַעֲבָדוֹ		*of the king of Babylon and will serve him,*
וְהִנַּחְתִּיו עַל־אַדְמָתוֹ נְאֻם־יְהוָה		*I will let rest in its land, oracle of the Lord,*
וַעֲבָדָהּ וְיָשַׁב בָּהּ		*they will till it and dwell in it.*

---

16   The *waw* can also be given an explicative value ("namely that which"). The syntactic concatenation within v. 8 is altered by an anacoluthia or *casus pendens* (JM §156a): the second relative phrase (introduced by וְאֵת אֲשֶׁר) takes the subject of the initial proposition (הַגּוֹי וְהַמַּמְלָכָה), but that subject is then deprived of the support of a congruent syntactic function, gets expressed with a pronoun and, in fact, becomes the direct object of the clause supported by אֶפְקֹד (cf. A. Niccacci, *Sintassi del verbo ebraico nella prosa biblica classica*, SBFA 23, Jerusalem 1986, §§ 123–125). As I sought to highlight during the translation, this serves to emphatically distinguish the punishment destined for the nations who refuse to submit to Babylon (cf. T. Muraoka, *Emphatics Words and Structures in Biblical Hebrew*, Jerusalem – Leiden 1985, 155).

17   The transitive form of √תמם qal is unusual (the LXX has the intransitive form ἐκλίπωσιν), and has been cause for discussion between commentators, some of whom propose amending the reading תֻּמָּם according to the form that recurs in 24:10 ("[...] until their destruction"). On my part, I prefer to maintain the MT, considering that, in any case, another occurrence of the verb with transitive meaning is attested in Ps 64:7.

18   Together with the principal ancient versions (LXX, except the Origenian and Lucianean recensions, which translate using ἐνυπνίων ὑμῶν ["your dreams"], Vg, Syr; the Tg translates instead by paraphrasing: וּמְחלמי חלמיכון; "the dreams of your dreamers") and modern ones (cf. D. Barthélemy, *Critique textuelle*, 668–669), I consider the term חֲלֹמֹתֵיכֶם (lit.: "your dreams") like a *nomen agentis* ("your dreamers"; cf. also 29:8) inserted in a homogenous series of figures who were dedicated to divinatory practices. Based on some Mishnaic parallels, it is possible to think, along with A.B. Ehrlich, *Randglossen zur Hebräischen Bibel: textkritisches, sprachliches und sachliches. Vierter Band: Jesaia, Jeremia*, Leipzig 1912, 312–313, of the name of a profession based on the verbal adjective חָלוֹם (cf. JM §50b).

Jer 27–28: A first approach to the textual data

וְאֶל־צִדְקִיָּה מֶלֶךְ־יְהוּדָה דִּבַּרְתִּי[19] **12** *I spoke already[19] to Zedekiah king of Judah*
כְּכָל־הַדְּבָרִים הָאֵלֶּה לֵאמֹר *according to all these words:*
הָבִיאוּ אֶת־צַוְּארֵיכֶם בְּעֹל מֶלֶךְ־בָּבֶל *place your neck under the yoke of the king of Babylon,*
וְעִבְדוּ אֹתוֹ וְעַמּוֹ וִחְיוּ *serve him and his people and you will live!*

לָמָּה תָמוּתוּ אַתָּה וְעַמֶּךָ **13** *Why would you and your people want to die*
בַּחֶרֶב בָּרָעָב וּבַדָּבֶר *by the sword, famine, and plague,*
כַּאֲשֶׁר דִּבֶּר יְהוָה אֶל־הַגּוֹי *as the Lord has spoken concerning the nation*
אֲשֶׁר לֹא־יַעֲבֹד אֶת־מֶלֶךְ בָּבֶל *that will not serve the king of Babylon?*

וְאַל־תִּשְׁמְעוּ אֶל־דִּבְרֵי הַנְּבִאִים **14** *Therefore do not listen to the words of the prophets*
הָאֹמְרִים אֲלֵיכֶם לֵאמֹר לֹא תַעַבְדוּ אֶת־מֶלֶךְ *that are telling you: 'You must not serve the king of*
בָּבֶל כִּי שֶׁקֶר הֵם נִבְּאִים לָכֶם *Babylon!'. For they are prophesying a lie to you!*

כִּי לֹא שְׁלַחְתִּים נְאֻם־יְהוָה **15** *I have not sent them at all, oracle of the Lord,*
וְהֵם נִבְּאִים בִּשְׁמִי לַשָּׁקֶר *but they prophesy falsely in my name,*
לְמַעַן הַדִּיחִי אֶתְכֶם וַאֲבַדְתֶּם *so that I cast you out and you shall perish,*
אַתֶּם וְהַנְּבִאִים הַנִּבְּאִים לָכֶם *you and the prophets who prophesy to you.*

וְאֶל־הַכֹּהֲנִים וְאֶל־כָּל־הָעָם הַזֶּה דִּבַּרְתִּי **16** *I spoke also to the priests and to all the people,*
לֵאמֹר כֹּה אָמַר יְהוָה אַל־תִּשְׁמְעוּ אֶל־דִּבְרֵי *saying: Thus says the Lord: do not listen to the words*
נְבִיאֵיכֶם הַנִּבְּאִים לָכֶם לֵאמֹר *of your prophets who prophesy to you:*
הִנֵּה כְלֵי בֵית־יְהוָה *'Behold, the vessels of the house of the Lord*
מוּשָׁבִים מִבָּבֶלָה עַתָּה מְהֵרָה *will soon be brought back from Babylon';*
כִּי שֶׁקֶר הֵמָּה נִבְּאִים לָכֶם *for these prophesy lies to you.*

אַל־תִּשְׁמְעוּ אֲלֵיהֶם עִבְדוּ אֶת־מֶלֶךְ־בָּבֶל **17** *Do not listen to them! Serve the king of Babylon*
וִחְיוּ לָמָּה תִהְיֶה הָעִיר הַזֹּאת חָרְבָּה *and you shall live! Why should this city be laid waste?*

וְאִם־נְבִאִים הֵם וְאִם־יֵשׁ דְּבַר־יְהוָה **18** *If they really are prophets and the word of the Lord*
אִתָּם יִפְגְּעוּ־נָא בַּיהוָה *is with them, let them instead intercede with the Lord*
צְבָאוֹת לְבִלְתִּי־בֹאוּ[20] הַכֵּלִים הַנּוֹתָרִים *of hosts so that[20] the vessels remaining*
בְּבֵית־יְהוָה וּבֵית מֶלֶךְ *in the house of the Lord and in the house of the king*
יְהוּדָה וּבִירוּשָׁלַם בָּבֶלָה *of Judah and in Jerusalem not go[20] to Babylon!*

---

19 I render the meaning of the perfect דִּבַּרְתִּי thus, intending Jeremiah's speech to Zedekiah and then to the priests as a citation (of a fact already occurred) inserted within the message that God orders be communicated to the sovereigns of the neighbouring states through their ambassadors.

20 "So that [...] they *do* not *go*": לְבִלְתִּי־בֹאוּ. A problematic verb form (it itself, an imp. 2nd pers. m. pl.), which G. FISCHER, *Jeremia 1–25*, 51 counts amongst the "unübliche Konstruktionen" typical of the book of Jeremiah. It can be interpreted as a perfect (בָּאוּ), vocalised however as an imperfect, which is the form that would be expected here, as in Exod 20:20 and 2 Sam 14:14 (cf. GK §72o; 76g), even if after לְבִלְתִּי, an infinitive would be called for (cf. JM §124e; 160l; but consider also the particular case attested in 23:14: לְבִלְתִּי־שָׁבוּ; and cf. E. JENNI, *Die hebräischen Präpositionen*. Band 3: Die Präposition Lamed, Stuttgart 2000, 297, who proposes amending this last form with the imperfect יָשׁוּבוּ, and בֹאוּ in 27:18 with יָבֹאוּ). The cause is probably the omission, by haplography, of an original יְ (יָבֹאוּ לְבִלְתִּי). W. Rudolph, in the BHS (cf. ID., W. RUDOLPH, *Jeremia*, 177), suggests the option of reading the infinitive form בֹא attested in a few mss (as opposed to A.B. EHRLICH, *Randglossen*, 313, for whom a scribal error of haplography can hardly explain such a reading). For a brief statistical-semantic survey of the use combined with the preposition לְ with the negation בְלְתִי in the book of Jeremiah, see the note by H. MIGSCH, «*l*=*bilti* im Jeremiabuch», *BN* 157 (2013) 111–114.

308 Jer 27–28. The world beneath the yoke of the king of Babylon

כִּי כֹה אָמַר יְהוָה צְבָאוֹת	19	*For thus says the Lord of hosts*
אֶל־הָעַמֻּדִים וְעַל־הַיָּם[21] וְעַל־הַמְּכֹנוֹת		*concerning the pillars, the 'sea',[21] the stands*
וְעַל יֶתֶר הַכֵּלִים הַנּוֹתָרִים בָּעִיר הַזֹּאת		*and the rest of the vessels remaining in this city:*
אֲשֶׁר לֹא־לְקָחָם נְבוּכַדְנֶאצַּר מֶלֶךְ בָּבֶל	20	*those that Nabuchadnezzar king of Babylon did not*
בַּגְלוֹתוֹ[22] אֶת־יְכָנְיָה[23] בֶן־יְהוֹיָקִים		*take, when he deported[22] Jeconiah,[23] son of Jehoiakim*
מֶלֶךְ־יְהוּדָה מִירוּשָׁלַם בָּבֶלָה		*king of Judah, from Jerusalem to Babylon*
וְאֵת כָּל־חֹרֵי יְהוּדָה וִירוּשָׁלָם		*along with all the nobles of Judah and Jerusalem.*
כִּי כֹה אָמַר יְהוָה צְבָאוֹת	21	*Indeed, thus says the Lord of the hosts,*
אֱלֹהֵי יִשְׂרָאֵל עַל־הַכֵּלִים הַנּוֹתָרִים		*God of Israel, concerning the vessels remaining*
בֵּית יְהוָה וּבֵית		*in the house of the Lord and in the house*
מֶלֶךְ־יְהוּדָה וִירוּשָׁלָם		*of the king of Judah and in Jerusalem:*
בָּבֶלָה יוּבָאוּ וְשָׁמָּה	22	*they will be taken to Babylon and there they will*
יִהְיוּ עַד יוֹם פָּקְדִי אֹתָם		*remain until the day that I will visit them,*
נְאֻם־יְהוָה וְהַעֲלִיתִים		*oracle of the Lord, and I will bring them back and*
וַהֲשִׁיבֹתִים אֶל־הַמָּקוֹם הַזֶּה		*restore them to this place".*

2.2. Jer 28: Hebrew text, translation, and philological-exegetical notes

Ch. 28

וַיְהִי בַּשָּׁנָה הַהִיא בְּרֵאשִׁית מַמְלֶכֶת	1	In that same year, in the beginning of the reign of
צִדְקִיָּה מֶלֶךְ־יְהוּדָה בַּשָּׁנַת[24] הָרְבִעִית		Zedekiah, king of Judah, in the fourth year,[24] in the
בַּחֹדֶשׁ הַחֲמִישִׁי אָמַר אֵלַי חֲנַנְיָה		fifth month, it came to be that Hananiah,
בֶן־עַזּוּר הַנָּבִיא אֲשֶׁר מִגִּבְעוֹן		son of Azzur, the prophet of Gabaon, said to me
בְּבֵית יְהוָה לְעֵינֵי הַכֹּהֲנִים		in the house of the Lord, in front of the priests
וְכָל־הָעָם לֵאמֹר		and all the people:
כֹּה־אָמַר יְהוָה צְבָאוֹת אֱלֹהֵי יִשְׂרָאֵל לֵאמֹר	2	*"Thus says the Lord of hosts, God of Israel:*
שָׁבַרְתִּי אֶת־עֹל מֶלֶךְ בָּבֶל		*I have broken the yoke of the king of Babylon!*

---

21 This is the so-called "sea" of bronze that Solomon had built, according to 1 Kgs 7:23, a great reservoir that probably symbolised the cosmic ocean.

22 Irregular form of inf. hi. without the initial ה (cf. 24:1; 43:3).

23 Case of Q (יְכָנְיָה) / K (יְכוֹנְיָה). The name of this king, here according to the Q in the abbreviated form with respect to that in 2 Kgs 24:6, 12; Jer 37:1; 1 Chron 3:1 (יְהוֹיָכִין, "Jehoiachin"), recurs in the HB in different variants.

24 Case of Q (בַּשֶּׁנָה) / K (בִּשְׁנַת). I follow the K (cf. 32:1; 46:2; 51:59; Dan 9:1). Verse 1 of the MT is overloaded compared to the LXX, which omits בַּשָּׁנָה הַהִיא בְּרֵאשִׁית מַמְלֶכֶת צִדְקִיָּה and instead keeps the temporal notation of "fourth year of Zedekiah king of Judah" (ἐν τῷ τετάρτῳ ἔτει Σεδεκία βασιλέως Ιουδα). According to N. SARNA, «The Abortive Insurrection», 289–290 (who echoes the Judaic interpretive tradition dating back to Kimchi), the apparent irreconcilability between the two temporal references in the MT (בְּרֵאשִׁית מַמְלֶכֶת on the one hand, and בַּשָּׁנָה הָרְבִעִית on the other) can be resolved if the "fourth year" is understood with respect to the cycle determined by the falling of the sabbatical year, which began in 602 (a date obtained by confronting Jer 34:8–22 with Deut 15).

Jer 27–28: A first approach to the textual data

בְּעוֹד שְׁנָתַיִם יָמִים אֲנִי מֵשִׁיב אֶל־הַמָּקוֹם הַזֶּה
אֶת־כָּל־כְּלֵי בֵּית יְהוָה
אֲשֶׁר לָקַח נְבוּכַדְנֶאצַּר מֶלֶךְ־בָּבֶל
מִן־הַמָּקוֹם הַזֶּה וַיְבִיאֵם בָּבֶל

3 *Within two years I will restore to this place*
all the vessels of the Lord's house,
which Nabuchadnezzar, king of Babylon, took away
from this place and took to Babylon.

וְאֶת־יְכָנְיָה בֶן־יְהוֹיָקִים
מֶלֶךְ־יְהוּדָה וְאֶת־כָּל־גָּלוּת יְהוּדָה
הַבָּאִים בָּבֶלָה אֲנִי מֵשִׁיב
אֶל־הַמָּקוֹם הַזֶּה נְאֻם־יְהוָה
כִּי אֶשְׁבֹּר אֶת־עֹל מֶלֶךְ בָּבֶל

4 *Also Jeconiah himself, son of Jehoiakim,*
king of Judah, and all the exiles from Judah
who went to Babylon, I will bring back
to this place, oracle of the Lord,
for I will break the yoke of the king of Babylon".

וַיֹּאמֶר יִרְמְיָה הַנָּבִיא
אֶל־חֲנַנְיָה הַנָּבִיא לְעֵינֵי הַכֹּהֲנִים
וּלְעֵינֵי כָּל־הָעָם הָעֹמְדִים
בְּבֵית יְהוָה

5 Then the prophet Jeremiah responded
to the prophet Hananiah in front of the priests
and in front of all the people who were standing
in the house of the Lord:

וַיֹּאמֶר יִרְמְיָה הַנָּבִיא
אָמֵן כֵּן יַעֲשֶׂה יְהוָה
יָקֵם יְהוָה אֶת־דְּבָרֶיךָ[25] אֲשֶׁר נִבֵּאתָ
לְהָשִׁיב כְּלֵי בֵית־יְהוָה
וְכָל־הַגּוֹלָה מִבָּבֶל
אֶל־הַמָּקוֹם הַזֶּה

6 The prophet Jeremiah said:
"*Amen! May the Lord do this!*
May the Lord fulfill that[25] *which you have prophesied,*
so that the vessels of the house of the Lord
and all the exiles can return from Babylon
to this place!

אַךְ־שְׁמַע־נָא הַדָּבָר הַזֶּה אֲשֶׁר אָנֹכִי דֹבֵר
בְּאָזְנֶיךָ וּבְאָזְנֵי כָּל־הָעָם

7 *But now hear what I have to say*
to you ears and to the ears of all the people:

הַנְּבִיאִים אֲשֶׁר הָיוּ לְפָנַי וּלְפָנֶיךָ
מִן־הָעוֹלָם וַיִּנָּבְאוּ אֶל־אֲרָצוֹת
רַבּוֹת[26] וְעַל־מַמְלָכוֹת גְּדֹלוֹת
לְמִלְחָמָה וּלְרָעָה[27] וּלְדָבֶר

8 *The prophets who came before me and you*
from ancient times prophesied against many
countries[26] *and against great kingdoms,*
war, calamity,[27] *and plague.*

הַנָּבִיא אֲשֶׁר יִנָּבֵא לְשָׁלוֹם
בְּבֹא דְּבַר הַנָּבִיא יִוָּדַע
הַנָּבִיא אֲשֶׁר־שְׁלָחוֹ יְהוָה בֶּאֱמֶת

9 *As for the prophet who prophesies peace: only when*
his word shall come to pass shall he be recognised as a
prophet that has truly been sent by the Lord".

וַיִּקַּח חֲנַנְיָה הַנָּבִיא אֶת־הַמּוֹטָה
מֵעַל צַוַּאר יִרְמְיָה הַנָּבִיא
וַיִּשְׁבְּרֵהוּ[28]

10 Then the prophet Hananiah took the (yoke) collar
from the neck of the prophet Jeremiah
and broke it.[28]

---

25 Lit.: "your words that you have prophesied".
26 Here, unlike in 27:7, in light of the testimonies of biblical prophetism (in which the oracles against the nations are addressed to *many* nations and not only those having a greater geopolitical weight), it seems appropriate to me to emphasise the numerical dimension of the adjective רַב. Otherwise, the expression that follows (מַמְלָכוֹת גְּדֹלוֹת) would result as pleonastic.
27 Some modern versions, based on not a few Hebrew mss, read the term רָעָב ("hunger") instead of רָעָה ("calamity"), probably for assimilation to the recurring tripartite series דֶּבֶר + רָעָב + חֶרֶב ("sword; hunger; famine"; cf. e.g. 14:12; 21:7, 9; 24:10; 27:8, 13; etc.). Regardless, it should also be noted that in 28:8, in place of חֶרֶב, there is מִלְחָמָה. Cf. D. BARTHÉLEMY, *Critique textuelle*, 671–672.
28 The 3rd pers. m. sing. suffix does not correspond to the feminine substantive מוֹטָה (cf. 27:2). The final ו is most probably a dictography.

310   Jer 27–28. The world beneath the yoke of the king of Babylon

וַיֹּאמֶר חֲנַנְיָה לְעֵינֵי כָל־הָעָם לֵאמֹר   **11**   Then Hananiah in front of all the people said:
כֹּה אָמַר יְהוָה כָּכָה אֶשְׁבֹּר אֶת־עֹל   *"Thus says the Lord: in this way I will break the yoke*
נְבֻכַדְנֶאצַּר מֶלֶךְ־בָּבֶל בְּעוֹד שְׁנָתַיִם יָמִים   *of Nabuchadnezzar king of Babylon within two years*
מֵעַל־צַוַּאר כָּל־הַגּוֹיִם   *from the neck of all the nations!"*
וַיֵּלֶךְ יִרְמְיָה הַנָּבִיא לְדַרְכּוֹ   And the prophet Jeremiah went his way.

וַיְהִי דְבַר־יְהוָה אֶל־יִרְמְיָה   **12**   But the word of the Lord came unto Jeremiah
אַחֲרֵי שְׁבוֹר חֲנַנְיָה הַנָּבִיא אֶת־הַמּוֹטָה   after the prophet Hananiah had broken the collar
מֵעַל צַוַּאר יִרְמְיָה הַנָּבִיא לֵאמֹר   from the neck of the prophet Jeremiah:

הָלוֹךְ וְאָמַרְתָּ אֶל־חֲנַנְיָה לֵאמֹר   **13**   *Go and tell Hananiah:*
כֹּה אָמַר יְהוָה   *Thus says the Lord:*
מוֹטֹת* עֵץ שָׁבָרְתָּ*[29]   *"You have broken*[29] *crossbars*[30] *of wood,*

---

29   Lit.: "you have broken" (שָׁבָרְתָּ) [...] "and you have done" (וְעָשִׂיתָ) [...]. Both the *qatal* forms provide the reader with retrospective or "recuperated" information (cf. A. NICCACCI, *Sintassi*, §§ 14–25; 164). The paratactic relationship between the respective main phrases (x-*qatal* [protasis] + waw-x-*qatal* [apodosis]), mediated by a simple *waw*, however, has, in my opinion, an implicit significance that is both *consecutive* and *causal*. The first phrase, in fact, recalls the act of Hananiah, the second, instead, its consequence (or, one could say that the first indicates the cause of that which is affirmed in the following principal one). The relationships of coordination and subordination, in the majority of cases, are actually equivalents on a semantic level, and this allows for their interchangeability in many languages (cf. R. SIMONE, «Espaces instables entre coordination et subordination», in: *La Parataxe*. Tome 1: Entre dépendance et intégration, *eds.* M.-J. BÉGUELIN – M. AVANZI – G. CORMINBOEUF, Berne 2010, 231–253). In translation, one thus has a sufficient margin for manoeuvre to emphasise one or the other semantic nexus according to one's judgement. It should be emphasised that these semantic implications are not predetermined from the linguistic point of view, but rather generated by the *pragmatic* context of reference (instituted by the dynamic of the clash between Jeremiah and Zedekiah and exceeding the single verse). I have preferred to explicate the consecutive value that I recognise in the sequence שָׁבָרְתָּ + x + וְ + עָשִׂיתָ ("you have broken [...] *but thus [doing]* you have done"), but it would be possible, alternatively, to emphasise the *causal* importance of the first perfect (שָׁבָרְתָּ), translating it, e.g. with a gerund ("*breaking* the bars of wood you have made bars of iron") that corresponds to an introductory clause, e.g. with "*since*" or "*seeing as*". This consecutive or cause-effect relationship is accentuated in the MT by the chiastic arrangement of the two phrases. For this type of causal or consecutive relationship between clauses, which assume, respectively, the function of protasis and apodosis through a "*waw* of apodosis" or copulative *waw* (וְעָשִׂיתָ), see JM §170*c*; 176*a-e*; WO § 32.3; 38.4*a* (cf. also the subsequent n. 31).

30   At this point, it is opportune to note the variety of terms used by the MT to refer to that which, in chs. 27–28, many modern versions almost always choose to translate uniformly with the generic term "yoke", probably to render the symbolic intention of the story more explicit to the reader and to avoid that it be rendered opaque by an excessively technical translation. In fact, the vocabulary used seems to denote a precise knowledge of the object in question, but this creates a certain difficulty during translation, even if it does not in the least impede the comprehension of the metaphoric meaning. The most recurrent (and clear) lemma is עֹל, and it is used in 27–28 (27:8, 11, 12; 28:2, 4, 11, 14), every time in a figurative sense, to indicate the power of the king of Babylon (the LXX always renders it with ζυγός). What is probably

וְעָשִׂיתָ ²⁶תַחְתֵּיהֶן	*but by doing so, you have made*[31]
מֹטוֹת בַּרְזֶל	*crossbars of iron in place of them.*

---

intended by this is the "yoke", complete with all its elements. When instead, in the text, attention is paid to the "yoke" or rather, to the "collar (of the yoke)", a concrete object in relation to the symbolic gesture of Jeremiah, other vocabulary words are used in alternation, sometimes in the singular, other times in the plural, with a coherence that is not always immediately evident: 27:2 speaks of מוֹסֵרוֹת "halters, tethers, ties, ropes" and of מֹטוֹת, which I have translated with the plural "poles" (the LXX translates with the pl. of κλοιος, "collar"; the Vg with *catenas,* "chains"), probably in reference to the pegs, bars, or wooden posts that are inserted in special holes lengthwise with respect to the principal axis of the yoke, which would then be positioned to the right and left of the neck of the beast of burden, to then be secured by cords or other straps (to get an approximative idea, see also G. SCHUMACHER, «Der arabische Pflug», *ZDPV* 12 [1889] 157–166; L. TURKOWSKI, «Peasant Agriculture in the Judean Hills», *PEQ* 101 [1969] 21–33, 101–112, esp. p. 30 and the Figures: *b* on p. 29 and *g,h* on pg. 102). In 28:10, 12, what Jeremiah wears on his neck and what Hananiah breaks is called מוֹטָה (while the LXX, in vv. 10, 12, 13 still uses, as in 27:2, the pl. of κλοιος, a singular that for the synecdoche (cf. Isa 58:6) should be referred to as "collar" (made up of מוֹסֵרוֹת and מֹטוֹת). In v. 13, in fact, the plural מֹטוֹת returns, which some read as a singular ("yoke"), despite the attestation of the plural form in 27:2 and the indication in Lev 26:13; Ezek 34:27 (from which it can clearly be gathered that the yoke can be composed of different מֹטוֹת; cf. also Ezek 30:18). Commentators have attempted to overcome these difficulties both by hypothesising a "generic plural" (for v. 13) and by seeking to precisely determine the elements that made up the agricultural instrument in question. For more information, see W.L. HOLLADAY, *Jeremiah 2*, 119–120; A. BAUMANN, «מוט», *ThWAT* IV, 728–734; H. SCHMOLDT, «עֹל», *ThWAT* VI, 79–83; C.L. TYER, «Yoke», *ABD* VI, 1026–1027; P.J. KING, *An Archaeological Companion,* Louisville 1993, 159–162; and the meticulous analysis of Å. VIBERG, *Prophets in Action.* An Analysis of Prophetic Symbolic Acts in the Old Testament, CB.OT 55, Stockholm 2007, 130–140, whose semantic analysis with which I substantially concur, myself distinguishing between the "collar" (the concrete and compositive object fabricated by Jeremiah with cords and pieces of wood, a part of which was then broken by Hananiah) and the "yoke" in its entirety, as an agricultural instrument, which 27–28 refers to in a metaphorical sense. Making, regardless, an important distinction: as I will elaborate later (cf. § 4.1.4), the instrument in question could also recall, in an allusive sense, the instruments utilised in ancient times to control and transport prisoners and slaves, and this would bestow the symbolic vector of the "yoke" with a twofold referential value (the isotopy of the animal/agricultural world and that of humankind in relation to war and slavery).

31   Following the LXX, which anticipates, with the 1ˢᵗ pers. sing. (ποιήσω), the meaning of the verb τίθημι in the following v. 14 (where the subj. of the action is YHWH), not a few modern versions opt, in fact, for a textual facilitation ("I will do" rather than "you have done"). For my part, I prefer to keep the reading of the MT, not only for its support of Vg, Syr, and Tg, but also for exegetic reasons (cf. ch. V, § 3.2.8). The gesture of Hananiah, in fact, constitutes an *intensification* of the rejection of the word of truth announced by Jeremiah. To this, while preserving the reading of the MT, an *exacerbation* of the subjugation to the foreign power announced by the prophet of Anathoth corresponds almost as a counterpoint.

312   Jer 27–28. The world beneath the yoke of the king of Babylon

כִּי כֹה־אָמַר יְהוָה צְבָאוֹת אֱלֹהֵי יִשְׂרָאֵל	**14**	*For thus says the Lord of hosts, God of Israel:*
עֹל בַּרְזֶל נָתַתִּי עַל־צַוַּאר כָּל־הַגּוֹיִם הָאֵלֶּה		*I placed a yoke of iron on the neck of all these nations*
לַעֲבֹד אֶת־נְבֻכַדְנֶאצַּר		*that they shall serve Nabuchadnezzar,*
מֶלֶךְ־בָּבֶל וַעֲבָדֻהוּ		*king of Babylon, and indeed they shall serve him!*
וְגַם אֶת־חַיַּת הַשָּׂדֶה נָתַתִּי לוֹ		*Even the wild animals I have given him."*
וַיֹּאמֶר יִרְמְיָה הַנָּבִיא	**15**	Then the prophet Jeremiah said
אֶל־חֲנַנְיָה הַנָּבִיא		to the prophet Hananiah:
שְׁמַע־נָא חֲנַנְיָה לֹא־שְׁלָחֲךָ יְהוָה		*"Listen Hananiah! The Lord has not sent you,*
וְאַתָּה הִבְטַחְתָּ אֶת־הָעָם הַזֶּה עַל־שָׁקֶר		*and you induce these people to trust in a lie!*
לָכֵן כֹּה אָמַר יְהוָה הִנְנִי מְשַׁלֵּחֲךָ	**16**	*Therefore thus says the Lord: Behold, I will send you*
מֵעַל פְּנֵי הָאֲדָמָה הַשָּׁנָה		*away from the face of the earth. This very year*
אַתָּה מֵת כִּי־סָרָה דִבַּרְתָּ		*you will die, for you have encouraged rebellion*
אֶל־יְהוָה		*against the Lord."*
וַיָּמָת חֲנַנְיָה הַנָּבִיא בַּשָּׁנָה הַהִיא	**17**	The prophet Hananiah died that very year,
בַּחֹדֶשׁ הַשְּׁבִיעִי		in the seventh month.

2.3. Contextual insertion and delimitation of the communicative unit

Already, in ch. I, I presented a general mapping of the book of Jeremiah, highlighting the most relevant macro-units and their articulation. This reconnaissance allowed me to emphasise the presence of some interesting semiotic interactions between the different textual portions (and some of their support columns), and to infer that a specific communicative intentionality of a symbolic redactional sort had informed the overall structure of the work. Once having assessed the specific dislocation of the various texts pertaining to the theme of surrender to the king of Babylon, it was then possible to detect significative elements of meaning of an orientative nature for an initial hermeneutical approach.

A study of the immediate and proximate literary context of 21:1–10 then allowed us to verify *in situ*, that is, in a limited section of the book of Jeremiah, how these organisational criteria operate in a similar manner on the local level as well, in the arrangement of smaller units. Indeed, the presence of "semiotic *arcatas*" that link, over varied distances, broad sections or load-bearing chapters of the book (as in the case of ch. 1; 25 and 52) occurs yet again on a reduced scale, but in a way that is more complex, in the section comprised of chs. 21–24, where the initiating position of 21:1–10 plays a key role in relation to all of the following units. Indeed, the semiotic *arcatas* that reach the subsequent texts at varying distances and interface with them, establishing hermeneutical relationships relevant for an overall understanding, originate herein.

Analogous compositional phenomena can be detected in the case of chs. 27–28 as well. Despite being two autonomous textual units,[32] together, they constitute a broader block, which, in turn, interacts with the subsequent chapter (Jer 29, this too endowed

---

32   See e.g. T. SEIDL, *Texte und Einheiten*, 19–24, 65, who believes they have a different origin (p. 271); as does A. GRAUPNER, *Auftrag und Geschick des Propheten Jeremia. Literarische Eigenart, Herkunft und Intention vordeuteronomistischer Prosa im Jeremiabuch*, BTSt 15, Neukirchen-Vluyn 1991, 61.

Jer 27-28: A first approach to the textual data   313

with its own relative independence),[33] delineating a circumscribed literary unit on
an even higher level.[34] This unifying framework is made up of a common historical
contextual setting (the time of King Zedekiah) for the words and gestures of Jeremiah
and by the repetition in different (isomorphic) forms of the same prophetic message
regarding submission to the king of Babylon, proclaimed in open contrast to the false
prospects of hope sustained by the false prophets.[35] What comes before these chapters
and what follows, apart from the unsurprising reuse and relative development of previous thematics,[36] seems to distance itself fairly distinctly, both for motives that are
formal and content-related motives and for actual dating. Chapter 26, in fact, takes
place at the time of Jehoiakim and the scene recounted therein is indubitably ascribable to that precise period (as opposed to the incongruous relationship between 27:1
and the following verses), while a new literary unit placed immediately after ch. 29,
the "book of consolation" (chs. 30-31), contains oracles in poetry and has no explicit
temporal anchoring. Actually, by keeping in mind another, distant communicative
unit (chs. 37-38), we will discover that the heuristic importance of the category of
"semiotic *arcata*" holds still more surprises. I will only deal with this, however, in the
following chapter, as it relates to the contextualisation of 38:14-28a (cf. ch. V, §§ 2.4-5).

Within the unit comprised of chs. 27-29, signalled by minor, though also significative,[37] linguistic elements, the particular independence of ch. 29 need regardless

---

33   Cf. T. SEIDL, *Texte*.1. Teil, 89-90.
34   As e.g. W. RUDOLPH, *Jeremia*, 172-173; A. WEISER, *Das Buch Jeremia.* II, 236-237;
     W. THIEL, *Jeremia 26-45*, 5; R.P. CARROLL, *Jeremiah*, 523-524.
35   To this, linguistic motivations are also added, which are emphasised by some com-
     mentators. See e.g. W.L. HOLLADAY, *Jeremiah 2*, 114, and also J.R. LUNDBOM, *Jeremiah
     21-36*, 304, who points to how, from the redactional point of view as well, there is no
     consensus in attributing ch. 27 to one of the classic "sources" of S. Mowinckel, unlike
     ch. 28, which is commonly assimilated to the material in "source" B (biographic prose
     of Baruch or, in any case, deemed to depend in some manner from an eyewitness).
36   The problematic dating of 27:1, however one is to understand it (as a scribal error
     or as a symbolic clue to be deciphered), constitutes a connection with ch. 26 that is
     only formal (cf. 26:1). Above all, what should be underscored is the mention made of
     the priests, the prophets, and the people (27:9, 13, 14, 16, 18; etc.; cf. 23:34; 26:7; etc.);
     cf Nebuchadnezzar as true servant of YHWH (27:6; cf. 25:9); of the deportation of
     Jehoiachin (27:10, 15; cf. 24:1); of the theme of false prophecy (27:10, 15; 28; cf. 23:9-
     40); of the alternative between death and life (27:13, 17; cf. 21:8); and of the threat of
     the catastrophe (27:17; cf. 22:5). Cf. T. SEIDL, *Formen und Formeln*, 180; G. FISCHER,
     Jeremia 26-52, 47.
37   Cf. what was found in note 13 in relation to the particular spelling of the names of
     Jeremiah and Nebuchadnezzar, of which the occurrence (8x each) is concentrated
     right in section 27:1-29, 3. The phenomenon, according to G. FISCHER, *Jeremia
     26-52*, 48, would be most certainly intentional (even if rather enigmatic) and can-
     not be adequately explained by the traditional hypothesis of literary criticism. For
     his part, J. KRISPENZ, *Literarkritik und Stilstatistik im Alten Testament.* Eine Studie
     zur literarkritischen Methode, durchgeführt an Texten aus den Büchern Jeremia,
     Ezechiel und 1 Könige, BZAW 307, Berlin – New York 2001, 109-115; ID., «Namen im
     Jeremiabuch. Ein Vergleich zwischen Jer 1-10 und Jer 26-35», in: *Sprachen – Bilder –
     Klänge*. Dimensionen der Theologie im Alten Testament und in seinem Umfeld, eds.
     C. KARRER-GRUBE *et al.*, AOAT 359, Münster 2009, 39-53 (here, p. 39), traces the

314   Jer 27–28. The world beneath the yoke of the king of Babylon

be recognised, as it contains Jeremiah's letter to those in exile.[38] For this very reason, Jer 29 merits a separate study. Chapters 27–28, on the other hand, are strictly linked: they deal with two episodes (cf. 27:1 and 28:1) that are distinct yet contiguous, be it for their dating (both take place during the year 594,[39] a short time from the uprisings reported in the Babylonian Chronicles, which exploded in Babylon against Nebuchadnezzar the year spanning the end of 595 and beginning of 594),[40] and for the theme of the yoke and clash with Hananiah developed in ch. 28, which clearly presuppose what is recounted in ch. 27.

2.4. Compositional arrangement

On the basis of the most significative rhetorical phenomena, the following structuralisation can be defined.[41] This presents a textual whole endowed with a coherent, balanced articulation and, at the same time, allows for the focalisation of the semiotic elements that are significative for an initial hermeneutical act.

---

phenomenon instead to the *casual* distribution of simple orthographical variants and denies that they have any likely impact on the identification of Jer 27–29 as independent literary stratification (as is instead sustained by W. RUDOLPH, *Jeremia*, 172–173, and the many scholars who maintain his same position). On the contrary, according to the recent and well-documented study of diachronic linguistics signed by A.D. HORNKOHL, *Ancient Hebrew Periodization*, 68: "the linguistic distinctiveness of Jer 27–29 is strong evidence of their independence", and although some typical characteristics of late Hebrew can be noted, these are, for the author, very reduced in number in 27–29, and so these "cannot substantiate a date of composition later than the Restoration". In any case, in my opinion, the thematic connection remains the strongest argument (or at least, the most evident) and I will address (in the following chapter of the present dissertation) the particular relation between chs. 27–29 and the preceding ch. 26 from precisely this point of view.

38 Cf. 29:1: "These are the words of the "letter" that Jeremiah sent [...]"; וְאֵלֶּה דִּבְרֵי הַסֵּפֶר אֲשֶׁר שָׁלַח יִרְמְיָה.

39 G. FISCHER, *Jeremia 26–52*, 50, who maintains the reference to Jehoiakim, places ch. 27 in the year 608, thus creating a temporal short-circuit between the incorrect dating of 27:1 and the events narrated in the ch. itself, clearly set under the reign of Zedekiah. According to this author, the dates should be understood only as symbolic indications (their scope would be that of demonstrating how both the kingdoms were subject to the Babylonian power), but then to contextualise the passage, he gives his preference to the year 608. This approach does not seem congruous to me. Supposing, and not granting, the symbolic value of reference to Jehoiakim, this should be assumed as such, opting for a correct temporal placement for its dating, rather precisely deducible (and compatible with the extrabiblical sources) from the events narrated in 27–28.

40 Cf. H. SCHMIDT, «Das Datum», 138–144; W.L. HOLLADAY, *Jeremiah 2*, 118, 127. For greater details on the reconstruction of the historical context of reference, see ch. II, § 2.2.2. of my dissertation.

41 Also in this case, to favour the identification of the principal phenomenon of textual composition (emphasised by the repetition of lexemes and/or syntagms) I propose a translation that is more literal than that offered previously.

Jer 27–28: A first approach to the textual data   315

2.4.1. Rhetorical analysis of Jer 27. Universal perspective and particular focalisation

I	A	1 In the beginning of the reign of Jehoiakim [Zedekiah], son of Josiah, king of Judah, this word came to Jeremiah from the Lord:
	Ia	2 «**THUS SAYS THE LORD**: Make straps and (yoke) crossbars and put them on your neck; 3 then send them to the king of Edom, to the king of Moab, to the king of the sons of Ammon, to the king of Tyre, and to the king of Sidon, through the ambassadors that are coming to Jerusalem to ZEDEKIAH, KING OF JUDAH; 4 and command them for their masters:
	Ib	**THUS SAYS THE LORD** *of hosts, the God of Israel:* Thus you shall say to your masters: 5 I made the earth, humankind and the animals that are on the face of the earth, with my great power and by my outstretched arm, and I give it to whomever seems right in my eyes. 6 And now I have given all these lands into the hand of Nebuchadnezzar, king of Babylon, my *servant* (√עבד); *even the beasts of the field I have given to him* to *serve* him (√עבד). 7 And so all the nations *shall serve* (√עבד) him, his son and his son's son, until the time comes for him and his own land as well; then *he will be made a slave* (√עבד) by great nations and powerful kings. 8 And it shall come to pass that the nation or kingdom that will not want *to serve him* (√עבד), Nebuchadnezzar king of Babylon, and that will not want to place its neck under the yoke of the king of Babylon, by sword, famine and plague will I punish that nation, **ORACLE OF THE LORD**, until I have completely destroyed them by his hand.
		9 So you *must not listen* to your prophets, nor to your diviners, nor your dreamers, nor your enchanters, nor your sorcerers, who say to you: "*You must not serve* (√עבד) *the king of Babylon!*". 10 For they are prophesying lies to you, so you will be driven out of your land, for I cast you out and you shall perish. 11 But the nation that **will place** (√בוא) **its neck under the yoke of the king of Babylon** and *will serve* (√עבד) him, I will let rest in its land, **ORACLE OF THE LORD**, they *will till* (√עבד) it and dwell in it.

IIa		12 **I SPOKE** already (דִּבַּרְתִּי) to ZEDEKIAH KING OF JUDAH according to all these words: **place** (בוֹא√) **your neck under the yoke of the king of Babylon,** *serve* him (עבד√) and his people and you will live! 13 Why would you and your people want to die by the sword, famine, and plague as the Lord has spoken concerning the nation that will not *serve* (עבד√) the king of Babylon?
		14 Therefore *do not listen* to the words of the prophets that are telling you: "*You must not serve* (עבד√) *the king of Babylon!*". For they are prophesying a lie to you! 15 I have not sent them at all, **ORACLE OF THE LORD**, but they prophesy falsely in my name, so that I cast you out and you shall perish, you and the _prophets_ who prophesy to you.
II		16 **I SPOKE** (דִּבַּרְתִּי) also to the priests and to all the people, saying: **THUS SAYS THE LORD**: *do not listen* to the words of your _prophets_ who prophesy to you: "Behold *THE VESSELS* (כְּלֵי) of the *HOUSE OF THE LORD* (בֵּית יְהוָה) will soon be brought back from Babylon"; for these prophesy lies to you. 17 **Do not listen to them!** *Serve* (עבד√) *the king of Babylon* and you shall live! Why should this city (הָעִיר הַזֹּאת) be laid waste? 18 If they really are prophets and the word of the Lord is with them, let them instead intercede with the LORD OF HOSTS so that the *VESSELS* (הַכֵּלִים) REMAINING (יתר√) in the *HOUSE OF THE LORD* (בֵּית יְהוָה) and in the *HOUSE OF THE KING OF JUDAH* (וּבֵית מֶלֶךְ־יְהוּדָה) *and in JERUSALEM* (וִירוּשָׁלַם) NOT GO TO BABYLON!
	IIb	19 For **THUS SAYS THE LORD** *of hosts* concerning the pillars, the "sea", the stands and the REST (יֶתֶר) of the *VESSELS* (הַכֵּלִים) REMAINING (יתר√) in this city (הָעִיר הַזֹּאת): 20 those that Nabuchadnezzar king of Babylon did not take, when he deported Jeconiah, son of Jehoiakim king of Judah, from Jerusalem to Babylon along with all the nobles of Judah and Jerusalem. 21 Indeed **THUS SAYS THE LORD** *of the hosts, God of Israel*, concerning the *VESSELS* (הַכֵּלִים) REMAINING (יתר√) in the *HOUSE OF THE LORD* (בֵּית יְהוָה) and in the *HOUSE OF THE KING OF JUDAH* (וּבֵית מֶלֶךְ־יְהוּדָה) *AND IN JERUSALEM* (וִירוּשָׁלַם): 22 THEY WILL BE TAKEN TO BABYLON and there THEY WILL REMAIN (יתר√) until the day that I will visit them, **ORACLE OF THE LORD**, and I will BRING THEM BACK AND RESTORE THEM TO THIS PLACE».

Here, I have illustrated the principal motifs that, in my opinion, justify the textual organisation of ch. 27 in *two* principal parts (I and II), in turn subdivided into two subparts (Ia-Ib and IIa-IIb).

Each unit, in both its principal parts and respective subparts, has a clear *initial term* composed of precise *verba dicendi* (אמר√ and דבר√) that assume an evident introductive function of a structural nature. In the first part, and in each of the two subparts (Ia: vv. 2–4a[42] and Ib: vv. 4b-11), the initial term is composed of the well-known messenger formula כֹּה־אָמַר יְהוָה ("thus says the Lord"; cf. vv. 2 and 5). Between Ia and IIb, the phrases "and commands (צוה√ pi.) them concerning their masters (אֶל־אֲדֹנֵיהֶם)" and

---

42 Verse 1 is to be considered as a whole with the first passage, but I prefer to emphasise it (A) by placing it in relation to 28:1 (B). Indeed, both verses, redactional in nature, have a clear function for both chs. 27 and 28 and refer to each other, placing the episodes at the beginning of the reign of Zedekiah (with the emendation of 27:1; cf. n. 6).

"Thus you will say (אמר√) to your masters (אֶל־אֲדֹנֵיכֶם)" should be noted as having the function of *middle terms* (*catchwords* or *Stichworte*).

Instead, in v. 12, there is an important caesura, marked by the initial term given by the perfect דִּבַּרְתִּי ("I spoke"), which in v. 16 also marks the beginning of the subpart IIb (vv. 16–22), also accompanied at the beginning of the II part, in v. 12, by the syntagm צִדְקִיָּהוּ מֶלֶךְ יְהוּדָה ("Zedekiah king of Judah"). This is how the message of Jeremiah is introduced, first addressed to Zedekiah, and then to the priests and all the people (v. 16).

The expression נְאֻם־יְהוָה ("oracle of the Lord") with the value of *final term* (cf. vv. 11, 15, 22) also marks both the closure of parts IIa (v. 11) and IIb (v. 22), and of some subparts (vv. 5–8; 9–11 in Ia; 12–15 and 19–22 in IIb). Within part IIb, once again, we find the *Botenformel* (in vv. 16, 19, 21) with a subsidiary dividing function (cf. the smaller units of vv. 16–18 and 19–22).[43] The position of the imperative in 2nd pers. pl. אַל־תִּשְׁמְעוּ calling to "not listen to" the false prophets and their message should also be noted. This is even repeated four times (vv. 9, 14, 16, 17) with the function of *initial term* identifying the beginning of IIb (vv. 16 and 17) and the smaller units given by vv. 9–11; 14–15.

Finally, I will note that the messenger formula is extended twice by the locution [יְהוָה] צְבָאוֹת אֱלֹהֵי יִשְׂרָאֵל ("[Lord] of hosts, God of Israel"), at precisely the beginning of part Ib (v. 5) and practically at the end of IIb (v. 21), thus rhetorically highlighting the unity of Jeremiah's discourse, which encompasses and threads through units Ib, IIa, and IIb.

Other significative elements, present in both parts of the text with unifying value (*catchwords*) and as clues to the main theme, are the strong presence of עבד√ ("I serve; to serve, make subservient, cultivate"; 12x, in vv. 6–14, 17) tied to the figure of the king of Babylon, and of נבא√ ("to prophetise"), a root always placed in syntagmatic relation to the lexeme שֶׁקֶר ("falsehood"; vv. 10, 14–16).

As thematic clues (expressed by specific lexical elements) that provide a transition to the content-related data in Jer 27, I will point out the counterposition between *negative event – positive event* attested in both the parts: In part I by בַּחֶרֶב וּבָרָעָב וּבַדֶּבֶר ("with the sword, hunger, and plague") + פקד√ ("to punish"), תמם√ ("to exterminate"; v. 8), נדח√ ("to banish"), אבד√ ("to die"; v. 10), to which are placed in opposition נוח√ ("to let rest"), עבד√ ("to cultivate"), ישב√ ("to inhabit"; v. 11); in part II with מות√ ("to die")

---

43 Part IIb is also characterised, in the two minor units that comprise it (vv. 16–18 and 19–22), by the recurrence of the term הַכֵּלִים ("the vessels") in vv. 16, 8, 19, 21, almost always placed in reference (except in v. 19) to the בֵּית־יְהוָה ("house of the Lord"). In particular, with the function of *final terms,* they appear at the end of the above-mentioned units of a lower level, following lexical elements in the same order, with a structural function (cf. vv. 18, 21): יְהוָה צְבָאוֹת ("Lord of hosts") + הַכֵּלִים ("the vessels") + יתר√ ("to remain") + בְּבֵית־יְהוָה ("in the house of the Lord") + וּבֵית מֶלֶךְ־יְהוּדָה ("and in the house of the king of Judah") + וִירוּשָׁלָם ("and in Jerusalem"). Also of note is the oppositive relation between the "to remain" (יתר√; vv. 18, 19) of the furnishings in the house of the Lord with their "to be taken (בוא√) to Babylon" and their "to remain" (יתר√) there, and between the term "Babylon" (v. 18; used again, in any case, in v. 22), with the term "this place" (i.e. Jerusalem, and specifically, the "house of the Lord", the destination of the return of the same furnishings; v. 22). The function of the *catchwords* can instead be identified in the expressions הָעִיר הַזֹּאת ("this city") and in יתר√ (together with the noun יֶתֶר), which recur in vv. 17 and 19.

318   Jer 27–28. The world beneath the yoke of the king of Babylon

בַּחֶרֶב בָּרָעָב וּבַדֶּבֶר + ("with the sword, hunger, and plague"; v. 13) + √נדח ("to banish"), √אבד ("to die"; v. 15), √היה + [...] + חָרְבָּה ("to be reduced to ruins"; v. 17), √בוא ("to be taken [to Babylon]"), √היה ("to remain" [in Babylon]; v. 22), counterbalanced by √פקד ("to visit"),[44] √עלה ("to bring up out of"), √שוב ("to make return/restore"; v. 22). It should be noted that the two final positive outcomes mark both part I and part II.

From the point of view of the development of the – rather complex – discourse, I will highlight the following ordered articulation:

+ Part Ia (vv. 2–4a): after the title (v. 1), the Lord's command is presented with regard to the symbolic gesture to enact on the part of the prophet and concerning the words that should accompany it.

+ Part Ib (vv. 4b–11): this is the discourse to be addressed directly to the ambassadors who, in turn, are to report it to their respective sovereigns. In the first of the secondary units (vv. 4b–8), the design of YHWH on the *contemporary history* is presented, by which the world is delivered into the power of the king of Babylon, while in the second (vv. 9–11), its *operational consequence* is derived, condensed in the imperative of not listening to voices to the contrary and of unconditional submission.

+ Part IIa (vv. 12–15): is the same message regarding submission to the king of Babylon reported in the first sub-unit (vv. 12–13) as it was previously addressed to Zedekiah and followed in the second sub-unit (vv. 14–15) by the pressing invitation to not give credence to the deceitful hopes divulged by the false prophets.

+ Part IIb (vv. 16–22): is dedicated to the priests and the rest of the people. These are other recipients who the same prophetic ministry has already reached. The first second-level unit (vv. 16–18) opens directly with the imperative to "not listen", having the false prophets as its object once again, while the second sub-unit (vv. 19–22) predicts the requisition of the furnishings remaining in the temple.

An *overview* of the various elements enables us, moreover, to highlight this balanced division (of a thematic nature, but founded on formal elements as well) of the text[45]: part I (with its relative sub-units) opens onto an extranational horizon (which I conventionally indicate as a *universal* perspective or dimension), while part II (with its two sub-units) focalises attention on the immediate recipients of the Jeremianic message (King Zedekiah; cf. v. 12: part IIa; the priests and all the people; cf. v. 16: part IIb), in other words, the kingdom of Judah in its various social and institutional components (*particular* perspective).

---

44   Interesting is the counterposition created by the use of the same verb √פקד, which, in part I, v. 8 means to make himself present in a punitive sense (i.e. to punish), while in part II, v. 22 means to make himself present in the salvific sense (to free, to bring the people back from exile).

45   I will look at these more closely in § 2.4.3, keeping the structure of ch. 28 in mind as well.

2.4.2. *Rhetorical analysis of Jer 28. Resumption of the particular perspective and return to the universal dimension*

I	**B**	1 *IN THAT SAME YEAR* (בַּשָּׁנָה הַהִיא), in the beginning of the reign of Zedekiah, *KING OF JUDAH*, in the fourth *YEAR* (שָׁנָה), *IN THE* fifth *MONTH* (בַּחֹדֶשׁ), it came to be that *HANANIAH*, son of Azzur, the *PROPHET* of Gabaon, said to me in the *HOUSE OF THE LORD* (בֵּית יְהוָה), in front of all the priests and *ALL THE PEOPLE*:
	Ia	2 "**THUS SAYS THE LORD** *of hosts, God of Israel*: **I break** (√שׁבר) the **yoke** (עֹל) **of the king of Babylon!** 3 *WITHIN TWO YEARS* I *will restore* (√שׁוב) to this place (הַמָּקוֹם הַזֶּה) all the *VESSELS* (כְּלִים) of the *LORD'S HOUSE* (בֵּית יְהוָה), which Nabuchadnezzar, king of Babylon, took away from this place (הַמָּקוֹם הַזֶּה) and had carried to Babylon, 4 just as I will *bring back* (√שׁוב) to this place (הַמָּקוֹם הַזֶּה) also Jeconiah himself, son of Jehoiakim, king of Judah, and all the exiles from Judah who went to Babylon, <u>**ORACLE OF THE LORD**</u>, for **I will break** (√שׁבר) the **yoke** (עֹל) **of the king of Babylon.**"
	Ib	5 Then the **prophet Jeremiah** responded to the **prophet Hananiah** in front of the priests and in front of *ALL THE PEOPLE* who were standing in the *HOUSE OF THE LORD* (בֵּית יְהוָה): 6 The **prophet Jeremiah** said: "Amen! May the Lord do this! May the Lord fulfil that which you have prophesied, *restoring* (√שׁוב) from Babylon in this place (הַמָּקוֹם הַזֶּה) all the exiles and the *VESSELS* (כְּלִים) of the *HOUSE OF THE LORD* (בֵּית יְהוָה)! 7 But now hear what I have to say to your ears and to the ears of all the people: 8 The prophets who came before me and you from ancient times prophesied against many countries (אֲרָצוֹת רַבּוֹת) and against great kingdoms (מַמְלָכוֹת גְּדֹלוֹת) war (מִלְחָמָה), calamity (רָעָה), and plague (דֶּבֶר). 9 As for the prophet who prophesies peace (שָׁלוֹם): only when his word shall come to pass shall he be recognised as a prophet truly **SENT** (√שׁלח) by the Lord."
	Ic	10 Then the **prophet Hananiah** took the collar (מוֹטָה) from the neck of the **prophet Jeremiah** and **broke it** (√שׁבר). Then Hananiah in front of *ALL THE PEOPLE* said: 11 "<u>*THUS SAYS THE LORD*</u>: in this way **I will break** (√שׁבר) **the yoke** (עֹל) **of Nabuchadnezzar king of Babylon** *WITHIN TWO YEARS* (שְׁנָתַיִם) time from the neck *of all the nations* (כָּל־הַגּוֹיִם)!". And the **prophet Jeremiah WENT** (√הלך) *on his way* (לְדַרְכּוֹ).

(Apparent) end of the clash – new revelative event – epilogue

II	**IIa**	12 But the word of the Lord came unto **Jeremiah** after the **prophet Hananiah had broken** (√שבר) the collar (מוֹטָה) from the neck of the **prophet Jeremiah**: 13 "Go and tell Hananiah: **THUS SAYS THE LORD: you have broken** (√שבר) crossbars (מוֹטֹת) of wood, but by doing so, you have made crossbars (מוֹטֹת) of iron in place of them. 14 For **THUS SAYS THE LORD** *of hosts, God of Israel:* I placed a yoke (עֹל) of iron on the neck of <u>*all these nations*</u> (כָּל־הַגּוֹיִם) that they shall serve (√עבד) Nabuchadnezzar, king of Babylon, and indeed they shall serve him (√עבד)! **Even the wild animals I have given him.**"
	IIb	15 Then said the **prophet Jeremiah** to the **prophet Hananiah**: "Listen Hananiah! The Lord **HAS NOT SENT YOU** (√שלח), and you induce these people to trust in a lie! 16 Therefore *__THUS SAYS THE LORD:__* Behold, **I WILL SEND** (√שלח) you away from the face of the earth. This very *YEAR* (שָׁנָה) you will die (√מות), for you have *spoken* (√דבר) rebellion against the Lord." 17 The **prophet Hananiah** died (√מות) *THAT YEAR* (בַּשָּׁנָה הַהִיא), in the seventh *MONTH* (בַּחֹדֶשׁ).

Chapter 28, whose unitariness is well signalled in vv. 1 and 17 by the *inclusion* established by the temporal notations בַּשָּׁנָה הַהִיא ("in that year") and בַּחֹדֶשׁ ("in the month") + numeral, and by the repetition of the name of the (false) prophet Hananiah[46] (*extreme terms*), is also divisible in *two principal parts* (I and II), in turn subdividable into *three* (Ia-Ib-Ic) and *two* (IIa-IIb) *subparts* each. This articulation corresponds to the different stages of the clash between Jeremiah and Hananiah. Verse 1 (denominated B), being a temporal introduction in which terms and syntagms that already appeared in 27:1 reappear, such as בְּרֵאשִׁית מַמְלֶכֶת, ("beginning of the kingdom") + [name of the king] + מֶלֶךְ־יְהוּדָה ("king of Judah"), establishes a semiotic *arcata* with v. 1 of the preceding chapter (A), signalling the thematic-narrative continuity between the two scenes.

Let us now look at the most significative clues that can legitimise this structuralisation and highlight the thematic-formal articulations that are most important.

+ Part I (vv. 1–11) is identified at the beginning, besides by the just mentioned temporal indication, by the following elements, having the function of *initial terms*: in v. 1 the name Hananiah and his title of נָבִיא ("prophet"), in v. 2, the messenger formula כֹּה־אָמַר יְהֹוָה (extended here) and √שבר ("I break/will break") + עֹל ("yoke"). Other elements have a delimiting function instead, as *extreme terms*: the term עַם ("people") in vv. 2 and 10, the temporal notation that appears in v. 3 and then in v. 11 בְּעוֹד שְׁנָתַיִם יָמִים ("within two years") and the phrase √שבר ("I break/will break") + עֹל ("the yoke") + מֶלֶךְ בָּבֶל ("of the king of Babylon"), a proposition that is twice repeated (vv. 2 and 4) and then returns at the close in v. 11. Also of note to that effect is the oppositional relationship between the indication of the place (with theological significance) where the scene takes place, expressed by the syntagm בְּבֵית יְהֹוָה ("in the house of the Lord"), and Jeremiah's abandonment of it to go √הלך + לְדַרְכּוֹ ("on his way"), an act that puts an end to the narrative tension of this first part.

---

46 Note also that the text opens with a locutory act on the part of Hananiah (qualified as a "prophet" without any value judgement, as opposed to the LXX), introduced by √אמר, and closes with a reference to the same subject and same act (judged, in the end, as a lie [v. 15: שֶׁקֶר] and instigation to rebellion [v. 16: סָרָה]) with another *verbum dicendi*, this time √דבר (v. 16).

Jer 27–28: A first approach to the textual data   321

This movement verb calls attention to some lexemes from the same semantic field that act as *final terms* of the two parts: for part I, in addition to √הלך in v. 11, also √שלח ("to send") in v. 9 should be mentioned, while as *final terms* at the conclusion of part II, in vv. 15 and 16, √שלח appears 2x.

Part I can be further subdivided into three subparts: Ia (vv. 2–4), with the *Botenformel* כֹּה־אָמַר יְהוָה as *initial term* and the expression נְאֻם־יְהוָה ("oracle of the Lord") as *final term*; Ib (vv. 5–9) and IIc (vv. 10–11), with the expressions "prophet Hananiah" and "prophet Jeremiah", and also כָּל־הָעָם ("all the people") as initial terms for both.

+ Part II (vv. 12–17) opens with a *Wortereignisformel*[47] that can be placed in dialectic relation to the communicative act of Hananiah at the beginning of part I (this likewise having been presented as an event of revelation by YHWH). In addition to the above-mentioned *final terms* (vv. 15 and 16: √שלח), part II is also delimited by the reuse of elements already highlighted in the opening of part I, having the value of *initial terms*: in v. 12, the lexemes נָבִיא ("prophet") and the name "Hananiah", the synonymical (with respect to that in v. 2) expression √שבר ("to break") + מוֹטָה ("to collar [with a yoke]"), replicated in another analogous variant in v. 13 with √שבר + מוֹטֹת ("crossbars"). The same v. 13 sees the return of the messenger formula כֹּה־אָמַר יְהוָה (without any extension). In the same passage (in v. 14), the *Botenformel* reappears with the extension "[Lord] of hosts, God of Israel" ([יְהוָה] צְבָאוֹת אֱלֹהֵי יִשְׂרָאֵל), which, with the recurrence in v. 2 of the selfsame expression, serves as an inclusion for the entire chapter.

Here as well, the couples of "prophet Hananiah" and "prophet Jeremiah" return as *initial terms*, on the basis of which (other than for thematic reasons), a further subdivision of part II can be made in another two minor units: IIa (vv. 12–14) and IIb (vv. 15–17).

From the content-related point of view, the development of the story is coherent: intervention of the prophet Hananiah (B + Ia); personal response of Jeremiah (Ib); symbolic counter-gesture of Hananiah and confirmation of his proclamation (Ic); word of the Lord addressed to Jeremiah, introduced by a *Wortereignisformel* (II) which, (a) confirms the design of God on the nations and their subjugation to the king of Babylon (IIa: vv. 12–14), and (b) becomes a condemnatory judgement against the false prophet (IIb: vv. 15–17). Moreover, mention should be made of the close relationship established between the end of part I (v. 9), which sets out the criterion of the *fulfilment* of the word spoken by the prophet, this being a sure parameter of reference for its discernment and recognition in history, and the end of part II (v. 17), where we see narrated the actual realisation of the prophetic word of Jeremiah, who had preannounced the death of the (false) prophet Hananiah (cf. Deut 18:20–22).

Even the *overall vision* of this chapter, considered above all on the basis of the criteria of a formal nature that have been highlighted, allows for the identification of a balanced division of the text that plays out along the same perspectival lines as those in ch. 27, though in reverse order[48]: the first two subparts (IIa and IIb), in fact, have the *particular* situation of Judah (the exiles and the temple furnishings) as their

---

47   Cf. T. SEIDL, «Die Wortereignisformel in Jeremia. Beobachtungen zu den Formen der Redeeröffnung in Jeremia, im Anschluss an Jer 27,1.2», *BZ* 23 (1979) 20–47.

48   Consider, amongst the various formal elements that can be highlighted (in reference to the temple and the vessels), the significant expression "this place" (הַמָּקוֹם הַזֶּה) in vv. 3(3x) and 4 (part I), and in v. 6 (part II).

322   Jer 27–28. The world beneath the yoke of the king of Babylon

object, while the third subpart (Ic) and the whole of II part brings the attention back to the *universal* dimension of the dominion of the king of Babylon.

This formal structuralisation is confirmed by an important *narrative caesura* situated between v. 11 and v. 12. This is also signalled in various ways by all of the most ancient and important manuscripts that have been handed down to us. Given the important exegetic implications of the phenomenon, I will return to discuss the subject in further depth in § 5.3.3. Here, I will limit myself to emphasising that the two parts highlighted by the rhetorical analysis correspond, from the point of view of the thematic-narrative dynamism of the text, to *two distinct scenes*[49]: as I have highlighted in the breakdown, a *first moment* is easily recognisable, in which the scene is dominated by the "evenly matched" clash between Hananiah and Jeremiah, consisting in part I. Instead, following v. 11, there is a considerable change of scene, with a duly marked, unprecedented revelatory event. It is a decisive *second narrative moment*, consisting of the II part, in which Jeremiah is the object of a revelatory event and subject of an about-face that concludes, as the narrator notes, with the unmasking and defeat of Hananiah.

2.4.3. Elements of unity and overall structure of chs. 27 and 28. Jerusalem and the nations, true and false prophecy

Various clues that are significative for rhetorical analysis confirm that chs. 27–28 can be studied as a relatively independent unit with respect to its immediate literary context (notwithstanding the relations it has with ch. 29 and the immediate context in general), and they solicit an act of reading capable of adequately highlighting the reciprocal and harmonious intersecting of the fundamental thematic lines that structure this unit and give order to its various components.

The *formal element* that appears to assume the function of *initial term,* as was already highlighted, is the temporal notion that acts as an *incipit* to the two chapters (A: 27:1 and B: 28:1). Despite the uncertainty of the textual transmission of 27:1, the configuration of a relationship of consequential succession can be recognised clearly (also on the basis of other internal data) between the two scenes of Jer 27 and 28.

This relationship is further reinforced by the repeated use of the expressions "this place" (הַמָּקוֹם הַזֶּה; cf. 27:22; 28:3, 4, 6); "the furnishings" (הַכֵּלִים; cf. 27:16, 18, 19, 21; 28:2, 5); "house of the Lord" (בֵית־יְהוָה; cf. 27:16, 18, 21; 28:1, 2, 5, 6); and of "to make return" (√שׁוב hi.; cf. 27:22; 28:3, 4), having the function of being *catchwords* between the end of ch. 27 (part IIb) and the beginning of ch. 28 (part Ia and Ib). The same elements, considered from a thematic point of view jointly with specification of the recipients of the Jeremianic message (the king Zedekiah, the priests, and all the people of Judah) that takes place in 27:12, 16 (thus contextualising the whole content of part II of ch. 27), indicate the *particular* frame of reference for this prophetic oracle.

Other important evidence of a *formal connection,* which also attest to the profound *thematic unity* given by the complementary *universalistic perspective* contained in the prophetic controversy underway, can be identified in the literal repetition of the

---

49   As is also highlighted by G. FISCHER, *Jeremia 26–52,* 67, who draws a distinction between a "Konfrontation zwischen Hananja und Jeremia" (vv. 1–11) and the "Gottes Wort durch Jeremia an Hananja" (vv. 12–17).

locution "I have given him even the wild animals of the field" (וְגַם אֶת־חַיַּת הַשָּׂדֶה נָתַתִּי לוֹ), which, positioned in 27:6 (part Ib) and 28 (part IIb), creates an inclusion of the whole unit chs. 27–28, and in the expression "all the nations" (כָּל־הַגּוֹיִם), which recurs both in 27:7 (part Ib) and in 28:11, 14[50] (parts Ic and IIa). Also significative to that effect is the formal correspondence between the following expressions, which are linked by a clear synonymic parallelism: גּוֹיִם רַבִּים וּמְלָכִים גְּדֹלִים ("great nations and powerful kings") in 27:7 (part Ib) and אֲרָצוֹת רַבּוֹת וְ[...] מַמְלָכוֹת גְּדֹלוֹת ("many countries and [...] great kingdoms") in 28:8 (part Ib).

Also to be noted is the inclusion and oppositive relationship created by use of the term מוֹטוֹת in 27:2 and in 28:13: in the first occurrence, at the beginning of the textual unit given by chs. 27–28, reference is made to the bars of a common *wooden* yoke, while, in closing, the same term is employed to indicate the bars of a metaphorical *iron* yoke imposed by God upon all the nations (in 28:14, we find the synonymical expression עֹל בַּרְזֶל instead). This oppositive relationship is clearly highlighted, moreover, in 28:13 through the counterpositioning of the expressions מוֹטֹת עֵץ and מֹטוֹת בַּרְזֶל.

On the level of the *thematic connection* between the two chapters, emphasis should be given to the symbolic gesture of the yoke requested of Jeremiah in 27:2–3 (followed by the explicative word of the message), that is, in the beginning of part I. In counterposition to this, in fact, in 28:10 (i.e. in the beginning of part Ic of this ch.), is the symbolic gesture of Hananiah, who breaks the "yoke" carried by Jeremiah and accompanies this action with a "prophetic" counter-word, a sign diametrically opposed to that of Jeremiah.

On precisely the basis of the various elements gathered, still from the point of view of the underlying thematic unity of chs. 27–28, an *internal structuralisation of a concentric type* can be highlighted, constituted by the fundamentally oppositive (and thematically complementary) relationship between the *universal* and *particular* perspectives by which the question of the Babylonian domination is presented according to the (controversial) prophetic reading of the design of God. This structuralisation can be presented schematically:

Jer 27		A	(v. 1)
	Universal perspective	Ia	(vv. 2–4a)
	Universal perspective	Ib	(vv. 4b-11)
	PARTICULAR PERSPECTIVE	IIa	(vv. 12–15)
	PARTICULAR PERSPECTIVE	IIb	(vv. 16–22)
Jer 28		B	(v. 1)
	PARTICULAR PERSPECTIVE	Ia	(vv. 2–4)
	PARTICULAR PERSPECTIVE	Ib	(vv. 5–9)
	Universal perspective	Ic	(vv. 10–11)
	Universal perspective	IIa-b	(vv. 12–17)

---

50 Note also the numerous synonimical variants (and the list of nations presented in 27:3–4): "all these lands" (כָּל־הָאֲרָצוֹת הָאֵלֶּה; 27:6); "land" (אֶרֶץ + suff. 3rd m.s.; 27:7); "the nation or kingdom" (הַגּוֹי וְהַמַּמְלָכָה; 27:8); "the nation" (הַגּוֹי; 27:8, 11, 13); "land" (אֲדָמָה + suff. 2nd m.s. in 27:10 and with suff. 3rd m.s. in 27:11).

324   Jer 27–28. The world beneath the yoke of the king of Babylon

As is summarised in the breakdown, which highlights the different textual perimeters, the call to submission put forth by Jeremiah is initially placed in relation to the *nations* (cf. 27:2–11: parts Ia and Ib), and only successively has the *particular* case of the kingdom of Judah in its various components (cf. 27:12–22: parts IIa and IIb) as its specific subject. Chapter 28, on the other hand, inverts the order, beginning with the resumption of the *particular* perspective on the part of Hananiah and Jeremiah (cf. 28:2–9: parts Ia and Ib),[51] to then returning to the *universal* one regarding the hegemony of Babylon over the nations (cf. 28:10–17: parts Ic and IIa-b). Thus, the *particular* question about the fate of the kingdom of Judah in relation to the Babylonian power remains at the (thematic and structural) centre, and this suggests that the evocation of the nations and their destiny has its own special significance in relation to the fate of Jerusalem, which remains the immediate aim of the prophetic Jeremianic message.

2.5. Content-related synthesis and focalisation of thematic saliencies

A detailed approach to the text, with philological notes and a meticulous mapping of the compositional logic, helps to give an account (at least an initial one) of the complexity of the textual elements and their reciprocal relations. Before continuing, however, it is worthwhile to briefly summarise the contents of the pericopes being studied, retracing the articulation of the biblical text. In this manner, I can highlight the focal points that, in a variety of manners, will be subject to discussion and hermeneutical reflection in my study hereinafter (while also being traced back to synthetic thematic polarities).

Chapter 27 opens with the signalling of a new word event: YHWH asks Jeremiah to enact a *symbolic gesture*. The prophet is to make a yoke (collar) and place it on his own neck. This is a very important *semiotic device* of prophetic communication, a sign that must reach even the ambassadors of the surrounding kingdoms that have gathered together to see the king Zedekiah (vv. 1–4a).

The verbal explication of the Jeremianic message regards the dominant theme of chs. 27–28: the need to *submit to the king of Babylon. God the creator of the heavens and earth* and *the Lord of history* now delivers the dominion of the world to Nebuchadnezzar, at least until an appointed time. For this reason, all the nations must submit to him or be subjected to divine punishment (vv. 4b-11).

Other prophetic voices claiming to speak in the name of YHWH call for the opposite, promising that YHWH will liberate Judah and the nations from the Babylonian yoke: but these *should not be obeyed,* Jeremiah declares, because theirs are only lies. The same message is addressed to Zedekiah: these false prophets should not be obeyed. Instead, necks should be bent beneath the yoke of the king of Babylon. The alternative is death (vv. 12–15).

---

51   Even if, already in 28:8, the universal perspective would seem to be reintroduced with the expression "many countries and great kingdoms", it appears clear from v. 9, in reference to the prophecy of Hananiah regarding the return of the vessels to the temple and the deported, that all of part Ib can be ascribed to the particular perspective centred on the kingdom of Judah.

Similar words are also addressed to the priests and all the people: these figures should by no means be listened to, even if they promise the return of the *temple furnishings* stolen in 597 with confidence. If they were true prophets of the Lord, they would be interceding with him so that something even worse did not come about and even the remaining furnishings be taken to Babylon. But this catastrophe is precisely what Jeremiah predicts, thus alluding to a new exile: these furnishings will be taken and carried to Babylon, and will remain there until YHWH has not decided that they should be returned (vv. 16–22). The question of the *profound motivations* for such misfortune and for submission as the most appropriate response according to the will of YHWH remains implicit, but pressing. The contextual reference is to the *totality of the book* of Jeremiah, and above all, to its third part, dedicated to the *oracles against/about the nations*.

Chapter 28 presents itself in *continuity* with this communicative framework, both on the level of the *symbolic gesture of the* yoke and the *verbal explication* of the message it implies. A representative of the aforementioned false prophets enters the scene: *Hananiah*. The question of the *discernment between true and false prophecy* thus becomes thematised clearly. In front of the priests and all the people, Hananiah gives voice to "another YHWH", who instead promises the *return* of the temple furnishings, king Coniah (Jehoiachin), and all the deportees of 597, even giving a very precise deadline: *within two years* (vv. 1–4).

Jeremiah shows that he has no immediate word of rebuttal from YHWH. In fact, he responds by acknowledging that the fulfilment of the prophecy of Hananiah would be desirable indeed. He does, however, put forth, as a *criterion of discernment,* the fact that the ancient prophets were instead concordant on *threats of misfortune,* while *oracles of peace* (in themselves more suspicious, since too correspondent to human expectations) can only be recognised in the very moment of their *realisation* (vv. 5–9).

Hananiah reacts decisively (indeed, violently) and spectacularly: he snatches the yoke carried by Jeremiah and breaks it, thus putting forth a *symbolic counter-gesture* accompanied by another oracular word. He reiterates the deadline of two years for the end of the Babylonian domination not only over Judah but over *all the nations* as well (vv. 10–11). In front of all the people, Jeremiah appears to lose the challenge of credibility. He has no word of response to proclaim in the name of YHWH, and this evidence forces him to *surrender* and to retreat in *silence,* far from the public sphere (vv. 10–11).

Only after this "surrender" does a new divine word reach Jeremiah, commanding him to relay a precise response to Hananiah for his claims of truth: his symbolic-prophetic act (since false and an expression of rebellion) has actually produced *exacerbation* of the guaranteed domination of the king of Babylon over all the nations. In a certain sense, all of creation has been subjected to him by God's will (vv. 12–14). Because of his *false prophecy* and the misleading effects it has on the people, Jeremiah prophesies to Hananiah his death as an unequivocal sign. And this, as the narrator notes, comes about promptly, within the time set by the Jeremianic oracle (vv. 15–17).

326 Jer 27–28. The world beneath the yoke of the king of Babylon

3. "Make yourself straps and yoke crossbars and put them on your neck" (27:2). The general communicative importance of an emblematic symbolic gesture in the book of Jeremiah

3.1. Preliminary considerations: Verbal communication and non-verbal communication in studies on biblical prophetism

The command given to Jeremiah by YHWH ushers us into the thematic of the so-called "symbolic gestures"[52] attested both within and outside of[53] biblical prophetism. Proper

---

52 The terminology of reference used by scholars to identify this kind of non-verbal communication used by the prophets varies significantly. I will indistinctively use both the expression "gesture/symbolic act" (fairly consolidated, beginning with the study by H.W. ROBINSON, «Prophetic Symbolism», in: *Old Testament Essays*, ed. D.C. SIMPSON, London 1927, 1–17, and immediately comprehensible, even if more generic, insofar as it can refer to acts that are typical of other fields of interest, such as culture, where, however, conventionality and repeatability are in force), and "prophetic gesture" (more technical, but also semantically more opaque, since it requires further specification). I will state immediately that thus doing, I do not intend to limit myself to an identification of the phenomenon that is based only on a hypothetical literary schema (or genre) of reference (like that proposed by G. FOHRER, *Die Symbolischen Handlungen der Propheten*, AThANT 54, Zürich 1953, ²1968, 18–19; the first version of his work, the results of which then remained unaltered even in the successive editions, can actually be traced back to his dissertation, defended in 1944; cf. ID. «Die Gattung der Berichte über symbolische Handlungen der Propheten», *ZAW* 64 [1952] 101–120). My perspective is that of modern communication theories (cf. e.g. the synthesis on non-verbal communication by L. ANOLLI, *Fondamenti*, 153–188). Other authors identify the phenomenon with other expressions (which correspond to different categorisations as well, which I cannot stop to look at), amongst which: "pantomime", "mime", "signe en action", "Zeichenhandlungen", "prophetischen Analogiehandlungen", "prophetische Körperhandlungen", "sign-acts", "street theatre"; "prophetic drama", "games prophets play", etc.

53 For the NT, think, above of, of the gestures of Jesus (the meal with the sinners, the expulsion of the vendors from the temple, the dried up fig tree, etc.) and the gesture of the Agabus in Acts 21:10–11, who binds his own feet and hands to prophetically reveal Paul's imprisonment. Beyond the biblical world, see the emblematic case attested in J.-M. DURAND, *Archives épistolaires de Mari I/1*, ARM 26/1, Paris 1988, 434–435, no. 206, where, before an assembly of elders, at the city gates, an ecstatic "prophet" of the god Dagan (technically, a *muḫḫûm*) devours a raw (or rather, living[!] lamb, the way a ferocious animal would) as an anticipatory sign of a devouring disaster. To delve further in this regard, see M. ASTOUR, «*Sparagmos*, Omophagia and Ecstatic Prophecy at Mari», *UF* 24 (1992) 1–2; J.-G. HEINTZ, «La "fin" des prophètes bibliques? Nouvelles théories et documents sémitiques anciens», in: *Oracles et prophéties dans l'antiquité. Actes du Colloque de Strasbourg (15–17 juin 1995)*, ed. J.-G. HEINTZ, Paris 1997, 195–214 (the argument is treated on pp. 202–212). For the Greek world (the most renowned case is perhaps that of the cynical philosopher Diogenes, about whom it is told that, amongst other things, he went around with a lantern in full daylight in search of a "true man"), see P. WENDLAND, «Symbolische Handlungen als Ersatz oder Begleitung der Rede», *NJKA* 19 (1916) 233–245.

"Make yourself straps and yoke crossbars and put them on your neck" (27:2)   327

treatment of this would require a series of quite broad, articulated, in-depth studies, impossible to carry out herein.[54] It is, however, useful to evaluate, at least summarily, the consideration that has been reserved for the question within the strands of research that have marked the path of the study of biblical prophetism over the last one hundred and fifty years.

The majority of the contributions dedicated to prophetic literature have taken on a perspective that is prevalently *historical-literary*, and this translates into at least two different expressions: the compositive dynamics that generated the current prophetic books have been examined analytically (think of the diachronic approach typical of *Redaktionsgeschichte* or *Redaction Criticism*), and a *comparativist approach* has been developed, made possible by the progressive discovery of interesting (albeit limited) extrabiblical documentation relating to the divinatory-prophetic practices used in certain areas and socio-cultural contexts typical of the ancient Near East.[55]

The first thread of research, after having ascertained the impossibility of segmenting the texts into "authentic" or "non-authentic" parts or sayings in a way that is certain[56] regarding elusive figures of historic (especially pre-exilic) prophets,[57] brought about a renewed understanding of prophetic literature as a complex and almost uninterrupted process of rewriting, carried out over generations by translators, directing the attention of scholars towards the phenomenon that is referred to as "scribal prophecy.[58] The comparativist approach, on the other hand, favoured (and can favour,

---

54   Though it is generated by the present research, I will postpone treatment of this to successive research, which I intend to dedicate to an exploration of the semiotic dynamics running through and structuring the entire book of Jeremiah, rendering a complex and intriguing system of signification, which every reader is invited to enter from the outset (cf. Jer 1).

55   See e.g. M. Nissinen, *Prophets and Prophecy in the Ancient Near East*, SBLWAW 12, Atlanta 2003, 1–11. The perspectives of study are indicated as obligatory routes by M.J. de Jong, *Isaiah*, in these terms: "The route from the biblical texts to prophecy as a socio-historical phenomenon in pre-exilic Israel runs through exegesis and historical analysis on the one hand, and comparative study on the other" (p. 30).

56   Emblematic examples of this formulation are the already cited studies by B. Duhm (in: *Jeremia*, but see also, amongst his other works, Id., *Das Buch Jesaja*, HK 3.1, Göttingen 1892, ²1914; Id., *Israels Propheten*, Tübingen 1916, ²1922).

57   Figures who remain, for many, inaccessible, if not to be considered fictitious stylisations and thus mere literary characters elaborated by scribal circles in late (post-exilic, Persian, or Hellenistic) epochs. On this topic, see e.g. R.P. Carroll, «Inventing the Prophets», *IBSt* 10 (1988) 24–36; H.M. Barstad, «No Prophets? Recent Developments in Biblical Prophetic Research and Ancient Near Eastern Prophecy», *JSOT* 57 (1993) 39–60; J.-G. Heintz, «La "fin" des prophètes bibliques?», 195–214, and that which I have observed in the following note.

58   For a rapid consultation of the results (or the proposals) of this line of research, the introductions to the various prophets can be seen in the collective work of E. Zenger *et al.*, *Einleitung in das Alte Testament*, KStTh 1.1, Stuttgart 1995, ⁶2006. Amongst the many contributions, see also K. Schmid, «Innerbiblische Schriftauslegung. Aspekte der Forschungsgeschichte», in: *Schriftauslegung in der Schrift*. Festschrift für Odil Hannes Steck zu seinem 65. Geburtstag, eds. R.G. Kratz – T. Kruger – K. Schmid, BZAW 300, Berlin – New York 2000, 1–22; E. Ben Zvi, «The Prophetic Book. A Key Form of Prophetic Literature», in: *The Changing Face of Form Criticism for the Twenty-First Century*, eds. M.A. Sweeney – E. Ben Zvi, Grand Rapids 2003, 276–297;

328   Jer 27–28. The world beneath the yoke of the king of Babylon

with the necessary methodological attention) a proper contextualisation of biblical prophecy within the vaster socio-religious panorama to which it belongs, underscoring its transcultural nature.[59]

In both these lines of research, as in those that have run parallel to them since the second half of the twentieth century, animated by a merely synchronic-literary interest[60] in the prophetic texts, it should, in my opinion, be noted that an approach

---

U. Becker, «Die Wiederentdeckung des Prophetenbuches. Tendenzen und Aufgaben der gegenwärtigen Prophetenforschung», *BThZ* 21 (2004) 30–60; Id., «Die Entstehung der Schriftprophetie», in: *Die unwiderstehliche Wahrheit*. Studien zur alttestamentlichen Prophetie. Festschrift für Arndt Meinhold, eds. R. Lux – E.-J. Waschke, ABIG 23, Leipzig 2006, 3–20; J. Jeremias, «Der Rätsel der Schriftprophetie», *ZAW* 125 (2013) 93–117. In M.J. de Jong, «Biblical Prophecy – A Scribal Enterprise. The Old Testament Prophecy of Unconditional Judgement Considered as a Literary Phenomenon», *VT* 61 (2011) 39–70, one of the most recent contributions on the theme, reasserts that "biblical prophecy", in the textual expression in which it has been handed down to us, is the result of scribal activity (even if the specific reference of the author, while not negating on principle the presence of "genuine prophecy" in the HB [p. 42], is to the prophecy of "unconditional and total judgement" as a literary creation held to most certainly be *ex eventu*). There are, however, even more extreme positions taken, which, in their drastic scepticism, are, in my view, entirely unfounded. As e.g. that of P.R. Davies, «"Pen of iron, point of diamond" (Jer 17:1): Prophecy as Writing», in: *Writings and Speech in Israelite and Ancient Near Eastern Prophecy*, eds. E. Ben Zvi – M.H. Floyd, SBLSymS 10, Atlanta 2000, 65–81, who considers the whole of biblical prophecy not so much a literary attestation of a social phenomenon, but rather as a pure scribal *invention* elaborated concordantly.

59   Cf. G.T. Sheppard – W.E. Herbrechtsmeier, «Prophecy: An Overview», in: *The Encyclopedia of Religion*. Second Edition, XI, ed. L. Jones, New York – London 1987, ²2005, 7423–7429; M. Weippert, «Aspekte israelitischer Prophetie im Lichte verwandter Erscheinungen des Alten Orients, in: *Ad bene et fideliter seminandum*. Festgabe für Karlheinz Deller zum 21. Februar 1987, eds. G. Mauer – U. Magen, AOAT 220, Neukirchen-Vluyn 1988, 287–319. Particularly relevant for the study of biblical prophetism are the attestations of Mari and of Neo-Assyrian prophetism; see, e.g. for Mari, amongst the many contributions, J.-G. Heintz, «Prophetie in Mari und Israel», *Bib.* 52 (1971) 543–555; the collections of studies by A. Malamat, *Mari and the Bible*; M. Köckert – M. Nissinen, eds., *Propheten in Mari, Assyrien und Israel*, FRLANT 201, Göttingen 2003, and D. Charpin, «Le prophétisme dans le Proche-Orient d'après les archives de Mari (XVIIIe siècle av. J.-C.)», in: *Les recueils prophétiques de la Bible. Origines, milieux et contexte proche-oriental*, eds. J.-D. Macchi – C. Nihan *et al.*, MoBi 64, Genève 2012, 31–73 (in particular, pp. 63–73); for Neo-Assyrian prophecy: M. Nissinen, «Die Relevanz der neuassyrischen Prophetie für die alttestamentliche Forschung», in: *Mesopotamica – Ugaritica – Biblica*. Festschrift für Kurt Bergerhof zur Vollendung seines 70. Lebensjahres am 7. Mai 1992, eds., M. Dietrich – O. Loretz, AOAT 232, Neukirchen-Vluyn 1993, 217–258; M. Weippert, «Prophetie im Alten Orient», *NBL* III, 196–200. For the methodological implications, cf. C. Bonnet – P. Merlo, «Royal Prophecy in the Old Testament and in the Ancient Near East: Methodological Problems and Examples», *SEL VOA* 19 (2002) 77–86; P. Merlo, «Il profetismo», 55–83.

60   This was due to the influence of *New Criticism*, an interpretive trend interested in the study of the coherent meaning of the textual whole as it presents itself in the final form of the literary work (cf. e.g. A.W. Biddle – T. Fulwiler, *Reading, Writing,*

"Make yourself straps and yoke crossbars and put them on your neck" (27:2)   329

centred *prevalently* on the *discursive* or *conceptual aspects* of the prophetic message has remained unvaried. It is a fact that for many decades, studies dedicated to the question of the symbolic gestures were quite rare or even null. After the articulate contribution of Georg Fohrer,[61] which for years remained the sole monograph worthy of note on the theme,[62] only in fairly recent times have we witnessed a renewed interest in this non-verbal communicative modality.[63]

Regardless of this, a marked attribution of "marginality" seems to generally remain unmutated in the contemporary exegetic panorama regarding this phenomenon, perhaps given the fact that out of fifteen of the so-called literary prophets, an explicit

---

and the Study of Literature, New York 1989, 100; Y. AMIT, *Reading Biblical Narratives. Literary Criticism and the Bible*, Minneapolis 2001, 10–32).

61 Cf. G. FOHRER, *Die Symbolischen Handlungen.*

62 Preceded only by the contribution of A. VAN DEN BORN, *De symbolische handelingen der Oud-Testamentische Profeten,* Utrecht-Nijmegen 1935, the work of G. Fohrer has long been a point of reference, albeit with all its limitations, due essentially to the univocal nature of the methodological perspective employed (the *Formgeschichte*), which prevents symbolic gestures from being grasped in their fundamental anthropological and communicative context. And in any case, the fundamental assumption of the work itself is even debatable, namely the possibility of being able to trace these gestures with any certainty to a specific *Gattung* of reference (understood as a rigid model; see, in this regard L. RAMLOT, «Prophétisme», *DBS* VIII, 811–1222, particularly p. 971).

63 Amongst the most significant works (leaving out dictionaries and minor articles), one need regardless limit oneself to: GRUBER M.I., *Aspects of Nonverbal Communication in the Ancient Near East,* 2 vols., StP 12/I-II, Roma 1980; S. AMSLER, «Les prophètes et la communication par les actes», in: *Werden und Wirken des Alten Testament.* Festschrift für C. Westermann zum 70. Geburtstag, *eds.* R. ALBERTZ *et al.,* Göttingen 1980, 194–201; ID., *Les actes des prophètes,* EssBib 9, Genève 1985; D. CLERC, «Des actes pour parler», 107–147; W.D. STACEY, *Prophetic Drama in the Old Testament,* London 1990; R.R. HUTTON, «Magic or Street-Theater? The Power of the Prophetic Word», *ZAW* 107 (1995) 247–260; J.E. BOTHA, «Exploring Gesture and Nonverbal Communication in the Bible and the Ancient World: Some Initial Observations», *Neotest.* 30 (1996) 1–19; B. LANG, «Games Prophets Play: Street Theatre and Symbolic Acts in Biblical Israel», in: *The Games of God and Man.* Essays in Play and Performance, *ed.* K.-P. KÖPPING, Hamburg 1997, 257–271 (= in: B. LANG, *Hebrew Life and Literature.* Selected Essays of Bernhard Lang, MSSOTS, Farnham 2008, 185–195 [I quote from this edition]); M. MALUL, *Studies in Mesopotamian Legal Symbolism,* AOAT 221, Neukirchen-Vluyn 1988; P.A. KRUGER, «"Nonverbal communication" in the Hebrew Bible: A Few Comments», *JNSL* 24 (1998) 141–164; K.G. FRIEBEL, *Jeremiah's and Ezekiel Sign-Acts.* Rhetorical Nonverbal Communication, JSOT.S 283, Sheffield 1999; J KRISPENZ, «Leben als Zeichen. Performancekunst als Deutungsmodell für prophetische Zeichenhandlungen im Alten Testament», *EvT* 64 (2004) 51–64; Å. VIBERG, *Prophets in Action*; K. OTT, *Die prophetischen Analogiehandlungen im Alten Testament,* EWANT 185, Stuttgart 2009; J.-D. DÖHLING, «Prophetische Körper. Ein exegetisch-soziologiches Plädoyer zu einer vernachlässigten Dimension der sog. "prophetischen Zeichenhandlungen"», *BZ* 57 (2013) 244–271; L. GASPARRO, *La Parola, il gesto e il segno.* Le azioni simboliche di Geremia e dei profeti, Bologna 2015.

330 Jer 27–28. The world beneath the yoke of the king of Babylon

presence is attested in only five or six of these.[64] It should be noted, moreover, that for not a few scholars (even amongst those who made them their subject of research), these seem to have a function that is merely didactic and/or persuasive,[65] and hence entirely ancillary with respect to verbal communication, the importance of which, it seems to me, is generally overrated in contemporary exegetic analyses.

The cause for this imbalance can be ascribed to a number of factors, mainly attributable to those Platonic-Cartesian (and Enlightenment) aspects of western mentality that have led to an emphasis on abstract thought and a devaluation of the corporal dimension of the individual in all their complex codes of communication. Not by chance, our culture is considered by some to be entirely "scriptocentric", and rightfully so.[66] As a concause, since it seems to still have a (more or less) underlying effect on many exegetic approaches, a certain Protestant idiosyncrasy for all that which is "sacramentum" should also be added, that is, for gestures, "actions" of the body and their performative significance in relation to divine intervention, images (even in motion), and non-verbal or non-conceptual communication in general.[67]

---

64 Five, according to G. FOHRER, *Die Symbolischen Handlungen* (Hosea, Isaiah, Jeremiah, Ezekiel, Zechariah), six according to the study by W.D. STACEY, *Prophetic Drama* (which also includes Micah [1:8]).

65 See, e.g. the study by K.G. FRIEBEL, *Sign-Acts*, in which the symbolic gestures are reduced in a biased manner to this rhetoric function.

66 Cf. S. MADISON, *Critical Ethnography.* Method, Ethics, and Performance, Thousand Oaks 2005, ²2012, 185, who speaks of "scriptocentrism". Consider also the influence and socio-cultural transformations induced by the invention of printing with moveable characters, studied extensively in the by now classic works of M. McLUHAN, *The Gutenberg Galaxy.* The Making of Typographic Man, Toronto 1962; E.L. EISENSTEIN, *The Printing Press as an Agent of Change.* Communications and Cultural Transformations in Early Modern Europe, vols. I-II, Cambridge 1979.

67 A similar doubt meekly presents itself e.g. also in J. KRISPENZ, «Leben als Zeichen», 52: "Und doch bleibt ein leiser Zweifel: Ist die Bedeutung des Handelns nicht doch unterschätzt, wenn man es so sehr mit dem gesprochenen Wort gleichstellt? Passt die Handlung damit nicht zu gut ins protestantische Bild – und zu gut zum Geschäft alttestamentlicher Exegese, die darauf spezialisiert ist, Texte zu verstehen?". But then, if we draw up a definition of "magic", such as that in the recent study by R. SCHMITT, *Magie im Alten Testament*, AOAT 313, Münster 2004 ("Magie ist eine ritualsymbolische Handlung, die durchgeführt in einer adäquaten Situation, durch Nutzung bestimmter göttlich enthüllter Medien [Symbol, Wort und Handlung] und kosmischen wissens, ein bestimmtes Ergebnis vermittels symbolischer Antizipation der göttlichen Intervention erzieht"; here, pp. 92–93), after removing certain particulars (like "cosmic knowledge"), it is easy to liken (though improperly) the sacramental dimension typical to the Catholic tradition with the magical realm, with the relative assessments of their value. This aside, it should be noted, in any case, that precisely in the Catholic world, at least until the Vatican Council II, "supernatural" revelation was lead to be understood according to the model of verbal communication. H. FELDER, *Apologetica sive theologia fundamentalis* [²1923], 28, e.g. expressed himself in this manner: "Revelatio supernaturalis [...] est manifestatio veritatis religiosae facta per Verba Dei ad hominem", and such the well-known manual by C.P. PESCH, *Praelectiones dogmaticae* [⁷1924], n. 151: "Revelatio naturalis fit per facta, revelatio supernaturalis per verba". I take both citations from H. DE LUBAC, *La révélation divine,* Paris 1968, ³1983, 40, who appropriately makes a marginal note: "[...] l'insistance sur *les paroles,*

3.2. For an interdisciplinary revaluation of the synergetic unity between gesture and word

The inquiry carried out in the present dissertation thus far has already suggested (and further elements will be put forth to corroborate this interpretation) how the theme of the Jeremianic call to surrender to Babylon is intentionally charged with dense interweavings of meanings that interact with multiple dimensions (from the political to the theological, symbolic, anthropological, etc.). A study founded on research methodologies oriented solely in a diachronic sense, whether these be historical-archaeological or exclusively critical-literary in nature, does not, therefore, seem to be able to adequately account for the complexity of its object. I believe that it be necessary to integrate, as I have been doing from the outset of my study, an *interdisciplinary* methodological sensibility (and wherever possible, effective practical application), which can help to better comprehend the peculiar nature of this topic of study without, obviously, circumventing the essential textual grounding that remains my singular point of departure.

It is clear, in fact, that every prophetic message, including that which is also conveyed through gestures or dramatisations, reaches us today not as spectators of an *occurrence* (of which, at most, the biblical page is narrative memory or re-elaboration, if not fictitious representation), but as readers of a *written text*[68] (with its particular history of composition). Therefore, while the literary dimension for us today is simply *unavoidable* and *coextensive* for the reception of the prophetic announcement, thus rendering the relative methods of approach essential, the writing itself can and intends to reach all of its potential readers/recipients with a communication that is virtually "multidimensional".

In other words, the *medium* through which the message reaches us remains the text, which can express itself either as a written text and/or heard text, engaging predominantly the channels of perception of sight and/or hearing. Nonetheless, precisely for its intrinsic nature, based on the communicative force of its language, the written text – though not without the active participation of its recipient – allows, in a certain sense, the reader/listener to enter into *his own* world, a multidimensional world in which all the senses can be reawakened and all the stories experienced anew. What comes about, rather than be a re-presentation, is instead practically more of a re-creation, an ever-shaping of itself *in fieri* of a new universe born of the *fulfilment* of what the text (and the story told by it) carried in its womb as hope (cf. e.g. Jer 52:31–34; Luke 4:21). It is a reciprocal merging of horizons, that of the *interpres* and the *interpretandum*, of multiple and never entirely foreseeable outcomes.[69]

---

au détriment des actes, supposait une moindre intelligence du caractère spécifique de la révélation, ainsi qu'une méconnaissance de la signification profonde du mot même de 'Parole de Dieu'".

68 I specify this since, from the semiotic point of view I refer to, by *text*, what is generally intended is "every portion of the sensual world on which we decide to exercise our interpretive activity" (translated from U. VOLLI, *Semiotica*, 135). Thus, also acts, images, musical compositions, cinematographic productions, dance performances, etc. are texts in so far as productions of meaning expressed by a "sign system" (cf. D. GRONOWSKI, *Comunicazione*, 38–39).

69 The reference is to the hermeneutical categories of "accomplissement" (des Écritures) that supports the project of biblical theology of P. Beauchamp (see in particular his

This communication is given and presents itself not only as an interweaving of words charged with pragmatic efficacy (while, however inevitably, being so),[70] but as the reproposal, in fragmented form, of the global *narrative plot*[71] of the Scripture (*textus*, in fact), constituted by the transmission-"attestation"[72] of correlated and intimately connected *actions and words*.[73] Words that are actions, and not only information, and actions that *are* words in which *the* Word echoes.[74] A saying (and a giving of oneself) in gestures and words that are thus not only *action*, but also (create) *inter-action* on various levels. What is at play, in other words, is the complexity of a relational *sender-recipient* engagement, in both the horizontal (between human beings) and vertical (between the human and transcendent) dimensions.

This communicative-revelative dynamism, as was already mentioned in the General Introduction, expresses itself according to varied modulations within the biblical prophetical phenomenon, but is particularly exalted in the book of Jeremiah, beginning with its literary organisation (especially in the arrangement elaborated by the MT). In fact, juxtaposed here, and in my opinion intentionally, are a first, *prevalently* oracular-poetic part (1–25) and a second part (26–45), in which the narrative form dominates instead. *Sayings* and *(f)acts* of Jeremiah, to which the twofold connotation of the lexeme דָּבָר in the initial syntagm of 1:1 (דִּבְרֵי יִרְמְיָהוּ) alludes, in an undifferentiated or better still, complementary way,[75] contribute to express a single prophetic message.

---

two volumes of *L'un et l'autre Testament*) and those of "Horizontverschmelzung" and "Wirkungsgeschichte", developed by H.-G. Gadamer (see above all his well-known work *Warheit und Methode*, in: ID., *Gesammelte Werke*. Band 1, Hermeneutik I: Wahrheit und Methode. Grundzüge einer philosophischen Hermeneutik, Tübingen 1960, ⁶1990, 305–312 [283–291], 380 [356], etc.).

70 As is taught by the linguistic pragmatic inaugurated by J.L. Austin (cf. J.O. URMSON – M. SBISÀ, *eds.*, *How To Do Things With Words*).

71 I keep in the background the concept of "récit totale" developed by P. Beauchamp and already mentioned in the General Introduction, in § 3.2, n. 78.

72 The "text" is to be understood therefore both according to its formal aspect as a "textile" (*textus*) that combines different elements, and in its "prophetic" presence as "testifier" (*testis*), of a revelatory fact (according to the twofold etymological reference – the second, however, purely suggestive or pseudoetimological, even if widely used in antiquity; cf. L. CANTONI – N. DI BLAS – S. RUBINELLI – S. TARDINI, *Pensare e comunicare*. Introduzione al critical thinking, Milano 2008, 166).

73 The dogmatic constitution *Dei Verbum* of the II Vatican Council recognises in this dynamic of reciprocity and complementarity between events and words ("gestis verbisque") the essence itself of the modality chosen by God to communicate himself to humankind: "Haec revelationis oeconomia fit gestis verbisque intrinsece inter se connexis, ita ut opera, in historia salutis a Deo patrata, doctrinam et res verbis significatas manifestent ac corroborent, verba autem opera proclament et mysterium in eis contentum elucident" (§ 2). In addition to the now classic and already cited H. DE LUBAC, *La révélation divine*, for some recent contributions on the topic, one can look at R. FERRI – P. MANGANARO, *eds.*, *Gesto e parola*. Ricerche sulla rivelazione, Roma 2005.

74 But also the "counter-Word", cf. e.g. Wis 1:16.

75 Although I am forced to choose one side or the other of this semantic plexus in translation, and indeed, there is no shortage of authors who emphasise the characteristic of factuality as opposed to that of mere verbal communication, in my opinion, it is

"Make yourself straps and yoke crossbars and put them on your neck" (27:2)   333

Not only the single gestures attributed to the prophet, but the *history* of his body rises to a revelative place of particular importance: the body elected, shaped, and thrown into the fray of history as a word of flesh, body humiliated, wounded and astonishingly saved, become a living image, "symbol", of the visible journey of the divine word in the world (cf. 26). And it is, in its own way and *in some respects* an analogical prolepsis of the destiny of Jerusalem[76] (and of the Christ, and in Him, of every believer).

I am convinced that it be fitting to *programmatically* take on the task of including, in the exegetic work on prophetic literature, a proper study of this semiotic-symbolic interconnection between body, existence, and prophetic word. This means that my study cannot prescind from dedicating serious attention, insofar as this is feasible in the current context, to the *world of signs, gestures, and symbolic interactions* that intimately structure the complex system of communications that the book of Jeremiah is, drawing as well from the pre- or extralinguistic, because the verbal cannot exist alone without the non-verbal. The semantic density and communicative dynamism of these signification devices give greater substance than that which this particular expressive modality of biblical revelation may seem to do at first glance, and they innervate in a particular way in the corporeal existence of whomever, like the prophet, is called to announce (and to *become* with their own life) a word of YHWH for their people. The response to this appeal thus cannot but foresee the engagement of the same channel of communication.[77] To deliver one's own "body". Whether this be the body of the social-state, or, above all, the visibilisation and actualisation of the dimension of the בָּשָׂר of the very *being* in this world. We have already seen this in Jer 21:1–10, and will have the opportunity to discuss it again in the following chapter, studying Jer 38:14–28a.

3.3. From the sign of the yoke to the (symbolic) act of surrender to Babylon

As confirmation of what I have just stated, I will point out that the message of surrender, in its first explicit chronological appearance attested by chs. 27–28, assumes first of all, a *non-verbal* communicative dimension: the preparation, sending, and assuming the burden of one or more yokes. The request of YHWH manifests itself within the historical horizon *beginning with the obedience of the prophet himself* to His command, obedience that becomes an external gesture, a total (or "clausal"[78])

---

    precisely this polysemy that provides the correct hermeneutical key to the book right from its *incipit.*

76 Focusing on this aspect is the study by M. Cucca, *Il corpo e la città. Studio del rapporto di significazione paradigmatica tra la vicenda di Geremia e il destino di Gerusalemme*, StRic.SB, Assisi 2010.

77 On the relationship between reading the body and reading "Scripture" (understood in a broad sense, with reference to the normative texts of religions), see D. Cave, «Reading the Body, Reading Scripture: The Implications of Neurobiology on the Study and Interpretation of Scripture», in: *Religion and the Body*. Modern Science and the Construction of Religious Meaning, eds. D. Cave – R. Sachs Norris, NBS.SHR 138, Leiden – Boston 2012, 15–35.

78 Just as words truly "live" only in a clause in which they are articulated (and find themselves separated, artificially, only in lexicons and dictionaries), likewise human gestures are composed of concatenations of movements carried out in space and time (I will borrow the expression used by M. Jousse, *L'anthropologie du geste*, Paris

334   Jer 27–28. The world beneath the yoke of the king of Babylon

gesture that is constituted by a series of coordinated actions, consequential amongst themselves and traversed by a sense of unity, aiming to indicate, in the surrender to the king of Babylon, the authentic hope of life and salvation carried in the womb of the present καιρός:

> *Make for yourself* [עֲשֵׂה לְךָ] straps and [yoke] crossbars and *place them* [וּנְתַתָּם] on your neck; then *send them* [וְשִׁלַּחְתָּם] to the king of Edom, to the king of Moab, to the king of the sons of Ammon, to the king Tyre and to the king of Sidon [...] (cf. 27:2–3).

The word that commands the gesture also requires the verbal explication of its profound meaning, but only afterwards:

> [...] and *command* [וְצִוִּיתָ] them for their lords: "*Thus says* [כֹּה־אָמַר] the Lord of hosts, the God of Israel [...]" (cf. 27:4).

YHWH manifests himself from the beginning as a speaking God.[79] The spoken word upon the bare materiality of the gesture and the concrete elements engaged in the symbolic act recalls the creative power of the word of YHWH who, by naming, creates, and by speaking upon the originary *vacuum,* populates it with forms and meaning.[80] Because the meaning, the Word, for the story of the Genesis, exists *before* all else. And it is only this Word which, by pronouncing itself and naming, instils the meaning and his light there where before (in an apparent "before"), there was nothing but *unformed and deserted* land (תֹהוּ וָבֹהוּ), with the darkness that covered the abyss (Gen 1:2).

Something analogous happens for the prophetic acts placed before their recipients, outside of and within the text. First, a gesture is seen, one that seems to be non-sense, a formless materiality, out of context. Something folly to laugh at and mock. Then, suddenly, the word that rips through the appearance creates a light of meaning. And nothing is as it was before. Something new has been created-revealed. This is why these symbolic gestures, with Danielle Clerc, can be called "signes de l'action créatrice de Dieu".[81] Once again, on the interweaving between word and silence, the same author writes:

> L'acte du prophète et le récit qu'il en fait plantent le décor, révèlent un état de fait: comme au début de la Genèse, "la terre était déserte et vide"..., il y avait "pas-encore-la-terre", ...ainsi le prophète met en scène "ce-n'est-plus-une-ceinture", "Jérusalem-la-non-réparable", "Pas-mon-Peuple", "Pas-ma-Bien-Aimée", etc. Le prophète plante ce décor totalement absurde avec un engagement si total, si sérieux, qu'il en devient parfois ridicule, voire suspect.

1974, 126–127). The adjective "clausal" is used here in an analogous sense to the conceptualising function of language in the field of communication, described e.g. by L. ANOLLI, «Inquadramento storico e teorico sulla comunicazione», in: *Psicologia della comunicazione, ed.* L. ANOLLI, Strumenti, Bologna 2000, 3–32 (here, p. 27).

79   Cf. P. BEAUCHAMP, «Au commencement, Dieu parle, ou les sept jours de la création», *Études* 365 (1986) 105–116; J.-P. SONNET, «Du personnage de Dieu comme être de parole», in: *Bible et théologie.* L'intelligence de la foi, *ed.* F. MIES, LeR 26, Bruxelles 2006, 15–36; P. BOVATI – P. BASTA, *"Ci ha parlato per mezzo dei profeti".* Ermeneutica biblica, Lectio 4, Roma – Cinisello Balsamo 2012, 35–39.

80   On this subject, see S. NIDITCH, *Chaos to Cosmos.* Studies in Biblical Patterns of Creation, SPSHS 6, Chico 1985 (esp. pp. 11–24).

81   D. CLERC, «Des actes pour parler», 112. And not by chance, the "God creator" theme is central precisely in chs. 27–28, as we will see in the following paragraph.

"Make yourself straps and yoke crossbars and put them on your neck" (27:2)   335

Et l'oracle vient soudainement, verdict dont le tranchant fait taire les rieurs, parole qui organise le sens: ce chaos, Dieu en fait un espace habitable (ce qui ne signifie pas toujours agréable). Au moment de l'oracle explicatif – la Parole sur l'acte – il advient réellement quelque chose de radicalement neuf, même si extérieurement rien ne se manifeste et si, par conséquent, le refus et la dénégation sont encore non seulement possibles, mais surtout raisonnablement plausibles. La Parole se détache sur fond de silence.[82]

Yes, the word detaches itself, emerges from deep within the silence, and for this, the prophet *in primis* will be asked to enter into this mystery (cf. 28:11, and what I will study in-depth in § 5.3). Once the complete linguistic-communicative act (union of the verbal and non-verbal)[83] has taken place, a fruitful hermeneutical circle between gesture and word is established, but it need be underlined that, at first, it is not the gesture that explains the word: it is the word that is added and joined to the gesture.[84] First, the impact of history and life, the factual word, then, the verbal word that illuminates or interrogates its meaning. The prophetic mimesis is also the reproposal of the dynamic intrinsic to human knowledge and divine revelation. It is an introduction to the "semiotic" of creation and the "contextual pragmatic" of the relationship with YHWH.

Certainly, the precedence of the gesture over the word *also* corresponds to a wise strategy of communication: the message is vital because it can save, but it can do so only if it moves from within, if it persuades the will of the recipient to embrace it freely. Nevertheless, the action completed by Jeremiah in obedience is not reducible to a mere dramatisation of prophetic speech: it is not only a rhetorical device nor a simple brief caption that explains the orality. It is, rather, in its originary sense, σύμβολον: a broken part of that which needs to be reconjoined with its missing half,[85] a "gestural

---

82   *Ibid.*, 111–112.
83   The paraverbal dimension of communication concerning prosody, tone, tempo, timbre, and vocal volume need be, for obvious reasons, omitted.
84   The anteriority granted to the gesture in relation to the word (that explains it), attested not only here but also in other texts in which scenes with symbolic actions are described (cf. e.g. Jer 13:1–11; 16:1–13; 19:6–44; 43:8–13; 51:63–64; Ezek 3:22–5:17; 12; 21; 24:15–27; etc.), could also be symptomatic of the phases through which human language evolved. According to the cognitivist M.C. CORBALLIS, *From Hand to Mouth. The Origins of Language*, Princeton 2002, who researched, for the first time systematically, an intuition that was not new (already expressed in the celebrated work by P. WATZLAWICK – J.H. BEAVIN – D.D. JACKSON, *Pragmatics of Human Communication. A Study of Interactional Patterns, Pathologies, and Paradoxes*, New York 1967), the origin of language is to be found not in the first vocalisations but in primordial forms of communication of a mimetic nature.
85   Obviously, the reference is to the primitive meaning of the Greek lexeme σύμβολον (from σύμ-βαλλω, "I throw/put/join together") as is attested e.g. in Plato (*Symposium*, 191d) and Aristotle (*Ethica Eudemia*, 1239 b31), where it alludes to the *tessera hospitalis*, to wit, a sign of recognition made up of the two broken halves of an object (a shell, ring, etc.) exchanged between single individuals or more complex social realities united by a mutual agreement or alliance. These are two divided parts, which, fit together, recompose the original unit, or far from one another, become a place of resonance and proof of the presence of the missing part, which it constitutively recalls.

336   Jer 27–28. The world beneath the yoke of the king of Babylon

verb" that calls for 1) an oral word from the prophet himself, to recompose a single communicative *act* and the unaltered meaning of a single message that is also, at the same time, an occurrence[86]; 2) a gesture of response, with symbolic-performative value, of which the prophetic communication is an authoritative appeal, mimetic prolepsis, and obediential response in itself (for, in this manner, the prophet makes true his adherence to the One who has elected and sent him).

It is not, therefore, merely an exercise of rhetorical technique (τέχνη ῥητορική),[87] but a profound anthropological engagement naturally involved in biblical revelation both on the level of the sender (God and his mediations[88]) and the recipient of the

---

Although it is generally good to be wary of a (sole) etymological reference regarding the precise comprehension of a term (whose most accurate semantic identity is to be traced instead by the relation it has with its linguistic context), this reference, even in the most varied (and contradictory) acceptations assumed in the history of thought, continues to indicate the fundamental semantic platform implicated in the concept of "symbol", that is, the *instance of reference* that is specified as the establishment of a *relationship of meaning* (between the signifier and the signified). In this case, I allude to a meaning that, while not immediately recognisable, is essential for the prophetic act: its yearning not only to be reunited with the oral word, which is explicative, but to the act that the communicative gesture in its totality (of verbal and non-verbal) invokes and commands as an adequate response (submission-surrender) on the part of the recipient/s.

86   Keeping the pragmatic function of language in mind, I can already allude to the fact that the gesture of the yoke and the word that accompanies it not only constitute an *informative* message (offering a reliable reading of history), but make "happen" or give form to an *act of injunction* or *appeal* demanding an obedient response that puts the lives of the recipients at stake. And this is in order to generate a different course of history, a new event.

87   Understanding the phenomenon of "symbolic gestures" only as having a persuasive function means equating them *tout court* to a communicative technique, which is actually the *ars rhetorica* of its threefold deliberative, epideictic, and judicial characteristics. And by (Aristotelian) definition, this τέχνη (which Plato downgrades to ἐμπειρία, "ability"; cf. *Gorgias*, 452d–455a) is not interested in the ἀλήθεια, but only in discovering, observing, and mastering "in any given case the available means of persuasion" (cf. *Ars Rhetorica*, I, 2, 1355b20) to convince the listener, on the basis of the possible or the probable (cf. *Ibid.*, I, 1357b). This is a reductive perspective that, in my opinion, impedes full comprehension of the most profound importance of meaning inherent to the revelative dynamism typical of prophetic communication actuated in gestures and words. Not merely strategy, a simple repertoire of measures to reach an end, it is instead revelation of the intimate nature of human-divine dialogue, its channels of communication, the diverse anthropological dimensions involved, and its communical objective that can be actualised only in truth.

88   It should be observed that between prophetic communication and the locutionary act of the rhetorician, there is a fundamental difference that concerns their fountainhead, and thus the role of the person communicating itself, its intentionality, and the type of discursive efficacy put into effect. While in the "mundane" context, the rhetorician is usually, in fact, both the origin and transmitter of the message, the biblical prophet is instead described as a messenger (think e.g. of the well-known introductory formula כֹּה אָמַר יְהוָה, already identified by L. KÖHLER, *Deuterojesaja stilkritisch untersucht*, BZAW 37, Giessen 1923, 102–109, and denominated "Botenformel" by H. WILDBERGER, *Jahwewort und prophetische Rede bei Jeremia*. Inaugural-Dissertation

"Make yourself straps and yoke crossbars and put them on your neck" (27:2)   337

communicative event (the human being). Involvement or *interaction* that is to be understood as a bidirectional dynamism of call and response (from God to the human being and vice versa), the scope of which is not only to convey *information* or produce *persuasion,* but to actualise or re-establish *communion* (which is then nothing but expression of the biblical concept of justice).[89] Thus the presence, the face, and the voice of He who alone is Father (Jer 3:4, 19, 22), Holy (Jer 50:29; 51:5; cf. Is 6:3; etc.), the Righteous One (Jer 12:1), and the Groom-Lover of Israel (Jer 2:2, 32; 3:1, 20; cf. Ezek 16; Hos 1–3; etc.) is manifested in history.

The action and speaking coincide in a gesture that becomes intensely "symbolic": because, in a certain sense, even the word *spoken* alone, with its inevitable "volatility" (*verba volant!*), albeit endowed with pragmatic efficacy, would suffer a certain degree of incompleteness if it were only proclaimed and not already substantially experienced. On the other hand, the reception of the Jeremianic command (to submit to the Babylonian yoke, surrender) would be likewise incomplete, "missing" (and in fact, rendered vain) if it were only heard and not actuated, that is, not embraced and not transformed in decisions, choices, and concrete gestures; in this case, the renunciation of political independence from the Babylonian empire and payment of the heavy tribute owned (cf. Jer 27–28), or the opening of the assailed city gates to go out towards the generals of Nebuchadnezzar to hand themselves over, without conditions and without being subject to the conditionings of the fear of dying (cf. Jer 21:1–10; 38:14–28a).

In this communicative context, the act of surrender can take on different forms, but not all are reducible to their factual terms in a political sense, but connoted with *symbolic importance,* an importance that also chs. 27–28, after 21:1–10, contribute to delineate. Beginning from the fact that "symbolic" does not mean ahistorical, abstract, ineffective. Anything but. The meaning itself of an entire history of covenant between YHWH and his people is at stake.

---

zur Erlangung der Doktorwürde der Theologischen Fakultät der Universität Zürich, Zürich 1942, 48–77), to not be identified with the ultimate origin of the message. It is YHWH who commands to speak and to enact symbolic gestures. He is therefore the true sender, and the communicative act of the prophet is to be fit into the context of his particular vocation, so it is as if he were sequestered, "set aside" (cf. Jer 1:5; √קדשׁ *hi.*), not only to speak, but also to *become* a message, even without full awareness of the actual reach of this semiosis. Think e.g. of the symbolic purchase of the field ordered of Jeremiah (cf. Jer 32): having carried out the mandate, evidently (by how the text presents the scene) without the prophet having understood the meaning, he directly addresses YHWH expressing his dismay for what he was asked to do, since he perceives it as senseless. Even while being careful to not fall into a mechanical conception of prophetic communication, as if the prophet were but a mere instrument in the hands of YHWH and not creatively participating with his humanity in the communicative event, these considerations make a solely "rhetorical" reading of the symbolic gesture appear rather reductive.

89   Cf. P. Bovati, *Ristabilire la giustizia,* 7–10, 21–23, 92–93, 76–77, 151–152, 194–196, 316, 361–362.

3.4. From semantics to pragmatics. Beyond the information, the relation. To surrender "prophetically"

What I have just summarily described can be defined as a *model of semiotic interaction*[90] with *pragmatic* efficacy: a sign placed before the eyes of its actants as an ostensive stimulus, on both an intradiegetic and extradiegetic level, reveals an *informative intention* and a *communicative intention* at the same time.[91] In other words, it synergically provides a series of (visual) information, *calls for* an interpretation (both on the part of the prophetic verbal language and on the part of the recipients), *actuates* an appeal, and *indicates* and *awaits* a likewise significative *gesture of response*.

We are clearly beyond a simply semantic level of analysis of symbolic gestures, in which what counts are, above all, the relations between the individual lexemes or syntagms that structure their literary configuration and respective meanings. The issue is instead that of raising the question of the communicative function of the gesture.

> Per scoprire la verità di un testo o il suo senso completo è necessario tener conto di quegli elementi che soggiacciono o interagiscono nel processo tra i partners: chi è il soggetto della comunicazione e con chi sta comunicando; in qualche contesto avviene la comunicazione; cosa si vuole trasmettere, quale effetto si cerca di ottenere, con quali soluzioni e valori l'emittente mira a far identificare i lettori.[92]

It is from the interweaving of these interactions that the meaning takes shape, without being given in a preconceived way by the single lexical elements of the text and by their significance understood in a *dictionary* sense. By way of language, whether verbal or non-verbal, actions are produced, events are determined. Every author calls their reader to the genesis of the meaning, appealing to their communicative and pragmatic competence, their *encyclopaedic* knowledge. And in this way, meaning is generated to the measure in which all the actants involved (on an intradiegetic and extradiegetic level) bring their own contribution, both on the level of interpretive cooperation[93] and

---

90   Every communicative event can be defined as a process of an exchange of meanings between at least two agents mediated by shared signs and by a common basis (implicit or explicit) of semiotic rules. Semiotic interactions thus regard the act of an interpretant (not to be understood here in the technical sense intended by C.S. Peirce), that is, of a person or even a computer, to comprehend (features of) phenomena in the real world like a message (with all that this implicates on a pragmatic level).

91   Cf. C. BIANCHI, *Pragmatica cognitiva*, 115.

92   "To discover the truth of a text or its complete meaning, it is necessary to take into consideration the elements underlying or interacting in the process between the partners: the one who is the subject of the conversation and the one with whom they are communicating; the communication comes about in some context; that which wants to be transmitted, the desired effect, with what solutions and values the emitter aims to have the reader identify." (translation from M. GRILLI, «Autore e lettore: il problema della comunicazione nell'ambito dell'esegesi biblica», *Gr.* 74 [1993] 447–459 [here, p. 454]).

93   I refer once again to the "principle of cooperation" of communicative exchanges (and to the "conversational maxims") formulated by H.P. Grice (cf. General Introduction, § 3.3.6, nos 123 and 126). On the notions of (pragmatic) context and of interpretive cooperations applied in the biblical exegetic field, see M. GUIDI, *"Così avvenne la generazione"* (esp. pp. 39–136).

"Make yourself straps and yoke crossbars and put them on your neck" (27:2)   339

actantial response. To the measure in which they share and determine a communicative context together,[94] both of the linguistic and extralinguistic sort.

In this sense, the gesture-message (the ostension of the yoke borne across the shoulders) is a deliberately evident, blatant *clue*, which not only metaphorically refers in an immediate way to the gesture of response that is expected (submission), but signals other less pronounced paths that, via inference, refer to an entire lattice of intratextual semiotic relationships, where the promise of a broader meaning is preserved. It is a discreet invitation that encourages pursuing a path of research along the lines of the complex dynamics of signification and communication contained in the book of Jeremiah.

Herein, I can only offer some brief observations in this regard. In anticipation, however, of the results of another parallel study of mine,[95] I can already say that this dramatisation of the prophetic word can be recognised as a portion of solid ground emerging from a vaster symbolic world, structured in multiple levels of signification. One can speak of a genuine Jeremianic *semiosphere*,[96] which, in the panorama of exegetic studies on the book of Jeremiah to date, still remains for the most part submerged and hidden, certainly disarticulated in isolated texts, in fragments of scenes, mimes, visions, and other elements of signification too often deprived of the organic and reasoned synthesis of an overall view[97] that embraces the Jeremianic work in its entirety.

At first instance, thus, by way of the gesture of the yoke, as if through one of its many entry doors, the "world of the text" reveals itself for us to be like a world of cross-references, analogies, signs, metaphors, and symbols, instituted to *stimulate*

---

94   I make a distinction between "literary context" and "communicative context". While the first is made up of "l'ensemble des unites constituant l'unité supérieure qui englobe la péricope envisagée" (R. MEYNET, *Lire la Bible*, 161–162, the second "is the situation of reference in which a linguistic act is made, and in which the dialogic cooperation between the sender and the receiver is called to take place" (translated from M. GRILLI, «Parola di Dio e linguaggio umano», 533).

95   Cf. that presented synthetically in ch. VII.

96   It is the Russian semiologist Jurij Michajlovič Lotman who, analogically recalling the concept of the biosphere of Vladimir Ivanovich Vernadskij (cf. ID., *Biosfera*, Moskvà 1967), identifying the habitat of the living, defines the universe of human communication "semiosphere" insofar as a complex cultural system in which ideas, signs, symbols, relations, etc. circulate and "live". This is a semiotic area or a condition of possibility formed by elements of meaning that are, in turn, organised in specific systems of relative pertinence, that is, in other semiospheres (original Russian edition: J.M. LOTMAN., «O semiosfere», *SSS* 17 [1984] 5–23 (Eng. tr. by W. Clark in: «On the Semiosphere», *SSS* 33 [2005] 205–229; Ita. tr. in: S. SALVESTRONI, *ed.*, *La semiosfera*. L'asimmetria e il dialogo nelle strutture pensanti, Venezia 1985, ²1992, 55–76). I thus take on the book of Jeremiah as a defined textual entity, a coherent semiotic universe, that is, as a *semiosphere* (to be conceived, in any case, as an open system constitutively interfacing both with other textualities and with the semiotic world of the reader).

97   This is the impression that I gain from the existing studies on the subject, where approaches are used that address the issue of "symbolic gestures" usually from unilateral perspectives, without these being contextualised within the development of the "symbolic fact" (or better still, semiotic-pragmatic or, in general, communicative) within the book of Jeremiah.

340   Jer 27–28. The world beneath the yoke of the king of Babylon

inferences, describe and provoke "dramatic" relational dynamics, concatenated by a syntax that is necessary to comprehend and respect, obedient to a grammar to which the book itself offers the keys, little by little.

On a closer look, however, the gesture of the yoke is not only *one* of the doors, but rather a *fundamental symbolic junction* through which one can gain access to the dynamic of signification implicated in the other symbolic gestures, and to which one need return to recuperate the keys to the semiotic code that structures the action called for by the prophet. On the one hand, the prophetic gesture of the yoke raises the question of the semiotic statute and of the taxonomy of the various symbolic gestures, attested both within the literary perimeter of the book and outside of it. From this point of view, considering the *index of anthropological impact*[98] of the gestures of prophetic signification as a fundamental criterion, that of the yoke is perhaps not amongst the strongest.

On the other hand, it is precisely this symbolic gesturality that is entrusted to convey the call for more decisive obedience in the imminence of the end of Jerusalem. The gesture of the yoke not only shows a *content,* but it also presents itself as a *prolepsis* in a mimetic (analogical) form of the symbolic value intrinsic in every concrete modality of its realisation (the submission to Babylon before the siege, surrender during the siege, acceptance of the exile on the part of the deported of 597, and not-escaping to Egypt after the assassination of Gedaliah). Indeed, this form of semiosis places the question of the surrender within the ambit of *intersubjective relations,* preventing its reduction to a merely conceptual or informative level.[99] As modern theories of communication highlight,[100] in fact, non-verbal language is, above all, of an *analogic* and continuous type, unfit for transmitting knowledge, abstract ideas, or qualitative semantic aspects.[101] For these functions of communication, verbal language results as being much more effective, since it is foremost of a *digital* sort, that is, one having discrete units.[102] Symbolic gestures, therefore, since they relate to the sphere of analogical

---

98   This is, in my opinion, the most decisive discriminant criterion for an adequate taxonomy of symbolic gestures. These range from prevalently didactic acts, to understanding and assigning highly relevant anthropological aspects. From this as well, it can be seen that these are not reducible to either a rhetorical or even ancillary function, let alone be simply communicative towards an external listener. Some actions requested by YHWH take the form, in fact, of genuine life choices, which involve all existence, permanent and irrevocable in nature. See e.g. Jer 16:1–9; Ezek 24; Hos 1–3. I will return to this topic in ch. V, § 5.3.3.3.

99   Cf. L. ANOLLI, *Fondamenti,* 187: "The human species, just as other animal species, uses NVC [non-verbal communication] for essentially relational reasons. [...] In communication and through communication, we create and play out our relations with others."

100   Starting with the landmark study in cognitive pragmatics by P. WATZLAWICK – J.H. BEAVIN – D.D. JACKSON, *Pragmatics.*

101   The translation of non-verbal language comes about according to a variety of expressive modalities. It can regard the vocal system (paralinguistic and extralinguistic aspects, such as those that are prosodic, like intonation, intensity, and the speed of speech), the kinesic one (gaze, facial expression, gestures, body posture), that of haptic contact (communication through touch), and that of proxemics (the regulation of physical distance between communicants). Cf. L. ANOLLI, *Fondamenti,* 153–188.

102   The differences between verbal and non-verbal communication are often depicted in the oppositive relationship between *digital* and analogical, between *denotative*

"Make yourself straps and yoke crossbars and put them on your neck" (27:2)   341

language of an ostensive type, present themselves on the plane of expression that relates to the *quality of the relation* between the subjects involved in the communicative act. For this reason too, they are actions that always provoke a reaction, never indifferent to the one who is their recipient.

> Car il est plus aisé de refuser d'écouter une parole que de refuser de voir un geste. Face au geste, l'interlocuteur est assailli à la fois par l'oeil et par l'oreille. Il est acculé à sortir de son apathie muette pour reprendre, ne serait-ce que par une question étonnée, le dialogue auquel il se refusait. Le geste vise une zone plus profonde de la vie intérieure de l'interlocuteur, au-delà des mots et des formules qui sont devenues inefficaces.[103]

It is therefore rather ingenuous to measure the importance of symbolic gestures by quantifying the literary space that they occupy in the prophetic corpus.[104] Describing a prophetic act is simple; it can be done in only a few words. A simple narrative brushstroke and a rapid glance offered to the reader can suffice, but its communicative impact can be worth far more than many speeches and verbal articulations, leaving a deep impression on the actants[105] that does not leave them indifferent, in one sense or another; or, even further, implicating a kind of existential involvement that affects both the person who puts it forth and those called on to assume its meaning. Take, for example, specifically the gesture of the yoke within the extension of the narrative frame of chs. 27–28, and its context expands to all those texts that refer, directly or indirectly, to the theme of the surrender to the king of Babylon. Consider then how the whole destiny of Jerusalem comes to depend, from a certain point on, upon this choice. Well: the gesture of the yoke in itself is described (in the form of a command) in just one verse! Its semiotic reverberation, however, establishes the entire communicative density of chs. 27–28 and echoes throughout many other texts (the theme of the yoke and its broken straps already appears in 2:20 and 5:5, that is, in the part traditionally considered to be the most "authentic", in the heart of the oracular teaching).

> (which regards "what is said") and *connotative* (the "how" it is said) functions, between the *arbitrary* and *conventional* aspect, which would be specifically the first, and that *motivated* and *iconic*, typical of the second. These distinctions are to be assumed with a certain amount of caution, since they are of relative value (it suffices to think of the phenomenon of phonosymbolism, in which arbitrary elements and evocative significance coexist). In the two forms of communication, at times, a certain intertwining between the different aspects occurs (see, in this regard, L. ANOLLI, *Fondamenti*, 156–157).

103   Cf. D. CLERC, «Des actes pour parler», 111.
104   I note, in any case, incidentally, that symbolic gestures have a remarkable extension in the book of Jeremiah, both in terms of textual space and of the time frame involved in their realisation as compared to attestations in other prophetic books. Of all of them, the yoke specifically has the broadest length of text that relates to it. This is not only because it lies at the centre of the plot of two entire chapters, but also because Jer 27–28, though it narrates two contiguous episodes, relates to different moments and traces a duration of the symbolic gesture that is of a certain extent (even if still less than Jer 13 or 16:1–9).
105   I stress the term "actants", as opposed to the limited term of "spectators" (or "audience").

342 Jer 27–28. The world beneath the yoke of the king of Babylon

The correct *semantics*[106] of one of the more decisive messages of the prophet Jeremiah and the description, at least on an embryonic level, of a "relational *pragmatic* of salvation"[107] inscribed in the text and offered to readers of all epochs as a hermeneutical-theological criterion will reveal themselves – I hope – to be the gift and conquest that the whole work invites us to penetrate. In the light of this broader context, which weaves a genuine lattice of semiotic-symbolic interactions, to surrender, as an act resignified by the Jeremianic request, will mean surrendering "prophetically": to discern the meaning of the present moment and assume it in obedience.

3.5. When words are no longer enough. The time of crisis and urgency of its language

But what time are we talking about? Let me return for a moment to the question of the marginalisation of symbolic gestures. There are those who tend to attribute the phenomenon to the influence of an unspecified "gusto de la época", by which they would thus be conferred a merely "relative" importance. Given then that they are recorded, above all, amongst the prophets of the seventh and sixth centuries, this would demonstrate the "papel secundario dentro del modo de expresarse de los profetas".[108] The lack of dedicated attention in the exegetical world would thus be justified by their "rôle non pas primordial, mais tout occasionnel, périphérique"[109] within prophetic biblical phenomenon.

In reality, the perspective shifts radically if, even while taking into account the communicative codes typical of their socio-cultural matrix (in the ethno-anthropological sphere, this is referred to as "performance culture"[110] or "performancekultur"[111]), these are instead seen as an extreme attempt at communication at dramatic points in time, that is, as a particular "langage pour un temps de crise".[112]

---

106 That is, what it *signifies* to surrender to the king of Babylon on the logical-conceptual level.
107 That is, what that gesture *actualises* on the level of intersubjective (historical-theological) impact in the relationships between YHWH and his people (on an intra-diegetic level), and between the text and the reader (on an extradiegetic level). I are speaking on the "embryonic level" because I am convinced that it is necessary to place this inquiry within the context of a broader and more articulated study, aimed at explicating the complex interweavings of signic-symbolic interactions that run throughout and structure the whole book of Jeremiah.
108 I cite the emblematic words of J.L. Sicre Díaz, *Introducción al profetismo bíblico*, Estella 2011, 122.
109 The expression is that of L. Ramlot, «Prophétisme», 970, who goes so far as to equate, in my opinion regrettably, the symbolic gesturality of the biblical prophets to that of the Greek theatrical art (p. 973).
110 Cf. B.J. Hibbitts, «"Coming to Our Senses". Communication and Legal Expression in Performance Cultures» *ELJ* 41 (1992) 873–960 (here, pp. 882–883); D.S. Madison, *Critical Ethnography*, 165–198.
111 Cf. A. Nünning, *Grundbegriffe der Kulturtheorie und Kulturwissenschaften*, SlgM 351, Stuttgart 2005, 172–173.
112 Cf. D. Clerc, «Des actes pour parler», 113–114. Along these interpretive lines, we also find K. Ott, *Analogiehandlungen*, 164–165, though this form of expression does not address the dimension of the anthropological impact, which, in my view, is fundamental.

"Make yourself straps and yoke crossbars and put them on your neck" (27:2)   343

To say that symbolic gestures reflect the flavour of a specific epoch implicitly asserts a truth, however partial: to understand their scope, it is necessary to engage the question of their spatial-temporal contextualisation seriously, that is, to correlate the instance of the discernment of their meaning to a precise *hic et nunc*. In effect, in the intradiegetic dimension of the Scripture, one notices that the recourse to symbolic gestures on the part of the prophets is concentrated in particular historical moments: at *the time of the crisis of meaning*, the time of the "end" (threatened, announced, actuated, and suffered in the form of exile). It is by no chance, therefore, that precisely the books of Jeremiah and Ezekiel, excellent witnesses to the period of the catastrophe, contain, in absolute terms, the greatest number of non-verbal forms of communication.[113] If we then refer to symbolic gestures as semiotic devices that are merely literary in nature, produced after the catastrophe of 721 or of 587 (or sometime later) we find ourselves in the exilic or post-exilic epoch, that is, in a context where an entire people retrospectively reflected on the meaning of the tragedy that had struck. In fact, the point of view does not change. For this reason, the aforementioned reductionist interpretation seems unconvincing.

The crisis in question takes shape in the prophetic corpus as a relational crisis that relates to the bond of covenant between YHWH and his people, and its expression is broken down over on multiple levels. The aspect that is most critical is probably that of *language*. In fact, the prophets strongly denounce the aberration this has been subjected to, and most insidiously of all, in precisely the principal channels of human-divine communication. Aspects such as the cult, prophecy, wisdom, and royal institution become vectors not of communication with YHWH, but of lies and of sin masquerading as justice and truth instead. And this comes about, in fact, under the aegis of the cult, the word of the prophets and wise men, in name of the monarchic-Davidic authority instituted by God. The temple discourse in Jer 7:1–15 and 26 is emblematic of this.[114] We are dealing with the opacification of language. Empty formulas and rituality fill the mouths and gestualities of the culture, but they have now become entirely ineffective and *insignificant*. That is to say, they no longer act as signs; they no longer provide a reference to something that is true, real, or effective. And thus, they can no longer generate *salvation*. And so, it is now disaster that intervenes, precisely to serve salvation. Because still, as at the time of Isaiah, "this people draws near with their mouth and honours me with their lips, whilst their hearts are far from me" (Isa 29:13).

[8] Behold, you trust in *false words* (דִּבְרֵי הַשֶּׁקֶר), that *cannot profit*[115] (לְבִלְתִּי + √יעל hi.):

---

113   Cf. K.G. FRIEBEL, *Sign-Acts*, 14.

114   But think also of the question of the intercession that is denied, denouncing precisely the peoples' vain penitentiary rites during the drought (cf. B. ROSSI, *L'intercessione nel tempo della fine*, 233–239, 299–300), or the oracle against Israel in Amos 2:6–16, centred on unveiling the injustice concealed behind an apparent (merely legalistic) observance of the prescriptions of the *Tôrâ*.

115   The semantic of √יעל hi. definitely has to do, primarily, with the generic concept of "advantage/profit/benefit". But there is no lack of contexts specifying the nuance of this personal interest expressed by √יעל hi. by placing it right beside the concept of salvation (and right beside √יצע), obtained-from or hoped-for from YHWH or from the gods (cf. e.g. Isa 30:5–6 [2x] in relation to the salvific aid from Egypt that is attended in vain; 47:12; 57:12 with the following v. 13, where √יצע appears; Jer 16:19;

344   Jer 27–28. The world beneath the yoke of the king of Babylon

⁹ steal, kill, commit adultery, burn incense to Baal, go after other gods that you have not known. ¹⁰ And then you come and you stand before me in this temple, which bears my name, and *you say* (וַאֲמַרְתֶּם): *"We are saved!"* (√נצל hi.), only to go right back to commit all these abominations again (Jer 7:8–10).

But it is no longer the time of Isaiah. *Now*, in Jeremiah's time, the climax has been reached, the point of no return is here. So a linguistic shock is necessary – the coming about of the disaster is itself one, and in the most eminent way – to radically call into question not so much and not only the individual, but rather an entire communicative system based on a lie that would otherwise nourish itself indefinitely. *"Transgress"* becomes the watchword to which the prophet is called by God to yield obedience. That is, to pass beyond the threshold of "common sense", of that meaning that is recognised and accepted by all as a given, righteous, and normal expression of correct interpersonal interrelation in the social realm.

The entire system of signification of meaning in Israel is reopened for discussion by the prophet with his gestures and words. Starting from Jerusalem, a fundamental semiotic junction, of which the (threat of) destruction is, first of all, (the spectre of) the death of the most sacrosanct and solid devices through which meaning is kept in custody: the remembrance of the miracles of the Exodus, which shall not be repeated (cf. 21:1–10; 45), the end of the Davidic dynasty, which will not contradict the promises upon which it relied (cf. 2 Sam 7:1–17; Ps 132:10–18 and Jer 14:13), the end of the cultual celebration of the covenant, and the loss of the land, as the end of the visibility of the election and of the alliance with God (cf. 52:1–30).

If humankind has learned to hide from the truth, obscuring its falsehood, crimes, and injustice behind (social, cultual, legal) "norms", then it will be precisely these norms that will be shattered. As will the other structures that have been warped to play this perverse game (the temple and the cult, the monarchy, the possession of the land). To put on display the unfolding tragedy that no one wants to see. So that humankind can come out of hiding. And be saved. Every metaphor, after all, to be so, and in order to be recognised as such, must *transgress* the common norms of ordinary language.¹¹⁶ And the prophets are called to this dangerous game, which borders on the frontiers of the absurd.¹¹⁷ So that Meaning is given the possibility of regaining citizenship in its own home, in human space and time.

23:32 [2x]; Prov 11:4 in connection to the same root). One could thus comprehend (more than render in translation) the expression לְבִלְתִּי הוֹעִיל as "[untruthful words] that do not *save*", marking the idea of implicit salvation, reinforced by the connection with the profession of untruthful faith of the people cited by Jeremiah in v. 10 (נִצַּלְנוּ; "we are saved!").

116 On the metaphorical process as "transgression catégoriale", cf. P. RICŒUR, *La métaphore vive*, Paris 1975, 31–34, 192, 250–251, 316–317, etc. The recouping of a conception of metaphor no longer limited to the (restricted) sphere of rhetoric's stylistic figures is mainly thanks to cognitive linguistics. For a cognitive approach to the metaphorical phenomenon in the book of Jeremiah (with particular reference to the poetic oracles), see the study by J.Y. JINDO, *Biblical Metaphor Reconsidered. A Cognitive Approach to Poetic Prophecy in Jeremiah 1–24*, HSM 64, Winona Lake 2010 (for the theoretical foundations in particular, pp. 24–53).

117 Cf. D. CLERC, «Des actes pour parler», 114.

"Make yourself straps and yoke crossbars and put them on your neck" (27:2)   345

Symbolic gestures have a subversive nature precisely for this destabilising finality (cf. 16:10–13). They are a sometimes-paroxysmal intensification of communication that deliberately seeks a *breaking point*.[118] Even by remaining silent, even by prohibiting the prophet from interceding (cf. 7:16; 11:14; 14:11). Even in the silence of the tragedy of exile. They wound no one physically, but strike at the very heart of a system upon which all depend and from which everyone extracts some gain. This is why everyone feels threatened and the prophet gets contested (cf. ch. 28!) and persecuted like a public enemy (cf. 20:1–2; 26:8; 38:4).

Symbolic gestures are without a doubt *effective acts*, but not in the sense that they can be traced back or assimilated to magic gestures, as in the well-known position taken by G. Fohrer.[119] The intention is precisely the opposite, at least in prophetic literature influenced by the Deuteronomistic, exilic, or post-exilic school in general. Over-simplifying, we can say the practice of magic, not unknown to Israel and for a certain time, not even seen with suspicion[120] (probably until the time of Isaiah), seeks to penetrate the secret forces that govern the world in order to submit them to human desires. Its efficacy is innate to the practice itself (though generally not without the participation of gods). The gestures performed make up a consolidated repertoire. The *classic* prophet instead takes action in obedience to YHWH, a God perceived as mysterious (cf. Judg 13:18; Isa 45:15), whose intents, if not revealed, escape the grasp of the human intellect (cf. e.g. Jer 32:16–25). The prophet is asked to perform gestures that are *unprecedented*,[121] and he knows that these gestures are effective, but only for the power of the word of God. The initiative is His. The prophet expresses precisely that which is given him in faith, with gestures and with words: YHWH *is not manipulable* by the human being, he is not a vain idol made in the image of his maker, nor is he a projection of his logic or desires.

It is freedom that at times remains silent and other times speaks, in varied, often-unpredictable ways. In events that occur or in human words. But it is a freedom that enters into history with the pretence of having the keys to its meaning, that meaning which alone can provide life, more than bread, affections, and dignity can. And which must communicate itself with *urgency*. And by communicating, it *changes reality*. Whether its message is heard or rejected (cf. 28:13–14). Once again, therefore, I must underscore that the rhetorical function of this form of non-verbal language

---

118   Cf. S. AMSLER, «Les prophètes», 200.
119   Cf. G. FOHRER, *Die Symbolischen Handlungen*, 9–19, 94–98, 121–124.
120   In this sense, the following, e.g., can be subject to discussion: Gen 30:37–43; Num 5:21–28; 1 Kgs 17:21; 2 Kgs 4:34; 5:11–14; etc. The most recent research, depending on the different cultures of reference, tends to highlight the existence of overlapping areas between the sphere usually considered to pertain to "religion" and that of "magic". On this topic, see also the extensive, up-to-date monograph by R. SCHMITT, *Magie*.
121   "[…] they never belong to a known and pre-established repertoire of gestures and customs, but are invented for the occasion. The prophet is his own author of the script; no script is provided by the culture in which he performs. He is an imaginative and creative performer rather than a professional magician who relies on traditional tricks and rituals others cannot do or dare not attempt" (B. LANG, «Games Prophets Play», 193).

346   Jer 27–28. The world beneath the yoke of the king of Babylon

of the prophets' gestures is not the only one, nor should it alone be considered the decisive one.

The crisis of meaning that these interrogate regards, *in primis*, the *ethic-religious* dimension. And yet, as I have already highlighted, since this crisis reaches its peak precisely at the time of Jeremiah (under the reign of Zedekiah), manifesting itself as a crisis of (verbal) language, that is where it breaks through the (non-verbal) language of the crisis as well: in particular, the gesture of celibacy (16:1–4), with the refusal of other fundamental codes of sociability (16:5–9), and the negation of intercession (7:16; 11:14; 14:11). It is the proleptic visibilisation of the end. And then the gesture of the yoke, less strong from the point of view of anthropological impact, but more than decisive, since it is a radical shift of the semiotic register: from here on, one passes from the ethical-religious dimension to the *political dimension*.[122]

That the prophet take on the language of politics would actually seem to be an entirely *ordinary* fact if we consider the historical forms of divinatory-prophetic mediation attested in the context of the ancient Near East.[123] Indeed, if we were to want to momentarily assume a merely historical-literary research perspective (typical, e.g. of the approach of M.J. de Jong), we could ask if specifically the message of surrender would not be more plausibly attributable to a sixth-century historical figure by the name of Jeremiah holding a prophetic function at the court of Jerusalem, than would all the other oracles attributed to him, traditionally considered more authentic than the part in prose, which presents him to us as having a political option to propose.

And yet, this message is truly emblematic and extra-*ordinary* within the context of the book of Jeremiah[124] precisely because in the current literary configuration of the book, the prevalent (if not absolute) content of the Jeremianic oracles is of an ethical-religious sort. And so, it is precisely of this dimension that the need to surrender to Babylon declared with the gesture of the yoke at the time of Zedekiah denounces *complete failure*. At this point, Israel is irrecoverable (cf. 6:27–30). Or rather, it will be recoverable only if it will know how to freely assume, in obedience and with awareness, its own failure, with all the mortal consequences of this, and this by way of the political-prophetic choice indicated by Jeremiah: *surrender to the king of Babylon*, a gesture that coincides with the symbolic acceptance of the "end" in all its forms.

---

122   This is to be understood, obviously, in the theonomous sense: it remains a dimension placed in relation with the divine will, albeit in different modalities and to different extents (cf. General Introduction, § 1.4.1).

123   See, on this topic in particular, M.J. DE JONG, *Isaiah*, 300–313.

124   Even if, I repeat, what is hermeneutically most relevant with respect to the anthropological impact of this communicative dynamic, is celibacy.

4. "Bend your neck beneath the yoke of the king of Babylon!" (27:12). Between wisdom and prophecy: Surrender as a universal theology of history

4.1. The response to the design of God anticipated and requested by means of the gesture of the yoke. Semantic-pragmatic analysis

4.1.1 The gesture of the yoke and its literary structure

The *literary structure* of the text presenting the symbolic gesture can be classified, with G. Fohrer, under the schema "*order*" (of implementation) ["Befehl"] (vv. 1–3) – "*meaning*" (of the gesture) ["Deutung"] (vv. 4–22).[125] As we have seen (cf. § 3.4), the disproportion between the two moments, as far as their textual extension is concerned, has nothing to do with a presumed minor importance of the non-verbal communication with respect to the verbal one, but rather reflects the different semiotic register that these activate (analogical/digital).

After having mentioned the semiotic-relational dimensions implicated in the analogic communication typical of a symbolic gesture that engages the corporeity of the prophet and the same actants to whom the message is intended, let me now concentrate my attention on the (digital-conceptual) content of the communication. It is only for analytical reasons that I reserve it specific attention, for in truth, it should always be conceived as a synergic fact having verbal and non-verbal elements, even in the narrative dimension in which it presents itself today to the reader/listener.

4.1.2. The gesture of the yoke and its historical context

The *historical context,* starting from the textual and extratextual clues available, is attributable to a period of great instability in the Syro-Palestinian area,[126] which, from 605, at the expense of the Egyptian dominion over the region, had passed under the Babylonian hegemony. After the *débâcle* endured by the kingdom of Judah in 597,

---

125 According to G. Fohrer, *Die Symbolischen Handlungen*, 18–19, the fundamental elements that, in the MT, configure attestations of symbolic gestures as a literary genre would be the following: (1) *order* (Befehl) with regard to the fulfilment of the gesture; (2) *report* (Bericht) on its actualisation; (3) *meaning* (Deutung) of the gesture made. The author's categorisation is solely of the literary-formal type (according to the method of the *Formgeschichte*) and this has, consequently, an approach to the phenomenon that is very limited. In this way, the peculiarities typical of non-verbal communication, which are not exhausted by their textual description, nor can they be reduced, therefore, to a rigid literary/formulaic schema are not taken into account (by this configuration, G. Fohrer, e.g. does not classify Jer 35; Ezek 6:11; 21:19–22 as "symbolic gestures", but just as "symbol-like behaviour" ["symbolähnliches Tun"; p. 72]). Obviously there are many differences between the various types of non-verbal communication associated with biblical prophetism, but the literary form cannot be taken on its own, in my opinion, as a valid criterion for organising an adequate taxonomy of the phenomenon, even if one limits oneself to its literary attestations.

126 For further details, herein overlooked, see what has already been said in ch. II, § 3.2.2.

348   Jer 27–28. The world beneath the yoke of the king of Babylon

the king Jehoiakim remained prisoner in Babylonia, along with the most influential strata of the population deported there. In Jerusalem, fomented in this by numerous prophets and by an intense nationalism, many probably see in him the legitimate king and await his rapid return. In any case, King Zedekiah (perhaps in spite of himself) and the ruling class demonstrate a strong anti-Babylonian and pro-Egyptian orientation.

Autonomistic expectations and/or desires seem to be on the verge of being fulfilled when the Babylonian empire suddenly finds itself in difficulty, on both the external and internal fronts. From outside, they undergo an attack by the Elamites, while internally, an insurrection breaks out against Nebuchadnezzar. We are between the end of 595 and beginning of 594. The revolt, though quite serious, is stifled, but this is not enough to hold that it be out of time, unrealistic, or historically completely hypothetical[127] for a strategic consultation to be held amongst the nearby or neighbouring vassal states with the kingdom of Judah (Edom, Moab, Ammon, Tyre, and Sidon),[128] whose ambassadors meet together in Jerusalem either the following year, in 594 (vv. 1.3) or already in 597, in the very first months of the reign of Zedekiah (according to another possible reconstruction).[129] It is in this circumstance, and certainly not at the time of Jehoiakim, that the injunction and execution of the symbolic gesture of the yoke (and of the yokes) can most plausibly be collocated.[130]

As I specified in ch. II, § 1, I have adopted these facts in my analysis not only for their general level of plausibility (in my opinion, not indifferent, despite the difficulties tied to the chronological sequencing of the events), but above all for their value as a realistic and pertinent *pragmatic context* with regard to a better comprehension of the Jeremianic message in chs. 27–28 (and 29).

4.1.3. Two literary resonances: The relationship with 1 Sam 11:7 and 1 Kgs 22:11

The symbolic gesture requested of Jeremiah by YHWH, concerning the rudimentary assembly of one or more yokes (or yoke collars), the performance to be carried out

---

127   G. Fischer, e.g., who considers all the historical data contained in the book of Jeremiah to be fictitious cloaking of its theological-literary message, does not insist on the question much. This is dropped, since it could not be reconstructed with any certainty (G. FISCHER, *Jeremia 26–52*, 51). A criterion that is hardly achievable in an absolute way, not only for every historical investigation on my text, but also for any reconstruction of the past, especially that farther away from us and less documented.

128   As can be noted in G.L. KEOWN – P.J. SCALISE – T.G. SMOTHERS, *Jeremiah 26–52*, 48–49, these five kingdoms were vassal states or allies of the kingdom of Judah at the time of David. Furthermore, aside from Sidon, they had also provided the raw materials and skilled labour for the construction of Salomon's temple (cf. 1 Kgs 5; 7:13–51; Sam 8:11–14).

129   This would be that proposed by N. SARNA, «The Abortive Insurrection», 281–294, already mentioned in ch. II, § 2.2.2.

130   *Pace* R.D. WELLS, Jr., «Dislocation in Time and Ideology in the Reconception of Jeremiah's Words: The Encounter with Hananiah in the Septuaginta *Vorlage* and the Masoretic Text», in: *Uprooting and Planting*, 322–350, which, in my opinion, inappropriately seeks to explain the textual difficulty tied to the presence of the name "Jehoiakim" (instead of that of Zedekiah) in 27:1, asserting that the gesture had been ordered in 609 and carried out only after 597.

"Bend your neck beneath the yoke of the king of Babylon!" (27:12) 349

with these objects, and the sending of them to the ambassadors, should not be considered an allegorical-imaginary fact (cf. Jer 25:15) or a sequence of actions situated in a visionary context (as, e.g. takes place in Ezek 37). The analogy with 1 Sam 11:7[131] does not leave much doubt in this regard. Nor is it a symbolic gesture whose formal aspect has an obscure interpretation, since it arises on a semantic-pragmatic line very similar to that attributed, for example, to the prophet Zedekiah in 1 Kgs 22:11. Corroborated by the message of the other court prophets (cf. v. 12), Zedekiah appears to be occupied with gestures and words to reassure Ahab, the king of Israel, of the victorious outcome of the military campaign he wishes to undertake against the Aramaeans along with Giosafat, king of Judah.

[11] Zedekiah, son of Chenaanah, who *made himself* ($\sqrt{}$עשׂה+ ל + suff. 3rd pers. m. sing.; cf. Jer 27:2) *horns of iron* (קַרְנֵי בַרְזֶל), and proclaimed: "Thus says the Lord: With these shall you gore the Arameans until they are destroyed". [12] All the prophets were prophesying the same: "Attack Ramoth Gilead: you will succeed! The Lord will hand it over to the king" (1 Kgs 22:11–12).

There are some important both formal and content-related common elements: the fact that it is the prophet himself who makes a concrete object (a pair of horns[132] of *iron*; cf. Jer 28:13–14) and that he carry it upon himself, the word that invests the object of symbolic significance, explaining its meaning and asking the interlocutor to act accordingly, and the fact that he presents himself as a legitimate, authoritative spokesperson for YHWH. Obviously the narrator does not say here that it is YHWH who commands the gesture (even if then, in 1 Kgs 22:19–23, he surprises us by saying to Michea that YHWH himself has allowed a spirit of untruth to falsely inspire the king's prophets). In a similar way, however, a political act is requested and encouraged (apparently) motivated by its positive objectives concerning the welfare of the state.[133] The content of the prophetic request linked to this verbal and non-verbal communication holds the opposite meaning of Jeremiah's yoke: in our case, the question is that of *submitting to the enemy*, not of fighting and winning over him. It is precisely on the content of this message that we need focus our attention.

---

131 Let us return to and explore what was already mentioned (in n. 4): it is narrated here that King Saul, in order to call together the Israelites to defend Jabes Galaad, a city besieged by Naas, king of the Ammonites, sends a pair of oxen that he had quartered to all the tribes with a specific verbal message: "Whoever does not come out to follow Saul and Samuel, so shall be done to his oxen" (v. 7). The narrator points out that Saul performs this symbolic act while gripped by the spirit of God (v. 6: "The spirit of God [רוּחַ־אֱלֹהִים] then rushed [$\sqrt{}$צלח] upon Saul [...]"), and that it was right after the liberation of Jabes that Saul comes to be fully recognised as the first king of Israel. It is an indication that assimilates this gesture to those typical of the prophets, considering that in the previous chapter (cf. 1 Sam 10:5–6, 1–13), using the same expression, it is explicitly said that Saul is endowed with the spirit and "acts as a prophet" (1 Sam 10:6, 10: $\sqrt{}$נבא hithp.) while amidst a group of prophets. Cf. G. FISCHER, *Jeremia 26–52*, 51.

132 On the use of these particular "props" on the part of the prophets, see P.E. DION, «The Horned Prophet (1 Kings XXII 11)», *VT* 49 (1999) 259–261.

133 According to M.J. DE JONG, *Isaiah*, 313, 456–458, the finality and meaning of the entire *historical* prophetic phenomenon in the ancient Near East (particularly in regard to prophecy in Assyria, Judah, and Israel) would be precisely this.

350   Jer 27–28. The world beneath the yoke of the king of Babylon

4.1.4. The lexicon and tool of the yoke in Jer 27–28 in the light of the cultural context of the ancient Near East: Between agricultural frame and military frame

I have already dwelled on a basic focalisation of the material aspect of the object assumed by the prophetic communication (i.e. the yoke [מוֹטָה/עֹל], or more precisely: the "collar" [of the yoke], composed of מוֹסֵרוֹת and מֹטוֹת) in the philological-exegetical notes marginally presented with the translation of chs. 27–28.[134] As we have seen, the text presents terminology that is not entirely clear on a first reading, and this can bring about, or has brought about, a certain degree of confusion in commentaries.[135] Further in-depth consideration would be possible in this regard.[136]

Herein, let me just add a few more indications to better understand the meaning, potentially polysemic, with which reference to this instrument is taken on within the context of the Jeremianic message. For this purpose, I will seek to briefly place the lexical data (and their respective contexts of use attested in the HB)[137] in relation

---

134   Cf. n. 30 and Figs. 19 and 20 on the following pages.

135   This is the case e.g. with K.G. Friebel, *Sign-Acts*, 140, where the author believes that Jeremiah is asked to manufacture a complete yoke (עֹל), which, to his understanding, would consist in the union of a horizontal bar (מוֹטָה) and ropes to fasten it (מוֹסֵרוֹת). Actually, in vv. 2–3, there is no mention of the term עֹל and even if in 28:10, 12, reference is made to the gesture of Hananiah as aiming to break a single מוֹטָה, immediately following, it reads: "you broke bars (מֹטוֹת) of wood". The physical instrument carried by Jeremiah is therefore a "collar", consisting in individual elements of wood and rope, while the complete yoke (עֹל), designed mainly for the use of paired animals, also provides for a robust horizontal axis, to which elements or thinner bars (מֹטוֹת) are fixed and positioned around the necks of the animals and fixed with ropes (מוֹסֵרוֹת), together with another longitudinal one, connected to the wagon or plough to be pulled (see also the detailed criticism of K.G. Friebel presented by Å. Viberg, *Prophets in Action*, 136, which I share). Also M. Ceccarelli, *Il profeta rifiutato*, 208, strangely first correctly identifies the מֹטוֹת with "the bars that fix the yoke around the animal's neck", but then improperly adds "and that we can translate with halters (It: 'capestri')". Now, in Italian, the term "capestro" (from the Lat. *capistrum*) never refers to rigid elements such as "bars", but rather to flexible belts or straps, such as head collars or generically, to ropes or ties used for bridling or tying oxen or other animals by the head (or also human beings, in reference to the execution noose or to other forms of forceful treatment).

136   For a whole series of more technical questions concerning ancient means of transport and traction utilised to make use of the strength of beasts of burden (typically horses, donkeys, oxen), in both civil and military use, see the collection of studies contained in M.A. Littauer – J.H. Crouwel, *Selected Writings on Chariots and Other Early Vehicles, Riding and Harness*, ed. P. Raulwing, CHANE 6, Leiden – Boston – Köln 2002 (with a rich presentation of images). Also to be borne in mind is the detailed and well-documented study by A. Ruwe – U. Weise, «Das Joch Assurs und *jhwhs* Joch. Eine Realienbegriff und seine Metaphorisierung in neuassyrischen und alttestamentlichen Texten», *ZABR* 8 (2002) 274–307 (on the use of the collar-shape yoke in particular, cf. pp. 277–288).

137   For עֹל see Clines VI, 398–400; for מוֹטָה Clines V, 172; for מוֹסֵרָה Clines V, 178.

with the pertinent semantic *frame*[138] of reference underlying them, upon which I will appropriately focalise by making use of some iconographic findings that come from the historical-cultural context of the ancient Near East (cf. Fig. 18).

Fig. 18. A pair of yoked (and emaciated, due to the siege undergone by the city) oxen pull a wagon of prisoners led into exile by the Assyrians. The two rigid components of the yoke are distinguishable: the horizontal bar and one of the vertical ones. Detail of the bas-relief of the taking of Lachish, from the time of Sennacherib (701–681) discovered in the royal palace of Nineveh (W. ORTHMANN, Der Alte Orient, 322, Fig. 233a; similar images in ANEP, Fig. 156 and 167, 367).

---

138 I refer to the theoretical framework of *Frame Semantics* theorised, above all, by the American linguist Charles J. Fillmore (especially in ID., «Frame Semantics and the Nature of Language», in: *ANYAS [Conference on the Origin and Development of Language and Speech]* 280 (1976) 20–32; ID., «Frame Semantics», in: *Linguistics in the Morning Calm*. Selected Papers from SICOL-1981, ed. LINGUISTIC SOCIETY OF KOREA, Seoul 1982, 111–137; ID., «Frames and the Semantics of Understanding», *QSem* 6 [1985] 222–254). For a general overview, see C.J. FILLMORE, «Frame Semantics», in: *Cognitive Linguistics: Basic Readings*, ed. D. GEERAERTS, CLRes 34, Berlin 2006, 373–400 and C.J. FILLMORE – C. BAKER, «A Frames Approach to Semantic Analysis», in: *The Oxford Handbook of Linguistic Analysis*, eds. B. HEINE – H. NARROG, Oxford 2010, 313–340). In this hermeneutical horizon, as one of its most famous maxims ("meanings are relativized to scenes") states, it is assumed that the understanding of the meaning of each lexical unit is not distinguishable from the scene ("frame") of reference presupposed by it. The meaning of a linguistic form, in other words, is not reducible simply to a list of truth-conditional elements, according to the postulate of compositional semantics. For Frame Semantics, the meaning of a lexeme is to be placed in relation to the schematisations of the experience of the world made by the speakers. A *frame* is a minimal narrative structure in which all elements are interconnected: "By the term 'frame' I have in mind any system of concepts related in such a way that to understand any one of them you have to understand the whole structure in which it fits; when one of the things in such a structure is introduced into a text, or into a conversation, all of the others are automatically made available" (C.J. FILLMORE, «Frame Semantics», 373). In this sense, Frame Semantics is "the study of how linguistic forms *evoke* or activate frame knowledge, and how the frames thus activated can be integrated into an understanding of the passages that contain these forms" (C.J. FILLMORE – C. BAKER, «A Frames Approach», 317). In the context of the

352   Jer 27–28. The world beneath the yoke of the king of Babylon

The image of the yoke has an entirely particular relevance in Jeremiah. The term
עֹל recurs 10x (2:20; 5:5; 27:8, 11, 12; 28:2, 4, 11, 14; 30:8) out of the total 40 attestations
present in the MT; מוֹטוֹת/מוֹטָה instead 5x (27:2 [pl.]; 28:10, 12 [sing.], 13[2x in the pl.])
out of a total of 12 occurrences. This second term, in the singular or plural, aside from
the case of the "crossbars of iron" (מֹטוֹת בַּרְזֶל) in 28:13, is used to describe the *material
composition* of the object, which, in chs. 27–28, is always used to *figuratively* refer to the
Babylonian power, both by Jeremiah and Hananiah. It is hence upon this term that we
need concentrate our attention, taking into account three contextual frameworks, which
I will interrelate: (a) that which is extrabiblical; (b) that which is biblical (MT); and (c) that
which is specifically Jeremianic (both within and beyond the unity given by chs. 27–28).

In order to render more pertinent the reference to other attestations, linguistic or
extralinguistic (i.e. of a pragmatic nature), we need keep in mind that the term עֹל in
Jer 27–28 is found inserted in syntagmatic relations supported by specific verbs that
define their context of use, along with others having a synonymic value (paradigmatic
axis) that correlates to the first ones, but of no lesser importance. Let us look at them:

	Syntagmatic axis	Paradigmatic axis
27:8	נתן√ + צַוָּאר (+ suff.) + בְּ + עֹל *to place* one's (own) neck in the yoke (of the king of Babylon)	עבד√ *to serve* (the king of Babylon)
27:11, 12	בוא√ hi. + צַוָּאר (+ suff.) + בְּ + עֹל *to introduce* one's (own) neck in the yoke (of the king of Babylon)	עבד√ *to serve* (the king of Babylon)
28:14	עֹל בַּרְזֶל + נתן√ + עַל + צַוָּאר a yoke of iron *to place* on the neck (of the nations)	
28:2, 4, 11	שבר√ + עֹל *to break*[139] the yoke (of the king of Babylon)	vv. 3, 4: שׁוב√ hi. *to bring back* (vessels and exiles)

On the one hand, there is the Jeremianic message, with the imperatives that ask to
place/introduce the neck in/under the yoke of Babylonia (27:8, 11, 12) or the (prophetic)
perfect that refers to YHWH as the subject that imposes it upon the nations (28:14).
To these actions, the verb עבד ("to serve"; 11x in 27:6, 7, 8, 9, 11, 12) is correlated with
synonymic value,[140] always having the Babylonian power as its object. On the other
hand, there is Hananiah who proclaims a message with a strong oppositional value,
attributing to the selfsame YHWH the will to *break* (שׁבר√; 6x in 28:2, 4, 11–14, 17) the
yoke of Babylon and thus to bring back (שׁוב√) from the exile the temple furnishings
and the deported of 597. The image of the "yoke" is thus invested by two symbolic
meanings that are radically antagonistic, depending on the verbs implicated.

---

following analysis, the linguistic notion of *frame* then finds an even more marked
relevance for the reference I will make to some "type" scenes attested by ancient
depictions coming from the cultural context of the ancient Near East.

139   The verb שׁבר has as object also the terms מוֹטָה (28:10, 12: a "bar" of the yoke and, by
synecdoche, the yoke itself) and מֹטוֹת (28:13; the "bars" of the collar-yoke).

140   Others verbs prove to be correlated, but have the value of governing subordinate
clauses that indicate the *consequences* of the act of submission to the Babylonian
yoke or of its breaking.

Fig. 19. *Animals (definitely) yoked pulling a plough. Detail of the bas-relief of the tomb of Paheri (XVIIIth Dynasty, 1550–1350) in El Kab (from The New York Public Library Digital Collections; cf. also ANEP, Fig. 84 and 91).*

It would seem obvious that the use of the term be metaphorical, but Daniel Bourguet is not convinced of this. He has dedicated an extensive monograph to the study of metaphors in the book of Jeremiah.[141] Let us therefore take a better look at the terms in question, because there are some interpretive implications to this that concern my theme.

The term עֹל/על (to which מוֹטָה, in singular or plural, can refer by synecdoche [cf. 28:10, 12] or as it relates to the wooden parts that make up the same על [cf. Lev 26:13; Ezek 34:27]) clearly designates the yoke imposed on beasts of burden to exploit their strength (and to be able to use them in pairs), both for the moving of people and/or things (by use of carts, for both civil and military use[142]; cf. Fig. 18) and in order to carry out demanding, essential agricultural activities[143] (cf. Num 19:2; Deut 21:3; 1 Sam 6:7; and also 4QJub^h 37:22) like the tillage and ploughing of the soil (cf. Fig. 19). From here, it is easy to comprehend why in many, if not all, ancient cultures, the image of the yoke was widely utilised to refer, in a metaphorical sense, to the concept of servitude, dominion, or dependence in general (also voluntary and in a positive sense) on someone else. In the MT, in fact, the metaphorical uses are much more frequent than the literal references,[144] even if D. Bourguet maintains that when the terms על and מוֹטָה are applied to human beings, one cannot properly (or in any case) speak of metaphorisation, but rather of metonymic use (the concrete for the abstract).[145] There would be,

---

141 D. BOURGUET, *Des Métaphores de Jérémie*, EtB 9, Paris 1987 (regarding the question of whether or not the image of the yoke is metaphoric, cf. pp. 420–424).
142 Also for ceremonials; cf. A. RUWE – U. WEISE, «Das Joch Assurs», 277.
143 Cf. O. BOROWSKI, *Agriculture in Iron Age Israel*, Winona Lake 1987, 51–52.
144 Out of 40 occurrences of the term על only those just cited refer to the agricultural tool. The other 37 in my opinion all imply a metaphorical use of the term, to indicate either submission or deference to the power/authority of someone.
145 See also, more recently, B.A. FOREMAN, *Animal Metaphors and the People of Israel in the Book of Jeremiah*, FRLANT 238, Göttingen 2011, 190–195, who substantially follows the opinion of D. Bourguet, highlighting, however (rightly) the clear metaphoricity of the expression "to break the yoke".

he claims, extrabiblical traces (cf. Fig. 20) and some textual clues that would suggest a literal reference when, in the MT, the image of the yoke is associated with human beings in correlation √עבד ("to serve"; cf. Gen 27:40; Lev 26:13; Deut 28:48; 1 Kgs 12:4, 7; Ezek 34:27) and/or with the term סֵבֶל ("weight", "burden", "load"; cf. Isa 9:3; 10:27; 14:25).[146] This would be a yoke similar to that used for animals, physically imposed on slaves or prisoners of war (cf. Fig. 21).

Fig. 20. A row of prisoners of war of Nubian origin immobilised by collars/halters and other bindings. From the rock carvings at the monumental temple complex built by Ramses II at Abu Simbel (©Shutterstock, with permission; cf. similar images in ANEP, fig. 1, 7, 8, 9, 32, 51).

Fig. 21. Prisoners of war lead away in a row, naked and restrained at neck height by long parallel bars (ancient Akkadian period, Nasrije, Iraq, ca. 2415–2290); from E. STROMMENGER, Fünf Jahrtausende Mesopotamien. Die Kunst von den Anfängen um 5000 v.Chr. bis zu Alexander dem Grossen, München 1962, pl. 118; W. ORTHMANN, Der Alte Orient, Fig. 103.

---

146 Connected, in turn, to the סִבְלוֹת, that is, to the "forced labour" (or "corvée") to which the Israelites in Egypt were obliged (cf. Exod 1:11; 2:11; 5:4–5; 6:6–7).

"Bend your neck beneath the yoke of the king of Babylon!" (27:12)   355

The same author then observes that in Jeremiah, there is never any mention of the animal as a metaphorising element (at least not in an explicit sense) when the image of the yoke is used in reference to Israel or other people (as in Jer 27–28). This leads him to hypothesise that the theme of the yoke may refer to two different isotopies: that of the animal, on the one hand (in reference to beasts of burden), and that of prisoners or slaves on the other, proposing, in our case, the second possibility. The avenue is quite an interesting one, but his argumentation does not seem to me to be entirely cogent in relation to the interpretation of the Jeremianic symbolic gesture.

The fact that Jeremiah does not explicitly make reference to the metaphorising element does not seem, in itself, to be nullifying, given the pervasiveness of the natural symbolic world in general and of animals in particular in the ancient collective imagination (and of the related human activities with their respective *frames*).[147] Moreover, if one reads the text carefully, the animal isotopy is called into question right in 27:5–6, when it is recalled that YHWH, creator of the animal world as well (v. 5: הַבְּהֵמָה), has subjugated even the "beasts of the field" (v. 6: חַיַּת הַשָּׂדֶה) to the Babylonian king Nebuchadnezzar, "so they will serve him" (לְעָבְדוֹ), that is, one can more specifically understand: "so they will work for him". The connotation of על in an agricultural sense would thus be the subtext, not even so implicitly. On the other hand, it is attested that on slaves and prisoners, as a security measure for control over them or for their relocation from one place to another, something similar to a yoke could be inflicted on the neck (the closest lexical reference in this case seems to be the term מוֹטָה). As far as we know, these were often collars[148] and other bindings (cf. Fig. 20), or rather long parallel poles to which the prisoners were harnessed in single file (cf. Fig. 21). Amongst the Assyrian bas-reliefs, however, there is a well-defined image in which armed soldiers are seen escorting a group of prisoners lined up in a row (cf. Fig. 22). They have their arms tied behind their backs, but at neck height, each one of them is immobilised by an instrument that, in all effects, resembles a "yoke collar". The description of the object that YHWH asks the prophet Jeremiah to realise, and with which Hananiah interacts, seems to have traits that are *very similar* to this depiction. It need be emphasised, however, that the reference to instruments similar to the "yoke" in this iconographic context of an Assyrian matrice is preponderantly applicable to the relocating of prisoners and not to their permanent *status* as people subject to slavery.

---

147   The concept of *frame*, as a "cognitive context" made up of a structured system of interdependent concepts by which an experience is organised, is broader than that of "isotopy" (which refers to a set of redundant semantic categories – since they appear repeatedly – useful for recognising the interpretive coherency of a text).

148   *HALAT*, 783, the entry על, points out that in Arabic, the term *ġullu* refers to the iron rings placed around the necks of prisoners. The Assyrian bas-reliefs attest to even more cruel practices: for the transfer of prisoners of war, a type of harpoons or hooks/grapples were thrust through their lips (cf. Amos 4:2 as well as 2 Kgs 19:28; Isa 37:29; Ezek 19:4; 38:4). See e.g. the image of Esarhaddon who keeps two subjugated kings on a leash (using rings thrust through their lips) in A. PARROT, *Ninive et l'Ancient* Testament, CAB 3, Neuchâtel 1953, 47 (Fig. 14) and an analogous one in A. PARROT, *Babylone et l'Ancient Testament,* CAB 8, Neuchâtel 1956, 73, Fig. 36).

Fig. 22. Assyrian soldiers escorting prisoners in neck stocks that resemble yokes (from A. PARROT, Assur, Paris 1961, 120, Fig. I).

Fig. 23. Two (yoked?) slaves who pull a plough. Detail of the bas-relief of the tomb of Paheri at El Kab (from The New York Public Library Digital Collections; cf. ANEP, Fig. 85). The scene is placed immediately to the right and on the same level as that of Fig. 20, where the yoke is not clearly visible, even if its presence can be held certain.

Nonetheless, based on at least one attestation of Egyptian origin, it is equally plausible that instruments of the sort (to which the HB, in any case, never makes mention in a material or literal sense as to something analogous), could be employed on men forced to perform work usually carried out by beasts, such as the ploughing of fields (cf. Fig. 23: the manner in which the men are tied to the plough they pull is not visible, but neither can the yoke to which the animals are tied be clearly distinguished in Fig. 19, though it is *undoubtedly present*) or hauling of wagons (by soldiers: which can be seen in a detail of the celebrated Assyrian bas-relief portraying the complex, ferocious military operations of the taking of Lachish[149]; cf. Fig. 24).

---

149 Cf. D. USSISHKIN, *The Conquest of Lachish*, 74, Fig. 63 (right side). The detail to which I refer is enlarged in the sketch on p. 116 of the same work, which I reproduce here

"Bend your neck beneath the yoke of the king of Babylon!" (27:12)

Fig. 24. Sketch of a detail of the bas-relief representing the taking of Lachish. Assyrian soldiers who pull a royal carriage using a very decorated yoke (from D. USSISHKIN, The Conquest of Lachish, 116). The context is that of the presentation of the war booty plundered from the city just conquered to the Assyrian sovereign (cf. ANEP, Fig. 85). The scene is contiguous, even if placed on a lower level than that of Fig. 18.

Given these interconnections, which are symbolic and material at the same time, distinguishing definitely between the two isotopies, and the relative *frames* underlining the lexicon attested, seems to me to be an arbitrary operation, or at least an impervious one. It is quite probable, in my view, that the metaphoric use of the image of the yoke and its relative vocabulary had its metaphorising origin (or *source domain*, according to the cognitivist vocabulary) in the *frame* of the agricultural use of beasts of burden, that is, that most common and universally prevalent. This does not exclude that, other than the generic concept of work and (agricultural) service, the *frame* of the world of war or slavery and/or imprisonment, with its concrete implications (and nevertheless, in reference to a transitory condition),[150] is also actually or directly involved when referring to the yoke in a context similar to the Jeremianic one.[151]

In relation to the theme of surrender, we could say, in synthesis, that considered in the perspective of the agricultural frame, what is emphasised by the yoke is the dimension of "service" (in this metaphorical context, the person who surrenders labours for the one who has subjected them, as in Jer 29, where the well-being of Babylon is favoured, inviting the people to "serve" the dominators), while in relation to the *frame*

---

in Fig. 24. Obviously, it is a very different context from the *frame* of slavery. See also the analogous image reproduced in A. PARROT, *Assur*, 123, Fig. B.
150 That is, the transfer of prisoners. From this point of view, tied to a condition that is more *permanent* (that of the intended purpose of use with animals), the agricultural *frame* certainly has a more marked connotation.
151 In this sense, also E. SILVER, «Performing Domination», 186–216, when he asserts that the idea of the "yoke" also expresses "an operating theory of sovereignty. It associates a power relationship which would otherwise be viewed as exploitative with a practice of thoughtful, even laborious cultivation" (p. 206). Regardless, the horizon of meaning pertinent to my theme needs to be broadened further, as I demonstrate in the following paragraphs.

358   Jer 27–28. The world beneath the yoke of the king of Babylon

of war (and the *sub-frame* of captivity), what is more marked is the humiliation, loss of autonomy, and fact of being at the mercy of the victor.[152]

Let me now concentrate on the figurative use of these references, in the light of the context of the ancient Near East.

4.1.5. The figurative use of the yoke and its various frames of reference in the context of the ancient Near East

The expressions attested in Jer 27–28 are common in sources from the ancient Near East, where the Akkadian equivalent of עֹל, that is, the term *nīru*[153] (along with the semantically related *abšānu*,[154] *šigaru/sigaru*,[155] *ṣimittu*,[156] *ḫullu*,[157] and also *gišgiššu*; cf. also the verb *ṣamādu*[158] "to yoke, to harness", having both animals and people as object), is often used in figurative reference to the submission (and thus, humiliation)[159] imposed by the sovereigns (or the gods) on vassals or conquered peoples (and also on their attempts at rebellion or voluntary subordination).[160] In the corpus of the fourteenth century letters of El-Amarna, for example, where we find attested the Semitic-western substantive **ǵullu* ("yoke"; *nīru* is glossed in one case [EA 296,38] with the term *ḫullu*, which, in turn, can be found in yet another text [EA 257,15,])[161] the speaker twice expresses his submission to a more powerful king declaring that he

---

152   It is important to underscore this connotation, for commentators often limit themselves to referring, in Jer 27–28, to the agricultural metaphor (as is still found, recently, in W.L. Kelly, *How Prophecy Works. A Study of the Semantic Field of* נביא *and a Close Reading of Jeremiah 1:4–19, 23:9–40 and 27:1–28:17*, FRALANT 272, Göttingen 2020, 218–219).

153   Cf. *CAD*, *N*, vol. XI, 260–263 («nīru A»).

154   Cf. *CAD*, *A*, vol. I – part I, 65–66 (lit.: "cord, rope". This rope is an integral part of the yoke, which can be understood from the term by synecdoche).

155   Cf. *CAD*, *Š*, vol. XVII – part II, 408–411 (the term refers to the shackles and/or collars used for prisoners of war or for animals).

156   Cf. *CAD*, *S*, vol. XVI, 198–199 (this is the horizontal bar of the yoke).

157   Cf. *CAD*, *Ḫ*, vol. VI, 230, the entry «ḫullu B», attested only 2x in the Amarna letters, with clear metaphorical significance.

158   Cf. *CAD*, *Ṣ*, vol. XVI, 89–92.

159   Even in the Latin sources, the yoke is an instrument and symbol of humiliation and dishonour for the defeated; we are reminded of this by Gaius Julius Caesar with regard to a crushing defeat suffered by the Romans in Gaul in 107: "Caesar, quod memoria tenebat L. Cassium consulem occisum exercitumque eius ab Helvetiis pulsum et sub iugum missum concedendum non putabat [...]" (Caesar, *De bello gallico*, I,7; cfr. Caesar, *The Gallic War*. With an English Translation by H.J. Edwards, LCL 72, London – Cambridge (MA) 1917, 13).

160   Subjection to a "yoke" as an equivalent to "power" is common in expressions concerning the dominion of a sovereign or main divinity of reference (the expression "yoke of the king X" is a frequently used expression, or, more specifically, "the yoke of Assur" in the Neo-Assyrian sources); cf. A. Ruwe – U. Weise, «Das Joch Assurs», 281–290 (on the image as used from the point of view of the subjected vassal, see p. 290).

161   Cf. D.S. Vanderhooft, «Wadi el-Ḥôl Inscription 2 and the Early Semitic Alphabetic Graph **ǵ*, **ǵull*, "yoke"», *HeBAI* 2 (2013) 125–135 (with illustrations).

"Bend your neck beneath the yoke of the king of Babylon!" (27:12)   359

will place his neck beneath his *hullu* ("yoke.")[162] These metaphorical references, whose pragmatic implications cannot be negated, even if they require specification,[163] become (increasingly) frequent in Neo-Assyrian and Neo-Babylonian inscriptions, especially from the middle of the eighth century.[164]

It should be highlighted that the image of the yoke is also tied (in isomorphic semiosis) to the image of another gesture of total obeisance, like that of *kissing the feet* of the superior authority. Also, the fact of remaining yoked means, amongst other things, paying a *tribute* owed to the supreme sovereign "year by year".[165] Sennacherib (705/704–681) explicitly denounces the non-compliance of this obligation on the part of King Hezekiah, upon whom he himself subsequently imposes both gestures:

> [I ruined the wide district of the recalcitrant (and) strong land Judah] (and) I made Hezekiah, its king, bow down at my feet so that he (now) pulls [my] yok[e.][166]

These data highlight some concrete aspects implicated in the Jeremianic request and invested by the prophetic communicative context by a symbolic meaning that assumes the political one and inserts it, transcending it, into a theological dimension. In Jer 27–28, one could think of the act of payment of the tributes that are owed, elsewhere, such as in 38:14–28a, to other concrete gestures of deference, submission, and surrender, such as going out to meet the enemy generals, surrendering to them, prostration before and kissing of the feet of Nebuchadnezzar, the complete handing over of all of the goods in possession, etc.

Amongst the many other literary and iconographic attestations, it is worth mentioning what is reported in the Rassam Cylinder found in the North Palace of Ashurbanipal (669–630/629) in Nineveh (modern-day Kouyunjik in Iraq) and contained its annals.[167] In the tenth column (lines 17–39), the literal reference of yoking and metaphorical reference to submission overlap in a single event, since it reports the

---

162   Thus, according to the translation by W.L. MORAN, *The Amarna Letters*, Baltimore 1992, 310 [EA 257]: "As I have placed my [n]eck in the yoke that I carry, may the king, my lord, know that I serve him [with com]plete devotion"; 338–339 [EA 296]: "And Indeed, now that I have *[p]la[ced]* the [...] of the yoke: *hu-ul-lu* of the king, my lord, on my neck, I carry it."

163   On the relationship between the metaphorical language and the possible pragmatic inferences, see R.W. GIBBS – M. TENDAHL – L. OKONSKI, «Inferring Pragmatic Messages from Metaphor», *LPPrag* 7 (2011) 3–28.

164   See in this regard M. ANBAR, «To Put One's Neck under the Yoke», in: *Essays on Ancient Israel in Its Near Eastern Context. A Tribute to Nadav Na'aman, eds.* Y. AMIT *et al.*, Winona Lake 2006, 17–19, and A. RUWE – U. WEISE, «Das Joch Assurs».

165   This is highlighted by A. RUWE – U. WEISE, «Das Joch Assurs», 284–286, in reference to the third military campaign of Sennacherib and to the exercise of Esarhaddon's rule.

166   Inscription engraved on a colossus (cf. A.H. LAYARD, *Inscriptions in the Cuneiform Character, from Assyrian Monuments,* London 1851, pls 59–62) from which I take the translation offered by RINAP 3/2, 48, no. 42,10b-11a. Cf. also TUAT I/4, 390 and ARAB II § 327 (see also TUAT I/4, 391, where we find added the translation of a shorter variant [inscription by Nebi-Yunus].

167   See M. STRECK, *Assurbanipal und die letzten assyrischen Könige bis zum Untergange Niniveh's.* II. Teil: Texte. Die Inschriften Assurbanipals und der letzten assyrischen Könige, VAB 7/II, Leipzig 1916, ²1975, 82–85; E.F. WEIDNER, *Reliefs der assyrischen*

360   Jer 27–28. The world beneath the yoke of the king of Babylon

fact of four kings defeated and subjected by Assurbanipal being *physically* forced to pull his ceremonial quadriga in the place of his team of horses in a celebrative-cultual context in honour of a divinity.

Nevertheless, it appears that only in a precious Mari attestation, aside from those contained in the HB (specifically in Jer 27–28; but cf. also 1 Kgs 12:11, 14; //2 Chr 10:11.14; Isa 47:6; Lam 1:14; Sir 33:27), do we find the image of the yoke to which submission is requested correlated explicitly to *castigation* or to *punishment* threatened in the case of refusal. Yašin-Dagan, general of the ruler of Elam writes to Hammurabi, king of Babylon in these terms on behalf of his king (we are in the ninth year of Zimri-Lim, king of Mari [i.e. between 1765 and 1764]):

> [...] (a) Les villes d'Ešnunna que tu détiens ne sont-elles pas miennes? (b) Évacue-les et *soumets-toi à mon joug!* (literally: *ki-ša-ad-ka a-na ni-ri-ia šu-ri-ib*, "Your neck to my yoke you submit") (c) Sinon, je pillerai ton pays de fond en comble. (d) L'armée fera route depuis Mankisum, elle franchira le fleuve à cet endroit. (e) À la tête de mes armées, je franchirai le fleuve et j'envahirai ton pays. .[...][168]

The paradigmatic context is determined by: (a) a *representative* or *assertive* linguistic act[169] that has the *illocutionary point* of affirming an actual fact, that is, the military occupation of Hammurabi of cities not his own (according to the speaker), and contemporaneously of conditioning the attitude of the interlocutor, because it is endowed with the *illocutionary force* of an *accusation* and of *vindication*, (b) an act with the illocutionary point of a *directive* sort, aimed at obtaining unconditioned submission to the yoke/dominion of the king of Elam, (c + e) the *commissive* act that *threatens punishment* as a gesture of retaliation in the event of disobedience, in turn made effective by (d) a proleptic description, that is, by a *representative* act (this, as well, having the value of a *threat*) concerning its material fulfilment.

It will be useful to keep this data in mind for a comparison with the pragmatic context of Jer 27–28. I will note at once that in Jeremiah as well, the call to submission is presented as an inevitable fact, and is motivated. Indeed, it is followed by a grave threat

---

Könige. Erster Teil. Die Reliefs in England, in der Vatikan-Stadt und in Italien, AfO 4, Berlin 1939, 53, 161.

168   Still unpublished letter (A. 3618), though partially translated and edited by D. CHARPIN, «Hammu-rabi de Babylone et Mari: Nouvelle Sources, Nouvelles Perspectives», in: *Babylon*. Focus Mesopotamischer Geschichte, Wiege früher Gelehrsamkeit, Mythos in der Moderne: 2. Internationales Colloquium der Deutschen Orient-Gesellschaft 24.–26. März 1998 in Berlin, *ed.* J. RENGER, CDOG 2, Saarbrücken 1999, 111–130 (here, p. 122).

169   For a classification of the illocutory significance of linguistic acts, I refer to the taxonomy proposed by J.R. SEARLE, «A Taxonomy of Illocutionary Acts», in: *Language, Mind, and Knowledge, ed.* K. GUNDERSON, Minneapolis 1975, 344–369 (= ID., «A Classification of Illocutionary Acts», *LangS* 5 [1975] 1–23; = ID., *Expression and Meaning*, Cambridge 1979, 1–29). This is based on three evaluative dimensions: *illocutionary point, direction of fit*, and *differences in expressed psychological states* as beliefs, intentions, desires. On this basis, the following types of locutionary acts can be distinguished: representative, directive, commissive, expressive, and declarative. I share the author's critique expressed on pp. 350–354 regarding the classification proposed by J.L. Austin, the latter having been conceived more as a working hypothesis.

"Bend your neck beneath the yoke of the king of Babylon!" (27:12)   361

(repeated several times, cf. 27:8, 10, 13, 15, 17) in the event of non-compliance, as in the text just mentioned. The motivations put forth are different, however: in Jeremiah, the necessity of submission seems to be tied only to the inscrutable divine design over history (cf. 27:5–7), at least at first sight.[170] In the Mari text, the question is instead that of restoring justice that has been violated (i.e. the right asserted by the sovereign of Elam on certain urban centres).

Another reference to be mentioned, though one of a more allusive type, concerns the conquest policy of Nebuchadnezzar pursued with determination and success in the Levant. In this regard, the sovereign expresses himself thus in auto-celebration, in the inscription from Wadi Brisa in reference to the peoples under submission (cf. WBC VIII 27–37)[171]:

> [...] I made them bow their neck to Babylon.[172]

The *frame* implicated here is still the same as in the previous cases. It should be noted, however, that in the context of the ancient Near East, reference to the yoke does not only have a negative significance tying it to asymmetrical power struggles of a political-military nature.[173]

In fact, in a proverb[174] rediscovered in a collection that is Assyrian but of clear Babylonian origin, we see called into question the theme (and therefore the relative frame) of *love of election*. The context is the socio-cultural one of interpersonal relations[175]:

---

170 I will deal with this question in § 4.2.
171 Herein, I report only the expression of greatest interest to us. A more extensive reference to the whole passage will be useful in § 4.2 when I treat the universal rule of Nebuchadnezzar.
172 WBC VIII 33 (R. Da Riva, *The Twin Inscriptions*, 61).
173 For the Neo-Babylonian period, in this respect, an expression of Nabopolassar that refers to his act of liberation from under Assyrian rule could always be cited: "[...] I chased them out of Akkad and I had (the Babylonians) *throw off their* (the Assyrians') *yoke*" (*ni-ir-šu-nu ú-ša-ad-di*). For the edition of the text and its translation, see S. Langdon, *Die neubabylonischen Königsinschriften*, VAB 4, Leipzig 1912, 66–69 and more recently, R. Da Riva, *The Inscriptions of Nabopolassar*, 59, 62 (her translation used here). The phrase with which Nabopolassar celebrates the liberation of Babylon from Assyrian rule is repeated twice in two different inscriptions, that of é.PA.GÌN.ti.la (NaplC12 1,21; pp. 59, 62) and that of Imgur-Enlil (NaplC32 I 28–33; II 1–5; pp. 94, 96).
174 The fact that it is a "proverb", that is, the popular expression of a sapiential truth that is widespread in the Mesopotamic milieu (or in the ancient Near East in general), gives this single attestation a significance of meaning that is even broader than, or equally significant to, the numerous claims of another sort taken from the Neo-Assyrian imperial annals.
175 Cf. W.G. Lambert, *Babylonian Wisdom Literature*, Oxford 1960, 227, col. II: 21–22. The Editor notes that the series of proverbs in this collection were most probably quite popular in Assyria (we are probably in the Middle Assyrian period). Others, however, believe that they are not proverbs but a very courteous and persuasive dialogical exchange between an Amorite man and his wife (p. 225). While this may not apply to the entire collection, the sayings that precede and follow this quote do

362   Jer 27–28. The world beneath the yoke of the king of Babylon

ša ta-ra-am-mi **21** Whom you love,
ù ni-ra tu-šá-aṭ **22** you bear (his) yoke.

Amongst the scarce Neo-Babylonian sources, Nebuchadnezzar himself uses this positive image twice in the Wadi Brisa inscription (which, however, testimonies his aggressive expansionist policy in the Levant) in reference to his devotion and obedience to the main Babylonian divinities. The underlying *frame* is therefore the cultic one.

Referring to Marduk and Nabu, it reads (cf. section WBA III 1–28, WBA III 29–34 = WBC Ib 1*-4*):

> My heart moves me (to strive) for their hearts' happiness; the (my) neck is bent to pull their chariot pole. They indeed are the great gods, the lords of destinies, who appointed me [...].[176]

The same image appears again further on, in the context of the message that concludes the inscription (cf. WBC X 13–40) to express the resolution of perennial fidelity and obedience toward the god Marduk:

> I am your faithful governor, let me tow your chariot pole until I become satisfied with extreme old age [...].[177]

In summary, one can say that the "yoke" and its complex "ties"[178] fasten different concepts together in significant relationships: slavery and service, freedom and dependence, love and prevarication, respect and infidelity. From the concreteness of this instrument and the cultural *frames* underlying it (socio-political-military and cultual), different and even antagonistic meanings and symbolisations branch out over the context of the ancient Near East. Its figurative reference is almost like a crossroads placed before human free will, or better still: it is a semiotic code capable of visually expressing conflicting outcomes and possibilities as this volition unfolds in its historical dimension.

4.1.6. *The image of the yoke in the HB and in the book of Jeremiah. Paths of meaning between slavery, liberation, transgression, and new promises*

Even from its first pages, in the HB, the image of the yoke is associated metaphorically (or via metonymy, even if this is less likely) to the concept of slavery, while the possibility of its breaking or removal (again, figuratively speaking) is tied to the opposite notion of freedom. Nonetheless, it should be stressed that even in the biblical literary

---

seem to trace back easily to that interpersonal context (which, in any case, can still make use of proverbial expressions).

176   WBA III 1–9 (I refer again to the edition by R. Da Riva, *The Twin Inscriptions*, 43–44).
177   WBC X 33–35 (R. Da Riva, *The Twin Inscriptions*, 63).
178   Plato defined analogy as "the most beautiful bond" (δεσμῶν [...] κάλλιστος), for its capacity to hold together entire different and even apparently incompatible semantic dimensions (*Timaeus*, 31c). The reference I allude to is therefore not only that of the material "ties" of the yoke, but to its multifarious metaphoric potential.

"Bend your neck beneath the yoke of the king of Babylon!" (27:12)   363

perimeter, in and of itself, this metaphorical context does not have a negative sense (or one that is positive only by its negation) *a priori*. This also applies for the two syntagmatic constructions placed in oppositional relation in Jer 27–28: "to carry", "to place", or "to break"; (etc.) the yoke can have opposite meanings, negative or positive, depending on the contexts of use.

According to the theoretical perspective of *componential analysis*,[179] based on the classic conception of the categories, we can identify, as necessary, sufficient traits for the focalisation of the figurative concept "to carry the yoke", not so much a generic form of action of [SUBMISSION] immediately marked by the trait [VIOLENT ENSLAVEMENT] caused by a stronger subject over a weaker subject,[180] but rather an action describable in its essential aspects as a [RELATIONAL INVOLVEMENT] of a person and their strength within the [OPERATIONAL DESIGN OF ANOTHER SUBJECT] (personal or figurative). On this underlying semantic, derived from the study of available biblical and extrabiblical attestations, other specifications or, technically,

---

179 The key assumption of this method of semantic analysis, or semantic feature analysis, is that the meaning of a word can be analysed by being broken down into its essential minor units or contrastive elements (organised in a matrix), called components (or semantic traits, features, semes, markers). Despite the limitations and the criticisms of this methodology, it remains, in many ways, of considerable heuristic value still today. In this regard, for a syntetic presentation, see R.M. KEMPSON, *Semantic Theory*, CTL, Cambridge 1977, 18–22; D.A. CRUSE, *Lexical semantics*, CTL, Cambridge 1986, 31–33; R. CARTER, *Vocabulary*. Applied Linguistic Perspectives, London – New York 1998, 30–33; D.A. CRUSE, *Meaning in Language*. An Introduction to Semantics and Pragmatics, OTLing, Oxford 1999, 2011³, 219–228; G. BASILE – F. CASADEI – L. LORENZETTI – G. SCHIRRU – A.M. THORNTON, *Linguistica generale*, MaU 93, Roma 2010, 333–344. My present discussion of semantics does not call for *prototypical semantics* to be brought into question. This approach is more effective than componential (or trait) analysis at accounting for various semantic phenomenon that depend on the vagueness of natural languages (in which the boundaries between different categories lack distinction) or on so-called "semantic anomalies" like metaphor or polysemy (cf. P. VIOLI, *Significato ed esperienza*, 151–207; F. CASADEI, *Lessico e semantica*, Roma 2003, 91–114).

180 It should be noted, incidentally, that the semiosis of the analogy implicated in the image of the yoke ("human being in relation"/"subjugated animal") does not generally find a positive translation according to the encyclopedia and the sensitivity of the modern reader. This is especially true for the analogy, very common in the ancient Near East, between the figure of the shepherd in relation to his flock and the function of the sovereign in relation to his subjects. If today, no one shows particular enthusiasm in being compared to a yoked animal or to a "sheep", and thus in conceiving oneself as being inserted in a "gregarious" dimension, it is because the original pragmatic context has been obscured (and transformed). In fact, in antiquity, particularly with this last analogy, the intent was, above all, to emphasise (even simply as imperial propaganda) the obligation placed in those invested with authority to care for and responsibility to guide the people that had been entrusted to them by their gods. In this positive sense, the image is also widely used in the NT, where Christ is the good shepherd who gives his life for his sheep (John 10:11; see Rev 7:17, where the shepherd is the Lamb) and the true Moses who, by donating the true Law, asks to assume his "yoke" (ζυγός), which is characterised in Mat 11:30 (cf. 1 Kgs 12:4), not coincidentally, as "sweet" (χρηστός) and "light" (ἐλαφρόν).

364   Jer 27–28. The world beneath the yoke of the king of Babylon

other markedness[181] (usually of the binary type) are then founded, determined by the context ([+/– FREE or IMPOSED]; [+/– DESIRED]; [+/– CONVENIENT]; [+/– ONEROUS]; etc.). Amongst these differentiations, let us look at those most relevant to my topic.

In Gen 27:40, Isaac preannounces to his son Esau that he will have to serve (√עבד) his brother, but also that by fighting against him, he will be able to rip off (√פרק) the yoke from his neck. Instead, in Lev 26:13, a decisive text of reference for my topic, the *founding* event of the Exodus is described as a liberation from the condition of slavery, represented by the image of being yoked:

> I am the Lord, your God, who brought you out (√יצא hi.) of the land of Egypt, so that you are no longer their slaves (עֲבָדִים); I broke (√שבר) the crossbars (מֹטֹת) of your yoke (עֻלְּכֶם) and made you walk with heads held high.

The whole exodical path can thus be synthesised in the passage from harsh Egyptian slavery (עֲבֹדָה; cf. e.g. Exod 1:14; 2:23; 5:9; etc.) to freely serving YHWH (עֲבֹדָה; cf. Exod 12:25–26; 13:5; 27:19; etc.).[182] It is not a transition from one slavery to another, nor from an external constraint to a freedom understood as pure individualistic volition (auto-nomy) or as utopian, disintegrating absolute freedom. It is rather a liberating release from an inhuman service in order to protend one's own being and personal history towards a donation of self that truly fulfills human nature, possible only in the reciprocity of that love that has God as origin, foundation, and means (theo-nomy). Understood in this relational framework, where subjects are bound by reciprocal relations of mutual recognition and promotion, service is the reason for the very existence of Israel. Because in biblical revelation, liberty, without relationship and without responsability, makes no sense.

On the basis of this expressive model of the originary salvation, other salvific interventions of YHWH in the history of Israel can also be understood, such as that preannounced in the Proto-Isaiah, where the Lord breaks the yoke of the foreigners

---

181   The notion of "markedness" derives from phonology where, between two phonemes, that which has a sound trait that lacks in the other is referred to as "marked". Analogously, in semantics, unmarked forms are also the most basic ones, those having, in other words, a broader meaning than those that are marked (e.g. the lexeme "man" [*unmarked*, with wider referential potential] than the lexeme "woman" [*marked*]). See also G. BASILE – F. CASADEI – L. LORENZETTI – G. SCHIRRU – A.M. THORNTON, *Linguistica generale*, 337.

182   In this regard, see the well-known contribution of G. AUZOU, *De la servitude au service*. Étude du livre de l'Exode, ConBi 3, Paris 1961, and in particular his concluding message: "Le service de Dieu est la réponse du peuple de l'Alliance au Seigneur qui s'est révélé à lui et qui lui a parlé. C'est la vie dans l'Alliance. Tout jusqu'ici, dans l'histoire que nous avons suivie, était ordonné à cette vie. Si Dieu a libéré son peuple, aussi bien de la servitude étrangère que des liens qui entravaient son cœur, s'il l'a convié a une Rencontre qui doit changer le cours de son histoire et l'histoire même du monde, c'est pour lui permettre de se donner parfaitement à ce service, dans lequel il trouvera l'accomplissement de son destin et la plénitude de la vie. Tel est, nous en sommes convaincus au terme de notre étude, le message essentiel du livre de l'Exode" (p. 377).

"Bend your neck beneath the yoke of the king of Babylon!" (27:12)   365

who oppresses his people.[183] The echo of the Neo-Assyrian expressions as well as their reworking or "process of transference"(*Umbuchungsprozess*),[184] is evident:

> For you have *smashed* (√חתת ni.) the yoke (על) that burdened him, the crossbar (מַטֵּה) on his shoulder and the rod that oppressed him, as on the day of Midian (Isa 9:3). So it will be that day, that his burden (סֹבֶל) *will be removed* (√סור) from your shoulders and his yoke (על) from your neck; the yoke (על) *shall be destroyed* (√חבל pu.) before the abundance[185] (Isa 10:27).

> *I will crush* (√שבר) the Assyrian in my land and I will trample him on my mountains; then his yoke (על) *shall be removed* (√סור) from them, and his burden (סֹבֶל) from their[186] shoulders (Isa 14:25).

It is in precisely this Isaianic tradition that the message of "salvation" of the prophet Hananiah, in opposition to the Jeremianic request, appears to draw its inspiration. I will discuss this briefly in § 5.2.2, in the context of the clash between the opposed prophetic messages of Jeremiah and Hananiah. For now, I will highlight that in the passages cited thus far, to be burdened with the yoke has a negative meaning, marked by traits [+ IMPOSED/ONEROUS] to which the powerful intervention of YHWH who frees from its weight and from its constrictive duress corresponds in a positive sense. Instead, in other texts, the image of the yoke has an entirely opposite significance: to carry it is a title of honour, and the traits that appear are [+ FREE/DESIDERED/CON-VENIENT]. Breaking it, on the other hand, means betraying a relationship of mutual trust. For example, particularly in reference to obedience to God and observance of the *Tôrâ*, carrying the yoke with its bonds is a path to life (cf. Jer 5:5[187]; and also Hos 11:4; Zep 3:9[LXX]; Lam 3:27; Sir 51:26).[188]

---

183   See also Hos 11:4, a text that is partially corrupt and not easily translated, in which, however, the image of the yoke (from which one is freed or which gets imposed, depending on the political-religious terminology common to analogous Neo-Assyrian attestations and in reference to the bonds of love of YHWH) seems to be central (cf. A. RUWE – U. WEISE, «Das Joch Assurs», 294–297).

184   I refer to the notion highlighted by J. ASSMANN, *Herrschaft und Heil*. Politische Theologie in Altägypten, Israel und Europa, München – Wien 2000, 49–52.

185   In the MT מִפְּנֵי־שָׁמֶן; lit.: "because of fat/oil". The enigmacity of this expression has resulted in the second part of the v. getting amended by many commentators, though without well-founded necessity (cf. D. BARTHÉLEMY, *Critique textuelle*, 77–78). The Hebrew text, though difficult, is well established. It is probably a proverbial saying or an expressive variant on the theme of liberation from the yoke (W.A.M. BEUKEN, *Jesaja 1–12*, HThKAT, Freiburg im Breisgau 2003, 273 [with explanations on p. 276], e.g. translates: "[...] da weicht seine Last von deiner Schulter, sein Joch wird von deinem Hals weggerissen *und der Jochriemen von der fetten Vorderfront*" [my italics]). I will not address this issue in detail because it falls beyond my argument.

186   The MT has the sing. (שִׁכְמוֹ): "from *his* shoulders". It probably intends to recall the analogous expression in Isa 9:3.

187   According to W.L. HOLLADAY, *Jeremiah 1*, 97, reference is being made here to the "weight" of the *Tôrâ*.

188   The metaphor of observance of the *Tôrâ* as the embracing of a salvific yoke (cf. e.g. *Berachot*, 12b, 13b, 14b, etc., also in reference to the "Kingdom of Heaven") is quite widespread in rabbinical teaching. Those who carry this yoke experience freedom: "[...] those who embrace the yoke of the *Tôrâ* are free from the yoke of the

366   Jer 27–28. The world beneath the yoke of the king of Babylon

A text having the value of an important semiotic nexus can be found right in the book of Jeremiah. It is Jer 2:20, a verse translated by modern versions in a way that is perhaps too uniform or offhanded,[189] as if the subject of the first two phrases were clearly Israel. Thus, it could instead be translated keeping with a flat reading of the MT but already highlighting two possible ways of understanding its second part (cola c-e and, particularly, colon d):

כִּי מֵעוֹלָם	a	Truly from times of old
שָׁבַרְתִּי[190] עֻלֵּךְ	b	I have broken[190] your yoke,
נִתַּקְתִּי[191] מוֹסְרֹתַיִךְ	c	I have torn[191] your bonds,
וַתֹּאמְרִי	d	but [and] you said:
לֹא אֶעֱבֹד[192]	e	"I do not want to serve" ["I will not transgress."][192]
כִּי[193] עַל־כָּל־גִּבְעָה גְבֹהָה		And in fact [but instead][193] on every high hill
וְתַחַת כָּל־עֵץ רַעֲנָן		and under every green tree
אַתְּ צֹעָה זֹנָה		you lay down like a prostitute.

The subject taking action in the beginning would thus be YHWH (as it also is in the Targum and the Peshitta). Keeping to this reading of the MT,[194] the meaning is clear, at least until colon c: the Exodus is still seen as a sovereign act of YHWH who liberates his people from the yoke and ties of Egyptian slavery.[195] In response, utterly

---

  state and from the yoke of civil duties [or worldly concerns]. Anyone who rejects the yoke of the *Tôrâ*, will be imposed with the yoke of the state and the yoke of civil duties [or worldly concerns]" (*Pirqe Avot*, 3,5/6; cf. BLACKMAN P., *Mishnayot.* Vol. IV: Order Nezikin, New York 1963, 508; it is interesting to note a distant echo in this saying of the Jeremianic discourse, since the "state" that imposes its yoke is surely meant to be understood as a "foreign state"; cf. also *Bereshit Rabba,* LXVII,7). In Gen 49:14–15, Jacob blesses the tribe of Issacar by comparing it to a "robust donkey" who "bent his back to carry the burden". For the Jewish tradition, Issacar is the tribe that consecrated itself to the study of the *Tôrâ*, burdening itself with its yoke like a sturdy donkey loaded with a heavy fardel (cf. *Bereshit Rabba,* XCVIII,12 and Rashi again in Gen 49:14–15). For its obstinacy and ability to carry considerable weight, in Judaism the donkey has risen to be a symbol of faithful and perseverant study of the law of God. Cf. S.D. MCBRIDE, «The Yoke of the Kingdom. An Exposition of Deuteronomy 6:4–5», *Interp.* 27 (1973) 273–306 (for the relation to the book of Jeremiah, see pp. 287–306).

189 In this regard, see A.B. BOZAK, «Heeding the Received Text: Jer 2,20a, A Case in Point», *Bib.* 77 (1996) 524–537, who first and foremost notes: "Although modern translations of the book of Jeremiah present a clear and apparently undisputed version of Jer 2,20, the meaning of this verse is not as transparent as the reader would be led to believe" (p. 524).

190 As in the MT, but the LXX reads συνέτριψας ("you have broken").

191 As in the MT. The LXX instead reads διέπασας ("you have torn").

192 In the case of Q (אֶעֱבוֹר)/K (אֶעֱבֹד).

193 On the diverse meanings that the particle כִּי can assume in this context, see A.B. BOZAK, «Heeding the Received Text», 526–527.

194 It is the one I personally prefer, with A.B. BOZAK, «Heeding the Received Text», 525.

195 Cf. P.C. CRAIGIE – P.G. KELLEY – J.F. DRINKARD, *Jeremiah 1–25,* 36–37.

"Bend your neck beneath the yoke of the king of Babylon!" (27:12) 367

ungrateful, Israel refuses to serve (colon d: K √עבד) Him from whom it has received the gift of freedom, the only true God (cf. Jer 10:10),[196] and prostitutes itself to the false gods of the land of Canaan instead. Reading the K, this would seem to be confirmed by the parallelism created with the following v. 21, where the amorous and gratuitous care of YHWH for his vineyard is counterposed with the unusual deterioration of the latter in "degenerate branches of a bastard vineyard". Instead, with the Masoretic Q (√עבר), followed by the Targum and the Peshitta, an admirable intention of fidelity would be emphasised, in the perspective of Jer 2:2 (where it is affirmed that at first, in the desert, Israel had followed the Lord).

The perspective is entirely inverted, on the other hand, if one considers, as in the LXX,[197] the first two governing verbal forms (שָׁבַרְתִּי and נִתַּקְתִּי) to be like ancient feminine forms of perfect qal in second person singular[198] (cf. 2:33): only the invincible rebel spirit of Israel would thus result as "originary". This is the translation followed by the majority of commentators and in modern versions.

כִּי מֵעוֹלָם	a	For truly from long ago
שָׁבַרְתִּי עֻלֵּךְ	b	you broke off your yoke,
נִתַּקְתִּי מוֹסְרֹתַיִךְ	c	you tore off your bindings,
וַתֹּאמְרִי	d	and you said:
לֹא אֶעֱבֹד[199]	e	"I do not want to serve."[199]
כִּי עַל־כָּל־גִּבְעָה גְּבֹהָה		And indeed on every high hill
וְתַחַת כָּל־עֵץ רַעֲנָן		and under every green tree
אַתְּ צֹעָה זֹנָה		you have laid down as a prostitute.

Beyond the characteristic productivity of meanings typical of poetic language,[200] it is precisely the polysemic symbolic significance of the yoke that has produced, in my opinion, these possibilities or outcomes of translation and suggestions of counterposed emendations. And this from the old versions. In any case, this text should be considered to be closely connected to 5:5 (and both of these, in turn, to 27–28)[201]:

---

196 On this subject, I note the valuable contribution of A. FAVALE, *Dio d'Israele e dei popoli*. Anti-idolatria e universalismo nella prospettiva di Ger 10,1–16, AnBib 211, Roma 2016.

197 Cf. W. McKANE, *Jeremiah*, I, 40; B. BECKING, «"I Will Break his Yoke from off your Neck". Remarks on Jeremiah xxx 4–11», in: *New Avenues in the Study of the Old Testament. A Collection of Old Testament Studies*, ed. A.S. VAN DER WOUDE, OTS 25, Leiden 1989, 63–76, here pp. 75–76 (reworked and republished in: ID., *Between Fear and Freedom*. Essays on the Interpretation of Jeremiah 30–31, OTS 51, Leiden – Boston 2004, 135–164).

198 As e.g. it is held to be by W.L. HOLLADAY, *Jeremiah 1*, 52 (cf. GK §44h; JM §42f).

199 According to the K.

200 Rightly recalled in this case by A.B. BOZAK, «Heeding the Received Text», 531.

201 Also to be considered pertinent are the expressions עַם־קְשֵׁה־עֹרֶף ("a stiff-necked people") in Exod 32:9; 33:3, 5; etc. and עֵגֶל לֹא לֻמָּד ("untrained calf") in Jer 31:18 (cf. W.L. HOLLADAY, *Jeremiah 2*, 190: "The assumption of the image is that the calf is 'trained' for the yoke"), to look at in relation to Hos 4:16; 10:11.

368 Jer 27–28. The world beneath the yoke of the king of Babylon

אֵלְכָה־לִּי אֶל־הַגְּדֹלִים   **a**   Therefore, I will go to the leaders
וַאֲדַבְּרָה אוֹתָם   **b**   and I will speak to them
כִּי הֵמָּה יָדְעוּ דֶּרֶךְ יְהוָה   **c**   <u>for they know the way of the Lord</u>,
מִשְׁפַּט אֱלֹהֵיהֶם   **d**   the justice of their God.
אַךְ הֵמָּה יַחְדָּו שָׁבְרוּ עֹל   **e**   But they alike had <u>broken off the yoke</u>,
נִתְּקוּ מוֹסֵרוֹת   <u>they had torn off the bindings.</u>

Jeremiah 5:5 is a significant text both because it explicates that the breaking of the yoke concerns the rejection of the law of God, and for motives of a rhetorical-structural nature, in reference to the strategic dislocation of the textual isotopies that are most significative in regard to the object of my dissertation's study. The theme of the yoke appears, in fact, in 2:20, 5:5, and 30:8 with precise lexical and syntagmatic references: in the whole HB, it is only in these passages (aside from the case of Nah 1:13) that the parallelism √שבר + עֹל (to break the yoke) – נתק √ pi. + מוֹסֵרוֹת (to tear the bindings) appears.[202]

The first two texts situate themselves at roughly the two extremities of one of the most important literary units of the first part of the book of Jeremiah (presented in chs. 2–6),[203] covering the oracles commonly considered to be the oldest and most "original". Whereas in 30:8 (where the same lexical elements are organised according to a chiastic arrangement), we find ourselves in the "Book of Consolation", that is, in the heart of the Jeremianic message, virtually on the other side of the disaster that is threatened, announced, and takes place in the other texts.

My research started off with the empiric focalisation of some texts that are key for the theme of surrender to the king of Babylon. But as I now move forward bit by bit, we can recognise how still other important textual hubs can be punctuated, and these do not limit themselves to the second part of the book. The same isotopy emerges, therefore, along a logical-thematic continuum that, at times in a way that is marked way and others almost as an undercurrent, proves to be a decisive interpretive key to the *entire* Jeremianic message, however much it has been, thus far, somewhat underestimated.

---

202   In this regard, see the studies by C. HARDMEIER, «Die Redekomposition Jer 2–6» (esp. pp. 38–39); ID., «Geschichte und Erfahrung in Jer 2–6: Zur theologischen Notwendigkeit einer geschichts- und erfahrungsbezogenen Exegese und ihrer methodischen Neuorientierung», *EvT* 56 (1996) 3–29 (above all, pp. 27–28); ID., «Wahrhaftigkeit und Fehlorientierung bei Jeremia: Jer 5,1 und die divinatorische Expertise Jer 2–6* im Kontext der zeitgenössischen Kontroversen um die politische Zukunft Jerusalems», in: *Exegese vor Ort*. Festschrift für Peter Welten zum 65. Geburtstag, *eds.* C. MAIER – R. LIWAK – K.-P. JÖRNS, Leipzig 2001, 121–144 (esp. pp. 128–130). In my opinion, however, the unit 2–6 is by no means a "Prozeßrede", as the author defines it, but should be considered in the logic of the bilateral controversy (רִיב), to be carefully distinguished from forensic judgement (מִשְׁפָּט).

203   For the general structuring of the book, refer back to ch. I, § 4.

"Bend your neck beneath the yoke of the king of Babylon!" (27:12)   369

4.1.7. The "iron yoke" and the curse of Deut 28:47–48. Levels of meaning and possible paths of salvation

From this intertextual confrontation, it can already be noted that the Jeremianic request for submission to the king of Babylon takes the shape of an *overturning* of the originary liberation that is the foundation of Israel's very identity. This eventuality is already presented in Deut 28:47–48, in the context of the blessings and curses connected to whether or not the clauses of the Covenant between YHWH and Israel have been observed.

> [47] Because you have not served (עבד√) the Lord, your God, with joy and a glad heart in the abundance of all things, [48] you shall serve (עבד√) your enemies, who the Lord will send against you, amidst hunger, thirst, nakedness, and the lack of all things; and he shall place (נתן√) an *iron yoke* (עֹל בַּרְזֶל) on your neck (עַל־צַוָּארֶךָ), until he has destroyed you.

To what we already saw when treating Jer 21:1–10 in relation to Deut and the punitive consequences prescribed in the alliance pact in the case of infedelity (cf. ch. III, § 4.2.1), I can add and further specify here that for Israel, the Jeremianic announcement of the universal bestowal of power to Nabuchadnezzar takes the shape of being part of the fulfillment of the curses threatened in Deut 28:15–68.

That the image of the imposition of the "iron yoke" (עֹל בַּרְזֶל) corresponds to a curse and not simply to a generic service or enslavement to the foreigner is implied by the semiosis generated by the "yoke" element combined with the attribution of its manufacture in iron, which can plausibly be retained as entirely unsuitable.[204] To burden an animal with an imaginary yoke made entirely of iron, thus one exceedingly heavy, would mean defeating the very purpose of the yoking (having the aim of transportation or tillage), since it would mean the draught animal being subjected at length to *unbearable* and *exhausting* fatigue (cf. in fact, Deut 28:48: "[...] until he has destroyed you [עַד הִשְׁמִידוֹ אֹתָךְ]"). Moreover, this image contrasts with that of the standard yoke (of wood), as regards the possibility of its being broken. In fact, amongst the various meanings connected to iron in the HB,[205] this metal also refers to a bond of

---

204   The material used in the construction of the yoke seems to have been only wood (cf. A. RUWE – U. WEISE, «Das Joch Assurs», 293).

205   As pointed out by J.F.A. SAWYER, «The Meaning of *barzel* in the Biblical Expressions "Chariots of Iron", "Yoke of Iron", etc.», in: *Midian, Moab and Edom. The History and Archaeology of Late Bronze and Iron Age Jordan and North-West Arabia*, eds. J.F.A. SAWYER – D.J.A. CLINES, JSOT.S 24, Sheffield 1983, 129–134, as opposed to the occurrences where bronze or other metals are mentioned, for the most part in the HB, a whole series of negative ideas are associated with iron (to that effect, the expression עַמּוּד בַּרְזֶל ["pillar of iron"] in Jer 1:18 goes against the current). Even the term בַּרְזֶל ("iron"), unlike the more traditional נְחֹשֶׁת ("bronze"), seems to be of foreign origin, having no identifiable Hebrew or Semitic etymology. The technique used for its production most certainly is not of Israeli origin (where it is practiced initially with poor results) and, not coincidentally, "iron" is often placed in relation to foreign or hostile populations (cf. Deut 3:11; 4:20; Josh 16:16–18; 1 Sam 17:7; Amos 1:3; Isa 10:34; Jer 15:12 ["iron from the North"]; Dan 2:40). It is then associated with images evoking obstinacy, oppression, hostility, battles, killings, and torture. Consider, in addition to the aforementioned text of 1 Kgs 22:11, the Egyptian slavery described as coming out of a כּוּר הַבַּרְזֶל ("iron blast furnace"; cf. Deut 4:20; 1 Kgs 8:51; Jer 11:4),

370   Jer 27–28. The world beneath the yoke of the king of Babylon

subservience that is *infrangible* (cf. Eccles 28:20). And yet, precisely in the voluntary and conscious acceptance of the yoke of Babylon, which therefore consists in renoucing ones own political projects to become an integral part of the operative design of a foreign sovereign, Jeremiah announces the possibility of overcoming the curse itself. An overcoming that is feasible on *two levels.*

First level. Premise: to be forced to serve foreigners is *already* a curse (cf. Deut 28:48 and Jer 5:19[206]). Overcoming: recognition of it as such, that is, in the light of the Covenant, and acceptance of it as just punishment means escaping distruction and embarking on the path of the blessing (cf. 27:12, 15–17).

Second level. Premise: refusal of the yoke (of wood), that is, this first level of the curse, understood as *subservience* to the power of Babylon, means aggravating the curse itself, permitting for its total fulfilment, and thus enduring another kind of yoke; that of iron prescribed in Deut 28:47–48, which leads to *annihilation.* True fulfilment of the curse, which is alluded to by the "iron yoke", will be actualised, in fact, only in case of *extreme disobedience* (cf. 28:13–14). It is extreme here too in two senses: (a) because the object of the Jeremianic message of surrender is no longer, as was already demonstrated in ch. III, § 4.2.1, an obedience of an ethical-religious sort, but is rather a specific act to be carried out within the the contingent historical-political scenario, though it will have the same salvific implications that concern fidelity to the Covenant, regardless; (b) because, as I have observed, enslavement to the foreigner is already a punitive consequence of infidelity to the Covenant. To reject the meaning of this event thus constitutes a final act of obstinate disobedience. Also on this second level, however, which we enter in Jer 27–28 by way of the paradigmatic gesture of Hananiah who breaks the yoke of Jeremiah and refuses its message in the name of his falsehood (cf. 28:10), not all is lost. The *overcoming* of the curse can still be actualised on two other levels and in two moments:

- Until the final instant, until the edge of the abyss, God offers the possibility of salvation to whomever seeks it. Another significant paradigm, the final discussion between Jeremiah and Zedekiah, shows this clearly (cf. 38:14–28a).[207] But even in history's gloomiest outcome, when even this last offering is in fact refused (cf. 38:28a), even in this eventuality, the definitive triumph of the "night" of meaning has not yet taken place (cf. 13:16; 39:4; 52:7). It is not yet the absolute end.

---

the terrible רֶכֶב בַּרְזֶל ("iron chariots" for war of the Canaanites; cf. Josh 17:16–18; Judg 1:19; 4:3.13), and the devastating kingdom תַּקִּיפָה כְּפַרְזְלָא ("*strong as iron,* just as iron breaks in pieces and shatters everything else"; cf. Dan 2:40), from the dream of Nebuchadnezzar, to the punisher שֵׁבֶט בַּרְזֶל ("scepter/iron rod"; cf. Ps 2:9) to strike the enemy nations, to the בַּרְזֶל ("iron" translatable as "the irons", to wit, the chains of slavery and captivity; cf. Ps 107:10; 105:18), and to the various work tools the defeated enemies of David are obliged to use (cf. 2 Sam 12:31). In short: "All the evidence suggests that the word *barzel,* in most of the Biblical passages where it occurs, was an emotive term, with unmistakably hostile and aggressive associations" (p. 131).

206   "And when you will ask: 'Why has the Lord our God done all these things to us?', say to them: 'As you have abandoned (√עזב) me and have served (√עבד) foreign gods in your land, so shall you serve (√עבד) foreigners in a land not yours'."

207   I will devote myself to the study of 38:14–28a in ch. V of the present dissertation.

"Bend your neck beneath the yoke of the king of Babylon!" (27:12)   371

- It is already presented in our text: even if disaster and eradication must take their course, YHWH will return to give grace to his people once again. Despite this being a salvific act that is entirely undeducible from the premises. If he has visited (√פקד) it for punishment (27:8; cf. also 5:9, 29; 6:6, 15; 9:8; 11:12, etc.), he will visit it (√פקד) for his salvation as well (cf. 27:22; cf. also 29:10; 30:20 [the punitive visit against the oppressors of Israel]; 32:5 [it is even said of Zedekiah that he will be "visited", despite his fatal disobedience and the subsequent punishment for it]; etc.). For, as the situation of the Jeremianic prophetic body itself demonstrates, exposed to death and miraculously saved, even history, at least that of the people as such, will continue. And as long as there will be a "history", in the logic of the *rîb* that expresses the meaning of all of God's action in the time of humanity,[208] hope will not fail. This is clearly deduced from the announcement in Jer 30:8 which I will pick back up in the context of what I will develop in the final paragraph (cf. in particular § 5.1.2), dedicated to the conflict between the opposing prophetic-salvific perspectives.

4.2. The universal dominion of YHWH, the world subjected to the yoke of the king of Babylon: Sapiential dimension and prophetic dimension

4.2.1. The ante factum of Jer 21:1–10. A historical-theological flashback essential for the foundation and comprehension of the theme of surrender to the king of Babylon

Following the current narrative flow of the book, the theme of surrender to Babylon assumes an unexpected proleptic position for the reader. We saw it when studying Jer 21:1–10 (cf. ch. III, § 3): it is a sort of *flash-forward* that modifies the development of the *fabula*, from both the logical and chronological points of view. Even though, in the case of the book of Jeremiah and its complex semiotic phenomenon, this categorical grid typical of narrative analysis is not altogether satisfactory,[209] we can nonetheless affirm with a certain approximation that with chs. 27–28, we find ourselves instead before the ante factum (or *flashback*) that provides the conceptual foundation of the Jeremianic message.

---

208 On the subject, see P. Bovati, *Ristabilire la giustizia*, 361–362; M. Cucca – B. Rossi – S.M. Sessa, *"Quelli che amo io li accuso"*. Il rîb come chiave di lettura unitaria della Scrittura. Alcuni esempi (Os 11,1; Ger 13,1–11; Gv 15,1–11/Ap 2–3), CSB.SB, Assisi 2012, 15–33; P. Bovati, *Vie della giustizia secondo la Bibbia*. Sistema giudiziario e procedure per la riconciliazione, Bologna 2014, 69–96.

209 As we have seen, these are categories which must be taken on with a certain degree of caution. In fact, the Jeremianic work, despite having large narrative sections, cannot be reduced *tout court* to the genre of story. Not only because there are equally large parts in which the oracular genre predominates in poetic form, but also because the rhetorical positioning of the texts (as I noted, in the case of Jer 21:1–10 in relation to the broader unit 21–24) also responds to other semiotic criteria. Consider the phenomenon of "semiotic *arcatas*", which I talked about in chs. I, § 2.4 and III, §§ 3.2.3–4, and which place significant textual units in relation to others even when distant and of different literary genres.

372   Jer 27–28. The world beneath the yoke of the king of Babylon

But to be more precise, we can say that what we have is *an* ante factum and *a* fundamental perspective of meaning. The elements provided by 21:1–10, in fact, given their
reference to previous parts of the book and to other founding biblical texts, already
provided important information on the motivations for the prophetic injunction. We
will see moreover that, at least at first glance, the call for submission to Babylon is
not uniquely founded on the literal data offered in Jer 27–28. Before examining this
further (cf. § 4.3), the question is, in any case, now that of underscoring that the logic
of the Jeremianic prophetic communication is founded on a dual assumption having
a *founding value*: YHWH is the creator God and the Lord of universal history. It is
in this light that the particular situation of Israel is also enlightened with meaning,
receiving significance and direction.

4.2.2. *The theme of creation in the HB and the book of Jeremiah.* The status quaestionis

While in Jer 21:1–10, we found ourselves suddenly amidst the turmoil of a story nearing its epilogue and, within this story, in a specific narrative fragment of it, the horizon
now expands instead to a universal dimension, both of the cosmic and intrahistorical
type. Just as the rhetorical analysis of chs. 27–28 (§ 2.4) already demonstrated, the
question is not that of a change of register that replaces the first, but of the development of an interactive relationship between the particular and the universal, between
"the great history of Nebuchadnezzar"[210] and the small history of the kingdom of Judah
and the people in the Syrian-Palestinian region.

For a long time, especially due to the influence of the arguments adopted by Gerhard
von Rad,[211] it was believed that the fulcrum of the faith of Israel concerned, above all,
the traditions of the Exodus and the covenant at Sinai. The proclamation of YHWH
as creator of the universe was held to be something secondary and tardive, a theme
that had only been integrated later, under Assyrian and/or Babylonian influence,[212]

---

210   It is A. Neher, in his brief but evocative commentary on the book of Jeremiah,
        who counterposes (explicitly only in the final summary) "la grande histoire de
        Nabuchodonosor" with "la petite histoire de Jérusalem".
211   I refer to the subordination of the theme of creation to the theology of salvation
        and the hypothesis of "historical belief" centred on the memory of the events of the
        Exodus. The best known is his renowned *Theologie des Alten Testaments* (esp. pp. 149–
        167 of the first volume: Die Theologie der geschichtlichen Überlieferungen Israels,
        München 1957, [10]1992) and hence, the paradigm of the *Heilsgeschichte* ("salvation
        story"). But the question of the relationship between election and faith in the crea-
        tor God had already been posed programmatically in an article by the same author
        published in 1936 (cf. G. von Rad, «Das theologische Problem des alttestamentlichen
        Schöpfungsglaubens», in: *Gesammelte Studien zum Alten Testament*, ed. G. von Rad,
        TB 8, München 1958, 136–147) and, even earlier, in an article by K. Galling, «Jahwe
        der Weltschöpfer», ThBl 35 (1925) 257–261. Another classic contribution from the
        German world on the theology of creation in the OT is that by C. Westermann,
        Schöpfung, ThTh 12, Stuttgart 1971.
212   This is the thesis held in the brief note by B. Lang, «Ein babylonisches Motiv in
        Israels Schöpfungsmythologie (Jer 27,5–6)», BZ 27 (1983), 236–237, in reference
        to the subject of creation contained in the book of Jeremiah. Along the line of the

"Bend your neck beneath the yoke of the king of Babylon!" (27:12) 373

above all during the post-exilic period.[213] The most pertinent texts in this sense were identified in the first two chapters of the Genesis, Isaiah, the book of Psalms, Job, and Proverbs. Jeremiah himself was considered by G. von Rad to be primarily a preacher of doom and intrahistorical salvation. And this further obscured the relevance of the Jeremianic references to the creative power of YHWH. Amongst the prophets, in fact, the most significant contribution to the creation theme is still found by most scholars in the pages of the so-called "Deutero-Isaiah" (Isa 40–55),[214] where faith in the oneness of the God of Israel is developed in an anti-idolatrical register and there is also great insistence on the concept of YHWH as the redeemer of Israel.

In the context of the subsequent reaction to this perspective, the work of H. Weippert in 1931[215] marked a remarkable attempt to rebalance the previous evaluations,[216]

---

position taken by H.W.F. SAGGS, *The Encounter with the Divine in Mesopotamia and Israel*, London 1978, who, in regard to Jer 27:5–6, believes that: "Jeremiah was taking over for Yahweh claims he found already made for Marduk of Babylon" (p. 43).

213 Others had already moved in this direction. But the first and most significant example of a synthesis of biblical theology dealing with the topic of creation only secondarily (i.e. in the second part of his tripart study) is that of W. EICHRODT, *Theologie des Alten Testaments*. Teil II: Gott und Welt, Teil III: Gott und Mensch, Leipzig 1935, Stuttgart ⁴1961 (in this edition, it is found on pp. 1–156).

214 Until not long ago, the basic assumption was that this composition be post-exilic. Actually, recent studies have demonstrated that the theme of creation runs like filigree throughout the entire book of Isaiah, which should be considered a homogeneous work, and not be divided artificially into distinct blocks.

215 H. WEIPPERT, *Schöpfer des Himmels und der Erde*. Ein Beitrag zur Theologie des Jeremiabuches, SBS 102, Stuttgart 1981. As far as the resumption of interest regarding the theme of creation is concerned, there are also notable contributions by, amongst others, H.H. SCHMID, «Schöpfung, Gerechtigkeit und Heil. "Schöpfungstheologie" als Gesamthorizont biblischer Theologie», *ZThK* 70 (1973) 1–19 (with a programmatic title and which actually risks reacting with an equally unilateral counterposition: "Das alles zusammengenommen besagt: Der Schöpfungsglaube, das heisst der Glaube, dass Gott die Welt mit ihren mannigfaltigen Ordnungen geschaffen hat und erhält, ist nicht ein Randthema biblischer Theologie, sondern im Grunde ihr Thema schlechthin" [p. 15]); G.M. LANDES, «Creation and Liberation», *USQR* 33 (1978) 78–99 (disputes the late dating of the creation motifs put forth by G. von Rad); R. KNIERIM, «Cosmos and History in Israel's Theology», *HBT* 3 (1981) 59–123 (= in: ID., *The Task of Old Testament Theology*. Substance, Method and Cases, Grand Rapids 1995, 171–224); and the contributions of L.G. PERDUE, *Wisdom & Creation*. The Theology of Wisdom Literature, Nashville 1994 (with specific reference to the sapiential dimension); ID., *The Collapse of History*. Reconstructing Old Testament Theology, Minneapolis 1994, 113–150 (pp. 141–150 are dedicated to the theology of creation in Jeremiah); S. PAAS, *Creation and Judgement* (in-depth and well-documented monograph on the argument; deals with Amos, Hosea, and Isaiah); K. SCHMID, «Himmelsgott, Weltgott und Schöpfer. "Gott" und der "Himmel" in der Literatur der Zeit des Zweiten Tempels», *JBTh* 20 (2005) 111–148.

216 There is no doubt, as has been observed by W. BRUEGGEMANN, «The Loss and Recovery of Creation in Old Testament Theology», *ThTo* 53 (1996) 177–190 (cf. also ID., «Jeremiah: Creatio in Extremis», in: *God Who Creates*. Essays in Honor of W. Sibley Towner, ed. W.P. BROWN – S.D. McBRIDE Jr., Grand Rapids 2000, 152–170, here pp. 166–167), that such assessments, unilaterally accentuating the tie between creation theology and soteriology, were likely to suffer from some precomprehensions of

374 Jer 27–28. The world beneath the yoke of the king of Babylon

contributing specifically to highlighting of the importance of the notion of God the creator in the book of Jeremiah, where a series of tests express motives analogous to those contained in Deutero-Isaiah.[217] Regardless, and despite subsequent contributions[218] that have rightly taken on this perspective as their own, highlighting other interesting correlations (such as that with creative power, intrahistorical dynamics of justice and salvation, and sapiential themes),[219] the theological implications deriving from the Jeremianic theme of the relation between the God of Israel and the creation remain, in my opinion, still rather underestimated.[220] Today, a monograph dedicated exclusively to this important thematic and to its complex function as a structural thematic node in the book of Jeremiah is still lacking.

---

the German socio-cultural and political context of the 1930s, in which the ecclesial reality had to cope with the ideological cult of land (homeland) and race of national-socialism. In this context, the work of G. von Rad and many other scholars "articulated a radical either/or of history versus nature, monotheism versus polytheism, and ethical versus cultic categories" (p. 179).

217 H. Weippert identifies three typologies of texts, some of which even pre-date the Deutero-Isaianic ones: (1) a series of older (Jeremianic) vv.: 2:13; 4:23–28; 5:21–25; 14:19–22; 18:1–12; 31:35–37; 32:38–40; (2) other late-Jeremianic texts: my own 27:5–6 and 32:27; (3) post-Jeremianic and post-exilic passages: 33:19–22:23–26. Her approach is that typical of that of redactional criticism, and for this very reason, her results are, in my opinion, unconvincing (as I observed in the General Introduction, § 1.4.2), for the high degree of hypotheticality that distinguishes this kind of analysis, especially with regard to the book of Jeremiah.

218 In particular, amongst the various contributions, see L. WISSER, «La création dans le livre de Jérémie», in: *La création dans l'Orient Ancien*. Congrès de L'ACFEB, Lille (1985), *eds.* F. BLANQUART – L. DEROUSSEAUX, LeDiv 127, Paris 1987, 241–260; D. RUDMAN, «Creation and Fall in Jeremiah X 12–16», *VT* 48 (1998) 63–73; W. BRUEGGEMANN, «Creatio in Extremis»; T.E. FRETHEIM, *God and World in the Old Testament*. A Relational Theology of Creation, Nashville 2005, 171–181 (cf. alos ID., *Creation Untamed*. The Bible, God, and Natural Disasters, Grand Rapids 2010); H. LALLEMAN-DE WINKEL, «Jeremiah, Judgement and Creation», *TynB* 60 (2009) 15–24; M.G. KLINGBEIL, «Creation in the Prophetic Literature of the Old Testament: An Intertextual Approach», *JATS* 20 (2009) 19–54; J.R. LUNDBOM, *Jeremiah Closer Up*, 42–57; A. FAVALE, *Dio d'Israele e dei popoli*, 497–503.

219 See in particular, e.g. L.G. PERDUE, *The Collapse of History*, 141–150, which articulates these three relations: (1) creation and history; (2) creation and the destiny of humanity; (3) creation and wisdom.

220 In this regard, one could perhaps still cite the assertion of R. RENDTORFF, «Some Reflections on Creation as a Topic of Old Testament Theology», in: *Priests, Prophets and Scribes*. Essays on the Formation and Heritage of Second Temple Judaism in Honour of Joseph Blenkinsopp, *eds.* E. ULRICH *et al.*, JSOT.S 149, Sheffield 1992, 204–212: "Nevertheless, creation to this day has been one of the 'proverbial step-children' in the recent discipline of Old Testament theology" (p. 205).

"Bend your neck beneath the yoke of the king of Babylon!" (27:12)   375

4.2.3. A notion having foundative value in the book of Jeremiah. The status creationis

In itself, the theme of creation explicitly occupies only vv. 5–8 of ch. 27 (and, in a more direct manner, only v. 5; cf. however, also 28:14). It is a textual perimeter that is quite narrow. But in this regard, one can say something similar to what was observed for the injunction of the symbolic gesture of the yoke, which, while confined within vv. 2–3, we still see giving meaning to the entire development of the literary unit of chs. 27–28. Its physical length does not coincide in the least with its relevance. Indeed, the relation seems inversely proportional.

The creative act, despite being represented as an act of word in the story of the Genesis, cannot properly be the object of speech. Certainly, in Gen 1–2, it is, but only as a mythical-analogical approximation. And this word or conceptual discourse defers to the image, which is a non-verbal reality, even if one recalled by the locutionary act. Two chapters: few words, in any case, that fundamentally hold together the entire literary monument of the Scripture, impressing the dynamism in the universal story that projects it towards its Fulfilment. It attempts to describe with symbols a fact that, in its essence, remains a mystery,[221] just as the creation (and thus, the intimate identity) of the woman for the man while sleeping and hence unable to take or possess that prodigious event that is the constitution of the one other than himself remains a mystery (cf. Gen 2:21–24). It is not by chance that in the book of Jeremiah (cf. 31:22b), the new creation characterising the re-establishment of Israel ("for the Lord *creates* [√ברא] a new thing on earth") be connected to the enigmatic event by which "the woman shall encompass the man" (נְקֵבָה תְּסוֹבֵב גָּבֶר).

We are therefore in the presence of the theme that provides grounding for the entire Jeremianic discourse as well. Not only for what is developed in chs. 27 and 28, or for the question of the surrender to Babylon, though this unfolds over broader textual territories. The creative power of God underlies and gives meaning to the entire communicative dynamism that is the book of Jeremiah, and, in general, to the whole *status* of the actants in play, which is hence a *status creationis*. After all, it is precisely the creative act of YHWH, motivated, in turn, by a non-deductible and gratuitous elective choice of a paternal nature, to be, from the beginning, placed at the origin of the prophetic body (1:5)[222] and his

---

221 This absolute indescribability of the Origin is somewhat reflected in the awareness of modern physics, which, at the moment, postulates the impossibility that human (theoretical) knowledge cut through the so-called "Planck barrier", that is, the state of the universe in the very first stages of the Big Bang, when its age was less than 10^{-43} seconds and size less than 10^{-33} centimetres (cf. J.D. BARROW, *Impossibility. The Limits of Science and the Science of Limits*, Oxford 1998, 182).

222 "Before I *formed you* in the womb I (re-)cognised you (יְדַעְתִּיךָ) [...]." I translate "formed you", reading the MT according to the Q אֶצָּרְךָ from √יצר "to give form", a root that evokes the act of creation (cf. e.g. Gen 2:7–8) and significantly appears in a similar context of divine election "from the womb" (מִבֶּטֶן) in Isa 44:2, 24; 49:5 (cf. also Ps 139:16). It should in any case be noted that also the K אֶצֹּורְךָ from √צור IV ("vb. fashion, delineate"; cf. *BDB*, 849), in the context, can be traced back to the same semantic field, even though the verb צור never has YHWH as its subject in the HB. For further development of this topic, refer to S.M. SESSA, «"Prima di formarti nel grembo materno ti ho (ri-)conosciuto" (Ger 1,5). La rivelazione del senso del nascere. Alcuni aspetti

376   Jer 27–28. The world beneath the yoke of the king of Babylon

mission,[223] and further still: of his sovereign power over the nations and over history (cf. 1:10) as the visibilisation of the same creative power of God and of his universal lordship. Creation and history can be differentiated only to better understand their interaction:

> The dichotomy between creation and history, while heuristically useful in describing Jeremiah's understanding of God, leads to serious misunderstanding, if the two dimension of divine lordship and activity are placed in opposition, or if history is given priority. It because Yahweh is creator that he expresses his divine sovereignty over history. Yahweh's covenant with and through Israel binds him, not only to all other peoples, but also to the entirety of all creation.[224]

4.2.4. A creation that is complete and thus continually underway, in a fragile equilibrium. Creatio continua *and the risk of de-creation*

A clarification is necessary: the creation on which relations and disputes between God, his people, and the nations are interwoven is not a sort of static cosmic order, established once and for all. There are, of course, fixed, immutable laws, which are taken as an analogous reference for other realities constituted as equally immutable, though at times less visible (cf. 33:20–26) or entirely invisible,[225] as far as their steadfastness throughout time is concerned. And in Gen 2:1–4a, after the creation of man and woman, and once cosmic order has been established, "completion" is spoken of (v. 1: כלה√ pu.; v. 2: כלה√ pi.), as is "cessation, rest" (vv. 2 e 3: שבת√). However, *precisely* these laws and the existing relations between all created elements foresee the intrahistorical God-humankind-world interaction. By placing the books of Genesis and Jeremiah in mutual dialogue, we see that biblical creation, still not made explicit as a *creatio ex-nihilo* (as in 2 Ma 7:28; Rom 4:17; cf. John 1:3–4; Col 1:15–17), must instead be conceived as a *creatio continua.*[226] And all the more so if we consider the tight aforementioned interconnection between the lordship of YHWH over creation and human history.

In this *creatio continua,* human beings are called to a very high responsibility of collaboration, which qualifies them, in a certain sense, as co-creators and sovereigns, and not as inert guardians of an already perfect and intangible masterpiece, only to be contemplated from a distance and relegated to an inaccessible immobility. According to the Genesis accounts, creation can truly express its greatest potential only if it

---

biblici», in: *Venire al mondo: i luoghi dell'invisibile,* eds. P. GRASSI – S. MODICA, QNB 7, Rosolini 2013, 21–37.

223   Cf. L.G. PERDUE, *The Collapse of History,* 147.

224   *Ibid.,* 145.

225   The biblical tradition has preserved the Jeremianic oracle of 33:20–26 (and not only) through the centuries, despite all the apparent historical rejections. In a Christian perspective, everything has found fulfilment in Christ.

226   This is rightly highlighted in some translations of the famous incipit of the Genesis, which base themselves on a more respectful reading of the syntax of the biblical text. See e.g. the proposal and related philological-exegetic comment by F. GIUNTOLI, *Genesi 1–11. Introduzione, traduzione e commento,* NVBTA 1.1, Cinisello Balsamo 2013, 72–73: "Quando Dio cominciò a creare il cielo e la terra [...]".

"carries the yoke" of humanity, that is, if it receives a co-creator intentionality from it. The dominion is not a tyrannical one, seeing as the reference is to the human being created in the image of God, and therefore called to govern as God governs: in communion (the human being is fulfilled and generates life as man and woman), with the mansuetude of the word[227] (which is meaning, communication, performative force), and according to justice (which is the promotion of good and recognition of the face of the other).

All this is good and is beauty, the true, great beauty (cf. Gen 1:4, 10, 12, 18, 21, 25, 31). But it is also a delicate balance. It is precisely this order that is at risk: there is, in fact, a concrete danger that creation can not only be seriously upset, but practically be de-created, if its co-creator decides to recant his *status*, refusing the cosmic order that is based on a relationship of divine-human covenant.[228] My reference to the creation stories in Genesis was not a casual. They are referred to explicitly in the book of Jeremiah itself, which, in precise antithetical reference to Gen 1, effectively shows the dramatic eventuality that is inherent to the sublime gift of the liberty donated: it is possible for human beings to render themselves de-creators (cf. Jer 4 and, in particular, vv. 23–29) and for YHWH to allow for creation (or, historically, a part of it) to be radically destructured, reverting to being "vacuous and empty" (תֹּהוּ וָבֹהוּ; cf. Gen 1:2 and Jer 4:23). This is what will happen to the land of Israel and its inhabitants if they do not accept to bow their necks beneath the yoke of the king of Babylon. I will take a closer look at this in the following paragraphs.

4.2.5. "I made the earth, the human beings, and the animals [...]" (27:5a). YHWH: The only God creator of the universe (sapiential dimension)

Let us now focus on the most pertinent textual elements, which we will then see in the context of the other principal references to the creation contained in the Jeremianic work. The root that expresses the creative act in our text is עשׂה in qal pf., having as its object "the earth" (הָאָרֶץ), "the men" (הָאָדָם), and "the animals" (הַבְּהֵמָה). The same verb is attested in 10:12 again for "the earth" (אֶרֶץ); in 14:22 in reference to "to give rain" (נשׁם √ part.) and to the "showers" (רְבִבִים), through the pronominal locution "all these things" (כָּל־אֵלֶּה); in 32:17 in reference to "the heavens" (הַשָּׁמַיִם) and to "the earth" (הָאָרֶץ); in 33:2 with suff. f. 3rd pers. sing. in reference to the "earth" (cf. LXX: κύριος ποιῶν γῆν); and also in 9:23 referring to "goodness" (חֶסֶד), "right" (מִשְׁפָּט), and "justice"(צְדָקָה). This does not, therefore, concern the more technical root בָּרָא[229] of Gen 1:1, 21, 27; 2:3;

---

227 Cf. P. BEAUCHAMP, «Création et fondation de la loi en Gn 1,1–2,4a. Le don de la nourriture végétale en Gn 1,29s», in: *La création dans l'Orient Ancien*, 139–182 (here, pp. 168–169); P. BEAUCHAMP – D. VASSE, «La violence dans la Bible», *CEv* 76 (1991) 10–11.

228 This is how the Jewish tradition expresses itself in this regard, recalling and re-elaborating the biblical attestation: *Pirke Aboth*, 1,2: "The world stands on three things: on the *Tôrâ*, on divine service, and on deeds of kindness." The reference to the theme of ecology is increasingly relevant, as is suggested in the contribution by K. CLAYVILLE, «Ecological Hermeneutics and Jeremiah», in: *The Oxford Handbook of Jeremiah, eds.* L. STULMAN – E. SILVER, Oxford 2021, 637–647.

229 When the MT resorts to the qal or ni., the subject is always and only YHWH (cf. K.-H. BERNHARDT, «בָּרָא III. Bedeutung», *ThWAT* I, 774–777 [here, p. 774]; R.C. VAN LEEUWEN, «ברא», *NIDOTTE* I, 728–735 and esp. pp. 731–732).

378   Jer 27–28. The world beneath the yoke of the king of Babylon

5:1; etc. (which, in the book of Jeremiah is, in any case, reserved in 31:22 for the creation of "a new thing" [חֲדָשָׁה], and, thus, new in a radical sense, shadowed in the somewhat enigmatic aforementioned expression "the woman shall encompass the man"
[נְקֵבָה תְּסוֹבֵב גָּבֶר]), but instead a very generic verb, which is, however, used many times
as its synonym (or in synonymic parallelism) in similar contexts (cf. e.g. Isa 41:20;
43:1, 7; 45:7, 12, 18; Amos 4:13; 5:8).

For a basic configuration of the semantic field of reference, other than this root,
which is used extensively in different contexts, one need also bear in mind √יצר ("to
form"; cf. 1:5 Q; 18:6: the analogy "potter" [יוֹצֵר]-clay/YHWH-nations); √צור IV ("to
form"; cf. 1:5 K); √שׂים; ("to place the sand as a boundary" [to the sea] in 5:22); √כון
hi. ("to establish", the "world" [תֵּבֵל] in 10:12 and "the earth" [הָאָרֶץ] in 33:2); √נטה ("to
stretch out" the "heavens" [שָׁמַיִם]) in 10:12 [and cf. other verbs correlating to the act of
creation in v. 13: √נתן; √עלה hi.; √יצא hi.]; the nominal phrase אִם־לֹא בְרִיתִי יוֹמָם וָלָיְלָה ("if
I had not [*made*] my covenant with heaven and earth") and √שׂים ("to establish" [the
laws of heaven and earth]) in 33:25. Also to note, then, is √מלא ("to fill"; 23:24), a verb
that in the HB is attested only in the book of Jeremiah in reference to the theme of
creation. YHWH, while remaining transcendent (מֵרָחֹק; "from afar"), fills heaven and
earth with his presence (מִקָּרֹב; "from close by"). He is therefore present in all human
affairs (cf. 23:23–24). Particular importance should be given to 10:12, a verse that
highlights the *sapiential dimension* of this important theme[230]:

עֹשֵׂה אֶרֶץ בְּכֹחוֹ	a	He has made the earth by his power,
מֵכִין תֵּבֵל בְּחָכְמָתוֹ	b	has established the world by his wisdom,
וּבִתְבוּנָתוֹ נָטָה שָׁמָיִם	c	and by his wisdom has spread out the skies.

Creation and sapiential themes are interconnected in many ways in the book of
Jeremiah.[231] The variety of expressive registers and communicative contexts (here, e.g.
in the context of the anti-idolatrical polemic, cf. v. 11) has, as a common horizon of
meaning, the fact that reference is made to a *perennial order* established by YHWH.[232]
And when "forever" is spoken of, when reference is made to acts of God in achronic
or panchronic terms, without reference to the archetypes upon which the Law is
formed and without the urgency of the prophetic "moment", we find ourselves within
a discourse typical of wisdom.[233]

---

230   For the contextualisation of this v. in the context of the anti-idolatric controversy
       in Jer 10:12–16, which is aimed at the false wisdom of the "manufacturers of the
       divine", see D. RUDMAN, «Creation and Fall», 63–73, and, above all, A. FAVALE, *Dio
       d'Israele e dei popoli*, 497–500.
231   For a quick overview, see e.g. L.G. PERDUE, *The Collapse of History*, 148–150.
232   P. BEAUCHAMP, *L'un et l'autre Testament*, 109: "La Sagesse, ainsi que les proverbes
       eux-mêmes, est sans âge. Elle se vit comme ce qui continue depuis toujours, depuis
       aussi longtemps que les hommes et les femmes enseignent à leurs fils à se réjouir et
       à se détourner des mêmes choses ou, du moins, à être hommes. Par sa permanence
       et sa quotidienneté, elle pose, au niveau de l'existence profane, la question de l'âge
       du monde.".
233   Cf. P. BEAUCHAMP, *L'un et l'autre Testament*, 136.

"Bend your neck beneath the yoke of the king of Babylon!" (27:12)   379

This sapient order and its perennial stability is potentially recognisable by all, through human intelligence. The same intelligence that characterises the typical *universal* perspective of the theme. It is by no chance that precisely through "sapience", Israel shares a series of truths with the other nations that are mediators of life. And it is by no chance, therefore, that the international dimension of chs. 27–28 has, as its foundation, a cosmic gaze over what unites life and the history of all peoples. With some fundamental elucidations, however. Let us have look at them.

What is striking on a pragmatic level in 27:5 is undoubtedly the emphatic value of the locution אָנֹכִי עָשִׂיתִי ("It was *I* who made"), with the personal pronoun relating to a finite verb (a structure replicated in the following v. 6).[234] It is an act of speech of the representative-assertive type, by which YHWH proclaims himself to be sole creator of the universe. The communicative impact is amplified by the pragmatic context of utterance.[235] The peculiar illocutionary force generated is due to the fact that this affirmation is directed at the representatives (and through them, to their respective sovereigns) of foreign lands (v. 4), each with their own gods, their own beliefs, and their own cosmogonies of reference. The explicit assertion, "It was *I* who made", thus *implies*[236] a polemic "it was not your gods", and going further, demanding[237] *universal* obedience (submission!) and recognition of limitless power to a divinity who is apparently completely "*local*", afferent to a small people of an equally not particularly significant state entity having very few or wholly utopian imperialistic goals (cf. Ezek 47:13–20; Mic 5:3; Ps 72:8). But there is more to it. Just think of how Nebuchadnezzar addresses his god Marduk in two exemplary epigraphic attestations:

> Ich bin der Fürst, der dir dienstwilling ist, das Geschöpf deiner Hand. Du hast mich geschaffen, die Königswürde über die Gesamtheit der Völker hast Du mir anvertraut.[238]

---

234 Cf. GK §135 a; JM §146 a; T. MURAOKA, *Emphatics Words*, 53; T. SEIDL, *Formen*, 62–89.

235 In this case, I refer to both of the notions of context defined by C. BIANCHI, *Pragmatica del linguaggio*, 24: i.e. 1) to the *semantic context* or *objective situation of utterance*, "which is limited to determining the content of a small number of variables and, in in particular, to establish the identity of the speaker and interlocutors, the time and place of the referral, and so on") and 2) to the pragmatic context, "which corresponds to the network of beliefs, intentions, activities of the interlocutors, and contributes to the determination of thier communicative intentions").

236 The notion of (conversational) "implicature" and the relationship between verbal and non-verbal communication are of fundamental importance in modern theories of communication, and particularly so for pragmatics in the linguistic field. I will better address the question, drawing on additional hermeneutical cues, in the following chapter of the present dissertation, dedicated to the final dialogue between Jeremiah and Zedekiah (38:14–28a).

237 T. MURAOKA, *Emphatics Words*, 48: "[...] the personal pronoun with verbum finitum serves to express an intense concern with, special interest in, or concentrated, focused consciousness of, the object referred to by the pronoun on the part of the speaker or writer. And moreover, sometimes the speaker or writer wants a listener or reader to share his concern, interest, or consciousness, which derives from the very nature of linguistic activity."

238 Translation from S. LANGDON, *Die neubabylonischen Königsinschriften*, 122–125 (with Akkadian text; no. 15, col. I: 61–65).

380   Jer 27–28. The world beneath the yoke of the king of Babylon

O Marduk, weitschauender Herr der Götter, großmächtigster Fürst! Du hast mich erschaffen, die Königsherrschaft über die Gesamtheit der Völker hast du mir anvertraut.[239]

If one considers, as B. Lang points out,[240] that Jeremiah is using the same literary motif that was utilised in Babylon to affirm the creative power of Marduk, the "YHWH – foreign deities" counterposition is even more significative and paradoxical. The motive is clear: on the one hand, the need to submit to Babylon is affirmed, while on the other, any and every value of its deities is *de facto* negated (as is done explicitly, after all, in other parts of the book; cf. e.g. the anti-idolatry controversy in ch. 10).

And yet, this YHWH[241] declares that he and only he is creator of all that exists (cf. 33:2; cf. 10:12–13 =51:15–16; 32:17), the "God of all flesh" (32:27: אֱלֹהֵי כָּל־בָּשָׂר; cf. 25:31; 45:5), the "king of the nations" (10:7: מֶלֶךְ הַגּוֹיִם).[242] As object of the creative act, "the earth (הָאָרֶץ), the men (הָאָדָם), and the animals (הַבְּהֵמָה) that are on the face of the earth (עַל־פְּנֵי הָאָרֶץ)" are mentioned.[243] The fact that, aside from the land, reference is not made to the heavens and the waters of the sea with its creatures does not mean that there be a limitation to his *sphere of action* (cf. Isa 45:12). One need only consider other significant Jeremianic texts where the same merism of Gen 1:1 appears: "the heavens and the earth"[244] (הַשָּׁמַיִם וְאֵת הָאָרֶץ) to express the creative power of YHWH[245] (cf. 23:24; 32:17; 33:25) or the impotence of the foreign deities (cf. 10:11 [in Aramaic: שְׁמַיָּא וְאַרְקָא]; cf. also 51:48). In this case, it is rather a question of a *concentration of relevancy*.[246]

---

239   *Idem*, 141 (no. 15, col. IX: 47–51); cf. A. FALKENSTEIN – W. VON SODEN, *Sumerische und akkadische Hymnen und Gebete*, BAW, Zurich 1953, 283; M.-J. SEUX, *Hymnes et prières aux dieux de Babylonie et d'Assyrie*, LAPO, Paris 1976, 506.

240   B. LANG, «Ein babylonisches Motiv», 236–237.

241   In relation to this international context, however, it does not seem pertinent to emphasise, as does G. FISCHER, «Gottes universale Horizonte. Die Völker der Welt und ihre Geschichte in der Sicht des Jeremiabuches», in: *"Ricercare la sapienza di tutti gli antichi" (Sir 39,1). Miscellanea in onore di Gian Luigi Prato*, eds. M. MILANI – M. ZAPPELLA, SRivBib 56, Bologna 2013, 313–328 (p. 325), that the proper name of the God of Israel, YHWH (יְהוָה), recurs 726x in the book of Jeremiah, that is, more than in any other book, since it is also the largest in the HB. If we instead calculate the percentages of the occurrences of יְהוָה in relation to the sum of the words in each biblical book, Jeremiah ranks in tenth position out of thirty-six (in first place is the book of Haggai). It could be interesting, however, to compare it with Ezekiel (which ranks much lower, in twentieth position), Job (third to last position), and Daniel (in last place).

242   Note that in the entire HB, this appellation occurs here only.

243   The LXX, on the other hand, mentions only the "earth" (γῆ).

244   As was pointed out by F. HARTENSTEIN, «JHWH, Erschaffer des Himmels. Zu Herkunft und Bedeutung eines monotheistischen Kernarguments», *ZThK* 110 (2013) 383–409, the confession of faith regarding YHWH as (sole) creator of the "heaven" (or of the "heavens"), is a theme developed monotheistically above all in late texts ("Deutero-Isaiah" and P) of the exilic and post-exilic period, to be compared with the Babylonian myth of Enūma eliš.

245   The idea of totality is also conveyed by the "distance-closeness" polarity in 23:23–24 (on the various interpretations of this, see W.M. LEMKE, «The Near and Distant God. A Study of Jer 23:23–34 in its Biblical Theological Context», *JBL* 100 [1981] 542–551).

246   Consider also Gen 2:19–20, where aquatic animals are not mentioned.

"Bend your neck beneath the yoke of the king of Babylon!" (27:12)   381

From the point of view of the kingdom of Judah, the chess board upon which the geopolitical balances of the ancient Near East are played out in the sixth century, where opposing empires and counterposed deities[247] challenge each other with their armies, claims to power and possession, is indeed all *terrestrial*. And so the basis and very object of this game, the land, is traced back to its sole proprietor and maker. Ultimately, to its true sovereign.[248] The land, above all that of Israel, is the נַחֲלָה ("inheritance") of YHWH.[249] And it is, at the same time, the stage of an infinite drama that sees men (v. 5. הָאָדָם) fight against men in the name of their supposed entitlement. Well, even these players (be they victims, losers, or momentary winners) are like the land (in fact, they are Adam, the "earthy one": הָאָדָם; for he was indeed drawn from the dust [עָפָר] of the soil; cf. Gen 1:26; 2:7): a work and property of God, the sole proprietor with absolute rights over it and all it contains (cf. Lev 25:23; Deut 10:14; Ps 24:1; 89:12).

But there are also the beasts that circulate and play their own part upon this troubled stage. The animal dimension expressed by the term בְּהֵמָה, especially outside of the book of Jeremiah, is sufficiently reassuring: it *generally* means "livestock", herds, and domestic animals.[250] Peaceful living beings subject to human beings and their necessities become "source domain" for significant metaphors.[251] In truth, this existential closeness, highlighted in Gen 1:24–31 by the fact that men and terrestrial animals are created on the same day (the sixth) and share a (albeit not identical) vegetarian diet, also conceals something disturbing. Many other metaphorical references likewise confirm this presentiment.[252] Indeed, there is also a whole dimension of hostility in that which moves upon the earth and makes up the bestial realm evoked by the word בְּהֵמָה (cf. Gen 3).[253]

---

247   In the ancient Near East, wars between nations are (also or above all) wars between gods; cf. A. van der Deijl, *Protest or Propaganda*. War in the Old Testament Book of Kings and in Contemporaneous Ancient Near Eastern Texts, SSN 51, Leiden – Boston 2008, 663.

248   Cf. N.C. Habel, *The Land Is Mine*. Six Biblical Land Theologies, OBT, Minneapolis 1995, 33–35, 75–96. The land, as the main strategic resource and source of wealth and prosperity, is the central object of every royal ideology of the ancient Near East (cf. pp. 17–32, where 1 Kgs 3–10 is commented).

249   Cf. W. Zimmerli, «The "Land" in the Pre-Exilic and Early Post-Exilic Prophets», in: *Understanding the Word*. Essays in Honor of Bernhard W. Anderson, eds. J.T. Butler – E.W. Conrad – B.C. Ollenburger, JSOT.S 37, Sheffield 1985, 235–254.

250   Cf. *BDB*, 96; G.J. Botterweck, «בְּהֵמָה», *ThWAT* I, 523–536; N. Kiuchi, «בְּהֵמָה», *NIDOTTE* I, 612–613. In Gen 1:24 (cf. Gen 2:20), three classes of terrestrial living creatures are distinguished (נֶפֶשׁ חַיָּה): the "cattle" (בְּהֵמָה), the "reptiles" or "creeping things" (רֶמֶשׂ), and the "beasts of the earth" (חַיְתוֹ־אֶרֶץ), which, after the sin of humanity, as the tale in the Genesis seems to imply (cf. Gen 1:30), become ferocious carnivores. Elsewhere, animals are distinguished in only two classes: the beasts of the field and the birds of the sky (cf. Gen 2:19).

251   For the book of Jeremiah, see B.A. Foreman, *Animal Metaphors*, above all, pp. 35–161, 190–195.

252   Cf. B.A. Foreman, *Animal Metaphors*, 162–189.

253   On the depiction of violence through use of the beastly image, a powerful metaphor for expressing the relationship between human beings and violence, see P. Beauchamp, «Création et fondation de la loi», 139–182; P. Beauchamp – D. Vasse, «La violence dans la Bible», 7–15.

382   Jer 27–28. The world beneath the yoke of the king of Babylon

The animal is so close to the human being that the Scripture gives us a glimpse of it as a threat poised at his threshold[254] under another name (חַטָּאת; "sin"; Gen 4:7),[255] capable of contending for his inhabitable space, even his very home (cf. Jer 50:39; Isa 13:21–22; 34:11.14; Zeph 2:14; Ps 102:7; Rev 18:2). Close enough to devour and swallow him (cf. Gen 9:5; 37:33; 1 Kgs 14:11; Josh 2:1; Tob 6:2; etc.). So close, that the animal can be man himself (cf. Gen 49:9, 14–15, 17, 21, 27; Deut 33:17, 20, 22; etc.)[256] or man can become an animal (cf. Ezek 19; 22:25; Dan 4:22, 30; Ps 7:3; 22:14; etc.).[257]

In fact, in the book of Jeremiah, where the term בְּהֵמָה recurs 18x, at least two different semiotic registers can be noted, depending on the contextual use. Quite frequent is the couple "men" (אָדָם) – "animals" (בְּהֵמָה), which is always in reference, in a literal sense, to the whole of the more evolved living beings (cf. 7:20; 21:6; 27:5; 31:27; 32:43; 33:10[2x]; 33:12; 36:29; 50:3; 51:62). Object of creation or destruction, they share the same fate. When, however, the stereotypical locution of "animals of the earth" [בֶּהֱמַת הָאָרֶץ] (cf. 7:33; 15:3; 16:4; 19:7; 34:20) is used, this is not to make reference to harmless mammals, but rather to evoke dramatic scenes, far from idyllic and dominated by the savage ferocity of carnivorous animals (cf. also 5:6; 15:3). So then, when in 27:5 where we find an expansion of the same locution ("animals that are on the face of the earth" [בְּהֵמָה אֲשֶׁר עַל־פְּנֵי הָאָרֶץ]), reference is being made, in all probability, in the figurative sense, *also* to state entities and empires that devour each other (cf. Jer 5:6; 51:34; Nah 2:12–14; Dan 7:5, 7; etc.), mauling human flesh without respite.[258]

Earth, human beings, animals: a chain of subjects in reciprocal relation, all interconnected realities, starting with the Sole unifying principle that is their Origin. They are almost "symbiotic"[259] realities, actants participating in a single destiny (cf. 12:4), for

---

254   Cf. P. BEAUCHAMP – D. VASSE, «La violence dans la Bible», 7.
255   Given the extreme difficulty of this verse, "glimpse" is without a doubt a pertinent clarification.
256   Obviously according to an analogical transposition common to all ancient (and modern) cultures. It suffices to recall the fables of Aesop and Phaedrus.
257   The man-animal similitude is so evocative in the Scripture that a master of patristic exegesis, Origen, had to defend the use of biblical images of animal isotopy (in homily XVI based on Jer 16:16–17,1), which could have exposed him to an accusation of professing metensomatosis. This doctrine, common in the philosophical conceptions of his time, "theorised the transmigration of the soul into successive and different bodies according to the level of purification achieved, without excluding, according to Origen, even reincarnation in the bodies of animals") (translated from E. DAL COVOLO – M. MARITANO, Omelie su Geremia. Lettura origeniana, BSRel 165, Roma 2001, 51).
258   Note, in this regard, P. BEAUCHAMP, «Création et fondation de la loi», 139–182: "Narrativement, la multiplicité ethnique, même si elle n'est pas causée par la violence ni par le péché, est nécessairement soumise à la régulation légale de la violence par la contreviolence. Entre les nations, sous le régime post-diluvien, l'effusion de sang n'est pas l'objet d'un interdit divin explicite, seule est exclue la haine avec ce qu'elle implique d'ambivalence. [...] c'est surtout dans les rapports entre les nations que nous est familier le spectacle de l'une dévorant les autres comme les fauves dévorent les plus faibles" (here, pp. 167–168).
259   N.C. HABEL, The Land Is Mine, 95, affirms this in regard to the relationship between God, Israel, and the land.

"Bend your neck beneath the yoke of the king of Babylon!" (27:12)   383

better or for worse.[260] A biblical awareness that reflects a common consciousness in the ancient Near East, as Hans Heinrich Schmid underscored in this regard:

> Unter dem Begriff der "Schöpfung" finden somit im altorientalischen Raum – abgekürzt gesagt – die kosmische, die politische und die soziale Ordnung ihre Einheit. [...] im ganzen Alten Orient, einschließlich Israels, ein Vergehen im Bereich des Rechts ganz selbstverständlich seine Folgen auch im Raume der Natur (Dürre, Hungersnot) oder der Politik (Feindbedrohung) zeitigen kann: Recht, Natur und Politik sind nur Aspekte der einen, umfassenden Schöpfungsordung.[261]

The creative act is evoked with a stereotyped expressive register that recalls (or that is also used in regard to) the founding event of the Exodus: בְּכֹחִי הַגָּדוֹל וּבִזְרוֹעִי הַנְּטוּיָה ("by my great power and by my outstretched arm"; the locution is found formally identical only in Deut 9:29; 2 Kgs 17:36; Jer 32:17). While in most of its occurrences, the underlying (also extrabiblical) context is that of the deity who inflicts punitive wounds[262] on his enemies (as we saw when studying 21:1–10), in the book of Jeremiah, this reference is juxtaposed and correlated to an entirely different use (which, without a doubt, has logical precedence over the other context), aimed at giving greater emphasis to the creative act of YHWH, as manifestation of his divine power (here, and in 32:17). Power that can de-create (cf. 1:10: "eradicate [√נתש] and demolish [√נתץ], destroy [√אבד hi.], and tear down [√הרס]") what he created, but for this very reason, he is also capable of re-creating life (cf. 1:10: "to build [√בנה] and plant" [√נטע]), that is, something humanly unimaginable (cf. 32:27), where the eyes of human beings fail to perceive anything but rubble, despair, and death.

4.2.6. *"And I give it to whomever seems right in my eyes" (27:5b). YHWH, creator and Lord of history (sapiential dimension and prophetic aperture)*

In the Jeremianic text we are looking at, the theme of YHWH as creator is called into question not only to confess an ahistorical truth (of a sapiential nature), which, understood as thus, would risk remaining on an abstract level, but also to strongly affirm (on a prophetic level) the exercising of a global lordship over the whole of human history.[263] The phrase in 27:5b acts as a hinge between these two dimensions.

Giving voice to YHWH's self-revelation as creator of the world, Jeremiah echoes a theological tradition that is *well known* to his listeners, and not only on the level of the narrative world.[264] Contrary to what was considered in the past, and despite the

---

260 In 12:4, e.g. what happens to the land is a reflection of what the prophet himself experiences, but also of what the people experience (cf. 14:2). See T.E. FRETHEIM, *God and World*, 175 and C.J. DEMPSEY, *Hope Amid the Ruins*. The Ethics of Israel's Prophets, St. Louis 2000, 74–88 (who, on p. 87, speaks of "systemic connection"), for an overview of prophetic texts regarding the deadly effect of sin on the land (cf. Isa 6:8–13; 13:9–13; 24; 33:7–9; 34:8–12; Jer 7:16–20; 12:4; 23:9–11; Hos 4:1–3; Jl 1:15–18; Amos 4:6–10; 8:4–8; Zeph 1:2–6).
261 H.H. SCHMID, «Schöpfung», 4.
262 This is highlighted in the study by K. MARTENS, «"With a Strong Hand», 123–141.
263 Cf. L. WISSER, «La création dans le livre de Jérémie», 252–253.
264 Therefore, Jeremiah should also be borne in mind when S. PAAS, *Creation and Judgement*, 150, asserts that "the creator functions of YHWH, viewed by so many as a

384   Jer 27–28. The world beneath the yoke of the king of Babylon

scarcity of attestations available to date,[265] the question regards a theme that is *in itself* most probably pre-exilic, even if it obviously went through subsequent developments and re-elaborations.[266] Besides the evidence consisting of possible Canaanite extraction, Egyptian influences, and epigraphical discoveries,[267] this is mainly suggested by the data derived from the biblical text, as Stefan Paas highlighted in his study.[268]

Along the lines of what I specified on a methodological level since the part of my dissertation dedicated to the historical contextualisation of the message of the surrender, and as I have also clarified in the present chapter, I recognise there to be a particular heuristic value in the reconstruction of a possible pragmatic context for the Jeremianic text through the evaluation of possible interconnections between a possible Jeremianic world (the world of the text) and extrabiblical (i.e. extratextual) data. For this reason, it is worth mentioning two inscriptions that were rediscovered alongside other graffiti and briefer texts (at least five) on the wall of a cave utilised as a tomb dating back to the eighth or seventh century, that is, to the time of the Assyrian invasion of the kingdom of Judah, on the site of Khirbet Beir Lei, a few kilometres east of Lachish, in the Sefela.

The texts are not easy to read,[269] but it seems quite probable that the first be a doxology in honour of YHWH, the God of Israel, proclaimed lord/creator of the universe and the second, a prayer that invokes his rescue. I will first look at inscription A, according to a reconstruction of the Hebrew text and the most accredited translation proposed[270]:

---

product of (post-)exilic monotheism, could actually have been ascribed to him already earlier. In any event, there is little or no reason to assume that Amos, Hosea and Isaiah were making unusual statements when they called *YHWH* Creator. A god other than YHWH (who could also be called El) was probably not considered. Needless to say, this does not mean that the *content* of such references was also self-evident".

265   As is justly noted by S. PAAS, *Creation and Judgement*, 18: "The *argumentum e silentio* of the relevant Old Testament evidence (meagre as it is), is an insufficient basis for the conclusion that belief in YHWH as Creator of the world was not found in pre-exilic Israel."

266   In addition to the development of "Deutero-Isaiah", also consider the psalms that celebrate YHWH as king of the gods and nations (cf. e.g. Ps 29; 47; 89:9–14; 97; 98; 99). Cf. H.-J. KRAUS, *Prophetie in der Krisis*. Studien zu Texten aus dem Buch Jeremia, BSt 43, Neukirchen-Vluyn 1964, 68–69.

267   S. PAAS, *Creation and Judgement*, 49–52. See, in particular, the inscription studied, amongst others, by P.D. MILLER Jr., «El, the Creator of Earth», *BASOR* 237 (1980) 43–46, in which, according to the reconstruction proposed, the expression "creator of the earth" can be read, referring to YHWH. The question, in any case, remains controversial.

268   For the Canaanite background and possible Egyptian influences, see S. PAAS, *Creation and Judgement*, 121–143. As far as the study of biblical attestations is concerned (cf. pp. 20–49), the belief held (and conclusion drawn) by the author is that the first Old Testament references to the faith of Israel in YHWH as creator come from the beginning of the age of the monarchy (pp. 49, 437).

269   Their first publication was done by J. NAVEH, «Old Hebrew Inscriptions in a Burial Cave», *IEJ* 13 (1963) 74–92. More recently, by the same author, see ID., «Hebrew Graffiti from the Temple Period», *IEJ* 51 (2001) 194–207.

270   We refer above all to J. RENZ, *Die althebräischen Inschriften*, 248. See also the translation and comment by W.W. HALLO – K.L. YOUNGER, Jr., eds., *The Context of Scripture*. Monumental Inscriptions from the Biblical World, vol. II, Leiden 2000, 179–180 and S. AḤITUV, *Echoes from the Past*, 233–234.

יהוה אלהי כל הארץ ה 1 YHWH (is) the God of the whole land, the
רי : יהוה ׃ לאלהי ׃ ירשלם 2 highlands of Judah belong to the God of Jerusalem

Inscription B could provide some significant clues for the definition of the pragmatic context of reference (and of utterance) of both texts, in addition to those deducible from the study of the inscriptions in relation to the site and to their presumable dating. A possible reading and translation of the graffiti reads[271]:

פקד יה אל חנן: נקה יה[271] יהוה 1 Intervene YH, merciful God! Absolve o[272] YHWH!

Fig. 25· Sketch of inscriptions A and B engraved on the western wall of the burial antechamber in Khirbet Beit Lei (from F.M. Cross, «The Cave Inscriptions», 300; J. Renz, Texte und Tafeln, tab. XXV).

Both inscriptions seem to have no direct relationship to the funerary semiotics of the cave[273] (which would appear to be more ancient and originary), both on the level of content (especially the first) and style (these are improvised texts, written without particular expertise or aesthetic concerns), and for the palaeographic dating. Praise and invocation of aid from YHWH as God of Israel (through the unusual expression "God of Jerusalem"; cf. 2 Chron 32:19; Esd 2:8; 7:17) seem to be attributed to refugees

---

271 Cf. J. Renz, *Die althebräischen Inschriften*, 248; W.W. Hallo – K.L. Younger, Jr., eds., *The Context of Scripture*, II, 180; S. Aḥituv, *Echoes from the Past*, 235 (also for reference to different proposed readings by other scholars).
272 Along with S.L. Gogel, *Epigraphic Hebrew*, 231 (cf. n. 340), I consider the lexeme יה here to be an interjection with vocative value and not an apocopated form of the divine Tetragrammaton (the occurrence of which, in the first phrase, is not certain, given that it could be the result of a cancellation of the last two consonants).
273 F.M. Cross Jr., «The Cave Inscriptions from Khirbet Beit Lei», in: *Near Eastern Archaeology in the Twentieth Century.* Essays in Honor of Nelson Glueck, ed. J.A. Sanders, Garden City 1970, 299–306.

386   Jer 27–28. The world beneath the yoke of the king of Babylon

fleeing from distressing events.[274] What? Several scholars hold that these are those from the beginning of the sixth century, namely precisely the historical context with which we are dealing. From the communicative point of view, it can be seen that the content of the inscriptions (which could be also a single text, as proposes Meindert Dijkstra,[275] amongst others; cf. Fig. 25) does not consist in abstract statements of doctrinal truths. They are professions of faith and invocations[276] made *in times of crisis*, which reread dramatic historical events in the light of the certainty that human events are under the authority of YHWH, confessed creator of the world and righteous Lord of history. And it is precisely for this that he is invoked as saviour.[277]

These references can help bring the pragmatic context of 27:5b into focus more effectively. The locution וּנְתַתִּיהָ לַאֲשֶׁר יָשַׁר בְּעֵינָי ("and I give it to whomever seems good/righteous in my eyes") in reference to the earth, though then actually in reference to the initial triad (earth, human beings, and animals), places the *freedom* and *intentionality* of God in relation to the destiny-destination of creation (cf. Gen 1:26–29; 2:19–20; 9:2–3; Ps 115:16) in the foreground, and thereby to the unfolding of human lordship over the world (cf. Dan 4:14, 22, 29; 5:21 in precise reference, through an analogous expression, to the overthrowing of the power of Nebuchadnezzar). With them, the *memory* of an originary act of entrustment effected by the creator and saviour of Israel is also renewed. Not only that of the Genesis, which is universal, but also that which is particular, in which YHWH one day freely entrusted/gave (√נתן; cf. e.g. Gen 17:1; 13:15, 17; etc.; Exod 6:4.8; 12:25; 13:5, 11; etc.; Deut 4:21, 28; etc.; Josh 1:2, 3, 6; etc.) the land of Canaan (and not others, destined for other peoples; cf. Deut 2:19) to an enslaved people fled from Egypt. In that circumstance, it was other people who should have understood that their land was being handed over to others and they should have been subjected themselves to the yoke of Israel (cf. Josh 2:8–14; Deut 20:10–15[278]; and of the king David; cf. 2 Sam 22:48; Ps 18:48; 144:2) in order to stay alive. But now, it

---

274 On caves as a place of refuge in the HB, see e.g. Gen 19:30; Judg 6:2; 15:8; 1 Sam 14:11; 24:4; 2 Sam 23:13 (cf. Ps 57:1; 142:1, in which the theme of David taking refuge in the cave is tied precisely to the plea to YHWH); Jer 49:16; etc.

275 M. DIJKSTRA, «I Have Blessed You by YHWH of Samaria and His Asherah: Texts with Religious Elements from the Soil Archive of Ancient Israel», in: *Only One God? Monotheism in Ancient Israel and the Veneration of the Goddess Asherah*, eds. B. BECKING *et al.*, BiSe 77, Sheffield 2001, 17–44: "(A) Yhwh is the God of the whole earth/ The land(?) of Judah belongs to him, the God of Jerusalem (B) See the attacked(?) city; have mercy on the innocent(?), o Yhwh (C) Save, [o Y]hwh! (D) The conjurer may curse him/ with the curse of the righteous against violation(?)" (here, p. 37).

276 Cf. S.L. GOGEL, *Epigraphic Hebrew*, 288, 411.

277 This is particularly highlighted by A. LEMAIRE, «Prières en temps de crise: les inscriptions de Khirbet Beit Lei», *RB* 83 (1976) 558–568. The same applies to the inscription C that the same author translates as "Deliver (us) O Lord" (p. 302).

278 In the theological design of Deut, only "far" cities are offered such a possibility. To those of the "neighbouring" peoples, on the other hand, who constitute a threat to the faith of Israel, the prescription of "extermination" had to be applied. In any case, in the book of Joshua (cf. Josh 2:8–14) Rahab rises to be a paradigmatic figure of salvation (for those who were, in any case, destined for the end) obtained through *discernment* (of *history*, and, in this case, of the actual designation of the land decided

"Bend your neck beneath the yoke of the king of Babylon!" (27:12)   387

is Israel who must submit if it wants to be saved. Even now, God gives the earth to those who appear good in his eyes! In his indisputable justice.

Free, non-negotiable, but also entirely unmotivated? In other words: the earth is given "to who looks good" or "who is right" in his eyes? Is it truly just free election, irrespective of any "merit", or is it rather a choice that recognises and rewards, in the one chosen, that they be "right" (יָשָׁר)? At first glance, a careful reading of the Hebrew text would negate the second hypothesis. In fact, the syntagm a יָשָׁר + בְּעֵינֵי + suff. or name (functioning as indirect object) calls for separate lexicographical consideration from the more common semantic of the adjective יָשָׁר (meaning "straight, flat, smooth" [cf. 31:9] or figurative sense "upright, righteous, etc."). The expression, which involves the organs of sight, calls in question first of all the subject's capacity of evaluation and thus the criteriology that orients its decision-making powers, including the whole consequent broad spectrum of possible outcomes of this.[279] The question is thus not that of opting for those who are "right", but of freely choosing according to one's own criteria, whether these be of an ethical-moral nature or not. Emphasis need once more be given, however, to the pragmatic impact of the context, by which the figure of Nebuchadnezzar, in the book of Jeremiah and implicitly in our own text, unquestionably plays a specific juridic/judiciary role (which is that of executor of the just sentence of YHWH) towards the kingdom of Judah. The Hebrew expression, in itself of an idiomatic type, can be read therefore as an allusive indication with an *ethical* value, in reference precisely to the king of Babylon as a "king of justice"[280]. It is not surprising then that the Tg take this potential line of interpretation decisively, rendering the phrase with "I have given it to *whomever is right* [לדכשר] before me". My own translation ("to whomever seems right in my eyes") respects the idiomatic sense, but does not preclude the second path of meaning. This, rather, would have resulted had I rendered the phrase with the more obvious "to who seems just in my eyes". It need be considered that the reading of the Tg, which forces the allusion to the justice of the king of Babylon so it becomes a universal principle, consequently generating an unsustainable theology of history: to affirm that whoever holds the power can automatically claim indisputable proof of morality. With its formulation, the MT, wisely avoids this outcome.

Jeremiah 27:5b, while remaining, on the one hand, a sapiential affirmation – is a kind of axiom with perennial or atemporal validity, expressed by a perfect (וּנְתַתִּיהָ) that could be defined as "gnomic"[281] – introduces a principle of radical relativisation of

---

by God) and *submission* (to the people to whom the earth had been delivered, and therefore to the *meaning* of present history revealed by God).

279   See L. ALONSO SCHÖKEL, «יָשָׁר III», *ThWAT* III, 1062–1069 (in particular, coll. 1067–1068).

280   Precisely for his extraordinary virtue as legislator and just judge, almost as if he were a new Hammurabi, he is praised in a cuneiform text of great interest (BM 45690), according to the study by W.G. LAMBERT, «Nebuchadnezzar King of Justice», *Iraq* 27 (1965) 1–11 (in particular, p. 3); and see also D.J. WISEMAN, *Nebuchadrezzar and Babylon*, 98–104 (in particular, p. 101).

281   Cf. GK 106*k*; WO 30.5.1c. The notion of "gnomic perfect", derived, by analogy, from that of the Greek "gnomic aorist", even if it was not subject to specific study, is used by various grammars when reference is made, with a *qatal*, to a general and permanent truth known experientially, as e.g. a proverb or another statement holding atemporal significance (cf. J. LYONS, *Semantics*, 681; J. BYBEE – R. PERKINS – W. PAGLIUCA,

388   Jer 27–28. The world beneath the yoke of the king of Babylon

the complex intrahistorical dynamics of human events that raises a question about events in the present. Everything is, in fact, *relative* to the design of YHWH and his justice. Events, circumstances, decisions, conquests and breakdowns, empires and cyclical about-faces. Even silence, or the apparent absence of God. Everything is to be reconsidered in relation to a will that is creative, transcendent, and absolute. And precisely because the criteria of this projectuality are not revealed immediately (or punctually), the urgency of the crisis generated by historical upheavals reactivates the *memory* (of the great works of God; cf. e.g. Exod 32:11; Judg 6:6–10; 1 Kgs 8:50–51; Neh 9; etc.), provokes the *discernment* (of what God is doing now; cf. e.g. Jer 14:19; Ezek 11:15; 33:24), and at the same time leaves room for *intercession* (to stay alive; cf. e.g. 2 Kgs 19:2–4; Jer 14:22; 21:1–2[282]; 32:17–27; 33:1–3). But, above all, it requires the intervention of the *prophetic word,* which is together memory, discernment, intercession, and an appeal to human freedom.

In this sense, the veil stretched like a backdrop across the scenes of history had already been partially raised in ch. 18, thanks to a spinning wheel and hands immersed in damp clay. To comprehend how God functions and his basic criteria with respect to the nations and their destiny, it actually sufficed to descend with Jeremiah down into the potter (יֹצֵר)'s workshop and to observe the artisan craft (cf. 18:7–10). Just as the potter acts "as it seems good to his eyes" (cf. 18:4: כַּאֲשֶׁר יָשַׁר בְּעֵינֵי) in order to achieve a beautiful work, that truly corresponds to his intentions,[283] likewise, divine liberty is not senseless whim or a mystery that is entirely inscrutable. It is, in turn, relative to human free will (cf. 26:14–15, where in v. 14, the same expression that is in 27:5b recurs substantially, in the phrase that Jeremiah addresses to his interlocutors after having announced the word of the Lord: עֲשׂוּ־לִי כַּטּוֹב וְכַיָּשָׁר בְּעֵינֵיכֶם ["do with me what is good and right in your eyes"]; cf. also 40:4–5). It is a will of a coming good that seeks acceptance in order to come about. The cosmic order and ethic (or social) order remain interconnected.[284]

The Evolution of Grammar. Tense, Aspect and Modality in the Languages of the World, Chicago 1994, 126, 319).

282   It is precisely this possibility, intrinsic to the institution of the Covenant, that YHWH denies the prophet Jeremiah at a certain point. It is a question, in fact, in my opinion, of a radicalisation of the intercessionary function of the prophet himself, called on to make a disturbing gesture for the salvation of his people. As an extreme attempt to unmask the falsehood of a people who, without converting, believe that they have a right to obtain grace from God.

283   It should be noted that the potter's intentions concern the realisation of an artefact that is already, in and of itself, a semiotic hub rich with anthropological references, relevant in various extents to the dimension of inter-human and human-divine relationality.

284   While distinguished and clarified differently by different scholars, a perception of this interdependence typifies sapiential reflection throughout the entire ancient Near East. See, in this regard, the contributions of H.H. Schmid, *Gerechtigkeit als Weltordnung.* Hintergrund und Geschichte des alttestamentlichen Gerechtigkeitsbegriffes, BHTh 40, Tübingen 1968; J. Krašovec, *La justice (ṣdq) de Dieu dans la Bible hébraïque et l'interprétation juive et chrétienne,* OBO 76, Freiburg 1988; J. Assmann, *Ma'at: Gerechtigkeit und Unsterblichkeit im Alten Ägypten,* München 1990.

"Bend your neck beneath the yoke of the king of Babylon!" (27:12) 389

What seems good/right in the eyes of YHWH (cf. also 34:15) has got nothing to do with any form of "divine imperialism"[285] expressed in nationalistic terms. It is rather the ineludible recognition of a *limit*, as an intrinsic necessity, both of the order of creation, understood as impersonal nature (cf. 5:22: וּבֻל ["boundary, confines"]) and of the human sphere, in all of its interpersonal expressions (socio-political-religious). In this second respect, the Jeremianic text underscores two aspects:

1) To recognise and accept this limit in its historical manifestation and (above all) its divine origin and intentionality is *mediation of life* itself (cf. 27:11–12, 17). To reject it, on the contrary, causes death, annihilation (cf. 27:8, 10, 13, 17; 28:15–17). Indeed, even worse: it causes creation to be plunged (back) into chaos,[286] subjecting it to radical, dramatic dismantling, and everything goes back to being תֹּהוּ וָבֹהוּ, that is, "waste and void" (cf. Gen 1:2; Jer 4:22–29 and 5:23–25; 9:10–11; 12:4, 7–13). For those who experience first-hand the devastating impact of war on social order, this is not just a mythology. That which the grimmest repertoire of human consciousness can evoke becomes actualised by infuriated throngs of enemy armies capable of devastating and annihilating an entire natural[287] and cultural ecosystem (and even if this is simply the urban fabric of a small town or the modest territorial and institutional horizons of the kingdom of Judah, it is still a complete, vital microcosm; cf. 12:9–12).

This is why war and the hostile forces of the nations are often represented in the context of the ancient Near East (in the context of royal ideology, especially Babylonian) as being the threatening resurgence of the originary chaos, that of a monster (Tiamat) who, despite having been killed at the beginning of time, seems to present itself repeatedly in history under other forms, determined to take back for itself, once and for all, that which the world-ordering deity had, in times immemorial (mythological), violently subtracted from it.[288] In the Babylonian view, it is the young god Marduk, already the slayer of Tiamat, who undertakes the pursuit of this fight.

---

285 Which is spoken about by J.J.M. ROBERTS, « The End of War in the Zion Tradition. The Imperialistic Background of the Old Testament Vision of Worldwide Peace», in: *Character Ethics*, 119–128 (here, p. 124).

286 Cf. M. BAUKS, «"Chaos" als Metapher für die Gefährdung der Weltordnung», in: *Das biblische Weltbild und seine altorientalischen Kontexte*, eds. B. JANOWSKI – B. EGO, FAT 32, Tübingen 2001, 431–464; D.T. TSUMURA, *Creation and Destruction*. A Reappraisal of the Chaoskampf Theory in the Old Testament, Winona Lake 2005.

287 Cf. T.E. FRETHEIM, *God and World*, 158, who defines 4:22–26 as "one of the most vivid biblical portrayals of environmental catastrophe". The systematic destruction of trees, vineyards and cultivated fields was a habitual war practice of the Babylonians, especially during sieges (what happened to the kingdom of Judah is emblematic; cf. J.W. BETLYON, «Neo-Babylonian Military Operations other than War in Judah and Jerusalem», in: *Judah and the Judeans*, 263–283). The instructions outlined in Deut 20:19–20 in case of a wartime siege are completely opposed and demonstrate a sensitivity that today we would call "ecological" (cf. M. HASEL, *Military Practice and Polemic*. Israel's Laws of Warfare in Near Eastern Perspective, Berrien Springs 2005, 95–123).

288 For a general overview of the topic, see M. BAUKS, «Chaoskampf», WAM, 94–98. In this regard, look at H.H. SCHMID, «Schöpfung», 3: "Sowohl in Mesopotamien als auch in Ugarit und in Israel erscheint der Chaoskampf nicht nur in kosmologischen, sondern ebensosehr – und im Grunde gleich ursprünglich – auch in, wenn man so sagen darf, politischen Zusammenhängen. Von der Zurückwerfung und Vernichtung

390   Jer 27–28. The world beneath the yoke of the king of Babylon

And every war undertaken by his protégé, Nebuchadnezzar, cannot but be configured as a battle against the selfsame enemy with its manifold intrahistorical faces.[289]

A paradoxical conflict of interpretations[290]: on the one hand, the kingdom of Judah, which finds itself invaded by foreign nations, feels assailed and threatened by the very same chaos (cf. Isa 17:12–14; 51:9–10; Ps 46:2–8 and Ps 77:17–20 as a rereading of the Exodus event), an image of that primordial chaos that, in some biblical traditions, YHWH had defeated (cf. Ps 29:10, 74:12–17; 93; Job 26:10–14; etc.)[291]. On the other, Nebuchadnezzar, seeing his mission as ordinator of a world threatened by rebellion and betrayal, believes and knows himself to be the bearer of a divine right who wants to and must restore harmony to the cosmos.[292] An assignment that is annually and solemnly renewed in the temple complex of Ésagila in Babylon on the fifth day of the great Akitu festival.

In Jer 27, however, there is a radical reversal, under these premises: what had been interpreted in the traditional vision as the threat of chaos is presented as an order of YHWH. And now we can reread 21:1–10 in this light and underscore some other paths of interpretation that would otherwise not be immediately demonstrable: by besieging Jerusalem, Nebuchadnezzar thinks he is obeying Marduk (cf. Ezek 21:26–27), but according to Jeremiah, he is obeying the true God and his design for justice (cf. 27:6) under this appearance. What Israel perceives as the looming and assault of chaos is actually order advancing, that of the Babylonian god Marduk (and YHWH, in the guise of his likeness and intentions), believed in and venerated in Babylon precisely as a victorious warrior against chaos. And Jerusalem has become its emblem, because, as Jeremiah forcefully denounces, everything in it has become injustice and oppression, upheaval of the laws of God (cf. 3:3; 5:1, 25; 6:7–8; 20:8; 22:17; etc.).

In the theological perspective of the book of Jeremiah, only the end of Babylon (cf. e.g. 50:2[293] in the context of chs. 50–51) and the reconstruction of Judah and Jerusalem (cf. e.g. 31:10–11[294] in the context of chs. 30–32) will finally reveal the One true Lord of history.

---

        der Feinde und damit von der Aufrechterhaltung der staatlichen Ordnung ist immer wieder in den Farben des Chaoskampfes die Rede. Die Feinde sind nichts anderes als Manifestationen des Chaos, das es zurückzudrängen gilt".

289   Cf. R. Da Riva, *The Twin Inscriptions*, 18–19 and WBC VIII 27–37 (p. 61).

290   On the resemblances between the respective "divine profiles" of YHWH and Marduk (from marginal deities to the claim of absolute sovereignty over the cosmos), see S.W. Flynn, *YHWH is King*. The Development of Divine Kingship in Ancient Israel, VT.S 159, Leiden – Boston 2014, 119–125.

291   Cf. M. Bauks, «"Chaos" als Metapher», 431–464.

292   Cf. M. Kessler, *Battle of the Gods*. The God of Israel versus Marduk of Babylon. A Literary/Theological Interpretation of Jeremiah 50–51, Assen 2003.

293   "Proclaim this amongst the people and let it be known, raise a banner, let it be known and do not hide it! Say: 'Babylon is captured. Bel is put to shame, Marduk is shattered, his images are put to shame, his idols are shattered'."

294   "[10] Hear, you nations, the word of the Lord, declare it to the distant islands and say: 'The one who scattered Israel now gathers him and keep him as a shepherd does his flock'. [11] For the Lord has redeemed Jacob, saved him from the hands of one stronger than he."

"Bend your neck beneath the yoke of the king of Babylon!" (27:12)   391

2) There is a *fixed limit* to every human power structure, whether it be foreign or even "consecrated" by election (as in the case of Israel) or similar authoritative divine accreditations (cf. 27:6). The next historical manifestation in the development of the story (which I will discuss in the next paragraph) is foreseen in 27:7 under this general principle. And yet even from this specific case, one can deduce additional elements of meaning on a universal level and thereby complete the framework of the sapiential dimension to which Jeremiah refers. If YHWH consigns the power to a single individual (and/or to a given nation), this does not occur, however, once and for all, but "until the time [also] comes for his country" (עַד בֹּא־עֵת אַרְצוֹ). At the expiry of the predetermined time frame (the reference to the time span of three generations ["he, his son and the son of his son"] in 27:7 has clear conventional value and no specific historic testimony in actual events,[295] just as the corresponding term of seventy years in 25:11–12), this power, in turn, will then have to submit to a force greater than itself. Ultimately, the sense of history according to the Jeremianic perspective is that nothing, aside from YHWH, is absolute. And that everyone ("every flesh"; cf. 45:5: כָּל־בָּשָׂר) must eventually be destabilised (by "disaster"; רָעָה) and submit to someone else. Even death itself.[296]

"And I give it to whomever seems right in my eyes." A statement that thus remains *sapiential* in nature and breadth, but which enables a transition to a *prophetic* focalisation on the present history. This aperture in meaning consists in the question that this affirmation of principle implicitly (but necessarily) elicits in the reader/listener. YHWH decides the destiny of peoples and bestows the power to those he wants, always, as he deems right. But *now*, to whom has the empire of the world, and thus universal authority, been delivered?

4.2.7. "And now I have delivered all these lands into the hand of Nebuchadnezzar, my servant" (27:6a). YHWH: The Lord of this history (prophetic dimension)

Distinguishing between the sapiential sphere and the prophetic perspective means dealing with two different modalities of relating to the *temporal dimension*. This is highlighted, with his unmistakable acumen, by P. Beauchamp, who also cites the peculiar (and fundamental) positioning of the Law within this hermeneutical perspective:

> Le rapport au temps n'est pas le même pour la Loi, les prophètes, les Sages. Le législateur antidate les lois sans plus de délibération qu'il n'en faut à un notaire pour changer de style. Il cache l'origine sous l'image du commencement. Le prophète à l'inverse dénude les conditions d'émergence de la parole et son moment, selon le paramètre universel, l'exposant à tous, du temps des astres et de l'histoire. Le sage tient un discours achronique ou panchronique. La Loi pose un *avant*: toute loi est ramenée à une ère archétypale et tout archétype est le lieu d'une loi. Le prophète pose un *maintenant*, le Sage un *toujours*.[297]

---

295   Cf. G. FISCHER, *Jeremia 26–52*, 53–54.
296   This extraordinary outcome, which will dealt with to its fulfilment in the NT (cf. 1 Cor 15:26), is already seen as a figure in the book of Jeremiah, in reference to the re-establishment of the fortunes of the people subjected to the catastrophe of the exile.
297   P. BEAUCHAMP, *L'un et l'autre Testament*, 136.

392 Jer 27–28. The world beneath the yoke of the king of Babylon

After having exalted the creative power of YHWH and correlated it with the constants of the exercise of divine lordship over history (27:5),[298] the Jeremianic text vehemently assumes a typical *prophetic register* (27:6). And thus the initial premise, which in itself already forces the nations to globally reconsider their political-religious points of reference,[299] deflagrates on the communicative level with all of its pragmatic power (or illocutionary force), outright determining the *meaning* of the present moment, the *historical key players* implicated, and the necessary *response* of obedience, required as the only mediation for life.

Now. Not yesterday, not tomorrow. *All these countries*, precisely your lands,[300] your lives, your future. *Nebuchadnezzar*, not the ruler of Egypt who you hope will help you, not your kings or your generals. *Now YHWH delivers everything into the hands*[301] *of the young king of Babylon*. Prophetic deixis, we could call it.

The perfect נָתַתִּי used by Jeremiah in 27:6 is particularly significant, on both the semantic and rhetorical level (given that it recurs in 27:5 [נְתַתִּיהָ], 2x in v. 6 [נָתַתִּי], and in 28.14 [נָתַתִּי], albeit loosely, at the beginning and at the end of Jeremiah's prophetic interventions in the 27–28 unit). In the process of translating into the English language, it is possible to render נָתַתִּי both in the present tense ("I consign/give") and the present perfect ("I consigned"), and in some cases, even in the future tense ("I will consign"). It would be a case of the so-called "prophetic perfect",[302] a phenomenon

---

298 In Israel, that YHWH be the Creator, implies the fact that he be the Lord of history as well, and from this profound interconnection "man gewinnt den Eindruck, daß JHWH's 'Schöpfer-sein' und sein 'Herr-sein' untrennbare Aspekte des Erlösungswerkes JHWH's sind, das sich in der Schöpfung des Kosmos offenbarte und sich seither in vielerlei Gestalt innerhalb des Kosmos manifestiert" (C. Houtman, *Der Himmel im Alten Testament*. Israels Weltbild und Weltanschauung, OTS 30, Leiden 1993, 96). We are, therefore, quite far from the notion of the Enlightenment of "God the Watchmaker" (think of the conception expressed e.g. by Robert Boyle [1627–1691]), by which God would have created a perfectly autonomous process (natural laws) that no longer require any proximity or divine intervention.

299 Even if, in principle, this discourse is acceptable to everyone, at least in Jerusalem.

300 I will specify that the term "lands" that I use to translate אֲרָצוֹת, as the immediate Jeremianic context (and not only) suggests, should be referred in first instance to certain territorial expanses understood in a generic sense (as a habitable platform), and not to the structured state entities installed in them. These are rather indicated 2x by the term גּוֹיִם ("nations") in v. 7 (and in the sing. in the following vv. 8, 11, 13 and 28:14), and in 26:6; 33:9; 44:8 are called גּוֹיֵי הָאָרֶץ ("nations of the earth"). For further, in-depth lexicographic study, see J. Bergman – M. Ottosson, «אֶרֶץ», *ThWAT* I, 418–436.

301 I have already dealt with the so-called *Übergabeformel* when commenting 21:1–10 in ch. III of the present dissertation (cf. § 4.1.3).

302 Cf. e.g. GK §106n; Cf. JM §111h; WO § 30.5.1e; etc. (also called *perfectum confidentiae* or "perfect of certainty"). See, in this regard, the much more up-to-date and in-depth study by M. Rogland, *Alleged Non-Past Uses of Qatal in Classical Hebrew*, SSN, Assen 2003, 53–114. The author, rightly highlighting the complexity of the phenomenon tied to the temporal (and therefore also semantic) determination of the diverse uses of the *qatal* in oracular (often Jeremianic) contexts, advises to avoid limiting oneself to the generic, put-in-quotes "perfect prophetic", and to attempt a more precise and punctual hermeneutic (of a grammatical or stylistic type, in his opinion; one also semantic in character, I would add), attentive to the context of use, which is after

"Bend your neck beneath the yoke of the king of Babylon!" (27:12)   393

long discussed since the medieval Jewish commentators, which deserves a slightly more distinctive semantic evaluation here, given the (pragmatic) context and thanks to that context itself.

Each of the three translation solutions can, in principle, be valid, since they emphasise different temporal references (with corresponding semantic repercussions) virtually contained in the Hebrew verb form.[303] None, however, expresses them all at the same time. Having to choose, it would perhaps at first be best to accord preference to the present tense of נָתַ֫תִּי in 27:6a, given the illocutionary strength of a performative type generated by the temporal deixes of the adverb עַתָּה ("now I consign") typical of direct discourse.[304] This particle, however, linked to the *waw*-conjunctive, not only has temporal value, but is also used in the sense of logical consequence ("and thus [...]"). Considering the frequency with which the text insists on the use of √נתן in the *qatal*, it would still be possible in translation to vary the temporal yield for the other occurrences of the verb, precisely to recover or integrate those values of meaning that would otherwise remain unexpressed. The same applies to the two occurrences of נָתַ֫תִּי in 28:14, a verse that from a rhetorical point of view is exactly *pendant* to 27:6. For this reason, the second occurrence of נָתַ֫תִּי, referring to wild animals (27:6b), should be translated using the present perfect tense ("I consigned").

Actually, for a translation wanting to render a more dynamic equivalence of וְעַתָּה, v. 6 could be translated in a way that would make the use of the present perfect less strident[305]: "*As for the present moment* (or: *and therefore*): I have consigned all these countries into the hands of the king of Babylon. Even the fierce beasts I have consigned to him, to serve him." Even aside from the question of rendering וְעַתָּה, for my translation of נָתַ֫תִּי in 27:6, I prefer this temporal option. Indeed, if YHWH proclaims the act of consignment, it is because he decided it beforehand, and prophetic oracles often describe divine decision[306] (precisely through the particular use of the *qatal*)[307] as something so certain that it must be considered, in fact, as having *already occurred* (or, in any case, as having already been decreed on the celestial plane, even if not yet realised on the terrestrial plane). This is reinforced by the communicative context implied

---

    all, quite varied. I will return to make reference to his contribution, which mainly interprets the "perfect prophetic" as a reference to visionary experiences placed in the past with respect to their speaker (cf. pp. 71–72), when I comment on the pf. הִרְאַ֫נִי in 38:21 in the next chapter of my dissertation.

303   See M ROGLAND, *Alleged Non-Past Uses of Qatal*, 3–4, where precisely the form נָתַ֫תִּי (di Pr 4,2) is taken as an example of the three possible (or controversial) temporal renderings, referring to the past or understood as "prophetic", "gnomic", or even "performative" depending on the scholar.

304   Cf. T. KRONHOLM, «עת», *ThWAT* VI, 463–482 (עַתָּה is discussed in col. 475–476).

305   Though seemingly incongruous, the coordination between the temporal deictic value referring to the present in וְעַתָּה and that rendered in the (simple) past by נָתַ֫תִּי could fall into the so-called "idiomatic tense mismatches" (an expression of Vincent DeCaen, cited in M. ROGLAND, *Alleged Non-Past Uses of Qatal*, 92), a not uncommon phenomenon attested in many languages.

306   At least, in those that are not limited to reporting visions set in the past with respect to the enunciative act of the prophet (cf. M. ROGLAND, *Alleged Non-Past Uses of Qatal*, 71–92).

307   Cf. *Ibid.*, 53–56, 92–95.

394   Jer 27–28. The world beneath the yoke of the king of Babylon

in the narrative dimension, which refers to a message whose ultimate recipients are not the ambassadors of the nations but their respective sovereigns (cf. 27:4), who can be reached only some time later. It is therefore logical to presume that the oracle was conceived to present the decree of YHWH as one already enacted and operative at the time of its subsequent reception.

If we were not intended to recognise a special grammatical category in this "prophetic perfect", it would seem rather reductive to understand it merely as a *rhetorical device*, as P. Joüon and T. Muraoka[308] (and others) suggest. This communicative form, apart from having a probable persuasive potential, seems to convey, above all, a significant *theological datum*, which specifically regards divine lordship over history.

To a superficial gaze, human vicissitudes proceed according to their own laws or to dynamics subjected exclusively to choices or entirely contingent facts. And yet, prophetic communication reveals that things are not that way at all. Prophetic communication makes that word, in itself inaudible, that once pronounced (e.g. נָתַתִּי; "I gave") irreversibly determines the history it judges or redeems, resonate in the ears of the actants of the historical drama themselves. Emblematic examples of this are the episode of the rejection of the king Saul and election of David. Both the first divine decision (cf. 1 Sam 15:23b, 26, 28, 35) and the second (cf. 1 Sam 16:1, 12–13) are expressed privately to Samuel and announced (and carried out) by him only before those directly involved (including, *first and foremost*, the reader). Even though the word of YHWH pronounced on the story is revealed, the latter actually seems to continue its course in a way that is completely indifferent to such an announcement, as if nothing had changed. And yet, by patiently following the unfolding of facts through the complex and mysterious interaction between human and divine free will, the reader is led to discover that from precisely that instant, events were directed towards a specific purpose, despite the factual ebb and flow. Until the decisive point when the story, pregnant with that divine word, before the eyes of the reader, comes to the (pre-)announced fulfilment of that word itself. Saul is disgraced and David becomes the king of Israel. The same hermeneutical frame explains the prophecy of Jer 36:30, unfinished if taken by the letter (in fact, Jehoiachin succeeds Jehoiakim before Zedekiah does, and they have no part in the end prophesied to him; cf. 2 Kgs 24:6), but significant from a theological point of view: parallel to the announcement of the incursion of a new world power in the person of Nebuchadnezzar, YHWH manifests that he had already decreed, in the fourth year of Jehoiakim (and in the context of the rejection of the prophetic word in ch. 36), the end of the Davidic dynasty.[309]

This is the general theological horizon into which the use of the "prophetic perfect" in the Jeremianic text in question can reasonably be inserted. But there are complicating elements which, without contradicting that overall interpretation, introduce complex variants. Indeed, even false prophecy uses the same "prophetic perfect" and, in its own way (cf. § § 4.1.7 and 5.3 in regard to 28:13–14), the word of falsehood is

---

308   Cf. JM §111*h*, according to which the prophetic perfect "is not a special grammatical perfect, but a rhetorical device".

309   Cf. K. Schmid, «Nebuchadnezzar, the End of the Davidic Rule, and the Exile in the Book of Jeremiah», in: *The Prophets Speak of Forced Migration*, eds. M.J. Boda *et al.*, SBL.AIL 21, Atlanta 2015, 63–76.

"Bend your neck beneath the yoke of the king of Babylon!" (27:12)   395

anything but ineffective. From the point of view of true prophecy, on the other hand, what seems inescapably decreed can actually be retracted up to the very threshold of its fulfilment. Once again for the mysterious, unpredictable outcome of the interaction between divine free will and human response.[310] I will address this briefly when commenting 38:17 in the following chapter of the present dissertation.

The transition from the sapiential motif, which remains perennially valid and is thus rendered with the present tense ("I have made the earth [...] and I give it to whomever seems right in my eyes"), to the prophetic perspective, which reveals the implementation of a "punctual" decision ("*now* I have given all these lands into the hand of Nebuchadnezzar), has a notable communicative impact, as I have highlighted. And yet, as if the destabilising effect of this illocutionary act, which manages to consolidate in itself the representative, declarative, commissive, and directive dimensions,[311] were not enough, YHWH adds or renews, for Nebuchadnezzar, the title of עַבְדִּי ("my servant"), endowing it with significance that is clearly provocative.[312]

The fact is, as we have seen,[313] that even without this lexical explication, the king of Babylon had already been "consecrated" in this role in 21:7. His is an investiture comparable to that of a faithful "vassal",[314] a title that (remaining within the context of the book) sets him on the same level as David (cf. 33:21), the prophets, Jeremiah in particular (cf. 7:25; 25:4; 26:5; 29:19; 35:15; 44:4), and Israel itself (cf. 30:10; 46:27). Not to mention the "servant of the Lord" par excellence, Moses (cf. Exod 4:10; 14:31; Num 12:8; Deut 34:5; etc.), who, at the time, had the task of *freeing* the people of God from Egypt (cf. Exod 3:8–10), and also his successor, Joshua.[315] Nebuchadnezzar, on the other and, is the servant who must *subjugate* Israel and in whom the manifestation of an unprecedented meaning of history (in which the intercession of the same Moses

---

310 A well-known example is the theological message of the book of Jonah, centred entirely on this paradoxical dynamic, disconcerting for the prophet himself (cf. Jon 3:4, 10; 4).

311 Cf. J.R. SEARLE, «A Taxonomy of Illocutionary Acts», 344–369 (esp., pp. 354–361).

312 To such an extent that e.g. W.M. LEMKE, «Nebuchadrezzar My Servant», 45–59, goes so far as to propose the implausible hypothesis that this be a scribal error. This embarrassment is already present in the LXX (if, on the contrary, it is not an exaggeration of the MT with respect to an earlier Hebrew text), since the epithet is absent in two of the three Greek versions (cf. 25:9; 43:10[=50:10^{LXX}]; while in 27:6[=34:5^{LXX}], it is rendered with its intensity toned down by the locution δουλεύειν αὐτῷ). On this theological propensity, see the additional annotations by H.J. STIPP, *Das masoretische und alexandrinische Sondergut des Jeremiabuches*. Textgeschichtlicher Rang, Eigenarten, Triebkräfte, OBO 136, Freiburg 1994, 118–119; ID., «Linguistic Peculiarities of the Masoretic Edition of the Book of Jeremiah: An Updated Index», *JNSL* 23 (1997) 181–202 (here, p. 189).

313 See what has already been said about this in ch. III, § 4.1.3, n. 168 (and corresponding bibliographic references).

314 As in Z. ZEVIT, Z., «The use of '*bd*», *JBL* 88 (1969) 74–77, who speaks, in my opinion inappropriately, of a "non-theological" meaning of the term עָבֵד. The vassal of a sovereign was required to provide his superior with the military assistance with his army, but it is clear that the use is nonliteral here (Nebuchadnezzar forged no binding alliance with YHWH).

315 Cf. P. BÉRÉ, *Le second Serviteur de Yhwh. Un portrait exégétique de Josué dans le livre éponyme*, OBO 253, Göttingen 2012.

396   Jer 27–28. The world beneath the yoke of the king of Babylon

and Samuel would now be useless; cf. 15:1; Ezek 14:14) is to be recognised, readable by legal categories (as we will better see in § 4.3).

The title עַבְדִּי appears for the first time in 25:9, in an analogous (and programmatic) international context, and will be repeated in 43:10, at the ideal closure of a large semiotic *arcata* (the entire section of 26–45 *also* closes[316] with mention of Nebuchadnezzar in 44:30) that places an entire story under the divine authority delegated by YHWH to the king of Babylon. In fact, with ch. 25, the first great phase of the prophetic ministry ends (marked by a non-listening; cf. 25:3) and another opens, the decisive one (of the necessary submission to the punitive instrument of YHWH). At the same time, the first part of the book ends and a new section is announced. From this "symbolic column" of the book that is ch. 25, a semiotic arc extends, marked by the figure of Nebuchadnezzar and his punitive function (already announced, for that matter, in a way that is veiled, in the first great bearing structure of the book, ch. 1, in vv. 1:14–15, and taken back up as a final seal in ch. 52[317]). Beginning and end are thus placed under the human-divine authority of the king of Babylon.

"Nebuchadnezzar, *my servant*": God interacts in history by means of human agents,[318] including the great world powers.[319] A deduction of the theology of history that is perhaps elementary, apparently obvious.[320] But with shocking consequences.[321] A real puzzle of discernment having possible outcomes that are in opposition, even for those who try to evaluate the possible theological and political implications.[322]

---

316   Without forgetting the other great semiotic *arcata* that connects, through the dynamic figure of the prophet-disciple relationship (Jeremiah-Baruch), chs. 26 and 45 (identifying the second part of the second section of the book of Jeremiah given by 26–35 and 36–45).

317   Not before it has been reiterated, with chs. 50–51, that the same fate is also reserved for Babylon.

318   For the book of Jeremiah, concentration is focused on this theme with interesting reflections by T.E. FRETHEIM, *Jeremiah*, 35–39; ID. «The Character of God in Jeremiah», in: *Character and Scripture. Moral Formation, Community, and Biblical Interpretation*, ed. W.P. BROWN, Grand Rapids 2002, 211–230 (in particular, pp. 219–223); ID., *God and World*, 161–162.

319   See, in this regard, the overview by L. ROST, «Das Problem der Weltmacht in der Prophetie», *ThLZ* 90 (1965) 241–250 (on Jer 27 in particular, pp. 246–247), which rightly highlights the theological-hermeneutical implications of the phenomenon.

320   Not for all commentators, apparently (see e.g. R.P. CARROLL, *Jeremiah*, 294; W. BRUEGGEMANN, *Jeremiah*, 54, 70, 176, 193, etc.; L. STULMAN, *Order Amid Chaos*, 123).

321   The advent of Nebuchadnezzar's universal domination (with the victory at Karkemish in 605, in the fourth year of Jehoiakim) coincides with the announcement of the end of the Davidic dynasty proclaimed in 22:30 and 36:30 (see, in this regard, K. SCHMID, «Nebukadnezars Antritt der Weltherrschaft und der Abbruch der Davidsdynastie. Innerbiblische Schriftauslegung und universalgeschichtliche Konstruktion im Jeremiabuch», in: ID., *Schriftgelehrte Traditionsliteratur. Fallstudien zur innerbiblischen Schriftauslegung im Alten Testament*, FAT 77, Tübingen 2011, 223–241 [in particular, p. 235]).

322   On the evolution of the interpretive processes concerning the figure of Nebuchadnezzar, see J. STÖKL, «Nebuchadnezar: History, Memory, and Myth-Making in the Persian Period», in: *Remembering Biblical Figures in the Late Persian and Early*

"Bend your neck beneath the yoke of the king of Babylon!" (27:12)   397

A proper indecipherable enigma or a principle of ideological aberrations, if taken simplistically.

One sees a man, a compatriot, or even a close relative with no title or authority (cf. 1:1–3, 6) and is called to acknowledge in him the voice of the God who made heaven and earth and to whom all things and people owe obedience, being the Origin and life of every being. He is a prophet. But he could be simply an impostor (28:10–11), a public danger (cf. 20:1; 26; 38:4, 25), and a shame for his clan (cf. 11:18–21; 12:6). On the horizon, "from the north" (מִצָּפוֹן),[323] a place that is practically mythological and evokes obscure imminent threats (cf. 1:14; 4:6; 6:1, 22[324]; etc.), a new power can be seen rising, a "hammer" (מַפֵּץ) that mercilessly crushes any opposing force and claims absolute dominion in the name of its gods (cf. 50:23; 51:20–23). Is it an enemy to fight, a mortal menace from which, yet again, YHWH will liberate his chosen people, if appropriately invoked (cf. 21:2)? He is known to be a Chaldean prince, to a king who comes from ancient and remote regions, from an alien world: *Nabû-kudurrī-uṣur*.[325]

But in this theophoric, foreign-sounding, incomprehensible, and unrepeatable name (cf. the two variants of the MT: נְבוּכַדְרֶאצַּר; נְבֻכַדְרֶאצַּר; the rendering in the LXX: Ναβουχοδονοσορ), which is identifiable as a prayer or profession of idolatrous faith ("Nabû protect my son/my heir!"), one may instead be called upon to acknowledge a "familiar" authority and a design that transcends all these human evaluations. "Nebuchadnezzar, *my servant*": YHWH is not only the "up close" (מִקָּרֹב) God, known and reassuring (cf. 23:23). He is also the God "from afar" (מֵרָחֹק).[326] So far as to sound like Marduk, so unpredictable as to elect, as his servant, king (and executor) of justice[327] and practically a new David (which anticipates, paradoxically, the one promised; cf. 23:5–6; 30:9), an "outsider"[328] with respect to the history of the people of YHWH, a

---

Hellenistic Periods. Social Memory and Imagination, eds. D.V. EDELMAN – E. BEN ZVI, Oxford 2013, 257–269.

323   Cf. B.S. CHILDS, «The Enemy from the North», 187–198.

324   On Jer 6, see esp. J. BOU RAAD, *Malheur annoncé, malheur dénoncé. Étude rhétorique de Jérémie 6*, Amchit [Lebanon] 2008.

325   Cf. D.J. WISEMAN, *Nebuchadrezzar and Babylon*, 2–3; M.P. STRECK, «Nebukadnezzar II», 196 (see also n. 36 of ch. II, § 2.1.2); H.D. BAKER – J.A. BRINKMAN, «*Nabû-kudurrī-uṣur*», 841–842.

326   Cf. G. FISCHER, «"Bin ich ein Gott aus der Nähe...?". Jer 23,23 und das Wesen von Theologie», in: ID., *Der Prophet wie Mose*, 284–286 (= in: C. MATHIS – P. OBERHOFER – F. SCHUCHTER, eds., *Tage kommen. Zukunft der Theologie*, Ulithiana 3, Innsbruck 2000, 65–67).

327   F. COXON, «Nebuchadnezzar's Hermeneutical Dilemma», *JSOT* 66 (1995) 87–97 (esp. pp. 93–96), highlights that, in spite of the negative traits that characterise the figure of Nebuchadnezzar in the popular imagination, both Babylonian sources and biblical ones (including my own text), give a portrait connoted by a (divine) idea of justice.

328   According to the terminology used by L. STULMAN, «Insiders and Outsiders in the Book of Jeremiah: Shifts in Symbolic Arrangements», *JSOT* 66 (1995) 65–85, which rightfully specifies: "The position of Babylon is nearly inverted in the world of Jeremiah. Babylon the outsider or barbarian is afforded semiotically the favoured status of insider" (p. 71). The image of YHWH that emerges from the book of Jeremiah is that of a God that cannot be confined to any fixed category once and for all, nor is he an "insider", for he is not controllable or manipulable by anyone (cf. p. 82).

398   Jer 27–28. The world beneath the yoke of the king of Babylon

foreign sovereign[329] consecrated to an idol and against whom one is willing to resist to the end to not bow one's neck beneath his yoke. And yet, only by doing what Jeremiah does, burdening himself with this symbol of surrender and enslavement as an example for all, can one be saved.

The close relationship between YHWH and Nebuchadnezzar is also expressed in the Jeremianic text by the frequent overlapping of subjects for the same verbs and the same metaphors.[330] The actions of YHWH and those of Nebuchadnezzar can often be overlapped, as is emblematically affirmed in 27:8 (עַד־תֻּמִּי אֹתָם בְּיָדוֹ; "until he has not completely destroyed them by his hand"; think also of the subjects who fight against Jerusalem: cf. 21:5 [√לחם ni. with subj. YHWH] with 21:2 [√לחם ni. with subj. Nebuchadnezzar], and 21.6 [√נכה hi. with subj. YHWH] with 21:7 [√נכה hi. with subj. Nebuchadnezzar.])[331] And yet, the king of Babylon is anything but a puppet in the hands of the God of Israel.[332] He may use his manoeuvring space improperly, and will be called to answer for this (cf. Isa 47:6; Jer 25:11–14; Zac 1:15). The fact remains that *now*, YHWH is in action. In him and with him. And even in spite of him. Despite that, otherwise put, in this complex interaction between two freedoms, it is the face of God that risks being obscured, seeing as how, on the historical plane, the ruthlessness of Nebuchadnezzar can be erroneously attributed to YHWH (cf. 13:14 with 21:7). That is, it can if one does not grasp that behind these historical upheavals and the typical language of the prophetic *rîb*, divine *páthos* trembles, a sovereign God cries[333] with his prophet over the misery of his unfaithful people and for the disaster that strikes the nations (cf. 9:9; 14:17; 48:32).

---

329   The "foreigner" (who is "raised up" [√עור hi.] against Babylon as well; cf. 51:11) is effective mediation of YHWH's intervention in a salvific sense as well (though, in the end, the role of Nebuchadnezzar is also salvific). In the book of Jeremiah, consider the paradigmatic figure of Ebed-melech (cf. 38:7–13; 45), and in the book of Isaiah, of the Persian king, Cyrus the Great (cf. Isa 44:28; 45:1; Exod 1:1–3; 2 Chr 36:22–23). On the topic of the foreigner in the book of Jeremiah, see G. Fischer, «"Mein Diener Nebukadnezzar"», 334–336.

330   See the schematic comparison between the actions of God and those of Nebuchadnezzar/Babylon in T.E. Fretheim, *Jeremiah*, 36; Id. «The Character of God in Jeremiah», 220–221.

331   Another interesting superimposition that can be cited here regarding the technical (in jurisprudence) locution √דבר pi. + מִשְׁפָּט + אֶת + pers. pron. suff. ("to pronounce, hand down a sentence against someone"; cf. P. Bovati, *Ristabilire la giustizia*, 62, 167–168, 320–321), presented with programmatic value in 1:16 (cf. also 4:12) with YHWH as its subject and attested in 2 Kgs 25:6, Jer 39:5; 52:9 in the context of the trial set up by Nebuchadnezzar against the unfaithful vassal Zedekiah.

332   In this manner, also T.E. Fretheim, *God and World*, 161–163, 338, n. 4.

333   G. Fischer, *Theologien des Alten Testaments*, NSK.AT 31, Stuttgart 2012, 87–89, speaks of YHWH as "Der weinende König der Nationen". The author takes the topic up again in his more in-depth study: Id., «Il Dio che piange. Una chiave per la teologia del libro di Geremia», in: *La profezia tra l'uno e l'altro Testamento. Studi in onore del prof. Pietro Bovati in occasione del suo settantacinquesimo compleanno, eds.* G. Benzi – D. Scaiola – M. Bonarini, AnBib.St 4, Roma 2015, 233–244.

"Bend your neck beneath the yoke of the king of Babylon!" (27:12) 399

Fig. 26. Colossal relief of a hero (perhaps the epic Gilgamesh, ancient king of Uruk) who subdues a lion and grasps a snake (Khorsabad, throne room of the palace of Sargon II [721–705]; photo from A. PARROT, Assur, Figg. 36 and 38, pp. 32–33; for the same iconographic motif in the Persian era, see Fig. 244 on p. 196).

Fig. 27. Detail of a bas-relief depicting King Ashurnasirpal II in a lion hunting scene (ninth century, Nimrud; from A. PARROT, Assur, Fig. 64, pp. 55–57).

Fig. 28. Bas-relief mural in polychrome bricks of roaring lion (from ORTHMANN, Der alte Orient, pl. XXIV; cf. ANEP, Fig. 762, p. 237). About 120 similar figures (along with those of other animals) decorated the processional route of Babylon, from which one entered the imposing city gate of Ishtar, the goddess of love and war, whose symbol was the lion itself (cf. A. PARROT, Assur, Fig. 85, p. 76 and also ANEP, 160–164, 177). Even if the complex, built by Nebuchadnezzar, is from a few years after the fall of Jerusalem, the deportees of the kingdom of Judah most certainly have contemplated them at length. In Jer 4:7, the Babylonian power is identified with the mortal threat of the lion leaping on its prey (cf. also 5:6; 25:38).

"Even the beasts of the field I have given him, to serve him" (27:6b; cf. 28:14; and Fig. 26). We have already seen (in § 4.2.5) that in 27:5, with the animal image (בְּהֵמָה), the brutal force of nations struggling against each other is probably also evoked. It should be pointed out here that the locution חַיַּת הַשָּׂדֶה ("beasts of the field"; which couples with the analogous expression בֶּהֱמַת הָאָרֶץ or בְּהֵמָה אֲשֶׁר עַל־פְּנֵי הָאָרֶץ) is even more explicit in this sense because in 12:9 (cf. also Ezek 31:6, 13; 34:5, 8; 39:4, 17; Hos 2:14; 13:8), it refers to ferocious and/or predatory animals as elements for metaphorising the state entities that devastate the kingdom of Judah (even in their instrumental function as the punitive activity of YHWH). These are forces capable of radically destructuring the existing order, both natural and social, by way of *war*. But even these "animals", if tamed, can serve (√עבד) their masters.

It may seem incongruous to evoke the image of wild beasts (and of ferocious ones, in particular) and to link this to a duty that only domesticated animals can perform. But all this emphasis on the consigning of the animal world into the hands of the king of Babylon would be even stranger if they were only harmless quadrupeds of burden that can be subjected by anyone without any particular divine investiture (cf. Figs. 27–28). Of course, one can allude to the universal dominion of Nebuchadnezzar over *all of creation*, if one thinks of a founding text like Gen 1:26, 28. This interpretative line is even more plausible in the light of Dan 2:37–38, where the intention is that of highlighting the universal nature of the power conceded to Nebuchadnezzar (in addition to the beasts of the field, winged animals are also mentioned), as 28:14, moreover, seems to do. Probably, however, keeping to the Jeremianic context, it is more correct to affirm that in 27:6b, two isotopies (both animals) intertwine and overlap, providing the basis for a figurative discourse with two different but complementary perspectives[334]: the

---

334 That the present Jeremianic oracle moves within the symbolic sphere, referring to animals to indicate the universal breadth of Nebuchadnezzar's domination, is also clearer when considering 36:29, where on the contrary – but evidently here in the

"Bend your neck beneath the yoke of the king of Babylon!" (27:12)   401

isotopy of victorious dominion over ferocious animals, that is, over the warlike nations or defeated rebels,[335] and that of the service provided by subjugatable animals (horses, oxen, etc.), referring to the same nations, subordinate and transformed into tributary vassals (cf. 28:14).[336] The transition from v. 6 to v. 7, marked by a ו, which may well have a consecutive value (וְעָבְדוּ אֹתוֹ כָּל־הַגּוֹיִם; lit.: "and [thus] will serve him all the nations"), and in which the national entities are immediately mentioned, supports this interpretation. The term הַגּוֹיִם ("nations") thus becomes the semiotic concentration of the semantic significance contained in the preceding expressions (the first, literal and the second, figurative) כָּל־הָאֲרָצוֹת הָאֵלֶּה ("all these countries/territories") and חַיַּת הַשָּׂדֶה ("[ferocious] beasts of the field").

It should additionally be noted[337] that the Assyrian-Babylonian royal ideology makes extensive reference to the common literary and iconographical motif of the mythical "master of animals",[338] that is, the power granted by a divinity to the king (or hero) over the animal world (cf. Fig. 29), an emblematic sign of the fullness of his authority[339] (and also his virility). Very common, also in figurative attestations, is the theme of the king's hunting parties for wild game in general, but above all, the theme of the *lion* hunt, eloquent symbol[340] of dominion over the fiercest and most feared animal force.[341] In itself, it is a figurative motif typical of neo-Assyrian rather than

---

literal sense –it is not enslavement that is alluded to, but rather the *extermination* of "men and animals" (אָדָם וּבְהֵמָה) as a destructive effect of the Babylonian war offensive.

335 It should be noted that, especially in the event of victory over distant and exotic countries, it was not uncommon for the tributes owed by the submissive peoples to include specimens characteristic of their local fauna. Emblematic is the case of the black obelisk of Salmaneser III, where, in the third scenic register from the top, various animals are depicted, of which the explanatory epigraph that gives voice to the sovereign reads: "I received tribute from Egypt: two-humped camels, a water buffalo (lit. 'a river ox'), a *rhinoceros*, an antelope, female elephants, female monkeys, (and) apes" (RIMA 3, A.0.102.89).

336 These vassals also had an obligation, if necessary, to serve the wartime cause of their lord. As we have seen in the historical part (cf. ch. II, § 2.2.11), e.g. in order to weaken the kingdom of Judah, Nebuchadnezzar also used incursions of Aramean, Moabite, and Ammonite contingents.

337 As pointed out by B. LANG, «Ein babylonisches Motiv», 237.

338 Cf. O. KEEL, *Jahwes Entgegnung an Ijob*. Eine Deutung von Ijob 38–41 vor dem Hintergrund der zeitgenössischen Bildkunst, FRLANT 121, Göttingen 1978, 86–125 (with an iconographic repertoire); D.B. COUNTS – B. ARNOLD, *eds.*, *The Master of Animals in Old World Iconography*, Archaeolingua 24, Budapest 2010.

339 Cf. B. LANG, *Kein Aufstand*, 100–101.

340 In Mesopotamia, the lion was considered "a recipient of *melam*, the peculiarly effulgent awesomeness which characterizes its bearer as more than human" (B.A. STRAWN, *What is Stronger than a Lion?* Leonine Image and Metaphor in the Hebrew Bible and the Ancient Near East, Fribourg 2005, 215). On the transcultural significance of this symbol, see also K. ULANOWSKI, «The Metaphor of the Lion in Mesopotamian and Greek Civilization», in: *Mesopotamia in the Ancient World*. Impact, Continuities, Parallels. Proceedings of the Seventh Symposium of the Melammu Project Held in Obergurgl, Austria, November 4–8, 2013, *eds.* R. ROLLINGER – E. VAN DONGEN, MSym 7, Münster 2015, 255–284.

341 Consider the formidable hunting exploits that Tiglath-Pileser I (1114–1076) attributed to himself: "Tiglath-pileser, valiant man, armed with the unrivalled bow, expert in

Fig. 29. Two seals depicting the Neo-Assyrian-Babylonian hero (winged and not) firmly grasping two goats. There is some debate over whether this iconographic motif intends to express an act of conquest or rather pacification/protection of the animal world (images taken from O. KEEL, Jahwes Entgegnung an Ijob, 98, to whom is due the introduction of the expression "Herr der Tiere" in the exegetic field).

neo-Babylonian iconography.[342] Yet it is not by chance that precisely in the Levant, that is, in the territories exempt from both Egyptian and Assyrian influences, this be used also by Nebuchadnezzar amongst other symbologies of propagandistic importance. The image of himself that the sovereign intended to carve in the collective imagination, having himself portrayed on sculptural representations placed in strategically important locations, is precisely that of the sovereign heir and supplanter of the

---

the hunt [...] I killed ten strong bull elephants in the land Harrān and the region of the River Habur (and) four live elephants I captured. I brought the hides and tusks (of the dead elephants) with the live elephants to my city Assur. By the command of the god Ninurta, who loves me, I killed on foot 120 lions with my wildly outstanding assault. In addition, 800 lions I felled from my light chariot. I have brought down every kind of wild beast and winged bird of the heavens whenever I have shot an arrow" (RIMA 2, A.0.87.1 vi 55–57, 70–84). It is significant that this reference to the hunting feats immediately follows and precedes the narration of the victorious wars waged by the Assyrian king against his enemies.

342 As can be seen in E. BRAUN-HOLZINGER – E. FRAHM, «Liebling des Marduk – König der Blasphemie. Große babylonische Herrscher in der Sicht der Babylonier und in der Sicht anderer Völker», in: *Babylon. Focus Mesopotamischer Geschichte, Wiege früher Gelehrsamkeit, Mythos in der Moderne: 2. Internationales Colloquium der Deutschen Orient-Gesellschaft 24.–26. März 1998 in Berlin*, ed. J. RENGER, Saarbrücken 1999, 131–156 (here, p. 141).

Fig. 30. Bas-relief of Ashurbanipal who pierces a lion with a sword (year 645 ca., North Palace, Room S at Ninive; BM 124875; from R.D. BARNETT, Sculptures from the North Palace of Ashurbanipal at Nineveh (668–627 B.C.), London 1976, tablet L; cf. also tablet LIX.

Assyrian power, intent, in at least two examples, to fight a rampant lion (see Fig. 30; also think of King David in 1 Sam 17:37).[343]

The symbolic significance of the killing of the lion was most certainly also ritualistic. If the sovereign measures himself against this fearsome animal and dominates over his beastly rage (in some images, not only from his war chariot, as in Fig. 27, but also in heroic full contact,[344] as seen in Fig. 30, and with regard to Nebuchadnezzar in Fig. 31), it is because he himself is the true lion that enemies must obey and fear.[345] Think of 50:17 (cf. 2:15; 4:7; 5:6; 25:38; 51:34, 38), where the Assyrian and Babylonian kings are depicted as devouring lions, or of the parabolic tale of the final episodes of

---

343   I refer to the two motifs represented in the inscriptions WBA e WS 1. See, in this regard, R. DA RIVA, «A Lion in the Cedar Forest. International Politics and Pictorial Self-Representations of Nebuchadnezzar II (605–562 BC)», in: *Studies on War in the Ancient Near East. Collected Essays on Military History*, ed. J. VIDAL, AOAT 372, Münster 2010, 165–191 and also ID., «Enduring Images of an Ephemeral Empire: Neo-Babylonian Inscriptions and Representations on the Western Periphery», in: *Mesopotamia in the Ancient World*, 603–629; R. DA RIVA, *The Twin Inscriptions*, 94.
344   See e.g. A. PARROT, *Assur*, Fig. 177B, p. 192.
345   On the validity of this analogical relation, see M.-A. ATAÇ, *The Mythology of Kingship in Neo-Assyrian Art*, Cambridge 2010, 15–16, 18–20, who highlights the intentional correspondence (in the case of the panels in the North-West palace of Ashurnasirpal II at Nimrud) between the scenes of libation over animals killed by the sovereign and those of the prostration of defeated enemies: "This positioning of the scenes clearly reveals not only how the royal hunt may be seen as analogous to the royal battle but also how the prostrate enemy is placed in a position analogous to that of the slain animals subject to the libation" (p. 19). As the author points out, the same phenomenon can be noted on the black obelisk of Shalmaneser III in reference to the prostration of Jehu, king of Judah, before the Assyrian ruler.

Fig. 31. Bas-relief in stone of Nebuchadnezzar with a rampant lion at Wadi es-Saba' (WS1). From R. DA RIVA, «A Lion in the Cedar Forest», 190.

the reign of Judah in Ezek 19:1-9, centred on the leonine metaphor with the referents reversed (and therefore having the relative capture of the "lion"-kings of Judah by the king of Babylon).

And if such beasts, from the largest to the smallest (cf. Amos 1:11; Israel included; cf. Num 23:24; 24:8-9; Deut 33:17; Ezek 19; Mic 5:7; etc.), are subjected to a sole yoke that subdues their instinctual aggression, the result can be called, in a certain sense, "peace"[346] (cf. 27:11 [to be left on its soil, to cultivate and inhabit it] and v. 12 [to live]; 28:9 [peace, well-being]). Even if everything is subjected to an imperial entity that is, this too, in its turn and in its time, a beast destined to be devoured by yet other, stronger beast-empires (think of the significance of the dream of the golden statue in Dan 2:31-45,[347] or the visions of Dan 7 concerning the four "beasts"/kings or empires that come up out of the sea), this is because *no human reality, however powerful, can escape the mystery of the end*.

---

346 Something similar to the proverbial "pax romana" (an expression first used in A.D. 64 by SENECA, *De providentia*, IV,14), as the status of the historical period (from 27 B.C. to A.D. 180) described in terms of civilization, order, justice, and harmony between the different peoples subject to the Roman Empire. The historian Tacitus denounced the underlying ambiguity tied to the use of violence and desire to exploit the resources of others with famous words (put in the mouth of Calgacus, the leader of the Caledonians, in his address to his soldiers before the final battle against the Romans): "Auferre trucidare rapere falsis nominibus imperium, atque ubi solitudinem faciunt, pacem appellant" (TACITUS, *Agricola*, 30).

347 Cf. R.G. KRATZ, *Translatio imperii. Untersuchungen zu den aramäischen Danielerzählungen und ihrem theologiegeschichtlichen Umfeld*, WMANT 63, Neukirchen-Vluyn 1991 (which addresses Jer 27-28 on pp. 190-195).

"Bend your neck beneath the yoke of the king of Babylon!" (27:12)   405

In the context of the Jeremianic oracle, however, reference is made to a "peace" (שָׁלוֹם) that carries a punitive meaning, not to the easy one announced by Hananiah (28:9), which can afford to disregard every act of obedience to God and makes the assumption that it can feed on a hypothetical power vacuum caused by a disengagement (or collapse) of the Babylonian empire. In any case, if we read the comprehensive prophetic announcement of the book of Jeremiah as a vectorial quantity, that is, seizing in it a meaning that unifies and provides a unitary basis for its various theological perspectives, it will not be difficult to prove that it is precisely by accepting in faith the prophetic meaning of this "now" that one enters (and is called to enter) to a symbolic dimension far deeper than the question as it relates to the material maintenance of its own economic and social *status quo*. But it is worth dedicating some further study to this topic.

4.3. Jer 27–28: To submit without any motivation? A pragmatic-intertextual solution perspective

4.3.1. The terms of the problem

Though the necessity of submission to Babylon is placed in relation to the creative sapience of YHWH and his lordship over human history, in Jer 27–28, the criteria underlying the divine intentionality underway and the reason for the prophetic request are not made explicit.[348] It is, nevertheless, erroneous to deduce from this that accepting the Babylonian yoke be an entirely arbitrary injunction or, in other words, a free, sovereign divine decision that cannot be traced back to any intelligible motivation (even looking at the whole book of Jeremiah). This hermeneutical perspective,[349] which, rather than make clarifications refuses to examine the "motives" of the Jeremianic position, aggravates the problem on two fronts:

1) on the *theological side*, because it sketches a face of a God who, while vindicating absolute lordship over the world, would govern history in a completely senseless or incomprehensible way,[350] an outcome that is in stark contrast with the general intent informing the book of Jeremiah, aimed entirely at offering traces of meaning in order to understand the catastrophe of the exile;
2) on the *anthropological side*, because both the kingdom of Judah and the nations (and ultimately, the reader themself) would not only find themselves before a request that is already in itself exceedingly costly (to completely renounce one's own independence and projects of political self-determination, let alone trust in one's respective protector deities), but should agree to it even for no specific reason, under penalty of the strictest punishment. This consequence as well, in which the human being would be reduced to that of material executor of divine precepts, contrasts with the general nature of biblical prophetism (and with the book of

---

348   The expression נְתַתִּיהָ לַאֲשֶׁר יָשַׁר בְּעֵינָי in 27:5 can also, and with good reason, be related to the analogous reference to the work of the potter in 18:1–10 (cf. § 4.2.6).
349   See what has been observed in the General Introduction, § 1.4.1, in ch. II, § 3.3.1, and in ch. III, § 4.1.3.
350   And what "seems to be" to Job (e.g. in Job 9), for the fact of not understanding how/ why God acts in certain ways in history.

406 Jer 27–28. The world beneath the yoke of the king of Babylon

Jeremiah, in particular), which, while affirming the transcendence and liberty of God, lavishes considerable sapiential energy on a communicative level to convincing the interlocutor of the wisdom of granting obedience to YHWH (cf. Hos 14:10).

Aside from what was previously noted, it can be specified here that, in addition to the supposed absence of textual clues, the other principal argument put forth to support the thesis by which submission to Babylon could not be placed in relation to the idea of *divine retribution* relates to the fact that the Jeremianic request is addressed in 27–28 not only to the kingdom of Judah, but to other nations as well.[351] The implicit postulate is that it would make no sense to speak of punishment for foreign peoples unrelated to the Mosaic Covenant. The logical conclusion is that submission would simply be a fact of political opportunism (even if presented religiously as an order of YHWH), that is, nothing more than a contingent condition for the welfare of one's (own) nation.[352]

I reiterate that this is, in my opinion, an unsustainable position, proved wrong, in this case, both by serious consideration of how the communicative system established by this textual section is configured (cf. § 4.3.2) and by the thematic development concerning the nations and the lordship of YHWH over the world in the book of Jeremiah (cf. § 4.3.3), with particular reference to the "oracles against the nations" contained in chs. 46–51, but also attested elsewhere (cf. § 4.3.4). A critical confrontation with this position will, in any case, allow me to bring into focus the relation between the "cosmic God" underlying chs. 27–28 and the "ethical God", presupposed not only by the book of Jeremiah, but by all biblical Revelation (cf. § 4.3.5).

4.3.2. Still on the decisive importance of the communicative context for a correct exegesis: Dramatisation, pragmatics, intertexuality. And a pertinent example

As announced prior in the General Introduction, special attention to the pragmatic dimension of the communication has accompanied my path of study constantly, even if this has been recalled explicitly only in the most opportune cases. This methodological perspective has allowed me to avail myself in a pertinent way of a notion of "context" that is of a linguistic-cognitive matrix, based on the dynamic correlation between: (1) a concept of communication that is not reduced to the theory of code (i.e. as a linear transmission of information), but is understood rather as a *manifestation and inferential recognition of intentions*; (2) a theory of (semantic) signification based on a conception of "text" as a *deliberate provocation to the interpretative cooperation* addressed to the "reader".

---

351 "[...] rien dans les textes ne suggère que la soumission à la Babylonie soit le châtiment de la rupture de son alliance avec Yahvé, voire d'une quelconque autre faute de Juda. Une telle interprétation est même exclue du fait que, d'après Jr 27,11 la soumission à la Babylonie est une obligation de tous les peuples, et pas soulement de Juda. Elle n'est pas un châtiment" (F.J. GONÇALVES, «Isaïe, Jérémie», 295). The other (and last) argument boils down to the fact that in Jer 27–28, the topic of chastisement refers only to the possibility of rejecting the Babylonian yoke and not to other, previous faults.

352 Cf. F.J. GONÇALVES, «Isaïe, Jérémie», 295–296.

"Bend your neck beneath the yoke of the king of Babylon!" (27:12)   407

If it is true, therefore, that no communication is ever absolute but is rather comprised of a sequence of exchanges that creates a semiotic network of presuppositions upon which each successive step of dialogue is articulated, one cannot underestimate, in the case of Jer 27–28 as well, the *conversational dynamic* established by the narrative structure through which the Jeremianic message is conveyed, nor the platform of implicit cognitive data that configures its context of reference. This dialogical dimension, in which, from a narrative point of view, the dramatisation of the global message of the text (*showing*) prevails over the descriptive level (*telling*), can be considered a communicative strategy aimed to engage the reader themself in the actantial dynamic of the whole book of Jeremiah.[353] Such engagement presupposes, as the reading gradually advances, the assimilation of all those elements that are most relevant to define the contextual frame in order to understand each successive stage.[354] In other words, it must be a given that it not be possible to think of adequately grasping the content-related density of the Jeremianic message in Jer 27–28 (as in the other pericopes covered by my study) without taking into account the global thematic-narrative development, and particularly those sections that are not purely oracular and poetic.[355]

I am talking about a hermeneutical approach that in some way, at least in the case of the book of Jeremiah, recoups and provides a greater basis for an *intertextual*

---

353   While taking into account the heterogeneous nature of the book, as regards the genres employed, which cannot be identified *tout court* with the development of a narrative (just think of the section dedicated to the oracles against the nations), I believe that with different modulations, the actantial paradigm of the renowned semiologist A.J. Greimas can be applied to each and every part. This interpretive model involves the identification of oppositional relationships between six fundamental actants or narrative roles that are: the *subject* (the one who performs the action), the *object* (which is the goal of the action), the *helper* (the figure that helps the subject), the *opponent* (the one who hinders the subject), the *sender* (i.e. the principal of the subject to the principle of the narrative), and the *recipient* (the one to whom the object or target of the communication is ultimately entrusted, who is, after all, the reader himself). For the justification and in-depth study of this technical terminology, see his essays: "La structure des actants du récit. Essai d'approche générative", and "Les actants, les acteurs et les figures", reproduced, respectively, in A.J. GREIMAS, *Du sens*. Essais sémiotiques, Paris 1970, 249–270, and in *Du sens II*. Essais sémiotiques, Paris 1983, 49–66, and the synthetic definitions contained in the two volumes by A.J. GREIMAS – J. COURTÉS, eds., *Sémiotique*. Dictionnaire raisonné de la théorie du langage, Paris 1979–1986.

354   As justly noted by D. CLERC, «Des actes pour parler», 120–121: "[...] le prophète n'intervient pas au nom d'un Dieu inconnu qui interpellerait pour la première fois son peuple. Jérémie et ses interlocuteurs ont en commun un certain nombre de présupposés qui forment ensemble une compréhension particulière du monde et de l'histoire, de l'action de l'homme et de Dieu en leur sein."

355   One can thus apply, in a broader sense, that which is affirmed by H. Weinrich in reference to the grammatical formalisation of textual linguistics: "a grammar which does not accept units beyond the sentence can never even notice let alone resolve the most interesting problems of linguistics" (the sentence translated here appears only in the preface to the Italian edition (Bologna 1978, p. 5) of his classical work, namely: H. WEINRICH, *Tempus*. Besprochene und erzählte Welt, Stuttgart 1964, München ⁶2001).

408   Jer 27–28. The world beneath the yoke of the king of Babylon

reading[356] that programmatically proposes to place different texts in dialogue with one another. Given the nature of the Jeremianic corpus, and the atomizing tendency of many exegetic studies, the question is not that of dealing (only) with the relation of reciprocal references (by way of quotations, allusions, or otherwise) between the different books and biblical literary genres, but rather of evaluating the network of semiotic relationships created by the totality of the single micro or macro textual units that comprise the current MT of the book of Jeremiah.[357]

The concept of intertexuality, in fact, given its genericity and the semantic amplitude with which scholars refer to it, still needs an operative definition in the field of exegesis.[358] It should be emphasised, however, that this is *primarily* a phenomenon that is quite common and simply ineludible, since it is implicated in every communicative event, starting primarily from the most ordinary and everyday.[359] And thus it will be all the more pertinent in a literary production[360] (which is always, in many ways, a reflection of this human reality), and in a special way in the Jeremianic texts of a narrative nature, which bring onto the scene of the text complex communicative exchanges composed of an intertwining of gestures and words, relative to multiple actants.

As an instructive example of the issue we are addressing, two inscriptions of Nabopolassar,[361] father of Nebuchadnezzar, can be compared, in which a question

---

356   On the notion of intertextuality as a literary theory (the term was taken from a programmatic essay by Julia Kristeva, an elaboration stemming from the contribution of the Russian critic Mikhail Bakhtin), see the introduction by A. Bernardelli, *Che cos'è l'intertestualità*, Bussole 466, Roma 2013.

357   Think, e.g. of the narration of Jer 36 concerning the generation and development of the "prophetic scroll". There is no doubt that the second scroll, the one rewritten after the destruction of the first, is a precise emblem of the intertextual process. Another macroscopic example is ch. 52, a text that takes up 2 Kgs 25, making it a not-indifferent element of meaning in the general structure of the book of Jeremiah.

358   Cf. G.A. Philipps, «Sign/Text/Différence. The Contribution of Intertextual Theory to Biblical Criticism», in: *Intertextuality*, eds. H.F. Plett, RTT 15, Berlin – New York 1991, 78–97. For its application to the book of Jeremiah, see the observations of R.P. Carroll, «Intertextuality and the Book of Jeremiah: Animadversions on Text and Theory», in: *The New Literary Criticism and the Hebrew Bible*, J.C. Exum – D.J.A. Clines, eds., JSOT.S 143, Sheffield 1993, 55–78. In particular, on the intertextual nature of the Jeremianic work, R.P. Carrol decidedly asserts: "There are so many intertextual element *within the book itself* that is difficult to know where to start in the argument. [...] all testify to the intertextual nature of the book" (p. 64). For a couple of specific examples, see the contributions of B.D. Sommer, «New Light on the Composition of Jeremiah», *CBQ* 61 (1999) 646–666, and of R.E. Clements, «Prophecy Interpreted: Intertextuality and Theodicy – A Case Study of Jeremiah 26:16–24», in: *Uprooting and Plantig*, 32–44.

359   On this topic, see e.g. B. Gasparov, *Speech, Memory, and Meaning*. Intertextuality in Everyday Language, TL.SM 214, Berlin – New York 2010.

360   "Literature is not exhaustible, for the sufficient and simple reason that no single book is. A book is not an isolated being: it is a relationship, an axis of innumerable relationships" (Jorge Luis Borges, cited by R.P. Carroll, «Intertextuality», 55).

361   I refer once again to the recent edition, edited by R. Da Riva, *The Inscriptions of Nabopolassar*, 8, 25–26 (on these pp., the passages of interest to us have been cited in translation and commented). On the phenomenon of intertextuality, in reference to the inscriptions of Nabopolassar and Neriglissar, she dedicates her entire § 1.3

"Bend your neck beneath the yoke of the king of Babylon!" (27:12)

analogous to that in Jer 27–28 is addressed: the Babylonian submission to the heavy Assyrian yoke. The self-congratulations of Nabopolassar, who prides himself on having freed Babylon from the Assyrian domination, explicitly mentions the motive that would explain why his country had to remain subjected to the foreigners for a long time, that is, for the *punitive wrath of the deity/deities*, only in the first inscription (NaplC32 I 28–31).

> [...] the Assyrian, who had ruled Akkad *because of divine anger*, and had oppressed the people of the country with his heavy yoke, [...].

In the second inscription (NaplC12/1 17–18), the same thing is taken up with almost the same words, but no motivation is given:

> [...] the Assyrian, who from distant days had ruled the entire people, and had oppressed the people of the country with his heavy yoke, [...].

It should be pointed out that the two inscriptions share an important set of common characteristics[362]: both come from Babylon, are datable between 622 and 612, and have a clear archaeological context of reference. Even the material support and handwriting are quite similar. As can be seen, therefore, an intertextual comparison allows for that which is stated in the second inscription to be inserted in its most appropriate pragmatic (and ideological) context. If we limit ourselves to considering the texts in a way that is isolated, without tracing any productive relations on the level of signification, we would be able to state, improperly, that the Babylonian submission is understood and described on NaplC12/1 17–18 as a merely factual historical occurrence, without being framed in any conception of history and without being traced, in the present case, to the concept of "divine punishment". As instead, in the light of a broader (and more pertinent) contextual understanding, it actually is.

4.3.3. "Drink!" (שְׁתוּ) [...] "You shall surely drink!" (שָׁתוֹ תִשְׁתּוּ). The nations faced with the (motivated) imperative of surrender to Babylon

A non-atomistic approach to the meaning (both of the lexicon and the literary motifs configured with it) implies that the theme of the "nations" developed in Jer 27–28 need be considered in the light of its other occurrences in the broader picture of the book of Jeremiah. Chapter 1 should be kept in mind and, in particular, ch. 25 and the section dedicated to the oracles on the nations in chs. 46–51. The structural importance of chs. 1 and 25 has been reported several times over the course of the present dissertation (cf. ch. I, § 4.1). Let me now focalise briefly only on the textual elements that are

---

(pp. 20–29). In addition to the three levels of intertextual relationships, all of them of only a formal type (word/s, sentences, broader structures, even concerning the whole composition), postulated mainly in reference to ancient texts on the basis of the indications of A. Seri, «Borrowings to Create Anew: Intertextuality in the Babylonian Poem of "Creation" (Enūma eliš)», *JAOS* 134 (2014) 89–106, it is, in my opinion, necessary to also take into consideration points of contact both of a content-related and conceptual nature.

362   As is highlighted by R. Da Riva, *The Inscriptions of Nabopolassar*, 25.

410 Jer 27–28. The world beneath the yoke of the king of Babylon

most significant for my argument,[363] organising them according to four themes that cross through the three parts ch. 25 can be divided into: (a) vv. 1–14; (b) vv. 15–29; (c) vv. 30–38:

1) *Announcement of punishment and historical materialisation of the disaster*. In 1:14–16, the "disaster" (רָעָה) is heralded as looming from the "north" (צָפוֹן) and is configured as the emission of "judgements" (מִשְׁפָּטִים) of YHWH implemented through the devastating invasion of a coalition of foreign people (מִשְׁפְּחוֹת), which is not better specified. In ch. 25, the theme of the nations returns and gets linked to the historical identity of the ruler of those people, who is also the executor of the divine "judgement": the king of Babylon (cf. vv. 1 and 9; already named however in 20:4, 21:2, 4, 7, 10; 22:25; 24:1). The tie between ch. 25 and the unit given by chs. 27–28 is significant, established through the locution נְבוּכַדְרֶאצַּר מֶלֶךְ־בָּבֶל עַבְדִּי ("Nebuchadnezzar, king of Babylon, my servant"), which recurs identically in 25:9 and 27:6 (but consider also the emphatic value of the expression גַּם־הֵמָּה ["even they"] in 25:14, referring to the Chaldeans, punitive instrument and themselves object of the divine punishment, which has the same function as that attested in 27:7b [וְגַם־הוּא] concerning the country and/or the king of Babylon). The war theme is closely connected to that of "divine judgement" in both Jer 1 and Jer 25. It is, after all, a very common correlation in the context of the ancient Near East,[364] and it is logical to presuppose it as a horizon of meaning in chs. 27–28 as well, without necessarily considering it to be a late insertion.

2) *Universal and totalising breadth of the disaster*. Both the textual units Jer 25 and Jer 27–28 give the disaster a "universal" dimension, albeit under two different perspectives: a historical (and therefore relative,[365] in Jer 27–28) one, and another more symbolic (and therefore truly universal and absolute, in Jer 25). While the two must certainly be distinguished, at the same time, they still need to be kept in reciprocal relation. If we consider ch. 1 as well, we notice, actually, a (non-linear) progression in the presentation of the theme. The dubious universalism of 1:14, whereby the catastrophe announced seems to regard "only"[366] the totality of the inhabitants of the land (כָּל־יֹשְׁבֵי הָאָרֶץ) of the kingdom of Judah, reveals the true global proportions elsewhere.

In 27–28, the Jeremianic message of submission extends, beyond all the components of the people of God, to the principal *bordering* or *neighbouring* nations (though neither Egypt nor the Philistic city-states are mentioned, probably for the reasons we

---

363 For a synthetic presentation, see W. WERNER, *Das Buch Jeremia*. Kapitel 25–52, NSK. AT 19/2, Stuttgart 2003, 11–17.

364 War and judgement can be a metaphor for each other, depending on the contexts, as is pointed out by P. BOVATI, *Ristabilire la giustizia*, 270–271. On war and its outcome as a manifestation of divine judgement on the contenders, see M. LIVERANI, *Guerra e diplomazia nell'antico Oriente (1600–1100 a.C.)*, Collezione storica, Bari 1994, 134. Cf. Ps 7 and Ps 76 as emblematic examples.

365 Cf. P.A. RAABE, «The Particularizing of Universal Judgment in Prophetic Discourse», *CBQ* 64 (2002) 652–674.

366 In truth, every *relative* totality, whether from a quantitative, spatial, or temporal point of view, still has, on a symbolic level, a truly *universal* significance, precisely as an *emblematic sign* of totality.

"Bend your neck beneath the yoke of the king of Babylon!" (27:12)   411

have already seen[367]). This extranational extension, *historically* marked by a reference to only some foreign nations (those involved in the anti-Babylonian unrest at a given historical juncture), is also present in ch. 25 (in v. 9 "all the nations" [כָּל־הַגּוֹיִם] "around/ bordering" [סָבִיב] are talked about; cf. also v. 11; and it is specified that these are the nations to which the prophet is sent; cf. vv. 15:17), but it is brought to a truly universal and totalizing dimension, of a *symbolic* type: v. 13 speaks in the absolute sense about "all the nations" (כָּל־הַגּוֹיִם) and the list presented includes all the state entities forming part of the geopolitical world in which the kingdom of Judah is inserted, within the polarity of Egypt and Babylon, the two maximum powers of the time. Significant for its universality, the pleonastic expression of v. 26: "all the kingdoms (כָּל־הַמַּמְלָכוֹת) of the land/world (הָאָרֶץ) that are on the face of the earth (עַל־פְּנֵי הָאֲדָמָה)"; while in vv. 29–32, it is specified that the "sword" (v. 29: חֶרֶב) and the roar (v. 30: שָׁאֹג) of YHWH are directed against "all the inhabitants of the earth" (2x; vv. 29, 30: כָּל־יֹשְׁבֵי הָאָרֶץ), they reach "to the end of the Earth" (v. 31: עַד־קְצֵה הָאָרֶץ; cf. vv. 32–33) and his judgement concerns the nations, indeed, it is addressed "against every flesh" (v. 31: לְכָל־בָּשָׂר).

Within this framework, ch. 45, another text of great strategic importance (in both the MT and LXX, but according to two different logics), which closes the whole second part of the book of Jeremiah, is mentioned. And well here too, the "disaster" (v. 5: רָעָה) assumes a universal dimension, since it extends to "all the earth" (v. 4: כָּל־הָאָרֶץ), making direct reference to Judah but with a potentially much wider aperture of meaning, and strikes "all flesh" (v. 5: כָּל־בָּשָׂר), that is, every living being (cf. Gen 6:13).

Still in ch. 25, it should likewise be noted that the "universal" dimension in a symbolic sense is strengthened by that of the "totality", expressed in v. 9 (cf. 30:11) as a totality of *extermination* (√חרם hi.) and as *definitiveness* or *perpetuity* (עוֹלָם; cf. 51:26, 62 and 49:33 with the sing. שְׁמָמָה instead of the intensive pl. of previous occurrences; cf. also Ezek 35:9) of the condition of opprobrium, horror, and ruin caused by divine retribution.[368] In synthesis, the historical contextualisation of the Jeremianic message

---

367   Cf. ch. II, § 2.2.2, n. 90.

368   Historically unfulfilled, not after the seventy years after the Jeremianic prophecy (cf. 25:11–12; 29:10; cf. 27:7), nor in the time during which numerous scholars place the composition of the book of Jeremiah (fourth century): a sign of the intentional symbolic value with which this oracle was proclaimed, written, and transmitted. Another piece of evidence of the symbolic perspective of ch. 25 can be seen in the alphabetic codification (which rabbis call *atbash*; for more detailed study, see J.R. LUNDBOM, *Jeremiah 21–36*, 266 and, in particular, M. LEUCHTER, «Jeremiah' 70-Year Prophecy and the Atbash Codes», *Bib.* 85 [2004] 503–522) to which the name of Babylon is subjected in v. 26 (and in 51:45), where Nebuchadnezzar is called the "king of Sheshak" (מֶלֶךְ שֵׁשַׁךְ). In the case of Babylon, which had thus become a universal symbol of evil (cf. J. HILL, *Friend or Foe?*, 107–108), it is worth noting that, though after the end of the Babylonian empire this city remained famous for centuries, it was indeed a time of perennial devastation (as it was for Nineveh, moreover, another city-symbol reproached by many prophets). And it is the state in which it is found to date, unlike other glorious ancient cities, whose original sites, while having naturally changed over time, have been inhabited uninterruptedly to this day. In retrospect, it can be said that the fate of Babylon became, in fact, a sign of warning that what it represented and represents has no future in history, of which God is Lord. This "symbolic" value of Babylon, moreover, is consecrated and relaunched for time to come in the book of Revelation at the closing of the New Testament canon.

412   Jer 27–28. The world beneath the yoke of the king of Babylon

of chs. 27–28 must therefore be seen certainly in the light of the meaning of history revealed programmatically and symbolically in ch. 25 (and confirmed, as final inclusion, by ch. 45).

3) *The injunction to surrender: two different communicative registers.* For the configuration of this theme as well, analogous observations should be made about the correlation between the two textual units, continuing to keep in mind their specific natures (the first of a poetic, symbolic, and programmatic sort, the second of a narrative, historical, and accurate nature). In 27–28, the message of Jeremiah is very clear on a conceptual-propositional level, even if mediated by the symbolic gesture of the yoke: the nations are called to renounce their political independence and to subject themselves to the design of YHWH, who wants them subjugated to the king of Babylon. In ch. 25, a completely *metaphorical* register is used, that of the "cup of the wine of wrath"[369] (כּוֹס הַיַּיִן הַחֵמָה) of God, for the nations to gulp down (vv. 15–28; cf. Isa 51:17–23; Ezek 23:28–35; Hab 2:15–17), and the *universal* dimension is more highly accentuated (of the dominion and divine "judgement"). Regardless, on close look, we can say that we are before an isomorphic[370] presence of the same theme, that of surrender, to be understood as an act of acceptance of God's righteous punishment.

The nations, in fact, and Judah included, are not simply faced with an ineluctable incident. Let me specify. Actually, it is as such (cf. v. 28: שָׁתוֹ תִשְׁתּוּ; "you shall surely drink"), only that an appeal is made to the freedom of the subjects involved calling for conscious consent, and in the framework of the Jeremianic theological message, this is not irrelevant. Indeed, this is the meaning of the imperative שְׁתוּ ("drink!") and the sequence of those that follows, connected paratactically שְׁתוּ וְשִׁכְרוּ וּקְיוּ וְנִפְלוּ וְלֹא תָקוּמוּ ("drink and become intoxicated, vomit, fall,[371] and not rise again"), referring in v. 27 to the cup (and

---

369   See, in this regard, T. SEIDL, *"Der Becher in der Hand des Herrn".* Studie zu den prophetischen "Taumelbecher"-Texten, ATSAT 70, St. Ottilien 2001; and also, more generally, G. FUCHS, *Der Becher des Sonnengottes.* Zur Entwicklung des Motivs "Becher des Zorns", BVBib 4, Münster 2003 (the pages dedicated to Jeremiah are pp. 94–112, where it is underscored, amongst other things, that the literary motif [of mythological and extrabiblical origin] of the "the cup of the wine of the wrath of YHWH" should be placed relation to the universal dimension of his lordship over history [pp. 98–99]).

370   I have already used this category a number of times, but here it calls for clarification. In semiotics, "isomorphism" refers to the similarity or formal identity as much as to the appearance or structure between signs belonging to codes or different semiotic levels, as e.g. in the case of the traceable isomorphic relationship between Roman and Indo-Arabic numerals (I refer to the definition proposed by M. DANESI – U. ECO *et al., Encyclopedic Dictionary of Semiotics, Media, and Communications,* Toronto 2000, 123; cf. also A.J. GREIMAS – J. COURTÉS, *Sémiotique,* 197). That which the sign of the yoke expresses in and of itself, and the same interactive model triggered (i.e. the issuance of the message as meaning [semantic aspect] and the simultaneous invocation of response [pragmatic aspect] already analogically anticipated in the message itself), we will find codified in other texts and in other ways (especially in Jer 29 and in 42–43:7) but with the same semantic structure (and pragmatic or illocutionary/perlocutionary force).

371   It should be noted that the verb נָפַל (lit.: "to fall"; which recurs also in v. 34) is used in the technical sense to express the act of surrender in some texts that are key for

"Bend your neck beneath the yoke of the king of Babylon!" (27:12)   413

the consequences of the consumption of its content), which metaphorises acceptance of the disaster decreed by YHWH. Confirmation comes from what is negatively
expressed in the following v. 28: "if they then will refuse to take (וְהָיָה כִּי יְמָאֲנוּ לָקַחַת־הַכּוֹס)
from your hand the drinking cup [...]". If in 27–28, the gesture of the yoke is placed
on a virtually historical level, in Jer 25, it is instead a symbolic type of communicative
act, that is, a translation in metaphorical terms of the divine command itself (and its
fulfilment) concerning the message of surrender to Babylon.

4) *The disaster as punishment of YHWH.* It is easy to ascertain that in Jer 25, the
universal disaster destined to strike Judah and all the other nations is explicitly justified as fulfilment of *divine punishment.* This is revealed in the motif of the cup of the
wrath of YHWH,[372] but is explicitly affirmed in regard to the people of God (v. 2: "all
the people of Judah and the inhabitants of Jerusalem" [כָּל־עַם יְהוּדָה וְאֵל כָּל־יֹשְׁבֵי יְרוּשָׁלַם])
already in the opening, where an assessment is made of the long Jeremianic ministry
(twenty-three years, up to the turning point of the fourth year of Jehoiakim, which
corresponds to the first year of the reign of Nebuchadnezzar) and obstinacy in *non-
listening*[373] is stigmatised, both in the face of Jeremiah's appeals for conversion (v. 3),
and towards the whole lot of prophets sent by YHWH (v. 4). The question of the
disobedience regards the fundamental ethical norms that substantiate the Covenant
relationship (cf. vv. 5–7) and the anti-idolatrical injunctions in particular.

The nations per se cannot be charged with infidelity, since they are collocated outside of this relational, normative framework (which implies exposure to the accusation
and divine punishment; cf. e.g. Deut 7:6–15; 8:5.11–20; Amos 3:2; Ps 50; etc.). They are,
however, punished as well, but on the basis of general ethical motives, the universal
value of which is clearly recognised (cf. Amos 1–2 as "first text", almost programmatic).[374] Moreover, based on the theological coordinates of the book of Jeremiah, it
is coherent to believe that if YHWH is the creator God and Lord of all the earth and

---

my research, such as 21:9 (in syntagmatic relation with the preposition עַל); 37:13
(with no syntagmatic relations), 14 (still with עַל); 38:19 (with אֶל); 38:9 (2x, with and
without עַל); 52:15 (2x, with and without אֶל). Cf. also 36:7, linked to לִפְנֵי יְהוָה, with
the meaning, "humiliate oneself before YHWH". Perhaps, analogously, the verb קוּם
("to raise yourselves back up") can allude to the "raising" of a rebellion. "Fall and do
not raise yourselves back up" could therefore mean: "surrender, without attempting
an uprising".

372 Cf. G. FUCHS, *Der Becher des Sonnengottes,* 99–106. On the more general theme of the
wrath of YHWH in the book of Jeremiah, see S. JOO, *Provocation and Punishment.* The
Anger of God in the Book of Jeremiah and Deuteronomistic Theology, BZAW 361,
Berlin – New York 2006 (on Jer 25:1–14 on pp. 187–201; with a synthetic appendix
of typical expressions on pp. 271–276).

373 Note the insistence of the motif: an identical locution is repeated in vv. 3-4:
וְלֹא שְׁמַעְתֶּם ("but you have not listened"); again in v. 4: וְלֹא־הִטִּיתֶם אֶת־אָזְנְכֶם לִשְׁמֹעַ ("and
you have not bent your ear to listen"); v. 7: וְלֹא־שְׁמַעְתֶּם אֵלַי ("but you did not listen to
me"); v. 8: יַעַן אֲשֶׁר לֹא־שְׁמַעְתֶּם אֶת־דְּבָרָי ("for you have not listened to my words").

374 In other collections of oracles against the nations, the motivation (of an ethical
nature) of announced misfortune emerges as well. In any case, the very presence of
the oracles against the nations in the prophetic books highlights the conception of
YHWH as "more than simply the national God of Israel" (R.E. CLEMENTS, *Prophecy
and Tradition,* Southampton 1975, 58).

414   Jer 27–28. The world beneath the yoke of the king of Babylon

all of history, then He himself is the source of the law (and the "judge") for all the nations. And so the Chaldeans and their sovereign, punitive instruments elected for the re-establishment of divine justice, will themselves be subjected to punishment (cf. v. 12): YHWH *shall punish* (√פקד), "their crimes" (עֲוֺנָם) and (cf. v. 14) *shall repay* them (√שלם pi.) "according to their actions and works of their hands" (כְּפָעֳלָם וּכְמַעֲשֵׂה יְדֵיהֶם). But what about all the other nations?

The disaster that is prophesied about them takes the shape of a *punishment* carried out by YHWH as well. God is beginning to chastise his elected city, upon which his name is invoked (a prerogative that, in theory, should put it in a state of favour; see e.g. 1 Kgs 8:28–53; 9:3; Jer 7:4.11). All the more reason why foreign and idolatrous peoples cannot be considered exempt (cf. 25:29: "and you will remain unpunished? You will not remain unpunished!" [וְאַתֶּם הִנָּקֵה תִּנָּקוּ לֹא תִנָּקוּ]; cf. Amos 1:2–2:16). Verse 31 is even more explicit about the meaning of the history underway: YHWH is carrying out his judgement against all the inhabitants of the earth, a process that "regards every flesh" (לְכָל־בָּשָׂר) and that delivers to "the wicked" (הָרְשָׁעִים) the sword. It is worth noting, however, that in the final phase (cf. vv. 34–36), it is specified that those stricken are (above all?) "the shepherds" (vv. 34 and הָרֹעִים), the "leaders of the flock" (אַדִּירֵי הַצֹּאן), that is, the ruling class of the nations. And this is a fact that can be taken as a key element for looking at the oracles on the nations (in particular, those in chs. 46–51, but not only), in search of greater specification regarding the "fault" for which YHWH confers a universal dimension on his punitive action.

4.3.4. A look at the oracles on the nations

To get a first idea of the faults attributed to the nations[375] to justify the punishment pronounced against them, one must *first and foremost* consider the pertinent oracles found in the first of the book of Jeremiah.

In 9:24–25, we find an interesting case straight off, though not without a lack of textual difficulties. Punishment is announced for some foreign nations (cf. v. 25), amongst which Edom, Ammon, and Moab (called into question again in 27:3),[376]

---

375   On the thematic of the nations in the book of Jeremiah, see, amongst others, P. ACKROYD, *Exile and Restoration. A Study of Hebrew Thought of the Sixth Century* B.C., OTL, London 1968, 219–225; G. FISCHER, «Jer 25 und die Fremdvölkersprüche. Unterschiede zwischen hebräischem und griechischem Text», *Bib.* 72 (1991) 474–499 (= in: ID., *Der Prophet wie Mose*, 3–23); W. WATTS, «Text and Redaction in Jeremiah's Oracles against the Nations», *CBQ* 54 (1992) 432–447; B. HUWYLER, *Jeremia und die Völker*. Untersuchungen zu den Völkersprüchen in Jeremia 46–49, FAT 20, Tübingen 1997; G. FISCHER, «Gottes universale Horizonte», 313–328; M.P. MAIER, *Ägypten*; J. HWANG, «The *Missio Dei* as an Integrative Motif in the Book of Jeremiah», *BBR* 23 (2013) 481–508; O. KAISER, *Der eine Gott Israels und die Mächte der Welt*. Der Weg Gottes im Alten Testament vom Herrn seines Volkes zum Herrn der ganzen Welt, FRLANT 249, Göttingen 2013, 73–94.

376   The first nation named in 9:25 is Egypt, followed by Judah. From the parallelism with 27:2, in fact, only the Arab tribes would be left out. Indeed, even if Egypt is not mentioned in 27:2, one can reasonably assume, as we have seen, that its covert direction or at least a promise of military support was behind the anti-Babylonian summit.

"Bend your neck beneath the yoke of the king of Babylon!" (27:12)   415

which appear to be placed on the same level as "Judah" (political term), also referred to here as "house of Israel" (a term connoted in the religious sense) in two fundamental respects. These too practice circumcision, and yet, just like the people of God, even these circumcised men are judged by YHWH to be only "circumcised (limitedly) on the foreskin" (מוּל בְּעָרְלָה), while remaining to all effects "uncircumcised" (עֲרֵלִים), just like the Israelites, who are "uncircumcised at heart" (עַרְלֵי־לֵב; cf. 4:4, 6:10).

Chapter 10 is also significant. It is a composite (and later) unit, but is focalised on sharp criticism of the nations and their vain idolatry (cf. 14:22). The "house of Israel" (v. 1) is invited to not learn their conduct (vv. 2–3), implicitly judged as guilty,[377] because precisely due to their ridiculous falsehood (their idols) they will be put to shame, when "punishment" (v. 15: פְּקֻדָּה; cf. vv. 10–11) will be inflicted on the false gods. Divine wrath is invoked on the nations and on the people who do not recognise YHWH and do not invoke his name (which is already a basis of fault; but cf. 16:19–20), on account of the evil done to "Jacob" (v. 25) over the course of history.[378]

In 18:7–10, it can clearly be seen that the action of YHWH in the history of the nations is placed in oppositive relation to their "wickedness" (v. 8: רָעָה) and to their non- "listening/obedience" (v. 10: √שׁמע) to the "voice" (קוֹל) of the Lord. It would be interesting to examine what "voice" is being referred to here, even if from the general context of the book, the existence of a sort of universal moral law seems to be presupposed, through which God enters into relation (speaks) to every nation. Only conversion can prevent them from being uprooted, demolished, and destroyed (v. 8).[379]

Another pertinent text is 12:14–17. The theme of the fault of the nations is taken back up (called, in v. 14, "my wicked neighbours" [שְׁכֵנַי הָרָעִים.]), understood as the damage caused to the inheritance of Israel (v. 14) and as "not listening" (v. 17: √שׁמע). In addition, the accusation of having taught (v. 17: √למד pi.) the people of YHWH to swear (√שׁבע ni.) in the name of Baal is specified. And yet, after the punishment, a *salvific horizon* is envisioned (vv. 15–16), and even admission into the relational perimeter of the Covenant, a sort of integration into the people of God. This highlights the positive purpose of all the punitive action of YHWH as the Lord of history.

Special attention should be devoted to the third part of the book of Jeremiah, entirely concerning the oracles on the nations. Unfortunately, due to their supposed "secondary" nature,[380] exegetes too often marginalise this section in order to favour a global understanding of the Jeremianic work. The literary unit is homogeneous as far as content is concerned, thematised beginning with its "title" in 46:1 (absent in the LXX,

---

377   Cf. A. FAVALE, *Dio d'Israele e dei popoli*, 264–323.
378   The final v. is clearly post-exilic (cf. the reference to the devastation of the dwelling), but this does not prevent from seeing a global reference to the sufferings endured by Israel at the hand of the nations throughout the course of its history.
379   Cf. M.E. BIDDLE, «Contingency, God and the Babylonians: Jeremiah on the Complexity of Repentance», *RevExp* 101 (2004) 247–265 (here esp. pp. 250–251).
380   Personally, I agree with W. Watts, when he asserts, at the conclusion of his contribution: "The OAN should no longer be dismissed as a secondary scribal addition, but should be taken into account in descriptions of the composition and editing of Jeremiah as an integral part of the book's second edition, and perhaps its first. This, in turn, means that these oracles should also be integrated into interpretations of the message of the book as a whole and given the attention which their prominent positions in both the LXX and MT suggest they deserve" (ID., «Text and Redaction», 447).

416   Jer 27–28. The world beneath the yoke of the king of Babylon

which places this section after 25:13a).[381] The strategic relationship that chs. 46–51 have with the beginning and the end of the first part is evident in the MT: in 1:5, 10, Jeremiah is sent to the nations, and what is announced in the form of a summary in ch. 25 is then detailed by a series of well-aimed oracles, whose sequence is substantially respected with respect to the timetable (beginning with Egypt and closing with Babylon, though for the other nations named, there are some discrepancies in the order).[382]

These correlations reinforce the plausibility of an intertextual reading that highlights the most congruous textual horizon, made up of multiple interrelations between difference communicative units, within which to comprehend the sense of the action taken and of the divine command announced by Jeremiah in 27–28. All the more so if we consider that, from a chronological point of view, staying with the textual clues, most of the oracles on the nations[383] should precede the prophetic call for submission to Babylon (cf. 27:1) by almost ten years (cf. 45:2; 46:2; 47:1). The relationship established between these phases of prophetic communication would thus be that between a remote *announcement* (of the punishment, with its motivations) and proclamation of its imminent *fulfilment* (with its respective request for acceptance, that is, of surrender to his agent in history, who is the king of Babylon). Moreover, on the level of temporal sequentiality of the narrative that can be deduced by the available clues as well, it must be presupposed that the actants implicated in 27–28 had knowledge of the preceding oracles concerning the nations (or at least some of them).[384]

Let us now take a quick look at the sequence of the oracles, highlighting only the textual elements that I hold to be most pertinent with regard to the topic being addressed.

---

381   According to a number of scholars, the disposition attested by the LXX would be traceable back to an older stage in the history of the composition of the book of Jeremiah. See e.g. J.G. JANZEN, *Studies in the Text of Jeremiah*, HSM 6, Cambridge (MA) 1973, 115–116; E. Tov, «Some Aspects of the Textual and Literary History of the Book of Jeremiah», in: *Le livre de Jérémie*, 145–167 (here, p. 152, n. 20); ID., «The Literary History of the Book of Jeremiah in the Light of Its Textual History», in: *Empirical Models*, 211–237 (here, p. 217, n. 23); P.-M. BOGAERT, «De Baruch à Jérémie. Les deux rédactions conservées du livre de Jérémie», in: *Le livre de Jérémie*, 168–173 (here, pp. 169, 172); B. GOSSE, «La place primitive», 389–391; W. WATTS, «Text and Redaction», 442. Then again, the books of Isaiah and Ezekiel also place their oracles against the nations in the central part (cf. Isa 13–23; Ezek 25–32). See also the more recent review by M. HARAN, «The Place of the Prophecies against the Nations in the Book of Jeremiah», in *Emanuel*. Studies in Hebrew Bible, Septuagint, and Dead Sea Scrolls in Honor of Emanuel Tov, *eds.* S.M. PAUL *et al.*, VT.S 94, Leiden 2003, 699–706.

382   The situation in the LXX differs greatly, presenting another distribution of the oracles. For a comparative schema, see J.M. ABREGO, *Jeremías*, 168.

383   Obviously, the oracles against Babylon in chs. 50–51 (cf. 51:59) should be excluded.

384   Cf. B. HUWYLER, *Jeremia und die Völker*, 307–315. By the same author, keep in mind also ID., «Jeremia und die Völker. Politische Prophetie in der Zeit der babylonischen Bedrohung (7./6. Jh. v. Chr.)», *ThZ* 52 (1996) 193–205. The oracle against Elam (49:34–49) is instead clearly dated at the beginning of the reign of Zedekiah (cf. v. 32).

"Bend your neck beneath the yoke of the king of Babylon!" (27:12)   417

On Egypt (46:2–28): the defeat of the Egyptian army at Karkemish by Nebuchadnezzar, King of Babylon, is announced. The rout is much more resounding than anticipated: it is not just the fatal outcome of a battle, but also annihilation of Egypt's boasting and haughty expansionist aims. Indeed, it is the "warriors" (v. 5, 12) who are defeated and fall, the most agile (v. 6), a nation that overflows like the Nile with the intention of covering the earth and wiping out the cities and their inhabitants (v. 8). For YHWH, it is a "day of vengeance" (v. 10: יוֹם נְקָמָה) in which he *takes revenge* (√נקם ni.) on enemies, who are exposed to dishonour and shame (vv. 12, 24), while the valiant warriors are thrown to the ground (v. 15: √סחף ni.)[385] and the pharaoh ridiculed (v. 17), the hired mercenaries become fattened calves ready for slaughter: the day of the disaster has come, the time of their punishment (v. 21). Those to be punished are the god Amon, Egypt, its other gods and its (deified) kings,[386] the pharaoh and those who trust in him (v. 25). It is clear from this picture that the objective of YHWH's punishment is the *downsizing of human presumptuousness* (the classic *hýbris*) and *confidence in the power of one's self or of another* (as well as in false deities), and that this dimension of values is, by nature, universal. Extermination is announced only for nations where Israel has been dispersed (v. 28). For Egypt (v. 26), as for Israel itself (vv. 27–28), the punishment suffered paves the way for a *salvific restoration.* This particularity is to be highlighted, because it shows that the divine action is understood as not being arbitrary: the punishment is motivated and is a transitional phase that has, as its purpose, life and good.

On the Philistines (47): the enemy announced always comes from the north. No specific fault is emphasised, aside from perhaps, but only incidentally, the futility of the cult practice of "making incisions" (√גדד hithpo.) on the body in reference to the survivors of Ascalon (v. 5). It should be borne in mind, however, that this is historically one of Israel's most hated enemies. And also, on that very basis, the surprisingly compassionate tone of v. 8. I will mention that reference is not made to the Philistines in 27:3 because, in all likelihood, they had already been hard hit by Nebuchadnezzar.

On Moab (48): Unlike Egypt and the Philistines, Moab is instead mentioned in 27:3. It is significant, therefore, that in this long oracle, what was previously noted in reference to Egypt be confirmed and amplified: the "punishment" or the divine "judgment" (v. 21: מִשְׁפָּט; v. 44: פְּקֻדָּה) is aimed at the *humiliation* of human (*vain*) *glory.* To this is added, as a specific imputation, the *having magnified* (*themselves*) against YHWH (vv. 26, 42: √גדל hi.) and *having considered Israel* as an "*object of ridicule*" (v. 27: שְׂחוֹק). Right off, in v. 1, the shame caused by the punishment is mentioned (2x: √בוש hi.) and, at the beginning of v. 2, it is proclaimed in a concise way that "the glory of Moab is no longer" (אֵין עוֹד תְּהִלַּת מוֹאָב).[387] That this reference is being

---

385   According to another possible interpretation of the expression נִסְחַף אַבִּירֶיךָ: "your powerful (bull) is thrown to the ground" (or, revocalising the MT נִסְחַף with the LXX: "Apis flees" [נָס חַף]). The reference in this case, using *pluralis maiestatis* and also staying to the MT, would not be to the crushed warriors, but to the god Apis, who was depicted by the image of the bull (see e.g. ANEP, 190, Fig. 570).

386   This is probably the allusion, since the kings (the various pharaohs) and gods of Egypt are named as part of a single category. On the question of the divinisation of the Egyptian sovereigns, see R.J. LEPROHON, «Royal Ideology and State Administration in Pharaonic Egypt», in: *Civilizations of the Ancient Near East*, vol. I, *ed.* J.M. SASSON, New York 1995, 278–287 (in particular, pp. 275–275).

387   The term תְּהִלָּה indicates the "praise" and thus the "glory" and "fame".

418   Jer 27–28. The world beneath the yoke of the king of Babylon

made not to the effect of the punishment, but to the *cause* of it, is stated explicitly in v. 7: "because (כִּי יַעַן) you have placed trust (√בטח) in your works (בְּמַעֲשַׂיִךְ)[388] and in your treasures (וּבְאוֹצְרוֹתַיִךְ)[389]". Moab is sure of itself since its youth (v. 11), and this reinforced perception, however erroneous, will be shattered by the exile (v. 12). It is useless to boast of being valiant warriors (v. 14), the best young men of Moab will be slaughtered, "says the King, whose name is YHWH of hosts" (v. 15: נְאֻם־הַמֶּלֶךְ יְהוָה צְבָאוֹת שְׁמוֹ). And again, references to the haughty greatness of Moab that will be humiliated are multiplied: v. 17: "the mighty sceptre" (מַטֵּה־עֹז), "the glorious staff" (מַקֵּל תִּפְאָרָה) it will be broken (√שבר ni.); v. 18: it will have to come down (√ירד) "from glory"(מִכָּבוֹד); v. 25: "the horn of Moab" (קֶרֶן מוֹאָב) will be cut off (√גדע ni.) and "its arm" (זְרֹעוֹ) broken (√שבר ni.), and again in v. 29, the finger is pointed at "the pride of Moab" (גְּאוֹן־מוֹאָב), pride beyond bounds (גֵּאֶה מְאֹד), his loftiness (גָּבְהוֹ), his pride (גְּאוֹנוֹ), his scorn (גַּאֲוָתוֹ), the insolence of his heart" (רֻם לִבּוֹ); v. 30: "his arrogance" (עֶבְרָתוֹ), his insubstantial boasting. Then, in v. 35, the anti-idolatry criticism is made explicit. Despite the disasters that are announced, the oracles against Moab *conclude positively*, with the promise that YHWH will bring back its exiles (v. 47). In the light of this context, can it really be affirmed that the Jeremianic call for submission to the king of Babylon be wholly unmotivated?

On the children of Ammon (49:1–6): the Ammonites, a population related to Moab, are also explicitly mentioned in 27:3. And the disaster that is pronounced against them (v. 2) is also clearly traced here to their guilt, which is dual in nature: v. 1: for having taken possession (lit.: "to have taken as inheritance"; √ירשׁ) of cities and territories belonging to Israel and having settled there (√ישׁב); and, in v. 4: its useless self-celebration (√הלל hithp.) and vain trust (√בטח) in its own riches and presumed invulnerability ("who will come against me?"; מִי יָבוֹא אֵלָי). But even in this case, the oracle concludes with a *positive look* to the future (v. 6): YHWH will bring back their deportees.

On Edom (49:7–22): Edom, as well, is implicated in 27:3. The fault sanctioned is perceptible in the initial rhetorical questions in v. 7 about where its "sapience" (חָכְמָה) has gone and whether "the advice to the intelligent" (עֵצָה מִבָּנִים) has failed (√אבד). Explicitly, in v. 16, blame is given to the error caused by their ability to instil "terror" (תִּפְלַצְתְּ), "pride" (זְדוֹן) of the heart (לֵב) and vain confidence in places of refuge thought to be inaccessible. The punitive act is recalled in v. 8 ("the time of his punishment"; עֵת פְּקַדְתִּיו) and in v. 12 with √נקה, first in negative form ("do you think you're going unpunished? You will not go unpunished!"; נָקֹה תִּנָּקֶה לֹא תִנָּקֶה), and then through the evident intertextual reference (which betrays the original positioning of the oracles against the nations attested in the LXX with respect to the MT) to the need to drink from the cup of wrath announced in 25:15–28 ("you shall surely drink!"; שָׁתֹה תִשְׁתֶּה; cf. 25:28: "you will drink inevitably"; שָׁתוֹ תִשְׁתּוּ). As retaliation, YHWH will make

---

388   With the generic term מַעֲשֶׂה, one can allude to an entire category of works grouped together for their dependence on the human capacity to make an impact on the real: achievements of a military nature, such as walls, fortresses, weapons; trade, riches, idols, etc., but in an abstract sense, one can also refer to productive efforts. Ultimately, it means all that which can feed the illusion of one's own power and security.

389   The אוֹצָרוֹת can also be the "warehouses", with reference to a broader reference to the capacity to accumulate goods and/or supplies in sight of the difficulties of life (cf. e.g. Mal 3:10; 2 Chr 11:11; etc.).

"Bend your neck beneath the yoke of the king of Babylon!" (27:12)   419

Edom small (v. 15: קָטֹן + √נתן + suff.) amongst the nations, and make it "despicable" (בזה√ qal pass.) amongst the assembly of men. Here, too, we find a sign of hope for the future (cf. v. 11).

On Damascus (49:23–27): a brief oracle of condemnation on the capital of Syria. No specific charges are made, although in closing (v. 27), the foretold disaster is expressed in a formulary very similar to that of Amos 1:14[390] (and note that in the oracles against the nations of Amos, every punishment is strictly correlated to specific faults, even in the case of Damascus; cf. Amos 1:3: precisely against Gilead, Israeli territory). It should furthermore be recalled that this is one of Israel's arch enemies (cf. 1 Kgs 11:23–25; 15:18–20; 20; 22; etc.) and that at the time of Jeremiah, allying itself with the Babylonians, it took part in the war offensive against Judah (cf. 2 Kgs 24:2).

On Kedar and the kingdoms of Asor (49:28–33): the introduction of v. 28 speaks of the disaster as having been already realised by Nebuchadnezzar. Also significant here is the emphasis on the supposed security of this "tranquil nation that lives in safety" (v. 31: גּוֹי שְׁלֵיו יוֹשֵׁב לָבֶטַח). The disaster is in fact conceived as retribution (cf. v. 32) because it concerns various nomadic desert populations (also identified with the Midianites and Amalekites) engaged not only in the commerce, but also in the pillaging (cf. Judg 6:1–6) of those same animals that are taken from them by force.

On the Elam (49:34–39): unique amongst the prophets, only Jeremiah addresses a specific oracle (dated at the beginning of the reign of Zedekiah, when it had already been defeated by the Assyrians in ca. 640) to the distant nation of Elam, probably for the role it played in the political chessboard of the Near East in the seventh century. This, like the role of Babylon that I look at below, would suggest that the ultimate intent of these oracles be that of sketching a complex profile of God's wrath on every (historical) form of injustice. In v. 35, it is announced that their "bow" (קֶשֶׁת), and "the mainstay of their might" (רֵאשִׁית גְּבוּרָתָם) will be broken (√שבר), but in closing, their return from the exile is also prophesied (v. 39).

On Babylon (50–51): of these numerous oracular pronouncements collected in the last two chapters of the section on (or rather, in this case *against*) Babylon,[391] I will highlight two fundamental thematics, both concerning the nexus between fault and punishment: 1) the punishment is eternal, definitive, without remission, and without apertures of hope for the future (cf. 50:13, 21, 26, 40; 51:3, 8–9, 37–39, 43, 58, 62–64). As I have already observed, this is due to the process of symbolisation in place, whereby Babylon becomes the emblem of absolute evil, which, as such, must be entirely eradicated. 2) The cause of the "revenge of YHWH" (50:15: נִקְמַת יְהוָה; 50:18, 27–28; 51:6, 11, 36) is widely illustrated and need not be elaborated. Once again, it has to do with human haughtiness, expressed in idolatry (50:2, 38; 51:17–18, 44, 47, 52), offense, and hostility against YHWH (50:14, 24, 29), prevarication, violence, and arrogance (50:15, 32; 51:13, 25), especially against the people of God (50:17, 33; 51:24, 34–35, 49–51). It is worth noting, in any case, that the call to leave and flee

---

390   But cf. also Jer 17:27; 21:14; 50:32.
391   I have always understood and translated the title of the section and the introductory indication of the recipients of the various oracles (in which the prepositions אֶל/עַל/ לְ + obj. are used without distinction) with "on" (as in, "with regard to"; etc.) taking into account the fact that, on several occasions, a positive future after the disaster is also announced. In the case of Babylon, however, the outlook is entirely negative.

420 Jer 27–28. The world beneath the yoke of the king of Babylon

from Babylon (cf. 50:8; 51:6, 45) is in *pendant* to that addressed to the inhabitants of Jerusalem concerning the act of surrender, especially in 21:8–10. As I have noted, for the symbolic network established and evoked in 21:1–10 (cf. ch. II), Jerusalem becomes an icon of irreparable corruption, destined to the fate that once befell the idolatrous populations of the land of Canaan, given to the Israelites.

In summary: the calamity preannounced against the foreign nations in the book of Jeremiah, and in the section of chs. 46–51 in particular, is almost always linked to a punitive act of YHWH determined by reprehensible acts or attitudes, which are not detailed nor traced back in an obvious manner to the relational framework of the Covenant. For the same reason, there are no exhortations to conversion, though there is no lack of personal-affective involvement of YHWH in the fate of the various nations, for whom in several cases, salvific restoration is promised. The punishment, in almost all of the cases, is more or less explicitly motivated, and concerns above all what in the Greek world is defined as *hýbris*. And it is significant that more than idolatry (cf. 46:15; 48:35, in reference to Babylon cf. 50.2.38; 51.17–18.44.47.52), the root cause of the anticipated misfortunes is precisely that of human arrogance (cf. 46:17, 25; 48:7, 11, 14, 25–26, 29–30, 35, 42; 49:4, 7, 16, 31, 35; 50:14, 24–27, 29–32; 51:7, 13, 25–26, 30, 41, 53, 55–56, 58).[392]

It should therefore come as no surprise that, in this context, the placing of the kingdom of Judah before a request for submission is not done with an explicitly anti-idolatric function. Even from the fact that the end does not have the final word, with the exception of the case of Babylon, what emerges is that the general purpose of divine action is for man to return to the truth of his condition as a creature. And the recovery of that truth, eclipsed by (self-)idolatrous lies, is salvific mediation, (tormented) transition in the direction of life (cf. 12:14–17; 46:26; 48:47; 49:6, 11, 39). It is therefore clear that in the light of this intertextual context, it is absolutely improper to say that in 27–28, the act of submission to Babylon and thus acceptance of the downsizing of one's power, is a completely unjustified act without any connection to the notion of (just) punishment.

It is by no coincidence, then, that in 3:17; 31:7–10; 33:9, the nations are called to gather together in the name of YHWH to hear and praise the story of the salvation of the people of God, the "rest of Israel" (31:7: שְׁאֵרִית יִשְׂרָאֵל), and that Jerusalem be presented as the "throne of YHWH" (3:17: כִּסֵּא יְהוָה) and Jacob as the "first of the nations" (3:17: רֹאשׁ הַגּוֹיִם),[393] especially in a *paradigmatic* sense.[394] Looking at the prophetic story of this people, beloved but unfaithful, humiliated yet saved, the nations will also be able to recognise the meaning of their own history and stop walking (3:17: √הלך) according to "the stubbornness of their evil heart" (שְׁרִרוּת לִבָּם הָרָע).

---

392 As noted as well by T.E. FRETHEIM, *God and World*, 341, n. 34. Arrogance and self-confidence are actually, in any case, a way to deny that history is being led by a divine sovereign. This "idolatric" manner of living is "judged" by the true God so as to reveal its lack of consistence. To recognise this is to embark on the path of salvation.

393 This expression is one that is found, other than in 31:7, only in 2 Sam 22:44 (Ps 18:44). The reference to the royal authority granted by YHWH to David over the nations is transferred or extended in Jeremiah to the whole people of God (cf. G. FISCHER, *Jeremia 26–52*, 149).

394 For the same reason, Babylonia will instead be the "last of the nations" (cf. 50:12: אַחֲרִית גּוֹיִם).

"Bend your neck beneath the yoke of the king of Babylon!" (27:12)   421

4.3.5 YHWH in Jer 27–28: A cosmic God or an ethical God? The prophetic synthesis of the Jeremianic message

If it is incorrect to consider the Jeremianic message in chs. 27–28 in a way that is detached from the punitive significance of the disasters announced against the foreign nations, it need however be underlined that this *ethical dimension* must be regained *inferentially*. This is certainly not the style that typifies Deuteronomist theology, with its incessant explicit reference to the linear concatenation between crime, punishment, conversion, and salvation. Here, just as in all the other attestations of the call to surrender to the king of Babylon, the text is reticent: it does not directly call into question ethical principles, crimes, or punishments, because it only gives clues or, in any case, presupposes the capacity of the reader to arrive at an overall vision within which the single elements of meaning can be put into place. Even more: it provokes and requires a hermeneutical act, rather than offer it as already completed or unequivocal.

The interpretive deduction that reduces the question of the surrender to the sphere of the Realpolitik is not the only one possible on the front of the absolutisation of the textual data of Jer 27–28 (if one were to want to perforce assume that it have intertextual incommunicability with rest of the book). This entirely "horizontal" perspective, that is, one flattened to a political dimension with no possibility of transcendence (at least, that which would be implicated by an ethical dimension, denied on the basis of an atomistic reading of the text), can express itself with the same presuppositions also in a radically "vertical" way, leaving the human dimension with no prospect of a cognitive grasp on the meaning of the divine action.

In addition to what has been noted previously on the subject of divine arbitrariness (cf. § 4.3.1), it is interesting to mention the hermeneutical approach represented by André Neher. This illustrious Jewish scholar lays his thesis out in reference to 21:8–10, but it is opportune to take it up now, for it is even more provocative in the context of 27–28, where, before the prophetic dimension and detailed focalisation on a single tile in the great, historical mosaic, attention is called to a sapiential dimension of a superhistorical, universal, cosmic amplitude. An even more fertile ground if you want to exalt the Absolute, beginning from the implications of the choice called for "now" by Jeremiah.

> Ce choix est véritablement intraduisible en termes d'éthique ou de politique. Pour le rendre intelligible, il faut recourir à un autre langage, à un système référentiel exclusivement axé sur Dieu. Les chemins de la vie et de la mort sont ici tracés par l'unique volonté de Dieu et l'exigence du choix n'a de fondement que dans cette volonté. Quel que soit le scandale de l'exigence divine, et fût-elle en contradiction évidente avec la morale naturelle et avec l'étique politique, on lui doit obéissance parce qu'elle émane de l'absolu, de Dieu.[395]

The ethical dimension, but this time also that which is purely political, are to be excluded in the name of *absolute* necessity of obedience to God. There is some truth in this reading. But there is also, in my opinion, a clear imbalance in favour of a transcendence that does not seem to leave any room for that need (and offering) for meaning which, in the totality of Scripture and the book of Jeremiah itself, abound. In other words, according to A. Neher, remaining in the Jeremianic perspective, one

---

395   A. NEHER, *L'essence du prophétisme*, Paris 1955, 220.

422 Jer 27–28. The world beneath the yoke of the king of Babylon

should give up finding or understanding the reasons for the divine imperative, and would, in fact, put (at least) in parentheses that notion of "justice" that is, in itself, essential to the biblical fabric and not detachable without a price from the (ethical-cultural) regulatory framework of the *Tôrâ*.[396] The image of YHWH sketched by Jer 27–28 would thus be that of a cosmic God, creator, Lord of history, life, and death. An absolutely transcendent God. One who obliges by virtue of who he is. Not, however, an ethical God[397] who presides over and regulates the moral order, since no such law seems to be evoked as the basis of the Jeremianic injunction.

Indeed, as is apparent from a more appropriate contextualisation of Jeremiah's message, the nexus between justice and life/death, creation and history, the divine request and the human ability to understand its meaning, is the semiotic texture that underlies the text that we are studying. Of course, the "justice" referred to here is not shaped in identical terms, in relation to Israel and the nations, because the people of YHWH are bound by the Covenant and judged on the basis of that. It is the theme of the creator God that reminds us that if there is a single Lord of history, then there is also a created moral order[398] valid for all, that exposes the nations equally to judgment,

---

396 This was effectively underscored by G. VON RAD, G., *Theologie des Alten Testaments*, I, 382: "Es gibt im Alten Testament keinen Begriff von so zentraler Bedeutung schlechthin für alle Lebensbeziehungen des Menschen wie den der צְדָקָה. Er ist der Maßtab nicht nur für das Verhältnis des Menschen zu Gott, sondern auch für das Verhältnis der Menschen untereinander bis hin zu der belanglosesten Streiterei, ja auch für das Verhältnis des Menschen zu den Tieren und zu seiner naturhaften Umwelt. צְדָקָה kann man ohne weiteres als den höchsten Lebenswert bezeichnen, als das, worauf alles Leben, wenn es in Ordnung ist, ruht".

397 On the distinction between cosmic divinities and ethic divinities, I turn to the considerations of R. PETTAZZONI, *L'onniscienza di Dio*, Torino 1955, 43–44, who specifies: "On the one hand, we have the world and the origin of the world, which is the specific object of those attributes that lead up to creative activity; on the other, man and his behaviour, which are the specific object of omniscience and all the attributes which go with it. On the one hand, the creation of the world-order and its preservation *in status quo* is the primary condition, the guarantee, of the existence of the universe, its duration and stability; on the other, we have the foundations of the social order and its repair when it has been violated by men and their misdoings. To violation of the rules of tribal life, conceived as a suspension of human order and a temporary relapse into the chaos of primaeval barbarism, corresponds a suspension of the cosmic order and a reversion to the primaeval chaos through the unchaining of the elements of violence contained in atmospheric phenomena and the cataclysms which follow. These two religious tendencies may now and then converge, and the attributes of the two corresponding groups be concentrated in the person of a single supreme Being who is the eternal and impassible Creator and at the same time omniscient, watchful, and avenging. Thus Yahweh, who created the world, also sends the Deluge. But in other cases the tendencies are felt and satisfied separately, and so we get Creators who are not omniscient, such as Mother Earth, nor good (Coyote), and so on, or on the other hand omniscient Beings who avenge but are not creators, such as Zeus, Jupiter, Helios and others" (Eng. tr. from ID., *The All-Knowing God. Researches into Early Religion and Culture*, Translation by H.J. Rose, London 1956, 24–25). See also the critical re-elaboration of the subject in A. RIZZI, *Pensare dentro la Bibbia*, NBSR 23, Roma 2010, 114–123.

398 Cf. T.E. FRETHEIM, *God and World*, 166.

"Bend your neck beneath the yoke of the king of Babylon!" (27:12)　　　423

and at the same time guarantees the possibility of their salvation as well (and that of the whole world).[399]

Both the ethical and political dimensions in Jer 27–28 are not expunged but *relativised* and subjected or traced back to *obedience to the meaning of the "moment"* (cf. 27:6). Of course, in the background are the fiery oracles of threat and condemnation of the crimes committed by the nations, and the pervious infidelity of Israel that has now reached a point of *no return*. Just as the announcement of the "end" is now without appeal as well,[400] and will, in some form, have to come about. And that is why, on the edge of the abyss, everything is suspended, ethics and political logic: what matters to Jeremiah is no longer to accuse, to recriminate, to insist on the denunciation of sin.[401] The ethical framework of reference, which in Israel is codified (or decoded) by the regulatory complex of the Covenant, is not abolished, obviously. But its essential, foundational, and originary dimension is restored: *the obedience of faith*. In YHWH as God of creation, history, and life. The obedience of faith that precedes and founds every ethical behaviour, the spiritual attitude that gives or should give meaning, in Israel, to every political action.

The horizontal (political) dimension and the vertical dimension (in both the sense of divine transcendence in itself, and insofar as this is the generator of an ethical norm, both within the Covenant and outside of it) are inextricably intertwined in Jer 27–28, though in certain respects, the vertical one prevails. Not in an ethical sense, but not in the perspective of an obliging and indecipherable Absolute either. It is, rather, an absolute (or better still, prophetic) reading of history offered to the limitations of the human being, who is called upon to assume it with his freedom, but not without his sense of reason. The mystery and drama of prophecy is fundamentally this. It is, after all, the entire book of Jeremiah that seems to have been built from the beginning to transform the reader into a reader-prophet. It is no coincidence, in fact, that no other biblical text insists so much on the necessary travail of the discernment of Meaning, on the question of true and false prophecy, on the urgency of speaking out and (actively) deciding, on the basis of the clues and witnesses that emerge from the narrative flow.

It is for this reason that the dramatic clash[402] between Jeremiah and Hananiah in ch. 28 takes place in front of a *mute* public, and practically appears to take place off the stage of the storytelling framework in order to get close to the reader. The scene is dominated only by the Word and its "counter-Word". The recipient *type* of the prophetic imperative, as a single figure and image of human consciousness before the appeal of God, will enter the scene in 38:14–28a, under the narrative guile of King Zedekiah.

399　Cf. *Ibid.*, 180–181.

400　Cf. Jer 5:31.

401　This interpretation presupposes that the "diachrony" of the narrative structure and sequence of events, and the theological development of the book of Jeremiah are seen (or at least taken as "given") as a coherent communicative whole. It is clear that on the basis of a consideration of the diachronic dimension of the historical-critical type, one could hypothesise (albeit with some difficulty in finding grounds) a history for the composition of the text in which the development itself could be interpreted rather as a juxtaposition of different ideologies or theological-political understandings, which could then be traced back to subsequent reworkings and scribal/editorial redactions. This question will be addressed in the following section.

402　Cf. S.A. Nitsche, «Prophetische Texte als dramatische Texte lesen», in: *Lesarten der Bibel. Untersuchungen zu einer Theorie der Exegese des Alten Testaments, eds.* H. Utzschneider – E. Blum, Stuttgart 2006, 155–181.

424   Jer 27–28. The world beneath the yoke of the king of Babylon

He will inevitably have to speak up and contend with the Word. Indeed, it will be he himself who requests it, summoning it (38:14), wrought with anguish over the (inevitable) "now". And together with him and his choice, along with its consequences, the model reader, as well as the empirical one, will be forced to reckon.

5. "They prophesy lies to you, do not listen to them!" (27:16–17). True and false prophecy in the face of crisis and threat of the end

5.1. True and false prophecy in the book of Jeremiah: A fallacious distinction or fallacious negationist argumentation?

5.1.1. The problematic position of M.J. de Jong

The theme of true and false prophecy in the HB (and in the book of Jeremiah as well, particularly in regard to ch. 28[403]) has been the subject of numerous contributions, upon which it will not be possible to dwell here in detail.[404] In any case, it should be

---

403   See M. Buber, «False Prophets (Jeremiah 28)», in: *On the Bible*. Eighteen Studies by Martin Buber, *ed.* N.N. Glatzer, New York 1982, ²2000, 166–171 (translation of a brief essay from 1940); T.W. Overholt, «Jeremiah 27–29: The Question of False Prophecy», *JAAR* 35 (1967) 241–249; Id., *The Threat of Falsehood*. A Study in the Theology of the Book of Jeremiah, SBT 16, London 1970, 24–48; D. Lys, «Jérémie 28 et le problème du faux-prophète, ou la circulation du sens dans le diagnostic prophétique», *RHPR* 59 (1979) 453–482; H. Mottu, «Jeremiah vs. Hananiah. Ideology and Truth in Old Testament Prophecy», in: *The Bible and Liberation*. Political and Social Hermeneutics, *ed.* N.K. Gottwald, Maryknoll 1983, 235–251; R. Brandscheidt, «Der prophetische Konflikt zwischen Jeremia und Hananja», *TThZ* 98 (1989) 61–74; C.R. Seitz, *Theology in Conflict*, 205–214; S. Herrmann, «Jeremia vor Chananja. Die angebliche Krise des Propheten», in: *Von Gott reden*. Beiträge zur Theologie und Exegese des Alten Testaments, *eds.* D. Vieweger – E.-J. Waschke, Neukirchen-Vluyn 1995, 117–122; A. Osuji, «Jer. 28 (MT) and the Question of Prophetic Authenticity (From the Ideological to the Narratological)», *EstBib* 63 (2005) 175–193; Id., «True and False Prophecy», 437–452; M. Kőszeghy, *Der Streit um Babel in den Büchern Jesaja und Jeremia*, BWANT 173, Stuttgart 2007, 128–163; R.D. Wells, Jr., «Dislocations», 322–350; A. Osuji, *Where Is the Truth?* Narrative Exegesis and the Question of True and False y in Jer 26–29 (MT), BEThL 214, Leuven 2010; D. Epp-Tiessen, *Concerning the Prophets*. True and False Prophecy in Jeremiah 23:9–29:32, Eugene 2012; J. Jeremias, *Theologie des Alten Testaments*, GAT 6, Göttingen 2015, 171–187. See also E. Di Pede, «Quando Geremia fa il falso profeta: la tentazione dei Recabiti (Ger 35) come riflessione sulla vera e falsa profezia», *RivBib* 63 (2015) 307–326.

404   To indicate those most important in the history of interpretation: G. von Rad, «Die falsche Propheten», *ZAW* 51 (1933) 109–120; H. Bacht, «Wahres und falsches Prophetentum», *Bib.* 32 (1951) 237–262; G. Quell, *Wahre und falsche Propheten*. Versuch einer Interpretation, BFChTh 46/1, Gütersloh 1952; E. Jacob, «Quelques remarques sur les faux prophètes», *ThZ* 13 (1957) 479–486; J.L. Crenshaw, *Prophetic Conflict*. Its Effect Upon Israelite Religion, BZAW 124, Berlin 1971; A. Jepsen, «Gottesmann und Prophet. Anmerkungen zum Kapitel 1. Könige 13», in: *Probleme biblischer Theologie*, 171–182; L. Ramlot, «Prophétisme», 1040–1050 (III: Les faux prophètes); F.-L. Hossfeld – I. Meyer, *Prophet gegen Prophet*. Eine Analyse der

"They prophesy lies to you, do not listen to them!" (27:16-17)   425

alttestamentlichen Texte zum Thema: Wahre und falsche Propheten, BiBe 9, Fribourg 1973 (on Jeremiah, pp. 57–112); J. ALONSO DÍAZ, «El discernimiento entre el verdadero y el falso profeta según la Biblia», *EE* 49 (1974) 5–17; G. MÜNDERLEIN, *Kriterien wahrer und falscher Prophetie. Entstehung und Bedeutung im Alten Testament*, EHS.T 33, Bern – Frankfurt – Las Vegas 1974, ²1979; A. GONZÁLEZ, «Verdaderos y falsos profetas», in: *Profetas verdaderos, profetas falsos*, eds. A. GONZÁLEZ – N. LOHFINK – G. VON RAD, Salamanca 1976, 13–76; J.L CRENSHAW, «Prophecy, False», *IDBSup*, Nashville 1976, 701–702; J.A. SANDERS, «Hermeneutics in True and False Prophecy», in: *Canon and Authority*. Essays in Old Testament Religion and Theology, eds. G.W. COATS – B.O. LONG, Philadelphia 1977, 21–41; W. VOGELS, «Comment discerner le prophète authentique?», *NRTh* 99 (1977) 681–701; I. MEYER, *Jeremia und die falschen Propheten*, OBO 13, Freiburg – Göttingen 1977, 15–45; S.J. DE VRIES, *Prophet Against Prophet*. The Role of the Micaiah Narrative (I Kings 22) in the Development of Early Prophetic Tradition, Grand Rapids 1978; M. McNAMARA, «Critères de discernement en Israël. Vrais et faux prophètes», *Concilium* 139 (1978) 11–22; W. GROSS, «Lying Prophet and Disobedient Man of God in 1 Kings 13: Role Analysis as an Instrument of Theological Interpretation of an OT Narrative Text», *Semeia* 15 (1979) 97–135; F.-L. HOSSFELD, «Wahre und falsche Prophetie in Israel», *BiKi* 38 (1983) 139–144; B.S. CHILDS, *Old Testament Theology in a Canonical Context*, Philadelphia 1986, 133–144; G.T. SHEPPARD, «True and False Prophecy within Scripture», in: *Canon, Theology, and Old Testament Interpretation*. Essays in Honor of B.S. Childs, eds. G.M. TUCKER *et al.*, Philadelphia 1988, 262–282; C. SCHNEIDER, *Krisis des Glaubens*. Zur Frage der sogenannten falschen Prophetie im Alten Testament, ThA 46, Berlin 1988; D.W. VAN WINKLE, «1 Kings XIII: True and False Prophecy», *VT* 39 (1989) 31–43; A. IBÁÑEZ ARANA, «Jeremias y "los profetas"», *ScrVict* 35 (1988) 5–56, 233–319; ID. «Los criterios de profecía», *Lum.* 39 (1990) 193–250; D.G. DEBOYS, «1 Kings XIII – A "New Criterion" Reconsidered», *VT* 41 (1991) 210–212; A. ÁLVAREZ VALDÉS, «El enfrentamiento entre profetas y falsos profetas», *RevBib* 53 (1991) 217–229; R.J. COGGINS, «Prophecy – True and False», in: *Of Prophet's Visions and the Wisdom of Sages*. Essays in Honour of R. Norman Whybray on His Seventieth Birthday, eds. H.A. McKAY – D.J.A. CLINES, JSOT.S 162, Sheffield 1993, 80–94; P.T. REIS, «Vindicating God: Another Look at 1 Kings XIII», *VT* 44 (1994) 376–386; H.-J. HERMISSON, «Kriterien "wahrer" und "falscher" Prophetie. Zur Auslegung von Jeremia 23,16–22 und Jeremia 28,8–9», *ZThK* 92 (1995) 121–139 (= ID., *Studien zu Prophetie und Weisheit*. Gesammelte Aufsätze, eds. J. BARTHEL – H. JAUSS – K. KOENEN, FAT 23, Tübingen 1998, 59–76); R.R. WILSON, «Interpreting Israel's Religion. An Anthropological Perspective on the Problem of False Prophecy», in: ID., *Sociological Approaches to the Old Testament*, GBSP, Philadelphia 1984, 67–80 (= in: *"The Place is Too Small for Us"*. The Israelite Prophets in Recent Scholarship, ed. R.P. GORDON, SBTS 5, Winona Lake 1995, 332–344); M. NISSINEN, «Falsche Prophetie in neuassyrischer und deuteronomistischer Darstellung», in: *Das Deuteronomium und seine Querbeziehungen*, ed. T. VEIJOLA, SESJ 62, Helsinki – Göttingen 1996, 172–195; B. HERR, «Der wahre Prophet bezeugt seine Botschaft mit dem Tod. Ein Versuch zu 1 Kön 13», *BZ* 41 (1997) 69–78; J.E. BRENNEMAN, *Canons in Conflict*. Negotiating Texts in True and False Prophecy, New York 1997; A. LANGE, *Vom prophetischen Wort zur prophetischen Tradition*. Studien zur Traditions- und Redaktionsgeschichte innerprophetischer Konflikte in der Hebräischen Bibel, FAT 34, Tübingen 2002; M.A. SWEENEY, «The Truth in True and False Prophecy», in: *Truth*. Interdisciplinary Dialogues in a Pluralistic Age, eds. C. HELMER – K. DE TROYER, StPT 22, Leuven 2003, 9–26 (= ID., *Form and Intertextuality in Prophetic and Apocalyptic Literature*, FAT 45, Tübingen 2005, 78–93); R.W.L. MOBERLY, *Prophecy and Discernment*, CSCD 14, Cambridge 2006; R.E. CLEMENTS, «Prophecy Interpreted», 32–44; W.J. WESSELS, «Prophet versus Prophet

426   Jer 27–28. The world beneath the yoke of the king of Babylon

noted that a prevailing tendency exists in the history of interpretation, one that is, in fact, assumed and fixed *a priori*, by which the oppositive categories of "true" and "false" prophecy are commonly applied. While this does not generally hold the significance of attributing values but remains merely descriptive (above all in reference to the biblical communicative context, particularly of a Deuteronomic matrice), this methodological perspective is looked upon with suspicion or even rejected by some scholars[405] and has been radically put into question in an article by M.J. de Jong[406] on precisely Jer 28:8–9.

---

in the Book of Jeremiah: In Search of the True Prophets», *OTEs* 22 (2009) 733–751 (on Jer 23:9–40); W.H. Schmidt, «"Über die Propheten". Streit um das rechte Wort Jer 23,9–32», in: *Geschichte Israels und deuteronomistisches Geschichtsdenken*. Festschrift zum 70. Geburtstag von Winfried Thiel, eds. P. Mommer – A. Scherer, AOAT 380, Münster 2010, 241–258; R. Willi, «"Anhaltspunkte" zur Unterscheidung von wahrer und falscher Prophetie aus der Perspektive des Alten Testaments», *FKTh* 26 (2010) 96–106; J.T. Hibbard, «True and False Prophecy: Jeremiah's Revision of Deuteronomy», *JSOT* 35 (2011) 339–358; A. Catastini, «Who Were the False Prophets?», *Hen.* 34 (2012) 330–366; D. Epp-Tiessen, *Concerning the Prophets*; J. Jeremias, «Remembering and Forgetting: "True" and "False" Prophecy», in: *Remembering and Forgetting in Early Second Temple Judah*, eds. E. Ben Zvi – C. Levin, FAT 85, Tübingen 2012, 45–54; W.J. Wessels, «True and False Prophets: Who is to Decide? A Perspective from Jeremiah 23:9–40», *JSem* 21 (2012) 137–156; S.B. Tarrer, *Reading with the Faithful*. Interpretation of True and False Prophecy in the Book of Jeremiah from Ancient to Modern Times, JThIS 6, Winona Lake 2013; T. Römer, «Comment distinguer le vrai du faux prophète?», in: *Comment devient-on prophète?*Actes du colloque organisé par le Collège de France, Paris, les 4–5 avril 2011, eds. J.-M. Durand – T. Römer – M. Bürki, Göttingen 2014, 109–120; F. Arena, *Prophetic Conflicts in Jeremiah, Ezekiel, and Micah*. How Post-Exilic Ideologies Created the False (and the True) Prophets, FAT 2. Reihe 121, Tübingen 2020.

405 See, e.g. G. Garbini, *History and Ideology*, 116–117; R.P. Carroll, «Poets Not Prophets: A response to "Prophets through the Looking-Glass"», *JSOT* 27 (1983) 25–31, Id., «Whose Prophet? Whose History? Whose Social Reality? Troubling the Interpretative Community Again. Notes Towards a Response to T.W. Overholt's Critique», *JSOT* 48 (1990) 33–49 (esp. p. 38); M. Nissinen, «Die Relevanz der neuassyrischen Prophetie», 250–251.

406 M.J. de Jong, «The Fallacy». Even more recently, along a similar line of reasoning is the contribution by F. Arena, *Prophetic Conflicts*, 181–188, which however, in my opinion, does not have the same argumentative weight. From the difficulties in establishing solid criteria for who were true and false prophets, the author concludes that this differentiation was not part of the socio-politico-religious context to which the Book of Jeremiah refers. This seems to me a *non sequitur*. Additionally, the author *en passant* states that in Jeremiah there is no sign of the Deuteronomic criterion (Deut 18:18–22) of "fulfilment" ("[it] is never employed in Jeremiah", p. 182), but then corrects himself in n. 6 saying that it is actually attested in Jer 28, but adding that this criterion is "quickly dismissed". On the contrary, one should note that this criterion not only forms the foundation of the canonisation of the whole Jeremianic tradition, but it is clearly found even in more decisive contexts then Jer 28, as in Jer 37,19 e 32,24. The book of Jeremiah has no need to make more explicit what is already absolutely clear (and one should not be surprised by this; cf. p. 183): false visions and prophecies by the antagonists of Jeremiah are such because they have deceived the people in explaining the true meaning of the unfolding history (instead attested by Jeremiah).

"They prophesy lies to you, do not listen to them!" (27:16–17)   427

According to him, it would be a fallacious conceptual instrumentation, since it lacks any historical foundation and moreover is not so relevant in the textual perimeter of the HB, whose texts regarding to the prophetic phenomenon would have been misinterpreted as a result of the influence of an impertinent reading of Deut 18:15–22 (which instead makes the question of discernment between true and false prophecy a decisive problem). His argumentation can be summarised in the following synthetic and consequential points:

1) The idea of there being an oppositional distinction between "true and false" prophecy would not be verifiable in ancient Near East sources, and this despite the author himself mentioning the divinatory practice of verifying oracular communication through *extispicium* common in Mari. According to him then, the cases of "false prophecy" reported by M. Nissinen,[407] in which the sovereign shows concern about oracles adverse to him, would only regard the need to adopt effective countermeasures for dealing with their potentially dangerous (but not false) content.[408]

2) Even in the case of Israel and Judah, reiterating the need to distinguish the historical-social phenomenon of prophecy from the literary image of it that emerges from the biblical texts, it would be incongruous to speak of "false prophecy". Amongst the functions of the historical prophet, in fact, who the author fundamentally sees as dedicated to the custody of the collective well-being (to wit, the established order), was that of making threats of disaster precisely so that they would not come about. A prophecy of the sort could never have been "false". Their fulfilment was, in fact, conditioned on the execution of specific divine wishes.

3) Given these premises, the author has no difficulty in declaring the categorical distinction between true and false prophecy fallacious. Given that the opposition between false prophets announcing peace and true prophets prophesying the irrevocable end of the established order would be only a later construction in the biblical literature, he proposes to demonstrate how the present interpretation of Jer 28:8–9, identified as an emblematic text, is vitiated by this perspective which he considers prejudicial.[409]

4) In his opinion, 28:8–9 belongs to an ancient stage of the compositional history of the Jeremianic work, prior to what would later make the historical Jeremiah, interested (only) in the welfare of the state like the ("pro-society") prophets of Mari or Neo-Assyrian prophets, a prophet adverse to the established order of his time, (improbable, and indeed *ex eventu*) announcer of the irrevocable ("contra-society") judgment of YHWH.[410]

---

407   See M. Nissinen, «Falsche Prophetie», 172–195 (in abbreviated form, Id., «Prophecy Against the King in Neo-Assyrian Sources», in: *"Lasset uns Brücken bauen"*. Collected Communications to the 15th Congress of the International Organization for the Study of the Old Testament, *eds.* K.-D. Schunk – M. Augustin, Cambridge 1995, Frankfut am Main 1998, 157–170), for whom it is clear that in the Neo-Assyrian empire as well, the question of false prophecy was a burning one and that, as in the OT, it was not only a theoretical question, but a topmost political risk ("ein estrangiges politische Risiko") requiring urgent measures (p. 172).

408   Cf. M.J. de Jong, «The Fallacy», 2–4.

409   These recall the doubts also expressed over "traditional" interpretation by R.W.L. Moberly, *Prophecy and Discernment*, 100–109.

410   Cf. M.J. de Jong, «The Fallacy», 4, 27.

428 Jer 27–28. The world beneath the yoke of the king of Babylon

5) Verse 8 ("*From ancient times, the prophets who came before me and you prophesied against numerous countries and against great kingdoms, of war, calamity, and pestilence*") would have nothing to do with the "true prophets of judgment", because this kind of prophecy would not actually be so ancient (the reference is to the expression מִן־הָעוֹלָם, rendered as "from time immemorial"). It would therefore concern not the content of the Jeremianic message, but rather that of Hananiah(!) against Babylon (which, in fact, would fall within the group of powerful kingdoms ordinarily object of the prophecies of doom).[411]

6) Verse 9 ("*As for the prophet who prophesies peace: only when his word is fulfilled will he be recognised as the prophet that the Lord has truly sent*") would regard the possibility of a prophecy of peace (שָׁלוֹם) and not the criteria for its falsification (in the Popperian sense, I would say). Moreover, it should not be considered related to the principle of fulfilment enucleated in Deut 18:21–22, given the small ("not so impressive")[412] number of close lexical contacts. As for parallelism with v. 8 (which cites *foreign nations* as the object of prophetic communication), this would concern not Hananiah's reassuring message towards the kingdom of Judah (nor that of the so-called "false prophets" mentioned in the book Jeremiah, who never address a foreign nation in positive terms), but rather that of Jeremiah towards Babylon(!), according to that which is announced to the exiles of 597 in 29:5–7.

As can be seen, the most common (and, in my opinion, obvious) interpretation is entirely inverted. But is it really a plausible reading of the textual data, when these are considered in the light of their communicative context?

5.1.2. Some critical notes

As we can see, the question of the comparison between true and false prophecy is strictly linked to the policy to be held before the Babylonian power. Amongst the various issues raised by the author, all worthy of consideration, I will limit myself for now to a critical assessment of the arguments put forth to deny the oppositional categorisation between true and false prophecy in reference to the text we are presently studying.

1) That the question of discernment between "true and false prophecy" was important in the world of the Mari is precisely demonstrated by the habitual practice of subjecting the prophetic oracles to ("objective") external verification through *extispicium*. It is therefore irrelevant that a technical categorical distinction not be found on a lexical level (and in a limited documental context). That then M.J. de Jong himself recalls this practice,[413] rightly pointing out its purpose ("this was to check whether the oracle and its interpretation were trustworthy"), only to then infer the opposite ("The idea that certain kinds of prophetic messages were 'false', and others 'true', however, is lacking") is surprising.[414] Actually, what can be affirmed is that there be

---

411 Cf. *Ibid.*, 7, 13–14.
412 Cf. *Ibid.*, 11–13.
413 Cf. *Ibid.*, 2.
414 Even more surprising is the fact that the author himself remembers, as is clearly attested in at least one case (cf. S. PARPOLA, *Letters from Assyrian and Babylonian Scholars*, SAA 10, Helsinki 1993, 143, text 179, l. 19–23 *verso*), that even the

"They prophesy lies to you, do not listen to them!" (27:16-17)   429

no attestation of an explicit lexicalization, certainly not the underlying idea. Indeed, from the examples of a Neo-Assyrian matrix adopted by M. Nissinen, the same conclusion can be deduced.

The error of M.J. de Jong here is due to a perspectival reduction, by which he seems to intend the question of "true or false prophecy" simply as a categorisation that concerns the prophecy's realisation or not. As M. Nissinen,[415] on the other hand, clearly points out, in the self-understanding of the political-religious institutions of the ancient Near East, this criteria concerned also (or primarily) the *orthodoxy* or not of an oracular communication. If it was believed that the *content* of a prophecy were to undermine the ideological foundations upon which the state was based, and hence the authority of the sovereign himself (legitimated *ex ante* by the will of the deities), it was natural that it would be perceived as a threat, but precisely for its intrinsic *falsehood*. This is the same criteriology that is clearly exposed in Deut 13:2–6 (a prophet or dreamer who induces people to follow foreign gods, even by virtue of a sign or prodigy, is to be deemed false for this very reason[416] and deserving of death) and is basically the same reason that justifies the violent and indignant reaction to the Jeremianic message (in Jer 26:8–9, above all). The only horizon of meaning in which a distinction between "true and false" prophecy would fall would be that in which the prophetic phenomenon be entirely absorbed within a magical vision of reality, so only the "intrinsic force" of the oracular words would count in order to manipulate world events and people, and not their truth. But this is not the case. The magical dimension is most certainly present in the socio-cultural context of the ancient Near East, but not in terms that identify magic with prophecy. There is an area where specialists in the field are recognised as having the ability to use occult forces to influence the real, but there is also another, in which the destiny of humankind depends instead upon the assumption of what is right and true, and which, in its contingent aspects, above all, can be the object of (divine) revelation only through diversified divinatory practices (amongst which, those that are prophetic).

2) It is clear that the oracles of doom linked to the non-compliance of the divine will are infalsifiable if the conditions they impose are implemented.[417] This is precisely their goal: to provoke a saving change and not to be realised. An obvious example is

---

"verification" through *extispicium* could itself be subject to falsification or not (cf. M.J. DE JONG, «The Fallacy», 2, n. 20).

415   Cf. M. NISSINEN, «Falsche Prophetie», 174–176.

416   Here again: even though the term שֶׁקֶר ("falsity") does not recur, it is clear that what is being discussed is specifically idolatric lies and those who propagate them. It suffices to look a few vv. earlier, in Deut 12:30: "be careful *to* not *be caught in a trap* (√נקשׁ ni.)". What is a trap (מוֹקֵשׁ), if not the material realisation of deceit? (cf. Deut 7:16, 25; 32:37–39; always in relation to the idolatric danger).

417   The case of prophecy against Jehoiakim in 36:30 is, instead, a particular case, which would seem to have failed, revealing itself thus to be "false" (both with regard to the manner of his death and for the fact that, even if only for three months, his son Jehoiachin did succeed him on the throne of Judah). But it is precisely through provocations like this that the book of Jeremiah invites the reader to comprehend what is intended by "true prophecy" within it, entering into a level of meaning (symbolical-theological) that is deeper than the literal level. We have already seen this with regard to 21:1–10. For further study on the question of 36:30, see K. SCHMID, «Nebukadnezar», 233–241.

430 Jer 27–28. The world beneath the yoke of the king of Babylon

the oracle of Micah recalled in Jer 26:18–19.[418] But that is not the point. It is the oracles of "peace", that is, those that reassure the recipients in the face of some danger without asking them for any ethical-cultual obligation in response, that be regardless amenable to verification. Precisely because they promise the fulfilment of a positive fact unconditionally. This is the case of the "false prophets" of the book of Jeremiah (cf. 6:14; 8:11; 23:17; 29:8–9, 21–23, 31–32) and of Hananiah in particular.

3) If it is fallacious to adduce unrealised oracles of doom as negative evidence, then it is likewise, in my opinion, too simplistic to identify *tout-court* the biblical oracles of doom as "oracles of irrevocable judgment",[419] to then classify them as *ex eventu* prophecies of a scribal matrix and reduce the question of "true or false prophecy" to that of being a tardive literary artefact. It is logical that following the exilic catastrophe, the stigmatisation of false messages of hope and the memory of threats of doom (as can be evinced from the LXX[420]) be emphasised, but one can neither stop at the letter of the individual oracles, nor believe that the interpretation of facts according to the "blame-punishment" scheme be only a later reworking. It suffices to take, as an example, the words of Micah in Jer 26:18: to the letter, they would seem to be a hopeless verdict, but the following v. 19 clearly shows that those words were also understood in a conditional sense.

It is, rather, the ultimate goal of the prophetic message that need be kept in mind, for this is always (from both the historical and literary points of view) aimed at salvation (in some form) and not at a useless (or merely exemplary or anecdotal) pre-view and (pre-announcement) of the end, even when the literal surface of the text seems to say the contrary (emblematic, for its "international" scope, Jon 3:4, 10). Telling of this horizon of meaning is the prophetic "perhaps" (אוּלַי; Ezek 12:3; Amos 5:15; Sof 2:3; Lam 3:29), which is present at key points in the book of Jeremiah (cf. 26:3; 36:3, 7) and which, as I have noted elsewhere (cf. ch. III, 3.1.3, n. 44), in any case, seems to announce the disaster in two stages: at first, it is conditional on conversion, while from a certain point on, given the pervicaciousness of the people, it is announced as inevitable. And yet, it is precisely the theme of surrender to the king of Babylon, as we will better see in the next chapter of the present dissertation, that shows a salvation that is possible up to the extreme limit of the befalling of the "end" (cf. 38:17–20). It is very strange then that the author considers the interpretation of the end of the reign of Judah offered by the book of Jeremiah according to the conceptual scheme of "fault-punishment" to be a necessarily tardive reworking[421] when he himself rightly

---

418 Cf. P. ROTA SCALABRINI, «Geremia e i suoi predecessori», in: *Processo esegetico ed ermeneutica credente: una polarità intrinseca alla Bibbia*. XL Settimana Biblica Nazionale (Roma, 8–12 settembre 2008), eds. E. MANICARDI – G. BORGONOVO, RStB 22, Bologna 2010, 25–42 (here, pp. 29–31).

419 Cf. M.J. DE JONG, «The Fallacy», 5. Cf. also ID., «Biblical Prophecy – A Scribal Enterprise», 39 and *passim*: "unconditional and total judgement".

420 Which, all told, actually shows an accentuation of the question that took place in not in immediately "post-exilic" times, but rather during a phase of the tradition even further from the event.

421 "The later revision of the early traditions decisively re-shaped the 'prophecies' of Jeremiah, by interpreting the disasters as Yahweh's punishment of the sins of Judah" (M.J. DE JONG, «The Fallacy», 5).

"They prophesy lies to you, do not listen to them!" (27:16–17)   431

recalls that it was a widespread hermeneutical model of history, innervated in the atavistic mentality of the whole ancient Near East.[422] It is truly quite unlikely that it be an extemporised post-exilic reminiscence.

4) To concentrate on 28:8–9 without adequate contextualisation of the logic of the Jeremianic message within the sequence of dialogical exchanges that structure ch. 28 (to be considered, regardless, in close relationship, both in form and content, to the preceding ch. 27) is misleading. And the considerations regarding the history of the composition proposed by the author, rather than rely on objective textual clues of a textual nature (extrabiblical attestations punctually compared to the LXX, which is even often referred to), are of an entirely conjectural nature and are based on an interpretation of thematic elements that is debatable. Let's look at why.

5) Setting aside the question of antiqueness or not of the prophecy of doom, which would merit a discourse of its own, the fallacy of M.J. de Jong's interpretation of 28:8–9 lies entirely in a misunderstanding of the dominant *communicative focus*[423] in ch. 28 (which, in turn, need be placed in close relation to ch. 27 more than to ch. 29, which – while part of a wider unit – regards a less pertinent situation). He understands v. 8 as if it were in reference to the prophecy of Hananiah, while from the structure and logic of the discourse, it can clearly be understood that Jeremiah is referring to what he himself prophesied to the nations and the kingdom of Judah. It is the call for submission to the king of Babylon that is presented as the "disaster" to be accepted, or risk that an even graver disaster come about: total destruction. The error, once again,

---

422 Cf. M.J. DE JONG, «Biblical Prophecy – A Scribal Enterprise», 42; ID., «The Fallacy», 5, 24–25.

423 Linguists, by the term "focus", refer to those communicative processes by which an interlocutor is able to emphasise certain information at the expense of others (cf. J. LYONS, *Semantics*, 503: "In any question that we might put relating to the components or circumstances of a situation, there is something that is presupposed and something that is in focus"). It is not a question of formalising the centrality of a discursive theme, but of the modality by which the speaker manifests their particular perspective on the same central themes disclosed to the listener-reader. Every language has multiple strategies for emphasising one piece of information over others, even without altering the syntactic disposition of the words (think, e.g. of intonation), which remains a very effective method for highlighting the focal point (as rhetorical analysis also points out). For further study in this regard, see H. WEIL, *The Order of Words in the Ancient Languages Compares with that of the Modern Languages*, Boston 1887; J. VACHEK, ed., *The Linguistic School of Prague*. An Introduction to Its Theory and Practice, Bloomington 1966; J. FAIRBAS, «Some Aspects of the Czechoslovak Approach to Problems of Functional Sentence Perspective», in: *Papers on Functional Sentence Perspective*, ed. F. DANES, The Hague 1974, 11–37; W. CHAFE, «Giveness, Contrastiveness, Definiteness, Subjects, Topics, and Point of View», in: *Subject and Topic*, ed. C.N. LI, New York 1976, 25–56; S. DIK, *Functional Grammar*, Amsterdam 1978, Dordrecht ³1981; S.C. DIK – M.E. HOFFMANN – J.R. DE JONG – S.I. DJIANG – H. STROOMER – L. DE VRIES, «On the Typology of Focus Phenomena», in: *Perspectives on Functional Grammar*, eds. T. HOEKSTRA – H. VAN DER HULST – M. MOORTGAT, Dordrecht 1981, 41–64; S.C. DIK, *The Theory of Functional Grammar*. Part I: The Structure of the Clause, FGS 20, Dordrecht 1989, Berlin – New York ²1997; D.L. PAYNE, ed., *Pragmatics of Word Order Flexibility*, Amsterdam 1992.

432 Jer 27–28. The world beneath the yoke of the king of Babylon

lies in a reading of the textual data that is purely formal (of both vv. 8–9), which, in itself, in effect, could even suit his interpretation, but only if decontextualised and considered in a way that is detached from their pragmatic dimension.[424]

Actually, Jeremiah is proposing, and not without difficulty and a certain degree of embarrassment (as a number of authors point out) a double (interdependent) criterion of discernment of the true prophecy. The *first* regards the recognition of an extraordinary thematic *convergence*: the true prophets have always announced a *negative* message. True prophecy, Jeremiah says, has always[425] been that of misfortune. But "true" in what sense? Not (always) in the sense of fulfilment (because this was precisely what it wanted to avoid), but certainly in that of the instances of conversion it had wanted to generate. This is the dynamic to be taken seriously every time for adequate discernment, and obviously Jeremiah refers to what he said in ch. 27, since Hananiah's speech (and the gesture of the breaking of the yoke) presupposes it clearly. This true prophetic message in v. 8 refers to the threatening prospect of "war, calamity, and pestilence" (מִלְחָמָה וּלְרָעָה וּלְדָבֶר). Here is the *key* textual element, which allows us to grasp the true focus of the Jeremianic discourse (and therefore, by opposition, also that of Hananiah). The expression in fact remodulates and recalls the triad of disasters announced *by Jeremiah himself* in 27:8 against all the nations mentioned: namely "sword, hunger, plague" (חֶרֶב וּבָרָעָב וּבַדֶּבֶר). It is certainly true that it is not correct to make two stand-alone categories of "peace" or of "disaster": prophesying peace for one kingdom often meant decreeing disaster for another, and vice versa. But here, it is important to distinguish the principal *focus* from that which underlies it, the objective of the oracular discourse from its collateral implications.

6) The *second* criterion regards the eventuality of a prophecy of "peace". For this to be true, and along with it, the prophet who announces it, it must *come about*. Or

---

424 As is rightfully pointed out by L. ANOLLI, *Fondamenti*, 117–118, "Meaning is not a mental entity that is *static, univocal, and abstract*, but is rather *dynamic, motivated and concrete*, since it is a contingent result of an exchange and collaboration between speakers in the use of specific (linguistic and extralinguistic) signs in an immediate context. [...] A focalisation of the meaning is an active, dynamic, and reciprocally shared process that takes time and concerns not only an attention to that which has been said but also to the perspective through which that which has been said in that circumstance is to be understood. Therefore, the meaning is generated by the manner in which the communicative focus takes shape through the belief system, moved by the scopes and intentions of the participants, guided by a certain flow of ideas" (my translation).

425 It is precisely to this accentuation of the dimension of *totality* (of time, senders, and recipients) that expressions referring to "old times" (or time immemorial) and foreign nations are to be traced, be they "numerous countries" or "great kingdoms". If this symbolic dimension is not grasped, one falls into the error of wanting to take a census of the names of prophets, epochs, prophecies, and their respective nations (and to invert, as does M.J. de Jong, the relation between the subject and the content of the prophecies), which does not seem to be quite the intentionality of the sentence. What Jeremiah wants to emphasise, in fact, is the *constant* (negativity) that accompanies true prophecy, and the exceptionality or problematic nature of the prophecy of peace.

"They prophesy lies to you, do not listen to them!" (27:16–17)   433

rather: it can be certified as true (and truly sent by YHWH the respective prophet) "when it comes about"[426] (v. 9: בְּבֹא דְבַר), a phrase that is to be read according to the meaning that would be attributed to it by almost all of the speakers (of then and now), that is, interpreting the "hidden" conditional[427] in this as if it were a corresponding biconditional: "*if, and only if* it comes about".[428] It is also a question in this case of implementing (amongst the other possibilities) a pragmatic approach to the text in the exegetic stage.[429]

Jeremiah is by no means against what Hananiah proposes per se. On the contrary, he considers it a highly desirable prospect (cf. 28:6). First thing, however, given the premise of v. 8, this cannot come about by contradicting or eliminating the message of doom. The structure of the book of Jeremiah itself, as I have highlighted (cf. ch. I), and in particular the very message of "handing oneself over to the king of Babylon", is but the proclamation of a peace generated from within disaster by means of God's creative power. This is why Jeremiah himself will prophesy salvation with words similar to those of Hananiah (cf. 30:8, 10) or with gestures of hope that are seemingly rash (cf. ch. 32). The context will be totally different: he does not announce an easy consolation, but invites accepting the disaster and its meaning, for only from this obedience and after this travail, will YHWH create something new on earth (cf. 31:22, 31–33). The *focus* of the announcement of peace mentioned in 28:9 is not at all the well-being of Babylon that Jeremiah asks to pray for in 29:7. As proof of the logic of the Jeremianic prophecy just illustrated, in ch. 29, it is understood that yes, Jeremiah can announce peace (conditional on another form of "surrender", that of real acceptance of God's punishment: cf. 29:6–7, 10, 28), but only because the disaster for the exiles has already

---

426   Even if this raises the question of *how* this is to be recognised in the moment it is announced.

427   See in this regard (*pace* M.J. DE JONG, «The Fallacy», 12) the cases of hidden conditionals (common to all languages) analysed by L.R. HORN, «From *if* to *iff*: Conditional Perfection as Pragmatic Strengthening», *JPrag* 32 (2000) 289–326 (here, pp. 319–320).

428   *Pace* M.J. DE JONG, «The Fallacy», 12–13 and 14 n. 48. This is the linguistic phenomenon of *conditional perfection*, that is, the tendency of speakers to "render a conditional perfect", that is, to interpret a conditional "as if it were a corresponding biconditional" (C. BIANCHI, *Pragmatica cognitiva*, 96–102, my translation). Experimental studies show that it is a tendency that is practically generalised, which cannot be disregarded even in the exegetic stage: 80 % to 90 % of the subjects would consider the inference from "if the word of the prophet is realised, it will be known that it is was actually sent by YHWH" to "if the word of the prophet does not come true, it will be known that it was not actually sent by YHWH" perfectly legitimate. The conditional of the first sentence, in other words, conveys the content expressed by the biconditional: "*if and only if* the word of the prophet is realised will one know that it was indeed sent by YHWH".

429   In this regard, in fact, L.R. HORN, «From *if* to *iff*», 321, emphasises that "the tendency to read sufficient conditions (e.g. the protasis of *if p then q*) as necessary-and-sufficient conditions (*iff p, q*) involves not the semantics of what conditionals *say* but the pragmatics of what speakers can be rationally assumed to *implicate* (or to *sous-entendre*)".

434   Jer 27–28. The world beneath the yoke of the king of Babylon

been fulfilled, it is underway! In 28:9, on the contrary, the peace spoken about is that which Hananiah prophesies, *at no expense*,[430] for the kingdom of Judah. That which contrasts head-on with the disaster of the Babylonian yoke carried symbolically on Jeremiah's neck. In both cases, the principle of fulfilment announced in Deut 18:15–22 remains a significant point of reference, aside from the formal number of lexical contacts. The fate of Hananiah stands out as a *sign of death*, while the salvation of the prophetic body (cf. 26:24; 38:7–13; 39:11–14; 40:1–6) anticipates, in a *sign of life*, the fulfilment of the salvific promises for all the people, the realisation of which must however wait not "within two years",[431] but at least after the seventy years announced by Jeremiah (Jer 25:11–12; 29:10; Dan 9:2; 2 Chr 36:21; cf. Isa 23:15, 17). The symbolic appearance of this numerical figure, well known also in extrabiblical contexts,[432] should not be seen as contradicting its historical confirmation/reference (cf. § 2.1, n. 6).

In summary, I can only reiterate how fundamental it is in exegesis to have, in addition to a rigorous framing of formal data, a correct definition of the *communicative context* within which these are inserted and from which they receive adequate pragmatic pertinentisation, so as to avoid critical misunderstandings of approach and aberrant interpretive conclusions.

5.2. "Do not listen to your prophets…" (27:9): The Jeremianic prophetic message and its implications

5.2.1. *To obey (the Word) means to dis-obey (other words)*

From the theological elements of the Jeremianic message highlighted so far,[433] by which YHWH claims his universal lordship over creation and thus the liberty to enter the history of humankind indicating the way to life in obedient listening (27:1–8), stems an *inevitable corollary*.[434] This divine intentionality that reveals here and now the *meaning of history* makes an appeal to those who are animated by altogether other intentions and other logic (e.g.: 1:16; 2:5, 8, 11, 13, 18; 14:10; etc.; Isa 55:8; 65:2; Ps 96:2; Rom 11:33). The *Word* and its human mediation par excellence in the AT, that is, the prophet, judges the present and comes into conflict with *other words* and *other perceptions of meaning*, oftentimes countervailing, and its authoritative strength clashes with other powers (cf. 1:18–19; 2:8, 26; 4:9; 8:1; 18:18; 32:32; etc.) who in turn claim the right to judge and demand to be heard and obeyed, often in the name of the same God (cf. 29:24–28). And it is for this very reason that the established socio-political-religious system can feel threatened right at its foundations and react violently (cf. e.g. 20:1–2; 26:8–9, 11; 37:12–15; 38:1–6, 25, 27).

---

430   At least, on a level of recognition of one's own sin (which is, after all, the central prophetic perspective of the book of Jeremiah). Because from the point of view of the political agenda, given the historical context that can be intuited in the light of 27:3, what would be implied is active involvement in an anti-Babylonian rebellion.

431   I already looked at the meaning and possible implications of this temporal limit in ch. II, § 2.2.2.

432   Cf. K. SCHMID, «Nebukadnezar», 236–237.

433   But also from biblical revelation as a whole.

434   *Pace* W. MCKANE, *Jeremiah*, II, 702.

"They prophesy lies to you, do not listen to them!" (27:16–17)   435

On the other hand, it should be noted that the process (cf. ch. 26) to which the prophet (and the scroll that represents him; cf. ch. 36) is subjected is first and foremost a sign that the strenuousness of discernment to identify the *true word* with which to read one's own story and to which deliver one's life is *ineludible*, because believing a *mendacious word* is not some harmless intellectual option, but can rather lead to catastrophic consequences. The Deuteronomic injunction concerning the elimination of the false prophet from amidst the people (cf. 13:2–6; Deut 18:20 with Jer 28:16–17) is the expression first of all symbolic, of that which concretely, at the present time, Jeremiah, with great insistence, asks be done: do not let themselves be seduced by the "lie" (שֶׁקֶר; 4x: 27:14, 16; 28:15), however reassuring, do not listen (אַל־תִּשְׁמְעוּ; "do not listen!"; 4x, an actual *refrain*: cf. 27:9, 14, 16,17) to other words (i.e. other prophetic-divinatory mediations), eliminate them from their guiding points of reference in order to discern the meaning of the present history correctly, and thus access goodness and salvation.

It is significant that in no other text of the HB as in the book of Jeremiah[435] – particularly with the trial in ch. 26, its isomorphic parallel in ch. 36, and above all, with the confrontation-clash between Jeremiah and Hananiah in ch. 28 – is the question of whether or not prophetic communication be true so extensively and dramatically thematised.[436] The titles of "false prophet" or "false prophets" (ψευδοπροφήτης/ ψευδοπροφῆται), endowed with a specific hermeneutical value, with which the LXX (9x in Jeremiah[437] and 1x in Zechariah) often renders the more generic (and relatively rare) socio-religious qualification of "prophet/prophets" (נְבִיא/נְבִיאִים) of the Jeremianic MT are eloquent signs of this.[438] But even more relevant for my study is the fact that

---

435 Aside from the book of Jeremiah (6:13–15; 23:13–32; 27:14–17; 28; 29:8–9; 15:21–23), the conflict between true and false prophecy is well attested in Ezek 13; Mic 3:5–12. Other important references can be found in Deut 13:2–6; 18:15–22; 1 Kgs 18:21–40; 22:5–28.

436 Despite their being mentioned immediately after the "prophets" (cf. 27:9) as accredited interlocutions amongst the people, other mediations of a divinatory nature ("soothsayers" [קֹסְמִים], "dreamers" [חֲלֹמוֹת], "magicians" [עֹנְנִים] e "sorcerers" [in the HB only the sing. כַּשָּׁף and the pl. with suff. are attested]) seem to be discarded *a priori*. The direct antagonist of the prophet Jeremiah is not a magician, a sorcerer, etc., but just another "prophet".

437 In Jer 6:13; 33:7, 8, 11, 16; 34:7; 35:1; 36:1, 8 (of 56 occurrences of the term נָבִיא in the Jeremianic MT [of a total of 95], normally translated with the corresponding προφήτης in the LXX of Jeremiah). On the various implications on the level of narrative strategy, dependent upon the qualification of "prophet" (נָבִיא) given to Hananiah in the incipit of ch. 28 of the MT (28:1), or of "false prophet" (ψευδοπροφήτης) in the LXX (35:1), see E. Di Pede, «La manière de raconter et l'enjeu du récit: Jérémie présente Ananias en Jer 28,1 MT et 35,1 LXX», BibInt 16 (2008) 294–301.

438 And it does so with its own logic, which seems to mark the discriminating importance of the principle of fulfilment of Deut 18:22. Cf. A. Pietersma – M. Saunders, «To the Reader of Ieremias», in: *A New English Translation of the Septuagint and the Other Greek Translations Traditionally Included under that Title*, eds. A. Pietersma – B.G. Wright, Oxford 2007, 876–881 (here, p. 877). The same term is used in other extrabiblical Judaic texts (cf. e.g.: TesXII.Jud XXI,9; Philo of Alexandria, *De specialibus legibus*, IV,51; Flavius Josephus, *Bellum iudaicum*, VI,5,285 and *passim*; etc.)

436   Jer 27–28. The world beneath the yoke of the king of Babylon

this problem concerns precisely the theological-political theme of submission to the king of Babylon, thus revealing its decisive importance within the book of Jeremiah (and not only), in a historical context that sees the kingdom of Judah faced with the concrete threat of the "end". Or, retrospectively, before the theological enigma of the waning of the visibility of the divine promises.

5.2.2. The truth of the prophetic mission as an authentic relation to the Origin

In Jer 27–28, the question of the truth or not of the prophetic word is expressed not only via reference to the *content-related fact* of its message or its *fulfilment*, but also by the problematisation of its *relational dimension* (inasmuch as it is a word presented as being spoken in the name of Another). In order to recognise the authority it demands, it is of paramount importance to actually know *whence* it has come, what its *origin* be.

Aside from any attempt at self-accreditation with the audience, in an "objective" sense, the true prophet is (only) the one who has been *sent* by YHWH, while the false prophet is the one who has not received this mission, and *therefore* speaks falsely and deceptively in the name of the God of Israel. On closer inspection, the entire book of Jeremiah, while not the only one, intends to found its authority on precisely this criterion from its inception, since it opens with the "vocation story" of 1:4–19, which has an evident legitimising function. But even this (self-)attestation, putting itself, after all, before the judgment of its interlocutors of all times, makes the whole work a single prophetic proclamation on whose origin, ultimately, the reader-listener themself must place judgement.

In 27:15, immediately following the negative imperative to not listen to any prophetic message expressed in words contrary to submission to the king of Babylon (cf. 27:14, 16: for this is tantamount to prophesying [√נבא ni.] a "lie" [שֶׁקֶר]), Jeremiah gives voice to YHWH who explains the reason: "because *I did not send them*, oracle of the Lord" (כִּי לֹא שְׁלַחְתִּים נְאֻם־יְהוָה). With the root שלח, which recalls the trilateral relationship between the sender, messenger, and recipient of the message, both within the human context (cf. e.g. Gen 32:4, 6, 19; 37:13–14, 32; Prov 25:13; 26:6; etc.) and a human-divine one (cf. e.g. Exod 3:10, 12–15; 4:13; Isa 6:8; Jer 1:7; etc.), what is essentially called into question is the ability to lay claim or not, "according to truth" (28:9: בֶּאֱמֶת)[439] to one's relation to the Origin itself of every word, and of every life and existing reality. The theme of *creation* as an absolute principle (cf. 1:5) is thus fused in Jer 27–28 with that of history and the origin of true prophecy (cf. √שלח in Sal 104:10, 30 with 105:17, 26; 107:20; 147:15, 18; Prov 9:1–3), becoming its foundation and principle. This, too, is also an additional layer of meaning with which the category of *ante factum* is dealt in Jer 27–28.

In Jeremiah, the root שלח is attested 89x, that is, more than in any other book of the HB (followed by Exodus, with 74 cases).[440] Of these occurrences, a good 53 refer to

---

and in the NT (cf. Matt 7:15; 24:11, 24; Mark 13:22; Luke 6:26; Acts 13:6; 2 Pet 2:1; 1 John 4:1; Rev 16:13; 19:20, 20:10).

439   The desire to separate the question of the divine origin of the messenger (√שלח) from the theme of the truth/reliability (אֱמֶת) of their message in order to negate the relevance of the thematic polarisation of "true-false prophecy" (as in, e.g. W.L. KELLY, *How Prophecy Works*, 250, 253–254), frankly seems quite forced to me.

440   These are absolute figures, and are to be interpreted as such. If, on the other hand, the percentages of occurrences are compared in relation to the number of words that

"They prophesy lies to you, do not listen to them!" (27:16–17)　　437

the sending of a "messenger" (or a person in charge of a mission, even in a figurative sense, as punitive instruments of God), of which 42 have as a logical, grammatical, and syntactic subject[441] or as "subject of depth" (that is as final recipient) YHWH.[442] Let us see all the Jeremianic occurrences and the distribution of their syntagmatic relationship with the various objects and recipients of reference schematically:

√חלש	OCCURRENCES	SUBJECT	OBJECT	RECIPIENT
	1:7; 19:14; 25:15, 17; 26:12, 15; 42:21; 43:1; 43:2 (with negation לא)[443]	YHWH	Jeremiah	Israel[444]
	7:25(2x); 25:4(2x); 26:5(2x); 28:9; 29:19(2x); 35:15(2x); 44:4(2x)		The (true) prophets	Israel
	14:14, 15; 23:21, 32; 27:15; 28:15; 29:9 (all with negation לא)[445]		The (false) prophets	Israel
	23:38		Message	(False) prophets
	42:5		(Jeremianic) Oracle	Israel

---

make up the respective books, the relationship is inverted, with the book of Exodus in eighth position and Jeremiah in ninth (preceded, in order, by Obad; Mal; 2 Kgs; 2 Sam; 1 Sam; Est; and Amos).

441　For these categorisations and additional specifications, cf. J. LYONS, *Semantics*, 500–511.

442　From a strictly formal, that is, grammatical-syntactic, point of view, in four cases (27:3; 29:1, 28, 31[2x]), the subject is not YHWH, but his prophet Jeremiah. According to the text, however, Jeremiah acts on the behalf of He who sent him, to wit, as a "surface subject" (or at least apparently so), making YHWH the (true) "underlying subject" of the phrase, insofar as He is the originating cause of the prophetic message. For an in-depth look at the question from a theological point of view, see E.K. HOLT, «Word of Jeremiah–Word of God: Structures of Authority in the Book of Jeremiah», in: *Uprooting and Planting*, 172–189, where the linear relationship (or of overlapping-coincidence) between God, the word of God, and the prophet Jeremiah (and Baruch) is interpreted as a (cascading) metaphorical expansion of divine communication (cf. p. 188). These different categorical perspectives of the linguistic field (even if applied herein in an analogous manner) are very important in the exegetic field as well, so as to not risk being bound by a traditional definition of "subject" ("he who performs the action"), at this point unsustainable since it refers to an incongruous notion of agentivity of the nominal syntagm.

443　Here, it is the leaders Azariah and Johanan, and "all the insolent men" who accuse Jeremiah of not being sent by YHWH.

444　Given the synthetic purposes of the outline, I use this "umbrella" term as a vague category, without further (and, in other contexts, appropriate) clarifications, to refer generically to the people of the Covenant.

445　The Lord states that he has not sent these prophets to announce his word (in 28:15, it is Jeremiah who personally accuses Hananiah).

√שלח	OCCURRENCES	SUBJECT	OBJECT	RECIPIENT
	8:17; 16:16(2x); 24:10; 29:17 25:9, 16, 27 48:12 49:37 51:2		Punitive agents	Israel Israel and the nations Moab Elam Babylon
	27:3 29:1, 28, 31(2x)	Jeremiah (YHWH)	Yokes Message ("letter")	to the ambassadors to the exiles of 597
	42:6, 9, 20	The leaders	Jeremiah (mediator)	YHWH
	2:10; 9:16; 14:3	Others	Various	Various

As can be observed, in the book of Jeremiah, the theme of sending (expressed by the root שלח) and thus that of the origin of the message and/or messenger is an eminently *theological* question. The reference (or not) to YHWH is central and determinant, both in the case of the ministry of Jeremiah and other true prophets (and for the punitive actions of God, which always have a semiotic-communicative significance), as well as when false prophets are stigmatised (*via negationis*). On this basis, Jeremiah himself is explicitly accused of false prophecy in 43:2 by the people who want to flee to Egypt in fear of the Babylonian retaliation. We are in a context in which, even after the fall of Jerusalem, the decisive theme of the Jeremianic prophecy is once again surrender to Babylon. It is precisely the *origin* of his message that is radically questioned (cf. 43:2: "the Lord our God did not *send* you"; לֹא שְׁלָחֲךָ יְהוָה אֱלֹהֵינוּ) because as a pretext, it is identified as having a source that is human, all too human (not YHWH, but the scribe-secretary Baruch, with his manipulative intentions).[446] And with this, Jeremiah is placed on the same level as the false prophets.[447]

And indeed, at a first glance, or considered in the light of an exegesis focalised only on formal references of a lexical nature, his message may well lay itself open to such criticism. Indeed, while if Hananiah's words give the impression that a new Isaiah has appeared to renew the salvific reassurances of the ancient prophet (cf. Isa 9:3; 10:27; 14:25),[448] then Jeremiah, on the other hand, does seem to assume the malevolent (and outrageous) role of the Assyrian emissary in the scenario of 2 Kgs 18:13–19:37, and in political circumstances that are not all that different. The "great cupbearer" (רַב־שָׁקֵה)

---

446 And it is therefore understandable why those who reject Jeremiah's message mention YHWH by calling him "our God" (אֱלֹהֵינוּ). The logic is perverse, because it is over-turned, but stringent: to follow a false prophecy means to obey a false god as well. The LXX does not have this emphasis (οὐκ ἀπέστειλέν σε κύριος πρὸς ἡμᾶς). The text of 4Q72a[Jerᵈ], l. 1 (Jer 43:2–3) lacks almost all of v. 2, but, according to the reconstruction by E. Tov (DJD XV, 203–204 pl. XXXVII), which takes into account the margins of the fragment and the space of the missing letters, appears to presuppose the lesson attested by the MT.

447 Cf. G. FISCHER, *Jeremia 26–52*, 418–419; 428.

448 Cf. in this regard what is highlighted in § 4.1.6.

"They prophesy lies to you, do not listen to them!" (27:16–17)　　　439

Sennacherib (cf. 2 Kgs 18:19), from beneath the walls of an anguished Jerusalem, had once sought, on behalf of his great sovereign, to discourage the leaders and all the people with strong words and images, inviting them to renounce every vain resistance and urging them to docile submission, because Egypt's aid would have proved to be a delusion (cf. 2 Kgs 18:19–27, 33–35).[449] A devious figure, who along with ostentatious assurance presented himself as being interested in Jerusalem's true good, promising – along with an inevitable *exile* – *peace* and prosperity (cf. 2 Kgs 18:31–32). Indeed, an obligatory path of peace, since willing or unwilling, they would have had to bend to the indomitable power of Assyria regardless, as YHWH himself had decreed (cf. 2 Kgs 18:25).

The narrator made the "great cupbearer" speak as such, placing the question of the *provenance* of the communication at the centre and tracing it back not so much or not only to Sennacherib (cf. 1 Kgs 18:19 and 27 [√חלש]), but ultimately to the Lord himself (cf. 1 Kgs 18:25). In this manner, he presented the reader with the possibility that Assyria was nothing more than an instrument of YHWH and, in fact, he assigned the figure of the Assyrian messenger a major *prophetic* connotation,[450] given the circumstances (which will then, by the outcome of the episode, be revealed as deceptive). It was the same significance of prophecy that now, at the time of the Babylonian threat, the tones and contents of the oracle of Jeremiah seemed to take on. For this reason, it would have been easy, sooner or later, to directly accuse the prophet of Anathoth of being an undercover agent paid by the enemy power, or at least a defeatist and traitor to the nation, with the inevitable consequences (which, in fact, will come about in Jer 26:8–11; 37:13; 38:1–4; cf. 43:1–4). It is rather obvious, then, that a *true* prophet is seen in Hananiah instead, at least by those who understood the mystery of the *origin* of the prophetic message as only a fact of *tradition* of what was already known, and not of *creative fidelity*[451] modulated in its expressions and its indications by God's auto-revelation in the mutable historical, theological, and political context of Israel and the peoples.

449　Cf. B.S. CHILDS, *Isaiah and the Assyrian Crisis*, SBT.SS 3, London 1967, 78–93, according to whom the discourse of the great cupbearer reflects a historical reality.

450　See D. RUDMAN, «Is the Rabshakeh also among the Prophets? A Rhetorical Study of 2 Kings XVIII 17–35», *VT* 50 (2000) 100–110, who highlights the "prophetic" language used by the Assyrian official, even if he maintains that his prophetic function should be seen only its functional relation to Sennacherib, who would claim to have a divine status superseding that of YHWH and the gods of all foreign peoples. In my opinion, on the other hand, according to 1 Kgs 18:25, the question is more complex (as is complex, in fact, the question of the text's unity, the articulation of his discourse, developed with several contrasting communicative registers to effect): the great cupbearer seems to also present himself as an authentic messenger ("prophet") and interpreter of the very will of YHWH.

451　Cf. in this regard, T.W. OVERHOLT, *Channels of Prophecy*. The Social Dynamics of Prophetic Activity, Minneapolis 1989, 71: "The people choose their prophets; that is, they attribute authority to them, because they perceive in the proclamation continuity with the cultural traditions sufficient to make what they say intelligible and at the same time innovations sufficient to offer the possibility of a new interpretation that will bring order out of what is perceived as chaos."

440 Jer 27–28. The world beneath the yoke of the king of Babylon

It is not difficult, then, to realise that in Jer 27–28, the (pragmatic) *context* is entirely different than at the time of Isaiah, and that its correct assumption determines a righteous (intradiegetic) discernment and more adequate exegetic reading.

5.3. "And the prophet Jeremiah went on his way" (28:11). Jeremiah's "surrender" before Hananiah: A "symbolic gesture" even more eloquent than that of the yoke

Amongst the many elements regarding the theme of "true/false prophecy" in Jer 27–28 that could be studied[452] or highlighted, I choose to focus on an aspect that is particularly significant for the development of my study because it allows me to identify an important semiotic arcata that links it to Jer 38:14–28a, the subject of the next chapter of the present dissertation. This regards the reaction, or rather the choice of *non-reaction*, on the part of Jeremiah to the imperious speech, followed by a likewise striking symbolic counter-gesture, of which the leading player is the prophet Hananiah (cf. 28:10–11), Jeremiah's antagonist and "counter-word".

5.3.1. *The preparation of the scene. MT and LXX: Two different paths of meaning towards the same mystery of the "surrender"?*

From a chronological point of view, the scene in ch. 28 of the MT clearly ties back to that in ch. 27 through the temporal notation in v. 1 (בַּשָּׁנָה הַהִיא, "in that year"), though it is not easy to harmonise the chronological relation with precision, given the textual difficulties I have highlighted (cf. nos. 6 and 24). The thematic continuity, also underlined by the reference to the *cultual* dimension symbolised[453] by the "furnishings of the house of the Lord" (כְּלֵי בֵית־יְהוָה; cf. 27:16, 18, 19, 21–22 with 28:1, 2, 6) and their fate is, however, evident. The arrival of the prophet Hananiah on the scene constitutes in fact the *reaction* to the Jeremianic message announced through the symbolic gesture

---

452   Think e.g. of the theme of intercession in favour of the "temple furnishings" in 27:18, and of YHWH's word on the same furnishings in 27:21–22 (which the prophetic intermediation should oppose), just as of the implications of theology of history that I mentioned, starting from 28:13–14, which show how false prophecy, in its oppositional tension to the true divine word, can be capable, in spite of itself of altering (in a negative sense) the development of events.

453   As I emphasised in §§ 2.4.1–3, the theme of the "temple furnishings" (starting with its lexical aesthetic) already has an important semiotic value on the level of the structuration of the unity of Jer 27–28, because it acts as a thematic and formal connection between the two chapters. If, in the first place, the international political dimension is called into question mainly through *animal symbolism* and the reference to divine authority over *creation*, which can place the power over the world in the hands of those it desires (cf. 27:5–8; 28:14), on the other hand, the metonymic relationship that is established between the fate of the kingdom of Judah (considered in its singularity) and the furnishings of the temple (cf. 27:18–22; 28:3, 6) should be noted. It is a relationship that, unlike that established in the symbolic sphere of the *animal* world in relation to the nations, expresses instead a purely *cultual*, and thus also *cultural*, dimension. The value of meaning of these furnishings, a (sacred) sign of the promise of YHWH and his presence in its sanctuary, should also be emphasised.

"They prophesy lies to you, do not listen to them!" (27:16–17)   441

of the yoke and the place of the confrontation does not remain as undetermined as in ch. 27, but is instead specifically the area of the temple of Jerusalem (cf. 28:1).

The oppositional relationship between the conflicting prophetic words concerning the political stance to be taken in the geopolitical scenario of the time was already present in 27:9–22 as a sort of prelude to the frontal confrontation in ch. 28. It should be observed, however, that the LXX seems to accentuate this fundamental contrast further and intentionally, at least according to a line of reading of the Greek text that I will highlight insofar as it is possible: in the communicative context of 34:18–19[LXX] (=27:18–19[MT]), the words of Jeremiah can (also) be read as a *challenge* to a direct *interlocutory confrontation* openly addressed to the false prophets.

Let me place in parallel,[454] in particular, v. 18 of the respective chapters of the MT and LXX, because precisely here, a remarkable "momentum" is imprinted on the act of reading, that is, a concentration of presuppositions and expectations that, in the LXX, with Jeremiah's reaction to the words and gestures of the "false prophet", will render more destabilising the impact on the reader. But also the MT, with its premise regarding prophetic intercession, will contribute in no small way to problematise (or rather, to direct and deepen) the hermeneutics of the message and mission entrusted to the prophet Jeremiah.

27:18[MT]	=	34:18[LXX]	
וְאִם־נְבִאִים הֵם	If they are prophets	εἰ προφῆταί εἰσιν	If they are prophets
וְאִם־יֵשׁ דְּבַר־	and if there is the word	καὶ εἰ ἔστιν λόγος	and if there is a word
יְהוָה אִתָּם	of the Lord with them,	κυρίου ἐν αὐτοῖς	of the Lord in them,
יִפְגְּעוּ־נָא בַּיהוָה	*may they intercede with the Lord*	ἀπαντησάτωσάν	*may they face*
צְבָאוֹת לְבִלְתִּי־בֹאוּ	*of hosts so that they don't go*	μοι.	*me.*
הַכֵּלִים הַנּוֹתָרִים	the vessels remaining		
בְּבֵית־יְהוָה	in the house of the Lord		
וּבֵית מֶלֶךְ	and in the house of the king		
יְהוּדָה וּבִירוּשָׁלָ͏ִם	of Judah and in Jerusalem		
בָּבֶלָה	*to Babylon.*		

As can be seen, the difference between the MT and the LXX is surprising,[455] not least because the opening sentence is indeed the same. The question is that of understanding whether the text of the MT is the explanatory development of a semantic nucleus that one could consider as being barely mentioned in the LXX and its *Vorlage* (i.e. an intercessorial "confrontation" with YHWH), or, as I would suggest, if the perspective of the Greek text can be understood in a way that is completely different from the outset (as a public "confrontation" with Jeremiah). In this sense, it is indubitably necessary to study the semantics of the verb ἀπαντάω, but it is crucial to determine the deictic of the personal pronoun μοι, that is, to assess whether the object of the action indicated

---

454   To even better illustrate the similarities and differences between the two texts, I offer a literal translation here that seeks to simulate the syntax of the respective texts as well.

455   Cf. W. McKane, *Jeremiah,* I, 693.

442 Jer 27–28. The world beneath the yoke of the king of Babylon

by the verb ἀπαντάω relates to YHWH, in the name of whom Jeremiah claims to speak from v. 16 on, or to the prophet himself. Let us explore this second option.

It is well known that in the complex communicative flow of the Jeremianic oracles, it is not always easy to distinguish the different speakers, precisely because of the scarcity or ambiguity of the personal deictics assigned to organise the roles of the participants in the discourse. And so the subjects speaking can change abruptly, the different voices overlap and follow in uninterrupted succession, and it is quite often unclear where the word of YHWH is being relayed and where, instead, Jeremiah is speaking in the first person.[456] I believe that this same phenomenon could be occurring in this case.

The *Botenformel* in v. 16 (כֹּה אָמַר יְהוָה; "so says the Lord"), provided that it not be intended to be understood simply as a "formula of legitimisation" of a Jeremianic word (of the tradition),[457] introduces the divine discourse in the first person contained in this verse. In the following vv. 17–18, one might instead think that it be Jeremiah himself communicating his personal thoughts, commenting on the just proclaimed words of YHWH. It would seem rather strange otherwise that God speak of himself a good three times in the third person ("if there is *the word of the Lord in them*, may they intercede *with the Lord* of hosts so that the vessels left *in the house of the Lord*[458] do not go". The divine word, on the other hand, would resume in v. 19, introduced by a new *Botenformel* preceded by an explicative-causal כִּי ("*because* so says the Lord" [...])[459] almost as if it were, in turn, a confirmation-comment on the words of the prophet.

According to this perspective, in the Greek version Jeremiah not only places the question of *discernment* in the foreground, but also seems to orient the solution more decisively and "dramatically". If, in fact, the deictic function of the pronoun μοι refers to Jeremiah, the prophet becomes the subject that provokes false prophets to a kind of showdown ("may they face me"), soliciting or invoking a public confrontation which, given the assuredness ostentated, seems to already announce a victorious outcome in his favour. While both Jeremiah and Hananiah present themselves as prophets of the self-same YHWH, according to this line of reading, one cannot help but think of the decisive challenge between the prophet Elijah and the prophets of Baal (cf. 1 Kgs 18) summoned by King Ahab on Mount Carmel, but precisely Elijah's orders (in 1 Kgs 18:19):

> *So now summon to gather to me* (וְעַתָּה שְׁלַח קְבֹץ אֵלַי) all of Israel, along with the four hundred and fifty prophets of Baal and the four hundred prophets of Asherah, who eat at the table of Jezebel!

---

456 The phenomenon and its complexity are highlighted by, amongst others, W.L. HOLLADAY, *Jeremiah 1*, 137; the complete monograph of M.E. BIDDLE, *Polyphony*, and G. FISCHER, *Jeremia 1–25*, 54–55; R.P. CARROLL, «The Polyphonic Jeremiah: a Reading of the Book of Jeremiah», in: *Reading the Book of Jeremiah*, 77–85.

457 See, in this regard, S.A. MEIER, *Speaking of Speaking*, 273–298; A. WAGNER, *Prophetie als Theologie. Die so spricht Jahwe*-Formeln und das Grundverständnis alttestamentlicher Prophetie, FRLANT 207, Göttingen 2004, 285–286; 322–324.

458 The expression "house of the Lord" (בֵּית יְהוָה), rather than "my house" (cf. e.g. Num 12:7; Isa 56:7; Jer 12:7; Ezek 23:39; 44:7; 1 Chr 28:6; etc.: בֵּיתִי) is, however, also used when it is more likely to be YHWH who is speaking in first person, as in vv. 16 and 21.

459 Cf. *Ibid.*, 227.

"They prophesy lies to you, do not listen to them!" (27:16–17)   443

The scene on Carmel, presenting itself as an ordeal, has an evident (analogical) juridic-judicial connotation,[460] as if it were a public trial carried out in the presence of all the people between Elijah and the other prophets, with a *notitia criminis* concerning an accusation of false cult and/or false prophecy (and consequently, with the title of true prophet(s) or false prophet(s) to the "defendants"), having as its judge not the highest authority of reference on earth (i.e. the king), himself also a stakeholder in the case, but the "true God" (who will have to reveal Himself as either the God of Israel or the Baal of the Phoenician queen).

The semantics of the verb used by Jeremiah in 34:18^{LXX} in imperative form can go in the same direction: in a generic sense, when the subject is personal, $\dot{\alpha}\pi\alpha\nu\tau\dot{\alpha}\omega$ means "moving from one place to another to *encounter* a person".[461] As always, however, it is the communicative context of a *pragmatic* nature that best specifies the most pertinent connotation. In classical Greek, $\dot{\alpha}\pi\alpha\nu\tau\dot{\alpha}\omega$ (+ dative) is frequently utilised in a *hostile sense*, mainly to refer to an *event of war* or *violent* (often punitive) *act* carried out against an adversary. It is attested several times in this context-determined sense in the LXX (cf. e.g. 1 Sam 15:2; 22:17, 18; 2 Sam 1:15; 1 Kgs 2:32, 34; Hos 13:8; etc.).[462]

It is thus not surprising that it also often be used in a *judiciary context*,[463] given the well-known semantic contiguity and process of cross-metaphorisation between the *forensic field* (and also that of the verbal confrontation that typifies a *quarrel*) and the scenario of *war*.[464] I believe this can also be, in an analogous sense (as in the scene of Elijah on Carmel), the nuance generated by the *focus* of the communicative context in 34:18–19^{LXX}, the basis of which is clearly polemic. The "cataloguing" of Hananiah as a "false prophet" ($\psi\epsilon\upsilon\delta\upsilon\pi\rho\upsilon\varphi\dot{\eta}\tau\eta\varsigma$)[465] by Jeremiah himself in the first person as the intradiegetic narrator in 35:1^{LXX} ($\epsilon\dot{\iota}\pi\acute{\epsilon}\nu$ $\mu\omicron\iota$ =28:1^{MT}: אָמַר אֵלַי),[466] is

---

460   Amongst the many elements that could be referred to, cf. e.g. P. BOVATI, *Ristabilire la giustizia*, 205, n. 12.

461   Cf. STEPHANUS, 1174–1177 (in particular, col. 1176–1177); LIDDELL-SCOTT, 178; MONTANARI, 254.

462   Cf. LUST, 60; MURAOKA, 64: "1. *to come face to face with*; [...] 4. *to present oneself* [...] for a public meeting; [...] 5. *to treat, deal with* [...] with harmful intent".

463   Also in Classical Greek, LIDDELL-SCOTT, 178 highlights its frequent legal use: "3. *meet in open court* [...] *present oneself* at the trial; etc.", also reiterated in LIDDELL-SCOTT(RS), 40: "counter an argument [...]; of a jury, *face, deal with* a line of argument", and MONTANARI, 254: "presentarsi: $\pi\rho\dot{\omicron}\varsigma$ $\tau\dot{\eta}\nu$ $\delta\dot{\iota}\varkappa\eta\nu$ (al processo); [...]; comparire in tribunale".

464   For the HB, cf. P. BOVATI, *Ristabilire la giustizia*, 273.

465   It is worth noting here that the expression "false prophet" ($\psi\epsilon\upsilon\delta\upsilon\pi\rho\upsilon\varphi\dot{\eta}\tau\eta\varsigma$) in the Greek text, while not having a precise correspondence in the HB, is instead attested in Qumran. The fragment written in Aramaic 4QList of False Prophets (cf. DJD XIX, 77–79, pl. XI) presents a list of "false prophets" (נביא [ש]קרא; an expression absent from the MT) of the biblical tradition, amongst which some figures mentioned by the book of Jeremiah appear precisely in the context of the question of whether to "consign oneself (or not) to the king of Babylon". They are [Aha]b son cf K[o]liah", "[Zede]kiah son of Ma[a]seiah", "[Shemaiah the Ne]hlemite"), and, in vv. 8–9, "[Hananiah son of Az]ur, [a prophet from di Gib]eon" himself. Even though only two letters have been preserved in these last two verses, "the reconstruction is relatively certain" (p. 79).

466   In 28:1–4, the narrator is Jeremiah himself (internal focus), while from v. 5 on, Jeremiah speaks in third person and the voice of the heterodiegetic narrator is

444 Jer 27–28. The world beneath the yoke of the king of Babylon

consistent with this perspective. Defining Hananiah from the beginning of the chapter as a "false prophet" would therefore not be an accidental narrative step in the LXX to be devalued with respect to the logic of the MT (by which, instead, Hananiah is a "prophet" [נָבִיא] like Jeremiah, without other "premature" specifications), but a device that goes to emphasise the Jeremianic *débâcle*[467] that follows in a different way.

Nonetheless, how can the marked differences between the MT and LXX (and its *Vorlage*) be justified when the protasis that precedes the semantic divarication of the following apodosis (intercession/confrontation-clash) is substantially identical? An important clue to the solution of the problem comes to us from the lexicon of the LXX compiled by J. Lust, E. Eynikel, and K. Hauspie, where, in the aforementioned part,[468] it is noted that the verb ἀπαντάω[469] followed by a dative referring to a person is a Semitism that corresponds to the Hebrew syntagm √פגע + בְּ. In effect, this correlation can be found many times (though not always).

With this in view, in any case, to understand the use of the verb in Jer 34:18^{LXX}, other texts where the syntagm √פגע + בְּ appears can be considered relevant (in both a figurative and literal sense), such as Num 35:19, 21: here the blood avenger can kill the murderer (i.e. the culprit) when he *encounters* him (translated in the LXX with συναντάω); Josh 2:16: those pursuing the (guilty, for the inhabitants of Jericho) spies of Israel can *encounter* them and capture them (LXX: συναντάω); Judg 8:21: Gideon is incited to *kill* two assassins (LXX: συναντάω); etc. On the level of *verbal confrontation*, reference can be made to Rut 1:16, where the Moabite asks her mother-in-law to not insist with further *dialectical pressure* in the attempt (which she judges as useless) to convince her to remain in her country (translated in the LXX with ἀπαντάω). The syntagm is used in a similar sense to express the futility of *prayer* in Job 21:15 (here again, translated in the LXX with ἀπαντάω).

And after this semantic *détour*, we find ourselves right in the book of Jeremiah where it is used to express the *intercessoral interposition*[470]: in 7:16, YHWH forbids the prophet to "insist with the prayer of intercession" (which the LXX renders with μὴ προσέλθῃς μοι περὶ αὐτῶν) and the nuance implicated in this kind of prayerful dialogue seems to be just that of a *hostile confrontation* in which one intends to *face* an "enemy" to win over him (according to the numerous attestations of this use in the

---

heard again (external focus). The unity with ch. 27 is strengthened by this narrative strategy.

467 It is suggestive, moreover, in the perspective of the LXX, to also bear in mind the occurrence in Jdth 7:15, in which ἀπαντάω (+ ἐν εἰρήνῃ) is used in reference to the act of *surrender* (though with a different syntagmatic construction). Jeremiah then asks for the adversaries to go to him for a confrontation and to "surrender themselves" to his superior prophetic ministry, while it is he himself who will instead have to exit the scene, fulfilling a gesture of "surrender" in front of the antagonist, Hananiah.

468 Lust, 60.

469 Cf. also Hatch – Redpath, 117.

470 In reference to the use of √פגע within the semantic field of prayer, see J.F.A. Sawyer, «Types of Prayer in the Old Testament. Some Semantic Observations on Hitpallel, Hithannen, etc.», *Semitics* 7 (1980) 131–143 (here, pp. 135–136); P. Maiberger, «פגע», *ThWAT* VI, 501–508 (here, pp. 505–506); B. Rossi, *L'intercessione nel tempo della fine*, 55–56.

"They prophesy lies to you, do not listen to them!" (27:16–17)   445

MT) In 15:11, Jeremiah recalls his *intercession* in favour of his enemies (the LXX refers to this intercessory act with the verb παρίστημι) and in 36:25, some court dignitaries *try to convince* King Jehoiakim to not burn the prophetic scroll (here, the LXX resorts to ὑποτίθημι). But the most significant datum is that, returning to the starting point, the construct √פגע + בּ recurs right in our own text, in 27:18.

We can presuppose therefore that the differences between the MT and LXX both derived from an identical *Vorlage* that had the same syntagm √פגע + בּ, or more precisely, √פגע + בי, which would have been read בי = μοι in the LXX (cf. בְּיהוָה צְבָאוֹת instead, in the MT). Its basic meaning (to meet someone, *confront them*) is made explicit in an intercessory sense in MT, but in the LXX, for its elliptical form, it remains open to two different semantic-pragmatic finalisations:

If [they] are prophets and if there is the/a word of the Lord with/in them,

יִפְגְּעוּ־נָא THEY CONFRONT בַּיהוָה צְבָאוֹת *the Lord of hosts*	ἀπαντησάτωσάν THEY CONFRONT μοι *me*
⇩	⇩
MT: CONFRONTATION WITH YHWH/ INTERCESSION	LXX: CONFRONTATION WITH YHWH/ INTERCESSION? PUBLIC CONFRONTATION WITH JEREMIAH/ "ORDEAL"?

Instead of the self-confident ostentation expressed by Jeremiah, which becomes a provocation for dialectical confrontation before of a public audience, in the MT, the prophet of Anathoth indicates another (dual) criterion of verification: true prophets can be distinguished from the fact that 1) they are aware (of divine intentions since they become participants)[471] regarding the present historical situation (the removal of the remaining temple furnishings, with all that this entails; cf. 27:19–22),[472]

---

471 Cf. Amos 3:7. The root פגע used in the context of intercession always conveys the semantic notion of "proximity" (specifically, of the person praying with YHWH; cf. E. ROSSI, *L'intercessione nel tempo della fine*, 55–56).

472 The topic warrants further study, but here I can limit myself to making only the following observations. In the perspective of the current communicative context of ch. 27 (MT), Jeremiah's speech suggests that, even in the case of submission to the king of Babylon, YHWH has already decided to allow a further, radical depredation of the temple (so much so that it could suggest the very cessation of the cult of the temple of Jerusalem, if the reference to sacred furnishings, columns, and the "sea" of bronze are read in a literal sense). But one could also understand the divine decree proclaimed by Jeremiah in 27:19–22 as a punitive effect of the rejection of submission and of the lie told by the false prophets (as reported in Jeremiah) in 27:16.

446   Jer 27–28. The world beneath the yoke of the king of Babylon

and 2), they oppose these intentions, or seek to oppose them, by virtue of their connatural *intercessorial function*,[473] to persuade YHWH to act otherwise on behalf of the people.

But at this point, some questions should arise in the reader of the book of Jeremiah (MT). It is clear that by calling into question the subject of intercession, Jeremiah makes it a decisive criterion for discernment (that of "fulfilment" is no less so, but will only be cited in 28:9). Yet it is precisely of Jeremiah, in 7:16; 11:14; 14:11 that any intercession is repeatedly prohibited by YHWH, and in 15:1, it seems to be permanently declared useless. Certainly, by way of contrast, the prohibition emphasises that this function, repeatedly requested (cf. 21:2; 37:3, 7 and 42:2, 4, 20), is really decisive for prophetic identity in the theological horizon of the book[474] (and beyond it; think of 2 Mac 15:14, where it becomes the identifying trait of his figure). But this does not detract from the fact that it is precisely Jeremiah who insists on this subject, indeed, it makes it even more paradoxical.

Trying to fill the blank spaces that the text creates with a whole series of *presupposed assumptions*[475], which it seems to deliberately deliver to the perspicacity of the reader, we can explicate the *unspoken* (but understood) in the Jeremianic discourse thus: "If they are true prophets, then they should have already known the intentions of YHWH, and they should have already addressed them with a prayer of intercession. But, above all, they should have come up against, as I have, the Lord's repeated and adamant refusal". In other words, the true prophet should have already made, or should still make, an act of submission and surrender before YHWH himself![476] What (the literary figure of) Jeremiah in ch. 27 does not seem to suspect in the least is that another form of delivery or acceptance of "surrender" will be asked of him personally. And right in front of an antagonistic prophet who, in the name of the selfsame Lord, proclaims a message entirely opposite to his own.

---

473   On the general topic of prayer in the prophets, see A.F. WILKE, *Die Gebete der Propheten*. Anrufungen Gottes im "corpus propheticum" der Hebräischen Bibel, BZAW 451, Berlin – Boston 2014. On the close correlation between the prophetic ministry and the intercessorial interposition between God and the people, see, e.g. A.B. RHODES, «Israel's Prophets as Intercessors», in: *Scripture in History and Theology*. Essays in Honor of J.C. Rylaardsam, *eds.* A.L. MERRILL – T.W. OVERHOLT, Pittsburgh 1977, 107–128; BALENTINE, S.E., «The Prophet as Intercessor: a Reassessment», *JBL* 103 (1984) 161–173 (p. 164: [...] the prophet is perhaps more accurately described as simply one figure among several who from time to time exercises the privilege of «praying for» another person"). In particular, on Jeremiah, see B. ROSSI, *L'intercessione nel tempo della fine*, 97–118.

474   In this sense and with more or less marked underscoring, W. RUDOLPH, *Jeremia*, 99; A.B. RHODES, «Israel's Prophets», 119; S. MANFREDI, *Geremia il profeta simbolo della nazione*. Contributo di teologia biblica per una teologia della profezia, Estratto dalla Dissertazione per il Dottorato, Palermo 1984, 69–70; L. STULMAN, *Order Amid Chaos*, 143. Along more general lines, J. KÜGLER, «Fürbitte», *HGANT*, 197.

475   In the following chapter of the present dissertation, I will devote specific theoretical insight on this topic, which is very important in communication theories and in cognitive pragmatics in particular.

476   Indeed, "if they are prophets", they should have understood that the furnishings taken to Babylon are already a reality to be accepted and surrendered to. Paradoxically, precisely the acceptance of this would make another deportation unnecessary. Indeed, the possible prophetic intercession consists in this.

"They prophesy lies to you, do not listen to them!" (27:16–17)   447

As can be seen, also in the MT (or at least according to the "intercessory" line of reading), the scene that will take place before the reader's eyes in ch. 28 is prepared differently, but not at all less effectively (and indeed, less obviously) than in the text of the LXX (read instead as a personal challenge launched to the false prophets by Jeremiah). In conclusion, therefore, I can state that, stemming from an identical premise, the text of the LXX and that of the MT can be considered the origin of two different paths of meaning; but also that both these perspectives ultimately flow into the same mystery of the "surrender" that entirely dominates the unit of chs. 27–28 (and the broader unit of chs. 27–29), despite its being modulated according to different registers in a reciprocal analogous relation.[477]

Hence, to integrate the explanatory framework of what has been highlighted thus far:

If [they] are prophets and if there is the/a word of the Lord with/in them,	
יִפְגְּעוּ־נָא בַּיהוָה צְבָאוֹת THEY CONFRONT *the Lord of hosts*	ἀπαντησάτωσάν μοι THEY CONFRONT *me*
⇩	⇩
MT: CONFRONTATION WITH YHWH/ INTERCESSION	LXX: PUBLIC CONFRONTATION WITH JEREMIAH/ "ORDEAL"?
⇩	⇩
SURRENDER (OF JEREMIAH) BEFORE YHWH	SURRENDER OF JEREMIAH BEFORE HANANIAH

5.3.2 The public dispute with Hananiah

In ch. 27, the only voice that resonates directly on the scene is that of Jeremiah. The opposing prophetic word remains in the background and it is known to us because he cites it himself (cf. 27:14) in order to counter it with the call to submission to Babylon. In ch. 28, on the other hand, the antagonistic salvific message storms in forcefully through the figure of Hananiah (חֲנַנְיָה, moreover, means "YHWH is/has been gracious"),[478] whose presentation in the MT (cf. 28:1) marks the question of "origin"

---

477 The submission-surrender of a political nature is also and above all a theological fact, and the "surrender" of the individual in the context of the prophetic intercession before YHWH recalls that in the sphere of dialectical confrontation before another prophet, and both are a sign of the surrender of the entire nation (or of all nations) to the righteous punishment of God mediated by the empire of Babylonia.

478 Cf. M. NOTH, *Die israelitischen Personennamen*, 35, 187; J.D. FOWLER, *Theophoric Personal Names*, 345. The name חֲנַנְיָה (here, in its short form) is attested in several archaeological finds, amongst which some jar handles from the sixth/seventh centuries B.C. found precisely on the site of ancient Gibeon, the birth city of the prophet Hananiah (cf. J. RENZ, *Die althebräischen Inschriften*, 257–261).

448 Jer 27–28. The world beneath the yoke of the king of Babylon

while at the same time leaving it pending: he is the "*son* of Azzur" (בֶּן־עַזּוּר)[479] and is "the prophet (הַנָּבִיא), *the one who comes from Gabaon*" (אֲשֶׁר מִגִּבְעוֹן)[480] But *where does* his message *come from* (cf. § 5.2.2)? As has already been noted, in the LXX, Hananiah is immediately identified negatively as a "false prophet", revealing the final verdict of 28:15–17 in advance.

One should, however, be cautious in believing that the MT intentionally wants to keep readers on hold and subject them to "un travail de discernement pour reconnaître le vrai prophète et se positionner à ses côtés".[481] It should also be further clarified that the notation of the LXX does not "désamorce immédiatement les questions suscitées par le récit massoretique",[482] but is rather an emphasis that, as I previously stated, has a direct repercussion on the unsettling effect of Jeremiah's retreat in 28:11. In fact, the (Model) reader of both the LXX and the MT, having reached this point in the book of Jeremiah, knows at least two fundamental things quite well, ever since ch. 1: how the whole story ends (the fall of Jerusalem, exile, and end of the kingdom of Judah), and that Jeremiah is a true prophet, because he was sent by YHWH and his word is fulfilled.[483] So once again,[484] interest is focused on the "how" of the whole affair, or rather, on the traces of meaning that can be highlighted retrospectively in a story that could otherwise appear to be absolute non-sense. And the reader is urged to trace the regularities, the paradigms that are valid for rereading the past and the present, so that the future may be not only vain hope or new looming anguish.

And so here is the scene where this tension reaches its *climax*. The place where it occurs, which is highly symbolic, makes the issue a theological one, first and foremost, and not (only) a political one. We are in the area of the temple of the Lord, and the context is public: along with the priests, all the people are present (cf. 28:1), in continuity with 27:16–22. Hananiah takes up what Jeremiah stated in ch. 27 and attacks him frontally, countering with a word that is entirely opposite. But not before he has solemnly declared the *divine origin* of his message using the well-known *Botenformel* in an expanded form (28:2a: "כֹּה־אָמַר יְהוָה צְבָאוֹת אֱלֹהֵי יִשְׂרָאֵל; so says the Lord of hosts, God of Israel"). Jeremiah announces in the name of YHWH the need for submission, Hananiah gives voice to a Lord who says the opposite instead: the yoke of Babylon

---

479 The term עַזּוּר means "helper" or "[person] who has been helped" (cf. *HALAT*, 768).

480 Even Gibeon, city of Benjamin, not far from either Jerusalem (9 km to the North; if the identification with El-Ǧīb is correct) or Anathoth, according to Josh 21:17, was, just as the latter (cf. Josh 21:18; Jer 1:1), a priestly city. These are data that make it even clearer that the question of the *origin* of the prophetic message is not presented as matter of easy discernment.

481 As in E. Di Pede, «La manière de raconter», 300.

482 *Ibid.*, 298.

483 Despite its being a study of narrative analyses, the contribution of E. Di Pede («La manière de raconter») seems to bank on the fragmentary conception of meaning that often dominates many studies of a historical-critical matrix that are concentrated on the history of the composition of biblical texts. In fact, it does not seem to take into adequate account the unity of the Jeremianic work (as a book), making ch. 28 into almost a story in its own right, with no relation to everything that precedes it (apart from ch. 27, to which it refers).

484 The narrative dynamic is always that which I have highlighted with the proleptic function of 21:1–10 in ch. III, § 3 of my dissertation.

"They prophesy lies to you, do not listen to them!" (27:16–17)   449

will be broken (28:2b). And not only that: the furnishings of the temple of the Lord will be brought back to Jerusalem (28:3), and together with them, the (true?) king, Jehoiachin (Jeconiah) will return from Babylon, along with all the deportees of 597. As if this were not enough, and in a tone of open defiance to Jeremiah's position, Hananiah shows that he does not at all fear the principle of "fulfilment", because he does not resort to stereotypical temporal, symbolic, and indefinite locutions ("seventy years", or "three years"; etc.), but fixes an extremely precise, verifiable deadline within a limited time frame: two years.[485]

Jeremiah's response (28:5–9), both for the reader and within the scene of the story, appears rather lacklustre, or, to be more benevolent, rather calm. The prophet from Anathoth seems intimidated in any case. Compared to the criterion designated for identifying "true prophets", which he himself placed in 27:18 and which was evidently rejected by Hananiah (intercession), and by YHWH himself(!),[486] Jeremiah reuses what was implicitly evoked by his opponent, which seems to take its cue from a much more solid and traditional principle: the word of the true prophet *comes to be* (cf. Deut 18:21–22). His version, nevertheless, is more elaborate, because it inserts a distinction and a probabilistic element: between the word of peace and that of misfortune, focus should be placed on the second, and precisely the prophet who announces it should be expected to be the one who is real, *still before* any fulfilment. The reason is clear: its scope is to exhort conversion, so that the threatened disaster does not become a reality. For the message of peace, on the other hand, since it can lead to a false security irrespective of any ethical-moral instance, it is necessary to wait and verify its realisation. In truth, his self-defence is rather bland and seems to ignore illustrious exceptions (specifically, some famous oracles of Isaiah, of which Hananiah himself seems to be the one to actualise), invoking an almost indeterminate suspension of judgment. And this while the political situation is in turmoil and Hananiah, against this backdrop much to his advantage, speaks of an imminent deadline.

It is striking that Jeremiah no longer flaunts the self-confidence of the previous scene. Given the premise of ch. 27, in fact, and that the reader knows that Jeremiah was sent by YHWH, one could have certainly expected a much more vigorous, indignant reaction. But not in the least. Instead, it is Hananiah who raises the bar of the confrontation, which from verbal becomes almost *physical*. To Jeremiah's words, he also presents a symbolic counter-gesture, which is coloured by a certain undeniable *violence* that, not without reason, is emphasised twice (cf. 28:10, 12). Hananiah rips the yoke (collar) from Jeremiah's neck and breaks it in front of everyone, following this with a word by which he reaffirms his peremptory prophecy and its rapid fulfilment. The (Model) reader already knows the outcome of the whole story, as I mentioned. But who could have expected that a true prophet, certain of the investiture and help of his God, sure of the truth of his message, would remain unwarlike in the face of such lies and prevarication? But that is precisely what happens. Not a single word in response:

---

485 I have already had an opportunity to reflect on the probable meaning of this deadline, considered in the context of the geopolitical events of its time, in ch. II, § 2.2.2 of my dissertation.

486 At least in some cases, or at a certain historical-theological moment.

וַיֵּלֶךְ יִרְמְיָה הַנָּבִיא לְדַרְכּוֹ **11** And the prophet Jeremiah went his
פ own way *silent pause*

5.3.3. The "surrender" of Jeremiah: The mystery of God's silence and the submission to the enemy

Between the end of v. 11 and the beginning of v. 12, in the Hebrew manuscript tradition, there is a sort of hiatus, a communicative shock marked by an empty space or, in the more "recent" editions, by a single letter (פ), which signals a *p^etûḥâ*. More precisely, going to look at the oldest and most important Jewish manuscripts that have come down to us, I can note that in the Leningrad code (L; Firkovich B19A; A.D. 1008/1009), which is the basis of the BHK³ (but not BHK¹⁻²),[487] BHS and BHQ editions, between the two vv., a half-line in white was left by the ancient scribe (cf. Fig. 32), a sign that identifies, as appropriate, the beginning of a new textual portion (*pārāšâ*) with the transition ("opening": *p^etûḥâ*) to another topic, or to a verse that is so important (whether the one before or after the marked boundary, if not both) that it must be highlighted by an adequate pause in the flow of the text. The separation between what for us are chs. 28 and 29 is, instead, a whole blank line.

Fig. 32. D.N. FREEDMAN et al., eds., The Leningrad Codex. *The Facsimile Edition*, Grand Rapids 1998, 533 (folio 261, recto). See also H.L. STRACK, ed., The Hebrew Bible – Latter Prophets: The Babylonian Codex of Petrograd, *New York 1971, 85b*.

---

487 The first and second edition (BHK¹⁻²) was edited by R. Kittel, and not based on L, but on the "textus receptus" edited by Jacob ben Chayim, which is the basis of the so-called Second Rabbinic Bible of 1524/1525.

Fig. 33. M.H. Goshen-Gottstein, ed., The Aleppo Codex. Provided with Massoretic Notes and Pointed by Aaron Ben Asher, Jerusalem 1976, 294 (רצד).

In the code of Aleppo (A; dated to A.D. 925 ca.), which is the basis for the project of the HUB (Hebrew University Bible), the solution for continuity is even more evident: between the two verses, there is even a groove etched by an empty line, quantitatively the same boundary that separates ch. 28 (or, more precisely, the episode of the conflict between Jeremiah and Hananiah) from the following letter of Jeremiah to the exiles of 597 (cf. Fig. 33).

Even the most ancient Masoretic witness in our possession, the code of the prophets from Cairo (C; 895/896), marks the same scenic-textual fault line, continuing the narrative that follows v. 11 only after forcing the reader's eyes to cross an empty line (cf. Fig. 34),[488] with all the enigmatic significance tied to the silent appeal for an adequate interpretation.

However minimal or broad and obvious, either as a space[489] or a graphic sign, this suspension or lack of writing contributes to the construction of the meaning.[490] It is a particular form of "textualisation",[491] that is, one of the possible semiotic modalities of

---

488　The separation between the two vv. that can be appreciated in this facsimile is respected by the edition of F. Pérez Castro, *ed., El Codice de Profetas de el Cairo*. Tomo V: Jeremias, TECC 37, Madrid 1987, 144, where the white space left between vv. 11 and 12 corresponds to a whole line of text.
489　E. Tov, *Scribal Practices*, 143, 155–156.
490　For a semiotic approach to this phenomenon, which highlights how much a graphic support is involved in the dynamic of rebuilding the meaning of the linguistic text written on it, see R. De Angelis, «L'esplicitazione dell'esperienza grafica. Lo *spazio bianco* come caso esemplare», in: *I segni dell'esperienza. Saggi sulle forme di conoscenza*, eds. A. Canzonieri – G. Gallo, BiTSt 693, Roma 2011, 77–89.
491　See, in this regard, the entry «Textualisation», in A.J. Greimas – J. Courtés, *eds., Sémiotique*, 391–392; and also R. De Angelis, «Sur la matérialité du texte. La

452 Jer 27–28. The world beneath the yoke of the king of Babylon

manifestation of a "text" (understood as a semantic representation of the discourse, in itself independent from its various, additional and possible written, figurative, musical, etc. concretisations). With this expressive form, reference is effectively made to a significative fracture in the narrative *continuum*, that is, a logical space that, long before us, authoritative readers and transmitters have considered necessary to point out.

Amongst the ancient scribes were not only mere copyists but also attentive interpreters of the text, listeners of prophets, and (writer) prophets themselves. Many studies highlight this, and this attitude is also reflected in the divisions of the text into sections and paragraphs, witnessed by the manuscripts that have been handed down to us.[492] Simple signs like a white space and consequent (and much more recent) graphic insertion of a *pᵉtûḥâ* (or a *sᵉtûmâ*),[493] although rather subjective scribal (and editorial)[494] interventions, are metacommunications on the biblical page with a serious tradition behind them,[495] not to be undervalued in the exegetic setting.[496] The intentional subdivision of text was in fact not only a medieval scribal practice, but was also commonly done in antiquity. In addition to the biblical sources, this is attested by various extrabiblical texts of cultual origin coming from Babylon and Ugarit.[497]

---

textualisation», in: *Directions actuelles en linguistique du texte*. Actes du colloque international. Le texte: modèles, méthodes, perspectives, *eds.* L. FLOREA *et al.*, Cluj-Napoca 2010, 95–106.

492 For a synthetic presentation of the question, see E. Tov, *Textual Criticism of the Hebrew Bible*. Second Revised Edition, Minneapolis ²2001, 50–53 (first edition 1992).

493 It appears to be clear by now that a sharp functional distinction between *pᵉtûḥâ* and *sᵉtûmâ* (opening and closing of the paragraphs/sections) is no longer sustainable (cf. M.C.A. KORPEL – J.C. DE MOOR, *The Structure of Classical Hebrew Poetry: Isaiah 40–55*, OTS 41, Leiden 1998, 1–9).

494 For a synthetic list of the division markings for the book of Jeremiah, which takes into account the Qumran mss, see J.R. LUNDBOM, *Jeremiah* 37–52, 568–576, where it is noted that the acronyms פ for a *pᵉtûḥâ* (section "opening") and ס for *sᵉtûmâ* (section "closing") were first introduced in place of the empty spaces left in the ancient mss in an edition of Isaiah and Jeremiah from 1492 (p. 568).

495 Note, regarding this, E. Tov, *Scribal Practices*, 51: "The subdivision itself into open and closed sections reflects exegesis on the extent of the content units [...]. It is possible that the subjectivity of this exegesis created the extant differences between the various sources. What in one Masoretic manuscript is indicated as an open section may appear in another as a closed section, while the indication of a section may be altogether absent in yet a third source. Nevertheless, a certain uniformity is visible in the witnesses of M."

496 It should be noted that for a long time, in the exegetic field, the question of the demarcation of textual units in the OT was fairly neglected (one could, regardless, point out C. PERROT, «Petuhot et Setumot. Étude sur les alinéas du Pentateuque», *RB* 76 (1969) 50–91; J.M. OESCH, *Petucha und Setuma*. Untersuchungen zu einer überlieferten Gliederung im hebräischen Text des Alten Testaments, OBO 27, Freiburg – Göttingen 1979). Recently, a specific area of study, called "delimitation criticism" has taken shape, suggesting the relevance of such research (cf., e.g. amongst the numerous contributions, M.C.A. KORPEL – J.C. DE MOOR, *The Structure*; M.C.A. KORPEL, *The Structure of the Book of Ruth*, Pericope 2, Assen 2001, and the collection of studies published in M.C.A. KORPEL – J. OESCH, *Delimitation Criticism. A New Tool in Biblical Scholarship*, Pericope 1, Assen 2000).

497 Cf. M.C.A. KORPEL, «Unit Delimitation in Ugaritic Cultic Texts and Some Babylonian and Hebrew Parallels», in: M.C.A. KORPEL – J. OESCH, *Delimitation Criticism*, 141–160.

"They prophesy lies to you, do not listen to them!" (27:16–17)   453

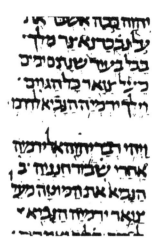

Fig. 34. D.S. LÖWINGER, Codex Cairo of the Bible. From the Karaite Synagoge at Abbasiya, Jerusalem 1971, 397.

Fig. 35. Given that chs. 27–28 are missing from 4QJer^a, as an example of text segmentation, shown here is a fragment containing Jer 18:15–19:1. In this case as well, the interruption marked by the space left empty (between v. 17 and 18; l. 3; but also between the end of ch. 18 and the beginning of 19, at l. 12, though more difficult to note) is hermeneutically significant (cf. 4Q70[Jer^a], in: DJD XV, 165, pl. XXVIII, col. XII, fr. no. 29).

454   Jer 27–28. The world beneath the yoke of the king of Babylon

As far as the literary material from Qumran is concerned[498] and, in particular, the fragments that relate to the book of Jeremiah found there, based on the textual configuration of an important witness such as 4QJer[a] (cf. Fig. 35)[499] (and other fragments), I can state with certainty that the division in paragraphs was practiced *at least* from the period that straddled the end of the third and the beginning of the second century B.C. (the time span within which the manuscript is dated),[500] although there are more than a few differences from the Masoretic tradition with regard to paragraph subdivisions (along with a series of correspondences).[501] In any case, it is a phenomenon that interrogates the hermeneutical act.

The rabbinical tradition, in *Sifra*, the most ancient Midrash on the book of Leviticus (third century A.D.), and in the comment made by Rashi on this,[502] warns us, for example, that the segmentation of the *Tôrâ* intends to respect and reflect the modality of the dialogic exchange between YHWH and Moses.[503] The rhythm between word and suspension of discourse, represented by the divisions signalled in the written text, was necessary so that the interlocutor (who for Deut 18:15 is the prototype of every future *prophet*)[504] could better enter into the mystery that it was revealing to him,[505] that is, in the words of the *Sifra*, "It was so as to give Moses a pause to collect his thoughts between the statement of one passage and the next, between the presentation of one topic and the next",[506] a fact that, as both the *Sifra* and Rashi specify, is absolutely necessary even in an ordinary and entirely human transmission of a teaching. This is also already a valuable indication.

And yet, there is something more in the break present in our text than a rhythm of speech and silence as would be expected in normal conversation, or even in a discursive act of a teacher striving for fruitful instruction. Certainly, for Jeremiah as well, the question here is one of being taught, just as it is now for the reader, even more so. But it is undeniable that it has to do with a *dramatic* suspension, not a pleasant or opportune pause in an intense, content-rich discourse. So it is appropriate to enter

---

498   See, in this regard, E. Tov, *Scribal Practices*, 131–166.

499   Cf. 4Q70[Jer[a]], in: DJD XV, 145–170, pls XXIV-XXIX.

500   For the different proposals for the dating of the scroll 4QJer[a], see DJD XV, 150. In any case, as stated by F.M. Cross and D.N. Freedman, it is one of the oldest specimens of the Qumran texts.

501   Cf. E. Tov, *Scribal Practices*, 50.

502   See A.M. Silbermann, *Chumash with Targum Onkelos, Haphtaroth and Rashi's Commentary Translated into English and Annotated*, Jerusalem 5745 [A.D. 1984], 2.

503   I refer to the study by Y. Sagiv, «"To Give Moses a Pause...": New Examples of Biblical Textual Divisions as Reflected in Rabbinic Literature and a Suggested Connection to the Calendar Debate», *Textus* 24 (2009) 205–220 (here, pp. 209–210).

504   Moses, for Num 12:6–8, is also more than a prophet; he is the revealer par excellence, the one who enjoys an unparalleled privileged intimacy with YHWH.

505   "And give him a chance to absorb what he had just been taught before continuing on. Most of the Torah was given to Moshe during the relatively short time before the sin of the ten spies [...]" (A. Davis, ed., *The Metsudah Chumash/Rashi*, III ויקרא Vayikro, Brooklyn 1998, 1, n. 1).

506   *Sifra: Parashat vayyiqra dibura denedabah*, 1 (parashah 1), 3.2.B (the translation is by J. Neusner, *Sifra. An Analytical Translation*, vol. I, BJSt 138, Atlanta 1988, 69).

"They prophesy lies to you, do not listen to them!" (27:16–17)   455

this "aperture" (*peꞇûḥâ*) signalled by the MT without being in too much of a hurry to proceed forward, at least not in a rereading. For to fully appreciate it, according to a narrative approach to the book, precisely a rereading is what one is invited to do, calling the memory back to the "principal" moment of the whole affair.

After the peremptory intervention of Hananiah, Jeremiah remains without words, one would almost say *without the Word*. He had tried to refute Hananiah's first speech in some way, but futilely. And then, it could be sensed already that the previous immediacy and assuredness of his speech had grown faint. His had been solid reasoning, even reasonable and comprehensible. But nothing more. After Hananiah's second reply, which was even more decisive than the first, Jeremiah is left alone, dishonoured,[507] with the pieces of his wooden yoke shattered by the *violence* of the adversary's gesture (cf. 28:10). And he almost seems to search in vain for traces on his mouth of that originary contact with the hand of YHWH that had made him forget all his inadequacy of speech and authority (cf. 1:6–10). Nothing.

Truly then, he was right to say to the Lord, moaning in fear and anguish, "I do not know how to speak" (1:6: לֹא־יָדַעְתִּי דַּבֵּר). He had even obeyed and had gone (1:8: √הלך) wherever the Lord had wanted, to proclaim his word, and now, precisely for that word, he found himself standing before Hananiah. If the Word had been placed on his lips, it would have sufficed to open it and let it vent, without fear. Also because the most important promise would have been fulfilled: "they will make war against you but will not win you, for I am with you to save you" (1:19). And what more opportune moment than this public confrontation with a false prophet, before the eyes of all, to show that God had made him like an iron column, a wall of bronze, and unassailable fortified city (cf. 1:18; 15:20)?

But now no encouragement comes from YHWH, no help, and no sign of comfort or even simple *presence*. So then truly, was YHWH no more than "a traitorous stream, a waterway that you can't count on"? (אַכְזָב מַיִם לֹא נֶאֱמָנוּ; cf. 15:18).[508] The divine promise of assistance and victory, solemnly made to Jeremiah (and the reader) in ch. 1, *seems* at the moment to fall into a void and not be realised at all. It was not and will not be the last time (cf. 20:1–2; 26; 36; 38:1–13; 43:1–7). In the Confessions, Jeremiah himself notes that his words do not come true (and that God, therefore, is not "reliable"; cf. 15:18; 17:15; 20:8). It is also the inglorious overturning of the Carmel scene. The indolence of the people is the same as that which leads to the frontal clash between Elijah and the prophets of Baal and Asherah (cf. 1 Kgs 18:21): no one takes a stand,[509] no one

---

507   On the importance of this theme for the question of the credibility of the prophetic word, see W.L. KELLY, «Prophets, Kings and Honour in the Narrative of 1 Ks 22», in: *Prophecy and Prophets in Stories*. Papers Read at the Fifth Meeting of the Edinburgh Prophecy Network, Utrecht, October 2013, *eds.* B. BECKING – H.M. BARSTAD, OTS 65, Leiden – Boston 2015, 64–75.

508   The LXX translates ὕδωρ ψευδὲς οὐκ ἔχον πίστιν (misleading water[course], devoid of reliability), rendering the expression even more disturbing, because it recalls the title of ψευδοπροφήτης, with which, in 34:1ᴸˣˣ, the false prophet Hananiah is stigmatised. The reference, as already in the MT, can also be to the unreliability of a *mirage*.

509   The *non-reaction* is that of all the people and of very distinct categories of people who represent the most important classes. Indeed, the number of references to the

456   Jer 27–28. The world beneath the yoke of the king of Babylon

assumes the responsibility of a response, at least not until the powerful manifestation of YHWH confirms the authority of his emissary.[510]

Here, however, the outcome is disastrous, and God seems entirely absent from the scene where, in his name, two perspectives from which to read history, diametrically opposed but both decisive, are revealed to the people. And so we see Jeremiah abandon the confrontation and go (28:11: √הלך) "on his way" (לְדַרְכּוֹ). The Hebrew expression לְדַרְכּוֹ, with or without the lexicalisation of the governing verb of motion (usually √הלך), is rather vague, but generally in reference to the moving of a subject toward the place decided solely by his own intention (cf. Gen 32:2; 33:16; Num 24:25; Judg 19:27; 1 Sam 26:25; 1 Kgs 1:49; Isa 53:6). It is therefore a very different movement from the one *commanded* (or forbidden) by YHWH to his interlocutors and to Jeremiah in particular in important moments in his ministry (cf. e.g. 1:7; 13:1; 16:5, 8; 18:2; 19:1; 26:2; 29:5–7).

Jeremiah goes away *in silence*. A silence that depends on the mystery of YHWH's silence. Both that of Jeremiah and that of God are, in any case, to be understood as forms of *communication* (intra and extradiegetic). This is a pragmatic dimension of the conversational dynamism with a broad spectrum of communicative functions codified differently depending on the contexts, which the studies of sociolinguistics, even in the biblical field,[511] have clearly highlighted.

Left speechless, the prophet seems to not know what to answer. Or rather, I would say, he *decides* not to answer. The text deliberately does not say so explicitly, and the narrator does not give us access to the emotions or intentions of the character, avoiding, as he usually does in the narrative parts of the book of Jeremiah, any internal focalisation. We are in the scene as well; we are one of the people or priests. And we are stimulated to read the situation, in the same way that the ancient manuscripts, with their interruption, deliberately put us in front of something unspoken that asks to be interpreted taking into account the pragmatic dimension of communication and not only the literality of the text, an open boundary inviting us to see beyond and to speak

---

recipients of the Jeremianic message is remarkable, in both chs. 27 and 28: the ambassadors who came to Jerusalem, and therefore their kings and respective nations, King Zedekiah, the priests, Hananiah (who represents all false prophets), and all the people of Judah, who Jeremiah now addresses in a particular way.

510 The existence and transmission itself of the book of Jeremiah attests this extratextual recognition, while in the flow of the narration, it can only be presupposed, beginning from the positive figure of Ebed-melech.

511 See e.g. the contribution of C.L. MILLER-NAUDÉ, «Silence as a Response in Biblical Hebrew Narrative: Strategies of Speakers and Narrators», *JNSL* 32 (2006) 23–43, who studies silence, understood as a response in a conversational setting. For other studies on the topic, cf. e.g. F. SPINA, «*A Prophet's "Pregnant Pause"*: Samuel's Silence in the Ark Narrative (1 Samuel 4:1–7:12)», *HBT* 13 (1991) 59–73; P. BARRADO, «El silencio en el Antiguo Testamento: aproximación a un símbolo ambiguo», *EstBib* 55 (1997) 5–27; S.J. BÁEZ, *Tiempo de callar y tiempo de hablar. El silencio en la Biblia Hebrea*, Roma 2000; W. DIETRICH, «Vom Schweigen Gottes im Alten Testament», in: *Gott und Mensch im Dialog*. Festschrift für Otto Kaiser zum 80. Geburtstag, *ed.* M. WITTE, BZAW 345/II, Berlin – New York 2004, 997–1014; M.C.A. KORPEL – J.C. DE MOOR, *The Silent God*, Leiden – Boston 2012.

"They prophesy lies to you, do not listen to them!" (27:16–17)   457

out.[512] It is not surprising that this empty space is sometimes (or often) filled unduly with the precomprehensions of each interpreter.[513] It is a space left to the disciples of the prophet.[514] And it is, in any case, the entirety of the book of Jeremiah that will help to grasp the most adequate meaning, since the Jeremianic text is the rereading of a history, which itself wants to be reread over and over again, so that the complexity of the interweaving of the meanings it contains can be appreciated.

5.3.4. "Whoever consigns themself [...] will live!" (21:9). Yet another (different) paradigmatic anticipation of a possible path of salvation within the horizon of the end of Jerusalem

The prophet, if we follow the logic of the (discontinuous) narrative flow from the time of its fountainhead (Jer 1), is repeatedly asked by YHWH to trust him and to continue to believe, until he accepts the experience of a momentary lack of visibility of the divine promises (cf. Jer 15:19–21; 20; 26:8–11; 36; 37:13; 38:1–4; 43:1–4). And this even when the non-visibility is so destabilising that it seems to be *entirely* identified with the failed fulfilment of the word of God, plummeting the whole prophetic experience of obedience into a *non-sense* to which death itself is preferable or, even more radically, to have not come out of the maternal womb into life (cf. 1:5 with 20:14–18). Once again, in the experience of Jeremiah, the configuration of a hermeneutical paradigm capable of rereading (or anticipating), *in some respects*, the story of all of Jerusalem and the people of Israel itself[515] is rendered visible to the reader.

In this case, Jeremiah is induced by the silence of God to fall silent himself, to remove himself from the public confrontation and withdraw. Thus (almost) accepting a defeat, since before the rhetorical force of Hananiah's proclamation, which even the reader (together with the Jeremiah-character) well knows to be false, he has nothing to use to counterattack. Hananiah has the last word. To emphasise lapidarily that "the prophet Jeremiah went on his way", however, means pointing to another specific level of contrast between the prophet of Anathoth and his antagonists, those prophets who in 23:25–26,

---

512 As is underscored by M. Miccio, *Ascoltare il silenzio*. Manuale di sociologia della comunicazione, Milano 2011, 8, silence "è un'arma retorica carica di significato al pari delle parole, ma più bisognosa di interpretazione" ("is a rhetorical weapon loaded with meaning equal to words, but in greater need of interpretation").

513 E. Di Pede, «La manière de raconter», 300, thinks, e.g. that Jeremiah decided to leave because he understood that countering would be useless, also considering the lack of reaction by those present (more or less along the same lines as J.R. Lundbom, *Jeremiah 21–36*, 337; R.W.L. Moberly, *Prophecy and Discernment*, 108). This is not, in my opinion, the motivation that the text suggests, when included in the general context of the book of Jeremiah and, in particular, in its thematisation of the "surrender".

514 For some interesting insights into the relation between the theme of the prophet's silence, the role of the "disciple", and the process of canonisation of the written prophetic word, see D. Janthial, «La parole prophétique: du rejet à la canonisation», *NRT* 136 (2014) 3–25 (esp. pp. 15–17, 24–25).

515 Again, see M. Cucca, *Il corpo e la città*. But also look at the critical observations and developments on the subject of the Jeremianic silence in ch. V, § 3.1.1 of my dissertation (esp. in n. 56, also in comparison to the silence of Jesus on trial).

458   Jer 27–28. The world beneath the yoke of the king of Babylon

30–32 are accused of founding their purported authority and social recognition on words stolen from others, and not on the authentic, sovereign revelation of YHWH:

> [25] I have heard what the prophets say who prophesy in my name, when they say; "I had a dream, I had a dream!". [26] How long shall there be prophets who prophesy lies, divulging as prophesy the deceit of their own heart? [...] [30] Therefore, behold, I am against the prophets (עַל־הַנְּבִאִים) who steal (√גנב pi.) from each other (אִישׁ מֵאֵת רֵעֵהוּ) my words – oracle of the Lord. [31] Behold, I am against the prophets – oracle of the Lord – who use their own tongues to declare oracles. [32] Behold, I am against the prophets of false dreams – oracle of the Lord – who tell them and lead astray my people with their lies and their boasting. I did not send them (√שׁלח), nor did I give them any command (√צוה pi.); they are of no benefit at all to these people. Oracle of the Lord.

The word of Jeremiah, contrary to that of the prophets of lies, does not have its original wellspring in he himself, nor is it the repetition of "stolen" words, that is, taken violently from other authentic prophets (so as to authenticate itself with that which is recognised as having prestige and authority). It is precisely his obvious inadequacy (cf. 1:6) that reveals that Another speaks in him and through him (in gestures and words). But this is revealed even further by the silence of Jeremiah who, *submitting* in fact to the adversary and his word, and exiting the scene, performs, above all, before the eyes of the attentive reader a "symbolic gesture"[516] of submission-surrender that while perhaps less flashy, has an even stronger force of impact than does that of the yoke. Indeed, we could say that precisely this gesture makes that of the yoke explicit, in the sense that it makes us understand the *surrender as silence* before the intrusion of evil on history.[517]

This act of *renouncing the power of the word* (and of public recognition) from the semiotic(-sociolinguistic) point of view actually guarantees a space of meaning for the word itself, which thus refuses to adulterate itself in the forms of lies, resorting to fantasies and the self-deception of one's heart (cf. 23:26). The choice is not an easy one, nor is it without consequences. It must certainly be placed in comparison with what follows the request of an oracle addressed to Jeremiah by the leaders of the people at another dramatic moment, even if it is after the destruction of Jerusalem. We are in Jer 42:1–6. Even though the need for a clear response from Jeremiah is urgent, he once again proves, in spite of himself, that he is not the *principle* (origin, source) of the prophetic communication. The divine word is not at his disposal, but is given gratuitously.[518] Just as it, likewise, is free to be silent. The response of YHWH does not

---

516   I speak of "symbolic gesture" obviously according to an analogous relationship. The question of gestures and symbolic structures in the book of Jeremiah merits an in-depth monographic study, which I cannot develop herein.

517   The partial or temporary defeat of Jeremiah is also reflected in the Confessions. In ch. 20, in particular, there is a void that is no less dramatic than that in 28:11. And in this, a theological-literary characteristic of the book of Jeremiah is confirmed, which I have noted from the outset of my research (cf. ch. 1, § 2.1): the constitutive relationship between narrative texts and texts having a more poetic form, two styles through which the totality of the Jeremianic message is spoken and articulated.

518   I therefore do not agree with R.W.L. MOBERLY, *Prophecy and Discernment*, 108, n. 16, who considers the two situations to not be comparable, since, in his opinion, Jeremiah would be placed before an entirely new situation (for which a specific

"They prophesy lies to you, do not listen to them!" (27:16–17)   459

berd to the anxiety and expectations of the calls for it, not even those of Jeremiah. And this is why the prophetic communication takes ten days to come (42:8–22). After these have passed, amongst other things, the applicants' inclinations seem to have rad_cally changed, if before, they had not been completely concealed (cf. ch. 43). As if, at this point, the appropriate time for the Word had already passed, the one arbitrarily fixed by humankind, not the one revealed or established by God.

Yet the experience of this otherness, while not easy, proves to be an obligatory step. Every false right must be surrendered and deposed. Only after the acceptance of this hiatus of extraordinary symbolic relevance, in Jer 28,12–17 as well, the voice of YHWH is made audible once again and, on the mouth of Jeremiah, becomes powerful prophecy that wipes out Hananiah's lie (cf. vv. 15–17) in his very person and in a much shorter time than the term fixed by his false prediction for the end of Babylonian hegemony.[519] In 28:16, the root שלח ("to send") is used in the piel, already utilised several times previously (cf. 28:9, 15, and even earlier in 27:3, 15). The word play created between "to send" the yoke (27:3), the being or not being "sent" by YHWH (27:15; 28:9, 15), and the punishment by which Hananiah is "sent" away from the face of the earth (28:16), on the one hand highlights a kind of *fitting punishment* (to presume to have been sent by YHWH – to be sent away by YHWH), on the other, it configures a curious *inclusion* between the beginning and end of the 27–28 unit, marked by the use of √שלח in the intensive form of the piel (which is located precisely at the opening in 27:3, while the other occurrences are in qal).

This "revenge" takes place in the *sign* of the "fulfilment" of the true prophetic word and in the accomplishment of what Deut 18:19–22 prescribes: the prophet who has the presumption to proclaim a word in the name of YHWH that does not have its origin in him, must die. And the (retrospective) criterion is precisely that of *realisation* (v. 22: √יהוה + √בוא) of what has been prophesied or not. Contrary to what the Deuteronomic prescription suggests, however, it is not a human court that executes a judgment on the false prophet (and not even the prophet himself, as happens with Elijah and the prophets of Baal in 1 Kgs 18:40, not without the help of those present), but it is YHWH himself who eliminates from the face of the earth the one who pushed the people of God towards rebellion and to trust in the lie (28:15–16). The prophet remains devoid of a power of his own: his only strength is obedience to the Lord of history. Whether he remains silent or publically demonstrates who his real envoy is. Precisely this outcome generates the *rereading* of 28:11 that I proposed.

---

divine revelation would have been necessary). In truth, it is new only in appearance. The question remains that of what stance to take before the Babylonian empire and its historical-theological role before YHWH, and the situation is analogically comparable to that seen previously (both with regard to Jerusalem under Zedekiah, and with regard to the exiles of 597). Indeed, one should be surprised by precisely the fact that, while the response of the prophet is entirely predictable (to the reader *in primis*), here, he renounces using even a single human word, even if, in theory, he would be legitimated in doing so, given his preceding prophetic experience (cf. 1:13: שׁקֵד), reasonable deductions on the subject, and demanded so by the urgency of the moment.

519   As notes e.g. L.C. ALLEN, *Jeremiah*, 318, who points out the irony of the fact.

460   Jer 27–28. The world beneath the yoke of the king of Babylon

The *convergence* or overlapping of the *moment of surrender* with that of *victory* is reaffirmed by another symbolic device, on another communicative level: that which requires the ability in an attentive reader to see an overview, the perspicacity to grasp points of contact between distant and seemingly unrelated textual elements ("semiotic *arcatas*", as I called them when I addressed the orientative hermeneutical coordinates in ch. II, § 2.4). The episode of the clash between Jeremiah and Hananiah, in fact, despite the textual difficulties that I have identified (cf. n. 24), is dated in 28:1 to the "fourth year" of Zedekiah (בַּשָּׁנָה הָרְבִעִית). This is the same year that Jeremiah, after having written on a scroll all the disasters prophesied against Babylon, hands it over to Seraiah, ordering him to make a symbolic gesture of great expressive strength (51:59–64): having reached the capital of the kingdom of Nebuchadnezzar along with the delegation of King Zedekiah, he should read its contents publicly and then throw the scroll into the Euphrates tied to a stone, decreeing the end of Babylon irrevocable. Even in this way, but on a different semiotic level, the coincidence of the acceptance of Babylonian domination with the proclamation of its defeat is thus signified.

As can be observed, the theme of "consignation" studied in 21:1–10 becomes more profound, revealing an admirable synthesis between the sapiential dimension and the prophetic one of revelation in the multifaceted prophetic symbolic gesture of surrender: surrendering to God is mediation of life, *always*. Even handing oneself over to the Babylonians is, but only *right now*. And only because by handing oneself over, first and foremost, to the Creator and Lord of history is one called to prophetically assume and signify in *this* way the meaning of *this* moment in time.

6. Conclusions: Jer 27–28 as an analepsis and multileveled paradigm with respect to the injunction of the surrender in Jer 21:1–10 and 38:14–28a

The topic we are studying is contained mainly in narrative portions. But the book of Jeremiah is *not* a story. Or rather, it is not *only* a story. Through the jagged surface of the text, a *plot* is certainly intuitable, but it is so complex that it risks bordering on chaos, also because it regards not only the organisation of the temporal development, but also the juxtaposition of genres and textual units that are quite diverse. More than be before a story, in fact, one can seem from the outset to be lost in a collection of disparate oracles. And yet, a little at a time, it is possible to trace a *fabula*, an orderly sequence of events that tends towards an end point that is, however, only indicated on the horizon in the oracles of consolation (or is hushed entirely regarding the final fate of the prophet).

Surprised by the unexpected proleptic insertion of Jer 21:1–10, the reader is later presented, in chs. 27–28, a textual unit that consists of two narrative moments, characterised by a clearly *analeptic function*. This *flashback* is necessary for the execution of the plan of the story to appear in a way that is understandable, but at the same time it also performs a *proleptic function* (in a theological-pragmatic sense, and therefore *paradigmatic*, and not narrative) in order to arrive armed with appropriate hermeneutical keys to open the subsequent narrative sections (above all, 38:14–28a). The particular positioning of Jer 27–28 therefore allows for the retrieval of information given first in presuppositions, according to *different levels of meaning*. First of all, the *historical-temporal* one. I have already focused on this extensively in chapter III of

Conclusions 461

the present dissertation. But, as was announced in the introduction, according to the path taken so far, other aspects can be highlighted herein.

In Jer 27–28, men, animals, nations, and prophets are placed within the horizon of the (*trés*) *longue durée* of history, set under the lordship of YHWH, the creator God. Against the background of the creation and the rhythms of the complex intrahistorical dynamics (the *longue durée*),[520] the destiny of the nations and societies is evoked. The reference to this universal dimension allows for a significant *focus* (by *contrast*)[521] on a fragment of *événementielle* history. Precisely what appears to be least influential to the gaze of a seasoned historian instead stands out in the book of Jeremiah as the most decisive place for understanding the (universal) Meaning being revealed (in the particular details). It is not the story of the powerful. Or not only. Not primarily. Great kingdoms, foreign nations, and the kingdom of Judah itself are involved. But it speaks of the meaning of history (of a single history and of all histories) that is offered indiscriminately to the discernment of all (to the nations, their ambassadors and their kings, to the king of Judah, its leaders and priests, and to all people and single individuals), presenting itself as a way of life to be assumed in obedience to the true word of God. A word that the book of Jeremiah attests be found on the mouths of concrete, fragile human beings, subject, like this man from Anathoth, to lashes and imprisonment, and even worse, themselves exposed to a refusal of the prophetic vocation and the temptation to reject the very meaning of their having come into the world (cf. 1:5 with 20:7–9, 14–18). Meaning is given in the fragment of detail, the book of Jeremiah strongly affirms. The Absolute is in the folds of history, of this history. The Meaning is here, now, before the nations, the kingdom of Judah, Jerusalem, its king, and all its inhabitants. A *stand must be taken*. If one does not decide, it will be done for them, regardless, as the course of events, in the place of those who would have had the privilege to exercise their freedom, heads into the night (cf. 13:16; 38:28).

A careful reading of the text (§ 2), together with a focalisation of its rhetorical articulation (cf. § 2.4), founded on the oppositive and complementary relationship between the *universal* semantic axis and the *specific* one, has thus not only allowed us a first examination, but has also indirectly highlighted how the *temporal dimension* is also called into account according to these two perspectives. And what decisive meaning can be revealed in it, and need be freely assumed. But other dimensions of meaning have emerged from the study of Jer 27–28, all of which can be framed, according to other levels, in the category of the *ante factum* (understood, however, in an analogical sense, starting from the narrative plan). Let us pick them back up synthetically.

---

520 By the term *longue durée,* the French Annales school of the historians (*École des Annales*) refers to a historiography with an interdisciplinary approach (directed mainly by social sciences) that programmatically privileges the study of long-standing historical structures rather than the sequence of circumstantial events (*histoire événementielle*).

521 On the diverse typologies of *focus*, on a linguistic level, see S.C. Dik – M.E. Hoffmann – J.R. de Jong – S.I. Djiang – H. Stroomer – L. de Vries, «On the Typology», 41–74; S.C. Dik, *Functional Grammar*.

462 Jer 27–28. The world beneath the yoke of the king of Babylon

6.1. Jeremiah beneath the yoke: A symbolic paradigmatic gesture to signify and physically take on the meaning of history in obedience to YHWH

Long underestimated in studies of biblical prophetism, which have mainly focused on the historical-literary and conceptual aspects of texts, the so-called "symbolic gestures" of the prophets have recently been the subject of renewed interest according to various lines of perspective. Regardless, their marginalisation with respect to verbal communication seems to generally remain, the latter favoured by the indisputable communicative superiority of discursive language (digital mode), at least as far as the level of productivity of conceptual meaning is concerned. Yet, as the most modern theories of communication increasingly highlight, communicating is an extremely complex phenomenon, in which the *relational* dimension is of fundamental importance and is conveyed above all by *non-verbal* language (analogical mode).

The prophetic Jeremianic message of "delivering oneself to the king of Babylon" and the way it is presented in Jer 27–28 on the basis of a synergy between gestures and words (cf. § 3), from its first emergence in the text (in a chronological sense), calls both dimensions into account, and thus requires an *interdisciplinary approach*. In fact, the prophetic body, placed at the centre of the scene of the text, assumes much more than a rhetorical-didactic function. In a *paradigmatic* way, that is, in order of a more adequate understanding of the entire subject, it poses before the eyes of the reader, as an ineluctable question, the *semiotic-symbolic interaction* between bodily existence and prophetic word, both in its proposing itself as a place of revelation for the Meaning (of history) and as an obligatory path for it to be taken on in response to the divine word.

Through the symbolic gesture of the yoke, Jeremiah actualises and renders visible his *status* as one who is "delivered" to obedience to YHWH first of all. The response requested of both the people of Judah and the foreign nations must also be placed on the same relational level, in Israel expression of the communal need for the Covenant. The rules that must inform the requested obedience are thereby contained in the symbolic grammar of this body language, which is of an eminently pragmatic nature (i.e. one determined by the communicative context). This will need to be implemented on an existential and political level this is concrete, and be elaborated in specific actions that concern both the body of the social-state and that of the individual, not least (as we shall see in the following chapter) with the "prophetic" act of *surrender* to the king of Babylon (cf. 38:14–28a). In other words, bearing in mind the symbolic perspective that emerges from the "total" Jeremianic message, said in gestures and words, allows one to better understand not only "how the Lord speaks",[522] within and beyond the book of Jeremiah, but also "how to respond to the Lord". The invitation is to enter into a prophetic-obediential dimension expressed in the "flesh", that is, in the body and with the body, involving the entire existential dimension of the human being.

---

522 In this sense, the so-called "messenger formula" shows an opening up of horizons of meaning that is much wider than a merely historical-literary understanding, along the lines – and *beyond* – of the theological dimension highlighted by A. WAGNER, *Prophetie als Theologie* (for whom, rightfully, the prophets are not mechanical repeaters of the divine word, but re-elaborators inspired by previous traditions).

6.2. YHWH as creator and Lord: Origin and foundation of a universal theology of history and paradoxical salvation, between a sapiential horizon and a prophetic focalisation

To have paid special attention to the form, and thus to the more specific identification of the instrument employed by the Jeremianic prophetic communication in 27–28 (cf. § 4.1) was not an idle or secondary matter ("zweitrangig").[523] It is in fact directly tied to the possibility of adequately focusing the underlying semantic *frame* both to the literal reference of the technical vocabulary and to the figurative value of the expressions concerning the image of the yoke.[524] In this sense, reference to documentation from the area of the ancient Near East, Neo-Assyrian and Neo-Babylonian, is very important for understanding the biblical texts that make use of the same image. The socio-cultural background is similar, and this has allowed us to refer to a wider encyclopaedic base (in the semiotic sense), which, in turn, allows us to appreciate the peculiar communicative intentions of the biblical page.[525] The yoke (imposed, carried, or broken, seen both from the perspective of the animal and human textual isotopies as well as from the agricultural or military *frame*) can be referred to, in any case, according to two, generally opposing, modes, a *negative* one and a *positive* one.

What is striking in the book of Jeremiah is twofold: (1) on the one hand, the rhetorical dislocation of the theme of the yoke makes it possible to appreciate its strategic importance. This allows me to observe that my theme is truly a thin red line that runs through the whole book, winding along its structural communicative articulations. In addition to this perspective, we can see that (2) in precisely the message of surrender to Babylon, we reach a kind of *coincidentia oppositorum*: the *negative* value of bearing the yoke, memory of Egyptian slavery or of fulfilment of the Deuteronomic curse, coincides with the *positive* one of observance of the word YHWH, which is always the path of goodness and salvation. In the ostensive and symbolic act of the yoke carried on the shoulders of the prophet, who asks, on the level of story, for an analogous assumption to be undertaken, modulated in political terms, a radical change

---

523   This is maintained e.g. by K. Ott, *Analogiehandlungen*, 154, who, if on the one hand rightfully believes it be impossible to form an exact idea of the instrument in question, still does not grasp that the terminology utilised in Jer 27–28 can recall, at the same time, animal isotopies (with the commonly understood yoke) and the human one (slavery, captivity, and their related instruments) and thus have interesting interpretive consequences.

524   A simplistic approach to the question leads to unfounded or completely conjectural conclusions, spoiled by their own subjective (encyclopaedic) concept of "yoke", such as the even suggestive one by Keown, G.L. – Scalise, P.J. – Smothers, T.G., *Jeremiah 26–52*, 48 (taken up by T.E. Fretheim, *Jeremiah*, 380), who, having in mind a "classic" yoke for two animals, believes that Jeremiah, by loading it onto his shoulders, left an empty place that would have ideally been taken on by his interlocutors.

525   Thus, in synthesis, A. Ruwe – U. Weise, «Das Joch Assurs», 307: "Der assyrische Kontext der Metapher wird nicht einfach übernommen oder kopiert. Vielmehr, so kann man mit aller Vorsicht sagen, bildet das neuassyrische Joch-Verständnis den Erfahrungshintergrund für einen kontrastierenden Umgang mit der Joch-Metaphorik in der *jhwh*-Volk-Beziehung, der dann nach dem Schwinden des assyrischen Kulturdrucks weiter eigene Wege in der Verwendung des Begriffes geht".

464   Jer 27–28. The world beneath the yoke of the king of Babylon

of perspective is produced. The history of Israel is the story of a people born from an act of liberation. It is precisely this people who is now called on to accept the enslavement of the foreign yoke as an "obligatory" path of meaning in order to not leave the very same story of life and liberty.

Another essential distinctive feature of Jer 27–28 is that the demand for submission is rooted in a foundation that is absolutely originary, and is inserted in a theology of history with universal breadth dominated by a divine will that knows no boundaries (§ 4.2). YHWH is in fact proclaimed *creator* and thus *Lord of the history of the nations*. Not only of those historically involved in the summit of Jerusalem before Zedekiah (594) or in the Babylonian advance in the Syro-Palestinian corridor (starting from 605). The necessity of submission and the threat of disaster acquires, in the Jeremianic message, a global symbolic value and concerns "every flesh", presenting itself therefore as an interpretive cipher that interrogates every human story. But it is in a fragment of history that this symbolic dimension is revealed, manifesting, in a certain sense, its *perennial value* (sapiential dimension), and in another sense, its *evenemential materialisation*, inimitable, in a here and now that is different from all other moments, that can only be an object of revelation (prophetic dimension). The appropriate human response is indicated in a gesture and a political-prophet choice that, in another pragmatic context (think of Isaiah during the Syrian-Ephraimite War), could have translated into all-out resistance, but which *now* takes the shape of "submission" to Nebuchadnezzar. At the time of Jeremiah, accepting the controversial *pax Babylonica* of this Hammurabi *Redivivus*[526] is not an apodictic necessity devoid of motivation. It has to do, for all nations, with the concrete acceptance of their own creaturely finitude, but also, more dramatically, with the divine instrument charged to *humiliate* all human *delusion of omnipotence* (§ 4.3) and to return Israel to the truth of its history.

Of course, this "now" implies, on the other hand, a *not now*. And this too is, in itself, a sapiential dimension, for there is a time, a "now" to fight and another to surrender (cf. Eccl 3:8). Knowing that there is not just one possibility is wisdom itself. Deciding whether in the urgency of the present one should surrender to the enemy or if it is best to resist or more advantageous to fight can still be, in certain cases, an issue of human shrewdness, of wise strategy. But to know how to discern the sense of time revealed by God here and now, know how to take on, within a relationship of response, obedience, and trust within the Covenant framework, and to have the courage to point it out to others at the risk of one's life, is solely a matter of *prophecy*. Thus, as bearer of this symbolic universe looking out upon human history from the eternal to transfigure it, Jeremiah will present himself before King Zedekiah in 38:14–28a, in their final, decisive discussion, upon which the entire destiny of Jerusalem will depend.

If in Jer 27–28, which is the first explicit, public attestation, chronologically speaking, of the call to surrender to the king of Babylon, the theme stands out against the grandiose background of a universal dimension and is introduced on the *stage* of the text while exalting the creationary power of YHWH and his lordship over all of history, this does not come about without a fundamental motive. And now we can get a greater sense of the motive. It is the establishment of a *principle*

---

526   As Nebuchadnezzar, with good reason, is defined by W.G. LAMBERT, «Nebuchadnezzar King of Justice», 3–4.

Conclusions 465

(origin, source) and *foundation* for the entire Jeremianic prophetic discourse of "delivering oneself to the king of Babylon". After the theme of surrender was presented in Jer 21:1–10 in the narrow perspective of the small history of Judah and within the gloomy horizon of its tragic failure before the God of the Covenant and the Exodus, this particular dimension is taken up again, but articulated and placed in relation to the theme of God the creator and Lord of the world and of all the nations. In Jer 27–28, together with the actants, before a man burdened with a yoke across his neck, as if he were a beast of burden: and now, we realise that the communicative dynamic of a symbolic-prophetic nature that renders this bizarre act a sensible gesture, and not ridiculous folly, depends first of all on faith in the power of YHWH. It is his creative word that makes Jeremiah's body in action the (mimetic) preview and (theological-symbolic) paradigm of the *condition of possibility* of the future of everyone, in the precise historical moment underway. There is, therefore, a Word that gives meaning to things, beyond all appearances.

Faced with the irreparability and inevitability of the end, *to remember* that YHWH is the creator God (cf. Jer 32:17.27) and the Lord of history will perhaps be the only stable foundation on which one can rely so as not to be overwhelmed by the non-sense generated from the systemic collapse of one's own world; the only narrow opening through which can pass the tenuous hope that the *end* not be the last word on this whole history,[527] even if culpable and a failure. Because only a God who is the guardian of the secret germination of life in all its forms, capable of shaping the wonders of the world and presiding over the highly complicated interweaving of human history, can build and plant a new world after or within his own (self)dissolution. That a prophet, that is, one who hears the Word, be "delivered" as accompaniment along this troubled path as a forerunner, whether he be an historical figure or a book named after him, is sign that again, this new Exodus will be rendered possible precisely by obediently handing oneself over to the revealed Meaning.

6.3. Between Word and anti-Word: Criteria for discernment of the meaning of history, before it is (once again) too late

In almost any communicative-situational context, a word that purports to read the meaning of events *according to truth* (cf. § 5) never has only a referential (or descriptive) function on the state of worldly objects, but generates a linguistic act with considerable

---

527 In this sense, this perspective provides greater grounds for the incisive synthesis of D. CLERC, «Des actes pour parler», 112, in reference to the relation between the symbolic gestures of the prophets and the drama of the exile: "Pour ceux qui reconnaissent ces actes comme signes de l'action créatrice de Dieu, ils sont comme des viatiques pour traverser les silences, les doutes, le rejet et la mort. Pour les traverser, non pour les éviter. Pour tous les prophètes proches de la crise de l'Exil, les relations entre Dieu et son peuple en sont à un tel degré de délabrement et de mensonge qu'elles sont devenues irréparables: le délai de conversion expire, la patience est à bout. Le seul recours qui reste à l'espérance, c'est que Dieu est créateur. Le jugement est un moment – noir mais inevitable – des relations entre Dieu et les hommes. Reconnaître que la réalité donne radicalement tort à tout homme, c'est peut-être, dans les grandes crises, le seul moyen de rester humain et d'espérer, malgré tout, devant Dieu."

466 Jer 27–28. The world beneath the yoke of the king of Babylon

illocutionary value,[528] which in the case at hand translates as the more or less explicit call to some form of "obedience" to the same meaning. This adhesion can take many forms and the call to it elicits various sorts of responses, even ones that are entirely negative. In any case, it is rather obvious that taking a statement for real corresponds with the negation (or, in biblical terms, with "non-listening"; cf. 27:9, 14, 16, 17) of its opposite. With this, I have repeatedly highlighted, over the course of my study, an indispensable expression of the performative-pragmatic dimension of human language, which can never be reduced to a series of formulations with mere constative value.[529] To speak is always also *to do*, to have an affect on the real, to provoke or solicit consequences in a relational sphere.

All the more reason, even at the level of the socio-cultural context,[530] the prophetic word, biblical or extrabiblical (whether this be a historical fact or a fictitious literary production), insofar as a proposal of *authoritative* revelation, implies in fact the need not only of obedience to precise indications, but also the rejection of other contrary words (i.e. "untrue", and not only adverse, as if they were a kind of magical power to be countered). And this makes it entirely logical that on the historical-phenomenological level, even before in the field of exegetic studies, in the historical-religious context of the ancient Near East, on the *conceptual level*, a line of demarcation between "true" and "false" prophecy was introduced, without this (always) having necessarily had a translation on a precise (and/or attested) *linguistic-lexical level*. The fact that this categorical distinction is by no means *fallacious* (according to the opinion of M.J. de Jong), and instead has an historical grounding, emerges from a pertinent reading of the available documentary sources (scarce, amongst other things) that does not limit itself to *solely formal* substantiation of a technical vocabulary.[531]

---

528 Amongst the many possible authors of reference, I reaffirm the ineluctability with regard to any interpretive act of the texts (verbal and non), together with the Dutch linguist T.A. VAN DIJK, *Text and Context*. Explorations in the Semantics and Pragmatics of Discourse, New York 1977, ⁶1992, 2: "[...] an utterance should not only be characterized in terms of its internal structure and the meaning assigned to it, but also in terms of the act accomplished by producing such an utterance. This PRAGMATIC level of description provides crucial conditions for reconstructing part of the conventions that make utterances acceptable, viz their APPROPRIATENESS with respect to the communicative context. In other words, pragmatic rules, which are also conventional and hence known by the language users of a speech community, determine the systematic use of utterances."
529 Cf. C. BIANCHI, *Pragmatica del linguaggio*, 61–64.
530 On the relevance of cultural context, see T.A. VAN DIJK, *Society and Discourse*. How Social Contexts Influence Text and Talk, Cambridge 2009, 154–212.
531 Not a few exegetic studies still base themselves, in fact, on an (unexpressed) conception of communication understood only as an encoding and decoding of information. This is the so-called "code model", whereby there would be conventional meanings perfectly retranslatable by the recipient of a message on a purely semantic basis. This model is actually insufficient, and needs to be integrated with processes of an *inferential* nature, given that "la rappresentazione semantica di una frase (la sua codifica) spesso non coincide affatto con i pensieri che possono essere espressi proferendo quella frase" ("the semantic representation of a phrase [its code] does often not coincide at all with the thoughts that can be expressed uttering that phrase") (translated from C. BIANCHI, *Pragmatica del linguaggio*, 100–126; here, p. 100).

Conclusions 467

In the specific case of Jer 27, and particularly in ch. 28, the impression is that more than a few exegetes, having probably comprehended the question of discernment between true and false prophecy in too simplistic terms, "solve" the hermeneutical knot posed by the comparison between prophets who proclaim and call for completely opposite things in the name of the same YHWH by resorting to an "Alexandrian solution": that is, denying the problem altogether.[532] Or by invoking here as well a formal explanation of the theme as in Deut 18:18–22. For this reason, Jer (27–)28 would concern, in other words, not the theme of discernment, but only the ideologically oriented presentation of a conflict between prophets.[533] In short: a story having nothing to do with indicating any interpretative criteriology for distinguishing the true prophetic word from the false one, despite recognising and highlighting before the reader's eyes that the fate of Jerusalem and the whole nation is specifically depends on the recognition and assumption of one rather than the other.

In truth, as I have attempted to demonstrate thus far (and as we will see even better in the next chapter), no part of the book of Jeremiah should be considered in isolation with respect to its overall semiotic architecture. Since the (Model) reader already knows the outcome of the story of the kingdom of Judah, their attention can be oriented to focus only on the *modalities* that produced it, and on how it could have been avoided (in the interest of the present and future). It is a rereading that dramatises, in narrative form, the interpretive travail that involved, in some measure, all the people of Israel. And the book of Jeremiah shows that Israel did not find itself before an ineluctable fate, seeing as its liberty of choice was solicited again and again to respond and choose, to the very end, the possible good.

---

532 As, e.g. R.W.L. MOBERLY, *Prophecy and Discernment*, 105, who thinks it be an error 'to assume that a narrative about prophetic conflict must also be about prophetic discernment", only to then indicate, as exemplary references, Amos 7:10–17 and 1 Kgs 13, which he says would be stories centred solely around the theme of "conflict". Actually, these specific examples demonstrate that the question of discernment is placed before the eyes of the reader regardless as being ineludible and decisive, even if complex. It can certainly be said that the elements provided are not clear, exhaustive, or even decisive, just as, after all, Deut 18:18–22 is not either, being a text that explicitly poses the problem, indicating a (unsatisfactory) resolution. The lack of a systematic framework or of criteria that is convincing in my eyes should not be confused with the problem not presenting itself at all in texts such as these (and Jer 28). Also because, taken in an absolute sense, and ultimately – no criterion is a conclusion that can be drawn precisely from how a question is presented, even in the texts just mentioned – *only a prophet can recognise another prophet* (cf. F. BEAUCHAMP, *Parler d'Écritures saintes*, Paris 1987, 63; P. BOVATI, «Alla ricerca del profeta. II. Criteri per discernere i veri profeti», *RCI* 67 (1986) 179–188 [= ID., «Alla ricerca del profeta. Criteri per discernere i veri profeti», in: *"Così parla il Signore"*. Studi sul profetismo biblico, *ed.* S.M. SESSA, Bologna 2008, ²2011, 37–52]; P. BOVATI – P. BASTA, *"Ci ha parlato per mezzo dei profeti"*, 111–137). And it is precisely to this "prophetic" discernment that the reader is called.

533 And it would be logical, taking on this prospective unequivocally, to resolve the question summarily, along the line of R.P. CARROLL, *Jeremiah*, 550: "The redaction is committed to Jeremiah, *therefore Hananiah is false*."

468   Jer 27–28. The world beneath the yoke of the king of Babylon

This is why the scene of the confrontation between Jeremiah and Hananiah is carefully prepared, in both the MT and LXX, which are careful to provide elements of narrative tension presented in an order that emphasises the twists and turns of ch. 28. While tracing out two different paths of meaning, both perspectives flow in a surprising way along the same *Leitmotiv* of the Jeremianic message of "surrender": the true prophets are those who should intercede for the temple furnishings, and it is of Jeremiah himself that (in MT) words of intercession are prohibited. The prophet of Anathoth confidently challenges the false prophets to a dialectical confrontation for decisive action (in the LXX), but then it is he who falters and retreats mutely and (apparently) defeated from the scene, having no further arguments. Too many empty, false, and useless words have now contaminated the history of the people of the Covenant, infecting and devastating the relational fabric with the other, the brother, and the Other who is the Origin of all things and the sense of its very existence. So if YHWH asks his prophet to surrender in this mystery of silence, it is because all of Jerusalem is *now* called to enter, through surrender, into the deep unknown of this cathartic silence. This is precisely where room can be left once more for the only true and life-giving Word, which creates and can re-create all things (cf. Lam 3:26–29, where the choice to remain silent correlates to the metaphor of the yoke and hope of the Lord's salvific intervention).

The comparison is obviously an analogous one, since relationships are drawn between pragmatic situations that are different, and yet these relationships an underlying logic even more clear: in ch. 28, the man Jeremiah, who accepts to be *reduced to silence* (as the ancient manuscripts themselves highlight graphically in their own way) and in this manner gesture, in spite of himself (cf. 16:1–13) the (provocative) withdrawal of YHWH from history,[534] is par excellence, in a paradigmatic sense, the one "delivered" to YHWH and to men, in faith and obedience, in a journey of humiliation and fruitful suffering. Precisely for this, he becomes, by the free action of God, the visible word of humanity "saved" from death, he who indicates to all of Israel (and to the reader) a possible path of salvation even in the darkest hour of the history of Jerusalem.

Actants and readers are placed before opposing prophetic words in which the Word is hidden and at the same time, revealed: the interpretive difficulty is evident, indeed, it is *emphasised*, and it is not overcome with an enucleation of clear, distinct criteria that solve the problem in the present beyond reasonable doubt. What matters, however, is that the text help to *thematise* the hermeneutical knot before the reader's conscience, the only one with the responsibility of uttering the final word, when they finds themself impersonated in the character-type of Zedekiah placed before an urgency of a final decision that can no longer be delayed.

So Jer (27–)28 does not wrap up the whole story or the full process of discernment, but just one of its phases. Not, however, before a decisive *criterion* has been indicated, despite the thorny difficulties of interpretation that rise to the surface: the true prophet is the one who allows themself to be led by faith through the mystery of a radical *handing over* of themself, precisely in God's silence, not backing down in the face of death (symbolic or not), and also accepting the loss of visibility of divine promises, without wanting to replace them with their own word or other hopes. We are not actually

---

534   Cf. D. Clerc, «Des actes pour parler», 131.

far off from the Deuteronomic principle of "fulfilment" (Deut 18:18–22), reiterated moreover by the conclusion in ch. 28. The question is that of its specific expression in more elaborated complexity. Indeed, the word of God comes to fulfilment beyond limited human expectations. And it is realised according to a *scalar perspective*, that is, by degrees along a temporal *continuum*. In Jer 28, we are presented with one of these phases that mark the life of the prophet Jeremiah. It is this living paradigm that will present itself before Zedekiah in 38:14–28a (and therefore in the reader's present time), to call, in turn, for total delivery, before it is (once again) too late.

Chapter V
Jer 38:14–28a.
Jeremiah and Zedekiah: The final colloquy.
A paradigmatic dramatisation
of human-divine communication

The unformulated primal theological principle of the Garden of Eden story about the divine-human relationship, namely that created man has been provided by the Creator's breath with real power of decision and so is able actually to oppose YHVH's commanding will – this mysterious article of faith rises now to awfully practical force. The divine demand for human decision is shown here at the height of its seriousness. It is to this personal decision of man with its part in the power of fate-deciding that the prophetic announcement of disaster calls. The alternative standing behind it is not taken up into it; only so can the prophet's speech touch the innermost soul, and also be able to evoke the extreme act: the turning to God.[1]

1. Introduction

In Jer 38:14–28a, the narrative tension built over the course of all the preceding chapters reaches its dramatic peak and the theme of surrender to the king of Babylon reveals itself, yet again and indeed this time definitively, to be the most crucial theological-political question of the entire book of Jeremiah. While in 21:1–10, the prophet from Anathoth was consulted by some of the king's emissaries, and 27–28 returned to the general backstory in the context of a *public confrontation* before a *large,* virtually international, *audience,* now the whole destiny of Jerusalem is played out in a final *secret colloquy* between the *individual figures* of the king and the prophet, in a face to face between Jeremiah and Zedekiah, albeit still before the eyes of the selfsame reader. To the Davidic sovereign desiring a prophetic word of hope, the way of life gets indicated here and now in the shape of a specific action: to go forth from the besieged city and deliver himself into the hands of the generals of the king of Babylon. This is the only way that he and the entire people will gain access to salvation, expressing obedience to the meaning of history revealed by YHWH in the unrepeatability of the present.

After having focalised the dislocation of the textual isotopy and some fundamental hermeneutical-literary coordinates of the theme of surrender to the king of Babylon (ch. I), we studied its historical context and the implications of this (ch. II). From the exegesis of 21:1–10 (ch. III), some important general theological repercussions emerged, and in 27–28 (ch. IV), we were placed before the multi-levelled *ante factum* of the Jeremianic injunction proclaimed on the scene of the text for the first time through the symbolic gesture of the yoke. Both the rhetorical-narrative positioning of 38:14–28a and its recapitulatory (while not entirely conclusive) nature[2] now invite

---

1 M. Buber, *The Prophetic Faith*, 103–104.
2 Because actually, the theme re-presents itself, in another context, in 42–43:7.

a treatment of the theme concentrated on study of the semantic-pragmatic dimension of the gesture of surrender requested of the king Zedekiah by the prophet in the most decisive moment in Jerusalem's history. Given its peculiar characteristics, this dramatisation appears to assume a *paradigmatic significance*. This is the principal path down which our exploration will lead us.

The study developed in the present chapter will hence proceed through the following stages:

I. *Jer 38:14–28a: text and context* (§ 2). As usual, I will present the Hebrew text, furnished with opportune critical notes and my translation alongside (§ 2.1). The textual unit will then be considered in relation to its immediate contextual placement (§ 2.2) and its internal articulation (§ 2.3). I will then subsequently widen the perspectival *focus* to study the contextual question over a wider scale, that is, to verify if any clues can be detected that justify speaking of there being a "redactional" symbolic intentionality in the structuralisation of the section comprised of chs. 26–45. I will highlight, in this sense, some particular long-distance relationships (semiotic *arcatas*) and interesting thematical-formal regularities that relate to the 38:14–28a unit and chs. 27–28 (§ 2.4). On this basis, I will then propose a new overall vision of the whole second section of the book of Jeremiah (§ 2.5).

II. *Exegetic focalisation of the most relevant aspects*. The subsequent stage will consist in exegetic study of the unit under examination, according to its internal tripartition (§ 3). This will be, above all, a question of grasping the significance of meaning of the call to surrender within the communicative exchange that takes place between Jeremiah and Zedekiah (§ 3.1) and the responsorial dynamic that this provokes, from resistances rooted in a fear of death (in its symbolic forms) to encouragement of the prophetic word, which does not hide the disastrous consequences of choosing the contrary (§ 3.2). Finally, I will briefly linger on the conclusive part of their meeting, a sinister prelude to the dramatic outcome of the whole story of the kingdom of Judah (§ 3.3).

2. A first approach to the textual data

In this initial approach to the textual data, I will once again limit myself to accompanying the usual presentation of the Hebrew text and my translation alongside it with some explicative notes. In several cases, these are intended primarily as introductive signallings of salient aspects. Where opportune, an in-depth analysis of these will then be deferred to the more specific treatment I will later develop.

2.1. Hebrew text, translation, and philological-exegetical notes

14	וַיִּשְׁלַח הַמֶּלֶךְ צִדְקִיָּהוּ וַיִּקַּח	King Zedekiah sent to get
	אֶת־יִרְמְיָהוּ הַנָּבִיא אֵלָיו	the prophet Jeremiah and had him come to him,
	אֶל־מָבוֹא הַשְּׁלִישִׁי אֲשֶׁר בְּבֵית יְהוָה	at the third entrance of the house of the Lord.
	וַיֹּאמֶר הַמֶּלֶךְ אֶל־יִרְמְיָהוּ	The king said to Jeremiah:
	שֹׁאֵל אֲנִי אֹתְךָ דָּבָר	"*I want to ask you a word*[3]:
	אַל־תְּכַחֵד מִמֶּנִּי דָּבָר	*don't keep any hidden from me!*"
15	וַיֹּאמֶר יִרְמְיָהוּ אֶל־צִדְקִיָּהוּ	Jeremiah responded to Zedekiah:
	כִּי אַגִּיד לְךָ	"*If I proclaim [it] to you,*
	הֲלוֹא הָמֵת תְּמִיתֵנִי	*will you not perhaps have me die?*
	וְכִי אִיעָצְךָ	*And if I give you counsel,*
	לֹא תִשְׁמַע אֵלָי	*you will not listen to me!*".
16	וַיִּשָּׁבַע הַמֶּלֶךְ צִדְקִיָּהוּ אֶל־יִרְמְיָהוּ	But the king Zedekiah swore to Jeremiah
	בַּסֵּתֶר לֵאמֹר חַי־יְהוָה	in secret: "[*As it is true that*] *the Lord is living*
	אֵת אֲשֶׁר עָשָׂה־לָנוּ אֶת־הַנֶּפֶשׁ הַזֹּאת	*who*[4] *gave us this life;*
	אִם־אֲמִיתֶךָ וְאִם־אֶתֶּנְךָ בְּיַד	*I will not have you die nor will I hand you over*
	הָאֲנָשִׁים הָאֵלֶּה אֲשֶׁר מְבַקְשִׁים אֶת־נַפְשֶׁךָ	*to those men who want your life!*".
17	וַיֹּאמֶר יִרְמְיָהוּ אֶל־צִדְקִיָּהוּ	So Jeremiah said to Zedekiah:
	כֹּה־אָמַר יְהוָה אֱלֹהֵי צְבָאוֹת אֱלֹהֵי יִשְׂרָאֵל	"*Thus says the Lord, God of hosts, God of Israel:*
	אִם־יָצֹא תֵצֵא אֶל־שָׂרֵי	*If you will really go out to meet the leaders*
	מֶלֶךְ־בָּבֶל וְחָיְתָה נַפְשֶׁךָ	*of the king of Babylon*[5] *your life will be saved,*
	וְהָעִיר הַזֹּאת לֹא תִשָּׂרֵף בָּאֵשׁ	*this city will not be burned with fire*
	וְחָיִתָה אַתָּה וּבֵיתֶךָ	*and you and your household shall live;*
18	וְאִם לֹא־תֵצֵא	*but if you do not go out*
	אֶל־שָׂרֵי מֶלֶךְ בָּבֶל	*to meet the leaders of the king of Babylon,*
	וְנִתְּנָה הָעִיר הַזֹּאת בְּיַד הַכַּשְׂדִּים	*then this city will be handed over to the Chaldeans*
	וּשְׂרָפוּהָ בָּאֵשׁ	*who will burn it with fire*
	וְאַתָּה לֹא־תִמָּלֵט מִיָּדָם	*and you shall not escape their hands*".
19	וַיֹּאמֶר הַמֶּלֶךְ צִדְקִיָּהוּ אֶל־יִרְמְיָהוּ	The king Zedekiah said to Jeremiah:
	אֲנִי דֹאֵג אֶת־הַיְּהוּדִים	"*I am afraid of the Judeans*
	אֲשֶׁר נָפְלוּ אֶל־הַכַּשְׂדִּים	*who have deserted to the Chaldeans:*
	פֶּן־יִתְּנוּ אֹתִי בְּיָדָם	*lest it not happen that they hand me over to them*
	וְהִתְעַלְּלוּ־בִי	*and they mistreat me!*".

---

3 Implied: "on the part of the Lord". A fully satisfying translation of this phrase cannot be found in English, given the ambivalence of the Hebrew term דָּבָר, which can be rendered with both "word" and "thing/fact", and which constitutes the direct object of the two propositions having the king as their locutor. Given the context, I prefer to shift the balance of the semantic of the text to the side of the "word-oracle", reserving further considerations for exegetic study (cf. also n. 6).

4 The *Masora parva* prescribes not reading the K (cf. BHS: *delendum*). For W. RUDOLPH, *Jeremia*, 242, it would only be a scribal error, but cf. 27:8, where the same marker of the direct object precedes the pronoun אֲשֶׁר (cf. C.F. KEIL, *Biblischer Commentar über den Propheten Jeremia und die Klagelieder*, Leipzig 1872, 391). According to E.F.C. ROSENMÜLLER, *Scholia*, II, 193, it would instead be a way to emphasise the subj. (YHWH) referred to by אֲשֶׁר.

5 Surrender is to be made to the generals/leaders (שָׂרִים) of the king of Babylon. Nebuchadnezzar, in fact, was not conducting the military operations of the siege in person, but was instead at his general quarters at Riblah (cf. 2 Kgs 25:1, 5–7, 18–21; Jer 39:5; 52:9–11:26–27). Cf. ch. II, § 3.3.1.

474 Jer 38:14–28a. Jeremiah and Zedekiah: The final colloquy

וַיֹּאמֶר יִרְמְיָהוּ **20** Jeremiah responded:
לֹא יִתֵּנוּ *"They will not hand [you] over!*
שְׁמַע־נָא בְּקוֹל יְהוָה *I beg you, listen to the voice of the Lord*
לַאֲשֶׁר אֲנִי דֹּבֵר אֵלֶיךָ* *in what I am saying to you[6]*
וְיִיטַב לָךְ *and [you will see that] it will go well for you*
וּתְחִי נַפְשֶׁךָ *and you shall live!"*

וְאִם־מָאֵן אַתָּה לָצֵאת זֶה הַדָּבָר* **21** *But if you refuse to go out, this is the word[7]*
אֲשֶׁר הִרְאַנִי* יְהוָה *that the Lord shows to me.[8]*

וְהִנֵּה כָל־הַנָּשִׁים אֲשֶׁר נִשְׁאֲרוּ **22** *Behold: all of the women who remain*
בְּבֵית מֶלֶךְ־יְהוּדָה מוּצָאוֹת *in the house of the king of Judah are led out*
אֶל־שָׂרֵי מֶלֶךְ בָּבֶל *to the leaders of the king of Babylon;*
וְהֵנָּה אֹמְרוֹת *and behold, they are saying:*
הִסִּיתוּךָ וְיָכְלוּ לָךְ *'They betrayed you, outdid you,*
אַנְשֵׁי שְׁלֹמֶךָ* *your trusted men[9]*;*
הָטְבְּעוּ* בַּבֹּץ רַגְלֶךָ *your feet sank[10] in the mud*
נָסֹגוּ אָחוֹר *[and they] turned their backs!'*

וְאֶת־כָּל־נָשֶׁיךָ וְאֶת־בָּנֶיךָ **23** *All of the women and your children*
מוֹצִאִים אֶל־הַכַּשְׂדִּים *shall be led out to the Chaldeans*
וְאַתָּה לֹא־תִמָּלֵט מִיָּדָם *and you cannot escape from their hands.*
כִּי בְיַד מֶלֶךְ־בָּבֶל תִּתָּפֵשׂ *Yes, you will be taken by the hand of the king of*

---

6 On the proposed translation, which seeks to emphasise the peculiar pragmatic force and possible theological density of this phrase, I will go into further detail ahead (in § 3.2.3).

7 In English, the phrase would be more obviously rendered with "this is *what* the Lord (shows to me)", but it would thus risk losing sight of a suggestive allusive reference that in Hebrew is suggested by the polysemy of the term דָּבָר. My translation, in fact, seeks to create in the English language an intentional sinesthetic dissonance between the audibility of the "word" and the visionary experience (√ראה hi.), thus recalling the דָּבָר (word/thing) asked of the prophet Jeremiah by Zedekiah in v. 14.

8 For the possibility (and the exegetic motive) of translating the perfect with the present in this case, see the considerations in § 3.2.6.

9 Lit.: "the men of your peace".

10 Following the LXX (καταλύσουσιν, which J. Ziegler corrects with καταδύσουσιν), Aq, Sym, and the Vg (*demerserunt in caeno et lubrico pedes tuos*), some commentators (e.g. B. DUHM, *Jeremia*, 306; D.P. VOLZ, *Jeremia*, 270; W.L. HOLLADAY, *Jeremiah 2*, 268) and some modern versions modify the vocalisation of the MT (that has an ho., as the Syr and Tg also presuppose) reading the verb as a hi.: הִטְבִּעוּ ("they made [them] sink"; cf. e.g. NEB: "they have let your feet sink in the mud"; RL: "[deine guten Freunde haben dich...] und in den Sumpf geführt"). With this facilitating solution, אַנְשֵׁי שְׁלֹמֶךָ would become the subject of the whole period and נָסֹגוּ אָחוֹר would be translated following the LXX: ἀπέστρεψαν ἀπὸ σοῦ ("they have turned away from you"); the Vg follows the LXX and translates: *recesserunt a te*). On the contrary, maintaining the MT, which reads הטבעו as an ho. ("they sank"), the subject of the phrase becomes רַגְלֶךָ ("your feet") and the implied subject of נָסֹגוּ אָחוֹר would still be identified in the expression אַנְשֵׁי שְׁלֹמֶךָ ("the men of your peace"). To me, this would seem to be the best

First approach to the textual data

וְאֶת־הָעִיר הַזֹּאת תִּשְׂרֹף[11]
בָּאֵשׁ

Babylon and <u>you will make</u> this city <u>burn</u>[11]
with fire!".

24 וַיֹּאמֶר צִדְקִיָּהוּ אֶל־יִרְמְיָהוּ
אִישׁ אַל־יֵדַע בַּדְּבָרִים־הָאֵלֶּה
וְלֹא תָמוּת

So Zedekiah said to Jeremiah:
"Let no one know these words
and you will not die.

25 וְכִי־יִשְׁמְעוּ הַשָּׂרִים
כִּי־דִבַּרְתִּי אִתָּךְ
וּבָאוּ אֵלֶיךָ וְאָמְרוּ אֵלֶיךָ
הַגִּידָה־נָּא לָנוּ מַה־דִּבַּרְתָּ אֶל־הַמֶּלֶךְ
אַל־תְּכַחֵד מִמֶּנּוּ וְלֹא נְמִיתֶךָ
וּמַה־דִּבֶּר אֵלֶיךָ הַמֶּלֶךְ

And if the leaders have come to know
that I have spoken with you
and they come to you and say to you:
'Go on, tell us! What did you say to the king?
Do not hide it from us and we shall not kill you',
and: 'What did the king say to you?',

26 וְאָמַרְתָּ אֲלֵיהֶם מַפִּיל־אֲנִי תְחִנָּתִי
לִפְנֵי הַמֶּלֶךְ לְבִלְתִּי הֲשִׁיבֵנִי
בֵּית יְהוֹנָתָן לָמוּת שָׁם

then you will say to them: 'I laid my plea
before they king to not send me back
to the house of Jonathan lest I die there'".

27 וַיָּבֹאוּ כָל־הַשָּׂרִים אֶל־יִרְמְיָהוּ
וַיִּשְׁאֲלוּ אֹתוֹ וַיַּגֵּד לָהֶם
כְּכָל־הַדְּבָרִים הָאֵלֶּה
אֲשֶׁר צִוָּה הַמֶּלֶךְ
וַיַּחֲרִשׁוּ מִמֶּנּוּ
כִּי לֹא־נִשְׁמַע הַדָּבָר

They came, [then], all the leaders to Jeremiah
and they question him, but he spoke to them
according to all those words
that the king had commanded;
so they ceased speaking with him
for nothing of the conversation had been heard.

28a וַיֵּשֶׁב יִרְמְיָהוּ
בַּחֲצַר הַמַּטָּרָה
עַד־יוֹם אֲשֶׁר־נִלְכְּדָה יְרוּשָׁלָ͏ִם[12]

And thus, Jeremiah remained
in the courtyard of the guard
<u>*until the day when Jerusalem was taken*</u>.[12]

---

solution. With D. Barthélemy, *Critique textuelle*, 718–720, I therefore hold that there is no well-founded reason to amend the MT.

11 Almost all commentators and modern version correct the MT on the basis of a few Hebrew mss, the LXX, the Syr and the Tg, revocalising the impf. 2nd per. sing. m. qal (תִּשְׂרֹף) like the ni. (תִּשָּׂרֵף) in v. 17. The Vg appears to follow the MT, but puts the verb in the 3rd per. sing.: "and he will burn this city with fire" (*et civitatem hanc conburet igni*). I, for my part, would prefer to maintain the MT, since it seems to be a witness of an interesting reading of the theology of history. I would therefore interpret the deontic modality of the impf. Hebrew תִּשְׂרֹף as an expression of a causal nuance (just like some translations cited by D. Barthélemy, *Critique textuelle*, 720), which implicates an underscoring of Zedekiah's culpability (cf. W. Rudolph, *Jeremia*, 242; in the MT, however, there are no attested uses of √שׂרף in either the hi. or pi.). On the motives for my choice, which presuppose the reference to the analogous question (both from the philological as well as the theological-exegetical point of view) in 28:13, see § 3.2.8.

12 In the MT, after a *sᵉtûmâ* that closes v. 28a (and recalls the one placed after v. 14, inviting the reader to consider 38:14–28a as a literary unit of its own), v. 28b continues thus: וְהָיָה כַּאֲשֶׁר נִלְכְּדָה יְרוּשָׁלָ͏ִם (lit.: "And it happens [for the use of וְהָיָה in place of וַיְהִי cf. also 3:9; 37:11, which the LXX translates with καὶ ἐγένετο], when Jerusalem was taken" [...]). Immediately following is a *pᵉtûḥâ* (and then a *sᵉtûmâ* in 39:14, at least according to codices A and C). Despite these indications of textual segmentation,

476   Jer 38:14–28a. Jeremiah and Zedekiah: The final colloquy

2.2. Immediate contextual placement (Jer 38) and unity of the composition being studied

The pericope under analysis, while endowed with its own relative thematic-formal autonomy, should be considered in close correlation to the one previous, 38:1–13, which narrates Jeremiah's preaching concerning the need for surrender to Babylon (vv. 1–3), the reaction of the leaders, who get permission from the king to put him to death and throw him in a cistern (vv. 5–6), and the prophet's salvation through the intervention of Ebed-melech, who intercedes for him with the king (vv. 7–13).

---

some commentators and some modern versions consider v. 28b to be a (second) conclusion of the passage we are studying, and translate with words similar to LND: "And he [Jeremiah] was there when Jerusalem was taken" (cf. e.g. BJ: "Et il y était quand Jérusalem fut prise"). Others, instead, consider v. 28b to be out of context, opting for its repositioning at the beginning of 39:3. The LXX (according to the Sinaiticus and Vaticanus codices), translates only וְהָיָה (καὶ ἐγένετο), incorporating it as the incipit of 46:1^{LXX} (=39:1^{MT}) and thus with an introductive function for the following textual unit. The Syr, along with some Hebrew mss, entirely omits v. 28b, probably for homeoteleuton (the last words of 28a and 28b [אֲשֶׁר נִלְכְּדָה יְרוּשָׁלָם] are identical), while the Vg and the Tg reflect the MT. As can be seen, the question is rather controversial and depends more on considerations of a critical-literary and exegetical nature than on difficulties tied to the transmission of the text (as is observed by D. BARTHÉLEMY, *Critique textuelle*, 723, to whom I defer for a broader and more detailed discussion of the problem, which I do not consider appropriate to develop further herein). I, for my part, believe that the MT (perhaps even deliberately) presents an elliptical phraseology that makes some lexical explicitation inevitable in translation, thus making the hermeneutical operation of the reader decisive. In this way, the reader is called to say the unsaid that they consider presupposed in the text, above all in reference to the verb וְהָיָה. There are, in my opinion, at least three possibilities to be considered: (1) If וְהָיָה refers to Jeremiah, the adverbial particle שָׁם needs to be introduced or, in any case, understood, as does LND. The prophet remains *there*, in the place of detention, until Jerusalem is conquered. In this manner, a semiotic *arcata* is created with the scene of his liberation in 39:14; (2) it could be an emphatic reference to what has just been narrated, given its decisive function in the narrative economy of the book: "and [*thus/this*] happens when Jerusalem was taken"; (3) a third possible reading links 28b to what follows: "(28b) And it happens, when Jerusalem was taken: (39:12) [*it was*] in the year [...] (39:3) and all the leaders of the king of Babylon entered [...]".Though it is not the only one, this solution is probably the best (thus, also D. BARTHÉLEMY, *Critique textuelle*, 725, and amongst the modern versions e.g. TOB; RL), also keeping in mind the aforementioned Masoretic indications. In 28a, all the dramatic tension of ch. 38 comes to a climax. The question prompted in the reader regarding the king's decision, on which the prophetic word makes the entire fate of Jerusalem depend, finds a bitter but suggestive response in 28a. Once again, the communicative-pragmatic power of the unsaid is used: it does not explain what Zedekiah has done, it mentions the catastrophic effects of his (non-) decision: Jerusalem goes to meet its fate. This is why the pause after 28a is truly significative. In this perspective, the phrase in 28b, precisely for its difficulty, acts as a hinge between the two moments (38:14–28a and 39:1–14) without clearly or unequivocally belonging to one textual unit or the other: it definitely does not stop the narrative flow, but rather opens it up (*pᵉtûḥâ*) to the dramatic description of the final events (even with a rapid flashback in 39:1 that picks up the thread of the events from the beginning of the Babylonian attack).

Chapter 38 presents itself as a *diptych* composed of two literary units (38:1–13 and 38:14–28a) that, despite being two distinct episodes, generate a consequential and coherent narrative flow. From the reciprocal relationship between these two scenes, as we shall see, significant elements of meaning can be deduced. For the time being, it suffices here to note the most salient thematic and formal clues highlighting this relationship:

1) the contrapositioning of the *public context* in which the Jeremianic message about surrender to Babylon resonates in 38:1–13 (cf. vv. 1, 4) and the *private* (indeed, secret) one described in 38:14–28a (cf. vv. 14, 16)[13];
2) the analogical correspondence between the image of the prophet Jeremiah thrown into the muddy cistern by his enemies in 38:1–13 (cf. v. 6: "In the cistern there was not water but *mire* [טִיט], and thus Jeremiah *sank* [√טבע] in the *mire* [טִיט]") and the "song of the women" that takes up the central part of 38:14–28a, which speaks of the feet of King Zedekiah sinking into the "mud" [בֹץ] because of the betrayal or prevarication of his fiduciaries or court ministers (cf. v. 22: "[...] your feet *sank* [√טבע ho.] in the *mud* [בֹץ] [and they] turned their backs!").

The most significant rhetorical element that indicates this dual delimitation (of ch. 38 as an independent unit formed, in turn, by two sub-units) is a conclusive sentence with a rhetorical function of *final term*: this marks a clear caesura with ch. 39 and, in turn, separates the pericope of 38:1–13 from our own. I am referring to the following expression, repeated to the letter in 37:21; 38:13b, and 38: 28aα: וַיֵּשֶׁב יִרְמְיָהוּ בַּחֲצַר הַמַּטָּרָה ("Thus Jeremiah remained in the courtyard of the guard). Its structuring function actually also concerns the organisation of the entire section and the respective sequences in chs. 37–38. A sentence with similar content concludes the unit of 37:11–16 as well. In particular, it should be noted that the placement of the verb וַיֵּשֶׁב, with Jeremiah as its subject (cf. 37:16b; 37:21b; 38:13b; 38:28a; 39:14b; 40:6b) marks the end of as many as six literary units.[14]

Other significant *final terms* to be highlighted for the general delimitation of ch. 38 are the lexemes עִיר ("city") and יְרוּשָׁלַם ("Jerusalem"), and the lexeme יוֹם ("day"), which set 37:21 and 38:28a in close relation. Also, the different syntagms that get constituted by the latter (לַיּוֹם; "every day" [a loaf of bread] and עַד־יוֹם; "until the day" [that Jerusalem was taken]) contribute, in their respective contexts, to define two temporal *arcatas* oriented to their *end*. In the first case, it is the provision of daily sustenance provided to the prophet in captivity as well as its *conclusion* (37:21a: עַד־תֹּם כָּל־הַלֶּחֶם מִן־הָעִיר; "until all the bread in the city was gone"). The depletion of basic food supplies for human survival in times of siege is a clear figure of the end of Jerusalem. In the second case, on the other hand, the final term is the fulfilment of the fate of the City itself, placed in relation to the end of Jeremiah's detention. Let us look at the textual scansion highlighted schematically:

---

13 Also of note is the alternation between *public* and *private* (*secret*) contexts that characterises the different scenes beginning from ch. 37: 37:1–10 (private consultation); 37:11–16 (public scene); 37:17–21 (secret encounter); 38:1–13 (public context, at least that relating to the preaching of the prophet); 38:14–28a (secret encounter).

14 As in G. WANKE, *Untersuchungen*, 94–95 and J.M. ABREGO, *Jeremías*, 65.

Jer 37:17–21	**SECRET** meeting (cf. v. 17) between Zedekiah and Jeremiah.
Final term	v. 21: "Thus Jeremiah remained in the courtyard of the guard."

Jer 38:1–13	Jeremiah asks (**PUBLICALLY**) for the surrender *of all the people* to the Babylonians and for this, gets thrown into the cistern by the "leaders", with the permission of Zedekiah. Jeremiah "SINKS in the MIRE"). He then gets LIBERATED through the intercession of Ebed-melech.
Final term	v. 13: "Thus Jeremiah remained in the courtyard of the guard."
Jer 38:14–28a	Zedekiah calls for Jeremiah: final (**SECRET**) dialogue *between the prophet and the king*. Jeremiah asks also Zedekiah to hand himself over to the king of Babylon, otherwise he himself "WILL SINK in the MUD".
Final term	v. 28aα: "Thus Jeremiah remained in the courtyard of the guard"; until the fall of the city.

Jer 38:28b–39:14	The taking of Jerusalem[15] and LIBERATION of Jeremiah.

Instead, as far as the specific delimitation of unit 38:14–28a is concerned, it should be observed that the initial verse (v. 14a) creates an inclusion with v. 28a. The introductory function of the first and conclusive function of the second are clear: they both frame[16] the dialogue between the king and the prophet and have some lexical elements in reciprocal reference, especially by analogy or antonymy. The narrative-spatial path they chart in reference to Jeremiah first shows the prophet being taken from prison and then brought back to the same place.

14a	King <u>Zedekiah</u> SENT (√שלח) TO *GET* (√לקח) the prophet <u>Jeremiah</u> (and HAD HIM COME)[17] to him, at the *third entrance* of the **house of the Lord**.
	- -
28a	Thus <u>Jeremiah</u> REMAINED (√ישׁב) in the *courtyard of the guard* Until the day when **Jerusalem** was *TAKEN* (√לכד).

---

15 In its turn, this pericope concludes in Jer 39:14b with a summary that is quite similar: "Thus he [Jeremiah] remained amongst the people" (וַיֵּשֶׁב בְּתוֹךְ הָעָם).

16 As we shall see, on the basis of other lexical relationships, I consider v. 27 to be an integral part of the final textual unit of our passage (vv. 24–27), even though this too does not lack a "conclusive" nature of its own and interrupts the dialogical exchange between the king and the prophet that runs from v. 14b to v. 26.

17 I believe that this locution, placed in parenthesis in the translation I have provided, can be an adequate rendering of the Hebrew expression that would literally read: "*The king Zedekiah sent to get* [...] *towards himself* (אֵלָיו), *towards* (אֶל) *the third entrance* [...]."

First approach to the textual data 479

While we may not perhaps be able to talk about actual proof of rhetorical organisation, it does nevertheless seem appropriate to point out the semantic relationships
between the lexical elements highlighted, accentuated, in my opinion, by the very
fact that the two units relate to one another as an "introduction" and a "conclusion".
In particular, attention should be given to the relations between: (1) proper names;
(2) verbs; (3) places. These are *three different semantic axes* that make up the basic
structure of the narration, and which already suggest an overall key of interpretation,
since the relation between the lexemes that represent them is dynamic.

1) The two proper names introduce the protagonists of the passage. The fact that in
   28a, that is, at the end of the narrative unit, only the name "Jeremiah" is repeated,
   in light of the unfolding of the story, is no accident.
2) To the verbs of movement that express the action of "to send to get" (√לקח + √שלח
   + אֶל) Jeremiah, the notion of "stasis" (through √ישב) rests in opposition, in reference to the very same subject. Bearing in mind the phrase repeated in 38:13b and
   38:28a, the trajectory of a path that begins from captivity and returns to captivity
   can actually be recognised.
3) Both at the beginning (v. 14a) and the end (v. 28a), significative spatial coordinates
   return, and a specific relationship can be highlighted between them. One is merely
   logistical in nature: "the third entrance" (מָבוֹא הַשְּׁלִישִׁי) – "the courtyard of the guard"
   (חֲצַר הַמַּטָּרָה); the other is connoted with a more theological-religious meaning: "the
   house of the Lord" – "Jerusalem".

2.3. Internal articulation of Jer 38:14–28a (rhetorical analysis)

It needs to be acknowledged that the interweaving of correspondences and lexical
references is very complex and it is not simple to present it in an arrangement that can
easily reconcile exhaustiveness and clarity. The text always surpasses its interpretations. I will therefore limit myself to isolating the phenomena that I consider most
relevant, primarily those that justify its subdivision into *three main units*:

	14	**KING Zedekiah sent** (√שלח) **TO GET** (√לקח) the prophet **Jeremiah** [and had him come] to him, at the third *entrance* of the house of the Lord.
I	15	The KING said to Jeremiah: «I want *TO ASK YOU* (√שאל) a word (דָּבָר): DO NOT HIDE FROM ME (√כחד pi.) any **word**! (דָּבָר)». Jeremiah responded to Zedekiah: «If I *inform* (√נגד hi.) you, will you not perhaps have me die? And if I give you counsel you will not listen to me!».
	16	But the KING Zedekiah swore to Jeremiah in **SECRET**: «[As it is true that] the Lord is living, who give us this life; I will not have you die nor will I *hand you over* (√נתן) to those men who want your life!».
	17	So Jeremiah said to Zedekiah: «Thus says the Lord, God of hosts, God of Israel: *If you will go out* (√יצא) *to meet the leaders for the* KING *of Babylon,* your life will be saved, **THIS CITY** (הָעִיר הַזֹּאת) will not be **burned with fire** (√שרף + בָּאֵשׁ) and you and your household shall live.
	18	But *if you do* not *go out* (√יצא) *to meet the leaders of the* KING *of Babylon,* then **THIS CITY** (הָעִיר הַזֹּאת) *will be handed over* (√נתן) to the Chaldeans who **will burn** it **with fire** (√שרף + בָּאֵשׁ) and you shall not escape **their hands**».

Jer 38:14–28a. Jeremiah and Zedekiah: The final colloquy

II	19	The **KING Zedekiah** said to **Jeremiah**: «I am afraid of the Judeans who have deserted to the Chaldeans: lest it not happen that they *hand me over* (√נתן) **into their hands** and they mistreat me!».
	20	Jeremiah responded: «They will not *hand* [you] *over!* (√נתן) Listen to the voice of the Lord in what I am saying to you and <u>it will go well for you and you will live!</u>
	21	But if you refuse to go out, this is the **word** (דָּבָר) that the Lord shows to me.
	22	Behold: **all the women** who remain in the house of the king of Judah *are led out* (√יצא ho.) *towards the leaders for the KING of Babylon* and they sing: "They betrayed you and outdid you the men of your peace; your feet are sunken in the mud [and they] turned their backs!" **All of your women** and your children *shall be led out* (√יצא hi.) *towards the*
	23	*Chaldeans* and you cannot escape **from their hands**.
		Yes, *you will be taken* (√תפשׂ ni.) **by the hand** of the **KING** of Babylon and **THIS CITY** (הָעִיר הַזֹּאת) **will be burned with fire** (√שׂרף + בָּאֵשׁ)».
III	24	So **Zedekiah** said to **Jeremiah**: «Let no one know of these **words** (דְּבָרִים) and you surely <u>will not die</u>.
	25	And if the leaders will have come to know that I have spoken with you and they come to you and say to you: "Go on, *inform us* (√נגד hi.)! What did you say to the **KING**? Do not hide (√כחד pi.) it from us and <u>we will</u> not <u>kill you</u>", and: "What did the **KING** say to you?",
	26	then you will say to them: "I laid my plea before **KING** to not send me back to the house of Jonathan to <u>die</u> there"».
	27	They came, [then], all the leaders to Jeremiah and **THEY ASKED HIM** (√שׁאל), but *he informed* them (√נגד hi.) according to those **words** (דְּבָרִים) that the **KING** had commanded him; so they ceased speaking with him because **the word/the thing** (דָּבָר) had not been heard.
	28a	And thus **Jeremiah** remained in the courtyard fo the guard until the day when Jerusalem was taken.

The internal three-part subdivision is highlighted by the *initial terms* "Zedekiah" + "Jeremiah" in vv. 14 (beginning part I), 19 (beginning part II), and 24 (beginning part III). The function of the *final terms* can instead be recognised in the expressions "this city" (הָעִיר הַזֹּאת) + "burn with fire" (√שׂרף + בָּאֵשׁ) in vv. 18 (end part I), 23 (end part II), to which the term "Jerusalem" + "conquered" (√לכד ni.) in v. 28a corresponds synonymically (marking the conclusive valence of part III).

Other internal rhetorical phenomena that confirm the tripartition proposed are the following:

In *part I* (vv. 14–18), the oppositive relationship between the term "entrance" (מָבוֹא) in v. 14, derived from the root בוא and the verb "to go out" (√יצא)[18] in vv. 17 and 18 can be highlighted. Despite the manifold attestation of the lexeme "king" (מֶלֶךְ), it can be considered the *extreme term* in vv. 14–15 and in vv. 17–18 (*part I*), and in vv. 19 and 29 (*part II*). In vv. 17–18, at the end of *part I*, the repetition of the phrase "exit" (√יצא) + "towards the leaders of the king of Babylon" (אֶל־שָׂרֵי מֶלֶךְ בָּבֶל) should also be noted, which then returns in the centre of *part II* (v. 22) where, at the end (v. 23), we have instead only the expression "king of Babylon" (מֶלֶךְ בָּבֶל).

Part II (vv. 19–23), which is linked to *part I* by the *middle terms* "the Chaldeans" (הַכַּשְׂדִּים) and "in/from their hands" (מִיָּדָם/בְּיָדָם),[19] is distinguished above all by the central placement of the vision with the "song of the women", which, in turn, has its fulcrum in the expression "the men of your peace" (אַנְשֵׁי שְׁלֹמֶךָ), marked by the inclusion given by the *extreme terms* of "all of your women" (כָּל־הַנָּשִׁים) + "are brought out" (√יצא ho. *and h..*). *Part I* and *II* also have the presence of the semantic field of *life* (promised) and *death* (suffered, inflicted, or avoided) in common.

Part III has the name "Jeremiah" and the lexemes "word/words" (דְּבָרִים/דָּבָר) as *extreme terms* in vv. 24 and 27, and is connected to *part I* by the verbs "to question" (√שאל) in vv. 14 and 27; "do (not) hide" (√כחד pi.) in vv. 14 and 25 (cf. also the phrase "no one knows" [אִישׁ אַל־יֵדַע] in v. 24); and "to inform" (√נגד hi.) in vv. 15 and 25.27. Also of note is the frequent attestation in all the units of the theme of "handing oneself over/going out towards" and the lexeme "king" (מֶלֶךְ), clear lexical evidence of how central the theme of the royal figure in relation to the prophetic word and its demands is in 38:14–28a. These rhetorical elements confirm a tripartite structure of the text that is also based on content-related criteria and on a narrative articulation that can be summarised as: I) the question of the king, objection, and first response; II) objection and new response (with expansion); III) injunction of secrecy on the part of the king, question of the leaders, Jeremiah back in prison.

2.4. Semiotics of the literary architecture (I): The long-distance relationship between Jer 26–27(-29) and the diptych of Jer 38 (v. 1–13 and 14–28a)

The book of Jeremiah, as I attempted to highlight in the chapter dedicated to the general hermeneutical-literary coordinates (ch. I), should not be considered a more or less random conflation of poetic texts and narrative sections devoid of a coherent organisation. Going beyond an initial impression, which can certainly disorientate the reader, bit by bit, as the gaze grows more attentive, one can at first glimpse and then gradually see *relations* and *regularities* become more marked and make more sense at both short and long distances, between both major and minor literary units.

---

18 Cf. e.g. Ps 121:8, where the opposition between the two roots is used in a common and significant merism: "The Lord will guard *your going out* (√יצא) and *your coming* (√בוא), now and forever."

19 These syntagmatic units also serve the function of *extreme terms* for the beginning (v. 19) and end (v. 23) of *part II*. Another middle term at a distance, which recurs 2x in *part I* (vv. 17–18), 1x in *part II* (v. 22) and again 2x in *part III* (vv. 25, 27) is the lexeme "leaders" (שָׂרִים).

482   Jer 38:14–28a. Jeremiah and Zedekiah: The final colloquy

For this reason, I spoke of "editorial semiotic intentions" and introduced the notion of "semiotic *arcatas*" as guiding concepts with heuristic valence.

In studying chs. 27 and 28, for example, not only did the tight relationship between them become clear, but so did (on a higher level of observation) their common belonging to an even broader unit given by chs. 27–29. Its delimitation downstream constitutes the beginning of a new unit (the "Book of Consolation" of chs. 30–31 [+ 32–33]), while upstream, with the narration of Jeremiah's Temple Sermon and the subsequent trial against him, we find ourselves in a vastly different context and even the thematic would appear to be different. *Would appear.*

Indeed, with ch. 27, we are no longer in the time of Jehoiakim, but in that of Zedekiah, and the prophet makes a symbolic public gesture to invite everyone to surrender to the king of Babylon. In ch. 26, however, Jeremiah's message, whilst threatening the destruction of the temple by an unnamed enemy, deals with a more ethical-religious question. Yet what seems to have no relation on a local level, when considered instead from a broader perspective, may turn out to have a semiotic relationship with another literary structure, the inner articulation of which is fundamentally clearer. This is precisely the case in the relationship between the two parts of ch. 38 and the two scenes in chs. 26 and 27, apparently unrelated. Let us look at why.

Let me return to the most obvious data that emerged from the analysis of the textual organization of ch. 38 and draw an interpretative consequence. Jer 38:1–13 and 38:14–28a form a diptych, and the analogical correspondence between Jeremiah's descent into the mire of the cistern (v. 6) and the sinking into the mud of the feet of Zedekiah sung by the women in the Jeremianic vision (v. 22) confirms this, inviting us to push beyond a simple ascertainment of the two units being placed in a narrative *continuum.* The question does not relate to merely this, but also the fact that the image of the prophet who presents himself before the king Zedekiah to address him in the final, decisive appeal for the duple handing over of himself (to YHWH and thus to the king of Babylon, his executor of justice) is that of a man who *incarnates himself the message he expresses.*[20] The events of his prophetic body just narrated in the previous scene are clearly, in themselves, a sign: Jeremiah is a figure of the human being handed over entirely in obedience to YHWH to the meaning of their story, which is that of being the defenceless word of God placed in the hands of humanity, with the promise that that word, which is now that very same person, will not be defeated. And this is what happens to him: his message is rejected, his body-message humiliated, wounded, and thrown into the pit of death. But from precisely there, from humanity's most absolute fear, he is saved.

Jeremiah presents himself this way before Zedekiah (and thus, *before the reader*). In his own story, there is already the sign that the word of YHWH is truly fulfilled (cf. 1:12) and he is truly indicating the meaning of present history to Zedekiah (and all the people) as well: it is necessary for them to *surrender to the king of Babylon*, symbolically accepting death, like Jeremiah, without letting themselves be overcome by fear (cf. 1:8, 17–19, and 38:19–20), certain that God will fulfil, through precisely this, his promise of life, for the king and for all of Jerusalem (cf. 38:17). So the diptych in ch. 38 is far more than a matter of rhetorical-textual organisation.

---

20   On this topic and for study of 38:1–13 in this sense, see M. Cucca, *Il corpo e la città*, 203–254.

Once the semiotic relationship has been recognised between *Jeremiah* as a living figure of the fulfilment of the divine word and his *interlocutors*, called to assume, in freedom, the same horizon of meaning, it is easier at this point to verify whether the same sign system is present elsewhere. Also because the repetition of the model would make the model itself even more significant. This is the case with the relationship between ch. 26 and the following ch. 27 (and therefore, with the unit given by chs. 27–29).

Even though these two scenes are placed on two different temporal planes, their interaction on a semiotic level appears to be the same. A first bit of evidence to be recovered on the symbolic level in favour of the relationship between chs. 26 and 27 is the anomaly of the MT, which, in 27:1, as we have seen (cf. ch. IV, n. 1), seems to misplace the episode at the time of the king Jehoiakim, thus almost identically (and, one could say, intentionally) copying the same incipit from ch. 26. In any case, between the two scenes, the same relationship shown between 38:1–13 and 38:14–28a is delineated: in ch. 26, Jeremiah is presented as the one who, in obedience to his mission, *does not fear* publicly exposing himself to a mortal risk (cf. 26:1–11), *handing himself over* (cf. 26:14) into the hands of the men who would like him dead. Subjected to the judgment of the established authorities and one step from a death sentence (cf. 26:20–23), he is *saved* unexpectedly (cf. 26:24), but according to the promises of divine assistance expressed programmatically in the vocational text (cf. 1:8, 17–19).

And so an unexpected connection with the following ch. 27 (and indeed, with the whole unit of 27–29, which actually concerns the same theme) appears thus: the prophet who places before the nations, King Zedekiah, the priests, and all the people the need for submission to the king of the Babylon as the path of life is the same one who has already first-hand analogically walked the same path of humiliation and self-surrender, returning as a living sign of the fulfilment of the word of YHWH. And so we find the same semiotic model *reduplicated over a distance*, which renders the relationship between the pragmatic dimension of the Jeremianic prophecy (rendered body in action) and the type of consent requested (a political gesture) even more narrow and significative.

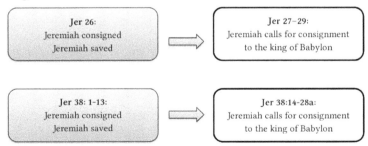

2.5. Semiotics of the literary architecture (II): A new overview of section chs. 26–45

The focalisation of the rhetorical-structural semiotic system that I highlighted in ch. 38, that is, the relationship between the figure of the *handed over* and *saved prophet*, and the call to *surrender to the king of Babylon* as the *path of salvation*, not only allows

484 Jer 38:14–28a. Jeremiah and Zedekiah: The final colloquy

for the same relationship (in an analogous sense) to be noted between chs. 26 and 27 (or with the unit of 27–29) but also, broadening the horizon, suggests a rereading of the entire textual organisation of the section given by the chs. 26–45 to see if the same symbolic redactional intent can possibly be traced. The answer, in my opinion, is that it can. So let us revisit the schema I proposed in chapter I of the present dissertation (cf. ch. I, § 4.2.1), integrating and explicating it with the signalling of other (unexpected) *regularities* that replicate the semiotic model identified on other textual levels.

26–45	
First sub-section *(26–35)*	**Second sub-section** *(36–45)*
26: at the time of *Jehoiakim*	36: at the time of *Jehoiakim*
JEREMIAH CONSIGNED AND *SAVED*	JEREMIAH-BARUCH-SCROLL CONSIGNED (BURNED) AND *SAVED* (REWRITTEN)
27: at the time of **Zedekiah**	37: at the time of **Zedekiah**
28: at the time of **Zedekiah**	38:1-13: at the time of **Zedekiah**
29: at the time of **Zedekiah**	*JEREMIAH CONSIGNED AND*
	SAVED BY EBED-MELECH
	38:13-28a: at the time of **Zedekiah**
JEREMIAH CALLS FOR CONSIGNMENT	JEREMIAH CALLS FOR CONSIGNMENT
30–31: without dating **THE NEW COVENANT**	38:28b–39:1-10: at the time of **Zedekiah** **END OF JERUSALEM** **END OF ZEDEKIAH**
32–33: at the time of Zedekiah **ORACLES OF SALVATION FOR JERUSALEM**	39:11-14: **SALVATION OF JEREMIAH** 39:15-18: ORACLE OF SALVATION FOR EBED-MELECH
34: at the time of **Zedekiah** vv. 1-7: message to Zedekiah (he will be CONSIGNED; the city will fall) vv. 8-16: Act of DISOBEDIENCE of Jerusalem vv. 17-22: PUNISHMENT ANNOUNCED	40–44: after **Zedekiah** (Gedaliah; etc.) 40: JEREMIAH FREED/SAVED (vv. 1-6) 41: Gedaliah killed: **anti-Babylonian act** 42: JEREMIAH ASKS FOR CONSIGNMENT 43: new **anti-Babylonian** DISOBEDIENCE 44: PUNISHMENT ANNOUNCED
35: at the time of *Jehoiakim* Example of OBEDIENCE of the Rechabites Confirmation of punishment for Jerusalem ANNOUNCEMENT OF SALVATION (for the Rechabites)	45: at the time of *Jehoiakim* JEREMIAH TO BARUCH: punishment is confirmed; invitation to Baruch to "HAND HIMSELF OVER" ANNOUNCMENT OF SALVATION (for Baruc)

THE TIME OF THE END (announced as irreversible and fulfilled)

First approach to the textual data 485

The structural complexity of the Jeremianic work according to the MT now appears even more evident, even with its present pagination limitations, which prevent a better graphical representation. As I specified on an introductory level when I addressed the methodological anchorage of my study and the fundamental literary coordinates of the book of Jeremiah, the apparently chaotic configuration of the work is actually due to a dense interweaving of co-dependencies mediated by thematic and formal references that are not immediately evident, and which respond to organisational principles that differ from our own.

Indeed, the question is that of unfolding the multiple intertextual connections between literary units placed in dialogue over differing distances from one another, in which the chronological criterion is either secondary (and is respected uninterruptedly only in chs. 40–44) or deliberately contradicted. The various textual units (from those that are smallest to those medium-sized, formed of aggregating minor units), whose origin and history of composition is debatable, result on the level of final macro-units (according to the current arrangement of the MT) as having undergone an organising force of some important "attractors".[21] The principal attractors, looking at the second section of the book of Jeremiah (chs. 26–45), are:

1) the thematic polarity of the "end" (38:28b–39:1–10) and the "new beginning" (chs. 30–31; 32–33 and 39:11–14),[22]

---

21 I employ this term in an analogical sense, borrowing it from the physical-mathematical field (and from its consequent application in chaos theory), where it refers to "a limiting set which is approached by a set of initial conditions (a subset of the attractor basin of non-vanishing measures) during the forwards evolution of a dissipative dynamic system. In addition, the attractor must be a *compact set* which is invariant with respect to the time evolution of the dynamic system in question, i.e. mapped onto itself through the dynamic flux, and which cannot be further divided into attractive subsets" (BARNERT, S., *et al.*, *Dictionary of Physics*, vol. I, London – New York 2004, 155). Think, for instance, of the dynamical system of the pendulum: the oscillatory movement tends to stabilise itself towards a single point of equilibrium (fixed point attractor).

22 The articulation between these two elements occurs on at least two distinct levels, as can be seen in the chart: a first relationship between the dimension of the disaster and that of unusual salvation is found between "the time of the end" (27–29 and 34), that is, those chapters dating from the time of Zedekiah (in which the end of Jerusalem and the kingdom of Judah is no longer threatened but simply predicted) and the chapters placed at the centre of this frame, that is, the "Book of Consolation" (30–31), with the announcement of the new covenant and other oracles of a salvific nature (32–33). A second level regards the structural relationship between the positive opening of this central part of the first subsection (26–35), framed by texts dating to the time of Jehoiakim, and that correspondent to the following subsection (36–45), signalled instead by the narration of the fall and the destruction of Jerusalem, and of the dramatic fate of Zedekiah and the royal household (38:28b–39:1–10) which, nonetheless, encloses (39:11–14) the structural relation between end and salvation. Here, in fact, the destruction of the temple is omitted (and will be only reported in ch. 52), the liberation of Jeremiah is narrated (as if he were the true substitute of the temple, the true place of the presence of YHWH in the present time of the history of Israel) and an oracle of salvation for Ebed-melech is formulated (39:15–18).

2) the polarity formed by the structural relationship between: (a) the Jeremianic paradigm of "to hand oneself over"-"to be saved" (a reality lived *in primis* by the prophet himself), and (b) that of the analogous request to "to hand oneself over" to the king of Babylon as a path of salvation. In this second "attractor", every single element (the handing over of oneself and the experience of salvation) reproduces the paradoxical juxtaposition of death and life of the first great "attractor".

In addition to the already highlighted semiotic *arcatas* by which a relationship can be drawn between the *paradigm* of the handed over and saved prophet and the *call* to surrender to the king of Babylon in order to experience an analogous salvation (26 and 27–29; 38:1–13 and 38:14–28a), similar links between other literary units positioned at strategic points can also be particularly noted:

+ *The large semiotic arcata connecting chs. 36–45.* Chapter 36 features the two paradigmatic figures of the "prophet" (Jeremiah) and the "disciple" (Baruch). It also introduces the great mediation of the prophetic word that is the literary body of prophecy, that is, the *scroll* (v. 2: מְגִלַּת־סֵפֶר), intended to represent-replace Jeremiah and survive the prophet himself. Indeed, this material form does take on or take the place of his physical presence because he is "prevented" (v. 5: עָצוּר)[23] from going to the temple for the public proclamation of the divine message. The analogous relationship that gets established between the body of the prophet and the "body" of the prophecy not only leaves unaltered the dynamic of the "handing over", but *extends* it, precisely involving both the "disciple" and the prophetic scroll in the mission and fate of the "prophet": both that of obedience to YHWH, in whose name one is defencelessly exposed before those in power (who are the recipients of the prophecy), and that of the promise of salvation, which now comes to be also realised for Baruch ("hidden" and protected by YHWH along with Jeremiah; cf. v. 26) and the scroll itself (burned and then rewritten; cf. vv. 28.32). As can be seen, a dynamic, complex paradigm is configured.

In ch. 45, the figures of the "prophet" (Jeremiah) and the "disciple" (Baruch) reappear, and the connection with ch. 36 is made immediately explicit (45:1). Indeed, while its temporal placement makes it appear to be entirely out of place after ch. 44, the literary unit presents itself as a kind of re-interpretative analysis of the whole scroll episode. In fact, there is a sudden return to the time of the king Jehoiakim, as in ch. 36, thus designing the semiotic space of a *frame*. The frame, much like the arch or other containment and/or conjoining structures is (also) a device used for putting something into focus, since it signals an inside and an outside, and helps to circumscribe a series of signs within a space, rendering them significant.[24] It should be specified, however, that here, while the theme of "surrender" most certainly returns, it does so calling into question the figure of the *disciple*, who, in turn, draws to himself that of the *reader* (Model): to Baruch, who suffers (for sharing of the fate of Jeremiah and for the historical moment), the prophet *addresses the invitation* to not expect a return of the great wonders of the Exodus (גְּדֹלוֹת)[25] but rather, on the contrary, to embrace

---

23 This being a sign of the death of the prophet and of the necessity that his word be reassumed and transmitted, both by the "disciple" and by the "literary body" of the prophecy.

24 Cf. C. GOTTARDI, «La porta, il ponte, l'architrave», 58.

25 Cf. J.M. ABREGO, *Jeremías*, 136–137.

the meaning of the present time (the end, the anti-Exodus) with the promise that he will be guaranteed "life as war booty" in every place he wanders within this (even existential) territory marked by universal devastation (45:5).

+ *The semiotic arcata that connects ch. 40 (vv. 1–6) to ch. 42*. The image of the surrendered prophet, lowered alive into the cistern as if into a funeral pit,[26] from which he is brought back and then saved constitutes, as we have said, a highly significant *hermeneutical paradigm*. This is also signalled by the fact that, from a rhetorical point of view, the literary unit of 38:1–13, according to its *local*[27] configuration, is found at the centre with respect to the section given by chs. 37–39. This can be seen in this simplified structuration[28]:

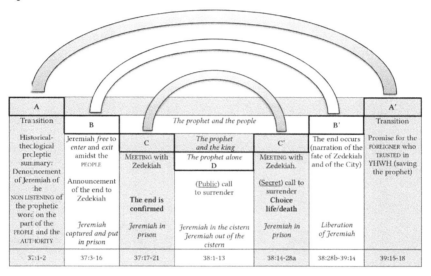

The powerful figure of the prophet saved from death (38:1–13), while referring back to the vocational promises of 1:8, 18–19 in the perspective of (their) fulfilment, already signalled moreover by the *plot resolution* in ch. 36, also assumes the role of

---

26 Cf. M. Cucca, *Il corpo e la città*, 255–300.
27 The fact that a relative autonomy, with a likewise autonomous rhetorical organisation, might be recognisable in chs. 37–39 should come as no surprise. This does not contradict the general structure of chs. 26–45 (with the respective subsections of chs. 26–35 and 36–45) that I presented schematically in the previous paragraph. On the contrary, it should be read within the latter as a further manifestation of a local "attractor", which, in this case, is the episode in 38:1–13. The complexity of the Jeremianic work is also due to these phenomena of possible overlapping of different structural configurations (and of many semiotic *arcatas*).
28 I have re-elaborated and simplified here the proposal of structuration of J.M. Abrego, *Jeremías*, 65–87, also taking into account its reproposal by E. Di Pede, *Au-de là du rejus*, 168. I hence defer to these authors for in-depth study of the formal and content-related correspondences that can be detected in the text.

being a symbolic structural pillar for other semiotic *arcatas* that extend to reach other, no less significant, texts. I am referring to the (re)incarceration-liberation polarity (of the prophet) in 38:28 and 39:11–14, and to that replicated in 40:1–6, where Jeremiah passes from being a shackled prisoner without any rights to being a free man, able to (once again) decide his own fate.

This other isomorphic re-presentation of the fundamental semiotic model in 38:1–13 (which – I reiterate – acts as a structural *pendant* to the call to surrender made to Zedekiah in 38.14–28a) also finds correspondence within its own literary context, with a similar call to "surrender" linked to a promise of salvation. Once again, Jeremiah becomes the living figure of his message. And on a closer look, it is indeed as a surrendered prophetic body exposed to death but saved by God that he presents himself again to the reader and to the survivors of the destruction of Jerusalem in ch. 42, when he repeats the call to "surrender to the king of Babylon" in obedience to YHWH, promising his salvific intervention (and threatening still further misfortune otherwise).

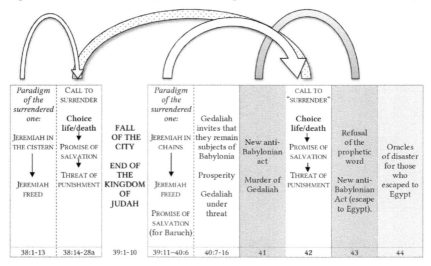

The issue is still, in another form, that of prophetically assuming the meaning of the selfsame "paradigm of the surrendered", not fearing the king of Babylon, not giving way to the project of flight to Egypt, remaining in the land of Israel, and trusting only in YHWH as the benevolent Lord of history. And returning once again in ch. 42, as in 38:14–28a, is the *alternative between the path of life and the path of death*, that is, between the choice to either surrender to the Babylonians or to *resist*, or rather, as in the case in ch. 42, to *flee to Egypt*, two only seemingly different ways to express the same rejection of the meaning of history revealed by YHWH in the here and now.

2.6. Content-related synthesis and focalisation of the thematic salencies

Following along the text's articulation, I will now synthesise the most important content-related data so as to bring into focus the thematic cores to which I will devote particular attention.

Exegetic focalisations 489

As we have seen, Jer 38:14–38a continues the narration of the first part of ch. 38. Jeremiah had been arrested for the subversive nature of his preaching about the need to surrender to the king of Babylon. Condemned by the leaders to starve to death in the darkness of a muddy cistern, he had been rescued by the intervention of Ebed-melech, and was confined to the prison atrium (vv. 1–13).

Our passage begins recounting King Zedekiah's willingness to *secretly consult* the prophet about the fate of the siege on Jerusalem. Jeremiah is reluctant, afraid to be put to death. The king makes an oath to protect the prophet, regardless of what he may have to relay to him on behalf of YHWH. Jeremiah's message remains the same: the only chance of salvation consists in *surrender to the king of Babylon*. The *alternative between the path of life and the path of death* that was addressed to all the people in 21:8–10 is now communicated to the royal figure alone, and expressed thereby in a *strictly personal sense*. The king, however, given the public nature of his *institutional function*, can guarantee salvation for himself and for all of Jerusalem with his obedience to the prophetic word. Otherwise, ruin is certain (vv. 14–18).

Faced with Jeremiah's request, Zedekiah confesses his *fear*. He is afraid of being handed over to the Jewish deserters and of being mistreated. The prophet reassures the king that this will not happen if (*by obeying*) *he will recognise* that it is YHWH himself who is now speaking to him through Jeremiah. He should instead be afraid of his own ministers, by whom he currently lets himself be conditioned. Indeed, if he does not consent to surrender, he will see the dramatic content of a *vision* that Jeremiah relays to him come true: the *women* of the house of the king are led to the Chaldeans and sing a *song of mockery* about Zedekiah that reveals the bitter *truth* of the situation. He himself will be captured by Nebuchadnezzar and the City will be set on fire. And *the fault will be his* (vv. 19–23).

Zedekiah *does not respond*. He only worries that nothing of the conversation he has had with the prophet gets leaked to his ministers. He obliges Jeremiah to remain in *silence*, indeed, to *lie*. Promptly interrogated by the court dignitaries, the prophet responds that he has asked the king to relieve his conditions of imprisonment. Jeremiah is then left alone and remains in the guard's yard until the day of the fall of Jerusalem, that is, until his prophecy is *fulfilled* (vv. 24–28a).

3. Exegetic focalisations

Let us now proceed, according to the tripartition of 38:14–28a that I highlighted, to the exegetic focalisation of some of the textual aspects that are most relevant to my topic of study. These are elements that I believe contribute to providing the basis for further reflective study in order to obtain a more adequate understanding of the Jeremianic call to surrender to the king of Babylon.

3.1. First part (vv. 14b-18): The need to surrender to the king of Babylon

3.1.1. The king (מֶלֶךְ) and the prophet (נָבִיא): The final and decisive secret consultation

The two main protagonists (actants) of the entire section are presented to the reader, from the incipit of the pericope, by their personal names and specific *thematic*

490   Jer 38:14–28a. Jeremiah and Zedekiah: The final colloquy

roles[29]: the *king* (מֶלֶךְ) Zedekiah and the *prophet* (נָבִיא) Jeremiah. The relationship between kings and prophets is a common fact in the extrabiblical sources documenting the prophetic phenomenon, since the latter were an integral part of the divinatory apparatus of the monarchical establishment. However, this documentation does not appear to provide evidence that there be a relationship as direct and personal[30] as that amply testified in the HB, and in our text in particular.

While in the biblical tradition, the prophet is the quintessential sign of the self-revelation of the word of YHWH in history, the king is chosen as the ultimate, decisive endpoint for this communicative appeal, precisely because in Israel (and in the ancient Near East in general),[31] he is also considered to be an *ideal* figure, almost an emblem of the fullness of the human condition,[32] the keystone of well-being and social stability. The king is the supreme military leader who must defend and guide the people to victory as well as the supreme judicial authority, who has "the duty of doing justice, possibly remedying the iniquity and neglect of the subordinates (Ps 72:1–4; 101; Prov 20:8; 31:4–9; etc..)"[33] In this regard, it suffices to recall, so as to remain within the

---

29 According to the surface narrative grammar (or more simply, the "narrativity") of A.J. Greimas, the "thematic role" is "la représentation, sous forme actantielle, d'un thème ou d'un parcours thématique (le parcours «pêcher», par exemple, peut être condensé ou résumé par le rôle de «pêcheur»" (A.J. GREIMAS – J. COURTÉS, eds., *Sémiotique*, 393).

30 As in M. NISSINEN, «Biblical Prophecy from a Near Eastern Perspective: The Cases of Kingship and Divine Possession», in: *Congress Volume Ljubljana 2007*, ed. A. LEMAIRE, VT.S 133, Leiden 2010, 441–468 (in particular, pp. 445–455). Although on this point, D. CHARPIN, «Prophètes et rois», 34, given the scarcity and nature of the documentation available to us, calls for more cautious judgment.

31 Cf. J.H. WALTON, *Ancient Near Eastern Thought*, 278–286.

32 "Le prophète a souvent pour vis-à-vis le roi, non que celui-ci appartienne à une espèce d'homme plus pécheresse, mais plus libre de pécher: le roi est comme délégué à une plénitude de la condition humaine parce qu'il dispose directement, comme un nouvel Adam, de l'universalité des biens et des noms. [...] Mais ce qui vaut de la figure du roi s'étend à la société: elle aussi est devant l'universalité des biens, dans la nudité du choix entre la vie et la mort" (P. BEAUCHAMP, *L'un e l'autre Testament*, 89–90). Cf. J.A. GRANT, *The King as Exemplar*. The Function of Deuteronomy's Kingship Law in the Shaping of the Book of Psalms, SBL.AS 17, Atlanta 2004.

33 Translated from P. BOVATI, *Vie della giustizia*, 45. With regard to the ideal emblematic programme of Ps 72, see in particular B. JANOWSKI, «Der andere König. Ps 72 als Magna Charta der judäischen Königsideologie», in: *Liebe, Macht und Religion*. Interdisziplinäre Studien zu Grunddimensionen menschlicher Existenz, Gedenkschrift für H. Merklein, eds. M. GIELEN – J. KÜGLER, Stuttgart 2003, 97–112. But also think of the symbolic value inherent to attributing to the ideal king Solomon, in addition to some psalms, the magnification of wisdom (Eccl, Sir, Wis) and the celebration of the loving encounter between man and woman (in Song, where the royal figure is directly invoked in reference to the relational dynamics being sung about). On the diversified concepts of kingship in the ancient world, see the studies collected in G.B. LANFRANCHI – R. ROLLINGER, eds., *Concepts of Kingship in Antiquity*. Proceedings of the European Science Foundation Exploratory Workshop (Padova, 28 november–1 december 2007), HANE.M 11, Padova 2010. On the relationship between human and divine kingship, and on the complex symbolic dimension implicated, see, in particular, R. JUNGBLUTH, *Im Himmel und auf Erden*. Dimensionen von Königsherrschaft im Alten Testament, BWANT 196, Stuttgart 2011.

perimeter of the Jeremianic text, the appeal addressed to the royal house in 22:3 to practice (√עשׂה) "righteousness and justice" (מִשְׁפָּט וּצְדָקָה) in the context of a prophetic oracle that renders the entire destiny of the Davidic dynasty dependent upon this obedience (cf. 22:1–9).

And so the theme of the surrender to Babylonia, after having already (potentially) regarded the *whole people* (in addition to the king and the priests) and the *public* dimension of the communication (cf. 21:1, 8–9; 27–28; 38:2; 37:3–16), now, at the most decisive moment in the history of Jerusalem, it becomes a prophetic word spoken in *secrecy* to a *single man*, to whom the equally "prophetic" gesture of surrender is shown as an extreme chance for salvation and for revelation of the meaning of an entire dramatic parabola of alliance.

From the point of view of the narrative flow, this is the last in a series of many communicative events of a prophetic nature that relate to the king Zedekiah,[34] either stemming from Jeremiah's initiative or solicited by Zedekiah himself (directly or vicariously) in the form of oracular consultations or as a request for YHWH's intercession regarding the dramatic political circumstance underway (cf. 21:1–10; 27:12–15; 32:3–5; 34:1–6, 8–22; 37:3, 7–10, 17–21; 38:14–28a). Let us take a schematic look at the consultations included within the thematic-narrative articulation of the surrounding and immediate context of chs. 37–39:

37:1–2	Proleptic summary[35]: enthronement of Zedekiah and global evaluation of his reign and of his epoch in relation to the (true) prophetic word: "[…] neither he, nor his ministers, nor the people of the land would listen to the words which the Lord spoke through Jeremiah the prophet" (v. 2).
37:3	Zedekiah sends messengers to Jeremiah (request for intercession)
37:4–5	Explicative pause relating to the historical context (suspension of the siege)
37:6–10	Response of Jeremiah to Zedekiah: announcement of the fall of Jerusalem
37:11–16	Jeremiah tries to leave the city, is arrested by Irijah under the accusation of treason. Jeremiah is flogged by the "leaders". *Jeremiah remains prisoner in the underground cistern*
37:17–21	*First* private colloquy between Zedekiah and Jeremiah: announcement of the capture of Zedekiah (the resumption of the siege is implicit) *Jeremiah remains in the prison courtyard*

---

34 Cf. E. Di Pede, «Jérémie et les rois de Juda, Sédécias et Joaqim», *VT* 56 (2006) 452–469; E. Chauty, *Qui aura sa vie comme butin?*, 306.

35 What I have already noted about the proleptic function of 21:1–10 (and, differently, also for chs. 27–28 in relation to 38:14–28a) is easy to recognise here as well, given that "Le procédé du sommaire proleptique est l'une des manières caractéristiques par lesquelles le récit déplace le suspense du «quoi» (que va-t-il se passer?) au «comment» (comment ce qui a été annoncé va-t-il se passer?)"; J.-P. Sonnet, «L'analyse narrative des récits bibliques», in: *Manuel d'exégèse de l'Ancien Testament*, eds. M. Bauks – C. Nihan, MoBi 61, Genève 2008, 47–94 (here, p. 64).

38:1-13	Jeremiah is thrown into the cistern by the "leaders". Salvation of Jeremiah by means of Ebed-melech (foreigner). *Jeremiah remains in the prison courtyard*
38:14-28a	*Second* and *last* private colloquy between Zedekiah and Jeremiah before the fall of Jerusalem: surrender indicated as the only path of salvation for the king and City *Jeremiah remains in the prison courtyard*
38:28b, 39:1-14	Description of the capture and destruction of Jerusalem. Jeremiah freed by the foreigners (Babylonians)
39:15-18	Oracle of salvation for Ebed-melech (the foreigner who trusted in YHWH)

A question highly debated amongst scholars[36] is the relationship between the facts narrated in ch. 38 and what was already presented to the reader in 37:11-21. Given the recognisable similarities,[37] some consider it to be a single biographical episode regarding the prophet, expressed, for various reasons, in two parallel accounts[38], while others point out the dissimilarities and are more inclined to draw a distinction between

---

36 Cf. H. MIGSCH, *Gottes Wort*, 61-84.
37 See e.g. the comparison between the two encounters between Jeremiah and Zedekiah proposed by H.K. HOLT, «The Potent Word of God: Remarks on the Composition of Jeremiah 37-44», in: *Troubling Jeremiah, eds.* A.R.P. DIAMOND – K. O'CONNOR – L. STULMAN, JSOT.S 260, Sheffield 1999, 161-170:

37:11-21:	*38:14-18:*

A The situation of Jeremiah:
  Accusation and imprisonment
B The King sends for Jeremiah to
  consult him
C Jeremiah presents his plea to
  the king
D New situation: the king complies
  with Jeremiah's request – and
  Jeremiah sits in the court of the
  guardhouse.
	A The situation of Jeremiah:
	  Accusation and imprisonment
	B The King sends for Jeremiah to
	  consult him
	C The king presents his plea to
	  Jeremiah
	D New situation: Jeremiah complies
	  with the king's request – and
	  Jeremiah sits in the court of the
	  guardhouse.

38 See, above all, C. STEUERNAGEL, *Lehrbuch der Einleitung in das Alte Testament. Mit einem Anhang über die Apokryphen und Pseudepigraphen*, Tübingen 1912, 557-558, and J. SKINNER, *Prophecy and Religion. Studies in the Life of Jeremiah*, Cambridge 1922, 258-259 (n. 1), whose opinion is followed or given serious consideration by others, such as e.g. H.G. MAY, «The Chronology of Jeremiah's Oracles», *JNES* 4 (1945) 217-227 (here, p. 220); J. BRIGHT, *Jeremiah* 232-234; J. THOMPSON, *The Book of Jeremiah*, NICOT, Grand Rapids 1980, 636-637; R.E. CLEMENTS, *Jeremiah*, 220, W. McKANE, *Jeremiah 2*, 968-971.

Exegetic focalisations   493

the two scenes, whilst substantially regarding them to be the interweaving of a single narrative continuum (*fabula*).[39]

Once again, it can be observed that the interpretation depends mainly on extra-textual factors, that is, on the pragmatic dimension implicated in the interpretive context hypothesised and assumed, *consciously or not*, by each interpreter. And this is so even when the problem and its solution are seen only on the basis of the composition's history and thus the attempt made is to highlight textual tensions and clues for textual criticism. It is clear, in fact (to take up one of the most critical points), that if the condition of imprisonment mentioned in 37:21 is understood in a rigid and literal sense, as if it were a prison regime of absolute isolation, it is not possible to accept that Jeremiah could have (continued to) proclaim his message "to all the people" (אֶל־כָּל־הָעָם), as can be seen from 38:1–4. If, on the other hand, as the text itself moreover suggests, in addition to a generic "prison" or, to the letter, "prison house" ([40]הַכְּלִיא בֵּית; cf. 37:4; 52:31), distinction is made between a place implying a state of total restriction (such as the "prison/underground cistern [הַבּוֹר בֵּית] with vaults [הַחֲנֻיוֹת][41]"; cf. 37:16, or "the cistern of Malchiah" [מַלְכִּיָּהוּ הַבּוֹר]; cf. 38:6), and a subsequent restrictive disciplinary action with a more bland limitation on personal freedom (as can be presupposed in reference to the "prison atrium" [הַמַּטָּרָה חֲצַר] located on the palace grounds; cf. 32:2; 37:21; 38:6, 13, 28a), the contradiction potentially vanishes.[42] In this sense, the locution

---

39   Think of, e.g. albeit using different arguments, A. WEISER, *Das Buch Jeremia*. II, 331, 338, W.L. HOLLADAY, *Jeremiah 2*, 282–283 and J.R. LUNDBOM, *Jeremiah 37–52*, 51, who, whilst noting the correspondence between Jeremiah's two incarcerations and consecutive "liberations" during the siege (37:12–21; 38:1–13) and the two accounts of liberation after Jerusalem is taken (39:11–14; 40:1–6), maintains that at this point, it is unlikely that these be parallel narratives "not only because the accounts in question can be explained as successive events, but more importantly, because there are too many differences in detail for them to be doublets, whether oral or literary".

40   The script of this term is rather undefined. The Q is הַכְּלוּא, but here, I follow the K.

41   As can be seen in W. McKANE, *Jeremiah 2*, 929–930, the locution וְאֶל־הַחֲנֻיוֹת employed in 37:16 to indicate the place of imprisonment (וְאֶל־הַחֲנֻיוֹת הַבּוֹר אֶל־בֵּית) is rather problematic, from both the grammatical and lexiographical (in fact, it is a *hapax legomenon*) points of view. My translation of the implicated lexeme (חָנוּת) is made plausible by the semantic relationship that can be reasonably hypothesised by the two analogous terms (one Syriac and the other Arabic) used in reference to the "vaulted cells", as is suggested respectively in *BDB*, 333 and *HALAT*, 320. Through the coordination expressed by the *waw*, which I intend here in an epesegetic sense (cf. D.W. BAKER, «Explicative *waw*», *EHLL* I, 890–892), what would thus be specified by the expression וְאֶל־הַחֲנֻיוֹת is a precise part of the underground location indicated by הַבּוֹר בֵּית. Cf. also M. CUCCA, *Il corpo e la città*, 260–264.

42   Even if the "penal" systems are (probably) not identical, an analogous comparison can perhaps be made between the regime of the *custodia militaris liberior* imposed on Paul (significantly different from the much more restrictive *custodia publica*), whose principal limitation consisted in the obligation to remain under fortress protection while still maintaining an ability to receive visits, or the obligation to move outdoors with one's right arm tied to the left arm of a soldier (cf. Acts 24:23). Also pertinent is the comparison with the concession of "house arrest" obtained in Rome, awaiting to appear before the imperial court (cf. Acts 28:16, 30). In this second case as well, Paul's freedom was only partially limited, given that over the course of the two years, he was able to proclaim the Gospel (which, then, I will highlight in specific reference

494   Jer 38:14–28a. Jeremiah and Zedekiah: The final colloquy

"all the people" (כָּל־הָעָם) in 38:1 can be understood, already with Carl Friedrich Keil,[43] as referring to all ordinary people, who – as Zedekiah does repeatedly, and in all likelihood also the members of the guard corps (cf. 38:4) – had wanted to hear (and divulge) Jeremiah's prophetic word about the destiny of Jerusalem.[44]

Although the phenomenon of binary repetition and the re-presentation of similar or identical texts is a peculiar characteristic (also) of the book of Jeremiah,[45] it is precisely the comparison between these attestations (cf., e.g. 7:1-15 and 26) and our present case that prevents the identification, on my part, of sufficient elements to be able to deny the possibility that there be a concatenation (even if non-linear) of different scenes along a single, reasonable narrative thread. Even taking my start from this position, which we do not need to explore now however, the point I am interested in underscoring is another: I do not think that it be possible to see, in the textual articulation of chs. 37–38, a convincing correspondence between the succession of events narrated and (some of) the consequent stages of a *unified* and *coherent* judicial process that would have been brought against Jeremiah.[46] It is clear that the context is judicial

---

to the situation of Jeremiah, was precisely the motive for which he was accused and incarcerated) to all the "notables of the Jews" and "to all those who went to him" (cf. Acts 28:17–31).

43   C.F. KEIL, *Jeremia*, 388.

44   Without underestimating the mediating role concerning the diffusion of the Jeremianic message that might have been filled precisely by the soldiers of the guard corps who were charged with surveillance of the place of captivity (cf. 38:4), that "courtyard of the prison" where, moreover, the celebration of an act of acquisition takes place in the presence of numerous witnesses without any problem (cf. ch. 32).

45   Cf. J.-D. MACCHI, «Les doublets dans le livre de Jérémie», in: *The Book of Jeremiah and its Reception. Le Livre de Jérémie et sa reception*, eds. A.H.W. CURTIS – T. RÖMER, BEThL 128, Leuven 1997, 119–150; H. PARKE-TAYLOR, *The Formation of the Book of Jeremiah*. Doublets and Recurring Phrases, SBLMS 51, Atlanta 2000.

46   As is instead sustained by M. CUCCA, *Il corpo e la città*, 203–254. The weakest point of the argumentation seems to me to be the interpretation given to 38:1. The premise upon which it stands is that of comprehending the prophet's imprisonment mentioned in 37:15–16 (following the arrest and charge of desertion) as a state of provisional restriction pending judgement. Even though in antiquity (especially in the Roman world), the state of captivity was generally not considered a form of punishment (although, in fact, many times it was, at least in Late Latinity, as the Ulpian rules seeking to put an end to the practice testify; cf. *Dig.* 48.18.8.9), in the book of Jeremiah itself, if one considers the case of Jehoiachin (whose captivity lasted 37 years) attested in 2 Kgs 25:27 and Jer 52:31 (and see even Ezr 7:26), this possibility must be admitted (along these lines, cf. L. GRIFFITH, *The Fall of the Prison*. Biblical Perspectives on Prison Abolition, Grand Rapids 1993, 89). Even recognising the temporary value of the arrest of Jeremiah, this does not, however, mean that it had any relation to an actual judicial process, as the author claims (likewise, also M. RONCACE, *Jeremiah, Zedekiah, and the Fall of Jerusalem*, LHBOTS 423, London – New York 2005, 79): the textual information is too scarce (if not contradictory) to affirm this, and, amongst other things, King Zedekiah has Jeremiah subsequently removed not to judge him, but to consult him, then mitigating his prison conditions (cf. 38:17–21). The link between this condition (seen as "provisional detention" [p. 234] pending judgement) and what is narrated in ch. 38 (seen as "forensic procedure" [p. 237] preceded by a "preliminary investigation" [p. 240] in vv. 1–3) is indeed the phrase in 38:1, translated as "*E*

Exegetic focalisations 495

and, here too, the underlying theme is that of the prophet under prosecution (as is exposed paradigmatically in ch. 36), but it seems rather forced to interpret the plot of chs. 37–38 as an orderly and *consequential* succession of the legal stages that typify (?) court proceedings (even if that attestation were understood to be fragmentary).

Regarding my own topic more closely, it seems inaccurate to speak of "(juridical) surrender"[47] in reference to the attitude held by the prophet in these circumstances, that is, in the face of the accusations made to him by the "leaders". If it is true, as I have highlighted, that in his figure what is really presented to the reader is the emblem *par excellence* of the one who has "surrendered" in faithful obedience into the hands of YHWH and, at the same time, still in obedience to Him, into those of humankind as well, then this does make sense of the textual evidence affirming that Jeremiah had renounced self-defence during legal proceedings.

Informed by the narrator of the real reasons why Jeremiah intends to leave Jerusalem (cf. 37:12),[48] the reader can perhaps be astonished, at least at first, when he

---

venne a conoscenza (וַיִּשְׁמַע) Sefatia [...] delle parole che Jeremiah *era solito dire* (מְדַבֵּר) a tutto il popolo [...]") and understood as a reassumption of the charges for which the prophet had been arrested by Irijah in 37:14 (p. 242), even if, actually, it can be seen that Jeremiah had *already* expressed himself clearly as "anti-national" in 37:7–10 (and also note that "Jehukal son of Shelemiah", probably a brother of the same Irijah in 37:13, is one of the "leaders" in question, and has already heard the Jeremianic message, given that he is part of the delegation of notables sent to the prophet in 37:3). In this manner, what seems to be laid out is an ordered succession of events. Regardless, the fact that one cannot speak of narrative linearity here on the level of plot, but instead of an analepsis, is attested clearly in 37:21, for the moment when food supplies run out in the city, if it does not coincide with the end of Jerusalem, it is to be placed in any case in the imminence of its fall, as can be seen from 52:6. What is heard by the "leaders", moreover, can be more easily understood in relation to the state of semi-freedom in which Jeremiah finds himself and to which he was, after all, relegated under partially restricted conditions not (at least initially) for his message, but for his attempt to leave the city (cf. 37:14–15).

47 As in M. Cucca, *Il corpo e la città*, 245.

48 The Hebrew text is not one of the clearest but, in my opinion, this does not permit us to stray very far from the comprehension of it expressed in all of the most important ancient (and modern) versions, which have understood there to be a reference made to a legal transaction of some real estate property. Instead, quite on the contrary, though in my opinion implausible, is the interpretation of W. McKane, *Jeremiah 2*, 926–928, who (on the basis of some lexicographical clues drawn from two minuscule codices and the proposal of Kimchi) believes the intention on Jeremiah's part to be readable as that of a furtive escape made from the city by mingling amongst the general population, thus lending greater weight to Irijah's accusations. W. McKane therefore translates v. 12 as: "Jeremiah purposed to leave Jerusalem to go to Benjamite territory, slipping out of the city among a crowd of other people" (p. 922). It is difficult, however, to think that the purchase of the field narrated in 32:6–44, chronologically *subsequent* to this episode (cf. 37:1–5 with 32:1–5), not be tied to this question in some way. If, in fact, the land transaction that Jeremiah consents to appears to be reasonable from the point of view of prophetic logic, it remains, on the contrary, absurd in the context of the siege, seeming entirely inexplicable how a relative of the prophet could have thought that in a situation similar Jeremiah might have agreed to the sale of some land. That is, in fact, unless the question didn't have to do with an issue that was outstanding, one that could be somehow tied to what is alluded to

496   Jer 38:14–28a. Jeremiah and Zedekiah: The final colloquy

hears the prophet defend himself from accusations by simply denying *sic et simpliciter* the charge made,[49] without providing any further explanation. But to infer, on this basis, that by doing so, Jeremiah would be "legally surrendering" is inaccurate. Upon more attentive consideration, it is indeed obvious to suppose that, in the logic of the narrative, it would have been a rather fragile (if not ridiculous) defensive argument for the prophet, known for his scandalous pro-Babylonian "anti-nationalist propaganda" (as it might have been simplistically interpreted) and thus for his announcement of the certain, imminent conquest of the kingdom of Judas by the Babylonians, to have defended himself by stating that he had wanted to go to sort out a family matter regarding the partition of earthly possessions.[50] It is, moreover, easy to observe that Jeremiah *always* defends himself from accusations made *directly* against him, both during the judicial proceedings in ch. 26 (cf. vv. 12–15), and in the face of the accusations of Irijah, and even before King Zedekiah[51] (cf. 37:14, 18–19). If it is presupposed that the motive moving the "leaders" to ask for the death of the prophet corresponds to a "debatement phase",[52] and that, based on this, it be highlighted that after this accusation, the text makes no reference to a self-defence on the part of Jeremiah (evident, in any case, both before and after these vv.), this does nothing but incur a sort of *petitio principii*: it establishes *a priori* that we find ourselves in the course of a regular trial, which should therefore provide a recognisable articulation of procedures, however, no defence is mentioned on the part of Jeremiah after the supposed "evidential phase" (corresponding to 38:1–3, where actually nothing is said except that the "leaders" come to know the Jeremiah message and that, on the basis of this, they then ask for the death of Jeremiah without addressing him in any way), and so it is implicitly inferred that we really are in a trial (which is actually just a hypothesis) in which the defendant "paradoxically" does not defend himself (which, instead, he does earlier, both in front of Irijah and then successively before the king, as I noted). In summary: from the textual clues, it is inferrable that we are in a trial, the defendant does not defend himself, and should do so since, in fact, being on trial, his silence is *therefore* significative. As can be seen, this is circular reasoning.

In fact, it is doubtful that the narrator wants to describe a judicial procedure (at least not one that is "regular"), precisely because (amongst other things) there is no direct accusation of Jeremiah, or at least, it is not at all evident that he is given a way to defend himself.[53] Ultimately, there is nothing in his attitude that suggests a kind

---

in 37:12. The impression that comes of it, yet again, is not so much that of a fictional narrative construction, but rather of an account that presupposes precise extratextual knowledge having a considerable pragmatic valence (for the purpose of a more precise historiographical contextualisation) that was, however, deemed unnecessary to include on the textual level.

49   As is underscored by M. RONCACE, *Jeremiah*, 48.
50   This is noted by M. Cucca himself (*Il corpo e la città*, 232).
51   Consider also the events narrated in ch. 36 and how, willingly, Jeremiah and Baruch evade the order of arrest promulgated by the king Jehoiakim and hide (vv. 19, 26).
52   Cf. M. CUCCA, *Il corpo e la città*, 243.
53   As is underscored by P. BOVATI, *Ristabilire la giustizia*, 236–237, not giving a defendant the opportunity to defend himself is a grave violation of the law and, consequently, one could add, a negation of the judicial power issued or embodied by the sovereign himself, as much as of precisely its purpose (the restoration of justice).

Exegetic focalisations   497

of "surrender" before his accusers.[54] The prophet hands himself over to his prophetic destiny, without backing down in the face of the (possibility of) death (symbolic or not), but not without doing everything possible to defend his actions and thus doing, save his life. The only, and here truly significant, "surrender" of Jeremiah during a public confrontation (as we saw studying ch. 28), is the one that follows the violent, polemical intervention of Hananiah.

I can therefore affirm that to place the fate of Jerusalem and its king, delivered into the hands of the king of Babylon, in an analogical relationship to the dramatic Jeremianic affair is doubtlessly a fruitful path for reflection that the text itself invites us to follow, on the condition, however, that the correct hermeneutical keys are assumed as well. Logical fallacies in these cases are always right around the corner, for if reasonable conclusions are to be drawn, every analogy has its own conditions of validity that must be respected. In this particular case, affirming the causal relationship between the need for surrender to Babylon as a way of salvation and the (supposed) necessity of Jeremiah's (legal) "surrender"[55] is simply a *non sequitur*. It is, in fact, erroneous analogical reasoning based on a relation of resemblance that is, on a closer look, not very pertinent.[56] Let me specify: the similarity of relations between Jeremiah and

---

54 In this sense (and contrary to what is instead affirmed by M. RONCACE, *Jeremiah*, 80, n. 51), his demeanour is not at all comparable to that held by Jesus before his accusers, who are astonished by his silence in the face of the (capital) accusations levelled against him (for a comparison, see S.M. SESSA, «"Non rispondi nulla?". Il silenzio di Gesù nel contesto processuale dei sinottici. Una "nuova" proposta interpretativa alla luce del *rîb* profetico», in: *La profezia tra l'uno e l'altro Testamento*, 285–309).

55 As in M. CUCCA, *Il corpo e la città*, 245: "if the 'surrendering' of the city to the Babylonian invader is necessary for its life to be saved (32:2b), then the (juridical) 'surrender' of the prophet is likewise indispensable during the trial against him, expressed, in fact, in the 'renouncement' of an intervention of defence" (my translation).

56 Likewise, the analogical relationship asserted also in the conclusions ("*Like* the prophet, in fact, *thus also* the people are brought to justice and, found guilty, struck with punitive measures"; p. 311), despite having defined its nature as "skew" as a justification (invoking the category of paradoxicality; cf. p. 312), appears to be inappropriate for that very reason if one wants to draw the conclusion that there be a significant paradigmatic relationship between the Jeremianic prophetic body and the city of Jerusalem *on this level* ("precisely in his being brought to justice and found guilty, the prophet fully assumes his 'symbolic' duty before the people assigned to him in the vocational incident"; pp. 310–311). An analogy, in order to be such, must express a resemblance of relationships. But the structure of reasoning, even if formally analogical in that sense, can lead to invalid conclusions if the relationship of resemblance is not subject to an acceptable "core of inference", that is, to a sufficient degree of relevance to guarantee its high probability, if nothing else (analogical reasoning, in fact, is not in every case assimilable to deductive reasoning and always requires an abduction). The fallacy of the analogous relationship established here thus consists in the establishment of a resemblance between semantic elements that do not meet this requirement, for both the *subjects* that carry forth the "judgement" and the respective "*judgements*" in themselves are completely different: the prophet is judged by the "leaders" (unjust men), but *unjustly* so, while Jerusalem is judged by YHWH (the just God), and *justly so*. YHWH does not at all ask Jeremiah to "take on himself (on his body) the path of humiliation of the guilty one" (p. 312), but rather to hand himself over to his prophetic mission, even if this will involve all kinds of adversity.

Jerusalem does exist and is indubitable (both subjects, e.g. undergo a "judgment"), but the level of similarity indicated does not hold. Jeremiah is not "judged" by YHWH, Jerusalem is. For "war" will be made against Jeremiah by his own fellow citizens (cf. 1:19), not by YHWH, who will, on the other hand, wage war against Jerusalem through Nebuchadnezzar (cf. 1:15–16; 21:5; etc.). Jeremiah must hand himself over, without fear, to the will of YHWH (and thus also to his enemies), and for this he will be saved, demonstrating that trusting God, by accepting in (and with) his own body the revealed meaning of the story underway, is the only path of salvation. Jerusalem, acknowledging its sin and trusting in YHWH's promise of salvation, will be saved if it delivers itself to its enemies in the same way, but the gesture of surrender that it is called to make expresses, on the one hand, the universal, timeless necessity of obedience to YHWH, while on the other, an *entirely different* meaning (that of recognising the failure of one's own history and accepting the just punishment that saves). The resemblance of the relationships, as can be seen, and as I am attempting to demonstrate with the present dissertation, therefore consists in the need to *obey* the meaning of history revealed by YHWH *here and now*. The symbolic device established in Jeremiah through what happens with his prophetic body (handed over in obedience to YHWH and to human beings, and for this reason, saved) is presented according to this perspective as a normative paradigm for the assumption of the (revealed) meaning of present history, not of every history or every moment, but of *this* very precise theological-political juncture.

3.1.2. The "surrendered" and taken (√לקח) prophet and the semiotics of space

I have already dealt with the historical context within which this last colloquy takes place (cf. ch. II, § 3.2.2). Here, it suffices to recall the particularly problematic *status* in which the new, young descendant king of David actually found himself after his placement on the throne by Nebuchadnezzar. This designation was intended to make him a perfect vassal, a king-lieutenant who should have guaranteed the fidelity of the kingdom of Judah to the Babylonian empire. On the other hand, Jehoiachin, who had become king before him upon the death of Jehoiakim, although having been immediately removed from the throne and kept in exile in Babylon, was still recognised

---

The promise is that he will come out alive. And even for this reason, Jeremiah does all that he can to defend himself from every accusation of fault, while remaining faithful to his mission. To glimpse in the story of the innocent, persecuted prophet a trace of meaning that illuminates the mystery of human suffering (in both the righteous and the wicked) is by all means suggestive and appropriate, but the interpretation being considered seems to depend more than anything on a rereading of the Jeremianic text influenced by the songs of the servant of YHWH, disrespectful to the theological elements contained in the book of Jeremiah itself (in which, in truth, the concept of vicarious atonement has not yet been reached, if not as a possibility). Amongst the numerous bibliographical references that could be cited concerning the conditions of validity of the use of analogical reasoning, seeing as, in the case at hand, this is carried out in context that is fundamentally juridical-judiciary, I will limit myself to F. Modugno, «L'analogia nella logica del diritto», *Rivista AIC* 1 (2011) 1–23, which refers to the masterful work by N. Bobbio in 1938 on analogy in the legal field (republished in N. Bobbio, *L'analogia nella logica del diritto*, Milano 2006).

Exegetic focalisations

by the same Nebuchadnezzar as a royal dignity, and it is likely that more than a few notables in Jerusalem still recognised him as the legitimate sovereign, awaiting his imminent return and re-enthronement (cf. 28:2–3, 6, 11). These were the same dignitaries who had fomented the rebellion by which Zedekiah had been found guilty before Nebuchadnezzar, whose armies had now been holding Jerusalem in the grip of a siege for months. From what can be seen by the context (cf. 37:11, 21; 38:28), the episode narrated in 38:14–28a takes place in the imminence of the end of Jerusalem, and Zedekiah, not knowing what to do, consults the prophet Jeremiah once again – for the last time.

As I already noted, Jeremiah is presented before the reader and before Zedekiah himself as a living representation of his message. Thrown into the cistern precisely for his invitation to surrender, he is saved only thanks to the intervention of a foreigner. His status as *surrenderer* into the hands of YHWH and human beings is clearly indicated from the beginning of the communicative exchange and that which precedes it. In 38:13, reference is made to his stable condition of captivity: "and so Jeremiah *remained* (וַיֵּשֶׁב) in the prison courtyard (בַּחֲצַר הַמַּטָּרָה)", an expression that in all of the HB, apart from one occurrence in Nehemiah (Neh 3.25; cf. also 12:39 where just the term מַטָּרָה appears), is attested solely and multiple times (11x) in the book of Jeremiah (cf. Jer 32:2, 8, 12; 33:1; 37:21 [2x]; 38:6, 13, 28; 39:14, 15). Zedekiah himself in 38:14 (as in 37:17; cf. 39:14) does not, therefore, send "to call for"[57] Jeremiah (cf. שָׁלַח√ + קרא√ in Gen 27:42; 31:4; 41:8; 41:14[58]; Exod 9:27; Num 16:12; 22:37; etc., where a relationship of greater respect is denoted), but sends (שָׁלַח√) for him "to be gotten" (לקח√), in compliance with his status as a *prisoner*.

> The syntagm in question is used in other contexts to indicate one subject's "taking" of another material object or person having a condition of inferiority or minority who cannot (any longer) practice self-determination, for having ceded (or have had to cede) control of their life to others (cf. שָׁלַח√ + לקח√ in Gen 3:22 [the man extends his hand[59] to take the fruit from the tree of life]; Jer 36:21 [the king sends someone to get the scroll]; Gen 20:2 [Sara taken by Abimelek; Gen 24:7, 40; 27:45; etc.]; 1 Sam 16:11 [Samuel asks Jesse to send for David, the youngest of the brothers; of Jesse instead it is said in v. 12 that he sends someone to "make him come" [בוא√ hi.][60]; cf. Gen 42:16; Exod 2:5; Deut 19:12; etc.]; Jer 25:9; 43:10 [God sends for the nations of the North and Nebuchadnezzar]; etc.). In fact, the biblical narrator points out that even after the fall of Jerusalem, the figure of Jeremiah (along with that of the scribe-disciple Baruch) is characterised by an existential form of *self-delivery*, freely chosen. Freed from captivity by the Babylonians, the prophet decides to remain with the survivors, renouncing a privileged condition in Babylon (cf. 39:11–14; 40:1–6).

---

57 This is instead the tenor of the Greek text in 45:15[LXX]: ἐκάλεσεν αὐτόν.

58 This case is one that is particularly interesting to place in parallel with our text, since the pharaoh sends for Joseph to be called from the underground prison precisely because he intends to decree his definitive liberation.

59 In this construct, commonly used in the HB, the verb does not so much mean "to send" someone to get something, but rather to "stretch out" the hand to grab something. In any case, the basic semantic core remains unvaried, since the question is still that of taking something or someone by way of an instrument.

60 Instead, in 1 Sam 19:14, 20; 20:30, the king Saul sends (or he is asked to send) some messengers to capture David.

500   Jer 38:14–28a. Jeremiah and Zedekiah: The final colloquy

Subjected to the will of the rebel "leaders", he is dragged to Egypt along with Baruch and the rest of the people.[61]

Zedekiah thus sends for Jeremiah to be brought from prison. For the reader, the motive is clear. It is his voice that – alone – accompanies, interprets, and illuminates, in a truthful and transcendent way, the meaning of the events that unfold over the course of the last years of the kingdom of Judah, events that, in the eyes of the historian, are instead attributable, on principle, to mere intra-worldly causes. This voice purports to

---

61   In H.-J. Stipp, «Legenden», he tries to deny that according to Jer 43:5–7, Jeremiah and Baruch were led to Egypt by force (as most, if not all commentators, take as undisputed), hypothesising that they too had been overwhelmed by fear of an imminent Babylonian retaliation (cf. p. 663), joined the rest of the people, and *freely decided* (were not *forced*, it is stressed) to flee to the pharaoh's protection. That the deportation is not forced, at least as far as the people remaining after the destruction of Jerusalem and the ensuing exile is concerned, is, in truth, quite clear from the context, where the intention to refuse the prophetic word of Jeremiah that called to remain in the land without fear of the king of Babylon appears to be unanimous. However, setting aside the questionable and conjectural arguments regarding the historical likelihood of the fact itself (cf. pp. 657–658), on which I cannot dwell at the moment, it is rather surprising to see that the author wants to support such a thesis (also) on the basis of the simplistic semantic evaluation that √לקח (with a human or divine subject and a person as object; cf. p. 659) would not *ever* implicate the use of force. Apart from the fact that this absolute negation is already contradicted a few lines later when Gen 14:12 is cited, the central issue is that, to defend the traditional reading of the text, there is no need to find a "violent" connotation of the root referring to the act of taking. In fact, the basic meaning of the active verb (and not only in Hebrew), remodulated according to various semantic nuances by the respective contexts of reference, usually (unless it means "to receive", "to accept") implies that it is an action carried out by a subject of authority or higher power towards another authority (and sometimes also dignitary) considered to be or actually inferior (in H. Seebass, «לקח», ThWAT IV, 588–594, the emphasis is placed on the responsibility or free initiative of the subject of the action expressed by the verb). In the specific case of Jer 43:5–7 (which recalls, at a short distance, the act of being the guide or leader of someone from one place to another, attested in the same context as Jer 41:16, also using √שוב hi.), it is not, therefore, decisive to postulate that √לקח would implicate an explicit physical coercion to affirm or deny, from the exegetic point of view, that Jeremiah and Baruch were lead to Egypt by force. Once again, a pragmatic consideration of the context is revealed to be necessary, since the letter – alone – remains, indeed, ambiguous. Precisely on the basis of the available elements, which highlight the protection granted to Jeremiah by the victors after the fall of Jerusalem (which, one can assume, would not have changed even after the assassination of Gedaliah, given his "pro-Babylonian" position in ch. 42), the radical disobedience of YHWH on the part of the survivors, and the permanently assumed statute of the prophet as a man "delivered" into the hands of God and human beings, one can easily think of the narration of the events in Jer 43:1–7 as a *coincidence* between the desire for extreme solidarity with his people on the part of the prophet (really quite implausible that the text allude to his having fear of the Babylonians) and the will of the fugitives to bring with them, independent of his will, the last remaining prophet of YHWH (bearing clearly in mind that this trait of Jeremiah is never negated, seeing as instead, Baruch is accused of having conditioned him).

Exegetic focalisations

501

give audible form to the word of YHWH itself, against the pretences of truth of other men who, like him, declare themselves prophets. And yet, in the travail of human evaluations, conditioned by the most diverse factors, the authority of this man's words seems to assert itself ever-increasingly: He pays for what he announces by risking his life, placing himself at odds with the dominant positions (cf. 7:1–15; 26), and what he says is put to the test in facts that are dramatically manifested to be more true than other, optimistic interpretations of the historical moment underway (37:19). Several times, King Zedekiah, over the course of his brief reign, is not only one of the recipients of Jeremiah's message (cf. 24:8; 27:12; 32:3–5; 34:17, 21), but he himself feels the need to ask for intercession or at least to have to confront or interpellate the word that comes from this prophet (cf. 21:1–2; 37:3, 17; 38:14) who *with his own body* has become the announcement of the *end* (cf. 16:1–9).

Placed before the question of decisive discernment, the political power feels that its habitual dependence on court scholars is insufficient and it is prompted to turn to the prophetic word, that which had already, several times, called it into question, and which the turns of events themselves were proving as superior over both the wisdom of the counsellors and the words of other prophets. The prophet in and of himself, even if he embodies a "counterpower",[62] has no power (of decision) and juridically is subjected to the king. And yet, it is the king who must (or should) submit to the prophet.[63] Indeed, his prospects of action are null without discernment, just as the discernment (offered by the prophetic word) can do nothing without obedient reception.

The decisive face-to-face takes place at the volition of Zedekiah in a place that will keep the meeting *secret*, at least as far as the contents of the dialogue are concerned. This, however, the narrator lets us infer only indirectly from the context (vv. 15a and 27), even though the pragmatic effect caused by the initial localisation (v. 14) leaves today's reader (and perhaps also almost all ancient readers) in the dark, even with regard to the exact place of the scene. It is not at all clear, in fact, what exactly is meant by the expression "*the third entrance* (מָבוֹא הַשְּׁלִישִׁי) of the house of the Lord" The presence of the article, commonly used in syntagms that localise doors or

---

62 On the figure of Jeremiah as a rebellious counterpower to the injustices of the royal power, see A. KABASELE MUKENGE, «La politique du prophète Jérémie: révolte ou résignation?», in: *Foi et politique dans la Bible*, ed., J.-L. VANDE KERKHOVE, Lubumbashi 2004, 61–81.

63 This is commented on by W. BRUGGEMANN, *To Build, to Plant*, 365, n. 41: "The same epistemological inversion takes place in the narratives of Joseph and Daniel, wherein the occupant of the throne must go outside his royal company to an uncredentialed Israelite to learn reality. In the same way, this king must go to the uncredentialed prophet to learn the truth. All these texts witness to the epistemological subversion that is present in the faith and in the text of Israel." This interesting reference is, however, only partially pertinent, since the king always depends on those who are wise (think of the emblematic figure of Ahitophel), but the relationship with prophets is different, because it is not always requested. I will note, furthermore, that, once the word of Jeremiah is realised, the anticipated truth reveals itself (or is summed up) in his vocation, according to which the prophet has received from God also the power over the kingdoms and "the kings of Judah"(cf. 1:10, 18). The power of radical intervention, the power to withstand any assault.

502   Jer 38:14–28a. Jeremiah and Zedekiah: The final colloquy

courtyards,[64] signals something quite specific. The LXX renders the expression with οἰκίαν ασελισηλ[65] ("house of Aselisel"), possibly referring to a different *Vorlage* that would have conveyed a proper name associated with a site near the temple (identified no better in the Greek version with "house").[66]

The conjectures of scholars aside,[67] I think the same uncertainty witnessed by the textual transmission may depend on a precise and particular originary element of logistical data. If, on the one hand, this notation constitutes a clue as to the proximity of the places and (presumably) also to the facts of the story on the part of the author, on the other, on the level of the effects the narration has on the reader (at least, on the modern one), it fixes the encounter in a dimension that is, I should say, "unique", since it is not perfectly localisable and yet, at the same time, it is dominated by the shadow of the *sacred*. Cognitive linguistics has long shown that a perception of spatial dimension affects semantic values, both through innate cognitive schemata (such as the subject's body schema) and through diversified cultural grids of reference. As U. Volli underscores, from a semiotic point of view, "lo spazio, oltre a fornire una topografia, *è soprattutto il supporto di un'assiologia*".[68]

Indeed, independent of the will of the king (moved purely by fear and the intent of secrecy), the place in itself seems to be the most suitable for the proclamation of the prophetic word, given its relationship of proximity to the *temple*, sacred space par excellence. Note that the temple is the place of the "word" in key points of the second section of the book of Jeremiah (chs. 26–45), that is, in 26:2 (the beginning of the first subsection of chs. 26–35), in 35:2 (the beginning of the chapter that marks the end of the same subsection), and also in 36:2 (the beginning of the second subsection given by chs. 36–45), through Baruch (since Jeremiah is prevented from accessing it in that circumstance).

As can be seen, the temple had been indicated to Jeremiah by YHWH as the ideal context for the prophetic proclamation and, in particular, for one of the most unprecedented and threatening oracles (cf. 7:1–15; 26:1–6), as if, once relations between the people of Israel and God had become perverted, the place of the highest sacredness itself had become "a den of bandits" (7:11; מְעָרַת פָּרִצִים), that is, an ideal refuge for the concealment of iniquity. So it could be significant to place the thematisation of this space, *sacred* and *secret* at the same time, in relation with what Jeremiah announces

---

64   See e.g. for the "doors": Ezek 9:2; 10:19; 11:1; etc.; Zac 14:10; for the "courtyards": 1Kgs 7:8, 12; Ezek 40:28; cf. GK 126w; JM §138c, 153fe; WO § 14.3.1d.

65   According to the text edited by A. Rahlfs. Instead, J. Ziegler, amongst the many other variants that attest an uncertain transmission, prefers ασελιοι.

66   Cf. J. ZIEGLER, *Beiträge zur Ieremias-Septuaginta*, MSU 6, Göttingen 1958, 79–80.

67   Extensive discussion of the problem already in E.F.C. ROSENMÜLLER, *Scholia*, II, 192–193. See also W. McKANE, *Jeremiah*, II, 956. Probably, as is suggested by J. BRIGHT, *Jeremiah*, 231, one should think of a private entrance for the king by which he could directly communicate between his palace and the area of the temple (cf. 2 Kgs 16:18).

68   "Space, in addition to providing a topography, *is above all the support of an axiology*." On space as a vehicle for textual meaning, see U. VOLLI, *Manuale di semiotica*, 158–167 (my translation from p. 161) and, in particular, the monograph by A. GIANNITRAPANI, *Introduzione alla semiotica dello spazio*, BTStu 833, Roma 2013. For a biblical theology of space, see the contributions collected in M. GOURGUES – M. TALBOT, eds., *Partout où tu iras*. Conceptions et expériences bibliques de l'espace, ScBib 13, Paris 2003.

Exegetic focalisations 503

at this decisive moment in the history of Israel, with the message made to resonate previously by Jeremiah himself (also through Baruch, in ch. 36) in the same place: even now, the nature of the Word that places man before the way of life and the way of death will be revealed, going to flush out evil (error, the lack of faith, self-deception, false prophecy) from precisely the space that is sacred, and which remains, in every age, also its best hiding place.

In this sense, it can also be reiterated that the prophetic nature of the book of Jeremiah appears not only in the poetic-oracular parts, but also in its taking on the task, through coordination between the narrative module (*telling*) and the scenic one (*showing*), of showing the reader the interpersonal, intimate dynamic between the self-revelation of YHWH (of which the prophet is the paradigmatic model) and the response of humankind (the ideal human being, i.e. the king). The place is inaccessible and the encounter is secret, yet everything is "prophetically" brought to light by the narrator for his reader, as if to highlight a "type scene" that, while on the one hand expresses the decisive fulfilment of all the previous face-to-face confrontations between the figure of the king and that of the prophet, on the other, invites us to draw a significative semiotic *arcata* connecting it to the equally paradigmatic "type scene" of Jeremiah's vocation in ch. 1.[69] Even the encounter between Jeremiah and Zedekiah (as I will try to highlight in § 3.2.4) analogously characterises itself as a special prophetic call (to obey the meaning of history), to be read in relation to the prototypical one that opens the entire book, giving it also the keys to interpretation that are most important.

3.1.3. The request of the king (שׁאל√) and relation between the urgency of salvation and need for truth

In many respects, knowledge is power, today as it was yesterday (cf. 1 Kgs 10:23–29; etc.). In the ancient Near East, the sovereign has control like none other over things and people by virtue of his authority, legitimised by the gods themselves, but ordinarily, he cannot access divine knowledge-power except through figures specialised in divinatory mediation. In the book of Jeremiah, starting from this common grounding, what is emphasised is the absolute freedom of YHWH's self-communication. Not only can the king not command the word of God at any time, but neither can the prophet, as we have already seen in my comment on ch. 28. The request of king Zedekiah in v. 14b brings us back into this theological and communicative horizon.

"I want to ask you (שׁאל) a *word* (דָּבָר): don't keep *any* (דָּבָר) hidden from me". In this verse, most modern translations prefer to translate the first occurrence of דָּבָר with "thing" or "question",[70] though the possibility of understanding the king's appeal in a technical sense as a request for a "word-oracle" on the part of God is accepted, and sometimes preferred.[71] Even though, on a pragmatic level, *in this case*, there is in fact

---

69 Cf. E. Di Pede, «Le prophète mis en scène: les récits de vocation comme scène type», in: *L'intrigue dans le récit biblique*. Quatrième colloque international du RRENAB, Université Laval, Québec, 29 Mai–1er Juin 2008, *eds.* A. Pasquier – D. Marguerat – A. Wénin, BETL 237, Leuven 2010, 127–140.

70 Cf. e.g. RSV; NEB; NAB; JPS, TOB, LB, EP.

71 Cf. W. Rudolph, *Jeremia*, 222; as a second possible translation, he adds as a note: "Ich frage dich um ein Wort (Jahwes)." Other modern versions that prefer that line: EÜ: "Ich

504   Jer 38:14–28a. Jeremiah and Zedekiah: The final colloquy

no difference between the concept of "word" and the generic concept of "thing" or "question" (since with דָּבָר, the speaker, in similar contexts, obviously wants to receive a verbal communication), my translation intends to accentuate the semantic field of the "word", here and also in the second phrase of the king, which instead everyone renders with "do not hide any from me (דָּבָר)". In fact, there are motives that, in my opinion, justify this accentuation rather than that commonly expressed by the greater part of modern translations.

The peculiarity of the Hebrew term דָּבָר is, to begin with, well known. In a single lexeme, it unites two concepts that, in English (as well as in many other modern languages) are made clearly distinct through the use of different terms: *words* and *facts* are, for those of us in the West, practically opposite realities. But for the Semitic mentality, this is not the case.[72] The same verb שָׁאַל, which already includes both the meaning of "to ask to know" and "to ask to obtain",[73] lends itself to be understood, depending on the context, as "to consult" God in order to have his "word" to help discern a situation in view of a decision on the part of humankind. With this accepted meaning, it is attested above all in the first book of Samuel (cf. 1 Sam 10:22; 14:37; 22:10, 13, 15; 23:2, 4; 28:6; 38:8), through a phraseology that seems to be technical (one asks *of* YHWH *by means* of a person). The one who is consulted is almost always introduced by the preposition בְּ, while, when the question has to do with obtaining (or knowing) something that is more generic, the person being addressed constitutes the direct object, and that about which one wants to be informed is preceded by לְ (cf. Gen 32:30; 43:7; Deut 4.32; 2 Kgs 8:6; Jer 6:16; Job 8:8). Occurrences where a direct object is inserted into the syntagmic construction are rare in both cases.[74]

As can be seen, not being able to ascribe with certainty v. 14b to either of the two frameworks delimited precisely by the different use of the prepositions, a possible overlapping of two semantic axes is created that is, perhaps, not entirely accidental. That, in the process of translation, the emphasis should be put, however, on the oracular "word" requested and uttered in the name of YHWH (compared to a generic "thing", which presupposes a specific question and an opinion that is simply human), is suggested, in my opinion, both by a confrontation with 37:17,[75] and from its symmetrical reuse found at the end of the narration, in 38:27, where, and I believe not coincidentally, the verb שָׁאַל and the term דָּבָר reappear, suggesting the presence of an intriguing semiotic *arcata*. This "strategic" positioning suggests that there be a path of interpretation provided to the reader intentionally, based on the ambivalence of √שׁאל and דָּבָר. If in fact, in closing, it reads: "They came, [then], all the leaders to Jeremiah and they questioned him (√שׁאל)" (v. 27a) and "no word (דָּבָר) had been heard", and not

---

    möchte dich nach einem Gotteswort fragen"; BJ: "Je veux te réclamer une parole; ne me la cèle pas!"

72   Cf. J. BERGMAN – H. LUTZMANN – W.H. SCHMIDT, «דָּבָר», *ThWAT* II, 89–133 (here, in coll. 111–114); J. BARR, *The Semantics*, 129–140.

73   Cf. G. GERLEMAN, «שׁאל», *THAT* II, 842–844.

74   For the first case, cf. Isa 58:2; Jer 50:5 (request for a thing or for information); for the second, cf. Deut 18:11; Josh 9:14; Isa 30:2 (personal direct object).

75   In a context quite similar to our own, we read: "King Zedekiah had him brought to his palace, and he asked him (√שׁאל) secretly, 'Is there any word (דָּבָר) from the Lord?'. Jeremiah answer: 'There is' and added: 'You shall be handed over to the king of Babylon!'." The reference to the "word-oracle" here is even more evident.

Exegetic focalisations 505

simply "nothing had been heard" (v. 27b), then what gets highlighted is that one of the dominant themes of the pericope is precisely the fate of the Word, requested, but not heard (listened to, obeyed) by anyone.

That Zedekiah makes specific reference in his question to precisely the request for an oracle pronounced in the name of God on the present historical moment (to wit, to a דָּבָר יְהוָה), is moreover evident from the fact that Jeremiah (after an initial objection) speaks to him immediately in the name of YHWH without waiting for the king to specify "what" he wants to ask (a legitimate expectation if we remain, instead, with the common translation, "I want to ask you something"). On the other hand, the injunction of the king, which seeks to insure that Jeremiah will speak with him frankly, is indubitably due to an awareness of having been, in fact, an enemy of the prophetic Word (in the wake of his predecessor Jehoiakim). His not-taking a position in favour of the (living) message of Jeremiah against other antagonistic "words" had already permitted, on the part of the "leaders", an attempt to suppress the prophet (cf. 37 11–15; 38:1–6).

In the logic of the narration, the king, knowing that he was fundamentally asking the prophet to expose himself to serious danger yet again, thinks that Jeremiah, having already been pushed to the limit, will prefer to protect himself with silence. It is at precisely this decisive hour, however, that the demand for a word of truth[76] appears to grow stronger. It is as if the nearing of the end were to bring out from the depths of the heart of humankind not only an extreme attempt to cling to life, but, and this need be distinguished, also the (perhaps dark) perception of the essential bond that unites life with truth. The king seems to understand that only a (true) word (however demanding and disturbing) coming from YHWH can still open a horizon of hope where, by now, only death looms.[77]

3.1.4. A space for the Word

The response of Jeremiah in v. 15 is, in turn, a question that assumes, *at least at a first glance*, the pragmatic form and force of a *rhetorical* question[78] ("If I proclaim [the word] to you, will you not perhaps have me die? And if I give you counsel, you will not listen to me!"). Even if, from the pragmatic point of view, the prototypical

---

76 And not only the hope for a more favourable oracle.
77 The case of 1 Kgs 22:1–28 is also very instructive in this regard. Here, too, in my opinion, something similar can be recognised: on the one hand, the royal power (Ahab and Jehoshaphat) before the question of discernment, on the other, the voice of the (400) prophets who announce a truth that conforms to human desires and the *uncomfortable* word of the only "non-aligned" prophet, Micaiah son of Imlah. When, upon being questioned, he speaks provocatively about what King Ahab wanted to hear himself told, the latter responds angrily: "*How many times must I adjure you to tell me nothing but the truth* (רַק־אֱמֶת) *in the name of the Lord?*" (1 Kgs 22:16). Here too: words of advice that are complaisant to human logic, (dark) perception of their insufficiency, (even darker and more contradictory) insistent request for a different (more "true", even if much less accommodating) truth.
78 Cf. K. SCHÖPSDAU, «Frage, retorische», HWR III, 445–454. On the pragmatic implications of the rhetorical questions in some of the sections in prose in the HB, see A. MOSHAVI, «Two Types of Argumentation Involving Rhetorical Questions in Biblical Hebrew Dialogue», Bib. 90 (2009) 32–46.

question conveys a request for information, there are other interrogative devices that intend for something different to be expressed. The pragmatic valence of the rhetorical question, in this case, is tantamount to the assertion "you will certainly have me die/be put to death".

This specification is necessary, seeing as הֲלֹא/הֲלֺא (the etymology of which is debated, as it appears to be a case of homonymy between two different lexemes, one that is equivalent to הִנֵּה, and the other composed of the particle הֲ + לֺא) can introduce, depending on the context, either a *negative interrogative phrase* or an *exclamation* or *affirmation* presented as a certainty.[79] It is not always easy to distinguish between the two possibilities and there are texts that remain ambiguous (one of the most famous is the "question" of the snake in Gen 3:1). The syntactic element that permits the disambiguation in this case is the subordinate conditional phrase introduced by כִּי, which precedes the main clause (cf. Obad 1:5; Ps 44:21−22).

The implicit assertion contained in the rhetorical question is, regardless, made explicit immediately by Jeremiah himself, accusing the king of not being willing to listen. On closer inspection, however, more than before a rhetorical question here (with the implied response made explicit by the prophet himself), we could specify that we are in the presence of a question that belongs to those classified as "conducive questions",[80] These "facilitating questions" are formulated to obtain a *particular* response. The expectations of the speaker can be varied and thus, likewise, the communication functions implicated by the question. In our case, the pragmatic valence assumes the force, in my opinion, not so much of an assertion, but of a *solicitation* to set aside any hostile intention and thereby be able to receive and accept the prophetic word. I will return to this point shortly.

From a syntactic point of view, the response of the prophet is made up of two hypothetical periods (a conditional subordinate clause, the protasis, and a main clause, the apodosis), which refer to each other reciprocally according to the device of synonymical parallelism.[81] Two verbs in the communication are juxtaposed with just as many radical negations:

---

79 As it is intended and has been translated in some modern versions (cf. JPS; TOB; EÜ; RL). On the question, see BLAU §§ 82; 103.3; JM §§161c; 164d; M.L. BROWN, «"Is it Not?" or "Indeed!": *HL* in Northwest Semitic», *Maarav* 4 (1987) 201−219; D. SIVAN − W. SCHNIEDEWIND, «Letting Your "Yes" Be "No" in Ancient Israel: A Study of the Asseverative לֺא and הֲלֺא», *JSSt* 38 (1993) 209−226; A. MOSHAVI, «Syntactic Evidence for a Clausal Adverb הֲלֺא in Biblical Hebrew», *JNSL* 33 (2007) 51−63 (the case of Jer 38:15 is mentioned on p. 58).

80 In this regard, see A. MOSHAVI, «"Is That Your Voice, My Son David?". Conducive Questions in Biblical Hebrew», *JNSL* 36 (2010) 65−81.

81 I borrow terminology that, in itself, identifies one of the most frequent and well-known literary processes of biblical poetry (see ch. 1, §§ 2.1; 2.4.1). My approach of the semantic sort, and if it is true, as asserted in M.Z. KADDARI, «A Semantic Approach to Biblical Parallelism», *JJS* 24 (1973) 167−175, that "poetical units even if they display metrical 'parallelism', are often deprived of all semantic parallelism", it is also possible to detect, as in this case, that even "non-poetical texts can be constructed in the style of semantic parallelism" (here, p. 175). It is in this perspective, e.g. that we find the contribution of E.A. MARTENS, «Narrative Parallelism and Message in Jeremiah 34−38», in: *Early Jewish and Christian Exegesis*. Studies in Memory of William Hugh Brownlee, *eds.* C.A. EVANS − W.F. STINESPRING, Atlanta 1987, 33−49.

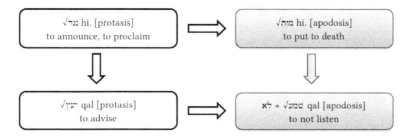

It seems that √נגד (hi.), compared to other *verba dicendi*, has the peculiarity of expressing the action of announcing something important to the recipient on the part of someone who comes from another place.[82] For its part, however, the root יעץ is tied to the meaning "to advise, to plan, to decide", whose own precise scope is situated within the fold of the sapiential tradition.[83] As such, it is taken up and used mainly by Isaiah, both in denouncing the vanity of human "advice" irrespective of YHWH (cf. Isa 7:5–7), both to extol the עֵצָה (the advice) of YHWH (cf. e.g. Isa 28:29). Both verbal roots are placed in relation here to a divine revelation, given that the content of the message is introduced in v. 17 with a solemn *Botenformel*.

According to a semantic approach to the phenomenon of *parallelismus membrorum* (by which *a single concept* is repeated twice, in slightly different forms, through different lexemes), it is possible to grasp a different nuance and mutual illumination in the juxtaposition made by Jeremiah of "to announce" (√נגד hi.) and "to make die" (√מות hi.), and between "to advise" (√יעץ qal) and "to not listen" (לא + √שמע qal). From a certain point of view, the relationship between the two phrases is *anti-climactic*, because since what is highlighted first is the announcement (of a divine word, cf. √נגד hi. in Jer 33:3; Amos 4:13) of what YHWH is putting into action and the consequent killing of the messenger, while on the other hand, the "advice" (to be understood as a truthful [operative] declaration, entrusted to the freedom of the interlocutor) is placed in relation to "non-listening". However, given that the "revelation"-announcement (√נגד hi.) is actually "advice" (√יעץ) that imposes a choice (of obedience or disobedience), the relationship can also be understood as a case of *hysteron proteron*[84]: "death" is spoken of first, but the conclusion that is most significant is the "not-listening", because the killing of the prophet is precisely the emblematic sign of the refusal to listen to the prophetic word.

I do not believe, as some have asserted,[85] that the objection to Zedekiah's question should to be simply attributed to fear provoked in Jeremiah as a result of the treatment

---

82 The prophet would be, par excellence, the man of the proclamation that comes from "another place", that is, from the intimacy of the divine. This observation about that root, however, while coinciding with the context of the prophetic proclamation that Jeremiah speaks about, does not find a consequent attestation within the prophetic literature, according to what is noted by C. WESTERMANN, «נגד», *THAT* II, 31–37.
83 Cf. H.-P. STÄHLI, «יעץ», *THAT* I, 748–753; L. RUPPERT, «יעץ», *ThWAT* III, 718–751.
84 On this figure, see ch. III, § 3.1.3, n. 46.
85 Cf. A. WEISER, *Jeremia*. II, 340–341; W. BRUEGGEMAN, *To Build to Plant*, 366: "He thought that speaking would bring jeopardy and so he preferred silence, because silence ostensibly maintains safety. It is better not to speak if the word only enrages

508   Jer 38:14–28a. Jeremiah and Zedekiah: The final colloquy

previously reserved for him (cf. 38:1–13). Indeed, in the logic of the narrative, he knows that it is precisely thanks to the favour of the king (albeit due to the intercession of Ebed-melech) that he was able to escape death and was extracted from the cistern-"burial" (cf. 38:7–13). Instead, Jeremiah intends to point out that the request of the king is *vitiated*, so any response would be not only *harmful*, but *useless*. The question is thus that of overcoming this *impasse*. As a consequence, the reticence expressed by the prophet can be understood as a reiteration on an intradiegetical level of the communicative effect that the extradiegetic narrator normally wants to produced in the reader by leaving intentional ellipses to arouse greater interpretive cooperation.[86]

Jeremiah, servant of the Word and having become himself a living word (through the symbolic gestures and, even more so, through his own story as a man who has handed himself over and been saved), is simply making a *last attempt*.[87] Contrary to what he will do with the "leaders" after the conversation with Zedekiah, consenting to the confinement to silence requested by the king and, in fact, abandoning them to the lie they do not want to get out of (cf. vv. 24–27), his objection seeks to create, in the person standing before him, a *space* for authentic communication, the minimum conditions necessary to receive what he has already announced, definitely for the last time before the catastrophe. He does so, first and foremost, by revealing to the very king who exhorts an oracle that which, in truth, he is far from wanting to accept as a normative truth coming from YHWH *for himself, here and now*.

In this apprehension revealed in the accusatory behaviour of the prophet resounds one of the most charged instances of *páthos* running through prophecy in Israel: the tension for the divine message to reach the heart of those who are called to receive it and obey it (to have life). All the prophetic traditions attest, according to multiple registers, the unfolding of this communicative effort, in which a Freedom is seen that becomes a call for communion in justice for still another freedom. It is the extreme attempt of the Truth to find space in the heart of humankind. Here, Jeremiah goes so far as to accuse King Zedekiah ("will you not perhaps have me die?" [...] "you will not listen to me!")[88] He does this not to condemn him and then isolate himself in a huffy

---

the government. The prophet is wisely restrained (v. 15). The prophet is not excessively courageous."

86 On this narrative technique, by which the unspoken in a story serves to manipulate the attention of the reader, increasing their interest and ability to respond to the textual provocations, see e.g. L. TOKER, *Eloquent Reticence*. Withholding Information in Fictional Narrative, Lexington 1993.

87 Moreover, as pointed out by J.R. LUNDBOM, «Jeremiah and the Break-Away from Authority Preaching», *SEÅ* 56 (1991) 7–28, the Jeremianic prophetic ministry is characterised by its dialogic dynamism. A comparison with other, more assertive styles of prophetic communication (as e.g. that of Amos, Hosea, Isaiah) confirms this impression.

88 The characteristic fact here is that the accusation directly regards the future, and only indirectly (logic dictates) a fait accompli (the non-listening as a general predisposition already documented by previous actions). In any case, the use of הֲלוֹא (or simply הֲ) may well introduce a criminal allegation in the form of a rhetorical question, as in Deut 32:6; 2 Sam 19:22; 1 Kgs 21:19; Isa 57:4b; Neh 2:19; cf. P. BOVATI, *Ristabilire la giustizia*, 64, n. 31 and the reference to H.A. BRONGERS, «Some Remarks on the Biblical Particle *hᵃlō'*», in: *Remembering All the Way*... A Collection of Old Testament Studies Published on the Occasion of the Fortieth Anniversary of the

Exegetic focalisations 509

silence, but rather to obtain a response, his reception, so that Jeremiah's even further "delivering of himself" to lend his voice to the word of God is not rendered futile.

3.1.5. The secret oath (√שׁבע). An underlying ambiguity

The word of the oath pronounced by Zedekiah (v. 16: introduced by √שׁבע ni.),[89] which would like to guarantee the most favourable condition for truth to be revealed, opens the way for the theme of "being delivered" or "surrendering". The king is directly involved, but so is the truth itself announced by the prophet Jeremiah. The act of taking the oath,[90] which is present whenever there is a need to validate a word given, has a reference to the sacred world as an essential characteristic. A deity is invoked not only as witness, but also as a judicial authority deputed to issue a conviction in case of perjury. It is a matter of voluntarily subjecting oneself to the threat of a malediction.[91]

There is an essential link between oath and imprecation (understood as submission to divine judgment),[92] Expressed in the form of conditional clauses, however, this relationship tends to tone itself down in commonly used formulas. The reason for this

---

Oudtestamentisch Werkgezelschap in Nederland, eds. B. ALBREKTSON et al., OTS 21, Leiden 1981, 177–189.

89 Cf. I. KOTTSIEPER, «שׁבע», ThWAT VII, 974–1000 (with bibliography).

90 Amongst the many contributions on this topic, see those of S.H. BLANK, «The Curse, Blasphemy, the Spell, and the Oath», HUCA 23 (1950–1951) 73–95; H.-J. KRAUS, «Der lebendige Gott», EvT 27 (1967) 169–200; M.R. LEHMANN, «Biblical Oaths», ZAW 81 (1969) 74–92; M. GREENBERG, «The Hebrew Oath Particle Ḥay/Ḥē», JBL 76 (1957) 34–39; in particular, for the use of אם in the oath, see H.S. GEHMAN, «The Oath in the Old Testament: Its Vocabulary, Idiom, and Syntax; Its Semantics and Theology in the Masoretic Text and the Septuagint», in: Grace upon Grace. Essays in Honor of Lester J. Kuyper, ed. J.I. COOK, Grand Rapids 1975, 51–63. More recently: Y. ZIEGLER, «"As the Lord Lives and as Your Soul Lives": An Oath of Conscious Deference», VT 58 (2008) 117–130; ID., Promises to Keep. The Oath in Biblical Narrative, VT.S 120, Leiden 2008, 87–122; B. CONKLIN, Oath Formulas in Biblical Hebrew, LSAWS 5, Winona Lake 2011, 27–30, 39.

91 In this regard, keep in mind the observations of H.G.L. PEELS, The Vengeance of God. The Meaning of the Root NQM and the Function of the NQM-Texts in the Context of Divine Revelation in the Old Testament, OTS 31, Leiden 1995, 237: "The curse played a significant role in the daily life of the ancient Middle East. In all areas of private as well as communal life (social-economic, juridical, cultic, political) the practice of cursing was applied. The curse was to bring the truth to light (in juridical procedures, e.g. in the ordeal), force obedience (with treaties and regulations), frighten off thieves, plunderers and vandals (with inscriptions on graves, boundary stones and buildings), guarantee honesty (in economic transactions), etc. The oath, which was uttered under a vast number of circumstances, is a form of self-cursing. The deity could also employ the curse as a preventive measure or in punishment." The author then underscores that this form of guarantee, understood as a "legal device", could be indicative of the lack of a strong central authority or developed legal apparatus (almost as if this were a further sign of weakness, therefore, of the status of King Zedekiah). Actually, it should be observed that these transactions were "private" in nature and not controlled by the state bodies (cf. n. 96).

92 Cf. S.H. BLANK, «The Curse», 90: "Thus, although the conditional curse is an essential part of the oath, the actual words of the curse, defining the calamity which is to befall the oath-taker if he has sworn falsely, are almost never spoken. They are evaded, as

can be seen in the almost magical fear that cloaks every formula wishing misfortune, considered dangerous even if only pronounced. It is my opinion that our case could be an example of a "truncated" formula, which omits the imprecatory part while still maintaining a trace of its original structure in the formulation.

The authenticating formula employed (חַי־יְהוָה), indubitably the most common of those possible (43x in the HB; also with the vocalization חֵי and three main variations: cf. Gen 42:16; 2 Sam 2:27 [cf. Amos 8:14]; Job 27.2–4; and 9x in the book of Jeremiah[93]), is elliptical and implies a inexplicit development that I expressed in translation with "[As it is true that] the Lord is living [...]". Literally, in a more expanded form, it would need to be translated and understood, in my interpretation, as: "[As it is true that] living is the Lord who gave us this life, [may this and that happen to me; that is, may I be cursed] if I make you die or if I hand you over to those men who seek your life." If this "self-imprecatory" development is not implied by the (topicalised) apodosis (or by the "authenticator"), the protasis is left hanging and remains hard to understand (cf., e.g. 1 Sam 19:6: "Living is the Lord/for the life of the Lord (חַי־יְהוָה), if he is put to death (אִם־יוּמָת)".

The appeal is addressed to YHWH the creator as the living (and true) God who possesses and gives life[94]: in the face of the threat of the end and the bursting through of the forces of chaos, what re-emerges from the depths, even with this expression, is faith in the creative power of YHWH.[95] Hence, it is a solemn appeal, but one that contains something contradictory in itself. The king is sincere, but a coward. The oath is *valid* (because it has evoked YHWH as its witness),[96] but is pronounced "in secret"

---

in the oath formula, or wholly suppressed, as in the truncated form of the oath. And this is done because of the fear that, even though the oath-taker is convinced of his innocence or sincere in his intentions, by some evil chance the words might nevertheless be realized. The words themselves are dangerous. A divine agency is indeed assumed in the oath formula; but the fear of the curse itself, of the very words of the curse, dictates the form of the formula."

93 Cf. 4:2; 5:2; 12:16; 16:14, 15; 23:7, 8; 38:16; 44:26 (cf. 22:24).

94 Whether חַי is to be understood as a verb ("the Lord *lives*") or as a substantive ("for *the life* of the Lord") is, in any case, in dispute; cf. H. Ringgren, «חָיָה», *ThWAT* II, 874–898 (here, col. 891–893).

95 I refer, in this regard, to what I developed in ch. IV (§§ 4.2 and 6.2) of the present dissertation.

96 *Pace* C. Russo, «Geremia e Sedecia: un dialogo impossibile e ironico alla vigilia della capitolazione. Analisi testuale di Ger 38,14–28a TM», in: «*Insegnaci a contare i nostri giorni e giungeremo al cuore della sapienza*» (Sal 90,12). Atti della XLV Settimana Biblica Nazionale (Roma, 10–14 settembre 2018), *eds.* D. Scaiola – F. Dalla Vecchia, RStB 32, Bologna 2020, 333–359 (here pp. 340–341). A. Weiser, *Jeremia*. II, 341, considers it "unofficial" because there are no (human) witnesses. Perhaps one could also say, while bearing in mind the king's fears towards his dignitaries, that in themselves, these are not required since the situation, in this case, is neither judicial nor cult-related, but rather "friendly" (in a broad sense), as in 1 Sam 20:17, where the context (cf. v. 11) suggests that the act of the oath that seals the pact between David and Jonathan is to be kept in an absolutely private sphere. The problem, in the case at hand, concerns the public function of the king and his responsibility regarding the fate of Jerusalem.

(בְּסֵתֶר)[97] which also renders it rather *ambiguous*, given the gravity of the moment. Also because there will be a sort of doubling[98] of the secrecy as a result of Zedekiah's injunction (vv. 24–26), by which he will demand that the prophet divulge nothing about their meeting. It is obvious that the king intends to safeguard his position from the preponderance of his notables, to evade being charged with hearing out, or worse yet, even consulting (one who is now considered to be) a traitor of the state.[99] But here, the question is not just that of sealing an agreement between two private parties for personal, undisclosable motives, but rather that of assuming full responsibility in the role of sovereign and leader of the people in one of the most critical moments in the history of Israel. It is not only the prophetic word that calls for this, it is the reality itself that demands it.

Zedekiah (and the reader along with him) actually knows full well that his question and the answer Jeremiah is about to give concerns the fate of an entire city, and will therefore require that a "public" stance be taken, just as the prophetic ministry of Jeremiah has, so far, been public. It is therefore not possible to leave everything in secrecy, if one truly wants to obey this prophetic word. The sphere in which the king intends to remain promises no good, and seems like a way to not pursue the truth. If even a declaration of the best intentions does not, in fact, guarantee the perseverance or actual acceptance of the indications that come from recognised mediators (cf. 42:1–6), all the more so, any initial reserve before the prophetic word and its implications runs the risk of pre-empting its subsequent and total rejection.

3.1.6. *The radicality of choice: More on the way of life and the way of death*

Jeremiah himself solemnly introduces the content of his response by using the well-known "messenger formula". In its simplest form, this coincides with the expression כֹּה־אָמַר יְהוָה ("thus says the Lord"), while the double expansion attested here (v. 17) seems to make an allusion, on the one hand, to the "warrior" qualification of the God who has the power to command and subjugate any enemy army (אֱלֹהֵי צְבָאוֹת: "God of hosts"),[100] and on the other (אֱלֹהֵי יִשְׂרָאֵל: "God of Israel"), to the ultimate recipient of the totality of the prophecy, that is, the entire people of the Covenant.

---

97 The MT seems to underscore this, seeing that the notation is omitted from the LXX (even if it can be learned all the same from v. 27).

98 As noted by C. Russo, «Geremia e Sedecia», 340.

99 As is rightly noted by W. Brueggemann, *To Build, To Plant*, 147.

100 Studies concerning the title אֱלֹהֵי צְבָאוֹת (279x in the MT, of which 77x in Jeremiah) are quite plentiful and orient an interpretation towards a contextual comprehension of the expression (for a brief summary, with bibliographical references, see e.g. M. Brettler, *God is King*. Understanding a Biblical Metaphor, JSOT.S 76, Sheffield 1989, 107–108). The title, that is, would have undergone an evolution that could be schematised in these terms: originally, its value was fundamentally cosmological, being linked in the East to the cosmic forces that in Israel are conceived as simple creatures subject to YHWH (cf. Ps 29; 103; 104; 148), subsequently, in the monarchical era, the title is coloured along a more historical vein, qualifying the powerful action of YHWH in the history of salvation. Finally, with the liturgical use, it becomes more generically consecrated within a sacred dimension that, without cancelling out the

In itself, in any case, this formula has the function of leading two different listeners/ readers (one intradiegetic and the other extradiegetic) to a dual source, a dual "beginning": the wellspring from which the word of Jeremiah flows, which is YHWH himself, and the initial, founding experience of the prophetic vocation (by which authoritative *emissaries* are appointed). But it is common knowledge that the *Botenformel* is an expressive module that abounds on the lips of false prophets as well, as we saw in ch. 28. In this sense, it becomes clear that the prophetic appeal to which it is attached is configured as a veritative demand, normative in nature, like an indication of salvation that need be accepted. It is not an apodictic demonstration. And indeed, if I were to limit myself to the prophetic communication in question, I could say that the interlocutor is given no other signs to believe than the message itself. But this would obviously be far too short-sighted a vision.

Actually, at this point, the reader, as well as the intradiegetic interlocutor, should well know that the Jeremianic "message" regards not only his words, but also his (symbolic) gestures, the story of his prophetic body, and the events of history. The "signs" to believe are certainly out there, at least, they are for those who do not want to shut their eyes to them. And it is Jeremiah himself, if his prior declaration of innocence (37:18) were not enough, who already reminded Zedekiah of the most obvious one:

"[...] where are your prophets who prophesied for you, saying: 'The king of Babylon will not attack you or this land'"? (37:19).

It is the criterion of the *fulfilment* of the prophetic word.[101] Certainly not to be taken to the letter, but nevertheless, at least in this case, verifiable without much effort: by now, false hopes have vanished. And in the void left behind by the deceptive human words, the possibility of discernment offered by the Word now unfolds (vv. 17–18).

What to human eyes appears to be simply an extreme reduction of the possibilities offered to political reasoning, which sees its manoeuvring room as having been limited to the sharply narrowed range of *just two* or three possible options (to resist, surrender, or flee[102]), the prophetic word knows how to lead it back, and indeed, always leads it back, to the decisive question of the faith of Israel: *to choose between listening or not listening to the voice of God*. Ultimately, these are fundamentally the *only two* options in the book of Jeremiah: to *adhere* to YHWH (cf. 13:11: √דבק)[103] and live in fidelity

---

other values (cosmic and military), declares the Temple and the Holy City as the home of the "king of Glory".

101 But this too remains ambiguous, in need of interpretation. And not just because it is fundamentally retrospective. Note, in particular, the resemblance, at least in a formal sense, with the motives for the *surrender* set forth by the "great cupbearer" of the King of Assyria below the walls of Jerusalem (cf. 2 Kgs 18:34).

102 The choices that affect the entire city are ultimately only two (either to surrender or to resist). The option to *escape*, on the other hand, can only be attempted by a very small number of people (cf. ch. II, § 3.2, in particular, nn. 119 and 120 for further study). And this is what Zedekiah will choose, in vain, along with his family members and a handful of soldiers (39:1–7; 52:6–11; cf. 2 Kgs 25:1–7; Ezek 12:12–14). For another biblical example, think of the case of the king of Judah, Amaziah (reported in 2 Kgs 14:19): when a conspiracy formed against him in Jerusalem, he escaped to Lachish where, however, he was chased down and overtaken, caught and murdered.

103 The same root recurs in 2 Kgs 18:6 to distinguish the upright behaviour of the king Hezekiah, in a context that is significant for our topic.

Exegetic focalisations 513

to the Covenant, or turn to other gods (i.e. to false life principles) and rot, become spoiled (cf. 13:7: √שחת ni., and vv. 9–10). The content of the oracle is structured as an *aut aut*, implicitly instituting an overlapping of the spheres of political action and religious action in a unifying perspective of the meaning imprinted on the history of Israel by its relationship with YHWH. For this reason, two different possibilities are re-presented, to which the same number of different outcomes correspond. There is the path of life or that of death (cf. 21:8–9).

This theme, even though it is not lexicalised here through the term דֶּרֶךְ ("path, road"),[104] is typical of both Deuteronomistic theology (cf. Deut 11:26–28; 30:15–20) and sapiential theology (cf. Prov 1:10, 15), and recurs clearly, as we have already seen, in 21 8: "And to this people you will say: Thus says the Lord: Behold, I set before you the way of life *(אֶת־דֶּרֶךְ הַחַיִּים)* and the way of death *(וְאֶת־דֶּרֶךְ הַמָּוֶת)*". Here too, the same choice: "Whoever remains in this city shall die by the sword, by famine and by plague; but whoever goes out and consigns himself to the Chaldeans who are besieging you shall live, and shall have his life as war booty" (21:9).

With regard to this schema of opposition, it is opportune to recall what I emphasised when studying ch. 28: the salvation promised by Jeremiah, unlike that divulged by the false prophets, does not negate the announcement of the disaster, nor does it play down the real situation of man (the sinner) before YHWH.[105] The fact is that this salvation is proclaimed precisely in close connection to the *negative* element: together or within the disaster itself. I will already note at this point that the path of life indicated by Jeremiah passes through a modality (surrender to the enemy) that, even if it does not coincide with death (in a physical sense), still requires the acceptance of its essential symbolic dimension: that of the "end".[106]

3.1.7. Going out (√יצא) towards the leaders of Babylon. Exodus, anti-Exodus, and new Exodus

If, in terms of the theme of submission to the king of Babylon, the oracle of Jeremiah is no different from those he had already repeatedly addressed to both the king and other recipients, it is, however, completely uncustomary if one considers not only the way faith was understood at his time (the traditional theology of the "impregnability of Zion"),[107] but also the oracles of all other prophets – present, past, and future.

There is a sole request, simple, precise, and unequivocal: *to surrender*. The act of handing oneself over to the Chaldeans is expressed, however, with a verb that paradoxically wants to make explicit non-passivity: the question is not that of opening the doors and letting the enemies in, but *to go out* (√יצא) of the city towards (אֶל) the "leaders of the king of Babylon" (שָׂרֵי מֶלֶךְ־בָּבֶל), that is, the generals and commanders

---

104 Cf. ch. III, § 4.2.1 (and n. 206, in particular).
105 On the contrary, it need be recognised that a surprising convergence exists between the true prophetic messages (albeit their having different bearers and recipients) with regard to their constant negativity. They talk repeatedly, though not only, obviously, about death (threatened or simply predicted).
106 And indeed, the king feels *fear*, which is the constitutive emotional response of the human being aroused by an (even unconscious) perception of one's possibly or having to die. I will study this topic further in §§ 3.2.1–2.
107 On this subject, we refer to what was studied in-depth in ch. II, § 3.2.2.1 point C.

514 Jer 38:14–28a. Jeremiah and Zedekiah: The final colloquy

leading the siege, while Nebuchadnezzar probably resided at the headquarters he had established in Riblah (cf. 39:5). For a more explicative translation having a dynamic equivalence, we could render the Hebrew expression as: "if you will *really* go out" (אִם־יָצֹא תֵצֵא). As such, the particular nuance that would be impressed on the conditional proposition by the construction with an absolute infinitive placed before the verb (cf. v. 17b) would be such as to amplify the root יצא, doubling it. On the basis of the context, the proposal does not seem to me to be an excessive one, even if it is only one possibility.[108] It could perhaps accentuate the fact that this decision must be taken on *responsibly.*[109]

The prophetic word of Jeremiah, whilst firmly placed in the very concrete context of the only two choices that were abundantly clear to both the king and his dignitaries, nevertheless, makes two completely different but equally concrete outcomes correspond to these that a simple political calculation could never have predicted with certainty:

ACTION		CONSEQUENCE
√יצא	to go out...	one's own life and the dynasty saved, the city intact
לא + √יצא	to not go out...	to not escape the Chaldeans, the city burned with fire

A sculptural representation of this alternative can be seen in the already repeatedly mentioned Assyrian bas-relief depicting the taking of Lachish by Sennacherib.[110] The complex, articulated depiction presents several scenic sequences, overlapping the successive temporal phases of the conquest in the unity of a single iconographic project that develops over several panels.

As C. Uehlinger points out,[111] those who created the work wanted to draw some clear distinctions between different categories of Jews: not only between the different typologies of soldiers and civilians, but also amongst those who are in charge or protagonists of the resistance against the Assyrians and the inhabitants who surrender and are led before the victorious sovereign (and then into exile). Amongst the long line of people (men, women, and children) leaving the city, there are no Israelite soldiers. Unlike other representations of similar subjects, here there are no scenes of mistreatment by the Assyrian military, whose presence is moreover limited in this context, and seems to have only a function of accompaniment. And it is interesting to note the emblematic contrapositioning that is highlighted in front of the monumental city gate (cf. Fig. 36), that is, the central axis of the entire composition: on one side are the

---

108 Cf. JM §123*d*: "Placed before the verb, the inf. abs. generally has a stronger nuance than when it follows it, and it is easy to see why, since putting an accusative before a verb reinforces the emphasis. [...] Fairly often the nuance added by the inf. is too light to be rendered without exaggeration in a literal translation. [...] It is only from the context that the nuance added by the infinitive can be deduced in each case." Another possibility would be a stereotypical use of the infinite absolute to reinforce the opposition between the two elements of a conditional clause, cf. JM §123*g*.

109 Cf. E.F.C. ROSENMÜLLER, *Scholia*, II, 193: "*Si exeundo exeas*, facta spontanea deditione [...]".

110 Cf. Fig. 13 in ch. II, § 2.3.1.

111 Cf. C. UEHLINGER, «Clio in a World of Pictures», 278–284.

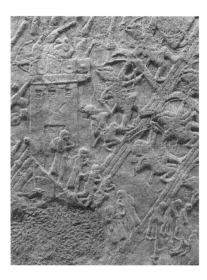

Fig. 36. The central axis of the composition of the taking of Lachish: on the one side, the civilians who leave the city to be deported, on the other, some leaders of the resistance who are impaled (photo from D. USSISHKIN, The Conquest of Lachish, 100, 103).

inhabitants who *go out in peace* carrying bundles typical of deportees, while on the other, a group of Jews (probably leaders or officers) are *impaled*. The propagandistic significance of the message is clear, and reflects the alternative presented in 2 Kgs 18:31–32a by the Assyrian "great cupbearer" below the walls of besieged Jerusalem: to consent to the surrender and then be deported to Assyria under the guarantee of life and of a future of well-being, or to persist in the resistance and be mercilessly killed.

Well, in a context that is similar, Jeremiah calls for surrender to the enemy. Rapidly reviewing the entire history of prophetism, it is impossible to find an adequate term of comparison. No prophet has ever indicated a similar political option as concrete adherence to the God of hosts and thus as a way to salvation. The most pertinent direct comparison, as we have seen, can be drawn not just with Isaiah,[112] but even more radically, with Moses himself, the man identified by the Deuteronomic tradition as YHWH's greatest prophet (cf. Deut 18:15; 34:10).

As for Isaiah and the prophetic ministry he led at the time of King Ahaz (ca. 735–715 or 736–729/725) and Hezekiah (ca. 715–687 or 728/725–700), a certain similarity can be seen (*mutatis mutandis*) in the historical-political context that acts as the background to his prophesising. Over the course of the Syro-Ephraimite War, King Rezin of Aram and King Pekach of Israel march against Jerusalem to lay siege to it; later, at the time of Hezekiah, it is then the Assyrians who attempt to take over the city in the same way under Sennacherib. In these cases as well, the political power is in serious trouble and possible allies are sought to face the threat, looking first to the Assyrians, then to

---

112   Cf. ch. II, § 3.3.1.

516   Jer 38:14-28a. Jeremiah and Zedekiah: The final colloquy

Egypt, depending on the historical circumstances of the present moment. The message of Isaiah is: no such alliance is necessary; if one has faith, YHWH himself will protect Jerusalem against the invader.[113] This prophetic proclamation is founded, in its very communication as the word of YHWH, on the repeatedly reiterated fact that the Lord himself has chosen Jerusalem (and its temple) as the home of his glory and object of his love and protection.

Just as it was difficult for Isaiah's contemporaries to accept his appeal to trust the salvific intervention of YHWH, renouncing the politics of alliances, also – paradoxically – in Jeremiah's time, it is precisely an emblematic representative of false prophetism, Hananiah, who makes himself the bold *de facto* propagator of this anti-Assyrian "Isaianic option" transposed in an anti-Babylonian key.[114] With him, many other (false) prophets (cf. 26:11; 27:9–10:14–17; 29:8; 37:19), along with other authoritative figures, hosted a far too easy hope, contributing to the choral, obstinate repetition and diffusion, always having the reassuring litany as its bottom line: "Temple of the Lord, Temple of the Lord, this is the Temple of the Lord!" (cf. 7:4). Taking unconditional divine protection as a given, the widespread belief was that nothing irreparable could ever take place: "To those who despise me, they say: 'The Lord has said: You shall have peace!' and to all those who walk according to the hardness of their heart: 'Misfortune shall not come upon you!'" (23:17). It is entirely logical, therefore, that Jeremiah's words had to have seemed, in his day, for what had become the traditional theology of the "impregnability of Zion", not only inappropriate, but even anti-national, irreverent, and blasphemous (cf. 20:1; 26:7–9; 38:4).

If we go back instead to the founding events narrated in the book of the Exodus and consider the figure of Moses, the liberator of the chosen people, the contraposition becomes even more marked and definitely intentional. There are those who have spoken of Jeremiah as an anti-Moses.[115] Indeed, there is no lack of antitheses: while Moses is the model of the intercessor and his intercession is fundamentally "provocated" by YHWH himself (cf. Exod 32:7–14:30–35), Jeremiah, on the other hand, is prohibited from any form of intercession (cf. 7:16; 11:14; 14:11; 15:1); Moses is the one at the hands of whom YHWH brings the people out of Egypt to leads them to the Promised Land, while Jeremiah is instead led by the rebels intent on returning

---

113   Obviously, this option is not exempt from problems of concrete political viability either (cf. J.M. ABREGO, *Los libros proféticos,* IEB 4, Estella 1993, 125–127).

114   When people believe they have become true disciples of a (past) prophet and think they have grasped the authentic message and honoured the prophet's memory by repeating the prophet's message slavishly (i.e. out of context), it is precisely then that they risk becoming killers of the "Prophecy" itself (that of today) of which those who they honour were the bearers (cf. Mt 23:19–32).

115   L. ALONSO SCHÖKEL, «Jeremías como anti-Moisés», 245–254 (I made mention of the question in ch. III, § 4.2.1). There is however, also no lack of striking similarities, as is pointed out by W.L. HOLLADAY, «The Background of Jeremiah's Self-Understanding: Moses, Samuel and Psalm 22», *JBL* 83 (1964) 153–164; ID., «Jeremiah and Moses: Further Observations», *JBL* 85 (1966) 17–27. See also, more recently, G. FISCHER, «Jeremiah – "The Prophet like Moses?"», in: *The Book of Jeremiah.* Composition, Reception, and Interpretation, *eds.* J. LUNDBOM – C.A. EVANS – B. ANDERSON, VT.S. 178, Leiden – Boston 2018, 45–66.

Exegetic focalisations

to Egypt, against the will of YHWH or as fulfilment of curses for the betrayal of the Covenant (cf. Deut 28:68).

Picking up on what Yair Zakovitch observes as an exemplary reference about some interesting narrative dynamics of the Genesis, we can thus say that we are in the strategic intertextual perspective that is typical to the Scripture, and which guides the interpretive act of the reader not through explicit or direct references, but rather through implicit allusions, in this case aimed at configuring a character as the antithesis of another one who is well known.[116] Here, however, the phenomenon of "reflection stories" pointed out by Y. Zakovitch is even more widespread, since it no longer regards the figure of Jeremiah alone. As J.M. Abrego highlights,[117] the same events that precede and immediately follow the fall of Jerusalem seem, in some ways, to propose once again the main scenes of the "founding story" (expressed in different traditions) of the exit from Egypt and entrance into the Promised Land, in the form, however, of an "anti-Exodus" that begins with the destruction of Jerusalem and end of the Davidic dynasty.[118] Let me re-elaborate and integrate his main observations, presenting them in a schematic form:

Jerusalem taken into possession (Exod 15:17; 2Sam 5:7), start of the Davidic dynasty and temple construction (2 Sam 7; 1 Chr 28–29)	Destruction of Jerusalem and the temple, until the Davidic dynasty (36:30; 37-39)
Entrance into the Promised Land (Josh; Judg)	Towards the exit from the Promised Land (41:10, 16-18)
Lack of bread and water during the journey; distrust of Moses; disobedience; turning back in the desert (Exod 15–17; etc.)	The "greatpool" of Gibeon. Pause in Bethlehem; distrust of Jeremiah; disobedience; decision to return to Egypt (41:12, 17; 42:1-22; 43:1-4)
Scourge (Exod 7:14–11:10) Exit from Egypt (Exod 14)	Announcement of the "scourge": sword, hunger, and plague (42:22; 44:27); return to Egypt (43:7)
Slavery; invocation of the name of the Lord (Exod 1–2); Moses' call and revelation of the Name (Exod 3)	The name of the Lord will cease to be invoked (44:26). Silence about the fate of Jeremiah

---

116 Y. ZAKOVITCH, «Through the Looking Glass: Reflections/Inversions of Genesis Stories in the Bible», *BibInt* 1 (1993) 139–152: "The new creation awakens in the reader undeniable associations to the source-story; the relationship between the new narrative and its source is like that between an image and its mirrored reflection: the reflection inverts the storyline of the original narrative" (p. 139). Fittingly, in this regard, J.P. SONNET, «Analyse narrative», 76–77, introduces the concept of "analogies", which, by nature, implicates "rapports de similitude et de contraste".

117 In J.M. ABREGO, *Jeremías*, 202–206, many interesting clues have been gathered together, the convergence of which clearly leads to thinking of an intentional antithetical reference to the event of the Exodus.

118 In 36:30, what is prophesied for the king Jehoiakim is an ignoble end and absence of any reigning heir. For the theological significance of this (historically problematic) Jeremianic prophecy, see K. SCHMID, «Nebuchadnezzar», 63–76.

518   Jer 38:14–28a. Jeremiah and Zedekiah: The final colloquy

These are resonances, references, and analogous relationships that I cannot now explore in detail,[119] but which unquestionably need to be integrated, at least herein, with what I highlighted about the inversion of the perspective of the Exodus with regard to the theme of "wonders" (נִפְלָאוֹת), the intervention of the powerful arm of YHWH against Jerusalem, and the function of the "scourge" (cf. ch. III, § 4).[120]

I will mention at least a few other possible correspondences, in the same perspective of the realisation of the curses prescribed in Deut 28 and the thematical-lexical elements that I have already treated. The most macroscopic one clearly regards the oppositional relationship between Moses and Jeremiah. The opposition is *relative*, insofar as Jeremiah is presented as having a whole series of characteristics that place him, from the outset, in continuity with the prophet Moses. It is clear, for example, that Jer 1, despite the common elements of the "vocation" literary genre (the call – objection – sign – sending), makes Jeremiah be thought of as the prophet "like Moses" that is announced and promised in Deut 18:15, 18. As for the people, however, whilst the children of Israel thrive and multiply in Egypt (cf. Exod 1:7), they are decimated, exiled, and stripped of everything as a consequence of their infidelity to the Covenant (cf. Jer 39), and the survivors who remain in the land find themselves poor (cf. Jer 39:10) and are reduced to little more than nothing (cf. Jer 42:2). The verb נָתַן also undergoes a remarkable referential reconfiguration: while YHWH, with the founding event "gives/donates" (√נתן) the land of Canaan to his people (cf. Exod 6:4, 8; 12:25; Deut 1:8, 20–21, 25; etc.), in the Jeremianic context, the same Lord of history "gives/hands over" (√נתן) the rebellious people, their leaders, their priests, and their prophets to the enemies who "want their lives" (cf. Jer 8:10; 12:7; 21:7; etc.). The entry into the Promised Land was also an act of conquest of urban and agricultural spaces (cf. Josh 1–6; etc.), while now, on the other hand, it is the people of God who see their vital environment invaded by foreigners who conquer their lands and topple their fortress-cities along with their inhabitants, one after another (cf. Jer 1:14; 4:7, 29; 8:16; 34:7; etc.).

In summary, it can regardless be affirmed that if there is a verb capable of adequately expressing the founding experience of the Exodus, it is most certainly represented by √יצא ("to exit"; "to go out"). The frequency with which this root recurs with this

---

119   E.g. according to J.M. ABREGO, *Los libros proféticos*, 171, n. 21, amongst the "innumerable *detalles*" (p. 203) that refer to the originary Exodus, the nouns "Bethlehem/house of bread" (41:17: בֵּית לֶחֶם) and "abundant waters" (41:12: מַיִם רַבִּים) would call to mind the controversy (*rîb*) of the people in the desert provoked by a lack of bread and water. Note, however, in particular the verbal coincidences pointed out by L. ALONSO SCHÖKEL, «Jeremías como anti-Moisés», 247–248, which is why it does not seem improper to establish a certain relationship between the stubborn will to go to Egypt of the remaining population and its leaders (against the prophetic word) and some episodes of rebellion in the desert. In particular, a comparison is made between: 1. the promise of obedience (cf. Jer 42:5–6 and Exod 19:8; 24:3, 7); 2. the negative formula "do not listen" (לִבְלְתִּי/לֹא + √שׁמע) + "the voice of the Lord" (בְּקוֹל יְהוָה) or "my/his voice" (בְּקֹלִי/בְּקֹלוֹ) (cf. Jer 42:13, 21; 43:4.7; 44:23 and Num 14:22; Deut 8:20; 9:23; 28:15, 45, 62); 3. mortal danger (cf. Jer 43:3 and Exod 16:3; Num 14:16; 16:13; 17:6; Deut 9:28).

120   For a discussion on the theological function of the "scourge", see the observations of J.M. ABREGO, *Jeremías*, 203, n. 392.

Exegetic focalisations 519

meaning, usually in construction with the preposition of motion from place מִן ("from") in reference to Egypt (מִצְרַיִם) is remarkable.[121] Jeremiah, at the historical juncture taking place, puts the revelatory-symbolic concentration of the will of YHWH on Zedekiah, but in general, for all the people of Israel, precisely in the verb of the origins, in the root יצא ("to go out") articulated with the preposition אֶל "towards"). The perspective of the Exodus *seems* to have been entirely inverted even from its fundamental semantic reference. It is not a question of paving the way for a path of freedom, but rather of handing oneself over into slavery. It is necessary to go out, yes, but out from the possession of the gifts of the Covenant in order to accept the "end" and subjugation to the enemy. Those who wish to persist in an attitude of obstinate resistance to defend their freedom, a freedom at this point devoid of its relationship to the Sinai pact and thus to its originary meaning, will have no future.

This antithesis is certainly shocking. It is for today's reader, and it is hard to recognise just to what extent it must have been so for the protagonists of those events or for the direct recipients of the Jeremianic text. And yet, on closer inspection, the sense of these oppositional references is precisely that of indicating (by contrast) a horizon of intelligibility where there would be otherwise nothing but an experience of a total disintegration of the meaning of one's (own) history. The book of Jeremiah thus not only *proposes* a single historical-literary figure (with his oracles) as being significative, but *is proposed* in its entirety as an act of prophetic reading of tragic, dark events, otherwise threatened by the void of non-sense. And all this clearly presupposes a knowledge of the traditions of the Exodus.[122]

Actually, as I have already noted, the notion of an "anti-Exodus" should be reserved for the "historical-symbolic" path that leads from the destruction of Jerusalem to the idolatry of Egypt. What Jeremiah calls for serves instead to open a new, however paradoxical, way *out* of a preannounced tragedy. And, therefore, it serves to set the conditions for that "new Exodus" that YHWH already promises within the chaotic, desperate horizon of the disaster of the final days of Judah (cf. 16:14–15; 23:7–8). Now, in any case, it is time to accept in faith the just punishment of God: that which YHWH

---

121 See, just to give an example, Exod 3:10. This is the first of these recurrences and regards precisely the mission that the Lord bestows upon Moses: "And now, go: I send you to the pharaoh to bring out (√יצא hi.) my people, the Israelites, from Egypt (מִמִּצְרַיִם)."

122 I therefore do not agree with the theory of E.K. Holt, «The Chicken and the Egg – or: Was Jeremiah a Member of the Deuteronomist Party?», *JSOT* 44 (1989) 109–122, who maintains, on the contrary, that it was the figure of Moses that was modelled after that of Jeremiah. In this regard, I will note that the quantity and surprising precision of the factual references contained in the Jeremianic text dedicated to the biographical events of the prophets, facts that do not at all seem to be, in themselves, strictly necessary for a mere theological-political finalisation of the story, lead to think of a first-hand witness, at least for the narrative parts, who was directly involved in the facts being described. That the book of Jeremiah be a mere historical fiction *ante litteram* seems to me highly unlikely, and there would be none alike in the HB in terms of the precise reuse of historical data. On the other hand, the antithetical references to the event of the Exodus presuppose therefore that these traditions not also be *tout court* post-exilic "inventions". But this direction of research would call for a comprehensive specific study, which for now falls beyond my intentions.

520   Jer 38:14–28a. Jeremiah and Zedekiah: The final colloquy

has planted must now be uprooted (cf. 1:10 with 45:4). Something new, if given, will be given gratuitously and will come afterwards, as a new act of creation.

3.1.8. The end is here, or not. An extreme possibility of salvation for the City as well?

The "uprooting" announced elliptically in chapter 1 (in v. 10), a programmatic start to the whole development of the book of Jeremiah, is already a rereading of what *actually* happened. Yet, as the continuation of the same prophetic text explains, it is also an intrinsic "necessity", *determined* by a history of failed covenant that by this point, has reached a point of no return. For the book of Jeremiah, "history of covenant" means history and drama of (more) freedom, interweaving narratives, upheavals and outcomes that are never entirely foreseeable. The "end" that Zedekiah faces (v. 18) is therefore not something that is *deterministic*. Otherwise there would not be a word interpellating his freedom and conscience even as far as the extreme limit that separates catastrophe from a narrow escape. At the same time, some form of traversing of this experience of *self-consignment* is necessary, just as it is necessary in any act of obedience.

What is surprising, in the present case, is to hear Jeremiah ask for obedience to YHWH not only by utilising the conditional form for the discourse that proposes two alternatives (v. 17: [...] אִם־יָצֹא תֵצֵא; v. 18: [...] וְאִם לֹא־תֵצֵא), but also by promising Zedekiah much more than "life as war booty" (cf. 21:9). When, after months and months of siege, stubborn resistance and rejection of any plea bargain of surrender to the enemy, no better prospect than preservation of personal physical safety could be imagined, what Jeremiah expresses *almost* seems to be express divine "repentance", tying even the integrity of Jerusalem to the king's surrender.[123] Or one could say that the righteous one ("who does justice": עֹשֵׂה מִשְׁפָּט), the one searched for in vain in 5:1 in order to grant forgiveness to the City, can now be identified in the king, if he were only to choose the *right* thing to *do* in this moment.

The call for surrender to the king of Babylon differs sharply from other prophetic messages, as we have seen, and indeed, seems to clearly contradict the very religious foundations of the people of the Covenant. While yes, within Jeremiah's own preaching, this oracle (vv. 17–18) is identical to the other interventions (as regards the general theme of the end and submission to Babylon), it is also surprisingly different, considering what had been previously announced about the fate of Jerusalem and the royal house itself: in 21:7, 10, the triple scourge of plague, famine, and sword, the extermination of the entire population including Zedekiah and his ministers, and the destruction of Jerusalem by fire were prophesied; in 34:2, 22, the theme was still the conquest and reduction to ashes of Jerusalem, destined to be deprived of all its inhabitants; in 37:8, 10, that is, only a few verses before the oracle we are now

---

123   In this regard, one could quote the phrase of M. Buber that I placed as exergue to the present chapter: "The true prophet does not announce an immutable decree. He speaks into the power of decision lying in the moment, and in such a way that his message of disaster just touches this power" (ID., *The Prophetic Faith*, 103). Actually, as I explicate in this same paragraph, something immutable, however, remains: the need to accept surrender and all that this signifies.

Exegetic focalisations 521

studying, the prophetic word had made the burning of the Holy City blaze twice more before the eyes of Zedekiah.

If, therefore, before this final colloquy between Jeremiah and Zedekiah, the end of Jerusalem and the Davidic dynasty itself seemed decreed and sealed by the judgement of God, it would now seem to all be up for discussion yet again[124]: if the king agrees to accept in faith the last chance offered to him, he will not only save his own life, but also his very dynasty and the entire City.[125] What would explain for this change?

The solutions proposed by literary criticism in such cases are far too obvious. Where there is tension, there must or may be fragmentation, a not entirely successful stitching together of texts and different sources. Synchronic readings, in some cases, are clearly forced, and in this regard, one could cite the textual question of Gen 37:18–28, the account of the symbolic end of another unfortunate "elected one" and his "prophetic visions": Joseph, also cast into the darkness of a cistern. It is textually clear that Jeremiah got pulled out on an order from Zedekiah (at most, from the point of view of textual criticism, one can ask if it really took thirty men, as the MT reports, or if three men sufficed).[126] Joseph, however, for Gen 37:25, 27, was to be *sold* to the Ishmaelites, only in v. 28, it is instead the Midianities who are mentioned (and who appear, rather, to *kidnap* him from the brothers), and it is they who sell him to the Ishmaelites. A clear contradiction. And here (and elsewhere), the best solution would seem to be the diachronic one,[127] but that is not always the case, and may be so even less than one thinks.

---

124 I place myself in a hermeneutical perspective different from that emblematically represented by R.P. CARROLL, *Jeremiah*, 97–107, who identifies in every difficulty and contradiction present in the book of Jeremiah the product of just as many political-religious ideologies.

125 According to R.P. CARROLL, *Jeremiah*, 97–107, this perspective is "utopian", as if Jeremiah were speaking in the name of his own personal fantasies or perhaps simply be an illustrious and convinced representative of the pro-Babylonian party. On the contrary, what is attested here, however paradoxically, is that the same prophecy "corrects" itself. I believe that questioning the how and why of this phenomenon is a part of the conscious assumption of the revelative (however apparently contradictory) dimension and that it is not anecdotal of the sacred text. Obviously, this does not mean validating a "naive" reading of the texts that does not take the results of literary criticism into account.

126 Cf. D. BARTHÉLEMY, *Critique textuelle*, 716. Most commentators and modern versions amend the MT reading as שְׁלֹשָׁה ("three") rather than שְׁלֹשִׁים ("thirty"), based on a single, late Hebrew ms, and thus without clear textual evidence. If, as it plainly seems, שְׁלֹשִׁים is the original reading, the reference is not only to the extraction of Jeremiah from the cistern, but also to the actual execution of the order of the king and protection of the prophet, who the notables wanted dead (cf. Acts 23:23, where a much larger and armed contingent is used to securely transfer Paul, a prisoner awaiting trial under his opponents' death threats). As is suggested by J.M. ABREGO, *Jeremías*, 72, n. 95, the expression could also refer not to a specific number of individuals, but rather to a sort of "special corps" of a military sort, such as the king's personal guard (cf. Ex 15:4; 2 Sam 23:9).

127 See, e.g. concisely, F. GIUNTOLI, *Genesi 11,27–50,26*. Introduzione, traduzione e commento, NVBTA 1.2, Cinisello Balsamo 2013, 235–238.

The intentional *juxtaposition* of differing elements is a phenomenon in the Scripture that is widely attested[128] on multiple levels, even though in the Hebrew language there is no lexical coding to identify this process of constructing meaning. And yet, and somewhat ironically if we like, the placing of one element beside another and allowing for the impact of the relation between the two to spark a question and its interpretation (for this, I have introduced the concept of "semiotic *arcatas*") is typical of this style of living literature, and is part of the character of a people, of its way of reasoning and recounting.[129] It is the reader who must speak their own mind, thus even coining or evoking verbs and delineating concepts that the letter of the text limits itself to merely suggesting. In the end, or from the start, the tensions (even those originally determined by diachrony) often times want to be much more than inevitable traces of a history of textual composition. They are devices for Meaning. It is narrative theology.

Remaining in the logic of the linear temporality of the *fabula*, in the case of the contrast between the prophetic promises expressed in 38:17, 20 and the threats of the oracles preceding, we are faced with a sudden change of perspective. To organise an event, decide on an action, and announce it. And then retract, correct, and reshuffle destinies and options. Are these not all articulations of the verb "repentance" (√נחם ni.)? This lexicalisation is clearly lacking, but perhaps we are not far here from the metaphorical representation to which this refers. Indeed, with this root,[130] in the semantic expressed (above all) by the conjugation to ni. and having YHWH as its subject,[131] one

---

128 Amongst the different texts that could be cited, cf. Deut 11:29; 27:12–13; 30, 15, 19; Josh 24:15; Isa 1:19–20; Ps 1; Ecc 15:16–20, where the juxtaposition is presented as an ethical-moral type of alternative; Jer 21:8 and the other Jeremianic texts on the submission-surrender to Babylon, where, according to my thesis, we move from the ethical sphere to a binary possibility situated on the symbolic-political plane; and Ecc 34:3; 42:24–25, where finally, or rather, returning to the principle (source, origin) and foundation of the phenomenon, the juxtapositions are contemplated as a reflection of the originary plan of God and structure itself of creation.

129 This is the basic argument of the challenging work of M. STERNBERG, *Hebrews between Cultures*. Group Portraits and National Literature, Bloomington 1998.

130 Only occasionally is √שוב also used.

131 In this regard, see also the monograph of Jörg Jeremias, recently republished and expanded (ID., *Die Reue Gottes*. Aspekte alttestamentlicher Gottesvorstellung, BThSt 31, Neukirchen-Vluyn 1975, 2002³), where, in the final synthesis, a distinction is made between two theological perspectives and their relative texts: a prophetic conception ("prophetische Konzeption"), which treats divine repentance regarding the threat of punishment that is then retracted, as in our case, and a historical-theological reflection ("geschichttheologische Reflexion"), where a repentance of YHWH is in question, always due to the (this time negative) response of humanity regarding a positive design of his. Cf. as well the contributions of H. VAN DYKE PARUNAK, «A Semantic Survey of NHM», *Bib.* 56 (1975) 512–532 (where, in a certain sense, the previous distinction can be found, made to derive from the basic semantic "retract a previously declared action"; cf. p. 525, where Jer 18:8, 10 is specifically cited as an emblematic text); T.E. FRETHEIM, «The Repentance of God. A Key to Evaluating Old Testament God-Talk», *HBT* 10 (1988), 47–70; D.C. RANEY, «Does YHWH *Naham*? A Question of Openness», *SBLSP* 42 (2003) 105–115; J.P. SONNET, «Narration biblique et (post)modernité», in: *La Bible en récits*. L'exégèse à l'heure du lecteur. Colloque international d'analyse narrative des textes de la Bible, Lausanne (mars 2002), *ed.* D. MARGUERAT, Genève 2003, ²2005, 253–263 (here, p. 259); ID., «God's Repentance

Exegetic focalisations

523

can enter better still into the heart of a great theological theme: the mystery of the divine will in its interaction with human beings and their (no less mysterious) will. Because even in this case, in the Scripture, divine repentance and non-repentance are juxtaposed, even when united by the same underlying motive unites them: God is not like human beings.[132] Limiting myself to the book of Jeremiah, I will note that the reader who has reached ch. 38 has already encountered this verb and its metaphorical usage, with the easing of emotional tension that it evokes in God himself, in truly significant passages.[133]

In 4:18 (cf. 20:16), a universal devastation is decreed for all the land that YHWH declares he does not want to regret (√נחם ni. in synonymic parallelism with שׁוּב√ + לֹא). No person in fact "regrets his wickedness" (8:6). But already from 15:6, addressing Jerusalem, YHWH threatens: "I am tired of repenting" (נִלְאֵיתִי הִנָּחֵם), making it clear that in reality, between guilt and punishment, or between threat of punishment and its actualisation, there has never been a relationship of cause and effect that is either logical or immediate. Many times, in fact, God has repented, retracing his steps, without destroying Jerusalem. At the very heart of the proclamation of the "re-establishment of fortunes" and the "new Covenant" (chs. 30–31) there is, moreover, forgiveness that is undeducible and humanly unmotivated. Even if it cannot truly be brought about without the participation of human freedom (cf. 31:19). It is in the potter's workshop, in any case, that a general law on the "repentance" of God is learned, concerning the fate of every nation (18:1–10)[134]: there are two types of unexpected change in the divine program, one that withdraws a blessing previously granted and another that, on the contrary, nullifies an already decreed punishment. It is not irrational whim: it is the inconceivable weight that human freedom exerts on the balance of the *krísis* (or of the מִשְׁפָּט; cf. 1:16) of God. In this perspective, it is attested in 38:17, 20 that the Word renders itself available to such an extent as to admit and indeed *desire* (cf. 5:1) a significant change of point of view, so as to be fulfilled in a new way. And this, according to a modality that does not renege its substance, for in the present case, two intimately connected constitutive elements are maintained integrally: the announcement of the

---

and "False Starts" in Biblical History (Genesis 6–9; Exodus 32–34; 1 Samuel 15 e 2 Samuel 7)», in: *Congress Volume Ljubljana*, 469–494.

132 Whether one says that YHWH cannot repent, as in Num 23:19; 1 Sam 15:29, or one affirms, on the contrary, as in Hos 11:8–9, that YHWH repents, the motive in these counterposed texts remains the same: YHWH is not (like) a human being (the question is that of the logic and cognitive potential of the metaphorical discourse, which, while negating the resemblance on a certain level, affirms it on another; cf. T.E. FRETHEIM, «The Repentance of God. A Key», 51–52).

133 *Significative*, not because a theoretical elucubration is being made, but because an attempt is being made to intuit something about the dynamics underlying an enormous catastrophe that while having already come about, remains always present in the consciousness of a people. In fact, nothing of what has passed, for a social or individual body, is simply tossed behind the back. The past continues to act in the present, consciously or not, and stirs up anxieties, puts forth questions, and asks for answers.

134 Cf. T.E. FRETHEIM, «The Repentance of God: A Study of Jeremiah 18:7–10», *HAR* 11 (1987) 81–92.

ineluctability of the end, in some symbolic (and therefore *real*) form, and the promise of life (as a *new beginning*).

But another question arises therefore: what does the prophetic word intend then when it threatens or announces the "end", whether this be the death of a king, extinction of a dynasty, decimation of a people, or ruin of a city? Does this last oracle of Jeremiah perhaps suggest that exile could still be avoided? I cannot answer this question (which is redactional, narrative and, not least of all, theological) with any certainty, but it seem to me that if one does not want to automatically trace every textual asperity to (more or less orderly) conflations of heterogeneous ideological positions, the track to follow is that of taking seriously the possibility that the text (MT) in its current form can convey an underlying meaning that is consistent. In this perspective, some elements for a possible interpretation that can be mentioned are: (a) that the "end", at a certain point in Jeremiah's preaching, is really a given fact; (b) that the chances for salvation that accompany it are expressed in their fundamental terms by the promise of preserving "life" (נֶפֶשׁ) as "war bounty" (לְשָׁלָל).

This last expression, which is also contained in the oracle of consolation reserved for Baruch in 45:5 (but already appeared in 21:9; 38:2, as we have seen, and also regards the fate of Ebed-melech in 39:18), would suggest that the promise of salvation itself made to Zedekiah in case of surrender wants to guarantee nothing more than the naked possession of life, without, however, ruling out the acceptance of some form of *death*.[135] We can perhaps say that the city can still be saved, and likewise the royal house, but through a modality that indicates precisely the contrary: exiting the City to surrender to the enemy is, *in fact*, a *symbolic* acceptance of the end. And the loss of power, with the exile, certainly seems to be the minimal form of a historical concretisation of this. I will clarify and develop the meaning of this statement over the course of the following stages of this research (cf. ch. VI, § 4.3).

3.2. Second part (vv. 19–23): Objection and response

3.2.1. Fear (√רא׳): The reaction of one, sign of objection of all

Biblical revelation in general and prophetic literature in particular deal with the encounter and communicative exchange between divine and human, providing multiple attestations of the resulting phenomenology. The prophetic word, specifically, asking to be believed and obeyed in the *hic et nunc* of its interlocutor as a norm-forming word of divine origin, often checkmates intelligence and the overall resilience of all other finite dimensions of the human being. The book of Jeremiah recalls this fact from its incipit (cf. 1:6): the fragile human creature, before the Mystery that reveals itself to orient and embrace existence, feels that surrendering in faith to the Other who speaks and who sends one forth regardless of any requisite for adequacy, involves leaving behind every foothold or security other than God himself. It is then understandable why an objection to the "call", which has its emotional manifestation in a sense of fear, arises almost spontaneously in more than a few "vocation stories" or wherever the biblical narrator presents us characters invested with a special mission by YHWH (cf. Exod 4:1–17; Josh 1:6–7, 9 [implicit objection]; Judg 6:13–15; 1 Sam 9:21; 1 Kgs 3:7; Isa

---

135 I will study this concept more in-depth in the following paragraphs.

Exegetic focalisations   525

6:5; Ezek 2:6.8 [there is an implicit allusion]; etc.) and indeed, seems to constitute the literary form deputed to synthesise in a paradigmatic form all the travail necessary for every human being in order to access divine truth. Let us hold this preliminary consideration in the background for the moment. I will return to it.[136]

Zedekiah seems to take the words of Jeremiah inviting the surrender seriously, if for none other than to evaluate the aspect of their concrete feasibility. Precisely for this reason, in his own way, he makes explicit the implications of the risk that a mere human calculation and vision cannot immediately get beyond. His objection is not, however, rational in nature, but is rather the emergence of an uncontrollable and tumultuous emotional world on the verbal plane: in 38:19, the king confesses with a sincerity, almost a candour, that is striking: "*I am afraid*" (אֲנִי דֹאֵג)[137]. If it is not merely an excuse or way of denying what the prophet has said, then it is an act of *private* humility that would seem to open the way to the *public* act of surrender called for by Jeremiah himself.

> The psychological background of the characters, with their emotional sphere, has always played an important role on the level of narrative, while it has long been excluded from the factors considered relevant for rigorous historiographical reconstructions. And yet, as controversial as they are, new approaches (like that of *psycohistory*) are gaining ground, seeking to show how relevant this sphere is within the horizon of historical change,[138] despite the inherent limit placed on this perspective of study by the nature and scarcity of available sources. While remaining, in our case, within the world of the text, we do not believe that such dynamics can be underestimated, especially in the perspective of cognitive pragmatics.[139]

---

136   Having already had the opportunity to dwell on the vv. that introduced the thematic of "handing oneself over to the king of Babylon", I will now proceed more expeditiously in the analysis of the remaining textual units (the second: vv. 19–23, and the third: vv. 24–27), emphasising only the exegetic questions most pertinent to my process of demonstration.

137   With regard to the emotional world in relation to its linguistic expressions in the Old Testament, from amongst the many possible contributions, see P.A. KRUGER «On Emotions and the Expression of Emotions in the Old Testament: A Few Introductory Remarks», *BZ* 48 (2004) 213–228; A. WAGNER, «Gefühl, Emotion und Affekt in der Sprachanalyse des Hebräischen», in: ID., *Emotionen, Gefühle und Sprache im Alten Testament*. Vier Studien, KUSATU 7, Waltrop 2006, 7–47. For a meticulous study of the linguistic material concerning the topic of fear in the HB, see the monograph of B. COSTACURTA, *La vita minacciata*. Il tema della paura nella Bibbia Ebraica, AnBib 119, Roma 1997.

138   "Especially in autocratic regimes, individual rulers had an enormous amount of power to shape the events of their times, and there can be little doubt that their actions, like those of any human being, were influenced by their emotions, passions, and fears" (I. KALIMI – S. RICHARDSON, «Sennacherib», 4).

139   Think e.g. of the recent contribution by E. FRAHM, «Family Matters», 163–222, which assumes a Freudian perspective for rereading, on the basis of available sources, the personality of the Assyrian sovereign in relation to the military choices adopted with regard to Jerusalem in his campaign against the kingdom of Judah in 701: "One does not have to be an orthodox Freudian to acknowledge the importance of emotions, passions, delusions, and outbursts of irrational sentiment as driving forces of human action and, consequently, of history" (p. 166).

526 Jer 38:14–28a. Jeremiah and Zedekiah: The final colloquy

The verb used to express the emotion of fear is rather rare and averts the reader that Zedekiah's situation dangerously risks moving away from that of the tree (mentioned by Jeremiah himself) that does not "fear" (cf. 17:8: יָרֵא√) the heat of the "year of drought", thanks to its ability to draw, from deep in the earth, water of trust in God. In the entire MT, the root דאג occurs only 13x, 7x in the qal form and 6x as a substantive (דְּאָגָה). Its basic meaning is "to be anxious" or "to be scared", and only the context and syntactic construction (with the preposition לְ or the sign of the accusative אֵת) allow one nuance or the other to be grasped. In our case, it is clear that it wants to indicate both the emotion of fear[140] and the object that provokes it: "I am afraid of the Judeans who have deserted to the Chaldeans: lest it does not happen that they hand me over to them and they mistreat me!"

It is a response that can, in turn, solicit a question in the reader: why does King Zedekiah say he fears those compatriots who have already passed to the Chaldeans (cf. 39:9; 52:15) as opposed to the king of Babylon himself, before whom, as his rebel vassal, he would have had to, without a shadow of a doubt, appear for judgement (cf. 39:5–7; 52:9–11)? A path that presents a solution can emerge from a careful analysis of Zedekiah's own words.

3.2.2. Humiliation (עלל√): A king's greatest fear

Just as v. 19 can commonly be understood,[141] Zedekiah himself imagines that his fate may be that of "being delivered" by the Babylonians into the hands of his former political opponents (pro-Babylonians) already passed over to the enemy and being mistreated and humiliated by them, becoming their laughingstock. The verb used is עלל (in po.), attested 30x in the MT, always in the intensive form. Depending on the context, its meaning fluctuates from a generic "to mistreat/torment" (1 Sam 6:6; Lam 1:12, 22; 2:20; 3:51), to a more specific "to make fun of" (cf. Exod 10:2; Num 22:29; 1 Sam 31:4 = 1 Chr 10:4), or "to physically abuse" (cf. Judg 19:25). The context most similar (and with an identical syntactic construction: verb in po. + prep. בְּ) seems to me to be the one already mentioned in 1 Sam 31:4, in which Saul, about to be overwhelmed by the Philistines, orders the squire to unfurl his sword and kill him before the enemy arrives. The motivation put forth is: "[...] so that those uncircumcised do not come, stab me, and... עלל√ (po. 3rd pl.) on me". Without wishing to produce undue and immediate contextual overlapping, the many elements of resemblance with the situation dreaded by Zedekiah induce a comparison, for which the trajectory of semantic clarification originates from the case of Saul in 1 Sam 31:4.

In fact, it is sufficiently clear that in this context, the verb does not refer to physical suffering, so it cannot simply be translated with a generic "to maltreat" or more specific "to torment", since the action expressed by עלל√ in this case has, as its object, a person who has already been killed (pierced: דקר√). Hence, the meaning "to take

---

140 This root appears twice in parallel to ירא√ in the book of Jeremiah (cf. 17:8; 42:16).
141 The opinion of A.B. Ehrlich, *Randglossen*, 341, according to whom the grammatical subject of יִתְּנוּ would not be the Chaldeans, but rather the Jewish deserters (based on an analogous idiomatic expression that can be found in Exod 5:21: "[...] to put a sword in their hands to kill us" (לָתֶת־חֶרֶב בְּיָדָם לְהָרְגֵנוּ), seems very unlikely to me.

Exegetic focalisations 527

fun, to vilify, to outrage" would appear more pertinent.[142] These are all actions that can well have as their object the body of an enemy who is hated, defeated, and killed. Given the relative similarity of the context, which implicates being left at the mercy of people animated by completely hostile intentions (although here, in comparison to Saul's case, they are his own compatriots and not foreign enemies), I think that Zedekiah can allude precisely to mistreatment that has the *humiliation* and reification of the person as its peculiar semantic trait.[143]

At first glance, it can be difficult to understand whether the scenario imagined by the king, that is, of victorious foreigners handing the rebel vassal over into the hands of the deserters so that they themselves might humiliate him in some way, might depend on a perception of reality that is indeed appropriate (but escapes us moderns, given our limited historical knowledge and hence extraneousness to the precise pragmatic context of reference),[144] or whether it is rather a prediction so rosy that it betrays an unmentionable terror of the worst (in other words, an atrocious punishment inflicted directly by Nebuchadnezzar, offended by the infidelity of the vassal and expenditure of energy and resources consumed for the reconquest of Jerusalem).[145]

It is nevertheless certain that the most considerable content of Zedekiah's objection has to do with the fear of humiliation rather physical death itself. It would be wrong, after all, to think that the pure biological fact of living can be identified with full realisation of the concept of "human existence". What constitutes the life of a person cannot be reduced to this (while it is, of course, its essential basis), because it includes more complex and specifically human values, such as dignity and honour, identity, love, etc. Confirmation of this, even within the HB, is given by the fact that when these constitutive elements, or at least values considered "vital", of the person are radically lost, often even pure survival is perceived as useless and, indeed, a source of greater pain.[146] The story of Saul's death is emblematic in this sense as well

---

142 Cf. some modern versions: EP: "[...] e facciano sevizie su di me"; EÜ: "[...] und sie würden mir übel mitspielen"; NAB: "[...] and make sport of me"; BJ; TOB: "[...] et ne se jouent de moi".

143 On the relevance of this topic in the biblical context in relation to the social sciences, see the studies collected in V.H. MATTHEWS – D.C. BENJAMIN, *Honor and Shame in the World of the Bible*, Semeia 68, Atlanta 1996.

144 In any case, one can keep in mind that which is deducible from the Neo-Assyrian attestations studied in D. NADALI, «Guerra e morte: l'annullamento del nemico nella condizione di vinto», *ScAnt* 11 (2001–2003) 51–70, here p. 51 (my translation): "Constantly following each assured, inevitable victory is a triumphal parade of the Assyrian army, led and represented by the great king of Assyria, and the procession of the defeated escorted before the sovereign as a sign of submission and humility; the cruel acts of torture and killing of the enemy are linked to practices widespread throughout the ancient Near East, becoming, in some cases, genuine codified iconological motifs rather than mere representations of violence."

145 In this regard, see also S. NIDITCH, «A Messy Business. Ritual Violence after the War», in: *Warfare, Ritual, and Symbol in Biblical and Modern Contexts, eds.* B.E. KELLE – F.R. AMES – J.L. WRIGHT, SBL.AIL 18, Atlanta 2014, 187–202.

146 I will cite some significant examples here. Abimelech has himself killed to avoid the dishonour of a death inflicted at the hand of a woman (Judg 9:54). Samson, with his death, vindicates the humiliation incurred by the Philistines (Judg 16:30). Saul's armour-bearer follows the example of his sovereign (1 Sam 31:5). Particularly

528   Jer 38:14–28a. Jeremiah and Zedekiah: The final colloquy

(cf. 1 Sam 31:3–4): a king seriously wounded in battle prefers to be killed by his squire or to kill himself rather than be humiliated by his uncircumcised enemies since he is a king consecrated by YHWH. The vilification of his corpse would have been inevitable in any case, but the choice made by Saul and highlighted by the narrator would still lay claim the inviolability of his royal freedom, which is elevated above the value of pure biological life, voluntarily depriving the hated Philistines of the pleasure of killing him directly. A valiant king or leader, if he cannot achieve victory on the field, cannot undergo the humiliation of *surrender* or retreat either. The biblical narrator suggests in Saul's case (and not only; Judg 16:30; 1 Mac 9:10; 2 Mac 6:18–31; 7) that a glorious death is preferable by far, and can remain as imperishable memory.[147]

This is, at least from an ideal point of view, a perspective that leads us from Saul to the almost "mythical" figure of the king Solomon, whose overall characteristic trait is that of magnificence, expressed in wisdom, justice, great riches, diplomatic skill, and military power, with which he guarantees the peace of the kingdom (cf. e.g. 1 Kgs 10).[148] This aura of "glory", in short, is an essential dimension of the royal ideology, a fundamental identifying value that Israel adopts, along with other important complementary aspects (that of the sacred, military, administrative, etc.), from the cultural context of the ancient Near East in its desire to be "like all the other peoples" (כְּכָל־הַגּוֹיִם; cf. 1 Sam 8:5).[149] With a particular distinctive trait, however, by which the

---

interesting, then, is the case of the suicide of Ahithophel, the counsellor of David (and then of his rebel son Absalom) whose word-counsel was so highly regarded for his wisdom that it was almost taken to be on the same level as the word of YHWH (cf. 2 Sam 16:23). The fact of having not been listened to on one occasion, in favour of the advice of another person of trust, induces him to plan and then carry out his suicide (cf. 2 Sam 17:1–23). Likewise worthy of note is the case of Zimri, who kills himself in the fire to avoid being captured (1 Kgs 16:18). Then, from another perspective, consider the punishment to which Nebuchadnezzar submits Zedekiah, the traitor and rebel vassal, according to what is recounted in 39:5–7; 52:9–11. Without underestimating the "conventional" nature of punishment, attested in similar cases in the Assyrian-Babylonian world (cf. ch. II, § 2.3.1, Fig. 14, where Sargon II can be seen gouging out the eyes of a conquered enemy king), it is not, however, difficult to make out there being a particularly cruel basic intent there, intensified in the case of Zedekiah by the fact that, killing his sons and heirs before his eyes, almost wanting to imprint this last horrible scene upon his memory forever, Nebuchadnezzar had wanted to inflict the maximum possible punishment, rendering the rest of his (physical) life a kind of death prolonged indefinitely in time.

147   Think of the elegy that David composes to celebrate Saul and Jonathan, the גִּבּוֹרִים ("mighty, warriors, or valiant men") fallen in battle (2 Sam 1:17–27). Cf. T.R. Preston, «The Heroism of Saul: Patterns of Meaning in the Narrative of the Early King», *JSOT* 24 (1982) 27–46: "Saul dies on the battlefield, doing the job he had been anointed and elected to do – leading the army of Israel against her enemies. Through all the reluctance, failure, and madness, he kept his bargain to the end, dying as the military king" (here, p. 37). See also R. Dolce, «Beyond Defeat. The Psychological Annihilation of the Vanquished in Pre-Classical Near Eastern Visual Communication», in: Krieg und Frieden im Alten Vorderasien, 237–267.

148   This echo reaches all the way to the NT, where Jesus refers to the renowned δόξα ("glory") of Solomon in Matt 6:29 and Luke 12:27.

149   In this regard, see the contribution of B.M. Levinson, «The Reconceptualization of Kingship in Deuteronomy and the Deuteronomistic History's Transformation of

Exegetic focalisations

body of the king, already a complex semiotic device in which representative dimensions of the divine world and the social body of the nation converge, also becomes the icon of the "body" itself of YHWH.[150]

The sacred conception of the Lord's anointed one found in Deuteronomic history (in reference, above all, to the stories of Saul, David, and Solomon) and in the poetic literature of the HB is, however, completely absent here. That is, it does not at all seem that Zedekiah fears the desecration of the sacred dimension of the "king" of Israel and wants to prevent this in his person. Indeed, the fundamental objection dominating the entire reaction of Zedekiah when faced with the prophet's request would be a concern to safeguard himself alone, and this is evident not only by the precise lexicalisation of the phenomenon attested by v. 19, but also by the third part of the text (vv. 24–27): here it is clear that the king fears even, on the part of his ministers, possible hostile consequences of being seen together with Jeremiah.

And so, what emerges clearly before the reader is a paradoxical oppositive relationship, as was noted by B. Duhm[151] with regard to the talks between Zedekiah and Jeremiah in chs. 37–38: on the one hand, the prophet, humiliated and disfigured by the suffering to which his body and, indeed, whole life has been subjected, a man reduced to a state of disgraceful captivity, delivered to the mercy of all, yet still free to announce the truth against all forms of power and authority,[152] steadfast in the fidelity to his mission; and on the other, the most powerful man in the kingdom of Judah, holding the fate of a people in his hand, yet a king who is uncertain and fearful, anxious to receive a word of hope that does not imply going through any crossing of misfortune or humiliation, little more than a shadow whispering in secrecy and trembling before the gazes of other men who should be his subjects, a person ultimately much more bound up than the prisoner who stands before him.

Humiliation is, in fact, a given for a king who has decided to capitulate. For Zedekiah, however, salvation is not far off; indeed, it is at hand. The king definitely has some tenacious opponents amongst the Jews who have already passed over to the enemy, and these are imagined as accusers who would have given the Chaldeans reason to rage against him. He confesses that he fears that his surrender, which at this point could be politically and externally configured as a search for a path of salvation *in extremis*, might expose him to total denigration. Yet the crucial point inherent to the Jeremianic request is precisely this: Zedekiah is called to deliver his deepest fears to God, accepting a form of abasement; otherwise, what he fears most is precisely what

---

Torah», *VT* 51 (2001) 513–534, which marks, against the background of numerous points of convergence, also interesting, however utopian, disassociations that can be found in the Deut and in the Dtr history regarding the downsizing of the royal power.

150 As in M.W. HAMILTON, *The Body Royal. The Social Poetics of Kingship in Ancient Israel*, BiInS 78, Leiden 2005: "In short, the royal body was an icon of Yahweh's body and therefore revelatory of the divine realm" (p. 273). On the semiotic dimension of the body of the king, see in particular pp. 111–116.

151 Cf. B. DUHM, *Jeremia*, 301.

152 According to a level of criticality, and hence with a modality that is unusual for the prophetic phenomenon attested elsewhere in the ancient Near East. For the prophetic criticism of the sovereign in this context, see M. NISSINEN, «Das kritische Potential in der altorientalischen Prophetie», in: *Propheten in Mari*, 1–32.

530   Jer 38:14–28a. Jeremiah and Zedekiah: The final colloquy

will come about (cf. Jer 1:17).[153] With a gesture that is no longer political but prophetic, one can then confess that with the Lord of history, even this desert can be crossed.

3.2.3. Nuances: To listen/to recognise (√שמע) the voice of God in the human word?

To Zedekiah's objection in v. 20, the prophet retorts: "They will not hand you over!" (לֹא יִתְּנוּ), thus inverting the perspective feared by the king as well as his phraseology. According to O. Lipschits,[154] by placing this reassurance on Jeremiah's lips, the ancient author wants to demonstrate the influence the prophet would have had on the group of deserters who had already passed over to the Chaldeans (cf. 38:19), thus alluding to the promise of his own intervention on behalf of the king. This certainly does not appear to be the perspective of the Jeremianic text, which, making no mention of this possibility, elsewhere decidedly brings the whole question back to a theological level: only through an intervention of YHWH on the heart of Nebuchadnezzar may those who deliver themselves (even after the end of Jerusalem) have their life saved (cf. 42:10–12). This also renders the demand for surrender a question that is not only political, but above all, theological. Jeremiah, on the other hand, in the continuation of his response, does not merely counterpose a prediction of the opposite sign. His appeal goes straight to the very heart of the whole question of biblical prophetism, re-presenting to the reader, at this decisive moment, not only the fundamental problem of discernment of the true word of YHWH, but also the paradoxical modality by which this reveals itself in history (a modality that had been the topic of the vocation story in ch. 1).

Everyone would like signs in order to believe, tangible and convincing evidence to give credit to a message heard from human lips but uttered in the name of God. Indeed, the stakes are very high: what depends on the correct discernment between true and false prophecy can be the fate of an entire people (cf. 5:10–14; 8:10–12; 14:13–16; 23:13–17). The sign *par excellence*, which stands before Zedekiah, and even more so before the eyes of the reader, is, however, Jeremiah himself: his prophetic body, wounded but not killed, thrown into the darkness of the cistern-tomb and from there "resurrected", is already a sign that one can go through the symbolic death of surrender in obedience to YHWH and from there, come out alive.

In the face of the recipient's reluctance, Jeremiah, aware that he has been assigned the imperative of the prophetic proclamation, can do nothing but reiterate the paradox of divine self-communication: a man is speaking, but one hears – one is called to hear – the voice of the Lord of history and the cosmos himself: "I beg you, listen (שְׁמַע־נָא) to the voice of the Lord (בְּקוֹל יְהוָה) *in what I am saying to you* (לַאֲשֶׁר אֲנִי דֹבֵר אֵלֶיךָ) and [you will see that] it will go well for you and you shall live!" This is how I have translated

---

153   In fact, as retaliation, Zedekiah will be humiliated by blinding and be deported to Babylon in chains like a slave. It should be noted that in the ancient Near East, mutilations were considered one of the most outrageous, humiliating punishments that could be inflicted (to such an extent that they were practiced in contempt even against depictions of defeated sovereigns. Many Assyrian bas-reliefs bear evident trace of this, as e.g. the face of Sennacherib in the renowned scene of the siege of Lachish).

154   Cf. O. Lipschits, *The Fall*, 94.

it. While the expressive modality of the first part of the sentence is commonly usage (cf. 26:13 in the pl.), what I have highlighted in italics appears as rather unusual, and I think that it may suggest the relevance of an important theological question (which is also reflected in the re-comprehension of the pragmatic strength of the previous invitation to "listen to the voice of the Lord").

In this sense, a comparison with the LXX is already indicative, because (a) on the one hand, the Greek version interprets the term קוֹל significatively, (b) on the other, it seems to simplify the overall meaning of the phrase of the MT, which in my opinion, dares to say something more in-depth than what may appear at first glance. Of course, these are nuances. And rather elusive nuances, which lay in the background. We are not in the domain of the incontrovertible and aggressive evidence of primary colours, but in the chromatic scale of more difficult-to-grasp semantic-pragmatic tones. But it is precisely in the context of what is not immediately visible or recognisable that the art of discernment is played out in the book of Jeremiah, especially with regard to the theme of surrender to the king of Babylon, that is, where from premises that are not entirely clear or certain, outcomes as far apart as life is from death can be derived nevertheless.

A) *From voice to word, an unusual translation.* In the LXX, the "voice" of the Lord becomes his "word" (λόγος; the Syriac has *mlt'*), and the choice is a surprising one: if we track down through all the other 17 occurrences in the MT where the same syntagm as in 38:20 with YHWH as its subject (√שמע + בְּ + קוֹל [+ suff.]) is attested, we notice that the LXX *never* translates קוֹל with λόγος. In 3:13, for example, even though in the MT the syntactic construction is in fact the same (בְּ + קוֹל + suff. 1st per. m. + √שמע; always in reference to the "voice" of YHWH), the LXX renders קוֹל with φωνή, marking thus, in this case, the physical-sonorous dimension of the locutionary act (obviously in a metaphorical sense), with respect to the communicative-conceptual dimension more immediately implied by the term λόγος. The same can be said for 3:25 ("*we have* not *listened* to [√שמע; LXX: ἀκούω] *the voice of the Lord* [בְּקוֹל יְהֹוָה; LXX: τῆς φωνῆς κυρίου"); 7:23 ("listen to [√שמע] my voice [בְּקוֹלִי; LXX: τῆς φωνῆς μου]"); and also for all other subsequent occurrences with the same syntagm[155]: 7:28; 9:12; 11:4; 18:10; 22:21; 26:13 [=33:13^{LXX}]; 32:23 [=39:23^{LXX}]; 40:3 [=47:3^{LXX}]; 42:6 [=49:6^{LXX}]; 42:13 [=49:13^{LXX}]; 42:21 [=49:21^{LXX}]; 43:4 [=50:4^{LXX}]; 43:7 [=50:7^{LXX}]; 44:23 [=51:23^{LXX}].

It would therefore seem that the LXX, intentionally choosing to translate λόγος instead of φωνή in 38:20, wants to highlight the content of the Jeremianic message (the need for surrender), the object upon which the pragmatic force of the imperative then goes, asking for obedient listening (using the verb ἀκούω). On the other hand, the fact that the term λόγος is used instead to render the Hebrew דָּבָר immediately brings us back to the wellspring event of the prophetic word (1:2: "to him was addressed the word of the Lord [דְּבַר־יְהֹוָה; λόγος τοῦ θεοῦ]") and thus to the incipit of the entire book of Jeremiah (cf. also 1:4). It is as if the entire meaning of the prophetic appeal to "conversion" were in some way summarised and concentrated in this last decisive announcement. The act of surrender is, once again, proposed by the book of Jeremiah as the synthetic cypher of the Jeremianic message in the face of the looming

---

155 In 35:8 (=42:8^{LXX}), the subject is another; 25:30 (=32:30^{LXX}), there is another construction, but here as well, the term קוֹל is rendered with φωνή.

532 Jer 38:14–28a. Jeremiah and Zedekiah: The final colloquy

threat of the end of Jerusalem. And this fact, yet again, cannot allow for its scope to be delimited within the trivialising boundaries of a gesture that is merely political, ideological, and thus anecdotal.

B) *The words are human, but it is the Lord who now speaks.* "Listen (to)/obey the voice of the Lord regarding what I tell you": this is the perspective of meaning taken by almost all the commentators and modern versions.[156] It is an interpretation that presents no problems. Perhaps one that is even too simple and obvious. And yet, for this very reason, it risks not doing justice to the particular pragmatic force that its communicative context suggests.

That the interpretation of the LXX is facilitative, given that it is easier to request that one "listen to the word of God" being announced than it is to invite someone to "listen" to their "voice" while only words of a human being are heard, seems confirmed by the rendering of the particular construction of the Hebrew phrase שְׁמַע־נָא בְקוֹל יְהוָה אֲנִי דֹּבֵר אֵלֶיךָ, which in Greek sounds straightforward like ἄκουσον τὸν λόγον κυρίου ὃν ἐγὼ λέγω πρὸς σε ("[listen to] the word of the Lord, *which I say to you*"). The Vulgate, while distancing itself from the LXX's translation of קוֹל with *vox*, equally tends toward simplification: "audi quaeso *vocem* Domini *quam ego loquor ad te* [et bene tibi erit et vivet anima tua]". After all, there is a similar (idiomatic) expression in Gen 27:8, where the pronominal syntagm לַאֲשֶׁר easily lends itself to that interpretation ("And now, my son, listen/obey [שְׁמַע] [to]my voice [בְּקֹלִי] *regarding what* [לַאֲשֶׁר] I command you"). But here, the speaker and the message are one in the same. And curiously, in this case, the LXX offers a translation that is different from that already seen in 38:20, that is: ἄκουσον μου καθὰ ἐγώ σοι ἐντέλλομαι, where the adverb καθὰ seems to be a lexical device more suitable for conveying the idea that the communicative focus of the phrase wants to emphasise the *conceptual content* of the paternal word that is the object of the request to listen/obey.

In Jer 38:20, by my interpretation, the possibility of highlighting something different opens up instead: A man is speaking, but in that word, one is invited to *recognise* (even before obeying) the *locutionary act* of God himself, who, in this precise moment, is making his voice audible through fragile human words. Otherwise stated, the pragmatic context of the dialogic exchange between Jeremiah and Zedekiah makes me lean towards this meaning of the phrase: "Please, *(listen=)recognise* the voice of the Lord *in what* I am saying to you!" Here, as elsewhere, the difference between saying and implying cannot be grasped by formal analysis of the lexicon,[157] but by consideration of the specific communicative context. Moreover, it is not difficult to recognise the semantic-pragmatic nuance of the act of "recognition" expressed by √שמע in other texts (and situations), such as, for example, 1 Kgs 14:6; Jer 5:21; 6:18; Isa 33:13 (in these last two cases, in significant parallelism with √ידע; cf. also Jer 32:8: "*Then I recognised*

---

156 Cf. e.g. amongst the modern versions: CEI; JPS; BJ; TNK; NAB; LT. significant exceptions are LND ("Deh, ascolta la voce dell'Eterno in ciò che ti dico"), TOB (Écoute la voix du SEIGNEUR dans ce que je te dis), and EÜ (Hör doch auf die Stimme des HERRN, in dem, was ich zu dir rede).

157 Where a more specific root does not appear, e.g. √ידע (cf. Deut 7:9; 8:5; 1 Sam 24:12; Jer 1:5; 2:23; 3:13; etc.) or נכר (cf. Gen 27:23; 31:32; Deut 21:17; 33:9; Isa 61:9; Lam 4:8; etc.), which would be much more easily translated with "you recognise".

Exegetic focalisations 533

[וָאֵדַע] that this was the word of YHWH"); and in a different way, in Isa 41:22; 42:18; 55:2; Song 2:14; 8:13.

3.2.4. Analogies (1:4–19 and 38:14–28a): A new "prophetic vocation"?

"[...] and it will go well for you and you shall live" (וְיִיטַב לְךָ וּתְחִי נַפְשֶׁךָ). Whilst considering other subsequent textual data that I will now disclose, with this reassurance, the text manages to accumulate a sufficient number of elements for the configuration and identification of an analogical relationship that is significant for my thematic. These are a series of clues that give cause to look at the possibility of there being a comparison with the vocational text that opens the whole book of Jeremiah (1:4–19, and above all, vv. 4–10, 18–19). Let us have a look at them.

In Jer 38:14–28a, from the point of view of the spatial-temporal context in general, and of the communicative situation in particular, we find ourselves in a *decisive moment*, marked by *secrecy* and by the *immediacy* of an interpersonal confrontation in which everything lies beneath the menacing shadow of the *"end"* (37:19; 38:2–3, 9, 14). Theirs is not an ordinary dialogic exchange, but a confrontation between a man who, risking his life, claims to introduce, as an authorised spokesman, a divine perspective and plan into the horizon of historical events, and another man who, whilst acknowledging this authority to certain degree, is reached by a message (38:14–16) that calls for *obedience*, and that, in turn, exposes to a *mortal risk* (38:17–18). The divine request is destabilising because it is felt to be disproportionate to the human abilities of the interlocutor, whose reaction is the psychosomatic one of *fear* (38:19). The *objection* is verbalised and somewhat justified, but the counter-response insists on the position that is being presented, adding further *reassurance* (38:20). In this case, the prophetic message is expanded through the account of a *vision* (38:21–23), which prefigures the disaster resulting from the opposite choice of disobedience.

To the reader, but first of all, of course, on an intradiegetic level, to Zedekiah himself, the figure of the prophet Jeremiah himself is indicated as a *sign* of guarantee. In the verses immediately preceding (38:1–13; but cf. also chs. 26 and 36), he was presented as the paradigm of reference for a human being who had handed himself over in obedience to YHWH and for this reason, been saved. Let me schematically synthesise the elements I have just brought into focus:

1.	Spatial-temporal context: *secrecy – immediacy – horizon of the "end"* (37:19; 38:2–3, 9, 14)
2.	Communicative situation: *consultation of the word of YHWH through the prophet* (38:14)
3.	*Call to obedience* in the name of YHWH, expressed in a conditional form (38:17–18)
4.	*Objection* of the interlocutor: fear and the motivation for it (38:19)
5.	*Reassurance* of the prophet, expressed as promised (38:20)
6.	*Sign* (implicit) of confirmation: the paradigmatic salvation of the prophetic body (26:24; 36:26; 38:1–13)
7.	*Vision* of threat (38:21–23)

534   Jer 38:14–28a. Jeremiah and Zedekiah: The final colloquy

What has been highlighted suggests the possibility of tracing an interesting semiotic *arcata* with 1:4–19, in the sign of an analogical relationship between some *profound structures* of signification that, in the two units, refer to each other reciprocally (by resemblance and/or opposition) and encourage advancement in the intelligence of the complexity of the prophetic phenomenon attested in the book. Jeremiah 1:4–19 is a text that, above all with regard to vv. 4–10, 17–19, is commonly ascribed to the so-called literary genre of "narrative of (prophetic) vocation", whose characteristic traits can be enucleated thus[158]:

1.	Immediate human-divine communicative event (Jer 1:4; cf. Isa 6:1–4; Ezek 1:1–28)
2.	Introductive word (Jer 1:5; cf. Isa 6:3–7; Ezek 1:28b-2:2; Isa 40:1–2)
3.	Call for obedience – charge entrusted (Jer 1:5b; cf. Isa 6:8–10; Ezek 2:3–5; Isa 40:3–5a)
4.	Objections put forth by the prophet (Jer 1:6; cf. Isa 6:11a; Ezek 2:6, 8 [implicit]; Isa 40:6–7)
5.	Reassurance on the part of YHWH (Jer 1:7–8; cf. Isa 6:11–13; Ezek 2:6–7; Isa 40:8–11)

---

158   Essentially, I have adopted and re-elaborated the schema (with relative biblical references) of N. Habel, «The Form and Significance of the Call Narratives», *ZAW* 77 (1965) 297–323 (pp. 305–309 specifically regard the vocation of Jeremiah). Also see, in this regard, what is proposed by E. Kutsch, «Gideons Berufung und Altarbau Jdc 6,11–24», *ThLZ* 81 (1956) 75–84 (= Id., *Kleine Schriften zum Alten Testament*. Zum 65. Geburtstag Ernst Kutsch, *eds.* L. Schmidt – K. Eberlein, BZAW 168, Berlin 1986, 99–109) who identifies three characteristic elements (1. The call of YHWH to a mission; 2. Fear and objection of the one called; 3. Divine response rejecting the objection, confirming the mission, and providing a sign of confirmation); G. del Olmo Lete, *La vocación del líder en el antiguo Israel*. Morfología de los relatos bíblicos de vocación, BSal.E 2, Salamanca 1973, calls for a distinction to be made, on the basis of formal and content-related reasons, between four different types of stories and, in synthesis, identifies three fundamental thematic polarities around which the minor motifs are organised (1. Theophania; 2. The mission, which arouses objection in the human being and, as a divine counter-response, a promise of assistance; 3. The sign given by YHWH as confirmation of a vocation); B.O. Long, «Prophetic Call Traditions and Reports of Visions», *ZAW* 84 (1974) 494–500 (with particular comparative reference to the pertinent attestations in the ancient Near East); S. Bretón, *Vocación y misión: Formulario profético,* AnBib 111, Roma 1987, 95–97 (holds that Jer 1:1–19 should be structured in five parts: 1. Introduction [vv. 1–3 + v. 4 as implicit theophania]; 2. Mission [vv. 5–8: dialogue, election, sending of the prophet]; 3. Investiture [vv. 9–10: gesture and formula]; 4. Visions [vv. 11–16]: setting and explanation of the message; 5. Confirmation [vv. 17–19]); P. Bovati, *Jeremiah 1–6*. Dispense PIB, Roma 2005–2006, 59–61 (proposes a tripartite structuring that I will return to further ahead); G.Y. Glazov, *The Bridling of the Tongue and the Opening of the Mouth in Biblical Prophecy*, JSOT.S 311, Sheffield 2001 (scrutinises, above all, the question of the objection to the call).

6.	Sign of confirmation[159] (Jer 1:9–10; cf. Isa 7,14; Ezek 2:8–3:11; 3:4–11)
7.	Report of *vision*[160] (Jer 1:11–16; cf. Isa 6:1–4; Ezek 1:1)

It should be pointed out that all the elements just reported must be assumed with prior awareness that one ought not make the mistake of identifying a literary genre with a standardised formulary made up of fixed locutions. Two or more texts can, in fact, have the same profound structure of signification whilst differing in terms of their surface-level expressive modules. Even with this caveat, the points of analogical referencing between the text that narrates the encounter between the prophet Jeremiah and the king Zedekiah (38:14–28a) and that between YHWH and Jeremiah are relevant. They are a series of analogical (even opposed) correspondences that can be examined in-depth, circumstantiated, and more thoroughly grounded, bearing in mind the synthetic tripartition proposed by P. Bovati[161] in reference to the literary genre of the story of prophetic vocation.[162]

A) God's imperative manifestation (1:5) and the injunction to surrender (38:17–18:20–23)

The founding event of the prophetic vocation (and mission) is dramatised in 1:4–19 according to a literary form that stages an *asymmetrical dialogic exchange*. The narrator thus expresses, first of all, that it is an *event of interpersonal communication*, and not the autonomous attainment of a higher self-awareness or a particularly enlightened consciousness of world events that arises from an intuition or by a rational process that is merely human in origin. Both texts emphasise the absolutely private and secret nature of the "colloquy", which only the narrator with his "omniscience" allow us to witness. With regard to the spatial-temporal context and the specific communicative situation, we note that to the *secrecy – immediacy – horizon of the "end"* triad that characterises the dialogic event of 38:14–28a, the opposite dimension of *origin* (the call is timeless; cf. 1:5) and *beginning* (the call takes place over time; cf. 1:10, 18: הַיּוֹם ["today"]), as well as that of the *"end"* (the call regards the announcement of divine judgments against the kingdom of Judah and the nations; cf. 1:14–16) corresponds in 1:4–19.

It should be noted that in 38:14–28a, we witness the *consultation of the word of YHWH through the prophet*, while in 1:1–19, the *prototypical immediacy* of divine

---

159 The sign that refers to the word (דָּבָר) that establishes the grounds for the mission indicated can be a symbolic gesture or a verbal act that enables the requested task (cf. N. HABEL, «The Form», 319–320).

160 To the six previous points, with respect to what is proposed by N. Habel, I think it is opportune to add a seventh, taking other contributions on the topic into account and referring, in particular, to the vocation of Jeremiah. Inserted significantly in the centre of the textual unit, the two visions included in the vocational story in ch. 1 are not so much found in a privileged position, but rather in a structuring "dialogical" relationship with the other two more specifically "vocational" parts placed at the extremities (1:4–10, 17–19).

161 Cf. P. BOVATI, *Jeremiah 1–6*, 59–61.

162 Having in mind, above all, 1:5–10.

self-communication to the man-prophet is attested instead. The relationship between the two moments is therefore scalar: the levels are different, but they are located along the same line. YHWH is obviously recognised in his transcendent nature with respect to Jeremiah, but this wellspring of alterity is reflected in the person themself of the one called, whose prophetic function serves to make divine transcendence as a normative source of action in a given historic moment present for Zedekiah.

The *imperative form* with which YHWH addresses his interlocutor asking for *obedience*, does not at all want to deny human freedom, but to signify that the divine word is the *norm* of living and the *foundation* itself of the identity of the envoy. That Jeremiah's free will is constantly in the balance between opposing possibilities is attested by that (literary) split in the intimate experience of his ministry that are the "confessions". The reader can thus enter into the heart of this drama, where the individual is confronted with the possibility of no longer speaking in His name (cf. 20:9), and of even going so far as to deny and in fact curse (cf. 20:14–18) the originary word that, before calling to prophecy, called into existence (making the two realities then coincide) through the exodus from the maternal womb.

I have already highlighted and studied the conditional form of the message of surrender in reference to the theme of the alternative between "two ways" and the Deuteronomic contraposition between blessings and curses implicated in the stipulation (and renewal) of the Covenant (cf. ch. III, § 4.2.1). Here, I will specify that, just as the divine imperative of the call expresses, in literary form, the normative nature of the Meaning revealed by the divine word (without denying human liberty), likewise, the binary perspective of the path of life and the path of death does not at all mean that it is a less cogent word: if one truly wants life, there is only one possibility now: to surrender. In this sense, the prophet's request is along the same lines as the divine imperative that originally reached Jeremiah himself, and which, parenthetically, a close look shows, contains a dramatic alternative as well: "do not be frightened before them, otherwise I will frighten you before them" (1:17b).

B) Resistance on the part of humankind as fear of "death" (1:6; 38:19)

Generally running alongside a biblical theophany is an involuntary psychosomatic alteration (sense of fear, loss of consciousness, paralysis, dismay, etc.) that occurs in a person reached by a manifestation of transcendence. But here, the specific theme is another: it is the consequent *verbalisation* of this instinctive reaction, which gives shape to a response of free and conscious *objection*, made explicit through several expressive modules. From the consciousness of the person called, an awareness of not being capable, through one's own human limits, of carrying out the divine demand emerges. The motivations may be manifold, but in the texts I am comparing, they are actually not so different: in both cases, the different lexical surfaces aside, the issue is that of the *fear* felt in the face of a *mortal risk*.

To be prophets means being called to speak the meaning of the present moment revealed by YHWH, lord and judge of history, against other meanings, other interpretations of the real, and other figures of authority (while these also lay claim to their own divine foundations). Jeremiah, in painful complaint, insists instead that he does not know how to speak (1:6). For this mission, this limit is a radical one. What is counterposed here is not, as in the case of Moses (cf. Exod 4:19), some speech defect or lack of sufficient rhetorical expertise. His is a problem of authority (as well as of truth)[163]: to be young (נַעַר) means not having sufficient qualifications to be able to make himself be heard, a requirement normally possessed by one who is "elderly" (זָקֵן), that is, a man of experience. On these fragile grounds, to presume to be recognised and obeyed as the bearer of a normative word for others means, in other words, exposing oneself to rejection, failure, defeat, and humiliation. And so, according to the perspective made explicit in the vocational text itself, it means having to face a "war/process" (cf. 1:17–19) that can have a *fatal outcome*. Indeed, Jeremiah, in addition to physical suffering, will experience such "shame" (בֹּשֶׁת) as to perceive his existence as senseless (cf. 20:8.18).

As we have already seen, Zedekiah's objection to the words of YHWH referred to him by the prophet Jeremiah is along the same lines. He is afraid of the *humiliation*, which is basically a reflection of a *fear of death*. Even Zedekiah, should he wish to obey, will be forced, in fact, to face those he feels to be his personal enemies (i.e. the "Jews who surrendered to the Chaldeans"; cf. 38:19) and by whom he fears being disgraced. One could object that while Jeremiah is asked for obedience affecting all existence (that of being a prophet) and that relates to, therefore, a rivelative dimension, Zedekiah, on the other hand, is shown nothing more than a political gesture. It should be observed, however, that this act calls into question *his entire life* and his royal status, involving, as well, *all the people* (it is the king who "burns the City"; cf. 38:23). I reiterate, in any case, that the type of relation I am attempting to establish is analogical, which means focalising a *resemblance of pertinent relations* (proportionality) placed on different (and seemingly entirely foreign) levels in such a way that the first element of comparison (called "source"), which is more familiar, might illuminate another ("target"), which is less clear, allowing elements of meaning to be identified in the latter that would otherwise be destined to remain in the shadows.

A close look shows that specific obediences are also asked of Jeremiah over the course of his ministry, including the famous "symbolic gestures". These are of a varied nature and importance as far as existential involvement is concerned, but are an important element of the prophetic mission because they show that revelatory communication passes not only through the verbal register, but through the physical-gestural dimension as well. These acts express the meaning of history from the perspective of God. What is asked of Zedekiah (and in fact of all the people), in my opinion, runs along the same lines, and that is what I am trying to demonstrate from the beginning of my research path. The question is not merely one of an anecdotal, sapiential, or ethical fact, but rather of expressing no less *prophetically*, through the political gesture of surrender, acceptance of the failure of his own history of Covenant and the consequent punishment, trusting the word of YHWH. This promises, by way of crossing through the symbolic form of "death" that the act of surrender intends to signify, salvation for the individual and for all of Jerusalem, and thus, another possible future.

---

163 Not knowing how to speak could also be understood as not knowing how to speak according to truth, even in reference to the objection of Isaiah, who confesses to having "unclean lips" (cf. Isa 6:5).

538   Jer 38:14–28a. Jeremiah and Zedekiah: The final colloquy

C) Divine confirmation (1:7–10) and prophetic reassurance (38:20)

The natural human resistance in the face of the divine word that puts pressure on creaturely limits and instincts of self-preservation does not mark the end of a dialogue, but rather finds a response that produces an *advancement* of the revelation itself. This applies both to the vocational text of 1:4–19 and, analogously, to the discussion between Jeremiah and Zedekiah. In both cases, though with different modulations of its surface form of expression, we have a *reassurance* that presents itself regardless *in primis* as a direct negation of the objection put forward by the interlocutor: "do not say: I am young" (1:7), "he will not deliver you to them" (38:19).

The following invitation to *not be afraid* addressed to Jeremiah is anchored in the *promise* of YHWH's action and protective presence, which will ensure that all that has been commanded can be achieved (cf. 1:7–10, 18–19). At this stage as well, the dialogic exchange typical of vocation stories attempts to express with stereotypical literary registers what cannot be reduced to either the literal representation of a discussion, or to a precise fact. As the book of Jeremiah attests, the objection to the divine plan and the force that counterbalances it are intimate, difficult to communicate experiences that run through all prophetic ministry. In any case, what is to be highlighted is that the revelation indeed progresses not in spite of the objection, but thanks to the objection itself, and that the difficulties put forth by the one called give YHWH the opportunity to add new elements of meaning to the communicative event in question.[164] And this occurs differently in both of the texts.

In Jeremiah's vocation there is also a *sign* of confirmation that, however, has nothing manifestly remarkable about it (YHWH touches his mouth and announces the "fortification" of his prophetic body) and, at this point, the two *visions* are introduced, which not only make the content of the message explicit, but paradigmatically define the synergy between word and vision in the perspective of preparing to *know how to discern* (cf. 15:19). The question, twice repeated, "what do you see, Jeremiah?" (1:11, 13) not only alludes, in my opinion, to some kind of training[165] in the exercise of prototypical prophetic ministry, but it is also a question that will be implicitly addressed to every person with whom the prophet will interact (think, above all, of the communicative dimension of the symbolic gestures), not the least, Zedekiah, who is, as well, in reality, an intradiegetic simulacrum of the reader themself, to whom the same question is addressed. In fact, what is at stake is the possibility of *becoming prophets*, recognising and obeying the true prophet placed in front of us.

The reassurance offered to Zedekiah follows the same symbolic guidelines emphasised in the vocational text. In addition to the direct denial of the objection, as we have noted, he too is implicitly offered a "sign" that *has nothing evidently miraculous* about it, and this sign is the prophet Jeremiah himself.[166] His constant presence in the midst

---

164   Cf. P. Bovati – P. Basta, *"Ci ha parlato per mezzo dei profeti"*, 92–93.

165   As suggests A. Neher, *Jérémie*, 19–54.

166   Even when in other vocational stories, the sign is indeed miraculous (cf. e.g. Exod 4:1–5; Judg 6:36–40), one must decipher its symbolic valence. As is, in fact, well emphasised by P. Bovati, *Jeremiah 1–6*, 60–61, "sarebbe ingenuo pensare che questo genere di eventi prodigiosi costituisca una sorta di oggettiva garanzia per chi dubita della esperienza interiore; senza la fede, infatti, anche il segno può essere contestato nella sua veridicità, oppure può apparire insufficiente se non è costantemente ripetuto. In Geremia, come in molti altri racconti di vocazione profetica, non abbiamo

Exegetic focalisations

539

of the drama that all the people are living,[167] the fulfilment of his word regarding the threat coming from the North, the story of his body delivered into the hands of men in obedience to God but always saved, even if through a humiliation, is, on the whole, the greatest guarantee that the path requested of King Zedekiah is not a deception, but rather the way of salvation for him and for all Jerusalem.[168] And the reason why now appears even more clearly: it is basically a question of reliving first-hand what has been asked of the prophet Jeremiah from the start of his vocation: to agree to express the meaning of the history underway with his own obedience.

The *visionary* element appears in 38:14–28a as well, in analogy to 1:4–19. With two (apparent) differences that seem to render the relationship impertinent: 1) in both cases, *only the prophet Jeremiah* is the subject of the visions, and 2) their content, on the one hand, makes explicit the *message to be transmitted* (cf. 1:11–12, 13–16), whilst on the other, it is, however, reported as a *threat* (38:21–23). In truth, even the two inaugural visions (the first centred on the fulfilment of the divine word, the other on the looming disaster coming from the North) can also be properly understood as threats, and even the vision of 38:21–23 should be translated, once accepted by the king, into a word to be transmitted, that order (first of all, to the reluctant "leaders") the surrender of the City.

In itself, however, that only Jeremiah "sees" something as coming directly from YHWH does not seem to be an apparent difference. And yet, it should be noted that the two "visions" in 1:11–12, 13–16 do not seem to be able to refer to anything transcendent or to an event that is entirely supernatural. It is more probably a question of seeing commonplace scenes, but with different eyes, prophetic eyes, that is, as having that capability of *analogical-prophetic reading of the real* that YHWH wants to teach. Also in 38:22–23, what is imposed on the "one called" (Jeremiah) and on those reached in a mediated way by the prophetic word (Zedekiah) is not so much a transcendental

---

nessun tipo di segno miracoloso. Chi acconsente alla missione si affida in realtà *sempre* ed esclusivamente alla *promessa*; al tempo stesso, ciò che sostiene, incoraggia, conferma la decisione di obbedire al mandato divino è l'esperienza *corporea* dell'intervento di Dio, vissuta come accrescimento di forza, ardimento e tenacia, una dotazione che consente di andare incontro al pericolo senza paura, un'anticipazione insomma del superamento degli ostacoli paventati" ("it would be naive to think that this kind of prodigious event were to constitute a kind of objective guarantee for those who doubt the inner experience; without faith, in fact, even the sign can be disputed in its veracity, or it may appear insufficient if it is not constantly repeated. In Jeremiah, as in many other tales of prophetic vocation, we have no kind of miraculous sign. Those who consent to the mission are in fact *always* and exclusively committed to the *promise*; at the same time, what supports, encourages, confirms the decision to obey the divine mandate is the *physical* experience of the intervention of God, lived as an increase in strength, daring and tenacity, an endowment that allows one to encounter danger without fear, an anticipation in short of overcoming the obstacles feared").

167 And even beyond: it is significant, after all, that in ch. 39, where the fall and destruction of Jerusalem is recounted, that there is no mention of the end of the temple. Its destruction will be mentioned only in closing, in ch. 52. As if to say that in the heart of the catastrophe, going beyond the temple, the permanence of the presence of YHWH is ensured by the presence of the prophet Jeremiah amidst the people.

168 It is like the "sign of Jonah" in Matt 12:39–40.

vision as it is an appeal to *know how to listen* (cf. 38:20) and thus to *know how to see* the meaning of history. Before Jeremiah's eyes are common objects and scenes, while in his "ears", there is a word that invites discernment. Analogously, before Zedekiah there is (only) a man speaking, one who speaks of what he has seen, and speaks to invite recognition, in all of this, of the word of YHWH that *lets him see* the meaning of what is happening and the outcome that will result from the king's choice. Implicitly, also to Zedekiah, as to the reader, "what do you see?" is asked. In the hope of being able to say: "you saw well" (cf. 1:12). But perhaps, at this point, Zedekiah will truly see well only when he will have to witness the most terrifying scene of his life, which will also be the last he ever sees with his eyes (cf. 39:6–7; 52:10–11).

3.2.5. Considerations: In view of further investigations

What emerges from the plausibility of the analogical relation highlighted between 1:4–19 and 38:14–28a can be understood, in summary, as a phenomenon of *transmission* and *extension of the charism characteristic of the prophetic mediator*.[169] Or more precisely, as one of its expressions. This development is, in fact, already visible in the paradigmatic relation that book of Jeremiah establishes between the "prototypical prophet" Jeremiah and the disciple Baruch (36; 45). And again, between Jeremiah, Baruch (and Seraiah in 51:59–64), and the prophetic scroll (cf. ch. 36), figures that are logically (and not for their importance) "secondary", destined to represent, under another form, the indestructible permanence of the prophetic word amidst the people of the Covenant and its universal truth. From the prophet to the disciples, from a prototypical prophecy to a discipular and scribal prophecy, made by the one who has received that message and is called to live it in first person: these are different phases that are however, placed along the continuum of a single flowing-forth of revelation springing from the selfsame source. On the other hand, on close consideration, a true prophet can only be recognised by *another "prophet"*.[170] The question certainly deserves ample in-depth consideration. In any case, I introduce this categorisation at least as a promising working hypothesis in view of more extensive investigations in this regard, convinced that there be, in the book of Jeremiah, a peculiar literary attestation (of a narrative sort) of a comprehensive phenomenon that relates to the totality of the prophetic tradition.

I will put forth an ulterior hermeneutical proposal, which can open up another interesting perspective of inquiry. It can be rightly seen that the expressive form of vocational stories responds to the canons of its relative literary genre (which, in turn,

---

169   In this regard, see P. Bovati, «"Figlio d'Adamo, nutri il tuo ventre e riempi le tue viscere con il rotolo che ti sto porgendo" (Ezek 3,3). L'ermeneutica della raccolta profetica come contributo all'approfondimento dell'ispirazione biblica», *Teol(M)* 36 (2011) 587–610.

170   This is the significant conclusion that can be drawn with P. Beauchamp, *L'un et l'autre Testament*, 100; *Parler d'Écritures saintes*, 63; P. Bovati, *"Così parla il Signore"*, 37–52; P. Bovati – P. Basta, *"Ci ha parlato per mezzo dei profeti"*, 78–137, from the study of the criteria of discernment between true and false prophecy. Only those who possess the same "spirit" that inspires the prophets and who obeys in their hearts are capable of recognising the genuineness of other words spoken from outside, by other people who declare themselves to be messengers of God.

Exegetic focalisations   541

contains and employs other minor genres). In this sense, it is clear that it should not be taken to the letter, but need be traced back to those profound, symbolic-existential dimensions I have tried to at least mention. But why not see in them, regardless, the reflection of a concrete experience like the consultation of prophets, which is well attested in Scripture and in the ancient Near East? In this manner, the correct terms of comparison could thus also be inverted: if it is enlightening to start from 1:4–19 to reinterpret the final colloquy between Jeremiah and Zedekiah according to these prophetic coordinates, then likewise, a comparison could also be drawn in the reverse sense. It is possible, in fact, that encounters of the sort, between a prophet and his interlocutor, called on to access the divine dimension by means of a human word, have provided a basic relational grammar (or *frame*, in terms of cognitive semantics) to express in a dialogical form and with a similar schema (imperative manifestation of the divinity, objection, reassurance) the originary theophanical irruption of God's word in the life of a person called to a prophetic life.

3.2.6. *Vision* (ראה√): *A communicative event in real time?*

The objection posed by King Zedekiah gives rise to a characteristic revelatory dynamic: the repetition and expansion of the prophetic word. This is a phenomenon that ch. 36 attests clearly. Jeremiah's response in particular is integrated with the account of a visionary event (38:21–23) defined by W. McKane as a "hypothetical vision".[171] The vision is doubtless "hypothetical", in regard to its anticipation of the detrimental effects that the king's refusal to perform the act of surrender would have, but it presents a sure fact that need be observed: this is not simply a visual experience, but also an auditory event communicating a verbal message.

"But if you refuse to go out, this is..." (v. 21). We could say, then, that more than be a generic "thing" (דָּבָר) ["this is what/this is the thing that...] or a uniquely visionary event (ראה√ hi.) ["this is the vision that...], in v. 21, Jeremiah speaks of what he has seen (or is seeing) as a "visual-word" coming from and shown by YHWH to facilitate the travail of discernment in which the king finds himself. We are within the same basic communicative horizon implicated by the דָּבָר requested by Zedekiah at the beginning (v. 14): the king asks "I want to ask you a *word* (דָּבָר) [...]" and Jeremiah's response, if it could have been understood before, at the most, as a simple repetition of what he had already given as a certain divine message, now takes the form typical of an oracle given and revealed by YHWH by means of his prophet in a precise manner: "If you refuse to go out, this is the *word* (דָּבָר) that the Lord *makes me see* (הִרְאַנִי): Behold all the women ... *they are led out* (מוּצָאוֹת) [...] and behold, *they are saying* (אֹמְרוֹת) [...]" (vv. 21–22).

As could already be noticed during the presentation of the text (§ 2.1), I have proposed an alternative translation compared to every other opinion of the major commentators on the matter. Based on the potential temporal references implied by the Hebrew verbs used, and also taking into account what is suggested by the rhetorical

---

171 W. McKane, *Jeremiah*, II, 958–959. Cf. P. Scalise, «Vision beyond the Visions in Jeremiah», in: "*I Lifted My Eyes and Saw*". Reading Dream and Vision Reports in the Hebrew Bible, *eds.* E.R. Hayes – L.-S. Tiemeyer, LHBOTS 584, London – New York 2014, 47–58 (here, pp. 52–53).

542   Jer 38:14–28a. Jeremiah and Zedekiah: The final colloquy

arrangement, mine underscores a "revelatory" nucleus coextensive to the present time of the speaker (vv. 22–23a), that is, a vision that is reported as a fact is taking place before the eyes (or mind) of the prophet-spectator in real time and not a visionary experience extracted from his memory and expressed in the future.[172] It is certainly possible (and recognised by scholars) to read all the verbs in vv. 22–23 in the future or the past,[173] but this does not seem to fully account for either the structure of the text, or the (apparently unjustified) repetition produced in this way in v. 23 (23b: "and you cannot escape from their hands"; 23c: "Yes, you will be taken by the hand of the king of Babylon."

Let me first of all present, in a way that is schematic, a more accurate rhetorical disposition of the textual-communicative unit constituted by Jeremiah's response to Zedekiah (vv. 20–23) in order to highlight the main structuring elements:

20b.d-e	A	*positive outcome* in case of obedience	*they will not hand [you] over [...]* *it will go well for you and you shall live*
21		subjective introduction to the vision	[...] this is the "word" that the Lord shows me
22a-b	B	**"objective" content of the vision**	**all THE WOMEN [...] will be led [...] and say [...]**
22c-f	C	SONG OF THE WOMEN	"THE MEN of your peace"
23a-b	B¹	**"objective" content of the vision**	**all YOUR WOMEN and your children [...] will be led** [...] and you cannot escape from their hands
23c-d	A¹	subjective confirmation of the vision and of the *negative outcome* in case of refusal	*Yes, you will be taken* by the hand of the king of Babylon and *you will make burn with fire this city*

The interpretations proposed by the modern versions, like my own alternative, depend on the interpretation given to the temporal reference of the qatal הִרְאַנִי (v. 21), the participles מוּצָאוֹת (vv. 22a, 23a), אֹמְרֹת (22b), and the yiqtol תִּמָּלֵט (v. 23b). The different possibilities on the level of translation depend on the fact upstream that, as all are well aware,[174] attempts at grammatical formalisation of the Hebrew language find

---

172   The standard rendering adopted by the major modern translations sounds like this: "[21] [...] this is what has *been shown* to me by the Lord. [22] Behold, all the women [...] *shall be led* to the leaders of the king of Babylon and they *will sing:* [...]. [23] All of your women and your children *shall be led out* towards the Chaldeans, and you *shall not escape* from their hands. You *shall be taken* by the hand of the king of Babylon and this city *shall be burned* with fire."

173   This is observed e.g. in particular with regard to the temporal valence of the participles, A. WEISER, *Jeremia*, II, 343, n. 1: "Man kann deshalb die zeitlosen Partizipialformen sowohl perfektisch als auch futurisch wiedergeben, je nachdem man mehr das Moment des Erlebnisses oder das der Verkündigung betonen will." It seems to me that the dimension of the present, that is, the possibility of contemporaneity with respect to the scene underway, should not be neglected either.

174   See e.g. the recent study (which begins with an extensive historical review of the principal theories) by J.A. COOK, *Time and the Biblical Hebrew Verb. The Expression of Tense, Aspect, and Modality in Biblical Hebrew*, LSAWS 7, Winona Lake 2012.

Exegetic focalisations 543

their greatest difficulty precisely in the comprehension of its verbal system. Indeed, it would seem that today, the research paths that have addressed this problem have reached a real impasse.[175] Aside from the scholastic simplifications or biased formulations that discard other perspectives *a priori*, the disaccord is considerable. There are, in fact, amongst scholars, those who believe that what the (finite) Hebrew verb primarily expresses is the *time*[176] (past or non-past, or, according to the trinary formula, past, present, and future), those, its *aspect* (conceptualised in binary terms as perfect or imperfect),[177] and who, more recently, a *relative time* (in reference to a time indicated within the discourse by another verbal form or other temporal indicators).[178] Even if I do not assume this as a conclusive theory of the Hebrew verbal system, this latter approach is, in my opinion, the most suitable both for exploring new paths of interpretation and, in particular, for establishing (or situating)[179] within a stronger theoretical framework the significance of meaning that I propose as a possibility yet to be considered as a translation.

In 38:21, the form הִרְאַנִי *seems* to have to necessarily be translated as "he made me see", with reference to a visionary event situated in the past and having a temporal aspect that is completed ("perfect") with respect to the time of its enunciation, as in 24 1. From my perspective, however, which at its root draws reference from the "Relevance Theory",[180] it is necessary to keep in mind the aims and elements of communication at play in the context of reference. So let us see if other, similar contexts can provide us with some useful indications.

The other relevant extra-Jeremianic attestations of the √ראה hi. perfect (qatal) with subj. YHWH + suff. 1st per. sing. on which our text seems to depend are those in Amos: they recur in a context of prophetic communication that is similar (cf. Amos 7:1, 4, 7; 8:1), and these, too, seem to refer only to the past. It is clear, in fact, that these cases concern visions situated in a temporal context that precedes the communicative situation of the speaker. However, despite the similarities, it should be noted that,

---

175 As observed by J.A. Cook, «The Hebrew Verb: A Grammaticalization Approach», *ZAH* 14 (2001) 117–143 (on p. 117).

176 Such as, e.g. J. Joosten, «Do the Finite Verbal Forms in Biblical Hebrew Express Aspect?», *JANES* 29 (2002) 49–70.

177 Cf. *Ibid.*, 21–35.

178 The pioneering contribution, which is, at the same time, also the most influential of this approach, is that of H. Reichenbach, *Elements of Symbolic Logic*, New York 1947, 286–299. In his system, there are three dimensions of temporality (E: event; R: point of reference; S: point of speech) and two possible types of relationships between them (simultaneity and anteriority). The whole thing gives rise to thirteen different possible combinations. Cf. B. Comrie, *Tense*, Cambridge 1985.

179 In fact, I will not be able to develop an exhaustive demonstrative system that employs the (even formal) resources of this perspective of analysis in a technical way.

180 For the "Relevance Theory" (already mentioned in the General Introduction in § 3.3.4) every speaker/writer elaborates presuppositions regarding the cognitive universe of the listener/reader and consequently selects the most appropriate linguistic instruments for communication. I will now limit myself to only briefly mentioning this interpretive direction of the phenomenon of communication, deferring further and more in-depth explanations to ch. VII, § 1.2, where the reference to this theoretic perspective will have more relevant implications for my study.

544   Jer 38:14–28a. Jeremiah and Zedekiah: The final colloquy

unlike our text, in Amos, the communicative context is not that of an intradiegetic dialogic exchange.

The case attested in 2 Kgs 8:10, 13 is, on the other hand, more similar to that in Jeremiah and seems less univocal than Amos' visions as far as the temporal reference is concerned. The concept of the relativity of time understood and expressed here is clear.[181] What Elisha refers to Hazael at two points as depending on two different visions, can help us understand, in fact, that the selfsame verbal expression (הִרְאַנִי in v. 10 and v. 13) can refer to different temporal planes, detectable only thanks to the pragmatic context of the communication underway. It is not as obvious, in the present case, that the account be of two visionary events situated in a homogeneous past, as should be seen in theory[182] from the recursiveness of the identical verbal form. It can also be a message dependent upon two "visions" that are essentially contemporary to their respective communicative phases.[183]

Another interesting comparison can be traced with the episode of the consultation of the prophet Michea, son of Imla, in 1 Kgs 22:7–28. Here, too, in my opinion, it is possible to detect temporal anchorings that are different, despite their being indicated with the very same verbal form in the "perfect". In 1 Kgs 22:17, 19, the qatal רָאִיתִי is used twice in reference to two visionary events that are different, though included within a single revelative phenomenon relevant to the situation currently underway. While, for the second, all modern translations agree on a surrender in the past ("I have seen/I saw"), for the first, they oscillate between the present ("I see") and the past. It is not easy to take a clear stance, since both possibilities can be congruent with the communicative context, even if the one most effective and coherent with the level of narrative dramatisation taking place would seem that of the surrender in the present "I see/I am seeing all the Israelites scattered upon the mountains [...]"

These considerations aside, one might wonder what other linguistic-grammatical tools (in addition to the participial forms)[184] would be available to a hypothetical narrator wanting to express in Hebrew the idea of a "vision" directly experienced by a character during a conversation with their interlocutor. We can uncover an answer

---

181 An example of such "relativity" of the verbal forms can be seen in the use of the wayyiqtol (actually a syntactic variant of the qatal) of √הלך in Gen 22:3. Assuming a rigid formal equivalence between the wayyiqtol and the idea of aspectual completeness, the verbal form וַיֵּלֶךְ would be translated as "and he went" [to the place indicated by YHWH], leaving it understood that the arrival of Abraham on Mount Moria had already happened. But by the immediate and proximal contextual indicators (cf. Gen 22:4), it can be clearly understood that the context instead obliges a translation that reads "and he walked" since the journey of Abraham is at its beginning.

182 And also in practice, according to many translations.

183 First communicative act (2 Kgs 8:10): "Elisha answered him: 'Go and tell him: you will surely recover. But the Lord *showed me/shows me* (הִרְאַנִי) that he will surely die'." Second communicative act (2 Kgs 8:11–13): "Then he fixed his gaze and stared at him steadfastly. Then the man of God wept." [...] "[...] the Lord *showed me* (הִרְאַנִי) that you will become the king of Syria." In this second case, the verb indicates the past, yes, but an immediate past, placed a minimal distance from the locutory act. It renders an account of a vision had during a dialogic exchange with Hazael, a context that is quite similar to the Jeremianic one.

184 Cf. Jer 1:11, 13: מָה־אַתָּה רֹאֶה ("what do you see/are you seeing?").

Exegetic focalisations 545

by observing another secret meeting, this one taking place on the night of Endor (cf. 1 Sam 28). The episode of the necromancer consulted by Saul at a time no less tragic than that experienced by Zedekiah and Jerusalem before the imminent defeat is, in my opinion, the most interesting attestation for putting my working hypothesis to the test, and decisively so, precisely because it sees a king appealing to a prophet in the imminence of a disaster. From the pragmatic context configured by the narration, it is clear that what the necromancer refers to Saul is not the content of a vision of the past, but of what she is seeing, or says she sees, right during their on-going conversation.[185] The verbal form used, twice, is the qatal √ראה in the qal form. In 1 Sam 28:12, in the first vision manifested to the prophet Samuel, the text expresses the dismay of the seer as: "The woman saw (וַתֵּרֶא) Samuel and cried [...]". The wayyiqtol of √ראה in qal is used here to refer to what has just been seen and thus expresses an immediate past. But soon thereafter, Saul urges on the necromancer, asking, "*What do you see/ are you seeing?* (מָה רָאִית)". To which the woman responds: "*I see/I am seeing* (רָאִיתִי) a divine *being risen/going up* (עֹלִים) from the earth".

It is clear, therefore, that not only the yiqtol (as e.g. in Num 24:17), but also the qatal of √ראה can be used under certain conditions to express the simultaneity of the visionary event.[186] This demonstrates the possibility of translating as "show me" or "it is showing me" the same qatal in the hi. form in Jer 38:21 as well, where a similar communicative situation[187] can be configured, accentuated, among other things, by the dual use of the deictic strength of וְהִנֵּה ("and behold [...]"; cf. v. 22).[188] Just as then, in 1 Sam 28:13, the participle עֹלִים that follows the qatal with the time reference highlighted indicates (or can indicate) something that is happening simultaneously, so the participles מוּצָאוֹת (Jer 38:22a, 23a), אֹמְרוֹת (v. 22b) can be translated not only with the future "they will be conducted" and "they will say", but with "they are conducted" and "they say", to describe a scene in the act of its unfolding before the eyes or mind of the prophet. As for the verb תִּמָּלֵט (v. 23b), usually translated in the future ("you will not escape"), it does not seem out of the question, as I have proposed, to attribute declarative epistemic deontic value, in reference to the necessity or inevitability of what will happen in Zedekiah, to an event that is contemplated as having actually already come about and communicated as a statement: "[...] you cannot escape".

Returning, in conclusion, to the proposed structuring, the plausibility of my interpretation can also be ascertained on the basis of the harmonious rhetorical disposition of the communicative unity that follows. The visionary event, in fact, as an irruption of the transcendent plane ("objective") on the historical horizon, is embedded between the words of the prophet Jeremiah that (subjectively) attest its reception (v. 21: "This,

---

185 In this sense, one could also "evoke" the vision of Baalam in Num 24, esp. the v. 17, and, as far as the NT is concerned, the vision of Stephen in Acts 7:56, his also being contemporaneous to the communicative situation in act.

186 For other cases where wayyiqtol and qatal are used in reference to the present or the future instead of the past, see JM §118o-s.

187 According to the perspective of H. Reichenbach, it can be said here that E ("event"), R ("point of reference"), and S ("point of speech") coincide.

188 While the particle הִנֵּה usually appears in relation to √אמר to introduce a direct discourse, וְהִנֵּה is instead particularly used together with verbs of vision and in the description of visions, dreams, and revelations; cf. T. ZEWI, «The Particles הנה and והנה in Biblical Hebrew», HebStud 37 (1996) 21–37.

546 Jer 38:14–28a. Jeremiah and Zedekiah: The final colloquy

the Lord makes me see [...]") and confirm, through the use of the emphatic–assertive כִּי,[189] its veracity (v. 38c: "Yes [כִּי], you will be handed over [...]").

3.2.7. Pre-vision (I): Weakness and truth

Let us now focus on the content of the Jeremianic vision. The narrator, as I have high-lighted, shows us the prophet in the act of not only reporting a scene, but of relating words he has heard (or is hearing). These do not come directly from the mouth of YHWH, but from some *women*, tenuous voices that in this scenario made up entirely of war cries, fears, and the decisions of men, would have less of a title of credit than others to be consulted and heard. Already, in 9:19–20,[190] in any case, they had been mentioned and reached by the word of God, precisely so they could carry out the painful revelative service of lamenting the pain over the end of Jerusalem to be taught to future generations. And once again in the book of Jeremiah, goodness and truth are revealed in a way that is as surprising as it is everyday (cf. 1:11–16), implicitly renewing the invitation to seek the Lord with all one's heart when he is near and can be found (cf. Isa 55:6; Jer 29:13) and to recognise the divine word where one would not expect it to be found (cf. 1:9, 11–16; 2:8; 26; 36; etc.; 38:20).

Truth and *weakness* are thus demonstrated as having a great deal in common. This relationship is suggested by the rhetorical arrangement of the text itself, where in v. 22, the term הַנָּשִׁים ("the women") and the participle מוּצָאוֹת ("they are led"), which incarnate the presence of a *helpless truth*, along with the term נָשֶׁיךָ ("your women") and the participle מוּצָאִים ("are led", in immediate syntactic reference to the coordinated lexeme בָּנֶיךָ; "your children") in v. 23, are an inclusion for the strophes that have as their subject אַנְשֵׁי שְׁלֹמֶךָ ("the men of your peace"), who, placed in relation to the act of "deceiving, instigating" (√סות hi.) and of "prevailing over" (√יכל), instead become a symbol of the *power* of the *deceiving lie*. This antithesis is reinforced by the fact that if the book of Jeremiah speaks of truth, it has no more explicit form than in the weakness of the prophetic body itself (both literary and physical).[191] The oppositional relationship is complete when one considers that the אַנְשֵׁי שְׁלֹמֶךָ can be identified, in my opinion, not only with the dignitaries or with the generic, trusted court counsellors, but with the false prophets themselves, Jeremiah's powerful enemies, whose lying proclamation is precisely that of שָׁלוֹם שָׁלוֹם ("peace, peace.!")[192]

---

189 Cf. A. SCHOORS, «The Particle כי», in: *Remembering All the Way...*, 240–276 (esp. pp. 243–253); T. MURAOKA, *Emphatics Words*, 158–164.

190 "[19] Hear therefore, oh women, the word of the Lord, may your ears receive the word of his mouth. Teach your children a wailing, and each other a lament. [20] For death has come up through our windows, has entered our citadels, to cut down children in the street, young people in the squares."

191 Think of the "passion" of the literary body in Jer 36 and to all of the sufferings and persecutions endured by Jeremiah himself. On this topic, see B. ROSSI, «Lo scritto profetico in Ger 36: tra fragilità e sovversione», in: *«Insegnaci a contare i nostri giorni e giungeremo al cuore della sapienza» (Sal 90,12)*. Atti della XLV Settimana Biblica Nazionale (Roma, 10–14 Settembre 2018), eds. F. DALLA VECCHIA – D. SCAIOLA, RStB 32, Bologna 2020, 199–219.

192 Cf., e.g. 8:11: "They heal the wound of my people, but only slightly, saying: Peace, peace! (שָׁלוֹם שָׁלוֹם), but there is no peace (שָׁלוֹם)." In this interpretive vein, C.F. KEIL, *Jeremia*, 392. Rather sceptical is J.R. LUNDBOM, *Jeremia 37–52*, 77, who instead

Exegetic focalisations   547

As was already highlighted,[193] the concept contained in and expressed by the root שׁלם seems to be one of the most richly nuanced of the whole OT, and it would be improper both to attribute a single valid meaning to it, always and regardless, as well as to ingenuously think that all meanings can be represented on each recurrence. Depending on the context, the basic idea can be: completeness, fulfilment, a state of fullness and unity, compensation for damage, reconciled relationship. For the term שָׁלוֹם in particular, it seems that the fundamental meaning can be expressed by the binomial "peace-prosperity", modulated and balanced in a different manner according to the case.[194] In many texts, שָׁלוֹם indicates not only a condition, but a relationship (cf. Gen 34:21; 1 Kgs 5:26) with regard to a people (cf. Deut 2:10; 21:13) or to two individuals (cf. Zec 6:13), coded in special cases with a treaty of alliance (בְּרִית).[195]

The text that comes closest to ours is definitely Abd 7:

"They have driven you to the border; all your allies (אַנְשֵׁי בְרִיתֶךָ) they have deceived you! (√נשׁא) They have overpowered you (√יכל) your friends (אַנְשֵׁי שְׁלֹמֶךָ), those who eat your bread plan to ambush you! – In him there is no intelligence."

It is therefore fairly clear who the men are referred to in v. 23, but we also know that the ideology corroborating their political option was that which had already for some time been advocated by the circle of "false" prophets (of the court).

The women led to the leaders of the king of Babylon are those of the court harem (together with their attendants) left or spared from the harshness of the siege, including the king's wives (named together with their children in v. 23a). The scene is not an unusual one in a context of war.[196] Amongst the various examples that could be given: many civilian prisoners, including women and children, are seen forming a long procession conducted before the victorious ruler, in the bas-relief of Shalmanassar III (859–825),[197] and in the famous depiction of the taking of Lachish by Sennacherib, where they can also be seen loaded on wagons taking them away from the conquered city.[198]

It is difficult to decide whether theirs is a song of ridicule or lament.[199] It is perhaps best to say that what is put on their lips is simply the truth revealed by YHWH about the situation underway and the inevitable consequences of rejecting the prophetic message. They speak, and their word takes on the indicative mood typical of prophetic

---

     underlines the irony that precisely those people most trusted by the king become the ones who betray him.

193   Cf. ch. II, § 3.2.2.1, n. 176 (highlighting the most important lexicographic contributions).

194   Well-being, material prosperity, and consequent attitude of satisfaction, physical health.

195   The semantic line joining שָׁלוֹם and בְּרִית can be traced either beginning from one term or the other: a relationship of שָׁלוֹם can be sealed by a בְּרִית, just as a בְּרִית can give life to a relationship of שָׁלוֹם. In these contexts, the latter lexeme would almost seem to be an official technical term; cf. G. VON RAD, «שָׁלוֹם im AT», 921.

196   As is rightly emphasised by J.R. LUNDBOM, Jeremiah 37–52, 78.

197   Cf. ANEP, 124, Fig. 358; 127, Fig. 365.

198   Cf. Fig. 18 (ch. IV, § 4.1.4) and D. USSISHKIN, The Conquest of Lachish, 77, 84–86. Likewise in another Assyrian bas-relief visible in ANEP, 128, Fig. 367.

199   For the opinions of the commentators, cf. W. MCKANE, Jeremiah, II, 959.

proclamation. The veil of appearance is torn and the reality of things is shown: the king has been deceived, and precisely by those who he considered friends.[200] Now there is nothing more painful than an evil that falls suddenly from where nothing but good was expected: this disaster has a lament and mockery all its own.

If, out of fear, the king does not trust God, then what will be realised is precisely his greatest fear, according to what was already been announced in warning to Jeremiah himself (cf. 1:17). In the HB, women applauding victory is a recurring motif: think of the song of Mary accompanied by the other women with dancing and the sounding of drums after the defeat of the Egyptians (cf. Exod 15:20–21), that of Deborah (cf. Judg 5), of Jephthah's daughter (cf. Judg 11:34), of the women celebrating David and Saul (cf. 1 Sam 18:6–7), or of Judith (cf. Judith 15:14–16:17). So Zedekiah, fleeing from humiliation, will find himself humiliated by a song (of defeat) intoned by those very same women who instead, in the tradition of Israel, extol the glory of a leader who is victorious. And so the theme of the "reversal" of fortunes returns yet again, in another respect, which, before the disaster has, above all, YHWH as its main object who, rather than fight to defend Israel, becomes its number one enemy (cf. 21:4–7 and what has already been highlighted in ch. III, § 4.1.3), and following the punitive event and seemingly definitive ruin, instead preannounces the otherwise inconceivable re-establishment of the Covenant, a return to the land, and the re-edification of Jerusalem and the temple (cf. 30:3, 18; 33:7, 11).

While these intertextual references help to better understand the content of the women's singing, other interesting data emerge by looking within the book of Jeremiah itself. The question once again regards the fact that certain communicative phenomena (only) become evident when semiotic *arcatas* are traced over a distance, even between different textual units. In the places where formal and/or semantic elements are presented, *regularities* can be found that serve, in fact, to render a message expressed on a different level than that which can be localised during a first act of reading. In this case, the content of the song of the women seems to further reinforce a dual relation that has already been highlighted: that between the first (vv. 1–13) and the second part of chapter 38 (vv. 14–28a), and that between the prototypical prophetic figure of Jeremiah and his interlocutor called to recognise and embrace, as "prophet", the same word.

A first, immediate allusion is to the unit immediately preceding that of 38:14–28a, that is, 38:1–13. Indeed, textual elements return that recall the descent of Jeremiah into the muddy cistern (38:6). Both Jeremiah and Zedekiah "sink" (√טבע) into the mud.

---

200   The accusation of the women is directed at the ministers, in order to not attack the king directly (and perhaps, therefore, not amount to the crime of "lese-majesty", as is noted by M.J. de JONG, *Isaiah*, 247–248, as regards the lack of any polemical reference to the king Hezekiah in the oracles of Isaiah concerning the events of 705–701). Also in the "Letter to God" by Esarhaddon, which I already cited in the historical part (cf. ch. II, § 3.3.2.5), the king of Shubria, who had disobeyed the command Esarhaddon, of whom he was a vassal, tries to justify himself by blaming the fault on his advisors, who were held to be guilty of having led him astray with their lies (cf. R. BORGER, *Die Inschriften Asarhaddons*, 103, Gbr. II, col. I: 20: "Meine fürstlichen Berater haben mir Lügen und Ruchlosigkeiten erzählt [...]"; RINAP 4, 82, nm. 33, col. I: 20: "The nobles, my advisors, spoke unwholesome lies to me [...]"; on this theme, see also G.B. LANFRANCHI, «Ideological Implications», 100).

Exegetic focalisations

While the regent verb is the same, the terms referring to "mud" are not identical (in 38.6: טיט [2x]; while in 38:22, the hapax בץ appears), but it is not hard to understand that the reality signified is the same,[201] even though טיט appears in two psalms that invoke or celebrate precisely the salvific intervention of YHWH for those who trust in him (cf. Ps 40:3; 68:15). The relationship, while it traces some significant analogies, is demarcated in an oppositional sense. Jeremiah placed his trust in God and was freed, but no one will pull Zedekiah out of the situation in which, human factors aside, ultimately his own disobedience has placed him. I am speaking about it as if it were a fact that had already occurred, but let us recall that the Jeremianic vision is conditional; it reveals dramatic facts that, while consequential and certain, are dependent upon the possibility of surrender being rejected.

Other interesting semantic references that intensify the analogic relationship I have highlighted can be detected between the "prophecy" of the women and the well-known passage of the "confessions" in 20:7–18. Both Jeremiah and Zedekiah fall prey to deception, prevarication, and ridicule.[202] And yet, while Jeremiah's experience is that of a man who *surrenders* to the will of YHWH, who exposes him to death but eventually saves him, Zedekiah, on the other hand, refuses to *hand himself over to the king of Babylon* for fear of humiliation, allows himself to be carried away by his ministers, and does not trust in YHWH, who reveals himself in Jeremiah. And for this, he heads straight for complete and total failure.

3.2.8. Pre-vision (II): Fire and responsibility

Let me now return briefly to the textual questions that concern vv. 22–23, already addressed in the presentation of the text in question, since further considerations can be made from a few clues therein.

In reference to the vocalisation of הטבעו (v. 22), I will reiterate that I see no valid reason to not accept the ho. form of the MT: "your feet *have sunk* in the mud". The meaning seems clear,[203] even admitting that the transition from one subject to another

---

201 On the meaning of the term בץ, there do not seem to be doubts. See in *HALAT*, 141 (which gives the translation "Schlammensand" for certain) the evident relationship between the Hebrew בץ and the related terms of other languages that mean "mud".

202 In fact, already in 20:7–8, 10, there are verbs present that speak of deception, violence, and prevarication of one subject on another. Jeremiah asserts (cf. 20:7) that he was seduced or deceived (√פתה pi.) by YHWH, and acknowledges that he had let himself be seduced/deceived, to have been forced (√חזק) by those who could prevail (√יכל) over him easily. Obeying YHWH had made him an object of ridicule and mockery on the part of all. It is significant that precisely his response to his vocation exposes him (cf. 20:8, 10), on the part of all his enemies (אֱנוֹשׁ שְׁלוֹמִי; "the men of my peace"), to desire his "fall" (צֶלַע), that he may be deceived (√פתה pu.), that he may be prevailed (√יכל) over, and that revenge (נִקְמָה + √לקח) may be taken on him. As can be seen, the semantic field has many traits in common with what is expressed in 38:22.

203 Even if this verb does not get traced back to the אַנְשֵׁי שְׁלֹמֶךְ as its subject, the historical situation may well suggest the vain help of Egypt; cf. D. BARTHÉLEMY, *Critique textuelle*, 719–720: "La situation historique s'accorde bien avec le hofal du *M: les alliés égyptiens de Sédécias ont séduit le roi en lui laissant espérer qu'ils l'aideraient s'il se trouvait en difficulté. Or ces alliés ont fait demi-tour (37,7) et ont abandonné

550   Jer 38:14–28a. Jeremiah and Zedekiah: The final colloquy

is rather abrupt. But this should come as no surprise, considering that 38:22–23 is regardless a brief insertion of a text with poetic characteristics into a narrative context.

A second, more interesting point, of a textual nature, instead concerns the form תִּשָּׂרֹף (v. 23b). To the letter, keeping to the MT, the complete phrase reads just as I have translated it: "and you *will burn* this city *with fire*". The rabbinical interpretation following Kimhi and Rashi already saw this as an underscoring of the king's personal responsibility for the destruction of the city. W. Rudolph suggests, both in his commentary[204] and in the critical apparatus of BHS in which he edited the part related to Jeremiah (though here, with some doubts), vocalising תִּשָּׂרֵף ("will be burned"), on the basis of a few manuscripts, the Peshitta, the Targum, and above all, the LXX (καὶ ἡ πόλις αὔτη κατακαυθήσεται). In fact, this is the reading that has reached almost all of the modern versions.[205] If the phrase is to be understood thus, however, the presence of the marker of the accusative would need to be explained. This would seem to invite us to not amend the MT and to instead read וְאֶת־הָעִיר הַזֹּאת as an object and not as the subject of the verb שׂרף. According to W. McKane,[206] this was an intrusion caused by the later rabbinical interpretation, while this time, Barthélemy's usually conservative approach (compared to the MT) stops only to maintain את, judged along with other authors to be admissible beside to the subject of a (correct) passive form.[207]

We find ourselves, in summary, before two different textual traditions, both authoritative, represented respectively by the MT and LXX. Both present evidence, but also some difficulties, albeit in reverse order. On the one hand, the LXX offers a reading that is perhaps too "pat", in the sense that it presents us with what we would have expected from the elements provided previously (cf. vv. 17–18). The doubt is that this is a harmonisation. Indeed, the MT seems to have evidence of precisely this right in its text[208]: not only the Masoretical vocalisation (well attested, against few other manuscripts), but also the same particle את, which, in most cases, indicates the direct object of the verb,[209] seems to actually call attention to the king's accountability with allegations,[210] as in the translation I have proposed. But the difficulty lies precisely

---

      Sédécias dans le bourbier où il s'est mis du fait de sa rivolte contre Nabuchodonosor (Ez 17,13–16)."

204   W. RUDOLPH, *Jeremia*, 242.

205   Cf. NEB: "(This city) will be burnt down"; RSV: "(This city) shall be burned"; RL: "(diese Stadt) wird [...] verbrannt werden"; TOB: "(la ville) est incendiée". Interestingly, the 1980 EÜ edition had: "diese Stadt aber wird man in Brand stecken", while the revised 2016 edition now has "diese Stadt aber wirst du im Feuer verbrennen". Cf. J. DE WAARD, *A Handbook on Jeremiah*, TCT 2, Winona Lake 2003, 149–150.

206   Cf. W. McKANE, *Jeremiah*, II, 961.

207   Thus, amongst others, also JM §128*b*.

208   And, in fact, already C.F. KEIL, *Jeremia*, 392 believed the emendation of the text to be inopportune.

209   There are, however, some exceptions, as has already been pointed to by P. VOLZ, *Jeremia*, 270. Cf. also JM §125*j*: "There are a certain number of cases where את precedes a noun which cannot be regarded, even virtually, as the object. These cases are difficult to explain [...]." In particular, see the following cases traced in the book of Jeremiah itself where את precedes the subject of the proposition: 35:14a; 38:4a; 50:20a.

210   According to A. VARUGHESE, «The Royal Family in the Jeremiah Tradition», in: *Inspired Speech*, 319–328, the Jeremianic tradition would impute the gravest

Exegetic focalisations 551

in this sudden shift in meaning (cf. v. 18) that does not seem to be in tune with the narrative flow.

The local management of the meaning, controlled by the flux of the communicative interactions between the interlocutors, could in fact initially suggest that my proposal be an exegesis that is "un peu trop subtile".[211] Here again, however, in my opinion, what remains crucial is that the gaze upon the text be capable of "hermeneutical memory" with respect to the narrative path already developed. And so, the possibility of tracing a new semiotic *arcata* between analogous situations that, placed in reciprocal relation, lose their bizarre *singularity* and instead configure an interesting *regularity*. The question is that of returning to ch. 28, and then to another text, already studied, that thematises the need for submission to the king of Babylon and stages a dialogue between Jeremiah and another interlocutor, the prophet Hananiah. In particular, in 28:13, as I underscored,[212] the accusation made by Jeremiah in the name of YHWH can be understood as a stigmatisation of Hananiah's responsibilities in the intensification of the disaster: "You have broken the crossbars of wood, but by doing so, *you have made* (וְעָשִׂיתָ) bars of iron in place of them".

If, therefore, one could agree in the abstract with the hypothesis[213] of a genesis of the reading of the MT from a probable Masoretic *rereading* influenced by the position of the particle את, what the distant relation just highlighted would suggest to us instead would be the presence of a "pre-Masoretic" communicative intentionality that instead conveys a theological *reinterpretation* of the responsibility of the individual *in the face of the prophetic appeal*. This would open an interesting path of reflection on the relationship between corporate responsibility and individual responsibility in the light of the general economy of the book of Jeremiah: while on the one hand, it is pointed out that personal choices have an impact that is significantly wider than that of one's individual fate (especially if this be a king or a prophet), on the other, in 31:29,[214] the emphasis seems to instead shift to individual responsibility, emphasising that a deliberate distance be taken from a traditional sort of sapiential vision where children suffer the effects of their fathers' faults.

Even though the theological line expressed in 31:29 would be secondary,[215] since it is dependent on Ezek 18:2 and, in general, on the context of Ezek 18 and the overall theological framework of this other prophetic book (in which this statement finds greater thematic and lexical relevance), the fact remains that in the current configuration of the Jeremianic work, a dialectic is introduced that invites more in-depth reflection. Here, it suffices to note that the involvement or not of the children in the faults of their fathers raises the issue of the effects of exercising human freedom

---

responsibility for the disaster of 587 to the Davidic sovereigns and the members of the royal family.

211 Cf. D. BARTHÉLEMY, *Critique textuelle*, 722: "Cette exégèse semble pourtant un peu trop subtile. Mieux vaut admettre avec Venema que 'la vocalisation massorétique a méconnu ici un cas de passif ayant maintenu le complément d'object (du verbe actif) introduit par la particule את'."
212 See ch. IV, § 2.2, n. 29 (and also § 4.1.7).
213 Cf. D. BARTHÉLEMY, *Critique textuelle*, 722.
214 "'In those days, they shall no longer say: 'The parents ate sour grapes and the children's teeth are set on edge'."
215 Cf. W.L. HOLLADAY, *Jeremiah 2*, 163.

in the face of *clearly codified and perpetually valid* questions of *"law and justice"* (מִשְׁפָּט וּצְדָקָה; cf. Ezek 18:5) according to the law of Israel (cf. Ezek 18:6–9) and that the (denied or affirmed) level of dependency is a temporal and intergenerational level.

The consequences of the responsibility invoked by our text (and by the case of Hananiah), even while implicitly affecting this last dimension as well, refer instead to the attitude of human freedom in the face of a *prophetic word that proposes to be decisive for the assumption of the meaning of history revealed by YHWH here and now*. The effects, more than being placed along a temporal axis, extend almost immediately to the fate of their own contemporaries. In this dialectic, it can also be noted, however, that the development of the biblical tradition moves forward prevalently through thematic-theological juxtapositions and not through synthetic re-elaborations, this operation being left to the hermeneutical act of the reader.

For our thematic, in any case, the matter is that of highlighting that the question of the fate of King Zedekiah, rather than being attributable to an unlikely "redactional debate",[216] reveals itself to be deeply intertwined with that of all of Jerusalem. What gets accentuated in a particular way are the sudden changes of scene and the interconnections that are dependent upon the unpredictable trajectories of human liberty. The reader, in fact, already knows the outcome of this dramatic story perfectly well, as well as the fate of Zedekiah, the different Jeremianic oracles that concern him aside. Calling into question the responsibility of human beings in the person of the last king of Jerusalem hence means underscoring the almost "cosmic" scope of human liberty and its capacity to redesign or disrupt the paths of history: to the last instant, nothing is fixed or predetermined in an entirely absolute way, because the human being is allowed to change even the very decisions of God.[217] The entire fate of Jerusalem is now placed back into the hands of a man (who believes he can do nothing), a man called to hand himself over freely to the enemies (who believe they prevail in all things; cf. 50:17, 23; 51:20–23). It is the only path of salvation that remains, for in reality, the question is that of surrendering oneself into the hands of God, the true Lord of history.

3.3. Third part (vv. 24–27): From the Word to words, towards the silence of the end

3.3.1. First impression: Vain wisdom and a futile interrogation

The entire third part of our pericope, recounting the king's ploy to keep secret the entire content of the colloquy with Jeremiah, gives the impression of being extraneous to the general topic of the text analysed thus far. Zedekiah interrupts the dialogue without offering any further response to the central question, and dwells at length

---

216   As is maintained by J. Applegate, «The Fate of Zedekiah».

217   In this perspective, it appears to be inopportune to speak of a "breakdown of the paradigm of human responsibility" (thus, J. Applegate, «The Fate of Zedekiah», 303) as an essential prerequisite for any hope of salvation according to the book of Jeremiah. This is an interpretation that, rather than make sense of the Jeremianic text, seems to want to unilaterally impose the logic of the Lutheran "sola gratia" on it.

Exegetic focalisations 553

on providing the prophet with vigilant instructions in anticipation of threatening interference from the court dignitaries.[218]

In a certain sense, however, we could observe, on the contrary, that there is a strong continuity between the second and third parts. The fear that the king confesses in v. 19 as the main obstacle to receiving the prophetic word indeed dominates all of Zedekiah's behaviour and multiplies his words in a way that is completely *irrelevant* to the indications of the prophetic message, to such an extent that his speech and specific instructions end up constituting quantitatively most of the textual fabric of the last unit (a good nine verbal forms can be counted in just v. 25).[219] I, on the other hand, will dedicate a less extensive comment to them than I have to the previous units. Just enough at least to highlight that what enters the scene in the (non-) response of the king is an intelligence that, the more it captures particular and meticulous aspects of the real, the more it loses sight of the overall meaning revealed in the present moment. Indeed, the king proves to be most concerned about his own personal safety and puts an articulated strategy into play to safeguard himself (and even the act of escape in 39:4 need be seen in this perspective), but this is *vain wisdom*, completely ruinous from the perspective of what truly matters at this theological-political juncture.

Zedekiah does not feel the need to respond affirmatively to Jeremiah's call, despite the urgency of the moment, but it is precisely this choice (and the text signals this to us almost in passing) that closes the narrative circle. And what is taking place is not a happy ending, as some lexical clues would also suggest. Indeed, from the "word" (דָּבָר) or "voice" (קוֹל) of God, requested and revealed through the prophet, object and subject of the first two parts (cf. vv. 14, 20; cf. 37:6),[220] it shifts to the "words" (דְּבָרִים) of humankind, placed in a much lower and even petty plane. Simple words seem to have become for the king the "Word" announced by Jeremiah (cf. v. 24). The prophet himself now speaks with the "words" (דְּבָרִים) of the king (v. 27), and only words to be censored come to needlessly interrogate the leaders (cf. 27), not an oracle that comes from YHWH.[221] Perhaps then, when the narrator concludes that "the word" (הַדָּבָר) had not been heard, he is not noting only that "*nothing* had been heard" of the conversation between the king and the prophet, but perhaps also involuntarily suggesting a bitter

---

218 As v. 19 already suggested, Zedekiah seems to fear some members of his own people (anti-Babylonian dignitaries) much more than he does the "official" enemy.

219 As is noted by G. FISCHER, *Jeremia 26–52*, 343, this can also be understood as a reflection of the tortuousness and complexity of the world of deception and lies.

220 In 37:2, however, reference is made to the prophetic message as "the words of the Lord" (דִּבְרֵי יְהוָה) pronounced through Jeremiah. This dual reference to the divine revelation, first in the singular and then in the plural, can lead to think of two complementary aspects that distinguish it: on the one hand, the uniqueness of the Word, expression of its transcendence, on the other, its repeated historical manifestations, which take the shape and voice of the multiple human words of prophets in general and of Jeremiah in particular. This relationship is already indicated in a programmatic way from the title of the book, where the "words/actions of Jeremiah" (דִּבְרֵי יִרְמְיָהוּ) are placed in tight correlation with the only "word of the Lord" (דְּבַר־יְהוָה) revealed to him (cf. 1:1, 2).

221 It is interesting to note that in closing there is a return of the same verb (√שאל) that had introduced the request on the part of the king for an oracle from Jeremiah.

554   Jer 38:14–28a. Jeremiah and Zedekiah: The final colloquy

ascertainment: it is "*the* word" of God that has not been heard or obeyed. Instead, "words" have prevailed, the reasonings and fears of humankind.

3.3.2. *Jeremiah and the silencing of the prophecy: Picking back up and developing a problematic theme*

"Let no one know about these words, and you will not die" (v. 24). The king's response to Jeremiah sounds ambiguous: is it a benevolent warning intended to shield the prophet from a mortal danger coming from others, or a personal threat? Perhaps even the king himself cannot make up his mind on this either. In any case, what is immediately called into question is the theme of *secrecy* that had been introduced from the very beginning, by the oath by which Zedekiah privately pledged to ensure the prophet's safety (v. 16). The king adds a clause that had not been agreed upon: Jeremiah will not be able to speak to anyone about the content of their encounter. And it is now clear that the protection offered concerned only the basic intention of the king, but did not preserve him from the hostile intentions of the ministers of the court who dominate over Zedekiah.[222] If the fact of the encounter cannot be kept hidden, the only defence the sovereign can pose against them is to obscure its contents, effectively forcing Jeremiah to lie. And so, the Babylonians besiege Jerusalem from the outside, the leaders besiege the king and the prophet from the inside, and the king himself puts pressure on the prophet. But it is Jeremiah's "surrendering" attitude that is most challenging to us, the only subject of the narration who does not seem to place any *resistance* now.

We had, in fact, already encountered the subject of the silence or "surrender" of the prophet before his opponents in the context of the public confrontation with Hananiah (cf. 28:11).[223] There, Jeremiah was seen deciding to not reply to his opponent, leaving in fact the whole scene saturated with an antithetical (pseudo-)prophetic word. Here, something similar happens, though also quite different and perhaps even more problematic. We are no longer in the presence of a silencing of the prophetic voice, as the prophet himself had done, but instead, on the part of Jeremiah, of acceptance of a silence desired by his interlocutor, who imposes a *substitution* of the prophetic word with his own human words.[224] The question is not, therefore, that of a potentially

---

222 In Dan 6:13–17, it is instead Darius the Mede who is subjected to pressure from his court dignitaries. In 2 Sam 21:17, the (in this case, positive) influence of the "men of David" (אַנְשֵׁי־דָוִד) over their sovereign is attested as he is pressured to not risk his life in battle.

223 Cf. ch. IV, § 5.3.

224 Actually, the king seems to be even more cunning (G. FISCHER, *Jeremia 26–52*, 343) because he puts in Jeremiah's mouth words of supplication that the prophet himself had addressed to him in another context (cf. 38:26 with 37:15, 20). It seems, in any case, ironic at the least that the words suggested by the king to Jeremiah as a path of *salvation* would contain the same verbal root (נפל√), though with a different syntagmatic construction (נפל√ part. hi. + תְּחִנָּה): "lay down, place before, the plea [in front of someone]"), utilised in 21:9 by Jeremiah to refer to the act of *surrender* (נפל√ + עַל־הַכַּשְׂדִּים): "fall, fall down before the Chaldeans"), that is, the only path of salvation put before Zedekiah himself. For a study of the vocabulary of the surrender, I will defer to ch. VI, § 3.5.

Exegetic focalisations 555

neutral silence (if this were ever even possible in the communicative field), but of an order to deliver compromising or completely false words.[225] Words no longer put on Jeremiah's mouth by YHWH, according to the paradigm of the originary vocational event (cf. 1:9),[226] but only by a man frightened by the truth (of the prophecy itself), unable to assume the responsibility before his adversaries of making a clear choice for the good of his people. With this, however, we are not outside of the prophetic phenomenon, for to speak of prophecy is to question the significance of the signs (first of all, those that are linguistic), and the signs can lend themselves to mediation of the truth or as a propagation of lies.[227]

To ask a prophet not to speak (v. 24), when his identity is founded precisely on the mystery of the word (cf. Deut 18:18; Jer 18:18), seems to be the intimation of a radical prohibition: that of *not being a prophet* (cf. Isa 30:10; Amos 2:12; 7:12–13:16; Mi 2:6). Already, the inhabitants of Anathoth had tried to stifle the prophetic word that came from the mouth of their fellow citizen, threatening him with death (cf. 11:21). Here, however, the vortex of the lie denounced by Jeremiah in 9:1–8, a man sent to reveal the truth in a society where everyone, including the prophets, speak falsities, seems to eventually swallow up even the prophet himself. The theme is not one to be underestimated.[228] The one who had gone through and overcome his fears, trusting the word of the Lord of history (cf. 27:5–6) and presenting himself as being strong only in His word against the most important authorities of the kingdom of Judah (cf. e.g. 1:4–10, 17–19; 20:1–2; 26; 27; 36; 37; 38:1–13), now seems to withdraw himself and be concerned only about his own safety at the cost of a dissimulating word. Obedience to YHWH presented him with a way to face a war (cf. 1:17–19), obedience to the king means that his opponents "ceased speaking with him" (v. 27: מִמֶּנּוּ וַיַּחֲרִשׁוּ). Or so it seems. Or perhaps there is something more, and a deeper rereading is possible? I believe that at least two important clarifications can be made in this regard.

Firstly, it should be noted that, beyond the possible moral implications,[229] the text poses the question above all of a prophetic word that *no longer exposes itself,* which

---

225 On this topic, see M.A. KLOPFENSTEIN, *Die Lüge nach dem Alten Testament. Ihre Begriff, ihre Bedeutung und ihre Beurteilung,* Zürich 1964.

226 "The Lord extended his hand and touched my mouth, and the Lord said to me: 'Behold, I place my words in your mouth'."

227 In this sense, U. Eco defined semiotics, a discipline having the study of signs as its object, as a "theory of the lie" (cf. U. ECO, *Trattato di semiotica generale,* Milano 1975, [16]1998, 17 [Eng. tr.: ID., *A Theory of Semiotics,* London 1976, 6]).

228 In my opinion, a text as allusive as the Jeremianic text, which continually provokes the reader to reflect upon and connect even distant thematic elements, does not need to further mark the importance of the question (as would be presumed, e.g. by G. WANKE, *Jeremia.* Teilband 2: Jeremia 25,15–52,34, ZBK.AT 20.2, Zürich 1995, 354).

229 For some interpreters (cf. R.W.L. MOBERLY, *Prophecy and Discernment,* 88–95, in dialogue with the position taken by R.P. Carroll), the lie of Jeremiah would be an immorality comparable to that for which the (false) prophets of Jerusalem are accused by Jeremiah himself (cf. 23:14–40). In my opinion, as can be seen from what I have highlighted in this paragraph, the issue is quite another. See also the opposition between the words of Micaiah and those of the other prophets regarding the king's military intentions 1 Kgs 22:20–23. The biblical narrator here makes Micaiah say that the deceitful response of the other prophets was caused not by their dishonesty but by the fact that a "spirit of lies" (שֶׁקֶר רוּחַ) had fallen upon them, sent by YHWH

remains silent about the truth of things in the face of an explicit *desire to oppose* the Word itself. Ultimately, this is the same communicative perspective with which our text opens (cf. v. 15): Jeremiah, though in a provocatory manner, is shown to be reticent about the king's request for an oracle, reproaching him for exactly the fierce and stubborn aversion he has suffered up to that point, even from him. But now, the case is even more serious, and the obscuring of the prophetic word becomes even more of a *sign of the* impending *end* (cf. Ezek 3:26; 24:27; 33:22). If, in addition to the linguistic and gestural expressions, silence can also be a significant form of communication in a dialogic exchange, especially in the prophetic sphere, what should be recognised in Jeremiah's behaviour is an implicit denunciation (signalled to the reader) that what we now face is a pervicacious and invincible will to reject the prophecy. The Jeremianic "silence", therefore, sounds like a judgment of condemnation for those who, like the "leaders" (שָׂרִים) of Judah, have closed all spaces off from the prospect of listening.

According to another perspective of meaning, not opposite but complementary to the first, one can also read a sign of deep divine compassion towards human frailty in the prophet's choice, that is, an *extreme form of condescension* that exceeds even the abstract principles of fidelity and truth (understood in the classic referential sense) in order to encourage the acceptance of good. As in ch. 28, where the silence of the prophet was aimed at preserving a horizon of meaning for the word, waiting for it to be transfigured anew in the Word of God and thus become a word of truth (cf. 28:11–12), in our text, the choice of Jeremiah preserves a margin of vital space intact for his interlocutor so a salvific acquiescence can germinate in it. It is in this sense that the prophet thinks not so only of his own safety, but also of the life of the king, threatened by his own ministers.

Jeremiah's lie is therefore only formal, and does not seem to have any moral relevance. The fact remains that the Jeremianic prophecy goes so far as to even disfigure its own face, indulging the king's request in order to grant a last, final *space of freedom* that allows Zedekiah to discern, decide, and determine without any further pressure, if not the helpless word of the captive prophet.[230] But the king does not decide.[231] And not deciding is already deciding. Because reality still needs to be confronted.[232] Events take their course, and the end really does come.

---

himself. The episode would merit specific commentary. Here, it suffices to note the not-immediate overlappability, in the biblical context (and particularly in the prophetic one), between lies and immoral conduct (cf. also 1 Kgs 13:18 and 2 Kgs 8:10).

230 The meekness of the prophet in this situation stands out even more when compared to the tenor of the words of the king (cf. vv. 14, 24) and his dignitaries (v. 25), a use that is very similar to that which resorts to imposition and intimidation (cf. G. FISCHER, *Jeremia 26–52*, 343).

231 The words come to mind with which the prophet Elijah stigmatises the indecision and ambiguity of the people, called upon to decide between Baal and YHWH (cf. 1 Kgs 18:21). The prophetic word illuminates a difference there where one does not want to see it: the path of life is not the path of death.

232 As rightly noted by W. BRUEGGEMANN, *To Build, To Plant*, 154: "In the world of prophetic reality, powerful leaders are offered an option of life, often an option that appears to be too costly politically. The prophetic word is uncompromising and unaccommodating of such political cost. A prophetic reading of reality finally makes no deals. It simply waits for reality to be faced."

3.3.3. Epilogue: The City falls, the Word is fulfilled, the end sets the Meaning free

"And so Jeremiah remained in the guard's yard *until the day Jerusalem was taken*" (v. 28a). For the last time, acting as the final term, we see the return of the already highlighted phrase that marked the structuring of chs. 37–38 along with the repetition of the verbal form וַיֵּשֶׁב with Jeremiah as its subject (cf. § 2.2). This time, however, a significant time limit is specified (עַד־יוֹם), which coincides with the fall of Jerusalem and the end of the kingdom of Judah (אֲשֶׁר־נִלְכְּדָה יְרוּשָׁלָם). The event marks an epochal turning point and is signalled, from the rhetorical point of view, by a *concentric composition*[233] that acts as a bridge between the end of ch. 38 and the beginning of ch. 39, where the narrator briefly summarises all the on-going drama, dwelling on the final moments and fate of Jeremiah (and Ebed-melech), with a comparison that is oppositive with respect to that of Zedekiah.

A)	28a	Thus, Jeremiah REMAINED in the courtyard of the guard	וַיֵּשֶׁב
B)		until the day *when Jerusalem was taken*.	אֲשֶׁר־נִלְכְּדָה יְרוּשָׁלָם
C)	28b	And it happened,	וְהָיָה
B')		*when Jerusalem was taken*.	כַּאֲשֶׁר נִלְכְּדָה יְרוּשָׁלָם
A')	39,1–3	In the ninth year [...] all the leaders of the king of Babylonia CAME (וַיָּבֹאוּ) and TOOK THEIR SEATS[234]	וַיֵּשְׁבוּ

The duration of the prophet's presence in a condition of captivity is the time granted to the king, a *prisoner* of his fear, to make a paradoxical choice of freedom. But it is not an infinite time. The insistent repetition, like a refrain, of the narrator's notation relating to Jeremiah's confinement in the prison courtyard also has an end, and this is significant. It is a reiteration that echoes the repetition of the infidelity of the people of YHWH, the repetition of the prophetic appeal, the repetition of the refusal to listen. As P. Beachamp notes, it is the *repetition* that generates the indifference, and it is the approaching of the end that re-establishes the Meaning of history in place, *freeing* it from the lie. It is a story of covenant, however things have gone up to this point.

> En face du maintenant comme différence, il est possible de vivre un maintenant indifférent, indifférent à l'accélération du mal et à l'épaississement du contentieux de l'alliance. Or mettre la relation entre Dieu et son peuple sous la raison de l'alliance, c'était poser que cette relation a sens; la vivre dans l'indifférence à son histoire età son moment, c'est y poser l'absence de sens. [...]. Cette conscience d'un temps gradué remplit le message prophétique. Ce temps gradué est un temps compté, en ce sens que c'est la fin qui rétablit le sens contre la dérision. L'alliance est un dialogue, qui ne peut se passer de vérité, fidélité, justice: quand celles-ci sont remises à un

---

233 Cf. G. FISCHER, *Jeremia 26–52*, 344.

234 In the opinion of more than a few commentators (who consider 39:1–2 to be a secondary addition), the phrase beginning in 38:28b (וְהָיָה כַּאֲשֶׁר נִלְכְּדָה יְרוּשָׁלָם) has its natural development or end point in 39:3.

558   Jer 38:14–28a. Jeremiah and Zedekiah: The final colloquy

> lendemain indéfini, le sens est réintroduit par le tragique. L'expérience humaine le dit et l'alliance n'a pas voulu parler à partir d'un autre lieu.[235]

On the ninth day of the month of Tammuz 586/587, after a long siege, a breach is opened in the wall of the city (cf. 2 Kgs 25:4; Jer 39:2; 52:7), the king and soldiers escape, and the armies of Babylon get the upper hand over the capital of the kingdom of Judah's resistance. About a month later, the seventh (2 Kgs 25:8) or the tenth day (52:12) of the month of Abib of the same year, Nebuzaradan, "the head of the guards" (רַב־טַבָּחִים) of Nebuchadnezzar destroys the temple and sets Jerusalem on fire. The fortunes turn: Jeremiah is freed from his condition of captivity (as is made explicit in 39:11–14; 40:1–6), while Zedekiah heads toward the *captivity* (and something even worse) that he had been threatened with as a consequence of his not-listening (38:18, 23). The fulfilment of the prophetic word coincides with its *liberation* and the revelation of its *power*. Power capable of destroying and eradicating, a creative force that, if it wants, can still build and plant something new (cf. 1:10; 24:6; 31:28).

It is significant that in ch. 39, in the framework of the narration of the end of Jerusalem, no mention is made of the destruction of the temple, holy site *par excellence* and sign of YHWH's presence amongst his people. It is not an oversight, given that in the parallel story at the conclusion of the whole book, its fate will be clearly mentioned, with a detailed list of the temple furnishings removed from there by the Babylonians and mention of the death penalty inflicted on some religious authority figures (cf. 2 Kgs 25:9, 13–18, 21; Jer 52:13, 17–24, 27). It is, rather, one of the clues that the book of Jeremiah has taught us to pay attention to. That Presence, even though Ezekiel saw it move away from the temple (cf. Ezek 10:18), seems to remain in another form in precisely the body of the prophet[236] handed over and saved from death, just as it remains, analogously, in the literary body of the prophecy that speaks of him and attests to his paradigmatic function. Still today.

4. Conclusions: The king and the prophet, a paradigmatic dramatisation of human-divine communication

Like other, extrabiblical experiences attested in the ancient Near East, also biblical prophecy set in the pre-exilic period has a structural relationship with the monarchical institution and with political events involving the fate of the state. It is therefore not surprising that from the book's title, the Jeremianic work engages the most important royal figures of the final years of the kingdom of Judah, and not only for motives of historical-temporal positioning. A great semiotic *arcata* immediately creates a bold bridge of signification between the beginning and the end of the book (ch. 52), where the names of the kings return (Zedekiah and Jehoiachin, in place of Jehoiakim) and, together with the event of the deportation, already tell the meaning of an entire history, its failure, and its hope beyond the failure.

---

235   P. Beauchamp, *L'un et l'autre Testament*, 103.

236   On this subject, see, in particular, the observations of G. Fischer, «"Ich Mache Dich… zur eisernen Säule" (Jer 1,18). Der Prophet als besserer Ersatz für den untergegangenen Tempel», *ZKTh* 116 (1994) 447–450.

The prophetic injunction to "deliver oneself to the king of Babylon" had to be, by necessity, a call upon the king himself first, especially since he himself had interrogated the prophet in the hope of receiving from him a favourable oracle in the context of the Babylonian invasion of the kingdom of Judah (cf. 21:1–10). The con-textual insertion (with regard to the section of chs. 21–24) of this consultation at a distance, as we have seen, thematises, more than anything else, at the level of structural semiotics, the key to a prophetic reading of the catastrophe already well known to the reader: it is the surrender, and the end that one should accept along with that surrender that penetrates the enigma of events. On the level of content, then, the royal interlocutor served to refract the presentation of the alternative between the path of life and that of death onto all his ministers and, above all, onto the entire people of Judah. With the diptych of 38:1–13 and 38:14–28a (cf. § 2.1–2), on the other hand, the king and prophet are deliberately placed *one in front of the other*, but one could also say *one against the other* and *one in favour of the other*. And all in favour of the hermeneutical act of the reader.

4.1. One in front of the other. Literary context and semiotic polarisations

In 38:1–13, the through line of the entire book of Jeremiah immediately resurfaces, that is, the radical oppositional relationship between life and death. The paths leading to them are not made explicit as in 21:8–10, where the direct reference is to the theme of surrender, but the horizon of meaning is the same. Jeremiah is the man delivered to an obedience to his ministry, asks for surrender to the king of Babylon and for this, is thrown into the cistern to die there. From the bottom of the pit of death, in a completely unexpected way, the path of salvation opens up before him, in accordance with the vocational promise in 1:8, 18–19. Yes, life and death are therefore in antithesis, but placed along the course of a freedom that has an orientation, on a journey. The king's own freedom is solicited in 38:14–28a to run along the same course, for the alternatives at stake are the same, only that what presents itself before him (and the reader) is the living *paradigm* of the Meaning that he is called to obey, namely Jeremiah, the man (self-)delivered and for this reason, saved.

On the level of *literary architecture* (cf. § 2.4–5), I have highlighted some structural regularities that connect over at a distance that allow us to identify a true and proper semiotic paradigm of reference underlying the comprehension of the message of Jeremiah: *whoever hands themself over will live*. This "paradigm of the delivered" is read on a first level of explicitness as: whoever hands themself over in (this precise) obedience to YHWH, *will live despite it all*. In this sense, the analogous dynamic found in the first instance in the relation between the diptych of ch. 38 and the polarity established between chapters 26 and 27 (cf. § 2.4) is indicative: also in Jer 27, what is presented on the scene of the text before Judah and all nations, with the call to the submission that saves, is the figure of the prophet just delivered into the hands of men in obedience to YHWH and for this, saved. This encouraging clue has led to the widening of the inquiry (cf. § 2.5) to the whole second part of the book of Jeremiah (26–45), where we can find a series of *analogous semiotic arcatas* (36 and 45; 40:1–6 and 42) and *two principal attractors* who preside over the general organisation of the whole section: 1) the thematic polarity of the "end" (38:28b–39:1–10) and the "new beginning" (chs. 30–31; 32–33, and 39:11–14); 2) the polarity formed by the structural relationship between: (a)

560   Jer 38:14–28a. Jeremiah and Zedekiah: The final colloquy

the Jeremianic paradigm of "delivering oneself"–"being saved", and (b) that of the analogous request to "deliver oneself" to the king of Babylon as a path of salvation. I have thus been able to present a reasoned structuring of both the local textual groupings and the entire second part of the book of Jeremiah.

4.2. One against the other, one for the other. Thematic-actantial polarisations, analogical relationships, and communicative dynamics

At the level of the thematic-narrative dynamic (cf. § 3), having found no good reason for identifying the stages of coherent judicial proceedings against Jeremiah in the textual scanning of chs. 37–38 (cf. § 3.1.1), I have instead emphasised the intrinsic necessity of the encounter between the king and the prophet, actants placed on the scene of the text as representatives of two distinct thematic-actantial roles. They cannot fail to meet but also to clash, they are placed one in front of the other as well as *one against the other* because both have a word to say about the fate of the people. Certainly, there is also a significant relationship between the fate of Jeremiah and that of Jerusalem, but it cannot be read in the sense of participation in a common judicial destiny without a precise distinction being made. Jeremiah is a figure of the one "delivered" in obedience to YHWH, for this, he faces death, and for this, he is saved. Jerusalem, on the other hand, is subjected to "judgment" for its infidelity and can save itself by going through misfortune along the course of meaning traced by the Jeremianic experience. But all this, as I said, is explicitly reiterated in a conclusive encounter between two distinct personal subjects. Where the ultimate destiny depends entirely on a discernment, on an obedience, and on a decision.

The prophet has or claims to have the word that can orient the action or events towards the meaning of history desired by YHWH, but he cannot do anything on a political level to save the people. The king has or would have this decision-making power, but if he wants to exercise it to accomplish good and not the ruin of the nation, he should obey the word of truth, discern it from the lie, and surrender to it. But indeed, between the king and the (true) prophet, barriers stand in the way, of other powers and other words that, on the one hand, intend to silence the adversarial prophetic word while, on the other, they try to bend the king to their wills. The king and the prophet are and remain one in front of the other, in a secret encounter, just like the call of YHWH and the consciousness of every single Israelite, who, in the king, finds the ideal essence of the human condition personified.

The king and the prophet are also one against the other because the former, when he does not persecute the prophet directly, if he does not accept his word, leaves him, in fact, at the mercy of his enemies (cf. 38:5), which the latter, instead, has never spared criticism, severe warnings, and threats to the crown (cf. chs. 21–24, in particular). Asking Jeremiah for yet another oracle, in return instead, in 38:15, Zedekiah sees his indecision be stigmatised as having a homicidal intent, even though, with this accusation, Jeremiah is actually seeking to create a final breach through which he can continue to reveal the salvific Word. And so, in this final encounter, not only is Jeremiah presented as a living figure of the very message he bears (cf. 38:1–13), but the process of communicating the prophetic word coming from YHWH and the possible modalities of its reception by humankind also become *dramatised* in a *paradigmatic* way. Zedekiah, in fact, just like Jeremiah before him, is called to overcome his fear,

Conclusions 561

to go through the symbolic death of surrender, trusting exclusively in the promise of YHWH's assistance. And here, the prophetic ministry proves to be entirely unbalanced *in favour* of the king and the welfare of the state, albeit in a way that is paradoxical.

The path of the surrender to Babylon takes the shape, in fact, of an option that is apparently anti-Isaianic, but even more so as an *inversion of the trajectory of the Exodus*. It is necessary to *leave* Jerusalem, which had been, with the land and the temple, the point of arrival and fulfilment of the founding *liberation*, to accept *to serve* the king of Babylon, subjecting himself to his yoke. An "anti-Exodus"? Formally, yes, but this expression should be reserved for the infaust journey taken by those who, following the catastrophe, opt to return to Egypt, disobeying the new prophetic indication to "deliver themselves" again to the king of Babylon, trusting in YHWH. On a close look, in fact, the path proposed by Jeremiah, precisely because it entails passing through a symbolic form of death (as through a new Sea of rushes), is the one that will render the "new Exodus" possible. Vocabulary that the book of Jeremiah effectively employs to announce, *after* the exile, the return and re-establishment of fortunes (cf. 16:14–15; 23:7–8), a possibility however that the call to surrender already prepares, directing the way.

In this encounter between the king and the prophet, where *in extremis* the salvation of the City would even be guaranteed (though the exile and the end of the Davidic monarchy do not appear to be excluded), what cannot be avoided is the *traumatic impact* with the transcendence that enters and reveals the meaning of history, asking to assume it, like the prophet, in one's own *body*. It is starting from the fear of Zedekiah, openly confessed on behalf of all, that I have drawn a comparison between the situation in which the king finds himself and the originary Jeremianic prophetic vocation. And we have seen how there are solid clues for tracing an analogical correspondence, in the sign of the need for an obediential discernment of the true word coming from YHWH and of a new "prophetic calling" to tell the meaning of the story underway. I therefore believe that we can speak about a phenomenon of *transmission* and *extension of the charism characteristic of the prophetic mediator.* But further investigations are needed in this direction.

If Jeremiah, by doing so, acts in favour of Zedekiah (and all of Jerusalem), then the latter also acts in favour of the prophet, though in a way that is ambiguous. The call for surrender remains unanswered. The king proves to be concerned that nothing of their conversation leak to his ministers. He protects it to protect himself, and thus, deep down, he protects himself from the Word itself, of which he requests *silence*. Not entering into the death that the prophetic word invited him to cross means, however, procuring it for himself and for all the people.

Ultimately, it can be said that the narrator, renouncing a presentation of the characters of the king and the prophet according to an expressive form of *telling*, which would involve making certain information explicit, moral judgments, intentions, etc., prefers to stimulate the hermeneutical act of the reader employing, once again, *external focalisation* and the procedure of *showing*. In this way, the actions and words of the characters are brought to the scene of the text, nothing more. The reader therefore knows and sees only that which the characters know and see, and becomes engaged in the same drama. But all of this provokes and favours its *hermeneutical pronouncement,* bearing in mind that the reader had already been invited, since the beginning of the book, to enter into the complexity of the Jeremianic semiosphere with some precise keys of interpretation. As we shall see (in ch. VII, § 2), these are two semiotic paradigms that tell how the Meaning is revealed and is to be assumed, that is, in the body and with the body, through a dynamism of education for discernment that gives shape to a *relational pragmatic of salvation.*

All of the readers of the Jeremianic text in fact already know the outcome of the story full well, even before reading or listening to the book of Jeremiah. But they do not really know *how* and *why* it came about as it did: so the invitation is not to collect bare factual information, but to question oneself about the meaning and to better understand the complex dynamic of revelation that was (and is) at stake. Because this does not end, and it challenges readers of all times, starting from a prophetic reading of the pertinent contexts.

PART III

"Whoever surrenders [...] shall live!"

HERMENEUTICS

Handing oneself over to the king of Babylon:
phenomenology and interpretation

> *You will say to this people: Thus says the Lord:*
> *Behold, I will set before you the path of life*
> *and the path of death:*
> *whoever remains in this city*
> *will die of the sword, of hunger, and of the plague:*
> *but whoever will go out and surrender to the*
> *Chaldeans laying you to siege shall live, and will*
> *have their own life as war booty (Jer 21:8–9).*

Chapter VI
The gesture of the surrender:
Phenomenology and symbolic apertures

Les symboles sont comme une parole de l'être.[1]

1. Phenomenology and symbolism. Starting from the linguistic and extralinguistic context

I have concluded the central part of my dissertation focusing on Jer 38:14–28a, that is, the text of the Jeremianic tradition that is perhaps the most emblematic with regard to the *dramatic necessity* of the act of surrender. The interpersonal communicative context, the representativity of the figures directly involved (the prophet and the king), the urgency of the moment established by the narrative (the proximity of the end), and the different anthropological dimensions called into question (the appeal to freedom, the fear of trusting, the relationship between truth and lies, etc.) make up a complex interweaving of significant thematics that relate to one another. The analytical study I have conducted thus far has allowed us to focus our attention on the most important elements of meaning innervated in the text. From this exegetic base, I will now focus my attention on the central thematic core around which everything revolves, for the gesture that Jeremiah requests is presented by the prophet as the most appropriate response, intimated by YHWH himself, to the significance of the historical events taking place. Understanding what it means to "hand oneself over to the king of Babylon" implicates, first of all, a *phenomenological study* of the theme that redimensionalises and reorients our modern precomprehensions regarding the notion of "surrender", valorising the contextual horizon in a pragmatic-cognitive sense. Beginning, therefore, from the most pertinent linguistic and extralinguistic references, it will be possible to better establish my interpretive proposal and configure a general hermeneutic of the Jeremianic message that takes into account the possible *symbolic apertures* activated by it.

2. Preliminary considerations: The surrender and its *frame* of reference in a pragmatic and symbolic perspective

For study of the "yoke" theme attested in chs. 27–28, I turned to the *Frame Semantics*[2] linguistic approach of Charles J. Fillmore, a theoretical system of a cognitive matrix that emphasises the existing continuity between language and experience, and thus the relevance of the "inferential model" over that of the classic "code model".

---

1   P. Ricœur, *Le conflit des interprétations*. Essais d'herméneutique, Paris 1969, 315.
2   For some essential data on this theory of the linguistic significance, see what has already been noted in ch. IV, § 4.1.4 (esp. in n. 138).

566 The gesture of the surrender

Communication takes place not through individual lexemes or statements, but rather through complex communicative units that lead to the individual *encyclopaedia* of each subject. The meaning of a lexeme must therefore be placed in relation with the capacity to frame individual semantic data within relevant schematisations of the world experience of the speakers (the "type scenes", or *frames*). A *frame* is a minimal narrative structure in which all the elements are interconnected, a logical-semantic unit that allows for the coherence or meaning of speech or text to be grasped. Therefore, it is not possible to focalise the significance of a lexeme (or of any linguistic expression) without this implicating inferential access to the entire encyclopaedic knowledge of the speaker (or interpreter) associated to that lexical data.[3] Semantics and pragmatics, according to this perspective, are indistinguishable.

The FrameNet project, developed by the International Computer Science Institute of Berkeley since 1997, is based on these fundamental assumptions.[4] It is the compilation of a lexical database for the English language (and, in parallel projects, also other languages) accessible online that, to date, associates more than 13,000 individual fundamental lexemes with about 1,200 different "semantic frames" and "semantic roles", in other words, to just as many contexts of use evoked by *lexical units* with their relative exemplifications (more than 200,000). For my research, it is interesting to keep in mind the treatment of the concept of surrender mediated by the lexeme "surrendering", because it offers us the focal point from which my underlying methodological perspective is generated.

> Here is a description of the *frame* of reference with its relative examples (shown without the various chromatic markings). Definition: "In this frame a Fugitive presents himself or himself to the Authorities to be subject to the criminal process". Examples: "The bank robber surrendered to Berkeley police. Norte is expected to surrender to police tomorrow on tax fraud charges". This is followed by reporting the *frame elements* (FE) that are central ("core FEs"), such as "Authorities" and "Fugitives" and the secondary frame elements ("non-core FSs"), which contribute to the configuration of the constitutive elements of the type-scene (Charges: The Charges is the offense for which the Fugitive is wanted; Explanation: This FE denotes a proposition from which the surrendering event logically follows; Manner: This FE identifies the Manner in which the Fugitive surrenders to the Authorities; Place is the location where the surrendering occurs; Time [Semantic Type: Time is when the Fugitive surrenders).

The network of semantic-pragmatic elements generated constitutes the underlying *frame* in which every individual component can find its right collocation, in synchronic reference to all the others. To speak of "surrender" means recalling that scene of reference. Clearly, the definition offered by FrameNet cannot be assumed as such in my research, but only as a methodological exemplification. The problem, in fact, is that the *frame*, precisely because it is produced by a weaving together of textual and extratextual elements, always depends on the historical-cultural context of the

---

3   Cf. I. Kecskes, «Encyclopaedic Knowledge and Cultural Models», in: *Cognitive Pragmatics, ed.* H.-J. Schmid, HP 4, Berlin – New York 2012, 175–200 (here, p. 180).

4   See in this regard, e.g. C.J. Fillmore – C.R. Johnson – M.R.L. Petruck, «Background to FrameNet», *IJL* 16 (2003) 235–250; C.J. Fillmore – C. Baker, «A Frames Approach», 791–816.

speakers. Interpreting an ancient text or a text generated by a different culture in general, means then attempting to reconstruct, using the historical-critical tools that are most adequate, the network of encyclopaedic interconnections implicitly recalled even by a single lexeme.

As regards the valorisation of the context of use in the field of biblical lexicographic, according to the indications of modern linguistics, one of the first notable attempts was, without a doubt, the dictionary developed by David J.A. Clines,[5] begun in 1993 and completed only in 2011 with its eighth volume. It is indubitably a very complex and laborious compilation, aimed at facilitating subsequent investigations. In my opinion, however, one of its greatest limitations lies in its restriction of the notion of context to a strictly linguistic-textual sphere. The notion of "surrender" then, being expressed in the HB with terminology that is varied, as we shall see, fails to find specific treatment in this great work, which focuses only on the lexemes of the Hebrew language considered the most meaningful.

It is therefore necessary to study the phenomenon of surrender by tracing and organising the relevant linguistic and (possibly) *extralinguistic* attestations, thereby attempting to reconstruct the framework of meaning that underlies the Jeremianic message and its implications. Political-theological implications, yes, but, even before that, *symbolic* and, in the final analysis, *prophetic* ones. To study the "letter" of the gesture of surrender means attempting to elaborate its phenomenology. To question its symbolic-prophetic significance, on the other hand, means tracing the proposal of a global hermeneutic of meaning that this gesture takes on in the discourse of Jeremiah, the prophet who dares to demand it of the people of his time, testifying with his life that *here* and *now* "thus speaks the Lord" (cf. 21:4, 8; 27:1, 16, 19, 22; 38:17, 20), and not just a man.

3. The (sub-)frame of the surrender in the context of the HB and the ancient Near East

Since symbolic meaning is formed and offers itself only *in* and *through* what we commonly define as "literal meaning" (which utilises analogy providing the analogous),[6] the first operation consists in defining and analysing the various elements that structure the semantic-pragmatic realm in which we are moving. Before entering into detail, however, I will present a simple working definition of the concept at hand. Surrender, in its "literal" or, better yet, *prototypical* meaning, can be described starting

---

5 D.J.A CLINES, *Dictionary of Classical Hebrew*, vols. I–VIII, Sheffield 1993–2011. For a critical review, see G.A. RENDSBURG, «Review Essay: The Sheffield Dictionary of Classical Hebrew», *AJS Review* 21 (1996) 111–118. For a study of cognitive pragmatics in the biblical field that draws more directly from *Frame Semantics,* I defer to the already cited work by di S.L. SHEAD, *Radical Frame Semantics and Biblical Hebrew. Exploring Lexical Semantics,* BiInS 108, Leiden – Boston 2011.

6 "Je suis porté par le sens premier, dirigé par lui vers le sens second; le sens symbolique est constitué par le sens littéral qui opère l'analogie en donnant l'analogue" (P. RICŒUR, *De l'interprétation.* Essai sur Freud, Paris 1965, 26). Cf. «Le symbole donne à penser», *Esprit* 27 (1959) 60–76; ID., *La métaphore vive*; S. MIGLIASSO, «Dal simbolo al linguaggic simbolico. L'interesse di una svolta nella teoria ermeneutica di Paul Ricoeur per un ermeneutica biblica creativa», *RivBib* 29 (1981) 187–203.

568   The gesture of the surrender

from our own experience, as a voluntary act by which a human subject (collective or individual), placed in a context of war and having recognised the disparity of forces involved, decides to capitulate before the enemy, that is, to hand themself (and all they possess) over in the hope of maintaining some form of good and avoiding the full totality of the disaster. Now let us look at the individual elements in the logical order deduced from the "precomprehension" of the *frame* through which we enter into dialogue with the biblical text.

3.1. The frame of war in the ancient Near East: Ideology and war typology

First of all, I will note that on the linguistic level, the basic semantic-pragmatic realm to which the *frame* of surrender should be properly attributed in the communicative context of the ancient Near East is that of the broader and more articulated *war conflict*, understood beginning from its generic and transcultural prototypical meaning of hand-to-hand combat and then projected on a vast scale and configured therefore as a military contraposition organised between two opposite subjects of a collective nature.[7] In this sense, surrender is more precisely configured as a sub-frame, one of several scenarios implicated in the principal *frame*. The objective of each of the subjects during wartime is to impose their own will on the other (the enemy) through the use of force, in all its possible variants and strategic modalities. It is from these basic semantic coordinates that all the degrees of extensional reference of the concept,[8] found not only in our modern languages but also in the ancient ones, derive.

Considering this operational definition, it should be emphasised that, in this case as well, the concept of a pragmatic-cognitive context is pivotal. It would be a methodological error, in fact, to study the ancient cultures in relation to an event of war only on the basis of our current conception of war, because we would risk drawing analogies that, while correct,[9] would be thoroughly unsuitable for fully understanding the phenomenon as it had been interpreted at the time of Jeremiah.

The modern understanding of war in the West was marked by the reflection of the Prussian general Carl von Clausewitz (1780–1831), for whom "war is nothing but the continuation of politics by other means".[10] Today we could say, on the contrary, that war is rather the failure of politics and its means, but in any case, it must be borne in

---

7   For a discussion of the defining difficulties related to the phenomenon of war in the ancient Near East, see F.R. Ames, «The Meaning of War: Definitions for the Study of War in Ancient Israelite Literature», in: *Writing and Reading War.* Rhetoric, Gender, and Ethics in Biblical and Modern Contexts, *eds.* B.E. Kelle – F.R. Ames, SBLSymS 42, Atlanta 2008, 19–31.

8   "The context of warfare, though, is virtually unrestricted because it encompasses military, civilian, domestic, political, religious, technological, economic and other realms of human existence, as well as factors such as geographical location, terrain, climate, and natural resources" (M.J. Fretz, «Weapons and Implements of Warfare», *ABD* VI, 893–895).

9   In the ancient Near East as well, soldiers went to combat, won or died, and armies needed generals, strategies, provisions, etc. (cf. W.J. Hamblin, *Warfare*, 12).

10   "Der Krieg ist eine bloße Fortsetzung der Politik mit anderen Mitteln" (C. von Clausewitz, *Vom Krieg*, München 2000, 44; I,1,24).

The (sub-)frame of the surrender in the context of the HB   569

mind that this famous definition, certainly reductive,[11] was elaborated by a veteran of the Napoleonic Wars at the height of the Age of Enlightenment, when even the way of fighting in orderly, counterposed rows, willing to be slaughtered by enemy fire without moving, reflected the mentality of the time precisely. In other cultures and in other ages, combat was, on the contrary, the supreme moment when the single individual could freely express his personal valour and thus his originality.

While this now classic definition makes sense in the modern context, in the cultural horizon of the ancient Near East, war was instead carried out through recourse to every possible magical-religious means. Rites, sacrifices, invocations of respective deities, and spells accompanied every choice of war. Inductions for campaigns, the departing of armies, the choice of the best road to take and most opportune manoeuvres to perform, everything was marked by a sense of the divine presence amongst the ranks positioned for combat.[12] The reason is simple: war was conceived as *the operational instrument through which the gods restored the cosmic order*, using human armies and divinely enthroned sovereigns to fight it out in their name.[13] Tragically, this definition is not so alien to the our own recent geopolitical scenario, where large scale killing in the name of one's own "God" has been resumed (in the form of islamistic terrorism attacks or in attempts to "export democracy"). This gives witness to the fact that, for better or worse, directly or indirectly, the religious factor proposes a vision of history that questions, at the root, the methodological (atheist) presupposition of scientific study of human phenomena as the single or preferential way for knowledge adequate to reality.

In any case, the anthropological relevance of war is such that it has in fact constituted the main object of historiographical research. The majority of historical data re-emerging from the past, both near and far, concern specifically the realm of war and its correlated events, including its final outcome, whether this be a surrender of one of the contenders or a resulting peace treaty. For the most correct reconstruction of a particular or general historical framework, again in this case, the linguistic attestations of literary sources concerning this phenomenon are to be placed in relation to

---

11 The problem of C. von Clausewitz, which can also be that of every interpreter of biblical text, was of not being aware of how much he was influenced by his own pragmatic-cognitive context, in this case, that of a professional class of officers at the service of a centralised European state. Otherwise, he would have been capable of realising, as was observed in this regard by J. KEEGAN, *Warfare,* that war "embraces much more than politics: that it is always an expression of culture, often a determinant of cultural forms, in some societies the culture itself" (p. 12).

12 Note, on this subject, A. FUCHS, «Assyria at War», 386: "Now, at the beginning of the 21st century, we might laugh at all of this apparently naïve mumbo jumbo. But even if the underlying assumptions were complete nonsense by our standards, these ideas and behaviours had massive repercussions in the real world. Certainly the rituals calmed fears, bolstered confidence, and convinced the soldiers to fight for a just cause, while the practice of secret knowledge must have strengthened confidence even in the most desperate situations. Without doubt, for a fighting force such morale boosts are at least as valuable as any superiority in numbers or technology. In those cases, therefore, the ideals shaped reality."

13 On the pertinence of this theme in my research, see what is highlighted in ch. IV, § 4.2.7.

those that are extralinguistic (or extratextual). And this applies all the more so to the ancient Near East,[14] where, in addition to the ideological-religious factor just mentioned, also the geographical context, distances, state and extra-state configurations, archaeological vestiges (especially figurative), and traces left on the ground help to provide us with an important contextual framework to make up for the gap wedged between the modern reader and the pragmatic-communicative presuppositions of ancient literary testimonies.[15]

Setting aside for now its instigating causes, but considering the *military power* of the subjects involved, the war scenario that can be outlined schematically starting from the sources of the ancient Near East and the pages of the Old Testament can be fundamentally of three types. It is useful to keep them in mind to best contextualise the phenomenon of surrender within the framework of the most frequent and well-known war scenarios in which the events referred to in the book of Jeremiah and prophetic request to "consign themselves to the king of Babylon" are included.

Fig. 37. Field battle scene coming from the palace of Sargon a Khorsabad. The Assyrian army overwhelms the enemies with horses and war chariots (detail from P. ALBENDA, The Palace of Sargon, King of Assyria. Monumental Wall Reliefs at Dur-Sharrukin, from Original Drawings Made at the Time of their Discovery in 1843–1844 by Botta and Flandin, Paris 1986, pl. 97).

a) *The field battle*. The players are two (or more) enormous opposing forces of a collective nature, of theoretically equivalent proportions, each determined to defend or impose their interests through the lethal use of physical force and most varied offensive military instruments. In this case, the most common clash is that of the open-field battle, where the dispute is usually resolved in a few hours, if only at the local level (cf. Fig. 37). Although the Bible refers to open-field battles often, it is still

---

14 Cf. I. EPH'AL, «On Warfare», 89.
15 Although focalised on a particular theme, there is general pragmatic importance to the observation of I. EPH'AL, «On Warfare», 93: "The Assyrian reliefs depict many details relating to fighting over cities. Likewise, we possess a considerable number of technical terms relating to this subject. What is still needed, however, is a systematic study of these terms and a coordination of the linguistic material with the visual sources. Such a study will deeper our understanding of the fighting method most frequently used by the empires under discussion."

The (sub-)frame of the surrender in the context of the HB   571

a relatively rare type of confrontation in extrabiblical attestations in the ancient Near East,[16] that, at least as far as the military operations of Assyrian armies are concerned, are mentioned by sources either before or after the account of a siege on a city.[17] It is, after all, more difficult to coordinate a surrender during a field battle. A surrender is generally decided by a commander, when he foresees or notices a defeat and can enforce his decision (cf. notwithstanding, the particular case of the raid mentioned in 2 Mac 12:10–12, to which I will return shortly).

b) *The siege.* If the disproportion of the conflicting forces is evident, those who find themselves in difficulty and under attack wind up preferring, by necessity, either an escape[18] or a defensive war, based on the resistance within fortified structures not easy to overtake.[19] In contrast to the field battle, where the force of the impact and speed of tactical manoeuvres are decisive factors, this form of combat is instead

---

16   We have few examples of depictions with scenes of open-field warfare, almost all from the time of Ashurbanipal. See, in this regard, D. NADALI, «La campagna di Assurbanipal contro gli Arabi: proposta di lettura delle dinamiche di una battaglia in campo aperto», *SMEA* 46 (2004) 59–78. His naval variant, which counts in ancient historic battles above all in the Greek and Roman sphere (but one could also cite the clashes between the Egypt of Ramses III and the Sea Peoples), is practically absent for obvious practical reasons in the geopolitical context now of interest to us. What can be noted from the written and figurative sources are, at most, Assyrian military interventions in the swampy areas near Babylon, or river battles (cf. J. SCURLOCK, «Neo-Assyrian Battle Tactics», in: *Crossing Boundaries and Linking Horizons.* Studies in Honor of Michael C. Astour, *eds.* G.D. YOUNG – M.W. CHAVALAS – R.E. AVERBECK, Bethesda 1997, 491–517, Fig. 7; R.D. BARNETT – E. BLEIBTREU – G. TURNER, *Sculptures from the Southwest Palace of Sennacherib at Nineveh,* London 1998, tabs. 237, 463), or, thanks to Philistine manual labour, naval operations against Elam throughout the Persian Gulf (cf. E. FRAHM, *Einleitung in die Sanherib-Inschriften,* AfO.B 26, Vienna 1997, 14).

17   Cf. D. NADALI, «Assyrian Open Field Battles. An Attempt at Reconstruction and Analysis», in: *Studies on War,* 117–152 (here, pp. 117–118).

18   Cf. S. ZAWADZKI, «Depicting Hostile Rulers in the Neo-Assyrian Royal Inscriptions», in: *From Source to History.* Studies on Ancient Near Eastern Worlds and Beyond, *eds.* S. GASPA et al., Münster 2014, 767–778: "Aware of their weakness in comparison with the Assyrian army, many local rulers avoided open battle, attempting to protect their most valuable assets by moving to safe, inaccessible places, like mountains, marshes, and seas" (here, p. 769).

19   For a specific study on this topic and of various obsidian techniques, aside from the classic Y. YADIN, *The Art of Warfare in Biblical Lands in the Light of Archaeological Study.* 2 vols., Jerusalem 1963 (in particular, pp. 293–374), see I. EPH'AL, *The City Besieged,* where the following detailed definition of this form of war combat is provided: "Siege is a form of warfare in which one of the combative sides defends itself within an area delimited by a system of obstacles, while the opponent attempts to penetrate these obstacles and to engage in hand-to-hand combat, in which its superiority is assured. Unlike pitched battle, which is generally dynamic and brief and in which mobility plays a significant role, siege warfare is protracted and static by nature" (p. 1). See also, beginning from the Achaemenid period, D.B. CAMPBELL, *Besieged,* as well as D. NADALI, «Attaccare e difendere un muro: una battaglia di confine», RS/C 2 (2011) 225–232.

mainly played out through the factor of *resistance*. For those defending, it suffices to resist just a little beyond how much the adversary can afford to sustain the siege (cf. Isa 22:8–11; 2 Chr 32:2–5). Indeed, for those who attack, a considerable investment of resources and time is required, especially if the defences of the besieged render the military techniques of the besieging army ineffective, and they must then stake everything on the effects of the starvation that results from isolating the city (cf. again Figs. 13 and 36).[20] This is the case in the siege of Jerusalem, which is the historical framework of the meeting between Jeremiah and Zedekiah. It is well known that the Babylonians only managed to gain the upper hand over the mighty defensive walls after 18 months of warfare,[21] including a temporary suspension of the blockade of the city for an urgent repositioning of the entire army due to the threat represented by an approaching Egyptian contingent (think of what is reported in Jer 37:5[22] and also in 2 Kgs 19:8–9). It is therefore the siege scenario that proves to be the most pertinent context for studying, from my perspective, the phenomenology of surrender.

c) *Raids*. This is the case with guerrilla warfare, a typical form of asymmetrical warfare in which the difference and disproportion of the forces makes neither the frontal clash with equal weapons nor siege techniques possible. Either because the attack forces are formed only of small groups, whose function is to deeply penetrate enemy territory causing havoc and demoralisation, or because the subject one wants to fight has no defined state configuration, as in the case of nomad tribes (or privateer contingents in sea combat). I have already cited *en passant* this scenario as well in the historical portion of my study,[23] in reference to Nebuchadnezzar's use of Chaldean contingents and tribal bands of raiders for punitive expeditions against the kingdom of Judah when he could not yet mobilise his army for a full-scale campaign. Another interesting case, since it is in direct relation to the act of surrender, is that mentioned in 2 Mac 12:10–12: here a substantial group of Arabic nomads suddenly attacks the men of Judah on the march, but without success. Overwhelmed by those they had attacked, they are forced to surrender and beg to be spared.

---

20   In an epoch not far from the one we are dealing with (between the fifth and sixth centuries A.D.), but in a completely different geographical-cultural context (that of China), Sun-Tzu wrote in his famous treatise on military strategy: "Thus the highest form of generalship is to baulk the enemy's plans; the next best is to prevent the junction of the enemy's forces; the next in order is to attack the enemy's army in the field; and the worst policy of all is to besiege walled cities. The rule is, not to besiege walled cities if it can possibly be avoided" (SUN-TZU, *Sun Tzu on the Art of War. The Oldest Military Treatise in the World*. Translated from the Chinese by L. GILES, London 1910, 17–18; III,3–4).

21   In this sense, the siege that Nebuchadnezzar carried out against Tyre should also be mentioned (cf. Ezek 29:18).

22   "Meanwhile, the pharaoh's army had set out from Egypt and the Chaldeans, who were besieging Jerusalem, as soon as they had heard this news, had withdrawn from Jerusalem."

23   See ch. II, § 2.2.1.

The (sub-)frame of the surrender in the context of the HB   573

3.2. The prodromes of a surrender: An enemy, a war, and a siege. Lexical traces of the biblical context

The event of war, an eloquent witness to the presence of violence in the history of humankind, is *frequently* attested in the Bible[24] according to its different typological manifestations, especially through the narrative module. The most notable verbal root on the lexicographical level is √לחם (in certain rare cases, and in the book of Jeremiah specifically, it is used to indicate the siege on a city; cf. 32:24, 29; 34:1, 22) and the most common lexeme derived is certainly the noun מִלְחָמָה (320x in the HB). Actually, the paradigmatic and syntagmatic lexical constellation that describes the phenomenon is quite vast and cannot be analysed here.[25] Let me just point out that amongst the phraseology utilised, we also see appear √יצא (often in construction with מִלְחָמָה or √לחם: "*to go out* to war or to fight"; cf. e.g. Judg 9:38–39; 1 Sam 8:20; etc.). It is useful to keep this in mind because the gesture of surrender is also expressed with the same root, which, as I already noted,[26] in the biblical context, and particularly that of Jeremiah, it rises to become the focal point in reference to the founding event of the Exodus. Obviously, it is necessary to distinguish between a direct reference and the allusive-symbolic potential of the use of the selfsame verbal root, but the possible semantic-symbolic resonances should not be underestimated.

The presence in the biblical text of the event of war and of violence in general is pervasive, and it is thus no wonder that in several cases, the gesture of surrender is attested (while obviously, not with the same frequency). In addition to the Jeremianic texts that I have already mentioned and which I will address again (cf. 21:9; 27:2–13, 16–17; 38:2–3),[27] allusion to it is also made in: 1 Sam 11:1–11; 2 Kgs 10:1–7; 18:13–16, 28–32; Jdt 2:10–11; 3; 5:4; 7:12–15:23–31; 1 Mac 6:49, 55–62; 11:49–51, 61–62,[28] 65–66; 13:45–46:50; 2 Mac 12:10–12.

Before dealing with the lexicon of surrender in detail, we can see from the point of view of synchronic semantics that the military context of such occurrences is expressed through a phraseology that refers to a characteristic *sub-frame* that acts as a prelude to the surrender itself: that of the *siege*.[29] I will therefore highlight the

---

24   Contributions in this regard abound and are certainly no novelty: cf. e.g. O. EISSFELDT, *Krieg und Bibel*, Tübingen 1915; H. FREDRIKSSON, *Jahwe als Krieger*, Lund 1945; H.E. DEL MEDICO, «Le rite de la guerre dans l'Ancient Testament», *Ethnog.* 45 (1947–1950) 127–170; C. HERZOG – M. GICHON, *Battles of the Bible*, London 1978. But see, in particular, ch. III, § 4.1.3 and the related bibliography cited therein.

25   I will defer, in this regard, to H.D. PREUSS, «מִלְחָמָה ;לָחַם», *ThWAT* IV, 914–926.

26   For this reference, I defer to what has already been observed in ch. III, § 4.1.2.

27   For a lexicographic study on the topic, one should also consider pertinent the texts of 2 Kgs 25:11 (//Jer 52:15); 37:13–14; 38:19; 39:9, which speaks about the phenomenon of *desertion*, which is none other than the *surrender* of individuals or small groups who decide to abandon their positions and pass over to the enemy. The concepts are partially overlapping, since Jeremiah's preaching concerned, without distinction, both the totality of the inhabitants of Judah and individual groups or subjects.

28   While I refer to this passage, I do so with many reservations, given that here, it is not easy to draw a clear distinction between a conditional surrender and a peace treaty (at least, not in vv. 55–62).

29   Sole exception: 2 Mac 12:10–12. Here, the acceptance of the surrender takes place as a result of a (failed) raid.

most significant syntactic-semantic structures having a direct cause-effect relationship with the subsequent phenomenon of "consigning oneself", referring in their turn to other pertinent war contexts as well. I will organise the data according to the linear temporal logic of the resulting *sub-frame*, that is, so that the order of the citations and the three groupings of the schema can reconstruct the different phases of the siege:

1) the movement of the *aggression*: the occupying force, equipped with overwhelming forces, sets off marching towards the objective, sets up camp near the city to be besieged, and
2) organises *control over the territory*, occupying the main access routes and cutting off to the enemy supply sources and thus, also routes for escape[30];
3) the most direct *war operations* are undertaken to get the better of the defensive apparatus and take over the city. The besieged, apart from the emotional implications (cf. e.g. 4:10, 13, 19; 6:1, 4), which I will highlight later (§ 3.4), take the necessary countermeasures and, if they can, counterattack even outside the walls.

	Subject	Predicate		Complement
Jer 4:16c	(the) besiegers (נֹצְרִים)	מִן + בוא√ + compl.	to come	*from a distant land*
Jer 37:19	Nebuchadnezzar	עַל + בוא√ + pron. suff. + obj.	to come *against*	*(Jerusalem) and the land*
Jer 6:3	The "shepherds" (the foreign kings)	אֶל + pron. suff. + בוא√	to go *against*	*Jerusalem*
2 Kgs 18:13	Sennacherib	עלה√ + עַל + obj.	to go up *against*	*the fortified cities of Judah*
1 Mac 6:48	The army units of Antiochus Eupator	ἀναβαίνω + εἰς συνάντησιν	to go up *to attack*	*the people of Judea*
Jdt 7:1	Holofernes (Nebuchadnezzar)	ἀναζεύγνυμι + ἐπί + obj.	to move *against*	*Bethulia*[31]
Jdt 7:1	Holofernes (Nebuchadnezzar)	ποιέω + πόλεμον + πρός + obj.	to make war *against*	*the children of Israel*
1 Mac 6:19	Judas Maccabeus	ἐξεκκλησιάζω + obj. + περικαθίζω + ἐπί + obj.	assemble to *besiege*	*The citadel (of Jerusalem)*
1 Mac 6:20	The people	συνάγω	to gather together	

---

30   Cf. I. EPH'AL, *The City Besieged*, 35–43.
31   Obviously, what is of interest to us is neither the historical accuracy nor the account, but rather the linguistic attestation of the fact.

	Subject	Predicate		Complement
Jdt 7:1, 7, 17	Holofernes (Nebuchadnezzar)	προκαταλαμβάνω + obj.	to seize	*the passes into the hills and the springs*
1 Sam 11:1	Nahash the Ammonite	√חנה + עַל + obj.	to encamp *against*	*Jabesh-gilead*
Jer 6:3	The enemy from the North	√תקע + עַל + pron. suff. + סָבִיב	to pitch *against* and *around*	*the tents (against Jerusalem)*
Jer 4 17a	The enemy from the North	√היה + עַל + pron. suff. + מִסָּבִיב	to place themselves *around*	*(Jerusalem)*
Jer 21:4	Nebuchadnezzar/ the Chaldeans	√צור + עַל + obj.	to besiege	*(Jerusalem)*
Jer 21:9	Nebuchadnezzar/ the Chaldeans	√צור + עַל + pron. suff.	to besiege	*(Jerusalem)*
2 Sam 20:15	The soldiers of Joab	√צור + עַל + pron. suff.	to besiege	*Abel-Beth-maacah*
1 Mac 6:20, 24	Judas Maccabeus	περικαθίζω + ἐπί + obj.	to besiege	*The citadel (of Jerusalem)*
1 Mac 6:26	Judas Maccabeus	παρεμβάλλω + ἐπί / εἰς + obj.	to surround	*The citadel (of Jerusalem)*
1 Mac 6:31, 48	Antiochus Eupator	παρεμβάλλω + ἐπί / εἰς + obj.	to surround	*Beth-zur, Judea, and Mount Zion*
Jdt 7:6	Holofernes (Nebuchadnezzar)	ἐξάγω + obj.	to lead out	*the cavalry*
Jdt 7:7	Holofernes (Nebuchadnezzar)	ἐπισκέπτομαι + obj.	to examine	*the approaches to the town*
Jdt 7:7	Holofernes (Nebuchadnezzar)	ἐφοδεύω + obj.	to reconnoitre	*the water springs*
Jdt 7:12	The soldiers of Holofernes	ἐπικρατέω + obj.	to take possession	*the spring*
Jer 6:6	The enemy from the North	עֵצָה + √כרת	to cut down	*the trees*
1 Mac 6:20	Judas Maccabeus	ποιέω + obj.	to build	*siege engines*
1 Mac 6:31	Antiochus Eupator	ποιέω + obj.	to build	*siege engines*
1 Mac 6:51, 52	Antiochus Eupator The besieged	ἵστημι + obj.	to set up	*siege engines*
2 Sam 20:15	The soldiers of Joab	√שׁפך + obj.	to throw up	*a siege mound*
Jer 6:6	The enemy from the North	√שׁפך + obj.	to throw up	*a siege mound*

Jer 4:16d	The enemy from the North	קוֹל + עַל + obj. + נתן√	to shout against	*the cities of Judah*
Jer 6:4	The enemy from the North	קדשׁ√ + עַל + pron. suff. + מִלְחָמָה	to consecrate the war against	*Jerusalem ("holy war")*
Jer 6:4	The enemy from the North	בַּצָּהֳרַיִם + עלה√ + קום√	to get up- and rush up-on *at noon*	*Jerusalem*
Jer 6:4	The enemy from the North	בַלָּיְלָה + עלה√ + קום√	to get up- and rush up-on *in evening*	*Jerusalem*
2 Mac 12:15	Judas Maccabeus	ἐνσείω + obj.	to rush furiously	*the walls*
2 Sam 20:15	The soldiers of Joab	נפל√ + שׁחת√ + obj.	to try to break down	*the walls*
Jer 21:2	Nebuchadnezzar/ the Chaldeans	עַל + לחם√ + pron. suff.	to fight	*(Jerusalem)*
1 Mac 6:31	Antiochus Eupator The inhabitants of Beth-zur	πολεμέω + obj.	to fight[32]	*against Beth-zur and against the assailants*
1 Mac 6:52	The besieged and the besiegers	πολεμέω + obj.	to fight	*one against the other*
1 Mac 6:63	Antiochus Eupator	πολεμέω + obj.	to fight	*Philip*
2 Mac 12:13	Judas Maccabeus	ἐπιβάλλω + ἐπί + obj.	to attack	*the city of Caspin*

As can be seen, the resulting virtual narrative sequence, trying to place the pertinent lexical elements of the various texts in a logical and time-consistent relationship, is segmented into very precise phases. In almost all of the attestations (apart from the episode in 1 Mac 11:41–51; in 2 Kgs 10:1–7, allusion is being made to the "fortified city" [v. 2: עִיר מִבְצָר] and other defensive devices), there are always military activities set in relation to *poliorcetics* (and therefore, also to the cutting off of access routes and

---

32 The verb πολεμέω recurs here 2x, in reference both to the attack of the besiegers and to the counterattack outside the walls on the part of the besieged (cf. Jer 21:4).

The (sub-)frame of the surrender in the context of the HB 577

possible supplies), and the figure (or "semantic role") that emerges as the propagating subject of the war manoeuvres is that of the *enemy*.

Depending on whether the perspective taken is that of the assailant or the assailed (a distinction that, outside of the biblical examples, is not always smooth), it can be defined as either the violent negator of a subject's essential goods (the right to life, freedom, possession, etc.) or as the obstacle that resists, to varying degrees, the achievement of one's own ends. In any case, whether seen as a mortal threat or prey to be conquered, its image gets warped according to propagandistic stylistic devices, and its defeat is desired by means of a most thorough subjugation (not least, that of physical elimination) or by the annihilation of its offensive potential.[33] The concept of "enemy" is lexicalised in the HB, above all, by the lexemes אֹיֵב/אֹיֵב (instead, אֵיבָה has the more abstract sense of "enmity"; cf. e.g. Gen 3:15; Ezek 25:15; etc.) plus their relative synonyms,[34] and can be both a single figure and a collective one. In Deuteronomistic history especially, and in the book of Jeremiah in particular (cf. e.g. our text of 21:1–10), the enemy is seen as an agent of YHWH evoked to punish the infidelity of his people to the covenant.

Speaking of war as armed confrontation, it is not arbitrary to point out that the very "letter" of this concept can immediately assume metaphoric values within biblical language (and not only) in reference to other areas of the human experience. In an analogous way, one can define as "war-battle" a bilateral dispute (*rîb*), a trial (*mišpaṭ*)[35] enmity, personal confrontations in general,[36] or ideological, commercial, or love rivalry, etc.[37] In each of these areas (or *frames*), the very idea of "surrender" can be applied, even if metaphorically, in a way that is pertinent. Of course, the face of the "enemy/adversary" also follows this semantic slippage, configuring its appearance

---

33 Cf. B. PONGRATZ-LEISTEN, «The Other and the Enemy in the Mesopotamian Conception of the World», in: *Mythology and Mythologies*. Methodological Approaches to Intercultural Influences, Proceedings of the Second Annual Symposium of the Assyrian and Babylonian Intellectual Heritage Project Held in Paris, France, October 4–7, 1999, *ed.* R.M. WHITING, MSym 2, Helsinki 2001, 195–231. In the later Neo-Assyrian inscriptions and figurative attestations, the figure of the enemy king falls into disrepute and, above all, gets stigmatised for his lack of courage and regal dignity, comparing particularly his *escape* before the pursuit of the Assyrian sovereign (think of the escape of Zedekiah from Jerusalem) to that of terrified wild animals (cf. S. ZAWADZKI, «Depicting Hostile Rulers»).

34 Cf. L. RUPPERT, *Der leidende Gerechte und seine Feinde*. Eine Wortfelduntersuchung, Würzuburg 1973; E. JENNI, «אֹיֵב», *THAT* I, 118–122; H. RINGGREN, «אֹיֵב» *ThWAT* I, 228–235.

35 Cf. P. BOVATI, *Re-Establishing Justice*, 293: "A trial is not really a battle, nor is an outbreak of war a trial, yet these two events, though separate, have mutual echoes. A trial resembles a battle, to the extent that it is a confrontation of two parties armed with arguments, proofs and convincing words, who run the risk of defeat, which is an embarrassing and sometimes fatal setback" (see also pp. 294–296).

36 Cf. B. COSTACURTA, *La vita minacciata*, 111.

37 I intentionally exclude as irrelevant for my discourse other contexts of signification, such as that of disease or a clash with ferocious animals or other forces of nature, which, in metaphorical language, can always be compared to battles and struggles (with the possible outcome of surrender).

578 The gesture of the surrender

in a diversified way according to context. The most interesting (and also unexpected) application that I would like to point out in the area of my study, in addition to that already mentioned in Jer 21:4–6 where YHWH fights against his own (unfaithful) people, is that consecrated by the book of Job, where the enemy of (the righteous) one seems to be YHWH himself.[38]

3.3. Imbalance of forces, negotiations, and admission of inferiority. The objective fact

Having focalised the fundamental elements (or *frame units*) that establish the scenario within which the gesture of surrender takes place, the next piece of data consists of another *objective* fact: the adversary is endowed with overwhelming power and is irresistible. If, at the beginning of the conflict, there was a supposed or temporary opposition between forces that were equal and opposed or, in any case, able to counterbalance one another,[39] now, one of these finds itself in a position to prevail over the other. Not only do the offensive or defensive weapons utilised come into play (although these will many times prove decisive, at least in individual episodes of conflict), but also strategic and tactical skills,[40] the exhaustion of vital resources, epidemics, a subjective perception of the war scenario (with which I will deal in the following paragraph), and conclusive episodes of other natures.[41]

---

38 Being unable to delve into this thematic herein, I will point out only that YHWH is portrayed as an enemy of the wicked and wickedness in many other passages, and as an enemy of his own people (for the same reason), above all in the prophetic writings. One example for all, Jer 30:14: "All your lovers have forgotten you, it is not you that they seek, for I have struck you as an *enemy* (אוֹיֵב) would strike, punishing you with the chastisement of (*one* who is) *cruel* (אַכְזָרִי). For your great guilt, because your sins are many." The fact, though, of YHWH being felt like an adversary by the righteous man as well, is thematised more clearly elsewhere, precisely in the book of Job (cf. e.g. Job 9:13–35; 13:21–28; 16:7–22; 19:6–22; 33:9–11). The fact that man and God can be each other's adversaries opens a path for reflection that is important: the theme of "surrender" can be placed in this relationship as well. Each of the two "combatants" asks the other to "hand themself over" and cease to resist, in order to establish their own will (cf. Gen 32:23–33). For the human being, the gesture of surrender is tantamount to the obedience of faith, while for God, it is the fulfilment of a supplication (even one that is intercessorial; cf. e.g. Ps 106:23).
39 Without this prerequisite, it is difficult for a real conflict to arise. Even modest state entities that decided to shake off the yoke of a great empire did so based on a reasonable political calculation that made success at least a possibility. History has demonstrated that it was not easy for the great Mesopotamian empires to manage to control vast expanses of territory and peripheral vassal kingdoms effectively and for long periods of time (cf. I. EPH'AL, «On Warfare», 96–97).
40 The *strategy* is the configuration, in view of an objective, of an intentionality or plan of action by which one seeks to scrupulously take into account all of the variables at stake, analysing the overall scenario in which one need operate, while the *tactic* is the operational consequence, that is, the specific methodology with which one intends to completely implement the strategy itself.
41 An ambush, a betrayal, a trap, or the intervention of YHWH itself (typically through catastrophic natural events) in the Bible can result in the sudden reversal of a war scenario.

The (sub-)frame of the surrender in the context of the HB 579

On the disproportion of strength between the Babylonian military apparatus[42] and that of the kingdom of Judah, there is not much to highlight, if not that in the event of conflict, states of these modest dimensions counted, more than anything, on political-military alliances (forming coalitions with other neighbouring state entities or securing the support of different superpowers interested in countering the influence of other adversary empires and increasing their own), the defensive capacity of their fortifications, and the availability of sufficient water and food reserves to resist until the enemy was forced to desist and retreat. An emplacement that is well-equipped can induce a mindset of security and ridicule towards enemies (as in 2 Mac 12:14)[43] just as, on the contrary, a sufficiently tenacious and aggressive siege force can afford to mock opponents, impose the conditions of an immediate surrender at will (think of the speech of the "great cupbearer" [רַב־שָׁקֵה] of Sennacherib below the walls of Jerusalem at the time of the king Hezekiah in 2 Kgs 18:17–37[44]), and lead to an objective deterioration of the situation of the besieged, to quite a dramatic extent.

During the siege, the unbalancing of forces is progressive and assumes a temporal progression that is more or less long depending on the resources available and defensive moves (and manoeuvres) taken. As far as the typology of armaments and military techniques is concerned, even before those actually utilised for the scope of storming the city,[45] one need consider the shock force of a highly specialised and organised army like the Assyrian and Babylonian ones, equipped with cavalry and war chariots. In their respective ages, these were the elements of force used to deter frontal attacks. Being forced to become entrenched in fortified cities (cf. Jer 4:5) and be besieged was already the result of a clear imbalance of forces: it meant not being able to face the enemy with equal weapons in an open field. Or if nothing else, recognition of this.[46]

---

42   See, in this regard, J. MACGINNIS, «Mobilisation and Militarisation in the Neo-Babylonian Empire», in: *Studies on War*, 153–163.

43   "Those inside, certain of the solidity of their walls and their supply of provisions, showed contempt for the men of Judah, insulting them, and even uttering blasphemies and pronouncing phrases that are not licit to repeat."

44   ῾19 [...] in whom do you trust to rebel against me? [...] 23 Now make a wager with my lord, king of Assyria; I will give you two thousand horses, if you are able to put your horsemen on them. [...].27 Did perhaps my lord send me to pronounce these words to your lord and to you and not instead to the men up on the wall, reduced to eating their excrement and drinking their urine with you?"

45   Depending on their functions, a distinction can be made between: (1) offensive weapons for close encounters or for distant targets (swords, daggers, clubs, spears, bows, slingshots); (2) various sorts of projectiles (javelins, arrows, stones); (3) mobile weapons (horses, wagons, siege machines); (4) defence weapons (from the shield to fortifications). For a detailed study on the subject, cf. R. MAXWELL-HYSLOP, «Daggers and Swords in Western Asia. A Study from Prehistoric Times to 600 B.C.», *Iraq* 8 (1946) 1–45; Y. YADIN, *The Art of Warfare*, 293–301; A. GOETZE, «Warfare in Asia Minor», *Iraq* 25 (1963) 124–130; R. GONEN, *Weapons of the Ancient World*, Jerusalem 1975. For an even more complete description in reference to the siege, see I. EPH'AL, *The City Besieged*, 68–107.

46   In this sense, the attack directed by the king Josiah against the Egyptian army of the pharaoh Necho in transit to the north seems to make little sense (cf. 2 Kgs 23:29–30; 2 Chr 35:20–24), if for only purely tactical considerations.

Fig. 38. Detail of the great bas-relief dedicated to the capture of Lachish in 701 by Sennacherib (from D. USSISHKIN, «Symbols of Conquest in Sennacherib's Reliefs of Lachish: Impaled Prisoners and Booty», in: Culture through Objects. Ancient Near Eastern Studies in Honour of P.R.S. Moorey, eds. T.F. POTTS et al., Oxford 2003, 207–217, Fig. 3).

The continual endeavour of battering rams and other means and techniques of attack, as well as the deprivation of the resources of provisions (cf. 2 Kgs 25:1; Jer 52:4; Ezek 4:1–3) could, in the long run, in many cases, gain the upper hand over the grandeur of city walls and resilience of people and soldiers.[47] At a certain point, clear signs denounced the imminent collapse: in addition to the structural damage of the fortifications and opening of breaches, for prolonged sieges, the indicators of the extreme situation were malnutrition, hunger and thirst, starvation, epidemics, and resulting decimations (which affected, *in primis*, the child population[48]), collapse of morale, deterioration of the social and economic fabric (inflation), the sale of children, and even acts of cannibalism. All phenomena attested in both the HB and extrabiblical sources.[49]

---

47 Cf. D.B. CAMPBELL, *Besieged*, 11–13.
48 Cf. R. DA RIVA, «La guerra en el Antiguo Oriente: el asedio a las ciudades y la penuria de la población», *Historiae* 5 (2008) 1–9.
49 Impressive in this regard is the description of Deut 28:47–57 (which is, in any case, a *tòpos* of the curse; Cf. D.R. HILLERS, *Treaty Curses*, 62–63). See also 2 Kgs 6:24–29; 18:27; Jer 19:9; 52:4–7; 1 Mac 6:52; 13:49. For further study on the matter, I defer to I. EPH'AL, *The City Besieged*, 57–68.

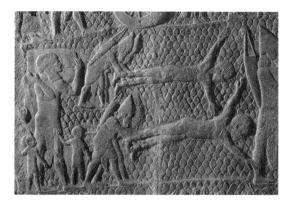

Fig. 39. From the bas-reliefs representing the storming of Lachish (from D. Ussishkin, The Conquest of Lachish, 86–87).

Before reaching this extreme limit or in anticipation of such an outcome, there was generally the possibility of opening negotiations.[50] In this case, we are in the realm of *conditional surrender*. The first to be interested in such an agreement, beyond the rhetoric of superiority or war propaganda, could have been the besiegers themselves (cf. 1 Sam 11:1–3) since, as I have already pointed out, conducting a siege required a major war effort, and a skilful agreement (cf. Prov 21:22; Ecc 9:14–16) could avoid unnecessary damage and loss on both sides. Sometimes the besieged, knowing or hoping to be rescued by friendly forces, could negotiate only to buy time. Or they could explicitly propose to the attackers to not to start the war until an agreed upon time, during which and not beyond, they would wait for the arrival of external aid. If this had not arrived by the fixed day, the besieged promised to surrender without resistance.[51] Negotiations or momentary ceasefires for specific humanitarian motives (such as the recovery, on both sides, of those killed or wounded) were possible in some cases even during clashes.

In order to induce this type of conditional surrender, the besiegers had two typologies of approaches, of opposite natures: that of *intimidations* or that of *reassurances*, each with their relative promises of clemency. While we can get from the written sources in our possession, both biblical and extrabiblical, an idea of the threats that might be directed at the besieged,[52] it is yet again the extralinguistic data

---

50 Cf. I. Eph'al, *The City Besieged*, 43–97. In 2 Sam 20:16–22 the intermediation is carried out by a wise woman of the besieged city.
51 For some extrabiblical examples, see I. Eph'al, *The City Besieged*, 43, n. 27. In Jdt 7:30–31; 8:9, 11 this sort of pact with YHWH is stipulated.
52 See e.g. in this regard, in the broader context of the war in general, D.T. Lamb, «"I Will Strike You Down and Cut Off Your Head" (1 Sam 17:46): Trash Talking, Derogatory Rhetoric, and Psychological Warfare in Ancient Israel», in: *Warfare, Ritual, and Symbol in Biblical and Modern Contexts*, eds. B.E. Kelle – F.R. Ames – J.L. Wright, SBL.AIL 18, Atlanta 2014, 111–130. A significative example is also offered by Flavius Josephus in his *De bellum iudaicum*, VII, 6.4.201–205: "Observing this Bassus proceeded to practise a ruse upon the enemy, desiring so to intensify their distress as to

582 The gesture of the surrender

coming from ancient figurative artefacts that can provide us with the most adequate idea of the concept of "intimidation" itself. In the famous scene of Sennacherib's siege of Lachish, amongst the various stages of war activities, for example, prisoners of war can be seen impaled in front of the city walls or skinned alive before the eyes of their families (cf. Figs. 38 and 39). For the emotional impact also resulting from such practices in the context of siege warfare, I will defer to the following paragraph.

The opposite communicative register was instead that of reassurances. With this second option, in address to the besieged, according to the corresponding Akkadian locutions, "kind words" would be pronounced.[53] This expression, similar to that in Hebrew offering "peace" (בְּרָכָה/שָׁלוֹם), attested for example in Deut 20:10 (אֶל + קְרָא√ + pron. suff. + שָׁלוֹם + לְ) and in 2 Kgs 18:31 (אֵת +עשׂה√ + pron. suff. + בְּרָכָה), is not to be confused with an informal act of generous benevolence or an offer of surrender without consequences. Anything but.[54] For my topic, it is important that this be emphasised, for even if there is no mention in the book of Jeremiah of any form of negotiation, either for the surrender of Jehoiachin that did occur (cf. 2 Kgs 24:10–12) or for that on the part of Zedekiah which lacked, dramatic results would have certainly not been absent in the case that an agreement of the sort had been met. The "great cupbearer" of Sennacherib, for example, who actually plays on both communicative registers (intimidation and reassurance), upon proposing an "easy" way to surrender to Hezekiah (or rather, directly to the people listening from the walls above), very clearly invites the acceptance in fact of a loss of all rights except that of one's own life, and of being led into exile far from their own land with all that follows (cf. 2 Kgs 18:31–32; Isa 36:15–16).[55]

This is how, in any case, the development of a wartime situation can take the shape of a situation in which the subject under attack (collective or individual) can find themself having to objectively recognise a radical *inferiority* before the enemy. Nonetheless, especially in a scenario dominated by the dynamics of a progressive exasperation of the conflict[56] in which the worst is feared, in addition to this outward or factual aspect, the *subjective* backlash must also be given due importance. Indeed,

---

compel them to purchase the man's life by the surrender of the fort; and in this hope he was not disappointed. For he ordered a cross to be erected, as though intending to have Eleazar instantly suspended; at which sight those in the fortress were seized with deeper dismay and with piercing shrieks exclaimed that the tragedy was intolerable" (FLAVIUS JOSEPHUS, *Josephus*, III, 562–563). Cf. also A. FUCHS, «Über den Wert von Befestigungsanlagen», *ZA* 98 (2008) 45–99 (p. 57).

53 Cf. I. EPH'AL, *The City Besieged*, 43–97 (for the Akkadian forms, see n. 31).

54 Cf. M. WEINFELD, «The Counsel of the "Elders" to Rehoboam and its Implications», *Maarav* 3 (1982) 27–53. In the case of Deut 20:10–11, those who accept "peace" are destined to forced labour.

55 "[...] even when mass deportation did not mean being reduced to the wretched state of slavery, its very nature implied the humiliation of lost personal identity" (R. DOLCE, «Beyond Defeat», 245).

56 See what has already been observed in ch. II, § 3.3.2.4, where I introduced the category of *escalation* to most adequately contextualise the political-military situation in which the Jeremianic message of surrender takes place.

The (sub-)frame of the surrender in the context of the HB   583

it is a determinative factor for explaining the gesture of surrender, which, like war, is always a phenomenon of an anthropological nature.

3.4. Mortal danger, fear, and desire for salvation. The subjective fact

In the field of study devoted to the military history of ancient civilizations, the conviction that the quality of weapons be the decisive factor for the outcome of battles has on not a few occasions induced an interpretative simplification. Some scholars have called this assumption into question, speaking critically of "technological determinism".[57] Indeed, in reality, without underestimating the relevance of the technological component of war, the development of war conflict does not depend only on predictable deterministic cause-and-effect relationships that can be reduced to matters of mere technological-military supremacy. And this is true as well in modern scenarios, which have even seen the introduction of weapons of mass destruction.

The *human factor* remains decisive and should not be ignored.[58] Consider the courage of the fighters, their training, resistance to fatigue, the discipline, stratagems, and above all, the complex and even contradictory ideological, emotional, and irrational dynamics in play. In particular, when the initial balance between the belligerent forces severely deteriorates in favour of one of the contenders, what is also created is a fundamentally important *subjective* implication that contributes to determining the exiguous range of final outcomes. The perception, real or induced, of the dramatic force of the moment generates, in fact, the emotion of *fear*,[59] which can lead to conflicting choices: to decide to surrender or be driven to not do so (to escape or to resist all-out),[60] as is evidenced in the case of Zedekiah or the Jerosolimitan ruling class in

---

57 In this sense, it is asserted that military tactics are determined by the military improvements implemented during the war scenarios. Their adaptation to the new weapons available would, in turn, decide the military superiority and ultimately be identifiable as the main cause for historical upheavals from a political, economic, and social point of view.

58 On this topic, see F. ECHEVERRÍA REY, «Weapons, Technological Determinism, and Ancient Warfare», in: *New Perspectives on Ancient Warfare*, eds. G.G. FAGAN – M. TRUNDLE, HW 59, Leiden – Boston 2010, 21–56.

59 According to the definition of U. GALIMBERTI, *Dizionario di psicologia*, Torino 1992, 659, fear is "a primary emotion of defense, provoked by a situation of danger that can be real, anticipated by prediction, evoked by memory, or produced by fantasy. Fear is often accompanied by an organic reaction, for which the autonomic nervous system is responsible, which prepares the organism for the emergency situation by predisposing it, though not in a manner that is specific, to the preparation of defenses that usually result in fight or flight behaviours [...]" (my translation).
For thematic treatment within the HB, I defer to the already cited study by B. COSTACURTA, *La vita minacciata*.

60 This alternative can be considered the political-military reflection of a basic physiological phenomenon well known in psychology as a *fight-or-flight response* (or also an *acute stress response*): it is an instinctive reaction to highly stressful situations caused by unexpected situations perceived as dangerous. Fear is distinct from anxiety because the first, unlike the second, takes place in the presence of an immediate threat that is concrete and well defined. Both, regardless, naturally serve an adaptive purpose, as they allow human beings to adapt to the conditions of the environment in which they find themselves. Cf. J. PANKSEPP, *Affective Neuroscience. The Foundations*

general, in the very pericope I examined (cf. Jer 38:19[61] and 39:4; 52:7; //2 Kgs 25:4; cf. also Isa 30:16; Ezek 12:12).

This natural emotional state, necessary for survival and cognitive development, arises whenever any threat presents itself to the subject in the form of a stimulus affecting their personal well-being (health, *status*, power, safety, etc.) and is perceived as concrete (even if it can be either real or imaginary, near or far, immediate or future), and it has the aim of triggering adaptive-defensive measures of various kinds. In this sense, one can say that it would always concern human beings both rationally and irrationally (and animals, only on an instinctive level) insofar as they are beings constitutionally subject to the *threat of death*. What makes the experience one that is entirely human and defines both its drama and its mystery, however, is that of consciously living its nature as something structurally destined to die, while at the same time experiencing an irrepressible *desire for life*.

The inexorable drawing near of a *mortal danger* due to an enemy's overwhelming force and the collapse of one's defensive possibilities gives rise to a phenomenology that is diversified. While in the extrabiblical sources, the impressive account of the psychosomatic effects of the Battle of Halule (of 691) between Assyria on one side and the Babylonians and Elamites on the other is worth mention,[62] for a context closer to our topic, it would seem pertinent (and sufficient for my intentions) to refer, above all, to Jer 4:5–31[63] (cf. also Isa 7:2). The text is a dramatic one, dominated by a tumult of emotions and reactions aroused by a terrifying event, whose disruptive force is rendered on an expressive level by the well-known lion metaphor referring to the aggressive power of Babylon: "Up leaps the lion (אַרְיֵה) from his thicket, the destroyer of nations has set out [...]" (4:7).

To be precise, this scene is not simply a description of the anguishing effects of a siege, but is instead an announcement of the invasion that will overwhelm the kingdom of Judah. The scourge is nevertheless presented in its entirety by the prophetic word according to the poetic-symbolic register, without making a distinction between the various moments implicated according to different temporal levels (invasion, siege, destruction of cities and of Jerusalem in particular). For this reason, I believe that some emblematic emotional traits attributable (also) to the final phase of the war against the kingdom of Judah can also be acknowledged.

---

of Human and Animal Emotions, New York 1998, 206–222; G.N. MELDOLESI, *Panico, ossessioni e fobie: psicobiologia dell'ansia*. Dalle origini del comportamento ai rapporti familiari, Milano 2011, 151–207.

61 The fear that animates Zedekiah, while having as its direct object the Jews who have passed over to the enemy ranks, expresses well the general anguish of the historical moment underway.

62 Beyond the inconclusive lots of the battle, the writer of Sennacherib's Annals enjoy describing the paralysing effects of terror aroused by the Assyrian power in the kings of Babylon and Elam: "The terror of my battle overturned their bodies like a *lû*-demon. They abandoned their tents and to save their lives trampled the bodies of their (fallen) soldiers, their hearts were beating like that of pursued young dove, they defiled with hot urine, voided their excrement in their chariots" (D.D. LUCKENBILL, *The Annals of Sennacherib*, 47, col. VI: 26; translation by S. ZAWADZKI, «Depicting Hostile Rulers», 771; cf. RINAP 3/2, 196).

63 Cf. B. COSTACURTA, *La vita minacciata*, 107–111.

The (sub-)frame of the surrender in the context of the HB   585

Jer 4:5–31 is a short but very dense text. In few verses and using icastic expressions, different subjects and diversified emotional states are staged, all having in common a reaction to an imminent mortal danger. All levels of Israelite society are involved: kings, leaders, priests, prophets, Jeremiah himself, all the people of Judah, and all of Jerusalem.

	Subjects involved	Vocabulary	Phenomenology
4:9	The king and leaders	לֵב + אבד√	The heart shall perish (dread)
4:9	The priests	שׁמם√	astonishment
4:9	The prophets	תמה√	wonder
4:10	Jeremiah	אֲהָהּ (interjection)	Ah!
4:13	Jeremiah	אוֹי (interjection) + לָנוּ	Woe unto us!
4:19	Jeremiah	מֵעַי מֵעַי	My bowels!
4:19	Jeremiah	קִירוֹת לִבִּי	The wall of my heart!
4:19	Jeremiah	חיל√ K	To be pained
4:19	Jeremiah	יחל√ Q	Expectation (effort to hold on)[64]
4:19	Jeremiah	המה√	Heart palpitations
4:19	Jeremiah	לֵב + המה√	The heart "roars"
4:19	Jeremiah	חרשׁ√ (II) + לא	Impossibility of keeping silent
4:29	The inhabitants of Judah	ברח√	General escape
4:29	The inhabitants of Judah	בֶעָבִים + בוא√	Go into darkness[65]
4:29	The inhabitants of Judah	בַכֵּפִים + עלה√	Climb up on the rocks
4:29	The inhabitants of Judah	כָּל־הָעִיר + עזב√	Abandon every city[66]
4:30	Jerusalem[67]	שָׁנִי + לבשׁ√	Dress in crimson
4:30	Jerusalem	עֲדִי־זָהָב + עדה√	Adorn oneself with gold

---

64   Probably, the יחל√ Q in the cohortative hi. impf. with 1st pers. sing. ("that I wait/ resist") alludes to the prophet's effort to resist the pain, holding it inside (as, e.g. J.R. LUNDBOM, *Jeremiah 1–20*, 352), though uselessly, as the following expressions in the same verse then attest (cf. also 20:9).

65   With probable reference to caves, woods, or other places of refuge.

66   This probably has to do with the abandonment of cities and villages that, deprived of adequate fortifications, were thus incapable of withstanding a siege.

67   Apostrophised with שָׁדוּד ("devastated", a problematic form, since grammatically it is vocalised in the MT as a masculine past participle), that as, as destined for devastation.

	Subjects involved	Vocabulary	Phenomenology
4:30	Jerusalem	עֵינַיִם + בַּפּוּךְ + קרע√	To put on make-up[68]
4:30	Jerusalem	יפה√	To pretty oneself
4:31	The daughter of Zion	חלה√ + קוֹל	The cry (voice) of one suffering
4:31	The daughter of Zion	בכר√ + צָרָה	The travail of one in labour
4:31	The daughter of Zion	יפח√	Panting
4:31	The daughter of Zion	פרש√ + כַּפַּיִם	To stretch out the hands
4:31	The daughter of Zion	אוֹי־נָא לִי (*interjection*)	*Woe is me!*

As can be noted from the proposed schematisation, individual subjects and their relative emotional-behavioural reactions can be isolated in an order. The political-religious establishment is dismayed, the inhabitants of the kingdom of Judah flee, hide, and seek shelter from the destructive fury of the enemy. Jerusalem, the capital under siege, is clenched with pain like that of childbirth. At the same time, according to another female metaphorical register, the prophet denies in advance that there be any chance of success in a hypothetical attempt to escape the end by resorting to weapons of seduction.[69] We can recognise here the manoeuvres of human wisdom to circumvent the drama underway (possible alliances, political-economic concessions, vain hopes),[70] but without knowing, however, how to recognise either the cause (its own infidelity to the Covenant), the actual entity (the enemies are determined to end it, we are at a point of no return), or the way that YHWH indicates to get through it (surrender).

Fear, expressing the force of the desire to live, instinctively seeks an extreme path of salvation in a situation that already appears to have no way out and conditions the scope of options still possible. If the dishonourable choice of escape is discarded[71] (cf. 2 Mac 12:21–22) along with all-out resistance (with sorties on the outside or combat from the walls) and suicide,[72] nothing remains but the acceptance of a surrender.

---

68   Lit.: "to make one's eyes bigger" with "mascara" (פּוּךְ).
69   See in this regard A. Bauer, «Dressed to be killed: Jeremiah 4.29–31 as an Example for the Functions of Female Imagery in Jeremiah», in: *Troubling Jeremiah*, eds. A.R.P. Diamond – K.M. O'Connor – L. Stulman, JSOT.S 260, Sheffield 1999, 293–305. Jeremiah's metaphorical allusion is a close reference to the behaviour of Jezebel as her end drew near at the hands of Jehu (cf. 2 Kgs 9:30–37).
70   Cf. Ezek 23:40–42.
71   Cf. I. Eph'al, *The City Besieged*, 107–108 and n. 215.
72   This paradoxical possibility is actually conceived to be sort of "vindication" or "salvation", insofar as it is intended to be an extreme gesture of redress or to avoid the most painful effects of the end, and reveals, in any case, that the desire for life does not coincide *tout court* with biological life (cf. the cases of suicide attested in the Bible: Jud 9:52–54; 16:30; 2 Sam 1:1–10; 1 Chr 10:1–6; 2 Sam 17:23; 1 Kgs 16:18; 2 Mac 14:37–46; Matt 27:3–5; Acts 1:18; cf. also the attempted suicide of the prison guard of Philippi

The Jeremianic option, however, as many of the elements highlighted thus far have allowed me to affirm and reiterate, is not referred to as a pragmatic choice dictated by a merely political assessment of the situation. Indeed, had it remained the only way forward, there would have been no need for a prophet to point out the evidence. Once again, we are invited to look at his figure as to the paradigmatic place where God performs both the drama and the salvation in advance. In 4:30, everything that afflicts the socio-religious body of Judah and the anguish of all Jerusalem is reflected in his body and his life. It is a corporeal-existential space transfigured into a place of prophecy, prophecy of the end but also of possible salvation through the handing over of oneself to the enemies. The importance of the meaning can already be sensed, but it becomes present, as with any symbol, through the flesh and materiality of a gesture of which, first of all, fundamental semantic-pragmatic coordinates need to be set.

3.5. The act of surrender

Let me now specifically address the "surrender" alternative and, by initially limiting myself to the biblical attestations noted above (§ 4.2.2), let's look at what actions are put into place to bring it about, and with what vocabulary words they are signified. Let me start with the texts that are most relevant to us, namely, those in the book of Jeremiah, and then consider some cases that are likewise interesting.

Jer 21:9; 37:13– 14; 38:2, 17– 19. While a behaviour denoting a stubborn will to resist is described in 21:9 and 38:2b with a verb expressing the condition of *being static*, that is, "to remain" (√ישׁב) in the city, the surrender in 21:9 (and the desertion in 37:13–15; 38:19) is instead configured as a *movement* having a dual orientation: outward and/or downwards. In fact, according to the basic semantic axes recalled by the relative syntagmas, it is a question of "going out towards" (√יצא + אֶל) the Chaldeans and of "falling down before" (√נפל + עַל) them, or into their hands. The same oppositive relationship is delineated in 38:17–18, where the gesture of "to hand oneself over" is expressed in a conditional clause, first with the verb יצָא strengthened by the infinitive absolute (v. 17b: [...] אִם־יָצֹא תֵצֵא אֶל), and then, in a second hypothetical period proposing the alternative to the contrary, that is, simply that of "to not go out" to the generals of the king of Babylon (v. 18a: [...] וְאִם לֹא־תֵצֵא אֶל). In v. 19b, the expression "to surrender to the Chaldeans", in reference to the Judean deserters, is rendered with √נפל in syntagmic construction with the preposition אֶל.

At first glance, it would seem that these observations could be rendered invalid insofar as the result of an "etymologising" hermeneutic perspective. Indeed, if we were in the presence of a *technical terminology* referring to the gesture of surrender, absolutising the meaning of the verbal roots that make up the two syntagmas would make little sense. Even in this case, however, consideration of the lexicon within a

---

in Acts 16:27–28). Aside from what was already observed in ch. III, § 4.2.2 (and the examples noted in n. 229), think also, in Old Testament times, of the collective suicide of the 960 rebels of Masada (with women and children). With this gesture, the insurgents, at least according to the account of Flavius Josephus (*De bellum iudaicum*, VII, 252–406), refusing to hand themselves over to the Romans, rejected an ignominious surrender and, at the same time, affirmed the dignity and irreducibility of their own political-religious convictions. There is no shortage of examples, in every age and culture, of suicides due to the unsustainability of shame or unfounded accusations.

588   The gesture of the surrender

broader horizon, one that is therefore also pragmatic-cognitive, allows me to put forth
an interpretation of the phenomenon that is more solid than a purely textual basis. In
truth, already on a lexicographic basis, we can gather some clues that are interesting.
It is not difficult to sense that the movement of "to go out towards" ("the Chaldeans"
or "the generals of the king of Babylon") expressed by √יצא + אֶל implicates, on the level
of presupposition of meaning, the encyclopaedic information relating to the *sub-frame*
of the siege, that is, a city surrounded by walls and equipped with at least one fortified
entrance structure under the control of the besieged, from which they decide to go out
to hand themselves over to their enemies or to respect a peace agreement, as in 1 Mac
6:57–62. The use of √נפל + עַל, on the other hand, requires some further clarification.

According to Wolfram von Soden,[73] נָפַל should be counted amongst the onomato-
poeic verbs, and he theorises that the initial נ has developed as a strengthening of
the root (other analogous cases would confirm this). The underlying anthropological
experience is the originary one caused by the force of gravity whereby bodies, when
they fall, impact the surface with a characteristic sound (cf. e.g. Gen 24:64; 2 Kgs 6:5;
Amos 9:9; Nat 3:12; etc.). Relevant syntagmatic constructs could be, amongst the different combinations possible, for example, √נפל + עַל (+ פְּנֵי/אַף + suff.)/(+ אַרְצָה)/(+ רַגְלַיִם +
suff.), which describe the act of falling to the ground and/or on one's own face (or nose)
or at the feet of someone as a sign of humble *prostration* in front of that person (and
also of YHWH himself) to whom one wants to pay homage and/or who is recognised
as having dignity superior to one's own. See, amongst the many cases, Gen 44:14;
50:18; 1 Sam 20:41; 25:24; 2 Sam 1:2; 14:4; 2 Kgs 4:37; Ps 45:6; etc. My theory is that this
type-scene be the one underlying, on the pragmatic-cognitive level, the "technical"
expression of the surrender (with the two interchangeable prepositions: √נפל + עַל/אֶל).
The latter would therefore be its standardised elliptical variant.

A significative piece of confirming evidence is gained by integrating the true-
conditional[74] semantic analysis with, in fact, an extralinguistic perspective. The context
of use of this syntagm is, indeed, in all likelihood, reconstructable, albeit with due
caution,[75] through the figurative attestations of an Assyrian matrix regarding the gesture of submission-surrender of one sovereign (and thus of a state) to another that is
recognised as superior. In all of these scenes, the one who recognises themself as won
over, subdued, or otherwise inferior to the authority before them,[76] prostrates themself

---

73   W. VON SODEN, *Grundriss der akkadischen Grammatik,* AnOr 33, Roma 1952, ³1995, 137.
74   Remember that, as is noted by C. BIANCHI, *Pragmatica del linguaggio,* 5–6, "semantics
      deals with [...] the *meaning* of the linguistic expressions – words or phrases – outside
      of the situations in which they are used. [...] The conventional meaning of an expres-
      sion is thus generally conceived as a set of *conditions*: the rules of Italian, for example,
      associate each word with a set of *applied conditions* (the conditions that an object
      must meet for the word to apply to it) and, in each phrase, a set of *conditions of truth*
      (the conditions that the world must meet for the phrase to constitute an appropriate
      description of the word, and be true"). My translation.
75   It is always necessary to discern between factual truths and stereotyped figurative
      literary styles, as notes e.g. A. FUCHS, «Assyria at War», 385. The fact remains, how-
      ever, that even a merely symbolic representation serves to illustrate the pragmatic-
      cognitive context that the speakers may have subtended in a given communicative
      situation.
76   It can also, in fact, be a common subject, such as a soldier, who pays homage to his
      superior.

Fig. 4C. Ḥanunū of Gaza, face down before Tiglath-Pileser III. Bas-relief from the Kalhu palace of the Assyrian king (British Museum, WA 118933; from R.D. BARNETT – M. FALKNER, The Sculptures of Aššur-Naṣir-Apli II (883–859 B.C.), Tiglath-Pileser III (745–727 B.C.), Esarhaddon (681–669 B.C.) from the Central and South-West Palaces at Nimrud, London 1962, pl. 95, b).

and "falls" with their face to the ground before the other. The oppositive relationship created between the vertical line drawn by the upright figure of the sovereign and the almost horizontal line of the submissive person is remarkable. This can be seen, for example, in the case of Ḥanunū king of Gaza,[77] shown while formally performing the act of submission to Tiglath-Pileser III (745–727), kneeling and falling face to the ground before him (who also places his right foot on his head and points a spear at him as a sign of humiliation and total control over his person; cf. Fig. 40). And again, regarding a historical context that is even more relevant to the biblical world (though a little later than that previous), one can consider the depictions visible on the famous Black Obelisk of Shalmanaser III (858–824) on display at the British Museum (ME 118885). In twenty panels divided into five series of scenes that unfold in succession across the four sides of the five-level monument, with admirable synergy between verbal and non-verbal communication, the thirty-one years of military campaigns of the Assyrian ruler and their consequent successes are evoked and celebrated. The unifying theme is the rich tribute offered in his honour by the subjected vassals. The first two cycles of scenes, starting from above, are of particular interest since they also show the physical gestures with which the defeated sovereigns submit to the great king of Assyria. The act of submission is depicted, as in the case of Ḥanunū, through a *voluntary* prostration, with knees and face to the ground. The first character is the king Sua of Gilzanu (a region of present-day north-western Iraq), while the second

---

[77] Cf. C. UEHLINGER, «Hanun von Gaza und seine Gottheiten auf Orthostatenreliefs Tiglatpilesers III», in: *Kein Land für sich allein. Studien zum Kulturkontakt in Kanaan, Israel/Palästina und Ebirnâri für Manfred Weippert zum 65. Geburtstag*, eds. U. HÜBNER – E.A. KNAUF, OBO 186, Fribourg – Göttingen 2002, 92–125.

is Jehu (cf. Fig. 41), king of Israel (named in the inscription as *Bīt-Ḫumrî*, to wit, "of the house of Omri").[78]

Fig. 41. Jehu, King of Israel, submits to Shalmaneser III. Black obelisk (ca. 827, British Museum, ME 118885 (Photo © Trustees of the British Museum).

There is, therefore, a series of non-semantic information that can plastically provide us with the pragmatic context in which the syntagm √נפל + אֶל/עַל is born and used in the military sphere. On the other hand, Horst Seebass, in his lexicographical study dedicated to נָפַל, notes, with regard to the syntagm in question, that almost all of its occurrences relate precisely to the context of the end of the kingdom of Judah and surrender-desertion option (cf. 2 Kgs 25:11 [//Jer 52:15]; 37:13–14; 38:19; 39:9).[79] In his view, then, the valence of such a gesture would be "neutral", in the sense that it would not convey a connotation that was either positive or negative. It would perhaps be best to specify that the theme of surrender is (always) at the centre of a conflict of interpretations in which each of the parties in question (or the narrator *in primis*) projects upon it their own value or disvalue judgement. And that in this sense, it can never be "neutral". While changing sides is presented as a positive fact in 1 Chr 12:20(2x), 21; 2 Chr 15:9, in the book of Jeremiah, it is clear that the official authorities consider it to be high treason. But it is typical of the Jeremianic prophetic word, according to the programmatic visions in 1:11–16, not so much to see different things than what all can see, but rather to see the same things *differently*, according to the perspective of YHWH. The same applies for another emblematic gesture that expresses the act of submission-surrender, that of the yoke.

---

78 This is the first iconographic attestation of an Israeli sovereign. For further study, see S.C. CURRY, «Jehu and the Black Obelisk of Shalmaneser III», in: *Scripture in History & Theology. Essays in Honor of J. Coert Rylaarsdam*, eds. A.L. MERRILL – T.W. OVERHOLT, Pittsburgh 1977, 71–105; O. KEEL – C. UEHLINGER, «Der Assyrerkönig Salmanassar III. und Jehu von Israel auf dem Schwarzen Obelisken aus Nimrud», *ZKTh* 116 (1994) 391–420 (pp. 406–419 in particular are dedicated to the significance of the gesture of prostration before the great king, with other figurative examples).

79 Cf. H. SEEBASS, «נָפַל», *ThWAT* V, 521–531.

Jer 27:2–13, 16–17. Here, as we have seen,[80] the symbol of the "yoke" (and the ropes) is introduced as a sign of the Babylonian domination, but with a dual meaning. The nuance that we grasp regards the meaning of the prophetic message that interprets it for its interlocutors. First of all, it is predicted as a fact decreed by YHWH, and therefore irrevocable, that all the kingdoms have *already* been virtually placed in the hands of Nebuchadnezzar: "*And so all nations will serve* (√עבד) *him* [...]" (cf. 27:7). The yoke, however, in addition to being exhibited as a plastic (and effective) representation of an ineludible fact, is proposed also as an instrument under which to *voluntarily* subject their own necks: "*Place* (√בוא hi., and in v. 8 √נתן) *your neck beneath the yoke of the king of Babylon, serve* (√עבד) *him and his people and you shall live!"* (cf. 27:12b). The surrender thus appears to be an act requested by YHWH himself and the reference to the yoke can be both metaphorical and metonymic. In an extrabiblical context, as has already been noted,[81] the symbolism of the yoke is widely used in the ancient Near East to refer to the act of submission-surrender imposed upon defeated enemies.

1 Sam 11:1–11. In this episode, Nahash the Ammonite encamps against Jabesh-gilead and declares himself willing to keep peace on the condition that he can gouge out the right eye of all the inhabitants (as a sign of the humiliation of all of Israel). The episode is a strange one: indeed, one may wonder whether this request is not to be understood as a way of rejecting any negotiation, and how a "condition" of the sort could ever be accepted. In any case, in v. 1, initially, a negotiation is attempted (requesting that a pact [בְּרִית + כרת √] be made, by which they be obliged to serve [√עבד] the enemy), then, in v. 3, the concept of "surrender" reappears as a hypothesis, described as "to go out towards" (√יצא + אֶל), and is conditioned on whether or not help can be received from a "saviour" (מוֹשִׁיעַ).

2 Kgs 18:13–16, 31–32. These are two separate, though contiguous, facts. The first: Hezekiah, having rebelled against Sennacherib, the king of Assyria, looks on helplessly as his punishment advances towards him, overtaking and occupying the fortified cities of Judah. Having perceived the impossibility of standing up to it, here is the act of surrender that takes shape in an articulated way:

1	Admission of culpability		v. 14b
	חָטָאתִי	*I have sinned* (√חטא)	
2	Supplication		v. 14c
	שׁוּב מֵעָלַי	*withdraw* (√שׁוב) *from me*	
3	Promise of obedience	*all that you will impose on me* (√נתן)	v. 14d
	אֵת אֲשֶׁר־תִּתֵּן עָלַי אֶשָּׂא	*I will accept it* (√נשׂא)	
4	The levying of the heavy tribute	*The king of Assyria imposes* (√שׂים) *on Hezekiah, king of Judah, three hundred*	v. 14e
	וַיָּשֶׂם מֶלֶךְ־אַשּׁוּר עַל־חִזְקִיָּה מֶלֶךְ־יְהוּדָה שְׁלֹשׁ מֵאוֹת כִּכַּר־כֶּסֶף וּשְׁלֹשִׁים כִּכַּר זָהָב	*talents of silver and thirty talents of gold*	

---

80   In ch. IV of the present dissertation. In this case as well, it has proven proficuous to integrate semantic analysis with a pragmatic-cognitive perspective.

81   Particularly in § 4 of ch. IV.

| 5 | Payment of the tribute [...] וַיִּתֵּן חִזְקִיָּה אֶת־כָּל־הַכֶּסֶף [...] בָּעֵת הַהִיא קִצַּץ חִזְקִיָּה | *Hezekiah delivers* (√נתן) *all the silver* [...] (of the temple and of the royal palace) *At that time, Hezekiah removed* (√קצץ) [...] (the precious overlaying of the doors and door jambs of the temple) | v. 15 v. 16 |

The following episode (from v. 17ss), according to the narrative concatenation of the current text, seems to be due to an afterthought on the part of Sennacherib: the act committed by Hezekiah is considered insufficient and what the king of Judah presumes to be able to preserve (independence and salvation of the city) is deemed inadmissible. The will of the Assyrian sovereign is made explicit through his "great cupbearer"[82]: Sennacherib demands the total subjugation and deportation of the people (cf. v. 32), but concedes the guarantee of life and future well-being in the event of a spontaneous *surrender*. Two locutions express the act requested: "to make peace" (√עשׂה + בְּרָכָה) and "to go out towards me" (√יצא + אֵלַי).

Jdt 2:10–11; 3:1–7; 5:4; 7:12–15, 23–31; 8:9. This entire (fictitious) story, from which we draw only some data of interest to us, would merit a separate study in direct comparison with the message of Jeremiah. Indeed, the prospects are exactly inverted: while the people of Bethulia, exhausted by the siege, would like to capitulate (and the leaders themselves, in a certain sense, set an *ultimatum* to God, after which they would open the doors to the enemy), the faith of the pious Judith ("the Jew") instead results in a deadly counteroffensive.[83] Here, the useless attempt at seduction mentioned by Jeremiah (in 4:30) becomes the deadly weapon that defeats the enemy (cf. Jdt 9:10, 13; 10–11; 12:15–20; 13:6–10, 16; 16:7–9). And while the enslavement demanded by the prophet is presented as the way of life and future blessing in the land of exile, the slavery that the inhabitants of Bethulia would encounter if they were to surrender is proposed by Judith as a source of dishonour and contempt (cf. Jdt 8:23). The hypothesis of surrender is regardless configured according to the following terminology (which I organise following a logic of semantic references):

| 2:10 | ἐκδίδωμι | *to hand oneself over* | opposed to "*to disobey*" (Jdt 2:11: ἀπειθέω) |
| 7:12 | ἐκδίδωμι | *to hand over* | the city |

---

82   It is interesting to note how his speaking below the walls of Jerusalem in Hebrew and not, as was custom, in Aramaic (the language of international diplomacy that the people of that time still neither understood nor spoke), was perceived by the authorities sent by Hezekiah as an additional shock wave, capable of causing the situation to precipitate (cf. vv. 26–28). This is a clear indication of how the word itself can be understood, for all intents and purposes, within the world of war as a determining factor.

83   I note the opposition here as well: while in Jer 4:30, the extreme attempt to remain alive becomes an act of seduction (or prostitution), here the same seductive force of femininity becomes instead the instrument of war used (in faith) to defeat the enemies. To seduce as a desperate gesture of surrender (in order to remain alive), to seduce in order to attack and kill the enemy.

7:26	ἐκδίδωμι	to hand over	the city to plunder (εἰς προνομὴν)
5:4	ἔρχρομαι + εἰς	to come out towards	
7:15	ἀπαντάω	to move oneself towards	in peace (ἐν εἰρήνῃ)
7:24	λαλέω + εἰρηνικά	to negotiate peace	
3:2a	παράκειμαι	to prostrate oneself	+ word of delivering life and goods (vv. 2b-4)
3:7	δέχομαι	to welcome	with songs, dances, etc.[84]

1 Mac 6:49, 55–62; 11:49–51, 61–62, 65–66; 13:45–46:50; 2 Mac 12:11. Given the dominant textual isotopy of these tales (the Maccabaian revolts), scenes of battles and sieges abound. Thus, it is not surprising that there are also gestures of surrender. As compared to the previous attestations, however, the frequency with which, in this context, verbs related to the use of the word are employed, usually to implore the adversary to have mercy, is striking.

1 Mac 11:62	ἀξιόω	to implore	to give (δίδωμι) the right (δεξιὰς)
1 Mac 12:66	ἀξιόω	to implore	to accept (λαμβάνω) the right (τοῦ δεξιὰς)
1 Mac 13:45	ἀξιόω	to implore	to give (δίδωμι) the right (δεξιὰς)
2 Mac 12:11	ἀξιόω	to implore	to give (δίδωμι) the right (δεξιὰς)
1 Mac 11:49	κράζω	to shout	with a plea (μετὰ δεήσεως)
1 Mac 13:45	βοάω	to shout	in a loud voice (φωνῇ μεγάλῃ)
1 Mac 13:50	βοάω	to shout	to accept (λαμβάνω) the right (δεξιὰς)
1 Mac 11:49–50	λέγω	to ask	to give (δίδωμι) the right (δεξιὰς)
2 Mac 12:11	ὑπισχνέομαι	to promise	livestock (βοσκήματα) and to be useful (ὠφελέω)
1 Mac 6:49	ἐξέρχομαι	to go out	of the city (ἐκ τῆς πόλεως)
1 Mac 13:45	ἀναβαίνω	to go up	with wives and children on the wall (ἐπὶ τὸ τεῖχος)
1 Mac 13:45	διαρρήγνυμι	to rip up	the clothes (τὰ ἱμάτια)
1 Mac 11:51a	ῥίπτω	to throw	the weapons (τὰ ὅπλα)

---

84 Such a "festive" welcome really seems to be the translation, in practical terms, of that degrading dressing up in the clothes of a prostitute alluded to by Jeremiah in regard to Jerusalem in 4:30.

3.6. Overview

As can be seen from all the passages cited, the terminology of "to hand oneself over" is quite varied, and every single lexical element contributes to the specification of some nuance of the semantic value of the expressions (content), according to the respective contexts of utterance (speaker, place, time). Without purporting to build a comprehensive systematic organisation of the data collected, I will limit myself to summarily reporting the semantic elements that are most relevant.

Depending on the literary context, a different and specific vocabulary appears that does not seem to consist only of expressions that are rigidly technical. The act of surrender can be expressed with verbs of motion to place referring, above all, to *going out* from the city where one is being besieged to head towards the enemy (to whom one decides to hand themself over), or with a verb that underlies the act of humiliation, prostration, recognition of one's inferiority and total acceptance of the power of the counterpart. In addition to the gestures, the *locutory act* also has an important function in some attestations. Through the *word*, those on the verge of surrender confess their own inferiority (or guilt, as in the case of Hezekiah) and plead with the aggressor to cease hostilities. In this manner, the whole phase of possible negotiations is invoked. Another fundamental semantic trait consists in the *handing over* of something valuable to the enemy; a gesture and object through which one symbolically expresses the handing over of one's own person. This is (at best) a tribute or other goods of various sorts, which can range from livestock to their own city, or life itself given into perpetual slavery. This last perspective of *handing oneself over* is expressed both in the book of Jeremiah and in extrabiblical contexts as a *subjugation* and *serving* of the foreigner by subjecting oneself to their "yoke". And this is why, in 27–28, the prophet visibilises and indicates emblematically, through the symbolic gesture of the yoke, what YHWH expects not only from the leaders of Judah, but from all the people. The prophetic symbolic gesture must therefore correspond with another "symbolic gesture", no less "prophetic". We will see in what sense it can be called "symbolic" and "prophetic" over the following stages of my study.

4. Structure of the symbol and polysemic apertures of meaning. Surrender as a "symbolic gesture"

4.1. Introductory hermeneutical notes: Literal meaning does not exist

Having traced a phenomenology of the act of surrender based on the semantic-pragmatic context beginning from the different linguistic and extralinguistic attestations available allows me to draw a provisional conclusion that, in turn, becomes the introductory premise for this next stage of study: *a literal meaning of surrender does not exist.* Let me clarify this statement, which is, at first glance, perhaps surprising.[85]

The distinction between *literal* meaning and *figurative* meaning was preceded by the corresponding distinction between *denotative* meaning and *connotative* meaning

---

85 For further study and specialised bibliographical referrals on the considerations that follow, I defer to L. ANOLLI, *Fondamenti*, 119–123.

in the works of John Stuart Mill (in 1843). If denotation is the stable, objective element of the meaning of a lexical unit, given by the primary ("obvious") correspondence between a word or enunciation and the object or concept denoted, connotation is instead the secondary meaning of a word or enunciation added to the primary one. Likewise, the classical notion[86] of literal meaning presupposes that words are like "neutral and objective semantic containers", and that their utilisation is sufficient to convey the meanings associated with them.[87] In this perspective, "the literal meaning concerns the *linguistic meaning* generated by the combination of the meanings of the individual words of the sentence and is the result of exclusively linguistic operations, such as phonological, lexical, and syntactic operations".[88] The figurative meaning would instead be a secondary reference of a metaphorical or symbolic type determined by particular expressive modalities. The cognitive dynamic that is determined has been described according to a three-step model, which involves (a) the comprehension of a phrase on a literal level, (b) verification, based on the context, of the literal meaning, (c) an acceptance of the literal meaning, if this makes sense in relation to the context, or a search for another (figurative or metaphorical) meaning that communicates a meaning that is more adequate in relation to the context itself.

In the exegetic field, it need be noted that this dichotomic way of understanding meaning has guided and influenced many interpretive contributions. The reason is simple: amongst the fundamental objectives of the historical-critical method is precisely that, insofar as it is "scientific exegesis", of investigating and determining the *literal meaning* of ancient texts in relation to their respective epochs of composition.[89]

---

86   M. ARIEL, «The Demise of a Unique Concept of Literal Meaning», *JPrag* 34 (2002) 361–402: "According to the classical definition (see Katz, 1977; Searle, 1978; Dascal, 1987) linguistic meaning is direct, grammatically specified, sentential, necessary, and context free" (p. 362).

87   For G.B. CAIRD, *The Language and Imagery of the Bible*, London 1980, Grand Rapids ²1997, "words are used literally when they are meant to be understood in their primary, matter-of-facts sense" (p. 133).

88   Translated from L. ANOLLI, *Fondamenti*, 119–120: "il significato letterale concerne il *significato linguistico* generato dalla combinazione dei significati delle singole parole della frase ed è il risultato di operazioni esclusivamente linguistiche, quali le operazioni fonologiche, lessicali e sintattiche."

89   The document of the Pontifical Biblical Commission *The Interpretation of the Bible in the Church* (of 1993), recalls (in I,A,4) that already, for the *Divino Afflante Spiritu* (but also for the Aquinate himself) "the search for the literal sense of Scripture is an essential task of exegesis". It then specifies that "in order to fulfil this task, it is necessary to determine the literary genre of texts", and that this is "something which the historical-critical method helps to achieve". The document then specifies (II,B,1) that the "literal sense" cannot be understood in a way that is reductionist. In addition to obviously rejecting the fundamentalist approach, which arbitrarily detaches the letter of the text from its historical development (I,F), the literal sense is distinguished from the metaphorical one, letting it be understood that the latter be "not that which flows immediately from a *word-to-word translation* (for example: «Let your loins be girt», Luca 12:35), but that which corresponds to the metaphorical use of these terms («Be ready for action »)" (II,B,1). The literal sense of the Scripture would thus be "that which has been *expressed directly* by the inspired human authors" that "one arrives at by means of a careful analysis of the text, within its literary and historical context. The principal task of exegesis is to carry out this analysis, making use of all

It is precisely this methodological assumption that should be revisited on the basis of the most recent linguistic-cognitive acquisitions. As a consequence, in fact, on the one hand, a problematic identification has been established between the degree of certainty of a textual analysis and its "literal" anchoring, while on the other, for a long time, there has been constant suspicion generated towards figurative, metaphoric, and symbolic meaning, almost as if this were, by its nature, to be left to the domain of subjectivity and thus be excluded from rigorous treatment insofar as it not be verifiable by adequate methodological-conceptual tools. Regarding these hermeneutical frameworks, it need be acknowledged, by now, that the traditional theoretical framework just outlined has been brought seriously into question, on both the linguistic and cognitive levels (assuming that these areas can actually be separated), since the validity of the classical notion of "literal meaning" has become the subject of fierce criticism from linguists and philosophers of language.[90]

Of course, the distinction between literal and figurative meanings still has a certain plausibility and operative usefulness,[91] but to speak of literal meaning presupposing the existence of an *objective* and *neutral* meaning that it would be suffice to decode on the linguistic level, seems unsustainable today. The recourse to the context is, in fact, fundamental even for an understanding of the "literal" meaning itself, given that meaning is a unitary reality in which "denotative" and "connotative" aspects converge in a way that is undisjointable. As for cognitive dynamics, it has been demonstrated that at the neurophysiological level, for the speakers there is, in fact, no distinction between a standardised meaning and a figurative one, and that a just understanding of which form is being used in the discourse requires the same time of processing and response.

In other words, the identification of a "literal" meaning, understood as a *typical enunciation* understandable based on a series of underlying assumptions, is structurally "already *the result of an option* and of a selective operation of interpretation".[92] The meaning is not a pre-established fact, but the product of an interaction between

---

the resources of literary and historical research, with a view to defining *the literal sense* of the biblical texts with the *greatest possible accuracy*". It is noted, however, that although "in general" the literal text is unique, references can be given by the inspired author on multiple levels of reality, as in the case of poetry (or also John 11:50, where two different literal meanings coincide: "Although this example may be extreme, it remains significant, providing a warning against adopting too narrow a conception of the inspired text's literal sense"). Despite the anti-reductionist warnings, as can be seen from the expressions I have highlighted in italics, a definition in the "literal sense" can be understood that comes close to what I have described, as much as it justly says that its complexity is such that it renders an adoption of the historical-critical method alone insufficient.

90 For a synthesis of the discussion and various positions taken, F. RECANATI, «Literalism and Contextualism: Some Varieties», in: *Contextualism in Philosophy*. Knowledge, Meaning, and Truth, *eds.* G. PREYER – G. PETER, Oxford 2005, 171–196. See also C. BIANCHI, *La dipendenza contestuale*. Per una teoria pragmatica del significato, Napoli 2001.

91 I refer to the "methodological contextualism" spoken about by F. RECANATI, *Literal Meaning*, Cambridge 2004, 160.

92 Translated from L. ANOLLI, *Fondamenti*, 121: "[the literarl meaning is] già *il risultato di un'opzione* e di un'operazione selettiva di interpretazione".

the preceding and current contexts of use. In this sense, the literal meaning of a text "does not exist",[93] if not as a possibility (amongst many) of attribution (or activation) of meaning operated by the interlocutor, both on the oral and written level (think of the "interpretive cooperation" of which U. Eco speaks).[94] Understanding the meaning of a text (of any kind) and also the communicative *intention* of the one speaking or writing is therefore the result of an *inference* based on available *clues* and the *encyclopaedia of knowledge* of those involved in the communication.[95] And it is not an "objective" fact.

The implications on my specific object of study translate into a methodological precaution: one must avoid projecting onto the concept of "surrender" expressed by the call of Jeremiah what, for us moderns, its "literal" meaning should be, understood as a semantic notion detached from *the context itself* within which the Jeremianic message is instead inserted as an organic whole. In addition to this fact, the decisive point is the following: the context is one that needs to be specified time after time, on various levels,[96] interconnected between them, and cannot be limited to the narrow semantic space of individual Jeremianic pericopes extrapolated perforce from their underlying communication horizon. There is the context of immediate utterance given by the communicative situation configured by the particular narrative arrangement, the following context given by the preceding and subsequent stages of the narration itself, the surrounding context represented by the "possible world" created by the entire Jeremianic work and its general structure (both on the level of overall disposition and underlying themes). There is then (or prior) the pragmatic-cognitive context given by the insertion in a determined extratextual historical reality, be it that of the events to which the Jeremianic texts refer, and that (not immediately coincident) of the time in which the texts were materially written or reread and reconfigured.

It would be an error of method, therefore, to automatically think of a simple, immediate, and therefore "safe" and "primary" literal meaning of the surrender, which would coincide only with its political aspect and instead reduce other possible symbolic-figural readings to secondary or inconsistent interpretations. I believe that the work done so far has already shown that in the gesture requested by Jeremiah, presented in 27–28 in the form of a symbolic-prophetic act (the yoke), multiple levels of meaning converge in an inseparable unity. The "literal" meaning that I have focalised so far has been of a semantic-pragmatic sort, but two other equally "literal" levels remain

---

93 The title I have chosen to give to the present paragraph also has more than one "literal" meaning. The deliberately peremptory affirmation by which "literal meaning does not exist" can be understood in an absolute sense or relative sense, and can be rejected or accepted, depending on whether one notion or the other of "literal meaning" is presupposed (without counting that the implied reference, which can be then seen in what I say afterwards, is to the literal sense of "handing oneself over to the king of Babylon"). In the one case and the other, they are always inferential operations that have their beginnings in a specific implicit context.

94 Above all in U. Eco, *Lector in fabula*.

95 Cf. C. Bianchi, *Pragmatica del linguaggio*, 106–109.

96 Always in the linguistic field, in controversy against the conception of context assumed in the classical paradigm of formal semantics, see e.g. C. Bianchi, «Three Forms of Contextual Dependence», in: *Modeling and Using Context*. Second International and Interdisciplinary Conference. Context '99, Trento, Italy, September 9–11, 1999, Proceedings, *eds.* P. Bouquet *et al.*, Berlin 1999, 67–76.

598   The gesture of the surrender

to be illustrated: the *symbolic* one and the *prophetic* one. The first, which I am now addressing, is given by the potential valences of meaning implicated by the materiality of the gesture, the second, which I will address in the next chapter, is determined by the communicative context established by the book of Jeremiah (both in the work as a whole, and in the narrative figure of the prophet).

4.2. The symbol is within the body of the "letter", not outside of it

To talk about symbolic meaning in terms of "literal meaning" seems to contradict one of the classic definitions of the "symbol" at its root,[97] that by to which, thanks to a *surplus of meaning*, a word, a gesture, or any communicative element can refer to something other than itself, that is, to a secondary or "figurative"[98] meaning with respect to the level of meaning that is primary or, indeed, "literal". According to the contextualist perspective that I have drawn from the linguistic field, we should instead say that, on the part of the interpreter, in the determination of a symbolic meaning, the same basic operation occurs as it does for any "literal" meaning: starting from the interaction between the element of meaning in play, one's cognitive encyclopaedia, and own inferential capacity, the interpreter activates or chooses to activate some of its "semantic opportunities". But the same goes for the emitter of a symbolic communication.

This means that the symbol already has *in itself*, in its literality, or better still, in its concreteness and in its being grounded in matter (whether this be natural or anthropological-cultural), the potential to refer to *other than itself*. This "other than itself" should therefore not be understood as something that is attributable from the outside, conventionally or arbitrarily.[99] We would be in the regime of allegory or signs. The symbol is *already* in the letter of the gesture, and is not a secondary meaning (if not only logically or at the level of abstraction).[100] Its materiality, that is, *does not*

---

97   For an updated synthesis on the theory of the symbol and symbolic language (also in relation to the "sign" and to "metaphor") in perspective of hermeneutics and biblical exegesis, see the valuable work of L. Gasparro, *Simbolo e narrazione in Marco*. La dimensione simbolica del secondo Vangelo alla luce della pericope del fico di Mc 11,12–25, Anbib 198, Roma 2012 (above all, pp. 21–92).

98   According to P. Ricœur, who articulates an important reflection on the relationship between symbol and metaphor (in many contributions, but especially in *La métaphore vive*), the symbol cannot be understood simply as the substitution for rhetorical purposes of a "literal" term with a "symbolic" one. In this manner, there would be no real semantic innovation, a process that instead occurs in the "living" metaphors (which are phrases more than single terms). Here as well, the contextual question is a decisive one. The metaphor manages to say something new about the reality by putting in an unresolvable tension (and thus, one that produces sense) two distinct meanings, two different interpretations of a phrase, one literal and one figurative. In the case of the symbol, on the other hand, according to this perspective, the second meaning is reachable only by traversing the primary one all the way to the end (cf. L. Gasparro, *Simbolo e narrazione in Marco*, 41).

99   Even though in the complex history of the notion of symbol there are hermeneutic traditions that understand it precisely as a conventional and arbitrary fact, that is, in a way entirely opposite to the definition that I assume.

100 In this sense, "pour celui qui participe à la signification symbolique, il n'y a pas deux significations, l'une littérale et l'autre symbolique, mais un seul mouvement qui nous

refer from a first sense to a second sense, but rather, that which we improperly call a "secondary sense" is *summoned, included, rendered present* and *incorporated* into the symbol.[101] With a difference from "concept" that is substantial: the symbol actualises a communicative dynamism of meaning that has the peculiarity of not exhausting it, not chaining it, and leaving it free to circulate. The secondary meaning, for those who understand the symbol, is or becomes the primary one. In this sense, to set reality and symbol in opposition, as is often done, is completely inappropriate.[102] To caress does not mean to touch an epidermis in a way that is superficial or only material, but to express affection, closeness, etc. to another person (which does not coincide with the skin itself, but to which the skin symbolically refers or, rather, makes, in fact, present). It is obvious that, at least for the one who makes the gesture, the meaning is not secondary, but exactly what is wanted to be communicated, mediated by the "letter" or materiality of the gesture.

The path generated by the symbol traces a line *from a visible fact to an invisible one*. The symbol makes the invisible present as a missing part, and missing not because it is not literal, but precisely because it is not immediately perceivable or material. In this sense, it is present at the very moment a symbolic reality is given. The broken part that the symbol is, therefore, is a constitutive invitation to *recompose the whole*. But the whole in the symbol is *already* given, because this whole is an inseparable and mysterious unity of visible and invisible. And it can be complete only in this form, according to this ontological modality, which unites the limited and unlimited. The structural fracture of the symbol therefore coincides with the fault between what is seen and what, though present, is not immediately seen.

It is not surprising, then, that the Scripture, and the prophets in particular, makes extensive use of symbols. And that even the symbolic gestures, contrary to what has often been said, take on great communicative importance.[103] It is precisely the prophet who sees and shows others the invisible. Of the boundless symbolic horizon of meaning, what is of particular interest to us for my topic is the sphere of corporeal gesturality. A crossroads of the senses, the body, according to this perspective, cannot be conceived as mere biological data to which, secondarily, figurative or symbolic meanings can perhaps be attributed from the outside. The body is, in itself, "symbolic irradiation". And as such, it becomes involved and oriented in the communicative dynamism of prophecy.

---

transfère d'un niveau à l'autre et qui nous assimile à la signification seconde grâce à – ou à travers – la signification littérale" (P. Ricœur, «Parole et symbole», 150).

101 In this sense, as is asserted by T. Fawcett, *The Symbolic Language of Religion. An Introductory Study*, London 1970, 27: "Symbols are not created, but born out of life."

102 "Ajoutons une précision tout à fait capitale. Dans le langage courant, le qualificatif 'symbolique' est parfois presque synonyme de 'irréel'. [...] Évidemment, appliquée à la Bible, une telle conception est catastrophique. Je dirais même plus: dans la Bible, une réalité symbolique s'appuie sur le réel, bien loin de le nier" (N. Guillemette, *Introduction à la lecture du Nouveau Testament. Au soir du troisième jour*, Paris 1980, 332).

103 For these observations, refer to ch. IV, §§ 3.1–2.

600 — The gesture of the surrender

L'antropologo M. Leenhardt, nel suo saggio *Do kamo. La persona e il mito nel mondo melanesiano,* ci racconta di un missionario che chiede all'indigeno: "Insomma non è forse la nozione di spirito che abbiamo portato nel vostro pensiero?" E l'indigeno: "Lo spirito? No, non ci avete portato lo spirito. Noi conoscevamo già l'esistenza dello spirito. Quello che ci avete portato è la nozione di corpo." Ma che nozione di corpo può aver portato il missionario che l'indigeno non conosceva? Se indaghiamo l'universo simbolico delle società primitive non tardiamo a renderci conto che per loro il corpo non è quell'entità anatomica che noi conosciamo come qualcosa di isolabile dalle altre entità che compongono il mondo oggettivo e che identifichiamo come sede della singolarità di ogni individuo; per loro il corpo è il centro di quell'irradiazione simbolica, per cui il mondo naturale e sociale si modella sulle possibilità del corpo, e il corpo si orienta nel mondo tramite quella rete di simboli con cui ha distribuito lo spazio, il tempo e l'ordine del senso. Mai quindi il corpo nella sua isolata singolarità, ma sempre un corpo comunitario, per non dire cosmico, dove avviene la circolazione dei simboli e dove ogni singolo corpo trova, proprio in questa circolazione, non tanto la sua identità, quanto il suo luogo.[104]

The richness and even the communicative surplus triggered by the symbolic body is due to the fact that *polysemy* is intrinsic to the concept of symbol and also constitutes its strength, intrigue, and beauty. While the technical signs in their perfect transparency aim simply to convey that which they signify and for which they are used,[105] symbolic language never coincides with the mere delivery of a fact or a clear and distinct Cartesian idea.[106] It goes far beyond, and, drawing on the *unconceptualised* universe of human experience, it bestows on a *concrete fact* and its verbal or non-verbal expression the power to analogically evoke dimensions of the real that are unexpected and profound, or at least not immediately reachable. This is also why symbols are timeless and transcultural. Ultimately, it is a dimension of nature that is

---

104 Translated from U. GALIMBERTI, *Il corpo*, Opere V, Milano 1983, [11]2002, 33: "The anthropologist M. Leenhardt, in his essay *Do kamo. The person and the myth in the Melanesian world* tells us of a missionary who asks the native: 'Is it not perhaps the notion of spirit that we have brought into your thinking?'. And the native: 'The spirit? No, you didn't bring us the spirit. We already knew the existence of the spirit. What you have brought us is the notion of body'. But what notion of the body might the missionary have brought that the native did not know? If we investigate the symbolic universe of primitive societies, we are not slow to realise that for them, the body is not that anatomical entity that we know as something insolable from the other entities that make up the objective world and that we identify as the seat of the singularity of each individual; for them, the body is the centre of that symbolic irradiation, by which the natural and social world is modeled on the possibilities of the body, and the body orients itself in the world through that network of symbols with which it distributed space, time and the order of meaning. Never, then, does the body in its isolated singularity, but always a community body, not to say cosmic, where the circulation of symbols takes place and where every single body finds, precisely in this circulation, not so much its identity, but its place."

105 Cf. P. RICŒUR, *Le conflit des interprétations*, 285–286.

106 Cf. U. GALIMBERTI, *Paesaggi dell'anima*, Milano 1996, 26: "The impossibility of defining the symbol with the logic of reason testifies to a linguistic impossibility intimately connected to the inability of reason to speak without suppressing the very source of its language" (my translation).

Surrender as a "symbolic gesture"   601

constitutive, understood as *created*: to make reference to its Origin, convey the meaning imprinted by the Word that evoked it, provide the intelligence with a direction towards which it may push. The symbol challenges, "gives rise to thought", and asks to be interpreted. Its deciphering is always a work in progress and is never complete, it is not an exclusive object of historical science, it cannot be proven as conclusive, but shown or suggested.[107]

If the symbol is in the letter of the body, this is also because the body itself is letter, verb, and communication of meaning. All the more so if, as in the case of Jeremiah, it is thrown into the scene of history and made word of YHWH to his people. But caution: it is not only the prophetic body that generates symbolic gestures or an entire symbolic-prophetic life. The gesture of the yoke asks, as a response, an equally symbolic-prophetic gesture of welcoming of the meaning of history. That of submission-surrender to Babylon. The prophetic body (performed) generates other prophetic bodies (and gestures).

4.3. Fundamental symbolic irradiations implicated by the act of surrender

4.3.1. *The symbol of the yoke and the yoke of the symbol*

The Jeremianic message that we are studying spurns abstract communication and is conveyed from the outset through the involvement of somatic symbolic structures. Even when it involves a more generic *submission* to the Babylonian power (in chs. 27–28), before it is an auditory word, it is a visual text unfolding before the eyes of the interlocutor. The human body that bears the yoke of a beast of burden certainly evokes a metaphorical language that is quite common in the ancient Near East. But the sphere of pre-linguistics imposes itself here with the concreteness of a prophetic dramatisation, which harnesses the strength of some fundamental symbolic dimensions and makes them detonate together. At least, according to two different levels of meaning.

First: *the human is mixed with the animal*. We can no longer speak only of the "symbol of the yoke", but also of the "yoke of the symbol", that is, of the yoke that the symbol is, since it manages to con-*join* different and even opposite worlds. Two symbolic spheres collide, merge, intertwine. And, under the same "yoke", they give life to something new. This is true even if the reference is to the *status* of prisoner of

---

107   To offer itself as an opportunity for holistic access to the Scripture (even only as literature), exegetic science cannot therefore limit itself to being an exercise of historical intelligence (philosophical and/or literary) that verifies its own validity on the basis of dictates of method that programmatically exclude the symbolic phenomenon. The biblical world, in fact, (as well as the rest of life) is woven with symbolic values that elude the statistics, immediate confirmation, and in general, a uniquely demonstrative procedure, and speak above all to sensitivity and intuition. This, however, does not impede rigorous study of the symbolic structures summoned by the single texts, focalising the perspectives of meaning that are most pertinent on the basis of the different contexts. It is not therefore a question of preferring one or the other form of knowledge, but of ordering them harmoniously with each other. See in this regard the study of the symbol in relation to the historical-critical method also in the reflections of L. Alonso Schökel, *Símbolos matrimoniales en la Biblia*, Estella 1997, 44–46.

war. It regards *in primis* humanity bound by bonds and bindings that radically reduce its capacity for action, as is the case for oxen or other animals. Movement is still possible, indeed, it is *obligatory*. But it is no longer the sovereign liberty of action of the humankind of the Genesis (nor that of a historical king) directing it. From being rulers of the animal world, those forced into a yoke find themselves regressing to the space of the fifth day of creation or to the first part of the sixth. That is, to obey, along with other animals, other human beings (cf. Gen 1:20–26). Having opened that semantic trajectory, the symbol immediately offers yet another, similar and, at the same time, of an opposite sign: the yoke is borne by *those who love*, can be an expression of choice, service, and voluntary dedication (cf. e.g. Exod 21:5).[108] Paradoxically, in fact, in the symbolic Jeremianic gesture, the one who bears the yoke is the prophet, and he does so as a *free* man. No human authority has forced him. It is he who has chosen to obey YHWH, it is he who, by obeying YHWH, is submitting to the yoke and to the judgment of others. We are thus already on a second level, which, according to the logic typical of the symbol, coincides with the first: the relationship between *constriction* and *freedom*.

The theme of free will is even more evident on the linguistic level, where the symbolic remains in any case underlying as a foundation for the metaphorical or figurative plane. The matter is that of *freely* putting one's own neck under or inside the yoke of the king of Babylon (cf. 27:8, 11, 12; etc.). The concrete translation on the political plane of this injunction still has a symbolic epicentre (implicit in Jeremiah): the payment of a *heavy tribute*. The fact that it is heavy does not negate that it is also a symbol. On the contrary. It reveals the specific weight of its corporeality. As they strip themselves of their treasures or of the goods of the people, and hand themselves over to a foreign ruler (cf. 2 Kgs 23:33, 35; 2 Chr 36:3; etc.), it is said that the authority no longer resides in either the royal palace or the temple, as it did at its origin. The "great king" is outside of the confines of his own state. The national king is a subject, more or less like all the others. He too must bend over and fall, face down, before a power that overwhelms and directs him. Exactly like beasts of burden.

4.3.2. *The gate and walls of the City. To go out and (to let) enter*

There is never any mention of doors or walls in the Jeremianic message of surrender. At least not in a form that is explicit. And yet, the reference to such symbolic elements is implicit in it, and it would be a mistake to ignore it. This is another characteristic of the symbolic dimension. A concrete fact refers not only to a symbol, but to a *contextual symbolic network*, to a "frame symbolics", we could say, consisting of the series of elements interconnected at the level of immediate relevance. And it could not be otherwise, if a fundamental characteristic of the symbol is its incarnation in all that can be clearly named and identified amongst the objects and phenomena of the world. The *frame semantics* can then be, at the same time, a *frame symbolics*, and vice versa.

As we have seen, in the lexicon of the Jeremianic surrender, the act of *going out* to meet the generals of the king of Babylon assumes a particular relevance. The intuition of the implicit elements of this type scene is immediate. One goes out *from* a circumscribed location, from an enclosed space, to enter another. Here, one goes out from a city, Jerusalem. One goes out from a city fortified by *walls*[109] laid to siege to

---

108   See what is observed in ch. IV, § 4.1.5.
109   Cf. A. Fuchs, «Befestigungsanlagen», 45–99.

place themself in the hands of the enemy leaders conducting the war manoeuvres. By necessity, one goes out of a *gate*, or the main gate (cf. 17:19), which, until then, has been kept barred and safeguarded. Gates and walls of defence are tightly interconnected elements, which together form a symbolic plexus richer than the individual elements considered independently.

The *gate* (שַׁעַר) is a liminal place, the threshold between two worlds. Ambivalent by nature,[110] it can be opened or closed, from inside or outside, though in antiquity, for obvious reasons, urbic doors were closed only from the inside. Depending on the point of view, it means protection, prohibition of access for strangers, or impediment, since it leaves out, excludes, or initially postpones to an exhibition of a sign of recognition. It can imprison in an enclosed space or be the object of attempted break-ins, if one wants to enter by force. It represents the line of demarcation between belonging and being excluded from a city community, whether this be permanent or temporary. In the ancient Near East, the city gate is a monumental entrance, the civic and public space par excellence, the place that is most crowded and controlled. The city gate represents the weakest part of the defensive wall, but precisely for this reason, it is also its most fortified part. It is necessary to allow the daily entry of goods for subsistence. It is the place of judgment and legal procedures of various natures, asylum, a theatre for executions, display of corpses of the condemned or the spoils of war, place of thrones and celebratory works of art, area subject to the protection of deities, place of assemblies and public proclamations, place for markets and transactions, and a social place for encounters.

Through a gate, one can pass, *enter* or *exit*. An immediate reference, of originary valence, it regards the entire experience of human life. Its structural caducity sketches not so much a transfer from one place to another, each distinct from the other, but a "symbolic excursion" that passes from the going out of the womb to a re-entering of the same cavity, even if this is called "land". Uterus and tomb, according to the logic of the symbol, overlap. And it is therefore not surprising that the book of Jeremiah itself includes, within these two coinciding polarities, the travails of the Jeremianic experience, maintaining a tension between the originary moment when the prophetic body is shaped in the womb (cf. 1:5) and his wish that this journey had never have begun, but instead been brought to a conclusion inside the womb itself at the outset (cf. 20:14–18). Job will put it even more explicitly (cf. Job 1:21), bringing the act of going out (√יצא) even closer to that of returning (√שׁוב) to the womb. Paradoxically, however, for Jeremiah, drawn out from the pit of death alive, this will be the experience of a new birth. The call to surrender is in the same horizon of meaning, since it

---

110   See in this regard e.g. E. OTTO, «שַׁעַר», *ThWAT* VIII, 358–403 e ID., «Zivile Funktionen des Stadttores in Palästina und Mesopotamien», in: *Meilenstein*. Festgabe für Herbert Donner, *eds.* M. WEIPPERT – S. TIMM, Wiesbaden 1995, 188–197 (a revised and updated version can be found in his collection of studies: ID., *Altorientalische und biblische Rechtsgeschichte*. Gesammelte Studien, Wiesbaden 2008, 519–530. On its symbolic-rememorative function in relation to the sculpting of the post-exilic social identity, see the recent contribution by C. WALSH, «Testing Entry: The Social Functions of City Gates in Biblical Memory», in: *Memory and the City in Ancient Israel, eds.* D.V. EDELMAN – E. BEN ZVI, Winona Lake 2014, 43–59.

604 The gesture of the surrender

is also a "going out" from the protective womb of the City to "enter" into a hostile or/ and foreign dimension, in which one finds oneself stripped of everything but *alive*, their naked "life" (נֶפֶשׁ) having been earned "as war booty" (לְשָׁלָל).

Another symbolic territory that can get across to the reader the evocation of the act of "going out" in relation to that of "entrance" takes instead a different appearance from that of the *return* (from the womb of the mother to the womb of mother earth) and assumes that of the *destination*, of the reaching of the final objective of a journey. It is the perspective, likewise "originary", within the sphere of the traditions of Israel, of the Exodus from the land of slavery of Egypt to the promised land of Canaan. As I have noted, the Jeremianic call to surrender, precisely by picking back up the same symbolic register, appears to entirely invert the coordinates and direction of that itinerary. There are, however, different levels of meaning: the going out from Jerusalem leads to the spoliation of the exile, but only so that one can reenter and return renewed (cf. 16:14–15; //23:7–8 and, in general, chs. 30–31 and 32–33); whereas the exit from the land of promise not requested by YHWH (when one should instead remain; cf. the events narrated in chs. 41–43) leads to re-entering Egypt, which represents the real failure or rewinding of the history of salvation to its zero point (cf. Deut 28:68), with the aggravation of free choice (which makes it a curse or self-condemnation, and not a state of unjust oppression that invokes a liberator).

To enter and to go out, therefore. The two concepts, if invoked by verbal roots placed in close correlation as anonyms of each other (usually √יצא and √בוא), indicate a state of total freedom (in reference to Jeremiah before his imprisonment, cf. 37:4, 12), and in the case of the kings, of full sovereignty:

> The Lord said to me: «Go to stand at the *gate* (שַׁעַר) of the Sons of the people, through which the kings of Judah *enter* (√בוא) and *exit* (√יצא), and all the *gates* of Jerusalem (17:19).

In particular, in 1 Sam 8:20, it is pointed out that *to go out to battle* at the head of the army is the specific task of the king, seen as the supreme military leader. The Jeremianic perspective of surrender therefore implicates the management of this symbolic place of transit and overturns the paradigm radically. One must go out not to fight and win: the king must lead everyone to *surrender*. The gate must be opened wide, even if this is undesired. Even if there is a ferocious enemy outside whose true intentions are not fully predictable, regardless of any possible prior stipulation of peace treaties (cf. 1 Mac 6:58–63; 11:50–53; 2 Mac 4:24; 14:19–22).

To go out of the gate (which marks the space for controlling the entrance or exit from the urban circuit) and handing themselves over to the enemy means allowing the enemy *to enter*, granting them the right to dispose of the fate of the city at will. Those who leave can no longer return, at least not like before. There are more than a few cases attested in the ancient Near East of rebellious rulers who are then reinstalled on the throne after their capitulation by the victors. Sovereigns "cloven" by war, re-entering their own domain only to reign as the lieutenants of another authority. That is not always the case. Often, though, one leaves the scene permanently, and others enter in place of the defeated. To be able to return as king to one's own city is a promise that sometimes only a prophet can have the courage to make (cf. 22:4).

4.3.3. The goods, the land, the temple, and the loss of possession

Surrendering to the enemy also implies a symbolic handing over of the city. Some might immediately object that it is not symbolic at all. But that would be like falling back into the misunderstanding, already noted, whereby the symbolic would not be real, concrete. And yet, the goods that are in fact handed over in the act of surrender are precisely that. By their moving from hand to hand, they call into question and render visible another essential dimension of human experience: *possession* (and loss of it). This expression of power concerns different subjects and can be exercised over a wide range of goods, and not only material ones.

It can be useful, in this regard, to recall the addressees who, in the book of Jeremiah, are asked to surrender and to thus identify some forms by which an exercising of the "power of disposal" relates to them. These are mainly *state and/or national entities* (foreign nations, the kingdom of Judah and its people, and the inhabitants of Jerusalem in particular; cf. 27:2–11, 16–17; 38:2–3; but cf. also 29:4–7; 42:7–18), the figure of the *king* (cf. 27:12–13; 38:17–23), and the *priests* (27:16). To these subjects, in different ways, we can connect the availability of various natures of *goods*, including, above all, the *land*, which for Israel is a sign of the Covenant, and the temple, sign of power over the cultic sphere, which, in Israel has its most significant materialisation in the "house of YHWH" (בֵּית־יְהוָה). It should also be emphasised that, with the act of surrender, one's own rights over *persons* subject to his own authority (wives, children, ministers, soldiers, slaves, etc.; cf. 6:12; 8:10; 38:22) also fall and are placed into the hands of the enemy.

It is no coincidence, in this perspective, that one of the most dramatic symbolic gestures demanded of Jeremiah by God is that of celibacy (cf. 16:1–9), that is, the renunciation of fundamental relationships, of having a *wife* and *children* of his own. The concept of dispossession is expressed here through the root לקח: it is that of "to not take for oneself" (v. 2: לֹא־תִקַּח לְךָ). The same verb is the Leitmotiv of the "the right of the king" (מִשְׁפַּט הַמֶּלֶךְ), preannounced by the prophet Samuel at precisely the crucial historical-theological moment of the advent of the monarchical power in Israel (cf. 1 Sam 8). If it is the act of "taking" (material goods and people) what characterises the figure of the king (and this reduces the Israelites to the rank of "slaves" [עֲבָדִים] according to 1 Sam 8:17), one can get an even better sense of the profound symbolic valence the Jeremianic injunction of surrender evokes (even in light of prophetic criticism of the abuses of the royal house; cf. 21:11–23.8). Not to mention the symbolic valence of the possession of the Promised Land and the circumstance of its loss (cf. 2:7, 15; 3:19; 4:7, 20–28; 5:19; 6:8, 12; 8:10; etc.).

> The anthropological theme of possession runs throughout the entire HB and has many other pertinent implications, which it will not be possible to explore here. In necessarily brief terms, it is regardless possible to draw a line that, by placing in intertextual relation some passages commonly recognised as being of fundamental importance to the biblical tradition, makes the following aspects related to "possession" evident: a) it is an essential (and not accidental) dimension of human existence and its positivity depends on its being desired by God for human beings (there is an actual order to "possess"); b) its truth consists in recognising it and in maintaining it within the logic of the gift that typifies the Covenant, whereby "possessing" need necessarily be open to some form of sharing (without this being identified with "dispossession"); c) to betray this logic means perverting the meaning of possession

606 The gesture of the surrender

and, at a particular moment in the history of Israel – when this "perversion" seems to reach its peak because of idolatry and a rejection of the prophetic word – to the order to "own", with Jeremiah, what follows is that of accepting to "be deprived of possession": it is an act of faith requested as a way to re-establish the authenticity of its originary meaning.

a) In the origin stories, it seems clear that the biblical perspective, according to which man gratuitously receives not only the goods of creation, but also himself and the only help that can free him from his solitude,[111] woman. The gift received establishes the (even mutual) possession, which, however, does not coincide with unlimited ownership. This expresses, that is, an effective power connected to the "availability" of everything that we generically call "good",[112] but excludes that absolute and exclusive right, which immediately belongs to God alone. The human being can eat the fruits of the tree of life, but not those of the tree of knowledge of good and evil (cf. Gen 2:9, 16), a sign of this intrinsic limit placed on the human condition, a limit that is itself also a gift, because it assumes the prophetic dimension of indicating the truth of a relationship.

To possess, that is, to enjoy an availability concerning that which is "good", is in any case a dimension so inherent to humanity that it appears almost simultaneously with the creative act of which it is object. Even in Gen 1:26, 28, its very existence appears to be aimed at "dominating" (√רדה) and "subjugating" (√כבש), expressions that denote the administration of a possession and the exercise of a sovereignty that are actualised, however, not tyrannically, but in the likeness of the governance of God, that is, through the meekness of the word.[113] This is symbolically explicated in the second story through the act of imposing names (cf. Gen 2:19–20). To possess is therefore a good reality, foreseen and desired by God for humankind, but subject to ambiguity.

b) In v. 29, it is expressly lexicalised (although in reference to nourishment) that the "good" does not find itself in the hands of humanity by chance; there was a movement, a transition from one hand to the other. It comes from God: "Behold, *I give you* (הִנֵּה נָתַתִּי לָכֶם) [...]", but it is tied to a command that demands obedience in faith (cf. Gen 2:16). Nevertheless, the "good" cannot be stopped on the palm or in the fist of a hand, but remains "good" only if its path continues, for that which the greatest and divine God gives in possession (in an analogous way) is his own ability to give what he possesses. Thus, man and woman, who are given their lives and to whom one is given to the other, will actualise this possession only by passing it on to their children.[114]

Another beginning includes and expresses the same movement. Abraham is elected and simultaneously the "possession" is annexed to this in the form of a promise (cf. Gen 15:7). Here too, the "good" receives its meaning only if inserted into the flow

---

111 According to the study by J.L. Ska, «"Je vais lui faire un allié qui soit son homologue" (Jon 2,18). A propos du terme '*ezer* – "aide"», *Bib* 65 (1984) 233–238, the term "help" (עֵזֶר) is placed precisely in reference to that mortal threat (solitude), from which only YHWH can liberate.

112 I obviously intend, with this term, to include by extension both material and spiritual realities.

113 Cf. P. Beauchamp, «Au commencement», 105–116.

114 And the children will close the circle by directing the good to God anew, in the symbolic form of sacrifice (cf. Gen 4:3).

Surrender as a "symbolic gesture" 607

of the gift that from God comes to the elected one and, from him, passes on to his offspring (cf. Gen 17:2–8). But there is also something new, a new way of actualising the believer's consent. Receiving what God freely gives as a gift as a "possession" means that something else must be left behind: it is necessary to leave one's own *land* in order to enter into that which God will then show (cf. Gen 12:1). Another founding event reveals the same logic, with an even more radical reference to the "land", understood as a perpetual inheritance to be transmitted from father to son, received as a gift from YHWH[115]: both as a *conquest* made possible by God alone (cf. Deut 6:10–12; 24:13; etc.) and as an inheritance (נַחֲלָה) *allotted* (גּוֹרָל) and shared by all (see Josh 14–19; Num 26:55–56). The global meaning of the history of Israel is enclosed in the binary schema of the tradition of the Exodus, which places the *going out* from Egypt in close relationship with the *entrance* into the land of Canaan, as fulfilment of the promises made to the fathers. This movement corresponds to the transition from the condition of the "slave" (עֶבֶד), who juridically does not possess even themself, and "immigrant" or "foreigner" (גֵּר), who has no home of their own, to that of a free resident with the right to live (√ישׁב) in their abode and in their land, a non-transferable symbol and sign of their inalienable dignity.

Entering the Promised Land therefore coincides with the order of God to "take in possession" (cf. e.g. Josh 1:6), an order that anyway comes after the long training of the desert: that is, after having realised the need *to leave behind them* the onions and watermelons of Egypt (cf. Num 11:5) and after learning, in a certain sense, to return to being children, receiving every day that manna from the hand of God that, at the very moment of its gathering means submitting to the law of the one who gives it.[116] And it can be no other way. How else would one know that it has to do with a new beginning, if that which is good were to lose its intimate relational valence as precisely all that which is recognised as a "gift"[117]? When Jeremiah proposes the naked possession of life ("as war booty") as a way of salvation, he can only allude to the reproposition of a similar condition, where the perversion of possession can be healed by the gratuitousness of the gift.

c) It is at this misrepresentation that the prophets point the finger, at a time when possession reaches the peak of opacity due to idolatry. The fulfilment of the event of the Exodus had taken place in the transition from the nomadic life represented by the "tent", to the stability of the dwelling, indicated by the solidity of the "house" or the "palace". But now the houses and the land are expropriated, the (royal) palace built on blood and by violence.[118] One no wonders any longer "where is the

---

115 For deeper study of the theological significance of this theme, see the extensive *excursus* on "the land (as inheritance) in Israel", to which I refer, in P. BOVATI, *Giustizia e ingiustizia nei libri profetici*. Dispense PIB, Roma 2004, 107–111.

116 "La manne est ce pain qui met sous la loi du donateur, et la Loi, qu'elle dit elle-même, est d'attendre tout de lui: ce qui est commandé, c'est de croire [...]" (P. BEAUCHAMP, *L'un et l'autre Testament*, 47).

117 Keep in mind in this regard the warnings formulated in Deut 9:4–6 (cf. also 1 Chron 28:8).

118 On this these, I defer to S.M. SESSA, «"Andranno in rovina le case d'avorio. Oracolo del Signore" (Am 3,15). Abitare il dono di Dio edificando sull'ingiustizia? Storie di progetti insensati», *PSV* 64 (2011) 47–67.

608 The gesture of the surrender

Lord?"[119] and the cult of Baal promulgates the harsh law of the idol[120]: By saying to the wood and stone "you are my father, you have generated me" (cf. 2:27), human beings worship themselves as they prostrate before the work of their own hands, and it is precisely for this lie that death abducts the fertility gifted by God (cf. 7:30–31). Injustice that loses sight of the meaning of the possessed good leads to the injustice that usurps that of others as well, and a sole *remedy* is indicated in both cases by the prophetic word: the privation of all possessions (cf. e.g. 8:8–10), to subtract the "good" from those who he had taken it away from the "movement" that had been imprinted on them from above, to reveal that outside of the logic of the Covenant (which is a logic of gratuitousness and fidelity), the usurped possession (of the earth, the house, and other gifts of God) becomes a mortal trap for those who own it. It is like a new desert for a new relationship with God (cf. 22:6; 31:2).

In the historical juncture that provides a frame for the texts of the Jeremianic invitation to surrender is the entire people of Israel, called upon to carry out a decisive act of *faith*, configured by Jeremiah as an actual gesture of *dispossession*, one as radical as the goods in question are fundamental. Indeed, what is at stake is their own identity (religious, national, and political). By handing themselves over to the king of Babylon, in fact, they are called to deprive themselves of the "visible" dimension of the promise of God, and this is accomplished by renouncing the tangibility of the *land* of Canaan (perennial pledge of the Covenant), the perseverance of the ruling *dynasty* of the descendants of David (sign of political independence), and the security offered by the *temple* of Jerusalem (sign of the sure presence of God amongst his people). However, as the study of the rhetorical organisation of the second part of the book of Jeremiah (chs. 26–45) let us foresee, in precisely the moment the end was announced, those oracles of consolation and hope are proclaimed (cf. Jer 30–31) revealing it, against all human logic, as a new beginning, a mortal wound inflicted for an unexpected *healing* (cf. 30:12–17), as a necessary privation in order to be able to once again *buy* (√קנה) "fields, houses, vineyards" (32:15).

The act of surrender, as a *voluntary* dispossession of goods, is perfectly inscribed in this salvific dynamic, for if the "good" were merely snatched away, evil would still remain rooted in its place and, on the contrary, one would see the cause of misfortune not in infidelity, but paradoxically in an idolatry that was not sufficiently convinced (cf. 44:18). This is why the injunction of this symbolic-prophetic gesture, to be translated into full and decisive submission to the king of Babylon and to the good of his kingdom, exceeds the phase of the siege and remains valid for both the exiles (cf. 29:4–7) and the residue population that remained in the land of Judah after the catastrophe[121] and attempted to take refuge in Egypt (cf. 42:10–18).

---

119 Cf. 2:5–8 and, in particular, v. 7: "I lead you to a generous land, so you could eat its fruits and goodness. But you, as soon as you entered, contaminated my land and turned my heritage into an abomination."

120 Cf. S. Petrosino, *L'idolo. Teoria di una tentazione dalla Bibbia a Lacan*, Altro discorso 4, Milano – Udine 2015.

121 And especially after the assassination of the new governor (Gedaliah) imposed by the Babylonians (cf. 41:1–3).

4.3.4. The stranger, his order, and his gods

Another aspect implicated by the gesture of surrender is its *theological* valence. We moderns would see only a political fact in it, with possible *social repercussions* (not at all to be underestimated, by the way, precisely for my theme). Orphans of the symbol, it is a struggle for us to understand that it is, instead (also) a theo-logy, that is, a discourse about God and about gods in general. If wars are the clash, before the tribunal of history and people, between opposing divine revindications of universal sovereignty,[122] the outcome of the battle necessary also becomes the affirmation of a "theological-dogmatic" truth. Amongst the many examples, we can again mention a direct attestation of Nebuchadnezzar from his inscription of Wadi Brisa (cf. WBC IX 13–58; WBC X 1–12).[123]

> With the strength of my lords Nabû and Marduk, I sent [*my armies*] regularly to Lebanon for battle. I expelled its (Lebanon's) enemy above and below and I made the country content.

To go out and surrender means entering the enemy's area of influence, into its symbolic territory, subjecting oneself to its laws and values. The (very likely) possibility of physical *deportation* into the imperial territory (first Assyrian and then Babylonian) then amplifies the symbolic scope of this event. The enemy is always perceived and represented by the royal ideology as a manifestation of the forces of chaos. And if the rebels are not defeated and killed in battle, the fortunate survivors are assimilated through massive transfers by mass and targeted relocations to other provinces,[124] that is, within the space governed by laws and gods that restore the order and civilisation that were upset. They are two effective ways to *suppress the diversity*.[125]

Surrendering to the enemy can mean admitting the weakness of one's own gods. For those who win, on the other hand, it is the manifest superiority of their own culture and national deities. Or of their just judgment on rebellious vassals and infidels to a treaty of alliance that had been stipulated previously. Not for nothing, as can be seen from the Assyrian depictions, as well as from the book of Jeremiah (cf. 48:7; 49:3), the deportation of a submissive population could often also implicate the bringing into exile of its gods[126] and destruction of its

---

122 I defer to what is developed in ch. IV, § 4.2.

123 I refer once again to the critical edition and translation of R. Da Riva, *The Twin Inscriptions*, 63.

124 To which can follow the reutilisation (and therefore, the reabsorption) within the imperial structure or through acclimatisation in auxiliary military corps of the army or by enrolment in various sectors of its bureaucratic apparatus.

125 See, on this topic, D. Nadali, «Guerra e morte», 51–70 (esp. pp. 56–57).

126 "The frequent collocation of the deportation of divine statues and the deportation of captured kings represented the decisive removal of the nuclear symbols of statehood" (S.W. Holloway, *Aššur Is King! Aššur Is King!* Religion in the Exercise of Power in the Neo-Assyrian Empire, CHANE 10, Leiden 2002, 195–196). See also M. Nissinen, «The Exiled Gods of Babylon in Neo Assyrian Prophecy», in: *The Concept of Exile in Ancient Israel and its Historical Contexts*, eds. E. Ben Zvi – C. Levin, BZAW 404, Berlin – New York 2010, 27–38; M.B. Hundley, *Gods in Dwellings*. Temples and Divine Presence in the Ancient Near East, SBLWAWS 3, Atlanta 2013, 205–206, 277–281, 329–331, 358–360.

610 The gesture of the surrender

temples.[127] The symbol once again: their statues are physically transported (or their earthly dwellings demolished), making not a naive identification, but rather a symbolic metaphor, and one that, in various respects, is no less effective.

For the Deuteronomistic tradition that echoes in Jeremiah as well, finding oneself worshipping foreign deities represents the fulfilment of a curse, and is, paradoxically, just punishment due to the fact of their having prostituted themselves to idolatry and betrayed the Covenant (cf. Deut 4:27–28; 28:36.64; Jer 16:13). The act of the surrender thus paves the way for the *voluntary* acceptance of this eventuality. In the context of the Jeremianic request, however, it is clear that the issue is that of accepting and making a precise act of reading of the history underway. Indeed, the call is not that of submitting to Nebuchadnezzar as a "servant of Marduk", but as a "servant of YHWH".

4.4. Overview

Focalising the structural elements of the (sub-) frame of the surrender in light of the data obtained from the HB and from other attestations from the ancient Near East (§ 3) has allowed me to configure a specific *phenomenology*. The act requested by Jeremiah thus found its initial contextualisation. In order to achieve a greater level of relevance in relation to the semantic-pragmatic framework evoked by the prophetic injunction, I then sought to trace the main *symbolic irradiations* implicated in the gesture of handing oneself over (§ 4), clarifying that, in itself, at the level of interpretive methodology, it is not possible to contemplate a "first" or "literal" meaning of the surrender, from which only successively would "secondary" or "symbolic" meanings be extrapolated or be applicable. The symbol, in fact, is already given entirely in the concreteness of the act (and of its respective semantic and symbolic frame) by which it is made present.

The main symbolic trajectories identified revolve around the following elements: the gate and walls of the city, the movement of entrance and exit, the dimension of possession and security (and loss of this) evoked by goods (material or otherwise), and in particular of the land (of Israel) and the temple of YHWH. Finally, surrendering to the enemy invokes the relationship with the foreigner, their system of values and their gods. It is starting from this sphere of relevance that the gesture of surrender demanded by Jeremiah will receive a further, definitive semantic-pragmatic delimitation of a signic-*prophetic* type. To identify this accurately, it will now be necessary to introduce a subsequent contextual level, that is, that configured by the complex communicative system established by the totality of the book of Jeremiah.

---

127 "Given their spatial-symbolic valence, the demolition of temples – along with the deportation and/or destruction of gods and other cultic items found within them – constitutes one of the most effective methods of conquering and remapping territories. Abundant material evidence witnesses directly to the violent treatment of monuments and statues" (J.L. WRIGHT, «The Deportation of Jerusalem's Wealth and the Demise of Native Sovereignty in the Book of Kings», in: *Interpreting Exile*, 105–133, here, p. 121).

Chapter VII
The surrender to the king of Babylon as a "symbolic-prophetic choice"

La mort et la vie dépendent de Dieu. Éviter la mort, choisir la vie, ce n'est pas déchif-frer en termes d'éthique les problèmes posés par l'histoire, c'est ressentir ce qu'il y a d'immédiatement divin dans ces problèmes. L'option n'est pas morale ou politique; elle est prophétique.[1]

1. The surrender to the king of Babylon as a "symbolic-prophetic choice" (and not only)

1.1. From the symbol to the (prophetic) sign. From the proposal to the (prophetic) response

After having studied the phenomenology of the gesture of surrender on the basis of the textual and extratextual attestations available and having explored the semantic potentials underlying a symbolic reading of it, all that remains is to thoroughly formulate an overall interpretation of the *prophetic perspective* with which Jeremiah marks this option in a specific way. In this stage, I will therefore make a transition in the analytical focus from the dimension of the *symbol* to that of the *sign*, which is defined in semiotics as "everything which can be taken as significantly substituting for something else".[2] If the symbol, according to the definition I have proposed, is to be understood never as an artificial construct but rather as the emergence to conscious-ness and language (in the form of metaphor) of what could be neither said otherwise nor confined within the univocity of the concept, then the sign, on the other hand, which, to be precise, is, in any case, not a static "thing", but rather a *relation*, establishes a relationship that is fairly stable within a particular context of utterance between the level of the expression and that of its content.[3]

---

1   A. NEHER, *L'essence du prophétisme*, 222.
2   U. ECO, *A Theory of Semiotics*, 7. For a more exhaustive definition that takes the various hermeneutical perspectives that this regards into account, see U. VOLLI, *Manuale di semiotica*, 16–36.
3   With this binary terminology, I give echo to the model of F. De Saussure, then reformu-lated by the Danish linguist Louis Trolle Hjelmslev, for whom the linguistic sign is the union given by the *signified* (i.e. the concept to which the sign refers) and the *signifier* (i.e. the vehicle through which the signified is evoked). I take as a given that to this schema, a third element need be added, which, in the triadic model used by C. Pierce to explain the semiosis, is called the "interpretant". There is no need here to elaborate further. It will suffice to say that "the process of production and circulation of meaning (*semiosis*) intervenes only when someone (an *interpreter*) establishes a link between a unit, which in this way becomes *expression* (a sound, an atmospheric phenomenon, an image, etc.), and a unit that acts as *content*" (translated from U. VOLLI, *Manuale di semiotica*, 21).

The area of communicative irradiation of a symbol is not reducible to the narrow literary boundaries of a specific pericope. Not only because it crosses beyond the cognitive modality of the concept, remaining, in itself, open to polysemic readings whithersoever it is found, but also because within broader textual perimeters, extending to include the entire canon, the symbol charts diversified courses with specific teleologies.[4] With regard to the symbolic elements that underlie the theme of the surrender, what I have just highlighted already reflects the need for a certain necessary focalisation. But it is when the prophet intends to communicate analogously through a coordination of gestures and words that the overflowing semantic richness of the symbolic dimension is then assumed, in order to be oriented according to specific signic trajectories. The symbol and the sign, distinct realities in themselves, are thus incorporated *into a single semiotic device*. I therefore prefer to define classic "symbolic gestures" in terms of "symbolic-prophetic gestures", emphasising the "multilevel" dimension of the object of study. This can be seen clearly by reconsidering the "symbolic-prophetic gesture" of the yoke (27–28), where the potential symbolic polysemy gets directed towards a precise content of signification, without this allowing the underlying symbolic level to become completely reabsorbed and exhausted by the signic dimension.

At this point, a step needs to be taken forward. It is my conviction that within the book of Jeremiah, the theme of the surrender plays out between *two* fundamental *polarities* that mediate a transition of meaning in two directions: from the *prophetic paradigm proposed* in the figure of the prophet (handed over, in obedience to YHWH, into the hands of human beings, burdened with a yoke, etc.) to the configuration of a *pragmatic response* requested as possible and opportune of the interlocutors reached by the Jeremianic message. On the one hand, therefore, Jeremiah, who performs the symbolic-prophetic gesture of the yoke, outstretched to signify the response that YHWH awaits from all the people, while on the other, the requested assumption of the communicative content conveyed by this gesture, through its pragmatic translation on the political level indicated by Jeremiah himself (in 21:1–10 and in 38:14–28a) in the terms of the surrender to Babylon. On the horizon of the end of Jerusalem, therefore, to the gesture "of *proposal*" of the yoke, corresponds (not as a *pendant* in a symmetrical sense, but according to an analogical relation) that "of *response*", indicated in the "symbolic-prophetic obedience or choice" of surrender.

To speak in these terms of what some would reduce to a simply factual, anecdotal, and hence political level, means introducing a new hermeneutical category. If it is true that *entia non sunt multiplicanda praeter necessitatem*, according to the well-known adage of Occam's razor, then I believe that precisely the complexity and articulation of the Jeremianic semiosphere suggests highlighting, for differentiation, a specific phenomenon of symbolic-sign relation having its own specific statute, not recognised

---

4   G. Borgonovo in *La notte ed il suo sole. Luce e tenebre nel Libro di Giobbe. Analisi simbolica*, AnBib 135, Roma 1995 (cf. pp. 328–331), speaks about the "tragitto simbolico"("symbolic journey"). But here, in addition to the typological dynamism of the Scripture re-highlighted by L. Alonso Schökel (cf. e. g. Id., *Il dinamismo della tradizione*, BCR 19, Brescia 1970, 51–52), one can recall, above all, the figurative approach of biblical theology elaborated by P. Beauchamp (cf., esp., Id., «L'interprétation figurative et ses présupposés», *RSR* 63 [1975] 299–312; Id., *L'un et l'autre Testament*. 2, 220–237).

The symbolic-prophetic choice 613

thus far by scholars. This would be a hermeneutical category whose heuristic value can highlight new aspects tied to the communicative dimension of biblical prophetism, and not only of the Jeremianic one.

1.2. The symbolic-prophetic sign and its context in the light of the inferential model of communication

The symbolic-prophetic sign identifies, renders pertinent the symbol, conveying and concentrating some of its essential semantic dimensions in a precise *hic et nunc*. This is exceedingly evident for the symbolic gesture of the yoke, which I have also called a proposal-gesture, but in my opinion, the same thing must be said in relation to the response-gesture of the surrender, which is precisely what is requested and expected by the prophetic intervention. It is, therefore, in a correct understanding of the communicative context within which the Jeremianic message is placed that its interpretation plays out as well.

The theme of surrender to Babylon has been and is still often reduced to a predominantly or merely political level perhaps precisely because in the texts with which I have dealt, and 21:1–10 and 38:14–28a in particular, the relational dimension of the analogical communication implicated by the gesture of surrender[5] has been underestimated and no clear and explicit indications put in Jeremiah's mouth have been recognised to make us think of an ulterior semantic valence. The criterion is a rather strange one, however, since it should have been deduced paradoxically that the very destruction of Jerusalem and end of the reign of Judah, that is, the most dramatic event in the history of Israel, it is not, in the immediate narrative context, traced back to any theological dimension (aside from the concluding insertion of ch. 52 with the hermeneutical note of v. 3).

If, in fact, we read the text of 39:1–14, that is, the immediate continuation of 38:14–28a with the same criteria of contextualisation, we must admit that there is no evident trace of a theological-prophetic interpretation of the catastrophic outcome of the Babylonian siege. The narration is focalised externally and proceeds with objective detachment, making no comment, drawing no moral deductions, nor calling into question any logic of remuneration justice, betrayal of the Covenant, or concept of punishment – nothing. The same could be observed with regard to the Jeremianic forbiddance to return to Egypt and the respective deadly threats (cf. 42:7–22; 43:2; etc.): one need at least keep texts like Exod 13:17; 14:13; Num 14:3–4; Deut 17:16; 28:68 in mind, and then consider the meaning of this choice in the general context of the respective textual areas (which are in mutual reference) in order to comprehend the (underlying) meaning of the prophetic words.[6] Put another way, it is actually not difficult to realise that the theological implications of these events, as in the case of

---

5   For the fundamental distinction between *digital* communication (which largely conveys conceptual content) and *analogical* communication (which modulates the relational aspect between the subjects involved), I will refer to what was developed in ch. IV, § 3.4 of the present dissertation.

6   The relational criticality (between YHWH and his people) intercepted by the call to surrender and its isomorphic translation represented by the command to not return to Egypt can also be inferred from the qualification given to Jeremiah's interlocutors (in 43:2: "proud men" [אֲנָשִׁים הַזֵּדִים]).

614   The surrender as a "symbolic-prophetic choice"

the call to surrender, are elsewhere and must be inferred from the relevant context of reference, the highlighting of which was and is one of the fundamental scopes of my dissertation.

The exegetic analysis that I conducted on 38:14–28a highlighted and valorised, from the hermeneutical point of view, two different contextual levels, to which I will now once again call attention. The first, of a *symbolic structural* nature, concerns the communicative intentionality that can be seen beginning from the peculiar insertion of the pericope in its near and immediate context (cf. § 2.2–5). The second consists in the *dialogical nature* of the text itself, which is, moreover, common to the other attestations of the theme of surrender studied (21:1–10; 27–28), and which requires the reader to enter into the mechanism of the production of meaning through the grammar of its expressive form, a literary mirror of ordinary *conversational dynamics*.[7] It is precisely this latter perspective that requires an exacting analysis of the textual aspects to be reunderstood and orientated by a theory of communication capable of taking into account the consequent implications. It is therefore necessary to move from a competence that is solely linguistic to a textual competence, that is, to a "linguistics of sense".[8] In other words, if the prophetic injunction to "hand oneself over to the king of Babylon" is not expressed in the abstract form of a treatise with postulates of departure and reasoned consequent deductive steps, but emerges as the object of a communicative exchange of a verbal ("digital-conceptual") and non-verbal ("analogical-relational") nature, an appropriate methodological profile must be assumed. I have already amply resorted to the pragmatics of communication (and to *Frame Semantics*) as a general direction of cognitive orientation that allows for an approach to human communication as a global event not reducible to individual words or utterances, but will now refer, in particular, to the *Relevance Theory*.[9]

---

7   On this topic, cf. J.T. WILLIS, «Dialogue between Prophet and Audience as a Rhetorical Device in the Book of Jeremiah», *JSOT* 33 (1985) 63–82; S.A. MEIER, *Speaking of Speaking*; M.D. ZULICK, «The Agon of Jeremiah: On the Dialogic Invention of Prophetic Ethos», *QJS* 78 (1992) 125–148; N. BONNEAU, «The Illusion of Immediacy. A Narrative-Critical Exploration of the Bible Predilection for Direct Discourse», *Theoforum* 31 (2000) 131–151; S.A. NITSCHE, «Prophetische Texte», 155–181.

8   Here, I pick up the concept of "Linguistik des Sinns" proposed by E. COSERIU, *Textlinguistik. Eine Einführung*, TBL 109, Tübingen ²1981, 51–153. The tracing back of the textual linguistics to the linguistics of sense is pertinent, for it can happen that one comprehends a communicative unity only from the semiotic point of view, that is, on the level of the signs that compose it (linguistic competence), without, however, understanding its overall sense, just as, on the contrary, it is possible to grasp the sense of a text (textual competence) without knowing how to exactly decipher all of the signs interwoven in it. It is possible, in other words, for a reader to understand, e.g. the sense of a dissertation or a novel without understanding the sporadic citations in the original language, or rather, as in the example that the author Karl Bühler himself evokes, it is possible for a person to understand that they are being insulted even if they do not understand the words that are being addressed to them (because completely invented; cf. pp. 66–67).

9   I have already mentioned this in the General Introduction, in § 3.3.4. Here, I will recall only the main text of reference: D. SPERBER – D. WILSON, *Relevance*. For a general overview, refer to C. BIANCHI, *Pragmatica cognitiva*, 103–170. According to the author, who, in any case, does not hide any incongruences and still unresolved descriptive

The symbolic-prophetic choice   615

It is well established by now that the discursive universe affects the formation of (not only linguistic) texts, especially those intending to reproduce a conversational dynamic. It is then logical that an understanding of a communicative unit demand that the circumstances in which an enunciation takes place, range of presuppositions of the interpreter, inferential dynamics required, relationship with other texts, and so on be taken into consideration. The Relevance Theory contrasts, as was already observed, with the classic *code model,* by which the communicative event would consist of a process of encoding and decoding data. This prefers a *model of inference,* taking it up and developing it starting from Grice's contribution,[10] by which human communication is mainly configured as a process of *collaboration* between the interlocutors engaged in the production and interpretation of *clues* or *evidence* (and the role of decoders becomes only auxiliary).

If the code model presumes the improbable need for the communicating subjects to share through and through the same context (perception of the physical environment, encyclopaedia, beliefs, memories, recollections, etc.), then for the inferential model, communication is instead successful if a process of *meta-representation* can be actualised, that is, a "reading the mind" of the interlocutor starting from the correct interpretation of the clues that he himself provides (on an explicit and implicit level), presuming that any communicative act, as such, intends to be pertinent.[11]

> In questa prospettiva, quando comunichiamo non codifichiamo pensieri, né dupli-chiamo i nostri pensieri nel nostro interlocutore, e nemmeno modifichiamo i suoi pensieri: quello che facciamo è modificare in modo intenzionale il contesto dei nostri interlocutori, il loro ambiente cognitivo e, in particolare, l'insieme di ipotesi che sono manifeste a noi e a loro – allo scopo di permetter loro di *leggerci nel pensiero*".[12]

---

difficulties, the *Relevance Theory* "today represents the most innovative and complete perspective on the nature of communication – a perspective that is closely tied to a mature and complete conception of cognition and the architecture of the mind" (my translation from p. 103).

10 These are the two key ideas taken up by H.P Grice: "A. Understanding is a process of acknowledging the communicative intentions of the speaker – a process that is inferentially implemented; B. The recipient is guided in the process of comprehension by certain expectations on the statement uttered by the speaker" (my translation from C. BIANCHI, *Pragmatica cognitiva,* 104).

11 "A subject produces a clue (even non-linguistic, as in the case of gestures or intentional facial expressions) of the meaning that they intend to communicate, and puts the interlocutor in a position to infer that meaning from that clue, from the information made available from the context, and from certain crucial expectations about the behaviour of the rational agents. A statement is nothing more than a complex clue of the meaning understood by the speaker (and not a coding of theirs)" (translated from C. BIANCHI, *Pragmatica cognitiva,* 104).

12 "In this perspective, when we communicate, we do not codify thoughts, nor duplicate our thoughts in our interlocutor, nor do we modify his thoughts: what we do is to intentionally modify the context of our interlocutors, their cognitive environment and, in particular, the set of hypotheses that are manifest to us and to them – in order to allow them to read our thoughts" (translated from C. BIANCHI, «Capire e farsi capire: pragmatica», in: *Filosofia della comunicazione, eds.* C. BIANCHI – N. VASSALLO, Bari 2005, 42–67, here, p. 59).

616 The surrender as a "symbolic-prophetic choice"

On the basis of this approach, we could reformulate the prophetic pretension of obedience as an ability to "read the mind" of YHWH, and the interpretive effort of intradiegetic or extradiegetic interlocutors (which are us) as an attempt to "read the mind" of Jeremiah (without distinguishing here between the literary-historical character and the homonymic book). We are not listening to an oral text and directly aired conversations, of course, but their written representation. This has consequences, but it does not alter, in my opinion, the underlying methodological assumptions, which require us to focalise our attention on the question of the *pertinent communicative context*,[13] which also occurs, after all, on the level of specialised studies, which, for obvious reasons, always have to do with exemplifications presented in written form.

The diversified attestations that have allowed us to describe a phenomenology of the gesture of surrender, and thus a sketch of its symbolic potentials, undoubtedly make up part of a pragmatic context of reference that orients the interpretive act, albeit at diversified levels. However, the elements most relevant on the basis of which the reader is made able to carry out those *inferences* allowing him to grasp what the speaker actually wanted to mean and to configure (*speaker's meaning*), beyond the "literal" meaning of the enunciations relating to the need to "hand oneself over to the king of Babylon" (*utterance's meaning*), can be more adequately highlighted in the light of the complex articulation of the *semiosphere* of the book of Jeremiah, whose hermeneutical access portal is its "opening" chapter. In other words, I believe that a rereading of the Jeremianic work, which is, on a close look, already Jer 1, allows us to realise how diversified the level of semiotic devices employed throughout the book (which is, in itself, a "world of signs", i.e. a semiosphere) are, and how their mutual relationship constitutes a sophisticated interweaving of references (i.e. clues) capable of configuring the *pertinent context* within which the reader can formulate an adequate interpretive act.

According to my thesis, which intends to propose an original interpretation of the act of surrender, it will be precisely through the *progressive differentiation* between the different semiotic-symbolic levels of the book that the specific profile of "handing oneself over to the king of Babylon" will emerge. The issue, therefore, is that of identifying *a category of signification* that has not, so far, been seen by scholars, but that is endowed, in my opinion, with a fertile hermeneutical valence. The development that follows does not constitute a long digression unrelated to the demonstrative logic of my work, but is (the sketch of) a necessary categorisation of the principle communication devices of the book of Jeremiah. The basic question about the meaning of the act of surrender will find a first response fulfilled, because it can be understood, at least initially, as a "symbolic-prophetic choice". Starting from here, in the following chapter, it will then be possible to clarify the conceptual delimitation and communicative meaningfulness of this notion even further.

---

13 "The role of the context is then precisely that of narrowing the communicative possibilities of a message, that is, essentially that of *reducing the risks* of communication" (translated from C. BIANCHI, «Capire e farsi capire», 50).

2. Incipit. Jer 1 as a "cognitive map" for access to the Jeremianic semiosphere

2.1. Point of departure

To varying degrees, all scholars recognise that Jer 1 has a programmatic function in relation to the book of Jeremiah in its entirety. And this is, indeed, undeniable. But in my opinion, there is more to the question. Almost like in a game of mirrors, as its exegetes explain it, Jer 1 has the ability to reveal the interpretive presuppositions informing their respective studies and commentaries dedicated to the book of Jeremiah.[14] In fact, already here, amongst the many questions that arise, we see present itself the problem of the articulation between the profile of the prophet presented by the book (anticipated in 1:4–19) and its historical anchorage (delineated immediately in the "title", in 1:1–3). In any case, as the *incipit* of the book in its present state, it is precisely this text that plays the decisive role in the hermeneutical act.[15] In Jer 1, a reading *alliance* (or contract)[16] gets established between the narrator (and whoever is behind them)[17] and the Model Reader,[18] and this is the point of departure of the textual strategy, which aims not only to turn the empirical reader into a competent one,[19] but also to stimulate them to take a stance, in the hope that in the end, they will correspond to the Model Reader to a certain degree themself.

---

14 Cf. R.P. CARROLL, «*Jeremiah Studies*», 126–127.

15 See e.g. A. DEL LUNGO, *Gli inizi difficili*. Per una poetica dell'Incipit romanzesco, Padova 1997; A. Oz, *The Story Begins*. Essays on Literature, New York 1999; A. DEL LUNGO, «La frontière du commencement. Transitions, transgressions», in: *Au commencement du récit*. Transitions, transgressions, ed. C. PÉRÈS, Collection Hispania, Carnières-Morlanwelz 2005, 9–15.

16 Cf. A. Oz, *The Story Begins*, 7: "Any beginning of a story is always a kind of contract between writer and reader." The introduction of the concept of "reading contract" is owed to E. VÉRON, «Quand lire, c'est faire: l'énonciation dans le discours de la presse écrite», in: *Sémiotique*, II, IREP, Paris 1984, 33–56. On the phenomenon of the "reading pact" see the classic contributions by P. LEJEUNE, *Le Pacte autobiographique*, Paris 1975; U. ECO, *Lector in fabula*; W. ISER, *Der implizite Leser*, München 1972; ID., *Der Akt des Lesens*. Theorie ästhetischer Wirkung, München 1976. For a recent and interesting application in the biblical field, which I take as a point of reference for this type of approach to the text, see J.-P. SONNET, «L'alliance de la lecture: lorsque la Bible refuse l'ésotérisme», in: *La Bible sans avoir peur*, ed. J.-F. BOUTHORS, Paris 2005, 129–151; and also, by the same author, the synthesis of the question presented in the introduction of the collection of essays on biblical narrative translated into Italian in *L'alleanza della lettura*. Questioni di poetica narrativa nella Bibbia ebraica, Lectio 1, Cinisello Balsamo 2011, 7–20.

17 Cf. U. ECO, *Lector in fabula*, 60–66. On the many narrative levels, and on the relationship between the narrator and the story told, see G. GENETTE, *Figures III*, Poétique, Paris 1972 (esp. pp. 225–267); ID., *Nouveau discours du récit*, Poétique, Paris 1983.

18 Cf. U. ECO, *Lector in fabula*, 55, 62. The Model Reader (W. Iser instead introduces the notion of Implied/Implicated Reader, which is not exactly the same thing) "is a textually established set of felicity conditions to be met in order to have a macro-speech act (such as a text is) fully actualized" (U. ECO, *The Role of the Reader*, 11).

19 "Thus it seems that a well-organized text on the one hand presupposes a model of competence coming, so to speak, from outside the text, but on the other hand works

It is my belief that in Jer 1, there is a desire to provide the reader not only with the even fundamental (and not at all obvious) literary coordinates for a unitary assumption of the book,[20] and even more so, an anticipation of the fundamental *topics* or first convenient narrative *Einkleidung*[21] to his message: Here, we are handed the access keys for an adequate reading itinerary. And it is precisely in regard to its decipherment that the stakes are high, for this is, in my opinion, to be understood, in its most exhaustive form, as a proposal for a specific itinerary of *prophetic formation*. And the text seeks readers willing to navigate it.

To fully acknowledge the programmatic nature of Jer 1 means, in other words, grasping in it not only a proleptically offered "rewriting" or "recapitulation",[22] but also

---

to build up, by merely textual means, such a competence" (U. Eco, *The Role of the Reader*, 8; cf. U. Eco, *Lector in fabula*, 56). The Model Reader does not coincide with the empirical/real Reader. It is an abstract role, that is, the recipient of the textual communication conceived by the empirical/real Author. Conversely, the Model Author, as an interpretive hypothesis derived from the textual data, should be distinguished from the empirical/real Author (cf. Eco, *Lector in fabula*, 62), a notion that is, in any case, problematic in the biblical field.

20   I am referring to the relationship between Jer 1 and the strategic points of the book, such as Jer 25; 51:64, and the conclusion of Jer 52.
     Some commentators limit the textual area circumscribed by the title to chs. 1–39, and what is contained in chs. 40–45 does not seem anticipated explicitly in the opening verses (even if it could be considered so, as the consequence of גְּלוֹת יְרוּשָׁלָ͏ִם). In spite of this, it seems evident to me that here we can detect a redactional intention at work, aimed to form (beginning from 1:1–3) a large inclusion that finds its closure in 51:64 (עַד־הֵנָּה דִּבְרֵי יִרְמְיָהוּ; "thus far the words of Jeremiah") and the insertion of ch. 52 (cf. 2 Kgs 24:18–25:30), which, re-narrating the fall of Jerusalem and the deportation (cf. Jer 39), imprints the theological seal of the category of "fulfilment" on what was announced in the opening.
21   Think of the contextualising relationship, from the historical point of view, between vv. 1–3 and 4–19. G. Fischer, assuming an exclusively literary point of view, understands the relationship between the text and the historical data contained therein (even when they prove to be reliable) as a fictitious "re-cloaking" due to the creativity of the author of the book (cf. Id., *Jeremia*, 117: "Jeremia und die Epoche des Untergangs Judas sind die *Einkleidung*, das Gewand, das der Autor von Jer seiner Botschaft gibt"). This position seems excessive to me. I would be inclined instead to apply to Jeremiah what Mark W.G. Stibbe states with regard to the question of the historicity of the Gospels: "Mark and John – indeed all the gospels – are fictionalized history, not historicized fiction" (M.W.G. Stibbe, *John as Storyteller*. Narrative Criticism and the Fourth Gospel, SNTSMS 73, Cambridge 1992, 75). On this question, see the introduction to the historical part (ch. II). Regarding the interesting analogy between the composition of Jeremiah and the composition of the Gospels, see J. Goldingay, *The Book of Jeremiah*, NICOT, Grand Rapids 2021, 12–16.
22   Some authors use metaphoric expressions for this that are, in my opinion, rather limiting. Alonso Schökel – J.L. Sicre Diaz, *Profetas I*, 423, speak e.g. about Jer 1 as "una composición estilizada que sirve da portada (i.e. a "frontispiece") que sintetiza aspectos sustanciales del libro"; S. Herrmann, *Jeremia*. Lieferung 1, BK 12 Neukirchen-Vluyn 1986, 51, utilises instead the musical metaphor of the "Ouvertüre" to generically underscore its introductive nature.

a peculiar implementation of that "principle of cooperation", already formulated by H.P. Grice and reworked by U. Eco,[23] upon which the communicative intent of human relations is based. In the case of Jer 1, I believe it can reasonably be inferred that this "principle of cooperation" is expressed *in a specific way*. The narrator intends to offer the (Model) Reader the essential elements of a project for educating the hermeneutical act and the intelligence of meaning (understood as a recognition of significances), destined to be translated into likewise sensible choices (significa*[c]tions*),[24] both within the textual dimension (in the character of Jeremiah; intradiegetic level) and beyond it (according to the actualising competence of the empirical reader; extradiegetic level).

In other words, we can say that Jer 1 intends to provide the reader with a "cognitive map"[25] that can guide them through the hermeneutical itinerary that awaits them. The map, however, is not the territory. It is not, therefore, a summary (important elements are lacking and there is no totality in a miniaturised form), but a *paradigm*,[26] understood to be a key to the reading (in itself, articulated and composed of semiotic paradigms in relation) of the whole communicative dynamic of the book. A large quantity of information and complex networks of semiotic relationships normally

---

23   Cf. General Introduction, § 3.3.6, nn. 125 and 128.

24   The (political) message of Jeremiah asks to be recognised in its (prophetic) meaning as a call of obedience to the meaning of the history revealed here and now, and urges for the performance of a corresponding act (the submission to Babylon) or series of actions (to build and inhabit homes, remain in the land; cf. 29:4–7; 42:7–22) invested with the same signifying power (prophetic obedience).

25   See, in this regard, the collection of studies contained in J. PORTUGALI, *ed., The Construction of Cognitive Maps*, GeoJL 32, Dordrecht 1996; and the contributions of J.D. NOVAK – D.B. GOWIN, *Learning How to Learn*, New York 1984, [21]2006; J.D. NOVAK, *Learning, Creating, and Using Knowledge*. Concept Maps as Facilitative Tools in School and Corporations, Mahwah 1998, [2]2010; R.L. SOLSO, *Kognitive Psychologie*, Heidelberg 2005, 242–290 (from the original English 2001 edition); R. TRIM, *Metaphor and the Historical Evolution of Conceptual Mapping*, London 2011.

26   The category of "paradigm" has, in the field of biblical studies, long taken on a particular gnoseological value (see e.g. the contribution of J. BLENKINSOPP, «Abraham as Paradigm in the Priestly History in Genesis», *JBL* 128 [2009] 225–241) and in reference to the prophetic experience of Jeremiah, it was already in some way thematised by several scholars (see e.g. J.M. BERRIDGE, *Prophet*, 148, a mere mention; S.H. BLANK, «The Prophet as Paradigm», in: *Essays in Old Testament Ethics*. J.P. Hyatt, *In Memoriam*, *eds.* J.L. CRENSHAW – J.T. WILLIS, New York 1974, 111–130, above all in reference to the inner labour attested in the "confessions"; W. BRUEGGEMANN, «The Book of Jeremiah. Portrait of a Prophet», *Interp.* 37 (1983) 130–145; T. POLK, *The Prophetic Persona*. Jeremiah and the Language of the Self, JSOT.S 32, Sheffield 1984. It should be noted that these contributions limited themselves to justifying their legitimacy in relation to some generic thematics, taking on this category in a rather uncritical way, that is, without exploring conditions of plausibility, different registers of meaning, and consequent hermeneutical repercussions within the Jeremianic text.

generate confusion and disorientation in those who do not have cognitive anchorages and principles of recognition for identifying structures of meaning and regularity of relationships ("cognitive mapping"). The metaphorical notion of a cognitive map should therefore be understood both as a *process* (as a modality of learning), which Jer 1 intends to support, and as a *result* (modality of knowledge). And in this sense, I consider Jer 1 to be already the result of a dynamic of "prophetic" recognition of the meaning of a sequence of events and a call to an inspired discernment addressed to the reader themself.

2.2. The form of the text and originary semiotic paradigms

Considering it to be the most correct structural mapping of the text in question, let us bear in mind the following general figure of Jer 1, derived from an application of the principles of rhetorical analysis.[27]

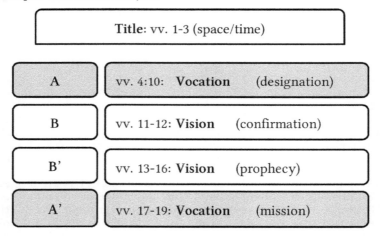

The communication of meaning[28] thematised in the book of Jeremiah has, in the first chapter, its fundamental grammar and ineludible door of access. Keeping in mind

---

27 The proposals for the structuring of the pericope do not find agreement amongst scholars. (cf. e.g. J.R LUNDBOM, *Jeremiah*, 127–130; ID., «Rhetorical Structures in Jeremiah 1», *ZAW* 103 [1991] 193–210 [in particular pp. 197–205]). Since I consider it the one best founded, for my analysis, I refer to the textual organisation presented in an articulate and rigorous way in P. BOVATI, *Geremia 1–6*, 74–83. In agreement with the identification of the same compositional structure, even if for different reasons, and not always equally convincingly, also W. RUDOLPH, *Jeremia*, 2–13 (who, actually, does not at all justify this subdivision); G. WANKE, «Jeremias Berufung (Jer 1,4–10). Exegetisch-theologische Überlegungen zum Verhältnis von individueller Äußerung und geprägtem Gut anhand eines Einzeltextes», in: *Alttestamentlicher Glaube und biblische Theologie. Festschrift für Horst Dietrich Preuß zum 65. Geburtstag*, eds. J. HAUSMANN – H.-J. ZOBEL, Stuttgart 1992, 132–144 (here, p. 134).

28 To be always understood bidirectionally: from YHWH to human beings and from human beings to YHWH.

the textual dynamism highlighted by the rhetorical analysis, it is possible to trace the essential coordinates of the book's theological-literary *setting*. In the parts that circumscribe the *word* that elects/shapes the prophetic *body* (1:4–10, 17–19) and the *vision* that interrogates the one called (1:11–16), the wellspring and programmatic point of *two* fundamental *semiotic paradigms* (or communicative modules) can be identified. They are models of production and recognition of meaning that allow for the identification of semiotic dynamics that alternate and intertwine along the entire textual axis of the book, while being particularly highlighted themselves in the sections that are narrative in nature.

In sum, we can say that the meaning of history revealed by the divine word: (a) must be assumed and signified with the "body", and (b) provides for a process of discernment that is activated through an intersubjective interaction. Let me explicate these hypotheses, which prospectively already show how the act of surrender is deeply embedded in these communicative processes.

a) "Before I formed you in the womb I knew you, before you were born I consecrated you, a prophet to the nations I appointed you" (1:5).

The *first paradigm*, of originary valence, regards the semiotic-structural modalities of *generation* and *assumption/signification* of meaning within the Jeremianic semiosphere. This coincides with the literary units in which the distinctive features of the Jeremianic prophetic vocation are presented (1:4–10, 17–19). It is a model of interpretation of the processes of signification developed within the work (but traceable in other prophetic and non-prophetic literature as well) that the text immediately presents to the reader starting from Jer 1. In v. 5, in particular, it refers to the living being that is formed in the maternal womb (בֶּטֶן) and thus the *historical-literary existence*[29] of the *person-prophet*, the paradigmatic dimension of the *assumption* and *signification* of meaning mediated by the prophetic ministry. The "body in the scene"[30] and the "scene of the body" is for me the synthetic cypher of that notion. It also encompasses those texts improperly called the "confessions"[31] (cf. 11:18–12:6; 15:10–21; 17:14–18; 18:18–23; 20:7–20), to be understood not as intimist withdrawals, but a verbalisation and visceral reaction to what the corporeal experience of the prophet suffers and communicates,[32] as a reflection (whether a welcoming or rejection) of divine *páthos* itself.

---

29 With this definition, I methodologically prescind from the debate over the historicity of the figure of Jeremiah, referring first of all to the literary world presented by the text and within which the biographical references of the life of the prophet from Anathoth are contextualised.

30 An expression that I take (along with other suggestions that are pertinent to my research) from the reflections of M.J. CONTRERAS LORENZINI, *Il corpo in scena. Indagine sullo statuto semiotico del corpo nella prassi performativa*, Bologna 2008; ID., «Il corpo del fare. Verso una definizione semiotica di pratica», *Studi Culturali* 6 (2009) 387–408.

31 By analogy with the famous "Confessions" of Saint Augustine.

32 Always remaining in a literary perspective, above all. Within this textual series, one could easily highlight a constellation of references to the concreteness of the corporeal experience, which metaphorically also become a language of the inner reality and inform, at the same time, the prayerful appeals to YHWH (called to "stay beside",

622   The surrender as a "symbolic-prophetic choice"

b) "You, Jeremiah, what do you see?" (1:11, 13).

The *second paradigm* is instead made explicit in the indication of *how*, essentially, that meaning (of history) can be read and identified by the prophet, by the recipients of his message, and therefore, ultimately, by the empirical reader. It is the Jeremianic paradigm of the *hermeneutic of meaning*: a dynamic of *recognition* or *discernment* that can only be given through an interpersonal communicative interaction in which the active unfurling of *human freedom* is required, invited by YHWH (via the prophet) in the shape of a response to a relational appeal.[33] With the second paradigm, what is shown is the dynamic that emerges, guiding the prophet to the fulfilment of their prophetic identity, as a subject capable of reading the Meaning revealed in history. The story of their own body, along with the *dābār* of the events of the world. A stage upon which God has always spoken. Awaiting the response of humanity.

3. In the semiosphere: First guidelines for mapping the symbolic levels of the book of Jeremiah. Towards the identification of a new hermeneutical category

Analytical study of the Jeremianic semiosphere, given its elevated degree of complexity, deserves a monographic treatment that is impossible to develop herein. As with Jer 1, I will anticipate and condense the most relevant and pertinent elements of my more extensive research now in the process of elaboration.

Usually, analytical study of the overall complexity resorts to processes of classification. Similarities and differences can help to focalise the properties of the objects of study. Nevertheless, the elaboration of a taxonomy is always a risky and questionable operation. One should, first of all, be vigilant about the principles established upstream, which are not always made explicit. One should make clear, in my opinion, limiting myself to an epistemological statement as simple as it is fundamental, that not everything is classifiable, that reality with its (even textual) phenomena hardly lets itself be entirely boxed in by rigid schemata. Having reiterated this, it need also be said that the criteria for developing a taxonomy can be manifold, complementary but also contradictory, limiting: at times, too inclusive and other times, overly exclusive. I will therefore limit myself to some fundamental differentiations that can serve as guidelines for further verifications and for the in-depth consideration necessary to structure a demonstrative system that is more rigorous.

---

and to not let his prophet "perish", experienced as a word of joy and nourishment to "devour" and verb of fire "shut away in the bones" and uncontainable, etc.). It is a dimension most significatively and effectively synthesised precisely by the (problematising) reference to that originary event of the vocation that invests the formation of the prophetic body in the womb and birth of Jeremiah (cf. Jer 15:10; 20:14–18).

33   Cf. C. LEVIN, «The "Word of Yahweh": A Theological Concept in the Book of Jeremiah», in: *Prophets, Prophecy, and Prophetic Texts*, 42–62 (for a study on the theological-redactional impact of the "word-event formula" on the composition of the book of Jeremiah, see also the previous contribution: ID., «Das Wort Jahwes an Jeremia. Zur ältesten Redaktion der jeremianischen Sammlung», *ZThK* 101 [2004] 257–280).

In this regard, rather than offer rigidly taxonomic intentions, it is useful to refer once more to the category of the "conceptual map", for this not only enables a focalisation of the hermeneutical function of Jer 1, but also allows me to provide reasoning for the plausibility of the operation that I intend to sketch out on the cognitive level as well. I have already introduced the concept of "linearisation" of the linguistic code in relation to "semiotic *arcatas*",[34] heuristic tools that allow for the tracing of semiotic relationships between textual units placed at a distance. Even in this perspective, here, relations are more complex, since they give life to reticulated forms (cognitive maps, to be precise) that do not always appear hierarchised, just as what occurs in the mental organisation of knowledge.

Natural languages are sequential and, likewise, textual forms of communication are structured on a linear basis. But this is not the case at the cognitive level, since every real interpretive act that is not a cold mnemonic repetition of data involves a reorganisation of concepts according to pertinent relations and criteria of priority. The book of Jeremiah unrolls and juxtaposes the elements of a communicative flow that can appear chaotic from this point of view. And so, as I have already had opportunity to point out, the order of the Jeremianic work needs to be reconstructed or underscored on another level. This is also true of the complexity of the symbolic-signic forms that structure it, whose relations and mutual dependencies must be the object of hermeneutical intelligence. Let me focalise at least a few elements, in view of the presentation and most appropriate contextualisation of the interpretative category that I intend to present to explain the gesture of surrender.

3.1. Level of microstructural signification. The prophetic language and the signs of the overflowing of meaning

It is from the beginning of the book of Jeremiah that something more emerges from the horizon of mere factual data, and it is precisely in the recognition and communication of this overflowing of meaning that the prophetic mission and appeal to the reader can be identified. An almond branch announces the fulfilment of the divine word and the explosion of life from the winter of death, from a boiling pot placed on the fire, the threat of the destruction of all of Jerusalem inundates. Concentrating attention initially on the elementary structuration of the interweaving of signification of the prophetic discourse, those elements that signal to the reader the impossibility of stopping at a merely "literal"[35] level of production of meaning need thus be highlighted. The theme is a complex one, in which diversified phenomena of signification interpenetrate, defining themselves on a case to case basis as analogies, similitudes, symbols, signs, etc. An *ad hoc* study should definitely be done. Let me therefore narrow

---

34 In ch. I, § 2.4.1. See, esp., n. 79.
35 As was already explained previously (cf. § 4.3), I maintain the distinction, on an operative-conventional level, between "literal meaning" and "figural meaning". In itself, in fact, "the symbolic value of the biblical text is not a second sense that overlaps with the literal one, but it is the *unicus sensus litteralis* in all its potential" (translated from L. GASPARRO, *Simbolo e narrazione in Marco*, 499).

the perspective, starting from a consideration of the prophetic language of the book of Jeremiah, which I could, to a large extent, define as "symbolic".

Symbolic language utilises images to convey abstract ideas or otherwise inexpressible experiences, and all biblical literature, not only that which is prophetic, is completely pervaded. The symbolic matrix of the Jeremianic work is therefore the backbone of all the other semiotic processes through which the reader is provoked to formulate their interpretive act, bearing in mind both the *archaeological* aspect of the symbol (its presence antecedent to the text to be interpreted) and the *teleological* one (its finalisation in relation to the configuration of a communicative event aimed at reaching readers of all time).

The first work to be done in this regard would be a reconnaissance of the *fundamental symbolic nuclei* of the book of Jeremiah, around which the minor symbolic constellations revolve. For my theme, as I have already highlighted, the symbol of the *yoke* is of great relevance, along with the meanings associated with it. It should be borne in mind that the emergence of that which is symbolic (which concerns the pre- and extralinguistic data)[36] is often signalled in the sphere of language by the use of ("living") *metaphor*.[37] This should be understood not as a simple substitution of one *term* for another, but as that intentional tension instituted by the locutor between two possible meanings of a *phrase* (between its "literal" and its "figurative" one) that generates the aperture of the meaning,[38] that is, a real cognitive gain that cannot be reduced to a mere rhetorical effect. Still remaining within my topic, one can think, for example, of the term "iron yoke" (עֹל בַּרְזֶל) in 28:13–14, in the context of the clash with the prophetic counter-message of Hananiah. The material impossibility of the expression (given that a yoke of iron would make ploughing virtually impracticable) directs comprehension of the meaning towards a metaphorical plane specified by the communicative context. A detailed study of the metaphors of the book of Jeremiah has already been attempted by D. Bourguet,[39] but in my opinion, the entire hermeneutical system would need to be revisited, on the basis of the most recent investigations of a cognitivist matrix on metaphor.

In addition to these two basic levels of signification (the symbol and the metaphor), there is then that of semiotic codifications that are grafted on the previous symbolic ramifications, but always on the level of the smallest units of speech, and always with

---

36 P. Ricœur defines the pre-linguistic dimension as the threshold between *bíos* and *lógos*: "La métaphore se tient dans l'univers déjà purifié du logos. Le symbole hésite sur la ligne de partage entre bios et logos. Il témoigne de l'enracinement premier du Discours dans la Vie. Il naît au point où Force et Forme coïncident" (cf. P. Ricœur, «Parole et symbole», 153).

37 According to the well-known definition of P. Ricœur in *La métaphore vive*.

38 "L'interprétation métaphorique consiste à transformer une contradiction, qui se détruit elle-même, dans une contradiction signifiante [...]. Nous sommes contraints de donner une signification nouvelle au mot, une extension de sens, grâce à qui nous pouvons «faire sens», là où l'interprétation littérale est proprement in-sensée" (P. Ricœur, *La métaphore vive*, 311). Cf. also P. Ricœur, «Biblical Hermeneutics», *Semeia* 4 (1975) 29–148 (in particular, pp. 75–76).

39 I have already cited his contribution: *Des Métaphores de Jérémie*. Cf. also the study on metaphorical images of animals in Jeremiah by B.A. Foreman, *Animal Metaphors*.

Towards the identification of a new hermeneutical category 625

the scope of stimulating the reader's interpretive cooperation.[40] There are at least two typologies of characteristics to be signalised: names and "symbolic" dates.[41]

In Jeremiah, one may note a use of names by which, intentionally, something other than what is immediately referred to wants to be communicated. This is evident, for example, when Nebuchadnezzar is mentioned using the unusual expression "king of Sesac" (מֶלֶךְ שֵׁשַׁךְ) in 25:26, where the name "Babylon" is encrypted; something similar can be said of the terms "Merataim" and "Pekod" in 50:21, "Zimrì" in 25:25, and probably also of the term "children of Benjamin" in 6:1. Even the particular names by which, in 22:11, 14, reference is made to the kings of Judah merit attention, and the proper name "Zedekiah" (צִדְקִיָּהוּ) itself is taken on in the first text I studied (21:1–10) not only to indicate a specific sovereign, but in its etymological meaning ("[my] justice [is] YHW[H]") to make semiotic reference to the prophetic promise of a new Davidic descendant depicted as a "righteous branch" (צֶמַח צַדִּיק) who will govern according to justice (cf. 23:5) at a time when Judah will be called "YHWH (is) our justice" (23:6: יְהוָה צִדְקֵנוּ).

Even the *dating* often seems to go beyond mere historical or anecdotal fact to configure semiotic temporalities (of a theological type). Starting with the "title" of the book, the duration of the Jeremianic prophetic ministry takes the shape, for the attentive reader, of a forty year time frame (from 627 to 587), which could very well symbolically[42] recall the time of the Exodus, the days granted to Nineveh for conversion in the book of Jonah, the work of the reform of Josiah, etc. Amongst the many other examples that could be cited,[43] undoubtedly encasing the valence of *axial* time is the "fourth year of the reign of Jehoiakim" (i.e. 605; cf. 25:1; 36:1; 45:1; 46:2; 51:59): at the very moment when Nebuchadnezzar ascends to the throne and imposes his power against Egypt and the entire Syrian-Palestinian strip, the last phase of the kingdom of Judah begins, and the end of the empire itself is foretold (cf. 51:59), the duration of which is still fixed symbolically at seventy years (cf. 25:11–12). Times and names generate a short-circuit of the meaning in 27:1, where in the MT, the time of Zedekiah to which the whole chapter refers becomes that of Jehoiakim. The mistake is too obvious to not think, at least as a working hypothesis, that there be a peculiar communicative intentionality.[44]

---

40 "Zu diesem Zweck greift er [the author of the book of Jeremiah] zusätzlich auf die Mittel der *Codierung und der Symbolnamen* zurück" (G. FISCHER, *Jeremia 1–25*, 53).

41 This is the expression with which phenomena of the sort are most commonly signalled. In the light of what I said previously, it can be understood that the use of the adjective "symbolic" takes on here the Percian meaning, which is exactly the opposite of the one I have assumed, in the wake of another interpretive tradition. Strictly speaking, the dimension is that of the "sign" and not that of the "symbol".

42 Cf. L. RYKEN – J.C. WILHOIT – T. LONGMAN III, *eds.*, *Dictionary of Biblical Imagery*, Downers Grove 1998, 305–306.

43 Cf. G. FISCHER, *Jeremia 1–25*, 80–82.

44 On the symbolic significance of this strange scribal "error", see, esp., G. FISCHER, *Jeremia 26–52*, 50, and what I observed in ch. IV, § 2.1, n. 6.

626   The surrender as a "symbolic-prophetic choice"

3.2. Level of macrostructural signification. The general architecture of the book and its semiotic *arcatas*

Part of the dynamics of signification just signalised, at the level of the smallest unit of the discourse would not be activated if another semiotic dimension, the macrostructural one, did not also come into play on a different level. Since the question regards the controversial opinion over the overall arrangement of the book of Jeremiah, as well as the strategic arrangement of the texts that relate to my topic of study, I have already dealt with it many times over the course of the present dissertation. So it is not necessary to insist upon it here yet again. It will suffice to recall what I tried to emphasise in ch. III with regard to the particular textual positioning of 21:1–10. The theme of the surrender to Babylon receives a double symbolic-prophetic marking: one configured starting from its microstructural symbolic fabric (through the reassumption and reorientation of the literary registers typical of "holy war", the Exodus, the two Deuteronomistic paths, etc.), the other by means of the multiple cross-references ("semiotic *arcatas*") to just as many thematic-lexical attractors situated on the opposite side of the selfsame literary unit given by chs. 21–24.

The reader's intelligence is therefore provoked by the Jeremianic work to extend to a global scale the question posed programmatically from the beginning to its textual simulacrum,[45] represented by the figure of the prophet Jeremiah: "what do you see?" (cf. 1:11, 13). The gaze, that is, cannot focalise only on the signic relationships established within the immediate contexts, but must be able to grasp the indications of meaning that spring forth from the relations over a distance, inclusions or diachronic juxtapositions that intentionally delude the (expected) confirmation of a linear chronological criterion.

3.3. Level of signification of the prophetic ministry. The figure of Jeremiah and his interlocutors

Amidst the extreme polarities that I have identified in the Jeremianic semiosphere, a whole series of intermediate semiotic devices "circulate", revolving around the figure of the prophet. Their common characteristic, therefore, is their anchoring to the dynamic-narrative dimension of the prophetic body placed on the scene of history. I will try to present them in summary form, highlighting those characteristic elements that allow for their identification and differentiation.

3.3.1. Symbolic-prophetic oracles

The multitude of individual symbolic elements scattered throughout the book of Jeremiah finds an initial organisation on the level of a well-defined textual unit within a minimal narrative frame in an oracular typology that, despite having a moderate decent textual extension and complex articulation, seems to have only one isotopic structuration[46]: the oracle of the "wine cup of wrath" (כּוֹס הַיַּיִן הַחֵמָה) of YHWH in

---

45 According to the terminology of the semiotic-enunciative model of communication.

46 Let us again remember that a textual isotopy is "the uniform reading of the story" (U. Eco, *The Role of the Reader*, 26; cf. U. Eco, *Lector in fabula*, 93: "la coerenza di un percorso di lettura"), that is, a semantic structure inherent to the text itself being considered.

Towards the identification of a new hermeneutical category   627

25:15–29.[47] Around this central symbol, many other related symbolic elements (the drunkenness, the sword, the scorn, etc.) are arranged, like the tiles of a mosaic.

All this lends to a suggestive communicative situation that is not comparable to the classic symbolic gestures, nor to the symbolic-prophetic visions. It is a *surreal* scene in which there are no personal physical actants provided for, not even potential ones (cf. on the other hand, the case of the clay jar in ch. 19), there are no anchorings to any realistic context, and the orders that YHWH imparts to the prophet are clearly to all be placed on the metaphorical plane. The same applies to the acts requested or attributed to the nations faced with the need to drink from the cup of wrath. A need that goes to take shape, it should be noted, of a reformulation of the theme of surrender to the king of Babylon actualised through other communicative registers. Jeremiah appears, in fact, as the mediation of the divine will for all peoples, according to the same universalist context highlighted on the political plane in chs. 27–28. This will is an expression of "anger" and therefore has its historical translation in calamitous events symbolised by the sword and made explicit in destruction, horror, ridicule, and curses. The punitive measures are announced as ineluctable, but the nations are asked to "drink" them, that is, to actively accept them from the "hand" of the prophet and submit to them. This is confirmed by the fact that the opposite attitude, that of those who refuse to drink from the cup, is reproved (cf. 25:28). In this case, one will have to "drink perforce". This is precisely what will happen in Jerusalem and to Zedekiah. Rejection of the cup will only render its contents bitterer.

One may wonder whether another symbolic-prophetic oracle can be detected in 13:12–14, a text that represents the same isotopic axis as the "wine". But here, it is dubious. It could be something similar to the imaginary-metaphorical scene of the cup of wrath, but it could also actually be interpreted as the description of a real scene, in which both levels (literal and figurative) of metaphorical communication play out. To find other examples of this oracular typology in which the prophetic word is pronounced in the context of a surreal scene, one need cross beyond the boundaries of the book of Jeremiah. At least one other pertinent example to this effect can be recognised in Zac 11:4–17.

3.3.2. Symbolic-prophetic visions

This theme is well known to scholars[48] and is of a typology fairly contiguous to the preceding. The discriminating element, beyond the level of "reality" of the scene that

---

47   I have already addressed this, according to another investigative perspective, in ch. IV, § 4.3.3.

48   See, in this regard, F. HORST, «Die Visionsschilderungen der alttestamentlichen Propheten», *EvT* 20 (1960) 193–205; B.O. LONG, «Prophetic Call»; ID., «Reports of Visions Among the Prophets», *JBL* 95 (1976) 353–365; S. NIDITCH, *The Symbolic Vision in Biblical Tradition*, HSM 30, Chico 1980; W. BEYERLIN, *Reflexe der Amosvisionen im Jeremiabuch*, OBO 93, Freiburg – Göttingen 1989; E. RUPRECHT, «Das Zepter Jahwes in den Berufungsvisionen von Jeremia und Amos», *ZAW* 108 (1996) 55–69; J. PSCHIBILLE, *Hat der Löwe erneut gebrüllt?* Sprachliche, formale und inhaltliche Gemeinsamkeiten in der Verkündigung Jeremias und Amos, BThSt 41, Neukirchen 2001; A. BEHRENS, *Prophetische Visionsschilderungen im Alten Testament*. Sprachliche Eigenarten, Funktion und Geschichte einer Gattung, AOAT 292, Münster 2002; A. SCHART, «Die Jeremiavisionen als Fortführung der Amosvisionen», in: *Schriftprophetie*, 185–202.

628 The surrender as a "symbolic-prophetic choice"

presents itself before the reader, is that the prophet clearly attests how YHWH "shows" something significant. The example that is the clearest are the visions that inaugurate the book of Jeremiah (1:11–12, 13–16) and the vision of the two fig baskets (ch. 24), but in my opinion, the ordinary "vision" of the actions of the potter (18:1–11)[49] can, without a doubt, also be mentioned. Usually, the accounts of visions attested in the HB are divided into two parts: the first with the presentation of the vision and its object, and a second, in which the dialogic exchange between YHWH (or an "angel interpreter") and the seer predominates, or instead, a monologue appears, in which YHWH himself introduces and explains the vision.

From a pragmatic point of view, according to Achim Behrens,[50] such visions (understood here in a supernatural sense and not as ordinary perceptual events) have a dual function: of an *announcement-appeal* and a *legitimisation* of the message and the visionary himself. In my opinion, this is not just an expedient to increase the communicative efficacy in didactic terms. As I have emphasised starting from the inaugural visions of the book of Jeremiah, the question is instead that of a *discernment of history* that is placed before the attention of the reader, who is called to personally participate in the recognition and construction of the meaning. This aspect will be amplified on the scenic-interactive level by subsequent semiotic devices, in which the prophetic body and that of his interlocutors is involved in an even more profound way. And bear in mind, in the background, the gesture of the yoke seen in relation to the act of surrender demanded by the prophet.

3.3.3. Symbolic-prophetic gestures (rhetoric-didactic and biographical)

I introduced the classic category of "symbolic gestures" already when addressing the gesture of the yoke in chs. 27–28.[51] These can be defined as *acts* carried out by the prophet on the orders of YHWH with a specific communicative intention addressed to specific interlocutors (sometimes, this is also the reader alone, and not their textual simulacrum), in which the non-verbal register is coordinated with the verbal one.[52] The message and the locutor in the "symbolic gestures" thus converge to configure a single event of communication.[53]

---

49   This is always based on the presupposition that it not be the level of "reality" that distinguishes the prophetic vision. In this case, the invitation to "see" is not lexicalised, as much as is, rather, the *event of the word* that follows (on the strategic positioning of this expression in Jeremiah, see J.I Lawlor, «Word Event in Jeremiah: A Look at the Composition's "Introductory Formulas"», in: *Inspired Speech*, 231–243). But it is clear that YHWH asks Jeremiah to go down into the potter's workshop to show him a very specific scene, upon which, secondarily, a divine word is grafted. Also the "visions" as supernatural events follow in this the same schema: first there is the visible perception, then the word that explains the meaning.

50   Cf. A. Behrens, *Visionsschilderungen*, 64–75.

51   In ch. IV, § 3 (with relative bibliographical indications, above all in § 3.1).

52   Similarly Å. Viberg, *Prophets in Action*, 27; K. Ott, *Analogiehandlungen*, 28.

53   There is some consensus in the tracing of "symbolic gestures" in the HB in the following texts: 1 Kgs 11:29–31; 19:19–21; 22:11; 2 Kgs 13:14–19; Isa 7:3; 8:1–4; 20:1–6; Jer 13:1–11; 16:1–9; 19:1–11; 27:1–12; 28:1–11; 32:6–15; 43:8–13; 51:59–64; Ezek 3:22–27 (with 24:25–27 and 33:21–22); 4:1–3, 4–8, 9–17; 5:1–17; 12:1–11, 17–20; 21:11–12:23–29; 24:1–14, 15–24; 37:15–28; Hos 1:2–9; 3:1–5; Zac 6:9–15.

Towards the identification of a new hermeneutical category   629

The question of their classification is rather complex, and does not find unanimity of consensus amongst scholars, given that each stems from different criteria of reference.[54] The variables to be taken into consideration for the drafting of a reasoned repertoire would be quite numerous and therefore would demand a dedicated study. It is, nevertheless, pertinent for my research to be able to distinguish them in two distinct groups: the symbolic-prophetic gestures of a *rhetorical-didactic* nature and those of a *biographical* nature.[55] I will specify that, with this distinction, I indicate not two dimensions that are completely separate or separable, but rather two different gradations of *impact* or *anthropological involvement*, according to a categorisation that I have already introduced.[56]

The predominant function of the former ones is to provide the verbal register with a non-verbal (and usually very elementary) scenic support that can better favour explicitness of the message as well as a greater persuasive efficacy. In this sense, the gesture of the broken jug (ch. 19), while certainly impressive, but also rather simple and of immediate reception, can be considered a standard exemplary reference. The latter ones amplify this communicative valence through a more marked anthropological involvement (according to various gradations), capable of breaking through, at least at the level of initial impact, even to the least responsive recipients. But not only that. It is an instance of meaning that goes beyond both the mere informational piece of data and its pure persuasive valence, since it calls into question not the singularity of an act delimited in narrow space-time coordinates or elementary didactic gestures, but *choices* that are *permanent, irreversible*, or *prolonged* that deeply impact the *personal experience* of the prophet (think of the Jeremianic celibacy, with the consequent renunciation of the blessing of offspring and parentage [16:1–9], to the marriage of Hosea [Hos 1:2–9; 3:1–5], the nudity of Isaiah [20:1–6], the loss of the wife of Ezekiel and his abstention from mourning [Ezek 25:15–24]; etc.).

3.3.4. *The celibacy of Jeremiah as an extreme symbolic-prophetic gesture*

In the perspective just highlighted, standing out with its unique, beyond characteristic profile, is the choice of celibacy requested of Jeremiah in 16:1–9 along with the other symbolic-prophetic acts.[57] First of all, more than gestures, these seem like nongestures, since what is asked of Jeremiah is a triple *abstention*: do not take a wife or have offspring (16:2), do not grieve (16:5), and do not participate in the moments of celebration (16:8). For this reason, K. Ott does not account for them in his "analogous gestures".[58] A choice that is actually quite problematic because, in his formalism, he appears not to grasp that the communicative valence of both the symbolic "gestures" and the symbolic "non-gestures" ordered of the prophet lies not so much in the visiblisation of a material act, but rather in the plastic manifestation (by addition or by subtraction) of a *decision*, of an *intentionality*, and ultimately, of a meaning of history to which one need respond here and now. They are not, therefore, only descriptions

---

54 For an overview of the main taxonomies, see Å. VIBERG, *Prophets in Action*, 45–46.
55 For a more articulated distinction, see e.g. that proposed by L. GASPARRO, *La Parola, il gesto e il segno*, 33–34.
56 In ch. IV, § 3.4.
57 On this topic, I refer once again to L. GASPARRO, *La Parola, il gesto e il segno*, 51–137.
58 Cf. K. OTT, *Analogiehandlungen*, 64.

630 The surrender as a "symbolic-prophetic choice"

or evocations of acts to be carried out, but freedom in action, which becomes revelation, provocation, and a call, in a socio-religious context woven with prescribed codes, norms, traditions, and expectations that, by contrast, allow for the emergence of a specific event of communication.

Jeremiah 16:1–9, while a text presenting *three prohibitions* commanded of the prophet, suggests, almost as a *mise en abyme*, performing the same hermeneutical operation that I am presently developing in reference to the Jeremianic semiosphere: to focalise the existing identity and reciprocal relationships between the various elements of signification in order to understand their communicative valence. It is not difficult, in this case, to realise that the central symbolic-prophetic gesture, around which the other two gravitate, is that of celibacy. Three commands, but a single message. No prophet in the OT receives a similar order from YHWH,[59] an injunction that seems entirely out of place, considering the fundamental importance of marriage and generativity in the socio-cultural context of the ancient Near East.

> La tradizione veterotestamentaria è unanime su questo dato. Essere senza figli è una situazione spregevole (Is 56,5), la sterilità sinonimo di maledizione (Gen 22,17; 1Sam 1,6–8) e la verginità motivo di lamento e di lutto (Gdc 11,37). Il matrimonio è ritenuto parte dell'ordine della creazione (Gen 1,27–28; 2,21–24) e la nascita di figli esprime la benedizione di Dio (Sal 127,3–5; 128,3–4), che ha comandato agli uomini: "siate fecondi e moltiplicatevi" (Gen 1,28; 8,17; 9,1.7). La generazione immette in un flusso di benedizione che scorre tra passato e futuro. Avere una discendenza è talmente essenziale nella mentalità biblica da dare adito alla creazione di leggi specifiche, come quella del levirato (Dt 25,5–10), per impedire che si muoia senza generare.[60]

To express this choice, it is even necessary to resort to a double periphrasis (do not take a wife and have no sons or daughters), for the Hebrew language lacks a suitable term. But it is precisely the perception of a dramatic *lack* that the symbolic-prophetic gesture of celibacy wants to indelibly impress upon the consciousness of the interlocutors. The "peace" (שָׁלוֹם), "mercy" (חֶסֶד), and "compassion" (רַחֲמִים) of YHWH for his people is going to *come less* (√אסף אָסַף +מִן + obj.; 16:5). A terrible event looms upstream. Starting in Hosea, the spousal metaphor is one of the most emblematic for expressing the relationship of Covenant[61] (cf. Hos 1–3; Isa 7–8; Ezek 16:8–13; Mal 2.14; Prov 2.17), but now its crisis is almost at a point of no return. A symbolic-prophetic gesture that is *extreme* is therefore necessary. So Jeremiah is asked to prophetically *take on* the fate

---

59 Cf. G. FISCHER, *Jeremia 1–25*, 521.

60 "The Old Testament tradition is unanimous on this fact. Being childless is a despicable situation (Isa 56:5), infertility synonymous with curse (Gen 22:17; 1 Sam 1:6–8), and virginity cause for lament and mourning (Judg 11:37). Marriage is considered part of the order of creation (Gen 1:27–28; 2:21–24) and the birth of children expresses the blessing of God (Ps 127:3–5; 128:3–4), who commanded that human beings: "be fruitful and multiply" (Gen 1:28; 8:17; 9:1, 7). The generation enters into a stream of blessings that flows between the past and the future. Having descendants is so essential in the biblical mentality that it gives rise to the creation of specific laws, such as that of levitate (Dt 25,5–10), to prevent one from dying without generating" (translated from L. GASPARRO, *La Parola, il gesto e il segno*, 67).

61 "Si l'amour du couple est, de par son essence, allégorie divine, on pouvait s'attendre à ce que la Bible parle le langage nuptial pour dire Dieu" (P. BEAUCHAMP, *L'un et l'autre Testament. 2*, 187). See also L. ALONSO SCHÖKEL, *Símbolos matrimoniales*, 41.

Towards the identification of a new hermeneutical category 631

of all the people himself, to anticipate it in his flesh, allowing life to be *permanently*[62] disrupted, so that the life of the people, his own, can be saved, even only *in extremis*.

3.3.5. A symbolic-prophetic life (vocation and "passion" of Jeremiah)

If, in the biblical context, the spousal metaphor is capable of expressing the totality of the meaning of a history (the relationship between YHWH and his people), its carnal configuration in the life of humanity, even in the paradoxical form of its negation, cannot but sequester and consecrate the complete space of existence for its prophetic purpose. In Jer 16,1–9, it is evident that Jeremiah is called upon to assume the fate of the people on their way to ruin. But the choices that he must signify have, in any case, a limited reference, to the *end*.

Nevertheless, this intensity of anthropological engagement suggests the possibility of a transition to an even higher level. To a global signification, in which human experience becomes prophetic experience,[63] that is, meaningful to others. And, in fact, based on the textual clues offered repeatedly in strategic sections of the book, the Jeremianic celibacy can be considered another clue and additional reference to a subsequent level of meaning, the extent of which actually encompasses all the (other) fundamental aspects of the life of the "body in the scene". From its absolute beginning (cf. 1:5) to its end (even only symbolic; cf. 20; 26:1–8; 38:1–6; etc.). Until its resurgence (cf. 26; 38:7–13). In this sense, the book of Jeremiah immediately invites the reader to understand the life of the prophet as a *total communication*.

The God who presides over the formation of the prophetic body reveals the ordinary naturalness of the event of birth as a prodigy who engages his creative hand, while announcing, at the same time, the significance of life and history, implicitly promising that all this will not end in the dissolution of non-sense. Writing such words while having, before one's eyes, the rubble of the destruction of Jerusalem, and in one's hands, the shreds of a covenant history, this is what it means to prophesy. In the book of Jeremiah, the prophet himself will be this living prophecy, both in the eyes of the reader and in relation to the other narrative figures (or textual simulacra), whom he will have to confront.

The space given to his biography is indicative and has no parallel in the other prophetic figures. What is also formally spelled out for Ezekiel ("I have placed you as a symbol [מוֹפֵת] for the house of Israel"; cf. Ezek 12:6) is already and even more valid for Jeremiah, called to become, like no one else, revelation of the divine word.[64]

---

62 In my opinion as well (along with L. GASPARRO, *La Parola, il gesto e il segno*, 68–69 and other commentators), the textual elements suggest this interpretation rather than a spatial-temporal relativisation of the Jeremianic celibacy.

63 Cf. J.L. SICRE, *Introducción al profetismo bíblico*, 124, who, in reference to Hosea, defines his symbolic gestures "como exposición dramática de su experiencia".

64 "Jeremiah constitutes the clearest biblical example of how all that pertains to the prophet is requisitioned by God to render him transparency of his Word. After him, such an identification will be fuller only in Jesus. It is no coincidence that Jeremiah is the prophet who prefigures him more than any other. The Word, which in the prophetic gesture assumes a physical form, reaches the culmination of its materialisation in the incarnation of the Son of God. The conjunction is finally complete: the message and the messenger interpenetrate to such an extent as to become a single thing (John

632   The surrender as a "symbolic-prophetic choice"

The "ordinary prodigy" of plasmation in the womb, which marks the entry into the universal company of humanity, is specified in the legal act of paternal recognition and in elevation to a symbolic function (cf. 1:5) that recalls, *in primis*, that of the first-borns in Israel (cf. Num 3:11–13), a memorial for everyone of the salvation operated by YHWH in the events of the Exodus (cf. Exod 13:2, 11–16; 22:28–29; 34:19–20; cf. also Hos 11:1; etc.). From here on, every other event assumes this level of meaning, not only his vocation and consecration, but also his prophetic apprenticeship, symbolic-prophetic gestures, celibacy, and even the crisis attested in the "confessions".

It is, above all, his "passion", however, that becomes the sign par excellence. Jeremiah's life and ministry had already been placed in connection with the "deportation of Jerusalem" (גָּלוֹת יְרוּשָׁלַם) from the beginning (cf. 1:3), but in his suffering and his unexpected escape from death, he becomes a symbol-prophet and "paradigmatic signification" (מָשָׁל) of the fate of all the people and the whole City.[65] The question, in my view, is that of analogous relations that have yet to be clarified in a way that is complete, despite the contributions that have already been developed. This does not detract from the fact that the judgment on Jerusalem and the prophecies of salvation concerning it cannot fail to be related to the forensic procedure suffered by the prophet in ch. 26, as well as by the "literary body" of the prophecy, that is, the scroll in ch. 36. The recursiveness of this paradigm then reaches a focal point with the symbolic-prophetic dynamic of "death" and "salvation from death" when, in front of the reader, Jeremiah is first lowered into the tank-tomb and then, from there, pulled out against all predictions (cf. 38:1–13), through the risky and voluntary engagement of Ebed-melech in the fate of the messenger of YHWH. It is precisely the entry upon the scene of this figure, who in some respects reduplicates that of the faithful helper Baruch, that allows us to focalise an ulterior plan of decisive paradigmatic signification, that of the call-response.

3.3.6. Symbolic-prophetic choices/acts of obedience requested of Jeremiah

Taking the life of the prophet on as a "total communication" leads us, as its interpretive repercussion, to consider as paradigmatic an unavoidable relational aspect, that which regards the dynamism of *appeal* and *response* between God and human beings, a principle fundamental to all biblical revelation. Placed upon the scene of history, the "prophetic body" is at this point a semiotic device that signifies, points to, refers to something other than itself, regardless of its will. This, however, should not be understood only in a unidirectional sense, as a trajectory that goes from YHWH, through the prophet, to the people. Prophetic communication is also, or at the same time, *metacommunication*, that is, a word on the communication taking place.

By repeating "thus says the Lord" (כֹּה אָמַר יְהוָה), Jeremiah reveals, at the same time, not only *what* the Lord says, but also *how* the Lord speaks of history *in* history. So the

---

    1:14: ὁ λόγος σὰρξ ἐγένετο)" (translated from L. Gasparro, *La Parola, il gesto e il segno*, 137).

65   On this theme, already suggested by Martin Buber (in: *The Prophetic Faith*, New York 1949, ²1960, 182), I refer, in particular, to the following contributions: S.H. Blank, «The Prophet as Paradigm», 111–130, above all in reference to the inner labour attested by the "confessions"; W. Brueggemann, «The Book of Jeremiah», 130–145; T. Polk, *The Prophetic Persona*; M. Cucca, *Il corpo e la città*.

Botenformel can be well understand as a "thus *speaks* the Lord",[66] considering not only the content of the message, but also the modality by which it gets channelled. A first level of metacommunication brings forth the importance of the bodily (symbolic-analogous) engagement in the revelatory event. In this sense, the medium is itself the message.[67] I have underscored this abundantly. Another aspect, however, regards the grammar of human-divine interaction, whereby what is revealed to humankind is not only who YHWH is or what he requests, but also *how*, concretely, to respond to him.

This category of signification shifts the attention, therefore, not only to the relationship between YHWH and the people, but to the relationship between YHWH and the prophet, to that which YHWH asks of the prophet and how the prophet is called, first of all and in a paradigmatic sense for others, to respond to God in a logic of alliance. The literary phenomenon of the "confessions" definitely directs attention to this aspect, which is not merely biographical or intimist, for it regards an interpersonal dynamic placed before the eyes of the reader so that they themselves can thematise their relationship with God. In this sense, some of the choices requested of Jeremiah by YHWH can be reread as paradigmatic typologies of the human-divine call and response dynamism that serves as a pertinent context for a more adequate understanding of the injunction of surrender to the king of Babylon.

If the programmatic anticipation is presented in the second semiotic model expressed in the vocational text (i.e. the concrete engagement of the pragmatic-body dimension; cf. § 5.3.2), its most emblematic realisation undoubtedly regards the prophet's consent to the divine command requesting that he get himself to the temple to threaten the destruction of the house of YHWH (7:1–15; 26). I have already cited the episode of the trial brought against Jeremiah for his subversive and blasphemous message. According to another perspective of reading, however, a different level of signification also emerges, in which what is being focalised is not so much the dynamic of the events arising from the announcement, but rather the conditions of the announcement's possibility itself: Jeremiah must assume in faith the same dynamic of *obedient delivery* that he will ask of his interlocutors. The surrender into the hands of men (26:14: "As for me, I am in your hands"), reveals and expresses, on the historical and concrete level, nothing other than an originary handing over into the hands of YHWH (cf. 26:2: "Go to the atrium of the Temple of the Lord and repeat [...] all the words that I commanded you to announce to them, omit not a word").

On the same level, of course, we see placed the prescription of *celibacy* along with other *gestures of abstention from social life* (16:1–9), but also the command to announce the *surrender* to Babylon either through the gesture of the yoke (27–28) or even just verbally (21:8–9; 38:1–3). If accepting celibacy means already taking on death (in a symbolic-prophet form), then asking others to take on a similar dimension (the surrender) places him back in the same situation of mortal risk that he experienced in ch. 26 (because he seems to be a traitor of the nation), but also in the same dynamic

---

66 Significant in this sense is the title chosen for the collection of studies on biblical prophetism by P. Bovati, *«Così parla il Signore»*.

67 This is primarily due to the contribution of M. McLuhan, *Understanding Media. The Extensions of Man*, New York 1964, who highlighted the extent to which the channel of transmission selected to communicate a message has the power of influencing the message itself. The famous assertion "the medium is the message" is his own.

634 The surrender as a "symbolic-prophetic choice"

of unexpected salvation (38:4–13; 39:11–14; 40:1–6). In addition to these choices that challenge Jeremiah's freedom, one could also mention the triple *prohibition to intercede* (cf. 7.16; 11.14; 14.11; 15.1), which would, in any case, merit special consideration in this respect as well.

In any case, as can be seen, this typology of requests that YHWH makes of the prophet is not of an ethical-moral type, nor does it concern the observance of some ritual or religious prescription. They are *precise* requests for obedience in which what is expressed is the meaning of his history as a person-prophet who has *handed himself over*, and for this very reason is *saved*. In other words, they are *symbolic-prophetic* choices. Only from the interaction between these two symbolic moments (the handing over of himself and undeducible salvation) can one truly appreciate the meaning of escaping death as promised by YHWH. This salvific outcome, in fact, is by no means an anecdotal or accidental event, but an occurrence placed in consequential relationship with the concrete trust and conscious assumption of the significance connected to the divine command.

3.3.7. Symbolic-prophetic choices/acts of obedience requested of the people

Once this new symbolic paradigmatic category has been identified in the person of the prophet, it is not difficult to trace what the corresponding symbolic level is on the side of the response requested of his interlocutors. This too must have its own precise delimitation on the level of story, along the same semiotic trajectory, and should be sought in the textual simulacra that interface with Jeremiah. There is no shortage of clues.

It is no coincidence that very unique *salvation* oracles (cf. 39:16–18; 45:5) are reserved for both Baruch and Ebed-melech, even amidst the inevitable drama of the events taking place. Both can be taken on as intradiegetic personifications (and as provocations for empiric readers) of those who have recognised, in Jeremiah, a true prophet and for this reason have obeyed, in an analogous and significant way, the *totality of the meaning of the history underway* revealed by YHWH, as the prophet had already done exemplarily in antecedence.

To assert that the essence of prophetic ministry consists in calling people to obedience according to the implications of the Covenant is certainly nothing new. It does not appear however that any in-depth interrogation has been done of the different forms of obedience required in Israel in relation to their symbolic significance. Nevertheless, important indications of meaning can be found in the reflections of P. Bovati on Deuteronomy about the modalities by which Scripture comes to thematise the need to reach a unifying principle regarding the "disparate variety of commandments" of the Law.[68] Three symbolic levels can thus be distinguished:

a) *The "principial" commandment*. This has the love of God as its direct object, and is synthetically formulated in the famous text of Deut 6:4–9: "Listen Israel: the Lord is our God, the Lord alone. You *shall love* the Lord your God with all your heart, with all your soul, and with all your strength [...]" (but cf. also 10:12, 15; 11:13, 15, 22; 13:4, etc.). This commandment is not identified with one of the many precepts to which obedience is required by virtue of the Covenant, but represents its source,

---

68 See, in this regard, P. Bovati, *Giustizia e ingiustizia nell'Antico Testamento*, 151–154.

the *principle* that gives meaning to all others, and which becomes true in their observance. The full meaning of the Law is thus placed outside of the Law[69] itself, in the unquantifiable dimension of the totality of love.

b) The *"tautological"* commandment. This can be found expressed according to varied synonymic modalities (cf. Deut 4:1.10; 6:1, 4a; etc.)[70]: "Observe (or: remember, listen, obey, practice, etc.) the Lord's command (or: his precepts, his norms, his words, etc.)". This imperative only affirms itself, that is, it places, as a unifying principle of the Law, the need to observe the Law itself. In other words, it does not require the observance of a certain behaviour, but clarifies that the fundamental commandment is that of obedience to YHWH. Every command and every act of obedience in this regard must be assumed in its symbolic valence capable of making the One who asks to be recognised and loved present.

c) The *commandment sign of the whole Law.* Here, we are on another level with respect to the previous ones, and the symbolic-communicative dimension evoked is highly pertinent to my discourse. Another way in which a focal point of the Law is identified in the Old Testament tradition is that by which, in precise historical-literary contexts, one of the many (even minimal) commandments arises with its specific symbolic weight as a semiotic device to express not so much the observance of that particular commandment in itself, but rather obedience to the *totality* of the Law. The question, in my opinion, is that of having the capability to read the real, which can easily be defined as *prophetic*, because it does not regard disquisitions on abstract and/or timeless principles, but discernment of the present hour seen from the perspective of YHWH. Ultimately, it is an inverse and complementary expression of the ability of the prophets to see, in certain behaviours, which are apparently good or even formally justified by the Law itself (cf. e.g. Amos 2:6–16), the signs of a radical betrayal of the spirit of the Covenant.

Some possible examples: at the time and in the book of Amos, the crucial issue is the re-establishment of law in the courts (cf. Amos 5:15) against the hypocrisy of cult offerings (cf. 4:4–5; 5:21–25) or soulless pilgrimages (cf. 5:5); just as for Isaiah (cf. Isa 1:11–15) and the other prophets who testimony to the same degenerate situation. After the exile, on the other hand, in another context, the matter seems almost inverted. It is in the reconstruction of the temple and other cultural obligations that a symbolic valence is identified, capable of expressing the meaning of a renewed relationship with YHWH (cf. Hag 1:3–11; Neh 10.32–40). Consider also the norm prohibiting mixed marriages (with foreign women), still in the time of Ezra-Nehemiah (cf. Ezra 9–10), a practice that gets stigmatised since it was believed to have jeopardised the Yahwist faith. At the time of the Maccabees, another pertinent focalisation can be witnessed: loyalty to the Covenant of the fathers is played out entirely in the observance of the norms on pure and unclean foods (cf. also Tob 1:10–12), and in order to not eat pork, even leads to martyrdom (2 Mac 7).

---

69 With this traditional denomination, dependent on the Greek text, I emphasise, in the present context, the normative nature of the *Tôrâ*.

70 As regards its presence in the Deut, see N. Lohfink, *Das Hauptgebot.* Eine Untersuchung literarischer Einleitungsfragen zu Dtn 5–11, AnBib 20, Roma 1963, 64–72, 90–97.

The content of the prophetic appeal in the book of Jeremiah is basically simple: *return to YHWH*. Its practical variations are, however, manifold, starting from the observation of a fact that is as simple as it is dramatic: no one wants to recognise that they are far from the God of the Covenant. And while the prophet, as in other cases, identifies and exposes the hypocrisy of his compatriots by stigmatising certain specific behaviours (the templar cult again as a way of hiding injustice [cf. 7:1–16; 26], having broken the oath by which the freeing of Jewish slaves was promised [34:8–22]; etc.), at the same time, he indicates different forms of obedience to express fidelity to the covenant and restore its salvific efficacy. These are, from one time to the next, and depending on the interlocutors to whom they are addressed (all the people or individual figures), *ethical-moral* (the commandments; cf. 5:8; 7:5–9; 26:13; etc.), *religious-cultual* (the rejection of idolatry; observance of the Sabbath; etc.; cf. 11:17; 17:19–27; etc.), or *symbolic-prophetic* prescriptions (writing and proclamation of the prophetic scroll asked of Baruch, the gesture asked of Seraiah; cf. 36; 51:59–64). Starting from this last dimension, the symbolic-prophetic profile characteristic of the most decisive choice indicated by the prophet in the horizon of the end of Jerusalem emerges: the surrender to Babylon. In my opinion, however, this is a choice that has its own very special level of signification, which, while being embedded in the symbolic-prophetic dimension, needs to be further specified.

4. The surrender as Prophetic-Obediential ConSign*A(c)tion (POC)*

4.1. A synthetic definition

The conceptual map that I have outlined in its basic aspects, while obviously requiring further in-depth study and clarification, already enables the highlighting of the specificity and relationships between different symbolic-semiotic categorical dimensions present in the book of Jeremiah (and beyond). I will now try to identify the *structuring elements* of the symbolic level that emerges for differentiation from those identified thus far. These configure the fundamental semantic axes of a new symbolic-semiotic category, to which I dedicated initial consideration as a "symbolic-prophetic obedience or choice" (cf. § 5.1–2), but which I will now denominate more precisely and technically with a neologism, that is, as "Prophetic-Obediential ConSign*A(c)tion*" (POC).[71]

---

71 From here on, to refer to the just announced notion, I will use prevalently the acronym POC, beside the simpler (though perhaps for this, less clear) expression "obedience or symbolic-prophetic choice". With this neologism, I refer back to an already existing term in the historic Italian vocabulary. According to the TLIO (Tesoro della Lingua Italiana delle Origini, accessible online), the now archaic term "*consegnazione*" (which is attested with diversified spellings: *consegnatione, consignagione, comsegnagion*; etc.) has three main meanings: (1) entrustment, handing over of an object or good; (2) assignment of a public role or a task; (3) inspection of soldiers and their enrolment. It is interesting that, in even further depth, the ancient *Dizionario universale, storico, e critico dei costumi, leggi, usi, ecc.*, vol. I, by J.-P. Costard *et al.*, translated from the original French in Italy in 1784, specifies on p. 265 that the "*consegnazione*", which translates the term "tradition" (as an "act of consigning something") in vol. IV on p. 422, took place according to the contexts by means of a symbolic gesture, that is, by

Prophetic-Obediential ConSign*A(c)tion* (POC) is:

1) a *choice*
2) signified through an *action* with profound *anthropological implications* (it is an attitude, a choice of life, or, at least, an act of considerable existential investment),
   a) of a historical-temporal nature (marked by a certain duration or by the irreversibility of the choice made)
   b) socio-affective in nature (touches the relational dimension and the sphere of emotions, feelings, and social roles)
   c) of a dramatic nature (may pose a fatal risk)
3) understood as *commanded by God* to the prophet or to the *people* (usually through the prophet) *precisely*, that is, it is not reducible only
   a) to *a political-military strategy*
   b) nor to *an ethical-moral attitude* (normative for every person)
   c) or *religious* of a *cultic* type
   d) nor for only *rhetorical-didactic* purposes
4) but which has the ability to *express* and *actualise* a *significant and prophetic performant option* in relation to its positioning within the relational perimeter of the Covenant taking place *in* history and in reference to the *meaning of the present history*, namely:
   a) it actually carries out an *obedience of faith* through which *one responds positively to God*, rendering the relationship of Covenant living and real
   b) it is actualised through *the concrete acceptance* (cf. number 2: action, attitude, choice of life...) *of a sense of present history revealed by God* for the recipients of the prophecy itself.

In the following paragraphs, I will detail the just highlighted elements of meaning, grouping them by logical-semantic areas of relevance. I will clarify immediately that these should not be considered in isolation or independently. It is their mutual interaction and semiotic synergy that helps define the POC as a categorical unit capable of coherently segmenting an important part of the Jeremianic semiosphere. This takes concrete and emblematic form in the act of surrender requested by Jeremiah in the face of the Babylonian power. To surrender, in the context of the book of Jeremiah, is therefore an example and, in my opinion, perhaps the one most paradigmatic, which, however, does not exhaust the phenomenon in question. Indeed, there are various ways to surrender, and other ways to express a POC attested both within and outside of the texts that I have dealt with in depth in the present dissertation (21:1–10; 27–28; 38:14–28a).

---

means of a knife, a clod of earth (for an inheritance), giving keys (to a barn containing sold wheat), simply showing an object, etc. This lexicographic basis lends itself to a resemantisation and to an *ad hoc* graphic recomposition. "ConSign*A(c)tion*" thus concentrates a network of meanings that seek to express the richness of meaning of the semiotic category I have identified and that I will explain in its constitutive elements: It is a choice that expresses a "consigning" (handing over) of oneself to God (and in obedience to Him, possibly also into the hands of human beings); it is an "action", that is, a concrete gesture, a choice of life, or in any case, an act-sign that "signals"/"marks" in the flesh whoever makes it and, at the same time, "points to", that is, signifies the assumption of the meaning of present history revealed by God.

4.2. A category to be understood in a prototypical sense

A caution of a linguistic nature is necessary. The recognition of the category for which I have isolated the defining elements in different textual areas, cannot be merely the result of an analysis based on criteria typical of *componential analysis*.[72] A more adequate reconnaissance of the POC should instead, in my opinion, be based on the *prototype semantics*, assumed in its extended theoretical version.[73]

Unlike *componential analysis*, whereby lexical meaning is to be understood as the set of necessary and sufficient conditions, prototype semantics[74] refers to the notion of "prototype". According to the most recent reworking of the theory, this should not be understood as the most representative concrete exemplar of a category but "as an abstract entity, constituted of a set of typical properties"[75] of a category, which serves as a focal point to represent the meaning of the word that it indicates. Starting from

---

72 By "traits" in linguistics, what is understood is the minimum unit of signification. On some general limitations of this kind of analysis, see J. Lyons, *Language and Linguistics. An Introduction*, Cambridge 1981, ⁹1992, 154.

73 For the summary that I will present, I refer above all to the following contributions (some specialised, others, those in Italian language, of a synthetic-introductive nature, useful for an initial approach to the question, but in my opinion, in general, not sufficient for adequately clarifying the argument in all of its aspects): G. Lakoff, *Women, Fire and Dangerous Things*. What Categories Reveal about the Mind, Chicago 1987; J.R. Taylor, *Linguistic Categorization*. Prototypes in Linguistic Theory, Oxford 1989, ²1995; P. Violi, *Significato ed esperienza*, 151–207; F. Casadei, *Lessico e semantica*, 91–114; D. Geeraerts, «Prospects and Problems of Prototype Theory», in: *Cognitive Linguistics: Basic Readings*, 141–165 (already published in: *Linguistics* 27 [1989] 587–612); L. Anolli, *Fondamenti*, 102–111; D. Geeraerts, *Theories of Lexical Semantics*, Oxford 2010, 182–203; G. Basile – F. Casadei – L. Lorenzetti – G. Schirru – A.M. Thornton, *Linguistica generale*, 344–363. Needless to say that, for reasons of space, I am obliged to present an exposition that is essential, both of the theory and the application that I will propose with regard to the theme being treated.

74 This, in sum, the main assumption of the theory at its inception, a work above all by Eleanor Rosch: "When describing categories analytically, most traditions of thought have treated category membership as a digital, all-or-none phenomenon. That is, much work in philosophy, psychology, linguistics, and anthropology assumes that categories are logical bounded entities, membership in which is defined by an item's possession of a simple set of criterial features, in which all instances possessing the criterial attributes have a full and equal degree of membership. In contrast, it has recently been argued [...] that some natural categories are analog and must be represented logically in a manner which reflects their analog structure" (E. Rosch – C.B. Mervis, «Family Resemblances: Studies in the Internal Structure of Categories», *CognPsy* 7 [1975] 573–605 [here, pp. 573–574]).

75 Translated from F. Casadei, *Lessico e semantica*, 99. See also L. Anolli, *Fondamenti*, 108. This is one of the aspects for which the extended theory of the prototype (developed since the 1990s) goes beyond the limits of standard theory, which lays itself open to criticism for creating some confusion between the concepts of *representativity* (i.e. the possession of the larger number of properties typical of a given category) and *belonging* to the category (which cannot be based only on vague criteria of resemblance).

The surrender as Prophetic-Obediential ConSignA(c)tion   639

this centre, more peripheral occurrences that manifest the semantic flexibility in various degrees can be connected.[76] Let me elaborate the argument.

Componential analysis, based on the classical theory of categories (which dates back to Aristotle, Porphyry, Boethius) conceives category as: (1) defined by a set of *necessary and sufficient traits* found in the essential properties of its members; (2) a *discrete unit*; (3) without internal structuring, therefore providing, only the case of a *clear* categorical *belonging* or of an equally *clear exclusion*. The result is a conception of the meaning that is univocal and determined in an absolute way by the constitutive traits attributed to each lemma. But this is ultimately untenable, because it does not account for, among other things, the gradualness of semantic properties (so-called semantic vagueness), the flexibility of meaning found in speakers' usage, and the extensive use of words (metaphorical, metonymic, figurative uses in general), which are fundamental characteristics of every natural language.

According to prototype semantics, on the other hand, which conceives categorisation as a process of cognitive optimisation and "economic" structuration of the perceived world,[77] the characteristics of a category understood in a prototypical sense are: (1) the possibility of blurred boundaries: so their members can have levels of *gradual membership*; (2) various degrees of *representativity*: the members participate differently in a set of *typical properties* of the category, which do not necessarily have to all be present simultaneously (technically, in linguistics, it is said that they are subject to exceptions and *cancellable*), even if participation in one or more (necessary, but not sufficient) *essential traits* cannot be lacking; (3) *absence* of a *set of necessary and sufficient properties* common to all members of the category; (4) possible presence of *referential polysemy* with univocal semantics.[78]

---

76 Note D. GEERAERTS, «Prospects», 156: "Cognitive Linguistics is not only interested in what constitutes the centre of a category, but also in how this centre can be extended towards peripheral cases, and how far this extension can go."

77 For this reason, one should speak about this (with G. Lakoff), more than as "prototype", as "prototypical effects", thus intending prototypicity as "a superficial manifestation, a product of the nature of the cognitive patterns we use to make sense of our experience of the world" (translated from F. CASADEI, *Lessico e semantica*, 104). The prototype effect manifests itself, in fact, differently according to the different linguistic categories.

78 E.g. as notes D. GEERAERTS, «Prospects», 149–150, the category "bird" (*bird* in reference to the English language speakers that the author has in mind) refers to very different animals (*referential polysemy*) but is, in general, perceived as being well defined, that is, of a discrete type (having a *univocal semantic*): "At least with regard to our own, real world, the denotation of *bird* is determinate; educated speakers of English know very well where birds end and non-birds begin. They know, for instance, that a bat is not a bird but that a penguin is. [...]. As it functions now, [...], in present-day English, *bird* is denotationally clearly bounded, the archaeopteryx notwithstanding. [...] the existence of prototypicality effects in clearly bounded concepts such as *bird* implies that a strict distinction has to be made between degree of membership and degree of representativity. Membership in the category *bird* is discrete; something is or is not a bird. But some birds may be birdier than others: the swallow does remain a more typical bird than the ostrich" (pp. 149–150). The category of POC, on the other hand, on the basis of my interpretation, does refer to other likewise diverse forms, but these are not always immediately identifiable: It is, in fact, not immediate that the choices Jeremiah asks the exiles of the first deportation and of those who escaped the

640 The surrender as a "symbolic-prophetic choice"

4.3. Some possible examples of reference (in view of further research)

As can be seen, by listing the above characteristics, I have highlighted the possibility or not of their presence. The very notion of prototypicality, in fact, must be understood in a prototypical sense,[79] that is, as a category defined by various properties (1. blurred boundaries; 2. inclusion of more or less representative members; 3. absence of a set of necessary and sufficient properties simultaneously shared by all members; 4. referential polysemy with univocal semantics) that *do not necessarily all have to be present* at the same time. There are, therefore, categories with different degrees of prototypicality, depending on how many typical properties (of the prototypical category) they possess.

I believe that these clarifications, whilst on the one hand, help to focalise the categorial definition that I have identified and adopted, also allow for further development of my research, as already mentioned. Within the book of Jeremiah, it is possible to discover a twofold *isomorphic* manifestation of the theme of surrender to Babylon in two other prophetic demands: (a) that of renouncing a rapid return from the land of exile, addressed to the deportees of 597 (cf. ch. 29), to be expressed in a series of actions that can be defined precisely as POC: building houses and living them, planting vegetable gardens, getting married, generating sons and daughters, praying for the well-being of Babylon; (b) that of not fearing retaliation by the king of Babylon after the murder of the governor Ghedaliah, appointed for the survivors of the catastrophe of the kingdom of Judah, deciding to remain in the Land without fleeing to Egypt and trusting in the protection of YHWH (cf. 42:7–22).

Outside of the book of Jeremiah, despite their apparent historical-literary diversity, the category of POC could give new depth of meaning to gestures or choices between which nothing or little of analogous is usually noticed, and which do not seem comparable to the Jeremianic option of surrender. Amongst the many examples that might be mentioned are, for example, the word of YHWH that asks Jacob to return to his land, where he would probably find his brother Esau with his ancient fratricidal intentions (cf. Gen 32:10–12); the command to go to battle and conquer the land of Canaan (and, in an oppositive sense, the refusal to do so out of fear), and the subsequent prohibition to fight and order to turn back into the desert (cf. Num 13–14; Josh 1; etc.); the unusual request made by Elijah to the widow of Sarepta ("first, though, prepare a small bread cake for me and bring it to me [...]"; cf. 1 Kgs 17:14–15); Hosea's marriage to a prostitute (cf. Hos 1–3); Isaiah's invitation to resist the Assyrian threat (which is the opposite of what Jeremiah asks in another context, to not make alliances and to trust in YHWH during the Syro-Ephraimite war (cf. Isa 7); the nudity requested of Isaiah himself (cf. Isa 20); the mourning of Ezekiel and the forbiddance of weeping (cf. Ezek 24:15–27); the prophetic indication given to Jehoshaphat to defeat the enemies (cf. 2 Chr 20:1–25), and so on. Indeed, this is quite a promising development of the present research, which could even better demonstrate the heuristic valence of the POC.

---

destruction of the kingdom of Judah to make be included in the category of POC, that is, that they be identified as variations on the theme of "consigning onself to the king of Babylon" (of which I will speak further in the following paragraph).

79 Cf. D. GEERAERTS, *Theories*, 187–192.

Chapter VIII
The surrender to the king of Babylon as "Prophetic-Obediential ConSign*A(c)tion*" (POC)

La liberté n'a de porte qu'une traversée effective de la mort, qui devient vie: trajet impensable si quelqu'un d'autre que l'homme ne le conduit. Il ne s'agit pas d'une identité des contraires, mais de leur coïncidence. Cette coïcidence a lieu seulement «maintenant.»[1]

1. A hermeneutical synthesis as a new working hypothesis

The category that emerged from my investigation of the symbolic levels of the book of Jeremiah, providing, with its constituent semantic elements, a battery of criteria for its identification and verification, has two important hermeneutical and operational consequences. It encourages testing of the heuristic valence of this notion on other areas of the Scripture, and allows me to attempt an interpretation of my object of investigation from a point of view alternative to the historical and historical-literary ones, which have revealed to be insufficient, in my opinion, in accounting for its wealth of meaning. For reasons of space and pertinence, I will obviously concentrate on the second possibility.

After having isolated by differentiation[2] the phenomenon of "Prophetic-Obediential ConSign*A(c)tion*" from other semiotic dynamics, what remains is to analyse in detail the semantic axes that identify this proposed category, to see what aspects of my topic of study become particularly enlightened by it. I will take my start from the elements cited in the synthetic formulation of the POC. It is within this that the most significant elements of the phenomenon highlighted are coordinated, that is: the dynamism of the *symbolic signification*, engagement of the *body in action*, and prophetic dimension of *obedient listening*.

Symbolic signification. This is, first of all, a dynamism of signification, that is, of a relationship of structural reference to something other than itself contained in the particular form of a "sign". Properly speaking, what is in question in my case is that type of reference rooted *in primis* in the dimension of the *symbol*. It is, therefore, not a question of a relationship established in a purely conventional or arbitrary way, nor is it simply a signic function understood as a mere reference between a signifier and its meaning. It is also, in itself, without further specifications, detached from evaluative ethical-moral characterisations.[3]

---

1 P. BEAUCHAMP, *L'un et l'autre Testament*. 2, 31.
2 As I have already observed, it has been possible to proceed herein with only a rough taxonomic organisation that is quite simplified. It is, nevertheless, valid as a working guideline for more in-depth and exhaustive research, which I will defer to subsequent study.
3 It is clear, in any case, that in the book of Jeremiah, the POC of submission-surrender to Babylon implicates a moral value, as an obediential response to the word of YHWH

As I pointed out (cf. § 4.3.2), in the symbol, the signified reality is not only indicated or represented, but is given, in a certain sense, as being *already present*. It is already here, in the symbol itself, and together, it projects itself and leads *beyond* the symbol. The symbolic fact does not provide the meaning in a way that is exhaustive; it renders it present, yes, but in its irreducible inexhaustibility. The symbol, experimented through the senses, can be conceptualised, like the sign, but only in a way that is utterly partial, provisional, never completely satisfactory. It is good to keep this in mind; otherwise it would be not a symbol, but (only) a sign. The symbol "donne à penser", that is, expresses a richness of meaning that presents itself with questioning force before the subjectivity of the interpreter. It is pro-poses itself in a way that is permanent, for it cannot be grasped once and for all. While it communicates a meaning, a conceptual actuality, it also delivers an opening, establishes a channel of communication between two worlds, which are rendered present to one another. The signification that I allude to is thus that of the symbolic power highlighted by the philosophical reflection of P. Ricœur. It is not the abstractism of the symbolic conception of Peircean semiotics, for which the symbol is pure convention.[4]

The "body" in action. Another characteristic of the signification implicated in the phenomenon of the POC is its *corporeal anchorage*. The body, understood as visible humanity on the scene of history, is called into question here in a direct way, both as a body "acted upon" and as an "agent" body: acting by the hand of God, by a combination of natural and historical-cultural conditionings, put into motion by the very freedom of human consciousness, which, within the limits of its creaturehood and the contextual conditionings of existence, retains its capacity for self-determination. In other words, it is the historical dimension of the biblical human being, seen in their intrinsic fragility. A fragility, however, able to bear and carry the vertigo of freedom, that capable even of hosting divine transcendence: the design of YHWH, his will, and his self-communication, which reaches the individual in the spatial-temporal horizon in which he is given to live.

It is therefore the signification that is put into effect by the action. Human activity, represented and evoked by the text, comes to or returns to life in the act of its reading or hearing. It can, in a certain sense, be *seen*. Like the symbolic gestures of the prophets narrated in the prophetic pages: visible words or visibilisations of the word (understood as messages, communication), which polarise (above all) sight and sound around the event of the communication of meaning.

For this same reason, the graphic form that I have adopted to define the category of "Prophetic-Obediential ConSign*A(c)tion*" is almost a *mise en abyme* of the very phenomenon it wants to describe, because it maintains in a single unit (the reference

---

proclaimed by his prophet. This is clarified by the outcome of the "consignation", that is, life, while the opposite produces death.

4   "In the terminology of the Peirceian tradition [...] a signic relationship is instead called symbolic when, in its absence, there would be no link at all between signifier and the signified. In other words, a symbol (in Peirce's terminology) has no motivation that is other than historical or conventional: It is, in short, opaque or arbitrary. [...] but it is a somewhat unfortunate terminology, because in the literary and religious tradition, by symbol something very different is meant, that is, a strongly motivated sign, rich with emotional and narrative implications" (translated from U. VOLLI, *Manuale di semiotica*, 29).

A choice. A free choice carried out in a story of revelation   643

to) an *audible form* (by analogy with the verbal message of the prophets of a digital and linear type) and a *graphic form* (by analogy with their gestural mimesis).[5] This is to recall the difference and connection between the fundamental concepts of the sign (which supposes for us a reorientation of an underlying symbolic dimension), the signified, the signifier, the act of signification, and the actant/acting body, and to express, starting from the act of reading/listening, the dimension tied to the sense of sight typical of this prophetic semiotic. Signification, thus understood, is for me, therefore, a Sign*A(c)tion*, a lemma assumed as a neologism and an unusual graphic form that intends to communicate something other (and new) with respect to the only audible form, in which traditional significances are sedimented.

Prophecy and obedience. This Sign*A(c)tion* is then connoted in a sense that is *prophetic* and *obediential* together. These dimensions are decisive and will thus be the object of specific, in-depth treatment in subsequent paragraphs (cf. §§ 6.4.1–2). I will anticipate here that the dynamic of signification I am referring to is that typical of *biblical* prophetism. This essentially has to do with the human time that is *history*, seen through the eyes of YHWH and conceived as a space of revelation of his presence and desire for self-communication within the framework of a relationship of alliance. In this signification, what is expressed is the central dimension of human-divine communication, that of obedient listening.

Let me now take up the elements typical of the POC listed synthetically in the previous paragraph, showing how they can make sense of the Jeremianic call for surrender to the king of Babylonia.

2. A choice. A free choice carried out in a story of revelation

By defining the POC as, first of all, a "choice", what is called into question is the "dramatic" dimension of biblical history. It should be recalled that this "history" is one that is quite particular, that is, it is a story of *revelation*.[6] According to the experience of Israel, God can only be known[7] because he himself has decided to reveal himself and does so. And only stemming from this self-communication can a person commit to choose him, in freedom. Given, then, that it is only in the temporal flow of events that the human being experiences freedom, biblical revelation is essentially *historical*.[8]

---

5   Every word can have a graphic form and an audible form. Depending on cultures or contexts, both are given, or at times not. A word can be only an audible form in a non-written language, or can be communicated, depending on the context, only in audible form or only in graphic form.

6   The revelation of the "name" of God (cf. Exod 3:13–15), as an emblematic paradigm of this process, is not the proclamation of his existence but of his proper name. A name that designates him as a subject and not as an object. The intentionality at the base of divine self-communication is not of the informative but rather the communal type. God calls and chooses for a particular relationship in which the universal meaning of history is reflected.

7   Not to be understood in an intellectualistic sense.

8   In this sense, one can also say that "truth" is historical, in the sense that one can tap into it through many truths and particular experiences, without this taking away from the fact that it be absolute. And indeed, an absolute that is always extracted and revealed in particulars, in that which is finite, in limits.

This revelative dynamic brings into play the freedom of God who, offering himself, gives space to that of the *homo respondens* (because *responsabilis*), at the same time, projecting these events onto the scene of the text like onto a stage. It is thus a "sacred representation" that can lend itself to an (analogical) comparison with the Greek categories that define the theatrical art, a representation of history seen through the eyes of a different culture. And so, this history of revelation is neither a *comedy* nor a (real and true) *tragedy*: it is neither simple ordinariness, lightness of living, and determinism of good with a guaranteed happy ending, nor the inevitable hastening of events towards the catastrophe of the end without remedy or hope.[9] It is indeed a "drama" of freedom, with its possible and hoped-for fulfilment in the embrace of communion of the Covenant.

In the microcosm of the Scripture, the world of humanity is hosted in all its profound dynamics, with innumerable nuances, and revealed to be a space of human and divine freedom.[10] Choosing, deciding, or simply living means having the *actual* possibility of opting, in self-awareness, for at least one alternative from amongst two or more different roads. In the Greek world, the gods dominate humanity, but they have only limited power. Above them, Fate (Μοῖρα) and its blindness dominates. It is true, one should not exaggerate, as has often been done: gods and destiny are not at all the puppeteers of humankind. Constant recourse to divinatory practices demonstrates this.[11] And yet, at times, there is a strong sense that everything is ultimately governed and heteroimposed by this impersonal Necessity. The decisions of human beings, their desire for freedom, and manifestations of power risk being just illusions in motion. If they are not, and precisely Greek tragedy seems to highlight this, the risk is that

---

9 This is also reflected in the particular style of the biblical narrations. As has long been noted by E. Auerbach, *Mimesis. Die Darstellung der Wirklichkeit in der abendländischen Literatur*, Bern 1946, in the biblical world, the classic distinction between the elevated style of tragedy or epic drama and that of the "humble" comedy and satire does not exist.

10 Cf. P. Bovati, *I giorni di Dio*, Sestante 32, Milano 2013, 19: "The Scripture denounces, accuses, warns, shakes; it speaks of sin and responsibility, but also of remedies and of hope tied to change. Because it believes in the *freedom* of man, though fragile and uncertain; it believes that man has the potential to build the future, just as he unfortunately has the power to vote everything to destruction. Precisely the notion of brief time, limited time, time that passes inexorably introduces, as a consequence, the concept of responsibility (Rom 13:11–12; 1 Cor 7:29). The word of the prophet shows the concrete places in which the covenant has been betrayed; it reveals the ways in which the bond with God the Father and with his brothers has been broken [...]. It is necessary to believe in the freedom of the human being in order to correct evil and give hope to sinners. And in the Bible, radical confidence in the intimate strength of the human creature, in the never-extinguished possibility of returning to do good, is the basis of a positive reading of history. Time is a formidable opportunity, always given, given to everyone, to begin again, to recreate once again the space of the primigenial garden" (my translation).

11 K. Beerden, *Worlds Full of Signs. Ancient Greek Divination in Context*, RGRW 176, Leiden – Boston 2013, 221–222. The attestations of this practice in the Greek world, according to the author, allow for the conclusion that the common person had a variegated idea of the future, not very distinct from our own: "they too usually saw their future(s) as open-but-not-empty" (p. 222).

A choice. A free choice carried out in a story of revelation 645

human freedom will seek alibis behind the wills of the deities or of fate. Even beyond such conceptions of life and the world, this doubt is also reproposed, in a certain sense, by modern neurosciences.[12] The biblical perspective is thus far from obvious. In the world of the Iliad, Patroclus and Hector cannot choose: they must both die because it *has been decreed* thus.[13] While before Zedekiah, on the other hand, the path of life and the path of death are placed. Many things will be taken from his control and the punitive event will be inevitable, but up to the end, he will have an alternative before him and can decide for life.

Deciding means cutting off all other possibilities. Choosing, electing, is the same as discarding all the other elements placed on the storyboard. What the neurosciences undoubtedly demonstrate is that this process is strongly influenced by emotional-affective dynamics.[14] The rationalisation of the choice comes only later, even though emotions and affections can convey veritative content.[15] In the Scripture, the role of freedom is perhaps more evident than elsewhere. Also because, otherwise, the notion of covenant between YHWH and his people, decisive in the context of biblical

---

12 If a reductionist approach to the question of free will is assumed, the tendency is inevitably that of arguing that freedom, as an event of conscious self-determination (and thus also of moral responsibility) is only a cerebral illusion, seeing as it would be nothing more than a deterministic effect of electrochemical impulses. See, in this regard, the emblematic (and much debated) positions of S. SMILANSKY, *Free Will and Illusion,* Oxford 2000; D.M. WAGNER, *The Illusion of Conscious Will,* Cambridge (MA) 2002; B. LIBET, *Mind time.* The Temporal Factor in Consciousness, Cambridge (MA) 2004, according to whom some studies in the neuroscientific field would demonstrate that actions "happen to us" rather than be caused by us. From some experiments, it would seem, in fact, that the brain decides what to do a few milliseconds before the subject becomes aware. Contrariwise, in an anti-reductionist reading, the results of more recent research and positions of other scholars, such as e.g. T. O'CONNOR, *Persons and Causes.* The Metaphysics of Free Will, New York 2000; J. DUPRÉ, *Human Nature and the Limits of Science,* Oxford – New York 2001; J.R. SEARLE, *Freedom and Neurobiology.* Reflections on Free Will, Language, and Political Power, New York 2007; etc. The debate, therefore, remains open.
13 "But it was destructive Fate and the son of Leto who slew me, and of men Euphorbus, while thou art the third in my slaying. And another thing will I tell you, and do you lay it to heart: surely you shall not yourself be long in life, but even now does death stand hard by you, and resistless fate, to be slain at the hands of Achilles, the incomparable grandson of Aeacus." Thus "prophesies" Patroclus, near death, to Hector, as he took his life (*Iliad,* XVI, 849–854; translation from HOMER, *Iliad.* Books 13–34. With an English Translation by A.T. Murray, Revised by William F. Wyatt, LCL 171, Cambridge (MA) – London 1999, 224–225.
14 See e.g. with regard to the "emotional brain", the chapter dedicated to emotions and sentiments in the famous neuroscience manual by Eric R. Kandel: J.E. LEDOUX – A.R. DAMASIO, «Emotions and Feelings», in: *Principles of Neural Science, eds.* E.R. KANDEL, *et al.,* New York 1981, [5]2013, 1079–1094, which concludes saying: "The loss or impairment of the neural processes responsible for feelings diminishes the ability to anticipate and plan behavior" (p. 1092).
15 Cf. M.R. WYNN, *Emotional Experience and Religious Understanding.* Integrating Perception, Conception and Feeling, Cambridge 2005 (esp. pp. 93–122).

646   The surrender as "Prophetic-Obediential ConSignA(c)tion"

revelation[16] would be non-sense. In biblical law, unlike Mesopotamian law, there is, in principle, no difference between free men and slaves. The true difference is between YHWH and his people. All hold responsibility for the demands of the Covenant,[17] not just the sovereign.

And so there is an insistent re-proposition, throughout the pages of the Scripture and, particularly in the book of Jeremiah, of the choice between the two paths, the way of life and the way of death (on this theme, see what was developed in ch. III, § 4.2.1). The alternative is presented before the Covenant is entered into, but remains ever present in every age, in the form of fidelity or infidelity that measures the resilience of the choices made through the flux of time, both towards men and towards YHWH (cf. e.g. Jer 15:17; Ps 1; 26:5; Prov 4:14; Eccl 15:16–20; etc.).

In the case of the surrender to Babylon, this dimension is highlighted in a particular way and from multiple perspectives: first of all, the political one, which involves both the decision-making power of a few figures of authority and the destiny and freedom of all the people of Israel and of entire nations. We are on the chessboard where the great empires of the time face each other off: Egypt, Assyria, and Babylon. And yet, in the context of their great manoeuvres, even the small kingdoms of the Syrian-Palestinian buffer zone are faced with choices. Despite the intrahistorical dynamics, with their stringent links of cause and effect, no one gets crushed irregardless and in an entirely passive way by their destiny.[18] And so alliances are formed or repudiated, defeats and invasions suffered, rebellions fomented. And the prices for these are paid. Even the small kingdom of Judah (as we saw in ch. II) is placed before choices. Almost as if to reflect the binary alternative typical of Deuteronomistic and wisdom literature, starting from 605 (i.e. with the victory of Nebuchadnezzar over Egypt at Carchemish), the possible options are only two: submit (and then remain submissive) to the Babylonian yoke, or try to either reject it or shake it off after it had been loaded on their neck.

---

16   Amongst the numerous contributions on the notion of covenant in the biblical field, I will point to the classic work of a systematic approach by W. EICHRODT, *Theologie des Alten Testaments*. Teil I: Gott und Volk, Leipzig 1933, Stuttgart ⁵1957 (including two other parts [Teil II: Gott und Welt; Teil III: Gott und Mensch] contained in the volume already cited prior), and the essay by P. BEAUCHAMP, «Propositions» 161–194 (ID., *Pages exégètiques*, LeDiv 202, Paris 2005, 55–86).

17   See, in this regard, S.M. PAUL, *Studies*, 37–40. Amongst other things, the author underscores that: "Unlike Mesopotamia where the king alone was chosen by the gods and granted the gift of the perception of the *kīnātu* [the 'right'], God selects the entire corporate body of Israel to be the recipients of his law. His care and concern extend to all members of this community and not merely to one chosen individual. Thus everyone is held personally responsible for the observance of the law. This leads, in turn, to the concept of individual and joint responsibility" (here, p. 38).

18   Obviously, it should be specified that such freedom could be expressed more fully only at the level of top government. A king and his entourage, faced with an overwhelming and oncoming threat of war, could find their own safety and refuge by escaping, as is often attested in the historical sources of the ancient Near East. The same possibility was not reserved for the local population in general. An exceptional case is represented in the remarkable description of the escape of some two hundred brave citizens of the city of Plataea besieged by the Peloponnesians (THUCYDIDES, *Historiae,* III, 20–24; cf. ch. II, § 4.2.2.5 of the present dissertation).

From the point of view of Jeremianic theology, which does not reject the political sphere but rather rereads it from a prophetic perspective, the alternative is the same, but the meaning differs profoundly. The option to choose is indicated for everyone unequivocally: submission to the king of Babylon must be made. This choice alone means, here and now, *hitching* one's destiny to the salvific design of YHWH, who will, in any case, go forward, with or without the response of humankind (cf. chs. 30–31 and 32–33). Only going out to meet the generals of the king of Babylon with no hope but the naked possession of life (cf. the expression נֶפֶשׁ + suff. + לְשָׁלָל ["life as war booty"] in 21:9; 38:2; 39:18; 45:5, commented in ch. III § 4.2.2), for a providential intervention of the Lord of Hosts (and not for diplomatic-political calculations), means reading and interpreting, according to truth and justice, the authentic meaning of history, of this history.

What is surprising is to see the extent to which this appeal for freedom gets pushed. Following the dramatic thread of events that lead to the end of Jerusalem, the possibility of the choice is pushed to the cusp of the abyss, much further than the human wisdom of the leaders and court counsellors, or even the king himself, conceived possible for a decision-making process.[19] And even beyond that which the prophetic condemnation had, at a certain point, predicted as inevitable. If there is nothing left to do, what more can be done? If YHWH has already decreed the end, what remains to be chosen, even upon hearing the fiery oracles of the prophet?

What remains is *to listen to the very end*. For if there is a word that still resonates in Jerusalem, even if only by silent physical presence inside a prison or at the bottom of a slimy well, all cannot be lost. And, in fact, Jeremiah repeats it over and over again, to the extreme, in the imminence of the end, on the edge of the chasm. In the final "secret" colloquy that the narrator has us witness between the king Zedekiah and the prophet Jeremiah, it will be stated clearly: Even when there is no more choice, if there is a prophetic word, one can still choose. One can still carry out this act of prophetic-obedient ConSign*A(c)tion* that is surrender, by handing over one's life above all to YHWH, and acknowledging the failure of one's own history of convenant. From here, it could all begin again. But this must be chosen, desired. It comes by accepting in freedom one's own (symbolic) death in order to have back from God life and a future.

3. Signified by an action with profound anthropological implications

The choice requested by Jeremiah does not just regard an existential or intimistic dimension, but must take the shape of a very precise gesture. From the outside, it may seem like just a political act, while in fact, it is a theo-logical event. Indeed, it says something *from* and *about* God.[20] It presents itself along the line of human-divine communication that passes through the signs of history and the *body's capacity for signification*. We are leaning, therefore, towards the field of analogical communication

---

19 From what can be deduced from the book of Jeremiah, the pro-Egyptian faction never seems to question the anti-Babylonian option, not even in the imminence of the foreseeable tragic outcome of the siege of Jerusalem. It is almost as if resistance to the end were, at that point, a *mandatory choice*.

20 Cf. E. Chauty, *Le livre de Jérémie: signifier la Parole*, CEv 199, Paris 2022.

648   The surrender as "Prophetic-Obediential ConSignA(c)tion"

as opposed to digital communication. The first, as I have observed, concerns, above all, the relational realm, while the second, the conceptual one, mediated by orality. It has to do, therefore, more generally, with a concrete choice, an attitude or way of acting, which has visible effects on the world scenario (that of the text or beyond the text).

Even the so-called "symbolic gestures" are virtually, or at a first glance, on the same level. However, from what it has been possible to point out, this historical-literary phenomenon is actually a complex, variegated microcosm of semiotic-symbolic factors that I have tried to organise according to my first taxonomy, to be thought of, in reality, as a conceptual map (with a hierarchical structure and intercrossing links).

For me, the most significant criterion for establishing at least one important level of classification is the *anthropological impact index*. Despite the formal similarities of a literary nature, even common sense should suggest that there are essential differences between shattering a jug in front of witnesses and taking on celibacy as a radical option or refusing to participate in the celebratory rites of life (marriage and mourning) that do not allow such gestures to be placed on the same categorial level. A thorough analysis confirms this impression, and renders the gaze capable of noticing other important and different levels of impact of the prophetic gesture on the human dimension of the subject who makes it (and upon those called to respond to the appeal it presents). In the case of the POC, these are not symbolic-prophetic gestures having an almost exclusively didactic-rhetorical meaning that are exhausted in external acts, but rather something that, at different levels, *puts at stake the very life* of those who have to put that choice into place. In some cases, like that of celibacy in 16:1–4, one can speak of a real *life choice*.

When does this situation occur? Its identification cannot be based on an unequivocal criterion, but rather on the convergence of certain fundamental elements, since there are many variables to be taken into account. Some general indications, however, can be given, so a *prototypical* categorial consideration need be borne in mind. The anthropological effect of the choice can, in fact, regard *diverse levels* of existential impact, often correlated and partially overlapping. In order to talk about POC, not all of these must be present at the same time or with the same representative force. Amongst the most important criteria, however, it is necessary to emphasise: the involvement of the *corporeal dimension* (to be expressed at least as an implication of the historical-temporal dimension and as an existential precariousness subject to the risk of death), of the *cognitive* one, and of the socio-affective sphere. While the cognitive realm will be called into question in relation to the prophetic scope of the POC (cf. § 6.4), I will now focus on the other areas, which also remain decisive.

3.1. Historical-temporal implications. The duration or irreversibility of the choice presented

A fundamental anthropological fact concerns the historicity of human existence, which places a subject in a constitutive relationship with their past and with the cultural tradition from which and in which they were generated. It is from this starting basis that one can become, in turn, principle (origin, source) for a transmission of values and transformation of reality. The whole journey of the human being is realised between the memory of what has been and the desire for what can or will be, in a future to be understood either as a coming about of the uncontrollable, or as a projection and project of oneself and the world towards a coming fulfilment. In Israel,

Signified by an action with profound anthropological implications   649

this orientation of existence is particularly accentuated, and surpasses the notion of "eternal return" that could arise from the experience of the rhythms of the sky and seasons. The very notion of a universal story, with its starting point, direction, and future Fulfilment (take the apocalyptic, even just remaining within the OT) is the horizon for the entire biblical world. In a context of beliefs in which all human life plays out within a limited time frame, while the possibility of a life in the afterworld, alluded to by the category of the *šᵉ'ôl*, is for a long time only glimpsed and, in any case, thought of almost as a non-life, this dimension is even more relevant. Prophecy and history are intimately correlated, starting from these premises.

There are some commands received by Jeremiah whose fulfilment involves individual acts and a narrow time frame, while of others, one of the distinguishing traits is the *permanence* in time of the attitude to be adopted. Consider, for example, the injunction to not intercede in favour of the people (cf. 7:16; 11:14; 14:11; 15:1). This is given peremptorily by means of expressions that do not seem to allow for or provide deadlines. In truth, it is clear that the end of Jerusalem, the realisation of the punitive threat, or acceptance of the surrender deplete the need and meaning of the prohibition.[21] And, in fact, Jeremiah does not hesitate to intercede for the people at its very request by his leaders in 42:4. But despite this, it is undeniable that YHWH asks Jeremiah for an obedience that implicates the prolonging in time (in itself, without predetermined deadlines) of a significant behaviour, one that is *prophetic*.

Even more evident, as we have seen, is the case of the imperatives of 16:1–9. No temporal limit is explicitly indicated. As with the prohibition of intercession, it would appear, at first glance, that these "symbolic gestures" (which, in my opinion, should be redefined and or looked at in confrontation with the category of the POC) cease to fulfil their function of meaning with the end of Jerusalem. The punishments threatened and presented to the people by Jeremiah in a vivid and scandalous way come about with the ruin of the kingdom of Judah. Actually, for celibacy, an indefinite duration can be postulated, that extends beyond the punitive event. Not only because, unlike the intercessorial function, the Jeremianic text does not explicitly guarantee any restoration of the situation precedent to the divine command, but also for the fact that, in the case of celibacy, the level of anthropological incidence regards the body and its function of *memoriative permanence*.

Jeremiah repeatedly announces the end of the time of celebration and joy, the loss of the happy voice of the bride and groom (cf. 7:34; 16:9; 25:10). But the book of Jeremiah, beyond the looming of these disasters, in precisely its central part, *already* proclaims the advent of a new pact and sings of the newfound exultation of wedding joy that will still be celebrated in Israel (cf. 33:10–11). This will happen, however, in future times that are not those in which Jeremiah lives, not even after the fall of Jerusalem. Amongst the rubble of the Holy City, times of mourning are suffered, as are violence, terror, days of tears for a lack of meaning and for the silence of God, but it is also possible to enter into a grace of time still freely given for them to find themselves again (cf. 41–43:1–7). The prophet, moreover, cannot in any way personally take on the divine invitation, which he himself transmitted to the exiles of 597, to resume the celebration of life in the land of exile (cf. 29:4–7). Having remained voluntarily amongst the survivors in Israel, he must endure from his own compatriots,

---

21   Cf B. Rossi, *L'intercessione nel tempo della fine*, 366–368.

650   The surrender as "Prophetic-Obediential ConSignA(c)tion"

deportation that leads him not towards Babylon, where YHWH promises new life and a new future, but towards Egypt (cf. 43:6–7), where they were not supposed to return (cf. Deut 17:16). It is almost as though his destiny were that of total solidarity, with all its consequences, with a people determined to descend into the abyss of extreme rejection of the word of God (cf. 44:7–30).[22] The meaning of celibacy, therefore, as a sign of the (escaped or suffered) "end" engraved in the flesh, remains as a memory and, again, as threatening anticipation of the punishment that hangs over the hardness of heart of those who refuse to obey the prophet, even after all the trials and signs that had been had up to that point.

In the case of the surrender in Babylon, it is clear that Jeremiah does not ask for an act with scant temporal repercussions. It is not a question of submitting to the enemy yoke for a shrewd political calculation and by doing so, negotiating, for a few days or a few months, or a few years of servitude, a future of foreseeable well-being. The surrender to Babylon, according to Jeremiah, must be *unconditional*. The duration of the Babylonian empire is in the hands of the Lord of history (cf. 27:7), and is prophetically fixed at seventy years (cf. 25:11–12), a symbolic figure indicating the entire span of a human life (cf. Ps 90:10[23]). This will also be the temporal extent of the exile, according to 29:10. No subjective guarantee of return from this choice is given per se. To some, it will be granted, but only in the last stretch of a life that has been, at that point, lived entirely in exile, and therefore in the form of an attestation that connects the past to the present in a single design. Indeed, it is no coincidence that, according to Ezra 3:12–13 (cf. Hg 2:3), amongst the exiles repatriated to Jerusalem, only the surviving elders are present at the beginning of the work on the new temple, when tears of pain and cheers of joy blend together, witnesses of the lost splendour of the ancient Solomonic building erected in honour of YHWH and then destroyed by Nebuchadnezzar. But also of the fulfilment of the words of the Lord's prophets.

3.2. Socio-affective implications. The intensity of the relational repercussions

Starting from the human being-there in the world and flow of history, the whole socio-affective dimension unfolds, without which its nature would be completely incomprehensible. Emotional experience is rooted in the interactive matrix of the relationships that constitute the very identity of the son of man, made, for Gen 1:26–27, in the image and likeness of God. And it is clear that for biblical revelation, the relationship that expresses the uniqueness of that subject in the creative design is their originary relationship with God, experienced as a fumbling along in the journey of the peoples, but revealed in full in the history of the chosen people.

Feelings, emotions, and passions,[24] while finding different realisations, expressions, considerations, and codifications in every culture, remain a complex phenomenic array that founds the subjective (psychic) experience of each individual and renders

---

22   On this topic, see S.M. Sessa, «Accompagnare il destino di un popolo: il profeta Geremia», *Credere Oggi* 222 (2017) 87–96.

23   "Seventy is the sum of our years, or eighty, if we are strong."

24   For differential semantics, see M. Cerulo, *Il sentire controverso. Introduzione alla sociologia delle emozioni*, BiTSt 482, Roma 2010.

Signified by an action with profound anthropological implications   651

it dynamic. The body is its first witness, both outward in front of the world, and before personal consciousness, starting from the movements of the "heart".[25] Here, the rationalising self is called to confront the enigmas of the world, and the darkest and most unknown part of the self, that which startles emotionally and reacts in an uncontrolled way, that raises unexpected and irrepressible desires or needs from deep down, highly intense and violent impulses that interrogate the subject or are filtered and interpreted by the socio-cultural context of reference.

The study of emotional states, axiological taxonomy, and cultural codifications attested on the linguistic level in the HB (and in the totality of the Scripture) seems to me to have long been ignored by the exegetes,[26] even if there is no shortage indeed of hermeneutical approaches to the biblical texts of a sociological matrix. While sociology has developed a specific branch of study dedicated to the emotional sphere since the 1970s,[27] in the biblical field, the social dimension and the emotional-affective world seem to remain separate areas in which interconnections are not highlighted enough.

It is certain that in itself the Bible does not have a psychologising nature, nor is it legitimate to introduce a modern awareness of intrapsychic dynamics into it irrespective of the hermeneutical mediations of exegetical sciences. However, there is no doubt

---

25   In this sense, S. SCHROER – T. STAUBLI, *Die Korper-Symbolik der Bibel*, Darmstadt 1998, 75, speak of the organs of the "biblical body" as "Seismographen des Gefühls".

26   For an example of the contrary, cf. S. ACKERMAN, «The Personal is Political: Covenantal and Affectionate Love (*'āhēb,'ahăbâ*) in the Hebrew Bible», *VT* 52 (2002) 437–458, where the political implications on the lexical level are studied. For an example that relates to the NT, cf. A. MIRANDA, *I sentimenti di Gesù. I verba affectuum dei Vangeli nel loro contesto lessicale*, StBi (Bo) 49, Bologna 2006. The document of the Pontifical Biblical Commission, *The Interpretation of the Bible in the Chrurch*, explains itself thus in part I, D, also underscoring the importance of the symbolic dimension for exegesis: "In order to communicate itself, the word of God has taken root in the life of human communities (cf. Sir 24:12), and it has been through the psychological dispositions of the various persons who composed the biblical writings that it has pursued its path. It follows, then, that the human sciences – in particular sociology, anthropology and psychology – can contribute toward a better understanding of certain aspects of biblical texts. [...] Psychological and psychoanalytical studies do bring a certain enrichment to biblical exegesis in that, because of them, the texts of the Bible can be better understood in terms of experience of life and norms of behavior. [...] Psychology and, in a somewhat different way, psychoanalysis have led, in particular, to a new understanding of symbol. The language of symbol makes provision for the expression of areas of religious experience that are not accessible to purely conceptual reasoning but which have a genuine value for the expression of truth. For this reason, interdisciplinary study conducted in common by exegetes and psychologists or psychoanalysts offers particular advantages, especially when objectively grounded and confirmed by pastoral experience."

27   Think of the pioneering contribution of Arlie Russell Hochschild, whose name is tied to the birth of the sociology of emotions. His programmatic manifesto is contained in the essay A.R. HOCHSCHILD, «Work, Feelings Rules, and Social Structure», *AJS* 85 (1979) 551–575. This branch of sociology aims to study the relationship that emotions and sentiments have with the dynamics of social communication. For a thorough presentation, see M. CERULO, «Ogni comprensione è sempre emotiva. Arlie Russell Hochschild e la nascita della sociologia delle emozioni», in: *Lavoro emozionale e struttura sociale*, ed. A.R. HOCHSCHILD, Roma 2013, 3–34.

652   The surrender as "Prophetic-Obediential ConSignA(c)tion"

that the emotional-affective scope of human actions and choices finds widespread reverberation on the level of the text and is the object of a specific communicative intentionality, expressed on both the verbal and non-verbal levels. Also because, in the perspective of biblical revelation and particularly within prophetic literature, human feelings and emotions somehow express the "feelings" and "emotions" of God himself[28] in his relating to the world of human beings and especially to the covenant partner, taking on a significant revelative (i.e. theological) valence. There are therefore deep connections between the emotional-affective sphere and interpersonal relationships that cannot fail to leave traces within the text, even without being called into question directly.

Generally, when in the presence of a POC, it is also this socio-affective relational dimension that is touched very deeply. Consider, for example, the prophet Hosea who is asked to assume the role of a betrayed husband by marrying a prostitute, that is, a woman who is, in herself, symbol of the infidelity (cf. Hos 1–3). As a POC, and not only as a generic symbolic gesture, in my opinion, the attitude that Ezekiel is called to assume needs to be interpreted: after the sudden death of his wife (cf. Ezek 24:15–24), who is named, and not coincidentally, by YHWH in his dialogue with the prophet as the "delight of your eyes" (מַחְמַד עֵינֶיךָ), Ezekiel is asked to lay a levee to the rush of tears and to make no gesture of mourning. The social dimension and the personal sphere find themselves to be still intertwined. Thus, with all of his person, the deepest and most sensitive part of his being, the prophet will become a resounding sign for his people.

Another case that can fall into the category of the POC, illustrating this aspect (along with that previous, related to the temporal dimension), is the request made to Isaiah in Isa 20. The prophet, who is after all already dressed in a sack (שַׂק), with sandals on his feet, is asked by YHWH to go away barefoot and naked for three full years, to become in front of everyone, "sign and symbol/omen (אוֹת וּמוֹפֵת) for Egypt and Ethiopia" (Isa 20:3). It is easy to imagine how many and what are the anthropological implication of a social and intrapsychic nature of such an injunction, starting from the emotion of "shame", expression of the sense of defeat, helplessness, confusion, and disappointment (cf. Isa 20:5; Jer 20:8, 18; etc.).

The most emblematic example in the book of Jeremiah still remains the series of acts requested of the prophet in 16:1–9, above all the injunction of celibacy. While affective involvement does not appear to be directly called into question (at least not on the linguistic level), indeed it is, in the strongest way possible, since it is precisely in this horizon that the "symbolic gestures" requested of the prophet reveal their full subversive charge against the established socio-cultural codes, in which the choice not to marry, and to not take part in the rites of mourning and nuptial bliss is apparently completely absurd and incomprehensible, if not irreverent.[29]

---

28   In this, the book of Jeremiah is rich with significant attestations in which the figure and voice of the prophet are intentionally placed as fading and blending with the figure and voice of YHWH. See e.g. what is noted in G. FISCHER, «Il Dio che piange», 233–244.

29   The consequences on the emotional sphere of the prophetic vocation, which also includes obedience to such demanding injunctions and *compassion* for the misfortune that falls on Judah and Jerusalem, emerge clearly in other texts. Think of the feelings of solitude, anguish, of the reproach from the people and his most intimate

Signified by an action with profound anthropological implications   653

In the case of the surrender to Babylon, this anthropological dimension is touched on several levels. A first distinction concerns the generic concept of "submission", which should not be superimposed *tout court* with the more specific concept of "surrender". I have already explained this elsewhere.[30] The message of Jeremiah, unified in terms of symbolic-communicative intentionality, calls for a response that comes about or should come about on the historical-political/existential level in at least two forms, dependent on the historical-symbolic context of reference. The first form of the Jeremianic message can be traced back to the broader concept of "submission". Asked of the kingdom of Judah and of "all the land" (cf. 27–28) immediately after Nebuchadnezzar's victory in Karkemish, it evidently regards the radical reconfiguration of the social role of the political authorities involved, both against the external enemy and the communities of which they are the leaders and representatives. On the individual level, however, this message has an immediate impact on Jeremiah himself, who becomes its bearer. What is to put into question here is his claim to truth, that is, his social image as a true prophet who asks for a response of obedience and therefore public recognition on the part of his fellow citizens (this theme is developed in ch. 27 by way of the clash between the Jeremiah and Hananiah).

The second form, that of the "surrender", is presented in a peculiar way: both in 21:1–10, a text that introduces us to the drama of the siege of Jerusalem, and in 38:14–28a, where the scene of the dialogue between the prophet and the king directly calls into question the subjectivity of the person reached by the prophetic word. It can be deduced from the context that in both texts, the question is no longer a generic one of "submitting themselves", but rather that they "surrender to" to an enemy determined to put an end, once and for all, to the rebellion of the vassal kingdom of Judah. This presupposes a hastening of events and the reaching of a point of no return, before which a position must be taken.

Significantly, precisely here, the affective and emotional dimension is also made explicit at the textual level and is correlated to the social dimension. The responsibility of the single subject manifests itself in its structural interconnection with familial relations and with the social fabric of the city community: if you surrender, "*this city* (הָעִיר הַזֹּאת) will not be burned with fire, and *you* and *your household* (אַתָּה וּבֵיתֶךָ) shall live". This is what prophet promises the king. "I am afraid/I am anxious" (אֲנִי דֹאֵג) Zedekiah responds (cf. 38:19) to the words of Jeremiah, who presses him further to trust, to obey YHWH who now speaks to him through him (cf. 38:20).

The object of the fear is precisely indicated: "I am afraid *of the Jews who surrendered to the Chaldeans* (אֶת־הַיְּהוּדִים אֲשֶׁר נָפְלוּ אֶל־הַכַּשְׂדִּים) *that it does not come about that they hand me over to them* (פֶּן־יִתְּנוּ אֹתִי בְּיָדָם) and *mistreat me* (וְהִתְעַלְּלוּ־בִי)" (38:19). Fear of losing control over events, anguish over what might happen to one's personal physical integrity, but even more, to one's own personal and social image (hence, the perception of *shame*): just enough to see that the choice indicated by the prophet, as a POC, strongly involves deep dimensions of interpersonal, intrapsychic, and corporeal experience, the social role, the self-image, emotions, and feelings. After all, it will be precisely the atrocious punishment that Nebuchadnezzar will inflict on Zedekiah that

---

family members, of (self)commiseration, etc. attested e.g. in 8:23; 13:17; 14:17; 15:17; 20:7–18, etc.

30   See, in this regard, ch. IV dedicated to Jer 27–28.

654   The surrender as "Prophetic-Obediential ConSignA(c)tion"

dramatically thematises this socio-affective dimension once again (cf. 39:6–7). His children, that is, his direct inheritors and descendants, will have their throats slashed before his eyes, and this will be the last image imprinted in his heart. Blinded, he will be taken prisoner to Babylon until the end of his days.

3.3. Dramatic implications. The entity of the mortal risk

Directly related to the previous dimension is the factor of *risk* associated with the POC. What I have just highlighted immediately enables us to not identify the mortal danger that can result from this type of signification with a dimension that is exclusively *physical-biological.* As I noted in reference to the objection of Zedekiah (cf. § 3.2.2), for the human being, the experience of dying is tied not only to the physical disintegration of its living corporeal structure, but is also given in the symbol, and thus in a no less real and effective way, according to other, more spiritual dimensions as well. Self-image, one's social role, relationships that are betrayed, broken, or denied, personal failure, etc., are all aspects that fall within the dimension of "death". They are by no means secondary realities, since on not a few occasions, precisely their failure (or the risk of their failing) renders physical death something pronounceable or less grave for the subject. Nevertheless, it should be pointed out that exposing oneself to a POC can also involve a real danger of significant importance, it can signify *putting one's life on the line.* The life of the physical-body, the only one that the biblical person of the OT conceives and has at his disposal.

The criterion concerning the elevated degree of existential "dramatic force" created by the involvement in particular situations of a semiotic-prophetic valence may be an indicative symptom of the presence of the phenomenon of signification that I have identified as POC. Let us first look at some examples outside of the book of Jeremiah.

Emblematic, because it offers an oppositive comparison with the thematic of the surrender in Babylon, is what Isaiah asks of Acaz in the context of the so-called Syro-Ephraimite War. It is exactly the contrary of what Jeremiah will ask of Zedekiah. For Isaiah, in the face of the looming political-military threat, one must not flee or surrender but *resist,* trusting in the salvific intervention of YHWH (cf. Isa 7:1–16; 8:1–8; 30:15–18). In other words, "believing", in this case, is equivalent to not doing, with waiting and letting God act. Here, too, the emotional sphere is evoked, linked directly to the fear of succumbing. The temptation is to stem the threat by seeking the military aid of Assyria, the powerful and cumbersome neighbour, a decisive player, at that time, in the geopolitical scenario of the entire ancient Near East. In these terms, we move purely on a horizontal and political level. What Isaiah is asking for challenges this perspective head-on. For precisely this reason, he appears to expose the king Acaz to death, already implied by the narrator when he makes the intentions of the assailants explicit:

> Let us go up against Judah, terrorise it, let us open a breach (in its walls) and conquer it for ourselves,[31] and we will install the son of Tabeel as the king there (Isa 7:6).

---

31   I render the richness of meaning contained in the expression נַבְקִעֶנָּה אֵלֵינוּ as two distinct verbs ("to open a breach", "to conquer").

Signified by an action with profound anthropological implications   655

The risk of being eliminated, as a consequence of the option of faith and obedience towards YHWH, is a symptom of the presence of a POC, to be verified obviously on the basis of other elements.

Going backwards through the Scripture, to reach the prophetic figure par excellence, that of Moses, we can rediscover another manifestation of the POC in Num 13:17–14:11. Here too, we are in a context of war, but once again, obeying YHWH takes a different form. On the threshold of the Promised Land, the divine order[32] is to *fight* and *conquer* the cities of the enemies. The fact is that the proportion of forces on the ground is perceived by the Israelites as entirely disadvantageous, the possibility of victory a chimera, and the danger of dying more real and imminent than ever:

> And why is the Lord leading us to that land to die by the sword? Our wives and our children will be prey. Would it not be better for us to return to Egypt? (Num 14:3).

I will note *en passant* that in this case as well, we can recognise the engagement of the emotive sphere (cf. Num 13:31: the discouragement; Num 14:1–2: outcry, cries of anguish, tears, and regret) and socio-affective sphere (the mortal threat that those called to act perceive as looming over their own identifying and fundamental relationships: between husbands and wives, between fathers and sons).

Going back to the book of Jeremiah, as I have already mentioned, one can identify a POC that relates to the prophet himself in the episode of the famous temple speech (7:1–15 26), a text that, for obvious formal reasons, is not considered by exegetes to be a symbolic gesture. I believe, however, that a valence of meaning that exceeds a mere rhetorical-didactic reading can be recognised in it, which does not permit the hermeneutics of the text to be reduced to the conceptual content of its message.[33] The body as a semiotic-symbolic device is, in fact, involved fully, from the first verses:

> *Stay/stand* (עֲמֹד) at the gate of the temple of the Lord and there *proclaim* (וְקָרָאתָ) this message (אֶת־הַדָּבָר הַזֶּה) [...] (7:2)

> Thus says the Lord: *Stay/stand* (עֲמֹד) in the courtyard of the temple of the Lord and *announce* (וְדִבַּרְתָּ) to all the cities of Judah who come to bow down in the temple of

---

32   Not explicit, but clearly implied, as is well understood in the light of the words of YHWH in Num 14:11: "Then the Lord said to Moses: 'Until when will this people spurn me? How long will they not trust me after all the signs I have performed amongst them?'".

33   An interesting path for reflection, which I cannot develop herein, would be that which regards the dual attestation of the episode, in which the conceptual-conversational elements and the symbolic-narrative ones seem to be intentionally positioned and distributed in different ways in the two texts. In 7:1–15, the preponderance of the narrative development of the first elements is evident, while in ch. 26, the narrative development of the story prevails. In my opinion, the logic underlying this communicative operation regards the entire structure of the book of Jeremiah, and in particular, the nature of the first two big textual blocks: the first (1–25) containing, above all, the "words of Jeremiah", that is, the texts of an oracular and poetic nature, and the second (26–45), regarding "the actions" of the prophet, that is, the narration of the events that connect the story of his body to the destiny of Jerusalem. That this be a single communicative-prophetic event is expressed, in any case, already in the "title" of the book, through the ambivalence of the expression דִּבְרֵי יִרְמְיָהוּ ("words/acts/facts of Jeremiah").

656 The surrender as "Prophetic-Obediential ConSignA(c)tion"

the Lord all the words that I have commanded you to announce to them; do not leave out even a word (26:2).

Such corporeal involvement is not only given by the fact that the divine word must resonate through his mouth. The body is not a mere support for the oral message here (and neither will be the scroll in ch. 36). What is expressed by *that body* (with its origin, its provenance, and the meaning of its presence)[34] put in *that place* (considered sacred and inviolable) and what follows, all this is part of the unfolding and structuration of a powerful, complex dynamism of signification, verbal and non-verbal, that transcends the formal boundaries of the pericopes that contain it.[35]

The consequences of this communicative impact are immediate and clear, and relate to Jeremiah himself: "When Jeremiah had finished reporting what the Lord had commanded him to say to all the people, priests, prophets, and all the people arrest him, saying, '*you must die*' (מוֹת תָּמוּת)" (26:8). The prophetic body is subjected to trial and the death sentence seems to be already written. But the Jeremianic message reaches its maximum expressive force when the POC is made explicit in 26:14 by these other words: "[...] as for me, *here I am in your hands!* (וַאֲנִי הִנְנִי בְיֶדְכֶם)". Thus the actual stakes contained and implied in the opening verses cited above (7:2; 26:2) are revealed. The prophetic body is a *body handed over* (by YHWH) and at the same time, a body that

---

34 Jeremiah is presented from the "title" of the book (according to the MT, confirmed by the Vg) and from its first verse (Jer 1:1) as one of the descendants "of the priests of Anathoth [מִן־הַכֹּהֲנִים אֲשֶׁר בַּעֲנָתוֹת], in the territory of Benjamin" (בְּאֶרֶץ בְּנְיָמִן). The LXX marks his origin even further, not limiting itself to a reference to his ancestry, but indicating Anathoth as the place of his dwelling ([...] ἐκ τῶν ἱερέων ὃς κατῴκει ἐν Αναθωθ ἐν γῇ Βενιαμιν. In the often deliberately allusive style of the Scripture, it does not seem inappropriate to me to see a reference, one not even too veiled, to the story of this sacerdotal family descending from Abiathar. To this priest, according to what is reported in 1 Kgs 2:26–27, Solomon had denied the right in perpetuity to exercise the functions in Jerusalem (where he himself erected the temple of YHWH), with the obligation of residing in his lands of Anathoth. This punitive measure (Abiathar had sided with Adonai in the delicate phase of the succession to the throne of David; cf. 1 Kgs 1:7, 25) is seen explicitly as the fulfilment of a curse of the Lord on the house of the priest Eli, begun with the catastrophe of the sanctuary in Shiloh. Abiathar, son of Ahimelech (survivor of the massacre of the priests of Nob, whose sanctuary, not far from Jerusalem and Anathoth, from that point on, are never again mentioned; cf. 1 Sam 22:20) was one of Eli's descendants. In the body and story of Jeremiah, while the reference is kept allusive (given the lack of absolutely certain facts), some element of meaning can be seen so concentrated there that they render his speech at the temple particularly threatening and subversive, and better explain the violent reaction of the clergy of Jerusalem *in primis* (amongst which, some of his fiercest adversaries will be); cf. 19:1–20:6 and also 29:24–32), but also the prophets and the people who witness his prophetic proclamation (cf. 26:8). Jeremiah, in fact, carries upon himself the story of his family, rendering visible the concrete possibility of the loss of the sacerdotal prerogative and a recurrence of the selfsame rejection on the part of God (cf. 7:29 with 6:30). He is a burdensome memory of the destruction of a sanctuary of YHWH as famous as that of Shiloh, which he himself explicitly recalls as an example of the destruction threatened of the temple of Jerusalem (7:12–14; 26:6).

35 Above all, in reference to ch. 26 and its relationship to the following chs. 27–28, as I noted in ch. V, § 2.4.

Signified by an action with profound anthropological implications   657

hands itself over (freely). It is the realisation of a choice, of an obedience, the offering of a revelation about the meaning of the present and future history, the indication of a path that is accessible to all the people.

The fulfilment of the message, however, is made clear by the unexpected conclusion of the trial: Jeremiah escapes death, against all odds. His fate of unhoped-for salvation can be that of all the people, of the king, the leaders, and the priests, when for Jerusalem there seems to no longer be any possibility of avoiding the catastrophe. If only they understood the semiotic-symbolic (and theological) importance of what is placed in front of them. I think that we can understand it, in the wake of the elements of meaning scattered precisely for this purpose by the text and its "author". This is why I think it is possible to identify an emblematic example of POC in 7:1–15; 26, requested and actualised *by the prophet* himself. Starting from his own obedience and the realisation of its salvific efficacy, he will be able to authoritatively propose and demand it in other respects to his interlocutors as well when the need to surrender to Babylon occurs. An intradiegetic level that bounces beyond the boundaries of the narrated story to reach readers of all time and extradiegetically interrogate them.

The dramatic dimension is a central implication in the theme of handing oneself over to the king of Babylon. Jeremiah asks everyone, from the king to the ruling class to all the people for unconditional surrender to the generals of the king of Babylon, beyond all political calculation and all human hope of survival. As I have pointed out,[36] there is, in itself, no certain guarantee that such a gesture will insure the salvation of the City and its rulers. After all, the prophet Jeremiah himself does not promise it at no cost, but only through the symbolic acceptance of death and the recognition of their own sin. It is at best, as I have already noted, the naked possession of life (life "as war booty" [לְשָׁלָל]; cf. 21:9; 38:2; 39:18; 45:5). Perhaps, at times, it would seem possible to avoid the destruction of Jerusalem and end of the Davidic dynasty (cf. 38:17.20), but certainly not the exile, with all that this entails.

It is clear, for example, from 2 Kgs 18:31–32 (Isa 36:16–17) that surrender means undergoing *deportation*, and being deported – even though life can continue in exile – means losing ties to the land and (the risk of) dissolving national identity, constituted necessarily, at least in the monarchical era, by the indivisible relationship between deities-people-land.[37] This eventuality is reinforced by the common belief diffused throughout the ancient Near East that each territory corresponded to a specific "area of competence" reserved for some local deities, as can also be deduced from the fact that the populations deported in Israel after the disaster of 721 start to also worship YHWH,[38] contaminating themselves culturally (cf. 2 Kgs 17:24–41). In fact, the deportations also had the scope of undermining and breaking up the cultural-identifying integrity of the submitted peoples, and, since for the ancient mentality, the power of the deities had territorial limitations (cf. 1 Sam 4:5–8; 1 Kgs 20:23.28), such measures prevented a favourable influence of the losers.[39]

---

36   In ch. II of my present dissertation.
37   Cf. D.I. BLOCK, *The Gods of the Nations*, 20.
38   In v. 26, it says that the deported populations do not know אֶת־מִשְׁפַּט אֱלֹהֵי הָאָרֶץ, that is, "the right (the cult) of the local God (lit.: of the land)".
39   Cf. D.I. BLOCK, *The Gods of the Nations*, 116–117.

Even from these observations, it can be understood that the Jeremianic promise to have life saved "as was booty", that is, the naked possession of one's physical existence, makes the request for surrender coincide not with an easy expedient of salvation, but with the call to accept a *symbolic form of death.* It is therefore easy to understand why this option gets opposed by the entire ruling class holding the political fortunes of Jerusalem in hand from 597 onwards, even though, as is so in any case, cases of desertion are not lacking. The reaction of King Zedekiah is emblematic: before the Jeremianic request, he explicitly confesses his fear of being mocked specifically at the hands of those who have already surrendered to the Chaldeans (cf. 38:19).

4. Commanded by God to the prophet or the people at a precise point in time

The POC is a communicative act with performance valence, a free choice that actualises a response to what is recognised as an *imperative request* coming from YHWH. It is not, therefore, a mere piece of advice, warning, admonition, or encouragement. The injunction is addressed *to the prophet* themself or, through their person or the events of history, to *another subject* (single or collective).

Another peculiar characteristic of this form of call to freedom and discernment is its *timely* nature. This concerns the reading and (prophetic) assumption of the meaning of a precise time, chain of events, relational (human-divine) dynamic inserted in a circumstantialised spatial-temporal context. It does not stem from human prudence or a sapiential attitude. It is not something routinely prescribed. It is not perspicacity or a prophetic indication of a strategic-political nature. It is not a concern of the ethical-religious sphere, of moral norms, or cultural prescriptions. Certainly, the signic-symbolic structure on which the POC is based at times risks being confused with one or another of these dimensions, but it is never reducible to that "literal" level. A whole series of clues make possible and require a higher level of inferential reading, of a symbolic-prophetic type.

Let us now take a closer look at what semiotic and semantic-pragmatic areas are excluded from the dynamism of meaning expressed in each POC, and from my theme in particular, in order to let the peculiarity of the POC of the surrender to the king of Babylon emerge by differentiation. Keep in mind that the dimensions I will deal with always concern prophetic forms of communication and the respective possible content-related modulations of their subject matter.

4.1. Beyond the strategic-political dimension

> [...] So they consulted the Lord again: "Did the man come here?".
> The Lord answered: "*Behold, he is hiding amongst the baggage*" (1 Sam 10:22).

Using the practice of drawing lots, the prophet Samuel proceeds with a progressive selection that leads to the identification of Saul, son of Kish, as the king chosen by YHWH and requested by the people. But he cannot be found. It is implicit that what reveals his presence in the camp and his hiding place is prophetic (if not divinatory) mediation. From what we can ascertain on the basis of the biblical and extrabiblical attestations regarding the socio-religious context of the ancient Near East, this and other similar practical purposes must have been quite common amongst the functions recognised in the "prophets" (as in divinatory practices in general as well).

From this pragmatic point of view, one should note the divine commands (or instances perceived as such) that relate to the more properly strategic-political or military realm in general, a context in which making of right decisions at the right time is vital.[40] The human perspicacity of the figure of the counsellor (יוֹעֵץ) of the court (think e.g. of Ahitophel and Hushai, advisors to David and Absalom; cf. 2 Sam 15:12, 31–34), even when they enjoyed very high consideration,[41] was readily flanked by mediators specialised in divine will (again in the case of David, it suffices to recall the prophets Gad [also called חֹזֶה, "seer/visionary"] and Nathan; cf. 1 Sam 22:5; 24:11; 2 Sam 7:2; 1 Kgs 1:32; 1 Chron 29:29; etc.).[42] Let us look at some very clear cases that relate to this prophetic function.

> [18] The Israelites set out, came to Bethel and consulted God, saying: "Who of us shall go first to go to battle against the sons of Benjamin". The Lord answered: "*Judah will go first*". [...] [23] The Israelites went up and wept before the Lord until evening and inquired of the Lord, saying: "Shall I continue to fight against Benjamin, my brother?". The Lord answered: "*Go up against them*". [...]. [27] The Israelites inquired of the Lord – the ark of the covenant of God in that time was there [28] and Phinehas, son of Eleazar, son of Aaron, was serving before it in those days – and they said: "Shall I still continue to go out to battle against the son of Benjamin, my brother, or shall I cease?". The Lord answered: "*Go, for tomorrow I will hand them over to you*".[29] So Israel set up an ambush around Gibeah [...] (Judg 20:18–48).

> The prophet Gad said to David: "*Do not remain in this stronghold any longer. Depart and go to the land of Judah*". David departed and went into the forest of Hereth (1 Sam 22:5).

---

40 One of the most common functions of extrabiblical prophetism and, in general, that of the divinatory practices widespread in the ancient Near East with which one seeks or recognises a channel of communication between the world of humanity and that of the divine, is that of being the authoritative source of useful information for making important choices. This is particularly true for the figure of the sovereign and those holding the highest positions of government. Personal ruin or ruin of the kingdom can depend on wrong decisions. For this reason, both the uncertainties of the variables at stake and the limited predictive capability of human wisdom lead to a search for every other possible means to overcome these difficulties. Even when one is sure to be able to avail oneself of a prophetic channel, things do not always go as desired (cf. e.g. the case of 1 Sam 14:36–37: "[36] Then Saul said: 'Let us go down to follow the Philistines this very night, and ransack them until morning and not let a single on of them escape'. They replied: 'Do what you think best'. But the priest said: 'Let us consult God'. [37] So Saul inquired of God: 'Shall I go down in pursuit of the Philistines? Will you consign them into the hands of Israel?'. But that day he received no response").

41 Emblematic in this regard, the note of the narrator in 2 Sam 16:23: "In the time in which Ahitophel was counsellor (√יעץ), his counsel (עֵצָה) had the same value [as the word] as he who had consulted (√שאל) the word of God. Such was every counsel of Ahitophel both to David and Absalom."

42 One can sense, in any case, the existence of different fields of "specialisation". In the events concerning the conspiracy of Absalom, e.g. prophetic figures with a specific role do not appear. But at the root of these, is the prophetic word of Nathan who throws revealing light upon on the causes and meaning of this crisis of the reign of David (cf. 2 Sam 12:7–12).

660   The surrender as "Prophetic-Obediential ConSignA(c)tion"

[19] David inquired of the Lord, asking: "Shall I attack the Philistines? Will you deliver them into my hands?". The Lord answered David: *"Go ahead, for I will surely deliver the Philistines into your hands"*. [20] David went to Baal-Perazim and there, Davide defeated them [...]. [22] The Philistines came up then again and deployed themselves in the valley of Rephaim. [23] Davide inquired of the Lord, who told him: *"Do not go; circle behind them and come at them from the balsam trees. [24] When you hear the sound of marching in the tops of the balsam trees, strike out swiftly,* for then will go out before you to defeat the army of the Philistines". [25] David did as the Lord had commanded him, and defeated the Philistines from Gibeon as far as Gezer. (2 Sam 5:19–25; cf. 1 Chron 14:8–17).

[21] Then the king of Israel went out and struck the horses and chariots and inflicted a great defeat on Aram. [2] Then the prophet came near to the king of Israel and said to him: "Go, strengthen yourself; know and see what you should do, for *next year the king of Aram will come up against you"* (1 Kgs 20:21–22).

[15b] While the minstrel played his instrument, the hand of the Lord was upon Elisha. [16] He announced: "Thus says the Lord: *Dig many trenches in this valley.* [17] Indeed, the Lord says: You will not see wind, you will not see rain, and yet this valley will fill with water; you will drink, your cattle and your animals. [18] This is a small thing in the eyes of the Lord: he will also hand Moab over to you. [19] You shall strike every fortified city and every main city, you shall fell every good tree and stop up every spring of water, you shall ruin all the fields filling them with stones". [...]. [24] Then they went to the camp of Israel. But the Israelites rose up and attacked the Moabites, who ran away from them. They followed them and defeated the Moabites (cf. 2 Kgs 3:15b-24).

[8] The king of Aram waged war against Israel, and in counsel with his officials said that he would camp in a certain place. [9] The man of God (אִישׁ הָאֱלֹהִים)[43] sent a message to the king of Israel: *"Beware that you do not pass by this place, for the Arameans are going down there"*. [10] The king of Israel sent scouts to the place indicated by the man of God and with regard for his warning, and was on his guard, more than once or twice.

[11] Greatly disturbed in his heart for this fact, the king of Aram called together his offers and told them: "Can you not tell me who amongst us is for the king of Israel?". [12] One of the officers answered: "No, oh king, my lord, but Elisha, the prophet (נָבִיא) of Israel, can tell the king of Israel the very words that you speak in your bedroom" (2 Kgs 6:8–12).

This typology of prophetic-divinatory communication, even if inserted in elaborate narrative frames, closely recalls the tenor of the oracles found in the royal archive of the Mari, dating back to the eighteenth century B.C. To proceed with such a comparison, some preliminary warnings are certainly required.[44] Faced with a different

---

43   This expression is not included by J. Stökl, *Prophecy in the Ancient Near East. A Philological and Sociological Comparison*, CHANE 56, Leiden – Boston 2012, 157–202, amongst the terms used in the HB to indicate the "prophets", but in this passage at least, the identification with the figure of the נָבִיא is clear.

44   Documentation that relates to prophetism, for instance, is much less extensive compared to that of a juridic nature, and the respective contexts of production and transmission should be evaluated carefully. On the difficulties and criteria for a plausible comparativistic methodology, keep in mind once again C. Bonnet – P. Merlo, «Royal Prophecy».

literary genesis[45] but on the basis of a similar institutional context (the Mari letters pertain to the prophetic correspondence addressed to the royal figure, that of the king Zimri-Lim, engaged in various military campaigns), it appears that the latter give evidence of, more than anything, a prophetism of a type that is "practical, utilitarian, functional, devoid of any moral or theological concern".[46] The cases adopted by M.J. de Jong to corroborate his case for a Jeremiah that is solely historical "pro-society" (in contrast to his post-exilic "contra-society" reconfiguration) go in the same direction as well,[47] but risk making comparativism a way of denying the arising of a substantial differentiation, which, as far as the unequalable vitality manifested by the historical path of the prophetic phenomenon in Israel as a whole is concerned, cannot be denied. Here, similarities and differences may perhaps (also) be explained in a historical-evolutionary sense, but it is, in my opinion, inaccurate to identify an absolute line of demarcation between pre-exile and post-exile, as if it had only been possible in Israel after the catastrophe of Jerusalem to conceive of a prophetism capable of being "pro-society" in a paradoxical way, according to the Jeremianic perspective of the surrender to Babylon.

The prophetic mediation that transmits an order from YHWH relating to actions with pragmatic purposes of a strategic nature is also attested in the HB, as we have seen. There are messages reported by the consulted prophets that *have no primary symbolic relevance*, but that merely provide *practical indications* (albeit "prophetic" ones, since they get attributed to YHWH as their primary source) to win a war or resolve other emergencies. The impression is that it be almost a vestige of a rather "primitive" prophetism,[48] which had remained within a conception of prophetic mediation that was much more elaborated from the theological-literary point of view, and which has evolved with time (but not only after the exile). One could cite at least two emblematic cases in the HB, amongst the many possible, in which the strategic-political element is flanked by a more profound valence of meaning. These are already paradigms of that semiotic-symbolic plus-valence that informs the peculiarity and richness of the communicative horizon typical of biblical prophetism.

---

45 The Mari letters mostly resemble first-hand documents, reports drawn up over a short span of time, sometimes immediately after the oral proclamation of the prophecies. These are prophetic oracles that "seem to be raw reports without any trace of later selection or elaboration, literary, moral or theological" (cf. C. BONNET – P. MERLO, «Royal Prophecy», 80).

46 Thus writes L. CAGNI, Le profezie di Mari. TVOA.M 2.2, Brescia 1995, 33, who adds: "[...] contrary to that which characterises the biblical world". It should be noted, however, that the context of these prophetic communications is rather circumstantial. Given the scarcity of documentation available, it is hard to assert categorically that no instances of a different nature were present in any measure. A more moderate stance may be advisable, as is found in M. NISSINEN, *Ancient Prophecy*. Near Eastern, Biblical, and Greek Perspectives, Oxford 2017, 261–263.

47 Cf M.J. DE JONG, «Rewriting the Past», 128–132.

48 Or, according to some, in the perspective of M.J. de Jong, more correspondent to the reality historically more widespread in the ancient Near East. Without indulging in "genetic comparativism" (cf. C. BONNET – P. MERLO, «Royal Prophecy», 77–80), I will limit myself here to noting the difference, in the amount of implications of meaning, that is registrable between the various types of prophetic communication attested, within the HB first of all.

662   The surrender as "Prophetic-Obediential ConSignA(c)tion"

In 1 Kgs 22:1–6, for example, Ahab and Jehoshaphat turn to the prophets to know if war can be waged against Aram, for the question of their yearned (re)conquest of Ramoth-gilead. Here, an interesting difference can be noted between a "corporate" prophetism, which is limited not just to pandering to the wishes of the king, but also to providing uniquely practical indications (vv. 1–6), accompanied by didactic "symbolic gestures" (v. 11) as well, and a prophetism in the minority (represented by Micah) that is far from complaisant, which establishes a communication that is much more complex (vv. 7–38) and also less obvious: first, Micah pretends to pander to the other prophets and to the desires of the king with an attitude that is, to say the least, provocative (since contrary to his usual style; cf. v. 8), then presents his interlocutors with a very elaborate interpretive picture of events that reveals the true and surprising dynamics of the story. He then concludes with an indication-warning that cannot be reduced to an equal alternative and is contrary to that of the court prophets. The valence of meaning appears more serious and profound, as can be seen after all, from the conclusion of v. 38, which ties Ahab's death to his previous actions and to the fulfilment of the words of YHWH spoken against him by the prophet Elijah in 1 Kgs 21:18–19.

An even more interesting example is the one offered in 2 Chron 20:1–25. Although it belongs to a different theological-literary project, it places the episode in direct temporal succession to that narrated in the First book of Kings.[49] The situation is this: the king Jehoshaphat finds himself under attack by a coalition of Moabites, Ammonites, and Meunites from Edom. After a heartfelt prayer to YHWH (the underlying question is emblematic; "[...] and we do not know what to do"; [וַאֲנַחְנוּ לֹא נֵדַע מַה-נַּעֲשֶׂה]; cf. v. 12), he receives an oracle of encouragement with precise tactical advice for handling the enemy (cf. v. 16–17). Actually, it can be noted, in this case, that these are not *only* practical indications relating to a special military strategy. Indeed, it would appear quite the contrary: it is a non-strategy. What is explicitly requested, in fact, is the assumption of a concrete *behaviour* of faith (cf. vv. 15:17: do not give in to fear, go out to meet the enemies, remain still) that actually *signifies* the meaning of the history underway (cf. v. 15: the war concerns YHWH), expresses total trust in YHWH (cf. v. 21: the singers of divine praise precede the soldiers), and thus allows the God of Israel to manifest his providential power (cf. v. 17:22–24). In other words, here we are more on the semiotic-symbolic side of the "Prophetic-Obediential ConSign*A(c)tion*".

The POC is precisely this: it can regard, in its literal, pragmatic dimension, an attitude or a choice that can be framed *at first glance* within the logic of political-military (or, at times, diplomatic) strategy aimed at winning a war or resolving a difficult situation in this area, coming either from a only human sapiential source or from a prophetic figure. However, a series of textual clues makes it possible to understand that the question is not that of a prudential form of problem resolution, nor a prophetic indication of a pragmatic nature aimed to substitute the human limits of knowledge or prediction of events. Deeper levels of meaning are at stake, which highlight the *symbolic* nature of what is ordered by the Lord of history. These amount

---

49   Which is then, besides, taken back up in 2 Chron 18, though without the final theological note regarding the fate of Ahab.

Commanded by God to the prophet or to the people at a precise point in time   663

to a "symbolic-prophetic choice", the repercussions of which, on the hermeneutical plane, reveal to be intriguing, and all to be investigated.

4.2. Beyond the ethical-moral dimension

Another important distinction should be drawn with regard to a communicative instance that has, for some time, been regarded by German exegesis of a Protestant matrix (especially in the nineteenth century) as an essential characteristic of the mediating function of the biblical prophets. The question is that of the ethical-moral dimension.[50] For this interpretive tradition, the prophet appeared to be representative of an authentic spiritual renewal,[51] himself the forger of the moral conscience of the people of Israel[52] and its "pure

---

50 Eckart Otto notes, despite the interest in the topic, the scarcity of studies on ethics, in both the German and English-speaking worlds, (cf. ID., «Hebrew Ethics in Old Testament Scholarship», in: *Psalmody and Poetry in Old Testament Ethics*, ed. D.J. HUMAN, New York 2012, 3–13). For some recent contributions of an orientative nature, see e.g. the collection of studies by K.J. DELL, ed., *Ethical and Unethical in the Old Testament*. God and Humans in Dialogue, LHBOTS 528, New York – London 2010, and in particular, amongst the most recent contributions: K. SCHMID, «Monotheismus und politische Ethik. Die politische Determination biblischer Gottesvorstellungen und ihre ethischen Implikationen», in: *Moral und Angst*. Erkenntnisse aus Moralpsychologie und politischer Theologie, eds. P. AERNI – K.-J. GRÜN, Göttingen 2011, 157–170; ID., «Genealogien der Moral. Prozesse fortschreitender ethischer Qualifizierung von Mensch und Welt im Alten Testament», in: *Gut und Böse in Mensch und Welt*. Philosophische und religiöse Konzeptionen vom Alten Orient bis zum frühen Islam, eds. H.G. NESSELRATH – F. WILK, ORA, Tübingen 2012, 83–102; E. OTTO, «The Study of Law and Ethics in the Hebrew Bible/Old Testament», *HBOT* III/2, 594–621 (with an ample bibliography); J. BARTON, *Ethics in Ancient Israel*, Oxford 2014. It is possible to introduce a technical distinction between the concept of *morality*, understood as intuitive and universal knowledge of the distinction between good and evil (and thus as the set of values, norms, and customs of an individual or community), and that of *ethics*, reserved for the speculative reflection of the morality itself. In my treatise, in reference to the biblical context I am dealing with, it seems most convenient to consider the two terms as essentially synonymous. One should furthermore keep in mind that looking at the world of the Scripture, the classical distinction between law and morality, and (typical of Roman law) between sacred law (*fas*) and profane law (*ius*), is not a simple one in the first case and does not have much sense in the second. This is due to the fact that the entire law of Israel is attributed to God as its origin, and every human reality is, in a certain sense "sacred", even if at times, the OT attests some distinctions between the two. Hence, while substantially true, the judgement of S M. PAUL, *Studies*, 37 remains too *tranchant*: "[In Biblical law the] whole of one's life is now directly related to the will of God. The distinction between *jus* and *fas* known to Roman law is non-existent").

51 See e.g. H. EWALD, *Die Propheten des Alten Bundes*, Erster Band, Stuttgart 1840, 1–64, who in any case underscores the political implications of this instance as well.

52 Even if this absolutisation is inaccurate, there is no doubt that the theme of the "conscience" is constitutive of biblical prophetism, as has always been recognised on the part of the Catholics. It is worth citing, in this regard, the study by A. ULEYN, *Actualité de la fonction prophétique*. Psychologie pastorale et culpabilité, Paris 1966, aimed at

664   The surrender as "Prophetic-Obediential ConSignA(c)tion"

religion"[53] that distinguished it from every other "clerical" form of extrabiblical religiosity. Their historical position was therefore to be relocated not after, but *before* the elaboration of the *Tôrâ*, being the true founders of the *ethical monotheism* of the religion of Israel.[54] Their call for fidelity to YHWH, in terms of a sincere spirituality that condemned the empty formalism of the temple cult,[55] made them appear like forerunners of the sixteenth century reformers, bitter enemies of what, by logical consequence, was considered the legalistic, ritualistic ("Proto-Catholic") degeneration of later Judaism.

Aside from the fact that this line of interpretation has highlighted, more than anything, the ethical-moral paradigm of reference of the respective commentators,[56] it should be noted that the wave of the aforementioned approach has recently come to touch upon the theme of the surrender to the king of Babylon in a study signed by the Benedictine biblist Joseph Jensen.[57] In it, there is a tendency to regard the call for submission as an *ethical* overcoming of the populist nationalism of a religious matrix fomented by the false prophets. Jeremiah would thus represent the purification of a certain early prophetism instigative of violence (the author recalls the case of Samuel commanding Saul to eliminate the Amalekites; cf. 1 Sam 15:1–3), and a warning against the permanent risks to which every society governed by religious principles would be subject.[58]

In the POC, there is perhaps nothing further than this ethical-moral perspective, if understood as a totalising dimension or sole key to reading the prophetic phenomenon. Indeed, the POC's reason for being, configured by the gesture of surrender to the king of Babylon, is based precisely on the failure of any attempt at moralisation. In the book of Jeremiah, as in the other prophetic books, there are numerous oracles based on the ethical-moral instance. Just think, for example, wanting to remain in the narrative sphere, of the ethical appeals contained in the speech delivered at the temple (cf. 7:5–7). And yet, a point is reached where the conversion of the people is useless for the purpose of the salvation of Jerusalem, given the hastening of events, marked from a certain point on[59] as being unstoppable. But the prophetic function does

---

showing how the dynamics of the conscience can be described and understood more adequately by taking precisely the figure of the prophet as a model of reference.

53   It suffices to recall the position of E. RENAN, *Histoire du peuple d'Israël*, II, livre IV, cap. VI ("Prépondérance du rôle des prophètes en Israël. Progrès du monothéisme. Mosaïsme"), Paris 1891, 483: "C'est par le prophétisme qu'Israël occupe une place à part dans l'histoire du monde. La création de la religion pure a été l'oeuvre, non pas des prêtres, mais de libres inspirés. Les *cohanim* de Jérusalem, de Babel, n'ont été en rien supérieurs à ceux du reste du monde; souvent même l'oevre essentielle d'Israël a été retardée, contrariée par eux."

54   Think, in particular, of the works by A. KUENEN, *De profeten en de profetie onder Israël*. Historisch-dogmatische studie, Leiden 1875; J. WELLHAUSEN, *Prolegomena zur Geschichte Israels*, Berlin 1882, ⁶1905, 363–424.

55   Cf. B. DUHM, *Die Theologie der Propheten als Grundlage für die innere Entwicklungsgeschichte der israelitischen Religion*, Bonn 1875; ID., *Israels Propheten*, Tübingen 1916, ²1922.

56   As was noted e.g. by J. BLENKINSOPP, *Prophecy and Canon. A Contribution to the Study of Jewish Origins*, Notre Dame 1977, 108.

57   Cf. J. JENSEN, *Ethical Dimensions*.

58   Cf. *Ibid.*, 141–142.

59   In my opinion, the decisive event that acts as a clear point of division, is narrated in Jer 36. It is the radical refusal of the prophetic word (and prophetic body) enacted at

Commanded by God to the prophet or to the people at a precise point in time   665

not cease for this. The threatening drama reveals instead its inexhaustible reserve of communicative devices,[60] proof of an indomitable divine desire for communion and salvation, an identifying sign of the God of the Covenant who has revealed himself to Israel in its travailed experience.

The POC is therefore not something that conforms to the ethical-moral normative dimension for every individual (at least in Israel, under the Covenant). It is not a call to respect one's neighbour, or to the divine right in one of its expressions. The need to surrender to the Babylonians proclaimed by Jeremiah is not a command prescribed by any tablet of the Law. On the contrary, it appears, in itself, to be an indication that is entirely opposed to the prophetic function of safeguarding the state[61] and to the common sense of any true God-fearing person (an attitude that, in Israel, could not but coincide with a good deal of nationalism). In this regard, the following observations of P. Beauchamp are particularly pertinent to the POC:

> Il est parfaitement fondé de rappeler que les prophètes, rencontrant l'obstacle des lois cérémonielles, et tout particulièrement du sacrifice, lui opposent les lois de la moralité générale et des devoirs envers le prochain. Mais il y aurait déformation du prophétisme à oublier que les textes convergent pour opposer au sacrifice avant toutes choses une attitude de présence à Dieu. Selon 1 S 15,22, il s'agit de préférer au sacrifice cette "écoute" active et "attentive" de la parole divine que les traductions appellent "obéissance", ou bien, selon Os 6,6, de fidélité à l'alliance et connaissance de Dieu, – et Michée 6,8 ajoute à la justice et l'amour le "marcher avec Dieu". En outre, et c'est ici le principal, ces mêmes prophètes ne fondent cette préférence qu'en retrouvant le chemin du récit perdu: rappel du passé dans Jérémie, Amos, Osée, Michée. [...]. De cette fidélité prophétique au récit, une importante conclusion découle. L'obéissance dont il s'agit n'est pas celle qui consiste en l'application des normes morales générales. Elle est celle qui intime de faire, sur le chemin de l'histoire, *le pas particulier que Dieu veut.* Cette volonté-là n'est point exprimée dans la loi mais plutôt cachée par elle. Elle consiste à faire un acte non parce qu'il est vertueux, mais *parce qu'il est voulu de Dieu et à se porter ainsi au-delà de la loi.*[62]

The fact remains that in particular cases, the POC can assume, in its "literal" expression, precisely the configuration typical of a moral act. Even in this case, however, it

---

the time of Jehoiakim with the incineration of the scroll containing all the words of Jeremiah. From this point on, the *threat* of the (avoidable) "end" turns into the *prediction* of its ineluctable fulfilment (cf. 36:29–31).

60   The rhetoric of violence, which is difficult to comprehend today, also depends on this logic. On this topic, see the contribution by A. KALMANOFSKY, «Poetic Violence in the Book of Jeremiah», in: *The Oxford Handbook of Jeremiah, eds.* L. STULMAN – E. SILVER, Oxford 2021, 328–342.

61   One of the conclusions reached by the study of M.J. DE JONG, *Isaiah*, is summarised as follows: "Both the Assyrian prophets and Isaiah functioned as *guardians of the state* and fiercely turned against those perceived as enemies of the state" (p. 456, my emphasis). The ideological support assured to the royal dynasty, as the author himself had already noted, in the wake of studies by A. MALAMAT, «A Mari Prophecy», 79–82), and T. ISHIDA, *The Royal Dynasties*, 90–92, is characteristic of the *historical prophets* (to be distinguished from the figures of the "classical prophets", seen as later literary profiles) both in Israel (cf. 2 Sam 7:5–17) and in Mari and Assyria (cf. p. 33).

62   P. BEAUCHAMP, *L'un et l'autre Testament.* 2, 407–408 (my emphasis).

666   The surrender as "Prophetic-Obediential ConSignA(c)tion"

is the pragmatic elements provided by the context that point towards this further type of signification of meaning that is the POC. In other words, I believe that in certain historical-literary contexts, a *single* ethical commandment can assume the (prophetic) function of being a sign of observance of the *whole* Law, but always in a particular circumstance or historical contingency. I have already highlighted this in § 5.4.3.7.

4.3. Beyond the religious dimension of the cult

Rejecting the presuppositions central to the above-mentioned approach, which saw in the prophets the founders of Israel's ethical monotheism, other scholars successively pointed out how they were, instead, tied to the tradition,[63] implicated in the sphere of the cult[64] and mediation of the Mosaic law (cf. e.g. Deut 18:15–19). Their theological-literary position thus returned to be dependent upon that of the *Tôrâ*, the ecstatic experience was redimensionalised,[65] and real and true (canonical) prophets of the "cultic" type (such as Joel, Habakkuk, Aggeus, and Zacharias) were identified. Thanks to this rereading, the prophets are no longer seen today as enemies of the cult,[66] or as founders of a (new) ethical religion, but as actualisers and developers of the previous religious tradition.

One of the obligations of every sovereign of the ancient Near East, including the kingdom of Judah, was to take care of the maintenance of the cultic apparatus according to the canons of a certain "orthodoxy" and traditional orthopraxy. As a place of intersection between the divine and human worlds, the temple of the divinity in particular had its (at least apparently) own irreplaceability. It is therefore not surprising that amongst the messages of which the prophets make themselves bearers, many concern the sovereign in his relationship with the cultic sphere. The prophetic

---

63   Think, in particular, of both the first volume of G. VON RAD, *Theologie des Alten Testaments*, and the second (which I have already had the opportunity to cite), dedicated to the prophetic traditions (*Die Theologie der prophetischen Überlieferungen Israels*).

64   Amongst these, in particular S. MOWINCKEL, *Prophecy and Tradition;* ID., *Religion und Kultus*, Göttingen 1953; A.R. JOHNSON, *The Cultic Prophet in Ancient Israel*, Cardiff 1944; ID., *The Cultic Prophet and Israel's Psalmody*, Cardiff 1979; A. HALDAR, *Associations of Cult Prophets among the Ancient Semites*, Uppsala 1945; I. ENGNELL, *The Call of Isaiah*. An Exegetical and Comparative Study, Uppsala 1949 (places Isaiah's vocation in a precise cultural context, the feast of the new year); H.G. REVENTLOW, *Liturgie;* G.W. AHLSTRÖM, *Joel and the Temple Cult of Jerusalem*, VT.S 21, Leiden 1971.

65   More recently re-evaluated. See N.G. HOLM, «Ecstatic Research in the 20th Century – An Introduction», in: *Religious Ecstasy*, ed. N.G. HOLM, Uppsala 1982, 7–26; P. MICHAELSEN, «Ecstasy and Possession in Ancient Israel: A Review of Some Recent Contributions», *SJOT* 3 (1989) 28–54.

66   Cf. e.g. J.W. HILBER, «Psalm CX in the Light of Assyrian Prophecies», *VT* 53 (2003) 353–366; ID., *Cultic Prophecy in the Psalms*, BZAW 352, Berlin 2005; VAN DER TOORN, K., *Scribal Culture*, 183 (with particular reference to Amos and Jeremiah). According to the study by M.J. DE JONG, *Isaiah*, the prophetic figures who appeared in Assyria and in the kingdom of Judah have in common the fact of being often tied to the cult and to a specific temple (cf. p. 457: "Although prophets for the delivery of divine messages were not exclusively bound to the temple, the main institutional embodiment of prophecy seems to have been the temple").

Commanded by God to the prophet or to the people at a precise point in time   667

communications contained in the Mari letters and the neo-Assyrian collections,[67] for example, in addition to dealing with political-military issues, on several occasions, provide explicit directives referring to temple maintenance and issues that relate to the cult in general.[68] There is also no lack of reproaches of the sovereign, accused in some cases of negligence towards cultic obligations to be performed to some deities.[69]

As an emblematic case in the HB, on the other hand, it suffices to think of Josiah's whole reform of the Yahwist cult, provoked – according to the biblical narration – both by the discovery of the book of the *Tôrâ*, and by the prophetic interpretation of this event, reread in the light of past and present history (cf. 2 Kgs 22:14–23:25; 2 Chron 34:22–35:19).[70]

Proceeding through subsequent differentiations towards the specific conceptual content of the POC, it need be specified that even this religious dimension, which is expressed through a complex normative and ritualistic system and is the object of divine imperatives transmitted by the prophets, is to be excluded. Certainly, there are prophetic messages in the HB that contain injunctions relating to the cult, and there is no doubt that every ritual aspect already has a strong symbolic valence to it. But the prime objective of the POC is not to prescribe or call to a "religious" way of life, whether this be cultual or ritualistic, in accordance with the expressive tradition of Israel. At least if we look at its dynamism of signification in the light of its essential communicative-pragmatic purpose.

Even in the cultual realm, in fact, just as in the ethical-moral sphere, nothing prevents the POC from *also* taking on the factual configuration of religious behaviour. This fact is not paradoxical or contradictory to what I am saying, since typical of the POC is its rooting in the concreteness of human action. The difference, or the plus-valence of meaning, is once again indicated by the pragmatic context, vital situation, sense of time to be assumed, in freedom and in obedience, *in a given historical circumstance.*

Consider also the highly symbolic value that the observance of the Shabbat assumes, or the norm on pure and unclean foods during the dramatic juncture of the persecution of Antiochus IV Epiphanes at the time of the Maccabees (cf. e.g. 1 Mac 1:43; 2:32–38[71]; 2 Mac 7), the practice of burial in the land of exile in the book of Tobias (cf.

---

67   The Mari letters have almost all been published and translated in the already cited edition by J.-M. DURAND, *Archives épistolaires de Mari*, 377–452. Other texts, including Neo-Assyrian ones, with transliteration and translation, can be found in M. NISSINEN, *Prophets.* The Neo-Assyrian prophecies were published in S. PARPOLA, *Assyrian Prophecies,* SAA 9, Helsinki 1997.

68   See e.g. the oracles ARM 26 194; 218; 220; 221; SAA 9 1.4; 1.10; etc.

69   See e.g. the oracles ARM 26 203; 215; 217; 218; SAA 9 3.5; etc.

70   On the religious and political motives for the reform under Josiah, see N. NA'AMAN, «The King», 131–168 (in particular, pp. 140–141, 165–166).

71   That the choice to get killed rather than go to combat on a Sabbath day can be understood in this episode as a POC is demonstrated by the opposite decision made by Mattathias and his companions immediately afterward (cf. 1 Mac 2:39–41). They too, while intending to remain with all their strength unconditionally faithful to the *Tôrâ*, decide to express this fidelity by going to combat even on Saturday. What is at stake, therefore, is a different ("prophetic") interpretation of the meaning of the time and events in which one's own story plays out.

668   The surrender as "Prophetic-Obediential ConSignA(c)tion"

Tob 1:11–12),[72] or even still, the reconstruction of the temple of YHWH after the exile, at the time of Nehemiah and the prophet Haggai (cf. Hag 1:3–11). In order to grasp the profound meaning of these, without their being reduced to a superficial reading limited to simply noting their cultual pertinence (and the symbolic value "immanent" to the norm in itself), I believe that, in the light of the pragmatic context highlighted by the textual data, it can be useful to apply the interpretive category of the POC.

4.4. Beyond the rhetorical-didactic dimension

Another communicative instance that can be recognised as taking place in biblical prophetism regards the objective of persuading the audience, and its ability to transmit a message that is clear and comprehensible, at times didactic, far from the ambiguity typical of other divinatory mediations (omens, dreams, ambiguous oracular answers, riddles, etc.). The prophet is indubitably an authoritative figure, but, as a rule, has no power of governance.[73] If the teaching of the *Tôrâ* is the prerogative of the priest (כֹּהֵן), and counsel (עֵצָה) concerns the sage (חָכָם), then the prophet is, instead, the person of the דָּבָר (cf. 18:18). The only weapon they possess is their word, a word whose strength is given by their claim to normativity, by the degree of authority given by its verification/falsification on the level of history, but also by the rhetorical strategies they assume, in both their oral version and literary (or scribal) one.

This aspect of prophetic communication is of a different nature than the previous ones. While those regard the different possible *content*, that is, the semantics of the prophetic message (and thus of the POC as well), this refers to the *form* and the pragmatic *purpose* underlying the particular forms of expression adopted by the prophetic language, both verbal and non-verbal. There is no doubt that the prophets are (presented as) masters of effective communication. They are as the individual characters, both in the narrative framework in which they are inserted and in the oracles attributed to them. They are as the authors and as the (no less prophetic) transmitters of the books that bear their names. They are normally not so, however, merely because they are "scribal technicians" of communication. The question is not one of specialists who put themselves at the service of just any communicative instance.

A potentiality is nothing without an intentionality that can make it express, develop, and direct itself towards an objective. And the biblical prophets are communicators *out of passion*, or better yet, communicators *of* a passion that bursts into history. The instance that animates the prophet attested in the HB, to put it with Abraham Joshua

---

72   The refusal to eat pork or the burial of one's dead compatriots at the risk of one's own life become gestures and decisions that go beyond the intrinsic value of the observance of a ritual norm. The much broader meaning of absolute faith in the God of Israel and one's own identity is expressed, with a heightened degree of anthropological impact (the risk of life). It can be observed that, in these cases, the injunction of a prophet and the explicit imperative of YHWH is lacking. What is pointed out concerning the prototypicity of the category of the POC in § 3.3.1 applies in this regard.

73   I refer both to the "writing prophets" of the HB and to the figures of prophetic mediation attested in the ancient Near East, within and beyond the borders of Israel. It is known that Abraham, Moses (eminently), and David, figures having an authority of "governance", were considered prophetic figures in post-exilic times.

Heschel, is the very *páthos*[74] of God who desires to communicate, save, forge, and renew alliance. This is this reason why he cries, grows silent, whispers, evokes, tells, admonishes, and condemns, moans, cries, and rejoices. His speech cannot be limited to a cataloguising of formularies or specific or identifying literary genres. The prophet deploys a very vast range of communicative registers. In principle, excluding none. And in doing so, it is not aesthetic purposes that drive him, but the fire burning in his bones (cf. 20:9), God's tireless attempt not to win but to convince his partner in the Covenant to recognise the Origin that gives life, the Face of the groom of Israel. In order for the listener to truly listen, and thus be able to assume the prophetic discourse, embrace it, obey it, and live.

Studies on this argument as it relates to prophetic literature are many.[75] For the interpretative line I have taken on in my research, it is interesting to refer, once again, in particular, to the work of K.G. Friebel regarding the "symbolic gestures" of the prophets,[76] since the POC is intimately connected to it. As I have already had the opportunity to note, his key to interpretation is principally of a rhetorical type and is motivated by the fact that, in his opinion, the prophetic recourse to non-verbal communication models would be motivated by rhetorical-didactic purposes.

While not negating this fundamental purpose, from my point of view, on the other hand, the reduction of symbolic gestures to this level is entire inaccurate. In addition to the rhetorical dimension, their *performative* pragmatic valence must also be given just emphasis. The question is not that of evoking magical dynamisms but of ascertaining the communicative logic of the Covenant between YHWH and his people. There are symbolic gestures that not only signify but *actualise*, produce a specific event in the very instant they are performed. Obedience is not just a thought, it is an act, it is a *fact*. Or a series of concrete acts made over time.

Consider still Jeremiah's temple speech (7:1–15; 26): while it may or may not convince the listeners (both on the intradiegetic level and otherwise), the *fact* remains that Jeremiah *handed himself over* in obedience to God into the hands of men. This is the fact that the story presents and this realises his prophetic identity beyond any

---

74 The work in which he developed this hermeneutical category, the "theology of *páthos*", is A.J. HESCHEL, *The Prophets*, New York 1962 (above all, on pp. 221–323).

75 Just to give some minimal bibliographic indications of a general nature, I will cite the pioneering works of C. WESTERMANN, *Grundformen prophetischer Rede,* BEvT 31, München 1960, [5]1978; M. WEINFELD, «Ancient Near Eastern Patterns in Prophetic Literature», *VT* 27 (1977) 178–195, the collection of essays in D.J.A. CLINES – D.M. GUNN – A.J. HAUSER, eds., *Art and Meaning*. Rhetoric in Biblical Literature, JSOT.S 19, Sheffield 1982, and the more recent contributions of K. MÖLLER, *A Prophet in Debate*. The Rhetoric of Persuasion in the Book of Amos, JSOT.S 372, Sheffield 2003; E.R. WENDLAND, *Prophetic Rhetoric*. Case Studies in Text Analysis and Translation, Lakewood 2009, [2]2014; G. EIDEVALL, *Sacrificial Rhetoric in the Prophetic Literature of the Hebrew Bible*, New York 2012. For the book of Jeremiah in particular, see W. BRUEGGEMANN, «Jeremiah's Use of Rhetorical Questions», *JBL* 92 (1973) 358–374; J.R. LUNDBOM, Jeremiah; T. POLK, *The Prophetic Persona*; E.D. LEWIN, «Arguing for Authority»; A.R. DIAMOND, Confessions; D.F. MURRAY, «The Rhetoric of Disputation: Re-examination of a Prophetic Genre», *JSOT* 38 (1987) 95–121; M.D. ZULICK, «The Agon of Jeremiah», 125–148.

76 Cf. K.G. FRIEBEL, *Jeremiah's and Ezekiel Sign-Acts*.

670   The surrender as "Prophetic-Obediential ConSignA(c)tion"

possible persuasive outcome of the speech pronounced. His gesture, configured by the synergy between those words spoken in that place, has and wants to have a disruptive force, on the level of communicative efficacy. But we are dealing with more than just this aspect. In other words, what we are before are more than simple rhetorical devices. These are *paradigms of response* to the God of the Covenant.

The POC is decidedly positioned in this perspective. This should be emphasised, especially with regard to the POCs asked of the prophets, because they can be misunderstood as configurations of symbolic gestures of an exclusively rhetorical nature. Almost as if what counted was only *impressing* the listener or actant. And hence, the reader as well. This purpose certainly underlies, to varying degrees, every communicative event. But here, something else is involved: let us see what.

5. Expression of a significative and prophetic option (regarding the Covenant and the meaning of history)

5.1. It is an obedience of faith (within a history of covenant)

Each POC is configured as a *response* to the God of the Covenant that is free and *positive*. The communicative context presupposed, in other words, is the "history of salvation", that is, the relationship between YHWH and his people (and all of humanity), testified by the flux of tradition, which, over time, has assumed written form and normative value for biblical Israel and beyond.[77]

In this context, it is clear that YHWH's self-revelation to humanity in history (and in creation) has an eminently communal intent. The multiplex attestation of the Scripture on the theme shows without a shadow of a doubt that, to this gratuitous initiative, the most adequate manner of response by the human being is faith, listening, and obedience (cf. § 5.4.3.7). The question is that of a responsorial dynamism that is expressed in various forms, but in the OT, above all, in the observance of the *Tôrâ* and in obedience to the voice of the prophets and sages of Israel who make reference and actualise the authentic demands of precisely the *Tôrâ*. The capacity to give free assent, as we have already seen (cf. § 6.1), is an essential prerequisite.

If the founding event of the Exodus[78] is narrated through symbolic imagery typical of the mystery of birth (for it is coming out of Egypt through the waters of the sea

---

77   As I specified in the introductory portion (ch. I, § 3.2), there are several hermeneutical levels that can be assumed, according to starting premises, research objectives, and respective textual contexts found pertinent. My underlying hermeneutical perspective embraces the unity of the OT and NT given by the assumption in faith of Christ as *fulfilment* of this salvific trajectory. For methodological reasons, however, my interest is concentrated on the OT and, in particular, on the HB, in which, always from a canonical point of view, the unity of these textual entities is configured by the tradition that sees in them the attestation of precisely a "history of covenant".

78   The event of the Exodus is founder precisely because it does not presuppose either the identity of a people or its freedom. It is the gratuitous act of YHWH that founds both the identity and freedom itself of Israel. In other words, one can say that YHWH, punishing the pharaoh who, for fear of being overwhelmed, enslaves and kills the descendants of Abraham, places himself in the opposite condition: that of being able to be refused and eliminated from the relational horizon of Israel.

Expression of a significative and prophetic option 671

that Israel is born as a people), then with the ideal moment of the stipulation of the Covenant, what is entered instead is, so to speak, adulthood or the possibility of it.[79] Hence, the vocabulary characteristic of this phase is drawn from the world of law and justice, to be understood not so much as the due respect for an abstract norm, but as a desire to promote and recognise the face of the (O)other, in a project of communion, in the diversity of individual subjects.[80]

In truth, there would be many other specifications to be made in this regard for a more adequate thematisation. I will limit myself therefore to a terminological focalisation with an allusive-evocative valence, which can immediately give echo to the intrinsic richness of meaning in the concept. In reference to the free response of the biblical human being to the God that reveals himself, a synthetic expression that is, in my opinion, fairly happy, is that of "obedience of faith",[81] with both subjective and objective valence (the faith that obeys and the obedience that is faith in action). This is, in fact, capable of recalling and articulating central meanings for this issue, linked in the HB, above all, to the roots שמע (listen, obey, etc.) and אמן (being stable, certain, believe, trusting, having trust, etc.).

The specific object of the action of consent included in the category of the POC will be the subject of the next paragraph. Here, my intent is to underscore that each POC has within it the *performative*[82] strength to make the relationship of Covenant alive

---

79 As observes P. Beauchamp, the whole journey across the emptiness of the desert can be configured as a repeated attempt to stimulate the freedom of Israel towards an entrance into adulthood: "Ce vide ne produit rien, rien que le désir d'en sortir, de franchir la discontinuité qui sépare l'enfant de l'homme, frontière que la décision seule trouve" (*L'un et l'autre Testament*, 46).

80 Making reference to Emmanuel Lévinas (*Totalité et infini. Essai sur l'extériorité*, Nijhoff 1961, ³1968), thus expresses, in this regard, P. BOVATI, *Vie della giustizia*, 26: "*Justice* is an ethical concept that defines the human being as one capable of relating to another according to truth. One's *being just* (or unjust) will be judged not on the basis of the compliance (or not) to a norm, even if this were a categorical imperative or apodictic law, but rather on the basis of the ability to recognise the face of the other." The biblical notion of justice, in fact, "implicates a relation between two (or more) subjects endowed with the inner principle of freedom, with all that this entails as a responsibility" (translated from P. BOVATI, «"Quando le fondamenta sono demolite, cosa fa il giusto?" (Sal 11,3). La giustizia in situazione di ingiustizia», in: *La giustizia in conflitto*. XXXVI Settimana Biblica Nazionale [Roma, 11–15 settembre 2000], ed. R. FABRIS, Bologna 2002, 9–38 [here, p. 12]).

81 It is not found as such in the HB, but the expression ὑπακοὴν πίστεως echoes both in Rom 1:5, where Paul speaks, in fact, about the salvific purpose of the apostolate, aimed at arousing amongst all peoples a free response to the design of God revealed in Christ, and in Rom 16:26, where it refers precisely to the dynamism of the prophetic revelation of the OT (cf. also 2 Cor 10:5–6). The same synthetic formulation is authoritatively taken up by the Second Vatican Council in *Dei Verbum*, 5: "Deo revelanti praestanda est *oboeditio fidei* [...], qua homo se totum libere Deo committit 'plenum revelanti Deo intellectus et voluntatis obsequium' praestando et voluntarie revelationi ab Eo datae assentiendo" (my emphasis).

82 On the performative efficacy of the prophetic word, capable of creative (or destructive) force on the events of human history, see e.g. 1 Sam 3:11; 1 Kgs 12:15; Isa 55:10–11; Jer 1:11–12; Ezek 13:6; etc.

670   The surrender as "Prophetic-Obediential ConSignA(c)tion"

and *present* (according to "love" [חֶסֶד; cf. 2:2; אַהֲבָה; 31:3], "truth [אֱמֶת], righteousness [מִשְׁפָּט], and justice" [צְדָקָה]; cf. 4:2). This capacity is not intrinsic to the act itself, as it would be from a certain point of view if it were an ethical-religious norm accepted and recognised as coming from YHWH and valid in perpetuity,[83] but gets attributed to it independently with respect to the normative framework codified by the precepts of the *Tôrâ*.[84] It is YHWH himself, usually through the mouth of the prophet, who identifies it as the obediential path to be accepted in faith in a specific historical moment.[85]

The indication is not an arbitrary or irrational one: The POC is presented rooted in the logic of the Covenant and the order of the real that can be experienced by all. The human intelligence is recognised as having a (discreet) ability to grasp these dynamics and factualities.[86] The theme of "handing oneself over to the king of Babylon" is an eloquent example of this, since the Jeremianic option can be confused as being a prudential form of only a political nature, detached from transcendence. My thesis, as I have thus far tried to support, is that precisely in the gesture of surrender to the king of Babylon, carried out in obedience to the prophetic word, the book of Jeremiah identifies the most extreme path and most unexpected possibility of reintegration into the vital dynamism of the Covenant.

It is important to note in the scope of my research that both the characteristic vocabulary and emblematic examples to which I could refer other than that of the surrender, orient the configuration of this (indicated and awaited) response not so much towards a merely legalistic observance or intellectual adherence to an abstract series of dogmatic truths, as much as instead to a personal involvement, to be translated and lived out in concrete acts. "I am a jealous God" (אֵל קַנָּא), YHWH repeats several times (cf. e.g. Exod 20:5; 34:14; Deut 4:24; etc.): everything that gets put before this interpersonal relationship takes on the connotations of the vain idol and configures the sin of adultery, even if this can be concealed precisely by a formalistic ritual observance and a historical decontextualisation of the "articles" of the Israeli faith (cf. e.g. 7:1–15, and particularly v. 4).

Talking about "obedience of (or to) faith" in relation to a category that wants to distinguish itself from other systems of signification might seem, at first glance, fairly generic and not relevant. Let us remember, however, that this expression does not apply to the conceptual levels that I discarded earlier. It is an obedience of faith that is not actuated (only) on either an ethical or cultic level (like an observance of the

---

83   In the context or in a specific context of the Israeli religion.

84   Even if, as I have said previously, it is not to be ruled out that the POC might, at times, coincide or overlap with an ethical norm. In this case, the valence of meaning of the precept is not given so much by the precept itself as by its prophetic-obediential valence conferred by the historical juncture.

85   The generative source of the significance of creatural entities, and of the meaning of history for the Scripture is the provident *intentionality* of God (cf. A. MURATORE, «Simbolo, mistero e mito: il quadro epistemologico», in: *La conoscenza simbolica*, eds. C. GRECO – A. MURATORE, Cinisello Balsamo 1988, 9–39 [here, p. 20]).

86   Although limited, since creatural, human intelligence is sufficient, according to the Scripture, both to advance in knowledge of the realities of the world, and to interact according to wisdom (חָכְמָה) with the Wisdom (which, for the NT, will be the *lógos*) of God himself. The human ability to *intus-legere* is, in fact, sign of the human being created in the image and likeness of his Creator.

Expression of a significative and prophetic option

Tôrâ), it is not resolved nor should it be identified as a political, diplomatic, or strategic choice, and does not have political objectives as its priority (though it does not exclude them). Its objective is to intercept the profound meaning of history, *hic et nunc*. The spatial-temporal coordinates therefore configure the originary dimension in which the covenant relationship unfolds, and manifest the elective place of the revelation of the Meaning for all prophetic literature. This explains why the various attestations of POC, and in particular that of the surrender to Babylon, all either appear in narrative texts or are attached to them in a way that is decisive (as e.g. 21:1–10).

5.2. It is the emergence of the unsaid (the foreigner who saves)

One of the most emblematic elements of meaning for my path of investigation can be derived from the oracle of salvation concerning Ebed-melech (39:15–18), to which I have referred a number of times, precisely for its particular communicative and theological relevance. From the words Jeremiah addresses to the courageous official of the king, what emerges, in fact, is all of the submerged force of the unsaid. And it becomes clear the extent to which a part of the Jeremianic prophetic message is to be found not simply on the level of the mere formal evidence of the enunciations, but on that of the clues and necessary inferences that the author expects of their Model Reader.

Indeed, according to an exclusively factual reconnaissance, the narrative that sees Ebed-melech protagonist of the *in extremis* salvation of the prophet (38:1–13) makes no pronouncement at all regarding his emotional-intentional sphere, nor does it in any way highlight a direct connection between his actions and YHWH or the implications of the Covenant. His would seem to be described only as a "philanthropic" act, moved by even laudable human compassion, but without any other significant impact. Nothing is explicitly said about the question of discernment between true and false prophecy or about whether or not he recognises the authenticity of the Jeremianic ministry and normativity of his message. Moreover, though the phenomenon does not concern this text alone, according to the LXX, both Ebed-melech and Zedekiah do not even refer to Jeremiah giving him the title of "prophet" (נָבִיא) as in the MT (cf. 38:9–10 with 45:9–10^{LXX}). For the court eunuch, he is simply "this man" (cf. 45:9^{LXX}: τὸν ἄνθρωπον τοῦτον). And, an even more significant piece of data (both in the MT and the LXX), it is not ever said that Ebed-melech followed the prophet's directions on the factual level, passing over to the Chaldeans. Perhaps he may not have been physically able to do so (cf. 39:17a), but that is of no interest to the narrator who, in any case, does not count him amongst the deserters.

Instead, what is striking is that at a certain and not random distance (a phenomenon that I have called "semiotic *arcatas*"), there is a text placed in which Jeremiah dedicates an oracle of salvation to him, motivated not so much by a formal reference to the episode of his liberation but to the *invisible* (or implied) act of his *faith in YHWH* (cf. 39:18: "[...] because *you trusted in me*" [כִּי־בָטַחְתָּ בִּי]). A faith, therefore, signified precisely by that gesture, and a gesture, the interest taken in the prophet's liberation, which, according to the profile of the POC, must have cost him no small amount in terms of personal exposure to the risk of a violent rejection by the king or retaliation from Jeremiah's enemies (who become *ipso facto* his own enemies: cf. 39:17: "the men whom you dread" [הָאֲנָשִׁים אֲשֶׁר־אַתָּה יָגוֹר מִפְּנֵיהֶם]).

674 The surrender as "Prophetic-Obediential ConSignA(c)tion"

Here, what emerges in all its strength is the communicative dimension of the unsaid that underlies every textuality,[87] and does so especially, in my opinion, throughout the entire book of Jeremiah, where the reader is constantly provoked to retrace their steps to *reread* the (textual and extratextual) reality in a new and more "prophetic" way. Another clear example in this sense, of great relevance for the validation of my underlying thesis, is the reduplication of the same phenomenon of "emergence of the implicit meaning" that takes place, and it cannot be by chance, again on the thematic axis of "handing oneself over to the king Babylon". As I have already noted,[88] when Jeremiah, before the fleeing survivors, isomorphically reformulates the same "pre-catastrophe" injunction to submit without fear to Nebuchadnezzar (cf. 42:9–12), he adds a theological motivation that, retrospectively, explicates a significant unsaid, which remained implicit in his preceding oracles on the same question:

I will have (נתן√) mercy (רַחֲמִים) so (Nebuchadnezzar) will have mercy (רחם√) on you and will let you return to your land (v. 12).

The Jeremianic option is thus confirmed once again not as a sapiential way to save the salvageable nor as a mere political opinion but as an event of revelation of the meaning of history, the necessary assumption of which determines a positive outcome of the drama underway, guaranteed only by the direct intervention of YHWH. From a pragmatic point of view, without going into too far into technical aspects, I can say that the two enunciations in question (39:17; 42:12) act as "activators of the presupposition" of "existence",[89] and that these presuppositions are of an informational (explicative) nature with regards to all the other texts with which they are, in different ways, connected from the isotopic point of view (because they share the same theme of "handing oneself over to the king of Babylon").

What has been said so far reveals Ebed-melech's gesture as an *obedience of faith*, a structuring element of a POC, but this factor is not yet decisive for my discourse. Other elements, however, are: (a) the *context* of the utterance of the promise; (b) the content of the promise as a *liberation*; (c) the configuration of the liberation according to the perspective indicated by the locution "*your life as war booty*" (נַפְשְׁךָ לְשָׁלָל).

---

87   On this topic of great interest, see in particular M. Sbisà, *Detto non detto. Le forme della comunicazione implicita*, Bari 2007, ²2010. As the author notes in the opening, implied communication is that uneliminable part of presuppositions and understandings that accompanies every communicative event: "The issue is not a marginal one compared to the general issue of communication. Presuppositions and implications are everywhere. They contribute significantly to the meaning of our linguistic communications or, more precisely, to the texts"; "Often, in fact, the lack of understanding in a linguistic communication depends precisely on the lack of understanding of what it implies or presupposes" (translated from p. 5).

88   Cf. ch. III, § 4.2.2.

89   They reveal as fundamental presuppositions that: (1) in freeing Jeremiah, Ebed-melech performed an act of faith in YHWH (recognising Jeremiah as a true prophet); (2) the injunction to surrender requires entering a theological dimension of the meaning of history, in which it is YHWH who reveals himself as sole Lord, changing the heart of the king of Babylon and thus making the surrender a path of salvation (to be interpreted, indeed, theologically). For other considerations on the figure and role of Ebed-melech, see: C.J. Sharp, *Jeremiah 26-52*, IECOT, Stuttgart 2022, 253-255.

a) The context is clear: it is that of the fulfilment of the prophetic threat concerning the destruction of Jerusalem (cf. 39:16). The connection with the theme of surrender to Babylon is immediate, not only because it concerns, in a generic way, the extreme path of salvation proposed in this contextual framework, but because Jeremiah's words to Ebed-melech depend on a divine communication received "when he was still a prisoner in the courtyard of the prison" (cf. 39:15), that is, in the typical context in which our theme is placed in the final days of Judah.

b) As far as the contents of the oracle are concerned, it should be noted that YHWH, by way of the mouth of Jeremiah, promises "liberation" (cf. 39:18: "I will certainly free you" [מַלֵּט אֲמַלֶּטְךָ]), thus presupposing an at least analogous commonality between the situation of his prisoner prophet and that of Ebed-melech. Not only on a superficial or factual level, but on the level of participation in the same bipolar paradigmatic dynamic of "*consignment* to YHWH"/"*salvation* undeducible from human factors". Just as Jeremiah is a prisoner for having surrendering himself in obedience to YHWH and, for the same reason, will be saved, according to the divine promise, so will Ebed-melech, having placed himself in a position of mortal risk for having trusted in YHWH (saving Jeremiah), precisely as a consequence of the same obedience of faith, also be saved. But in a meaningful modality. Let's have a look at it.

c) The salvation promised to Ebed-melech is configured in such a way that its implicit reference cannot go unnoticed by the attentive reader. It is substantially the same promise of salvation that is guaranteed to those who, by obeying the Jeremianic message in faith, will decide to "hand themselves over to the king of Babylon". Two textual elements are indicative of this. Promised to Ebed-melech in 39:17, in addition to liberation, is: "you will not be handed over (לֹא תִנָּתֵן בְּיַד) to the men you fear (הָאֲנָשִׁים אֲשֶׁר־אַתָּה יָגוֹר מִפְּנֵיהֶם)". The very same expressions and same vocabulary with which Jeremiah invites Zedekiah to surrender are utilised, when in 38:20, he assures him: "you will not be handed over [to them]" (לֹא יִתֵּנוּ), referring to the king's *fear* of being handed over to the Jews who had passed over to the Chaldeans (cf. 38:19). But it is, above all, the promise to have "life" (נֶפֶשׁ) saved "as war booty" (לְשָׁלָל; cf. 39:18) that makes the reference to the theme of surrender unequivocal, rendering an additional wealth of meaning explicit. As I have observed,[90] the expression in question makes up part of a construct that has no other parallels in the HB and is attested only 4x in Jeremiah (21:9; 38:2; 39:18; 45:5). In the *first two* cases, the context is the same Jeremianic injunction of surrender to Babylon, accompanied, in fact, by the promise of having life saved. The recipients are *collective* subjects, that is, all the people (21:8). In the *other two* cases, however, in an oppositional relationship that is, in my opinion, not accidental, the subjects are *single* characters, Ebed-melech and Baruch. Even in the case of Baruch, the context is that of the end of Jerusalem, and the prophet invites his faithful aide to accept the on-going drama in faith, thus placing an isomorphic equivalence to the act of surrender. In this overall context, it seems clear that the promise made to Ebed-melech should also be read from the same perspective. A further positive relationship is given by the fact that the first two attestations (21:9 and 38:2) fall in the context of an appel that is not yet known whether it will find a positive response in the internal logic

---

90   Cf. ch. III, § 4.2.2.

676   The surrender as "Prophetic-Obediential ConSignA(c)tion"

of the story, while the other two are promises made to those who have already
implemented the choice of embracing the figure of the prophet (and thus his message). Baruch did not part from Jeremiah, and Ebed-melech put his life in danger to
save him from death.[91] But even here, there is interplay with the references making
explicit what in the text connected by a semiotic *arcata* is implied. The choice of
Ebed-melech is explicit as is his faith, while the choice of Baruch in the text in
question is implicit (one must keep ch. 36 in mind, or read between the lines of ch.
45 to understand that the fidelity of Baruch is taken as certain).

From these data, which bring forth a richness of meaning not immediately visible
from the textual surface, we believe that we can trace a *significant inference*: in the
Jeremianic perspective, surrendering means having faith in YHWH, and having faith
in YHWH taking on the isomorphic forms of the surrender (like the salvation of the
prophet) leads into the same salvific promise addressed to those who surrender to
the king of Babylon. This correlation stems from an intertextual dialogue: on the one
hand, the promises made to Ebed-melech place his figure on the same thematic horizon
as the subjects who are called upon to surrender to Babylon, while on the other, the
motivation for the oracle of salvation addressed to him, that is, his faith in YHWH,
focalises the essentiality of the symbolic-prophetic dimension of the Jeremianic message about "handing oneself over to the king of Babylon".

The oracle to Ebed-melech gives rise to a decisive dimension of meaning in this
sense: surrendering is *not (only) a material fact*. Going out to meet the generals of the
king of Babylon because it is perhaps more politically convenient is not what matters (cf. 21:8–10; 38:1–3, 17–18, 20–23), nor should one build houses, inhabit them,
take wives, or raise children in exile for a mere economic calculation (cf. 29:1–7).
The question is not that of remaining in the land and not fleeing to Egypt for an
irresponsible underestimation of the risk-benefit ratio with respect to the threat of
Babylonian retaliation (cf. 42:7–16). Ultimately, it is one thing only: *to trust in God*,
taking on the meaning of the history revealed by him here and now. Ebed-melech
did not surrender or was not able to do so (and with him, probably a large part of the
population), but his gesture towards Jeremiah expressed the same central semantic-
pragmatic nucleus of "handing himself over to the king of Babylon". And perhaps,

---

91   Perhaps herein is the difference between the gesture of Ebed-melech and that of
Ahikam son of Shaphan, who was also responsible for the salvation of the prophet
in another dramatic circumstance, that of the forensic proceedings brought against
Jeremiah in ch. 26. According to 26:24, Ahikam intervenes in favour of Jeremiah *in
extremis*, and prevents him from being condemned to death. His position in the royal
entourage seems to be much more privileged than that of Ebed-melech. In fact, he
already has a leading role at the time of Josiah, when the scroll of the law is found in
the temple and the consultation with the prophetess Huldah becomes necessary (cf.
2 Kgs 22:12–14; 2 Chron 34:20–22). Jeremiah does not reserve for him an oracle similar
to that which he addresses to Ebed-melech, even if then, after the fall of Jerusalem,
we find a son of his, Gedaliah, elevated to the dignity of governor of the territory
of Judea at its base in the new political-administrative centre of Mizpah. Another
hypothesis: probably Ahikam, who should have already been elderly if he was one
of Josiah's ministers, had already died of natural causes or been deported with the
other notables in 597.

considering the complexity of the symbolic-semiotic references that structure the book of Jeremiah, neither the name or provenance of this character is a random fact.

Ebed-melech (עֶבֶד־מֶלֶךְ) means "servant of the king", and its obvious reference is to his role as a functionary of King Zedekiah. The nucleus of the Jeremianic message, on the other hand, consists in agreeing to "serve" (√עבד) another king, "the king of Babylon" (cf. 27–28). Which king, then, did Ebed-melech really serve when he forced the hand of Zedekiah so that the prophet who demanded the surrender to the king of Babylon would be freed? The question is not that of an explicit dimension on the level of the textual surface, but rather of a reorientation of the transitive action implicated by the verb "to serve" (√עבד). A reorientation in the right direction.

Another aspect: Ebed-melech is also called "the Cushite" (הַכּוּשִׁי), that is, "the Ethiopian" (39:16). The salvation of Jeremiah in the case of 38:1–13 comes not from a compatriot of his, but, in fact, from a *foreigner*, who Zedekiah had *listened to*. Similarly, the salvation of Jerusalem depends on obedient *listening* to *another* through whom YHWH speaks (Jeremiah; cf. 38:20) and on submission to another foreigner, the king of Babylon. But "foreigner" or "stranger" is also the meaning of the surrender for an exclusively formal reading of the texts we have studied, a meaning that nevertheless asks for the right of citizenship in the hermeneutical act. For it is this "foreigner" who saves Jeremiah and with him, the very hermeneutical act, by proper discernment of the prophetic word. And so thus, the POC is also configured as an "emergence/emergency", again in the dual sense of *urgent appeals* to respond to on the interpretive level, and *explications* of a "foreign" meaning that consigns itself in the symbol, a meaning perhaps not immediately visible, but expression of a significative, prophetic option.

5.3. It is the acceptance and concrete manifestation of the meaning of history (revealed by God here and now)

The insertion of the POC in the narrative dimension of the Scripture, which, along with P. Beauchamp, I intend as not divisible in individual isolated episodes but as a "total narrative" that strains towards Fulfilment, is strictly tied to an approach to the mystery of the revelation that is centred on the dynamics of the signification of the *symbol* itself. The value of a story is not reducible, in fact, to its possible conceptual translations. The narrative system, made up, above all, of images in movement, assumes the open structure typical of the symbol and its inexhaustible provocative force for the hermeneutical act. No formulation can exhaust what is evoked in it, no speculative objectification can, on par with the symbol, make present and accessible the mystery of God's communication to humanity. However, it is the very nature of the prophetic word, as we have seen, to convey the centrifugal, polysemic force of the symbol towards a concretisation of meaning, indicated in a specific and multilevel reality like the "symbolic-prophetic" gestures (cf. § 5.4). In our case, it is the choice to "hand oneself over to the king of Babylon".

A POC is thus given, both within and outside of the biblical narrative, when it can be recognised that a specific divine intentionality invests a specific choice, attitude, or life option with a symbolic-prophetic valence able to adequately signify (i.e. in a "prophetic" way) *the meaning of a time, event, situation, or entire story revealed by God*. Through the structuring and indication of a POC, in other words, God addresses the individual, providing them with the criteria of intelligence of their collocation and existence in that history.

The obedience of faith that is at stake in every POC is therefore an intrahistorical act that has, at the same time, the ability to both signify and to (re)configure its own positioning within the relational perimeter of the Covenant, as well as to signify the concrete acceptance of the meaning of the (present) history revealed by God for the same recipients of the prophecy in a given spatial-temporal context. It is a free assent to what YHWH has operated or is operating in significant and decisive events here and now, events that actualise the profound meaning of the founding stories of the faith and identity of Israel. In the specific case of the surrender to Babylon, what is in question, in some respects, is the overturning of those originary events through the signification of the recognition of a history of failed alliance, the acceptance of just punishment for their own faults, and of the *end*, even if in the symbol. The specification of the semantic and pragmatic density contained and condensed in this symbolic-prophetic gesture has been the object of my investigation.

The POC therefore presupposes a *discernment* of a *prophetic* nature, because it is precisely the prophet who is able to perceive the Invisible in action in the history that is visible to all. It need be underscored here that the definition of "prophet" should not be limited to the "classic" figure of the prophet typical of common imagination in reference to biblical texts. It has to do not only with those who indicate or call for a particular form of obedience in the name of YHWH, like the POC, but also – and from my point of view, for all the more reason – those who *recognise* the prophet as such, and receive the prophet's pretension to be abided as an indication of the true meaning of the history in progress, to be welcomed and lived. One is a prophet, by extension of the originary concept, who freely and consciously makes a Prophetic-Obediential ConSign*A(c)tion*. The book of Jeremiah, in my opinion, attests quite well to this phenomenon, of which P. Beauchamp could write:

> le prophète n'est que l'avant-garde d'un peuple où chacun est appelé à la même représentativité, au même contact immédiat avec la parole.[92]

To sum up what has been said in these last three paragraphs, we can see that, endowed with this semiotic-symbolic device, the very meaning of the word "history" takes on three different meanings, on three different, all interconnected, levels:

(a) history in the most common and generic sense, as a spatial-temporal dimension in which world events and the concatenation of human decisions occur;

b) history as the temporal unfolding of the Covenant between YHWH and his people;

c) history as a personal story in search of its meaning within the first two histories, profoundly interlaced between them.

The POC, therefore, indicated, requested, and assumed prophetically, indicates *to* a subject, or *for* a (single or collective) subject, the meaning of their personal history in a given segment of human history, the meaning of which is revealed in the light of the history of the Covenant.

---

92 P. Beauchamp, *L'un et l'autre Testament*, 92.

General conclusions (and apertures)
"But what will you do when the end comes?" (Jer 5:31)

Die Grenzen zwischen Widerstand und Ergebung sind also prinzipiell nicht zu bestimmen; aber es muß beides da sein und beides mit Entschlossenheit ergriffen werden. Der Glaube fordert dieses bewegliche lebendige Handeln. Nur so können wir die jeweilige gegenwärtige Situation durchhalten und fruchtbar machen.[1]

1. The whole meaning (of history) in a (symbolic-prophetic) gesture

1.1. Final synthesis: The gesture of surrender and its communicative context

In the global communicative context of the book of Jeremiah, which is dominated by the prospect of the end of Jerusalem, *the gesture of surrender to the king of Babylon should be understood as a "symbolic-prophetic choice" revealed by YHWH here and now that expresses and assumes the meaning of the history underway.* To surrender, therefore, means *recognising* the end of a history marked by the failure of the Covenant, *accepting* the rightful chastisement of God who reveals the relational truth of this situation, and *opening oneself* in faith to the possibility of a path of salvation that is destined, in a way that is undeducible, for a New Covenant. This is the result of my research in a nutshell. There are manifold hermeneutical implications of this assumption, starting from a renewed awareness of how relevant *contextual dependence* is for correct comprehension of every act of communication, and particularly those that are implicated, described, or elicited in the biblical text.

So taking a different perspective from those adopted thus far, I will start off by briefly mentioning the background horizon in which the Jeremianic call for surrender is collocated, that is, the *thematic context* through which its peculiar meaning can be inferred, exemplified, and illuminated starting with an oracle from the "first" preaching done by Jeremiah: 5:20–31 (§ 1.1). I will then, on a second level of complexity, explicate the results from my path of research that have stemmed from the thesis I have sought to sustain (§ 1.2), in any case bearing in mind that the whole third part of the present dissertation has already been dedicated to articulating the various aspects of my interpretative proposal in detail. In the paragraphs that follow (§§ 2–5), I will instead try to focalise some of its most important hermeneutical repercussions, while at the same time suggesting some new possible paths of inquiry to be explored. I will

---

1   From a letter by Dietrich Bonhoeffer to his friend Eberhard Bethge, written from Tegel Prison on 21 February 1944 (cited here from D. Bonhoeffer, *Widerstand und Ergebung. Briefe und Aufzeichnungen aus der Haft, eds.* C. Gremmels *et al.*, DBW 8, Gütersloh 1998, 334).

680   General conclusions (and apertures)

thus avoid simply reproposing the content of the conclusions of the various chapters (of the first and second parts of the dissertation), which can be referred to directly for the specific syntheses they offer.

1.2. The configuration of the background context: Facing the failure of the Covenant and imminence of the end

Human transgressions have upset the order of creation, evil has broken all bounds, and every limit is shattered. Brothers prey and are preyed upon by other brothers, the people of God have stopped fearing their God and live in houses filled with deceit, where falsehood resides undisturbed. The rights of the weakest are trampled; there are those who brazenly get fat and rich from an abuse of power. This is why, in the book of Jeremiah, YHWH exclaims, "should I not punish them?" in the face of such senseless perversion of justice (cf. 5:20–29).

Yet, something still worse contaminates the sacred space circumscribed by the Covenant, corrupting the very meaning of the founding event of the Exodus and the human-divine relations that originated from this. The whole earth is shaken. From the perspective of YHWH, the source of the Word of truth that reveals, saves, and frees, the facts are horrendous, frightening, and bleak ones: The proclamations of the prophets have been reduced to the propagation of falsehoods; they no longer prophesy in the name of YHWH but in the name of what is false (v. 31: בַּשֶּׁקֶר; and therefore, of Baal; cf. 2:8; 23:13). The priests, the guardians of the sacred themselves, are dependent on this and even more insane is that people *love* all this! (cf. 5:30–31).

In order to plant and build something new, first, the pre-existing order needs to be eradicated and demolished, especially if it is a perverse system based on a disorder with the intent of self-legitimisation obstinately rooting itself in the nerve centre of the sacred: This is what the vocational text of Jer 1:10 programmatically announced. This is why the decisive question in 5:31 extends from the impassioned oracular unit of 5:20–31 to the extreme opposite end of the book of Jeremiah: "but what will you do when the end comes? (וּמַה־תַּעֲשׂוּ לְאַחֲרִיתָהּ)". Literally: "but what will you do *at its end*?"

Is it the end of the land of God, forced to witness all this devastation? (cf. v. 30). The end of a well-being that bases itself on the malady of others? (cf. vv. 26:28; etc.). The end of the prophets and their lies? (cf. 23:9–40). Of the priests, of "faithful", and of "their" temple, having at this point become a den of thieves? (cf. 7:1–15; 26). The end of Jerusalem itself, the city of the promises made to the Davidic dynasty? Is it then the end of its king and its inhabitants? (cf. 7:34; 13:9–10; 15:7; 19:8–9; 22:6, 30; 36:30; etc.). In this indeterminacy, the horizon of the catastrophe gradually widens to assume the dimension of a totality. It is the *end of everything*, to be understood above all as a global crisis of meaning, for the disaster will fall upon "every flesh" (cf. 45:5). And, in fact, it will have to be faced by everyone and *in primis*, by the reader/listener of the book.

In reality, not all is lost: In the oracular unit (6:1–8) that follows, a glimmer can already be glimpsed. However, it will be only a potential path of salvation *in extremis* and under certain conditions: that there be placed no opposition or condition. The destruction will, in fact, irrupt from the North. Jerusalem will be stormed mercilessly. The generals of the enemy forces will hurl their armies against the City walls, day and night until they overwhelm it and decimate it. They have the permission of YHWH, for at this point, all that is in it is oppression and violence. To resist and wait for aid, human or divine, will be to no avail: Nothing is left but *to decide to go out from*

The whole meaning (of history) in a (symbolic-prophetic) gesture   681

Jerusalem, leaving behind, as indefensible, a city that is destined for punishment. For how can those who love evil be saved, if not by shattering the false promises of good in which they believe?

So "seek refuge, children of Benjamin, *outside of Jerusalem!* (מִקֶּרֶב יְרוּשָׁלַם): lit. "out *of the centre, of the middle* of Jerusalem" (6:1). Evil must disappear in its entirety, as at one time YHWH had decreed of the end, obliteration (*herem*) of the Canaanite cities imbued with idolatry and nefariousness. This call to leave Jerusalem, along with the invitation to sound the alarm about the oncoming disaster, is still accentuated with brusque, dashing impressionistic brush strokes, lacking precise contours, typical of the more poetic texts, as are most of those scattered throughout the first section of the book (1–25).

Already in ch. 21, however, as we have seen, this indication takes on the distinctive outline of a clear theological-political choice: For Jeremiah, it is necessary *to go out to encounter the generals of the king of Babylon and surrender* (cf. 21:8–10), precisely because YHWH is about to *turn back* the weapons with which the besieged try to counter the enemies outside the walls, in order to hurl them against the "*heart*", the "*centre*" of Jerusalem (cf. 21:4: אֶל־תּוֹךְ הָעִיר הַזֹּאת). In the second part of the book (26–45), in the narrative texts, the call for surrender will be more specified and contextualised. And an attentive reader will be able to discover, amongst other things, that precisely the territory of Benjamin will be spared from the Babylonian fury, becoming, along with the city of Mizpah, the new administrative centre and point of confluence for the survivors (cf. 40:6; etc.). To surrender here and now is therefore a *path of life* and *prophetic interpretation* of the meaning of the history in progress. But in the historical-theological context just outlined, a synthesis of what I have explicated in my study, what, more precisely, does that gesture actually mean? Let us look at it schematically.

1.3. The pragmatic orientation of the gesture: The surrender as signification and assumption of the meaning of history

The horizon of the end, whether this is understood as an enigma to be answered retrospectively, a looming divine threat, or an ineluctable punitive event, is sign of a *crisis of the Covenant* and is a *central thematic pole* of the book of Jeremiah. The undeducible possibility of *salvation* that starts precisely from this disaster constitutes the other, indisjointable aspect of the same polarity, which serves, along with the theme of the catastrophic fate of Jerusalem, as a principle of attraction and organisation for the entire work. At least at a certain point, in fact, the question is no longer that of avoiding catastrophe and death but rather of going through it trusting in God alone and in his prophet. It is an extreme possibility of salvation that is offered *within the disaster* and not prescinding from it, as the false prophets had instead envisioned.

The deliberate insistence on the *contextual dimension* and its expressive disposition of a "dramatic" nature that I have just presented again, according to a different thematic angle than that explored in the body of the dissertation and according to one of its possible levels,[2] intends to account for the pertinent historical-theological

---

2   The contextual dimension to which I have referred over the course of my research can be broken down according to different levels of pertinence: historical, literary, structural, pragmatic, etc.

682 General conclusions (and apertures)

scenario within which the Jeremianic call acquires its specific signification. This signification is not reducible to a solely *political-strategic* level. The injunction of "handing oneself over to the king of Babylon", in other words, is not to be understood as only a suggestion of a way to save the salvageable or indication of a strategy that, in similar cases, tends to be a reliable one. The interpretation, in my opinion reductive, of the surrender-option as a purely anecdotal fact dictated mostly by Realpolitik motives can only be founded on an a-contextual reading of the Jeremianic attestations limited, in fact, to its linguistic forms detached from their own (literary and pragmatic) context of reference.

Insofar as we have been able to define the relevant context of the prophetic Jeremianic communication, the meaning of the act of surrender has become increasingly clear. If, in the book of Jeremiah, a political event like the invasion of Babylon is read in a precise theological key, that is, as a punitive measure decided by YHWH because of Israel's infidelity (or for the salvific humiliation of the nations), it would seem congruous to expect that the political act of response to such an emergency, also desired by YHWH, should be understood according to analogous relational coordinates. For this reason, according to the data highlighted in my research, the act of "handing oneself over to the king of Babylon" in the horizon of the end of Jerusalem and in obedience to the divine command revealed in a *precise* manner by Jeremiah, is equivalent to placing a "prophetic choice" that *signifies* and *takes on* the meaning of the history in progress, redefining the roles of its protagonists: YHWH is the universal Lord, and those who surrender recognise this lordship and the intentionality of the actions he takes *hic et nunc*. We are in the *pragmatic* sphere of communication. More precisely, therefore, as can be inferred from the *communicative context* instituted by the entire book of Jeremiah, the question is that of configuring a "symbolic-prophetic" choice, which I have defined in a technical sense as a "Prophetic-Obediential ConSignA(c)tion" (POC).

On the fecundity of this *new hermeneutical category*, which helps to identify other devices of signification in other biblical texts, I will return later (§ 3). What need be highlighted now, on the other hand, is that in the prophetic injunction of surrender, the meaning of the history in place (a) is identified with a precise *content*, and (b) assumes a specific *modality* of expression.

a) Deciding for *submission* to Babylon and obeying the prophetic word, for the people of YHWH, means first of all r*ecognising* their sin to the core, *accepting* the consequent rightful divine punishment, and thus opening themselves to an unusual path of *salvation*. And even though they are outside of the Mosaic Covenant, the foreign nations are involved as well (cf. chs. 27–28), since the Jeremianic message takes on a universal valence (cf. ch. 25). The issue is that of accepting the humiliation of one's pride and due punishment for one's own misdeeds. But also, for these peoples in general, through the difficult passageway of submission (or of other equivalent symbolic forms), a salvific restoration is foreseen (cf. 9:24–25; 10; 18:7–10; 12:14–17; and chs. 46–49). The preponderance of Babylon itself will have a limited operational time, for it too will be, in turn, annihilated by still other powers (cf. 50–51). With the difference that, surging as a symbol of evil, Babylon will never again rise from its ruin (cf. 51:64).

The act of *surrender*, called for specifically in the imminence of the end, when Jerusalem is already besieged, intensifies that dimension of meaning. In addition to not

"What do you see, Jeremiah?" Contextual pertinence and interpretive cooperation   683

being an option of a merely strategic-political nature, it is not a choice reducible to an ethical-moral level, or a religious level that is cultish in nature, nor can it be confined on the rhetorical-didactic one. To surrender is *to accept* the failure of one's history of alliance with YHWH, *to renounce* the visibility of its promises, and *to open oneself* to the possibility that these can be accomplished in a whole new way. In this decisive time, all are called to a gesture of *self-consignment* and *dispossession*, and the prophet Jeremiah, first of all. The people of God, who had been born going out of Egypt with the divine gesture of liberation from the enslavement of the pharaoh, must now accept *voluntary enslavement* to another foreign ruler as the path to a new Exodus (only the most obstinate post-catastrophe rebellion will configure an actual anti-Exodus with a true return to Egypt). The event of the Exodus had been sealed by the Covenant and taking into secure possession of the land of Canaan, but now that the Covenant itself has been rejected by a history of infidelity that has reached a point of no return, the prophetic word that calls for actually renouncing the *land* as sign of the Covenant and fulfilment of the liberating journey of the Exodus, the *temple of YHWH* as a sign of his stable presence in the midst of his people, to the *Davidic dynasty* as a guarantee of political independence. According to the Jeremianic perspective, precisely by accepting God's punitive action as revelation of the gravity of the evil committed, one can access a paradoxical path of salvation that contemplates the promise of *mere possession of life* (life "as war booty") as an otherwise unthinkable possibility of a radical new beginning destined for a New Covenant.

b) The mediation of this complex signification is neither abstract faith nor an automatism detracting responsibilisation, but the physicality of a gesture invested with a symbolic-prophetic meaning. Jeremiah, by loading the (collar of the) yoke upon himself, proposes this by means of a *concrete symbolic gesture* (and, as I have pointed out, to conjugate gestural materiality and symbolic dynamics is by no means an oxymoron), sign of the requested enslavement to the foreign power. The anticipated response must be configured, in its turn, in the concreteness of a choice (political submission), which, in the final phase of the kingdom of Judah, while Jerusalem is under siege by the Babylonian armies, must translate itself into a *gesture of the body* (to leave Jerusalem and surrender to the enemy). Moreover, the corporeal dimension, with all its profound symbolic valences, had already been presented on the scene of the text starting from the vocational text of ch. 1, where the coincidence between the word of YHWH and the story of the prophetic body is established programmatically. We have seen this confirmed on several occasions, especially when Jeremiah "gave himself over" into the hands of men in the context of the Temple speech, and up until, when called for a last colloquy by Zedekiah (38:14–28a), he presented himself before the king (and the reader) as the *paradigm* of the human being *consigned* (to the enemies, in obedience to YHWH), and for this, *saved* (cf. 26:14, 24; 38:1–13).

2. "What do you see, Jeremiah?" Contextual pertinence and interpretive cooperation

The assumption of the book of Jeremiah as a complex phenomenon of (prophetic) communication, world of signs/symbols, and network of intertextual and extratextual references, has led me to focus my attention on the *processes of signification* and

684 General conclusions (and apertures)

inference that govern the interpretive act, making use of the most recent contributions that relate to the various fields of study involved. In particular, having focalised the fundamental importance of *contextual dependence* underlying the generative dynamics of the meaning restored the vocational text of Jer 1:4–19, and the entire Jeremianic semiosphere, with new hermeneutical strength.

Here I have emphasised the permanent invitation to *interpretive cooperation*, that is, incitement to dare an act of reading capable of combining the adventure "of thought and feeling",[3] critical rigour, challenges of the intuition, and patient assumption of the necessary demonstrative processes. Indeed, every textuality originates and is inevitably marked by the whole series of *presuppositions* that inhabit its author, and the cognitive horizon of the world in which it is inserted. These inscribe *white spaces* within the textual fabric that the correct interpretation of the reader/listener is called to later fill in, while remaining, however, within the limits set by the text itself. Only through this work of relational recomposition between the *said* and *unsaid* is the hermeneutical act realised in full.

"What do you see, Jeremiah?": the programmatic question addressed to the prophet-reader by God at the gateway to the complete Jeremiah work, already suggests, with its *dialogical dimension* and *recursiveness* (1:11, 12; cf. 15:19; 24:3), that action be taken to ("prophetically") identify, one time after the next, the correct criteria of *pertinence* to enable an adequate understanding of the self-revelation of God in history, in the words and life of the prophet, and in the very structuring of the book. The *ostensive-inferential* communication is therefore expressly thematicised, directing the reader's attention, from the beginning, to a whole series of clues, signs, and other phenomena of signification exhibited on the scene of the text, that await a referent capable of inferring the pertinent meaning in them. So let us see at least the main *levels of contextual reference*, with their respective specificities and the consequent hermeneutical effects on the theme of the surrender, which I have developed the most with my research.

2.1. The surrender and the literary context (between synchrony and diachrony)

2.1.1. Synchronic level

The current arrangement of the book of Jeremiah is undoubtedly one of its most complex and debated problems. To know whether the individual textual units (and therefore, also the various literary attestations of my theme) are simply part of a random and fragmented dissemination of traditions, insertions, and juxtaposed reworkings, aggregated without a unitary logic, or whether the whole thing is instead theologically oriented and regulated by structuring criteria is not irrelevant. My working hypothesis took this second direction and I believe I have pointed to several confirmative elements, which, in my specific case, also highlight the *strategic occurrence* of the theme

---

3 "Reading is first and foremost a perception of the gaze and of hearing, a delay on the sounds and colours of the word; but precisely this exactness of observation in the materiality of the text, amongst its particulars, opens up an interweaving of meaning and always implies an exploration of the invisible, in a conjoined adventure of sensitivity and thought" (translated from E. Raimondi, *Un'etica del lettore*, Bologna 2007, 32).

"What do you see, Jeremiah?" Contextual pertinence and interpretive cooperation   685

of the surrender and its considerable importance within the "hierarchy of *topics*"[4] of the Jeremianic work.

Certainly, the organisation of the work draws complex lines and implements ordering principles that include, but at the same time go beyond, those more suited to a modern Western sensitivity, such as the criterion of chronological arrangement. In this sense, if there are some conspicuous (or apparent) fractures (that go far beyond the relationship between the *fabula* and the *plot* established by the narrativity), it is precisely because on different levels, signs of *continuity*[5] can also be found. In the case of Jeremiah, we find ourselves not before a narrative plot (if not at the local level), but a positioning of major and minor units (as well as different genres and styles), connected remotely and more than a few times by a signification device that I have called a "*semiotic arcata*". Along the linearisation constituted by the textual signs that make up the Jeremianic "scroll", these are marked as "columns", significative thematic-formal references. After the "necessary failure" of a first reading founded on expectations too centred on the modern reader,[6] these invite the more attentive reader to trace and identify interpretatively those theological messages that turned out to inform the textual arrangement.[7] I have identified at least three fundamental areas of signification, which contribute to placing the act of the surrender (accepted or rejected) on the dramatic threshold that separates the path of life from that of death:

a) The most important semiotic-"redactional" intentionality concerns the polarity between the theme of the *end* and that of the *new beginning*, replicated at different levels. This proves to exert a decisive force of attraction and organisation, especially in the second part of the book (chs. 26–45), where it places the pole constituted of chs. 30–31 and 32–33 (nucleus of the subsection of chs. 26–35)

---

4   Cf. U. Eco, *Lector in fabula*, 91.

5   Besides, as is rightly observed by H.-G. Gadamer in response to J. Derrida (in an "improbable dialogue" between deconstruction and hermeneutics from 1981; I refer in particular to H.-G. GADAMER, «Und dennoch: Macht des Guten Willens», in: *Text und Interpretation*. Deutsch-französische Debatte mit Beiträgen von J. Derrida, Ph. Forget, M. Frank, H.-G. Gadamer, J. Greisch und F. Laruelle, *ed.* P. FORGET, UTB 1257, München 1984, 59–61), on the level of a text's coherence of meaning, one cannot speak of discontinuity or breakage (nor is it possible to give space to the communicative effect typical of works of art, produced precisely by the effect of breaking predetermined boundaries) if not within an intelligible horizon of meaning, that is, presupposing a continuity as the starting point for the interpretation. As far as the Jeremianic work is concerned, this basic background horizon is given by the unity of the "book" of Jeremiah itself, regardless of its internal organisation attested in the different traditions (MT and LXX).

6   Picking up *mutatis mutandis* on what U. Eco asserts with regard to the apparent strangeness of *Un drame bien parisien,* a narrative text published by Alphonse Allais in 1390, we could thus say of the book of Jeremiah as well that "it was written to be read (at least) twice. The first, by a naïve reader, the second, by a critical reader who interprets the failure of the endeavour of the first" (my translation from U. Eco, *Lector in fabula*, 194).

7   As a working hypothesis, I will point out that, at least in the book of Isaiah, one could attempt an analogous inquiry, also because, in this case, it can be compared with the physical support of the important, ancient Qumran scroll 1QIs[a] (ca. 125 B.C.), structured in 54 columns that contain all 66 chapters.

686 General conclusions (and apertures)

regarding the announcement of the saving restoration and the New Covenant in relation with the pole of 38:28b–39:1–10, a unit dedicated to the description of the disaster of Jerusalem. Chapter 39 is placed at the centre of the second subsection (chs. 36–45) but it duplicates the same polarity again within it (cf., in particular, ch. I, § 4.2 for more details). In this case, we can speak of the establishment of *structural paradigms*.

b) The second polarity, this too in a certain sense of the semiotic-structural type, also reflects that previous, at the *narrative level* and according to *two complementary planes*. On the first plane, I identified in the person of the prophet Jeremiah himself and in some significant events that concern him, the relationship between the act of his "*handing himself over*" and consequent *salvation*. This is the configuration of the *narrative paradigm* of the human being "*handed over*" to others in obedience to YHWH and for this, *saved from death*, even in its symbolic form of defeat (cf. 26; 28; 38:1–13; 39:11–14 and also 43.6[8]). It is a paradigm of *proposal* of the act of surrender. On the second plane, this binominal constitutes another polarity in relation to the prophet's interlocutors, represented as paradigms of *response* (negative or positive, depending on the case: those who "hand themselves over" access the promise of life, those who do not, head for a disaster): Ebed-melech (cf. 38:7–13; 39:15–18), Baruch (36; 45), King Zedekiah (38.14–28a; 39.1–7), and the leaders of the people who survived the destruction of Jerusalem (cf. 42–43).

c) A third important *structural signification* was identified in the first part of the book (chs. 1–25) and, specifically, in the final unit given by chs. 21–24(25). Clearly contravening the chronological order with the text of 21:1–10, the theme of the end and the demand for surrender is stated in the series of oracles that relates to the final exponents of the royal house. Amongst the different semiotic *arcatas* that connect various texts at a distance, the two *arcatas* that, starting from 21:1–10 reach 23:1–8 and as far as ch. 24, ideally include all the final events of the kingdom of Judah within the polarity of the *end* and the extreme possibility of *salvation*. In this sense, the call to surrender can be understood as the "*first*" word that expresses the meaning (and is to be taken on as such) of a whole story of infidelity and relational failure. Only by starting from an acceptance of the resulting disaster that reveals this situation can something new be born, and this positive aperture will be the *last* word of unit 21–24 (cf. 24) and the final seal put on the whole book of Jeremiah (cf. the sign of the reinthronement of the king Jehoiachin in 52:31–34).

2.1.2. Diachronic level

While my research perspective has privileged the final, or rather current, text of the book of Jeremiah according to the MT, it did not seem appropriate to ignore those hypotheses of compositional history having proximate or immediate repercussions on the theme of the surrender. According to a classical approach of literary criticism, in fact, which can be traced back at least to the classification by "sources" proposed by S. Mowinckel, the most "original" Jeremianic texts should be found amongst the "poetic" ones in the first section of the book (1–25), while the narrative parts,

---

8 Although in this case, the salvific perspective is guaranteed only for Baruch, in light of 45:5. The fate of Jeremiah remains a mystery.

"What do you see, Jeremiah?" Contextual pertinence and interpretive cooperation   687

positioned above all in the second part (26–45), would be considered "secondary". Even the prophetic injunction calling to "hand themselves over to the king of Babylon" should be seen as a thematic that occurred late with respect to the oracular content.

Today, one can see the structural crisis that the conceptual distinctions of "originality"/"non-originality" and between "poetry" and "prose" (and not only for the book of Jeremiah) have undergone. It is virtually impossible to distinguish in the biblical text supposed original sayings from subsequent reworkings, nor can a truly clear distinction be drawn between communicative units on the basis of literary registers that are more suited to our culture than to the Semitic one. Therefore, even establishing a chronological-authorial precedence of "poetry" versus "prose" suffers the same underlying problem. Amongst other things, as I have noted, the theme of surrender can already be glimpsed in the "poetic" oracles placed in the first chapters of the book (cf. 6:1–8, 22–30; cf. also ch. 25), and the first explicit instance of the theme is found in the first section (1–25), in a text (21:1–10) of which I have highlighted the notable hermeneutical implications. The ordering principles (or great "attractors") that I found highlighting the phenomenon of "semiotic *arcatas*", which pertain to the whole book on different levels, cause me to lean towards considering the Jeremianic work to be a substantially unitary reality, invested by a global communicative intentionality of a semiotic-structural nature.

In addition to the above, I have looked at how the recent contributions on this subject by M.J. de Jong completely overturn the classical perspective, and the note of "secondariness" with which the theo-political position present in several texts of the book of Jeremiah has often been marked. This scholar, basing himself on a comparativist methodology that is, in my opinion, not free from problematic issues,[9] believes that the indication regarding submission to Babylon can be safely traced within the function of guaranteeing the state and its institutions ("pro-society") typical of those historical forms of divinatory-prophetic mediation attested (very scarcely, in truth) in the context of the ancient Near East.

In this sense, the message of surrender would be the one announced by the "historic" Jeremiah, but with a merely practical interest with respect to the "well-being" of the state. The implausible threat (according to M.J. de Jong) of the end of the kingdom of Judah (also found in other prophets) would instead be only the retro-projection of a condemnation addressed indiscriminately to the society (and prophets) of the pre-exile by post-exilic intellectual circles. It should be remembered that this position takes its cues from a series of more dated contributions from other scholars (starting with K.-F. Pohlmann, C.R. Seitz, and C.J. Sharp) already oriented towards making distinctions

---

9   Undoubtedly, more than a few times, the phenomenological models elaborated with a comparativist methodology, which are used in the field of historical research (and that of the history of religions, in particular), can have and have a heuristic valence. Generally, however, it is necessary to proceed with great caution. The risk (amongst others) is that of reducing the unprecendented or immeasurable to the already known (and of forcibly "normalising" every exception, not only those that only are so in appearance), driven perhaps by an attraction to the procedure that is typical of experimental scientific disciplines, which seek to identify regularities in order to then trace back to the laws that determine them. Properly understood, comparitivism can help, on the contrary, to make the specific differences between the objects of study stand out (and thus, be studied).

688 General conclusions (and apertures)

and antithesis, in my opinion with excessive confidence, between various texts that would have been elaborated in a self-legitimative function by two different competing communities: the exilic (pro-Babylonian) one and the Jewish (pro-Egyptian) one that remained in the land after the Babylonian war operations.

While frictions and contrasts between the two communities are clearly attested (cf. Ezek 11:14–21; 33:23–29), amongst the corollaries to my research, many reservations derive with regard to such positions of literary criticism, especially in reference to the common criterion of theo-political "homogeneity" (affirmed or denied for selected texts), which would lead to the identification of a supposed pro-Babylonian party in opposition to a pro-Egyptian one, as well as to the presence of texts attributable to just as many underlying communities of transmitters in polemical opposition to each other within the book of Jeremiah itself. The not random complexity of the book's communicative system at the literary level, along with the fact that *the necessity of surrender concerns everyone* as a paradoxical path of "well-being", both the community formed in Babylon after 597 and the inhabitants of the kingdom of Judah and Jerusalem before and after the catastrophe, suggests the inadequate pertinence of these categorisations and a farewell to the political-religious criterion of *self-legitimisation* (through counterposing scribal manipulations) as an intentional, predominant subtext for the tensions or internal "contradictions" within the Jeremianic work.

Furthermore, assuming (and not conceding[10]) that the current composition of the book of Jeremiah should be placed around the fourth century (G. Fischer) or, for others, even later, it is not clear[11] to what political-religious end it would have served to

---

10 Think of the position of J.-H. Stipp, which I share, when he focalises Jeremiah's positive attitude towards Jerusalem: "One wonders what purpose this kind of eulogy could have served after the Babylonian empire had begun to crumble, let alone after its collapse. What we read here is much easier to motivate in an environment where the author was keen to soften the feelings of his addressees toward a Babylonian rule hat was firmly in place; in other words: where he wanted to promote a cooperative attitude towards those who continued to be their overlords. This, however, presumes a situation in which the Babylonian power still seemed invincible, which once again points to a date of origin in the early phases of the exilic period" (ID., «The Concept of the Empty Land in Jeremiah 37–43», 103–154 [here, p. 133]). See also K. SCHMID, «How to Date the Book of Jeremiah: Combining and Modifying Linguistic- and Profile-based Approaches», *VT* 68 (2018) 1–19.

11 The analogies alluded to by M. OEMING, «"See, We Are Serving Today" (Nehemiah 9:36): Nehemiah 9 as Theological Interpretation of Persian Period», in: *Judah and the Judeans in the Fourth Century B.C.E.*, eds. O. LIPSCHITS – G.N. KNOPPERS – R. ALBERTZ, Winona Lake 2007, 571–588 (on p. 581) seem weak to me because the context is too different, even if here one could open a path for a more detailed demonstration and evaluation on the topic. Even this author, in any case, believes that in the book of Nehemiah, as in those of Jeremiah and Ezra, objectives are not pursued for motives of propaganda or political-religious polemics (which, here, would be pro or anti-Persian): "Let us return to the beginning of this essay: is a text such as (Ezra and) Nehemiah entirely Persian propaganda? Considering the theological-religious dimension of the text described above, I believe it to be informed by a profound, almost radical piety. Whether this piety is pro-Persian or anti-Persian is not of primary importance. If we reduce Jeremiah's message to the statement that he was pro-Babylonian, then we will not have understood much of what Jeremiah was trying to say" (p. 583). In the same perspective see, more recently, the observations by

"What do you see, Jeremiah?" Contextual pertinence and interpretive cooperation   689

insist upon the need for submission to the Babylonian power (which already collapses with Cyrus in 538) when, with the Persians, an era of tolerance unfolds and, in the land of Israel, the Jewish community of the Second Temple is formed. This is not to mention, then, the Hellenistic period, definitely a theatre of violent oppression in the late era, but nothing at all comparable to the Babylonian domination. With the persecution of the Seleucid ruler Antiochus IV Epiphanes (187–163), the options become either that of *passive resistance*, that is, martyrdom, or *violent resistance* of organised rebellion.[12] In this context, the figure of Jeremiah referred to certainly does not invite surrender, on the contrary. In the tradition attested in 2 Mac 15:14–16,[13] if Jeremiah is still a *great intercessor* (though his intercession is denied several times in 7:16; 11:14; 14:11; cf. 15:1),[14] his political alternative is that of the *sword* ($\dot{\rho}$ομφαία). It is the exactly the opposite of the position attested in the book of Jeremiah (cf. e.g. 5:17^{LXX}; 6:25^{LXX}; 45:2^{LXX}; 49:16–17:22^{LXX}; etc.), even if, on closer inspection, in the light of the POC (cf. § 3:2), this indication of the Maccabean Jeremiah could also be the most correct "prophetic" translation of the call for surrender at the time of the Babylonian threat, since different situations and periods require different readings of history.[15] In this sense, an additional interesting path of reflection would be opened by comparing the late revival of the "orthodox" Jeremiah made by the book of Baruch, and investigating the nature and purpose of this re-presentation of the Jeremianic message of submission to Babylon (cf. Bar 1:11–12; 2:20–24; 6:2).

The fundamental fact that emerges from my study is, in any case, the full citizenship of the *theological question about the meaning of the end* within the textual perimeter and throughout the history of the composition of the book of Jeremiah. It is an instance of meaning and discernment that ultimately constitutes its very origin (in an era, in my opinion, very close to the facts, in the nucleus of its source tradition) and the driving

---

J. GOLDINGAY, *The Book of Jeremiah*, 17–20, who rightly remarks: "Whereas 'Whose interests does it serve?' has become a familiar question in the West in the context of conflicts over the past century, perhaps we are imposing it on Ezra and Jeremiah, and people were less preoccupied by power then modern Western people or could disagree without being in conflict" (p. 19).

12   Cf. J. SIEVERS, «Widerstand und Ergebung in den Makkabäerbüchern», in *Martyriumsvorstellungen in Antike und Mittelalter. Leben oder sterben für Gott?*, eds. S. FUHRMANN –R. GRUNDMANN, AGJU 80, Leiden – Boston 2012, 69–84. Precisely because it is resistance and refusal to submit to the impositions of foreigners, it does not seem altogether fitting to me to intend martyrdom as an act of surrender (cf. p. 82). See also A.E. PORTIER-YOUNG, *Apocalypse Against Empire*. Theologies of Resistance in Early Judaism, Grand Rapids 2011.

13   This is how the prophet is presented: "[14] Then Onias answering, said: «This man is one who loves his brothers, he who *prays* (προσευχόμενος; cf. Jer 39:16^{LXX}; 44:3^{LXX}; 45:2, 4, 20^{LXX}) much for the people and for the Holy City, Jeremiah, the prophet of God». [15] And Jeremiah, stretching out his right hand gave to Judas *a golden sword* ($\dot{\rho}$ομφαίαν χρυσῆν) pronouncing these words as he gave it: [16] 'Take the *holy sword* (ἁγίαν $\dot{\rho}$ομφαίαν) as a gift from God; with this *you shall destroy* (θραύσεις; cf. Jer 28:30^{LXX}) your enemies'."

14   Cf. B. ROSSI, *L'intercessione nel tempo della fine*.

15   Indeed, the Babylonian power did not intend to impose, as instead occurred under Antiochus IV, a repudiation of the traditions of the Fathers and therefore a rejection of the *Tôrâ*.

690 General conclusions (and apertures)

force that has allowed it to pass through the centuries, ever reaching and generating new readers troubled by these same questions. For after all, nothing is more timely and urgent than *crisis*, in all ages. And no one is more worth listening to than those who, from a crisis that plunges them into the anguish of death, came out alive.

2.2. The surrender and the pragmatic-cognitive context of the communication

I have taken it on and implemented it as the fundamental hermeneutical principle of our journey: *words are not enough*. And at times, to communicate, they don't even serve at all.[16] In other cases, even when one formally masters the same vocabulary as the communicative source, serious misunderstandings take place, since the same term can express different or completely opposite ideas or nuances, depending on the selection of different contexts of use, and on the presuppositions implied.

> Studiare i presupposti e i sottintesi, essere in grado di riconoscerli, stanarli, formularli esplicitamente è aumentare la nostra capacità di comprendere testi. È inoltre aumentare la nostra capacità di usarli, per apprendere le informazioni che ci danno ma anche, eventualmente, per metterli in discussione. Infine, è aumentare il nostro controllo sulla nostra stessa comprensione, ricondurla a delle regole, perché il riconoscimento di impliciti può e deve essere motivato.[17]

Some exegesis still struggles to recognise that the hermeneutical act turns out compromised if it limits itself to a purely formal inspection of grammatical, lexical, and syntactic data. The contribution of the linguistic dimension of communication is inextricable from the extratextual experience of the world, nor can it offer semantics that are not, at the same time, also pragmatics.[18] Concepts can not only find expression regardless

---

16 Cf. C. Bianchi, *Pragmatica cognitiva*, 216–217.
17 "To study the presuppositions and implications, be able to recognise them, flush them out, formulate them explicitly is to increase our ability to understand texts. It is, moreover, to increase our ability to use them, assimilate the information they give us, but also, potentially, to question them. In the end, it is to increase our control over our own understanding, bring it back to rules, because the identification of that which is implicit can and must be motivated" (translated from M. Sbisà, *Detto non detto*, 5).
18 It would seem that a misunderstood need for "scientific rigour" based implicitly on the communicative model called the "code model" has placed the exegete with regard to the biblical text (above all in reference to those passages which stage conversational exchanges, as in the case of the theme of the surrender) in a situation analogous to that of a person with Asperger's syndrome (a high-functioning autism) when they find themself engaged in understanding a sentence in a precise communicative situation. In fact, the situation is probably even worse. If, indeed, the exegete excludes *a priori* a meaning different from that of the explicit supposed "conventional" semantic meaning of the phrase (according to a very reductive idea of context), then they also preclude its correct comprehension, which derives only from a correct pertinentisation capable of going beyond the linguistic dimension. In the case of Asperger's syndrome, on the other hand, the person realises that an *inferential approach* is necessary, but also that they cannot manage to immediately access all the pertinent *presuppositions* involved (as neurotypical people usually do naturally) and so they must thus activate strenuous and not very productive processes of interpretation, attempting to test all the various congruous contexts possible with respect to the

"What do you see, Jeremiah?" Contextual pertinence and interpretive cooperation   691

of "technical" terminology and be determined on the basis of pertinent intratextual contexts, but are also communicated thanks to the encyclopaedic competence of the participants in the communicative event (whether this be oral or written). Ultimately, understanding meaning is a process of *recognition of intentions*, since "il senso di una espressione linguistica dipende dall'*uso* che dell'espressione si fa – dipende da ciò che con quell'espressione si vuole fare".[19] I have therefore abandoned the so-called "code" model, to adopt, when necessary, the basic approach typical of the *inferential model* or of "pertinence" (Relevance Theory). Let us now look at the most important implications that have derived from this.

2.2.1. The historical-literary context

The point of departure for my research has always remained the text. But the text itself, as an event of communication, as I have just called to mind, has proved to be traversed in every one of its expressions by presuppositions that refer to the extratextual dimension as to the reference necessary to provide for the constitutive fragmentariness and incompleteness of the linguistic meaning. The question of the historical context in relation to the theme of the surrender has highlighted this in a particular way.

The literary context of the book of Jeremiah abounds with explicit and implicit references to *knowledge of the world*, both that of the intradiegetic interlocutors and of the empirical author. The pragmatic perspective with which to take into hand the question of "historicity" in relation to the Jeremianic work and the weaving of this with its literary dimension has therefore appeared to me to be a promising path. In this sense, I could say that it is precisely the recent shift in paradigm, which has moved researchers' interest from the historical Jeremiah to the text of the book of Jeremiah (or to the "Literary Jeremiah"), that actually favours a critical return to questions regarding its historical anchoring. This can be studied at least on three levels, which I have borne in mind in the attempt to contextualise the Jeremianic call. This is necessarily integrated into a specific geopolitical scenario and presupposes an encyclopaedic knowledge of the world that, even while far from us, is clearly defined, and which can be the subject of diversified inquiries.

---

communicative situation underway. In this way, a dear, young friend speaks of his cognitive experience in one of his precious testimonies: "In the situation of a dialogue, one is required to mentally process an infinite amount of detail as quickly as possible and then discard the vast majority of it. The few significant details recognised must then be assembled, like a puzzle whose number of pieces is not known. As a result, one never knows whether the mental idea built is complete and effective enough to trigger context-appropriate behaviours. If the situation has already been experienced, we can imitate an already memorised model, otherwise, such a dramatically inductive mental process is truly dispersive and ineffective. That is why, in new situations, I am often mistaken in my behaviour" (translated from F. DE ROSA, *Quello che non ho mai detto. Io, il mio autismo e ciò in cui credo*, Cinisello Balsamo 2014, 44).

19   "The meaning of a linguistic expression depends on the *use* made of the expression – it depends on what one wants to do with that expression" (translated from C. BIANCHI, *Pragmatica del linguaggio*, 20). In this sense, "it is a founding thesis of the pragmatic perspective that enunciations have no conditions of truth determined in the abstract, once and for all beyond all contexts" (cf. *Ibid.*, 123–126; here, from p. 126).

692   General conclusions (and apertures)

a) Even though there are many clues scattered throughout the narrative texts that would suggest they be accounts by either direct or very close testimonies to the events themselves,[20] the intrinsic difficulty of investigations of this kind remains unaltered, despite the interest in them, and my attention has privileged a different perspective. That is, I have not dealt with the question of the historicity of the figure of Jeremiah, but have rather raised the problem of subjecting the Jeremianic indication to surrender to an *assessment of historical plausibility*.

Interpreters of Jeremiah often speak of the surrender-option as a happy strategic choice, as the best suggestion could be given to guarantee the salvation of Jerusalem. Submitting to Babylon first and then surrendering, once the siege has been laid, seems, in other words, the most logical and recommendable action that could be encouraged in the face of the overwhelming enemy power. The results of my research dispute this univocal attribution of *realism*. I emphasised, above all, the influence of prophetic figures in the decision-making circle of the institutional figures itself. Cross-checking biblical data with those extracted from extrabiblical sources from the ancient Near East, it became clear that the act of surrender, while in itself a way to negotiate conditions for survival (sparing the enemy further losses in terms of men, time, and means) was not at all a sure way to guarantee the salvation of either a besieged city or its leaders. Sometimes, of course, the outcome could be positive, but other times, completely catastrophic. In the case of Jerusalem then, due to the phenomenon of the *escalation* of the local conflict (in relation to the antagonistic pushing and shoving between the Babylonian and Egyptian empires), the hope that an act of surrender could have saved the situation had to be quite meagre. This would also account for the fact (within the book of Jeremiah), that the prophet appears to be the sole promoter of such an option, and that at least after 597 (the "time of Zedekiah"), there is no clear trace of the existence of any pro-Babylonian "party" in Jerusalem.

b) A historical-situational assessment cannot prescind from a focalisation of the impact of the Jeremianic message against the symbolic universe typical of the theological order upon which the ruling class of the time based its political positions. I therefore sought to investigate what were the essential assumptions that could animate the prophet's opponents (and who were, concretely, his adversaries or sympathisers). In sum, the so-called "*theology of the inviolability of Zion*" can be identified as the ideological basis that stigmatised the subversive force of his message and therefore,

---

20   With regard to this and contrary to the well known, sceptical position of R.P. Carroll, in favour of the historical reliability of the book of Jeremiah, L.L. GRABBE, *Ancient Israel*, 209, expresses himself thus: "there are a number of statements in Jeremiah about external events that could be based only on contemporary knowledge". In the heterogeneity of the Jeremianic material, the author highlights that "it seems likely that some of the data there can be explained best as coming from a contemporary writer. Unlike 2 Kings, however, the information is not likely to come from a chronicle. Although it refers to international events on occasion, a lot of it is highly individual to Jeremiah or those around him. The best explanation seems to be that a contemporary of Jeremiah's did write some sort of 'biography' of the prophet. If this suggestion does not commend itself, any alternative theory has to take account of how the book has some statements that match what we know of the wider history of the ancient Near East at the time" (p. 210).

"What do you see, Jeremiah?" Contextual pertinence and interpretive cooperation   693

by contrast, the extent of its (anti-)theological nature. For the inextricable relationship between politics and religion that typified societies of the ancient Near East, even according to this historical-literary perspective, it was thus possible to evince the profound *symbolic valence* of the act of surrender.

c) One final aspect to underscore, linked to those previous, concerns the methodology of historiographic investigation in the biblical field itself. According to the pragmatic perspective of communication, the relationship between the world and the text is bidirectional. If, in the previous paragraph, I have highlighted the impact of the words (of Jeremiah) on the world of his time, in terms of precise calls to be translated into actions, facts, and history (but also, as repulsion and consequent persecution by his opponents), then what need also be considered is the *dramatic effect* of the wartime events, not least that which depended on the predicament of the siege, on the various textual attestations, direct or implicit, in all its expressions.

I refer in particular to the repercussions on the *emotional sphere* (think, above all, of the impact of *fear*[21]), an anthropological dimension of absolute importance that seems to me to have been programmatically excluded from the historical-literary reconstructions of biblists, probably in the name of a very problematic concept of "objectivity". With my work, I have sought to highlight the hermeneutical reach of this factor, particularly in the part related to historical contextualisation (ch. II) and in the exegetic study of Jer 38:14–28a (ch. V), where the theme of fear before the spectre of humiliation in connection to the surrender-option is explicitly thematised, inviting the reader who empathises with Zedekiah to formulate an implicit but clear act of faith ("God is greater than what you fear").

In the perspective indicated, in my view, a new way of studying biblical texts would open in relation to (real or fictitious) historical situations to which they refer. In the historiographic field, on the other hand, it is increasingly being highlighted how emotionality in general, and fear in particular, influences the constitution of those symbolic universes that concretely shape the history of humanity and the literary texts that refer to this.[22] Knowledge of the world is always (also) an *emotional* fact, mediated, that is, by a series of reactions caused by a perception of external stimuli. The scientific rigour of a historical reconstruction cannot consist in their being ignored, but in giving them voice and consistency, also because already, on their own, they tend to configure stable structures or "*emotional regimes*",[23] which, in turn, have serious factual repercussions manifested in the evidence of human choices.

---

21   In this sense, one can say that fear is "a powerful driving force in the history of humanity" and that "its spectre cannot be ignored" (J. BOURKE, *Fear. A Cultural History*, Emeryville 2005, xii).

22   Fear as a historical-political factor, in reference to the modern era, had already been written about by G. LEFEBVRE, *La grande peur de 1789*, Paris 1932 and J. DELUMEAU, *La peur en Occident (XIVe–XVIIIe siècles). Une cité assiégée*, Paris 1978. See, in this regard, V. GIRONDA – M. TOLOMELLI, «Introduzione. Storia e emozioni: costruzioni sociali e politiche della paura», *Storicamente* 11 (2015) 1–8 (with essential bibliography), who speak of an "emotional turn" in reference to a recent historiographic tendency determined "to lead emotions back into the flow of history" (translated from p. 3).

23   I refer to the *emotional regime* concept of the historian and cultural anthropologist William M. Reddy, who defines it as follows: "The set of normative emotions and the

694 General conclusions (and apertures)

2.2.2. *The surrender and its phenomenology, between language and encyclopaedic experience*

Having established that the lexical units that substantiate the plot of the Jeremianic text should be considered not as semantically closed and autonomous devices of signification, but as access points to a specific encyclopaedic cognitive patrimony, I have attempted to configure, on these foundations, a study also of a *phenomenological* type.

In the texts of 21:1–10 and 38:14–28a, the Jeremianic option takes the form and dramaticism of the act of surrender, and not only that of more generic political submission to the Babylonian power as in the less anguished context of chs. 27–28. This has given me the ability to develop the question in a targeted phenomenological study since the theological-political implications of the prophetic call are highlighted by its precise and concrete *factual* dimension. As was for the study of the gesture of the yoke in ch. 28 (and to which I will return in § 2.3 with regard to the symbolic dimension), I made use of the cognitive approach of *Frame semantics* in the general framework of the inferential model of communication, convinced that the linguistic dimension cannot be separated from the experiential dimension, which refers to the semiotic Echian notion of "encyclopaedia" (which postulates knowledge as a network configuration of interconnected cognitive units).

The most pertinent schematisations of the experience of the world (the "type scenes", or *frames*) made by the speakers placed on the scene of the Jeremianic text were reconstructed as extensively as possible by channelling textual and extratextual data coming from the OT and other attestations typical of the ancient Near East. The result was a complex, articulated framework that configures the surrender as an act (or *sub-frame*) which, in turn, can be broken up into a syntax of its own that is, at the same time, variable depending on the different situations, always included within the symbolic microcosm (*frame*) of war.

The characteristic vocabulary was found to consist not only of expressions of a technical sort, but also of phraseology referring both to locutors and to a specific gestuality aimed to account for the anthropological-relational dimensions implicated. The figure of the enemy, event of war, scenario of the siege, imbalance of forces in the field, possible negotiations, risk of succumbing, desire for salvation, terror, all these emergencies of the human being contribute to determine a *pragmatic of surrender* and therefore, a more pertinent contextual framework to understand the message of Jeremiah. Amongst the most important characterising elements, I will note those of going out from the besieged city and the going towards humiliation, expressed with a gesture of prostration that shows recognition of one's inferiority and the superiority of the adversary. The distinctive trait of the surrender in the book of Jeremiah is without a doubt that of "handing oneself over", expressed in the act of leaving Jerusalem to accept submission to the yoke of the foreigner (with a possible dual, ambivalent *frame* of reference to animals and to the world of war).

---

official rituals, practices, and emotions that express and inculcate them, a necessary underpinning of any stable political regime" (W.M. REDDY, *The Navigation of Feeling. A Framework for the History of Emotions*, Cambridge 2001, 129).

2.3. The surrender in the context of the symbolic-pragmatic communication

2.3.1. Symbolic gestures and digital communication

Another area of detailed contextual study has been identified by my research, in the *non-verbal* register of the so-called "*symbolic gestures*" of the prophets, which are not mere rhetorical tools, but often also paradigms of revelation, as well as practices of radical protest and a breaking of communication and social conventions, suitable especially for rough times of the relational crisis between YHWH and his people, times that demand a decisive change of perspective on the on-going reality. This is a phenomenon that for a long time has been little studied by biblists, and that, still today, risks being undervalued, probably because at the "quantitative" level, its attestation is not comparable with that of the oracles (or narrative texts) in which the verbal (or digital) dimension of communication dominates. The fact is that precisely the peculiar characteristics of symbolic-prophetic communication render the words for its realisation relative or entirely superfluous, and very few of them suffice to describe such acts. Certainly, coordination between gestures and words is often necessary and expected by the device of the "symbolic gesture" itself, but the activated channels of communication stay on two different levels.

As I highlighted studying chs. 27–28, the message of submission to Babylon is presented precisely through this (dual) form. The prophetic locution explains only later what is first of all communicated through the gesture of the "yoke". I therefore highlighted, on the one hand, a type of communication that is mainly "digital", that is, characterised by the discrete traits typical of the verbal medium, and on the other, a communication that is prevalently "analog", less suitable for conveying conceptual information but very effective in the *intersubjective relational field*. This is why, in this communicative context, the thematic pole of the "surrender" is configured as a *relational pragmatic of salvation*. The question is not only that of accepting or changing theological-political ideas or truths, but of physically engaging in *significative* relationships, that is, performing acts that "give a sign", indicating and assuming in a prophetic way the meaning of the history underway. In this case, putting oneself in specific relation with the king of Babylon according to the indications of the prophet Jeremiah expresses a new relationship with YHWH himself. And so it is understandable how, from a pragmatic point of view, not only can "saying" become "doing", but how also "doing" (i.e. performing a concrete gesture in history) can and does actually become "saying", that is, express and realise a *new type of relationship*. The path of salvation, therefore, as the study of 38:14–28a specifically and paradigmatically revealed, is a path of pragmatic communication.

2.3.2. Symbolic irradiations of the literality

The necessity of the surrender, as we have seen, was presented in chs. 27–28 with a symbolic gesture of great symbolic-semiotic significance. Its translation into a concrete political act cannot but recall, in turn, the wealth of meaning of the *symbolic dimension of the communication*. And this is where my interpretive proposal has been focused, that is, starting from a reclaiming of the *heuristic valence* of the symbol, understood not as an arbitrary convention or even a pure surplus of meaning with respect to a supposed "literal" significance of the enunciation, but as a provocation to thought, grafted constitutively in the materiality of the events and elements of the world.

If literal significance is not reducible to a series of mere linguistic operations capable of accounting for a (non-existent) neutral and objective meaning but is already given as an interpretive selection starting from a given context, then it makes no sense, in itself, to refer to a "literal" meaning of the surrender or to then reduce it to a mere sapiential-strategic fact or intentionality generically interested in the well-being of the state. I thus placed the theme of the surrender in relation with its more pertinent semantic-pragmatic contextuality, and then proceeded to identify the levels of symbolic and prophetic meaning.

The first step in this direction led me to enucleate, in the body of the literality of the surrender, some symbolic polarities from which polysemic semantic virtualities irradiate: in particular, the symbol of the yoke, the gate and walls of the City from which one is called to go out, the goods, the land and the loss of possession, the figure of the foreigner, with their gods and their being the principle (source, origin) of a kind of cosmic "order" that comes to disturb the theological-political balance of the kingdom of Judah. The phenomenology of the surrender and the reconnaissance of its main symbolic potentials thus provided a foundation for the next step, the one that allowed me to study the *semiotic-prophetic orientation* actualised by the Jeremianic message in a precise theological-political context.

3. The surrender in the context of the Jeremianic semiosphere. A new interpretive proposal

3.1. The surrender as a "symbolic-prophetic gesture" of response

Dissatisfied with the hermeneutical proposals tending, in fact, to reduce the Jeremianic theme of "handing oneself over to the king of Babylon" to an anecdotal level (both on the historical side and the generically theo-political side), I have laid the foundation, with the exegetic study of the texts most pertinent to the theme of the surrender, for a new interpretative proposal. My working hypothesis was the conviction that this could be more appropriately reapprehended only starting from the *inferential model* of communication, and only if inserted into the complex *semiotic-symbolic* system that governs the communicative exchanges within the book of Jeremiah. Amongst the polyvalent symbolic dimensions inherent in the gesture of surrender, the prophetic perspective, in fact, selects some aspects, channelling them in a precise content of signification offered to interpretation (within and outside of the world of the narration). And in this way, the gesture of the yoke becomes a semiotic device that joins the effusive richness of the *symbol* and the communicative precision of the (*prophetic*) *sign*. For this reason, I have preferred to speak of the so-called "symbolic gestures" of the prophets as "symbolic-prophetic" gestures, where the attribute of "prophetic" refers precisely to this semiotic operation.

If the message of the surrender is presented from the (logical-temporal) beginning, in 27–28, according to this communicative dimension, this is not only for didactic-rhetorical reasons but because the whole Jeremianic work invites entering into a world of signs to be interpreted and also assumed. After the semantic-pragmatic dimension, a subsequent level of contextualisation was then that of establishing a first exploration of the Jeremianic *semiosphere,* starting from the cognitive map offered by Jer

The surrender in the context of the Jeremianic semiosphere 697

1:4–19. Proceeding through subsequent identifications and differentiations, I traced the boundaries and main contours of that complex territory. In particular, I came to lay down an initial taxonomy of the so-called "symbolic gestures" contained in the book of Jeremiah and to support the plausibility of an interdependence on the same semiotic plane between the gesture of *the call* to "hand oneself over to the king of Babylon" expressed by means of the yoke, and that of *the response*, to be carried out pragmatically by way of the act of surrender. It is in this sense that we can therefore speak of surrender as a "symbolic-prophetic" gesture of response: not because it is equivalent to the gesture of yoke, but because it is placed on the same *continuum* of signification that substantiates the dialogue between YHWH and his people in the context of the end of Jerusalem.

Loading himself with a yoke and its harnesses is not the act of a madman, but the prophetic interpretation of a history, a reference to submission to Babylon, a divine command. The surrender actualises that submission, signifying, at the same time, much more than a political act, since indeed, it also constitutes a symbolic-prophetic gesture (of another type) that presupposes and expresses obedience in faith to YHWH and acceptance of the meaning of the history in process revealed by him as a path of salvation through the crossing of a symbolic form of death. The matter is that of a typology of symbolic-prophet gesture that still has such peculiar characteristics as to merit identification through an even more specific categorisation.

3.2. The surrender as "Prophetic-Obediential ConSignA(c)tion" (POC)

Starting from the fundamental semiotic coordinates of access to the book, I have sketched some lines of inquiry for an *initial mapping of the Jeremianic semiosphere*, the specifications of which can already be indicated as a path for further, promising research. On this basis, I have identified in the Jeremianic call to surrender the configuration of what could initially be denominated an "obedience or symbolic-prophetic choice". With particular reference to the necessary revision of the current taxonomies by which the various "symbolic gestures" are classified today, this category emerges with an identity of its own that goes to structure a complex semiotic-symbolic device that I then more technically denominated as "Prophet-Obediential ConSign*A(c)tion*" (POC). The fundamental semantic axes of this category, to be understood in any case *prototypically*, can be synthesised as follows:

> The POC is a *choice* with profound *anthropological implications* (of a *historical-temporal, socio-affective*, and *dramatic* nature) signified through an *action*, perceived or described as *commanded by God* to the *prophet* or the *people* (usually through a prophet) *precisely* (not reducible, that is, to being only a winning political-military strategy, always-valid ethical-moral option, religious-cultual fact, or rhetorical-didactic device). This choice has the capacity to *express* and *actualise* a *significative and prophetic performant option* in relation to its own positioning within the relational perimeter of the Covenant in reference to the *meaning of the present history*, namely, it: a) realises, in fact, an *obedience of faith* through which one responds positively to God by rendering the relationship of Covenant alive and existant, and b) is actuated through a concrete acceptance of the meaning of the present history revealed by God for the recipients of the prophecy themselves.

698 General conclusions (and apertures)

The POC, as an interpretive category with heuristic valence, identifies a structure and dynamism of signification within a complex interweaving of communicative levels and channels. It gives unity of meaning and hermeneutical coordinates for a more adequate understanding of a semiotic-symbolic phenomenon, which in our case is the thematic of the surrender to the king of Babylon. While the gesture of surrender is a particularly representative example of this device, it is not alone. In my opinion, in fact, several other examples of POC can be seen both within and outside of the literary perimeter of the book of Jeremiah.

Showing the consistency, attestations, and hermeneutical implications of the phenomenon on a larger scale was not and could not have been the scope of the present phase of research. A broader and more circumstantial study of the complex system of the Jeremianic semiosphere should (and, in my view, certainly could) demonstrate its full plausibility and descriptive fecundity. Even while outlining its appearance, conditions of possibility, and verifiability, I have therefore presented it as a *working hypothesis* within the context of the objectives of the present dissertation. On the basis of the exegetic analysis carried out on the texts pertinent to my thematic, however, I can affirm that I have already verified the presence of the typical elements established in the POC category and thus, the heuristic valence of this hermeneutical hypothesis.

3.3. The surrender and its isomorphic manifestations (Jer 29; 42–43:7)

If the category of POC can identify and make explicit even outside of the book of Jeremiah the meaning of particular processes of "self-consignation" that make a "sign" through precise "actions" of a prophetic nature (ConSign*A(c)tions*, in fact), it is within the very literary world with which I have dealt that we can identify at least two important *isomorphisms* of the act of the surrender requested by the prophet. These are two texts that I already included amongst those pertinent to the theme of the surrender (cf. ch. I, § 3.2), but which, at the end of our journey, can be reconsidered as candidates for specific study that has not been possible to carry out herein. Let us focalise just a few salient points:

3.3.1. Eradication: Accepting the end of a history to inhabit a new relationship with God

In Jer 29, Jeremiah addresses, in written form, the exiles of 597, that is, that considerable group of prisoners that Nebuchadnezzar had deported from Jerusalem along with the precious temple furnishings after the surrender of the king Jehoiachin. From the book of Jeremiah, it is not clear why Jehoiakim's successor surrendered to the Chaldeans. There is no prophetic injunction referring to an act of the sort, and a purely political motive can be presumed.

Yet, in the critical context of the time of King Zedekiah, the Jeremianic call for surrender, with its prophetic profile, also reaches this community, which, with the exile, had already experienced a form of "surrender" and had thereby already crossed the symbolic threshold of death. For Jeremiah, the need for submission to Babylon remains the same for these exiles as well, even if they would have had to formally express themselves in a different way. One can, in fact, have lost essentially everything,

The surrender in the context of the Jeremianic semiosphere 699

without still ever having really "surrendered" in a "prophetic" way (i.e. according to the nature of the POC). In this case, again, there are false prophets to not be listened to.

To signify, in this context, acceptance of the meaning of history in progress revealed by YHWH, this must be translated into a series of specific acts that express an acceptance of "eradication" (cf. 1:10; 18:7; 45:4) as God's just punishment for infidelity to the Covenant. It is necessary to build houses and live there, to plant gardens and await the fruits, to accept a life far from one's homeland by marrying and bringing sons and daughters into the world of a foreign country. And, above all, it is necessary to seek the well-being of Babylon, praying for this nation that holds the immediate responsibility for one's own captivity (cf. 29:4–9). Only in this way can one insert one's freedom into the salvific project of YHWH (cf. 29:10–14), which, as he has uprooted so can he plant and build a totally renewed relationship with his people (cf. 24:6; 31:28).

3.3.2. Radication: Accepting to let oneself be planted anew in the land of the Covenant

In Jer 42–43:7, we are beyond the threshold of the catastrophe of Jerusalem. And yet, in spite of everything, there are still those who want to carry forth, in some way, the useless war against Babylon, in the name of hope or unrealistic rivalry. Gedaliah, the governor that the Babylonians had appointed over the survivors in Mizpah, is killed by deceit along with the garrison. The one responsible is Ishmael, a Davidic descendant (cf. 41:1). After seizing the population under Gedaliah's protection, he tries to lead her out of the land of Israel to the Ammonites, where he then takes refuge alone because a certain John, along with other leaders of armed gangs, intervenes to thwart his plan. At this point, though unrelated to the fact, the latter gather the people and prepare to flee to Egypt, fearing the revenge of Nebuchadnezzar.

After the storm of the "judgment" of God passed over Jerusalem, it seemed that one could begin to live again with the divine blessing on the land of the Fathers (cf. 40:12). Once again, however, a mortal danger must be faced. Once again, the question of discernment of the true prophetic word returns with regard to the Babylonian power and the meaning of the history in progress, although now, there are no other prophets on the scene to oppose Jeremiah. Once again, he is consulted and his message, presented by him solemnly as an event of revelation and not as a (heterodirected) opinion of a (pseudo) sapiential (cf. 43:2–3) nature, calls for *symbolic-prophetic obedience* (i.e. a POC) that translates the same fundamental theme of the "surrender" into a new gesture: it is necessary *to remain* in the land of Israel without fearing the Babylonians. If one wishes to enter into a new history of covenant, it is therefore necessary to allow oneself to be replanted by God in the "land" of the Covenant, which is obedient listening done "with all the heart" (cf. 1:10; 6:8; 12:15; 24:6–7). It is still necessary, that is, to "hand oneself over to the king of Babylon", and, once again, not because this would be the best possible strategy to avoid the worst (the danger of a ruthless retaliation is real), but to assume in faith the fact that YHWH has *now* (after the hour of "wrath") decided *to plant* and *to root* anew this portion of his people who survived the disaster and were not led into exile. For this reason, God himself commits to inspiring feelings of pity in the feared foreign ruler (cf. 42:12).

As I have noted, this important notation of divine intentionality sheds a retrospective light on previous Jeremianic indications: Surrendering signifies trusting in the Creator God and Lord of history who changes the hearts of human beings, directs

700 General conclusions (and apertures)

events, and reveals their meaning. But not without human free will: which paves for way for a series of repercussions on the theological level, which I will now mention.

4. Theological horizons on the threshold of the end

4.1. The urgency of the discernment, between true and false prophecy

The multidimensional complexity of the contextual horizon that I have studied calls into question, according to different perspectives, the interpretive cooperation of the reader/listener of the book of Jeremiah. On the intradiegetic level, everything is dramatised through the encounter and interpersonal confrontation between the prophet and his interlocutors, but it is in the clash between the opposing claims to prophetic authority on the part of Jeremiah and Hananiah (in chs. 27–28) in particular that the fundamental question is thematised: the urgency of *discernment between true and false prophecy*. This categorisation is not a fallacious one, introduced *ex post* in the book of Jeremiah with respect to the pre-exilic events to which it refers, but rather a problematic one innate to the biblical and extrabiblical phenomenon of prophetic communication.

In the theological structure of the Jeremianic work, however, given that the destruction of Jerusalem is a fact that has already happened in the moment the oracles are written or facts recounted, the recollection of the question is not reduced to attestations trapped in the past. Discerning remains an urgency *of the present*. The very existence of the book of Jeremiah is the result of an act of discernment conducted in the light of the Deuteronomic criterion of the *fulfilment* of the true prophetic word (cf. Deut 18:21–22). For this reason, proceeding through the reading beginning from ch. 1, it is clear that it passes from "what do you see, Jeremiah?", in fact, to the implicit "what do you see?" addressed to the interlocutors of the prophet, to ultimately reach the reader/listener of all times. With its complexity, the book of Jeremiah trains its interpreters to confront the complexity of the real. This is another way of saying that it can form other "prophets", other people capable of grasping the Meaning in its revelation *here and now*.

In the decisive clash between Jeremiah and Hananiah, the criterion of "fulfilment" is once again thematised, but with a series of interesting specifications that precisely concern the act of surrender. The Deuteronomic dictum enunciated a general principle but here, it is seen lowered into a historical juncture. It is precisely the dramaticism of this story that highlights its greatest limitation: it is a criterion that is only *retrospective*. But if it is *now* that one must decide, in the urgency of the present moment one cannot wait for the facts to unfold and then realise only in retrospect who was the true bearer of the divine word. The matter is one of life and death, not of intellectual curiosity.

On closer inspection, however, the criterion can somehow clasp even the *now* if it is assumed in its *scalar* or partial form. In the aforementioned episode, in fact, a word of Jeremiah (the death of Hananiah) is, in any case, fulfilled, and when the prophet finds himself before Zedekiah in the final, decisive colloquy, on which the fate of Jerusalem depends, other proofs of fulfilment have accumulated before the eyes of the king. The threat of the enemy from the North has come about, contrary to the words of the other prophets (cf. 37:19), Babylon has besieged the City (cf. 32:24), the

Theological horizons on the threshold of the end   701

pharaoh's army, from which salvation was hoped, had dissolved like a ghost, while the Babylonians returned to fight below the walls after a brief and illusory suspension of the warfare (cf. 37:3–10).

It is in the eyes of the reader, however, that another fact emerges with greater clarity: this very prophet who calls for the surrender, promising salvation in the name of YHWH, is a living *paradigm of the fulfilment* of this word. He himself, in fact, has repeatedly "handed himself over" and been saved (§ 2.1.1. b). And precisely in the confrontation-clash with Hananiah, as I have highlighted, he has been seen to be a man who agrees to "surrender" to defeat, entering the dark zone of the invisibility of the promises of God (marked even graphically, in my opinion, in the ancient Jewish manuscripts that I reported). Only by not retreating in the face of death and going through its *symbolic forms*[24] does one have access to life and that unusual victory whose spoils of war are life itself. Paradoxically Jeremiah does not carry out in the same external form that which he asks of others, that is, he does not surrender and hand himself over to the generals of the king of Babylon, precisely to demonstrate the semiotic-prophetic meaning of the act of surrender.[25]

4.2. For a theology of the history, between wisdom and prophesy

In a time of crisis and universal catastrophe, when the wonders (נִפְלָאוֹת) of the Exodus or great works (גְדֹלוֹת) of God have turned against his own people, and Jerusalem itself becomes the object of *ḥerem*, as the perverse Canaanite cities once had (cf. Gen 15:16; Exod 23:23; Lev 18:24; Deut 2:34; 7:2; 1 Kgs 21:26; etc.), the simple fact of staying alive should be regarded as the maximum aspiration possible (cf. 45:4–5). Yet, if the coming ashore of a crossing as dangerous and humiliating as is obedience to the Jeremianic call for surrender meant only obtaining life itself "as war booty" (לְשָׁלָל; cf. 21.9; 38.2; 39.18; 45.5), understood as a mere material fact, we would be before a rather modest promise

---

24   Cf. by contrast, e.g. other than Hananiah, also the prophet Uriah (cf. 26:20–23) and, above all, King Zedekiah (cf. 39:1–7; 52:1–11).

25   In this sense, it can be said that the act of surrender in the book of Jeremiah provokes a short-circuit in the argumentation by which, according to Jan Assmann, the theory of the so-called "Mosaic distinction" would find its foundation (cf. ID., *Moses der Ägypter. Entzifferung einer Gedächtnisspur*, München 1998 and *Die Mosaische Unterscheidung. Oder der Preis des Monotheismus*, München 2003). According to the renowned Egyptologist, the monotheistic revolution attributed to Moses would have given rise to a kind of "counter-religion", structurally violent and intolerant towards every other religious expression and consequently towards all other peoples, because in this would have been introduced (in addition to the usual polar categories of sacred and profane, pure and impure) the unprecedented contraposition between *true* and *false* (God and/or religion), and therefore between *friend* and *enemy*. As can be seen, the Jeremianic "claim" to truth does not at all translate into an identification of the other, the one who is different, that is Nebuchadnezzar and the Babylonian Empire as the "enemy" to fight, not even when Jerusalem is in fact attacked militarily and besieged. Instead of a hostile political attitude against the "enemies of YHWH", he asks, on the contrary, for submission to the servant of the god Marduk (saying that he is actually serving YHWH) and asks to pray for his well-being. For a critique of a more general theological nature, see J. RATZINGER, *Glaube, Wahrheit, Toleranz. Das Christentum und die Weltreligionen*, Freiburg im Breisgau 2003, 170–208.

702 General conclusions (and apertures)

and goal. Indeed, looking at it more closely, the guarantee of the naked possession of life in exchange for submission to a foreign power and renunciation of independence and national pride with its religious legitimation could be qualified, at least for those animated by great ideals, as quite a paltry option.

At the time of the Maccabaic uprisings (ca. 167–160 B.C.), surrender to the forced hellenisation amounts to betrayal, while facing death for sacred traditions is considered a great honour and example of encouragement for future generations (cf. 1 Mac 2:29–38; 9:1–22; 2 Mac 6:18–7:42; 14:37–46, even if the two books have different perspectives; cf. also the prodromes of the possibility of martyrdom present in Dan 3). In fact, the baton is passed on in the context of the second "end" of Jerusalem. During the first Jewish war (A.D. 66–70), according to the account of Flavius Josephus,[26] the Roman general Titus sought every way possible to convince the insurgents besieged in Jerusalem to surrender, given the senselessness of diehard resistance to the siege. Evidently, even though he considered those soldiers who had let themselves be taken alive unworthy to fight for Rome,[27] this did not seem to him like a *mors triumphalis*, while to the insurgents, it did. It was to all avail, however: the Second Temple was ultimately set on fire and Jerusalem suffered destruction. In the same context of war, the last rebels fought strenuously during the siege of Herod's fortress on the Dead Sea, to the point of self-inflicting death in order to not be dishonoured by defeat or surrender.[28] Of course, the historical reliability of the Flavian chronicle is disputable, but it is nevertheless a significant attestation of how the act of surrender could be seen as unacceptable in the name of values deemed superior to mere biological survival.

Jeremiah himself gives an eloquent demonstration of this. In the vocational context of Jer 1:4–19, like in the rejection of the call outlined in the most dramatic text of the Confessions in 20:7–18, the lexical expressions pertaining to the concept of "life", which are semantically underdetermined,[29] are best understood against the pragmatic background of the the war *frame* (cf. 1:17-19), but also in the light of the mysterious event of "coming into the world" (1:5; 20:13-18). The semiotic *arcata* traceable between the two texts is a notable hermeneutical provocation. If, in fact, in the first text, the creation of the human being in the womb, is *designated* from the most absolute origin by a *significant action* of YHWH, for whom it is indeed the life of Jeremiah itself, in his naked and primordial physicality incapable of speech (*in-fans*; cf. 1:6), that becomes the semiotic-symbolic (prophetic) device of the wealth of meaning of the divine word, then in the second case, on the contrary, it is the deprivation of the meaning (or lack of its perception) that makes the brute biological fact completely *senseless*, insofar as *insignificant*. It is evident that, in the painful Jeremianic experience,

---

26 I have dealt with this in the context of the category of "escalation" of the conflict in ch. II, § 3.3.2.4.

27 Cf. *Bellum iudaicum*, VI,7,362.

28 In reference to this episode, Ygael Yadin, ex-soldier and archaeologist, responsible for the most important excavation of Masada, conducted in the early days of the state of Israel with clear nationalistic intentions, "quotes the oath taken, in Masada itself, by the recruits of the Israeli armored units, who shout the verse of Isaac Lamdan: 'Never again will Masada fall!' " (translated from A. PAUL, «Masada: inchiesta su un suicidio collettivo», in: *Israele. Da Mosè agli accordi di Oslo, ed.* F. CARDINI, Storia e civiltà 46, Bari 1999, 163–182, here, p. 179).

29 Cf. C. BIANCHI, *Pragmatica cognitiva*, 180–183.

the mere willingness of life, deprived of all the value-related connotations considered indispensable, makes even non-birth invokable as a preferable situation. And yet, Jeremiah does not remove himself from history, but lives it to the full.

Indeed, the outcome of the act of "handing oneself over", expressly indicated in the book of Jeremiah, is a sort of zero point, almost a painful regress to the original nudity, a humiliation that makes *tabula rasa* of every human superstructure, however sacred and intangible it may be considered. But it is precisely here that its theological valence of a *sapiential* nature is revealed, both for the *foreign nations* and for the *people of God*. The universal and permanent dimension of the Jeremianic message is placed in the context of the exaltation of YHWH as Creator of the world, Lord of history, and thus solely responsible for every *translatio imperii* (cf. 27:5–7). If God is to carry on his work of "eradication" across the earth and misfortune to fall upon "every flesh" (45:4–5), even on Babylon, which seems irresistible, this means that every human power must recognise the time of its end, its intrinsic inconsistency before the divine lordship. It is a fact to be accepted, a fact of reality that repositions, according to justice, the creature with respect to the Creator. It is not just a matter of crime and punishment, if not for the fact that the dimension of guilt is somehow the daughter of an aberration of the gaze on the world and obfuscation of right knowledge of self.

As for the nations and the universality of the Jeremianic message, it can be observed that the inherent revelative purpose of a theology of history centred on the surrender is not that far removed from the gaining of awareness expressed in the famous incipit of *La crise de l'esprit* by Paul Valéry, written in the aftermath of the disaster of the First World War: "We others, civilisations, now know that we are mortal",[30] With the surrender, one would reach the same conclusion, definitely accepting a symbolic form of "death" as *finis historiae* but without passing however through the devastation of war (cf. 27:1; 38:17) or at least, without seeing war pass over it as with Jerusalem, which must be destroyed regardless (cf. 21:9–10; 38:2–3, 18, 23). Other than to the modern states, the reference of the author is *in primis* to the ancient times of the kingdoms of Elam, Nineveh, and Babylon. Not by chance. Since antiquity, as Emil M. Cioran noted in 1957, having in mind the recursiveness of the same sapiential lesson once again, in the gloomy scenarios of the Second World War, "every epoch is inclined to believe that it, in a certain sense, is the last"[31]: last for the fact that it is unconceivable for us, if not perhaps in the face of the evidence of the facts, that other models of civilisation can supplant us and do without us.

That is why such a strong bond is placed in the book of Jeremiah (and those who say bond, Plato recalls, say "analogy"), between the figure and the story of the prophet

---

30   «Nous autres, civilisations, nous savons maintenant que nous sommes mortelles». This phrase appears at the beginning of the first of the two "Letters from France" (*The Spiritual Crisis* and *The Intellectual Crisis*) that were published in an English translation in 1919 by the periodical *The Athenaeum*. The original French version was later printed under the title *La crise de l'esprit*, in *La Nouvelle Revue Française* (1919). My citation is from P. VALÉRY, «La crise de l'esprit (Essais quasi politiques)», in: *Œuvres*, ed. J. HYTIER, vol. I, Paris 1957, 988–1014 (here, p. 988).

31   "Chaque époque incline à penser qu'elle est en quelque sorte la dernière", from: E.M. CIORAN, *Essai sur la pensée réactionnaire. À propos de Joseph de Maistre*, Paris 1977, 49 (text originally published in 1957 as preface to a collection of writings by J. de Maistre).

704 General conclusions (and apertures)

from Anathoth, between Jerusalem and the nations. Often, only on the brink of the end, to cite P. Valéry again, is it possible to realise that a civilization, a kingdom, a City, carries within it the same fragility that marks every human life.[32] And yet, precisely because the paradigm placed is not simply sapiential, but *prophetic*, the gaze of the reader is invited to be fixed not so much on any person, but on any person who has become a prophet, a living sign of the undeducible entry of the divine into the world. From here, one can evince a theology of history, which, as in the case of the full significance of the gesture of surrender, appears to the reader-exegete of the prophetic book more clearly, more than it does on the rugged surface of the text.[33]

Jeremiah has consigned himself into the hands of men (cf. 26:14), accepted defeat, and the silence of God (cf. 20:7–18; 28:10–11; 37:11–16; 38:1–6; etc.), surrendered to the written text intended to supplant him, that prophetic scroll that announced the end to him, at the very moment in which by order of YHWH his words pierced through one semiotic dimension to another, and from that spoken to that written, from one hand to another, from mouth to ear (cf. ch. 36). But in all this, the life promised by God was concealed. To Him and to life, Jeremiah handed himself over, definitively. The path of humiliation, already traversed by the prophet from Anathoth (and then, by the mysterious servant of YHWH of the book of Isaiah), is then discovered to be a path of salvation, a path of the New Covenant. This is how we can open ourselves (foreign nations included) to the possibility of the end being a new beginning, and of God therefore operating a new creation, founded or foundable not on human pride but on the gift that renews the originary and undeserved giving of life itself.

4.3. The risks of a "theology of surrender" (without the option of "resistance")

The fact that Jeremiah identifies in the gesture of surrender the act of faith required so that history can have a continuation beyond the end does not authorise tracing an immediate and permanent equivalence between these two realities, *surrendering* and *trusting in YHWH*. The risk would be that of deducing a general theology of the surrender (wrongly) extensible to any reality that has to do with faith in its being faced with a precise option. This is not really the case, at least on a level of contraposition between alternatives having repercussions on a political and strategic level. Once the specific semiotic-symbolic dimension of the surrender has been identified and focalised, in fact, it must then be respected at its categorial level without making it too soon an all-encompassing disposition of the subject that translates into an *attitude* that is, so to speak, "sapiential". If we want to talk about an "ethics of surrender", this

---

32 As in P. Valéry: "Nous sentons qu'une civilisation a la même fragilité qu'une vie" (P. VALÉRY, «La crise de l'esprit», 988).

33 Cf. also K. SCHMID, «Nebukadnezars Antritt», 238–239. It should be noted that the theology of the history of the book of Jeremiah has nothing to do with a "Universaltheorie" in the Hegelian mould (see, in this regard, A. DEMANDT, *Philosophie der Geschichte. Von der Antike zur Gegenwart*, Köln – Weimar – Wien 2011, 322–333). The perspective on the "fulfilment" of past history is not that of those who presume to have identified the definitive hermeneutical key (generated by a *philosophical* rationality), but of those who, in the murky enigma of the end, identify and assume, *prophetically*, bright traces of meaning.

Theological horizons on the threshold of the end   705

must be done at another level of discourse (the human-divine relational one), as we shall see further on (in § 4.5.3).

It is precisely the tradition of biblical "wisdom"[34] that investigates the eternal, the great immutable laws as the simplest harmonies of life, and condenses them into maxims or "proverbs" that can transmit this form of knowledge from father to son.[35] However, in the face of the radical question of how to get out of fear and crisis in a specific situation, it seems improper to refer to the "letter" of a norm that tends to have a universal character. It would be likewise erroneous to derive and justify a general strategy applicable to any eventuality starting from a particular case (as e.g. that of 38:14–28a). This was the formal error of the false prophets, who, slavishly reproposing in their own days the message of Isaiah on the impregnability of Zion (always conditional on the faith) transformed it from a prophetic word into a sapiential disposition valid for all ages and under any (apparently) similar circumstances.

The question is not that of discrediting "wisdom" for the benefit of "prophecy" but of subordinating them both to that essential spiritual act (required of all) that is *discernment*. This is produced when amongst the various expressions of the true, one knows how to choose (in order to adhere to it) that which really assumes and interprets from the point of view of God my being here and now. This is, however, possible if one accepts the necessary labour obliging every human being to obey that truth that, to the extent to which it is revealed and intimately accepted, is recognisable even when announced from the outside in the contingency of time and space. Discerning is therefore an act that imposes itself for the very fact of being human beings. And it is required, as such, both by Prophecy (to be recognised and accepted) and Wisdom, for there is a time for one thing and a time for its opposite (cf. Ecc 3:1–8); there is, therefore, a time for *surrender* and a time for *resistance*.

It is interesting to cite, in this regard, as a further reflexive stimulus, a significant passage in which, in the letter of 21 February 1944 written by the prisoner D. Bonhoeffer, he wonders where the boundary is between "necessary resistance" and the equally necessary surrender to "destiny". Assuming Don Quixote as an emblem of resistance carried through to a point of non-sense ("indeed to madness") and Sancho Panza as a symbol of surrender, "the type of complacent and artful accommodation to things are they are", he infers a criterion of discernment that has a remarkable affinity with what has emerged from my study on the *prophetic* meaning of the "surrender" in Jeremiah. For D. Bonhoeffer, in fact, we

> must confront fate – to me the neuter gender of the word 'fate' (*Schicksal*) is significant – as resolutely as we submit to it at the right time. One can speak of 'guidance' only on the other side of the twofold process, with God meeting us no longer as 'Thou', but also 'disguised' in the 'It'; so in the last resort my question is how we are to find the 'Thou' in this 'It' (i.e. fate), or, in other words, how does 'fate' really become 'guidance'? It's therefore impossible to define the boundary between resistance and submission on abstract principles; but both of them must be there and must

---

34 I will refer to the acute reflections of P. BEAUCHAMP, *L'un et l'autre Testament*, 106–135.
35 The family, therefore, is the very place of the transmission of this patrimony. Prophecy, on the other hand, according to the Jeremianic attestation, seems to break the bonds established by this familial (and tribal) alliance. Indeed, this introduces a discontinuity that is not assimilable by traditional cognitive models (cf. 11,18–23; 12,6; 20,10).

706 General conclusions (and apertures)

be shown with determination. Faith demands this elasticity of behaviour. Only so can we stand our ground in each situation as it arises, and turn it to gain.[36]

The Jeremianic message, in an analogous way, is not an indeterminate indication addressed to everyone once and for all, almost as if it were an absolute moral norm or wisdom to be inherited and transmitted in crystallised form from time immemorial. The problem is precisely how to confront a specific and unrepeatable "event" (or "destiny"), in which a "guide" (the prophetic word) emerges revealing the presence of the "you" of God. This presence calls on human freedom to hand itself over in faith through an acceptance of the Meaning of the history in progress made present by the event itself. This is how communion with God and a new way of living the Covenant are realised.

If the act of handing oneself over is thus understood as obedience of faith to God expressed in concrete choices, this is a *universal necessity* and a *sapiential truth*. If handing oneself over to enemies is a political gesture that translates this obedience only here and now, it is instead a *prophetic fact*. Since one can also hand themself over to God and therefore fight; they can hand themself over and therefore resist.

4.4. Two paradigms of free will in the face of the end (human will and divine will)

Biblical history is like a tightrope between the freedom of choice of the human being and that of God. My research has repeatedly highlighted, from different angles, how strongly the call for the responsibilisation of human action emerges from the book of Jeremiah. The fate of Jerusalem and its inhabitants therefore rises to a parable of free will, a paradigm of its decisive valence, in one sense or another.

It should in any case be noted at this point, after all the journey made, that in the crepuscular context of the last years of the kingdom of Judah, the divine action towards the people takes on *two complementary perspectives*. These account for seemingly contradictory instances: (a) that of *human free will* called to answer and determine its destiny, and (b) that of the "necessity" of the salvific design, which will still go ahead regardless of the choices of human beings, as the ultimate expression of *divine will*.

Let me try to clarify.

a) The *first perspective* regards the interpersonal dynamics between YHWH and his people, always presented as two free subjects bound by a relationship of covenant whose stability and implementation lies in the hands of the two contracting parties. In this sense, YHWH is the one who, through the prophetic word, denounces the infidelity to the pact, invites conversion, threatens and/or announces destruction, and indicates and asks for the act of surrender as an extreme possibility of salvation. The scenario is a "dramatic" one because it presents on the scene of the text, focalising above all on the choices of *individual characters* (the prophet Jeremiah himself, the king Zedekiah, the scribe-secretary Baruch, the eunuch Ebed-melech, the ministers of the king, etc.), the unpredictable outcome of human free will, and

---

36 D. BONHOEFFER, *Letters and Papers from Prison*. With a New Introduction by Samuel Wells, London 2017, 69–70, from the letter to Eberhard Bethge dated 21 February 1944.

Theological horizons on the threshold of the end 707

therefore, at the same time, its tremendous greatness and fascinating mystery. *History is not already written*: Truly, the choices of men in the book of Jeremiah have the sovereign power to determine the course of events, even to upset the order of the cosmos and almost nullify the creative act (cf. 4:23–26). Human free will can turn a wooden yoke into an iron yoke (see 28.13), decide the fate of nations (cf. 18:1–12; 27:8, 11; etc.), and condition the action of God in one way or another. It can save God's envoy in place or on behalf of God (cf. 26:38; 36:19; 38:1–13) or save a city from fire when it was already destined for fire (cf. 38:17), but it can also transform a chance of salvation into an atrocious failure (cf. 38:18, 20–23; 39:1–10; 52:1–30).

b) The *second perspective* instead seems to ignore this interaction, for here, only divine freedom assumes the principal role, exerting absolute lordship over human history. In fact, despite the failure of the Covenant, pervasive refusal of the people to (ethical) conversion, rejection of the act of surrender as a path of salvation (as a POC), and consequent catastrophe with the destruction of Jerusalem and loss of all visible certainties of the political-religious identifying order of Israel (the kingdom of Judah, land of the promise, temple of YHWH, Davidic dynasty), God intends to carry forth his design of salvation. The book of Jeremiah places at its centre, in the midst of the desolation, the prophecies of consolation concerning the re-establishment of the fortunes of Jerusalem and the return from the exile as a New Exodus that, despite everything and regardless of any human choice, God will make the surviving people perform (cf. 30–31 and 32–33). In this sense, it reconnects to the Isaianic theology of the "remnant of Israel" (שְׁאָר יִשְׂרָאֵל), which survived the punitive chastisement in order to open itself up to a future of hope, by the sheer grace of YHWH (cf. Isa 10:20–27; 11:11–16; 37:32; etc.). Unlike the first paradigm, here, the active subject is YHWH alone, while the object of the divine action or the passive subject is always of a *collective* type: Jerusalem or the people of Israel in its various determinations.

Focalising the configuration of these (other) two paradigms highlights, yet again, how in the book of Jeremiah there are powerful devices of signification present, appointed to orient the search for meaning before the enigma of the end. In this case, their complementary relationship can help the reader to respond to a series of specific questions that may arise when they question the concrete feasibility of the Jeremianic option of surrender in relation to its theological valence.

In the context of the symbolic-prophetic frame that I have highlighted, what should one think, for example, of the hostage population inside the walls who, even if they wished, could not have surrendered anyway? (cf. in 37:11–16, the case of Jeremiah himself, arrested at the city gates on charges of desertion). If Jeremiah had prophesied extermination for those who had remained in Jerusalem or not submitted to Babylon (cf. 21:8–10; 27:12–13; 38:2), what about those who, even without giving up, survived? And those who surrendered (cf. 38:19; 39:9; 52:15) for reasons that were not theological, that is, not in obedience to the prophetic word but for a simple pragmatic calculation or personal gamble?

All these questions can be answered by reiterating the underlying intentionality that I found to be the driving force behind the Jeremianic work, that is, the search for general perspectives of meaning, as well as gradually focalising its different communicative levels. If the text, fundamentally, wants to establish interpretive paradigms

708 General conclusions (and apertures)

and not simply compile historiographic reconnaissances of factual truths of the past, this means that it is addressed to believers of all times who are called to measure themselves against these hermeneutical keys.

As I have observed, for example, the whole communicative structure of 21:1–10 veers from a simple *report* of a prophetic consultation towards a symbolic signification (also through the literary disposition of textual unit), and thus towards clear, totalising semantic oppositions: those who surrender are safe, those who remain in Jerusalem will be lost. But the reinterpreting reference is clearly that of the Deuteronomic theme of the two paths and it is obvious that this admits but two options, with no halftones. Moreover, the prophetic dismay attested for example in 5:1; 6:8; 9:1–4; etc., in the face of the ubiquity of evil and the fact that there would be no principle of justice left in Jerusalem, that is, not even a "righteous one" (as at least Jeremiah and his supporters, like Baruch and his brother Seraiah, Ebed-melech and Ahikam, son of Saphan, are presumed to have been) must be understood in the same symbolic-communicative perspective (with hyperbolic accents typical also of Semitic rhetoric).

In addition to the utilisation of specific communicative registers, which, to avoid interpretative aporias need be well understood, the configuration of the two paradigms outlined above enables just as many clarifications. On the one hand, it is possible to focalise the global meaning of the design of YHWH, which has its landing place in the mirable, undeducible event of the "resurrection" after "death". In this sense, the emblem is *the fate of Jerusalem,* understood both as a symbolic urban space and as a community exiled and brought back into the reedified City. It is an *impersonal paradigm,* since it does not involve the exercise of free will. Both Jerusalem, in fact, and the even meagre number of Israelites representative of the totality of the people, will be regardless the object of divine benevolence and will become, with or without their "assent", prophetic signs of the salvific gratuitousness operated by God (cf. chs. 24 and 30–33)[37] and directed ultimately to all, even to the nations. This, as I have pointed out, is the paradigm of *divine will.*

According to another perspective, on the other hand, that is, according to the paradigm of *human free will,* every single person is called to latch on, in freedom, to this salvific design, assuming, in discernment, the most pertinent "prophetic choices". Of this, Jeremiah himself (and not Jerusalem, therefore) is the emblem or most representative paradigm. If in fact for the paradigm of divine will the fate of the "resurrection" is a certain fact, then the real risk is that of remaining personally excluded from that

---

37 It is interesting to underscore here as well that the relationship between the paradigms is complementary and tightly interconnected. If, on the one hand, the gratuitous benevolence of YHWH towards the deportees, understood as a group or a totality, is insisted upon, then in any case the paradigm of the free personal response called upon to accept the divine gift is also included. The necessity of conversion and therefore the appeal to the freedom of individuals remains fundamental: cf. e.g.: 24:7: "I will give them a heart to know me, for I am the Lord; they shall be my people and I will be their God, *for they shall return to me with their whole heart*" (כִּי־יָשֻׁבוּ אֵלַי בְּכָל־לִבָּם); 31:18: "I heard Ephraim rocking in grief: you chastised me, and I was chastised like an untamed calf. *Bring me back and I will come back* (הֲשִׁיבֵנִי וְאָשׁוּבָה)". The same principle of individual responsibility, already very present in Deut 24:16, is clearly underscored in Jer 31:29–30 and widely taken up in the book of Ezekiel (cf. particularly ch. 18 and 33:12–20).

horizon And here, it becomes understandable in what sense one must "deliver themself to the king of Babylon": it is necessary to freely place that symbolic-prophetic gesture (POC) that interprets for each person the meaning of history according to truth, that gesture requested of all, but according to the modalities dictated by the context in which each person finds themself.[38]

This can also be understood by looking at "how" Jeremiah handed himself over, that is, without making the material gesture of surrender that he called for in the name of YHWH as access to salvation. In the same vein, another significant example of what I am saying is Ebed-melech: He too does not surrender (and could not have done so even if he had been willing) but still receives the same promises of salvation reserved for those who had surrendered in obedience to the prophetic word. By risking his life to save Jeremiah, he in fact (as we have seen) is the significance itself of the act of surrender. In other words, as YHWH himself reveals to him by the mouth of the prophet in 39:18, the motivation that would always resonate in his ears, verifying his liberation and salvation is this: "[...] because *you trusted in me*" [כִּי־בָטַחְתָּ בִּי]). The surrender, then, is not only a material fact, but is a symbolic-prophet gesture of faith, a specific way of living the Covenant.

4.5. "To hand oneself over to the king Babylon": The horizon of the end and its overcoming

Through the "symbolic gestures" of prophets, God exerts his creative power on the world which is always a power of word: A naked fact, a bare body, a shapeless and chaotic event gets re-semanticised, which is like saying *recreated*.

If the instrument of burden loaded on the shoulders of this man, Jeremiah, is no longer a yoke, but is the sovereign power granted by God to Babylon, to whom everyone must submit, even the disaster looming over the kingdom of Judah is no longer an anonymous event generated by the innumerable chaotic upheavals of a senseless history, but is the visibilisation of the inconsistency of human pride and the relational failure of the Covenant. It can no longer be said that going out from Jerusalem to meet the generals of the king of Babylon is just yet another re-presentation of one of the alternatives possible in similar critical junctures if it is God who asks for it as a "symbolic gesture of response".

The Word reorganises the meaning of reality, even if externally reality appears to remain the same. At least as long as the Word is fulfilled. Then, what seemed stable and eternal is undone, what appears to have no way out turns out to be the mediation

---

38 An emblematic example of this dual perspective is identifiable in the figure of the queen Esther. She finds her personal free will called upon to act (and to fulfil an authentic POC) by presenting herself before the king to intercede in favour of her people. The risk is a fatal one, a challenge before which one can be tempted to withdraw. This is when Mordecai shows Esther (and us readers) the intrahistorical dynamic of these two forms of free will: If she does not give her consent to participate in the salvific design of God with her free will, it will proceed regardless and be realised, but those who hold back from it will be lost: "Even if you now remain silent, relief and deliverance will come to the Jews from another source; but you and your father's house will perish. Who knows – perhaps it was for a time like this that you became queen?" (Est 4:14).

710   General conclusions (and apertures)

of an unexpected crossing from death to life. To surrender, *now*, means accepting this end and opening oneself to its paradoxical passing. *When there is no more choice, one can still choose.* Faced with the end, which seems to cancel every possible option, one can choose to enter it welcoming the mystery that inhabits it and that the prophet reveals. And so doing, even failure becomes salvation because of all the certainties that have collapsed only one remains for support: that of faith in God who can save from death, even through death. Amongst the various dimensions of the end-failure revealed as a boundary that the prophetic act of surrender (as POC) can make one pass through and overcome, let us see at least the most important separately (even though there are numerous interdependent relations).

4.5.1. The end of politics

The crepuscular hour of the siege of Jerusalem coincides with the crisis of all the political-military strategies devised to ensure the independence and well-being of the kingdom of Judah. But this end had been announced from the very first incursion of the injunction of surrender on the scene of the text and on the chessboard of the international strategy that they wanted to address in the court of King Zedekiah (cf. 27:1–4).

At the very moment when the foreign ambassadors forgathered in Jerusalem with their advice and tactics find themselves faced with those improvised agricultural instruments made of wood and ropes and hear the words that untie their weighty significance, what is announced is the end of politics[39] and its every religious legitimacy of a manipulative nature (cf. 27:5–22). It is the historic hour when one must simply submit, though not so much to Nebuchadnezzar as to he who, as Creator and Lord of history, has decreed his punitive function.

When the events precipitate, Jerusalem is extenuated by the siege and no Egyptian army takes any more interest in its fate, King Zedekiah has at this point exhausted almost entirely all political resources, every strategic means, and all that remains for him to do is to once again call for that prophet with the yoke to know if any possibility of salvation remains (cf. 38:14–28a). The mandate, however, remains the same: *hand themselves over to the king of Babylon.* This gesture preserves the entire specific semantic heritage of the political sphere (surrendering themselves means performing a *political act* that potentially marks the *political* [and otherwise] *end* of those who place it, with the hope that this will not happen), but since it must be assumed as a *symbolic-prophetic* act, symbolically, in fact, it also decrees the end: the path of life, well-being, and salvation of the City, Jeremiah says, in other words, to King Zedekiah, is *to accept that he is no longer the king.* If the political option fails, the

---

39   Biblical prophecy already contains in its essence this contrast between the self-referential ways of managing problems and the prophetic perspective that denounces their idolatrous implications: "These are two opposing voices in the biblical texts. A voice in defence of politics – that is, of prudence and calculation, these two embodied in the king and his counsellors; and a voice against politics, describing self-help as a form of idolatry, which is represented in prophetic poetry. The second voice is greater than the first in the Bible, but never yet in the world" (M. Walzer, «Prophecy and International Politics», *HPSt* 4 [2009] 319–328, here, p. 328).

Theological horizons on the threshold of the end 711

path of obedience of faith instead remains open. This transfigures from within the act of surrender into an efficacious gesture for the renewal of history.

4.5.2. The end of religion

Defining what "religion" is in the ancient Near East (and elsewhere) is not a simple undertaking,[40] since the phenomenon that the term would like to identify is extremely complex and variegated. If, by "religion", we mean, in a broad sense, everything that relates to the relationship between the human being (as an individual or social group) and divinity, it is obvious that the whole biblical tradition is the evident attestation of this reciprocity. Here, I intend to refer, within an operative definition that focalises its communicative dynamics,[41] to that degeneration of the relationship of Covenant often denounced by the prophets and in particular by Jeremiah himself in the famous temple speech (cf. 7:1–15; 26).

When the prophet is sent to stigmatise the vacuous, illusory confidence in the formality of ritual practices, which have become, at this point, a devious means of concealing the evil committed, obtaining guarantees of impunity and national well-being, the Israeli *religio* is reduced to pure negotiation according to the principle of *do ut des* that governs relations of a commercial nature. The problem, therefore, is not only the illicit worship of foreign deities (cf. 7:16–20), but of a cult that is no longer substantiated by an authenticity of the relation. This is clearly stated in 7:21–28, where not only is the profanation of sacrificial acts denounced with stinging irony, but the divine origin of those sacrifices that according to the tradition of the Exodus was prescribed by God himself to Sinai is formally denied! (cf. also Deut 5:22; Amos 5:25). Whether this be a rhetorical gimmick or not,[42] the fact remains that the only thing necessary is indicated as *obedient listening* to YHWH (cf. 6:10–20). For this reason, Jeremiah threatens the end of the Temple and the entire cultual system as an extreme means for recuperation of the essential: an authentic relationship with God.

Already, with his identity as a priest from Anathoth (cf. 1:1), he could most probably reawaken in his interlocutors (and his fellow citizens) the spectre of an ancient curse and national disaster tied to the destruction of the sanctuary of Shiloh (cf. 1 Kgs 2:26–27 with 1 Sam 3:11–14).[43] Called by YHWH as a priest without worship, without a temple, without a ministry, the drama of the curse rises with Jeremiah to be a prophetic word that presents the act of the surrender on the horizon of the end of all the sacred institutions of the Israelite cult as the last and only way to relate again, in a just way, *in extremis*, to the God of the Covenant.

Surrendering to the king of Babylon (*now*) signifies an acceptance of being before a God who cannot in any way be managed or conditioned through worship or through

---

40 See, in this regard, the synthetic review (with related critical observations) of Z. Zevit, *The Religions of Ancient Israel. A Synthesis of Parallactic Approaches*, London – New York 2001, 15–16.

41 Cf. *Ibid.*, 15: "Israelite religions are the varied, symbolic expressions of, and appropriate responses to the deities and powers that groups or communities deliberately affirmed as being of unrestricted value to them within their worldview."

42 Cf. J.R. Lundbom, *Jeremiah 1–20*, 481–482.

43 Cf. ch. VIII, § 3.3, n. 34.

712   General conclusions (and apertures)

one's own idea of religion. As was already made clear in 1 Sam 15:22–23, there is nothing more important to "offer" to access life than to perform that sabbatical act of "rest", of obedience, liberation, and depossession (cf. Exod 20:8–11; Deut 5:12–15) that is no longer a "do" but a renunciation of control, of every self-justification and self-salvation, to leave God still "free" to "rest" from all of his work (the wonders of the Red Sea will no longer be seen) and to act according to his absolutely free love that renews the ancient wonders of the Exodus in a way that is paradoxical. Even if in other forms, the Israelite religion will continue even after the exile and destruction of the Temple, this is clear.[44] But in Jeremiah, what gets established at this point is a permanent paradigm that postulates the "end", or better still, the symbolic-prophetic principle of the supersession of all its idolatric forms.

4.5.3. The end of ethics

> *Risolvi! [...] Ah! Tempo più non v'è!*[45]

So many prophetic appeals are similar to this modern, emblematic artistic-expressive synthesis of the ethical obligation. The urgency of conversion is all the more pressing as the window of time available for the virtuous exercise of freedom gets reduced. The choice of "good", even made *in extremis*, can ward off disaster or allow one to cross the mystery of death unscathed. Otherwise, in case of obstinate refusal, nothing remains but the end and the curse-"damnation".

Prophetic literature presents the history of Israel to us continually shaken by the cries, words, and gestures of envoys of YHWH who seek to lead the Covenant partner back along the path of life, that is, faithful observance of the divine commands. As I have been able to highlight with my research, the book of Jeremiah is well aware of the Deuteronomistic indications, with the stark alternative between life and death, between the choice of the blessing or the curse. In Deuteronomy itself, the ethical choice cannot lead across death (it will in later literature; Dan 12:2–3; Wis 3:1–8; 5:14–15; 2 Mac 7:9) but can make it be avoided *tout court*, as failure and punishment. Life promised as a consequence of fidelity is also understood, in and of itself, horizontally. In this sense, things do not change much in the book of

---

44 J. Assmann in *Das kulturelle Gedächtnis. Schrift, Erinnerung und politische Identität in frühen Hochkulturen*, München 1992, [7]2013, 196–207, rightly spoke of "religion as resistance" ("Religion als Widerstand") in reference, above all, to the Israeli religion of the Second Temple, understood as a factor in the preservation of one's own cultural identity. Yet, it can be observed that precisely an attitude of this sort, strongly "politicised" by the royal institution, had caused the disaster of the destruction of the kingdom of Judah and of Jerusalem. According to this perspective, the act of the surrender, on the contrary, amounted to a "religion of surrender" ("Religion als Übergabe"). For this very reason, it was seen as unacceptable by the political-religious entourage of Jerusalem. Indeed, it appeared to be the end or very negation of the ideological-religious pillars of the time.

45 "*Decide! [...] Ah! There is no more time!*". The Commander to Don Giovanni, in a last resort to induce the philanderer's conversion before the fatal moment of death, destined to crystallise and project into eternity the last possible choice (in *Don Giovanni* di Wolfgang Amadeus Mozart; libretto by Lorenzo Da Ponte, 1787).

Jeremiah, and this, for its reader, makes the mystery of his personal story and the secret in which God himself conceals the reasons for his decrees even more terrible and fascinating.[46]

The time of Jeremiah is nevertheless a time of total crisis for the ethical dimension as a path of salvation. His appeals during the time of Jehoiakim are numerous and insistent, and the threat of the end is always articulated in a request for moral conversion, understood as fidelity to the immutable, perpetually valid instructions of the *Tôrâ*. At the time of Zedekiah, though, a trespassing beyond the point of no return is determined, marked by a stubborn rejection of the prophetic appeal, which causes the threat of punishment to mutate into the proclamation of an end that is, in certain respects, irreversible. Precisely in this context, a reprise and paradoxical mutation of the Deuteronomistic alternative between the path of life and the path of death takes place in the preaching of Jeremiah. The call is addressed in 21:8–10 to all the people, while in 38:14–28a, right on the brink of the end, we witness the drama of freedom called to "decide for itself" before it is too late. The ethical horizon, however, no longer has any relevance at this point.[47] Thus, an extreme type of salvation is constituted, not reducible to its material form, accessible only through a symbolic-prophetic gesture (the POC), which could be the subject matter for a specific in-depth study in the field of moral theology.

If before, all the streets and squares of Jerusalem had been searched in vain for one who could obtain the pardon of YHWH on behalf of the whole City, identifying him in the unfindable profile of an irreproachable practitioner of justice (cf. 5:1), then now that man is discovered right amongst the heirs of the house and throne of David. In the end, he is there amidst those sovereigns publicly shamed by the prophet for their injustices! (cf. 21:11–23:2). In order to save himself and save the City, he is no longer asked to practice justice (all have failed), but to perform the symbolic-prophetic act of surrender.

If one can speak of ethics, at this point the question is precisely that of a mutual handing over of themselves, of God and of the human being, of one to the other and vice versa.[48] Signified contingently in the political gesture of the surrender, this act can now substitute every commandment and every word/promise of fidelity precisely because it resays its lost essence. At the least, it can open onto an unhoped-for

---

46 As noted efficaciously by G. von Rad regarding the travail of the prophetic ministry of Jeremiah: "Wie er, dem sein Amt so problematisch geworden ist, mit diesem ihn zerbrechenden Beruf doch in einem übermenschlich scheinenden Gehorsam seinen Weg hinaus in die Gottverlassenheit zu Ende gegangen ist, das bleibt Jeremias Geheimnis. Keinen Augenblick ist ihm der Gedanke gekommen, daß dieses sein mittlerisches Leiden vor Gott einen Sinn haben können. Und dies, daß Gott das Leben seines getreuesten Boten in eine so entsetzliche und durchaus unbegriffene Nacht hinausgeführt und aller Wahrscheinlichkeit nach dort hat zerbrechen lassen, das ist Gottes Geheimnis" (G. VON RAD, *Theologie des Alten Testaments*, II, 214).

47 Only for foreign nations does the call for submission to Babylon (cf. chs. 27–28) take on an ethical dimension as well, in an implicit reference to a sort of "Noahide covenant" of universal valence, which prescribes the prohibition of all injustice and pride.

48 According to this perspective, which outlines an "etica della consegna" in reference to the intersubjective recognition and interpersonal practices of mutual trust, see the reflections of P. RICCI SINDONI, *Etica della consegna e profetismo biblico. Geremia, Ezechiele, Giona, Abacuc, Tobia*, La dialettica 26, Roma 2007, 8–9 and *passim*.

714 General conclusions (and apertures)

overcoming of the failure of the Covenant.[49] Indeed, at this point, the moral dimension has been shelved. Only a new heart will be able to return to the matter (cf. Ezek 11:19; 18:31; 36:26–27). But for this, a new creation and new Covenant will be necessary (cf. Jer 31:22, 27–28, 31–43).

4.5.4. The end of rhetoric

When one wants to communicate effectively and persuasively, simple words arranged according to the logic and syntax of ordinary language are not enough. It takes a good deal of oratory technique, an ability to wield figures of words and thought, knowing how to imprint an emotional charge, pragmatic strength, sense of beauty, and ability to reason logically on the discourse. *Docere, movere,* and *delectare* are the classic objectives of the art of persuasion.

In a communicative context in which the word itself has lost its bite, for those who obstinately want to arouse attention and be heard, it becomes necessary to intensify the effort, resort to other registers, break consolidated cognitive patterns, surprise, shock. The first way to do this may be to simply renounce the word itself. Silence in certain contexts can then become an eloquent instrument of speech. On the prophet Ezekiel, a temporary paralysis of language is imposed (cf. Ezek 3:26), Jeremiah remains alone with his uncertain reasoning, without divine words of reply, after Hananiah's counter-response (cf. 28:11). God himself forbids him to exercise the force of persuasion towards himself, so that those who know of this dismissal of the prophetic intercessory role seriously question what is happening. The prophets, in the communicative passion they incarnate, resort to multifarious expressive devices, and in a certain sense are (despite themselves, at times) *masters of rhetoric.*

It is to the sphere of non-verbal communication that the "symbolic gestures" belong as well. Coordinated with the word more frequently in some cultures more than others, these are also means used effectively by prophets especially in times of *relational crisis* between YHWH and his people. In this sense, it is clear why some scholars have attributed a *rhetorical purpose,* above all, to them. However, I have noted that this is a reductive vision, not least because there are symbolic gestures that the prophets are called to perform in the absence of an audience, and which therefore concern they themselves and the extradiegetical narratee (the Model Reader) or the empirical reader.

The message of the surrender is presented from the (chronological, not literary) beginning with the symbolic gesture of the yoke, and if this were to be mainly a means of persuasion, then its resounding failure should be noted immediately. The fulfilment of the prophecy concerning Hananiah's death would be a more convincing argument, but the text of Jer 28 is silent on the communicative effects of Jeremiah's words and gestures in this episode. It does make clear, however, that it is misleading to follow the rhetoric track in order to adequately understand the meaning of the symbolic dimension involved in the presentation and assumption of the gesture of surrender. What matters instead is the *existential engagement* of the same subject who is called on to perform the gesture or embrace its meaning.

---

49   The rabbinical tradition attests to the conception of exile as a form of universal atonement for the sins of Israel, in other words, as an exceptional replacement of ethics and the cult as ordinary paths of salvation. See, in this regard, J. NEUSNER, *Jeremiah in Talmud and Midrash.* A Source Book, SJ(L), Lanham 2006, 348.

The last king of Israel and the fulfilment of the kingship 715

Once again, the issue is that of an *act of revelation* (of the meaning of history) and the configuration of a *possible paradigm of relationship* with God (in precisely this history) that can performatively change the course of events. With Ezekiel, YHWH will be more explicit: he will have to speak to his people, and whether they "listen or do not listen" is of no matter: "*they will know* that there is a prophet amongst them" (Ezek 2:5; cf. 2:7; 3:11). The important thing is not his capacity for persuasion but that he himself is the first to *obey* the divine word: "And you, son of man, listen to what I tell you; do not be as rebellious like this rebellious house; open your mouth and eat what I give you" (Ezek 2:8). What YHWH asks of Jeremiah from ch. 1 goes in the same direction: neither the success of the mission nor exemption from suffering is guaranteed, but rather that he will not be "won over" by his persecutors. In other words, it is already said that "whoever hands themself over will live". What is asked of him, in fact, is that he *hand himself over* to his mission, and precisely this surrender will be the most difficult thing for Jeremiah to complete, if we think of the inner drama attested by the Confessions. The impossibility (cf. 1:6) or renunciation of the rhetorical power of persuasion, if it is the sign of surrender, is also what is asked of Jerusalem. It will be needless to seek to attract the benevolence of the foreigners: embellishments and ornamentation of discourse aside: "they seek your life", says YHWH (cf. 4:30).

Faced with the imminence of the end, the act of surrender therefore configures a relational paradigm of *trusting obedience* and *unhoped-for salvation* that entirely exceeds the power or hope of being able to induce the adversary to change their mind about what would be most right to do. Jeremiah is in fact presented before the people, the leaders, and the king Zedekiah as a man who has "handed himself over". Only by trusting and obeying will they understand that he was right, or after the catastrophe. But they too are called to "hand themselves over to the king of Babylon". Only after this act can they have their lives saved, and only through the intervention of YHWH, not because surrender in itself has the value of being a *captatio benevolentiae* before the assailants. It is God who reserves the power to change the heart of Nebuchadnezzar to open an inconceivable path of salvation (cf. 42:12). The "end of rhetoric" in the sense described thus appears to have the scope of *revealing* something new about reality, configuring a specific *prophetic paradigm of faith* to be relaunched in the future of every generation that survived the disaster of disobedience. It is a revelation projected towards a fulfilment to come, as the rare but significant messianic-Davidic oracles of the book of Jeremiah let us foresee.

5. The last king of Israel and the fulfilment of the kingship (in the act of surrender)

Amongst the significative semiotic *arcatas* that connect the proleptic presentation of the surrender in 21:1–10 to the later text units, it is worth remembering, having reached the end of our journey, the connection between the figure of King Zedekiah (צִדְקִיָּהוּ: "*justice of YHWH*" or "*my justice is YHWH*") and the messianic promise of a *Davidic descendant* who will come to redeem the failure of the predecessors, in the name of a perfect exercise of kingship according to justice and in the context of the salvation of Judah-Israel freely actualised by God.

> [5] Behold, days are coming, oracle of the Lord, when I will raise up a righteous branch for David, who shall *reign as (true) king* (מֶלֶךְ מָלַךְ), he shall be wise and will do what is right and just in the land. [6] In his days, Judah shall be saved and Israel shall

716 General conclusions (and apertures)

dwell in security. This will be the name by which they call him: *"YHWH our justice"* (יְהוָה צִדְקֵנוּ) (23:5–6; //33:15–16).

Starting from the failure of the monarchical institution, represented by King Zedekiah placed before the announcement of the end and the injunction of surrender along with all the people, the expectation of a sovereign capable of realising the meaning of Davidic kingship within the framework of the Covenant is projected towards the days to come. And yet, there will be no more kings who can sit on the throne of David, for the kingdom of Judah itself will collapse, and will never be restored. Zedekiah is, in fact, the last king of Jerusalem, and it is, paradoxically, precisely he who seems to be asked to seal the Davidic dynasty through the act of surrender. Yet, what may seem like the incomprehensible negation of God's own promises (cf. 2 Sam 7) becomes, in the mystery, anticipation of their fulfilment.

On the one hand, in the dramatic fate of Zedekiah and the entire house of the kings of Judah, what is ironically fulfilled is the desire of the people who had wanted a king "like all (the other) peoples" (כְּכָל־הַגּוֹיִם; 1 Sam 8:5). Even the humiliating end of Zedekiah, in fact, goes to add itself to that of so many other foreign sovereigns fallen to disgrace during historical upheavals, and with him, a dynasty and kingdom disappear from the face of the earth, as had happened so many times and would still happen to so many other peoples. According to another perspective, however, precisely as a result of these events, the process of *resignification* of the monarchical power that had been started by YHWH himself from its inception in the time of the prophet Samuel with Saul, and even more with David, heads towards its complete fulfilment.[50]

It is necessary at this point, however, to further open the contextual and hermeneutical horizon to the unity of the One and the Other Testament. In the perspective of a teleological reading[51] of the two Testaments that sees in the Scripture a *"récit totale"* set in motion from the Genesis and striving towards its Christological fulfilment, what I have focalised can be understood as a "figure" (τύπος),[52] that is, the con-*figuration* of an intrinsic correlation between different narrative moments, as a device of signification that anticipates and invokes a fullness of meaning, denouncing itself at the same time as structurally deficient in relation to the fulfilment itself.

By opening a specific trail of investigation, one could then trace the path of the *"figure" of the surrender* through a whole series of texts, identifying them as correspondent to just as many narrative stages of the *récit totale*, in which the same

---

50 On the theme of the ambiguous beginning of the monarchy in Israel and its "prophetic" resignification, see S.M. SESSA, «"Dacci un re che ci governi!" (1Sam 8,6). L'avvento della monarchia in Israele e la sua ambiguità», e ID., «"Il Signore si è già scelto un uomo secondo il suo cuore"» (1Sam 13,14). La riconfigurazione profetica del potere regale in Israele», in: *Il Re delle schiere*. L'esercizio del re temporale e del Re eterno (ES 91–98), *ed.* D. LIBANORI, Cinisello Balsamo 2017, 17–44 and 45–78.

51 I again refer to the *critical* regrounding of the typological exegesis (in and of itself practiced within the Bible itself with its own modalities) elaborated by P. Beauchamp (cf. General Introduction, § 3.2, n. 76).

52 According to P. BEAUCHAMP, «Sens de l'Ecriture», *DCT*, 1084–1085 (here, p. 1084), the term tuvpo~ identifies "moins la copie ou reproduction d'un modèle (céleste ou autre) qu'un modèle de ce qui est encore à produire ('antitype')". In this sense, the figures are "attirés par cet avenir", and they establish a pro-tension of the texts that contain them towards their Fulfilment.

The last king of Israel and the fulfilment of the kingship   717

prototypical profile re-presents itself in an analogous way, advancing towards its *télos*. Here, it suffices to note, reaching the aim immediately, how in the "fullness of time" (Gal 4:4) what had been asked of the last king of Judah takes place precisely in its full and definitive form as the path of life for himself and for all the people: the symbolic-prophetic act of surrender.

This figure, in fact, is fulfilled completely in Christ, fully revealing its significance with which it was pregnant, and precisely in the supreme gesture of accepting a humiliating handing over of oneself into the hands of human beings in obedience to the Father, actualised "to gather together the children of God who were scattered" (cf. John 11:51–52 with precisely Jer 23:3.7–8!). Here, the "New Covenant" announced by Jeremiah is finally fulfilled (cf. Luke 22:20; 1 Cor 11:25; 2 Cor 3:6; Heb 8:13; 9:15). And it is done when the "King of the Jews", instead of fleeing to save himself (Jer 39:1–4; 52:6–8), in order to save his people goes out *freely* (cf. John 10:14–18) to encounter the enemies who had long been "besieging" him to capture him; when his legions do not intervene to free him (cf. Matt 26:53; John 18:36) and he asks his "soldiers" for the anger to be released and the sword to be put back in the sheath (cf. John 18:11); when a young man manages to escape naked from the hands of his enemies, thus indicating what Amos 2:16 has already announced: for the power of God, it is possible to cross the barrier of the end and enter into a paradoxical salvation that passes through a stripping down and return to an orginary nudity that promises and realises a new birth.

According to this key of interpretation, the last king of Judah should therefore have, by the act of surrender, prefigured the definitive King and his "just" way of reigning. It is precisely the failure of King Zedekiah, who does not hand himself over, that makes stand out, in any case, the obedience of the One who makes of his own consignation the cipher of his existence. Having recognised the coming and the meaning of the *present moment*, Christ does not place himself at the head of the resistance or trigger an armed rebellion against Rome. The surrender of the cross signals the *end of politics* and the human means by which power is exercised, both for good and for evil. He, "made to be sin" for us (cf. 2 Cor 5:21), dies abandoned by God and by men outside the Holy City in an impure place (cf. Heb 13:11–13), sign, in his body, of the *end of the Temple and of the religion* of blood and sacrificial rituals, a shadow of the truth (Col 2:16) and (often) a promise of salvation at a discount. He dies like an evildoer in a desecrated place, sharing the fate of the cursed in the horizon of the guilty failure of the observance of the Law and the *naufrage of ethics*. He also dies in the *silence* of God and for having reduced to silence the power of his word of truth, in which he did not seek recourse during the trial against him to defend himself against the false accusations of those who wanted him dead, much to the amazement of the high priest.[53] A word, therefore, unable (or not wanting to) persuade or convince anyone, or at least none of those who could save him from death, for any act in his own defence would have been immediately transformed into an act of indictment and condemnation (and thus victory) against the false witnesses.

Scorned and dishonoured by human beings, whose faults and their consequences he took upon himself, Christ enters into the mystery of a radical handing over of himself to the Father. And only when that mystery is carried out to the end (i.e. until death) is

---

53   Cf. S.M. Sessa, «"Non rispondi nulla?"», 285–309.

718 General conclusions (and apertures)

the kingdom of darkness defeated and its prince thrown out, the new Temple forever reedified, the Law fulfilled to perfection, and the hearts of human beings pierced along with his own, finally convinced, so life can enter them (cf. John 16:8; Acts 2:37; Rev 1:7).

At the time of the end of Jerusalem, Ebed-melech the Ethiopian, upon meeting Jeremiah, recognises the prophet of God delivered into the hands of men, and receives the promise of his own future salvation. At the moment of the figures' fulfilment, once again a foreigner becomes witness to the truth. The Roman centurion, seeing the signs of the end (cf. Luke 23:44–45) and the condemned man enter the abyss of death *handing his spirit over into the hands of the Father* (cf. Luke 23:46), unintentionally proclaims that the ancient search has finally been fulfilled:

Truly this man was righteous! (Luke 23:47; cf. Matt 27:54; Mark 15:39).

Indeed, at the time of Sodom and Gomorrah, ten righteous people would have sufficed to obtain mercy, but they could not be found (Gen 18:20–33). At the time of Jeremiah, one would have sufficed, just one (Jer 5:1), but even then, the search was in vain and Jerusalem was destroyed (Jer 5:1). But when the fullness of time had come, the only innocent one was finally found, and thanks to his handing over his life, the City could receive forgiveness and be saved.

Here, sapiential truths and prophetic revelation coincide in a single act of surrender. Handing himself over, the Son *reveals* to humankind the face of a loving Father who can be trusted, for he is capable of getting us across the mystery of the end towards a new creation. But it also expresses the meaning of the *present moment*: the moment to *assume*, completely and entirely, all the evil and sin of humanity with its bitter consequences, the moment to show the absolute, irrevocable gratuitousness of the love of God, the moment in which his divine power is manifested, the only one capable of giving life and resurrecting even the dead, of transforming every failure into a path of salvation, and every act of trusting surrender, or ConSign*A(c)tion*,[54] into a new and eternal Covenant.

---

54 God hands himself entirely over to humankind and humankind finally hands themselves back to the Father, recovering their regal dignity as Children of God. The fecundity of this mystery, destined to reach all humankind, will inform from a certain point on, our own language as well, even going so far as to resemanticise the symbolic-prophetic meaning of the same verb with which I indicated, from the beginning, the act of surrender. "*Consignation*", from a certain point on, will signify renewing and perpetuating in some way the imprint and meaning of the *signum crucis* as a memorial, pledge, and expectation of the Fulfilment. In fact, etymologically, the verb "to consign" (and others like it) derives from the Latin *consignatio*, a term originally typical of the commercial and juridical lexicon, but resemanticised by the Christian tradition to "indicate the symbolic gesture consisting in tracing with the right hand, the sign of the cross on the forehead of the neophyte in the moment in which they are confirmed in the faith [...]. By metonymy, the *consignatio* indicated both the *signum crucis* on the forehead (= consigned to Christ) and the transmission of that "consignment" to the neophyte. This has made possible, or in any case, at least strongly facilitated, the semantic transition of *consign* from 'sign' to a generic 'entrust'". See, in this regard, P. Martino, «Per la storia etimologica di *insegnare* e *consegnare*», in: *La croce, un simbolo attraverso i tempi e le culture*. Atti del Convegno delle Scienze Umanistiche nell'ambito della Pastorale Universitaria (Roma, LUMSA-EUR-SAPIENZA, 5–6 marzo 2012), *eds.* I. Becherucci – P. Martino, Roma 2013, 196–210 (here, p. 206).

ABBREVIATIONS AND SIGLA[1]

A	Aleppo Codex
A.	Siglum for the Mari Letters in the (Louvre) museum archives
AABS	Australian Association for Byzantine Studies
ABD	D.N. FREEDMAN, *ed., Anchor Bible Dictionary,* vols. I-VI, New York – London – Toronto – Sydney – Auckland 1992
ABIG	Arbeiten zur Bibel und ihrer Geschichte
ABR	*Australian Biblical Review*
AcChr	Academia Christiana
AD	Anno Domini
AfO	Archiv für Orientforschung
AfO.B	Archiv für Orientforschung. Beiheft
AGJU	Arbeiten zur Geschichte des antiken Judentums und des Urchristentums. Ancient Judaism & Early Christianity
AION	*Annali dell'Università degli Studi di Napoli "L'Orientale"*
AJS	*American Journal of Sociology*
ALASP	Abhandlungen zur Literatur Alt-Syrien-Palästinas und Mesopotamiens
AmA	*American Anthropologist*
AnBib	Analecta biblica
AnBib.St	Analecta biblica. Studia
AncB	Anchor Bible
ANEP	J.B. PRITCHARD, *The Ancient Near East in Pictures Relating to the Old Testament.* Second Edition with Supplement, Princeton 1954, ²1969
ANETS	Ancient Near Eastern Texts and Studies
ANVAO.HF	Avhandlinger i Norske Videnskaps-Akademi i Oslo – Historisk-filosofisk Klasse
ANYAS	Annals of the New York Academy of Sciences
AOAT	Alter Orient und Altes Testament

---

1   I have conformed the abbreviations of series of books and periodicals, insofar as possible, to S.M. SCHWERTNER, *IAT3*³. Internationales Abkürzungsverzeichnis für Theologie und Grenzgebiete. Zeitschriften, Serien, Lexika, Quellenwerke mit bibliographischen Angaben. 3., überarbeitete und erweiterte Auflage, Berlin – Boston ³2014.

AOS	American Oriental Series
Aq	Aquila's revision of the LXX
aram.	aramaic
ARM	Archives royales de Mari
ASNSP.L	Annali della Scuola Normale Superiore di Pisa. Classe di Lettere e Filosofia
ATD	Das Alte Testament Deutsch
AThANT	Abhandlungen zur Theologie des Alten und Neuen Testaments
ATSAT	Arbeiten zu Text und Sprache im Alten Testament
AUSS	*Andrews University Seminary Studies*
BA	*Biblical Archaeologist*
BAH	Bibliothèque archéologique et historique
BArR	*Biblical Archaeology Review*
BASOR	*Bulletin of the American School(s) of Oriental Research*
BAW	Die Bibliothek der Alten Welt
BBB	Bonner Biblische Beiträge
BBR	*Bulletin for Biblical Research*
BC	Before Christ
BCR	Biblioteca di cultura religiosa
BDB	F. Brown – S.R. Driver – C.A. Briggs, *The New Brown-Driver-Briggs-Gesenius Hebrew and English Lexicon with an Appendix Containing the Biblical Aramaic,* Oxford 1906, Peabody 1979
BE	Biblische Enzyklopädie
BET	Beiträge zur biblischen Exegese und Theologie
BEThL	Bibliotheca Ephemeridum Theologicarum Lovaniensium
BeTS(W)	Beiruter Texte und Studien. Würzburg
BEvT	Beiträge zur evangelischen Theologie
BFChTh	Beiträge zur Förderung christlicher Theologie
BHK^{1-2}	Biblia Hebraica (*ed.* R. Kittel, Leipzig 1906, 1913)
BHK^3	Biblia Hebraica (*eds.* R. Kittel – P. Kahle *et al.,* Stuttgart 1929–1937, ^{7}1972)
BHQ	Biblia Hebraica Quinta (*eds.* A. Schenker – Y.A.P. Goldman – A. van der Kooij – G.J. Norton – S. Pisano – J. de Waard – R.D. Weis, Stuttgart 2004-)

BHS	Biblia Hebraica Stuttgartensia (*eds.* K. ELLIGER – W. RUDOLPH *et al.*, Stuttgart 1967–1977, ^{5}1997)
BHTh	Beitrage zur historischen Theologie
Bib.	*Biblica*
BiBe	Biblische Beiträge
BibInt	*Biblical Interpretation*
BibOr	Biblica et orientalia
BiInS	Biblical Interpretation Series
BiKi	*Bibel und Kirche*
BiLi	*Bibel und Liturgie*
BiRe	*Bible Review*
BiSe	Biblical Seminar
BiTr	*Bible Translator*
BiTSt	Biblioteca di testi e studi
BJ	*La Bible de Jérusalem* (Paris 1973, Nouvelle édition revue et corrigée; Paris 1998)
BJSt	Brown Judaic Studies
BK	Biblischer Kommentar
BKAT	Biblischer Kommentar – Altes Testament
BLAU	J. BLAU, *A Grammar of Biblical Hebrew*, PLO.NS 12, Wiesbaden 1976, ^{2}1993
BN	*Biblische Notizen*
BSal.E	Bibliotheca Salmaticensis – Estudios
BSRel	Biblioteca di Scienze Religiose
BST	Basel Studies of Theology
BSt	Biblische Studien
BSTJ	*Bell System Technical Journal*
BThSt	Biblisch-theologische Studien
BThZ	*Berliner Theologische Zeitschrift*
BTS	Biblical and Theological Studies
BTStu	Biblioteca di Scienze e Studi – Scienze della Comunicazione
BVBib	Beiträge zum Verstehen der Bibel
BWANT	Beiträge zur Wissenschaft vom Alten und Neuen Testament

BZ	*Biblische Zeitschrift*
BZAR	Beihefte zur Zeitschrift für Altorientalische und Biblische Rechtsgeschichte
BZAW	Beihefte zur Zeitschrift für die alttestamentliche Wissenschaft
C	Cairo Codex of the Prophets
ca.	circa
CAB	Cahiers d'archéologie biblique
CAD	A.L. OPPENHEIM *et al.* eds., *The Assyrian Dictionary of the Oriental Institute of the University of Chicago*, vols. I-XXI, Chicago – Glückstadt 1956–2010
CB.OT	Coniectanea biblica – Old Testament Series
CBET	Contributions to Biblical Exegesis and Theology
CBQ	*Catholic Biblical Quarterly*
CBR	*Currents in Biblical Research*
CCE	Collana di Cultura Ebraica
CChr.SL	Corpus Christianorum. Series Latina
CDOG	Colloquien der Deutschen Orient-Gesellschaft
CEI	*La Sacra Bibbia* (second edition by Conferenza Episcopale Italiana, Roma 2008)
CEsL	*Castilla. Estudios de literatura*
CEv	Cahiers Évangile
CFi	Cogitatio fidei
ch(s).	chapter/chapters
CHANE	Culture and History of the Ancient Near East
Classici UTET.CG	Classici UTET. Classici greci
Classici UTET.CL	Classici UTET. Classici latini
CLRes	Cognitive Linguistic Research
col(l).	column/colums
ComT	*Communication Theory*
ConBi	Connaissance de la Bible
CR.BS	*Currents in Research: Biblical Studies*
CRThPh	Cahiers de la Revue de théologie et de philosophie
CSB.SB	Commenti e Studi Biblici. Studi Biblici

CSCD	Cambridge Studies in Christian Doctrine
CSHBS	Claremont Studies in Hebrew Bible and Septuagint
CSL	Current Studies in Linguistics
CTB	Calwer Taschenbibliothek
CTHPT	Cambridge Texts in the History of Political Thought
CTL	Cambridge Textbooks in Linguistics
CuaBi	*Cuadernos bíblicos*
DB (V)	F. Vigouroux, *ed., Dictionnaire de la Bible*, vols. I–V, Paris 1895–1912
DBS	L. Pirot *et al. eds., Supplément au Dictionnaire de la Bible*, vols. I–XIII, Paris 1928-.
DBW	Dietrich Bonhoeffer Werke
DCT	J.-Y. Lacoste, *ed., Dictionnaire critique de Théologie*, Paris 1998.
Dig.	*The Digest of Justinian*
dir. obj.	direct object
Diss.	Dissertation
DJD XIX	M. Broshi *et al. eds., Qumran Cave 4.* XIV: Parabiblical Texts. Part 2, DJD XIX, Oxford 1995
DJD XV	E. Ulrich *et al. eds., Qumran Cave 4.* X: The Prophets, DJD XV, Oxford 1997
DJD	Discoveries in the Judean Desert
DOI	Digital Object Identifier (followed by the code for the unique identification of articles published online, trackable through the International DOI Foundation [IDF] website at https://www.doi.org/)
EA	El-Amarna (with reference to the numbering of the letters presented in the edition by J.A. Knudtzon, *Die El-Amarna-Tafeln, mit Einleitung und Erläuterungen.* Herausgegeben von J.A. Knudtzon. Anmerkungen und Register bearbeitet von Otto Weber und Erich Ebeling, VAB 2/I, Leipzig 1915)
ed(s).	*editor/editors*
EE	*Estudios eclesiásticos*
EF	Fondazione Centro Studi Filosofici di Gallarate, *ed., Enciclopedia Filosofica*, vols. I-XII, Milano 2006
EHLL	G. Khan, *ed., Encyclopedia of Hebrew Language and Linguistics*, vols. I-IV, Leiden – Boston 2013
EHS.T	Europaische Hochschulschriften. Reihe 23, Theologie

EJ.SE	F. Skolnik *et al.* eds., *Encyclopaedia Judaica*. Second Edition, vols. I-XXII, Detroit 2007
ELJ	*Emory Law Journal*
EP	*La Bibbia*. Nuovissima versione dai testi originali (Roma 1983)
ErIsr	Eretz-Israel. Archaeological, Historical and Geographical Studies
EssBib	Essais bibliques
EstAT	Estudios del Antiquo Testamento
EstBib	*Estudios bíblicos*
et al.	*et alii (and others)*
EtB	Études Bibliques. Nouvelle série
etc.	et cetera
Ethnog.	*L'ethnographie. Société d'Ethnographie*
ETL	*Ephemerides Theologicae Lovanienses*
ETR	*Études théologiques et religieuses*
ETSMS	Evangelical Theological Society. Monograph Series
Études	*Études publiées par des Pères de la Compagnie de Jésus*
EÜ	*Die Bibel. Einheitsübersetzung der Heiligen Schrift*. Vollständig durchgesehene und überarbeitete Ausgabe (Stuttgart 2016)
EvT	*Evangelische Theologie*
f.	feminine
FAmb	Fontes Ambrosianae
FAT	Forschungen zum Alten Testament
FGS	Functional Grammar Series
Fig(s).	Figure/Figures
FJTC	Flavius Josephus: Translation and Commentary
FKTh	*Forum katholische Theologie*
fr.	fragment
FRLANT	Forschungen zur Religion und Literatur des Alten und Neuen Testaments
GAT	Grundrisse zum Alten Testament
Gbr.	Gottesbrief (Esarhaddon's "Letter to god"; in: R. Borger, *Die Inschriften Asarhaddons Königs von Assyrien*, AfO 9, Graz 1956, § 68)
GBSP	Guides to Biblical Scholarship. Philadelphia

GeoJL	The GeoJournal Library
GESENIUS	W. GESENIUS (eds. U. RÜTERSWÖRDEN – R. MEYER – H. DONNER), *Hebräisches und Aramäisches Handwörterbuch über das Alten Testament*, vols. I–VII, Berlin – Heidelberg [18]1987–2010
GESENIUS(T)	W. GESENIUS, *Thesaurus philologicus criticus linguae hebraeae et chaldaeae Veteris Testamenti*, vols. I-III, Lipsiae 1829–1853
GK	W. GESENIUS – E. KAUTZSCH, *Hebräische Grammatik*, Halle 1813, Leipzig [28]1909
GMTR	Guides to the Mesopotamian Textual Record
Gr.	*Gregorianum*
GSAT	Guide spirituali all'Antico Testamento
HAE	J. RENZ – W. RÖLLIG, *Handbuch der althebräischen Epigraphik*, Darmstadt 1995–2003
HALAT	L. KÖHLER – W. BAUMGARTNER, *Hebräisches und Aramäisches Lexikon zum Alten Testament*, Leiden [3]1967–1996
HANE.M	History of the Ancient Near East. Monographs
HAR	*Hebrew Annual Review*
HAT	Handbuch zum Alten Testament
HATCH – REDPATH	E. HATCH – H.A. REDPATH, *A Concordance to the Septuagint and the Other Greek Versions of the Old Testament (Including the Apocryphal Books)*, Oxford 1897–1906, Grand Rapids [2]1998
HB	Hebrew Bible
HBM	Hebrew Bible Monographs
HBOT	M. SÆBØ, *ed., Hebrew Bible/Old Testament*. The History of Its Interpretation, vols. I-V, Göttingen 1996–2015
HBT	*Horizons in Biblical Theology*
HDLA	Historical Dictionaries of Literature and the Arts
HdO	Handbuch der Orientalistik
HeBAI	*Hebrew Bible and Ancient Israel*
HeBAI	*Hebrew Bible and Ancient Israel*
HebStud	*Hebrew Studies*
Hen.	*Henoch. Studies in Judaism and Christianity from Second Temple to Late Antiquity*
HGANT	A. BERLEJUNG – C. FREVEL, *eds., Handbuch theologischer Grundbegriffe zum Alten und Neuen Testament*, Darmstadt 2006

hi.	hiphil
hishth.	hishthaphel
hithp.	hithpael
hithpo.	hithpolel
HK	Handkommentar zum Alten Testament
ho.	hophal
HP	Handbook of Pragmatics
HPSt	*Hebraic Political Studies*
HSM	Harvard Semitic Monographs
HThKAT	Herders Theologischer Kommentar zum Alten Testament
HTR	*Harvard Theological Review*
HUB	Hebrew University Bible
HUCA	*Hebrew Union College Annual*
HvTSt	*Hervormde Teologiese Studies/Theological Studies*
HW	History of Warfare
HWR	G. Ueding, *ed., Historisches Wörterbuch der Rhetorik*, vols. I-X, Tübingen – Berlin 1992–2012
IBSt	*Irish Biblical Studies*
ICC	International Critical Commentary
IDBSup	*Interpreter's Dictionary of the Bible – Supplement 1976*
IEB	Introducción al estudio de la Biblia
IECOT	International Exegetical Commentary on the Old Testament
IEJ	*Israel Exploration Journal*
IEKAT	Internationaler Exegetischer Kommentar zum Alten Testament
IJL	*International Journal of Lexicography*
imp.	imperative
inf. absol.	infinitive absolute
inf. constr.	infinitive construct
Interp.	*Interpretation. A Journal of Bible and Theology*
IOS	*Israel Oriental Studies*
IREP	Institut de recherches et d'études publicitaires
IRT	Issues in Religion and Theology

ITC	International Theological Commentary
IUO.SAMi	Istituto Universitario Orientale – Dipartimento Studi Asiatici. Series Minor
JAAR	*Journal of the American Academy of Religion*
JANER	*Journal of Ancient Near Eastern Religions*
JANES	*Journal of the Ancient Near Eastern Society*
JAOS	*Journal of the American Oriental Society*
JATS	*Journal of the Adventist Theological Society*
JBL	*Journal of Biblical Literature*
JBTh	*Jahrbuch für Biblische Theologie*
JCS	*Journal of Cuneiform Studies*
JETS	*Journal of the Evangelical Theological Society*
JHS	*Journal of Hebrew Scriptures*
JJS	*Journal of Jewish Studies*
JM	P. JOÜON – T. MURAOKA, *A Grammar of Biblical Hebrew*, SubBi 27, Roma 1991, ²2009
JNES	*Journal of Near Eastern Studies*
JNSL	*Journal of Northwest Semitic Languages*
JPrag	*Journal of Pragmatics*
JPS	The Jewish Publication Society (*Hebrew-English TANAKH,* The Traditional Hebrew Text and the New JPS Translation, Philadelphia 1985, ²1999)
JSem	*Journal for Semitics*
JSOT	*Journal for the Study of the Old Testament*
JSOT.S	Journal for the Study of the Old Testament – Supplement Series
JSSt	*Journal of Semitic Studies*
JThIS	Journal of Theological Interpretation Supplements
K	Ketib
KAI	H. DONNER – W. RÖLLIG, *Kanaanäische und Aramäische Inschriften,* I, Wiesbaden 1962, ²1966
KAT	Kommentar zum Alten Testament
KHC	Kurzer Hand-Commentar zum Alten Testament
KStTh	Kohlhammer Studienbücher Theologie
KuD	*Kerygma und Dogma*

KUSATU	Kleine Untersuchungen zur Sprache des Alten Testaments und seiner Umwelt
L	Codex Leningradensis (Firkovich B19A)
l./ll.	line/lines
LangS	*Language in Society*
LAPO	Littératures anciennes du Proche-Orient
LASBF	*Liber annus. Studium Biblicum Franciscanum*
LBSo	Linguistische Berichte Sonderheft
LCL	The Loeb Classical Library
LeDiv	Lectio divina
LeDiv.HS	Lectio divina. Hors série
LeR	Le livre et le rouleau
LeTh	Leitfaden Theologie
LettM	Le letterature del mondo
Levant	*Levant. The Journal of the Council for British Research in the Levant*
LHBOTS	Library of Hebrew Bible/Old Testament Studies (continuazione della serie JSOT.S)
Liddell-Scott	H.G. Liddell – R. Scott, *A Greek-English Lexicon*, Oxford 1843, ¹⁰1968
Liddell-Scott(RS)	H.G. Liddell – R. Scott – H. Stuart Jones – R. McKenzie, *A Greek-English Lexicon*. Revised Supplement, Oxford 1996
LIM	Linguistic Inquiry Monographs
lit.	literally
LND	*La Nuova Diodati* (Brindisi 1991)
LPPrag	*Lodz Papers in Pragmatics*
LSAWS	Linguistic Studies in Ancient West Semitic
Lum.	*Lumen. Revista de sintesis y orientación de ciencias eclesiásticas*
Lust	J. Lust – E. Eynikel – K. Hauspie, *A Greek-English Lexicon of the Septuagint*. Revised edition, Stuttgart 2003
LUT	Lutherbibel (Stuttgart 1984)
LXX	Greek text of the Septuagint (based on the Papyrus 965, and the Alexandrian, Sinaiticus, and Vatican mss)

m.	masculine
Maarav	*Maarav. A Journal for the Study of the Northwest Semitic Languages and Literatures*
MaU	Manuali universitari
MBa	Manuali di base
MDOG	Mitteilungen der Deutschen Orientgesellschaft
ML	Manuali Laterza
MoBi	Le monde de la Bible
MONTANARI	F. MONTANARI, *Vocabolario della lingua greca,* Torino 1995
ms(s)	manuscript(s)
MSSOTS	Monograph Series. Society for Old Testament Studies
MSU	Mitteilungen des Septuaginta-Unternehmens
MSym	Melammu Symposia
MT	Masoretic Text
MTK	*Materiale Textkulturen*
MURAOKA	T. MURAOKA, *A Greek-English Lexicon of the Septuagint,* Leuven 2009
n./nn	note/notes
NAB	*New American Bible* (Washington 1970, ³1991)
NaplC12	é.PA.GÌN.ti. inscription, Babylon (*ed.* R. DA RIVA, *The Inscriptions of Nabopolassar Amēl-Marduk and Neriglissar,* SANER 3, Göttingen 2013)
NaplC32	Imgur-Enlil inscription, Babylon [long version] (*Ibid.*)
NBE	Nueva Biblia Española
NBL	M. GÖRG – B. LANG, *eds., Neues Bibel-Lexikon,* vols. I-III, Düsseldorf – Zürich 1988–2001
NBS.SHR	Numen Book Series. Studies in the History of Religions
NBSR	Nuova Biblioteca di Scienze Religiose
NEA	*Near Eastern Archeaology*
NEB	*The New English Bible.* The Old Testament (Oxford – Cambridge 1970)
Neotest.	*Neotestamentica*
ni.	niphal
NICOT	The New International Commentary on the Old Testament

NIDOTTE	W.A. VanGemeren, *ed., New International Dictionary of Old Testament Theology and Exegesis*, Grand Rapids 1997
NJKA	*Neue Jahrbücher für das klassische Altertum, Geschichte, deutsche Literatur und für Pädagogik*
no(s).	number/numbers
NRSV	*New Revised Standard Version* (New York 1989)
NRTh	Nouvelle revue théologique
NSBT	New Studies in Biblical Theology
NSK.AT	Neuer Stuttgarter Kommentar. Altes Testament
NVBTA	Nuova Versione della Bibbia dai Testi Antichi
OBO	Orbis biblicus et orientalis
OBT	Overtures to Biblical Theology
OIP	Oriental Institute Publication
ORA	Orientalische Religionen in der Antike
ost.	Ostrakon/ostraka
OTEs	*Old Testament Essays. Journal of the Old Testament Society of South Africa*
OTL	Old Testament Library
OTLing	Oxford Textbooks in Linguistics
OTS	Oudtestamentische Studiën = Old Testament Studies
p./pp.	page/pages
part.	participle
PBSB	Petite bibliothèque des sciences bibliques
PEQ	*Palestine Exploration Quarterly*
Pericope	Pericope. Scripture as Written and Read in Antiquity
pers.	person
PHSC	Perspectives on Hebrew Scriptures and its Contexts
pi.	piel
PIATA	Publications of the Institute of Archaeology. Tel Aviv
PIB	Pontificio Istituto Biblico
pl.	plural
pl./pls	plate/plates

PLO.NS	Porta Linguarum Orientalium – Neue Serie
PNA 2/II	H.D. Baker, *ed., The Prosopography of the Neo-Assyrian Empire.* Volume 2, Part II: L-N, Helsinki 2001
P.OTS	Peshitta. The Old Testament in Syriac
PNA	K. Radner – H.D. Baker, *eds., The Prosopography of the Neo-Assyrian Empire*, vols. I-VI, Helsinki 1998–2011
po.	Poel
POC	Prophetic-Obediential ConSign*A(c)tion*
Poétique	Collection Poétique
pron.	pronominal
pu.	pual
PVTG	Pseudepigrapha Veteris Testamenti Graece
Q	Qere
QJS	*Quarterly Journal of Speech*
QNB	Quaderni Netini di Bioetica
QSem	*Quaderni di Semantica*
RB	*Revue biblique*
RBR	*Ricerche bibliche e religiose*
RBSem	Retorica biblica e semitica
RCI	*Rivista del clero italiano*
RevExp	*Review and Expositor*
RevSR	*Revue des sciences religieuses*
RGG⁴	H.D. Betz *et al.* eds., *Religion in Geschichte und Gegenwart.* Handwörterbuch für Theologie und Religionswissenschaft. Vierte, völlig neu bearbeitete Auflage, vols. I–IX, Tübingen ⁴1998–2007
RGRW	Religions in the Graeco-Roman World
RHPR	*Revue d'histoire et de philosophie religieuses*
RhSem	Rhétorique sémitique
RIMA 2	A.K. Grayson, *ed., Assyrian Rulers of the Early First Millennium BC I (1114–859 B.C.)*, RIMA 2, Toronto – London 1991
RIMA	The Royal Inscriptions of Mesopotamia
RINAP 1	H. Tadmor – S. Yamada, *The Royal Inscriptions of Tiglath-Pileser III (744–727 B.C.) and Shalmaneser V (726–722 B.C.), Kings of Assyria*, RINAP 1, Winona Lake 2011

732   Abbreviations and sigla

RINAP 3/2   A.K. GRAYSON – J. NOVOTNY, *eds., The Royal Inscriptions of Sennacherib, King of Assyria (704–681 B.C.)*, RINAP 3/2, Winona Lake 2014

RINAP 4   E. LEICHTY, *ed., The Royal Inscriptions of Esarhaddon, King of Assyria (680–669 B.C.)*, RINAP 4, Winona Lake 2011

RINAP   The Royal Inscriptions of the Neo-Assyrian Period

RivBib   *Rivista biblica*

Rivista AIC *Rivista Associazione Italiana dei Costituzionalisti*

RLA   E. EBELING – B. MEISSNER *et al. eds., Reallexikon der Assyriologie und Vorderasiatischen Archäologie*, vols. I–XIV, Berlin 1932–

RS/C   *Ricerche di S/Confine*

RSR   Recherches de science religieuse

RStB   Ricerche storico-bibliche

RSV   *Revised Standard Version* (New York 1952)

RTT   Research in Text Theory/Untersuchungen zur Texttheorie

S&HBC   Smyth & Helwys Bible Commentary

SAA 17   M. DIETRICH, *The Babylonian Correspondence of Sargon and Sennacherib*, SAA 17, Helsinki 2003

SAA 9   S. PARPOLA, *Assyrian Prophecies*, SAA 9, Helsinki 1997

SAA   State Archives of Assyria

SAAB   *State Archives of Assyria Bulletin*

SAHL   Studies in the Archaeology and History of the Levant

SAL   Scientific American Library

SANER   Studies in Ancient Near Eastern Records

SBB   Stuttgarter biblische Beiträge

SBFA   Studium Biblicum Franciscanum Analecta

SBL   Society of Biblical Literature

SBL.AIL   Society of Biblical Literature – Ancient Israel and Its Literature

SBL.AS   Society of Biblical Literature – Academia Series

SBL.SBL   Society of Biblical Literature – Studies in Biblical Literature

SBLDS   Society of Biblical Literature – Dissertation Series

SBLMS   Society of Biblical Literature – Monograph Series

SBLRBS   Society of Biblical Literature – Resources for Biblical Study

SBLSBS   Society of Biblical Literature – Sources for Biblical Study

SBLSP	*Society of Biblical Literature – Seminar Papers*
SBLSymS	Society of Biblical Literature – Symposium Series
SBLWAW	Society of Biblical Literature – Writings from the Ancient World
SBLWAWS	Society of Biblical Literature – Writings from the Ancient World Supplements Series
SBOT	The Sacred Books of the Old Testament
SBS	Stuttgarter Bibelstudien
SBT	Studies in Biblical Theology
SBT.SS	Studies in Biblical Theology. Second Series
SBTS	Sources for Biblical and Theological Study
SCAn	Smithsonian Contributions to Anthropology
ScAnt	*Scienze dell'Antichità*
ScBib	Sciences Bibliques
SchL	Schweich Lectures of the British Academy
ScrHie	Scripta Hierosolymitana
ScrVic⁺	*Scriptorium Victoriense*
SEÅ	*Svensk Exegetisk Årsbok*
SELVOA	*Studi Epigrafici e Linguistici sul Vicino Oriente Antico*
Sem.	*Semitica*
SemClas	*Semitica et Classica.* Revue internationale d'études orientales et méditerranéennes. International Journal of Oriental and Mediterranean Studies
Semeia	Semeia. An Experimental Journal for Biblical Criticism
SemeiaSt	Semeia studies. Society of Biblical Literature
SESJ	Schriften der Finnischen Exegetischen Gesellschaft
SGL	Scrittori greci e latini (Fondazione Lorenzo Valla)
SHCANE	Studies in the History and Culture of the Ancient Near East
SHR	Studies in the History of Religions
SIDA	Scripta Instituti Donneriani Aboensis
SJ(L)	Studies in Judaism (Lenham)
SJHC	Studies in Jewish History and Culture
SJOT	*Scandinavian Journal of the Old Testament*
SKI.NF	Studien zu Kirche und Israel. Neue Folge

SlgM	Sammlung Metzler
SMEA	*Studi Micenei ed Egeo-Anatolici*
SNTSMS	Society for the New Testament Studies. Monograph Series
SOTI	Studies in Old Testament Interpretation
SPSHS	Scholars Press Studies in the Humanities Series
SRivBib	Supplementi alla Rivista Biblica
SSN	Studia Semitica Neerlandica
SSS	*Sign Systems Studies*
StBi (Bo)	Studi biblici, Bologna
STEPHANUS	H. STEPHANUS (*eds.* L.A. DINDORF – W. DINDORF – K.B. HASE), *Thesaurus graecae linguae,* vols. I-IX, Parisiis 1831–1865
STLa	Saggi Tascabili Laterza
StOTB	Studies in Old Testament Biblical Theology
StP	Studia Pohl
StPT	Studies in Philosophical Theology
StRic.SB	Studi e ricerche. Sezione biblica
StSLL	Studies in Semitic Languages and Linguistics
StTDJ	Studies on the Texts of the Desert of Judah
StTh	*Studia Theologica – Nordic Journal of Theology* (*Scandinavian Journal of Theology*)
SubBi	Subsidia biblica
subj.	subject
suff.	suffix
SusBi	Sussidi Biblici
Sym	Revision of LXX by Symmachus
Syr	Syriaca. The Old Testament in Syriac according to the Peshitta Version
Syr.	*Syria. Revue d'art oriental et d'archéologie*
TasB	Tascabili Bompiani
TAVO	Tübinger Atlas des vorderen Orients
TB	Theologische Bücherei
TBL	Tübinger Beiträge zur Linguistik
TCT	Textual Criticism and the Translator

TECC	Textos y studios "Cardinal Cisneros"
Teol(M)	*Teologia.* Milano. Rivista della Facoltà Teologica dell'Italia settentrionale
TesXII.Jud	*Testament of Judah* (in: M. DE JONGE, *ed., The Testaments of the Twelve Patriarchs.* A Critical Edition of the Greek Text, PVTG 1/2, Leiden 1978)
Tg	Targum (*ed.* A. SPERBER, *The Bible in Aramaic.* Based on Old Manuscripts and Printed Texts. Volume III: The Latter Prophets according to Targum Jonathan, Leiden 1962, Leiden – Boston ³2004)
TGr.T	Tesi Gregoriana. Serie Teologia
ThA	Theologische Arbeiten
THAT	E. JENNI – C. WESTERMANN, *eds., Theologisches Handwörterbuch zum Alten Testament,* vols. I-II, München 1971–1976
ThBl	*Theologische Blätter*
ThLZ	*Theologische Literaturzeitung*
ThTh	Themen der Theologie.
ThTo	*Theology Today*
ThWAT	G.J. BOTTERWECK – H. RINGGREN *et al.* eds., *Theologisches Wörterbuch zum Alten Testament,* vols. I-X, Stuttgart 1970–2016
ThZ	*Theologische Zeitschrift*
TL.SM	Trends in Linguistics. Studies and Monographs
TOB	*Traduction oecuménique de la Bible* (Paris 1975)
TrEu	*Transeuphratène. Études sur la Syrie-Palestine et Chypre à l'époque perse*
TSSI	Textbook of Syrian Semitic Inscriptions
TThZ	*Trierer theologische Zeitschrift*
TVOA.M	Testi del Vicino Oriente Antico – 2, Letterature mesopotamiche
TynB	*Tyndale Bulletin*
UAVA	Untersuchungen zur Assyriologie und vorderasiatischen Archäologie
UF	*Ugarit-Forschungen*
USQR	*Union Seminary Quarterly Review*
UTB	Uni-Taschenbücher
v./vv.	verse/verses
VA	*Venezia Arti*
VAB	Vorderasiatische Bibliothek

736 Abbreviations and sigla

VACCARI *La Sacra Bibbia* tradotta dai testi originali con note a cura del Pontificio Istituto Biblico di Roma (Firenze 1957–1958)

Vg Vulgata

VJTR *Vidyajyoti Journal of Theological Reflection*

vol(s). volume/volumes

VStH *Vanderbilt Studies in Humanities*

VT *Vetus Testamentum*

VT.S Vetus Testamentum – Supplements

W&H Warfare and History

WAM M. FIEGER – J. KRISPENZ – J. LANCK, *eds.*, *Wörterbuch alttestamentlicher Motive*, Darmstadt 2013

WAr *World Archaeology*

WARENEP The Wellcome Archaeological Research Expedition to the Near East Publications

WBA Brisa Old-Babylonian Inscription

WBC World Biblical Commentary

WMANT Wissenschaftliche Monographien zum Alten und Neuen Testament

WO B.K. WALTKE – M. O'CONNOR, *An Introduction to Biblical Hebrew Syntax*, Winona Lake 1990

WS 1 Wadi es-Saba' Inscription

WuD *Wort und Dienst*

WUNT Wissenschaftliche Untersuchungen zum Neuen Testament

WW *Word and World*

WWeg *Wort auf dem Weg*

ZA *Zeitschrift für Assyriologie und Vorderasiatische Archäologie*

ZABR *Zeitschrift für altorientalische und biblische Rechtsgeschichte*

ZAH *Zeitschrift für Althebraistik*

ZAW *Zeitschrift für die alttestamentliche Wissenschaft*

ZBK.AT Zürcher Bibelkommentare AT

ZDMG *Zeitschrift der Deutschen Morgenländischen Gesellschaft*

ZDPV *Zeitschrift des Deutschen Palästina-Vereins*

ZKTh *Zeitschrift für katholische Theologie*

ZORELL   F. ZORELL, *Lexicon Hebraicum et Aramaicum Veteris Testamenti*, Roma 1968

ZThK   *Zeitschrift für Theologie und Kirche*

Bibliography

1. Hebrew text and ancient versions

1.1. Hebrew text

ELLIGER, K. – RUDOLPH, W., eds., *Biblia Hebraica Stuttgartensia*, Stuttgart 1967–1977.

FREEDMAN, D.N. *et al.*, eds., *The Leningrad Codex*. The Facsimile Edition, Grand Rapids 1998.

GOSHEN-GOTTSTEIN, M.H., ed., *The Aleppo Codex*. Provided with Massoretic Notes and Pointed by Aaron BEN ASHER, Jerusalem 1976.

LÖWINGER, D.S., *Codex Cairo of the Bible*. From the Karaite Synagoge at Abbasiya, Jerusalem 1971.

McCARTHY, C., ed., *Deuteronomy*, BHQ 5, Stuttgart 2007.

PÉREZ CASTRO, F., ed., *El Codice de Profetas de el Cairo*. Tomo V: Jeremias, TECC 37, Madrid 1987.

RABIN, C. – TALMON, S. – TOV, E., eds., *The Book of Jeremiah*. The Hebrew University Bible, Jerusalem 1997.

STRACK, H.L., ed., *The Hebrew Bible – Latter Prophets: The Babylonian Codex of Petrograd*, New York 1971.

ULRICH, E., *The Biblical Qumran Scrolls*. Transcriptions and Textual Variants. Vol. 2: Isaiah–Twelve Minor Prophets, Leiden – Boston 2013.

ULRICH, E., *et al.* eds., *Qumran Cave 4. X: The Prophets*, DJD XV, Oxford 1997.

WHITE CRAWFORD, S . – JOOSTEN, J . – ULRICH, E., «Sample Edition of the Oxford Hebrew Bible: Deuteronomy 32:1–9, 1 Kings 11:1–8, and Jeremiah 27:1–10 (34 G)», *VT* 58 (2008) 352–366.

1.2. Ancient versions

Greek version of the Septuagint

RAHLFS, A., ed., *Septuaginta*. Vol. II: Libri poetici et prophetici, Stuttgart 1935, [9]1984.

RAHLFS, A., *Septuaginta*. Id est Vetus Testamentum graece iuxta LXX interpretes. Editio altera quam recognovit et emendavit Robert Hanhart, Stuttgart 2006.

ZIEGLER, J., ed., *Jeremias, Baruch, Threni, Epistula Jeremiae*, Septuaginta, Vetus Testamentum Graecum. Auctoritate Societatis Litterarum Gottingensis editum XV Göttingen 1957.

Syriac version of the Peshiṭta (Jeremiah)

ALBREKTSON, B., *et al.*, *The Old Testament in Syriac according to the Peshiṭta Version*. Jeremiah – Lamentations – Epistle of Jeremiah – Epistle of Baruch – Baruch, P.OTS 3.2, Leiden 2019.

740 Bibliography

Aramaic version of the Targum (Latter Prophets)

MONACHI ABBATIAE PONTIFICIAE SANCTI HIERONYMI IN URBE ORDINIS SANCTI BENEDICTI, eds., *Liber Hieremiae et Lamentationes.* Biblia sacra iuxta latinam vulgatam versionem XIV, Romae 1972.

SPERBER, S., *The Bible in Aramaic.* Based on Old Manuscripts and Printed Texts. Vol. III: The Latter Prophets According to Targum Jonathan, Leiden 1962, Leiden – Boston ³2004.

Latin version of the Vulgate

WEBER, R. – GRYSON, R., eds., *Biblia Sacra Vulgata.* Editio quinta, Stuttgart 1969, ⁵2007.

2. Other sources

2.1. Texts from the ancient Near East

AḤITUV, S., *Echoes from the Past.* Hebrew and Cognate Inscriptions from the Biblical Period, Jerusalem 2008.

BORGER, R., *Die Inschriften Asarhaddons Königs von Assyrien*, AfO 9, Graz 1956.

CAGNI, L., ed., *Le profezie di Mari*, TVOA.M 2.2, Brescia 1995.

CROSS, F.M. «The Cave Inscriptions from Khirbet Beit Lei», in: *Near Eastern Archaeology in the Twentieth Century.* Essays in Honor of Nelson Glueck, *ed.* J.A. SANDERS, Garden City 1970, 299–306.

DA RIVA, R., *The Twin Inscriptions of Nebuchadnezzar at Brisa (Wadi Esh-Sharbin, Lebanon).* A Historical and Philological Study, AfO.B 32, Wien 2012.

DA RIVA, R., *The Inscriptions of Nabopolassar, Amēl-Marduk and Neriglissar*, SANER 3, Göttingen 2013.

DIETRICH, M., *The Babylonian Correspondence of Sargon and Sennacherib*, SAA 17, Helsinki 2003.

DOBBS-ALLSOPP, F.W. *et al.*, *Hebrew Inscriptions.* Texts from the Biblical Period of the Monarchy with Concordances, New Haven – London 2005.

DONNER, H. – RÖLLIG, W., *Kanaanäische und Aramäische Inschriften.* Band I: 5., erweiterte und überarbeitete Auflage, Wiesbaden 1962, ⁵2002.

DURAND, J.-M., *Archives épistolaires de Mari I/1*, ARM 26/1, Paris 1988.

GIBSON, J.C.L., *Hebrew and Moabite Inscriptions*, TSSI 1, Oxford 1971, ²1973.

GLASSNER, J.-J., *Mesopotamian Chronicles*, SBLWAW 19, Atlanta 2004.

GRAYSON, A.K., *Assyrian and Babylonian Chronicles*, Locust Valley 1975.

GRAYSON, A.K., ed., *Assyrian Rulers of the Early First Millennium BC I (1114–859 B.C.)*, RIMA 2, Toronto – London 1991.

GRAYSON, A.K. – NOVOTNY, J., eds., *The Royal Inscriptions of Sennacherib, King of Assyria (704–681 BC), Part 2*, RINAP 3/2, Winona Lake 2014.

HALLO, W.W. – YOUNGER, K.L., Jr., eds., *The Context of Scripture.* Monumental Inscriptions from the Biblical World, vol. II, Leiden 2000.

HALLO, W.W. – YOUNGER, K.L., Jr., eds., *The Context of Scripture.* Archival Documents from the Biblical World, vol. III, Leiden 2002.

Bibliography   741

KNUDTZON, J.A., *ed., Die El-Amarna-Tafeln, mit Einleitung und Erläuterungen.* Herausgegeben von J.A. Knudtzon, Anmerkungen und Register bearbeitet von Otto Weber und Erich Ebeling, VAB 2/I-II, Leipzig 1915.

LEICHTY, E., *ed., The Royal Inscriptions of Esarhaddon, King of Assyria (680–669 Bc),* RINAP 4, Winona Lake 2011.

LUCKENBILL, D.D., *The Annals of Sennacherib,* OIP 2, Chicago 1924.

MORAN, W.L., *The Amarna Letters,* Baltimore 1992.

NIESE, B., *ed., Flavii Iosephi Opera.* Vol. II. Antiquitatum Iudaicarum libri VI–X, Berolini 1885.

PARPOLA, S., *Assyrian Prophecies,* SAA 9, Helsinki 1997.

PARPOLA, S., *Letters from Assyrian and Babylonian Scholars,* SAA 10, Helsinki 1993.

PARPOLA, S. – WATANABE, K., *Neo-Assyrian Treaties and Loyalty Oaths,* SAA 2, Helsinki 1988.

RENZ, J., *Die althebräischen Inschriften.* Teil 1. Text und Kommentar, HAE 1, Darmstadt 1995.

RENZ, J., *Texte und Tafeln,* HAE 3, Darmstadt 1995.

SMELIK, K.A.D., *Writings from Ancient Israel.* A Handbook of Historical and Religious Documents, Edinburgh 1991 (originale olandese: Id., *Behouden Schrift: historische documentation uit het oude Israël,* Baarn 1984).

STUDEVENT-HICKMAN, B. – MELVILLE, S.C. – NOEGEL, S., «Neo-Babylonian Period Texts from Babylonia and Syro-Palestine», in: *The Ancient Near East.* Historical Sources in Translation, *ed.* M.W. CHAVALAS, Malden 2006, 382–406.

TADMOR, H. – YAMADA, S., *The Royal Inscriptions of Tiglath-Pileser III (744–727 BC) and Shalmaneser V (726–722 BC), Kings of Assyria,* RINAP 1, Winona Lake 2011.

TORCZYNER, H., *et al. eds., Lachish I (Tell ed-Duweir).* The Lachish Letters, WARENEP 1, London 1938.

WISEMAN, D.J., *Chronicles of Chaldean Kings (626–556 B.C.) in the British Museum,* London 1956.

WISEMAN, D.J., *The Vassal-Treaties of Esarhaddon,* London 1958.

2.2. Classical historiography

BEGG, C. – SPILSBURY, P., *eds., Flavius Josephus Judean Antiquities 8–10,* FJTC 5, Leiden 2001.

CAESAR, *The Gallic War.* With an English Translation by H.J. EDWARDS, LCL 72, London – Cambridge (MA) 1917.

ERODOTO, *Le Storie.* A cura di Aristide Colonna e Fiorenza Bevilacqua, vols. I–II, Classici UTET.CL, Torino 1996.

FLAVIO GIUSEPPE, *La guerra giudaica.* A cura di Giovanni Vitucci, vol. II (Libri IV–VII), SGL, Milano 1974.

FLAVIUS JOSEPHUS, *Josephus.* The Jewish War, Books IV–VII, With an English Translation by H.St.J. Thackeray, III, LCL 210, London – New York 1928.

742 Bibliography

FLAVIUS JOSEPHUS, *Judean Antiquities 8–10*. Translation and Commentary by C.T. BEGG – P. SPILSBURY, FJTC 5, Leiden – Boston 2005.

HERODOTUS, *The Persian Wars*. With an English Translation by A.D. GODLEY, I, Books I–II, LCL 117, London – Cambridge (MA) 1920, ²1981.

HERODOTUS, *The Persian Wars*. With an English Translation by A.D. GODLEY, III, Books V–VII, LCL 119, London – Cambridge (MA) 1938.

JACOBY, F., *Die Fragmente der griechischen Historiker*, vol. 3C, Leiden 1958, 364–395.

LIVY, *Livy*. With an English Translation in Fourteen Volumes, IX, Books XXXI–XXXIV, Translated by E.T. SAGE, LCL 295, Cambridge (MA) – London 1935, ²1985.

NIESE, B., *ed.*, *Flavii Iosephi Opera*. Edidit et apparatu critico instruxit Benedictus Niese, vol. II, Antiquitatum Iudaicarum Libri VI–X, Berolini 1885.

POLYBIUS, *The Histories*. With an English Translation by W.R. PATON, VI, LCL 161, Cambridge (MA) – London 1968.

PLUTARCO, *Vite*. Volume quinto. A cura di Gabriele Marasco, Classici UTET.CG, Torino 1994.

ROSÉN, H.B., *ed.*, *Herodoti Historiae*. Vol. I: Libros I–IV continens, Leipzig 1987.

SCRIPTORES HISTORIAE AUGUSTAE, *The Scriptores Historiae Augustae*. With an English Translation by D. MAGIE, III, LCL 263, Cambridge (MA) – London 1932.

TACITO, *Opere*. Annali, Storie, Germania, Agricola, Dialogo degli oratori. Traduzione di C. GIUSSANI, commento di Albino Garzetti, introduzione di Alain Michel, I millenni, Torino 1968.

TACITUS, *Tacitus*. In Five Volumes, IV, The Annals, Books IV–VI, XI–XII, with an English Translation by J. JACKSON, LCL 312, Cambridge (MA) – London 1937.

TACITUS, *The Annals*. Translated, with Introduction and Notes, by A.J. WOODMAN, Indianapolis – Cambridge 2004.

THUCYDIDES, *The War of the Peloponnesians and the Athenians*. Edited and Translated by J. MYNOTT, CTHPT, Cambridge 2013.

TITO LIVIO, *Storie*. Libri XXXI–XXXV. A cura di Piero Pecchiura, Classici UTET.CL, Torino 1970.

TUCIDIDE, *Il dialogo dei Melii e degli Ateniesi*. A cura di Luciano Canfora con testo a fronte, Venezia 1991.

VERBRUGGHE, G.P. – WICKERSHAM, J.M., *Berossos and Manetho, Introduced and Translated*. Native Traditions in Ancient Mesopotamia and Egypt, Ann Arbor 1996.

ZOSIMUS, *New History*. A Translation with Commentary by R.T. RIDLEY, AABS 2, Camberra 1982.

2.3. Other classics

ARISTOTLE, *Ethica Eudemia*. Recognoverunt brevique adnotatione critica instruxerunt R.R. WALZER et J.M. MINGAY, Praefatione auxit J.M. MINGAY, Oxford 1991.

HOMER, *Iliad*. Books 13–34. With an English Translation by A.T. MURRAY, Revised by William F. WYATT, LCL 171, Cambridge (MA) – London 1999.

PLATO, *Platonis opera*. Recognovit brevique adnotatione critica instruxit Ioannes Burnet. Tomus II tetralogias III–IV continens, Oxonii 1901.

PLATO, *Timaeus. Critias. Cleitophon. Menexenus. Epistles*. Translated by R.G. BURY, LCL 234, Cambridge (MA) 1929.

SENECA, *Dialoghi*. A cura di Paola Ramondetti, Torino 1999.

SUN-TZU, *Sun Tzu on the Art of War*. The Oldest Military Treatise in the World. Translated from the Chinese by L. GILES, London 1910.

2.4. Dead Sea texts

BROSHI, M. *et al.* eds., *Qumran Cave 4*. XIV: Parabiblical Texts. Part 2, DJD XIX, Oxford 1995.

CHARLESWORTH, J.H., *The Dead Sea Scrolls*. Hebrew, Aramaic, and Greek Texts with English Translations. Volume 7: Temple Scroll and Related Documents, Tübingen 2011.

MAIER, J., *The Temple Scroll*. An Introduction, Translation and Commentary, JSOT.S 34, Sheffield 1985.

2.5. Rabbinical and Jewish texts

BEKHOR, S. – HADAD DADON, A., *ed.*, *Genesi – Bereshit*, Milano 2006.

BLACKMAN P., *Mishnayot*. Vol. IV: Order Nezikin, New York 1963.

CATTANI, L., *ed.*, *Rashi*. Commento alla Genesi, Casal Monferrato 1985.

CAVALLETTI, S., *ed.*, *Il trattato delle benedizioni (Berakhot) del Talmùd babilonese*, Torino 1968.

DANIEL, S., *ed.*, *De specialibus legibus I et II*, Les œuvres de Philon d'Alexandrie 32, Paris 1972.

DAVIS, A., *ed.*, *The Metsudah Chumash/Rashi*, III ויקרא Vayikro, Brooklyn 1998. DE JONGE, M., *ed.*, *The Testaments of the Twelve Patriarchs*. A Critical Edition of the Greek Text, PVTG 1/2, Leiden 1978.

DE JONGE, M., *The Testaments of the Twelve Patriarchs*. A Critical Edition of the Greek Text, PVTG 1/2, Leiden 1978.

GOLDWURM, H. – SCHORR, Y.S. – MALINOWITZ, C., *eds.*, *The Schottenstein Edition Talmud Bavli* = תלמוד בבלי: The Gemara: The Classic Vilna Edition, with an Annotated, Interpretive Elucidation, as an Aid to Talmud Study, vols. I–LXXIII, Brooklyn 1990–2005.

NEUSNER, J., *Sifra*. An Analytical Translation, vol. I, BJSt 138, Atlanta 1988.

Pirqê Abôth. Traduzione dall'ebraico, introduzione e commento di Yoseph Colombo, CCE 9, Roma 1985.

SILBERMANN, A.M., *Chumash with Targum Onkelos, Haphtaroth and Rashi's Commentary Translated into English and Annotated*, Jerusalem 5745 [A.D. 1984].

WEINREB, T.H. *et al.* eds., *Koren Talmud Bavli*, vols. I–XLII, Jerusalem 2012.

3. Photographic Repertories

ALBENDA, P., *The Palace of Sargon, King of Assyria*. Monumental Wall Reliefs at Dur-Sharrukin, from Original Drawings Made at the Time of their Discovery in 1843–1844 by Botta and Flandin, Paris 1986.

BARNETT, R.D., *Sculptures from the North Palace of Ashurbanipal at Nineveh (668–627 B.C.)*, London 1976.

BARNETT, R.D. – BLEIBTREU, E. – TURNER, G., *Sculptures from the Southwest Palace of Sennacherib at Nineveh*, London 1998.

BARNETT, R.D. – FALKNER, M., *The Sculptures of Aššur-Naṣir-Apli II (883–859 B.C.), Tiglath-Pileser III (745–727 B.C.), Esarhaddon (681–669 B.C.) from the Central and South-West Palaces at Nimrud*, London 1962.

ORTHMANN, W., *Der Alte Orient*, PKG 14, Berlin 1975.

PARROT, A., *Assur*, L'univers des formes, Paris 1961.

PRITCHARD, J.B., *The Ancient Near East in Pictures Relating to the Old Testament*. Second Edition with Supplement, Princeton 1954, ²1969.

STROMMENGER, E., *Fünf Jahrtausende Mesopotamien*. Die Kunst von den Anfängen um 5000 v.Chr. bis zu Alexander dem Grossen, München 1962.

USSISHKIN, D., *The Conquest of Lachish by Sennacherib*, Tel Aviv 1982.

WISEMAN, D.J., *Illustrations from Biblical Archaeology*, Lodon 1958.

4. Instruments

4.1. Grammar and syntax books

BLAU, J. *A Grammar of Biblical Hebrew*, PLO.NS 12, Wiesbaden 1976, ²1993.

GESENIUS, W. (*eds.* U. RÜTERSWÖRDEN – R. MEYER – H. DONNER), *Hebräisches und Aramäisches Handwörterbuch über das Alten Testament*, Berlin – Heidelberg ¹⁸1987–2012.

GESENIUS, W. – KAUTZSCH, E., *Hebräische Grammatik*, Halle 1813, Leipzig ²⁸1909.

GOGEL, S.L., *A Grammar of Epigraphic Hebrew*, SBLRBS 23, Atlanta 1998.

JOÜON, P. – MURAOKA, T., *A Grammar of Biblical Hebrew*, SubBi 27, Roma 1991, ²2009.

NICCACCI, A., *Sintassi del verbo ebraico nella prosa biblica classica*, SBFA 23, Jerusalem 1986.

WALTKE, B.K. – O'CONNOR, M., *An Introduction to Biblical Hebrew Syntax*, Winona Lake 1990.

4.2. Dictionaries, encyclopedias, concordances, and other instruments

BARNERT, S., *et al.*, *Dictionary of Physics*, 4 vols., London – New York 2004.

BERLEJUNG, A. – FREVEL, C., *eds.*, *Handbuch theologischer Grundbegriffe zum Alten und Neuen Testament*, Darmstadt 2006.

Betz, H.D. *et al. eds., Religion in Geschichte und Gegenwart*. Handwörterbuch für Theologie und Religionswissenschaft. Vierte, völlig neu bearbeitete Auflage, vols. I–IX, Tübingen [4]1998–2007.

Clines D.J.A., *Dictionary of Classical Hebrew*, vols. I–VIII, Sheffield 1993–2011.

Cohen, M.E., *An English to Akkadian Companion to the Assyrian Dictionaries*, Bethesda 2011.

Ebeling, E. – Meissner, B., *et al. eds., Reallexikon der Assyriologie und Vorderasiatischen Archäologie*, vols. I–XIV, Berlin 1932-.

Fieger, M. – Krispenz, J. – Lanck, J., *eds., Wörterbuch alttestamentlicher Motive*, Darmstadt 2013.

Fondazione Centro Studi Filosofici di Gallarate, *ed., Enciclopedia Filosofica*, vols. I–XII, Milano 2006.

Freedman, D.N., *ed., Anchor Bible Dictionary*, vols. I–VI, New York 1992.

Gesenius, W, *Thesaurus philologicus criticus linguae hebraeae et chaldaeae Veteris Testamenti*, vols. I–III, Lipsiae 1829–1842.

Görg, M. – Lang, B., *eds., Neues Bibel-Lexikon*, vols. I–III, Düsseldorf – Zürich 1988–2001.

Greimas, A.J. – Courtés, J., *eds., Sémiotique*. Dictionnaire raisonné de la théorie du langage, vols. I–II, Paris 1979–1986.

Hatch, E. – Redpath, H.A., *A Concordance to the Septuagint and the Other Greek Versions of the Old Testament (Including the Apocryphal Books)*, Oxford 1897–1906, Grand Rapids [2]1998.

Jenni. E. – Westermann, C., *eds., Theologisches Handwörterbuch zum Alten Testament*, vols. I–II, München 1971–1976.

Karrer, M. – Kraus, W., *Septuaginta Deutsch*. Erläuterungen und Kommentare zum griechischen Alten Testament, Stuttgart 2011.

Khan, G., *ed., Encyclopedia of Hebrew Language and Linguistics*, vols. I–IV, Leiden – Boston 2013.

Köhler, L. – Baumgartner, W., *Hebräisches und Aramäisches Lexikon zum Alten Testament*, Leiden [3]1967–1996.

Liddell, H.G. – Scott, R., *A Greek-English Lexicon*, Oxford 1843, [10]1968.

Liddell, H.G. – Scott, R. – Stuart Jones, H. – McKenzie, R., *A Greek-English Lexicon*. Revised Supplement, Oxford 1996.

Lust, J. – Eynikel, E. – Hauspie, K., *A Greek-English Lexicon of the Septuagint*. Revised Edition, Stuttgart 2003.

Montanari, F., *Vocabolario della lingua greca*, Torino 1995.

Muraoka, T., *A Greek-English Lexicon of the Septuagint*, Leuven 2009.

Neusner, J., *Jeremiah in Talmud and Midrash*. A Source Book, SJ(L), Lanham 2006.

Oppenheim, A.L., *et al. eds., The Assyrian Dictionary of the Oriental Institute of the University of Chicago*, vols. I–XXI, Chicago – Glückstadt 1956–2010.

Pardee, D., *A Handbook of Ancient Hebrew Letters*. A Study Edition, SBLSBS 15, Chico 1982.

746 Bibliography

PARPOLA, S., ed., *Assyrian-English-Assyrian Dictionary*, Helskinki 2007.

PIROT, L. *et al.* eds., *Supplément au Dictionnaire de la Bible*, vols. I–XIII, Paris 1928-.

RADNER, K. – BAKER, H.D., eds., *The Prosopography of the Neo-Assyrian Empire*, vols. I–VI, Helsinki 1998–2011.

RENZ, R. – RÖLLIG, W., *Handbuch der althebräischen Epigraphik*, Darmstadt 1995–2003.

RYKEN, L. – WILHOIT, J.C. – LONGMAN III, T., eds., *Dictionary of Biblical Imagery*, Downers Grove 1998.

SÆBØ, M., ed., *Hebrew Bible/Old Testament. The History of Its Interpretation*, vols. I–V, Göttingen 1996–2015.

SKOLNIK, F., *et al.* eds., *Encyclopaedia Judaica*. Second Edition, vols. I–XXII, Detroit 2007.

STEPHANUS, H., (eds. L.A. DINDORF – W. DINDORF – K.B. HASE), *Thesaurus graecae linguae*, vols. I–IX, Parisiis 1831–1865.

STIPP, H.-J., *Deuterojeremianische Konkordanz*, ATSAT 63, St. Ottilien 1998.

TAWIL, H., *An Akkadian Lexicon Companion for Biblical Hebrew.* Etymological, Semantic and Idiomatic Equivalence with Supplement on Biblical Aramaic, Jersey City 2009.

TOV, E., *Revised Lists of the Texts from the Judean Desert*, Leiden – Boston 2010.

UEDING, G., ed., *Historisches Wörterbuch der Rhetorik*, vols. I–X, Tübingen – Berlin 1992–2012.

VANGEMEREN, W.A., ed., *New International Dictionary of Old Testament Theology and Exegesis*, Grand Rapids 1997.

VIGOUROUX, F., ed., *Dictionnaire de la Bible*, vols. I–V, Paris 1895–1912.

DE WAARD, J., A *Handbook on Jeremiah*, TCT 2, Winona Lake 2003.

ZORELL, F., *Lexicon Hebraicum et Aramaicum Veteris Testamenti*, Roma 1968.

4.3. Online/information technology resources

BibleWorks © 10: Software for Biblical Exegesis and Research (LLC, Norfolk 2015).

FrameNet Project. International Computer Science Institute (Berkeley, California: https://framenet.icsi.berkeley.edu/fndrupal/IntroPage).

The Semantics of Ancient Hebrew Database Project (http://www.sahd.div.ed.ac.uk/start). An International Collaborative Research Project (Bonn, Cambridge, Edinburgh, Florence, Oxford, Leiden, Rome *et al.*).

5. Commentaries and other studies

ABATE, E., *La fine del regno di Sedecia*, Madrid 2008.

ABREGO, J.M., *Jeremías y el final del reino.* Lectura sincrónica de Jer 36–45, Institución San Jerónimo, EstAT 3, Valencia 1983.

ABREGO, J.M., «El texto hebreo estructurado de Jeremías 36–45», *CuaBi* 8 (1983) 1–49.

ABREGO, J.M., *Los libros proféticos*, IEB 4, Estella 1993.

ACKERMAN, S., «The Personal is Political: Covenantal and Affectionate Love (ʾāhēb,ʾahăbâ) in the Hebrew Bible», *VT* 52 (2002) 437–458.

AEJMELAEUS, A., «Jeremiah at the Turning-Point of History: The Function of Jer. XXV 1–14 in the Book of Jeremiah», *VT* 52 (2002) 459–482.

AEJMELAEUS, A., «"Nebuchadnezzar, My Servant": Redaction History and Textual Development in Jer 27», in: *Interpreting Translation.* Studies on the LXX and Ezekiel in Honour of Johan Lust, eds. F. GARCÍA MARTÍNEZ – M. VERVENNE, BEThL 192, Leuven 2005, 1–18.

AGUILERA, A., «La fórmula "Templo de Yahvé, Templo de Yahvé, Templo de Yahvé" en Jer 7,4», *EstBib* 47 (1989) 319–342.

AHLSTRÖM, G.W., *Joel and the Temple Cult of Jerusalem,* VT.S 21, Leiden 1971.

AHLSTRÖM, G.W., *The History of Ancient Palestine from the Palaeolithic Period to Alexander's Conquest.* With a contribution by G.O. Rollefson, *ed.* D. EDELMAN, JSOT.S 146, Sheffield 1993.

AICHELE, G., *Sign, Text, Scripture.* Semiotics and the Bible, Sheffield 1997.

ALBALADEJO, T., *Teoría de los mundos posibles y macroestructura narrativa.* Análisis de las novelas cortas de Clarín, Alicante 1986.

ALBALADEJO, T., *Semántica de la narración.* La ficción realista, Madrid 1992.

ALBERTZ, R., «פלא», *THAT* II, 413–420.

ALBERTZ, R., *Religionsgeschichte Israels in alttestamentlicher Zeit.* Teil 1: Von den Anfängen bis zum Ende der Königszeit, ATD 8/1, Göttingen 1992.

ALBERTZ, R., *Die Exilszeit.* 6. Jahrhundert v. Chr., BE 7, Stuttgart 2001 [Eng. tr.: *Israel in Exile.* The History and Literature of the Sixth Century B.C.E., SBL.SBL 3, Atlanta 2003].

ALBREKTSON, B., «Prophecy and Politics in the Old Testament», in: *The Myth of the State, ed.* H. BIEZAIS, SIDA VI, Stockholm 1972, 45–56.

ALBRIGHT, W.F., «The Seal of Eliakim and the Latest Preëxilic History of Judah, with Some Observations on Ezekiel», *JBL* 51 (1932) 77–106.

ALBRIGHT, W.F., «King Joiachin in Exile», *BA* 5 (1942) 49–55.

ALETTI, J.-N. – GILBERT, M. – SKA, J.-L. – DE VULPILLIÈRES, S., *Vocabulaire raisonné de l'exégèse biblique.* Les mots, les approches, les auteurs, Paris 2005.

ALLEN, L.C., *Jeremiah.* A Commentary, OTL, Louisville 2008.

ALONSO DÍAZ, J., «El discernimiento entre el verdadero y el falso profeta según la Biblia», *EE* 49 (1974) 5–17.

ALONSO SCHÖKEL, L., *La palabra inspirada.* La Biblia a la luz de la ciencia del lenguaje, AcChr 27, Madrid 1964, ³1986.

ALONSO SCHÖKEL, L., *Il dinamismo della tradizione,* BCR 19, Brescia 1970.

ALONSO SCHÖKEL, L., «יָשַׁר III», *ThWAT* III, 1062–1069.

ALONSO SCHÖKEL, L., «Jeremías como anti-Moisés», in: *De la Tôrah au Messie.* Hom. à H. Cazelles, *eds.* M. CARREZ – J. DORÉ – P. GRELOT, Paris 1981, 245–254.

ALONSO SCHÖKEL, L., *Manual de poética hebrea,* Madrid 1987.

ALONSO SCHÖKEL, L., *Símbolos matrimoniales en la Biblia,* Estella 1997.

ALONSO SCHÖKEL, L. – SICRE DIAZ, J.L., *Profetas*. Introducciones y comentario. I. Isaias – Jeremias, NBE, Madrid 1980.

ALT, A., «Hic murus aheneus esto», *ZDMG* 86 (1933) 33–48.

ALTER, R., *The Art of Biblical Poetry*, New York 1985.

ALTHANN, R., «Zedekiah», *ABD* VI, 1068–1071.

ÁLVAREZ VALDÉS, A., «El enfrentamiento entre profetas y falsos profetas», *RevBib* 53 (1991) 217–229.

AMES, F.R., «The Meaning of War: Definitions for the Study of War in Ancient Israelite Literature», in: *Writing and Reading War*. Rhetoric, Gender, and Ethics in Biblical and Modern Contexts, *eds*. B.E. KELLE – F.R. AMES, SBLSymS 42, Atlanta 2008, 19–31.

AMIT, Y., *Reading Biblical Narratives*. Literary Criticism and the Bible, Minneapolis 2001.

AMSLER, S., «Les prophètes et la communication par les actes», in: *Werden und Wirken des Alten Testament*. Festschrift für C. Westermann zum 70. Geburtstag, *eds*. R. ALBERTZ *et al*., Göttingen 1980, 194–201.

AMSLER, S., *Les actes des prophètes*, EssBib 9, Genève 1985.

ANBAR, M., «To Put One's Neck under the Yoke», in: *Essays on Ancient Israel in Its Near Eastern Context*. A Tribute to Nadav Na'aman, *eds*. Y. AMIT *et al*., Winona Lake 2006, 17–19.

ANDERSON, J.A., *Communication Theory*. Epistemological Foundations, New York 1996.

ANOLLI, L., «Inquadramento storico e teorico sulla comunicazione», in: *Psicologia della comunicazione*, *ed*. L. ANOLLI, Strumenti, Bologna 2000, 3–32.

ANOLLI, L., *ed*., *Psicologia della comunicazione*, Strumenti, Bologna 2000.

ANOLLI, L., *Fondamenti di psicologia della comunicazione*, Manuali, Bologna 2006, [2]2012.

ANSORGE, U. – LEDER, H., *Wahrnehmung und Aufmerksamkeit*, Wiesbaden 2011.

APPLEGATE, J., «The Fate of Zedekiah: Redactional Debate in the Book of Jeremiah», *VT* 48 (1998) 137–160, 301–308.

ARENA, F., *Prophetic Conflicts in Jeremiah, Ezekiel, and Micah*. How Post-Exilic Ideologies Created the False (and the True) Prophets, FAT 2. Reihe 121, Tübingen 2020.

ARIEL, M., «The Demise of a Unique Concept of Literal Meaning», *JPrag* 34 (2002) 361–402.

ARNAUD, D., *Nabuchodonosor II roi de Babylone*, Paris 2004.

ARNOLD, B.T., «What has Nabuchadnezzar to do with David? On the Neo-Babylonian Period and Early Israel», in: *Mesopotamia and the Bible*. Comparative Explorations, *eds*. M.W. CHAVALAS – K.L. YOUNGER, Jr., JSOT.S 341, London 2002, 330–355.

ARNOLD, B.T. – MICHALOWSKI, P., «Achaemenid Period Historical Texts Concerning Mesopotamia», in: *The Ancient Near East*. Historical Sources in Translation, *ed*. M.W. CHAVALAS, Malden 2006, 407–430.

ASSMANN, J., *Ma'at: Gerechtigkeit und Unsterblichkeit im Alten Ägypten*, München 1990.

ASSMANN, J., *Das kulturelle Gedächtnis*. Schrift, Erinnerung und politische Identität in frühen Hochkulturen, München 1992, [7]2013.

ASSMANN, J., *Moses der Ägypter*. Entzifferung einer Gedächtnisspur, München 1998.

Assmann, J., *Herrschaft und Heil.* Politische Theologie in Altägypten, Israel und Europa, München – Wien 2000.

Assmann, J., *Die Mosaische Unterscheidung.* Oder Der Preis des Monotheismus, München 2003.

Astour, M., «*Sparagmos,* Omophagia and Ecstatic Prophecy at Mari», *UF* 24 (1992) 1–2.

Ataç, M.-A., *The Mythology of Kingship in Neo-Assyrian Art,* Cambridge 2010.

Auld, A.G., «Prophets and Prophecy in Jeremiah and Kings», *ZAW* 96 (1984) 66–82.

Auzou, G., *De la servitude au service.* Étude du livre de l'Exode, ConBi 3, Paris 1961.

Avioz, M., «The Historical Setting of Jeremiah 21:1–10», *AUSS* 44 (2006) 213–219.

Avis, P., *God and the Creative Imagination.* Metaphor, Symbol and Myth in Religion and Theology, London 1999.

Avishur, Y. – Heltzer, M., «Jehoiachin, King of Judah in Light of Biblical and Extra-Biblical Sources: His Exile and Release According to Events in the Neo-Babylonian Kingdom and the Babylonian Diaspora», *TrEu* 34 (2007) 17–36.

Bach, R., *Die Aufforderung zur Flucht und zum Kampf im alttestamentlichen Prophetenspruch,* WMANT 9, Neukirchen 1962.

Bach, H., «Wahres und falsches Prophetentum», *Bib.* 32 (1951) 237–262.

Badocco, C., «Precomprensione», *EF* IX, 8896–8897.

Báez, S.J., *Tiempo de callar y tiempo de hablar.* El silencio en la Biblia Hebrea, Roma 2000.

Bailey, R.C., «Prophetic Use of Omen Motifs: A Preliminary Study», in: *The Biblical Canon in Comparative Perspective.* Scripture in Context IV, eds. K.L. Younger, Jr. – W.W. Hallo – B.F. Batto, ANETS 11, Lewiston – Queenston – Lampeter 1991, 195–215.

Baker, D.W., «Explicative *waw*», *EHLL* I, 890–892.

Baker, H.D. – Brinkman, J.A., «*Nabû-kudurrī-uṣur*», *PNA* 2/II, 841–842.

Balentine, S.E., «The Prophet as Intercessor: A Reassessment», *JBL* 103 (1984) 161–173.

Balentine, S.E., «The Prose and Poetry of Exile», in: *Interpreting Exile.* Displacement and Deportation in Biblical and Modern Contexts, eds. B.E. Kelle – F.R. Ames – J.L. Wright, SBL.AIL 10, Atlanta 2011, 345–363.

Baltzer, K., *Das Bundesformular,* WMANT 4, Neukirchen-Vluyn 1960, ²1964.

Barr, J., *The Semantics of Biblical Language,* London 1961.

Barfado, P., «El silencio en el Antiguo Testamento: aproximación a un símbolo ambiguo», *EstBib* 55 (1997) 5–27.

Barrow, J.D., *Impossibility.* The Limits of Science and the Science of Limits, Oxford 1998.

Barstad, H.M., «No Prophets? Recent Developments in Biblical Prophetic Research and Ancient Near Eastern Prophecy», *JSOT* 57 (1993) 39–60.

Barstad, H.M., «History and Memory: Some Reflections on the "Memory Debate" in Relation to the Hebrew Bible», in: *The Historian and the Bible.* Essays in Honour of Lester L. Grabbe, eds. P.R. Davies – D.V. Edelman, LHBOTS 530, London – New York 2010, 1–10.

750   Bibliography

BARSTAD, H.M., «Jeremiah the Historian: The Book of Jeremiah as a Source for the History of the Near East in the Time of Nebuchadnezzar», in: *Studies on the Text and Versions of the Hebrew Bible in Honour of Robert Gordon*, eds. G. KHAN – D. LIPTON, VT.S 149, Leiden – Boston 2012, 87–98.

BARSTAD, H.M., «Who Destroyed Ashkelon? On Some Problems in Relating Text to Archaeology», in: *Let Us Go up to Zion*. Essays in Honour of H.G.M. Williamson on the Occasion of His Sixty-Fifth Birthday, *eds.* I. PROVAN – M.J. BODA, Leiden – Boston 2012, 345–357.

BARTHÉLEMY, D., *Critique textuelle de l'Ancien Testament*. 2. Isaie, Jérémie, Lamentations, OBO 50/2, Fribourg – Göttingen 1986.

BARTON, C.A., «The Price of Peace in Ancient Rome», in: *War and Peace in the Ancient World*, ed. K.A. RAAFLAUB, Malden – Oxford 2007, 244–255.

BARTON, J., «Historiography and Theodicy in the Old Testament», in: *Reflection and Refraction*. Studies in Biblical Historiography in Honour of A. Graeme Auld, *eds.* R. REZETKO – T.H. LIM – W.B. AUCKER, VT.S 113, Leiden – Boston 2007, 27–33.

BARTON, J., *Ethics in Ancient Israel*, Oxford 2014.

BASILE, G. – CASADEI, F. – LORENZETTI, L. – SCHIRRU, G. – THORNTON, A.M., *Linguistica generale*, MaU 93, Roma 2010.

BASTI, G., *Filosofia della Natura e della Scienza*. 1: I Fondamenti, Roma 2002.

BAUKS, M., «"Chaos" als Metapher für die Gefährdung der Weltordnung», in: *Das biblische Weltbild und seine altorientalischen Kontexte*, eds. B. JANOWSKI – B. EGO, FAT 32, Tübingen 2001, 431–464.

BAUKS, M., «Chaoskampf», WAM, 94–98.

BAUKS, M. – NIHAN, C., eds., *Manuel d'exégèse de l'Ancien Testament*, MoBi 61, Genève 2008.

BAUMANN, A., «מוט», *Th WAT* IV, 728–734.

BAUMANN, G., *The Written Word*. Literacy in Transition, Oxford 1986.

BEAUCHAMP, P., «Propositions sur l'alliance de l'Ancien Testament comme structure centrale», *RSR* 58 (1970) 161–194 (= Id., *Pages exégétiques*, LeDiv 202, Paris 2005, 55–86).

BEAUCHAMP, P., *L'un et l'autre Testament*. Essai de lecture, Paris 1976.

BEAUCHAMP, P., «Théologie biblique», in: *Initiation à la pratique de la théologie*. I: Introduction, *eds.* B. LAURET – F. REFOULÉ, Paris 1982, 189–237.

BEAUCHAMP, P., *Le récit, la lettre et le corps*. Essais bibliques, CFi 114, Paris 1982, ²1992.

BEAUCHAMP, P., «Au commencement, Dieu parle, ou les sept jours de la création», *Études* 365 (1986) 105–116.

BEAUCHAMP, P., «Création et fondation de la loi en Gn 1,1–2,4a. Le don de la nourriture végétale en Gn 1,29s», in: *La création dans l'Orient Ancien*. Congrès de L'ACFEB, Lille (1985), *eds.* F. BLANQUART – L. DEROUSSEAUX, LeDiv 127, Paris 1987, 139–182.

BEAUCHAMP, P., *Parler d'Écritures saintes*, Paris 1987.

BEAUCHAMP, P., «Préface», in: *L'analyse rhétorique*. Une nouvelle méthode pour comprendre la Bible, *ed.* R. MEYNET, Paris 1989, 7–14.

BEAUCHAMP, P., *L'un et l'autre Testament*. 2. Accomplir les Écritures, Paris 1990.

BEAUCHAMP, P., «Accomplir les Écritures. Un chemin de théologie biblique», *RB* 99 (1992) 132–162.

BEAUCHAMP, P., «Sens de l'Ecriture», *DCT*, 1084–1085.

BEAUCHAMP, P., «Lecture christique de l'Ancien Testament», *Bib.* 81 (2000) 105–115.

BEAUCHAMP, P. – VASSE, D., «La violence dans la Bible», CEv 76 (1991) [monographic issue].

BEAULIEU, P.-A., «נבופלאסר וקדמוניות בבל/Nabopolassar and the Antiquity of Babylon», in: *Hayim and Miriam Tadmor Volume*, eds. I. EPH'AL – A. BEN-TOR – P. MACHINIST, ErIsr 27, Jerusalem 2003, 9*-1*.

BECKER, U., «Die Wiederentdeckung des Prophetenbuches. Tendenzen und Aufgaben der gegenwärtigen Prophetenforschung», *BThZ* 21 (2004) 30–60.

BECKER, U., «Die Entstehung der Schriftprophetie», in: *Die unwiderstehliche Wahrheit. Studien zur alttestamentlichen Prophetie. Festschrift für Arndt Meinhold*, eds. R. LUX – E.-J. WASCHKE, ABIG 23, Leipzig 2006, 3–20.

BECKING, B., «"I Will Break his Yoke from off your Neck". Remarks on Jeremiah xxx 4–11», in: *New Avenues in the Study of the Old Testament*. A Collection of Old Testament Studies, ed. A.S. VAN DER WOUDE, OTS 25, Leiden 1989, 63–76 (reworked and republished in: Id., *Between Fear and Freedom*. Essays on the Interpretation of Jeremiah 30–31, OTS 51, Leiden – Boston 2004, 135–164).

BECKING, B., *Between Fear and Freedom*. Essays on the Interpretation of Jeremiah 30–31, OTS 51, Leiden – Boston 2004.

BEDFORD, P.R., «The Neo-Assyrian Empire», in: *The Dynamics of Ancient Empires. State Power from Assyria to Byzantium*, eds. I. MORRIS – W. SCHEIDEL, Oxford 2009, 30–65.

BEENTJES, P.C., «Inverted Quotations in the Bible: A Neglected Stylistic Pattern», *Bib.* 63 (1982) 506–523.

BEERDEN, K., *Worlds Full of Signs*. Ancient Greek Divination in Context, RGRW 176, Leiden – Boston 2013.

BEGIN, Z.B., «Does Lachish Letter 4 Contradict Jeremiah XXXIV 7?», *VT* 52 (2002) 166–174.

BEHRENS, A., *Prophetische Visionsschilderungen im Alten Testament*. Sprachliche Eigenarten, Funktion und Geschichte einer Gattung, AOAT 292, Münster 2002.

BENJAMIN, W., *Gesammelte Schriften*. Band 5: Das Passagen-Werk. 2 Teilbände, Frankfurt am Main 1991.

BEN-SHLOMO, D., «Results from Field IV: The Iron II and Later Periods», in: *The Smithsonian Institution Excavation at Tell Jemmeh, Israel, 1970–1990*, eds. D. BEN-SHLOMO – G.W. VAN BEEK, Washington 2014, SCAn 50, 403–641.

BEN-SHLOMO, D., «Tell Jemmeh, Philistia and the Neo-Assyrian Empire during the Late Iron Age», *Levant* 46 (2014) 58–88.

BEN ZVI, E., «The Prophetic Book. A Key Form of Prophetic Literature», in: *The Changing Face of Form Criticism for the Twenty-First Century*, eds. M.A. SWEENEY – E. BEN ZVI, Grand Rapids 2003, 276–297.

Béré, P., *Le second Serviteur de Yhwh.* Un portrait exégétique de Josué dans le livre éponyme, OBO 253, Göttingen 2012.

Berge, K., «Is There Hope in the Deuteronomistic History?», in: *New Perspectives on Old Testament Prophecy and History.* Essays in Honour of Hans M. Barstad, *eds.* R.I. Thelle – T. Stordalen – M.E.J. Richardson, VT.S 168, Leiden 2015, 264–277.

Berges, U., «Das Jesajabuch als literarische Kathedrale. Ein Rundgang durch die Jahrhunderte», *BiKi* 61 (2006) 190–197.

Bergman, J. – Lutzmann, H. – Schmidt, W.H. «דָּבָר», *ThWAT* II, 89–133.

Bergman, J. – Ottosson, M., «אֶרֶץ», *ThWAT* I, 418–436.

Bernardelli, A., *Che cos'è l'intertestualità*, Bussole 466, Roma 2013.

Bernhardt, K.-H., «בָּרָא III. Bedeutung», *ThWAT* I, 774–777.

Berridge, J.M., *Prophet, People, and the Word of Yahweh.* An Examination of Form and Content in the Proclamation of the Prophet Jeremiah, BST 4, Zürich 1970.

Bersani, L. – Dutoit, U., *The Forms of Violence.* Narrative in Assyrian Art and Modern Culture, New York 1985.

Betlyon, J.W., «Neo-Babylonian Military Operations other than War in Judah and Jerusalem», in: *Judah and the Judeans in the Neo-Babyloman Period, eds.* O. Lipschits – J. Blenkinsopp, Winona Lake 2003, 263–283.

Bettalli, M., «Il controllo di città e piazzeforti in Tucidide: l'arte degli assedi nel V secolo a.C.», ASNSP.L Serie III 23 (1993) 825–845.

Beuken, W.A.M., *Jesaja 1–12*, HThKAT, Freiburg im Breisgau 2003.

Beyerlin, W., *Reflexe der Amosvisionen im Jeremiabuch*, OBO 93, Freiburg – Göttingen 1989.

Bianchi, C., «Three Forms of Contextual Dependence», in: *Modeling and Using Context.* Second International and Interdisciplinary Conference. Context '99, Trento, Italy, September 9–11, 1999, Proceedings, *eds.* P. Bouquet *et al.*, Berlin 1999, 67–76.

Bianchi, C., *La dipendenza contestuale.* Per una teoria pragmatica del significato, Napoli 2001.

Bianchi, C., *Pragmatica del linguaggio,* Bari 2003, ⁸2010.

Bianchi, C., «Capire e farsi capire: pragmatica», in: *Filosofia della comunicazione, eds.* C. Bianchi – N. Vassallo, Bari 2005, 42–67.

Bianchi, C., *Pragmatica cognitiva.* I meccanismi della comunicazione, ML 273, Bari 2009.

Bianchi, F., «Godolia contro Ismaele. La lotta per il potere politico in Giudea all'inizio della dominazione neobabilonese (Ger 40–41 e 2Re 25,22–26)», *RivBib* 53 (2005) 257–275.

Biddle, A.W. – Fulwiler, T., *Reading, Writing, and the Study of Literature*, New York 1989.

Biddle, M.E., *Polyphony and Symphony in Prophetic Literature.* Rereading Jeremiah 7–20, SOTI 2, Macon 1996.

Biddle, M.E., «Contingency, God and the Babylonians: Jeremiah on the Complexity of Repentance», *RevExp* 101 (2004) 247–265.

BIEBERSTEIN, K., «Geschichten sind immer fiktiv – mehr oder minder. Warum das Alte Testament fiktional erzählt und erzählen muss», *BiLi* 75 (2002) 4–13.

BIRAN, A., «The Triple-Arched Gate of Laish at Tel Dan», *IEJ* 34 (1984) 1–19.

BIRNBAUM, S., «The Lachish Ostraca I», *PEQ* 71 (1939) 20–28, 91–110.

BLANK, S.H., «The Curse, Blasphemy, the Spell, and the Oath», *HUCA* 23 (1950–1951) 73–95.

BLANK, S.H., «The Prophet as Paradigm», in: *Essays in Old Testament Ethics.* J.P. Hyatt, *In Memoriam, eds.* J.L. CRENSHAW – T. WILLIS, New York 1974, 111–130.

BLAYNEY, B., *Jeremiah and Lamentations.* A New Translation with Notes Critical, Philological, and Explanatory, Oxford 1784, London ³1836.

BLENKINSOPP, J., *Prophecy and Canon.* A Contribution to the Study of Jewish Origins, Notre Dame 1977.

BLENKINSOPP, J., «Abraham as Paradigm in the Priestly History in Genesis», *JBL* 128 (2009) 225–241.

BLOCK, D.I., *The Gods of the Nations.* Studies in Ancient Near Eastern National Theology, ETSMS 2, Jackson 1988.

BLOCK, D.I., *The Book of Ezekiel.* Chapters 1–24, NICOT, Grand Rapids 1997.

BOBBIO, N., *L'analogia nella logica del diritto*, Milano 2006.

BODNER, K., *After the Invasion.* A Reading of Jeremiah 40–44, Oxford 2015.

BOGAERT, P.-M., «De Baruch à Jérémie. Les deux rédactions conservées du livre de Jérémie», in: *Le livre de Jérémie.* Le prophète et son milieu. Les oracles et leur transmission, *ed.* P.-M. BOGAERT, BEThL 54, Louvain 1981, 168–173.

BOITANI, P., *Prima lezione sulla letteratura*, Roma – Bari 2007.

BONHOEFFER, D., *Widerstand und Ergebung.* Briefe und Aufzeichnungen aus der Haft, *eds.* C. GREMMELS *et al.*, DBW 8, Gütersloh 1998 (Eng. tr.: D. Bonhoeffer, *Letters and Papers from Prison.* With a New Introduction by Samuel Wells, London 2017).

BONNEAU, N., «The Illusion of Immediacy. A Narrative-Critical Exploration of the Bible Predilection for Direct Discourse», *Theoforum* 31 (2000) 131–151.

BONNET, C. – MERLO, P., «Royal Prophecy in the Old Testament and in the Ancient Near East: Methodological Problems and Examples», *SELVOA* 19 (2002) 77–86.

BORDREUIL, P. – ISRAEL, F. – PARDEE, D., «Deux ostraca paléo-hébreux de la collection Sh. Moussaïeff», *Sem.* 46 (1996) 49–76 (Eng. tr.: Id., «King's Command and Widow's Plea: Two New Hebrew Ostraca of the Biblical Period», *NEA* 61 [1998] 2–13).

BORGONOVO, G., *La notte e il suo sole.* Luce e tenebre nel Libro di Giobbe. Analisi simbolica, AnBib 135, Roma 1995.

BORGONOVO, G., «Primo Testamento», in: *AsSaggi biblici.* Introduzione alla Bibbia anima della teologia, *ed.* F. MANZI, Milano 2006, 51–138.

BOROWSKI, O., *Agriculture in Iron Age Israel*, Winona Lake 1987.

VAN DEN BORN, A., *De symbolische handelingen der Oud-Testamentische Profeten*, Utrecht-Nijmegen 1935.

BOTHA, J.E., «Exploring Gesture and Nonverbal Communication in the Bible and the Ancient World: Some Initial Observations», *Neotest.* 30 (1996) 1–19.

754 Bibliography

BOTTERWECK, G.J., «בְּהֵמָה», *ThWAT* I, 523–536.

BOU RAAD, J., *Malheur annoncé, malheur dénoncé*. Étude rhétorique de Jérémie 6, Amchit [Lebanon] 2008.

BOURGUET, D., *Des Métaphores de Jérémie*, EtB 9, Paris 1987.

BOURKE, J., *Fear. A Cultural History*, Emeryville 2005.

BOVATI, P., *Ristabilire la giustizia*. Procedure, vocabolario, orientamenti, AnBib 110, Roma 1986, ²1997 (Eng. tr.: P. Bovati, *Re-Establishing Justice*. Legal Terms, Concepts and Procedures in the Hebrew Bible, JSST.SS 105, Sheffield 1994).

BOVATI, P., *Il libro del Deuteronomio (1–11)*, GSAT, Roma 1994.

BOVATI, P., *Geremia 30–31*. Dispense PIB, Roma 2001.

BOVATI, P., *Giustizia e ingiustizia nell'Antico Testamento*. Dispense PIB, Roma 2001.

BOVATI, P., «Deuterosi e compimento», *Teol(M)* 27 (2002) 20–34.

BOVATI, P., «"Quando le fondamenta sono demolite, cosa fa il giusto?" (Sal 11,3). La giustizia in situazione di ingiustizia», in: *La giustizia in conflitto*. XXXVI Settimana Biblica Nazionale (Roma, 11–15 settembre 2000), *ed.* R. FABRIS, Bologna 2002, 9–38.

BOVATI, P., *Giustizia e ingiustizia nei libri profetici*. Dispense PIB, Roma 2004.

BOVATI, P., *Geremia 1–6*. Dispense PIB, Roma 2005–2006.

BOVATI, P., «Alla ricerca del profeta. Criteri per discernere i veri profeti», in: Id., *"Così parla il Signore"*. Studi sul profetismo biblico, *ed.* S.M. SESSA, Bologna 2008, ²2011, 37–52 (rielaborazione parziale di Id., «Alla ricerca del profeta. II. Criteri per discernere i veri profeti», *RCI* 67 [1986] 179–188).

BOVATI, P., «Il centro assente. Riflessioni ermeneutiche sul metodo dell'analisi retorica, in riferimento specifico alle strutture prive di centro», in: *Retorica biblica e semitica 1*. Atti del primo convegno RBS, *eds.* R. MEYNET – J. ONISZCZUK, RBSem 1, Bologna 2009, 107–121.

BOVATI, P., «"Figlio d'Adamo, nutri il tuo ventre e riempi le tue viscere con il rotolo che ti sto porgendo" (Ez 3,3). L'ermeneutica della raccolta profetica come contributo all'approfondimento dell'ispirazione biblica», *Teol(M)* 36 (2011) 587–610.

BOVATI, P., «"Sterminerai ogni essere vivente (Gs 10,39)". La conquista della terra di Canaan», in: *Il Dio violento della Bibbia*, SusBi 116, Reggio Emilia 2012, 25–53.

BOVATI, P., *I giorni di Dio*, Sestante 32, Milano 2013.

BOVATI, P., *Vie della giustizia secondo la Bibbia*. Sistema giudiziario e procedure per la riconciliazione, Bologna 2014.

BOVATI, P. – BASTA, P., *"Ci ha parlato per mezzo dei profeti"*. Ermeneutica biblica, Lectio 4, Roma – Cinisello Balsamo 2012.

BOZAK, A.B., «Heeding the Received Text: Jer 2,20a, A Case in Point», *Bib.* 77 (1996) 524–537.

BRAND, F. – SCHALLER, F. – VÖLKER, H., *eds.*, *Transdisziplinarität*. *Bestandsaufnahme und Perspektiven*. Beiträge zur THESIS-Arbeitstagung im Oktober 2003 in Göttingen, Göttingen 2004.

BRANDSCHEIDT, R., «Der prophetische Konflikt zwischen Jeremia und Hananja», *TThZ* 98 (1989) 61–74.

BRAUN-HOLZINGER, E. – FRAHM, E., «Liebling des Marduk – König der Blasphemie. Große babylonische Herrscher in der Sicht der Babylonier und in der Sicht anderer Völker», in: *Babylon. Focus Mesopotamischer Geschichte, Wiege früher Gelehrsamkeit, Mythos in der Moderne: 2. Internationales Colloquium der Deutschen Orient-Gesellschaft 24.–26. März 1998 in Berlin*, ed. J. RENGER, Saarbrücken 1999, 131–156.

BREKELMANS, C.H.W., «חרם», *THAT* I, 635–639.

BREKELMANS, C.H.W., *De Ḥerem in het Oude Testament*, Nijmegen 1959.

BRENNEMAN, J.E., *Canons in Conflict. Negotiating Texts in True and False Prophecy*, New York 1997.

BRETÓN, S., *Vocación y misión: formulario profético*, AnBib 111, Roma 1987.

BRETTLER, M., *God is King*. Understanding a Biblical Metaphor, JSOT.S 76, Sheffield 1989.

BRIGHT, J., «The Date of the Prose Sermons of Jeremiah», *JBL* 70 (1951) 15–29 (= in: *A Prophet to the Nations*. Essays in Jeremiah Studies, eds. L.G. Perdue – B.W. Kovacs, Winona Lake 1984, 193–212).

BRIGHT, J., *A History of Israel*, London 1960, Louisville ⁴2000.

BRIGHT, J., *Jeremiah*, AncB 21, Garden City 1965.

BRIGHT, J., *Covenant and Promise*, London 1977.

BRONGERS, H.A., «Some Remarks on the Biblical Particle $h^a l\bar{o}$'», in: *Remembering All the Way... A Collection of Old Testament Studies Published on the Occasion of the Fortieth Anniversary of the Oudtestamentisch Werkgezelschap in Nederland*, eds. B. ALBREKTSON *et al.*, OTS 21, Leiden 1981, 177–189.

BROWN, M.L., «"Is it Not?" or "Indeed!": *HL* in Northwest Semitic», *Maarav* 4 (1987) 201–219.

BRUEGGEMANN, W., «Jeremiah's Use of Rhetorical Questions» *JBL* 92 (1973) 358–374.

BRUEGGEMANN, W., «The Book of Jeremiah. Portrait of a Prophet», *Interp.* 37 (1983) 130–145.

BRUEGGEMANN, W., «The Loss and Recovery of Creation in Old Testament Theology», *ThTo* 53 (1996) 177–190.

BRUEGGEMANN, W., *To Pluck Up, To Tear Down*. A Commentary on the Book of Jeremiah 1–25, ITC, Grand Rapids – Edinburgh 1988 (= Id., *A Commentary on Jeremiah*. Exile and Homecoming, Grand Rapids 1998, 1–228).

BRUEGGEMANN, W., *To Build, To Plant*. A Commentary on the Book of Jeremiah 26–52, ITC, Grand Rapids – Edinburgh 1991 (= Id., *A Commentary on Jeremiah*. Exile and Homecoming, Grand Rapids 1998, 229–502).

BRUEGGEMANN, W., «At the Mercy of Babylon: A Subversive Rereading of the Empire», *JBL* 110 (1991) 3–22.

BRUEGGEMANN, W., *Old Testament Theology*. Essays on Structure, Theme, and Text, ed. P.D. MILLER, Minneapolis 1992.

BRUEGGEMANN, W., «The "Baruch Connection": Reflections on Jer. 43: 1–7», *JBL* 113 (1994) 405–420.

756 Bibliography

BRUEGGEMANN, W., «Jeremiah: Creatio in Extremis», in: *God Who Creates*. Essays in Honor of W. Sibley Towner, *ed.* W.P. BROWN – S.D. MCBRIDE, Jr., Grand Rapids 2000, 152–170.

BRUEGGEMANN, W., *The Theology of the Book of Jeremiah*, New York 2007.

BRUNER, J., *Actual Minds, Possible Worlds*, Cambridge (MA) 1986.

BUBER, M., *The Prophetic Faith*, New York 1949, ²1960.

BUBER, M., «False Prophets (Jeremiah 28)», in: *On the Bible*. Eighteen Studies by Martin Buber, *ed.* N.N. GLATZER, New York 1982, 166–171.

BURKE, A.A., *Walled Up to Heaven*. The Evolution of Middle Bronze Age Fortification Strategies in the Levant, SAHL 4, Winona Lake 2008.

BYBEE, J. – PERKINS, R. – PAGLIUCA, W., *The Evolution of Grammar*. Tense, Aspect and Modality in the Languages of the World, Chicago 1994.

CAIRD, G.B., *The Language and Imagery of the Bible*, London 1980, Grand Rapids ²1997.

CAMPBELL, D.B., *Besieged*. Siege Warfare in the Ancient World, Oxford 2006.

CANFORA, L., *Storiografia greca*, Milano 1999.

CARDELLINI, I., «L'esilio. Un normale evento storico riletto con innovativa forza ideale», in: *Studi sul Vicino Oriente Antico*. Dedicati alla memoria di Luigi Cagni, *ed.* S. GRAZIANI, vol. III, IUO.SAMi 61, Napoli 2000, 1340–1343.

CARROLL, C.E., «Another Dodecade. A Dialectic Model of the Decentred Universe of Jeremiah Studies 1996–2008», *CBR* 8.2 (2010) 162–182.

CARROLL, R.P., *When Prophecy Failed*. Reactions and Responses to Failure in the Old Testament Prophetic Traditions, London 1979.

CARROLL, R.P., «Prophecy and Dissonance: A Theoretical Approach to the Prophetic Tradition», *ZAW* 92 (1980) 108–119.

CARROLL, R.P., *From Chaos to Covenant*. Prophecy in the Book of Jeremiah, New York 1981.

CARROLL, R.P., «Poets Not Prophets: A response to 'Prophets through the Looking-Glass'», *JSOT* 27 (1983) 25–31.

CARROLL, R.P., «Theodicy and the Community: The Subtext of Jeremiah v 1–6», in: *Prophets, Worship, and Theodicy*. Studies in Prophetism, Biblical Theology, and Structural and Rhetorical Analysis, and on the Place of Music in Worship. Papers Read at the Joint British-Dutch Old Testament Conference Held at Woudschoten, 1982, OTS 23, Leiden 1984, 19–38.

CARROLL, R.P., *Jeremiah*. A Commentary, OTL, London 1986.

CARROLL, R.P., «Inventing the Prophets», *IBSt* 10 (1988) 24–36.

CARROLL, R.P., «Prophecy and Society», in: *The World of Ancient Israel*. Sociological, Anthropological and Political Perspectives. Essays by Members of the Society for Old Testament Study, *ed.* R.E. CLEMENTS, Cambridge 1989, 203–225.

CARROLL, R.P., «Whose Prophet? Whose History? Whose Social Reality? Troubling the Interpretative Community Again. Notes Towards a Response to T.W. Overholt's Critique», JSOT 48 (1990) 33–49.

CARROLL, R.P., «Intertextuality and the Book of Jeremiah: Animadversions on Text and Theory», in: *The New Literary Criticism and the Hebrew Bible, eds.*, J.C. EXUM – D.J.A. CLINES, JSOT.S 143, Sheffield 1993, 55–78.

CARROLL, R.P., «Synchronic Deconstructions of Jeremiah: Diachrony to the Rescue», in: *Synchronic or Diachronic? A Debate on Method in Old Testament Exegesis, ed.* J.C. DE MOOR, Leiden 1995, 39–51.

CARROLL, R.P., «Surplus Meaning and the Conflict of Interpretations: A Dodecade of Jeremiah Studies (1984–95)», *CR.BS* 4 (1996) 115–160.

CARROLL, R.P., «Halfway through a Dark Wood: Reflections on Jeremiah 25», in: *Troubling Jeremiah, eds.* A.R.P. DIAMOND – K.M. O'CONNOR – L. STULMAN, JSOT.S 260, Sheffield 1999, 73–86.

CARROLL, R.P., «Century's End: Jeremiah Studies at the Beginning of the Third Millennium», *CR.BS* 8 (2000) 18–58.

CARROLL, R.P., «The Polyphonic Jeremiah: A Reading of the Book of Jeremiah», in: *Reading the Book of Jeremiah. A Search for Coherence, ed.* M. KESSLER, Winona Lake 2004, 77–85.

CARSTON, R., *Thoughts and Utterances.* The Pragmatics of Explicit Communication, Oxford 2002.

CARTER, R., *Vocabulary.* Applied Linguistic Perspectives, London – New York 1998.

CASADEI, F., *Lessico e semantica*, Roma 2003.

CASARI, R. *et al., eds., Testo letterario e immaginario architettonico*, Milano 1996.

CATASTINI, A., «Who Were the False Prophets?», *Hen.* 34 (2012) 330–366.

CAVE, D., «Reading the Body, Reading Scripture: The Implications of Neurobiology on the Study and Interpretation of Scripture», in: *Religion and the Body.* Modern Science and the Construction of Religious Meaning, *eds.* D. CAVE – R. SACHS NORRIS, NBS.SHR 138, Leiden – Boston 2012, 15–35.

CAZELLES, H., «La vie di Jérémie dans son contexte national et international», in: *Le livre de Jérémie.* Le prophète et son milieu. Les oracles et leur transmission, *ed.* P.-M. BOGAERT, BEThL 54, Louvain 1981, 21–39.

CAZELLES, H., *Histoire politique d'Israël.* Des origines à Alexandre le Grand, PBSB 1, Paris 1982.

CECCARELLI, M., *Il profeta rifiutato.* Studio tematico del rifiuto del profeta nel libro di Geremia, Roma 2003, ²2014.

CERULO, M., *Il sentire controverso.* Introduzione alla sociologia delle emozioni, BiTSt 482, Roma 2010.

CERULO, M., «Ogni comprensione è sempre emotiva. Arlie Russell Hochschild e la nascita della sociologia delle emozioni», in: *Lavoro emozionale e struttura sociale, ed.* A.R. HOCHSCHILD, Roma 2013, 3–34.

CHARPIN, D., «Hammu-rabi de Babylone et Mari: Nouvelle Sources, Nouvelles Perspectives», in: *Babylon.* Focus Mesopotamischer Geschichte, Wiege früher Gelehrsamkeit, Mythos in der Moderne: 2. Internationales Colloquium der Deutschen Orient-Gesellschaft 24.–26. März 1998 in Berlin, *ed.* J. RENGER, CDOG 2, Saarbrücken 1999, 111–130.

CHARPIN, D., «Prophètes et rois dans le Proche-Orient Amorrite», in: *Prophètes et rois. Bible et Proche-Orient, ed.* A. LEMAIRE, LeDiv.HS, Paris 2001, 21–53.

CHARPIN, D., «Le prophétisme dans le Proche-Orient d'après les archives de Mari (XVIIIe siècle av. J.-C.)», in: *Les recueils prophétiques de la Bible. Origines, milieux et contexte proche-oriental, eds.* J.-D. MACCHI – C. NIHAN *et al.*, MoBi 64, Genève 2012, 31– 73.

CHAUTY, E., *Qui aura sa vie comme butin?* Échos narratifs et révélation dans la lecture des oracles personnels de Jérémie, BZAW 519, Berlin 2020.

CHAUTY, E., *Le livre de Jérémie: signifier la Parole*, CEv 199, Paris 2022.

CHILDS, B.S., «The Enemy from the North and the Chaos Tradition», *JBL* 78 (1959) 187–198 (= in: *A Prophet to the Nations*. Essays in Jeremiah Studies, *eds.* L.G. PERDUE – B.W. KOVACS, Winona Lake 1984, 151–161).

CHILDS, B.S., *Isaiah and the Assyrian Crisis*, SBT.SS 3, London 1967.

CHILDS, B.S., *Old Testament Theology in a Canonical Context*, Philadelphia 1986.

CHRISTENSEN, D.L., *Transformations of the War Oracle in Old Testament Prophecy*. Studies in the Oracles against the Nations, HTR 3, Missoula 1975.

CIORAN, E.M., *Essai sur la pensée réactionnaire*. À propos de Joseph de Maistre, Paris 1977.

CLAASSENSIN, L.J., «Jeremiah. The Traumatized Prophet», in: *The Oxford Handbook of Jeremiah, eds.* L. STULMAN – E. SILVER, Oxford 2021, 358–373.

VON CLAUSEWITZ, C., *Vom Krieg*, München 2000.

CLAYVILLE, K., «Ecological Hermeneutics and Jeremiah», in: *The Oxford Handbook of Jeremiah, eds.* L. STULMAN – E. SILVER, Oxford 2021, 637– 647.

CLEMENTS, R.E., *Prophecy and Tradition*, Southampton 1975.

CLEMENTS, R.E., *Isaiah and the Deliverance of Jerusalem*. A Study of the Interpretation of Prophecy in the Old Testament, JSOT.S 13, Sheffield 1980.

CLEMENTS, R.E., «Jeremiah 1–25 and the Deuteronomistic History», in: *Understanding Poets and Prophets*. Essays in Honor of G.W. Anderson, *ed.*, A.G. AULD, JSOT.S 152, Sheffield 1993, 93–113.

CLEMENTS, R.E., *Jeremiah*, Interpretation, Atlanta 1988.

CLEMENTS, R.E., «Prophecy Interpreted: Intertextuality and Theodicy – A Case Study of Jeremiah 26:16–24», in: *Uprooting and Planting*. Essays on Jeremiah for Leslie Allen, *ed.* J. GOLDINGAY, LHBOTS 459, London – New York 2007, 32–44.

CLERC, D., «Des actes pour parler», in: *Jérémie*. Un prophète en temps de crise, *eds.* R. BLANCHET *et al.*, EssBib 10, Genève 1985, 107–147.

CLIFFORD, R.J., *The Cosmic Mountain in Canaan and the Old Testament*, HSM 4, Cambridge (MA) 1972.

CLINES, D.J.A. – GUNN, D.M. – HAUSER, A.J., *eds.*, *Art and Meaning*. Rhetoric in Biblical Literature, JSOT.S 19, Sheffield 1982.

COBLEY, P., *ed.*, *The Communication Theory Reader*, New York 1996.

COBLEY, P., *et al.*, *Communication Theories*, London 2006.

COGAN, M. «Judah under Assyrian Hegemony: A Reexamination of Imperialism and Religion», *JBL* 112 (1993) 403–114.

COGAN, M., *The Raging Torrent*. Historical Inscriptions from Assyria and Babylonia Relating to Ancient Israel, Jerusalem 2008.

COGGINS, R.J., «Prophecy – True and False», in: *Of Prophet's Visions and the Wisdom of Sages*. Essays in Honour of R. Norman Whybray on His Seventieth Birthday, *eds.* H.A. MCKAY – D.J.A. CLINES, JSOT.S 162, Sheffield 1993, 80–94.

CONKLIN, B., *Oath Formulas in Biblical Hebrew*, LSAWS 5, Winona Lake 2011.

CONRAD, E.W., *Fear not Warrior. A Study of 'al tîrā' Pericopes in the Hebrew Scriptures*, BJSt 75, Chico 1985.

CONRAD, J., «פֶּלֶא», *ThWAT* VI, 569–583.

CONTRERAS LORENZINI, M.J., *Il corpo in scena*. Indagine sullo statuto semiotico del corpo nella prassi performativa, Bologna 2008.

CONTRERAS LORENZINI, M.J., «Il corpo del fare. Verso una definizione semiotica di pratica», *Studi Culturali* 3 (2009) 387–408.

COOK, J.A., «The Finite Verbal Forms in Biblical Hebrew Do Express Aspect», *JANES* 30 (2006) 21–35.

COOK, J.A., *Time and the Biblical Hebrew Verb*. The Expression of Tense, Aspect, and Modality in Biblical Hebrew, LSAWS 7, Winona Lake 2012.

CORBALLIS, M.C., *From Hand to Mouth*. The Origins of Language, Princeton 2002.

CORNILL, C.H., *The Book of the Prophet Jeremiah*. Critical Edition of the Hebrew Text Arranged in Chronological Order with Notes, SBOT 11, Leipzig 1895.

CORNILL, C.H., *Das Buch Jeremia*, Leipzig 1905.

CORRE, A.D., «*'elle, hemma = sic*», *Bib.* 54 (1973) 263–264.

COSERIU, E., *Textlinguistik*. Eine Einführung, TBL 109, Tübingen ²1981.

COSTACURTA, B., *La vita minacciata*. Il tema della paura nella Bibbia Ebraica, AnBib 119, Roma 1998.

COUNTS, D.B. – ARNOLD, B., *eds.*, *The Master of Animals in Old World Iconography*, Archaeolingua 24, Budapest 2010.

COXON, P., «Nebuchadnezzar's Hermeneutical Dilemma», *JSOT* 66 (1995) 87–97.

CRAIG, R.T., «Communication Theory as a Field», *ComT* 9 (1999) 119–161.

CRAIG, R.T. – MULLER, H.L., *Theorizing Communication*. Readings Across Traditions, London 2007.

CRAIGIE, P.C. – KELLEY, P.G. – DRINKARD, J.F., *Jeremiah 1–25*, WBC 26, Dallas 1991.

CRENSHAW, J.L., *Prophetic Conflict*. Its Effect Upon Israelite Religion, BZAW 124, Berlin 1971.

CRENSHAW, J.L., «Prophecy, False», *IDBSup*, Nashville 1976, 701–702.

CRENSHAW, J.L., «Introduction: The Shift from Theodicy to Anthropodicy», in: *Theodicy in the Old Testament, ed.* J.L. CRENSHAW, IRT 4, Philadelphia 1983, 1–16.

CRENSHAW, J.L., «Theodicy and Prophetic Literature», in: *Theodicy in the World of the Bible, eds.* A. LAATO – J.C. DE MOOR, Leiden – Boston 2003, 236–255.

760   Bibliography

CRENSHAW, J.L., *Defending God.* Biblical Responses to the Problem of Evil, Oxford 2005.

CROSS, F.M., *Canaanite Myth and Hebrew Epic.* Essays in the History of the Religion of Israel, Cambridge (MA) 1973, [9]1997.

CROSS, F.M., «Introduction to the Study of the History of the Religion of Israel», in: *Inspired Speech.* Prophecy in the Ancient Near East. Essays in Honor of Herbert B. Huffmon, eds. J. KALTNER – L. STULMAN, JSOT.S 378, London – New York 2004, 8–11.

CROUCH, C.L., *War and Ethics in the Ancient Near East.* Military Violence in Light of Cosmology and History, BZAW 407, Berlin – New York 2009.

CRUSE, D.A., *Lexical semantics,* CTL, Cambridge 1986.

CRUSE, D.A., *Meaning in Language.* An Introduction to Semantics and Pragmatics, OTLing, Oxford 1999, 2011[3].

CUCCA, M., *Il corpo e la città.* Studio del rapporto di significazione paradigmatica tra la vicenda di Geremia e il destino di Gerusalemme, StRic.SB, Assisi 2010.

CUCCA, M. – ROSSI, B. – SESSA, S.M., *"Quelli che amo io li accuso".* Il *rîb* come chiave di lettura unitaria della Scrittura. Alcuni esempi (Os 11,1; Ger 13,1–11; Gv 15,1–11/Ap 2–3), CSB.SB, Assisi 2012.

CURRY, S.C., «Jehu and the Black Obelisk of Shalmaneser III», in: *Scripture in History & Theology.* Essays in Honor of J. Coert Rylaarsdam, eds. A.L. MERRILL – T.W. OVERHOLT, Pittsburgh 1977, 71–105.

CURZER, H.J., «Spies and Lies: Faithful, Courageous Israelites and Truthful Spies», *JSOT* 35 (2010) 187–195.

CZICHON, R.M., «Nebukadnezzar II. B. Archäologisch», *RLA* IX, 201–206.

DAL COVOLO, E. – MARITANO, M., *Omelie su Geremia.* Lettura origeniana, BSRel 165, Roma 2001.

DALLEY, S., «The Transition from Neo-Assyrians to Neo-Babylonians: Break or Continuity?», in: *Hayim and Miriam Tadmor Volume, eds.* I. EPH'AL – A. BEN-TOR – P. MACHINIST, ErIsr 27, Jerusalem 2003, 25*-28*.

DANDAMAYEV, M., «State Gods and Private Religion in the Near East in the First Millennium B.C.E.», in: *Religion and Politics in the Ancient Near East, ed.* A. BERLIN, Bethesda 1996, 35–45.

DANESI, M. – ECO, U., *et al., Encyclopedic Dictionary of Semiotics, Media, and Communications,* Toronto 2000.

DA RIVA, R., *The Neo-Babylonian Royal Inscriptions.* An Introduction, GMTR 4, Münster 2008.

DA RIVA, R., «La guerra en el Antiguo Oriente: el asedio a las ciudades y la penuria de la población», *Historiae* 5 (2008) 1–9.

DA RIVA, R., «A Lion in the Cedar Forest. International Politics and Pictorial Self-Representations of Nebuchadnezzar II (605–562 B.C.)», in: *Studies on War in the Ancient Near East.* Collected Essays on Military History, *ed.* J. VIDAL, AOAT 372, Münster 2010, 165–191.

DA RIVA, R., «Assyrians and Assyrian Influence in Babylonia (626–539 BCE)», in: *From Source to History*. Studies on Ancient Near Eastern Worlds and Beyond, *eds.* S. GASPA *et al.*, AOAT 412, Münster 2014, 99–125.

DA RIVA, R., «Enduring Images of an Ephemeral Empire: Neo-Babylonian Inscriptions and Representations on the Western Periphery», in: *Mesopotamia in the Ancient World*. Impact, Continuities, Parallels. Proceedings of the Seventh Symposium of the Melammu Project Held in Obergurgl, Austria, November 4–8, 2013, *eds.* R. ROLLINGER – E. VAN DONGEN, MSym 7, Münster 2015, 603–629.

DAVIES, P.R., «"Pen of iron, point of diamond" (Jer 17:1): Prophecy as Writing», in: *Writings and Speech in Israelite and Ancient Near Eastern Prophecy*, *eds.* E. BEN ZVI – M.H. FLOYD, SBLSymS 10, Atlanta 2000, 65–81.

DAY, J., *God's Conflict with the Dragon and the Sea*. Echoes of a Canaanite Myth in the Old Testament, Cambridge 1985.

DE ANGELIS, R., «Sur la matérialité du texte. La textualisation», in: *Directions actuelles en linguistique du texte*. Actes du colloque international. Le texte: modèles, méthodes, perspectives, *eds.* L. FLOREA *et al.*, Cluj-Napoca 2010, 95–106.

DE ANGELIS, R., «L'esplicitazione dell'esperienza grafica. Lo *spazio bianco* come caso esemplare», in: *I segni dell'esperienza*. Saggi sulle forme di conoscenza, *eds.* A. CANZONIERI – G. GALLO, BiTSt 693, Roma 2011, 77–89.

DEBOYS, D.G., «1 Kings XIII – A "New Criterion" Reconsidered», *VT* 41 (1991) 210–212.

VAN DER DEIJL, A., *Protest or Propaganda*. War in the Old Testament Book of Kings and in Contemporaneous Ancient Near Eastern Texts, SSN 51, Leiden – Boston 2008.

DELAMARTER, S., «"Thus Far the Words of Jeremiah": But Who Gets the Last Word?», *BiRe* 15 (1999) 34–45, 54–55.

DELL, K.J., *ed.*, *Ethical and Unethical in the Old Testament*. God and Humans in Dialogue, LHBOTS 528, New York – London 2010.

DEL LUNGO, A., *Gli inizi difficili*. Per una poetica dell'Incipit romanzesco, Padova 1997.

DEL LUNGO, A., «La frontière du commencement. Transitions, transgressions», in: *Au commencement du récit*. Transitions, transgressions, Collection Hispania, *ed.* C. PÉRÈS, Carnières-Morlanwelz 2005, 9–15.

DEL MEDICO, H.E., «Le rite de la guerre dans l'Ancient Testament», *Ethnog.* 45 (1947–1950) 127–170.

DELUMEAU, J., *La peur en Occident (XIVe-XVIIIe siècles)*. Une cité assiégée, Paris 1978.

DEMANDT, A., *Philosophie der Geschichte*. Von der Antike zur Gegenwart, Köln – Weimar – Wien 2011.

DE MAURO, T., *Minisemantica dei linguaggi non verbali e delle lingue*, STLa 87, Bari 1982, [10]2011.

DEMPSEY, C.J., *Hope Amid the Ruins*. The Ethics of Israel's Prophets, St. Louis 2000.

DE ROSA, F., *Quello che non ho mai detto*. Io, il mio autismo e ciò in cui credo, Cinisello Balsamo 2014.

DERVIN, B., *et al.*, *eds.*, *Rethinking Communication*. Volume 1: Paradigm Issues, Thousand Oaks 1989.

762 Bibliography

DE VRIES, S.J., *Prophet Against Prophet*. The Role of the Micaiah Narrative (I Kings 22) in the Development of Early Prophetic Tradition, Grand Rapids 1978.

DEZSŐ, T., «Neo-Assyrian Military Intelligence», in: *Krieg und Frieden im Alten Vorderasien*. 52e Recontre Assyriologique Internationale. International Congress of Assyriology and Near Eastern Archaeology, Münster 17.–21. Juli 2006, *eds.* H. NEUMANN *et al.*, AOAT 401, Münster 2014, 221–235.

DIAMOND, A.R., *The Confessions of Jeremiah in Context*. Scenes of Prophetic Drama, JSOT.S 45, Sheffield 1987.

DIETRICH, W., «Vom Schweigen Gottes im Alten Testament», in: *Gott und Mensch im Dialog*. Festschrift für Otto Kaiser zum 80. Geburtstag, *ed.* M. WITTE, BZAW 345/II, Berlin – New York 2004, 997–1014.

DIK, S.C., *Functional Grammar*, Amsterdam 1978, Dordrecht ³1981.

DIK, S.C., *The Theory of Functional Grammar*. Part I: The Structure of the Clause, FGS 20, Dordrecht 1989, Berlin – New York ²1997.

DIK, S.C. – HOFFMANN, M.E. – DE JONG, J.R. – DJIANG, S.I. – STROOMER, H. – DE VRIES, L., «On the Typology of Focus Phenomena», in: *Perspectives on Functional Grammar*, *eds.* T. HOEKSTRA – H. VAN DER HULST – M. MOORTGAT, Dordrecht 1981, 41–74.

DION, P.E., «Syro-Palestinian Resistance to Shalmaneser III in the Light of New Documents», *ZAW* 107 (1995) 482–489.

DION, P.E., «The Horned Prophet (1 Kings XXII 11)», *VT* 49 (1999) 259–261.

DI PEDE, E., *Au-de là du refus: l'espoir*. Recherches sur la cohérence narrative de Jr 32–45 (TM), BZAW 357, Berlin 2005.

DI PEDE, E., «Jérémie et les rois de Juda, Sédécias et Joaqim», *VT* 56 (2006) 452–469.

DI PEDE, E., «La manière de raconter et l'enjeu du récit: Jérémie présente Ananias en Jer 28,1 TM et 35,1 LXX», *BibInt* 16 (2008) 294–301.

DI PEDE, E., «Le prophète mis en scène: les récits de vocation comme scène type», in: *L'intrigue dans le récit biblique*. Quatrième colloque international du RRENAB, Université Laval, Québec, 29 Mai–1er Juin 2008, *eds.* A. PASQUIER – D. MARGUERAT – A. WÉNIN, BETL 237, Leuven 2010, 127–140.

DI PEDE, E., «Quando Geremia fa il falso profeta: la tentazione dei Recabiti (Ger 35) come riflessione sulla vera e falsa profezia», *RivBib* 63 (2015) 307–326.

VAN DIJK, T.A., *Text and Context*. Explorations in the Semantics and Pragmatics of Discourse, New York 1977, ⁶1992.

VAN DIJK, T.A., *Society and Discourse*. How Social Contexts Influence Text and Talk, Cambridge 2009.

DIJKSTRA, M., «I Have Blessed You by Yhwh of Samaria and His Asherah: Texts with Religious Elements from the Soil Archive of Ancient Israel», in: *Only One God? Monotheism in Ancient Israel and the Veneration of the Goddess Asherah*, *eds.* B. BECKING *et al.*, BiSe 77, Sheffield 2001.

DÖHLING, J.-D., «Prophetische Körper. Ein exegetisch-soziologiches Plädoyer zu einer vernachlässigten Dimension der sog. „prophetischen Zeichenhandlungen"», *BZ* 57 (2013) 244–271.

DOLCE, R., «Beyond Defeat. The Psychological Annihilation of the Vanquished in Pre-Classical Near Eastern Visual Communication», in: Krieg und Frieden im Alten Vorderasien, in: *Krieg und Frieden im Alten Vorderasien*. 52e Recontre Assyriologique Internationale. International Congress of Assyriology and Near Eastern Archaeology, Münster 17.–21. Juli 2006, *eds*. H. Neumann *et al.*, AOAT 401, Münster 2014, 237–267.

DOLEŽEL, L., *Heterocosmica*. Fiction and Possible Worlds, Baltimore – London 1998.

DONALD, M., «Material Culture and Cognition: Concluding Thoughts», in: *Cognition and Material Culture*. The Archaeology of Symbolic Storage, *eds*. C. RENFREW – C. SCARRE, Cambridge 1998, 181–187.

DONNER, H., *Israel unter den Völkern*. Die Stellung der klassischen Propheten des 8. Jahrhunderts v. Chr. zur Aussenpolitik der Könige von Israel und Juda, VT.S 11, Leiden 1964.

DONSBACH, W., *ed*., *International Encyclopedia of Communication*, Oxford 2008.

DORN, L., «The Unexpected as a Speech Device: Shifts of Thematic Expectancy in Jeremiah», *BiTr* 37 (1986) 216–222.

DUBBINK, J., «Jeremiah: Hero of Faith or Defeatist? Concerning the Place and Function of Jeremiah 20.14–18», *JSOT* 86 (1999) 67–84.

DUBOVSKÝ, P., *Hezekiah and the Assyrian Spies*. Reconstruction of the Neo-Assyrian Intelligence Services and its Significance for 2 Kings 18–19, BibOr 49, Roma 2006.

DUHM, B., *Die Theologie der Propheten als Grundlage für die innere Entwicklungsgeschichte der israelitischen Religion*, Bonn 1875.

DUHM, B., *Das Buch Jesaja*, HK 3.1, Göttingen 1892, [3]1914.

DUHM, B., *Das Buch Jeremia*, KHC 11, Tübingen – Leipzig 1901.

DUHM, B., *Israels Propheten*, Tübingen 1916, [2]1922.

DUPRÉ, J., *Human Nature and the Limits of Science*, Oxford – New York 2001.

DÜRING, B.S., «At the Root of the Matter. The Middle Assyrian Prelude to Empire», in: *Imperial Peripheries in the Neo-Assyrian Period*, *eds*. C.W. TYSON – V.R. HERRMANN, Louisville 2018.

DUSSAUD, R., «Le prophète Jérémie et les lettres de Lakish», *Syr.* 19 (1938) 256–271.

DUTCHER-WALLS, P., «The Social Location of the Deuteronomists: A Sociological Study of Factional Politics in Late Pre-Exilic Judah», *JSOT* 52 (1991) 77–94.

DYMA, O., «Wahre Geschichten: Zwischen Fiktionalität, Gattung, Weltbild und Geltungsanspruch», in: *Methodik im Diskurs*. Neue Perspektiven für die Alttestamentliche Exegese, BThS 156, Neukirchen-Vluyn 2015, 32–51.

ECHEVERRÍA REY, F., «Weapons, Technological Determinism, and Ancient Warfare», in: *New Perspectives on Ancient Warfare*, *eds*. G.G. FAGAN – M. TRUNDLE, HW 59, Leiden – Boston 2010, 21–56.

ECO, U., *Trattato di semiotica generale*, Milano 1975, [16]1998 (Eng. tr.: Id., *A Theory of Semiotics*, London 1976).

ECO, U., *Lector in fabula*. La cooperazione interpretativa nei testi narrativi, TasB 27, Milano 1979, [10]2006.

764 Bibliography

Eco, U., *The Role of the Reader*. Explorations in the Semiotics of the Text, Bloomington 1979.

Eco, U., *I limiti dell'interpretazione*, Milano 1990.

Ehrenreich, E., *Wähle das Leben!* Deuteronomium 30 als hermeneutischer Schlüssel zur Tora, BZAR 14, Wiesbaden 2011.

Ehrlich, A.B., *Randglossen zur Hebräischen Bibel: textkritisches, sprachliches und sachliches*. Vierter Band: Jesaia, Jeremia, Leipzig 1912.

Ehrlich, C.S., «Coalition Politics in Eighth Century b.c.e. Palestine: The Philistines and the Syro-Ephraimite War», *ZDPV* 107 (1991) 48–58.

Eichrodt, W., *Theologie des Alten Testaments*. Teil I: Gott und Volk, Leipzig 1933, Stuttgart ⁵1957; Teil II: Gott und Welt, Teil III: Gott und Mensch, Leipzig 1935, Stuttgart ⁴1961.

Eichrodt, W., *Der Prophet Hesekiel*, ATD 22, Göttingen 1966.

Eidevall, G., *Sacrificial Rhetoric in the Prophetic Literature of the Hebrew Bible*, New York 2012.

Eisenstein, E.L., *The Printing Press as an Agent of Change*. Communications and Cultural Transformations in Early Modern Europe, vols. I-II, Cambridge 1979.

Eissfeldt, O., *Krieg und Bibel*, Tübingen 1915.

Elgavish, D., «The Division of the Spoils of War in the Bible and in the Ancient Near East», *ZABR* 8 (2002) 242–273.

Engnell, I., *The Call of Isaiah*. An Exegetical and Comparative Study, Uppsala 1949.

Eph'al, I., «On Warfare and Military Control in the Ancient Near Eastern Empires: A Research Outline», in: *History, Historiography and Interpretation*. Studies in Biblical and Cuneiform Literatures, eds. H. Tadmor – M. Weinfeld, Jerusalem 1983, 88–106.

Eph'al, I., «Nebuchadnezzar the Warrior: Remarks on his Military Achievements», *IEJ* 53 (2003) 178–195.

Eph'al, I., «Esarhaddon, Egypt, and Shubria: Politics and Propaganda», *JCS* 57 (2005) 99–111.

Eph'al, I., *The City Besieged*. Siege and Its Manifestations in the Ancient Near East, CHANE 36, Leiden 2009.

Eph'al, I. – Tadmor, H., «Observations on Two Inscriptions of Esarhaddon: Prism Niniveh A and the Letter to the God», in: *Essays on Ancient Israel in Its Near Eastern Context*. A Tribute to Nadav Na'aman, eds. Y. Amit – E. Ben Zvi – I. Finkelstein – O. Lipschits, Winona Lake 2006, 155–170.

Epp-Tiessen D., *Concerning the Prophets*. True and False Prophecy in Jeremiah 23:9–29:32, Eugene 2012.

Erny, M., *Jeremias Königslogien*. Königstexte im Jeremiabuch, Diss. Univ. Basel [Locarno 2004].

Ewald, H., *Die Propheten des Alten Bundes*, 2 vols., Stuttgart 1840–1841.

Fabry, H.-J. – Blum, E. – Ringgren, H., «רַב», *ThWAT* VII, 294–320.

FAGAN, G.G., «"I Fell upon Him Like a Furious Arrow": Toward a Reconstruction of the Assyrian Tactical System», in: *New Perspectives on Ancient Warfare, eds.* G.G. FAGAN – M. TRUNDLE, HW 59, Leiden – Boston 2010, 81–100.

FALK, Z.W., «Religion and State in Ancient Israel», in: *Politics and Theopolitics in the Bible and Postbiblical Literature, eds.* H.G. REVENTLOW – Y. HOFFMAN – B. UFFENHEIMER, JSOT.S 171, Sheffield 1994, 49–54.

FALKENSTEIN, A. – VON SODEN, W., *Sumerische und akkadische Hymnen und Gebete,* BAW, Zurich 1953.

FANTALKIN, A., «Why Did Nebuchadnezzar II Destroy Ashkelon in Kislev 604?», in: *The Fire Signals of Lachish.* Studies in the Archaeology and History of Israel in the Late Bronze Age, Iron Age, and Persian Period in Honor of David Ussishkin, *eds.* I. FINKELSTEIN – N. NA'AMAN, Winona Lake 2011, 87–111.

FAVALE, A., *Dio d'Israele e dei popoli.* Anti-idolatria e universalismo nella prospettiva di Ger 10,1–16, AnBib 211, Roma 2016.

FAWCETT, T., *The Symbolic Language of Religion.* An Introductory Study, London 1970.

FENSHAM, F.C., «Malediction and Benediction in Ancient Near Eastern Vassal-Treaties and the OT», *ZAW* 74 (1962) 1–9.

FENSHAM, F.C., «Common Trends in Curses of the Near Eastern Treaties and *Kudurru-*Inscriptions Compared with Malediction of Amos and Isaiah», *ZAW* 75 (1963) 155–175.

FERRARIS, M., *La svolta testuale.* Il decostruzionismo in Derrida, Lyotard e gli "Yale Critics", Milano 1986.

FERRI, R. – MANGANARO, P., *eds., Gesto e parola.* Ricerche sulla rivelazione, Roma 2005.

FERRONI, G., *Profilo storico della letteratura italiana,* vol. I, Milano 1992.

FERRY, J., «"Je restaurerai Israël" (Jr 33,7.9.26). L'écriture de Jérémie 33», *TrEu* 15 (1998) 69–82.

FERRY, J., *Illusions et salut dans la prédication prophetique de Jérémie,* BZAW 269, Berlin – New York 1999.

FESTINGER, L., *A Theory of Cognitive Dissonance,* Stanford 1957.

FESTINGER, L., *Conflict, Decision, and Dissonance,* Stanford 1964.

FESTINGER, L. – RIECKEN, H.W. – SCHACHTER, S., *When Prophecy Fails.* A Social and Psychological Study of a Modern Group that Predicted the Destruction of the World, Minneapolis 1956, [2]2008.

FILLMORE, C.J., «Frame Semantics and the Nature of Language», *ANYAS (Conference on the Origin and Development of Language and Speech)* 280 (1976) 20–32.

FILLMORE, C.J., «Frame Semantics», in: *Linguistics in the Morning Calm.* Selected Papers from SICOL-1981, *ed.* Linguistic Society of Korea, Seoul 1982, 111–137.

FILLMORE, C.J., «Frames and the Semantics of Understanding», *QSem* 6 (1985) 222–254.

FILLMORE, C.J., «Frame Semantics», in: *Cognitive Linguistics: Basic Readings, ed.* D. GEERAERTS, CLRes 34, Berlin 2006, 373–400.

FILLMORE, C.J. – BAKER, C., «A Frames Approach to Semantic Analysis», in: *The Oxford Handbook of Linguistic Analysis, eds.* B. HEINE – H. NARROG, Oxford 2010, 313–340.

FILLMORE, C.J. – JOHNSON, C.R. – PETRUCK, M.R.L., «Background to FrameNet», *IJL* 16 (2003) 235–250.

FINKELSTEIN, I., «Archaeology as High Court in Ancient Israelite History: A Reply to NadavNa'aman», *JHS* 10 (2010) 1–8.

FISCHER, G., «Jer 25 und die Fremdvölkersprüche. Unterschiede zwischen hebräischem und griechischem Text», *Bib.* 72 (1991) 474–499.

FISCHER, G., *Das Trostbüchlein.* Text, Komposition und Theologie von Jer 30–31, SBB 26, Stuttgart 1993.

FISCHER, G., «"Ich Mache Dich... zur eisernen Säule" (Jer 1,18). Der Prophet als besserer Ersatz für den untergegangenen Tempel», *ZKTh* 116 (1994) 447–450.

FISCHER, G., *Jeremia 1–25,* HThKAT, Freiburg im Breisgau 2005.

FISCHER, G., *Jeremia 26–52,* HThKAT, Freiburg im Breisgau 2005.

FISCHER, G., *Jeremia.* Der Stand der theologischen Diskussion, Darmstadt 2007.

FISCHER, G., «Il libro di Geremia, specchio della cultura scritta e letta in Israele», *RivBib* 56 (2008) 393–417.

FISCHER, G., «"Bin ich ein Gott aus der Nähe...?". Jer 23,23 und das Wesen von Theologie», in: Id., *Der Prophet wie Mose.* Studien zum Jeremiabuch, BZAR 15, Wiesbaden 2011, 284–286 (= in: Mathis, C. – Oberhofer, P. – Schuchter, P., eds., *Tage kommen.* Zukunft der Theologie, Ulithiana 3, Innsbruck 2000, 65–67).

FISCHER, G., «Der Einfluss des Deuteronomiums auf das Jeremiabuch», in: *Deuteronomium – Torah für eine neue Generation, eds.* G. FISCHER – D. MARKL – S. PAGANINI, BZAR 17, Wiesbaden 2011, 247–269.

FISCHER, G., «"Mein Diener Nebukadnezzar". Zur Rolle von Fremden im AT», in: Id., *Der Prophet wie Mose.* Studien zum Jeremiabuch, BZAR 15, Wiesbaden 2011, 334–336 (= in: *WWeg* 293 [2004] 6–9).

FISCHER, G., «Partner oder Gegner? Zum Verhältnis von Jesaja und Jeremia», in: Id., *Der Prophet wie Mose.* Studien zum Jeremiabuch, BZAR 15, Wiesbaden 2011, 188–199 (= in: F. Hartenstein – M. Pietsch, *eds., "Sieben Augen auf einem Stein" [Sach 3,9].* Festschrift für Ina Willi-Plein zum 65. Geburtstag, Neukirchen 2007, 69–79).

FISCHER, G., *Der Prophet wie Mose.* Studien zum Jeremiabuch, BZAR 15, Wiesbaden 2011.

FISCHER, G., «Fulfiment and Reversal: The Curses of Deuteronomy 28 as a Foil for the Book of Jeremiah», *SemClas* 5 (2012) 43–49.

FISCHER, G., *Theologien des Alten Testaments,* NSK.AT 31, Stuttgart 2012.

FISCHER, G., «Gottes universale Horizonte. Die Völker der Welt und ihre Geschichte in der Sicht des Jeremiabuches», in: *"Ricercare la sapienza di tutti gli antichi" (Sir 39,1).* Miscellanea in onore di Gian Luigi Prato, *eds.* M. MILANI – M. ZAPPELLA, SRivBib 56, Bologna 2013, 313–328.

FISCHER, G., «Zurück nach Ägypten? Exodusmotivik im Jeremiabuch», in: *A Pillar of Cloud to Guide.* Text-Critical, Redactional, and Linguistic Perspectives on the Old Testament in Honour of Marc Vervenne, *eds.* H. AUSLOOS – B. LEMMELIJN, Leuven – Paris – Walpole 2014, 73–92.

FISCHER, G., «Il Dio che piange. Una chiave per la teologia del libro di Geremia», in: *La profezia tra l'uno e l'altro Testamento.* Studi in onore del prof. Pietro Bovati in occasione del suo settantacinquesimo compleanno, *eds.* G. BENZI – D. SCAIOLA – M. BONARINI, AnBib.St 4, Roma 2015, 233–244.

FISCHER, G., «וחפשי התורה לא ידעוני» The Relationship of the Book of Jeremiah to the Torah», in: *The Formation of the Pentateuch.* Bridging the Academic Cultures of Europe, Israel, and North America, *eds.* J.C. GERTZ *et al.*, FAT 111, Tübingen 2016, 891–911.

FISCHER, G., «Jeremiah – "The Prophet like Moses?"», in: *The Book of Jeremiah.* Composition, Reception, and Interpretation, *eds.* J. LUNDBOM – C.A. EVANS – B. ANDERSON, VT.S. 178, Leiden – Boston 2018, 45–66.

FLYNN, S.W., *YHWH Is King.* The Development of Divine Kingship in Ancient Israel, VT.S 159, Leiden – Boston 2014.

FOHRER, G., «Die Gattung der Berichte über symbolische Handlungen der Propheten», *ZAW* 64 (1952) 101–120.

FOHRER, G., *Die Symbolischen Handlungen der Propheten*, AThANT 54, Zürich 1953, [2]1968.

FOKKELMAN, J.P., *Reading Biblical Narrative.* An Introductory Guide, Louisville 1999.

FOKKELMAN, J.P., *Reading Biblical Poetry.* An Introductory Guide, Louisville 2001.

FOREMAN, B.A., *Animal Metaphors and the People of Israel in the Book of Jeremiah*, FRLANT 238, Göttingen 2011.

FOWLER, J.D., *Theophoric Personal Names in Ancient Hebrew.* A Comparative Study, JSOT.S 49, Sheffield 1988.

FRAHM, E., *Einleitung in die Sanherib-Inschriften*, AfO.B 26, Vienna 1997.

FRAHM, E., «Family Matters: Psychohistorical Reflections on Sennacherib and His Times», in: *Sennacherib at the Gates of Jerusalem.* Story, History and Historiography, *eds.*, I. KALIMI – S. RICHARDSON, CHANE 71, Leiden – Boston 2014, 163–222.

FRANZKOWIAK, J., *Der Königszyklus Jer 21,1–23,8.* Das vordeuteronomistische Traditionsgut und seine redaktionelle Bearbeitung, Diss., Stuttgart 1989.

FREDRIKSSON, H., *Jahwe als Krieger*, Lund 1945.

FRETHEIM, T.E., «The Repentance of God: A Study of Jeremiah 18:7–10», *HAR* 11 (1987) 81–92.

FRETHEIM, T.E., «The Repentance of God. A Key to Evaluating Old Testament God-Talk», *HBT* 10 (1988) 47–70.

FRETHEIM, T.E., *Jeremiah*, S&HBC, Macon 2002.

FRETHEIM, T.E., «The Character of God in Jeremiah», in: *Character and Scripture.* Moral Formation, Community, and Biblical Interpretation, *ed.* W.P. BROWN, Grand Rapids 2002, 211–230.

FRETHEIM, T.E., *God and World in the Old Testament.* A Relational Theology of Creation, Nashville 2005.

FRETHEIM, T.E., *Creation Untamed.* The Bible, God, and Natural Disasters, Grand Rapids 2010.

FRETZ, M.J., «Weapons and Implements of Warfare», *ABD* VI, 893–895.

768   Bibliography

FRIEBEL, K.G., *Jeremiah's and Ezekiel Sign-Acts*. Rhetorical Nonverbal Communication, JSOT.S 283, Sheffield 1999.

FRODEMAN, R., *Sustainable Knowledge*. A Theory of Interdisciplinarity, New York 2014.

FRYE, N., «Verse and Prose», in: *Princeton Encyclopedia of Poetry and Poetics, ed.* A. PREMINGER, Princeton 1965, [2]1974, 885–890 (Ita. tr.: Id., «Verso e Prosa», *Entymema* 5 [2011] 17–30).

FUCHS, A., «Über den Wert von Befestigungsanlagen», *ZA* 98 (2008) 45–99.

FUCHS, A., «Assyria at War: Strategy and Conduct», in: *The Oxford Handbook of Cuneiform Culture, eds.* K. RADNER – E. ROBSON, Oxford 2011, 380–401.

FUCHS, G., *Der Becher des Sonnengottes*. Zur Entwicklung des Motivs "Becher des Zorns", BVBib 4, Münster 2003.

FURLANI, G., «Le guerre quali giudizi di Dio presso i Babilonesi e Assiri», in: *Miscellanea G. Galbiati*, FAmb 27, Milano 1951, 39–47.

GADAMER, H.-G., *Gesammelte Werke*. Band 1, Hermeneutik I: Wahrheit und Methode. Grundzüge einer philosophischen Hermeneutik, Tübingen 1960, [6]1990.

GADAMER, H.-G., «Und dennoch: Macht des Guten Willens», in: *Text und Interpretation*. Deutsch-französische Debatte mit Beiträgen von J. Derrida, Ph. Forget, M. Frank, H.-G. Gadamer, J. Greisch und F. Laruelle, *ed.* P. FORGET, UTB 1257, München 1984, 59–61.

GALBIATI, G., «La guerra santa israelitica», *RBR* 18 (1983) 11–41.

GALIL, G., *The Cronology of the Kings of Israels and Judah*, SHCANE 9, Leiden – New York – Köln 1996.

GALIMBERTI, U., *Il corpo*, Opere V, Milano 1983, [11]2002.

GALIMBERTI, U., *Dizionario di psicologia*, Torino 1992.

GALIMBERTI, U., *Paesaggi dell'anima*, Milano 1996.

GALLING, K., «Jahwe der Weltschöpfer», *ThBl* 35 (1925) 257–261.

GARBINI, G., *Storia e ideologia nell'Israele antico*, Brescia 1986 (Eng. tr.: Id., *History and Ideology in Ancient Israel*, London 1988).

GARFINKEL, Y., «The Eliakim Na'ar Yokan Seal Impressions. Sixty Years of Confusion in Biblical Archaeological Research», *BA* 53 (1990) 74–79.

GASPAROV, B., *Speech, Memory, and Meaning*. Intertextuality in Everyday Language, TL.SM 214, Berlin – New York 2010.

GASPARRO, L., *Simbolo e narrazione in Marco*. La dimensione simbolica del secondo Vangelo alla luce della pericope del fico di Mc 11,12–25, Anbib 198, Roma 2012.

GASPARRO, L., *La Parola, il gesto e il segno*. Le azioni simboliche di Geremia e dei profeti, Bologna 2015.

GASS, E., «Nebukadnezzar ante portas – Zu den babylonischen Interessen in der südlichen Levante», *ZAW* 128 (2016) 247–266.

GEERAERTS, D., «Prospects and Problems of Prototype Theory», in: *Cognitive Linguistics: Basic Readings, ed.* D. GEERAERTS, CLRes 34, Berlin 2006, 141–165 (= in: *Linguistics* 27 [1989] 587–612).

GEERAERTS, D., *Theories of Lexical Semantics*, Oxford 2010.

GEHMAN, H.S., «The Oath in the Old Testament: Its Vocabulary, Idiom, and Syntax; Its Semantics and Theology in the Masoretic Text and the Septuagint», in: *Grace upon Grace*. Essays in Honor of Lester J. Kuyper, *ed.* J.I. COOK, Grand Rapids 1975, 51–63.

GENETTE, G., *Figures III*, Poétique, Paris 1972.

GENETTE, G., *Nouveau discours du récit*, Poétique, Paris 1983.

GENSINI, S. – CIMATTI, F., *eds.*, *Manuale della comunicazione*. Modelli semiotici, linguaggi, pratiche testuali, Roma 1999.

GERLEMAN, G., «נשא», *THAT* II, 842–844.

GERLEMAN, G., «שלם», *THAT* II, 919–935.

GESUNDHEIT, S., «The Question of LXX Jeremiah as a Tool for Literary-Critical Analysis», *VT* 62 (2012) 29–57.

GIANNITRAPANI, A., *Introduzione alla semiotica dello spazio*, BTStu 833, Roma 2013.

GIANTO, A., «Mood and Modality in Classical Hebrew», *IOS* 18 (1998) 183–198.

GIBBS, R.W. – TENDAHL, M. – OKONSKI, L., «Inferring Pragmatic Messages from Metaphor», *LPPrag* 7 (2011) 3–28.

GILLINGHAM, S.E., *The Poems and Psalms of the Hebrew Bible*, Oxford 1994.

GIRONDA, V. – TOLOMELLI, M., «Introduzione. Storia e emozioni: costruzioni sociali e politiche della paura», *Storicamente* 11 (2015) 1–8.

GITAY, Y., «The Poetics of Exile and Suffering: Memory and Perceptions. A Cognitive-Linguistics Study of Lamentations», in: *Exile and Suffering*. A Selection of Papers Read at the 50th Anniversary Meeting of the Old Testament Society of South Africa OTWSA/OTSSA, Pretoria August 2007, *eds.* B. BECKING – D. HUMAN, OTS 50, Leiden – Boston 2009, 203–212.

GIUNTOLI, F., *L'officina della tradizione*. Studio di alcuni interventi redazionali post-sacerdotali e del loro contesto nel ciclo di Giacobbe (Gn 25,19–50,26), AnBib 154, Roma 2003.

GIUNTOLI, F., *Genesi 1–11*. Introduzione, traduzione e commento, NVBTA 1.1, Cinisello Balsamo 2013.

GIUNTOLI, F., *Genesi 11,27–50,26*. Introduzione, traduzione e commento, NVBTA 1.2, Cinisello Balsamo 2013.

GLANZ, O., *Understanding Partecipant-Reference Shifts in the Book of Jeremiah*. A Study of Exegetical Method and Its Consequences for the Interpretation of Referential Incoherence, SSN 60, Leiden 2013.

GLATT-GILAD, D.A., «The Personal Names in Jeremiah as a Source for the History of the Period», *HebStud* 41 (2000) 31–45.

GLAZOV, G.Y., *The Bridling of the Tongue and the Opening of the Mouth in Biblical Prophecy*, JSOT.S 311, Sheffield 2001.

GOETZE, A., «Warfare in Asia Minor», *Iraq* 25 (1963) 124–130.

GÖRG, M., «Jeremia zwischen Ost und West (Jer 38,1–6). Zur Krisensituation in Jerusalem am Vorabend des Babylonischen Exils», in: *Künder des Wortes*. Beiträge zur Theologie der Propheten, *eds.* L. RUPPERT – P. WEIMAR – E. ZENGER, Würzburg 1982, 121–136.

GOLDINGAY, J., «Jeremiah and the Superpower», in: *Uprooting and Planting*. Essays on Jeremiah for Leslie Allen, *ed.* J. GOLDINGAY, LHBOTS 459, London – New York 2007, 59–77.

GOLDINGAY, J., *The Book of Jeremiah*, NICOT, Grand Rapids 2021.

GONÇALVES, F.J., «Isaïe, Jérémie et la politique internationale de Juda», *Bib.* 76 (1995) 282–298.

GONEN, R., *Weapons of the Ancient World*, Jerusalem 1975.

GONZÁLEZ, A., «Verdaderos y falsos profetas», in: *Profetas verdaderos, profetas falsos*, *eds.* A. GONZÁLEZ – N. LOHFINK – G. VON RAD, Salamanca 1976, 13–76.

GOOD, M., «The Just War in Ancient Israel», *JBL* 104 (1985) 385–400.

GOODY, J., *The Logic of Writing and the Organization of Society*, Cambridge 1986.

GOSSE, B., «La place primitive du recueil d'Oracles contre le Nations dans le livre de Jérémie», *BN* 74 (1994) 28–30.

GOTTARDI, C., «La porta, il ponte, l'architrave. L'idea di cornice nel sistema performativo», *VA* 27/24 (2014) 58–64.

GOTTWALD, N.K., *All the Kingdoms of the Earth*. Israelite Prophecy and International Relations in the Ancient Near East, New York 1964.

GOTTWALD, N.K., *The Politics of Ancient Israel*, Louisville 2001.

GOURGUES, M. – TALBOT, M., *eds.*, *Partout où tu iras*. Conceptions et expériences bibliques de l'espace, ScBib 13, Paris 2003.

GOWAN, D.E., *Theology of the Prophetic Books*. The Death and Resurrection of Israel, Louisville 1998.

GOZZOLI, R.B., *Psammetichus II*. Reign, Documents and Officials, GHP Egyptology 25, London 2017.

GRABBE, L.L., «The Kingdom of Judah from Sennacherib's Invasion to the Fall of Jerusalem: If We Had Only the Bible...», in: *Good Kings and Bad Kings*, LHBOTS 393, London – New York 2005, 78–122.

GRABBE, L.L., «"The Lying Pen of the Scribes?". Jeremiah and History», in: *Essays on Ancient Israel in Its Near Eastern Context*. A Tribute to Nadav Na'aman, *eds.* Y. AMIT – E. BEN ZVI – I. FINKELSTEIN – O. LIPSCHITS, Winona Lake 2006, 189–204.

GRABBE, L.L., *Ancient Israel*. What Do We Know and How Do We Know It?, London 2007.

GRANT, J.A., *The King as Exemplar*. The Function of Deuteronomy's Kingship Law in the Shaping of the Book of Psalms, SBL.AS 17, Atlanta 2004.

GRAUPNER, A., *Auftrag und Geschick des Propheten Jeremia*. Literarische Eigenart, Herkunft und Intention vordeuteronomistischer Prosa im Jeremiabuch, BTSt 15, Neukirchen-Vluyn 1991.

GREEN, A., «The Fate of Jehoiakim», *AUSS* 20 (1982) 103–109.

GREEN, G.L., «Lexical Pragmatics and Biblical Interpretation», *JETS* 50 (2007) 799–812.

GREEN, G.L., «Lexical Pragmatics and the Lexicon», *BBR* 22 (2012) 315–333.

GREENBERG, M., «The Hebrew Oath Particle *Ḥay/Ḥē*», *JBL* 76 (1957) 34–39.

GREENBERG, M., *Ezekiel 1–20*, AncB 22, Garden City 1983.

GREIMAS, A.J., *Du sens*. Essais sémiotiques, Paris 1970.

GREIMAS, A.J., *Du sens* II. Essais sémiotiques, Paris 1983.

GRICE, H.P., «Logic and Conversation», in: *Syntax and Semantics*. Vol. III: Speech Acts, eds. P. COLE – J. MORGAN, New York 1975, 41–58 (= in: H.P. Grice, *Studies in the Way of Words*, Cambridge 1989, 22–40).

GRICE, H.P., *Studies in the Way of Words*, Cambridge 1989.

GRICE, H.P., *The Conception of Value*, Oxford 1991.

GRICE, H.P., *Aspects of Reason*, eds. B. HALE – C. WRIGHT, Oxford 2001.

GRIFFIN, E., *A First Look at Communication Theory*, New York 1991, [8]2012.

GRIFFITH, L., *The Fall of the Prison*. Biblical Perspectives on Prison Abolition, Grand Rapids 1993.

GRILLI, M., «Autore e lettore: il problema della comunicazione nell'ambito dell'esegesi biblica», *Gr.* 74 (1993) 447–459.

GRILLI, M., «Parola di Dio e linguaggio umano. Verso una pragmatica della comunicazione nei testi biblici», *Gr.* 94 (2013) 525–547.

GRONOWSKI, D., *Introduzione alla teoria della comunicazione*, Roma 2010.

GROSS, W., «Lying Prophet and Disobedient Man of God in 1 Kings 13: Role Analysis as an Instrument of Theological Interpretation of an OT Narrative Text», *Semeia* 15 (1979) 97–135.

GRUBER, M.I., *Aspects of Nonverbal Communication in the Ancient Near East*, 2 vols., StP 12/I-II, Roma 1980.

GUIDI, M., *"Così avvenne la generazione di Gesù Messia"*. Paradigma comunicativo e questione contestuale nella lettura pragmatica di Mt 1,18–25, AnBib 195, Roma 2012.

GUILLEMETTE, N., *Introduction à la lecture du Nouveau Testament*. Au soir du troisième jour, Paris 1980.

GUNN, D.M. – FEWELL, D., *Narrative in the Hebrew Bible*, Oxford 1993.

HABEL, N.C., «The Form and Significance of the Call Narratives», *ZAW* 77 (1965) 297–323.

HABEL, N.C., *The Land Is Mine*. Six Biblical Land Theologies, Minneapolis 1995.

HALDAR, A., *Associations of Cult Prophets among the Ancient Semites*, Uppsala 1945.

HAMBLIN, W.J., *Warfare in the Ancient Near East to 1600 BC*. Holy Warriors at the Dawn of History, W&H, London 2006.

HAMILTON, M.W., *The Body Royal*. The Social Poetics of Kingship in Ancient Israel, BiInS 78, Leiden 2005.

HANSON, V.D., *A War Like no Other*. How the Athenians and Spartans Fought the Peloponnesian War, New York 2005.

HARAN, M., «The Place of the Prophecies against the Nations in the Book of Jeremiah», in: *Emanuel*. Studies in Hebrew Bible, Septuagint, and Dead Sea Scrolls in Honor of Emanuel Tov, eds. S.M. PAUL et al., VT.S 94, Leiden 2003, 699–706.

HARDMEIER, C., *Prophetie im Streit vor dem Untergang Judas*. Erzählkommunikative Studien zur Entstehungssituation der Jesaja- und Jeremiaerzählungen in II Reg 18–20 und Jer 37–40, BZAW 187, Berlin 1990.

772 Bibliography

HARDMEIER, C., «Die Redekomposition Jer 2–6. Eine ultimative Verwarnung Jerusalems im Kontext des Zidkijaaufstandes», *WuD* 21 (1991) 11–42.

HARDMEIER, C., «Geschichte und Erfahrung in Jer 2–6: Zur theologischen Notwendigkeit einer geschichts- und erfahrungsbezogenen Exegese und ihrer methodischen Neuorientierung», *EvT* 56 (1996) 3–29.

HARDMEIER, C., «Wahrhaftigkeit und Fehlorientierung bei Jeremia: Jer 5,1 und die divinatorische Expertise Jer 2–6* im Kontext der zeitgenössischen Kontroversen um die politische Zukunft Jerusalems», in: *Exegese vor Ort.* Festschrift für Peter Welten zum 65. Geburtstag, *eds.* C. MAIER – R. LIWAK – K.-P. JÖRNS, Leipzig 2001, 121–144.

HARTENSTEIN, F., «JHWH, Erschaffer des Himmels. Zu Herkunft und Bedeutung eines monotheistischen Kernarguments», *ZThK* 110 (2013) 383–409.

HASEL, M., *Military Practice and Polemic.* Israel's Laws of Warfare in Near Eastern Perspective, Berrien Springs 2005.

HAYES, E.R., *The Pragmatics of Perception and Cognition in MT Jeremiah 1:1–6:30.* A Cognitive Linguistics Approach, BZAW 380, Berlin – New York 2008.

HAYES, J.H., «The Tradition of Zion's Inviolability», *JBL* 82 (1963) 419–426.

HEINTZ, J.G., «Oracles prophétiques et "guerre sainte" selon les archives royales de Mari et l'Ancien Testament», in: *Congress Volume.* Rome 1968, *eds.* G.W. Anderson *et al.*, VT.S 17, Leiden 1969, 112–138.

HEINTZ, J.G., «Prophetie in Mari und Israel», *Bib.* 52 (1971) 543–555.

HEINTZ, J.G., «La "fin" des prophètes bibliques? Nouvelles théories et documents sémitiques anciens», in: *Oracles et prophéties dans l'antiquité.* Actes du Colloque de Strasbourg (15–17 juin 1995), *ed.* J.-G. HEINTZ, Paris 1997, 195–214.

HELFMEYER, F.J., «אות», *ThWAT* I, 182–205.

HERMISSON, H.-J., «Kriterien "wahrer" und "falscher" Prophetie. Zur Auslegung von Jeremia 23,16–22 und Jeremia 28,8–9», *ZThK* 92 (1995) 121–139 (= Id., *Studien zu Prophetie und Weisheit.* Gesammelte Aufsätze, *eds.* J. BARTHEL – H. JAUSS – K. KOENEN, FAT 23, Tübingen 1998, 59–76).

HERMISSON, H.-J., «Die "Königsspruch"-Sammlung im Jeremiabuch – von der Anfangs – zur Endgestalt», in: *Die Hebräische Bibel und ihre zweifache Nachgeschichte.* Festschrift für Rolf Rendtorff zum 65. Geburtstag, *eds.* E. BLUM – C. MACHOLZ – E.W. STEGEMANN, Neukirchen 1990, 277–299.

HERR, B., «Der wahre Prophet bezeugt seine Botschaft mit dem Tod. Ein Versuch zu 1 Kön 13», *BZ* 41 (1997) 69–78.

HERRMANN, S., *Geschichte Israels in alttestamentlicher Zeit,* München 1973.

HERRMANN, S., *Jeremia.* Lieferung 1, BK 12, Neukirchen-Vluyn 1986.

HERRMANN, S., «Jeremia vor Chananja. Die angebliche Krise des Propheten», in: *Von Gott reden.* Beiträge zur Theologie und Exegese des Alten Testaments, *eds.* D. VIEWEGER – E.-J. WASCHKE, Neukirchen-Vluyn 1995, 117–122.

HERZOG, C. – GICHON, M., *Battles of the Bible,* London 1978.

HESCHEL, *The Prophets,* New York 1962.

HESSE, F., *Die Fürbitte im Alten Testament*. Inaugural-Dissertation zur Erlangung der Doktorwürde der hohen Theologischen Fakultät der Friedrich-Alexander-Universität, Erlangen 1951.

HIBBARD, J.T., «True and False Prophecy: Jeremiah's Revision of Deuteronomy», *JSOT* 35 (2011) 339–358.

HIBBITTS, B.J., «"Coming to Our Senses". Communication and Legal Expression in Performance Cultures» *ELJ* 41 (1992) 873–960.

HIERONYMUS, *In Hieremiam prophetam libri VI, ed.* S. REITER, CChr.SL 74, Turnholti 1960.

HILBER, J.W., «Psalm CX in the Light of Assyrian Prophecies», *VT* 53 (2003) 353–366.

HILBER, J.W., *Cultic Prophecy in the Psalms*, BZAW 352, Berlin 2005.

HILL, J., *Friend or Foe? The Figure of Babylon in the Book of Jeremiah mt*, BiblInterp 40, Leiden – Boston – Köln 1999.

HILL, J., «Writing the Prophetic Word. The Production of the Book of Jeremiah», *ABR* 57 (2009) 22–33.

HILL, J., «The Dynamics of Written Discourse and the Book of Jeremiah MT», in: *Jeremiah (Dis)Placed*. New Directions in Writing/Reading Jeremiah, *eds.* A.R.P. DIAMOND – L. STULMAN, LHBOTS 529, London – New York 2011, 104–111.

HILLERS, D.R., *Treaty Curses and the Old Testament Prophets,* BibOr 16, Rome 1964.

HOCHSCHILD, A.R., «Work, Feelings Rules, and Social Structure», *AJS* 85 (1979) 551–575.

HOFFMAN, Y., «Reflections on the Relationship between Theopolitics, Prophecy and Historiography», in: *Politics and Theopolitics in the Bible and Postbiblical Literature, eds.* H.G. REVENTLOW – Y. HOFFMAN – B. UFFENHEIMER, JSOT.S 171, Sheffield 1994, 85–99.

HOGARTH, D.G., *Charchemish*. Part I: Introductory, London 1914.

HØGENHAVEN, J., «Prophecy and Propaganda. Aspects of Political and Religious Reasoning in Israel and the Ancient Near East», *SJOT* 1 (1989) 125–141.

HOLLADAY, W.L., «Prototypes and Copies: A New Approach to the Poetry – Prose Problem in the Book of Jeremiah», *JBL* 79 (1960) 351–367.

HOLLADAY, W.L., «The Background of Jeremiah's Self-Understanding: Moses, Samuel and Psalm 22», *JBL* 83 (1964) 153–164.

HOLLADAY, W.L., «Jeremiah and Moses: Further Observations», *JBL* 85 (1966) 17–27.

HOLLADAY, W.L., «The Recovery of Poetic Passages of Jeremiah», *JBL* 85 (1966) 401–435.

HOLLADAY, W.L., «A Fresh Look at "Source B" and "Source C" in Jeremiah», *VT* 25 (1975) 394–412.

HOLLADAY, W.L., *The Architecture of Jeremiah 1–20*, Lewisburg – London 1976.

HOLLADAY, W.L., *Isaiah: A Scroll of a Prophetic Heritage,* Grand Rapids 1978.

HOLLADAY, W.L., *Jeremiah 1*. A Commentary on the Book of the Prophet Jeremiah. Chapters 1–25, Hermeneia, Philadelphia 1986.

HOLLADAY, W.L., *Jeremiah 2*. A Commentary on the Book of the Prophet Jeremiah. Chapters 26–45, Hermeneia, Philadelphia 1989.

774 Bibliography

HOLLADAY, W.L., «Elusive Deuteronomists, Jeremiah, and Proto-Deuteronomy», *CBQ* 66 (2004) 55–77.

HOLLOWAY, S.W., *Aššur Is King! Aššur Is King!* Religion in the Exercise of Power in the Neo-Assyrian Empire, CHANE 10, Leiden 2002.

HOLM, N.G., «Ecstatic Research in the 20th Century – An Introduction», in: *Religious Ecstasy*, ed. N.G. HOLM, Uppsala 1982, 7–26.

HOLT, E.K., «The Chicken and the Egg – or: Was Jeremiah a Member of the Deuteronomist Party?», *JSOT* 44 (1989) 109–122.

HOLT, E.K., «Word of Jeremiah–Word of God: Structures of Authority in the Book of Jeremiah», in: *Uprooting and Planting*. Essays on Jeremiah for Leslie Allen, ed. J. GOLDINGAY, LHBOTS 459, London – New York 2007, 172–189.

HOOKER, P.K. – HAYES, J.H., «The Year of Josiah's Death: 609 or 610 BCE?», in: *The Land That I Will Show You*. Essays on the History and Archaeology of the Ancient Near East in Honour of J.M. Miller, eds. J.A. DEARMAN – M.P. GRAHAM, JSOT.S 343, Sheffield 2001, 96–103.

DE HOOP, R,., «Perspective after the Exile: The King, עבדי, "My Servant" in Jeremiah – Some Reflections on MT and LXX», in: *Exile and Suffering*. A Selection of Papers Read at the 50th Anniversary Meeting of the Old Testament Society of South Africa OTWSA/OTSSA, Pretoria August 2007, eds. B. BECKING – D. HUMAN, OTS 50, Leiden – Boston 2009, 105–121.

HORN, L.R. «From *if* to *iff*: Conditional Perfection as Pragmatic Strengthening», *JPrag* 32 (2000) 289–326.

HORNKOHL, A.D., *Ancient Hebrew Periodization and the Language of the Book of Jeremiah*. The Case for a Sixth-Century Date of Composition, StSLL 74, Leiden – Boston 2014.

HORST, F., «Die Visionsschilderungen der alttestamentlichen Propheten», *EvT* 20 (1960) 193–205.

HOSSFELD, F.-L., «Wahre und falsche Prophetie in Israel», *BiKi* 38 (1983) 139–144.

HOSSFELD, F.-L. – MEYER, I., *Prophet gegen Prophet*. Eine Analyse der alttestamentlichen Texte zum Thema: Wahre und falsche Propheten, BiBe 9, Fribourg 1973.

HOUTMAN, C., *Der Himmel im Alten Testament*. Israels Weltbild und Weltanschauung, OTS 30, Leiden 1993.

HUMPHREYS, W.L., *Crisis and Story*. An Introduction to the Old Testament, Mountain View 1990.

HUNDLEY, M.B., *Gods in Dwellings*. Temples and Divine Presence in the Ancient Near East, SBLWAWS 3, Atlanta 2013.

HUTTER, M., «Politik. III. Politik und Religion. 1. *Religionswissenschaftlich*», *RGG⁴* VI, 1453–1454.

HUTTON, R.R., «Magic or Street-Theater? The Power of the Prophetic Word», *ZAW* 107 (1995) 247–260.

HUWYLER, B., «Jeremia und die Völker. Politische Prophetie in der Zeit der babylonischen Bedrohung (7./6. Jh. v. Chr.)», *ThZ* 52 (1996) 193–205.

Huwyler, B., *Jeremia und die Völker.* Untersuchungen zu den Völkersprüchen in Jeremia 46–49, FAT 20, Tübingen 1997.

Hwang, J., «The *Missio Dei* as an Integrative Motif in the Book of Jeremiah», *BBR* 23 (2013) 481–508.

Hyatt, J.P., «Jeremiah and Deuteronomy», *JNES* 1 (1942) 156–173 (= Id., «Jeremiah and Deuteronomy», in: *A Prophet to the Nations.* Essays in Jeremiah Studies, *eds.* L.G. Perdue – B.W. Kovacs, Winona Lake 1984, 113–127).

Ibáñez Arana, A., «Jeremias y "los profetas"», *ScrVict* 35 (1988) 5–56, 233–319.

Ibáñez Arana, A., «Los criterios de profecía» *Lum.* 39 (1990) 193–250.

Irudaya, R., «A Prophetic Call against War. A Political-Theological Study of Jeremiah 21:1–14», *VJTR* 66 (2002) 796–808.

Iser, W., *Der implizite Leser,* München 1972.

Iser, W., *Der Akt des Lesens.* Theorie ästhetischer Wirkung, München 1976.

Ishida T., *The Royal Dynasties in Ancient Israel.* A Study on the Formation and Development of Royal-Dynastic Ideology, BZAW 142, Berlin 1977.

Jacob, E., «Quelques remarques sur les faux prophètes», *ThZ* 13 (1957) 479–486.

Jakobson, R., «Linguistics and Poetics », in: *Selected Writings III. Poetry of Grammar and Grammar of Poetry,* The Hague – Paris – New York 1981, 18–51.

Janowski, B., «Der andere König. Ps 72 als Magna Charta der judäischen Königsideologie», in: *Liebe, Macht und Religion.* Interdisziplinäre Studien zu Grunddimensionen menschlicher Existenz, Gedenkschrift für H. Merklein, *eds.* M. Gielen – J. Kügler, Stuttgart 2003, 97–112.

Janowski, B., *Konfliktgespräche mit Gott.* Eine Anthropologie der Psalmen, Neukirchen-Vluyn 2003, ²2006.

Janzen, J.G., *Studies in the Text of Jeremiah,* HSM 6, Cambridge (MA) 1973.

Jenni, E., «אוֹיֵב», *THAT* I, 118–122.

Jenni, E., «יצא», *THAT* I, 755–761.

Jenni, E., *Die hebräischen Präpositionen.* Band 3: Die Präposition Lamed, Stuttgart 2000.

Jensen, J., *Ethical Dimensions of the Prophets,* Collegeville 2006.

Jepsen E., «Gottesmann und Prophet. Anmerkungen zum Kapitel 1. Könige 13», in: *Probleme biblischer Theologie.* Gehrard von Rad zum 70. Geburtstag, *ed.* H.W. Wolff, München 1971, 171–182.

Jeremias, J., *The Cultic Prophet and Israel's Psalmody,* Cardiff 1979.

Jeremias, J., *Die Reue Gottes.* Aspekte alttestamentlicher Gottesvorstellung, BThSt 31, Neukirchen-Vluyn 1975, 2002³.

Jeremias, J., «Remembering and Forgetting: "True" and "False" Prophecy», in: *Remembering and Forgetting in Early Second Temple Judah,* eds. E. Ben Zvi – C. Levin, FAT 85, Tübingen 2012, 45–54.

Jeremias, J., «Der Rätsel der Schriftprophetie», *ZAW* 125 (2013) 93–117.

Jeremias, J., *Theologie des Alten Testaments,* GAT 6, Göttingen 2015.

776 Bibliography

JINDO, J.Y., *Biblical Metaphor Reconsidered.* A Cognitive Approach to Poetic Prophecy in Jeremiah 1–24, HSM 64, Winona Lake 2010.

JOB, J.B., *Jeremiah's Kings.* A Study of the Monarchy in Jeremiah, MSSOTS, Aldershot 2006.

JOHNSON, A.R., *The Cultic Prophet in Ancient Israel,* Cardiff 1944.

JONES, G.H., «The Concept of Holy War», in: *The World of Ancient Israel.* Sociological, Anthropological and Political Perspectives, *ed.* R.E. CLEMENTS, Cambridge 1989, 299– 321.

DE JONG, M.J., *Isaiah among the Ancient Near Eastern Prophets.* A Comparative Study of the Earliest Stages of the Isaiah Tradition and the Neo-Assyrian Prophecies, VT.S 117, Leiden – Boston 2007.

DE JONG, M.J., «Biblical Prophecy – A Scribal Enterprise. The Old Testament Prophecy of Unconditional Judgement Considered as a Literary Phenomenon», *VT* 61 (2011) 39–70.

DE JONG, M.J., «Why Jeremiah Is Not Among the Prophets: An Analysis of the Terms נביא and נביאים in the Book of Jeremiah», *JSOT* 35 (2011) 483–510.

DE JONG, M.J., «The Fallacy of "True and False" in Prophecy Illustrated by Jer 28:8–9» *JHS* 12 (2012) 1–29 [DOI: 10.5508/jhs.2012.v12.a10].

DE JONG, M.J., «Rewriting the Past in Light of the Present: The Stories of the Prophet Jeremiah», in: *Prophecy and Prophets in Stories.* Papers Read at the Fifth Meeting of the Edinburgh Prophecy Network, Utrecht, October 2013, *eds.* B. BECKING – H.M. BARSTAD, OTS 65, Leiden – Boston 2015, 64–75.

JOO, S., *Provocation and Punishment.* The Anger of God in the Book of Jeremiah and Deuteronomistic Theology, BZAW 361, Berlin – New York 2006.

JOOSTEN, J., «Do the Finite Verbal Forms in Biblical Hebrew Express Aspect?», *JANES* 29 (2002) 49–70.

JOUSSE, M., *L'anthropologie du geste,* Paris 1974.

JUNGBLUTH, R., *Im Himmel und auf Erden.* Dimensionen von Königsherrschaft im Alten Testament, BWANT 196, Stuttgart 2011.

KABASELE MUKENGE, A., «La politique du prophète Jéremie: révolte ou résignation?», in: *Foi et politique dans la Bible,* ed., J.-L. VANDE KERKHOVE, Lubumbashi 2004, 61–81.

KADDARI, M.Z., «A Semantic Approach to Biblical Parallelism», *JJS* 24 (1973) 167–175.

KAISER, O., *Der eine Gott Israels und die Mächte der Welt.* Der Weg Gottes im Alten Testament vom Herrn seines Volkes zum Herrn der ganzen Welt, FRLANT 249, Göttingen 2013.

KALIMI, I., *The Reshaping of Ancient Israelite History in Chronicles,* Winona Lake 2005.

KALIMI, I – RICHARDSON, S., «Sennacherib at the Gates of Jerusalem – Story, History and Historiography: An Introduction», in: *Sennacherib at the Gates of Jerusalem.* Story, History and Historiography, *eds.* I. KALIMI – S. RICHARDSON, CHANE 71, Leiden – Boston 2014, 1–7.

KALMANOFSKY, A., «Poetic Violence in the Book of Jeremiah», in: *The Oxford Handbook of Jeremiah, eds.* L. STULMAN – E. SILVER, Oxford 2021, 328–342.

KANG, S.-M., *Divine War in the Old Testament and in the Ancient Near East*, BZAW 177, Berlin 1989.

KASWALDER, P., «Re Ioiachin, una speranza perduta (2Re 25,27–30)», *LASBF* 54 (2004) 9–24.

KECSKES, I., «Encyclopaedic Knowledge and Cultural Models», in: *Cognitive Pragmatics*, ed. H.-J. SCHMID, HP 4, Berlin – New York 2012, 175–200.

KEEGAN, J., *A History of Warfare*, New York 1993.

KEEL, O., *Jahwes Entgegnung an Ijob*. Eine Deutung von Ijob 38–41 vor dem Hintergrund der zeitgenössischen Bildkunst, FRLANT 121, Göttingen 1978.

KEEL, O. – UEHLINGER, C., «Der Assyrerkönig Salmanassar III. und Jehu von Israel auf dem Schwarzen Obelisken aus Nimrud», *ZKTh* 116 (1994) 391–420.

KEIL, C.F., *Biblischer Commentar über den Propheten Jeremia und die Klagelieder*, Leipzig 1872.

KELLY, W.L., «Prophets, Kings and Honour in the Narrative of 1 Ks 22», in: *Prophecy and Prophets in Stories*. Papers Read at the Fifth Meeting of the Edinburgh Prophecy Network, Utrecht, October 2013, eds. B. BECKING – H.M. BARSTAD, OTS 65, Leiden – Boston 2015, 64–75.

KELLY, W.L., *How Prophecy Works*. A Study of the Semantic Field of נבא and a Close Reading of Jeremiah 1:4–19, 23:9–40 and 27:1–28:17, FRALANT 272, Göttingen 2020.

KEMPSON, R.M., *Semantic Theory*, CTL, Cambridge 1977.

KENNEDY, J.M., «Shaphan», *ABD* V, 1159.

KEOWN, G.L. – SCALISE, P.J. – SMOTHERS, T.G., *Jeremiah 26–52*, WBC 27, Dallas 1995.

KESSLER, K., *Das neuassyrische Reich der Sargoniden (720–612 v. Chr.) und das neubabylonische Reich (612–539 v. Chr.)*, TAVO Karte B IV 13, Wiesbaden 1991.

KESSLER, M., «Jeremiah 25,1–29: Text and Context. A Synchronic Study», *ZAW* 109 (1997) 44–70.

KESSLER, M., The Function of Chapters 25 and 50–51 in the Book of Jeremiah», in: *Troubling Jeremiah*, eds. A.R.P. DIAMOND – K. O'CONNOR – L. STULMAN, JSOT.S 260, Sheffield 1999, 64–72.

KESSLER, M., *Battle of the Gods*. The God of Israel versus Marduk of Babylon. A Literary/Theological Interpretation of Jeremiah 50–51, Assen 2003.

KESSLER, M., ed., *Reading the Book of Jeremiah*. A Search for Coherence, Winona Lake 2004.

KESSLER, R., *Der Weg zum Leben*. Ethik des Alten Testament, München 2017.

KILPP, N., *Niederreißen und aufbauen*. Das Verhältnis von Heilsverheißung und Unheilsverkündigung bei Jeremia und im Jeremiabuch, BThSt 13, Neukirchen-Vluyn 1990.

KING, L.W., *Bronze Reliefs from the Gates of Shalmaneser King of Assyria*, London 1915.

KING, P.J., *Jeremiah*. An Archaeological Companion, Louisville 1993.

KIUCHI, N., «בֶּהֱמָה», *NIDOTTE* I, 612–613.

KLINGBEIL, M.G., «Creation in the Prophetic Literature of the Old Testament: An Intertextual Approach», *JATS* 20 (2009) 19–54.

778 Bibliography

KLOPFENSTEIN, M.A., *Die Lüge nach dem Alten Testament.* Ihre Begriff, ihre Bedeutung und ihre Beurteilung, Zürich 1964.

KNIERIM, R., «Cosmos and History in Israel's Theology», *HBT* 3 (1981) 59–123 (= in: ID., *The Task of Old Testament Theology.* Substance, Method and Cases, Grand Rapids 1995, 171–224).

KOCH, K., « Ḫazzi-Ṣafôn-Kasion: Die Geschichte eines Berges und seiner Gottheiten», in: *Religionsgeschichtliche Beziehungen zwischen Kleinasien, Nordsyrien und dem Alten Testament.* Internationales Symposion, Hamburg, 17.-21. März 1990, *eds.* B. Janowski – K. Koch – G. Wilhelm, OBO 129, Freiburg – Göttingen 1993, 171–223.

KÖCKERT, M. – NISSINEN, M., *eds.*, *Propheten in Mari, Assyrien und Israel*, FRLANT 201, Göttingen 2003.

KÖHLER, L., *Deuterojesaja stilkritisch untersucht*, BZAW 37, Giessen 1923.

KONSTAN, D., *Pity Transformed*, London 2001.

KORPEL, M.C.A., «Unit Delimitation in Ugaritic Cultic Texts and Some Babylonian and Hebrew Parallels», in: *Delimitation Criticism.* A New Tool in Biblical Scholarship, Pericope 1, *eds.* M.C.A. KORPEL – J. OESCH, Assen 2000, 141–160.

KORPEL, M.C.A., *The Structure of the Book of Ruth*, Pericope 2, Assen 2001.

KORPEL, M.C.A., *The Silent God*, Leiden – Boston 2012.

KORPEL, M.C.A. – DE MOOR, J.C., *The Structure of Classical Hebrew Poetry: Isaiah 40–55*, OTS 41, Leiden 1998.

KORPEL, M.C.A. – OESCH, J., *Delimitation Criticism.* A New Tool in Biblical Scholarship, Pericope 1, Assen 2000.

KŐSZEGHY, M., *Der Streit um Babel in den Büchern Jesaja und Jeremia*, BWANT 173, Stuttgart 2007.

KOTTSIEPER, I., «עֶשֶׁק», *ThWAT* VII, 974–1000.

KRAŠOVEC, J., *La justice (ṣdq) de Dieu dans la Bible hébraïque et l'interpretation juive et chrétienne*, OBO 76, Freiburg 1988.

KRATZ, R.G., *Translatio imperii.* Untersuchungen zu den aramäischen Danielerzählungen und ihrem theologiegeschichtlichen Umfeld, WMANT 63, Neukirchen-Vluyn 1991.

KRAUS, H.-J., *Prophetie in der Krisis.* Studien zu Texten aus dem Buch Jeremia, BSt 43, Neukirchen-Vluyn 1964.

KRAUS, H.-J., «Der lebendige Gott», *EvT* 27 (1967) 169–200.

KREUZER, S., «Die Mächtigkeitsformel im Deuteronomium. Gestaltung, Vorgeschichte und Entwicklung», *ZAW* 109 (1997) 188–207.

KREUZER, S., «Die Verwendung der Mächtigkeitsformel außerhalb des Deuteronomiums. Literarische und theologische Linien zu Jer, Ez, dtrG und P», *ZAW* 109 (1997) 369–384.

KRISPENZ, J., «Grammatik und Theologie in der Botenformel», *ZAH* 11 (1998) 133–139.

KRISPENZ, J., *Literarkritik und Stilstatistik im Alten Testament.* Eine Studie zur literarkritischen Methode, durchgeführt an Texten aus den Büchern Jeremia, Ezechiel und 1 Könige, BZAW 307, Berlin – New York 2001.

KRISPENZ, J., «Die Einsetzung des Jeremia. Ambivalenz als Mittel der Sinnkonstitution», in: *Schriftprophetie*. Festschrift für Jörg Jeremias zum 65. Geburtstag, eds. F. HARTENSTEIN – J. KRISPENZ – A. SCHART, Neukirchen-Vluyn 2004, 203–219.

KRISPENZ, J., «Leben als Zeichen. Performancekunst als Deutungsmodell für prophetische Zeichenhandlungen im Alten Testament», *EvT* 64 (2004) 51–64.

KRISPENZ, J., «Namen im Jeremiabuch. Ein Vergleich zwischen Jer 1–10 und Jer 26–35», in: *Sprachen – Bilder – Klänge*. Dimensionen der Theologie im Alten Testament und in seinem Umfeld, eds. C. KARRER-GRUBE *et al.*, AOAT 359, Münster 2009, 39–53.

KRONHOLM, T., «עֵץ», *ThWAT* VI, 463–482.

KRUGER, P.A., «"Nonverbal communication" in the Hebrew Bible: A Few Comments», *JNSL* 24 (1998) 141–164.

KRUGER, P.A., «On Emotions and the Expression of Emotions in the Old Testament: A Few Introductory Remarks», *BZ* 48 (2004) 213–228.

KUENEN, A., *De profeten en de profetie onder Israël*. Historisch-dogmatische studie, Leiden 1875.

KUGEL, J.L. *The Idea of Biblical Poetry*, New Haven 1981.

KÜHNE, H. – STEUERWALD, H., «Das Nordost-Tor von Tell Mumbaqat», in: *Le Moyen Euphrate: Zone de contacts et d'échanges*. Actes du Colloque de Strasbourg 10–12 mars 1977, ed. J.C. MARGUERON, Leiden 1980, 203–215.

KUTSCH, E., «Gideons Berufung und Altarbau Jdc 6,11–24», *ThLZ* 81 (1956) 75–84 (= ID., *Kleine Schriften zum Alten Testament*. zum 65. Geburstag Ernst Kutsch, eds. L. SCHMIDT – K. EBERLEIN, BZAW 168, Berlin 1986, 99–109).

LACOMBE, P., *De l'histoire considérée comme science*, Paris 1994.

LAKOFF, G., *Women, Fire and Dangerous Things*. What Categories Reveal about the Mind, Chicago 1987.

LAKOFF, G., *Philosophy in the Flesh*. The Embodied Mind and Its Challenge to Western Thought, New York 1999.

LAKOFF, G. – JOHNSON, M., *Metaphors We Live By*, Chicago 1980.

LALLEMAN-DE WINKEL, H., *Jeremiah in Prophetic Tradition*. An Examination of the Book of Jeremiah in the Light of Israel's Prophetic Traditions, CBET 26, Leuven 2000.

LALLEMAN-DE WINKEL, H., «Jeremiah, Judgement and Creation», *TynB* 60 (2009) 15–24.

LAMB, D.T., «"I Will Strike You Down and Cut Off Your Head" (1 Sam 17:46): Trash Talking, Derogatory Rhetoric, and Psychological Warfare in Ancient Israel», in: *Warfare, Ritual, and Symbol in Biblical and Modern Contexts*, eds. B.E. KELLE – F.R. AMES – J.L. WRIGHT, SBL.AIL 18, Atlanta 2014, 111–130.

LAMBERT, W.G., *Babylonian Wisdom Literature*, Oxford 1960.

LAMBERT, W.G., «Nebuchadnezzar King of Justice», *Iraq* 27 (1965) 1–11.

LANDES, G.M., «Creation and Liberation», *USQR* 33 (1978) 78–99.

LANFRANCHI, G.B., «The Assyrian Expansion in the Zagros and the Local Ruling Elites», in: *Continuity of Empire (?)*. Assyria, Media, Persia, eds. G.B. LANFRANCHI – M. ROAF – R. ROLLINGER, HANE.M 5, Padova 2003, 79–118.

780   Bibliography

LANFRANCHI, G.B., «Ideological Implications of the Problem of Royal Responsibility in the Neo-Assyrian Period», in: *Hayim and Miriam Tadmor Volume, eds.* I. EPH'AL – A. BEN-TOR – P. MACHINIST, ErIsr 27, Jerusalem 2003, 100*-110*.

LANFRANCHI, G.B. – ROLLINGER, R., eds., *Concepts of Kingship in Antiquity.* Proceedings of the European Science Foundation Exploratory Workshop (Padova, 28 november–1 december 2007), HANE.M 11, Padova 2010.

LANG, B., *Kein Aufstand in Jerusalem.* Die Politik des Propheten Ezechiel, SBB, Stuttgart 1978.

LANG, B., «Ein babylonisches Motiv in Israels Schöpfungsmythologie (Jer 27,5–6)», *BZ* 27 (1983), 236–237.

LANG, B., «Games Prophets Play: Street Theatre and Symbolic Acts in Biblical Israel», in: *The Games of God and Man.* Essays in Play and Performance, *ed.* K.-P. KÖPPING, Hamburg 1997, 257–271 (= in: B. LANG, *Hebrew Life and Literature.* Selected Essays of Bernhard Lang, MSSOTS, Farnham 2008, 185–195).

LANGDON, S., *Die neubabylonischen Königsinschriften*, VAB 4, Leipzig 1912.

LANGE, A., *Vom prophetischen Wort zur prophetischen Tradition.* Studien zur Traditions- und Redaktionsgeschichte innerprophetischer Konflikte in der Hebräischen Bibel, FAT 34, Tübingen 2002.

LAWLOR, J.I., «Word Event in Jeremiah: A Look at the Composition's "Introductory Formulas"», in: *Inspired Speech.* Prophecy in the Ancient Near East. Essays in Honor of Herbert B. Huffmon, *eds.* J. KALTNER – L. STULMAN, New York 2004, 231–243.

LAYARD, A.H., *Inscriptions in the Cuneiform Character, from Assyrian Monuments*, London 1851.

LEDOUX, J.E. – DAMASIO, A.R., «Emotions and Feelings», in: *Principles of Neural Science, eds.* E.R. KANDEL *et al.*, New York 1981, [5]2013, 1079–1094.

LEFEBVRE, G., *La grande peur de 1789*, Paris 1932.

LEE, N.C. – MANDOLFO, C., eds., *Lamentations in Ancient and Contemporary Cultural Contexts*, SBLSymS 43, Atlanta 2008.

LEENE, H., «Blowing the Same Shofar: An Intertextual Comparison of Representations of the Prophetic Role in Jeremiah and Ezekiel», in: *The Elusive Prophets.* The Prophet as Historical Person, Literary Character and Anonymous Artist, *ed.* J.C. DE MOOR, OTS 45, Leiden 2001, 175–198.

VAN LEEUWEN, R.C., «ברא», *NIDOTTE* I, 728–735.

LEHMANN, M.R., «Biblical Oaths», *ZAW* 81 (1969) 74–92.

LEIBOVICI, M., «Nabuchodonosor», *DBS* VI, 286–291.

LEICHTY, E., «Esarhaddon's "Letters to the Gods", in: *Ah, Assyria...* Studies in Assyrian History and Ancient Near Eastern Historiography Presented to Hayim Tadmor, *eds.* M. COGAN – I. EPH'AL, ScrHie 33, Jerusalem 1991, 52–57.

LEICKA, G., *Dictionary of Ancient Near Eastern Architecture*, London 1988.

LEJEUNE, P., *Le Pacte autobiographique,* Paris 1975.

LEMAIRE, A., «Prières en temps de crise: les inscriptions de Khirbet Beit Lei», *RB* 83 (1976) 558–568.

LEMAIRE, A., *Inscriptions hébraïques.* Tome I: Les ostraca, LAPO 9, Paris 1977.

LEMAIRE, A., *ed.*, *Prophètes et rois*. Bible et Proche-Orient, LeDiv.HS, Paris 2001.

LEMAIRE, A., «Prophètes et rois dans les inscriptions ouest – sémitiques (IXᵉ–VIᵉ siècle av. J.-C.)», in: *Prophètes et rois*. Bible et Proche-Orient, *ed.* A. LEMAIRE, LeDiv.HS, Paris 2001, 85–115.

LEMKE, W.M., «Nebuchadrezzar My Servant», *CBQ* 28 (1966) 45–59.

LEMKE, W.M., «The Near and Distant God. A Study of Jer 23:23–34 in its Biblical Theological Context», *JBL* 100 (1981) 542–551.

LEMON, J.M., «Iconographic Approaches: The Iconic Structure of Psalm 17», in: *Method Matters*. Essays on the Interpretation of the Hebrew Bible in Honor of David L. Petersen, *eds.* J.M. LEMON – K.H. RICH, SBLRBS 56, Atlanta 2009, 143–168.

LENCHAK, T.A., *"Choose Life!"*. A Rhetorical-Critical Investigation of Deuteronomy 28,69–30,20, AnBib 129, Roma 1993.

LEPROHON, R.J. «Royal Ideology and State Administration in Pharaonic Egypt», in: *Civilizations of the Ancient Near East*, vol. I, *ed.* J.M. SASSON, New York 1995, 278–287.

LESÊTRE, H., «Sédécias», *DB(V)* V, 1556–1559.

LEUCHTER, M., «Jeremiah' 70-Year Prophecy and the Atbash Codes», *Bib.* 85 (2004) 503–522.

LEUCHTER, M., «The Temple Sermon and the Term מקום in the Jeremianic Corpus», *JSOT* 30 (2005) 93–109.

LEUCHTER, M., *The Polemics of Exile in Jeremiah 26–45*, Cambridge 2008.

LEVIN, C., *Die Verheißung des neuen Bundes*. In ihrem theologiegeschichtlichen Zusammenhang ausgelegt, FRLANT 137, Göttingen 1985.

LEVIN C., «Das Wort Jahwes an Jeremia. Zur ältesten Redaktion der jeremianischen Sammlung», *ZThK* 101 (2004) 257–280.

LEVIN, C., «The "Word of Yahweh": A Theological Concept in the Book of Jeremiah», in: *Prophets, Prophecy, and Prophetic Texts in Second Temple Judaism, eds.* M.H. FLOYD – R.D. HAAK, LHBOTS 427, London – New York 2006, 42–62.

LÉVINAS, E., *Totalité et infini*. Essai sur l'extériorité, Nijhoff 1961, ³1968.

LEVINE, B.A., «The View from Jerusalem. Biblical Responses to the Babylonian Presence», in: *The Babylonian World, ed.* G. LEICK, Abingdon 2007, 541–561.

LEVINSON, B.M., *Deuteronomy and the Hermeneutics of Legal Innovation*, New York – Oxford 1997.

LEVINSON, B.M., «The Reconceptualization of Kingship in Deuteronomy and the Deuteronomistic History's Transformation of Torah», *VT* 51 (2001) 513–534.

LEVINSON, S.C., *Presumptive Meanings*. The Theory of Generalized Conversational Implicature, Cambridge 2000.

LEWIN, E.D., «Arguing for Authority. A Rhetorical Study of Jeremiah 1.4–19 and 20.7–18», *JSOT* 32 (1985) 105–119.

LIBET, B., *Mind Time*. The Temporal Factor in Consciousness, Cambridge (MA) 2004.

LIND, M.C., *Jahweh Is a Warrior*. The Theology of Warfare in Ancient Israel, Scottdale 1980.

LINDENBERGER, J.M., *Ancient Aramaic and Hebrew Letters*, SBLWAW 14, Atlanta 1994, ²2003.

LIPIŃSKI, E., «The Egypto-Babylonian War of the Winter of 601–600 B.C.», *AION* 32 (1972) 235–241.

LIPSCHITS, O., «Nebuchadrezzar's Policy in "Ḫattu-Land" and the Fate of the Kingdom of Judah», *UF* 30 (1998) 467–487.

LIPSCHITS, O., *The Fall and Rise of Jerusalem*. Judah under Babylonian Rule, Winona Lake 2005.

LIPSCHITS, O. – BLENKINSOPP, J., eds., *Judah and the Judeans in the Neo-Babylonian Period*, Winona Lake 2003.

LITTAUER, M.A. – CROUWEL, J.H., *Selected Writings on Chariots and Other Early Vehicles, Riding and Harness*, ed. P. RAULWING, CHANE 6, Leiden – Boston – Köln 2002.

LITTLEJOHN, S.W. – FOSS, K.A., *Theories of Human Communication*, Belmont 1981, ¹⁰2011.

LITTLEJOHN, S.W. – FOSS, K.A., *Encyclopedia of Communication Theory*, Thousand Oaks 2009.

LIVERANI, M., «The Growth of the Assyrian Empire in the Habur/Middle Euphrates Area: A New Paradigm», *SAAB* 2 (1988) 81–98.

LIVERANI, M., *Guerra e diplomazia nell'antico Oriente (1600–1100 a.C.)*, Collezione storica, Bari 1994.

LIVERANI, M., *Oltre la Bibbia*. Storia antica di Israele, Bari 2003.

LIVERANI, M., *Antico Oriente*. Storia società economia, ML 17, Bari 1998, ²2011 (Eng. tr.: *The Ancient Near East*. History, Society and Economy, London – New York 2014).

LIWAK, R., *Der Prophet und die Geschichte*. Eine literar-historische Untersuchung zum Jeremiabuch, BWANT 121, Stuttgart 1987.

LOADER, J.A., «Understanding of Failure and Failure of Understanding: Aspects of Failure in the Old Testament», *HvTSt* 70 (2014) 1–11 [DOI: 10.4102/hts.v70i1.2657].

LOHFINK, N., *Das Hauptgebot*. Eine Untersuchung literarischer Einleitungsfragen zu Dtn 5–11, AnBib 20, Roma 1963.

LONG, B.O., «Prophetic Call Traditions and Reports of Visions», *ZAW* 84 (1974) 494–500.

LONG, B.O., «Reports of Visions Among the Prophets», *JBL* 95 (1976) 353–365.

LONG, B.O., «Social Dimensions of Prophetic Conflict», in: *Anthropological Perspectives on Old Testament Prophecy*, eds. R.C. CULLEY – T.W. OVERHOLT, Semeia 21, Chico 1982, 31–53.

LONGMAN, T. – REID, D.G., *God is a Warrior*, StOTB, Grand Rapids 1995.

LOTMAN, J.M., «O semiosfere», *SSS* 17 [1984] 5–23 (Eng. tr. by W. CLARK in: «On the Semiosphere», in: *SSS* 33 [2005] 205–229; Ita. tr. by S. SALVESTRONI, ed. *La semiosfera*. L'asimmetria e il dialogo nelle strutture pensanti, Venezia 1985, ²1992, 55–76.

LOWTH, R., *De sacra poesi Hebraeorum praelectiones academicae Oxonii habitae*, Oxford 1753.

DE LUBAC, H., *La révélation divine*, Paris 1968, ³1983.

LUNDBOM, J.R., *Jeremiah*. A Study in Ancient Hebrew Rhetoric, SBLDS 18, Missoula 1975, Winona Lake ²1997.

LUNDBOM, J.R., «Jeremiah and the Break-Away from Authority Preaching», *SEÅ* 56 (1991) 7–28.

LUNDBOM, J.R., «Rhetorical Structures in Jeremiah 1», *ZAW* 103 (1991) 193–210.

LUNDBOM, J.R., *Jeremiah 1–20*. A New Translation with Introduction and Commentary, AncB 21A, New York 1999.

LUNDBOM, J.R., *Jeremiah 21–36*. A New Translation with Introduction and Commentary, AncB 21B, New York 2004.

LUNDBOM, J.R., *Jeremiah 37–52*. A New Translation with Introduction and Commentary, AncB 21C, New York 2004.

LUNDBOM, J.R., «Delimitations of Units in the Book of Jeremiah», in: *The Impact of Unit Delimitation on Exegesis*, eds., R. DE HOOP – M.C.A. KORPEL – S.E. PORTER, Pericope 7, Leiden – Boston 2009, 146–174.

LUNDBOM, J.R., *Jeremiah Closer Up*. The Prophet and the Book, HBM 31, Sheffield 2010.

LYONS, J., *Semantics*, Cambridge 1977.

LYONS, J., *Language and Linguistics*. An Introduction, Cambridge 1981, ⁹1992.

LYS, D., «Jérémie 28 et le problème du faux-prophète, ou la circulation du sens dans le diagnostic prophétique, *RHPR* 59 (1979) 453–482.

MCBRIDE, S.D., «The Yoke of the Kingdom. An Exposition of Deuteronomy 6:4–5», *Interp.* 27 (1973) 273–306.

MCCARTHY, D.J., *Treaty and Covenant*. A Study in Form in the Ancient Oriental Documents and in the Old Testament, AnBib 21, Rome 1963, ²1978.

MACCHI, J.-D., «Les doublets dans le livre de Jérémie», in: *The Book of Jeremiah and its Reception*. Le Livre de Jérémie et sa reception, eds. A.H.W. CURTIS – T. RÖMER, BEThL 128, Leuven 1997, 119–150.

MACGINNIS, J., «Mobilisation and Militarisation in the Neo-Babylonian Empire», in: *Studies on War in the Ancient Near East*. Collected Essays on Military History, ed. J. VIDAL, AOAT 372, Münster 2010, 153–163.

MACHOLZ, G.C., «Jeremia in der Kontinuität der Prophetie», in: *Probleme biblischer Theologie*. Gehrard von Rad zum 70. Geburtstag, ed. H.W. WOLFF, München 1971, 306–334.

MCKANE, W., «The Construction of Jeremiah XXI», *VT* 22 (1982) 59–73.

MCKANE, W., *Jeremiah*. Volume I: Introduction and Commentary on Jeremiah I-XXV, ICC, Edinburgh 1986.

MCKANE, W., «Jeremia 27,5–8, Especially "Nebuchadnezzar, My Servant"», in: *Prophet und Prophetenbuch*. Festschrift für Otto Kaiser zum 65. Geburtstag, eds. V. FRITZ – K.-F. POHLMANN – H.-C. SCHMITT, BZAW 185, Berlin – New York 1989, 98–110.

MCKANE, W., *Jeremiah*. Vol. II: Commentary on Jeremiah XXVI–LII, ICC, Edinburgh 1996.

MCLUHAN, M., *The Gutenberg Galaxy*. The Making of Typographic Man, Toronto 1962.

MCLUHAN, M., *Understanding Media*. The Extensions of Man, New York 1964.

McNamara, M., «Critères de discernement en Israël. Vrais et faux prophètes», *Concilium* 139 (1978) 11–22.

Madison, D.S., *Critical Ethnography*. Method, Ethics, and Performance, Thousand Oaks 2005, ²2012.

Maiberger, P., «פָּנַע», *ThWAT* VI, 501–508.

Maier, C.M., *Jeremia als Lehrer der Tora*. Soziale Gebote des Deuteronomiums in Fortschreibungen des Jeremiabuches, FRLANT 196, Göttingen 2002.

Maier, C.M., *Jeremia 1-25*, IEKAT, Stuttgart 2022.

Maier, J., *The Temple Scroll*. An Introduction, Translation and Commentary, JSOT.S 34, Sheffield 1985.

Maier, M.P., *Ägypten – Israels Herkunft und Geschick*. Studien über einen theopolitischen Zentralbegriff im hebräischen Jeremiabuch, OBS 21, Frankfurt am Main 2002.

Malamat, A., «Mari and the Bible: Some Patterns of Tribal Organization and Institutions», *JAOS* 82 (1962) 143–150.

Malamat, A., «The Last Kings of Judah and the Fall of Jerusalem. An Historical-Chronological Study», *IEJ* 18 (1968) 137–156.

Malamat, A., «The Twilight of Juda: In the Egyptian-Babylonian Maelstrom», in: *Congress Volume*. Edinburgh 1974, eds. G.W. Anderson et al., VT.S 28, Leiden 1975, 123–145 (= in: Id., *History of Biblical Israel*. Major Problems and Minor Issues, CHANE 7, Leiden 2001).

Malamat, A., «A Mari Prophecy and Nathan's Dynastic Oracle», in: *Prophecy*. Essays Presented to Georg Fohrer on his Sixty-Fifth Birthday, 6 September 1980, ed. J.A. Emerton, BZAW 150, Berlin 1980, 68–82 (= in: Id., *Mari and the Bible*, SHCANE 12, Leiden 1998, 106–121).

Malamat, A., *Mari and the Bible*, SHCANE 12, Leiden 1998.

Malamat, A., «The Kingdom of Judah between Egypt and Babylon: A Small State within a Great Power Confrontation», in: Id., *History of Biblical Israel*. Major Problems and Minor Issues, CHANE 7, Leiden 2001, 322–337.

Malul, M., *Studies in Mesopotamian Legal Symbolism*, AOAT 221, Neukirchen-Vluyn 1988.

Manfredi, S., *Geremia il profeta simbolo della nazione*. Contributo di teologia biblica per una teologia della profezia, Estratto dalla Dissertazione per il Dottorato, Palermo 1984.

Manfredi, S., «Il tempo della guarigione. Studio della radice RP' "curare, guarire" in *Ier* 8,11.15.22», *Ho Theologos* 3 (1985) 203–230.

Martens, E.A., «Narrative Parallelism and Message in Jeremiah 34–38», in: *Early Jewish and Christian Exegesis*. Studies in Memory of William Hugh Brownlee, eds. C.A. Evans – W.F. Stinespring, Atlanta 1987, 33–49.

Martens, K., «"With a Strong Hand and an Outstretched Arm". The Meaning of the Expression בְּיד חזקה ובזרוע נטויה», *SJOT* 15 (2001) 123–141.

Martin-Achard, R., «Ésaïe et Jérémie aux prises avec les problèmes politiques. Contribution à l'étude du thème: Prophétie et politique», *RHPR* 47 (1967) 208–224

(= ID., *Permanence de l'Ancien Testament.* Recherches d'exégèse et de théologie, CRThPh 11, Genéve 1984, 306–322).

MARTINO, P., «Per la storia etimologica di *insegnare* e *consegnare*», in: *La croce, un simbolo attraverso i tempi e le culture.* Atti del Convegno delle Scienze Umanistiche nell'ambito della Pastorale Universitaria (Roma, LUMSA-EUR-SAPIENZA, 5–6 marzo 2012), eds. I. BECHERUCCI – P. MARTINO, Roma 2013, 196–210.

MATTHEWS, V.H., *More than Meets the Ear.* Discovering the Hidden Contexts of Old Testament Conversations, Grand Rapids 2008.

MATTHEWS, V.H. – BENJAMIN, D.C., *Honor and Shame in the World of the Bible,* Semeia 68, Atlanta 1996.

MAXWELL-HYSLOP, R., «Daggers and Swords in Western Asia. A Study from Prehistoric Times to 600 B.C.», *Iraq* 8 (1946) 1–45.

MAY, H.G., «The Chronology of Jeremiah's Oracles», *JNES* 4 (1945) 217–227.

MAYER, G., «דָּבַר», *ThWAT* II, 133–135.

MAYER, W., *Politik und Kriegskunst der Assyrer,* ALASP 9, Münster 1995.

MAZAR, A., *Archaeology of the Land of the Bible: 10,000–586 B.C.E.,* New York 1990.

MEIER, S.A., *Speaking of Speaking.* Making Direct Discourse in the Hebrew Bible, VT.S 46, Leiden 1992.

MELDOLESI, G.N., *Panico, ossessioni e fobie: psicobiologia dell'ansia.* Dalle origini del comportamento ai rapporti familiari, Milano 2011.

MERLO, P., «Il profetismo nel Vicino Oriente antico: panoramica di un fenomeno e difficoltà comparative», in: *Religione biblica e religione storica dell'antico Israele: un monopolio interpretativo nella continuità culturale.* Atti del XV Convegno di Studi Veterotestamentari (Fara Sabina, 10–12 Settembre 2007), ed. G.L. PRATO, RStB 21, Bologna 2009, 55–83.

MERRILL, E.H., «דָּרַך», *NIDOTTE* I, 989–993.

MERRILL WILLIS, A.C., *Dissonance and the Drama of Divine Sovereignty in the Book of Daniel,* LHBOTS 520, London – New York 2010.

MEYER, I., *Jeremia und die falschen Propheten,* OBO 13, Freiburg – Göttingen 1977.

MEYNET, R., *L'analyse rhétorique.* Une nouvelle méthode pour comprendre la Bible, Paris 1989.

MEYNET, R., *Lire la Bible,* Paris 1996, [2]2003.

MEYNET, R., *Traité de rhétorique biblique,* RhSem 4, Paris 2007, [2]2013.

MICHAELIS, J.D., *Observationes philologicae et criticae in Ieremiae Vaticinia et Threnos,* Goettingae 1793.

MICHAELSEN, P., «Ecstasy and Possession in Ancient Israel: A Review of Some Recent Contributions», *SJOT* 3 (1989) 28–54.

MICCIO, M., *Ascoltare il silenzio.* Manuale di sociologia della comunicazione, Milano 2011.

MICLIASSO, S., «Dal simbolo al linguaggio simbolico. L'interesse di una svolta nella teoria ermeneutica di Paul Ricoeur per un'ermeneutica biblica creativa», *RivBib* 29 (1981) 187–203.

786 Bibliography

MIGSCH, H., *Gottes Wort über das Ende Jerusalems*. Eine literatur-, stil- und gattungs-skritische Untersuchung des Berichtes Jeremia 34,1–7; 32,2–5; 37,3–38,28, ÖBS 2, Klosterneuburg 1981.

MIGSCH, H., «*l=bilti* im Jeremiabuch», *BN* 157 (2013) 111–114.

MILLAR, J.G., *Now Choose Life*. Theology and Ethics in Deuteronomy, NSBT 6, Leicester 1998.

MILLER, J.M. – HAYES, J.H., *A History of Ancient Israel and Judah*, Philadelphia 1986, Louisville ²2006.

MILLER, P.D., Jr., *The Divine Warrior in Early Israel*, HSM 5, Cambridge (MA) 1973.

MILLER, P.D., Jr., «El, the Creator of Earth», *BASOR* 237 (1980) 43–46.

MILLER, P.D., Jr., «The Theological Significance of Poetry», in: *Language, Theology, and the Bible*. Essays in Honour of James Barr, *ed.* S.E. BALENTINE – J. BARTON, Oxford 1994, 213–230.

MILLER-NAUDÉ, C.L., «Silence as a Response in Biblical Hebrew Narrative: Strategies of Speakers and Narrators», *JNSL* 32 (2006) 23–43.

MIRANDA, A., *I sentimenti di Gesù*. I *verba affectuum* dei Vangeli nel loro contesto lessicale, StBi (Bo) 49, Bologna 2006.

MITCHELL, T.C., «Judah until the Fall of Jerusalem (*c.* 700–586 B.C.)», in: *The Cambridge Ancient History*. The Assyrian and Babylonian Empires and other States of the Near East, from the Eighth to the Sixth Centuries B.C., vol. III/2, *eds.* J. BOARDMAN *et al.*, Cambridge 1991, 371–409.

MOBERLY, R.W.L., *Prophecy and Discernment*, CSCD 14, Cambridge 2006.

MODUGNO, F., «L'analogia nella logica del diritto», *Rivista AIC* 1 (2011) 1–23.

MÖLLER, K., *A Prophet in Debate*. The Rhetoric of Persuasion in the Book of Amos, JSOT.S 372, Sheffield 2003.

MORAN, W.L., «The End of the Unholy War and the Anti-Exodus», *Bib.* 44 (1963) 333–342.

MORO, A., *Dynamic Antisymmetry*, LIM 38, Cambridge (MA) 2000.

MORO, A., *The Boundaries of Babel*. The Brain and the Enigma of Impossible Languages, CSL, Cambridge (MA) 2008.

MORTARA GARAVELLI, B., *Manuale di retorica*, Milano 1988.

MOSHAVI, A., «Syntactic Evidence for a Clausal Adverb הלא in Biblical Hebrew», *JNSL* 33 (2007) 51–63.

MOSHAVI, A., «Two Types of Argumentation Involving Rhetorical Questions in Biblical Hebrew Dialogue», *Bib.* 90 (2009) 32–46.

MOSHAVI, A., «"Is That Your Voice, My Son David?". Conducive Questions in Biblical Hebrew», *JNSL* 36 (2010) 65–81.

MOTTU, H., «Jeremiah vs. Hananiah: Ideology and Truth in Old Testament Prophecy», in: *The Bible and Liberation*. Political and Social Hermeneutics, *ed.* N.K. GOTTWALD, New York 1983, 235–251 (= in: N.K. GOTTWALD – R.A. HORSLEY, *eds.*, *The Bible and Liberation*. Political and Social Hermeneutics, Revised Edition, Maryknoll 1993, 313–328).

Mowinckel, S., *Zur Komposition des Buches Jeremia*, Kristiania 1914.

Mowinckel, S., *Prophecy and Tradition*. The Prophetic Books in the Light of the Study of the Growth and History of the Tradition, ANVAO.HF 3, Oslo 1946.

Mowinckel, S., *Religion und Kultus*, Göttingen 1953.

Münderlein, G., *Kriterien wahrer und falscher Prophetie*. Entstehung und Bedeutung im Alten Testament, EHS.T 33, Bern – Frankfurt – Las Vegas 1974, ²1979.

Muilenburg, J., «Baruch the Scribe», in: *Proclamation and Presence*. Old Testament Essays in Honour of Gwynne Henton Davies, *eds.* J.I. Durham – J.R. Porter, Richmond 1970, 215–238 (= in: *A Prophet to the Nations*. Essays in Jeremiah Studies, *eds.* L.G. Perdue – B.W. Kovacs, Winona Lake 1984, 229–245).

Muraoka, T., *Emphatics Words and Structures in Biblical Hebrew*, Jerusalem – Leiden 1985.

Muratore, A., «Simbolo, mistero e mito: il quadro epistemologico», in: *La conoscenza simbolica*, *eds.* C. Greco – A. Muratore, Cinisello Balsamo 1988, 9–39.

Murray, D.F., «The Rhetoric of Disputation: Re-examination of a Prophetic Genre», *JSOT* 38 (1987) 95–121.

Na'aman, N., «The Historical Background to the Conquest of Samaria (720 BCE)», *Bib.* 71 (1990) 206–225.

Na'aman, N., «Nebuchadrezzar's Campaign in the Year 603 BCE», *BN* 62 (1992) 41–44 (= in: Id., *Ancient Israel and Its Neighbors*. Interaction and Counteraction. Collected Essays. Vol. I, Winona Lake 2005, 399–402).

Na'aman, N., «The Distribution of Messages in the Kingdom of Judah in Light of the Lachish Ostraca», *VT* 53 (2003) 169–180.

Na'aman, N., «Josiah and the Kingdom of Judah», in: *Good Kings and Bad Kings, ed.* L.L. Grabbe, LHBOTS 393, New York – London 2005, 189–247.

Na'aman, N., «The King Leading Cult Reforms in His Kingdom: Josiah and Other Kings in the Ancient Near East», *ZABR* 12 (2006) 131–168.

Na'aman, N., «Does Archaeology Really Deserve the Status of a «High Court» in Biblical Historical Research?», in: *Between Evidence and Ideology*. Essays on the History of Ancient Israel Read at the Joint Meeting of the Society for Old Testament Study and the Oud Testamentisch Werkgezelschap Lincoln, July 2009, *eds.* B. Becking – L.L. Grabbe, OTS 59, Leiden 2011, 165–184.

Nadali, D., «Guerra e morte: l'annullamento del nemico nella condizione di vinto», *ScAnt* 11 (2001–2003) 51–70.

Nadali, D., «La campagna di Assurbanipal contro gli Arabi: proposta di lettura delle dinamiche di una battaglia in campo aperto», *SMEA* 46 (2004) 59–78.

Nadali, D., «Assyrian Open Field Battles. An Attempt at Reconstruction and Analysis», in: *Studies on War in the Ancient Near East*. Collected Essays on Military History, *ed.* J. Vidal, AOAT 372, Münster 2010, 117–152.

Nadali, D., «Attaccare e difendere un muro: una battaglia di confine», RS/C 2 (2011) 225–232.

Naveh, J., «Old Hebrew Inscriptions in a Burial Cave», *IEJ* 13 (1963) 74–92.

Naveh, J., «Hebrew Graffiti from the Temple Period», *IEJ* 51 (2001) 194–207.

Neher, A., *L'essence du prophétisme*, Paris 1955.

788   Bibliography

NEHER, A., *Jérémie*, Paris 1960.

NEHER, A., *L'exil de la parole*. Du silence biblique au silence d'Auschwitz, Paris 1970.

NICHOLSON, E.W., *Preaching to the Exiles*. A Study of the Prose Tradition in the Book of Jeremiah, Oxford 1970.

NICOLESCU, B., «Transdisciplinarity – Past, Present and Future», in: *Moving Worldviews – Reshaping Sciences, Policies and Practices for Endogenous Sustainable Development*, eds. B. HAVERKORT – C. REIJINTES, Leusden 2006, 142–166.

NIDITCH, S., *The Symbolic Vision in Biblical Tradition*, HSM 30, Chico 1980.

NIDITCH, S., *Chaos to Cosmos*. Studies in Biblical Patterns of Creation, SPSHS 6, Chico 1985.

NIDITCH, S., «A Messy Business. Ritual Violence after the War», in: *Warfare, Ritual, and Symbol in Biblical and Modern Contexts*, eds. B.E. KELLE – F.R. AMES – J.L. WRIGHT, SBL.AIL 18, Atlanta 2014, 187–202.

NIEMANN, H.M., «Von Oberflächen, Schichten und Strukturen. Was leistet die Archäologie für die Erforschung der Geschichte Israels und Judas?», in: *Steine – Bilder – Texte*. Historische Evidenz außerbiblischer und biblischer Quellen, ed. C. HARDMEIER, ABIG 5, Leipzig 2001, 79–121.

NIHAN, C., «L'analyse rédactionnelle», *Manuel d'exégèse de l'Ancien Testament*, eds. M. BAUKS – C. NIHAN, MoBi 61, Genève 2008, 137–189.

NISSINEN, M., «Die Relevanz der neuassyrischen Prophetie für die alttestamentliche Forschung», in: *Mesopotamica – Ugaritica – Biblica*. Festschrift für Kurt Bergerhof zur Vollendung seines 70. Lebensjahres am 7. Mai 1992, eds., M. DIETRICH – O. LORETZ, AOAT 232, Neukirchen-Vluyn 1993, 217–258.

NISSINEN, M., «Prophecy Against the King in Neo-Assyrian Sources», in: *"Lasset uns Brücken bauen"*. Collected Communications to the XVth Congress of the International Organization for the Study of the Old Testament, eds. K.-D. SCHUNK – M. AUGUSTIN, Cambridge 1995, Frankfut am Main 1998, 157–170.

NISSINEN, M., «Falsche Prophetie in neuassyrischer und deuteronomistischer Darstellung», in: *Das Deuteronomium und seine Querbeziehungen*, ed. T. VEIJOLA, SESJ 62, Göttingen 1996, 172–195.

NISSINEN, M., «Spoken, Quoted, and Invented: Orality and Writtenness in Ancient Near Eastern Prophecy», in: *Writings and Speech in Israelite and Ancient Near Eastern Prophecy*, eds. E. BEN ZVI – M.H. FLOYD, SBLSymS 10, Atlanta 2000, 235–271.

NISSINEN, M., «Das kritische Potential in der altorientalischen Prophetie», in: *Propheten in Mari, Assyrien und Israel*, eds. M. KÖCKERT – M. NISSINEN, FRLANT 201, Göttingen 2003, 1–32.

NISSINEN, M., *Prophets and Prophecy in the Ancient Near East*, SBLWAW 12, Atlanta 2003.

NISSINEN, M., «Biblical Prophecy from a Near Eastern Perspective: The Cases of Kingship and Divine Possession», in: *Congress Volume Ljubljana 2007*, ed. A. LEMAIRE, VT.S 133, Leiden 2010, 441–468.

NISSINEN, M., «The Exiled Gods of Babylon in Neo Assyrian Prophecy», in: *The Concept of Exile in Ancient Israel and its Historical Contexts*, eds. E. BEN ZVI – C. LEVIN, BZAW 404, Berlin – New York 2010, 27–38.

Nissinen, M., *Ancient Prophecy*. Near Eastern, Biblical, and Greek Perspectives, Oxford 2017.

Nitsche, S.A., «Prophetische Texte als dramatische Texte lesen», in: *Lesarten der Bibel*. Untersuchungen zu einer Theorie der Exegese des Alten Testaments, *eds.* H. Utzschneider – E. Blum, Stuttgart 2006, 155–181.

Nobile, M., «Il profetismo biblico. Il dibattito su un tema ancora discusso», in: *"Ricercare la sapienza di tutti gli antichi" (Sir 39,1)*. Miscellanea in onore di Gian Luigi Prato, *eds.*, M. Milani – M. Zappella, SRivBib 56, Bologna 2013, 271–283.

Noth, M., *Die israelitischen Personennamen im Rahmen der gemeinsemitischen Namengebung*, Stuttgart 1928.

Noth, M., *Überlieferungsgeschichtliche Studien*. Die sammelnden und bearbeitenden Geschichtswerke im Alten Testament, Tübingen 1942, ^{2}1957.

Novak, J.D., *Learning, Creating, and Using Knowledge*. Concept Maps as Facilitative Tools in School and Corporations, Mahwah 1998, ^{2}2010.

Novak, J.D. – Gowin, D.B., *Learning How to Learn*, New York 1984, ^{21}2006.

Nünning, A., *Grundbegriffe der Kulturtheorie und Kulturwissenschaften*, SlgM 351, Stuttgart 2005.

Nurmela, R., *The Mouth of the Lord Has Spoken*. Inner-Biblical Allusions in Second and Third Isaiah, SJ(L), Lanham 2006.

Oates, J., «The Fall of Assyria (635–609 b.c.)», in: *The Cambridge Ancient History*. The Assyrian and Babylonian Empires and other States of the Near East, from the Eighth to the Sixth Centuries b.c., vol. III/2, *eds.* J. Boardman *et al.*, Cambridge 1991, 162–193.

Ockinga, B. «The Inviolability of Zion – a Pre-Israelite Tradition?», *BN* 44 (1988) 54–60.

O'Connor, K.M., «Do Not Trim a Word: The Contribution of Chapter 26 to the Book of Jeremiah», *CBQ* 51 (1989) 617–630.

O'Connor, K.M., «Jeremiah», in: *The Oxford Bible Commentary*, *eds.* J. Barton – J. Muddiman, Oxford 2001, 487–528.

O'Connor, K.M., «Surviving Disaster in the Book of Jeremiah», *WW* 22 (2002) 369–377.

O'Connor, K.M., «The Book of Jeremiah: Reconstructing Community after Disaster», in: *Character Ethics and the Old Testament*. Moral Dimensions of Scripture, *eds.* M.D. Carroll R. – J.E. Lapsley, Louisville 2007, 81–92.

O'Connor, K.M., *Jeremiah*. Pain and Promise, Minneapolis 2011.

O'Connor, M.P., *Hebrew Verse Structure*, Winona Lake 1980, ^{2}1997.

O'Connor, T., *Persons and Causes*. The Metaphysics of Free Will, New York 2000.

Oded, B., *Mass Deportations and Deportees in the Neo-Assyrian Empire*, Wiesbaden 1979.

Oded, B., *War, Peace and Empire*. Justifications for War in Assyrian Royal Inscriptions, Wiesbaden 1992.

Oded, B., «Where Is the "Myth of the Empty Land" to Be Found?», in: *Judah and the Judeans in the Neo-Babylonian Period*, *eds.* O. Lipschits – J. Blenkinsopp, Winona Lake 2003, 55–74.

790   Bibliography

O'Donovan, O., *The Desire of the Nations*. Rediscovering the Roots of Political Theology, Cambridge 1996.

Oeming, M., «"See, We Are Serving Today" (Nehemiah 9:36): Nehemiah 9 as Theological Interpretation of Persian Period», in: *Judah and the Judeans in the Fourth Century B.C.E.*, eds. O. Lipschits – G.N. Knoppers – R. Albertz, Winona Lake 2007, 571–588.

Oesch, J.M., *Petucha und Setuma*. Untersuchungen zu einer überlieferten Gliederung im h-ebräischen Text des Alten Testaments, OBO 27, Freiburg – Göttingen 1979.

O'Learhjby, S.D., «When Prophecy Fails and when It Succeeds. Apocalyptic Prediction and the Re-Entry into Ordinary Time», in: *Apocalyptic Time, ed.* A. Baumgarten, SHR 86, Boston 2000, 341–362.

Ollenburger, Ben C., *Zion, the City of the Great King*. A Theological Symbol of the Jerusalem Cult, JSOT.S 41, Sheffield 1987.

del Olmo Lete, G., *La vocación del líder en el antiguo Israel*. Morfología de los relatos bíblicos de vocación, BSal.E 2, Salamanca 1973.

Oppenheim, A.L., «Neo-Assyrian and Neo-Babylonian Empires», in: *The Symbolic Instrument in Early Times, vol. I: Propaganda and Communication in World History*, eds. H.D. Lasswell – D. Lerner – H. Speier, Honolulu 1979, 111–144.

Osuji, A., «Jer. 28 (MT) and the Question of Prophetic Authenticity (From the Ideological to the Narratological)», *EstBib* 63 (2005) 175–193.

Osuji, A., «True and False Prophecy in Jer 26–29 (MT). Thematic and Lexical Landmarks», *ETL* 82 (2006) 437–452.

Osuji, A., *Where is the Truth?* Narrative Exegesis and the Question of True and False Prophecy in Jer 26–29 (MT), BEThL 214, Leuven 2010.

Ott, K., *Die Prophetischen Analogiehandlungen im Alten Testament*, BWANT 185, Stuttgart 2009.

Otten, H., «Die inschriftlichen Funde», in: *Bericht über die Ausgrabungen in Boğazköy im Jahre 1954, MDOG* 88 (1955) 35–36.

Otto, E., «שַׁעַר», *ThWAT* VIII, 358–403.

Otto, E., «Zivile Funktionen des Stadttores in Palästina und Mesopotamien», in: *Meilenstein*. Festgabe für Herbert Donner, eds. M. Weippert – S. Timm, Wiesbaden 1995, 188–197.

Otto, E., *Altorientalische und biblische Rechtsgeschichte*. Gesammelte Studien, Wiesbaden 2008.

Otto, E., «Hebrew Ethics in Old Testament Scholarship», in: *Psalmody and Poetry in Old Testament Ethics, ed.* D.J. Human, New York 2012, 3–13.

Otto, E., «The Study of Law and Ethics in the Hebrew Bible/Old Testament», *HBOT* III/2, 594–621.

Overholt, T.W., «Jeremiah 27–29: The Question of False Prophecy», *JAAR* 35 (1967) 241–249.

Overholt, T.W., «King Nebuchadrezzar in the Jeremiah Tradition», *CBQ* 30 (1968) 39–48.

Overholt, T.W., *The Threat of Falsehood*. A Study in the Theology of the Book of Jeremiah, SBT, London 1970.

Overholt, T.W., *Channels of Prophecy*. The Social Dynamics of Prophetic Activity, Minneapolis 1989.

Oz, A., *The Story Begins*. Essays on Literature, New York 1999.

Paas, S., *Creation and Judgement*. Creation Texts in Some Eighth Century Prophets, OTS 42, Leiden 2003.

Pakkala, J., «Zedekiah's Fate and the Dynastic Succession», *JBL* 125 (2006) 443–452.

Palmer, A.L., *Historical Dictionary of Architecture*, HDLA 29, Lanham 2008.

Panier, L., «Semiotica e studi biblici. Evoluzioni metodologiche e prospettive epistemologiche», in: *Destini del sacro*. Discorso religioso e semiotica della cultura, eds. N. Dusi – A. Marrone, Meltemi.Edu 115, Roma 2008, 11–25.

Panksepp, J., *Affective Neuroscience*. The Foundations of Human and Animal Emotions, New York 1998.

Parker, R.A. – Dubberstein, W.H., *Babylonian Chronology 626 B.C. – A.D. 75*, Providence 1956.

Parker, S.B., «Official Attitudes toward Prophecy at Mari and in Israel», *VT* 43 (1993) 50–68.

Parker, S.B., «The Lachish Letters and Official Reactions to Prophecies», in: *Uncovering Ancient Stones*. Essays in Memory of H. Neil Richardson, ed. L.M. Hopfe, Winona Lake 1994, 65–78.

Parke-Taylor, H., *The Formation of the Book of Jeremiah*. Doublets and Recurring Phrases, SBLMS 51, Atlanta 2000.

Parpola, S., «Neo-Assyrian Treaties from the Royal Archives of Niniveh», *JCS* 39 (1937) 161–189.

Parpola, S., «International Law in the First Millennium», in: *A History of Ancient Near Easter Law*, ed. R. Westbrook, HdO 72, I, Leiden – Boston 2003, 1047–1066.

Parrot, A., *Ninive et l'Ancient Testament*, CAB 3, Neuchâtel 1953.

Parrot, A., *Samarie, capitale du royaume d'Israël*, CAB 7, Paris-Neuchâtel 1955.

Parrot, A., *Babylone et l'Ancient Testament*, CAB 8, Neuchâtel 1956.

Paul, A., «Masada: inchiesta su un suicidio collettivo», in: *Israele*. Da Mosè agli accordi di Oslo, ed. F. Cardini, Storia e civiltà 46, Bari 1999, 163–182.

Paul, S.M., *Studies in the Book of the Covenant in the Light of Cuneiform and Biblical Law*, VT.S 18, Leiden 1970.

Peels, H.G.L., *The Vengeance of God*. The Meaning of the Root NQM and the Function of the NQM-Texts in the Context of Divine Revelation in the Old Testament, OTS 31, Leiden 2.

Perani, M., ed., *The Ancient Sefer Torah of Bologna*. Features and History, SJHC 59, Leiden – Boston 2019.

Perdue, L.G., «Jeremiah in Modern Research: Approaches and Issues», in: *A Prophet to the Nations*. Essays in Jeremiah Studies, eds. L.G. Perdue – B.W. Kovacs, Winona Lake 1984, 1–32.

792   Bibliography

PERDUE, L.G., *Wisdom & Creation*. The Theology of Wisdom Literature, Nashville 1994.

PERDUE, L.G., *The Collapse of History*. Reconstructing Old Testament Theology, Minneapolis 1994.

PERROT, C., «Petuhot et Setumot. Étude sur les alinéas du Pentateuque», *RB* 76 (1969) 50–91.

PETROSINO, S., *L'idolo*. Teoria di una tentazione dalla Bibbia a Lacan, Altro discorso 4, Milano – Udine 2015.

PETTAZZONI, R., *L'onniscienza di Dio*, Torino 1955 (Eng. tr.: ID., *The All-Knowing God*, Researches into Early Religion and Culture, Translation by H.J. Rose, London 1956).

PHILIPPS, G.A., «Sign/Text/Différence. The Contribution of Intertextual Theory to Biblical Criticism», in: *Intertextuality, eds.* H.F. PLETT, RTT 15, Berlin – New York 1991, 78–97.

PIETERSMA, A. – SAUNDERS, M., «To the Reader of Ieremias», in: *A New English Translation of the Septuagint and the Other Greek Translations Traditionally Included under that Title, eds.* A. PIETERSMA – B.G. WRIGHT, Oxford 2007, 876–881.

PLANT, R.J.R., *Good Figs, Bad Figs*. Judicial Differentiation in the Book of Jeremiah, LHBOTS 481, London – New York 2008.

POHLMANN, K.-F., *Studien zum Jeremiabuch*. Ein Beitrag zur Frage nach der Entstehung des Jeremiabuches, FRLANT 118, Göttingen 1978.

POLK, T., *The Prophetic Persona*. Jeremiah and the Language of the Self, JSOT.S 32, Sheffield 1984.

PONGRATZ-LEISTEN, B., «The Other and the Enemy in the Mesopotamian Conception of the World», in: *Mythology and Mythologies*. Methodological Approaches to Intercultural Influences, Proceedings of the Second Annual Symposium of the Assyrian and Babylonian Intellectual Heritage Project Held in Paris, France, October 4–7, 1999, *ed.* R.M. WHITING, MSym 2, Helsinki 2001, 195–231.

PORTIER-YOUNG, A.E., *Apocalypse Against Empire*. Theologies of Resistance in Early Judaism, Grand Rapids 2011.

PORTUGALI, J., *ed., The Construction of Cognitive Maps*, GeoJL 32, Dordrecht 1996.

POSTGATE J.P., «The Land of Assur and the Yoke of Assur», *WAr* 23 (1992) 247–263.

PRESTON, T.R., «The Heroism of Saul: Patterns of Meaning in the Narrative of the Early King», *JSOT* 24 (1982) 27–46.

PREUSS, H.D., «יָצָא», *ThWAT* III, 795–822.

PREUSS, H.D., «לָחַם מִלְחָמָה», *ThWAT* IV, 914–926.

PROST, A., *Douze leçons sur l'histoire*, Paris 1996.

PSCHIBILLE, J., *Hat der Löwe erneut gebrüllt?* Sprachliche, formale und inhaltliche Gemeinsamkeiten in der Verkündigung Jeremias und Amos, BThSt 41, Neukirchen 2001.

DE PURY, A., «La guerre sainte israélite», *ETR* 56 (1981) 5–38.

QUELL, G., *Wahre und falsche Propheten*. Versuch einer Interpretation, BFChTh 46/1, Gütersloh 1952.

QUENEAU, R., *Exercices de style*, Paris 1947 (Ita. tr. by U. Eco: R. QUENEAU, *Esercizi di stile*, Struzzi 282, Torino 1983 and by S. Bartezzaghi: R. QUENEAU, *Esercizi di stile*, Tascabili 849, Torino 2001).

QUINN, J.D. «Alcaeus 48 (B 16) and the Fall of Ascalon (604 B.C.)», *BASOR* 164 (1961) 19–20.

RAABE, P.A., «The Particularizing of Universal Judgment in Prophetic Discourse», *CBQ* 64 (2002) 652–674.

VON RAD, G., *Der heilige Krieg im alten Israel*, AThANT 20, Zürich 1951, Göttingen ³1958.

VON RAD, G., «שָׁלוֹם im AT», *ThWNT* II, 400–405.

VON RAD, G., *Theologie des Alten Testaments*. Band I: Die Theologie der geschichtlichen Überlieferungen Israels, München 1957, ¹⁰1992.

VON RAD, G., «Das theologische Problem des alttestamentlichen Schöpfungsglaubens», in: *Gesammelte Studien zum Alten Testament, ed.* G. VON RAD, TB 8, München 1958, 116–147.

VON RAD, G., *Theologie des Alten Testaments*. Band II: Die Theologie der prophetischen Überlieferungen Israels, München 1960, ⁷1980.

RAIMONDI, E., *Un'etica del lettore*, Bologna 2007.

RAINEY, A.F., «The Fate of Lachish during the Campaigns of Sennacherib and Nebuchadrezzar», in: *Investigations at Lachish*. The Sanctuary and the Residency (Lachish V), *ed.* Y. AHARONI, PIATA 4, Tel Aviv 1975, 47–60.

RAINEY, A.F., «Watching out for the Signal Fires of Lachish», *PEQ* 119 (1987) 149–151.

RAITT, T.M., *Theology of Exile*. Judgment, Deliverance in Jeremiah and Ezekiel, Philadelphia 1977.

RAMLOT, L., «Prophétisme», *DBS* VIII, 812–1222.

RANEY, D.C., «Does YHWH *Naham*? A Question of Openness», *SBLSP* 42 (2003) 105–115.

RATZINGER, J., *Glaube, Wahrheit, Toleranz*. Das Christentum und die Weltreligionen, Freiburg im Breisgau 2003.

RECANATI, F., *Literal Meaning*, Cambridge 2004.

RECANATI, F., «Literalism and Contextualism: Some Varieties», in: *Contextualism in Philosophy*. Knowledge, Meaning, and Truth, *eds.* G. PREYER – G. PETER, Oxford 2005, 171–196.

REDDY, W.M., *The Navigation of Feeling*. A Framework for the History of Emotions, Cambridge 2001.

REDFORD, D.B., «New Light on Egypt's Stance towards Asia, 610–586 BCE», in: *Rethinking the Foundations*. Historiography in the Ancient World and in the Bible. Essays in Honor of John Van Seters, *eds.* S.L. MCKENZIE – T. RÖMER, Berlin 2000, 183–195.

REED, S., «Blurring the Edges: A Reconsideration of the Treatment of Enemies in Ashurbanipal's Reliefs», in: *Ancient Near Eastern Art in Context*. Studies in Honor of Irene J. Winter by Her Students, *eds.* J. CHENG – M.H. FELDMAN, Leiden 2007, 101–130.

REICHENBACH, H., *Elements of Symbolic Logic*, New York 1947.

REIMER, D.J., «The "Foe" and the "North" in Jeremiah», *ZAW* 101 (1989) 223–232.

REIMER, D.J., «Political Prophets? Political Exegesis and Prophetic Theology», in: *Intertextuality in Ugarit & Israel*. Papers Read at the Tenth Joint Meeting of The Society for Old Testament Study and Het Oudtestamentisch Werkgezelschap in Nederland en België, held at Oxford, 1997, *ed.* J.C. DE MOOR, OTS 40, Leiden 1998, 126–142.

REIMER, D.J., «Redeeming Politics in Jeremiah», in: *Prophecy in the Book of Jeremiah*, *eds.* H.M. BARSTAD – R.G. KRATZ, BZAW 388, Berlin 2009, 121–136.

REIS, P.T., «Vindicating God: Another Look at 1 Kings XIII», *VT* 44 (1994) 376–386.

RENAN, E., *Histoire du peuple d'Israël*, II, Paris 1891.

RENDSBURG, G.A., *Diglossia in Ancient Hebrew*, AOS 72, New Haven 1990.

RENDSBURG, G.A., «Review Essay: The Sheffield Dictionary of Classical Hebrew», *AJS Review* 21 (1996) 111–118.

RENDTORFF, R., «Some Reflections on Creation as a Topic of Old Testament Theology», in: *Priests, Prophets and Scribes*. Essays on the Formation and Heritage of Second Temple Judaism in Honour of Joseph Blenkinsopp, *eds.* E. ULRICH *et al.*, JSOT.S 149, Sheffield 1992, 204–212.

RENFREW, C., «Transformations», in: *Transformations*. Mathematical Approaches to Culture Change, *eds.* C. RENFREW – K.L. COOKE, New York 1979, 3–44.

RHODES, A.B., «Israel's Prophets as Intercessors», in: *Scripture in History and Theology*. Essays in Honor of J.C. Rylaardsam, *eds.* A.L. MERRILL – T.W. OVERHOLT, Pittsburgh 1977, 107–128.

RICCI SINDONI, P., *Etica della consegna e profetismo biblico*. Geremia, Ezechiele, Giona, Abacuc, Tobia, La dialettica 26, Roma 2007.

RICŒUR, P., «Le symbole donne à penser», *Esprit* 27 (1959) 60–76.

RICŒUR, P., *De l'interprétation*. Essai sur Freud, Paris 1965.

RICŒUR, P., *Le conflit des interprétations*. Essais d'herméneutique, Paris 1969.

RICŒUR, P., «Qu'est-ce qu'un texte? Expliquer et comprendre», in: *Hermeneutik und Dialektik*. Aufsätze II, *eds.* R. BUBNER – K. CRAMER – R. WIEHL, Tübingen 1970, 181–200.

RICŒUR, P., «Esquisse de conclusion», in: *Exégèse et Herméneutique*, *eds.* R. BARTHES *et al.*, Paris 1971, 286–287.

RICŒUR, P., «The Hermeneutical Function of Distanciation», *Philosophy Today* 17 (1973) 129–141.

RICŒUR, P., «Biblical Hermeneutics», *Semeia* 4 (1975) 29–148.

RICŒUR, P., *La métaphore vive*, Paris 1975.

RICŒUR, P., «Parole et symbole», *RevSR* 49 (1975) 142–161.

RICŒUR, P., *Temps et récit*. Tome I, Paris 1983.

RICŒUR, P., *La mémoire, l'histoire, l'oubli*, Paris 2000.

RIETZSCHEL, C., *Der Problem der Urrolle*. Ein Beitrag zur Redaktionsgeschichte des Jeremiabuches, Gütersloh 1966.

RINALDI, G., *Le letterature antiche del Vicino Oriente: sumerica, assira, babilonese, ugaritica, ittita, fenicia, aramaica, nord e sud-arabica*, LettM 29, Firenze 1968.

RINGGREN, H., «אָיַב» *ThWAT* I, 228–235.

RINGGREN, H., «חָיָה», *ThWAT* II, 874–898.

RIZZI, A., *Pensare dentro la Bibbia*, NBSR 23, Roma 2010.

ROBERTS, J.J.M., «Zion in the Theology of the Davidic-Solomonic Empire», in: *Studies in the Period of David and Solomon and Other Essays*. Papers Read at the International Symposium for Biblical Studies, Tokyo, 5–7 december, 1979, *ed.* T. ISHIDA, Tokio 1982, 93–108.

ROBERTS, J.J.M., «Solomon's Jerusalem and the Zion Tradition», in: *Jerusalem in Bible and Archaeology. The First Temple Period*, *eds.* A.G. VAUGHN – A.E. KILLEBREW, SBLSymS 18, Atlanta 2003, 163–170.

ROBERTS, J.J.M., «The End of War in the Zion Tradition. The Imperialistic Background of an Old Testament Vision of Worldwide Peace», in: *Character Ethics and the Old Testament. Moral Dimensions of Scripture*, *eds.* M.D. CARROLL R. – J.E. LAPSLEY, Louisville 2007, 119–128.

ROBINSON, H.W., «Prophetic Symbolism», in: *Old Testament Essays*, *ed.* D.C. SIMPSON, London 1927, 1–17.

ROFÉ, A., «The Arrangement of the Book of Jeremiah», *ZAW* 101 (1989) 390–398.

ROGLAND, M., *Alleged Non-Past Uses of Qatal in Classical Hebrew*, SSN, Assen 2003.

ROLF, E., *ed.*, *Pragmatik*. Implikaturen und Sprechakte, LBSo 8, Wiesbaden 1997.

RÖMER, T., *The So-Called Deuteronomistic History*. A Sociological, Historical and Literary Introduction, London – New York 2007.

RÖMER, T., «Comment distinguer le vrai du faux prophète?», in: *Comment devient-on prophète?*Actes du colloque organisé par le Collège de France, Paris, les 4–5 avril 2011, *eds.* J.-M. DURAND – T. RÖMER – M. BÜRKI, Göttingen 2014, 109–120.

ROM-SHILONI, D., «Facing Destruction and Exile: Inner-Biblical Exegesis in Jeremiah and Ezekiel», *ZAW* 117 (2005) 189–205.

ROM-SHILONI, D., «Group Identities in Jeremiah: Is It the Persian Period Conflict?», in: *A Palimpsest: Rhetoric, Ideology, Stylistics, and Language Relating to Persian Israel*, *eds.* E. BEN ZVI – D. EDELMAN – F. POLAK, PHSC 5, Piscataway 2009, 11–46.

ROM-SHILONI, D., «Ezechiel and Jeremiah. What Might Stand behind the Silence?», *HeBAI* 1 (2012) 203–220.

ROM-SHILONI, D., *Exclusive Inclusivity*. Identity Conflicts between the Exiles and the People Who Remained (6th–5th Centuries BCE), LHBOTS 543, London – New York 2013.

ROM-SHILONI, D., «From Prophetic Words to Prophetic Literature: Challenging Paradigms That Control Our Academic Thought on Jeremiah and Ezekiel», *JBL* 138 (2019) 565–586.

RONCACE, M., *Jeremiah, Zedekiah, and the Fall of Jerusalem*, LHBOTS 423, London – New York 2005.

ROSENMÜLLER, E.F.C., *Scholia in Vetus Testamentum*, VIII: Ieremiae vaticinia et Threnos, vol. I, Lipsiae 1826.

ROSENMÜLLER, E.F.C., *Scholia in Vetus Testamentum*, VIII: Ieremiae vaticinia et Threnos, vol. II, Lipsiae 1827.

ROSSI, B., *L'intercessione nel tempo della fine*. Studio dell'intercessione profetica nel libro di Geremia, AnBib 204, Roma 2013.

ROSSI, B., «Reshaping Jeremiah: Scribal strategies and the *prophet like Moses*», *JSOT* 44 (2020) 575–593.

ROSSI, B., «Lo scritto profetico in Ger 36: tra fragilità e sovversione», in: *«Insegnaci a contare i nostri giorni e giungeremo al cuore della sapienza» (Sal 90,12)*. Atti della XLV Settimana Biblica Nazionale (Roma, 10–14 Settembre 2018), *eds*. F. DALLA VECCHIA – D. SCAIOLA, RStB 32, Bologna 2020, 199–219.

ROST, L., «Das Problem der Weltmacht in der Prophetie», *ThLZ* 90 (1965) 241–250.

ROTA SCALABRINI, P., «Geremia e i suoi predecessori», in: *Processo esegetico ed ermeneutica credente: una polarità intrinseca alla Bibbia*. XL Settimana Biblica Nazionale (Roma, 8–12 settembre 2008), *eds*. E. MANICARDI – G. BORGONOVO, RStB 22, Bologna 2010, 25–42.

ROUILLARD-BONRAISIN, H., «Ésaïe, Jérémie et la politique des rois de Juda», in: *Prophètes et rois*. Bible et Proche-Orient, *ed*. A. LEMAIRE, LeDiv.HS, Paris 2001, 177–224.

ROVIRA, L., «"Share Them Out...". On the Mass Deportation of People according to the Texts of Mari (18th Century BC)», in: *The Other Face of the Battle*. The Impact of War on Civilians in the Ancient Near East, *eds*. D. NADALI – J. VIDAL, AOAT 413, Münster 2014, 25–36.

RUDMAN, D., «Creation and Fall in Jeremiah X 12–16», *VT* 48 (1998) 63–73.

RUDMAN, D., «Is the Rabshakeh also among the Prophets? A Rhetorical Study of 2 Kings XVIII 17–35», *VT* 50 (2000) 100–110.

RUDNIG, T.A. «"Ist denn Jahwe nicht auf dem Zion?" (Jer 8,19). Gottes Gegenwart im Heiligtum», *ZThK* 104 (2007) 267–286.

RUDOLPH, W., *Jeremia*, HAT 12, Tübingen 1947, ³1968.

RUSSO, C., «Geremia e Sedecia: un dialogo impossibile e ironico alla vigilia della capitolazione. Analisi testuale di Ger 38,14–28a TM», in: *«Insegnaci a contare i nostri giorni e giungeremo al cuore della sapienza» (Sal 90,12)*. Atti della XLV Settimana Biblica Nazionale (Roma, 10–14 settembre 2018), *eds*. D. SCAIOLA – F. DALLA VECCHIA, RStB 32, Bologna 2020, 333–359.

RÜTERSWÖRDEN, U., «שָׂרַף», *ThWAT* VII, 883–891.

RÜTERSWÖRDEN, U., «Der Prophet in den Lachish-Ostraka», in: *Steine – Bilder – Texte*. Historische Evidenz außerbiblischer und biblischer Quellen, *ed*. C. HARDMEIER, ABIG 5, Leipzig 2001, 179–192.

RUPPERT, L., *Der leidende Gerechte und seine Feinde*. Eine Wortfelduntersuchung, Würzuburg 1973.

RUPPERT, L., «יָעַץ», *ThWAT* III, 718–751.

RUPRECHT, E., «Das Zepter Jahwes in den Berufungsvisionen von Jeremia und Amos», *ZAW* 108 (1996) 55–69.

RUWE, A. – WEISE, U., «Das Joch Assurs und *jhwhs* Joch. Eine Realienbegriff und seine Metaphorisierung in neuassyrischen und alttestamentlichen Texten», *ZABR* 8 (2002) 274–307.

SACK, R.H., «Nebuchadnezzar», *ABD* IV, 1058–1059.

SACK, R.H., *Images of Nebuchadnezzar*. The Emergence of a Legend, Selinsgrove 1991, ²2004.

SACK, R.H., «Nebuchadnezzar II and the Old Testament: History versus Ideology», in: *Judah and the Judeans in the Neo-Babylonian Period*, eds. O. LIPSCHITS – J. BLENKINSOPP, Winona Lake 2003, 221–233.

SAGGS, H.W.F., *The Greatness that Was Babylon*. A Survey of the Ancient Civilization of the Tigris-Euphrates Valley, New York 1962, London ²1988.

SAGGS, H.W.F., *The Encounter with the Divine in Mesopotamia and Israel*, London 1978.

SAGGS, H.W.F., *The Might that Was Assyria*, London 1984.

SAGIV, Y., «"To Give Moses a Pause...": New Examples of Biblical Textual Divisions as Reflected in Rabbinic Literature and a Suggested Connection to the Calendar Debate», *Textus* 24 (2009) 205–220.

SANDERS, J.A., «Hermeneutics in True and False Prophecy», in: *Canon and Authority*. Essays in Old Testament Religion and Theology, eds. G.W. COATS – B.O. LONG, Philadelphia 1977, 21–41.

SARNA, N., «The Abortive Insurrection in Zedekiah's Day (Jer. 27–29)», in: *Studies in Biblical Interpretation*, ed. N. SARNA, Philadelphia 2000, 281–294 (= in: ErIsr 14 [1978] *89–*96 [Hebrew]).

DE SAUSSURE, F., *Cours de linguistique générale*, eds. C. BAILLY – A. SÉCHEHAYE, Paris 1916.

SAWYER, J.F.A., «Types of Prayer in the Old Testament. Some Semantic Observations on Hitpallel, Hithannen, etc.», *Semitics* 7 (1980) 131–143.

SAWYER, J.F.A., «The Meaning of *barzel* in the Biblical Expressions "Chariots of Iron", "Yoke of Iron", etc.», in: *Midian, Moab and Edom*. The History and Archaeology of Late Bronze and Iron Age Jordan and North-West Arabia, eds. J.F.A. SAWYER – D.J.A. CLINES, JSOT.S 24, Sheffield 1983, 129–134.

SBISÀ, M., *Detto non detto*. Le forme della comunicazione implicita, Bari 2007, ²2010.

SCALISE, P., «Vision beyond the Visions in Jeremiah», in: *"I Lifted My Eyes and Saw"*. Reading Dream and Vision Reports in the Hebrew Bible, eds. E.R. HAYES – L.-S. TIEMEYER, LHBOTS 584, London – New York 2014, 47–58.

SCHART, A., «Die Jeremiavisionen als Fortführung der Amosvisionen», in: *Schriftprophetie*. Festschrift für Jörg Jeremias zum 65. Geburtstag, eds. F. HARTENSTEIN – J. KRISPENZ – A. SCHART, Neukirchen-Vluyn 2004, 185–202.

SCHEARING, L.S. – MCKENZIE, S.L., eds., *Those Elusive Deuteronomists*. The Phenomenon of Pan-Deuteronomism, JSOT.S 268, Sheffield 1999.

SCHENKER, A., «Nebukadnezzars Metamorphose – Vom Unterjocker zum Gottesknecht», *RB* 89 (1982) 498–527.

SCHMID, H.H., *Gerechtigkeit als Weltordnung*. Hintergrund und Geschichte des alttestamentlichen Gerechtigkeitsbegriffes, BHTh 40, Tübingen 1968.

798   Bibliography

SCHMID, H.H., «Schöpfung, Gerechtigkeit und Heil. "Schöpfungstheologie" als Gesamthorizont biblischer Theologie», *ZThK* 70 (1973) 1–19.

SCHMID, K., *Buchgestalten des Jeremiabuches*. Untersuchungen zur Redaktions- und Rezeptionsgeschichte von Jer 30–33 im Kontext des Buches, WMANT 72, Neukirchen-Vluyn 1996.

SCHMID, K., «Innerbiblische Schriftauslegung. Aspekte der Forschungsgeschichte», in: *Schriftauslegung in der Schrift*. Festschrift für Odil Hannes Steck zu seinem 65. Geburtstag, *eds.* R.G. KRATZ – T. KRUGER – K. SCHMID, BZAW 300, Berlin – New York 2000, 1–22.

SCHMID, K., «Himmelsgott, Weltgott und Schöpfer. "Gott" und der "Himmel" in der Literatur der Zeit des Zweiten Tempels», *JBTh* 20 (2005) 111–148.

SCHMID, K., «Monotheismus und politische Ethik. Die politische Determination biblischer Gottesvorstellungen und ihre ethischen Implikationen», in: *Moral und Angst*. Erkenntnisse aus Moralpsychologie und politischer Theologie, *eds.* P. AERNI – K.-J. GRÜN, Göttingen 2011, 157–170.

SCHMID, K., «Nebukadnezars Antritt der Weltherrschaft und der Abbruch der Davidsdynastie. Innerbiblische Schriftauslegung und universalgeschichtliche Konstruktion im Jeremiabuch», in: ID., *Schriftgelehrte Traditionsliteratur*. Fallstudien zur innerbiblischen Schriftauslegung im Alten Testament, FAT 77, Tübingen 2011, 223–241 (= ID., «L'accession de Nabuchodonosor à l'hégémonie mondiale et la fin de la dynastie davidique. Exégèse intra-biblique et construction de l'histoire universelle dans le livre de Jérémie», *ETR* 81 [2006] 211–227).

SCHMID, K., «Genealogien der Moral. Prozesse fortschreitender ethischer Qualifizierung von Mensch und Welt im Alten Testament», in: *Gut und Böse in Mensch und Welt*. Philosophische und religiöse Konzeptionen vom Alten Orient bis zum frühen Islam, *eds.* H.G. NESSELRATH – F. WILK, ORA, Tübingen 2012, 83–102.

SCHMID, K., «Nebuchadnezzar, the End of the Davidic Rule, and the Exile in the Book of Jeremiah», in: *The Prophets Speak of Forced Migration*, *eds.* M.J. BODA *et al.*, SBL. AIL 21, Atlanta 2015, 63–76.

SCHMID, K., «Schrift und Schriftmetaphorik in der Prophetie des Jeremiabuches», in: *Metatexte*. Erzählungen von schrifttragenden Artefakten in der alttestamentlichen und mittelalterlichen Literatur, *eds.* F.-E. FOCKEN – M.R. OTT, MTK 15), Berlin – Boston 2016, 123–144.

SCHMID, K., «How to Date the Book of Jeremiah: Combining and Modifying Linguistic- and Profile-based Approaches», *VT* 68 (2018) 1–19.

SCHMIDT, H., «Das Datum der Ereignisse von Jer 27 und 28», *ZAW* 39 (1921) 138–144.

SCHMIDT, W.H., «"Über die Propheten". Streit um das rechte Wort Jer 23,9–32», in: *Geschichte Israels und deuteronomistisches Geschichtsdenken*. Festschrift zum 70. Geburtstag von Winfried Thiel, *eds.* P. MOMMER – A. SCHERER, AOAT 380, Münster 2010, 241–258.

SCHMITT, R., *Magie im Alten Testament*, AOAT 313, Münster 2004.

SCHMOLDT, H., «עלל», *ThWAT* VI, 79–83.

SCHNEIDER, C., *Krisis des Glaubens*. Zur Frage der sogenannten falschen Prophetie im Alten Testament, ThA 46, Berlin 1988.

SCHNIEDEWIND, *Society and the Promise to David*. The Reception History of 2 Samuel 7:1–17, New York 1999.

SCHNIEDEWIND, *How the Bible Became a Book*. The Textualization of Ancient Israel, Cambridge 2004.

SCHOORS, A., «The Particle יכ», in: *Remembering All the Way... A Collection of Old Testament Studies Published on the Occasion of the Fortieth Anniversary of the Oudtestamentisch Werkgezelschap in Nederland*, eds. B. ALBREKTSON *et al.*, OTS 21, Leiden 1981, 240–276.

SCHROER, S. – STAUBLI, T., *Die Korper-Symbolik der Bibel*, Darmstadt 1998.

VON SCHULER, E., *Die Kaškäer*. Ein Beitrag zur Ethnographie des alten Kleinasien, UAVA 3, Berlin 1956.

SCHULTZ, R.L., *The Search for Quotation*. Verbal Parallels in the Prophets, JSOT.S 180, Sheffield 1999.

SCHUMACHER, G., «Der arabische Pflug», *ZDPV* 12 (1889) 157–166.

SCHWALLY, F., *Der heilige Krieg im alten Israel*, Leipzig 1901.

SCURLOCK, J., «Neo-Assyrian Battle Tactics», in: *Crossing Boundaries and Linking Horizons*. Studies in Honor of Michael C. Astour, eds. G.D. YOUNG – M.W. CHAVALAS – R.E. AVERBECK, Bethesda 1997, 491–517.

SEARLE, J.R., «A Taxonomy of Illocutionary Acts», in: *Language, Mind, and Knowledge*, ed. K. GUNDERSON, Minneapolis 1975, 344–369 (= ID., «A Classification of Illocutionary Acts», *LangS* 5 [1975] 1–23; = ID., *Expression and Meaning*, Cambridge 1979, 1–29).

SEARLE, J.R., *Freedom and Neurobiology*. Reflections on Free Will, Language, and Political Power, New York 2007.

SEEBASS, H., «קְלַח», *ThWAT* IV, 588–594.

SEEBASS, H., «נֶפֶל», *ThWAT* V, 521–531.

SEIDEL, M., «Parallels between Isaiah and Psalms», *Sinai* 38 (1955–1956) 149–172, 229–240, 272–280, 335–355.

SEIDL, T., «Datierung und Wortereignis: Beobachtungen zum Horizont von Jer 27,1», *BZ* 21 (1977) 23–44, 184–199.

SEIDL, T., *Texte und Einheiten in Jeremia 27–29*. Literaturwissenschaftliche Studie. 1. Teil, ATSAT 2, St. Ottilien, 1977.

SEIDL, T., *Formen und Formeln in Jeremia 27–29*. Literaturwissenschaftliche Studie. 2. Teil, ATSAT 5, St. Ottilien, 1978.

SEIDL, T., «Die Wortereignisformel in Jeremia. Beobachtungen zu den Formen der Redeeröffnung in Jeremia, im Anschluss an Jer 27,1.2», *BZ* 23 (1979) 20–47.

SEIDL, T., *"Der Becher in der Hand des Herrn"*. Studie zu den prophetischen "Taumelbecher"-Texten, ATSAT 70, St. Ottilien 2001.

SEITZ, C.R., «The Crisis of Interpretation over the Meaning and Purpose of the Exile. A Redactional Study of Jeremiah xxi-xliii», *VT* 35 (1985) 78–97.

SEITZ, C.R., *Theology in Conflict*. Reactions to Exile in the Book of Jeremiah, BZAW 176, Berlin 1989.

Seitz, C.R., «The Prophet Moses and the Canonical Shape of Jeremiah», *ZAW* 101 (1989) 3–27.

Seitz, C.R., «Mose als Prophet. Redaktionsthemen und Gesamtstruktur des Jeremiabuches», *BZ* 34 (1990) 234–245.

Seitz, C.R., *Zion's Final Destiny*. The Development of the Book of Isaiah. A Reassessment of Isaiah 36–39, Minneapolis 1991.

van Selms, A., «The Name Nebuchadnezzar», in: *Travels in the World of the Old Testament*. Studies presented to Professor M.A. Beek on the Occasion of his 65th Birthday, *eds.* M.S.H.G. Heerma van Voss *et al.*, Assen 1974, 223–229.

Seri, A., «Borrowings to Create Anew: Intertextuality in the Babylonian Poem of "Creation" (Enūma eliš)», *JAOS* 134 (2014) 89–106.

Sessa, S.M., «"Andranno in rovina le case d'avorio. Oracolo del Signore" (Am 3,15). Abitare il dono di Dio edificando sull'ingiustizia? Storie di progetti insensati», *PSV* 64 (2011) 47–67.

Sessa, S.M., «"Prima di formarti nel grembo materno ti ho (ri-)conosciuto" (Ger 1,5)". La rivelazione del senso del nascere. Alcuni aspetti biblici», in: *Venire al mondo: i luoghi dell'invisibile*, *eds.* P. Grassi – S. Modica, QNB 7, Rosolini 2013, 21–37.

Sessa, S.M., «"Non rispondi nulla?". Il silenzio di Gesù nel contesto processuale dei sinottici. Una "nuova" proposta interpretativa alla luce del *rîb* profetico», in: *La profezia tra l'uno e l'altro Testamento*. Studi in onore del prof. Pietro Bovati in occasione del suo settantacinquesimo compleanno, *eds.* G. Benzi – D. Scaiola – M. Bonarini, AnBib.St 4, Roma 2015, 285–309.

Sessa, S.M., «"Dacci un re che ci governi!" (1 Sam 8,6). L'avvento della monarchia in Israele e la sua ambiguità», in: *Il Re delle schiere*. L'esercizio del re temporale e del Re eterno (ES 91–98), *ed.* D. Libanori, Cinisello Balsamo 2017, 17–44.

Sessa, S.M., «"Il Signore si è già scelto un uomo secondo il suo cuore"» (1 Sam 13,14). La riconfigurazione profetica del potere regale in Israele», in: *Il Re delle schiere*. L'esercizio del re temporale e del Re eterno (ES 91–98), *ed.* D. Libanori, Cinisello Balsamo 2017, 45–78.

Sessa, S.M., «Accompagnare il destino di un popolo: il profeta Geremia», *Credere Oggi* 222 (2017) 87–96.

Seux, M.-J., *Hymnes et prières aux dieux de Babylonie et d'Assyrie*, LAPO, Paris 1976.

Seybold, K., *Das davidische Königtum im Zeugnis der Propheten*, FRLANT 107, Göttingen 1972.

Seybold, K., *Der Prophet Jeremia*. Leben und Werk, CTB 416, Stuttgart – Berlin – Köln 1993.

Shannon, C.E., «A Mathematical Theory of Communication», *BSTJ* 27 (1948) 379–423, 623–656.

Shannon, C.E. – Weaver, W., *The Mathematical Theory of Communication*, Urbana 1963.

Sharp, C.J., *Prophecy and Ideology in Jeremiah*. Struggles for Authority in the Deutero-Jeremianic Prose, London – New York 2003.

Sharp, C.J., «Jeremiah in the Land of Aporia», in: *Jeremiah (Dis)Placed*. New Directions in Writing/Reading Jeremiah, *eds.* A.R.P. Diamond – L. Stulman, LHBOTS 529, London – New York 2011, 35–46.

SHARP C.J., *Jeremiah 26-52*, IECOT, Stuttgart, 2022.

SHEAD, S.L., *Radical Frame Semantics and Biblical Hebrew*. Exploring Lexical Semantics, BiInS 108, Leiden – Boston 2011.

SHEPPARD, G.T., «True and False Prophecy within Scripture», in: *Canon, Theology, and Old Testament Interpretation*. Essays in Honor of B.S. Childs, *eds.* G.M. TUCKER *et al.*, Philadelphia 1988, 262–282.

SHEPPARD, G.T. – HERBRECHTSMEIER, W.E., «Prophecy: An Overview», in: *The Encyclopedia of Religion*. Second Edition, XI, *ed.* L. JONES, New York – London 1987, ²2005, 7423–7429.

SICRE, J.L., «La monarquía y la justicia. La práctica de la justicia como elemento aglutinante en la redacción de Jr 21,11–23-8», in: *El misterio de la palabra*. Homenaje de sus alumnos al profesor D. Luis Alonso Schökel al cumplir veinticinco años de magisterio en el Instituto Bíblico Pontificio, *eds.* V. COLLADO – E. ZURRO, Madrid 1983, 193–206.

SICRE J.L., *Introducción al profetismo bíblico*, Estella 2011.

SIEVERS, J., «Widerstand und Ergebung in den Makkabäerbüchern», in: *Martyriumsvorstellungen in Antike und Mittelalter*. Leben oder sterben für Gott?, *eds.* S. FUHRMANN –R. GRUNDMANN, AGJU 80, Leiden – Boston 2012, 69–84.

SILVA, M., *Biblical Words and Their Meaning*. An Introduction to Lexical Semantics, Grand Rapids 1994.

SILVER, E., «Performing Domination/Theorizing Power: Israelite Prophecy as a Political Discourse beyond the Conflict Model», *JANER* 14 (2014) 186–216.

SIMIAN-YOFRE, H., *ed.*, *Metodologia dell'Antico Testamento*, StBi(Bo) 25, Bologna 1994.

SIMONE, R., «Espaces instables entre coordination et subordination», in: *La Parataxe*. Tome 1: Entre dépendance et intégration, *eds.* M.-J. BÉGUELIN – M. AVANZI – G. CORMINBOEUF, Berne 2010, 231–253.

SISSON, J.P., «Jeremiah and the Jerusalem Conception of Peace», *JBL* 105 (1986) 429–442.

SIVAN, D. – SCHNIEDEWIND, W., «Letting Your "Yes" Be "No" in Ancient Israel: A Study of the Asseverative לֹא and הֲלֹא», *JSSt* 38 (1993) 209–226.

SKA, J.-L., «Exode xiv contient-il un récit de "guerre sainte" de style deutéronomistique?», *VT* 33 (1983) 454–467.

SKA, J.-L., «"Je vais lui faire un allié qui soit son homologue" (Gn 2,18). A propos du terme '*ezer* – "aide"», *Bib.* 65 (1984) 233–238.

SKA, J.-L., *Le passage de la mer*. Étude de la construction, du style et de la symbolique d'Ex 14,1–31, AnBib 109, Roma 1986.

SKA, J.-L., *"Our Fathers Have Told Us"*. Introduction to the Analysis of Hebrew Narratives, SubBi 13, Roma 1990, ²2000.

SKA J.-L., «A Plea on Behalf of the Biblical Redactors», *StTh* 59 (2005) 4–18.

SOLSO, R.L., *Kognitive Psychologie*, Heidelberg 2005 (originale inglese: Id., *Cognitive Psychology*, Newton ⁶2001).

SMEND, R., *Jahwekrieg und Stämmebund*. Erwägungen zur ältesten Geschichte Israels, FRLANT 84, Göttingen 1963.

SMILANSKY, S., *Free Will and Illusion*, Oxford 2000.

SMIT, J.H., «War-related Terminology and Imagery in Jeremiah 15:10–21», *OTEs* 11 (1998) 105–114.

SMITH, D.L., «Jeremiah as Prophet of Nonviolent Resistance», *JSOT* 43 (1989) 95–107.

SMITH, D.L., *The Religion of the Landless.* The Social Context of the Babylonian Exile, Bloomington 1989.

SMITH, M., *Palestinian Parties and Politics That Shaped the Old Testament*, New York 1971.

SMITH, M.S., *The Laments of Jeremiah and their Contexts.* A Literary and Redactional Study of Jeremiah 11–20, SBLMS 42, Atlanta 1990.

SMITH-CHRISTOPHER, D.L., *A Biblical Theology of Exile*, Minneapolis 2002.

SOGGIN, J.A., «Der prophetische Gedanke über den heiligen Krieg, als Gericht gegen Israel», *VT* 10 (1960) 79–83.

SOGGIN, J.A., *Storia d'Israele.* Introduzione alla storia d'Israele e Giuda dalle origini alla rivolta di Bar Kochbà, BCR 44, Brescia 2002.

SOMMER, B.D., *A Prophet Reads Scripture.* Allusion in Isaiah 40–66, Stanford 1998.

SOMMER, B.D., «New Light on the Composition of Jeremiah», *CBQ* 61 (1999) 646–666.

SOMMER, B.D.«Dating Pentateuchal Texts and the Perils of Pseudo-Historicism", in: *The Pentateuch.* International Perspectives on Current Research, eds. T.B. DOZEMAN – K. SCHMID – B.J. SCHWARTZ, FAT 78, Tübingen 2011, 85–108.

SONNET, J.-P., «Narration biblique et (post)modernité», in: *La Bible en récits.* L'exégèse à l'heure du lecteur. Colloque international d'analyse narrative des textes de la Bible, Lausanne (mars 2002), *ed.* D. MARGUERAT, Genève 2003, ²2005, 253–263.

SONNET, J.-P., «L'alliance de la lecture: lorsque la Bible refuse l'ésotérisme», in: *La Bible sans avoir peur, ed.* J.-F. BOUTHORS, Paris 2005, 129–151.

SONNET, J.-P., «Du personnage de Dieu comme être de parole», in: *Bible et théologie.* L'intelligence de la foi, *ed.* F. MIES, LeR 26, Bruxelles 2006, 15–36.

SONNET, J.-P., «L'analyse narrative des récits bibliques», in: *Manuel d'exégèse de l'Ancien Testament, eds.* M. BAUKS – C. NIHAN, MoBi 61, Genève 2008, 47–94.

SONNET, J.-P., «God's Repentance and "False Starts" in Biblical History (Genesis 6–9; Exodus 32–34; 1 Samuel 15 e 2 Samuel 7)», in: *Congress Volume Ljubljana 2007, ed.* A. LEMAIRE, VT.S 133, Leiden 2010, 469–494.

SONNET, J.-P., *L'alleanza della lettura.* Questioni di poetica narrativa nella Bibbia ebraica, Lectio 1, Cinisello Balsamo 2011.

SPERBER, D. – WILSON, D., *Relevance.* Communication and Cognition, Oxford 1986, ²1995.

SPINA, F., «A Prophet's "Pregnant Pause": Samuel's Silence in the Ark Narrative (1 Samuel 4:1–7:12)», *HBT* 13 (1991) 59–73.

SPURR, D., *Architecture and Modern Literature*, Ann Arbor 2012.

STACEY, W.D., *Prophetic Drama in the Old Testament*, London 1990.

STAGER, L.E., «The Fury of Babylon: Ashkelon and the Archaeology of Destruction», *BArR* 22 (1996) 56–69, 76–77.

STÄHLI, H.-P. «יעץ», *THAT* I, 748–753.

STEELE, T., «Verse and Prose», *Princeton Encyclopedia of Poetry and Poetics*, eds. R. GREEN *et al.*, Princeton 1965, ⁴2012, 1507–1512.

STEEN, G.J., *Finding Metaphor in Grammar and Usage*. A Methodological Analysis of Theory and Research, Amsterdam – Philadelphia 2007.

STEINER, M.L., «Expanding Borders: The Development of Jerusalem in the Iron Age», in: *Jerusalem in Ancient History and Tradition*, ed., T.L. THOMPSON, JSOT.S 381, London –New York 2003, 68–79.

STEINMANN, J., *Le prophète Jérémie*. Sa vie, son œuvre et son temps, LeDiv 9, Paris 1952.

STENDEBACH, F.J., «שׁלוֹם», *ThWAT* VIII, 12–46.

STENGER, W., *Biblische Methodenlehre*, LeTh 18, Düsseldorf 1987.

STERN, E., *Archaeology of the Land of the Bible*. Vol. II: The Assyrian, Babylonian, and Persian Periods 732–332 bce, New York 2001.

STERN P.D., *The Biblical Ḥerem*. A Window on Israel's Religious Experience, BJSt 211, Atlanta 1991.

STERNBERG, M., «Proteus in Quotation-Land: Mimesis and the Forms of Reported Discourse», *Poetics Today* 3 (1982) 107–156.

STERNBERG, M., *The Poetics of Biblical Narrative*. Ideological Literature and the Drama of Reading, Bloomington 1985.

STERNBERG, M., «Telling in Time (I): Chronology and Narrative Theory», *Poetics Today* 11 (1990) 901–948.

STERNBERG, M., «Telling in Time (II): Chronology, Teleology, Narrativity», *Poetics Today* 13 (1992) 463–541.

STERNBERG, M., *Hebrews between Cultures*. Group Portraits and National Literature, Bloomington 1998.

STEUERNAGEL, C., *Lehrbuch der Einleitung in das Alte Testament*. Mit einem Anhang über die Apokryphen und Pseudepigraphen, Tübingen 1912.

STIBBE, M.W.G., *John as Storyteller*. Narrative Criticism and the Fourth Gospel, SNTSMS 73, Cambridge 1992.

STILLMAN, N. – TALLIS, N., *Armies of the Ancient Near East 3,000 BC to 539 BC*, Worthing 1984.

STIPP, H.-J., *Jeremia im Parteienstreit*. Studien zur Textentwicklung von Jer 26,36–43 und 45 als Beitrag zur Geschichte Jeremias, seines Buches und judäischer Parteien im 6. Jahrhundert, BBB 82, Frankfurt am Main 1992.

STIPP, H.-J., *Das masoretische und alexandrinische Sondergut des Jeremiabuches*. Textgeschichtlicher Rang, Eigenarten, Triebkräfte, OBO 136, Freiburg 1994.

STIPP, H.-J., «Zedekiah in the Book of Jeremiah: On the Formation of a Biblical Character», *CBQ* 58 (1996) 627–648.

STIPP, H.-J., «Linguistic Peculiarities of the Masoretic Edition of the Book of Jeremiah: An Updated Index», *JNSL* 23 (1997) 181–202.

STIPP, H.-J., «The Concept of the Empty Land in Jeremiah 37–43», in: *The Concept of Exile in Ancient Israel and its Historical Contexts, eds.* E. BEN ZVI – C. LEVIN, BZAW 404, Berlin – New York 2010, 103–154.

STIPP, H.-J., «Legenden der Jeremia-Exegese (II): Die Verschleppung Jeremias nach Ägypten», *VT* 64 (2014) 654–663.

STIPP, H.-J., *Jeremia 25–52,* HAT I/12,2, Tübingen 2019.

STIPP, H.-J., «Überlegungen zu ausgewählten Aspekten der Behandlung des Jeremiabuchs in der Monographie von Benjamin Ziemer "Kritik des Wachstumsmodells" (2020)», *BZ* 65 (2021) 191–215.

STÖKL, J., *Prophecy in the Ancient Near East.* A Philological and Sociological Comparison, CHANE 56, Leiden – Boston 2012.

STÖKL, J., «Nebuchadnezar: History, Memory, and Myth-Making in the Persian Period», in: *Remembering Biblical Figures in the Late Persian and Early Hellenistic Periods.* Social Memory and Imagination, *eds.* D.V. EDELMAN – E. BEN ZVI, Oxford 2013, 257–269.

STOLZ, F., *Jahwes und Israels Kriege.* Kriegstheorien und Kriegserfahrungen im Glauben des alten Israel, AThANT 60, Zürich 1972.

STOLZ, F., «Zeichen und Wunder. Die prophetische Legitimation und ihre Geschichte», *ZThK* 69 (1972) 125–144.

STRAWN, B.A., *What is Stronger than a Lion?* Leonine Image and Metaphor in the Hebrew Bible and the Ancient Near East, Fribourg 2005.

STRECK, M., *Assurbanipal und die letzten assyrischen Könige bis zum Untergange Niniveh's,* VAB 7/II, Leipzig 1916, [2]1975, 82–85.

STRECK, M.P. «Nebukadnezzar II. A. Historisch. Konig von Babylon (604–562)», *RLA* IX, 194–201.

STRONACH, D. – ROAF, M., *Nush-i Jan I.* The Major Buildings of the Median Settlement, Leuven 2007.

STULMAN, L., *The Prose Sermons of the Book of Jeremiah.* Redescription of the Correspondences with the Deuteronomistic Literature in the Light of Recent Text-critical Research, SBLDS 83, Atlanta 1986.

STULMAN, L., «Insiders and Outsiders in the Book of Jeremiah: Shifts in Symbolic Arrangements», *JSOT* 66 (1995) 65–85.

STULMAN, L., *Order amid Chaos.* Jeremiah as Symbolic Tapestry, BiSe 57, Sheffield 1998.

STULMAN, L., «The Prose Sermons as Hermeneutical Guide to Jeremiah 1–25: The Deconstruction of Juda's Symbolic World», in: *Troubling Jeremiah, eds.* A.R.P. DIAMOND – K. O'CONNOR – L. STULMAN, JSOT.S 260, Sheffield 1999, 34–63.

SWEENEY. M.A., «The Truth in True and False Prophecy», in: *Truth.* Interdisciplinary Dialogues in a Pluralistic Age, *eds.* C. HELMER – K. DE TROYER, StPT 22, Leuven 2003, 9–26 (= Id., *Form and Intertextuality in Prophetic and Apocalyptic Literature,* FAT 45, Tübingen 2005, 78–93).

SWEENEY. M.A., «Jeremiah's Reflection on the Isaian Royal Promise: Jeremiah 23:1–8 in Context», in: *Uprooting and Planting.* Essays on Jeremiah for Leslie Allen, *ed.* J. GOLDINGAY, LHBOTS 459, London – New York 2007, 308–321.

TADMOR, H., «Sennacherib's Campaign to Judah: Historical and Historiographical Considerations», *Zion* 50 (1985) 65–80 (Hebrew).

TALMON, S., «The Textual Study of the Bible – A New Outlook», in: *Qumran and the History of the Biblical Text*, eds. F.M. CROSS – S. TALMON, Cambridge 1975, 358–378.

TARREF, S.B., *Reading with the Faithful*. Interpretation of True and False Prophecy in the Book of Jeremiah from Ancient to Modern Times, JThIS 6, Winona Lake 2013.

TARSKI, A., *Logic, Semantics, Metamathematics*. Papers from 1923 to 1938, New York 1956, Indianapolis ²1983.

TATUM, L., «Jerusalem in Conflict: The Evidence for the Seventh-Century B.C.E. Religious Struggle over Jerusalem», in: *Jerusalem in Bible and Archaeology. The First Temple Period*, eds., A.G. VAUGHN – A.E. KILLEBREW, SBLSymS 18, Atlanta 2003, 291–306.

TAYLOR, J.R., *Linguistic Categorization*. Prototypes in Linguistic Theory, Oxford 1989, ²1995.

TAYLOR, M.A., «Jeremiah 45: The Problem of Placement», *JSOT* 37 (1987) 79–98.

THAMES, J.T., Jr., «A New Discussion of the Meaning of the Phrase *'am hā'āreṣ* in the Hebrew Bible», *JBL* 130 (2011) 109–125.

THELLE, R.I., «דרש את־יהוה. The Prophetic Act of Consulting Yhwh in Jeremiah 21,2 and 37,7», *SJOT* 12 (1998) 249–255.

THELLE, R.I., *Ask God*. Divine Consultation in the Literature of the Hebrew Bible, BET 30, Frankfurt am Main 2002.

THIEL, W., *Die deuteronomistische Redaktion von Jeremia 1–25*, WMANT 41, Neukirchen-Vluyn 1973.

THIEL, W., *Die deuteronomistische Redaktion von Jeremia 26–45*, WMANT 42, Neukirchen-Vluyn 1981.

THOMPSON, J.A., *The Book of Jeremiah*, NICOT, Grand Rapids 1980.

TIGAY, J., *The Evolution of the Gilgamesh Epic*, Philadelphia 1982.

TIGAY J., ed., *Empirical Models for Biblical Criticism*, Philadelphia 1985.

TOKER, L., *Eloquent Reticence*. Withholding Information in Fictional Narrative, Lexington 1993.

VAN DER TOORN, K., *Scribal Culture and the Making of the Hebrew Bible*, Cambridge (MA) 2007.

TOV, E., «Some Aspects of the Textual and Literary History of the Book of Jeremiah», in: *Le livre de Jérémie. Le prophète et son milieu. Les oracles et leur transmission*, ed. P.-M. BOGAERT, BEThL 54, Louvain 1981, 145–167.

TOV, E., «The Literary History of the Book of Jeremiah in the Light of Its Textual History», in: *Empirical Models for Biblical Criticism*, ed., J.H. TIGAY, Philadelphia 1985, 211–237.

TOV, E., *Textual Criticism of the Hebrew Bible*. Second Revised Edition, Minneapolis ²2001 (first edition 1992).

TOV, E., *Scribal Practices and Approaches Reflected in the Texts Found in the Judean Desert*, StTDJ 54, Leiden 2004.

TRIM, R., *Metaphor and the Historical Evolution of Conceptual Mapping*, London 2011.

TRÖLTSCH, E., «Das Ethos der hebräischen Propheten», *Logos* 6 (1916–1917) 1–28.

TRÖLTSCH, E., *Gesammelte Schriften*, vol. IV, Tübingen 1925.

TSUMURA, D.T., *Creation and Destruction*. A Reappraisal of the Chaoskampf Theory in the Old Testament, Winona Lake 2005.

TURKOWSKI, L., «Peasant Agriculture in the Judean Hills», *PEQ* 101 (1969) 21–33, 101–112.

TYER, C.L., «Yoke», *ABD* VI, 1026–1027.

UEHLINGER, C., «Gab es eine joschijanische Kultreform? Plädoyer für ein begründetes Minimum», in: *Jeremia und die "deuteronomistische Bewegung"*, ed. B. GROSS, BBB 98, Weinheim 1995, 57–89.

UEHLINGER, C., «Hanun von Gaza und seine Gottheiten auf Orthostatenreliefs Tiglatpilesers III», in: *Kein Land für sich allein*. Studien zum Kulturkontakt in Kanaan, Israel/Palästina und Ebirnâri für Manfred Weippert zum 65. Geburtstag, *eds.* U. HÜBNER – E.A. KNAUF, OBO 186, Fribourg – Göttingen 2002, 92–125.

UEHLINGER, C., «Clio in a World of Pictures – Another Look at the Lachish Reliefs from Sennacherib's Southwest Palace at Niniveh», in: *Like a Bird in a Cage*. The Invasion of Sennacherib in 701 BCE, *ed.* L.L. GRABBE, JSOT.S 363, Sheffield 2003, 221–305.

UFFENHEIMER, B., «The Religious Experience of the Psalmists and the Prophetic Mind», *Immanuel* 21 (1987) 7–27.

UFFENHEIMER, B., «Isaiah's and Micah's Approaches to Policy and History», in: *Politics and Theopolitics in the Bible and Postbiblical Literature*, *eds.* H.G. REVENTLOW – Y. HOFFMAN – B. UFFENHEIMER, JSOT.S 171, Sheffield 1994, 176–188.

ULEYN, A., *Actualité de la fonction prophétique*. Psychologie pastorale et culpabilité, Paris 1966.

UNTERMANN, J., *From Repentance to Redemption*. Jeremiah's Thought in Transition, JSOT.S 54, Sheffield 1987.

URMSON, J.O. – SBISÀ, M., *eds.*, *How To Do Things with Words*. The William James Lectures delivered at Harvard University in 1955, Cambridge 1962, [2]1975.

USSISHKIN, D., «Symbols of Conquest in Sennacherib's Reliefs of Lachish: Impaled Prisoners and Booty», in: *Culture through Objects*. Ancient Near Eastern Studies in Honour of P.R.S. Moorey, *eds.* T.F. POTTS *et al.*, Oxford 2003, 207–217.

USSISHKIN, D., «Sennacherib's Campaign to Philistia and Judah: Ekron, Lachish, and Jerusalem», in: *Essays on Ancient Israel in Its Near Eastern Context*. A Tribute to Nadav Na'aman, *eds.* Y. AMIT – E. BEN ZVI – I. FINKELSTEIN – O. LIPSCHITS, Winona Lake 2006, 339–357.

USSISHKIN, D., *Biblical Lachish*. A Tale of Construction, Destruction, Excavation and Restoration, Jerusalem 2014.

UTZSCHNEIDER, H. – NITSCHE, S.A., *Arbeitsbuch literaturwissenschaftliche Bibelauslegung*. Eine Methodenlehre zur Exegese des Alten Testaments, Gütersloh 2001.

VALÉRY, P. «La crise de l'esprit (Essais quasi politiques)», in: *Œuvres*, *ed.* J. HYTIER, vol. I, Paris 1957, 988–1014.

VANDERHOOFT, D.S., *The Neo-Babylonian Empire and Babylon in the Latter Prophets*, HSM 59, Atlanta 1999.

VANDERHOOFT, D.S., «Babylonian Strategies of Imperial Control in the West: Royal Practice and Rhetoric», in: *Judah and the Judeans in the Neo-Babylonian Period, eds.* O. LIPSCHITS – J. BLENKINSOPP, Winona Lake 2003, 235– 262.

VANDERHOOFT, D.S., «Wadi el-Ḥôl Inscription 2 and the Early Semitic Alphabetic Graph *ǵ, *ǵull, "yoke"», *HeBAI* 2 (2013) 125–135.

VAN DYKE PARUNAK, H., «A Semantic Survey of NḤM», *Bib.* 56 (1975) 512–532.

VAN SETERS, J., *In Search of History.* Historiography in the Ancient World and the Origins of Biblical Historiography, New Haven 1983, Winona Lake [2]1997.

VAN SETERS, J., «An Ironic Circle: Wellhausen and the Rise of Redaction Criticism», *ZAW* 115 (2003) 487–500.

VAN SETERS, J., «The Redactor in Biblical Studies: A Nineteenth Century Anachronism", *JNSL* 29 (2003) 1–19.

VAN SETERS, J., *The Edited Bible.* The Curious History of the "Editor" in Biblical Criticism, Winona Lake 2006.

VARUGHESE, A., «The Royal Family in the Jeremiah Tradition», in: *Inspired Speech.* Prophecy in the Ancient Near East. Essays in Honor of Herbert B. Huffmon, *eds.* J. KALTNER – L. STULMAN, JSOT.S 378, London 2004, 319–328.

DE VAUX, R., «Les ostraka de Lachis», *RB* 48 (1939) 181–206.

DE VAUX, R., «Jerusalem and the Prophets», in: *Interpreting the Prophetic Tradition, ed.* H.M. ORLINSKY, New York 1969, 277–300.

VERMEYLEN, J., *Le livre d'Isaïe.* Une cathédrale littéraire, LeDiv, Paris 2014.

VERNADSKIJ, V.I., *Biosfera*, Moskvà 1967.

VÉRON, E., «Quand lire, c'est faire: l'énonciation dans le discours de la presse écrite», in: *Sémiotique*, II, IREP, Paris 1984, 33–56.

VERSLUIS, A., «Devotion and/or Destruction? The Meaning and Function of חרם in the Old Testament», *ZAW* 128 (2016) 233–246.

VIBERG, Å., *Prophets in Action.* An Analysis of Prophetic Symbolic Acts in the Old Testament, CB.OT 55, Stockholm 2007.

VILLARD, P., «Les prophéties à l'époque Néo-Assyrienne», in: *Prophètes et rois.* Bible et Proche-Orient, *ed.* A. LEMAIRE, LeDiv.HS, Paris 2001, 55–84.

VIOLI, P., *Significato ed esperienza*, Milano 1997.

VITACOLONNA, L., *Per un paradigma semiotico del testo*, Chieti 1989.

VITACOLONNA, L., «Los textos literarios como mundos posibles», *CEsL* 16 (1991) 189–212.

VOGELS, W., «Comment discerner le prophète authentique?», *NRTh* 99 (1977) 681–701.

VÖLKER, H., «Von der Interdisziplinarität zur Transdisziplinarität?», in: *Transdisziplinarität. Bestandsaufnahme und Perspektiven.* Beiträge zur THESIS-Arbeitstagung im Oktober 2003 in Göttingen, *eds.* F. BRAND – F. SCHALLER – H. VÖLKER, Göttingen 2004, 9–28.

VOLLI, U., *Manuale di semiotica*, MBa 13, Bari 2000, [6]2007.

VOLZ, P., *Der Prophet Jeremia*, KAT 10, Leipzig 1922.

DE WAARD, H., *Jeremiah 52 in the Context of the Book of Jeremiah*, VT.S 183, Leiden 2020.

WAGNER, A., *Prophetie als Theologie*. Die *so spricht Jahwe*-Formeln und das Grundverständnis alttestamentlicher Prophetie, FRLANT 207, Göttingen 2004.

WAGNER, A., «Gefühl, Emotion und Affekt in der Sprachanalyse des Hebräischen», in: Id., *Emotionen, Gefühle und Sprache im Alten Testament*. Vier Studien, KUSATU 7, Waltrop 2006, 7–47.

WAGNER, A., «Der Parallelismus membrorum zwischen poetischer Form und Denkfigur», in: *Parallelismus membrorum, ed.* A. WAGNER, OBO 224, Göttingen 2007, 1–26.

WAGNER, D.M., *The Illusion of Conscious Will*, Cambridge (MA) 2002.

VAN DER WAL, A.J.O., «Toward a Synchronic Analysis of the Masoretic Text of the Book of Jeremiah», in: *Reading the Book of Jeremiah*. A Search for Coherence, *ed.* M. KESSLER, Winona Lake 2004, 13–23.

WALSH, C., «Testing Entry: The Social Functions of City Gates in Biblical Memory», in: *Memory and the City in Ancient Israel, eds.* D.V. EDELMAN – E. BEN ZVI, Winona Lake 2014, 43–59.

WALTON, J.H., *Ancient Near Eastern Thought and the Old Testament*. Introducing the Conceptual World of the Hebrew Bible, Grand Rapids 2006.

WALZER, M., «Prophecy and International Politics», *HPSt* 4 (2009) 319–328.

WALZER, M., *In God's Shadow*. Politics in the Hebrew Bible, New Haven – London 2012.

WANKE, G., *Untersuchungen zur sogenannten Baruchschrift*, BZAW 122, Berlin 1971.

WANKE, G., «Jeremias Berufung (Jer 1,4–10). Exegetisch-theologische Überlegungen zum Verhältnis von individueller Äußerung und geprägtem Gut anhand eines Einzeltextes», in: *Alttestamentlicher Glaube und biblische Theologie*. Festschrift für Horst Dietrich Preuß zum 65. Geburtstag, *eds.* J. HAUSMANN – H.-J. ZOBEL, Stuttgart 1992, 132–144.

WANKE, G., *Jeremia*. Teilband 1: Jeremia 1,1–25,14, ZBK.AT 20.1, Zürich 1995.

WANKE, G., *Jeremia*. Teilband 2: Jeremia 25,15–52,34, ZBK.AT 20.2, Zürich 1995.

WATTS, W., «Text and Redaction in Jeremiah's Oracles against the Nations», *CBQ* 54 (1992) 432–447.

WATZLAWICK, P. – BEAVIN, J.H. – JACKSON, D.D., *Pragmatics of Human Communication*. A Study of Interactional Patterns, Pathologies, and Paradoxes, New York 1967.

WEIDNER, E.F., *Reliefs der assyrischen Könige*. Erster Teil. Die Reliefs in England, in der Vatikan-Stadt und in Italien, AfO 4, Berlin 1939.

WEIDNER, E.F., «Jojachin, König von Juda, in babylonischen Keilschrifttexten», in: *Mélanges syriens offerts à Monsieur René Dussaud, eds.* F. CUMONT *et al.*, vol. II, BAH 30, Paris 1939, 923–935.

WEINBERG, J., «Gedaliah, the Son of Ahikam in Mizpah: His Status and Role, Supporters and Opponents», *ZAW* 119 (2007) 356–368.

WEINFELD, M., «Ancient Near Eastern Patterns in Prophetic Literature», *VT* 27 (1977) 178–195.

WEINFELD, M., «The Counsel of the "Elders" to Rehoboam and its Implications», *Maarav* 3 (1982) 27–53.

WEINFELD, M., «Divine Intervention in War in Ancient Israel and in Ancient Near East», in: *History, Historiography and Interpretation.* Studies in Biblical and Cuneiform Literatures, eds. H. TADMOR – M. WEINFELD, Jerusalem 1983, 121–147.

WEINRICH, F., *Der religiös-utopische Charakter der "prophetischen Politik"*, Giessen 1932.

WEINRICH, H., *Tempus.* Besprochene und erzählte Welt, Stuttgart 1964, München ⁶2001.

WEIPPERT, H., «Jahwekrieg und Bundesfluch in Jer 21 1–7», *ZAW* 82 (1970) 369–409.

WEIPPERT, H., *Die Prosareden des Jeremiabuches*, BZAW 132, Berlin 1973.

WEIPPERT, H., *Schöpfer des Himmels und der Erde.* Ein Beitrag zur Theologie des Jeremiabuches, SBS 102, Stuttgart 1981.

WEIPPERT, M., «"Heiliger Krieg" in Israel und Assyrien: Kritische Anmerkungen zu Gerhard von Rads Konzept des "heiligen Krieges" im alten Israel», *ZAW* 84 (1972) 460–493.

WEIPPERT, M., «Aspekte israelitischer Prophetie im Lichte verwandter Erscheinungen des Alten Orients», in: *Ad bene et fideliter seminandum.* Festgabe für Karlheinz Deller zum 21. Februar 1987, eds. G. MAUER – U. MAGEN, Neukirchen-Vluyn 1988, 287–319.

WEIPPERT, M., «Prophetie im Alten Orient», *NBL* III, 196–200.

WEIS, R.D. «The Structure of MT Jeremiah, with Special Attention to Chapters 21–45», in: *Partners with God.* Theological and Critical Readings of the Bible in Honor of Marvin A. Sweeney, eds. S.L. BIRDSONG – S. FROLOV, CSHBS 2, Claremont 2017, 201–224.

WEISER, A., *Das Buch Jeremia.* I: Kapitel 1–25,14, ATD 20, Göttingen 1952, ⁷1976.

WEISER, A., *Das Buch Jeremia.* II: Kapitel 25,15–52,34, ATD 21, Göttingen 1954, ⁴1966.

WELCH, A.C., *Jeremiah.* His Time and His Work, London 1928, Oxford ²1951.

WELLHAUSEN, J., *Prolegomena zur Geschichte Israels*, Berlin 1882, ⁶1905.

WELLS, R.D., Jr., «Indications of Late Reinterpretation of the Jeremianic Tradition from the LXX of Jer 21 1 – 23 8», *ZAW* 96 (1984) 405–420.

WELLS, R.D., «Dislocation in Time and Ideology in the Reconception of Jeremiah's Words: The Encounter with Hananiah in the Septuaginta *Vorlage* and the Masoretic Text», in: *Uprooting and Planting.* Essays on Jeremiah for Leslie Allen, ed. J. GOLDINGAY, LHBOTS 459, London – New York 2007, 322–350.

WENDLAND, E.R., *Prophetic Rhetoric.* Case Studies in Text Analysis and Translation, Lakewood 2009, ²2014.

WENDLAND, P., «Symbolische Handlungen als Ersatz oder Begleitung der Rede», *NJKA* 19 (1916) 233–245.

WERNER, W., *Das Buch Jeremia.* Kapitel 1–25, NSK.AT 19/1, Stuttgart 1997.

WERNER, W., *Das Buch Jeremia.* Kapitel 25,15–52, NSK.AT 19/2, Stuttgart 2003.

WESSELS, W.J., «Setting the Stage for the Future of the Kingship: An Ideological-Critical Reading of Jeremia 21:1–10», *OTEs* 17 (2004) 470–483.

WESSELS, W.J., «Prophets versus Prophets in the Book of Jeremiah: In Search of the True Prophets», *OTEs* 22 (2009) 733–751.

WESSELS, W.J., «Zion, Beautiful City of God. Zion Theology in the Book of Jeremiah», *VerEcc* 27 (2006) 729–748.

WESSELS, W.J., «True and False Prophets: Who is to Decide? A Perspective from Jeremiah 23:9–40», *JSem* 21 (2012) 137–156.

WEST, R. – TURNER, L.H., *Introducing Communication Theory*. Analysis and Application, New York 2000, [4]2010.

WESTERMANN, C., «Die Begriffe für Fragen und Suchen im Alten Testament», *KuD* 6 (1960) 2–30.

WESTERMANN, C., *Grundformen prophetischer Rede*, BEvT 31, München 1960, [5]1978.

WESTERMANN, C., *Jeremia*, Stuttgart 1967.

WESTERMANN, C., *Schöpfung*, ThTh 12, Stuttgart 1971.

WESTERMANN, C., «נגד», *THAT* II, 31–37.

WILCOXEN, J.A., «The Political Background of Jeremiah's Temple Sermon», in: *Scripture in History & Theology*. Essays in Honor of J. Coert Rylaarsdam, *eds.* A.L. MERRILL – T.W. OVERHOLT, Pittsburgh 1977, 151–165.

WILDBERGER, H., *Jahwewort und prophetische Rede bei Jeremia*. Inaugural-Dissertation zur Erlangung der Doktorwürde der Theologischen Fakultät der Universität Zürich, Zürich 1942.

WILKE, A.F., *Die Gebete der Propheten*. Anrufungen Gottes im "corpus propheticum" der Hebräischen Bibel, BZAW 451, Berlin – Boston 2014.

WILLI, R., «"Anhaltspunkte" zur Unterscheidung von wahrer und falscher Prophetie aus der Perspektive des Alten Testaments», *FKTh* 26 (2010) 96–106.

WILLIAMSON, H.G.M., *The Book Called Isaiah*. Deutero-Isaiah's Role in Composition and Redaction, Oxford 1994.

WILLIS, J.T., «Dialogue between Prophet and Audience as a Rhetorical Device in the Book of Jeremiah», *JSOT* 33 (1985) 63–82.

WILSON, R.R., «Interpreting Israel's Religion. An Anthropological Perspective on the Problem of False Prophecy», in: ID., *Sociological Approaches to the Old Testament*, GBSP, Philadelphia 1984, 67–80 (= in: *"The Place is Too Small for Us"*. The Israelite Prophets in Recent Scholarship, *ed.* R.P. GORDON, SBTS 5, Winona Lake 1995, 332–344).

WILSON, R.R., «Poetry and Prose in the Book of Jeremiah», in: *Ki Baruch Hu*. Ancient Near Eastern-Biblical and Judaic Studies in Honor of Baruch A. Levine, *eds.* R. CHAZAN *et al.*, Winona Lake 1999.

VAN WINKLE, D.W., «1 Kings XIII: True and False Prophecy», *VT* 39 (1989) 31–43.

WISEMAN, D.J., *Nebuchadrezzar and Babylon*, SchL 1983, Oxford 1985.

WISEMAN, D.J., «Babylonia 605–539 B.C.», in: *The Cambridge Ancient History*. The Assyrian and Babylonian Empires and Other States of the Near East, from the Eighth to the Sixth Centuries B.C., vol. III/2, *eds.* J. BOARDMAN *et al.*, Cambridge 1991, 229–251.

WISSER, L., «La création dans le livre de Jérémie», in: *La création dans l'Orient Ancien.* Congrès de L'ACFEB, Lille (1985), eds. F. BLANQUART – L. DEROUSSEAUX, LeDiv 127, Paris 1987, 241–260.

WOLFF, H.W., *Anthropologie des Alten Testaments,* München 1973.

WONG, G.C.I., «The Nature of Faith in Isaiah of Jerusalem», *TynB* 47 (1996) 188–190.

WONG, G.C.I., «Faith in the Present Form of Isaiah VII 1–17», *VT* 51 (2001) 535–547.

WOOD, J.T., *Communication Mosaics.* An Introduction to the Field of Communication, Boston 2006, ⁶2011.

WOOLLEY, C.L., *Charchemish.* Part II: The Town Defenses, London 1921.

WOOLLEY, C.L. – BARNETT, R.D., *Charchemish.* Part III: The Excavations in the Inner Town, and the Hittite Inscriptions, London 1952.

WRIGHT, J.L., «The Deportation of Jerusalem's Wealth and the Demise of Native Sovereignty in the Book of Kings», in: *Interpreting Exile.* Displacement and Deportation in Biblical and Modern Contexts, eds. B.E. KELLE – F.R. AMES – J.L. WRIGHT, SBL.AIL 10, Atlanta 2011, 105–133.

WYNN, M.R., *Emotional Experience and Religious Understanding.* Integrating Perception, Conception and Feeling, Cambridge 2005.

YADIN, Y., *The Art of Warfare in Biblical Lands in the Light of Archaeological Study,* 2 vols., Jerusalem 1963.

YAMADA, S., *The Construction of the Assyrian Empire.* A Historical Study of the Inscriptions of Shalmaneser III (859–824 B.C.) Relating to his Campaigns in the West, CHANE 3, Leiden 2000.

YDIT, M., «Av, The Ninth of», *EJ.SE* II, 714–716.

YOUNG, R.C., «When Did Jerusalem Fall?», *JETS* 47 (2004) 21–38.

YOUNGER, K.L., Jr., «Some Recent Discussion on the ḤĒREM», in: *Far from Minimal.* Celebrating the Work and Influence of Philip R. Davies, eds. D. BURNS – J.W. ROGERSON, LHBOTS 484, London – New York 2012, 505–522.

ZAKOVITCH, Y., «Through the Looking Glass: Reflections/Inversions of Genesis Stories in the Bible», *BibInt* 1 (1993) 139–152.

ZAWADZKI, S., «Depicting Hostile Rulers in the Neo-Assyrian Royal Inscriptions», in: *From Source to History.* Studies on Ancient Near Eastern Worlds and Beyond, eds. S. GASPA et al., Münster 2014, 767–778.

ZEHNDER, M., *Wegmetaphorik im Alten Testament.* Eine semantische Untersuchung der alttestamentlichen und altorientalischen Weg-Lexeme mit besonderer Berücksichtigung ihrer metaphorischen Verwendung, BZAW 268, Berlin 1999.

ZEHNDER, M., «Fluch und Segen in Buch Deuteronomium. Beobachtungen und Fragen», in: *Deuteronomium – Torah für eine neue Generation,* eds. G. FISCHER – D. MARKL – S. PAGANINI, BZAR 17, Wiesbaden 2011, 193–211.

ZENGER E., et al., *Einleitung in das Alte Testament,* KStTh 1.1, Stuttgart 1995, ⁶2006.

ZEVIT, Z., «The use of ʿbd as a Diplomatic Term in Jeremiah», *JBL* 88 (1969) 74–77.

ZEVIT, Z., *The Religions of Ancient Israel.* A Synthesis of Parallactic Approaches, London – New York 2001.

ZEWI, T., «The Particles הנה and והנה in Biblical Hebrew», *HebStud* 37 (1996) 21–37.

ZIEGLER, J., *Beiträge zur Ieremias-Septuaginta*, MSU 6, Göttingen 1958.

ZIEGLER, Y., «"As the Lord Lives and as Your Soul Lives": An Oath of Conscious Deference», *VT* 58 (2008) 117–130.

ZIEGLER, Y., *Promises to Keep.* The Oath in Biblical Narrative, VT.S 120, Leiden 2008.

ZIEMER, B., *Kritik des Wachstumsmodells.* Die Grenzen alttestamentlicher Redaktionsgeschichte im Lichte empirischer Evidenz, VT.S 182, Leiden 2020.

ZIMMERLI, W., *Ezechiel*, I. Teilband, BKAT 13/1, Neukirchen-Vluyn 1968.

ZIMMERLI, W., «The "Land" in the Pre-Exilic and Early Post-Exilic Prophets», in: *Understanding the Word.* Essays in Honor of Bernhard W. Anderson, *eds.* J.T. BUTLER – E.W. CONRAD – B.C. OLLENBURGER, JSOT.S 37, Sheffield 1985, 235–254.

ZULICK, M.D., «The Agon of Jeremiah: On the Dialogic Invention of Prophetic Ethos», *QJS* 78 (1992) 125–148.

ÖSTERREICHISCHE BIBLISCHE STUDIEN
Herausgegeben von Georg Braulik

Band 1 bis 13 sind erschienen im Verlag Österreichisches Katholisches Bibelwerk.

Band   1   Wilhelm Egger: Nachfolge als Weg zum Leben. Chancen neuerer exege-tischer Methoden, dargelegt an Mk 10,17-31. (vergriffen)

Band   2   Herbert Migsch: Gottes Wort über das Ende Jerusalems. Eine literar-, stil- und gattungskritische Untersuchung des Berichtes Jeremia 34,1-7; 32,2-5; 37,3-38,28.

Band   3   Walter Kirchschläger: Jesu exorzistisches Wirken aus der Sicht des Lukas. Ein Beitrag zur lukanischen Redaktion.

Band   4   Roland Schwarz: Bürgerliches Christentum im Neuen Testament? Eine Studie zu Ethik, Amt und Recht in den Pastoralbriefen.

Band   5   Roman Kühschelm: Jüngerverfolgung und Geschick Jesu. Eine exege-tisch-bibeltheologische Untersuchung der synoptischen Verfolgungs ankündigung Mk 13,9-13 par und Mk 23,29-36 par.

Band   6   Ryszard Rubienkiewicz: Die Eschatologie von Henoch 9-11 und das Neue Testament (aus dem Polnischen übersetzt von Herbert Ulrich).

Band   7   Birgit Langer: Gott als "Licht" in Israel und Mesopotamien. Eine Studie zu Jes 60,1-3,19f.

Band   8   Gerhard Langer: Von Gott erwählt – Jerusalem. Die Rezeption von Dtn 12 im frühen Judentum.

Band   9   Ursula Struppe: Die Herrlichkeit Jahwes in der Priesterschrift. Eine semantische Studie zu kebôd YHWH.

Band 10   Ingeborg Gabriel: Friede über Israel. Eine Untersuchung zur Friedens-theologie in Chronik I 10 - II 36.

Band 11   Gottfried Glaßner: Vision eines auf Verheißung gegründeten Jerusa-lem. Textanalytische Studien zu Jesaja 54.

Band 12   Martin Stowasser: Johannes der Täufer im Vierten Evangelium. Eine Untersuchung zu seiner Bedeutung für die johanneische Gemeinde.

Band 13   Michael Weigl: Zefanja und das "Israel der Armen". Eine Untersuchung zur Theologie des Buches Zefanja.

Seit 1996 erscheint die Schriftenreihe bei der Peter Lang GmbH, Internationaler Verlag der Wissenschaften in Berlin.

Band 14   Alfred Friedl: Das eschatologische Gericht in Bildern aus dem Alltag. Eine exegetische Untersuchung von Mt 24,40f par Lk 17,34f. 1996.

Band 15   Herbert Migsch: Jeremias Ackerkauf. Eine Untersuchung von Jeremia 32. 1996.

Band 16   Gianni Barbiero: Das erste Psalmenbuch als Einheit. Eine synchrone Analyse von Psalm 1-41. 1999.

Band 17   Reginaldo Gomes de Araújo: Theologie der Wüste im Deuteronomium. 1999.

Band	18	Jean-Marie Carrière: Théorie du politique dans le Deutéronome. Analyse des unités, des structures et des concepts de Dt 16,18-18,22. 2001.
Band	19	Agnethe Siquans: Der Deuteronomiumkommentar des Theodoret von Kyros. 2002.
Band	20	Markus Tiwald: Wanderradikalismus. Jesu erste Jünger – ein Anfang und was davon bleibt. 2002.
Band	21	Michael P. Maier: Ägypten – Israels Herkunft und Geschick. Studie über einen theo-politischen Zentralbegriff im hebräischen Jeremiabuch. 2002.
Band	22	Georg Braulik / Norbert Lohfink: Osternacht und Altes Testament. Studien und Vorschläge. Mit einer Exsultetvertonung von Erwin Bücken. 2., durchgesehene Auflage. 2003.
Band	23	Georg Braulik (Hrsg.): Das Deuteronomium. 2003.
Band	24	Miroslav Kocúr: National and Religious Identity. A Study in Galatians 3,23-29 and Romans 10,12-21. 2003.
Band	25	Rudolf Kutschera: *Das Heil kommt von den Juden* (Joh 4,22). Untersuchungen zur Heilsbedeutung Israels. 2003.
Band	26	Jerzy Seremak: Psalm 24 als Text zwischen den Texten. 2004.
Band	27	Hans Ulrich Steymans: Psalm 89 und der Davidbund. Eine strukturale und redaktionsgeschichtliche Untersuchung. 2005.
Band	28	Georg Braulik / Norbert Lohfink: Liturgie und Bibel. Gesammelte Aufsätze. 2005.
Band	29	Johannes Marböck: Weisheit und Frömmigkeit. Studien zur alttestamentlichen Literatur der Spätzeit. 2006.
Band	30	Ulrich Fistill: Israel und das Ostjordanland. Untersuchungen zur Komposition von Num 21, 21-36,13 im Hinblick auf die Entstehung des Buches Numeri. 2007.
Band	31	Theodor Seidl / Stephanie Ernst (Hrsg.): Das Buch Ijob. Gesamtdeutungen – Einzeltexte – Zentrale Themen. 2007.
Band	32	Blažej Štrba: *Take off your sandals from your feet!* An Exegetical Study of Josh 5,13-15. 2008.
Band	33	Georg Braulik / Norbert Lohfink: Osternacht und Altes Testament – Ergänzungsband. Vertonung des Vigilvorschlags durch Godehard Joppich. 2008.
Band	34	Dieter Böhler: Jiftach und die Tora. Eine intertextuelle Auslegung von Ri 10,6-12,7. 2008.
Band	35	Elisabeth Birnbaum: Das Juditbuch im Wien des 17. und 18. Jahrhunderts. Exegese – Predigt – Musik – Theater – Bildende Kunst. 2009.
Band	36	Irene Schulmeister: Israels Befreiung aus Ägypten. Eine Formeluntersuchung zur Theologie des Deuteronomiums. 2010.
Band	37	Herbert Migsch: Studien zum Jeremiabuch und andere Beiträge zum Alten Testament. 2010.
Band	38	Jaroslav Rindoš: *He of Whom It Is Written.* John the Baptist and Elijah in Luke. 2010.

Band	39	Hermann-Josef Stipp (Hrsg.): Das deuteronomistische Geschichtswerk. 2011.
Band	40	Georg Braulik: Psalmen beten mit dem Benediktinischen Antiphonale. 2011.
Band	41	Herbert Migsch: Die Kohärenzstörung in Jeremia 35,8-10. Eine exegesegeschichtliche Studie. 2011.
Band	42	Veronika Tropper: Jesus Didáskalos. Studien zu Jesus als Lehrer bei den Synoptikern und im Rahmen der antiken Kultur- und Sozialgeschichte. 2012.
Band	43	Gottes Wort im Menschenwort. Festschrift für Georg Fischer SJ zum 60. Geburtstag. Herausgegeben von Dominik Markl, Claudia Paganini und Simone Paganini. 2014.
Band	44	Marco Pavan: "He remembered that they were but flesh, a breath that passes and does not return" (Ps 78,39). The Theme of Memory and Forgetting in the Third Book of the Psalter (Pss 73-89). 2014.
Band	45	Michael Kodzo Mensah: *I turned back my feet to your decrees* (Psalm 119,59). Torah in the Fifth Book of the Psalter. 2016.
Band	46	Edmond Léonce Vieyra: L'Écriture dans la dynamique argumentative de 1 Corinthiens 1–4. 2016.
Band	47	Ludger Schwienhorst-Schönberger (Hrsg.): Das Hohelied im Konflikt der Interpretationen. 2017.
Band	48	Augustinus Friedbert Weber: Der Psalter als ein Weg des Aufstiegs in Gregor von Nyssas „In inscriptiones Psalmorum". 2017.
Band	49	Alexander Kraljic: Deuteronomium 10,12-11,32: Gottes Hauptgebot, der Gehorsam Israels und sein Land. Eine Neuuntersuchung. 2018.
Band	50	Melanie Peetz / Sandra Huebenthal (Hrsg.): Ästhetik, sinnlicher Genuss und gute Manieren. Ein biblisches Menü in 25 Gängen. Festschrift für Hans-Winfried Jüngling SJ. 2018.
Band	51	Konrad Kremser: Die Hochzeit des Königs. Exegetisch-theologische Untersuchungen zu Psalm 45. 2019.
Band	52	Johanna Friedl: Ein brüderliches Volk. Das ‚Bruder'-Konzept im Heilig-keitsgesetz und deuteronomischen Gesetz. 2021.
Band	53	Georg Braulik / Norbert Lohfink: Sprache und literarische Gestalt des Buches Deuteronomium. Beobachtungen und Studien. 2021.
Band	54	Edwin Rodrigues: Psalm of Praise for the Rescue of the Throat. Concatenation and *lectio continua* of Pss 33–34–35. 2022.
Band	55	Georg Braulik / Norbert Lohfink: Die Rhetorik der Moserede in Deuteronomium 1 – 4. 2022.
Band	56	Salvatore Maurizio Sessa: Surrender to the King of Babylon. Jeremiah's "Prophetic Choice" in the Face of Jerusalem's End (Jer 21:1-10; 27–28; 38:14-28a). 2024.

www.peterlang.com

www.ingramcontent.com/pod-product-compliance
Ingram Content Group UK Ltd.
Pitfield, Milton Keynes, MK11 3LW, UK
UKHW041325050325
4871UKWH00002B/25